With ThomsonNOW™ . . . You'll save time wh[...] we give each student *Personalized Study* help!

W9-CLP-484

Just what you need to do NOW!

Offering choice and flexibility, **ThomsonNOW™** for Weiten's *Psychology: Themes and Variations, Briefer Version,* Seventh Edition, saves you time with ready-to-go tests, automatic grading, and an easy-to-use grade book—while *also* providing your students with effective *Personalized Study* that will help them excel in your course.

Assignable diagnostic *Pre-Tests* and *Post-Tests*

After reading a textbook chapter, students take the chapter's online *Pre-Test*—which you can assign as homework—to get an initial assessment of their grasp of key concepts. **ThomsonNOW** automatically grades the *Pre-Test* and then provides *Personalized Study* guidance that focuses on the concepts revealed as needing further study. Each chapter's *Post-Test* (also assignable) measures students' mastery of the chapter once they have completed their *Personalized Study* plan for the chapter. *Tests written by Laura Gruntmeir, Redlands Community College.*

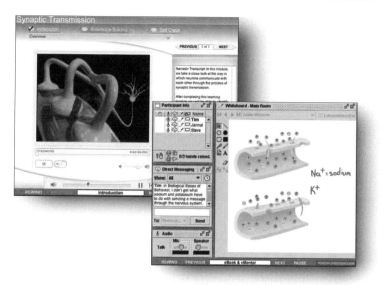

Personalized Study featuring interactive resources and live online tutoring

Personalized Study directs students to electronic text pages and online resources (incorporating video, animations, and demonstrations) that students need to review. If they need more help, they can click on the **vMentor™** icon and get live, online assistance from a psychology tutor.

A built-in gradebook—WebCT® and Blackboard® integration

When you assign **ThomsonNOW** to your students, the instructor gradebook makes it easy for you to monitor student progress. The *Pre-* and *Post-Tests* are automatically graded, with results flowing directly into the gradebook. If you use **WebCT** or **Blackboard,** we can provide integration that enables you to access the content capabilities of **ThomsonNOW** while using your familiar platform.

To include access to ThomsonNOW with each new textbook

Contact your Thomson Wadsworth representative or visit us online at www.thomsonedu.com/thomsonnow

PsykTrek™: A Multimedia Introduction to Psychology

Available on CD-ROM and online!

Intriguing . . . Interactive . . . Fully integrated with this textbook

With exceptional graphics, animations, video segments, and other interactive resources, **PsykTrek** guides students in actively exploring psychology's concepts and phenomena. Within its intuitive landscape, your students will take part in the action as they participate in classic experiments, manipulate visual illusions in ways that will make them doubt their own eyes, and learn about operant conditioning by actually shaping a virtual rat. Interactively partnering with this textbook, **PsykTrek's** unparalleled multimedia elements present the key concepts of introductory psychology in ways that are fascinating and *memorable*.

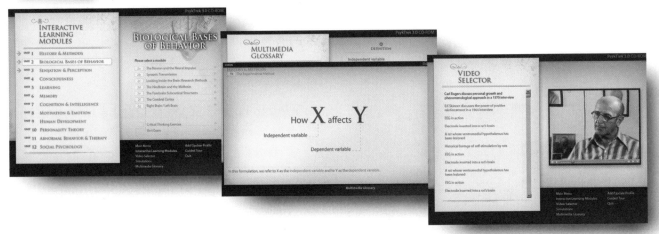

Integrated media teaches psychology's important concepts

- **Icons throughout every chapter** direct students to related study on **PsykTrek**.

- **Sixty-five learning modules, including three NEW modules,** use thousands of graphics, hundreds of photos and animations, and dozens of video segments to provide students with hands-on learning opportunities. New modules: "Forgetting," "Attachment," and "Conformity and Obedience."

- **Ten in-depth simulations** explore complex psychological phenomena—subjects such as memory, social judgment, and creativity—giving students an active role in experimentation.

- **A Video Selector** offers direct access to more than 35 video segments, which include footage from B. F. Skinner and cover interesting topics from this text, such as Little Albert and the Ames Room.

- **A multimedia glossary** includes detailed definitions of more than 800 terms, many with audio pronunciation and media elements.

It's easy to order PsykTrek packaged with every student text

Contact your Thomson Wadsworth representative for ordering information.

PsykTrek is compatible with Windows® 98, Windows® ME, Windows® XP, and newer Macintosh® operating systems.

Concise, current, conceptually integrated, and media linked

Weiten challenges students AND makes learning easy!

This *Briefer Version* of Wayne Weiten's *Psychology: Themes and Variations* is often described as a book that makes the challenging concepts and theories of psychology easy to learn. *How does Weiten do it?* By combining a superbly integrated thematic organization with many practical applications, examples, and a cohesive set of in-text learning aids, Weiten helps students see beyond the clutter to grasp the big-picture concepts and topics—the themes and variations on those themes—that are at the heart of psychology.

PLUS . . . PsykTrek™ ThomsonNOW™

and other innovative, fully integrated media tools and print resources to support your course. *See the front endpapers of this book and pages P-6 through P-8.*

In this new Seventh Edition of *Psychology: Themes and Variations, Briefer Version,* you'll find

- **Insights into important NEW research,** including more than 800 new references. *See page P-2.*

- **Visuals that teach, including striking NEW illustrations** by renowned biological/medical illustrator Fred Harwin. *See page P-3.*

- **Unifying themes** that clarify and capture psychology's essence. *See page P-4.*

- **Many applications and critical thinking tools** that enrich students' understanding of psychology. *See page P-5.*

THOMSON

WADSWORTH

Figure 3.9
MRI scans. MRI scans can be used to produce remarkably high-resolution pictures of brain structure. A vertical view of a brain from the left side is shown here.

(Dougherty & Rauch, 2003). This technology is exciting because it can provide both *functional* and *structural* information in the same image and moni-

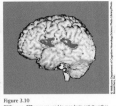

Figure 3.10
PET scans. PET scans are used to map brain activity rather than brain structure. They provide color-coded maps that show areas of high activity in the brain over time. The PET scan shown here pinpointed two areas of high activity (indicated by the red and green colors) when a research participant worked on a verbal short-term memory task.

tor changes in brain activity in real time. For example, using fMRI scans, researchers have identified patterns of brain activity associated with cocaine craving in cocaine addicts (Wexler et al., 2001).

Another new research tool in neuroscience is *transcranial magnetic stimulation (TMS)*, a technique that permits scientists to temporarily enhance or depress

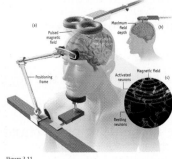

Another new research tool in neuroscience is *transcranial magnetic stimulation (TMS)*, a technique that permits scientists to temporarily enhance or depress activity in a specific area of the brain. With TMS, a magnetic coil mounted on a small paddle is held over a specific area of a subject's head (see Figure 3.11). By varying the timing and duration of magnetic

approach has been used to explore whether specific areas of the brain are involved in visuospatial processing (Sack et al., 2002), memory for objects (Olivieri et al., 2001), and language (Knecht et al., 2002).

Now that we have discussed a few approaches to brain research, let's look at what scientists have discovered about the functions of various parts of the brain. The brain is divided into three major regions: the hindbrain, the midbrain, and the forebrain. The principal structures found in each of these regions are listed in the organizational chart of the nervous system in Figure 3.5. You can see where these regions are located in the brain by looking at Figure 3.12.

Figure 3.11
Transcranial magnetic stimulation (TMS). In TMS, magnetic pulses are delivered to a localized area of the brain from a magnet mounted on a small paddle (a). The magnetic field only penetrates to a depth of two centimeters (b). This technique can be used to either increase or decrease the excitability of the affected neurons. The inset at bottom right depicts neurons near the surface of the brain being temporarily activated by TMS (c).

Source: Bremner, J. D. (2005). *Brain imaging handbook*. New York: W. W. Norton, p. 34. Illustration © by Bryan Christie Design

74   CHAPTER 3

Psychology Moves in a Positive Direction
1a

Shortly after Martin Seligman was elected President of the American Psychological Association in 1997, he experienced a profound insight that he characterized as an "epiphany." This pivotal insight came from an unusual source—Seligman's 5-year-old daughter, Nikki. She scolded her overachieving, task-oriented father for being "grumpy" far too much of the time. Provoked by his daughter's criticism, Seligman suddenly realized that his approach to life *was* overly and unnecessarily negative. More important, he recognized that the same assessment could be made of the field of psychology—that it, too, was excessively and needlessly negative in its approach (Seligman, 2003). This revelation inspired Seligman to launch an influential, new initiative within psychology that came to be known as the *positive psychology movement.*

Seligman went on to argue convincingly that the field of psychology had historically devoted too

---

- **New biological psychology coverage,** for example: new research on glial cells' contribution to communication in the nervous system; added coverage of transcranial magnetic stimulation; new research on the correlation between intelligence and brain size; new information on genetic bases for food preferences; and how experience and expectations influence perception.

- **Streamlined and updated evolutionary coverage,** such as why the human brain has evolved to organize color experience into four basic categories; the effects of ecologically relevant, conditioned stimuli; and mate poaching.

- **Greater attention to positive psychology throughout,** including a new section, "Psychology Moves in a Positive Direction," in Chapter 1.

- **Even more attention to cross-cultural and diversity topics,** including cultural similarities in patterns of sleeping and discussion relating Flynn effect to the controversy over cultural disparities in IQ scores.

- **Updated coverage of human memory,** including Kandel's Nobel-winning work on memory and synaptic transmission.

- **New discussion of media violence** as it relates to observational learning.

- **A new section on terror management theory,** a newly emerging theory that explores humans' unique awareness of the inevitability of death and the need to defend one's self-esteem, which protects against mortality-related anxiety.

NEW expertly rendered illustrations clarify complex concepts

Recognized for its didactic, comprehensive art program, Weiten's textbook helps to bring concepts into focus through an effective combination of color, narrative, and art—in visuals, schematics, and distinctive overview summaries.

NEW art that teaches, by Fred Harwin, award-winning medical illustrator

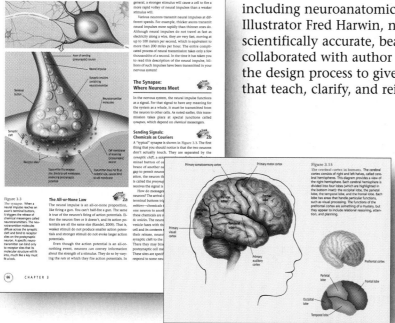

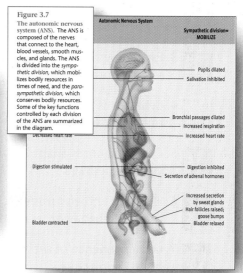

This Seventh Edition includes many new illustrations, including neuroanatomical and physiological graphics. Illustrator Fred Harwin, nationally renowned for his scientifically accurate, beautifully rendered work, has collaborated with author Wayne Weiten throughout the design process to give your students illustrations that teach, clarify, and reinforce!

Five *Illustrated Overviews* of key ideas

A hallmark of this book's art program, ***Illustrated Overviews*** help students understand how people, theories, research, and concepts fit together. Each of the book's five overviews effectively and dramatically combines tables, photographs, diagrams, and sketches into a clear visual sweep of information—revealing, at a glance, key concepts in the history of psychology, learning, personality theory, psychological disorders, and psychotherapy.

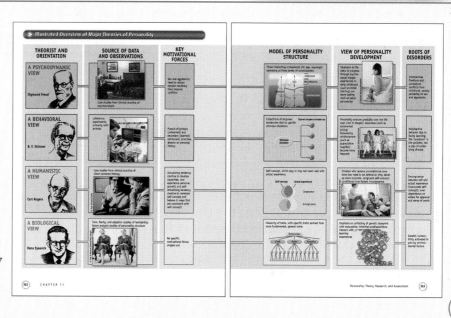

Seven unifying themes help students make sense of new information and research

Weiten consistently uses seven overarching themes to help students look at newly emerging facts and diverging research from broader, more meaningful perspectives. All seven themes are introduced in Chapter One, "The Evolution of Psychology." Then, relevant themes are discussed in each subsequent chapter. The result is a book that makes psychology both challenging to think about and easy to learn from—capturing the excitement of the field by emphasizing the ideas behind the facts.

Seven unifying themes

 1. Psychology is empirical.

 2. Psychology is theoretically diverse.

 3. Psychology evolves in a sociohistorical context.

 4. Behavior is determined by multiple causes.

 5. Our behavior is shaped by our cultural heritage.

 6. Heredity and environment jointly influence behavior.

 7. Our experience of the world is highly subjective.

Seven Unifying Themes

The enormous breadth and diversity of psychology make it a challenging subject for the beginning student. In the pages ahead you will be introduced to many areas of research and a multitude of new ideas, concepts, and principles. Fortunately, not all ideas are created equal. Some are far more important than others. In this section, I will highlight seven fundamental themes that will reappear in a number of variations as we move from one area of psychology to another in this text. You have already met some of these key ideas in our review of psychology's past and present. Now we will isolate them and highlight their significance. In the remainder of the book these ideas serve as organizing themes to provide threads of continuity across chapters and to help you see the connections among the various areas of research in psychology.

In studying psychology, you are learning about both behavior and the scientific discipline that in-

vestigates it. Accordingly, our seven themes come in two sets. The first set consists of statements highlighting crucial aspects of psychology as a way of thinking and as a field of study. The second set consists of broad generalizations about psychology's subject matter: behavior and the cognitive and physiological processes that underlie it.

Themes Related to Psychology as a Field of Study

Looking at psychology as a field of study, we see three crucial ideas: (1) psychology is empirical; (2) psychology is theoretically diverse; and (3) psychology evolves in a sociohistorical context. Let's look at each of these ideas in more detail.

PREVIEW QUESTIONS

- What is the purpose of the text's unifying themes?
- What are the first three themes that elucidate the nature of psychology?
- What are the remaining four themes that emphasize crucial insights about behavior?

The Evolution of Psychology 19

Reflecting on the Chapter's Themes sections with color-coded theme icons

Brightly colored theme icons appear in ***Reflecting on the Chapter's Themes*** sections located near the end of every chapter. These sections discuss connections between chapter topics and the unifying themes. The icons (color coded to be easily recognizable throughout the text) help ensure that students understand and link the themes discussed within the chapter.

Reflecting on the Chapter's Themes

Three of our seven themes stood out in this chapter: (1) heredity and environment jointly influence behavior, (2) behavior is determined by multiple causes, and (3) psychology is empirical. Let's look at each of these points.

In Chapter 1, when it was first emphasized that heredity and environment jointly shape behavior, you may have been a little perplexed about how your genes could be responsible for your sarcastic wit or your interest in art. In fact, there are no genes for behavior per se. Experts do not expect to find genes for sarcasm or artistic interest, for example. Insofar as your hereditary endowment plays a role in your behavior, it does so *indirectly*, by molding the physiological machine that you work with. Thus, your genes influence your physiological makeup, which in turn influences your personality, temperament, intelligence, interests, and other traits. Bear in mind, however, that genetic factors do not operate in a vacuum. Genes exert their effects in an environmental context. The impact of genetic makeup depends on environment, and the impact of environment depends on genetic makeup.

It was evident throughout the chapter that behavior is determined by multiple causes, but this theme was particularly apparent in the discussions of schizophrenia. At different points in the chapter we saw that schizophrenia may be a function of (1) abnormalities in neurotransmitter activity (especially dopa-

mine), (2) structural abnormalities in the brain identified with CT and MRI scans, and (3) genetic vulnerability to the illness. These findings do not contradict one another. Rather, they demonstrate that a complex array of biological factors are involved in the development of schizophrenia. In Chapter 13, we'll see that a host of environmental factors also play a role in the multifactorial causation of schizophrenia.

The empirical nature of psychology was apparent in the numerous discussions of the specialized research methods used to study the physiological bases of behavior. As you know, the empirical approach depends on precise observation. Throughout this chapter, you've seen how investigators have come up with innovative methods to observe and measure elusive phenomena such as neural impulses, brain function, cerebral specialization, and the impact of heredity on behavior. The point is that empirical methods are the lifeblood of the scientific enterprise. When researchers figure out how to better observe something, their findings usually facilitate major advances in our scientific knowledge. That is why the new brain-imaging techniques hold exciting promise for neuroscientists.

The importance of empiricism will also be apparent in the upcoming Personal Application and in the Critical Thinking Application that follows. In both applications you'll see the importance of learning to distinguish between scientific findings and conjecture based on those findings.

Heredity and Environment

Multifactorial Causation

Empiricism

The Biological Bases of Behavior 89

Many applications and critical thinking tools enrich students' understanding of psychology

CRITICAL THINKING *Application*

Analyzing Arguments: Making Sense out of Controversy

Consider the following argument: "Dieting is harmful to your health because the tendency to be obese is largely inherited." What is your reaction to this reasoning? Do you find it convincing? We hope not, as this argument is seriously flawed. Can you see what's wrong? There is no relationship between the conclusion that "dieting is harmful to your health" and the reason given that "the tendency to be obese is largely inherited." The argument is initially seductive because most people know that obesity is largely inherited, so the reason provided represents a true statement. But the reason is unrelated to the conclusion advocated. This scenario may strike you as odd, but if you start listening carefully to discussions about controversial issues, you will probably notice that people often cite irrelevant considerations in support of their favored conclusions.

This chapter was loaded with controversial issues that sincere, well-meaning people could argue about for weeks. Are gender differences in mating preferences a product of evolution or of modern economic realities? Is there a biological basis for homosexuality? Unfortunately, arguments about issues such as these typically are unproductive in

terms of moving toward resolution or agreement because most people know little about the rules of argumentation. In this application, we will explore what makes arguments sound or unsound in the hope of improving your ability to analyze and think critically about arguments.

The Anatomy of an Argument

In everyday usage, the word *argument* is used to refer to a dispute or disagreement between two or more people, but in the technical language of rhetoric, an *argument* consists of one or more premises that are used to provide support for a conclusion. *Premises* are the reasons that are presented to persuade someone that a conclusion is true or probably true. *Assumptions* are premises for which no proof or evidence is offered. Assumptions are often left unstated. For example, suppose that your doctor tells you that you should exercise regularly because regular exercise is good for your heart. In this simple argument, the conclusion is "You should exercise regularly." The premise that leads to this conclu-

sion is the idea that "exercise is good for your heart." An unstated assumption is that everyone wants a healthy heart.

In the language of argument analysis, premises are said to support (or not support) conclusions. A conclusion may be supported by one reason or by many reasons. One way to visualize these possibilities is to draw an analogy between the reasons that support a conclusion and the legs that support a table (Halpern, 2003). As shown in Figure 9.22, a table top (conclusion) could be supported by one strong leg (a single strong reason) or many thin legs (lots of weaker reasons). Of course, the reasons provided for a conclusion may fail to support the conclusion. Returning to our table analogy, the table top might not be supported because the legs are too thin (very weak reasons) or because the legs are not attached (irrelevant reasons).

Arguments can get pretty complicated as they usually have more parts than premises and conclusions. In addition, often are *counterarguments*, which are reasons that take support away from a conclusion. And sometimes the most important part of an argument is something that is not there—reasons that have been omitted, either deliberately or not, that would

Specific reasoning skills and how to use them on chapter material

Written by critical thinking expert Diane Halpern, a two-page *Critical Thinking Application* in each chapter focuses students on one or several specific reasoning skills. Rather than just think about the skills—such as understanding how reasons and evidence support or refute conclusions—students can *actually practice* them on chapter-related topics.

Table 9.1 Critical Thinking Skills Discussed in This Application

Skill	Description
Understanding the elements of an argument	The critical thinker understands that an argument consists of premises and assumptions that are used to support a conclusion.
Recognizing and avoiding common fallacies, such as irrelevant reasons, circular reasoning, slippery slope reasoning, weak analogies, and false dichotomies	The critical thinker is vigilant about conclusions based on unrelated premises, conclusions that are rewordings of premises, unwarranted predictions that things will spin out of control, superficial analogies, and contrived dichotomies.
Evaluating arguments systematically	The critical thinker carefully assesses the validity of the premises, assumptions, and conclusions in an argument, and considers counterarguments and missing elements.

Links to the personal, practical side of psychology

Throughout the text, **Personal Applications** summarize important research while illustrating how psychology is linked to students' everyday lives. These features offer practical information, and advice that students can put to use right away. Topics include improving everyday memory, understanding gender differences, and understanding eating disorders.

PERSONAL *Application*

Understanding Eating Disorders

Answer the following "true" or "false."

____ 1 Although they have only attracted attention in recent years, eating disorders have a long history and have always been fairly common.

____ 2 People with anorexia nervosa are much more likely to recognize that their eating behavior is pathological

____ 3 The prevalence of eating disorders is twice as high in women as it is in men.

____ 4 The binge-and-purge syndrome seen in bulimia nervosa is not common in anorexia nervosa.

than people suffering from bulimia nervosa.

All of the above statements are false, as you will see in this Application. The psychological disorders that we discussed in the main body of the chapter have largely been recognized for centuries and are generally found in one form or another in all cultures and societies. Eating disorders present a sharp contrast to this picture; they have only been

Psychological Disorders 427

A system of signposts guides students through every chapter

- **Preview Questions,** located at the beginning of each major chapter section, help students identify important ideas.

- **Concept Checks** sprinkled throughout each chapter challenge students to apply ideas rather than simply test rote memory.

- **An end-of-chapter *Review of Key Ideas*** is followed by **Key Terms** with page references to the chapter, enabling students to easily locate the definition in the context of the chapter's narrative for review.

PREVIEW QUESTIONS

- What are the subdivisions of the peripheral nervous system?

- What is the difference between afferent and efferent nerves?

- What does the autonomic nervous system regulate, and what are its subdivisions?

- What is the central nervous system made up of?

concept **check** 3.2

Linking Brain Chemistry to Behavior

Check your understanding of relations between brain chemistry and behavior by indicating which neurotransmitters or other biological chemicals have been linked to the phenomena listed below. Choose your answers from the following list: (a) acetylcholine, (b) norepinephrine, (c) dopamine, (d) serotonin, (e) endorphins. Indicate your choice (by letter) in the spaces on the left. You'll find the answers in Appendix A.

_____ **1.** A transmitter involved in the regulation of sleep, eating, and aggression.

_____ **2.** The two monoamines that have been linked to depression.

_____ **3.** Chemicals that resemble opiate drugs in structure and that are involved in pain relief.

_____ **4.** A neurotransmitter for which abnormal levels have been implicated in schizophrenia.

_____ **5.** The only neurotransmitter between motor neurons and voluntary muscles.

Preparation and presentation tools

Multimedia Manager with Instructor Resources CD-ROM: A Microsoft® PowerPoint® Tool

0-495-31934-1

Written by Brian Malley of University of Michigan, this one-stop resource helps you enhance your Microsoft® PowerPoint® lectures with integrated art and chapter-by-chapter lecture outlines, a bevy of video clips, and other integrated media. **Multimedia Manager** also contains the full *Instructor's Resource Manual* and *Test Bank* in electronic format.

ExamView® Assessment Suite

0-495-31931-7

Helps you to create customized tests in print or online in minutes! Contains all *Test Bank* questions in electronic format. You can easily edit and import your own questions and graphics, and edit and maneuver existing questions.

JoinIn™ on TurningPoint®

0-495-31935X

The easiest audience response system you'll ever use, **JoinIn™ on TurningPoint®** enables you to engage students and assess their progress with instant in-class quizzes and polls. You can pose book-specific questions and display students' answers seamlessly within the Microsoft® PowerPoint® slides of your own lecture, in conjunction with the "clicker" hardware of your choice. **JoinIn on TurningPoint** is compatible with major electronic grade book systems such as **WebCT**, **Blackboard**, and **ThomsonNOW.**

Instructor's Resource Manual

0-495-31929-5

Coordinated and written by Randolph Smith (Kennesaw State University) and housed in a convenient binder that you can personalize to your needs, the *Instructor's Resource Manual* includes a Resource Integration Guide, Lecture/ Discussion Topics, Demonstrations/ Activities, **PsykTrek**™ Integration, Suggested Readings, and Handouts. Additional essays by successful professors cover strategies for effective teaching, media for introductory psychology, cross-cultural comparisons, how to integrate writing into the curriculum, how to use the Web, how to use computers, and more.

Test Bank

0-495-31934-1

Written by Cheryl Hale, Jefferson Community College, each chapter of this *Test Bank* includes approximately 5–10 essay questions, 200 multiple-choice questions, 20 fill-in-the-blanks, and 20 true/false. Some multiple-choice questions are pulled from the *Study Guide,* making this a particularly cohesive package.

Animations, simulations, tutorials, online course management, web links, and more— all correlated with Weiten's text.

Available on CD-ROM and online!

PsykTrek™: A Multimedia Introduction to Psychology

Sprinkled throughout every chapter of this book, students will find **PsykTrek** icons, alerting them to topic-related multimedia on the CD-ROM. **PsykTrek** is a must-have for today's visually oriented learners. For more information, turn to the inside front cover of this book.

InfoTrac® College Edition with InfoMarks®

This exceptional online library places the full text of articles from more than 5,000 academic and popular magazines, newspapers, and journals at your students' fingertips.

Thomson™ NOW!

ThomsonNOW™ for Weiten's *Psychology: Themes & Variations, Briefer Version,* Seventh Edition

A time-saving tool for you and your students, **ThomsonNOW** is an intelligent, web-based study system and course management tool that provides a completely integrated package of diagnostic quizzes (by Laura Gruntmeir, Redlands Community College), Personalized Study, e-Book, Learning Modules, and an Instructor Gradebook that automatically captures and tracks student progress. For more information, turn to the inside front cover of this book.

WebTUTOR™ Advantage

WebTutor™ Advantage on WebCT® and Blackboard®

Save time managing your course, posting materials, incorporating multimedia, and tracking progress with this engaging, text-specific e-learning tool. Visit **http://webtutor.thomsonlearning.com.**

Book Companion Website

www.thomsonedu.com/psychology/weiten
Features a rich selection of teaching and learning resources, including chapter-by-chapter learning objectives, online tutorial quizzes, chapter-related web links, flash cards, critical thinking lessons, and more!

PLUS the Resource Integration Guide
An essential tool that helps you get maximum use from ALL resources available with Weiten's text.
Housed in the *Instructor's Resource Manual.*

Helping your students excel in psychology

Art and Lecture Outlines
0-495-31933-3
Written by Brian Malley, University of Michigan, this new supplement is designed for convenient note taking and review, and features printed Microsoft® PowerPoint® slides and selected textbook art—including new anatomical art by distinguished artist Fred Harwin. These slides match those featured in the instructor's **Multimedia Manager,** so students can spend more time listening and participating in class and less time writing.

Study Guide
0-495-31928-7
Written by Richard Stalling and Ronald Wasden, both of Bradley University, an author team with more than 30 years of experience as a team in writing study guides for introductory psychology texts, the *Study Guide* includes an engaging, multifeatured review of key ideas for each chapter (organized around learning objectives written by Wayne Weiten), a review of key terms, a review of key people, and a self-test for each chapter.

NEW! Bonus Modules
To enable you to customize your text, three bonus modules are available: "Industrial/ Organizational Psychology," "Careers in Psychology," and "Gender and Human Sexuality." These modules help you to tailor your course and enrich coverage for your students. Contact your Thomson Wadsworth representative to order the modules of your choice packaged with each student text.

Plus these great student tools . . . also available for packaging with each text

Writing Papers in Psychology, **Seventh Edition,** by Ralph L. Rosnow and Mimi Rosnow
0-534-53331-0

Writing With Style: APA Style Made Easy, **Third Edition,** by Lenore T. Szuchman
0-534-63432-X

Introduction to Positive Psychology, by William C. Compton. 0-534-64453-8

Careers in Psychology: Opportunities in a Changing World, **Second Edition,** by Tara L. Kuther and Robert D. Morgan. 0-495-09078-6

Challenging Your Preconceptions: Thinking Critically About Psychology, **Second Edition,** by Randolph A. Smith. 0-534-26739-4

Cross-Cultural Perspectives in Introductory Psychology, **Fifth Edition,** by William F. Price and Richley H. Crapo. 0-534-54653-6

Create your perfect course . . . with Thomson Custom Solutions!
The expert editorial team at Thomson Custom Solutions can help you create customized learning materials *tailor-fit* to the way you teach:

- **Customized Textbooks**—We'll guide you step by step in creating an affordable text by matching only the content you need to your course syllabus. Your custom text can include your original content such as course notes, handouts, regional or state material, and articles. Our flexible and attractive cover options will help make your project a hit with students.
- **Custom Media Solutions** ensure that technology works for you, matching the right technology to your course and text.
- **Custom Readers** enrich your course with selections from our Thomson Custom Solutions Collections, which feature readings, case selections, and exercises for a wide range of subjects.

For more information about our options and services, visit www.thomsoncustom.com
Or visit our powerful TextChoice book-building website at www.textchoice.com

Psychology
Themes and Variations
Briefer Version

7th EDITION

7th EDITION

Psychology
Themes and Variations
Briefer Version

Wayne Weiten

University of Nevada, Las Vegas

THOMSON ™
WADSWORTH

Australia • Brazil • Canada • Mexico • Singapore • Spain
United Kingdom • United States

Psychology: Themes and Variations
Briefer Version, Seventh Edition
Wayne Weiten

Publisher: Michele Sordi
Development Editor: Kirk Bomont
Assistant Editor: Dan Moneypenny
Editorial Assistant: Erin Miskelly
Technology Project Manager: Lauren Keyes
Marketing Manager: Kim Russell
Marketing Assistant: Natasha Coates
Marketing Communications Manager: Linda Yip
Project Manager, Editorial Production:
  Jennie Redwitz
Creative Director: Rob Hugel
Art Director: Vernon Boes

Print Buyer: Becky Cross
Permissions Editor: Linda Rill
Production Service: Tom Dorsaneo
Text Designer: Liz Harasymczuk
Photo Researcher: Linda L Rill
Copy Editor: Jackie Estrada
Illustrator: Carol Zuber-Mallison
Cover Designer: Liz Harasymczuk
Cover Image: © Flip Chalfant/Getty Images
Compositor: Thompson Type
Text and Cover Printer:
  Courier Corporation/Kendallville

© 2008, 2005 Thomson Wadsworth, a part of The Thomson Corporation. Thomson, the Star logo, and Wadsworth are trademarks used herein under license.

ALL RIGHTS RESERVED. No part of this work covered by the copyright hereon may be reproduced or used in any form or by any means—graphic, electronic, or mechanical, including photocopying, recording, taping, Web distribution, information storage and retrieval systems, or in any other manner—without the written permission of the publisher.

Printed in the United States of America
1 2 3 4 5 6 7 11 10 09 08 07

ExamView® and ExamView Pro® are registered trademarks of FSCreations, Inc. Windows is a registered trademark of the Microsoft Corporation used herein under license. Macintosh and Power Macintosh are registered trademarks of Apple Computer, Inc. Used herein under license.

© 2008 Thomson Learning, Inc. All Rights Reserved. Thomson Learning WebTutorTM is a trademark of Thomson Learning, Inc.

Library of Congress Control Number: 2006933858

ISBN-13: 978-0-495-10058-4
ISBN-10: 0-495-10058-7

Thomson Higher Education
10 Davis Drive
Belmont, CA 94002-3098
USA

For more information about our products, contact us at:
Thomson Learning Academic Resource Center
1-800-423-0563

For permission to use material from this text or product, submit a request online at
http://www.thomsonrights.com
Any additional questions about permissions can be submitted by e-mail to
thomsonrights@thomson.com

T. J.,
This one is for you

WAYNE WEITEN is a graduate of Bradley University and received his Ph.D. in social psychology from the University of Illinois—Chicago, in 1981. He currently teaches at the University of Nevada, Las Vegas. He has received distinguished teaching awards from Division Two of the American Psychological Association (APA) and from the College of DuPage, where he taught until 1991. He is a Fellow of Divisions 1 and 2 of the American Psychological Association. In 1991, he helped chair the APA National Conference on Enhancing the Quality of Undergraduate Educa-tion in Psychology and in 1996–1997 he served as President of the Society for the Teaching of Psychol-ogy. Weiten has conducted research on a wide range of topics, including educational measurement, jury decision making, attribution theory, stress, and cere-bral specialization. His recent interests have included pressure as a form of stress and the technology of textbooks. He is also the co-author of *Psychology Ap-plied to Modern Life* (Wadsworth, 2006) and the crea-tor of an educational CD-ROM titled *PsykTrek: A Multi-media Introduction to Psychology.*

Psychology is an exciting, dynamic discipline that has grown by leaps and bounds in recent decades. This progress has been reflected in the field's introductory texts, which have grown longer and longer. However, the length of the introductory psychology course generally has not changed. Hence, an increasing number of professors are reporting that they find it difficult to cover the wealth of material found in the typical introductory text. With this reality in mind, I decided to write a briefer version of *Psychology: Themes and Variations* to help meet the needs of those teachers who would like a challenging, but concise, introductory text.

If I had to sum up in a single sentence what I hope will distinguish this text, the sentence would be this: I have set out to create a *paradox* instead of a *compromise.*

Let me elaborate. An introductory psychology text must satisfy two disparate audiences: professors and students. Because of the tension between the divergent needs and preferences of these audiences, textbook authors usually indicate that they have attempted to strike a compromise between being theoretical versus practical, comprehensive versus comprehensible, research oriented versus applied, rigorous versus accessible, and so forth. However, I believe that many of these dichotomies are false. As Kurt Lewin once remarked, "What could be more practical than a good theory?" Similarly, is rigorous really the opposite of accessible? Not in my dictionary. I maintain that many of the antagonistic goals that we strive for in our textbooks only *seem* incompatible and that we may not need to make compromises as often as we assume.

In my estimation, a good introductory textbook is a paradox in that it integrates characteristics and goals that appear contradictory. With this in mind, I have endeavored to write a text that is paradoxical in three ways. First, in surveying psychology's broad range of content, I have tried to show that our interests are characterized by diversity *and* unity. Second, I have emphasized both research *and* application and how they work in harmony. Finally, I have aspired to write a book that is challenging to think about *and* easy to learn from. Let's take a closer look at these goals.

Goals

1. *To show both the unity and the diversity of psychology's subject matter.* Students entering an introduc-

tory psychology course often are unaware of the immense diversity of subjects studied by psychologists. I find this diversity to be part of psychology's charm, and throughout the book I highlight the enormous range of questions and issues addressed by psychology. Of course, our diversity proves disconcerting for some students who see little continuity between such disparate areas of research as physiology, motivation, cognition, and abnormal behavior. Indeed, in this era of specialization, even some psychologists express concern about the fragmentation of the field.

However, I believe that the subfields of psychology overlap considerably and that we should emphasize their common core by accenting the connections and similarities among them. Consequently, I portray psychology as an integrated whole rather than as a mosaic of loosely related parts. A principal goal of this text, then, is to highlight the unity in psychology's intellectual heritage (the themes), as well as the diversity of psychology's interests and uses (the variations).

2. *To illuminate the process of research and its intimate link to application.* For me, a research-oriented book is not one that bulges with summaries of many studies but one that enhances students' appreciation of the logic and excitement of empirical inquiry. I want students to appreciate the strengths of the empirical approach and to see scientific psychology as a creative effort to solve intriguing behavioral puzzles. For this reason, the text emphasizes not only *what* we know (and don't know) but *how* we attempt to find out. It examines methods in some detail and encourages students to adopt the skeptical attitude of a scientist and to think critically about claims regarding behavior.

Learning the virtues of research should not mean that students cannot also satisfy their desire for concrete, personally useful information about the challenges of everyday life. Most researchers believe that psychology has a great deal to offer those outside the field and that psychologists should share the practical implications of their work. In this text, practical insights are carefully qualified and closely tied to data, so that students can see the interdependence of research and application. I find that students come to appreciate the science of psychology more when they see that worthwhile practical applications are derived from careful research and sound theory.

3. *To make the text challenging to think about and easy to learn from.* Perhaps most of all, I have sought to create a book of ideas rather than a compendium

of studies. I consistently emphasize concepts and theories over facts, and I focus on major issues and tough questions that cut across the subfields of psychology (for example, the extent to which behavior is governed by nature, nurture, and their interaction), as opposed to parochial debates (such as the merits of averaging versus adding in impression formation). Challenging students to think also means urging them to confront the complexity and ambiguity of our knowledge. Hence, the text doesn't skirt gray areas, unresolved questions, and theoretical controversies. Instead, readers are encouraged to contemplate open-ended questions, to examine their assumptions about behavior, and to apply psychological concepts to their own lives. My goal is not simply to describe psychology but to stimulate students' intellectual growth.

However, students can grapple with "the big issues and tough questions" only if they first master the basic concepts and principles of psychology—ideally, with as little struggle as possible. In my writing, I never let myself forget that a textbook is a tool for teaching. Accordingly, I have taken great care to ensure that the book's content, organization, writing, illustrations, and pedagogical aids work in harmony to facilitate instruction and learning.

Admittedly, these goals are ambitious. If you're skeptical, you have every right to be. Let me explain how I have tried to realize the objectives I have outlined.

Special Features

This text has a variety of unusual features, each contributing in its own way to the book's paradoxical nature. These special features include unifying themes, Personal Application sections, Critical Thinking Application sections, a didactic illustration program, an integrated running glossary, Concept Checks, Preview Questions, and Practice Tests.

Unifying Themes

Chapter 1 introduces seven key ideas that serve as unifying themes throughout the text. The themes serve several purposes. First, they provide threads of continuity across chapters that help students see the connections among various areas of research in psychology. Second, as the themes evolve over the course of the book, they provide a forum for a relatively sophisticated discussion of enduring issues in psychology, thus helping to make this a "book of ideas." Third, the themes focus a spotlight on a number of

basic insights about psychology and its subject matter that should leave lasting impressions on your students. In selecting the themes, the question I asked myself (and other professors) was, "What do I really want students to remember five years from now?" The resulting themes are grouped into two sets.

Themes Related to Psychology as a Field of Study

Theme 1: Psychology is empirical. This theme is used to enhance the student's appreciation of psychology's scientific nature and to demonstrate the advantages of empiricism over uncritical common sense and speculation. I also use this theme to encourage the reader to adopt a scientist's skeptical attitude and to engage in more critical thinking about information of all kinds.

Theme 2: Psychology is theoretically diverse. Students are often confused by psychology's theoretical pluralism and view it as a weakness. I don't downplay or apologize for our field's theoretical diversity, because I honestly believe that it is one of our greatest strengths. Throughout the book, I provide concrete examples of how clashing theories have stimulated productive research, how converging on a question from several perspectives can yield increased understanding, and how competing theories are sometimes reconciled in the end.

Theme 3: Psychology evolves in a sociohistorical context. This theme emphasizes that psychology is embedded in the ebb and flow of everyday life. The text shows how the spirit of the times has often shaped psychology's evolution and how progress in psychology leaves its mark on our society.

Themes Related to Psychology's Subject Matter

Theme 4: Behavior is determined by multiple causes. Throughout the book, I emphasize, and repeatedly illustrate, that behavioral processes are complex and that multifactorial causation is the rule. This theme is used to discourage simplistic, single-cause thinking and to encourage more critical reasoning.

Theme 5: Our behavior is shaped by our cultural heritage. This theme is intended to enhance students' appreciation of how cultural factors moderate psychological processes and how the viewpoint of one's own culture can distort one's interpretation of the behavior of people from other cultures. The discussions that elaborate on this theme do not

Chapter	THEME						
	1 Empiricism	2 Theoretical Diversity	3 Sociohistorical Context	4 Multifactorial Causation	5 Cultural Heritage	6 Heredity and Environment	7 Subjectivity of Experience
1. The Evolution of Psychology	●	●	●	●	●	●	●
2. The Research Enterprise in Psychology	●						●
3. The Biological Bases of Behavior	●			●		●	
4. Sensation and Perception		●			●		●
5. Variations in Consciousness		●	●		●		●
6. Learning			●			●	
7. Human Memory		●		●			●
8. Cognition and Intelligence	●		●		●	●	●
9. Motivation and Emotion		●	●	●	●	●	
10. Human Development Across the Life Span		●	●	●	●	●	
11. Personality: Theory, Research, and Assessment		●	●		●		
12. Stress, Coping, and Health				●			●
13. Psychological Disorders			●	●	●	●	
14. Treatment of Psychological Disorders		●			●		
15. Social Behavior	●			●	●		●

simply celebrate diversity. They strike a careful balance—that accurately reflects the research in this area—highlighting both cultural variations and similarities in behavior.

Theme 6: Heredity and environment jointly influence behavior. Repeatedly discussing this theme permits me to explore the nature versus nurture issue in all its complexity. Over a series of chapters, students gradually learn how biology shapes behavior, how experience shapes behavior, and how scientists estimate the relative importance of each. Along the way, students gain an in-depth appreciation of what we mean when we say that heredity and environment interact.

Theme 7: Our experience of the world is highly subjective. All of us tend to forget the extent to which we view the world through our own personal lens. This theme is used to explain the principles that underlie the subjectivity of human experience, to clarify its implications, and to repeatedly remind readers that their view of the world is not the only legitimate view.

After introducing all seven themes in Chapter 1, I discuss different sets of themes in each chapter, as they are relevant to the subject matter. The connections between a chapter's content and the unifying themes are highlighted in a standard section near the end of the chapter, in which I reflect on the "lessons to be learned" from the chapter. The discussions of the unifying themes are largely confined to these sections, titled "Reflecting on the Chapter's Themes." I have not tried to make every chapter illustrate a certain number of themes. Rather, the themes were allowed to emerge naturally, and I found that two to five surfaced in any given chapter. The chart on page xi shows which themes are highlighted in each chapter. Color-coded icons near the beginning of each "Reflecting on the Chapter's Themes" section indicate the specific themes featured in each chapter.

Personal Applications

To reinforce the pragmatic implications of theory and research stressed throughout the text, each chapter includes a Personal Application section that highlights the practical side of psychology. Each Personal Application devotes two to five *pages* of text (rather than the usual box) to a single issue that should be of special interest to many of your students. Although most of the Personal Application sections have a "how to" character, they continue to review studies and summarize data in much the same way as the main body of each chapter. Thus, they portray research and application not as incompatible polarities but as two sides of the same coin. Many of the Personal Applications—such as those on finding and reading journal articles, understanding art and illusion, and improving stress management—provide topical coverage unusual for an introductory text.

Critical Thinking Applications

A great deal of unusual coverage can also be found in the Critical Thinking Applications that follow the Personal Applications. Conceived by Diane Halpern (Claremont McKenna College), a leading authority on critical thinking, these applications are based on the assumption that critical thinking skills can be taught. They do not simply review research critically, as is typically the case in other introductory texts. Instead, they introduce and model a number of critical thinking skills, such as looking for contradictory evidence or alternative explanations; recognizing anecdotal evidence, circular reasoning, hindsight bias, reification, weak analogies, and false dichotomies; evaluating arguments systematically; and working with cumulative and conjunctive probabilities.

The specific skills discussed in the Critical Thinking Applications are listed in the accompanying table, where they are organized into five categories using a taxonomy developed by Halpern (1994). In each chapter, some of these skills are applied to topics and issues related to the chapter's content. For instance, in the chapter that covers drug abuse (Chapter 5), the concept of alcoholism is used to highlight the immense power of definitions and to illustrate how circular reasoning can seem so seductive. Skills that are particularly important may surface in more than one chapter, so students see them applied in a variety of contexts. For example, in Chapter 7 students learn how hindsight bias can contaminate memory, and in Chapter 11 they see how hindsight can distort analyses of personality. Repeated practice across chapters should help students to spontaneously recognize the relevance of specific critical thinking skills when they encounter certain types of information. The skills approach taken to critical thinking and the content it has spawned are unprecedented for an introductory psychology text.

A Didactic Illustration Program

When I first outlined my plans for this text, I indicated that I wanted every aspect of the illustration program to have a genuine didactic purpose and that I wanted to be deeply involved in its development. In retrospect, I had no idea what I was getting myself into, but it has been a rewarding learning experience. In any event, I have been intimately involved in planning every detail of the illustration program. I have endeavored to create a program of figures, diagrams, photos, and tables that work hand in hand with the prose to strengthen and clarify the main points in the text.

The most obvious results of our didactic approach to illustration are the five Illustrated Overviews that combine tabular information, photos, diagrams, and sketches to provide exciting overviews of key ideas in the areas of history, learning, personality theory, psychopathology, and psychotherapy. But I hope you will also notice the subtleties of the illustration program. For instance, diagrams of important concepts (conditioning, synaptic transmission, EEGs, experimental design, and so forth) are often repeated in several chapters (with variations) to highlight connections among research areas and to enhance students' mastery of key ideas. Numerous easy-to-understand graphs of research results underscore psychology's foundation in research, and photos and diagrams often bolster each other (for example, see the treatment of classical conditioning in Chapter 6). Color is used carefully as an organizational device, and visual schematics help simplify hard-to-visualize concepts (see, for instance, the figure explaining reaction range for intelligence in Chapter 8). And in this edition we have strived to enhance the realism and pedagogical value of our drawings of the brain

Taxonomy of Skills Covered in the Critical Thinking Applications

Verbal Reasoning Skills

Understanding the way definitions shape how people think about issues	Chapter 5
Identifying the source of definitions	Chapter 5
Avoiding the nominal fallacy in working with definitions and labels	Chapter 5
Recognizing and avoiding reification	Chapter 8

Argument/Persuasion Analysis Skills

Understanding the elements of an argument	Chapter 9
Recognizing and avoiding common fallacies, such as irrelevant reasons, circular reasoning, slippery slope reasoning, weak analogies, and false dichotomies	Chapters 9 and 10
Evaluating arguments systematically	Chapter 9
Recognizing and avoiding appeals to ignorance	Chapter 8
Understanding how Pavlovian conditioning can be used to manipulate emotions	Chapter 6
Developing the ability to detect conditioning procedures used in the media	Chapter 6
Recognizing social influence strategies	Chapter 15
Judging the credibility of an information source	Chapter 15

Skills in Thinking as Hypothesis Testing

Looking for alternative explanations for findings and events	Chapters 1, 8, and 10
Looking for contradictory evidence	Chapters 1, 3, and 8
Recognizing the limitations of anecdotal evidence	Chapters 2 and 14
Understanding the need to seek disconfirming evidence	Chapter 7
Understanding the limitations of correlational evidence	Chapters 10 and 12
Understanding the limitations of statistical significance	Chapter 12
Recognizing situations in which placebo effects might occur	Chapter 14

Skills in Working with Likelihood and Uncertainty

Utilizing base rates in making predictions and evaluating probabilities	Chapter 12
Understanding cumulative probabilities	Chapter 13
Understanding conjunctive probabilities	Chapter 13
Understanding the limitations of the representativeness heuristic	Chapter 13
Understanding the limitations of the availability heuristic	Chapter 13
Recognizing situations in which regression toward the mean may occur	Chapter 14
Understanding the limits of extrapolation	Chapter 3

Decision-Making and Problem-Solving Skills

Using evidence-based decision making	Chapter 2
Recognizing the bias in hindsight analysis	Chapters 7 and 11
Seeking information to reduce uncertainty	Chapter 12
Making risk-benefit assessments	Chapter 12
Generating and evaluating alternative courses of action	Chapter 12
Recognizing overconfidence in human cognition	Chapter 7
Understanding the limitations and fallibility of human memory	Chapter 7
Understanding how contrast effects can influence judgments and decisions	Chapter 4
Recognizing when extreme comparitors are being used	Chapter 4

and other physiology. All of these efforts have gone toward the service of one master: the desire to make this an inviting book that is easy to learn from.

Integrated Running Glossary

An introductory text should place great emphasis on acquainting students with psychology's technical language—not for the sake of jargon, but because a great many of our key terms are also our cornerstone concepts (for example, *independent variable, reliability,* and *cognitive dissonance*). This text handles terminology with a running glossary embedded in the prose itself. The terms are set off in **blue boldface italics**, and the definitions follow in **blue**, **boldface roman** type. This approach retains the two advantages of a conventional running glossary: vocabulary items are made salient, and their definitions are readily accessible. However, it does so without interrupting the flow of discourse, while eliminating redundancy between text matter and marginal entries.

Concept Checks

To help students assess their mastery of important ideas, Concept Checks are sprinkled throughout the book. In keeping with my goal of making this a book of ideas, the Concept Checks challenge students to apply ideas instead of testing rote memory. For example, in Chapter 6 the reader is asked to analyze realistic examples of conditioning and identify conditioned stimuli and responses, reinforcers, and schedules of reinforcement. Many of the Concept Checks require the reader to put together ideas introduced in different sections of the chapter. For instance, in Chapter 4 students are asked to identify parallels between vision and hearing. Some of the Concept Checks are quite challenging, but students find them engaging and report that the answers (available in Appendix A in the back of the book) are often illuminating.

Preview Questions

To help students identify important ideas, each chapter includes five to eight sets of Preview Questions. Generally speaking, the Preview Questions are found at the beginning of each major section in a chapter, in the margin, adjacent to a level-one heading. Of course, some exceptions to this rule-of-thumb had to be made to accommodate very long or very brief sections under level-one headings. The Preview Questions are short, thought-provoking learning objectives that should help students focus on the key issues in each section.

Practice Tests

Each chapter ends with a 15-item multiple-choice Practice Test that should give students a realistic assessment of their mastery of that chapter and valuable practice taking the type of test that many of them will face in the classroom (if the instructor uses the Test Bank). This feature grew out of some research that I conducted on students' use of textbook pedagogical devices (see Weiten, Guadagno, & Beck, 1996). This research indicated that students pay scant attention to some standard pedagogical devices. When I grilled my students to gain a better undertanding of this finding, it quickly became apparent that students are very pragmatic about pedagogy. Essentially, their refrain was "We want study aids that will help us pass the next test." With this mandate in mind, I devised the Practice Tests. They should be useful, as I took most of the items from Test Banks for previous editions.

In addition to the special features just described, the text includes a variety of more conventional, "tried and true" features as well. The back of the book contains a standard *alphabetical glossary.* Opening *outlines* preview each chapter, and a thorough *review* of *key ideas* appears at the end of each chapter, along with lists of *key terms* (with page numbers indicating where the terms were introduced) and *key people* (important theorists and researchers). I make frequent use of *italics for emphasis,* and I depend on *frequent headings* to maximize organizational clarity. The preface for students describes these pedagogical devices in more detail.

Content

The text is divided into 15 chapters, which follow a traditional ordering. The chapters are not grouped into sections or parts, primarily because such groupings can limit your options if you want to reorganize the order of topics. The chapters are written in a way that facilitates organizational flexibility, as I always assumed that some chapters might be omitted or presented in a different order.

The topical coverage in the text is relatively conventional, but there are some subtle departures from the norm. For instance, Chapter 1 presents a relatively "meaty" discussion of the evolution of ideas in psychology. This coverage of history lays the foundation for many of the crucial ideas emphasized in subsequent chapters. The historical perspective is also my way of reaching out to the students who find that psychology just isn't what they expected it to be. If we want students to contemplate the mysteries of behavior, we must begin by clearing up the biggest mysteries of them all: "Where did these rats, statistics, synapses, and genes come from; what could they possibly have in common; and why doesn't this course bear any resemblance to what I anticipated?" I use history as a vehicle to explain how psychology evolved into its modern form and why misconceptions about its nature are so common.

I also devote an entire chapter (Chapter 2) to the scientific enterprise—not just the mechanics of research methods but the logic behind them. I believe that an appreciation of the nature of empirical evidence can contribute greatly to improving students' critical thinking skills. Ten years from now, many of the "facts" reported in this book will have changed, but an understanding of the methods of science will remain invaluable. An introductory psychology course, by itself, isn't going to make a student think like a scientist, but I can't think of a better place to start the process.

As its title indicates, this book is a condensed version of my introductory text, *Psychology: Themes and Variations*. I have reduced the length of the book from 323,000 words to 239,000 words. How was this reduction in size accomplished? It required a great many difficult decisions, but fortunately, I had excellent advice from a team of professors who served as consultants. About 40% of the reduction came from deleting entire topics, such as psychophysics, mental retardation, blocking in classical conditioning, and so forth. However, the bulk of the reduction was achieved by compressing and simplifying coverage throughout the book. I carefully scrutinized the parent book sentence by sentence and forced myself to justify the existence of every study, every example, every citation, every phrase. The result is a thoroughly *rewritten* text, rather than one that was *reassembled* through "cut and paste" techniques.

Changes in the Seventh Edition

A good textbook must evolve with the field of inquiry it covers. Although the professors and students who used the first six editions of this book did not clamor for alterations, there are some changes. One change consists of the second phase of our systematic effort to improve our drawings of physiology and neuroanatomy throughout the book. Over the course of the last several editions, as we added new physiological drawings from a variety of sources, our anatomical illustrations gradually became less consistent in style than I wanted them to be. To remedy this problem, we secured the services of Fred Harwin, a superb medical illustrator, who redrew all the physiological and neuroanatomical graphics in a consistent (and strikingly beautiful) style. Roughly two-thirds of these new illustrations appeared for the first time in the previous edition, and one-third are making their debut in this edition.

You will also find a variety of other changes in this edition, such as the inclusion of the bulleted lists of Preview Questions, which serve as engaging learning objectives, and a new color treatment of figure citations in the text that should make the book's graphics more salient to students. Also, the old "Putting It in Perspective" sections have been renamed to make their purpose more explicit to students. These sections are now titled "Reflecting on the Chapter's Themes."

Of course, the book has been thoroughly updated to reflect recent advances in the field. One of the exciting things about psychology is that it is not a stagnant discipline. It continues to move forward at what seems a faster and faster pace. This progress has necessitated a host of specific content changes that you'll find sprinkled throughout the chapters. Of the roughly 3000 references cited in the text, over 800 are new to this edition.

PsykTrek: A Multimedia Introduction to Psychology

PsykTrek is a multimedia supplement that will provide students with new opportunities for active learning and reach out to "visual learners" with greatly increased efficacy. *PsykTrek* is intended to give students a second pathway to learning much of the content of introductory psychology. Although it does not cover all of the content of the introductory course, I think you will see that a great many key concepts and principles can be explicated *more effectively* in an interactive audio-visual medium than in a textbook.

PsykTrek consists of four components. The main component is a set of 65 *Interactive Learning Modules* that present the core content of psychology in a whole new way. These tutorials include thousands of graphics, hundred of photos, hundreds of animations, approximately four hours of narration, over 35 carefully selected videos, and about 160 uniquely visual concept checks and quizzes. The *Simulations* allow students to explore complex psychological phenomena in depth. They are highly interactive, experiential demonstrations that will enhance students' appreciation of research methods. A *Multimedia Glossary* allows students to look up over 800 psychological terms, access hundreds of pronunciations of obscure words, and pull up hundreds of related diagrams, photos, and videos. The *Video Selector* allows students to directly access the video segments that are otherwise embedded in the Interactive Learning Modules.

The key strength of *PsykTrek* is its ability to give students new opportunities for active learning outside of the classroom. For example, students can run themselves through re-creations of classic experiments to see the complexities of data collection in action. Or they can play with visual illusions on screen in ways that will make them doubt their own eyes. Or they can stack color filters on screen to demonstrate the nature of subtractive color mixing. *PsykTrek* is intended to supplement and complement *Psychology: Themes & Variations*. For instance, after reading about operant conditioning in the text, a student could work through three interactive tutorials on operant principles, watch three videos (including historic footage of B. F. Skinner shaping a rat), and then try to shape Morphy, the virtual rat, in one of the simulations.

Other Supplementary Materials

The teaching/learning package that has been developed to supplement *Psychology: Themes and Variations, Briefer Version* also includes many other useful tools. The development of all its parts was carefully coordinated so that they are mutually supported.

Concept Charts for Study and Review

To help your students organize and assimilate the main ideas contained in the text, I have created a booklet of Concept Charts. This booklet contains a two-page Concept Chart for each chapter. Each Concept Chart provides a detailed visual map of the key ideas found in the main body of that chapter. These color-coded, hierarchically-organized charts create snapshots of the chapters that should allow your students to quickly see the relationships among ideas and sections.

Study Guide (by Richard Stalling and Ronald Wasden)

For your students, there is an exceptionally thorough *Study Guide* available to help them master the information in the text. It was written by two of my former professors, Richard Stalling and Ronald Wasden of Bradley University. They have over 30 years of experience as a team writing study guides for introductory psychology texts, and their experience is readily apparent in the high-quality materials that they have developed.

The review of key ideas for each chapter is made up of an engaging mixture of matching exercises, fill-in-the-blank items, free-response questions, and programmed learning. Each review is organized around learning objectives that I wrote. The *Study Guide* is closely coordinated with the *Test Bank*, as the same learning objectives guided the construction of the questions in the *Test Bank*. The *Study Guide* also includes a review of key terms, a review of key people, and a self-test for each chapter in the text.

Instructor's Resource Manual (coordinated by Randolph Smith)

A talented roster of professors have contributed to the *Instructor's Resource Manual* (*IRM*) in their respective areas of expertise. The *IRM* was developed under the guidance of Randolph Smith, the editor of the journal *Teaching of Psychology*. It contains a diverse array of materials designed to facilitate efforts to teach the introductory course and includes the following sections.

- The *Instructor's Manual*, by Randolph Smith (Kennesaw State University), contains a wealth of detailed suggestions for lecture topics, class demonstrations, exercises, discussion questions, and suggested readings, organized around the content of each chapter in the text. It also highlights the connections between the text coverage and *PsykTrek* content and features an expanded collection of masters for class handouts.

- *Strategies for Effective Teaching*, by Joseph Lowman (University of North Carolina), discusses practical issues such as what to put in a course syllabus, how to handle the first class meeting, how to cope with large classes, and how to train and organize teaching assistants.

- *AV Media for Introductory Psychology*, by Russ Watson (College of DuPage), provides a comprehensive, up-to-date, critical overview of educational films relevant to the introductory course.

- *The Use of Computers in Teaching Introductory Psychology*, by Susan J. Shapiro (Indiana University–East), offers a thorough listing of computer materials germane to the introductory course and analyzes their strengths and weaknesses.

- *Introducing Writing in Introductory Psychology*, by Dana Dunn (Moravian College), discusses how to work toward enhancing students' writing skills in the context of the introductory course and provides suggestions and materials for specific writing assignments chapter by chapter.

- *Crossing Borders/Contrasting Behaviors: Using Cross-Cultural Comparisons to Enrich the Introductory Psychology Course,* by Ginny Zahn, Bill Hill, and Michael Reiner (Kennesaw State University), discusses the movement toward "internationalizing" the curriculum and provides suggestions for lectures, exercises, and assignments that can add a cross-cultural flavor to the introductory course.
- *Teaching Introductory Psychology with the World Wide Web* by Michael R. Snyder (University of Alberta), discusses how to work Internet assignments into the introductory course and provides a guide to many psychology-related sites on the World Wide Web.
- *Using InfoTrac® College Edition in Introductory Psychology* by Randolph Smith discusses how to make effective use of the *InfoTrac College Edition* subscription that is made available to students with this text. *InfoTrac College Edition* is an online database of recent full-text articles from hundreds of scholarly and popular periodicals.

Test Bank (by Cheryl Hale)

We have assembled a large, diversified, and carefully constructed *Test Bank* revised by Cheryl Hale (Jefferson Community College). The questions are closely tied to the chapter learning objectives and to the lists of key terms and key people found in both the text and the *Study Guide*. The items are categorized as (a) factual, (b) conceptual/applied, (c) integrative, or (d) critical thinking questions. The test bank also includes a separate section that contains about 600 multiple-choice questions based on the content of *PsykTrek's* Interactive Learning Modules. Data on item difficulty are included for many questions.

Computerized Test Items

Electronic versions of the *Test Bank* are available for a variety of computer configurations. The ExamView®

software is user-friendly and allows teachers to insert their own questions and to customize those provided.

Challenging Your Preconceptions: Thinking Critically About Psychology, Second Edition (by Randolph Smith)

This brief paperback book is a wonderful introduction to critical thinking as it applies to psychological issues. Written by Randolph Smith (Kennesaw State University), this book helps students apply their critical thinking skills to a variety of topics, including hypnosis, advertising, misleading statistics, IQ testing, gender differences, and memory bias. Each chapter ends with critical thinking challenges that give students opportunities to practice their critical thinking skills.

Multimedia Manager Instructor's Resource CD-ROM: A Microsoft® PowerPoint® Tool (by Brian Malley, University of Michigan)

This lecture and class preparation tool makes it easy for you to assemble, edit, and present customized, media-enhanced lectures for your course using Microsoft PowerPoint. It includes chapter-specific lecture outlines and art from the text (all on readymade Microsoft PowerPoint slides), as well as video clips and other integrated media. This CD also contains the full Instructor's Resource Manual and the Test Bank.

Book Companion Website: www.thomsonedu.com/ psychology/weiten

This website features teaching and learning resources, including: chapter learning objectives, online tutorial quizzes with multiple-choice, true-false, and fill-in-the-blank questions, web links, flash cards, Critical Thinking Lessons, Concept Checks, InfoTrac® College Edition activities, and more.

> Acknowledgments

Creating an introductory psychology text is a complicated challenge, and a small army of people have contributed to the evolution of this book. Foremost among them are the psychology editors I have worked with at Brooks/Cole and Wadsworth—Claire Verduin, C. Deborah Laughton, Phil Curson, Eileen Murphy, Edith Beard Brady, and Michele Sordi—and the developmental editor for the first edition of this book, John Bergez. They have helped me immeasurably, and each has become a treasured friend along the way. I am especially indebted to Claire, who educated me in the intricacies of textbook publishing, and to John, who has left an enduring imprint on my writing.

The challenge of meeting a difficult schedule in producing this book was undertaken by a talented team of people coordinated by Tom Dorsaneo, who did a superb job of pulling it all together. Credit for the text design goes to Liz Harasymczuk, who was very creative in building on the previous design. Linda Rill handled permissions and photo research with enthusiasm and extraordinary efficiency, and Jackie Estrada did an outstanding job once again in copyediting the manuscript. Fred Harwin and Carol Zuber-Mallison made stellar contributions to the artwork, and the team at Thompson Type efficiently oversaw the composition process.

Several psychologists deserve thanks for the contributions they made to this book. I am grateful to Diane Halpern for her work on the Critical Thinking Applications; to Vinny Hevern for contributing the Web Links; to Marky Lloyd for writing the optional module on careers in psychology, to Frank Landy, Kecia Thomas, and Matthew Harrison for writing the optional module on I/O psychology; to Rick Stalling and Ron Wasden for their work on the *Study Guide;* to Bill Addison and Shirley Hensch for their work on the previous editions of the test bank; to Cheryl Hale for her work on the current edition of the test bank; to Randy Smith, Joseph Lowman, Russ Watson, Dana Dunn, Ginny Zahn, Bill Hill, Michael Reiner, Susan Shapiro, and Michael Snyder for their contributions to the *Instructor's Resource Manual;* to Randy Smith and David Matsumoto for contributing ancillary books; to Jim Calhoun for providing item analysis data for the test items; to Harry Upshaw, Larry Wrightsman, Shari Diamond, Rick Stalling, and Claire Etaugh for their help and guidance over the years; and to the chapter consultants listed on page xviii and the reviewers listed on page ix, who provided insightful and constructive critiques of various portions of the manuscript.

Many other people have also contributed to this project, and I am grateful to all of them for their efforts. Bill Roberts, Craig Barth, Nancy Sjoberg, John Odam, Fiorella Ljunggren, Jim Brace-Thompson, Susan Badger, Sean Wakely, Stephen Rapley, Joanne Terhaar, Marjorie Sanders, Kathryn Stewart, Lori Grebe, and Margaret Parks helped with varied aspects of previous editions. Eve Howard, Vernon Boes, Jennie Redwitz, Kirk Bomont, and Dan Moneypenny made valuable contributions to the current edition. At the College of DuPage, where I taught until 1991, all of my colleagues in psychology provided support and information at one time or another, but I am especially indebted to Barb Lemme, Alan Lanning, Pat Puccio, and Don Green. I also want to thank my former colleagues at Santa Clara University (especially Tracey Kahan, Tom Plante, and Jerry Burger), who were a fertile source of new ideas, and Mike Beede and Jeremy Houska at the University of Nevada–Las Vegas who helped with clerical work.

My greatest debt is to my wife, Beth Traylor, who has been a steady source of emotional sustenance while enduring the rigors of her medical career, and to my son T. J., for making dad laugh all the time.

Wayne Weiten

Chapter Consultants

Chapter 1
David Baker
University of Akron
Charles L. Brewer
Furman University
C. James Goodwin
Wheeling Jesuit University
David Hothersall
Ohio State University
E. R. Hilgard
Stanford University
Michael G. Livingston
St. John's University

Chapter 2
Larry Christensen
Texas A & M University
Francis Durso
University of Oklahoma
Donald H. McBurney
University of Pittsburgh
Wendy Schweigert
Bradley University

Chapter 3
Nelson Freedman
Queen's University at Kingston
Michael W. Levine
University of Illinois, Chicago
James M. Murphy
Indiana University–Purdue University at Indianapolis
Paul Wellman
Texas A & M University

Chapter 4
Nelson Freedman
Queen's University at Kingston
Kevin Jordan
San Jose State University
Michael W. Levine
University of Illinois, Chicago
John Pittenger
University of Arkansas, Little Rock

Lawrence Ward
University of British Columbia
Chrislyn E. Randell
Metropolitan State College of Denver

Chapter 5
Frank Etscorn
New Mexico Institute of Mining and Technology
Tracey L. Kahan
Santa Clara University
Charles F. Levinthal
Hofstra University
Wilse Webb
University of Florida

Chapter 6
A. Charles Catania
University of Maryland
Michael Domjan
University of Texas, Austin
William C. Gordon
University of New Mexico
Barry Schwartz
Swarthmore College
Deborah L. Stote
University of Texas, Austin

Chapter 7
Tracey L. Kahan
Santa Clara University
Ian Neath
Purdue University
Tom Pusateri
Loras College
Stephen K. Reed
San Diego State University
Patricia Tenpenny
Loyola University, Chicago

Chapter 8
John Best
Eastern Illinois University

David Carroll
University of Wisconsin, Superior
Charles Davidshofer
Colorado State University
Shalynn Ford
Teikyo Marycrest University
Tom Pusateri
Loras College
Stephen K. Reed
San Diego State University
Timothy Rogers
University of Calgary
Dennis Saccuzzo
San Diego State University

Chapter 9
Robert Franken
University of Calgary
Russell G. Geen
University of Missouri
Douglas Mook
University of Virginia
D. Louis Wood
University of Arkansas, Little Rock

Chapter 10
Ruth L. Ault
Davidson College
John C. Cavanaugh
University of Delaware
Claire Etaugh
Bradley University
Barbara Hansen Lemme
College of DuPage

Chapter 11
Susan Cloninger
Russell Sage College
Caroline Collins
University of Victoria
Christopher F. Monte
Manhattanville College
Ken Olson
Fort Hays State University

Chapter 12
Robin M. DiMatteo
University of California, Riverside
Jess Feist
McNeese State University
Regan A. R. Gurung
University of Wisconsin, Green Bay
Chris Kleinke
University of Alaska, Anchorage

Chapter 13
David A. F. Haaga
American University
Richard Halgin
University of Massachusetts, Amherst
Chris L. Kleinke
University of Alaska, Anchorage
Elliot A. Weiner
Pacific University

Chapter 14
Gerald Corey
California State University, Fullerton
Herbert Goldenberg
California State University, Los Angeles
Jane S. Halonen
Alverno College
Thomas G. Plante
Santa Clara University

Chapter 15
Jerry M. Burger
Santa Clara University
Stephen L. Franzoi
Marquette University
Donelson R. Forsyth
Virginia Commonwealth University
Cheryl Kaiser
Michigan State University

Reviewers for Briefer Version, 7th Edition

Kate Byerwater
*Grand Rapids Community
College*

Cheryl Camenzuli
Hofstra University

Elaine Cassel
Lord Fairfax Community College

Heather Chabot
New England College

Jennifer Clark
University of North Carolina

Kimberley Duff
Cerritos College

David Eckerman
University of North Carolina

Bob Fletcher
*Truckee Meadows Community
College*

Sheila Kennison
Oklahoma State University

Mark Krause
University of Portland

Marissa McLeod
Santa Fe Community College

Bonnie Nicholson
*University of Southern
Mississippi*

Susan Nolan
Seton Hall University

Caroline Olko
Nassau Community College

Bryan Raudenbush
Wheeling Jesuit University

Vickie Ritts
*St. Louis Community College-
Meramec*

Paul Vonnahme
New Mexico State University

Shelly Watkins
Modesto Junior College

Will Wattendorf
Adirondack Community College

Reviewers for the Previous Briefer Editions

Bart Bare
Caldwell Community College

Mitchell Berman
*University of Southern
Mississippi*

Chris A. Bjornsen
Longwood University

Charles B. Blose
MacMurray College

Frederick Bonato
Saint Peter's College

Edward Brady
Belleville Area College

Kate Byerwalter
*Grand Rapids Community
College*

James F. Calhoun
University of Georgia

Cheryl Camenzuli
Hofstra University

Elaine Cassel
Lord Fairfax Community College

Heather Chabot
New England College

Monica Chakravertti
Mary Washington College

Thomas Collins
Mankato State University

Luis Cordon
*Eastern Connecticut State
University*

Christopher Cronin
Saint Leo University

Robert DaPrato
Solano Community College

Peggy A. DeCooke
Purchase College SUNY

Joan Doolittle
*Anne Arundel Community
College*

Kimberly Duff
Cerritos College

David Eckerman
University of North Carolina

Kenneth Elliott
University of Maine, Augusta

Meredyth Fellows
West Chester University

Bob Fletcher
*Truckee Meadows Community
College*

Christina Frederick
Southern Utah University

Barry Fritz
Quinnipiac College

Ronald Gage-Mosher
Imperial Valley College

Linda Gibbons
Westark College

Richard Griggs
University of Florida

Robert Guttentag
*University of North Carolina,
Greensboro*

Cheryl Hale
Jefferson College

Jane Halonen
James Madison University

Kevin B. Handey
Germanna Community College

Patricia Hinton
Cumberland College

Stephen Hoyer
Pittsburgh State University

Allen I. Huffcutt
Bradley University

Nancy Jackson
Johnson & Wales University

Cindy Kamilar
Pikes Peak Community College

Margaret Karolyi
University of Akron

Sheila Kennison
Oklahoma State University

Mark Krause
University of Portland

Charles F. Levinthal
Hofstra University

Gary Levy
University of Wyoming

Laura Madson
New Mexico State University

Kathleen Malley-Morrison
Boston University

Deborah R. McDonald
New Mexico State University

Marisa McLeod
Santa Fe Community College

Le'Ann Milinder
New England College

Jack J. Mino
Holyoke Community College

Joel Morogovsky
Brookdale Community College

Dirk W. Mosig
*University of Nebraska at
Kearney*

David R. Murphy
Waubonsee Community College

Bonnie J. Nichols
*Mississippi County Community
College*

Bonnie Nicholson
*University of Southern
Mississippi*

Susan Nolan
Seton Hall University

Caroline Olko
Nassau Community College

Gayle Pitman
Sacramento City College

Edward I. Pollack
*West Chester University of
Pennsylvania*

Rose Preciado
Mount San Antonio College

Bryan Raudenbush
Wheeling Jesuit University

Elizabeth A. Rider
Elizabethtown College

Alysia Ritter
Murray State University

Vicki Ritts
*St. Louis Community College,
Meramec*

Jayne Rose
Augustana College

Ana Ruiz
Alvernia College

H. R. Schiffman
Rutgers University

Heide Sedwick
Mount Aloysius College

George Shardlow
City College of San Francisco

Randolph A. Smith
Ouachita Baptist University

Thomas Smith
Vincennes University

James L. Spencer
West Virginia State College

Tim Tomczak
Genesee Community College

Iva Trottier
Concordia College

Travis Tubre
*University of Southern
Mississippi*

Jim Turcott
*Kalamazoo Valley Community
College*

Mary Ann Valentino
Reedley College

Doris C. Vaughn
Alabama State University

Paul Vonnahme
New Mexico State University

Shelly Watkins
Modesto Junior College

Will Wattendorf
Adirondack Community College

Carol Winters-Smith
Bay Path College

Randall Wight
Ouachita Baptist University

Integrated Coverage of Evolutionary Psychology

Integrated Coverage of Cultural Factors

Integrated Coverage of Issues Related to Gender

Integrated Coverage of Neuroscience (in addition to material in Chapter 3)

About Our New Illustration Program

This edition marks the completion of the second phase of a new illustration program for the book's depictions of physiology and neuoranatomy. One of the author's major goals for this program was to enhance the stylistic consistency, realism, and educational clarity of the text's drawings of physiological structures and the human brain. After reviewing many medical illustrators' work, he decided to search for an artist whose work had caught his eye a number of years ago. Thanks to the power of the Internet, he was able to locate Fredric Harwin in Portland, Oregon, where he soon met with him and talked him into contributing his talent and expertise to future editions of *Psychology: Themes & Variations*.

As you will see in the upcoming pages, Harwin brings a unique and strikingly beautiful style to the challenge of illustrating neuroanatomy. *Airbrush Digest* magazine has called Harwin "an author, a teacher, an artist and a scientist—but above all, a man of vision; a visual communicator." *The New England Journal of Medicine* said of his work in the *Manual of Cardiac Surgery*, "The book is blessed with a medical illustrator who is not content with the watchful passivity of a photographer. He obviously shares with his surgical co-authors the 'continuing ability to create and accommodate.'" Featured in *Communication Arts* and on CNN, Harwin's talent and attention to detail have been widely recognized and lauded. He has even been the subject of an award-winning short documentary entitled "Ocularist," which premiered at the 2003 Sundance Film Festival.

Jeanne Koelling, a fellow medical illustrator and associate of Harwin Studios, assisted in this project in all areas, especially the electronic generation of the drawings. The three graphics on this page, which show how one drawing progressed from conceptual sketch to finished product, provide a "behind-the-scenes" look at how these stunning pieces of art were created.

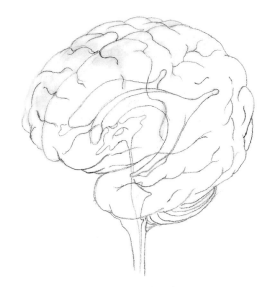

Step 1. Develop conceptual sketch based on the goals of the assignment (show four ventricles of human brain).

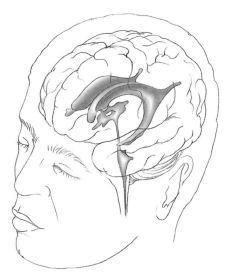

Step 2. Finalize monochromatic drawing based on client's input.

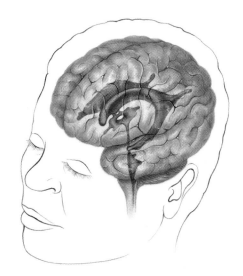

Step 3. Generate color illustration on a double-sided sheet of frosted mylar.

Brief Contents

CHAPTER 1

The Evolution of Psychology 1

© Caroline Schiff/zefa/Corbis

CHAPTER 2

The Research Enterprise in Psychology 32

© Josh Westrich/zefa/Corbis

CHAPTER 3

The Biological Bases of Behavior 62

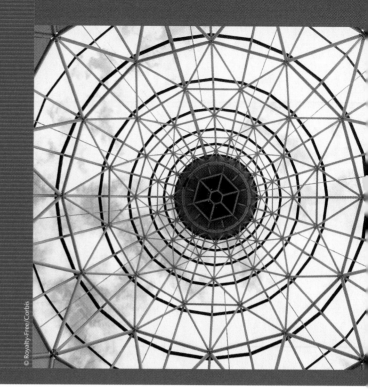

© Royalty-Free/Corbis

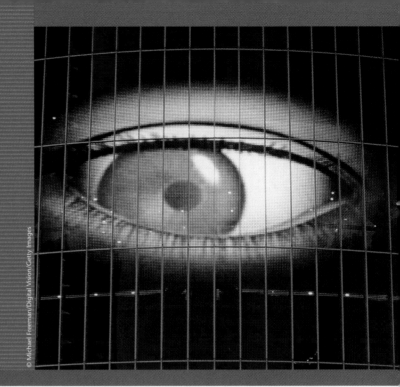
© Michael Freeman/Digital Vision/Getty Images

CHAPTER 4

Sensation and Perception 96

CHAPTER 5

Variations in Consciousness 136

© Nevada Wier/Corbis

© David H. Wells/Corbis

CHAPTER 7

Human Memory 204

© C. Lytle/zefa/Corbis

Cognition and Intelligence 234

© Anderson Ross/Blend Images/Alamy

NOTICE
TO RELEASE OPENED DOOR
FROM HELD POSITION
• OPEN DOOR FULLY
• CLOSE DOOR

UNLAWFUL TO PASS

CHAPTER 9

Motivation and
Emotion 272

© ER Productions/Corbis

CHAPTER (10)

Human Development Across the Life Span 304

© Reza/Webistan/Corbis

Personality:
Theory, Research,
and Assessment 338

© Bryan F. Peterson/Corbis

Stress, Coping, and Health 372

© Alan Schein Photography/Corbis

CHAPTER 13

Psychological Disorders 402

© Klaus Hackenberg/zefa/Corbis

© Dennis Cooper/zefa/Corbis

CHAPTER 15

Social Behavior 466

© Dennis Stock/Magnum Photo

Welcome to your introductory psychology textbook. In most college courses, students spend more time with their textbooks than with their professors, so it helps if students *like* their textbooks. Making textbooks likable, however, is a tricky proposition. By its very nature, a textbook must introduce students to many complicated concepts, ideas, and theories. If it doesn't, it isn't much of a textbook, and instructors won't choose to use it. Nevertheless, in writing this book I've tried to make it as likable as possible without compromising the academic content that your instructor demands. I've especially tried to keep in mind your need for a clear, well-organized presentation that makes the important material stand out and yet is interesting to read. Above all else, I hope you find this book challenging to think about and easy to learn from.

Before you plunge into your first chapter, let me introduce you to the book's key features. Becoming familiar with how the book works will help you to get more out of it.

Key Features

You're about to embark on a journey into a new domain of ideas. Your text includes some important features that are intended to highlight certain aspects of psychology's landscape.

Unifying Themes

To help you make sense of a complex and diverse field of study, I introduce seven themes in Chapter 1 that reappear in a number of variations as we move from chapter to chapter. These unifying themes are meant to provoke thought about important issues and to highlight the connections among chapters. They are discussed at the end of each chapter in a section called "Reflecting on the Chapter's Themes." Icons for the specific themes covered in a chapter appear near the beginning of these sections to help make the book's thematic structure more prominent.

Personal Applications

Toward the end of each chapter you'll find a Personal Application section that shows how psychology is relevant to everyday life. Some of these sections provide concrete, practical advice that could be helpful to you in your educational endeavors, such as those on improving academic performance, improving everyday memory, and achieving self-control. So,

you may want to jump ahead and read some of these Personal Applications early.

Critical Thinking Applications

Each Personal Application is always followed by a two-page Critical Thinking Application that teaches and models basic critical thinking skills. I think you will find that these sections are refreshing and interesting. Like the Personal Applications, they are part of the text's basic content and should be read unless you are told otherwise by your instructor. Although the "facts" of psychology will gradually change after you take this course (thanks to scientific progress), the critical thinking skills modeled in these sections should prove valuable for many years to come.

Web Links

To help make this book a rich resource guide, we have included dozens of Web Links, which are recommended websites that can provide you with additional information on many topics. The recommended sites were selected by Professor Vincent Hevern, who sought out resources that are interesting and that provide accurate, empirically sound information. The Web Links are dispersed throughout the chapters, adjacent to related topical coverage. Because web addresses change frequently, we have *not* placed the URLs for our Web Links in the book. If you are interested in visiting these sites, we recommend that you do so through the *Psychology: Themes & Variations, Briefer Version* home page at the Wadsworth Psychology Study Center website (www.thomsonedu.com/psychology/weiten). Links to all the recommended sites are maintained there, and the Wadsworth Webmaster periodically updates the URLs. Of course, you can also track down the recommended websites by using a search engine, such as Google.

Learning Aids

This text contains a great deal of information. A number of learning aids have been incorporated into the book to help you digest it all.

An *outline* at the beginning of each chapter provides you with an overview of the topics covered in that chapter. Think of the outlines as road maps, and bear in mind that it's easier to reach a destination if you know where you're going.

Headings serve as road signs in your journey through each chapter. Four levels of headings are used to make it easy to see the organization of each chapter.

Preview Questions, found at the beginning of major sections, can help you focus on the key issues in the material you are about to read.

Italics (without boldface) are used liberally throughout the text to emphasize crucial points.

Key terms are identified with ***italicized blue boldface*** type to alert you that these are important vocabulary items that are part of psychology's technical language. The key terms are also listed at the end of the chapter.

An *integrated running glossary* provides an on-the-spot definition of each key term as it's introduced in the text. These formal definitions are printed in **blue boldface** type. Becoming familiar with psychology's terminology is an essential part of learning about the field. The integrated running glossary should make this learning process easier.

Concept Checks are sprinkled throughout the chapters to let you test your mastery of important ideas. Generally, they ask you to integrate or organize a number of key ideas, or to apply ideas to real-world situations. Although they're meant to be engaging and fun, they do check conceptual *understanding,* and some are challenging. But if you get stuck, don't worry; the answers (and explanations, where they're needed) are in the back of the book in Appendix A.

Illustrations in the text are important elements in your complete learning package. Some illustrations provide enlightening diagrams of complicated concepts; others furnish examples that help flesh out ideas or provide concise overviews of research results. Careful attention to the tables and figures in the book will help you understand the material discussed in the text.

A *Chapter Review* at the end of each chapter provides a summary of the chapter's *Key Ideas,* a list of *Key Terms,* and a list of *Key People* (important theorists and researchers). It's wise to read over these review materials to make sure you've digested the information in the chapter. To aid your study efforts, the lists of key terms and key people show the page numbers where the terms or individuals were first introduced in the chapter.

Each chapter ends with a 15-item *Practice Test* that should give you a realistic assessment of your mastery of that chapter and valuable practice in taking multiple-choice tests.

An *alphabetical glossary* is provided in the back of the book. Most key terms are formally defined in the integrated running glossary only when they are first introduced. So if you run into a technical term a second time and can't remember its meaning, it may be easier to look it up in the alphabetical glossary.

A Few Footnotes

Psychology textbooks customarily identify the studies, theoretical treatises, books, and articles that information comes from. These *citations* occur (1) when names are followed by a date in parentheses, as in "Smith (2004) found that . . ." or (2) when names and dates are provided together within parentheses, as in "In one study (Smith, Miller, & Jones, 2005), the researchers attempted to . . ." All of the cited publications are listed by author in the alphabetized *References* section in the back of the book. The citations and references are a necessary part of a book's scholarly and scientific foundation. Practically speaking, however, you'll probably want to glide right over them as you read. You definitely don't need to memorize the names and dates. The only names you may need to know are the handful listed under Key People in each Chapter Review (unless your instructor mentions a favorite that you should know).

Concept Charts for Study and Review

Your text should be accompanied by a booklet of Concept Charts that are designed to help you organize and master the main ideas contained in each chapter. Each Concept Chart provides a detailed visual map of the key ideas found in the main body of that chapter. Seeing how it all fits together should help you to better understand each chapter. You can use these charts to preview chapters, to double-check your mastery of chapter content, and to memorize the crucial ideas in chapters.

PsykTrek: A Multimedia Introduction to Psychology

PsykTrek is a multimedia resource developed to accompany this textbook. It is an enormously powerful learning tool that can enhance your understanding of many complex processes and theories, provide you with an alternative way to assimilate many crucial concepts, and add a little more fun to your journey through introductory psychology. *PsykTrek* has been designed to supplement and complement your textbook. I strongly encourage you to use it. The CD icons that you will see in many of the headings in the upcoming chapters refer to the content of *PsykTrek*. An icon indicates that the textbook topic referred to in the heading is covered in the Interactive Learning Modules or Simulations found on *PsykTrek*. The relevant simulations (Sim1, Sim2, and so forth) and the relevant Interactive Learning Modules (1a, 1b, 1c, and so forth) are listed to the right of the icons.

A Word About the Study Guide

A *Study Guide* is available to accompany this text. It was written by two of my former professors, who introduced me to psychology years ago. They have done a great job of organizing review materials to help you master the information in the book. I suggest that you seriously consider using it to help you study.

A Final Word

I'm pleased to be a part of your first journey into the world of psychology, and I sincerely hope that you'll find the book as thought provoking and as easy to learn from as I've tried to make it. If you have any comments or advice on the book, please write to me in care of the publisher (Thomson Wadsworth, 10 Davis Drive, Belmont, CA 94002). You can be sure I'll pay careful attention to your feedback. Finally, let me wish you good luck. I hope you enjoy your course and learn a great deal.

Wayne Weiten

CHAPTER ①

The Evolution of Psychology

© Caroline Schiff/zefa/Corbis

What is psychology, and why is it worth your time to study? Let me approach these questions by sharing a couple of stories with you.

In 2005, Greg Hogan, a college sophomore, briefly achieved national notoriety when he was arrested for a crime. Greg wasn't anybody's idea of a likely criminal. He was the son of a Baptist minister and the president of his class. He played cello in the university orchestra. He even worked part-time in the chaplain's office. So it shocked everybody who knew Greg when police arrested him at his fraternity house for bank robbery.

It seems that Greg had faked having a gun and made away with over $2800 from a local bank. His reason? Over a period of months he had lost $5000 playing poker on the Internet. His lawyer said Greg's gambling habit had become "an addiction" (Dissell, 2005; McLoughlin & Paquet, 2005).

Greg ended up entering a clinic for treatment of his gambling problem. In a way, he was lucky—at least he got help. Moshe Pergament, a 19-year-old community college student in Long Island, New York, wasn't so fortunate. Moshe was shot to death after brandishing a gun at a police officer. Moshe's

gun turned out to be plastic. On the front seat of his car was a note that began, "Officer, it was a plan. I'm sorry to get you involved. I just needed to die." Moshe had just lost $6000 betting on the World Series. His death was what people in law enforcement call "suicide by cop" (Lindsay & Lester, 2004).

These stories are at the extreme edge of a trend that concerns many public officials and mental health professionals: The popularity of gambling—from lotteries to sports betting to online poker—is booming, especially among the young (D. Jacobs, 2004). College students seem to be leading the way. To some observers, gambling on college campuses has become an "epidemic" (Koch, 2005). Student bookies on some campuses make tens of thousands of dollars a year taking sports bets from other students. TV shows like *The World Series of Poker* are marketed squarely at college-student audiences. Poker sites on the web invite students to win their tuition by gambling online.

For most people, gambling is a relatively harmless—if sometimes expensive—pastime. However, estimates suggest that 5 or 6 percent of teens and young adults develop serious problems with gambling—two to four times the rate of older adults (Jacobs, 2004; Petry, 2005; Winters et al., 2004). The enormous growth of pathological gambling among young people raises a host of questions. Is gambling dangerous? Can it really be addictive? What is an

The perplexing problem of pathological gambling, which has increased dramatically among college students in recent years, raises a host of complicated questions. As you will see throughout this text, psychologists investigate an infinite variety of fascinating questions.

addiction, anyway? If pathological gamblers abuse drugs or commit crimes, is gambling the cause of their troubles, or is it a symptom of a deeper problem? Perhaps most critically of all, why do some people become pathological gamblers, while the great majority do not? Every day millions of people in the United States play the lottery, bet on sports, or visit casinos without apparent harm. Yet others can't seem to stop gambling until they have lost everything—their savings, their jobs, their homes, and their self-respect. Why? What causes such perplexing, self-destructive behavior?

Psychology is about questions like these. More generally, psychology is about understanding *all* the things we do. All of us wonder sometimes about the reasons underlying people's behavior—why it's hard to diet, why we procrastinate about studying, why we fall in love with one person rather than another. We wonder why some people are outgoing while others are shy. We wonder why we sometimes do things that we know will bring us pain and anguish, whether it's clinging to a destructive relationship or losing our tuition money in a game of Texas hold 'em. The study of psychology is about all these things, and infinitely more.

Many of psychology's questions have implications for our everyday lives. For me, this is one of the field's major attractions—*psychology is practical*. Consider the case of gambling. Pathological gamblers suffer all kinds of misery, yet they can't seem to stop. Listen to the anguish of a gambler named Steve: "Over the past two years I have lost literally thousands . . . I have attempted to give up time after time after time, but failed every time. . . . I have debts around my neck which are destroying mine and my family's life. . . . I just want a massive light to be turned on with a message saying, 'This way to your old life, Steve'" (SJB, 2006).

What is the best way to help someone like Steve? Should he join a group like Gamblers Anonymous? Would counseling work? Are there drugs that can help? By probing the whys and hows of human behavior, psychology can help us find answers to pressing questions like these, as well as better understand issues that affect each of us every day. You will see the practical side of psychology throughout this book, especially in the Personal Applications at the ends of chapters. These Applications focus on everyday problems, such as coping more effectively with stress, improving self-control, and dealing with sleep difficulties.

Beyond its practical value, psychology is worth studying because it provides a powerful *way of thinking*. All of us make judgments every day about why

people do the things they do. For example, we might think that pathological gamblers are weak-willed, or irrational, or just too dumb to understand that the odds are stacked against them. Or we might believe they are in the grip of an addiction that simply overpowers them. How do we decide which of these judgments—if any—are right?

Psychologists are committed to investigating questions about human behavior in a scientific way. This means that they seek to formulate precise questions about behavior and then test possible answers through systematic observation. This commitment to testing ideas means that psychology provides a way of building knowledge that is relatively accurate and dependable. It also provides a model for assessing the assertions we hear every day about behavior, as you'll see in upcoming chapters' Critical Thinking Applications.

In the case of gambling, for example, researchers have designed careful studies to probe the relationship of gambling problems to any number of possible influences, from childhood experiences to membership in a college fraternity. They have compared the way slot machines are set to reward players with frequent small payoffs to the way rats and pigeons learn to earn food rewards in the laboratory. They have used state-of-the-art scanners to image the brains of people performing tasks similar to placing bets. They have even looked at whether some people are predisposed by their genes to develop problems with gambling (Petry, 2005; Rockey et al., 2005, Szegedy-Maszak, 2005).

If there is one clear conclusion that emerges from these studies, it is that there is no simple answer to the mystery of pathological gambling. Instead, a full explanation of gambling problems will likely involve many influences that interact in complex ways (Derevensky & Gupta, 2004; Petry, 2005). As you'll see throughout this course, the same is true of most aspects of behavior. In my opinion, this is yet another reason to study psychology: It teaches us a healthy respect for the *complexity* of behavior. In a world that could use more understanding—and compassion—this can be an invaluable lesson.

As you go through this course, I hope you'll come to share my enthusiasm for psychology as a fascinating and immensely practical field of study. Let's begin our exploration by seeing how psychology has evolved from early speculations about behavior to a modern science. By looking at this evolution, you'll better understand psychology as it is today, a sprawling, multifaceted science and profession. We'll conclude our introduction with a look at seven unifying themes that will serve as connecting threads in the chapters to come. The chapter's Personal Application will review research that provides insights into how to be an effective student. Finally, the Critical Thinking Application will discuss how critical thinking skills can be enhanced.

> From Speculation to Science: How Psychology Developed

Psychology's story is one of people groping toward a better understanding of themselves. As psychology has evolved, its focus, methods, and explanatory models have changed. Let's look at how psychology has developed from philosophical speculations about the mind into a modern behavioral science.

The term *psychology* comes from two Greek words, *psyche*, meaning the soul, and *logos*, referring to the study of a subject. These two Greek roots were first put together to define a topic of study in the 16th century, when *psyche* was used to refer to the soul, spirit, or mind, as distinguished from the body (Boring, 1966). Not until the early 18th century did the term *psychology* gain more than rare usage among scholars. By that time it had acquired its literal meaning, "the study of the mind."

Of course, people have always wondered about the mysteries of the mind. To take just one example, in ancient Greece the philosopher Aristotle engaged in intriguing conjecture about thinking, intelligence, motives, and emotions in his work *Peri Psyches (About the Soul)*. Philosophical speculation about psychological issues is as old as the human race. But it was only in the late 19th century that psychology emerged as a scientific discipline.

A New Science Is Born

1a

Psychology's intellectual parents were the disciplines of *philosophy* and *physiology*. By the 1870s a small number of scholars in both fields were actively exploring questions about the mind. How are bodily sensations turned into a mental awareness of the outside world? Are our perceptions of the world accurate reflections of reality? How do mind and body interact? The philosophers and physiologists who were interested in the mind viewed such questions as fascinating issues *within* their respective fields. It was a German professor, Wilhelm Wundt (1832–1920), who eventually changed this view. Wundt mounted a campaign to make psychology an independent discipline rather than a stepchild of philosophy or physiology.

The time and place were right for Wundt's appeal. German universities were in a healthy period of expansion, so resources were available for new disciplines. Furthermore, the intellectual climate favored the scientific approach that Wundt advocated. Hence, his proposals were well received by the academic community. In 1879 Wundt succeeded in establishing the first formal laboratory for research in psychology at the University of Leipzig. In recognition of this landmark event, historians have christened 1879 as psychology's "date of birth." Soon after, in 1881, Wundt established the first journal devoted to publishing research on psychology. All in all, Wundt's campaign was so successful that today he is widely characterized as the founder of psychology.

Wundt's conception of psychology dominated the field for two decades and was influential for several more. Borrowing from his training in physiology, Wundt (1874) declared that the new psychology should be a science modeled after fields such as physics and chemistry. What was the subject matter of the new science? According to Wundt, it was *consciousness*—the awareness of immediate experience. *Thus, psychology became the scientific study of conscious experience.* This orientation kept psychology focused squarely on the mind. But it demanded that the methods used to investigate the mind be as scientific as those of chemists or physicists.

Wundt was a tireless, dedicated scholar who generated an estimated 54,000 pages of books and articles in his career (Bringmann & Balk, 1992). Studies in his laboratory focused on attention, memory, sensory processes, and reaction-time experiments that provided estimates of the duration of various mental processes (Fuchs & Milar, 2003). His hard work and provocative ideas soon attracted attention. Many outstanding young scholars came to Leipzig to study under Wundt. Many of his students then fanned out around the world, establishing laboratories that formed the basis for the new, independent science of psychology. The growth of this new science was particularly rapid in North America, where some 23 new psychological research laboratories sprang up between 1883 and 1893 at the universities shown in

PREVIEW QUESTIONS

- What were Wundt's key ideas and accomplishments?
- What were the chief tenets of structuralism and functionalism?
- What did Freud have to say about the unconscious and sexuality, and why were his ideas so controversial?
- What basic principle of behavior did Skinner emphasize?
- What did Skinner do to stir up controversy?
- What was the impetus for the emergence of humanism?

**WILHELM WUNDT
1832–1920**

"Physiology informs us about those life phenomena that we perceive by our external senses. In psychology, the person looks upon himself as from within and tries to explain the interrelations of those processes that this internal observation discloses."

Figure 1.1

Early research laboratories in North America. This map highlights the location and year of founding for the first 23 psychological research labs established in North American colleges and universities. Many of these labs were founded by the students of Wilhelm Wundt. (Based on Benjamin, 2000)

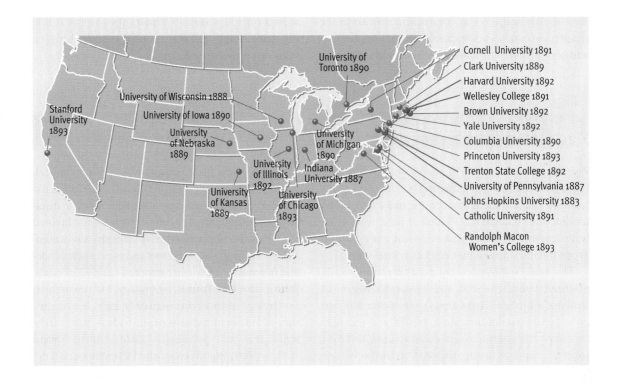

Web Link 1.1

Mind and Body: René Descartes to William James
Designed originally to celebrate psychology's first century as an independent discipline, this online exhibition traces three historical themes: the mind–body problem posed in the 17th century by philosopher René Descartes, the rise of experimental psychology, and the beginnings of psychology in America. **Note: The URLs (addresses) for the Web Links can be found on the website for this text (www.thomsonedu.com/psychology/weiten), or you can find them using a search engine such as Google.**

Figure 1.1 (Benjamin, 2000). Although psychology was born in Germany, it blossomed into adolescence in North America. Like many adolescents, however, the young science was about to enter a period of turbulence and turmoil.

The Battle of the "Schools" Begins: Structuralism Versus Functionalism

1a

When you read about how psychology became a science, you might have imagined that psychologists became a unified group of scholars who busily added new discoveries to an uncontested store of "facts." In reality, no science works that way. Competing schools of thought exist in most scientific disciplines. Sometimes the disagreements among these schools are sharp. Such diversity in thought is natural and often stimulates enlightening debate. In psychology, the first two major schools of thought, *structuralism* and *functionalism,* were entangled in the first great intellectual battle in the field.

Structuralism emerged through the leadership of Edward Titchener, an Englishman who emigrated to the United States in 1892 and taught for decades at Cornell University. Although Titchener earned his degree in Wundt's Leipzig laboratory and expressed great admiration for Wundt's work, he brought his own version of Wundt's psychology to America (Hilgard, 1987; Thorne & Henley, 1997). *Structuralism*

was based on the notion that the task of psychology is to analyze consciousness into its basic elements and investigate how these elements are related. Just as physicists were studying how matter is made up of basic particles, the structuralists wanted to identify the fundamental components of conscious experience, such as sensations, feelings, and images.

Although the structuralists explored many questions, most of their work concerned sensation and perception in vision, hearing, and touch. To examine the contents of consciousness, the structuralists depended on the method of *introspection,* or the careful, systematic self-observation of one's own conscious experience. As practiced by the structuralists, introspection required training to make the *subject*—the person being studied—more objective and more aware. Once trained, participants were typically exposed to auditory tones, optical illusions, and visual stimuli such as pieces of fruit and were asked to analyze what they experienced.

The functionalists took a different view of psychology's task. *Functionalism* was based on the belief that psychology should investigate the function or purpose of consciousness, rather than its structure. The chief architect of functionalism was William James (1842–1910), a brilliant American scholar (and brother of novelist Henry James). James's formal training was in medicine. However, he was too sickly to pursue a medical practice (he couldn't imagine standing all day long), so he joined the faculty of Harvard University to pursue a less grueling career

(Ross, 1991). Medicine's loss proved to be a boon for psychology, as James quickly became an intellectual giant in the field. James's landmark book, *Principles of Psychology* (1890), became standard reading for generations of psychologists and is perhaps the most influential text in the history of psychology (Weiten & Wight, 1992).

James's thinking illustrates how psychology, like any field, is deeply embedded in a network of cultural and intellectual influences. James had been impressed with Charles Darwin's (1859, 1871) theory of *natural selection.* According to the principle of **natural selection, inherited characteristics that provide a survival or reproductive advantage are more likely than alternative characteristics to be passed on to subsequent generations and thus come to be "selected" over time.** This cornerstone notion of Darwin's evolutionary theory suggested that the typical characteristics of a species must serve some purpose. Applying this idea to humans, James (1890) noted that consciousness obviously is an important characteristic of our species. Hence, he contended

that psychology should investigate the *functions* rather than the *structure* of consciousness.

James also argued that the structuralists' approach missed the real nature of conscious experience. Consciousness, he argued, consists of a continuous *flow* of thoughts. In analyzing consciousness into its "elements," the structuralists were looking at static points in that flow. James wanted to understand the flow itself, which he called the "stream of consciousness."

Whereas structuralists naturally gravitated to the laboratory, functionalists were more interested in how people adapt their behavior to the demands of the real world around them. This practical slant led them to introduce new subjects into psychology. Instead of focusing on sensation and perception, functionalists such as G. Stanley Hall, James McKeen Cattell, and John Dewey began to investigate mental testing, patterns of development in children, the effectiveness of educational practices, and behavioral differences between the sexes. These new topics may have played a role in attracting the first women into the field of psychology (see **Figure 1.2**).

WILLIAM JAMES 1842–1910

"It is just this free water of consciousness that psychologists resolutely overlook."

Mary Whiton Calkins (1863–1930)

Mary Calkins, who studied under William James, founded one of the first dozen psychology laboratories in America at Wellesley College in 1891, invented a widely used technique for studying memory, and became the first woman to serve as president of the American Psychological Association in 1905. Ironically, however, she never received her Ph.D. in psychology. Because she was a woman, Harvard University only reluctantly allowed her to take graduate classes as a "guest student." When she completed the requirements for her Ph.D., Harvard would only offer her a doctorate from its undergraduate sister school, Radcliffe. Calkins felt that this decision perpetuated unequal treatment of the sexes, so she refused the Radcliffe degree.

Margaret Floy Washburn (1871–1939)

Margaret Washburn was the first woman to receive a Ph.D. in psychology. She wrote an influential book, *The Animal Mind* (1908), which served as an impetus to the subsequent emergence of behaviorism and was standard reading for several generations of psychologists. In 1921 she became the second woman to serve as president of the American Psychological Association. Washburn studied under James McKeen Cattell at Columbia University, but like Mary Calkins, she was only permitted to take graduate classes unofficially, as a "hearer." Hence, she transferred to Cornell University, which was more hospitable toward women, and completed her doctorate in 1894. Like Calkins, Washburn spent most of her career at a college for women (Vassar).

Leta Stetter Hollingworth (1886–1939)

Leta Hollingworth did pioneering work on adolescent development, mental retardation, and gifted children. Indeed, she was the first person to use the term *gifted* to refer to youngsters who scored exceptionally high on intelligence tests. Hollingworth (1914, 1916) also played a major role in debunking popular theories of her era that purported to explain why women were "inferior" to men. For instance, she conducted a study refuting the myth that phases of the menstrual cycle are reliably associated with performance decrements in women. Her careful collection of objective data on gender differences forced other scientists to subject popular, untested beliefs about the sexes to skeptical, empirical inquiry.

Figure 1.2
Women pioneers in the history of psychology. Women have long made major contributions to the development of psychology (Milar, 2000; Russo & Denmark, 1987), and today nearly half of all psychologists are female. As in other fields, however, women have often been overlooked in histories of psychology (Furumoto & Scarborough, 1986). The three psychologists profiled here demonstrate that women have been making significant contributions to psychology almost from its beginning—despite formidable barriers to pursuing their academic careers.

Photos courtesy of the Archives of the History of American Psychology, University of Akron, Akron, Ohio

The impassioned advocates of structuralism and functionalism saw themselves as fighting for high stakes: the definition and future direction of the new science of psychology. Their war of ideas continued energetically for many years. Who won? Most historians give the edge to functionalism. Although the structuralists can be credited with strengthening psychology's commitment to laboratory research, functionalism left a more enduring imprint on psychology. Indeed, Buxton (1985) has remarked that "nowadays no one is called a functionalist in psychology, and yet almost every psychologist is one" (p. 138). Functionalism eventually faded as a school of thought, but its practical orientation fostered the development of two important descendants—behaviorism and applied psychology—that we will discuss momentarily.

Freud Brings the Unconscious into the Picture

Sigmund Freud (1856–1939) was an Austrian physician who early in his career dreamed of achieving fame by making an important discovery. His determination was such that in medical school he dissected 400 male eels to prove for the first time that they had testes. His work with eels did not make him famous, but his subsequent work with people did. Indeed, his theories made him one of the most influential—and controversial—intellectual figures of modern times.

Freud's (1900, 1933) approach to psychology grew out of his efforts to treat mental disorders. In his medical practice, Freud treated people troubled by psychological problems such as irrational fears, obsessions, and anxieties with an innovative procedure he called *psychoanalysis* (described in detail in Chapter 14). Decades of experience probing into his patients' lives provided much of the inspiration for Freud's theory. He also gathered material by looking inward and examining his own anxieties, conflicts, and desires.

His work with patients and his own self-exploration persuaded Freud of the existence of what he called the *unconscious*. According to Freud, **the unconscious contains thoughts, memories, and desires that are well below the surface of conscious awareness but that nonetheless exert great influence on behavior.** Freud based his concept of the unconscious on a variety of observations. For instance, he noticed that seemingly meaningless slips of the tongue (such as "I decided to take a summer school curse") often appeared to reveal a person's true feelings. He also noted that his patients' dreams often seemed to express important feelings that they were unaware of. Knitting these and other observations together, Freud eventually concluded that psychological disturbances are largely caused by personal conflicts existing at an unconscious level. More generally, his *psychoanalytic theory* attempts to explain personality, motivation, and mental disorders by focusing on unconscious determinants of behavior.

Freud's concept of the unconscious was not entirely new (Rieber, 1998). However, it was a major departure from the prevailing belief that people are fully aware of the forces governing their behavior. In arguing that behavior is governed by unconscious forces, Freud made the disconcerting suggestion that people are not masters of their own minds. Other aspects of Freud's theory also stirred up debate. For instance, he proposed that behavior is greatly influenced by how people cope with their sexual urges. At a time when people were far less comfortable discussing sexual issues than they are today, even scientists were offended and scandalized by Freud's emphasis on sex. Small wonder, then, that Freud was soon engulfed in controversy.

In part because of their controversial nature, Freud's ideas gained influence only very slowly. By 1920 psychoanalytic theory was widely known around the world, but it continued to meet with considerable resistance in psychology (Fancher, 2000). Why? The main reason was that it conflicted with the spirit of the times in psychology. Many psychologists were becoming uncomfortable with their focus on conscious experience and were turning to the less murky subject of observable behavior. If they felt that conscious experience was inaccessible to scientific observation, you can imagine how they felt about trying to study *unconscious* experience. Most psychologists viewed psychoanalytic theory as unscientific speculation that would eventually fade away (Hornstein, 1992).

They turned out to be wrong. Psychoanalytic ideas steadily gained acceptance around the world, influencing thought in medicine, the arts, and literature (Rieber, 1998). Then, in the 1930s and 1940s, more and more psychologists found themselves becoming interested in areas Freud had studied: personality, motivation, and abnormal behavior. As they turned to these topics, many of them saw merit in some of Freud's notions (Rosenzweig, 1985). Although psychoanalytic theory continued to generate heated debate, it survived to become an influential theoretical perspective. Today, many psychoanalytic concepts have filtered into the mainstream of psychology (Westen, 1998).

SIGMUND FREUD
1856–1939

"The unconscious is the true psychical reality; in its innermost nature it is as much unknown to us as the reality of the external world."

Understanding the Implications of Major Theories: Wundt, James, and Freud

Check your understanding of the implications of some of the major theories reviewed in this chapter by indicating who is likely to have made each of the statements quoted below. Choose from the following theorists: (a) Wilhelm Wundt, (b) William James, and (c) Sigmund Freud. You'll find the answers in Appendix A in the back of the book.

_____ **1.** "He that has eyes to see and ears to hear may convince himself that no mortal can keep a secret. If the lips are silent, he chatters with his fingertips; betrayal oozes out of him at every pore. And thus the task of making conscious the most hidden recesses of the mind is one which it is quite possible to accomplish."

_____ **2.** "The book which I present to the public is an attempt to mark out a new domain of science. . . . The new discipline rests upon anatomical and physiological foundations. . . . The experimental treatment of psychological problems must be pronounced from every point of view to be in its first beginnings."

_____ **3.** "Consciousness, then, does not appear to itself chopped up in bits. Such words as 'chain' or 'train' do not describe it fitly. . . . It is nothing jointed; it flows. A 'river' or 'stream' are the metaphors by which it is most naturally described."

Watson Alters Psychology's Course as Behaviorism Makes Its Debut

 1a, 5b

The debate between structuralism and functionalism was only the prelude to other fundamental controversies in psychology. In the early 1900s, another major school of thought appeared that dramatically altered the course of psychology. Founded by John B. Watson (1878–1958), *behaviorism is a theoretical orientation based on the premise that scientific psychology should study only observable behavior.* It is important to understand what a radical change this definition represents. Watson (1913, 1919) was proposing that psychologists *abandon the study of consciousness altogether* and focus exclusively on behaviors that they could observe directly. In essence, he was redefining what scientific psychology should be about.

Why did Watson argue for such a fundamental shift in direction? Because to him, the power of the scientific method rested on the idea of *verifiability.* In principle, scientific claims can always be verified (or disproved) by anyone who is able and willing to make the required observations. However, this power depends on studying things that can be observed objectively. Otherwise, the advantage of using the scientific approach—replacing vague speculation and personal opinion with reliable, exact knowledge—is lost. For Watson, mental processes were not a proper subject for scientific study because they are ultimately private events. After all, no one can see or touch another's thoughts. Consequently, if psychol-

ogy was to be a science, it would have to give up consciousness as its subject matter and become instead the *science of behavior.*

Behavior **refers to any overt (observable) response or activity by an organism.** Watson asserted that psychologists could study anything that people do or say—shopping, playing chess, eating, complimenting a friend—but they could *not* study scientifically the thoughts, wishes, and feelings that might accompany these behaviors. Obviously, psychology's shift away from the study of consciousness was fundamentally incompatible with psychoanalytic theory. By the 1920s Watson had become an outspoken critic of Freud's views (Rilling, 2000). Behaviorism and psychoanalysis would go on to have many heated theoretical debates in the ensuing decades.

Watson's radical reorientation of psychology did not end with his redefinition of its subject matter. He also took an extreme position on one of psychology's oldest and most fundamental questions: the issue of *nature versus nurture.* This age-old debate is concerned with whether behavior is determined mainly by genetic inheritance ("nature") or by environment and experience ("nurture"). To oversimplify, the question is this: Is a great concert pianist or a master criminal born, or made?

Watson argued that each is made, not born. He discounted the importance of heredity, maintaining that behavior is governed entirely by the environment. Indeed, he boldly claimed:

Give me a dozen healthy infants, well-formed, and my own special world to bring them up in and I'll guarantee

**JOHN B. WATSON
1878–1958**

"The time seems to have come when psychology must discard all references to consciousness."

Web Link 1.2

History & Philosophy of Psychology Web Resources
Professor Christopher Green of York University in Canada has assembled a wide range of web-based materials relating to psychology's theoretical and historical past, including a collection of sites focused on specific individuals. Web pages devoted to key figures mentioned in this chapter (such as Mary Whiton Calkins, William James, B. F. Skinner, and Margaret Floy Washburn) can be accessed here.

B. F. SKINNER 1904–1990

"I submit that what we call the behavior of the human organism is no more free than its digestion."

to take any one at random and train him to become any type of specialist I might select—doctor, lawyer, artist, merchant-chief, and yes, even beggar-man and thief, regardless of his talents, penchants, tendencies, abilities, vocations and race of his ancestors. I am going beyond my facts and I admit it, but so have the advocates of the contrary and they have been doing it for many thousands of years. (1924, p. 82)

For obvious reasons, Watson's tongue-in-cheek challenge was never put to a test. Although this widely cited quote overstated and oversimplified Watson's views on the nature-nurture issue (Todd & Morris, 1992), his writings contributed to the environmental slant that became associated with behaviorism (Horowitz, 1992).

Despite meeting with resistance and skepticism in some quarters, Watson's behavioral point of view gradually took hold (Samelson, 1981, 1994). Actually, psychology had already been edging away from the study of consciousness toward the study of behavior for two decades before Watson's influential campaign (Leahey, 1992). Among other things, this gradual transition to the study of behavior contributed to the rise of animal research in psychology. Having deleted consciousness from their scope of concern, behaviorists no longer needed to study human subjects who could report on their mental processes. Many psychologists thought that animals would make better research subjects anyway. One key reason was that experimental research is often more productive if experimenters can exert considerable *control* over their subjects. Otherwise, too many complicating factors enter into the picture and contaminate the experiment. Obviously, a researcher can exert much more control over a laboratory rat or pigeon than over a human subject, who arrives at a lab with years of uncontrolled experience and who will probably insist on going home at night. Thus, the discipline that had begun its life a few decades earlier as the study of the mind now found itself heavily involved in the study of simple responses made by laboratory animals.

Skinner Questions Free Will as Behaviorism Flourishes 1a, 10b

The advocates of behaviorism and psychoanalysis tangled frequently during the 1920s, 1930s, and 1940s. As psychoanalytic thought slowly gained a foothold within psychology, many psychologists softened their stance on the acceptability of studying internal mental events. However, this movement toward the consideration of internal states was dra-

matically reversed in the 1950s by the work of B. F. Skinner (1904–1990), one of the most influential of all American psychologists. In response to the softening in the behaviorist position, Skinner (1953) championed a return to Watson's strict stimulus-response approach. Skinner did not deny the existence of internal mental events. However, he insisted that they could not be studied scientifically. Moreover, he maintained, there was no need to study them. According to Skinner, if the stimulus of food is followed by the response of eating, we can fully describe what is happening without making any guesses about whether the animal is experiencing hunger. Like Watson, Skinner also emphasized how environmental factors mold behavior. Although he repeatedly acknowledged that an organism's behavior is influenced by its biological endowment, he argued that psychology could understand and predict behavior adequately without resorting to physiological explanations (Delprato & Midgley, 1992).

The fundamental principle of behavior documented by Skinner is deceptively simple: *Organisms tend to repeat responses that lead to positive outcomes, and they tend not to repeat responses that lead to neutral or negative outcomes.* Despite its simplicity, this principle turns out to be quite powerful. Working primarily with laboratory rats and pigeons, Skinner showed that he could exert remarkable control over the behavior of animals by manipulating the outcomes of their responses. He was even able to train animals to perform unnatural behaviors. For example, he once trained some pigeons to play a respectable version of table tennis (they pecked the ball back and forth on the Ping Pong table). Skinner's followers eventually showed that the principles uncovered in their animal research could be applied to complex human behaviors as well. Behavioral principles are now widely used in factories, schools, prisons, mental hospitals, and a variety of other settings.

Skinner's ideas had repercussions that went far beyond the debate among psychologists about what they should study. Skinner spelled out the full implications of his findings in his book *Beyond Freedom and Dignity* (1971). There he asserted that all behavior is fully governed by external stimuli. In other words, your behavior is determined in predictable ways by lawful principles, just as the flight of an arrow is governed by the laws of physics. Thus, if you believe that your actions are the result of conscious decisions, you're wrong. According to Skinner, we are all controlled by our environment, not by ourselves. In short, Skinner arrived at the conclusion that *free will is an illusion.*

As you can readily imagine, such a disconcerting view of human nature was not universally acclaimed.

Copyright © 1971 Time Inc. Reprinted by permission. Getty Images

B. F. Skinner created considerable controversy when he asserted that free will is an illusion.

Like Freud, Skinner was the target of harsh criticism. Much of this criticism stemmed from misinterpretations of his ideas that were reported in the popular press (Rutherford, 2000). Despite the controversy, however, behaviorism flourished as the dominant school of thought in psychology during the 1950s and 1960s (Gilgen, 1982).

The Humanists Revolt

1a, 10c

By the 1950s behaviorism and psychoanalytic theory had become the most influential schools of thought in psychology. However, many psychologists found these theoretical orientations unappealing. The principal charge hurled at both schools was that they were "dehumanizing." Psychoanalytic theory was attacked for its belief that behavior is dominated by primitive, sexual urges. Behaviorism was criticized for its preoccupation with the study of simple animal behavior. Both theories were criticized because they suggested that people are not masters of their own destinies. Above all, many people argued, both schools of thought failed to recognize the unique qualities of *human* behavior.

Beginning in the 1950s, the diverse opposition to behaviorism and psychoanalytic theory blended into a loose alliance that eventually became a new school of thought called "humanism" (Bühler & Allen, 1972). In psychology, **humanism is a theoretical orientation that emphasizes the unique qualities of humans, especially their freedom and their potential for personal growth.** Some of the key differences between the humanistic, psychoanalytic, and behavioral viewpoints are summarized in Table 1.1, which compares six contemporary theoretical perspectives in psychology.

Web Link 1.3

Museum of the History of Psychological Instrumentation
You can examine instruments and complex apparatus used by psychological researchers in the discipline's early decades in this "cybermuseum" maintained at Montclair State University.

Table 1.1 Overview of Six Contemporary Theoretical Perspectives in Psychology

Perspective and Its Influential Period	Principal Contributors	Subject Matter	Basic Premise
Behavioral (1913–present)	John B. Watson Ivan Pavlov B. F. Skinner	Effects of environment on the overt behavior of humans and animals	Only observable events (stimulus-response relations) can be studied scientifically.
Psychoanalytic (1900–present)	Sigmund Freud Carl Jung Alfred Adler	Unconscious determinants of behavior	Unconscious motives and experiences in early childhood govern personality and mental disorders.
Humanistic (1950s–present)	Carl Rogers Abraham Maslow	Unique aspects of human experience	Humans are free, rational beings with the potential for personal growth, and they are fundamentally different from animals.
Cognitive (1950s–present)	Jean Piaget Noam Chomsky Herbert Simon	Thoughts; mental processes	Human behavior cannot be fully understood without examining how people acquire, store, and process information.
Biological (1950s–present)	James Olds Roger Sperry David Hubel Torsten Wiesel	Physiological bases of behavior in humans and animals	An organism's functioning can be explained in terms of the bodily structures and biochemical processes that underlie behavior.
Evolutionary (1980s–present)	David Buss Martin Daly Margo Wilson Leda Cosmides John Tooby	Evolutionary bases of behavior in humans and animals	Behavior patterns have evolved to solve adaptive problems; natural selection favors behaviors that enhance reproductive success.

CARL ROGERS 1902–1987

"It seems to me that at bottom each person is asking, 'Who am I, really? How can I get in touch with this real self, underlying all my surface behavior? How can I become myself?'"

Humanists take an *optimistic* view of human nature. They maintain that people are not pawns of either their animal heritage or environmental circumstances. Furthermore, they say, because humans are fundamentally different from other animals, research on animals has little relevance to the understanding of human behavior. The most prominent architects of the humanistic movement have been Carl Rogers (1902–1987) and Abraham Maslow (1908–1970). Rogers (1951) argued that human behavior is governed primarily by each individual's sense of self, or "self-concept"—which animals presumably lack. Both he and Maslow (1954) maintained that to fully understand people's behavior, psychologists must take into account the human drive toward personal growth. They asserted that people have a basic need to continue to evolve as human beings and to fulfill their potentials.

Fragmentation, dissension, and a distaste for conducting research have reduced the influence of humanism in recent decades, although some advocates are predicting a renaissance for the humanistic movement (Taylor, 1999). To date, the humanists' greatest contribution to psychology has probably been their innovative treatments for psychological problems and disorders.

Psychology Comes of Age as a Profession

The 1950s also saw psychology come of age as a profession. As you know, psychology is not all pure science. It has a highly practical side. Many psychologists provide a variety of professional services to the public. Their work falls within the domain of *applied psychology,* **the branch of psychology concerned with everyday, practical problems.** This branch of psychology, so prominent today, was actually slow to develop. Although a small number of early psychologists dabbled in various areas of applied psychology, it remained on the fringes of mainstream psychology until World War II (Benjamin et al., 2003).

The first applied arm of psychology to achieve any prominence was *clinical psychology.* As practiced today, *clinical psychology* **is the branch of psychology concerned with the diagnosis and treatment of psychological problems and disorders.** In the early days, however, the emphasis was almost exclusively on psychological testing and adjustment problems in school children. Although the first psychological clinic was established as early as 1896, by 1937 only about one in five psychologists reported an interest in clinical psychology (Goldenberg, 1983).

Clinicians were a small minority in a field devoted primarily to research.

That picture was about to change with dramatic swiftness. The impetus was a world war. During World War II (1939–1945), many academic psychologists were pressed into service as clinicians. They were needed to screen military recruits and to treat soldiers suffering from trauma. Many of these psychologists (often to their surprise) found the clinical work to be challenging and rewarding, and a substantial portion continued to do clinical work after the war. More significantly, some 40,000 American veterans, many with severe psychological scars, returned to seek postwar treatment in Veterans Administration (VA) hospitals. With the demand for clinicians far greater than the supply, the VA stepped in to finance many new training programs in clinical psychology. These programs, emphasizing training in the treatment of

PREVIEW QUESTIONS

- What events stimulated the development of applied psychology and clinical psychology?

- What is the cognitive perspective, and when did it become important?

- What is the biological perspective, and when did it become important?

- What events sparked psychology's increased interest in cultural factors?

- What is the basic premise of evolutionary psychology?

- What was the impetus for the positive psychology movement?

concept check 1.2

Understanding the Implications of Major Theories: Watson, Skinner, and Rogers

Check your understanding of the implications of some of the major theories reviewed in this chapter by indicating who is likely to have made each of the statements quoted below. Choose from the following: (a) John B. Watson, (b) B. F. Skinner, and (c) Carl Rogers. You'll find the answers in Appendix A at the back of the book.

_____ **1.** "In the traditional view, a person is free. . . . He can therefore be held responsible for what he does and justly punished if he offends. That view, together with its associated practices, must be reexamined when a scientific analysis reveals unsuspected controlling relations between behavior and environment."

_____ **2.** "I do not have a Pollyanna view of human nature. . . . Yet one of the most refreshing and invigorating parts of my experience is to work with [my clients] and to discover the strongly positive directional tendencies which exist in them, as in all of us, at the deepest levels."

_____ **3.** "Our conclusion is that we have no real evidence of the inheritance of traits. I would feel perfectly confident in the ultimately favorable outcome of careful upbringing of a healthy, well-formed baby born of a long line of crooks, murderers and thieves, and prostitutes."

psychological disorders as well as in psychological testing, proved attractive. Within a few years, about half of the new Ph.D.'s in psychology were specializing in clinical psychology (Goldenberg, 1983). Assessing the impact of World War II, Routh and Reisman (2003) characterize it as "a watershed in the history of clinical psychology. In its aftermath, clinical psychology received something it had not received before: enormous institutional support" (p. 345). Thus, during the 1940s and 1950s the prewar orphan of applied/professional psychology rapidly matured into a robust, powerful adult.

Since the 1950s, the professionalization of psychology has continued at a steady pace. In fact, the trend has spread into additional areas of psychology. Today, the broad umbrella of applied psychology covers a variety of professional specialties, including school psychology, industrial and organizational psychology, and counseling psychology. Whereas psychologists were once almost exclusively research scientists, roughly two-thirds of today's psychologists devote some of their time to providing professional services.

Psychology Returns to Its Roots: Renewed Interest in Cognition and Physiology 1a

While applied psychology has blossomed in recent decades, scientific research has continued to progress. Ironically, two of the latest trends in research hark back more than a century to psychology's beginning, when psychologists were principally interested in consciousness and physiology. Today psychologists are showing renewed interest in consciousness (now called "cognition") and the biological bases of behavior.

Cognition **refers to the mental processes involved in acquiring knowledge.** In other words, cognition involves thinking or conscious experience. For many decades, the dominance of behaviorism discouraged investigation of "unobservable" mental processes, and most psychologists showed little interest in cognition (Mandler, 2002). During the 1950s and 1960s, however, research on cognition slowly began to emerge (Miller, 2003). Major progress in the study of cognitive development (Piaget, 1954), memory (Miller, 1956), language (Chomsky, 1957), and problem solving (Newell, Shaw, & Simon, 1958) sparked a surge of interest in cognitive psychology.

Cognitive theorists argue that psychology must study internal mental events to fully understand human behavior (Gardner, 1985; Neisser, 1967). Ad-

vocates of the *cognitive perspective* point out that our mental processes surely influence how we behave. Consequently, focusing exclusively on overt behavior yields an incomplete picture of why we behave as we do. Equally important, psychologists investigating decision making, reasoning, and problem solving have shown that methods *can* be devised to study cognitive processes scientifically. Although the methods are different from those used in psychology's early days, research on the inner workings of the mind put the *psyche* back in contemporary psychology. In fact, many observers maintain that the cognitive perspective has become the dominant perspective in contemporary psychology—and some interesting data support this assertion, as can be seen in **Figure 1.3** (Robins, Gosling, & Craik, 1999).

The 1950s and 1960s also saw many discoveries that highlighted the interrelations among mind, body, and behavior (Thompson & Zola, 2003). For example, researchers demonstrated that electrical stimulation of the brain could evoke emotional responses such as pleasure and rage in animals (Olds, 1956). Other work, which eventually earned a Nobel prize for Roger Sperry (in 1981), showed that the right and left halves of the brain are specialized to handle different types of mental tasks (Gazzaniga, Bogen, &

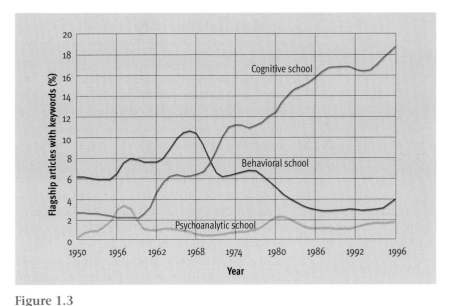

Figure 1.3

The relative prominence of three major schools of thought in psychology.
To estimate the relative influence of various theoretical orientations in recent decades, Robins, Gosling, and Craik (1999) analyzed the subject matter of four prestigious general publications in psychology, measuring the percentage of articles relevant to each school of thought. Obviously, their approach is just one of many ways one might gauge the prominence of various theoretical orientations in psychology. Nonetheless, the data are thought provoking. Their findings suggest that the cognitive perspective surpassed the behavioral perspective in influence sometime around 1970. As you can see, the psychoanalytic perspective has always had a modest impact on the mainstream of psychology.

Source: Adapted from Robins, R. W., Gosling, S. D., & Craik, K. H. (1999). An empirical analysis of trends in psychology. *American Psychologist, 54,* 117–128. Copyright © 1999 by the American Psychological Association. Reprinted by permission of the author.

Sperry, 1965). The 1960s also brought the publication of David Hubel and Torsten Wiesel's (1962, 1963) Nobel–prize–winning work on how visual signals are processed in the brain. These and many other findings stimulated an increase in research on the biological bases of behavior. Advocates of the *biological perspective* maintain that much of human and animal behavior can be explained in terms of the bodily structures and biochemical processes that allow organisms to behave. As you know, in the 19th century the young science of psychology had a heavy physiological emphasis. Thus, the renewed interest in the biological bases of behavior represents another return to psychology's heritage.

Although advocates of the cognitive and biological perspectives haven't done as much organized campaigning for their viewpoint as proponents of the older, traditional schools of thought, these newer perspectives have become important theoretical orientations in modern psychology. They are increasingly influential viewpoints regarding what psychology should study and how. The cognitive and biological perspectives are compared to other contemporary theoretical perspectives in **Table 1.1**.

Psychology Broadens Its Horizons: Increased Interest in Cultural Diversity

Throughout psychology's history, most researchers have worked under the assumption that they were seeking to identify general principles of behavior that would be applicable to all of humanity. In reality, however, psychology has largely been a Western (North American and European) enterprise with a remarkably provincial slant (Gergen et al. 1996). The vast majority of research has been conducted in the United States by middle- and upper-class white psychologists who have used mostly middle- and upper-class white males as subjects (Hall, 1997; Segall et al., 1990). Traditionally, Western psychologists have paid scant attention to how well their theories and research might apply to non-Western cultures, to ethnic minorities in Western societies, or even to women as opposed to men.

However, in recent years Western psychologists have begun to recognize that their neglect of cultural variables has diminished the value of their work, and they are devoting increased attention to culture as a determinant of behavior. What brought about this shift? The new interest in culture appears mainly attributable to two recent trends: (1) Advances in communication, travel, and international trade have "shrunk" the world and increased global interdependence, bringing more and more Americans and Europeans into contact with people from non-Western cultures; and (2) the ethnic makeup of the Western world has become an increasingly diverse multicultural mosaic, as the data in **Figure 1.4** show for the United States (Brislin, 1993; Hermans & Kempen, 1998; Mays et al., 1996).

These trends have prompted more and more Western psychologists to broaden their horizons and incorporate cultural factors into their theories and research (Adamopoulos & Lonner, 2001; Miller, 1999). These psychologists are striving to study previously underrepresented groups of subjects to test the generality of earlier findings and to catalog both the differences and similarities among cultural groups. They are working to increase knowledge of how culture is transmitted through socialization practices and how culture colors one's view of the world. They are seeking to learn how people cope with cultural change and to find ways to reduce misunderstandings and conflicts in intercultural interactions. In addition, they are trying to enhance understanding of how cultural groups are affected by prejudice, discrimination, and racism. In all these efforts, they are striving to understand the unique experiences of culturally diverse people *from the point of view of those people.* These efforts to ask new questions, study new groups, and apply new perspectives promise to enrich the discipline of psychology (Lehman, Chiu, & Schaller, 2004; Matsumoto, 2003; Sue, 2003).

Psychology Adapts: The Emergence of Evolutionary Psychology

A relatively recent development in psychology has been the emergence of *evolutionary psychology,* a new theoretical perspective that is likely to be influential in the years to come. Evolutionary psychologists assert that the patterns of behavior seen in a species are products of evolution in the same way that anatomical characteristics are. **Evolutionary psychology examines behavioral processes in terms of their adaptive value for members of a species over the course of many generations.** The basic premise of evolutionary psychology is that natural selection favors behaviors that enhance organisms' reproductive success— that is, passing on genes to the next generation. Thus, if a species is highly aggressive, evolutionary psychologists argue that it's because aggressiveness conveys a survival or reproductive advantage for members of that species, so genes that promote aggressiveness are more likely to be passed on to the next generation. Although evolutionary

Web Link 1.4

The Archives of the History of American Psychology (AHAP)
The Archives of the History of American Psychology (AHAP) at the University of Akron is a huge repository of information and materials on the history of psychology. Its website provides a well-organized overview of the archive's holdings and access to a number of photos of instruments and equipment used in psychological research.

psychologists have a natural interest in animal behavior, they have not been bashful about analyzing the evolutionary bases of human behavior. As La Cerra and Kurzban (1995) put it, "The human mind was sculpted by natural selection, and it is this evolved organ that constitutes the subject matter of psychology" (p. 63).

Looking at behavioral patterns in terms of their evolutionary significance is not an entirely new idea (Graziano, 1995). As noted earlier, William James and other functionalists were influenced by Darwin's concept of natural selection over a century ago. However, in the ensuing decades applications of evolutionary concepts to *psychological* processes were piecemeal, half-hearted, and not particularly well received. The 1960s and 1970s brought major break-throughs in the field of evolutionary *biology* (Hamilton, 1964; Trivers, 1971, 1972; Williams, 1966), but these advances had little immediate impact in psychology. The situation began to change in the middle to late 1980s. A growing band of evolutionary psychologists—led by David Buss (1985, 1988, 1989), Martin Daly and Margo Wilson (1985, 1988), and Leda Cosmides and John Tooby (Cosmides & Tooby, 1989; Tooby & Cosmides, 1989)—published widely cited studies on a broad range of topics, including mating preferences, jealousy, aggression, sexual behavior, language, decision making, personality, and development. By the mid-1990s, it became clear that psychology was witnessing the birth of its first major, new theoretical perspective since the cognitive revolution in the 1950s and 1960s.

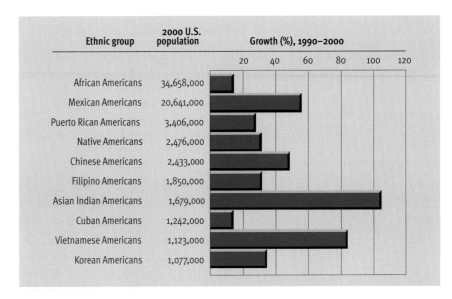

Ethnic group	2000 U.S. population	Growth (%), 1990–2000
African Americans	34,658,000	
Mexican Americans	20,641,000	
Puerto Rican Americans	3,406,000	
Native Americans	2,476,000	
Chinese Americans	2,433,000	
Filipino Americans	1,850,000	
Asian Indian Americans	1,679,000	
Cuban Americans	1,242,000	
Vietnamese Americans	1,123,000	
Korean Americans	1,077,000	

As with all prominent theoretical perspectives in psychology, evolutionary theory has its critics (Gould, 1993; Lickliter & Honeycutt, 2003; Plotkin, 2004; Rose & Rose, 2000). Among other things, they argue that many evolutionary hypotheses are untestable and that evolutionary explanations are post hoc, speculative accounts for obvious behavioral phenomena (see the Critical Thinking Application for this chapter). However, evolutionary psychologists have articulated persuasive rebuttals to these and other criticisms (Bereczkei, 2000; Buss & Reeve, 2003; Conway & Schaller, 2002), and the evolutionary perspective has become increasingly influential.

Psychology Moves in a Positive Direction

1a

Shortly after Martin Seligman was elected President of the American Psychological Association in 1997, he experienced a profound insight that he characterized as an "epiphany." This pivotal insight came from an unusual source—Seligman's 5-year-old daughter, Nikki. She scolded her overachieving, task-oriented father for being "grumpy" far too much of the time. Provoked by his daughter's criticism, Seligman suddenly realized that his approach to life *was* overly and unnecessarily negative. More important, he recognized that the same assessment could be made of the field of psychology—that it, too, was excessively and needlessly negative in its approach (Seligman, 2003). This revelation inspired Seligman to launch an influential, new initiative within psychology that came to be known as the *positive psychology movement*.

Seligman went on to argue convincingly that the field of psychology had historically devoted too

Figure 1.4

Increased cultural diversity in the United States. The 1980s and 1990s brought significant changes in the ethnic makeup of the United States. During the 1990s, the nation's Hispanic population grew by 45% and its Asian American population grew by 49%, while the white population increased by only 6%. Experts project that ethnic minorities will account for over one-third of the U.S. population within the next few decades. These trends have contributed to psychologists' increased interest in cultural factors as determinants of behavior. (Data from U.S. Bureau of the Census)

© Michael & Patricia Fogden/Corbis

The praying mantis has an astonishing ability to blend in with its environment, along with remarkably acute hearing and vision that permit it to detect prey up to 60 feet away and powerful jaws that allow it to devour its prey. They are so deadly they will eat each other, which makes sex quite a challenge, but males have evolved a reflex module that allows them to copulate successfully while being eaten (even after decapitation)! These physical characteristics obviously represent adaptations that have been crafted by natural selection over the course of millions of generations. Evolutionary psychologists maintain that many patterns of behavior seen in various species are also adaptations that have been shaped by natural selection.

1870   **1880**   **1890**   **1900**   **1910**   **1920**   **1930**

1875

First demonstration laboratories are set up independently by **William James** (at Harvard) and Wilhelm Wundt (at the University of Leipzig).

1905

Alfred Binet develops first successful intelligence test in France.

1914–1918

Widespread intelligence testing is begun by military during World War I.

1908

Margaret Washburn publishes *The Animal Mind*, which serves as an impetus for behaviorism.

1879

Wilhelm Wundt establishes first research laboratory in psychology at Leipzig, Germany.

1916

Lewis Terman publishes Stanford-Binet Intelligence Scale, which becomes the world's foremost intelligence test.

1909

1920s

Gestalt pychology nears its peak influence.

Sigmund Freud's increasing influence receives formal recognition as G. S. Hall invites Freud to give lectures at Clark University.

1881

Wilhelm Wundt establishes first journal devoted to research in psychology.

1890

William James publishes his seminal work, *The Principles of Psychology*.

1913

John B. Watson writes classic behaviorism manifesto, arguing that psychology should study only observable behavior.

1933

Sigmund Freud's influence continues to build as he publishes *New Introductory Lectures on Psychoanalysis*.

1883

G. Stanley Hall establishes America's first research laboratory in psychology at Johns Hopkins University.

1892

G. Stanley Hall founds American Psychological Association.

1914

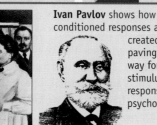

Leta Hollingworth publishes pioneering work on the psychology of women.

1904

Ivan Pavlov shows how conditioned responses are created, paving the way for stimulus-response psychology.

1940 **1950** **1960** **1970** **1980** **1990** **2000**

1941–1945

Rapid growth in clinical psychology begins in response to huge demand for clinical services created by World War II and its aftermath.

1953

B. F. Skinner publishes his influential *Science and Human Behavior*, advocating radical behaviorism similar to Watson's.

1954

Abraham Maslow's *Motivation and Personality* helps fuel humanistic movement.

1956

The cognitive revolution is launched at watershed conference where Herbert Simon, George Miller, and Noam Chomsky report three major advances in just one day.

1947

Kenneth and Mamie **Clark** publish work on prejudice that is cited in landmark 1954 Supreme Court decision outlawing segregation.

1963

Stanley Milgram conducts controversial study of obedience to authority, which may be the most famous single study in psychology's history.

1950

Erik Erikson writes *Childhood and Society* in which he extends Freud's theory of development across the life span.

1951

Carl Rogers helps launch humanistic movement with publication of *Client-Centered Therapy*.

Note:
The credits for copyrighted photos and illustrations on pages 14–15 can be found on page CR-1.

1961–1964

Roger Sperry's split-brain research and work by David Hubel and Torsten Wiesel on how cortical cells respond to light help rejuvenate the biological perspective in psychology.

1971

B. F. Skinner creates furor over radical behaviorism with his controversial book *Beyond Freedom and Dignity*.

1978

Herbert Simon wins Nobel prize (in economics) for research on cognition.

1974

Eleanor Maccoby and Carol Jacklin publish their landmark review of research on gender differences, which galvanizes research in this area.

1980s

Increased global interdependence and cultural diversity in Western societies spark surge of interest in how cultural factors mold behavior.

1981

Roger Sperry wins Nobel prize (in physiology and medicine) for split-brain studies.

Early 1990s

Evolutionary psychology emerges as a major new theoretical perspective.

1990s

The repressed memories controversy stimulates influential research by **Elizabeth Loftus** and others on the malleability and fallibility of human memory.

Late 1990s

Martin Seligman launches the positive psychology movement.

1988

Research psychologists form American Psychological Society (APS) to serve as an advocate for the science of psychology.

2000

Eric Kandel wins Nobel Prize (in physiology and medicine) for his research on the biochemistry of memory.

2002

Daniel Kahneman wins Nobel Prize (in economics) for his research on decision making.

The Evolution of Psychology   **15**

much attention to pathology, weakness, and damage, and how to heal suffering. He acknowledged that this approach had yielded valuable insights and progress, but he argued that it also resulted in an unfortunate neglect of the forces that make life worth living. Seligman convened a series of informal meetings with influential psychologists and then more formal conferences to gradually outline the philosophy and goals of positive psychology. Other major architects of the positive psychology movement have included Mihaly Csikszentmihalyi (2000), Christopher Peterson (2000), and Barbara Fredrickson (2002). Like humanism before it, positive psychology seeks to shift the field's focus away from negative experiences. As Seligman and Csikszentmihalyi (2000) put it, "The aim of positive psychology is to begin to catalyze a change in the focus of psychology from preoccupation with only repairing the worst things in life to also building positive qualities" (p. 5). Thus, *positive psychology* **uses theory and research to better understand the positive, adaptive, creative, and fulfilling aspects of human existence.**

The emerging field of positive psychology has three areas of interest (Seligman, 2003). The first is the study of *positive subjective experiences,* or positive emotions, such as happiness, love, gratitude, contentment, and hope. The second focus is on *positive individual traits*—that is, personal strengths and virtues. Theorists are working to identify, classify, and analyze the origins of human strengths and virtues, such as courage, perseverance, nurturance, tolerance, creativity, integrity, and kindness. The third area of interest is in *positive institutions and communities*. Here the focus is on how societies can foster civil discourse, strong families, healthy work environments, and supportive neighborhood communities.

Although it has proven far less controversial than evolutionary psychology, positive psychology has its critics. For example, Richard Lazarus (2003) has ar-gued that it is an oversimplification to divide human experience into positive and negative domains and that the line between these two domains is not as clear and obvious as most have assumed. Lazarus expresses concern that positive psychology may be little more than "one of the many fads that come and go in our field" (p. 93). Only time will tell, as positive psychology is still in its infancy. It will be fascinating to see whether and how this new movement reshapes psychology's research priorities and theoretical interests in the years to come.

Our review of psychology's past has shown how the field has evolved. We have seen psychology develop from philosophical speculation into a rigorous science committed to research. We have seen how a highly visible professional arm involved in mental health services emerged from this science. We have seen how psychology's focus on physiology is rooted in its 19th-century origins. We have seen how and why psychologists began conducting research on lower animals. We have seen how psychology has evolved from the study of mind and body to the study of behavior. And we have seen how the investigation of mind and body has been welcomed back into the mainstream of modern psychology. We have seen how different theoretical schools have defined the scope and mission of psychology in different ways. We have seen how psychology's interests have expanded and become increasingly diverse. Above all else, we have seen that psychology is a growing, evolving intellectual enterprise.

Psychology's history is already rich, but its story has barely begun. The century or so that has elapsed since Wilhelm Wundt put psychology on a scientific footing is only an eyeblink of time in human history. What has been discovered during those years, and what remains unknown, is the subject of the rest of this book.

> Psychology Today: Vigorous and Diversified

PREVIEW QUESTIONS

- What evidence suggests that psychology is a vigorous, growing discipline?
- What are the main areas of research in psychology?
- What are the four professional specialties in psychology?

We began this chapter with an informal description of what psychology is about. Now that you have a feel for how psychology has developed, you can better appreciate a definition that does justice to the field's modern diversity: **Psychology** **is the science that studies behavior and the physiological and cognitive processes that underlie behavior, and it is the profession that applies the accumulated knowledge of this science to practical problems.**

Contemporary psychology is a thriving science and profession. Its growth has been remarkable. One simple index of this growth is the dramatic rise in membership in the American Psychological Association (APA), a national organization devoted to the advancement of psychology. The APA was founded in 1892 with just 26 members. Today, the APA has over 90,000 members. Moreover, as **Figure 1.5** shows, APA membership has increased ninefold since 1950. In

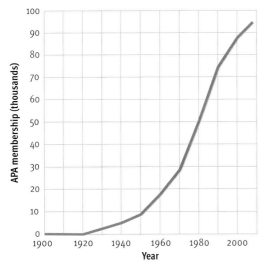

Figure 1.5

Membership in the American Psychological Association, 1900–2004. The steep rise in the number of psychologists in the APA since 1950 testifies to psychology's remarkable growth as a science and a profession. If graduate student members are also counted, the APA has over 155,000 members. (Adapted from data published by the American Psychological Association, by permission.)

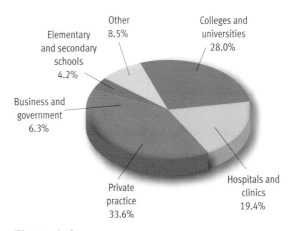

Figure 1.6

Employment of psychologists by setting. The work settings in which psychologists are employed have become very diverse. Survey data on the primary employment setting of APA members indicates that one-third are in private practice (compared to 12% in 1976) while only 28% work in colleges and universities (compared to 47% in 1976). (Based on 2000 APA Directory Survey)

Web Link 1.5

American Psychological Association (APA)
The APA website is a treasure trove of resources on psychology in all its rich diversity. The section for the public includes electronic pamphlets on practical topics such as depression, aging, and anger. A wealth of information on career possibilities in the field can also be found here.

the United States, psychology is the second most popular undergraduate major and the field accounts for about 9% of all doctoral degrees awarded in the sciences and humanities. The comparable figure in 1945 was only 4% (Howard et al., 1986). Of course, psychology is an international enterprise. Today, over 1900 technical journals from all over the world publish research articles on psychology. Thus, by any standard of measurement—the number of people involved, the number of degrees granted, the number of studies conducted, the number of journals published—psychology is a healthy, growing field.

Psychology's vigorous presence in modern society is also demonstrated by the great variety of settings in which psychologists work. The distribution of psychologists employed in various categories of settings can be seen in **Figure 1.6**. Psychologists were once found almost exclusively in the halls of academia. However, today only about one-fourth of American psychologists work in colleges and universities. The remaining three-fourths work in hospitals, clinics, police departments, research institutes, government agencies, business and industry, schools, nursing homes, counseling centers, and private practice.

Clearly, contemporary psychology is a multifaceted field, a fact that is especially apparent when we consider the many areas of specialization within psychology today. Let's look at the current areas of specialization in both the science and the profession of psychology.

Research Areas in Psychology

Although most psychologists receive broad training that provides them with knowledge about many areas of psychology, they usually specialize when it comes to doing research. Such specialization is necessary because the subject matter of psychology has become so vast over the years. Today it is virtually impossible for anyone to stay abreast of the new research in all specialties. Specialization is also necessary because specific skills and training are required to do research in some areas.

The seven major research areas in modern psychology are (1) developmental psychology, (2) social psychology, (3) experimental psychology, (4) physiological psychology, (5) cognitive psychology, (6) personality, and (7) psychometrics. **Figure 1.7** (on the next page) briefly describes each of these areas of inquiry.

Professional Specialties in Psychology

Within applied psychology there are four clearly identified areas of specialization: (1) clinical psychology, (2) counseling psychology, (3) educational and school psychology, and (4) industrial and organizational psychology. Descriptions of these specialties can be found in **Figure 1.8** on the next page. Clinical psychology is currently the most widely practiced professional specialty.

Web Link 1.6

Marky Lloyd's Career Page
For those who think they might want to find a job or career in psychology or a related field, Marky Lloyd of Georgia Southern University has put together a fine set of resources to help in both planning and making choices.

Web Link 1.7

A Student's Guide to Careers in the Helping Professions
Written by Melissa J. Himeline of the University of North Carolina at Asheville, this online guide provides detailed career information for 15 of the most important helping professions that psychology majors often consider entering.

Figure 1.7

Major research areas in contemporary psychology. Most research psychologists specialize in one of the seven broad areas described here. The figures in the pie chart reflect the percentage of academic and research psychologists belonging to APA who identify each area as their primary interest. (Based on 2000 APA Directory Survey)

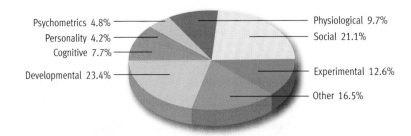

Area	Focus of research
Developmental psychology	Looks at human development across the life span. Developmental psychology once focused primarily on child development, but today devotes a great deal of research to adolescence, adulthood, and old age.
Social psychology	Focuses on interpersonal behavior and the role of social forces in governing behavior. Typical topics include attitude formation, attitude change, prejudice, conformity, attraction, aggression, intimate relationships, and behavior in groups.
Experimental psychology	Encompasses the traditional core of topics that psychology focused on heavily in its first half-century as a science: sensation, perception, learning, conditioning, motivation, and emotion. The name experimental psychology is somewhat misleading, as this is not the only area in which experiments are done. Psychologists working in all the areas listed here conduct experiments.
Physiological psychology	Examines the influence of genetic factors on behavior and the role of the brain, nervous system, endocrine system, and bodily chemicals in the regulation of behavior.
Cognitive psychology	Focuses on "higher" mental processes, such as memory, reasoning, information processing, language, problem solving, decision making, and creativity.
Personality	Is interested in describing and understanding individuals' consistency in behavior, which represents their personality. This area of interest is also concerned with the factors that shape personality and with personality assessment.
Psychometrics	Is concerned with the measurement of behavior and capacities, usually through the development of psychological tests. Psychometrics is involved with the design of tests to assess personality, intelligence, and a wide range of abilities. It is also concerned with the development of new techniques for statistical analysis.

Figure 1.8

Principal professional specialties in contemporary psychology. Most psychologists who deliver professional services to the public specialize in one of the four areas described here. The figures in the pie chart reflect the percentage of APA members delivering professional services who identify each area as their chief specialty. (Based on 2000 APA Directory Survey)

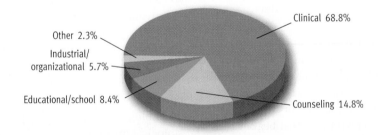

Specialty	Focus of professional practice
Clinical psychology	Clinical psychologists are concerned with the evaluation, diagnosis, and treatment of individuals with psychological disorders, as well as treatment of less severe behavioral and emotional problems. Principal activities include interviewing clients, psychological testing, and providing group or individual psychotherapy.
Counseling psychology	Counseling psychology overlaps with clinical psychology in that specialists in both areas engage in similar activities—interviewing, testing, and providing therapy. However, counseling psychologists usually work with a somewhat different clientele, providing assistance to people struggling with everyday problems of moderate severity. Thus, they often specialize in family, marital, or career counseling.
Educational and school psychology	Educational psychologists work to improve curriculum design, achievement testing, teacher training, and other aspects of the educational process. School psychologists usually work in elementary or secondary schools, where they test and counsel children having difficulties in school and aid parents and teachers in solving school-related problems.
Industrial and organizational psychology	Psychologists in this area perform a wide variety of tasks in the world of business and industry. These tasks include running human resources departments, working to improve staff morale and attitudes, striving to increase job satisfaction and productivity, examining organizational structures and procedures, and making recommendations for improvements.

concept **check** 1.3

Understanding the Major Research Areas in Contemporary Psychology

Check your understanding of the various research areas in psychology reviewed in this chapter by indicating which type of psychologist would be most likely to perform each of the investigations described below. Choose from the following: (a) physiological psychology, (b) cognitive psychology, (c) developmental psychology, (d) psychometrics, and (e) personality. You'll find the answers in Appendix A at the back of the book.

1. Researchers interviewed the parents of 141 children (all born in 1956) every few months throughout childhood. Questions dealt with various aspects of the children's temperaments. The conclusion was that most children fall into one of three temperamental categories: "easy," "difficult," or "slow to warm up."

_____

2. It was discovered that rats will work extremely hard (pressing a lever, for instance) to earn small amounts of electrical stimulation directed to specific areas of their brains. Research indicates that the human brain may also contain similar "pleasure centers."

_____

3. The Sensation Seeking Scale (SSS) was developed to measure individual differences in the extent to which people prefer high or low levels of sensory stimulation. People such as skydivers tend to score high on the SSS, while someone whose idea of a good time is settling down with a good book would tend to score low.

_____

Although it is useful to distinguish between research and professional specialties in psychology, it is important to note that many psychologists work on *both* research and application. Some academic psychologists work as consultants, therapists, and counselors on a part-time basis. Similarly, some applied psychologists conduct basic research on issues related to their specialty. For example, many clinical psychologists are involved in research on the nature and causes of abnormal behavior.

> Seven Unifying Themes

The enormous breadth and diversity of psychology make it a challenging subject for the beginning student. In the pages ahead you will be introduced to many areas of research and a multitude of new ideas, concepts, and principles. Fortunately, not all ideas are created equal. Some are far more important than others. In this section, I will highlight seven fundamental themes that will reappear in a number of variations as we move from one area of psychology to another in this text. You have already met some of these key ideas in our review of psychology's past and present. Now we will isolate them and highlight their significance. In the remainder of the book these ideas serve as organizing themes to provide threads of continuity across chapters and to help you see the connections among the various areas of research in psychology.

In studying psychology, you are learning about both behavior and the scientific discipline that investigates it. Accordingly, our seven themes come in two sets. The first set consists of statements highlighting crucial aspects of psychology as a way of thinking and as a field of study. The second set consists of broad generalizations about psychology's subject matter: behavior and the cognitive and physiological processes that underlie it.

Themes Related to Psychology as a Field of Study

Looking at psychology as a field of study, we see three crucial ideas: (1) psychology is empirical; (2) psychology is theoretically diverse; and (3) psychology evolves in a sociohistorical context. Let's look at each of these ideas in more detail.

PREVIEW QUESTIONS

- What is the purpose of the text's unifying themes?
- What are the first three themes that elucidate the nature of psychology?
- What are the remaining four themes that emphasize crucial insights about behavior?

Theme 1: Psychology Is Empirical

Everyone tries to understand behavior. Most of us have developed our own personal answers to such questions as why some people are hard workers, why some are overweight, and why others stay in demeaning relationships. If all of us are amateur psychologists, what makes scientific psychology any different or better? The critical difference is that psychology is *empirical*.

What do we mean by empirical? **Empiricism is the premise that knowledge should be acquired through observation.** This premise is crucial to the scientific method that psychology embraced in the late 19th century. To say that psychology is empirical means that its conclusions are based on direct observation rather than on reasoning, speculation, traditional beliefs, or common sense. Psychologists are not content with having ideas that sound plausible. They conduct research to test their ideas. Is intelligence higher on the average in some social classes than in others? Are men more aggressive than women? Psychologists find a way to make direct, objective, and precise observations to answer such questions.

The empirical approach requires a certain attitude—a healthy brand of skepticism. Empiricism is a tough taskmaster. It demands data and documentation. Psychologists' commitment to empiricism means that they must learn to think critically about generalizations concerning behavior. If someone asserts that people tend to get depressed around Christmas, a psychologist is likely to ask, "How many people get depressed? In what population? In comparison to what baseline rate of depression? How is depression defined and measured?" Their skeptical attitude means that psychologists are trained to ask, "Where's the evidence? How do you know?" If psychology's empirical orientation rubs off on you (and I hope it does), you will be asking similar questions by the time you finish this book.

Theme 2: Psychology Is Theoretically Diverse

Although psychology is based on observation, a string of unrelated observations would not be terribly enlightening. Psychologists do not set out to just collect isolated facts; they seek to explain and understand what they observe. To achieve these goals they must construct theories. **A *theory* is a system of interrelated ideas used to explain a set of observations.** In other words, a theory links apparently unrelated observations and tries to explain them. As an example, consider Sigmund Freud's observations about slips of the tongue, dreams, and psychological disturbances. On the surface, these observations appear unrelated. By devising the concept of the *uncon-*

scious, Freud created a theory that links and explains these seemingly unrelated aspects of behavior.

Our review of psychology's past should have made one thing abundantly clear: Psychology is marked by theoretical diversity. Why do we have so many competing points of view? One reason is that no single theory can adequately explain everything that is known about behavior. Sometimes different theories focus on different aspects of behavior—that is, different collections of observations. Sometimes there is simply more than one way to look at something. Is the glass half empty or half full? Obviously, it is both. To take an example from another science, physicists wrestled for years with the nature of light. Is it a wave, or is it a particle? In the end, it proved useful to think of light sometimes as a wave and sometimes as a particle. Similarly, if a business executive lashes out at her employees with stinging criticism, is she releasing pent-up aggressive urges (a psychoanalytic view)? Is she making a habitual response to the stimulus of incompetent work (a behavioral view)? Or is she scheming to motivate her employees with "mind games" (a cognitive view)? In some cases, all three of these explanations might have some validity. In short, it is an oversimplification to expect that one view has to be right while all others are wrong. Life is rarely that simple.

Students are often troubled by psychology's many conflicting theories, which they view as a weakness. *However, contemporary psychologists increasingly recognize that theoretical diversity is a strength rather than a weakness* (Hilgard, 1987). As we proceed through this text, you will learn how clashing theories have often stimulated productive research. You will also see how approaching a problem from several theoretical perspectives can often provide a more complete understanding than could be achieved by any one perspective alone.

Theme 3: Psychology Evolves in a Sociohistorical Context

Science is often seen as an "ivory tower" undertaking, isolated from the ebb and flow of everyday life. In reality, however, psychology and other sciences do not exist in a cultural vacuum. Dense interconnections exist between what happens in psychology and what happens in society at large (Altman, 1990; Danziger, 1990). Trends, issues, and values in society influence psychology's evolution. Similarly, progress in psychology affects trends, issues, and values in society. To put it briefly, psychology develops in a *sociohistorical* (social and historical) context.

Our review of psychology's past is filled with examples of how social trends have left their imprint on psychology. For example, Sigmund Freud's groundbreaking ideas emerged out of a specific sociohistorical context. Cultural values in Freud's era encouraged the suppression of sexuality. Hence, people tended to feel guilty about their sexual urges to a much greater extent than is common today. This situation clearly contributed to Freud's emphasis on unconscious sexual conflicts. As another example, consider how World War II sparked the rapid growth of psychology as a profession.

If we reverse our viewpoint, we can see that psychology has in turn left its mark on society. Consider, for instance, the pervasive role of mental testing in modern society. Your own career success may depend in part on how well you weave your way through a complex maze of intelligence and achievement tests made possible (to the regret of some) by research in psychology. As another example of psychology's impact on society, consider the influence that various theorists have had on parenting styles. Trends in childrearing practices have been shaped by the ideas of John B. Watson, Sigmund Freud, B. F. Skinner, and Carl Rogers—not to mention a host of additional psychologists yet to be discussed. In short, society and psychology influence each other in complex ways. In the chapters to come, we will frequently have occasion to notice this dynamic relationship.

Themes Related to Psychology's Subject Matter

Looking at psychology's subject matter, we see four additional crucial ideas: (4) behavior is determined by multiple causes; (5) behavior is shaped by cultural heritage; (6) heredity and environment jointly influence behavior; and (7) people's experience of the world is highly subjective.

Theme 4: Behavior Is Determined by Multiple Causes

As psychology has matured, it has provided more and more information about the forces that govern behavior. This growing knowledge has led to a deeper appreciation of a simple but important fact: Behavior is exceedingly complex, and most aspects of behavior are determined by multiple causes.

Although the complexity of behavior may seem self-evident, people usually think in terms of single causes. Thus, they offer explanations such as "Andrea flunked out of school because she is lazy." Or they assert that "teenage pregnancies are increasing

because of all the sex in the media." Single-cause explanations are sometimes accurate insofar as they go, but they usually are incomplete. In general, psychologists find that behavior is governed by a complex network of interacting factors, an idea referred to as the *multifactorial causation of behavior*.

As a simple illustration, consider the multiple factors that might influence your performance in your introductory psychology course. Relevant personal factors might include your overall intelligence, your reading ability, your memory skills, your motivation, and your study skills. In addition, your grade could be affected by numerous situational factors, including whether you like your psychology professor, whether you like your assigned text, whether the class meets at a good time for you, whether your work schedule is light or heavy, and whether you're having any personal problems. As you proceed through this book, you will learn that complexity of causation is the rule rather than the exception. If we expect to understand behavior, we usually have to take into account multiple determinants.

Theme 5: Behavior Is Shaped by Cultural Heritage

Among the multiple determinants of human behavior, cultural factors are particularly prominent. Just as psychology evolves in a sociohistorical context, so, too, do individuals. Our cultural backgrounds exert considerable influence over our behavior. What is *culture*? It's the human-made part of our environment. More specifically, ***culture* refers to the widely shared customs, beliefs, values, norms, institutions, and other products of a community that are transmitted socially across generations.** Culture is a very broad construct, encompassing everything from a society's legal system to its assumptions about family roles, from its dietary habits to its political ideals, from its technology to its attitudes about time, from its modes of dress to its spiritual beliefs, and from its art and music to its unspoken rules about sexual liaisons.

Much of one's cultural heritage is invisible (Brislin, 1993). Assumptions, ideals, attitudes, beliefs, and unspoken rules exist in people's minds and may not be readily apparent to outsiders. Moreover, because our cultural background is widely shared, we feel little need to discuss it with others, and we often take it for granted. For example, you probably don't spend much time thinking about the importance of living in rectangular rooms, trying to minimize body odor, limiting yourself to one spouse at a time, or using credit cards to obtain material goods and services. Although we generally fail to appreciate its in-

Web Link 1.8

Encyclopedia of Psychology
This "encyclopedia," developed by psychology faculty at Jacksonville State University, is actually a collection of over 2000 links to webpages around the world on psychological matters. The links related to the history of the field and careers in psychology are extensive, as are the links relating to theories and publications in psychology.

fluence, our cultural heritage has a pervasive impact on our thoughts, feelings, and behavior.

Let's look at a couple of examples of this influence. In North America, when people are invited to dinner in someone's home they generally show their appreciation of their host's cooking efforts by eating all of the food they are served. In India, this behavior would be insulting to the host, as guests are expected to leave some food on their plates. The leftover food acknowledges the generosity of the host, implying that he or she provided so much food the guest could not eat it all (Moghaddam, Taylor, & Wright, 1993). Cultures also vary in their emphasis on punctuality. In North America, we expect people to show up for meetings on time; if someone is more than 10 to 15 minutes late, we begin to get upset. We generally strive to be on time, and many of us are quite proud of our precise punctuality. However, in many Asian and Latin American countries, social obligations that arise at the last minute are given just as much priority as scheduled commitments. Hence, people often show up for important meetings an hour or two late with little remorse, and they may be quite puzzled by the annoyance of their Western visitors (Brislin, 1993). These examples may seem trivial, but culture can also influence crucial matters, such as educational success, physical health, and a variety of other things, as you will see throughout this book.

Although the influence of culture is everywhere, generalizations about cultural groups must always be tempered by the realization that great diversity exists within any society or ethnic group. Researchers may be able to pinpoint genuinely useful insights about Ethiopian, Korean American, or Ukrainian culture, for example, but it would be foolish to assume that all Ethiopians, Korean Americans, or Ukrainians exhibit identical behavior. It is also important to realize that *both differences and similarities in behavior occur across cultures*. As we will see repeatedly, psychological processes are characterized by both cul-

tural variance and invariance. Caveats aside, if we hope to achieve a sound understanding of human behavior, we need to consider cultural determinants.

Theme 6: Heredity and Environment Jointly Influence Behavior

Are we who we are—athletic or artistic, quick-tempered or calm, shy or outgoing, energetic or laid back—because of our genetic inheritance or because of our upbringing? This question about the importance of nature versus nurture, or heredity versus environment, has been asked in one form or another since ancient times. Historically, the nature versus nurture question was framed as an all-or-none proposition. In other words, theorists argued that personal traits and abilities are governed entirely by heredity or entirely by environment. John B. Watson, for instance, asserted that personality and ability depend almost exclusively on an individual's environment. In contrast, Sir Francis Galton, a pioneer in mental testing, maintained that personality and ability depend almost entirely on genetic inheritance.

Today, most psychologists agree that heredity and environment are both important. A century of research has shown that genetics and experience jointly influence individuals' intelligence, temperament, personality, and susceptibility to many psychological disorders (Grigerenko & Sternberg, 2003; Plomin, 2004). If we ask whether people are born or made, psychology's answer is "Both." This response does not mean that nature versus nurture is a dead issue. Lively debate about the *relative influence* of genetics and experience continues unabated. Furthermore, psychologists are actively seeking to understand the complex ways in which genetic inheritance and experience interact to mold behavior.

Theme 7: People's Experience of the World Is Highly Subjective

Our experience of the world is highly subjective. Even elementary perception—for example, of sights and sounds—is not a passive process. We actively process incoming stimulation, selectively focusing on some aspects of that stimulation while ignoring others. Moreover, we impose organization on the stimuli that we pay attention to. These tendencies combine to make perception personalized and subjective.

The subjectivity of perception was demonstrated nicely in a study by Hastorf and Cantril (1954). They showed students at Princeton and Dartmouth universities a film of a hotly contested football game between the two rival schools. The students were told to watch for rules infractions. Both groups saw the

Cultural background has an enormous influence on people's behavior, shaping everything from modes of dress to sexual values and norms. Increased global interdependence brings more and more people into contact with cultures other than their own. This increased exposure to diverse cultures only serves to underscore the importance of cultural factors.

© Steve Raymer/Corbis

same film, but the Princeton students "saw" the Dartmouth players engage in twice as many infractions as the Dartmouth students "saw" (and vice versa). The investigators concluded that the game "actually was many different games and that each version of the events that transpired was just as 'real' to a particular person as other versions were to other people" (Hastorf & Cantril, 1954). This study showed how people sometimes see what they *want* to see. Other studies have demonstrated that people also tend to see what they *expect* to see (Kelley, 1950).

Thus, it is clear that motives and expectations color our experiences. This subjective bias in perception turns out to explain a variety of behavioral tendencies that would otherwise be perplexing (Pronin, Lin, & Ross, 2002; Pronin, Gilovich, & Ross, 2004). Human subjectivity is precisely what the scientific method is designed to counteract. In using the scientific approach, psychologists strive to make their observations as objective as possible. Left to their own subjective experience, people might still believe that the earth is flat and that the sun revolves around it. Thus, psychologists are committed to the scientific approach because they believe it is the most reliable route to accurate knowledge.

Now that you have been introduced to the text's organizing themes, let's turn to an example of how psychological research can be applied to the challenges of everyday life. In our first Personal Application, we'll focus on a subject that should be highly relevant to you: how to be a successful student. In the Critical Thinking Application that follows it, we discuss the nature and importance of critical thinking skills.

concept **check** 1.4

Understanding the Seven Unifying Themes

Check your understanding of the seven key themes introduced in the chapter by matching the vignettes with the themes they exemplify. You'll find the answers in Appendix A.

Themes

1. Psychology is empirical.

2. Psychology is theoretically diverse.

3. Psychology evolves in a sociohistorical context.

4. Behavior is determined by multiple causes.

5. Our behavior is shaped by our cultural heritage.

6. Heredity and environment jointly influence behavior.

7. People's experience of the world is highly subjective.

Vignettes

a. Several or more theoretical models of emotion have contributed to our overall understanding of the dynamics of emotion.

_____

b. According to the stress-vulnerability model, some people are at greater risk for developing certain psychological disorders for genetic reasons. Whether these people actually develop the disorders depends on how much stress they experience in their work, their families, or other areas of their lives.

_____

c. Physical health and illness seem to be influenced by a complex constellation of psychological, biological, and social system variables.

_____

d. One of the difficulties in investigating the effects of drugs on consciousness is that individuals tend to have different experiences with a given drug because of their different expectations.

_____

PERSONAL *Application*

Improving Academic Performance

Answer the following "true" or "false."

_____ 1 If you have a professor who delivers chaotic, hard-to-follow lectures, there is little point in attending class.

_____ 2 Cramming the night before an exam is an efficient method of study.

_____ 3 In taking lecture notes, you should try to be a "human tape recorder" (that is, write down everything your professor says).

_____ 4 You should never change your answers to multiple-choice questions, because your first hunch is your best hunch.

All of the above statements are false. If you answered them all correctly, you may have already acquired the kinds of skills and habits that facilitate academic success. If so, however, you are not typical. Today, many students enter college with poor study skills and habits, and it's not entirely their fault. Our educational system generally provides minimal instruction on good study techniques. In this first Personal Application, I will try to remedy this situation to some extent by reviewing some insights that psychology offers on how to improve academic performance. We will discuss how to promote better study habits, how to enhance reading efforts, how to get more out of lectures, and how to improve test-taking strategies. You may also want to jump ahead and read the Personal Application for Chapter 7, which focuses on how to improve everyday memory.

Developing Sound Study Habits

Effective study is crucial to success in college. Although you may run into a few classmates who boast about getting good grades without studying, you can be sure that if they perform well on exams, they do study. Students who claim otherwise simply want to be viewed as extremely bright rather than as studious.

Learning can be immensely gratifying, but studying usually involves hard work. The first step toward effective study habits is to face up to this reality. You don't have to feel guilty if you don't look forward to studying. Most students don't. Once you accept the premise that studying doesn't come naturally, it should be apparent that you need to set up an organized program to promote adequate study. According to Siebert (1995), such a program should include the following considerations:

1. *Set up a schedule for studying.* If you wait until the urge to study strikes you, you may still be waiting when the exam rolls around. Thus, it is important to allocate definite times to studying. Review your various time obligations (work, chores, and so on) and figure out in advance when you can study. When allotting certain times to studying, keep in mind that you need to be wide awake and alert. Be realistic about how long you can study at one time before you wear down from fatigue. Allow time for study breaks; they can revive sagging concentration.

It's important to write down your study schedule. A written schedule serves as a reminder and increases your commitment to following it. You should begin by setting up a general schedule for the quarter or semester, like the one in **Figure 1.9**. Then, at the beginning of each week, plan the specific assignments that you intend to work on during each study session. This approach to scheduling should help you avoid cramming for exams at the last minute. Cramming is an ineffective study strategy for most students (Underwood, 1961; Zechmeister & Nyberg, 1982). It will strain your memorization capabilities, can tax your energy level, and may stoke the fires of test anxiety.

In planning your weekly schedule, try to avoid the tendency to put off working on major tasks such as term papers and reports. Time-management experts, such as Alan Lakein (1996), point out that many of us tend to tackle simple, routine tasks first, saving larger tasks for later when we supposedly will have more time. This common tendency leads many of us to repeatedly delay working on major assignments until it's too late to do a good job. You can avoid this trap by breaking major assignments down into smaller component tasks that can be scheduled individually.

2. *Find a place to study where you can concentrate.* Where you study is also important. The key is to find a place where distractions are likely to be minimal. Most people cannot study effectively while the TV or stereo is on or while other people are talking. Don't depend on willpower to carry you through such distractions. It's much easier to plan ahead and avoid the distractions altogether. In fact, you would be wise to set up one or two specific places used solely for study (Hettich, 1998).

3. *Reward your studying.* One reason that it is so difficult to be motivated to study regularly is that the payoffs often lie in the distant future. The ultimate reward, a degree, may be years away. Even more short-term rewards, such as an A in the course, may be weeks or months away. To combat this problem, it helps to give yourself immediate, tangible rewards for studying, such as a snack, TV show, or phone call to a friend. Thus, you should set realistic study goals for yourself and then reward yourself when you meet them. The systematic manipulation of rewards involves harnessing the principles of behavior modification described by B. F. Skinner and other behavioral psychologists. These principles are covered in the Chapter 6 Personal Application.

Improving Your Reading

Much of your study time is spent reading and absorbing information. These efforts must be active. Many students deceive themselves into thinking that they are studying by running a marker through a few sentences here and there in their book. If they do so without thoughtful selectivity, they are sim-

Figure 1.9
One student's general activity schedule for a semester. Each week the student fills in the specific assignments to work on during each study period.

Weekly Activity Schedule							
	Monday	**Tuesday**	**Wednesday**	**Thursday**	**Friday**	**Saturday**	**Sunday**
8 A.M.						Work	
9 A.M.	History	Study	History	Study	History	Work	
10 A.M.	Psychology	French	Psychology	French	Psychology	Work	
11 A.M.	Study	French	Study	French	Study	Work	
Noon	Math	Study	Math	Study	Math	Work	Study
1 P.M.							Study
2 P.M.	Study	English	Study	English	Study		Study
3 P.M.	Study	English	Study	English	Study		Study
4 P.M.							
5 P.M.							
6 P.M.	Work	Study	Study	Work			Study
7 P.M.	Work	Study	Study	Work			Study
8 P.M.	Work	Study	Study	Work			Study
9 P.M.	Work	Study	Study	Work			Study
10 P.M.	Work			Work			

Some locations are far more conducive to successful studying than others.

ply turning a textbook into a coloring book. Research suggests that highlighting selected textbook material *is* a useful strategy—if students are reasonably effective in identifying the main ideas in the material and if they subsequently review the main ideas they have highlighted (Caverly, Orlando, & Mullen, 2000).

You can use a number of methods to actively attack your reading assignments. One worthwhile strategy is Robinson's (1970) SQ3R method. **SQ3R is a study system designed to promote effective reading by means of five steps: survey, question, read, recite, and review.** Its name is an acronym for the five steps in the procedure.

Step 1: Survey. Before you plunge into the reading itself, glance over the topic headings in the chapter. Try to get a general overview of the material. If you know where the chapter is going, you can better appreciate and organize the information you are about to read.

Step 2: Question. Once you have an overview of your reading assignment, you should proceed through it one section at a time. Take a look at the heading of the first section and convert it into a question. Doing so is usually quite simple. If the heading is "Prenatal Risk Factors," your question should be "What are sources of risk during prenatal development?" If the heading is "Stereotyping," your question should be "What is stereotyping?" Asking these questions gets you actively involved in your reading and helps you identify the main ideas.

Step 3: Read. Only now, in the third step, are you ready to sink your teeth into the reading. Read only the specific section that you have decided to tackle. Read it with an eye toward answering the question you have just formulated. If necessary, reread the section until you can answer that question. Decide whether the segment addresses any other important questions and answer them as well.

Step 4: Recite. Now that you can answer the key question for the section, recite the answer out loud to yourself in your own words. Don't move on to the next section until you understand the main ideas of the current section. You may want to write down these ideas for review later. When you have fully digested the first section, you may go on to the next. Repeat steps 2 through 4 with the next section. Once you have mastered the crucial points there, you can go on again. Keep repeating steps 2 through 4, section by section, until you finish the chapter.

Step 5: Review. When you have read the entire chapter, refresh your memory by going back over the key points. Repeat your questions and try to answer them without consulting your book or notes. This review should fortify your retention of the main ideas. It should also help you see how the main ideas are related.

The SQ3R method should probably be applied to many texts on a paragraph-by-paragraph basis. Obviously, this approach will require you to formulate some questions without the benefit of topic headings. If you don't have enough headings, you can simply reverse steps 2 and 3. Read the paragraph first and then formulate a question that addresses the basic idea of the paragraph. Then work at answering the question in your own words. The point is that you can be flexible in your use of the SQ3R technique.

Using the SQ3R method does not automatically lead to improved mastery of textbook reading assignments. It won't be effective unless it is applied diligently and skillfully and it tends to be more helpful to students with low to medium reading ability (Caverly, Orlando, & Mullen, 2000). Any strategy that facilitates active processing of text material, the identification of key ideas, and effective review of these ideas should enhance your reading.

Besides topic headings, your textbooks may contain various other learning aids you can use to improve your reading. If a book provides a chapter outline, chapter summary, learning objectives, or preview questions don't ignore them. They can help you recognize the important points in the chapter. Graphic organizers (such as the Concept Charts available for this text) can also enhance understanding of text material (Nist & Holschuh, 2000). A lot of effort and thought goes into formulating these and other textbook learning aids. It is wise to take advantage of them.

Getting More out of Lectures

Although lectures are sometimes boring and tedious, it is a simple fact that poor class attendance is associated with poor grades. For example, in one study (see **Figure 1.10** on the next page), Lindgren (1969) found that absences from class were much more common among "unsuccessful" students (grade average C– or below) than among "successful" students (grade average B or above). Even when you have an instructor who delivers hard-to-follow lectures, it is still important to go to class. If nothing else, you can get a feel for how the instructor thinks, which can help you anticipate the content of exams and respond in the manner expected by your professor.

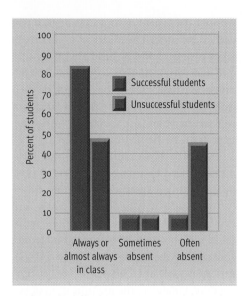

Figure 1.10

Attendance and grades. When Lindgren (1969) compared the class attendance of successful students (B average or above) and unsuccessful students (C– average or below), he found a clear association between poor attendance and poor grades.

Fortunately, most lectures are reasonably coherent. Studies indicate that attentive note taking *is* associated with enhanced learning and performance in college classes (Titsworth & Kiewra, 2004; Williams & Eggert, 2002). However, research also shows that many students' lecture notes are surprisingly incomplete, with the average student often recording less than 40% of the crucial ideas in a lecture (Armbruster, 2000). Thus, the key to getting more out of lectures is to stay motivated, stay attentive, and expend the effort to make your notes as complete as possible.

Books on study skills (Longman & Atkinson, 2002; Sotiriou, 2002) offer a number of suggestions on how to take good-quality lecture notes, some of which are summarized here:

• Extracting information from lectures requires active listening. Focus full attention on the speaker. Try to anticipate what's coming and search for deeper meanings.
• When course material is especially complex, it is a good idea to prepare for the lecture by reading ahead on the scheduled subject in your text. Then you have less brand-new information to digest.
• You are not supposed to be a human tape recorder. Insofar as possible, try to write down the lecturer's thoughts in your own words. Doing so forces you to organize the ideas in a way that makes sense to you.
• Asking questions during lectures can be helpful. Doing so keeps you actively involved in the lecture and allows you to clarify points that you may have misunderstood. Many students are more bashful about asking questions than they should be. They don't realize that most professors welcome questions.

Improving Test-Taking Strategies

Let's face it—some students are better than others at taking tests. **Testwiseness is the ability to use the characteristics and format of a cognitive test to maximize one's score.** Students clearly vary in testwiseness,

and such variations are reflected in performance on exams (Geiger, 1997; Rogers & Yang, 1996). Testwiseness is *not* a substitute for knowledge of the subject matter. However, skill in taking tests can help you show what you know when it is critical to do so (Flippo, Becker, & Wark, 2000).

A number of myths exist about the best way to take tests. For instance, it is widely believed that students shouldn't go back and change their answers to multiple-choice questions. Benjamin, Cavell, and Shallenberger (1984) found this to be the dominant belief among college *faculty* as well as students (see **Figure 1.11**). However, the old adage that "your first hunch is your best hunch on tests" has been shown to be wrong. Empirical studies clearly and consistently indicate that, over the long run, changing answers pays off. Benjamin and his colleagues reviewed 20 studies on this issue; their findings are presented in **Figure 1.12**. As you can see, answer changes that go from a wrong answer to a right answer outnumber changes that go from a right answer to a wrong one by a sizable margin. The popular belief that answer changing is harmful is probably attributable to painful memories of right-to-wrong changes. In any case, you can see how it pays to be familiar with sound test-taking strategies.

General Tips

The principles of testwiseness were first described by Millman, Bishop, and Ebel (1965). Here are some of their general ideas:

DOONESBURY

DOONESBURY © by G. B. Trudeau. Distributed by Universal Press Syndicate. Reprinted with permission. All rights reserved.

Figure 1.11

Beliefs about the effects of answer changing on tests. Ludy Benjamin and his colleagues (1984) asked 58 college faculty whether changing answers on tests is a good idea. Like most students, the majority of the faculty felt that answer changing usually hurts a student's test score, even though the research evidence contradicts this belief (see **Figure 1.12**).

Figure 1.12

Actual effects of changing answers on multiple-choice tests. When the data from all the relevant studies were combined by Benjamin et al. (1984), they indicated that answer changing on tests generally *increased* rather than *reduced* students' test scores. It is interesting to note the contrast between beliefs about answer changing (see **Figure 1.11**) and the actual results of this practice.

- If efficient time use appears crucial, set up a mental schedule for progressing through the test. Make a mental note to check whether you're one-third finished when a third of your time is gone.
- Don't waste time pondering difficult-to-answer questions excessively. If you have no idea at all, just guess and go on. If you need to devote a good deal of time to the question, skip it and mark it so you can return to it later if time permits.
- Adopt the appropriate level of sophistication for the test. Don't read things into questions. Sometimes students make things more complex than they were intended to be. Often, simple-looking questions are just what they appear to be.
- If you complete all of the questions and still have some time remaining, review the test. Make sure that you have recorded your answers correctly. If you were unsure of some answers, go back and reconsider them.

Tips for Multiple-Choice Exams

Sound test-taking strategies are especially important with multiple-choice (and true-false) questions. These types of questions often include clues that may help you converge on the correct answer (Mentzer, 1982; Weiten, 1984). You may be able to improve your performance on such tests by considering the following points (Flippo, 2000):

- Always read each question completely. Continue reading even if you find your anticipated answer among the options. There may be a more complete option farther down the list.
- Learn how to quickly eliminate options that are highly implausible. Many questions have only two plausible options, accompanied by "throwaway" options for filler. You should work at spotting these implausible options so that you can quickly discard them and narrow your choices.
- Be alert to the fact that information relevant to one question is sometimes given away in another test item.
- On items that have "all of the above" as an option, if you know that just two of the options are correct, you should choose "all of the above." If you are confident that one of the options is incorrect, you should eliminate this option and "all of the above" and choose from the remaining options.
- Options that represent broad, sweeping generalizations tend to be incorrect. You should be vigilant for words such as *always, never, necessarily, only, must, completely, totally,* and so forth that create these improbable assertions.
- In contrast, options that represent carefully qualified statements tend to be correct. Words such as *often, sometimes, perhaps, may,* and *generally* tend to show up in these well-qualified statements.

In summary, sound study skills and habits are crucial to academic success. Intelligence alone won't do the job (although it certainly helps). Good academic skills do not develop overnight. They are acquired gradually, so be patient with yourself. Fortunately, tasks such as reading textbooks, writing papers, and taking tests get easier with practice. Ultimately, I think you'll find that the rewards—knowledge, a sense of accomplishment, and progress toward a degree—are worth the effort.

Developing Critical Thinking Skills: An Introduction

If you ask any group of professors, parents, employers, or politicians, "What is the most important outcome of an education?" the most popular answer is likely to be "the development of the ability to think critically." *Critical thinking* **is purposeful, reasoned, goal-directed thinking that involves solving problems, formulating inferences, working with probabilities, and making carefully thought-out decisions.** Critical thinking is the use of cognitive skills and strategies that increase the probability of a desirable outcome. Such outcomes would include good career choices, effective decisions in the workplace, wise investments, and so forth. In the long run, critical thinkers should have more desirable outcomes than people who are not skilled in critical thinking (Halpern, 1998, 2003). Here are some of the skills exhibited by critical thinkers:

- They understand and use the principles of scientific investigation. (How can the effectiveness of punishment as a disciplinary procedure be determined?)
- They apply the rules of formal and informal logic. (If most people disapprove of sex sites on the World Wide Web, then why are these sites so popular?)
- They think effectively in terms of probabilities. (What is the likelihood of being able to predict who will commit a violent crime?)
- They carefully evaluate the quality of information. (Can I trust the claims made by this politician?)
- They analyze arguments for the soundness of the conclusions. (Does the rise in drug use mean a stricter drug policy is needed?).

The topic of thinking has a long history in psychology, dating back to Wilhelm Wundt in the 19th century. Modern cognitive psychologists have found that a useful model of critical thinking has at least two components: It consists of knowledge of the skills of critical thinking—the *cognitive component*—as well as the attitude or disposition of a critical thinker—the *emotional* or *affec-*

tive component. Both are needed for effective critical thinking.

The Skills and Attitudes of Critical Thinking

Instruction in critical thinking is based on two assumptions: (1) a set of skills or strategies exists that students can learn to recognize and apply in appropriate contexts, and (2) if the skills are applied appropriately, students will become more effective thinkers. Critical thinking skills that would be useful in any context might include understanding how reasons and evidence support or refute conclusions; distinguishing among facts, opinions, and reasoned judgments; using principles of likelihood and uncertainty when thinking about probabilistic events; generating multiple solutions to problems and working systematically toward a desired goal; and understanding how causation is determined. This list provides some typical examples of what is meant by the term *critical thinking skills*. Because these skills are useful in a wide variety of contexts, they are sometimes called *transcontextual skills*.

It is of little use to know the skills of critical thinking if you are unwilling to exert the hard mental work to use them or if you have a sloppy or careless attitude toward thinking. A critical thinker is willing to plan, flexible in thinking, persistent, able to

admit mistakes and make corrections, and mindful of the thinking process. The use of the word *critical* represents the notion of a critique or evaluation of thinking processes and outcomes. It is not meant to be negative (as in a "critical person") but rather is intended to convey that critical thinkers are vigilant about their thinking.

The Need to Teach Critical Thinking

Decades of research on instruction in critical thinking have shown that the skills and attitudes of critical thinking need to be deliberately and consciously taught because they often do not develop by themselves with standard instruction in a content area (Nisbett, 1993). For this reason, each chapter in this text ends with a "Critical Thinking Application." The material presented in each of these Critical Thinking Applications relates to the chapter topics, but the focus is on how to think about a particular issue, line of research, or controversy. Because the emphasis is on the thinking process, you may be asked to consider conflicting interpretations of data, judge the credibility of information sources, or generate your own testable hypotheses. The specific critical thinking skills highlighted in each Application are summarized in a table so that they are easily identified. Some of the skills will show up in multiple chapters because the

NON SEQUITUR

NON SEQUITUR © 2004 by Wiley Miller. Distributed by Universal Press Syndicate. Reprinted with permission. All rights reserved.

goal is to help you spontaneously select the appropriate critical thinking skills when you encounter new information. Repeated practice with selected skills across chapters should help you develop this ability.

An Example

As explained in the main body of the chapter, *evolutionary psychology* is emerging as an influential school of thought. To show you how critical thinking skills can be applied to psychological issues, let's examine the evolutionary explanation of gender differences in spatial talents and then use some critical thinking strategies to evaluate this explanation.

On the average, males tend to perform slightly better than females on most visual-spatial tasks, especially tasks involving mental rotation of images and navigation in space (Halpern, 2000; see **Figure 1.13**). Irwin Silverman and his colleagues maintain that these gender differences originated in human evolution as a result of the sex-based division of labor in ancient hunting-and-gathering societies (Silverman & Phillips, 1998; Silverman et al., 2000). According to this analysis, males' superiority in mental rotation and navigation developed because the chore of *hunting* was largely assigned to men over the course of human history, and these skills would have facilitated success on hunting trips (by helping men to traverse long distances, aim projectiles at prey, and so forth) and thus would have been favored by natural selection. In contrast, women in ancient societies generally had responsibility for *gathering* food rather than hunting it. This was an efficient division of labor because women spent much of their adult lives pregnant, nursing, or caring for the young and, therefore, could not travel long distances. Hence, Silverman and Eals (1992) hypothesized that females ought to be superior to males on spatial skills that would have facilitated gathering, such as memory for locations, which is exactly what they found in a series of four studies. Thus, evolutionary psychologists explain gender differences in spatial ability—like other aspects of human behavior—in terms of how such abilities evolved to meet the adaptive pressures faced by our ancestors.

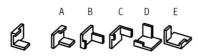

Figure 1.13

An example of a spatial task involving mental rotation. Spatial reasoning tasks can be divided into a variety of subtypes. Studies indicate that males perform slightly better than females on most, but not all, spatial tasks. The tasks on which males are superior often involve mentally rotating objects, such as in the problem shown here. In this problem, the person has to figure out which object on the right (A Through E) could be a rotation of the object at the left.

How can you critically evaluate these claims? If your first thought was that you need more information, good for you, because you are already showing an aptitude for critical thinking. Some additional information about gender differences in cognitive abilities is presented in Chapter 10 of this text. You also need to develop the habit of asking good questions, such as, "Are there alternative explanations for these results? Are there contradictory data?" Let's briefly consider each of these questions.

Are there alternative explanations for gender differences in spatial skills? Well, there certainly are other explanations for males' superiority on most spatial tasks. For example, we could attribute this finding to the gender-typed activities that males are encouraged to engage in more than females, such as playing with building blocks, Lego sets, Lincoln Logs, and various types of construction sets, as well as a host of spatially oriented video games. These gender-typed activities appear to provide boys with more practice than girls on most types of spatial tasks (Voyer, Nolan, & Voyer, 2000), and experience with spatial activities appears to enhance spatial

skills (Lizarraga & Ganuza, 2003). If we can explain gender differences in spatial abilities in terms of disparities in the everyday activities of males and females, we may have no need to appeal to natural selection.

Are there data that run counter to the evolutionary explanation for modern gender differences in spatial skills? Again, the answer is yes. Some scholars who have studied hunting-and-gathering societies suggest that women often traveled long distances to gather food and that women were often involved in hunting (Adler, 1993). In addition, women wove baskets and clothing and worked on other tasks that required spatial thinking (Halpern, 1997). Moreover—think about it—men on long hunting trips obviously needed to develop a good memory for locations or they might never have returned home. So, there is room for some argument about exactly what kinds of adaptive pressures males and females faced in ancient hunting-and-gathering societies.

Thus, you can see how considering alternative explanations and contradictory evidence weakens the evolutionary explanation of gender differences in spatial abilities. The questions we raised about alternative explanations and contradictory data are two generic critical thinking questions that can be asked in a wide variety of contexts. The answers to these questions do *not* prove that evolutionary psychologists are wrong in their explanation of gender differences in visual-spatial skills, but they do *weaken* the evolutionary explanation. In thinking critically about psychological issues, you will see that it makes more sense to talk about the *relative strength* of an argument, as opposed to whether an argument is right or wrong, because we will be dealing with complex issues that rarely lend themselves to being correct or incorrect.

Table 1.2 Critical Thinking Skills Discussed in This Application

Skill	Description
Looking for alternative explanations for findings and events	In evaluating explanations, the critical thinker explores whether there are other explanations that could also account for the findings or events under scrutiny.
Looking for contradictory evidence	In evaluating the evidence presented on an issue, the critical thinker attempts to look for contradictory evidence that may have been left out of the debate.

CHAPTER 1 *Review*

Key Ideas

From Speculation to Science: How Psychology Developed

● Psychology's intellectual parents were 19th-century philosophy and physiology, which shared an interest in the mysteries of the mind. Psychology was born as an independent discipline when Wilhelm Wundt established the first psychological research laboratory in 1879 at Leipzig, Germany. He argued that psychology should be the scientific study of consciousness. The new discipline grew rapidly in North America in the late 19th century.

● The structuralists believed that psychology should use introspection to analyze consciousness into its basic elements. Functionalists such as William James believed that psychology should focus on the purpose and adaptive functions of consciousness. Functionalism left a more enduring imprint on psychology.

● Sigmund Freud's psychoanalytic theory emphasized the unconscious determinants of behavior and the importance of sexuality. Freud's controversial ideas were met with resistance in academic psychology. However, as more psychologists developed an interest in personality, motivation, and abnormal behavior, psychoanalytic concepts were incorporated into mainstream psychology.

● Behaviorists, led by John B. Watson, argued that psychology should study only observable behavior. Thus, they campaigned to redefine psychology as the science of behavior. Emphasizing the importance of the environment over heredity, they often used laboratory animals as research subjects.

● The influence of behaviorism was boosted greatly by B. F. Skinner's research. Like Watson before him, Skinner asserted that psychology should study only observable behavior, and he generated controversy by arguing that free will is an illusion.

● Finding both behaviorism and psychoanalysis unsatisfactory, advocates of humanism, such as Carl Rogers and Abraham Maslow, became influential in the 1950s. Humanism emphasizes the unique qualities of human behavior and humans' potential for personal growth.

● Stimulated by the demands of World War II, clinical psychology grew rapidly in the 1950s. Thus, psychology became a profession as well as a science. This movement toward professionalization eventually spread to other areas in psychology. During the 1950s and 1960s advances in the study of cognitive processes and the physiological bases of behavior led to renewed interest in cognition and physiology.

● In the 1980s, Western psychologists, who had previously been rather provincial, developed a greater interest in how cultural factors influence thoughts, feelings, and behavior. This trend was sparked in large part by growing global interdependence and by increased cultural diversity in Western societies.

● The 1990s witnessed the emergence of a new theoretical perspective called evolutionary psychology. The central premise of this new school of thought is that patterns of behavior are the product of evolutionary forces, just as anatomical characteristics are shaped by natural selection. The turn of the century brought the emergence of the positive psychology movement.

Psychology Today: Vigorous and Diversified

● Contemporary psychology is a diversified science and profession that has grown rapidly in recent decades. Major areas of research in modern psychology include developmental psychology, social psychology, experimental psychology, physiological psychology, cognitive psychology, personality, and psychometrics. Applied psychology encompasses four professional specialties: clinical psychology, counseling psychology, educational and school psychology, and industrial and organizational psychology.

Seven Unifying Themes

● As we examine psychology in all its many variations, we will emphasize seven key ideas as unifying themes. Looking at psychology as a field of study, our three key themes are (1) psychology is empirical, (2) psychology is theoretically diverse, and (3) psychology evolves in a sociohistorical context.

● Looking at psychology's subject matter, the remaining four themes are (4) behavior is determined by multiple causes, (5) behavior is shaped by cultural heritage, (6) heredity and environment jointly influence behavior, and (7) people's experience of the world is highly subjective.

PERSONAL APPLICATION • Improving Academic Performance

● To foster sound study habits, you should devise a written study schedule and reward yourself for following it. You should also try to find one or two specific places for studying that are relatively free of distractions. You should use active reading techniques to select the most important ideas from the material you read. SQ3R is one approach to active reading that can be beneficial.

● Good note taking can help you get more out of lectures. It's important to use active listening techniques and to record lecturers' ideas in your own words. It also helps if you read ahead to prepare for lectures and ask questions as needed.

● Being an effective student also requires sound test-taking skills. In general, it's a good idea to devise a schedule for progressing through an exam, to adopt the appropriate level of sophistication, to avoid wasting time on troublesome questions, and to review your answers whenever time permits.

CRITICAL THINKING APPLICATION • Developing Critical Thinking Skills: An Introduction

● Critical thinking refers to the use of cognitive skills and strategies that increase the probability of a desirable outcome. Critical thinking is purposeful, reasoned thinking. A critical thinker is flexible, persistent, able to admit mistakes, and mindful of the thinking process.

● Evolutionary psychologists have attributed contemporary sex differences in spatial abilities to the sex-based division of labor in hunting-and-gathering societies. However, there are alternative explanations for these differences that focus on the sex-typed activities that modern males and females engage in. There also are contradictory data regarding the adaptive pressures faced by females and males in hunting-and-gathering societies.

Key Terms

Applied psychology (p. 10)
Behavior (p. 7)
Behaviorism (p. 7)
Clinical psychology (p. 10)
Cognition (p. 11)
Critical thinking (p. 28)
Culture (p. 21)
Empiricism (p. 20)
Evolutionary psychology (p. 12)
Functionalism (p. 4)
Humanism (p. 9)
Introspection (p. 4)
Natural selection (p. 5)
Positive psychology (p. 16)
Psychoanalytic theory (p. 6)
Psychology (p. 16)

SQ3R (p. 25)
Structuralism (p. 4)
Testwiseness (p. 26)
Theory (p. 20)
Unconscious (p. 6)

Key People

Mary Whiton Calkins (p. 5)
Sigmund Freud (p. 6)
Leta Stetter Hollingworth (p. 5)
William James (pp. 4–5)
Carl Rogers (p. 10)
Martin Seligman (pp. 13, 16)
B. F. Skinner (pp. 8–9)
Margaret Floy Washburn (p. 5)
John B. Watson (pp. 7–8)
Wilhelm Wundt (p. 3)

1. For which of the following is Wilhelm Wundt primarily known?
   A. The establishment of the first formal laboratory for research in psychology
   B. The distinction between mind and body as two separate entities
   C. The discovery of how signals are conducted along nerves in the body
   D. The development of the first formal program for training in psychotherapy

2. Leta Hollingworth is noted for:
   A. Being the first woman to receive a Ph.D. in psychology.
   B. Being the first woman president of the American Psychological Association.
   C. Founding one of the early psychology laboratories in America.
   D. Collecting objective data on gender differences in behavior.

3. Which of the following approaches might William James criticize for examining a movie frame by frame instead of seeing the motion in the motion picture?
   A. Structuralism
   B. Functionalism
   C. Dualism
   D. Humanism

4. Fred, a tennis coach, insists that he can make any reasonably healthy individual into an internationally competitive tennis player. Fred is echoing the thoughts of:
   A. Sigmund Freud.
   B. John B. Watson.
   C. Abraham Maslow.
   D. William James.

5. Which of the following approaches might suggest that forgetting to pick his mother up at the airport was Henry's unconscious way of saying that he did not welcome her visit?
   A. Psychoanalytic
   B. Behavioral
   C. Humanistic
   D. Cognitive

6. Which of the following is a statement with which Skinner's followers would agree?
   A. The whole is greater than the sum of its parts.
   B. The goal of behavior is self-actualization.
   C. Nature is more influential than nurture.
   D. Free will is an illusion.

7. Which of the following approaches has the most optimistic view of human nature?
   A. Humanism
   B. Behaviorism
   C. Psychoanalysis
   D. Structuralism

8. Which of the following historical events created a demand for clinicians that was far greater than the supply, leading to the emergence of clinical psychology?
   A. World War I
   B. The Depression
   C. World War II
   D. The Korean War

9. _____ psychology examines behavioral processes in terms of their adaptive value for a species over the course of many generations.
   A. Clinical   C. Evolutionary
   B. Cognitive   D. Physiological

10. The study of the endocrine system and genetic mechanisms would most likely be undertaken by a:
    A. clinical psychologist.
    B. physiological psychologist.
    C. social psychologist.
    D. educational psychologist.

11. The fact that psychologists do not all agree about the nature and development of personality demonstrates:
    A. that there are many ways of looking at the same phenomenon, illustrating theoretical diversity.
    B. the fundamental inability of psychologists to work together in developing a single theory.
    C. the failure of psychologists to communicate with one another.
    D. the possibility that personality may simply be incomprehensible.

12. A multifactorial causation approach to behavior suggests that:
    A. Most behaviors can be explained best by single-cause explanations.
    B. Most behavior is governed by a complex network of interrelated factors.
    C. Data need to be analyzed by the statistical technique called factor analysis in order for the data to make sense.
    D. Explanations of behavior tend to build up from the simple to the complex in a hierarchical manner.

13. Psychology's answer to the question of whether we are "born" or "made" tends to be that:
    A. we are "born."
    B. we are "made."
    C. we are both "born" and "made."
    D. neither is correct.

14. In regard to changing answers on multiple-choice tests, research indicates that _____ changes tend to be more common than other types of changes.
    A. wrong to right
    B. right to wrong
    C. wrong to wrong

15. Critical thinking skills:
    A. are abstract abilities that cannot be identified.
    B. usually develop spontaneously through normal content instruction.
    C. usually develop spontaneously without any instruction.
    D. need to be deliberately taught because they often do not develop by themselves with standard content instruction.

Answers

1 A p. 3	6 D pp. 8–9	11 A p. 20
2 D p. 5	7 A pp. 9–10	12 B p. 21
3 A p. 5	8 C pp. 10–11	13 C p. 22
4 B pp. 7–8	9 C p. 12	14 A pp. 26–27
5 A p. 6	10 B p. 18	15 D p. 28

PsykTrek

Go to the PsykTrek website or CD-ROM for further study of the concepts in this chapter. Both online and on the CD-ROM, PsykTrek includes dozens of learning modules with videos, animations, and quizzes, as well as simulations of psychological phenomena and a multimedia glossary that includes word pronunciations.

ThomsonNOW

www.thomsonedu.com/ThomsonNOW

Go to this site for the link to ThomsonNOW, your one-stop study shop. Take a Pre-Test for this chapter, and ThomsonNOW will generate a Personalized Study Plan based on your test results. The Study Plan will identify the topics you need to review and direct you to online resources to help you master those topics. You can then take a Post-Test to help you determine the concepts you have mastered and what you still need to work on.

Companion Website

www.thomsonedu.com/psychology/weiten

Go to this site to find online resources directly linked to your book, including a glossary, flash cards, drag-and-drop exercises, quizzes, and more!

CHAPTER 2

The Research Enterprise in Psychology

© Josh Westrich/zefa/Corbis

- Do adversaries in debates overestimate the gap between their views?
- How does anxiety affect people's desire to be with others? Does misery love company?
- Are there substantial differences among cultures when it comes to the pace of everyday life?
- What are the psychological characteristics of people who commit suicide?
- Are taller people more successful in life?

Questions, questions, questions—everyone has questions about behavior. The most basic question is: How should these questions be investigated? As noted in Chapter 1, psychology is empirical. Psychologists rely on formal, systematic observations to address their questions about behavior. This methodology is what makes psychology a scientific endeavor.

The scientific enterprise is an exercise in creative problem solving. Scientists have to figure out how to make observations that will shed light on the puzzles they want to solve. To make these observations, psychologists use a variety of research methods because different questions call for different strategies of study. In this chapter, you will see how researchers have used such methods as experiments, case studies, surveys, and naturalistic observation to investigate the questions listed at the beginning of this chapter.

Psychology's methods are worth a close look for at least two reasons. First, a better appreciation of the empirical approach will enhance your understanding of the research-based information you will be reading about in the remainder of this book. Second, familiarity with the logic of the empirical approach should improve your ability to think critically about research. This skepticism is important because you hear about research findings nearly every day. The news media constantly report on studies that yield conclusions about how you should raise your children, improve your health, and enhance your interpersonal relationships. Learning how to evaluate these reports with more sophistication can help you use such information wisely.

In this chapter, we will examine the scientific approach to the study of behavior, then look at the specific research methods that psychologists use most frequently. After you learn how research is done, we'll review some common flaws in doing research. Finally, we will take a look at ethical issues in behavioral research. In the Personal Application, you'll learn how to find and read journal articles that report on research. In the chapter's Critical Thinking Application, we'll take a critical look at the nature and validity of anecdotal evidence.

> **Looking for Laws: The Scientific Approach to Behavior**

Whether the object of study is gravitational forces or people's behavior under stress, *the scientific approach assumes that events are governed by some lawful order.* As scientists, psychologists assume that behavior is governed by laws or principles, just as the movement of the earth around the sun is governed by the laws of gravity. The behavior of living creatures may not seem as lawful and predictable as the "behavior" of planets. However, the scientific enterprise is based on the belief that there are consistencies or laws that can be uncovered. Fortunately, the value of applying this fundamental assumption has been supported by the discovery of a great many such consistencies in behavior, some of which provide the subject matter for this text.

Goals of the Scientific Enterprise

Psychologists and other scientists share three sets of interrelated goals: measurement and description, understanding and prediction, and application and control.

1. *Measurement and description.* Science's commitment to observation requires that a researcher figure out a way to measure the phenomenon under study. For example, a psychologist could not investigate whether men are more or less sociable than women without first developing some means of measuring sociability. Thus, the first goal of psychology is to develop measurement techniques that make it possible to describe behavior clearly and precisely.

2. *Understanding and prediction.* A higher-level goal of science is understanding. Scientists believe that they understand events when they can explain the reasons for their occurrence. To evaluate such understanding, scientists make and test predictions called hypotheses. A *hypothesis* is a tentative statement about the relationship between two or more variables. *Variables* are any measurable conditions, events, characteristics, or behaviors that are controlled or observed in a study. If we predicted that

PREVIEW QUESTIONS

- What are the goals of the scientific enterprise?
- What are the key steps required by a scientific investigation?
- What are the principal advantages of the scientific approach?

"IT MAY VERY WELL BRING ABOUT IMMORTALITY, BUT IT WILL TAKE FOREVER TO TEST IT."

ScienceCartoonsPlus.com

putting people under time pressure would lower the accuracy of their time perception, the variables in our study would be time pressure and accuracy of time perception.

3. *Application and control.* Ultimately, most scientists hope that the information they gather will be of some practical value in helping to solve everyday problems. Once people understand a phenomenon, they often can exert more control over it. Today, the profession of psychology attempts to apply research findings to practical problems in schools, businesses, factories, and mental hospitals. For example, a school psychologist might use findings about the causes of math anxiety to devise a program to help students control their math phobias.

How do theories help scientists to achieve their goals? As noted in Chapter 1, psychologists do not set out to just collect isolated facts about relationships between variables. To build toward a better understanding of behavior, they construct theories. A *theory* **is a system of interrelated ideas used to explain a set of observations.** For example, using a handful of concepts, such as natural selection and reproductive fitness, evolutionary theory (Buss, 1995, 1996) purports to explain a diverse array of known facts about mating preferences, jealousy, aggression, sexual behavior, and so forth (see Chapter 1). Thus, by integrating apparently unrelated facts and prin-

ciples into a coherent whole, theories permit psychologists to make the leap from the *description* of behavior to the *understanding* of behavior. Moreover, the enhanced understanding afforded by theories guides future research by generating new predictions and suggesting new lines of inquiry (Fiske, 2004; Higgins, 2004).

A scientific theory must be testable, as the cornerstone of science is its commitment to putting ideas to an empirical test. Most theories are too complex to be tested all at once. For example, it would be impossible to devise a single study that could test all the many aspects of evolutionary theory. Rather, in a typical study, investigators test one or two specific hypotheses derived from a theory. If their findings support the hypotheses, confidence in the theory that the hypotheses were derived from grows. If their findings fail to support the hypotheses, confidence in the theory diminishes, and the theory may be revised or discarded. Thus, theory construction is a gradual, iterative process that is always subject to revision.

Steps in a Scientific Investigation

Curiosity about a question provides the point of departure for any kind of investigation, scientific or otherwise. Scientific investigations, however, are *systematic*. They follow an orderly pattern, which is outlined in **Figure 2.1**. Let's look at how this standard series of steps was followed in a study of *naïve realism* conducted by David Sherman, Leif Nelson, and Lee Ross (2003). Sherman and his colleagues wanted to investigate whether adversaries in political debates overestimate the gap between their views.

Step 1: Formulate a Testable Hypothesis

The first step in a scientific investigation is to translate a theory or an intuitive idea into a testable hypothesis. Sherman et al. (2003) noted that in heated disputes people seem to assume that they see matters as they really are—that their perceptions are objective and accurate—and that their opponents' views are distorted by self-interest, ideology, or some other source of bias. The researchers call this belief in one's own objectivity and opponents' subjectivity "naïve realism." Based on their concept of naïve realism, Sherman and his colleagues speculated that in political debates people on both sides would tend to characterize their opponents as extremists and to overestimate the extent of their mutual disagree-

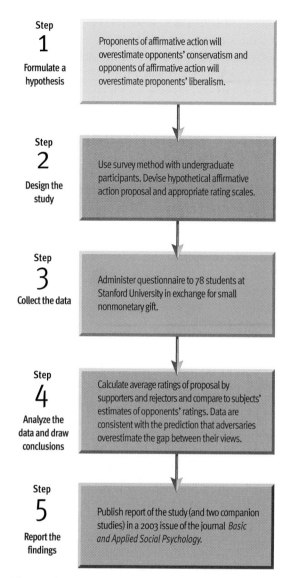

Step 1
Formulate a hypothesis

Proponents of affirmative action will overestimate opponents' conservatism and opponents of affirmative action will overestimate proponents' liberalism.

Step 2
Design the study

Use survey method with undergraduate participants. Devise hypothetical affirmative action proposal and appropriate rating scales.

Step 3
Collect the data

Administer questionnaire to 78 students at Stanford University in exchange for small nonmonetary gift.

Step 4
Analyze the data and draw conclusions

Calculate average ratings of proposal by supporters and rejectors and compare to subjects' estimates of opponents' ratings. Data are consistent with the prediction that adversaries overestimate the gap between their views.

Step 5
Report the findings

Publish report of the study (and two companion studies) in a 2003 issue of the journal *Basic and Applied Social Psychology*.

Figure 2.1

Flowchart of steps in a scientific investigation. As illustrated in the study by Sherman, Nelson, and Ross (2003), a scientific investigation consists of a sequence of carefully planned steps, beginning with the formulation of a testable hypothesis and ending with the publication of the study, if its results are worthy of examination by other researchers.

ment. To explore this line of thinking they chose to examine individuals' views on the contentious issue of affirmative action. Thus, they hypothesized that proponents of affirmative action would overestimate opponents' conservativism and that opponents of affirmative action would overestimate proponents' liberalism.

To be testable, scientific hypotheses must be formulated precisely, and the variables under study must be clearly defined. Researchers achieve these clear formulations by providing operational definitions of the

relevant variables. **An *operational definition* describes the actions or operations that will be used to measure or control a variable.** Operational definitions—which may be quite different from concepts' dictionary definitions—establish precisely what is meant by each variable in the context of a study.

To illustrate, let's see how Sherman and his colleagues operationalized their variables. They decided that the issue of affirmative action is too complex and multifaceted to ask people about their views of affirmative action *in general*. Each person would be judging something different, based on his or her highly varied exposure to affirmative action initiatives. To circumvent this problem they asked students to respond to a specific affirmative action program that supposedly had been proposed for their university. To get a precise measurement of participants' views, they asked the students to indicate their degree of support for the proposal on a 9-point scale anchored by the descriptions *definitely adopt* and *definitely reject*. Those checking 1 to 4 on the scale were designated as *supporters* of the proposal and those checking 6 to 9 on the scale were designated as *rejecters* (those who checked the midpoint of 5 were classified as *neutral*).

Step 2: Select the Research Method and Design the Study

The second step in a scientific investigation is to figure out how to put the hypothesis to an empirical test. The research method chosen depends to a large degree on the nature of the question under study. The various methods—experiments, case studies, surveys, naturalistic observation, and so forth—each have advantages and disadvantages. The researcher has to ponder the pros and cons and then select the strategy that appears to be the most appropriate and practical. In this case, Sherman and colleagues decided that their question called for *survey* research, which involves administering questionnaires or interviews to people.

Once researchers have chosen a general method, they must make detailed plans for executing their study. Thus, Sherman et al. had to decide how many people they needed to survey and where they would get their participants. ***Participants,* or *subjects,* are the persons or animals whose behavior is systematically observed in a study.** For their first study, Sherman et al. chose to use 78 undergraduates (45 women and 29 men) at Stanford University. Sherman and his colleagues also had to devise a plausible-sounding affirmative action proposal that students

Web Link 2.1

PubMed
Very few commercial databases of journal articles or abstracts in the health sciences are available online for no charge. However, the National Library of Medicine has opened the millions of items of MEDLINE's abstracts and references to anyone wanting to research within the scientific literature of medical journals, including some important psychology publications.

could evaluate. And they had to craft rating scales that would permit the assessment of subjects' political ideology and the subjects' perceptions of their opponents' political ideology.

Step 3: Collect the Data

The third step in the research enterprise is to collect the data. Researchers use a variety of *data collection techniques,* **which are procedures for making empirical observations and measurements.** Commonly used techniques include direct observation, questionnaires, interviews, psychological tests, physiological recordings, and examination of archival records (see **Table 2.1**). The data collection techniques used in a study depend largely on what is being investigated. For example, questionnaires are well suited for studying attitudes, psychological tests for studying personality, and physiological recordings for studying the biological bases of behavior. Depending on the nature and complexity of the study, data collection can often take months, and sometimes requires years of work. One advantage of the survey method, however, is that you can often collect data quickly and easily, which was true in this case. Sherman and his colleagues simply had their subjects complete a carefully designed questionnaire in their dorm rooms in exchange for a small non-monetary gift.

Step 4: Analyze the Data and Draw Conclusions

The observations made in a study are usually converted into numbers, which constitute the raw data of the study. Researchers use *statistics* to analyze their data and to decide whether their hypotheses have been supported. Thus, statistics play an essential role in the scientific enterprise. Based on their statistical

analyses, Sherman et al. (2003) concluded that their data supported their hypothesis. As predicted, they found that supporters of the affirmative action proposal greatly overestimated the conservativism of the rejectors and that the rejectors of the proposal greatly overestimated the liberalism of the supporters (see **Figure 2.2**). The data indicated that the ac-

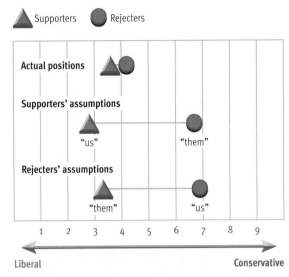

Figure 2.2
Results of the Sherman et al. (2003) study. As you can see, the actual liberal-conservative positions of the supporters and rejectors of the affirmative action proposal were not all that far apart (top row). However, when supporters of the proposal were asked to estimate the political ideology of other supporters as well as of those who rejected the proposal, they assumed that there was a huge gap between the two groups (middle row). Similarly, when those who were against the proposal were asked to make the same estimates (bottom row), they also overestimated the disparity between the two groups.

Source: Sherman, D. K., Nelson, L. D., & Ross, L. D. (2003). Naïve realism and affirmative action: Adversaries are more similar than they think. *Basic and Applied Social Psychology, 25,* 275–289. Copyright © 2003 Lawrence Erlbaum Associates, Inc. Reprinted by permission.

Table 2.1 Key Data Collection Techniques in Psychology

Technique	Description
Direct observation	Observers are trained to watch and record behavior as objectively and precisely as possible. They may use some instrumentation, such as a stopwatch or video recorder.
Questionnaire	Subjects are administered a series of written questions designed to obtain information about attitudes, opinions, and specific aspects of their behavior.
Interview	A face-to-face dialogue is conducted to obtain information about specific aspects of a subject's behavior.
Psychological test	Subjects are administered a standardized measure to obtain a sample of their behavior. Tests are usually used to assess mental abilities or personality traits.
Physiological recording	An instrument is used to monitor and record a specific physiological process in a subject. Examples include measures of blood pressure, heart rate, muscle tension, and brain activity.
Examination of archival records	The researcher analyzes existing institutional records (the archives), such as census, economic, medical, legal, educational, and business records.

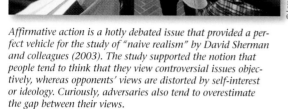

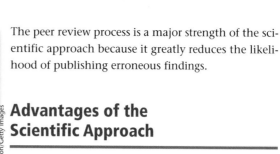

Affirmative action is a hotly debated issue that provided a perfect vehicle for the study of "naive realism" by David Sherman and colleagues (2003). The study supported the notion that people tend to think that they view controversial issues objectively, whereas opponents' views are distorted by self-interest or ideology. Curiously, adversaries also tend to overestimate the gap between their views.

tual (average) attitudes of the two groups really were not all that far apart, but each group *assumed* that their opponents held very dissimilar views. Obviously, insofar as this may be true of political debates in general, it sheds light on (1) why it is often so difficult for opposing sides to bridge the (perceived) gap between them, and (2) why people often have such pervasively negative views of their adversaries.

Step 5: Report the Findings

Scientific progress can be achieved only if researchers share their findings with one another and with the general public. Therefore, the final step in a scientific investigation is to write up a concise summary of the study and its findings. Typically, researchers prepare a report that is delivered at a scientific meeting and submitted to a journal for publication. A *journal is a periodical that publishes technical and scholarly material, usually in a narrowly defined area of inquiry.* The study by Sherman and his colleagues (2003) was published, along with two companion studies, in a journal called *Basic and Applied Social Psychology.*

The process of publishing scientific studies allows other experts to evaluate and critique new research findings. When articles are submitted to scientific journals they go through a very demanding *peer review process.* Experts thoroughly scrutinize each submission. They carefully evaluate each study's methods, statistical analyses, and conclusions, as well as its contribution to knowledge and theory. The peer review process is so demanding, many top journals reject over 90% of submitted articles! The purpose of the peer review process is to ensure that journals publish reliable findings based on high-quality research.

The peer review process is a major strength of the scientific approach because it greatly reduces the likelihood of publishing erroneous findings.

Advantages of the Scientific Approach

Science is certainly not the only method that can be used to draw conclusions about behavior. We all use logic, casual observation, and good old-fashioned common sense. Because the scientific method requires painstaking effort, it seems reasonable to ask what advantages make it worth the trouble.

Basically, the scientific approach offers two major advantages. The first is its clarity and precision. Commonsense notions about behavior tend to be vague and ambiguous. Consider the old adage "Spare the rod and spoil the child." What exactly does this generalization about childrearing amount to? How severely should children be punished if parents are not to "spare the rod"? How do we assess whether a child qualifies as "spoiled"? A fundamental problem is that such statements have different meanings, depending on the person. In contrast, the scientific approach requires that people specify *exactly* what they are talking about when they formulate hypotheses. This clarity and precision enhance communication about important ideas.

The second and perhaps greatest advantage offered by the scientific approach is its relative intolerance of error. Scientists are trained to be skeptical. They subject their ideas to empirical tests. They also inspect one another's findings with a critical eye. They demand objective data and thorough documentation before they accept ideas. When the findings of two studies conflict, the scientist tries to figure out why, usually by conducting additional research. In contrast, commonsense analyses involve little effort to verify ideas or detect errors.

All this is not to say that science has an exclusive copyright on truth. However, the scientific approach does tend to yield more accurate and dependable information than casual analyses and armchair speculation do. Knowledge of scientific data can thus provide a useful benchmark against which to judge claims and information from other kinds of sources.

Now that we have had an overview of how the scientific enterprise works, we can focus on how specific research methods are used. *Research methods consist of differing approaches to the observation, measurement, manipulation, and control of variables in empirical studies.* In other words, they are general strategies for conducting studies. No single

Web Link 2.2

PsycINFO Direct
The definitive resource for information on the scientific literature in psychology is the PsycINFO database of abstracts maintained by the American Psychological Association (see the Personal Application for this chapter). You may be able to access this database for free through your college library. If not, you can purchase access to PsycINFO Direct via the Internet. However, it would be wise to carefully plan your research in advance, as the cost is not cheap ($11.95 for a 24-hour period).

research method is ideal for all purposes and situations. Much of the ingenuity in research involves selecting and tailoring the method to the question at hand. The next two sections of this chapter discuss the two basic types of methods used in psychology: *experimental research methods* and *descriptive/correlational research methods*.

> Looking for Causes: Experimental Research

PREVIEW QUESTIONS

- What is the difference between an independent variable and a dependent variable?
- What is the purpose of experimental and control groups?
- What are extraneous variables and confounded variables?
- How can experiments vary in format?
- What are the strengths and weaknesses of experimental research?

Does misery love company? This question intrigued social psychologist Stanley Schachter. When people feel anxious, he wondered, do they want to be left alone, or do they prefer to have others around? Schachter's review of relevant theories suggested that in times of anxiety people would want others around to help them sort out their feelings. Thus, his hypothesis was that increases in anxiety would cause increases in the desire to be with others, which psychologists call the *need for affiliation*. To test this hypothesis, Schachter (1959) designed a clever experiment.

The *experiment* is a research method in which the investigator manipulates a variable under carefully controlled conditions and observes whether any changes occur in a second variable as a result. The experiment is a relatively powerful procedure that allows researchers to detect cause-and-effect relationships. Psychologists depend on this method more than any other. To see how an experiment is designed, let's use Schachter's study as an example.

Independent and Dependent Variables

The purpose of an experiment is to find out whether changes in one variable (let's call it *X*) cause changes in another variable (let's call it *Y*). To put it more concisely, we want to find out *how X affects Y*. In this formulation, we refer to *X* as the *independent variable* and to *Y* as the *dependent variable*.

An *independent variable* is a condition or event that an experimenter varies in order to see its impact on another variable. The independent variable is the variable that the experimenter controls or manipulates. It is hypothesized to have some effect on the dependent variable, and the experiment is conducted to verify this effect. **The *dependent variable* is the variable that is thought to be affected by manipulation of the independent variable.** In psychology studies, the dependent variable is usually a measurement of some aspect of the subjects' behavior. The independent variable is called *independent* because it is *free* to be varied by the experimenter. The dependent variable is called *dependent* because it is thought to *depend* (at least in part) on manipulations of the independent variable.

In Schachter's experiment, *the independent variable was the participants' anxiety level*. He manipulated anxiety level in a clever way. Subjects assembled in his laboratory were told by a "Dr. Zilstein" that they would be participating in a study on the physiological effects of electric shock. They were further informed that during the experiment they would receive a series of electric shocks while their pulse and blood pressure were being monitored. Half of the participants were warned that the shocks would be very painful. They made up the *high-anxiety* group. The other half of the participants (the *low-anxiety* group) were told that the shocks would be mild and painless. In reality, there was no plan to shock anyone at any time. These orientation procedures were simply intended to evoke different levels of anxiety. After the orientation, the experimenter indicated that there would be a delay while he prepared the shock apparatus for use. The participants were asked whether they would prefer to wait alone or in the company of others. *The subjects' desire to affiliate with others was the dependent variable.*

Experimental and Control Groups

In an experiment the investigator typically assembles two groups of subjects who are treated differently with regard to the independent variable. These two groups are referred to as the *experimental group* and the *control group*. **The *experimental group* consists of the subjects who receive some special treatment in regard to the independent variable. The *control group* consists of similar subjects who do not receive the special treatment given to the experimental group.**

In the Schachter study, the participants in the high-anxiety condition constituted the experimental group. They received a special treatment designed to create an unusually high level of anxiety. The participants in the low-anxiety condition constituted the control group. They were not exposed to the special anxiety-arousing procedure.

It is crucial that the experimental and control groups in a study be very similar, except for the different treatment that they receive in regard to the independent variable. This stipulation brings us to the logic that underlies the experimental method. If the two groups are alike in all respects *except for the variation created by the manipulation of the independent variable,* then any differences between the two groups on the dependent variable *must be due to the manipulation of the independent variable.* In this way researchers isolate the effect of the independent variable on the dependent variable. Schachter, for example, isolated the impact of anxiety on the need for affiliation. As predicted, he found that increased anxiety led to increased affiliation. As **Figure 2.3** indicates, the percentage of participants in the high-anxiety group who wanted to wait with others was nearly twice that of the low-anxiety group.

Extraneous Variables SIM 1, 1b

As we have seen, the logic of the experimental method rests on the assumption that the experimental and control groups are alike except for their treatment in regard to the independent variable. Any other differences between the two groups can cloud the situation and make it difficult to draw conclusions about how the independent variable affects the dependent variable.

In practical terms, of course, it is impossible to ensure that two groups of subjects are exactly alike in *every* respect. The experimental and control groups only have to be alike on dimensions that are relevant to the dependent variable. Thus, Schachter did not need to worry about whether his two groups were similar in hair color, height, or interest in ballet. Obviously, these variables weren't likely to influence the dependent variable of affiliation behavior.

Instead, experimenters concentrate on making sure that the experimental and control groups are alike on a limited number of variables that could have a bearing on the results of the study. These variables are called extraneous, secondary, or nuisance variables. *Extraneous variables* **are any variables other than the independent variable that seem**

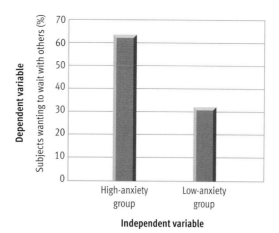

Figure 2.3
Results of Schachter's study of affiliation. The percentage of people wanting to wait with others was higher in the high-anxiety (experimental) group than in the low-anxiety (control) group, consistent with Schachter's hypothesis that anxiety would increase the desire for affiliation. The graphic portrayal of these results allows us to see at a glance the effects of the experimental manipulation on the dependent variable.

likely to influence the dependent variable in a specific study.

In Schachter's study, one extraneous variable would have been the participants' tendency to be sociable. Why? Because subjects' sociability could affect their desire to be with others (the dependent variable). If the participants in one group had happened to be more sociable (on the average) than those in the other group, the variables of anxiety and sociability would have been confounded. **A** *confounding of variables* **occurs when two variables are linked in a way that makes it difficult to sort out their specific effects.** When an extraneous variable is confounded with an independent variable, a researcher cannot tell which is having what effect on the dependent variable.

Unanticipated confoundings of variables have wrecked innumerable experiments. That is why so much care, planning, and forethought must go into designing an experiment. A key quality that separates a talented experimenter from a mediocre one is the ability to foresee troublesome extraneous variables and control them to avoid confoundings.

Experimenters use a variety of safeguards to control for extraneous variables. For instance, subjects are usually assigned to the experimental and control groups randomly. *Random assignment* **of subjects occurs when all subjects have an equal chance of being assigned to any group or condition in the study.** When experimenters distribute subjects into

Figure 2.4
The basic elements of an experiment. As illustrated by the Schachter study, the logic of experimental design rests on treating the experimental and control groups exactly alike (to control for extraneous variables) except for the manipulation of the independent variable. In this way, the experimenter attempts to isolate the effects of the independent variable on the dependent variable.

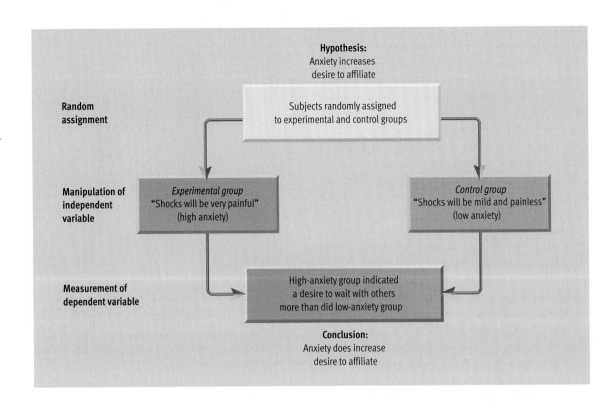

Hypothesis:
Anxiety increases
desire to affiliate

Random assignment

Subjects randomly assigned
to experimental and control groups

Manipulation of independent variable

Experimental group
"Shocks will be very painful"
(high anxiety)

Control group
"Shocks will be mild and painless"
(low anxiety)

Measurement of dependent variable

High-anxiety group indicated
a desire to wait with others
more than did low-anxiety group

Conclusion:
Anxiety does increase
desire to affiliate

Web Link 2.3

Psychological Research on the Net
This site, sponsored by the American Psychological Society, is a jumping-off point for people interested in participating in ongoing research projects that are collecting data over the Internet. Visitors will find a host of opportunities for taking part in genuine research.

groups through some random procedure, they can be reasonably confident that the groups will be similar in most ways.

To summarize the essentials of experimental design, **Figure 2.4** provides an overview of the elements in an experiment, using Schachter's study as an example.

Variations in Designing Experiments

We have discussed the experiment in only its simplest format, with just one independent variable and one dependent variable. Actually, many variations are possible in conducting experiments. *Sometimes it is advantageous to use only one group of subjects who serve as their own control group.* The effects of the independent variable are evaluated by exposing this single group to two different conditions: an *experimental condition* and a *control condition*. For example, imagine that you wanted to study the effects of loud music on typing performance. You could have a group of participants work on a typing task while loud music was played (experimental condition) and in the absence of music (control condition). This approach would ensure that the participants in the experimental and control conditions would be alike on any extraneous variables involving their personal characteristics, such as motivation or typing skill. After all, the same people would be studied in both conditions.

It is also possible to manipulate more than one independent variable or measure more than one dependent variable in a single experiment. For example, in another study of typing performance, you could vary both room temperature and the presence of distracting music as independent variables (see **Figure 2.5**), while measuring two aspects of typing performance (speed and accuracy) as dependent variables.

Advantages and Disadvantages of Experimental Research

The experiment is a powerful research method. Its principal advantage is that it permits conclusions about cause-and-effect relationships between variables. Researchers are able to draw these conclusions about causation because the precise control allows them to isolate the relationship between the independent variable and the dependent variable, while neutralizing the effects of extraneous variables. No other research method can duplicate this strength of the experiment. This advantage is why psychologists usually prefer to use the experimental method whenever possible.

For all its power, however, the experiment has limitations. One problem is that experiments are often artificial. Because experiments require great control over proceedings, researchers must often construct

Recognizing Independent and Dependent Variables

Check your understanding of the experimental method by identifying the independent variable (IV) and dependent variable (DV) in the following investigations. Note that one study has two IVs and another has two DVs. You'll find the answers in Appendix A in the back of the book.

1. A researcher is interested in how heart rate and blood pressure are affected by viewing a violent film sequence as opposed to a nonviolent film sequence.

IV _____

DV _____

2. An organizational psychologist develops a new training program to improve clerks' courtesy to customers in a large chain of retail stores. She conducts an experiment to see whether the training program leads to a reduction in the number of customer complaints.

IV _____

DV _____

3. A researcher wants to find out how stimulus complexity and stimulus contrast (light/dark variation) affect infants' attention to stimuli. He manipulates stimulus complexity and stimulus contrast and measures how long infants stare at various stimuli.

IV _____

DV _____

4. A social psychologist investigates the impact of group size on subjects' conformity in response to group pressure.

IV _____

DV _____

Distracting music

Present   Absent

Room temperature — Normal / High

Figure 2.5

Manipulation of two independent variables in an experiment. As this example shows, when two independent variables are manipulated in a single experiment, the researcher has to compare four groups of subjects (or conditions) instead of the usual two. The main advantage of this procedure is that it allows an experimenter to see whether two variables interact.

simple, contrived situations to test their hypotheses experimentally. For example, to investigate decision making in juries, psychologists have conducted many experiments in which participants read a brief summary of a trial and then record their individual "verdicts" of innocence or guilt. However, critics have pointed out that having a subject read a short case summary and make an individual decision is quite artificial in comparison to the complexities of real jury trials, which require group verdicts that are often the product of heated debates (Weiten & Diamond, 1979). When experiments are highly artificial, doubts arise about the applicability of findings to everyday behavior outside the experimental laboratory.

Another disadvantage is that the experimental method can't be used to explore some research questions. Psychologists are frequently interested in the effects of factors that cannot be manipulated as independent variables because of ethical concerns or practical realities. For example, you might want to know whether being brought up in an urban as opposed to a rural area affects people's values. An experiment would require you to assign similar families to live in urban and rural areas, which obviously is impossible to do. To explore this question, you would have to use descriptive/correlational research methods, which we turn to next.

PREVIEW QUESTIONS

- What is the difference between positive and negative correlations?
- How is correlation related to prediction and causation?
- How does naturalistic observation work?
- How can case studies be used to look for general principles of behavior?
- Why do researchers use surveys?
- What are the strengths and weaknesses of descriptive/correlational research?

As we just noted, in some situations psychologists cannot exert experimental control over the variables they want to study. In such situations, investigators must rely on *descriptive/correlational research methods*. What distinguishes these methods is that the researcher cannot manipulate the variables under study. This lack of control means that these methods cannot be used to demonstrate a cause-and-effect relationship between variables. *Descriptive/correlational methods permit investigators to see only whether there is a link or association between the variables of interest.* Such an association is called a *correlation,* and the results of descriptive research are often summarized with a statistic called the *correlation coefficient.* In this section, we'll take a close look at the concept of correlation and then examine three specific approaches to descriptive research: naturalistic observation, case studies, and surveys.

The Concept of Correlation 1d

In descriptive research, investigators often want to determine whether there is a correlation between two variables. **A *correlation* exists when two variables are related to each other.** A correlation may be either positive or negative, depending on the nature of the association between the variables measured. A *positive* correlation indicates that two variables co-vary (change together) in the *same* direction. This means that high scores on variable X are associated with high scores on variable Y and that low scores on variable X are associated with low scores on variable Y. For example, there is a positive correlation between high school grade point average (GPA) and subsequent college GPA. That is, people who do well in high school tend to do well in college, and those who perform poorly in high school tend to perform poorly in college (see **Figure 2.6**).

In contrast, a *negative* correlation indicates that two variables co-vary in the *opposite* direction. This means that people who score high on variable X tend to score low on variable Y, whereas those who score low on X tend to score high on Y. For example, in most college courses, there is a negative correlation between how frequently students are absent and how well they perform on exams. Students who have a high number of absences tend to get low exam scores, while students who have a low number of absences tend to earn higher exam scores (see **Figure 2.6**).

Strength of the Correlation 1d

The strength of an association between two variables can be measured with a statistic called the correlation coefficient. **The *correlation coefficient* is a numerical index of the degree of relationship between two variables.** This coefficient can vary between 0 and +1.00 (if the correlation is positive) or between 0 and −1.00 (if the correlation is negative). A coefficient near zero indicates no relationship between the variables. That is, high or low scores on variable X show no consistent relationship to high or low scores on variable Y. A coefficient of +1.00 or −1.00 indicates a perfect, one-to-one correspon-

Figure 2.6

Positive and negative correlation. Notice that the terms *positive* and *negative* refer to the direction of the relationship between two variables, not to its strength. Variables are positively correlated if they tend to increase and decrease together and are negatively correlated if one tends to increase when the other decreases.

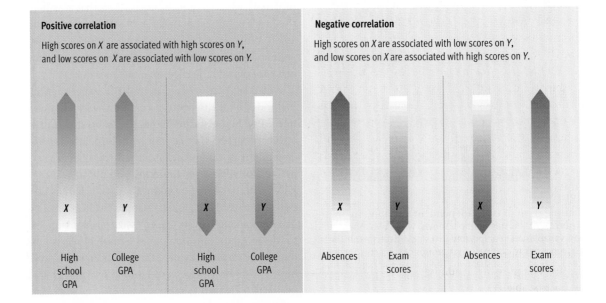

Positive correlation

High scores on X are associated with high scores on Y, and low scores on X are associated with low scores on Y.

X — High school GPA   Y — College GPA
X — High school GPA   Y — College GPA

Negative correlation

High scores on X are associated with low scores on Y, and low scores on X are associated with high scores on Y.

X — Absences   Y — Exam scores
X — Absences   Y — Exam scores

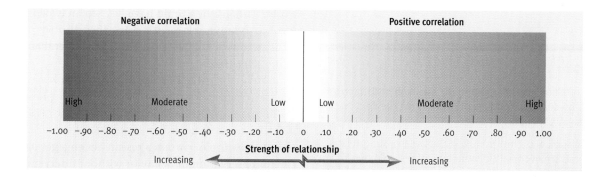

dence between the two variables. Most correlations fall between these extremes.

The closer the correlation is to either −1.00 or +1.00, the stronger the relationship (see **Figure 2.7**). Thus, a correlation of .90 represents a stronger tendency for variables to be associated than a correlation of .40. Likewise, a correlation of −.75 represents a stronger relationship than a correlation of −.45. Keep in mind that the *strength* of a correlation depends only on the size of the coefficient. The positive or negative sign simply indicates the direction of the relationship. Therefore, a correlation of −.60 reflects a stronger relationship than a correlation of +.30.

Correlation and Prediction

You may recall that one of the key goals of scientific research is accurate *prediction*. There is a close link between the magnitude of a correlation and the power it gives scientists to make predictions. *As a correlation increases in strength (gets closer to either −1.00 or +1.00), the ability to predict one variable based on knowledge of the other variable increases.*

To illustrate, consider how college admissions tests (such as the SAT or ACT) are used to predict college performance. When students' admissions test scores and college GPA are correlated, researchers generally find moderate positive correlations in the .40s and .50s (Gregory, 1996). Because of this relationship, college admissions committees can predict with modest accuracy how well prospective students will do in college. Admittedly, the predictive power of these admissions tests is far from perfect. But it's substantial enough to justify the use of the tests as one factor in making admissions decisions. However, if this correlation were much higher, say .90, admissions tests could predict with superb accuracy how students would perform. In contrast, if this correlation were much lower, say .20, the tests' prediction of college performance would be so poor that considering the test scores in admissions decisions would be unreasonable.

Correlation and Causation

Although a high correlation allows us to predict one variable on the basis of another, it does not tell us whether a cause-effect relationship exists between the two variables. The problem is that variables can be highly correlated even though they are not causally related.

When we find that variables *X* and *Y* are correlated, we can safely conclude only that *X* and *Y* are related. We do not know *how X* and *Y* are related. We do not know whether *X* causes *Y* or *Y* causes *X*, or whether both are caused by a third variable. For example, survey studies have found a positive correlation between smoking and the risk of experiencing a major depressive disorder (Breslau, Kilbey, & Andreski, 1991, 1993). Although it's clear that there is an association between smoking and depression, it's hard to tell what's causing what. The investigators acknowledge that they don't know whether smoking makes people more vulnerable to depression or whether depression increases the tendency to smoke. Moreover, they note that they can't rule out the possibility that both are caused by a third variable (*Z*). Perhaps anxiety and neuroticism increase the likelihood of both taking up smoking and becoming de-

"CONTRARY TO THE POPULAR VIEW, OUR STUDIES SHOW THAT IT IS REAL LIFE THAT CONTRIBUTES TO VIOLENCE ON TELEVISION."

Understanding Correlation

Check your understanding of correlation by interpreting the meaning of the correlation in item 1 and by guessing the direction (positive or negative) of the correlations in item 2. You'll find the answers in Appendix A.

1. Researchers have found a substantial positive correlation between youngsters' self-esteem and their academic achievement (measured by grades in school). Check any acceptable conclusions based on this correlation.

    _____ **a.** Low grades cause low self-esteem.

    _____ **b.** There is an association between self-esteem and academic achievement.

    _____ **c.** High self-esteem causes high academic achievement.

    _____ **d.** High ability causes both high self-esteem and high academic achievement.

    _____ **e.** Youngsters who score low in self-esteem tend to get low grades, and those who score high in self-esteem tend to get high grades.

2. Indicate whether you would expect the following correlations to be positive or negative.

    _____ **a.** The correlation between age and visual acuity (among adults).

    _____ **b.** The correlation between years of education and income.

    _____ **c.** The correlation between shyness and the number of friends one has.

compared the pace of life in 31 countries around the world. Perhaps they could have devised an experiment to examine this question, but they wanted to focus on the pace of life in the real world rather than in the laboratory.

To study the pace of life, Levine and Norenzayan had to come up with concrete ways to measure it—their operational definition of the concept. The measure they chose depended on *naturalistic observation*. **In *naturalistic observation* a researcher engages in careful observation of behavior without intervening directly with the subjects.** In this instance, the researchers observed (1) the average walking speed in downtown locations, (2) the accuracy of public clocks, and (3) the speed with which postal clerks completed a simple request. Their collection of data on walking speed illustrates the careful planning required to execute naturalistic observation effectively. In the main downtown area of each city, they had to find two flat, unobstructed, uncrowded 60-foot walkways where they could unobtrusively time pedestrians during normal business hours. Only adult pedestrians walking alone and not window shopping were timed. In most cities, the observations continued until 35 men and 35 women had been timed.

Levine and Norenzayan conducted their naturalistic observations in 31 countries, typically using the largest city in each country as the locale for their research. Their findings, based on all three measures, are summarized in **Figure 2.9** which ranks the pace of life in the countries studied. Their data suggest that the pace of life is fastest in the countries of Western Europe and in Japan. Using archival data, they also conducted correlational analyses to see whether variations in the pace of life were associated with factors such as climate, economic vitality, or population size. Among other things, they found that the pace of life was faster in colder climates and in countries that were more economically productive.

This type of research is called *naturalistic* because behavior is allowed to unfold naturally (without interference) in its natural environment—that is, the setting in which it would normally occur. The major

pressed. The plausible causal relationships in this case are diagrammed in **Figure 2.8**, which illustrates the "third variable problem" in interpreting correlations. This is a common problem in research, and you'll see this type of diagram again when we discuss other correlations. Thus, it is important to remember that *correlation is not equivalent to causation.*

Naturalistic Observation

Does the pace of everyday life vary substantially from one culture to the next? Do people operate at a different speed in say, Germany, as opposed to Canada or Brazil? Are factors such as economic vitality and climate related to differences in the pace of life? These are the kinds of questions that intrigued Robert V. Levine and Ara Norenzayan (1999), who

Figure 2.8

Three possible causal relations between correlated variables. If variables *X* and *Y* are correlated, does *X* cause *Y*, does *Y* cause *X*, or does some hidden third variable, *Z*, account for the changes in both *X* and *Y*? As the relationship between smoking and depression illustrates, a correlation alone does not provide the answer. We will encounter this problem of interpreting the meaning of correlations frequently in this text.

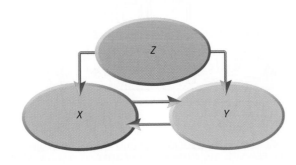

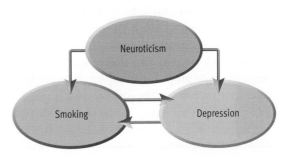

Naturalistic observation can be complex and challenging, as the study by Levine and Norenzayan (1999) illustrates. One of their measures of the pace of life in 31 cultures involved estimating people's walking speed in downtown locations. To reduce the influence of confounding factors, they had to find sidewalks that were unobstructed, uncrowded, not dominated by window shoppers, and so forth. Moreover, they had to find reasonably comparable locations in 31 very different types of cities.

strength of naturalistic observation is that it allows researchers to study behavior under conditions that are less artificial than in experiments. A major problem with this method is that researchers often have

trouble making their observations unobtrusively so they don't affect their subjects' behavior.

Case Studies

What portion of people who commit suicide suffer from psychological disorders? Which disorders are most common among victims of suicide? In health care visits during the final month of their lives, do people who commit suicide communicate their intent to do so? A research team in Finland wanted to investigate the psychological characteristics of people who take their own lives (Henriksson et al., 1993; Isometsa et al., 1995). Other researchers had explored these questions, but the Finnish team planned a comprehensive, national study of unprecedented scope. Their initial sample consisted of all the known suicides in Finland for an entire year.

The research team decided that their question called for a case study approach. **A *case study* is an in-depth investigation of an individual subject.** When this method is applied to victims of suicide, the case studies are called *psychological autopsies*. A variety of data collection techniques can be used in case studies. In normal circumstances, when the participants are not deceased, typical techniques include interviewing the participants, interviewing people who are close to the subjects, direct observation of the participants, examination of records, and psychological testing. In this study, the investigators conducted thorough interviews with the families of the suicide victims and with the health care professionals who had treated them. The researchers also examined the suicide victims' medical, psychiatric, and social agency records, as well as relevant police

Rank	Country	Rank	Country	Rank	Country
1	Switzerland	11	France	21	Greece
2	Ireland	12	Poland	22	Kenya
3	Germany	13	Costa Rica	23	China
4	Japan	14	Taiwan	24	Bulgaria
5	Italy	15	Singapore	25	Romania
6	England	16	United States	26	Jordan
7	Sweden	17	Canada	27	Syria
8	Austria	18	S. Korea	28	El Salvador
9	Netherlands	19	Hungary	29	Brazil
10	Hong Kong	20	Czech Republic	30	Indonesia
				31	Mexico

Figure 2.9

Ranking the pace of life in 31 cultures. Using naturalistic observation to collect their data, Levine and Norenzayan (1999) calculated estimates of the pace of life in 31 countries. Their rankings—from fastest to slowest—are shown here. As you can see, their findings indicate that the pace of life is fastest in Western Europe and Japan.

Source: Adapted from Levine, R. V., & Norenzayan, A. (1999). The pace of life in 31 countries. *Journal of Cross-Cultural Psychology, 30* (2), 178–205. Copyright © 1999 by Sage Publications. Reprinted by permission.

Web Link 2.4

PSYCLine: Your Guide to Psychology and Social Science Journals on the Web
Relatively few journals actually post their articles online for free. But, this searchable index to the online sites of more than 1900 psychology journals may lead you to recent tables of contents or abstracts or help you identify research resources on more unusual topics in psychology.

investigations and forensic reports. Comprehensive case reports were then assembled for each person who committed suicide.

These case studies revealed that in 93% of the suicides the victim suffered from a significant psychological disorder (Henriksson et al., 1993). The most common diagnoses, by a large margin, were depression and alcohol dependence. In 571 cases, victims had a health care appointment during their final four weeks of life, but only 22% of these people discussed the possibility of suicide during their final visit (Isometsa et al., 1995). Even more surprising, the sample included 100 people who saw a health professional on the same day they killed themselves, yet only 21% of these individuals raised the issue of suicide. The investigators concluded that mental illness is a contributing factor in virtually all completed suicides and that the vast majority of suicidal people do not spontaneously reveal their intentions to health care professionals.

Clinical psychologists, who diagnose and treat psychological problems, routinely do case studies of their clients. When clinicians assemble a case study for diagnostic purposes, they generally are *not* conducting empirical research. Case study *research* typically involves investigators analyzing a *series* of case studies to look for patterns that permit general conclusions.

Case studies are particularly well suited for investigating certain phenomena, such as psychological disorders. They can also provide compelling, real-life illustrations that bolster a hypothesis or theory. However, the main problem with case studies is that they are highly subjective. Information from several sources must be knit together in an impressionistic way. In this process, clinicians and researchers often focus selectively on information that fits with their expectations, which usually reflect their theoretical slant. Thus, it is relatively easy for investigators to see what they expect to see in case study research.

Surveys

Are taller people more successful in life? That would hardly seem fair, but folk wisdom suggests that height is associated with success. Some empirical studies of this issue have been conducted over the years, but many of them are extremely old and hobbled by a variety of methodological weaknesses. Hence, Timothy Judge and Daniel Cable (2004) set out to conduct a thorough investigation of the relationship between height and income. Their study depended on survey data. **In a *survey* researchers use questionnaires or interviews to gather information about specific aspects of participants' background and behavior.** In this case, Judge and Cable examined already-existing data that had been collected in four large-scale surveys that were concerned with other issues. Information on height and income were available for over 8000 participants from these studies.

What did the survey data reveal? In all four studies a modest association was found between height and income, with taller people earning more money. The association was not particularly strong, but it was not negligible. For example, based on their data, Judge and Cable estimated that a 6-foot-tall male would earn $166,000 more during a 30-year career than a similar man who was 5 feet 5 inches in stature. The relationship between greater height and greater income held for both men and women. The strength of the association varied somewhat across occupational areas. The height-income link was strongest for people in sales or management. The authors conclude that "our analyses revealed that height clearly matters in the context of workplace success" (p. 437). They discuss a variety of possible explanations for the association between height and earnings. Among other things, they note that taller people may develop higher self-esteem, which could foster better performance. Another possibility is that people just assume that taller individuals are more capable and competent and hence are more likely to buy products from them, hire them for good jobs, and promote them into even better positions. The exact mechanisms underlying the correlation between height and income are yet to be determined.

Surveys are often used to obtain information on aspects of behavior that are difficult to observe directly. Surveys also make it relatively easy to collect data on attitudes and opinions from large samples of participants. The major problem with surveys is that they depend on self-report data. As we'll discuss later, intentional deception, wishful thinking, memory lapses, and poorly worded questions can distort participants' verbal reports about their behavior (Krosnick, 1999).

Advantages and Disadvantages of Descriptive/Correlational Research

Descriptive/correlational research methods have advantages and disadvantages, which are compared to the strengths and weaknesses of experimental research in **Figure 2.10**. As a whole, the foremost advantage of these methods is that they give researchers a way to explore questions that they could not examine with experimental procedures. For example, after-the-fact analyses would be the only ethical way to investigate the possible link between poor maternal nutrition and birth defects in humans. In a similar vein, if researchers hope to learn how urban and rural upbringing relate to people's values, they have to depend on descriptive methods, since they can't control where subjects grow up. Thus, *descriptive research broadens the scope of phenomena that psychologists are able to study.*

Unfortunately, descriptive methods have one significant disadvantage: Investigators cannot control events to isolate cause and effect. *Consequently, descriptive/correlational research cannot demonstrate conclusively that correlated variables are causally related.* As an example, consider the cross-cultural investigation of the pace of life that we discussed earlier. Although Levine and Norenzayan (1996) found an association between colder climates and a faster pace of life, their data do not permit us to conclude that a cold climate causes a culture to move at a faster pace. Too many factors were left uncontrolled in the study. For example, we do not know how similar the cold and warm cities were. Climate could co-vary with some other factors, such as modernization or economic vitality, that might have led to the observed differences in the pace of life.

Figure 2.10

Comparison of major research methods. This chart pulls together a great deal of information on key research methods in psychology and gives a simple example of how each method might be applied in research on aggression. As you can see, the various research methods each have their strengths and weaknesses.

Overview of key research methods in psychology

Research method		Description	Example	Advantages	Disadvantages
Experiment 		Manipulation of an independent variable under carefully controlled conditions to see whether any changes occur in a dependent variable	Youngsters are randomly assigned to watch a violent or nonviolent film, and their aggression is measured in a laboratory situation	Precise control over variables; ability to draw conclusions about cause-and-effect relationships	Contrived situations often artificial; ethical concerns and practical realities preclude experiments on many important questions
Naturalistic observation 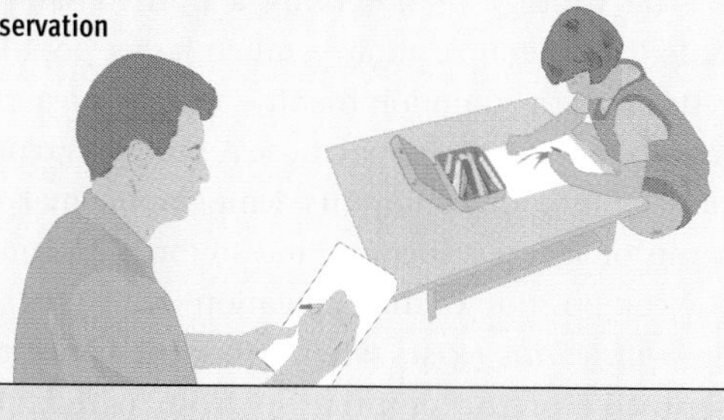		Careful, usually prolonged observation of behavior without direct intervention	Youngsters' spontaneous acts of aggression during recreational activities are observed unobtrusively and recorded	Minimizes artificiality; can be good place to start when little is known about phenomena under study	Often difficult to remain unobtrusive; can't explain why certain patterns of behavior were observed
Case studies 		In-depth investigation of a single participant using direct interview, direct observation, and other data collection techniques	Detailed case histories are worked up for youngsters referred to counseling because of excessive aggressive behavior	Well-suited for study of certain phenomena; can provide compelling illustrations to support a theory	Subjectivity makes it easy to see what one expects to see based on one's theoretical slant; clinical samples often unrepresentative
Surveys 		Use of questionnaires or interviews to gather information about specific aspects of participants' behavior	Youngsters are given questionnaire that describes hypothetical scenarios and are asked about the likelihood of aggressive behavior	Can gather data on difficult-to-observe aspects of behavior; relatively easy to collect data from large samples	Sef-report data often unreliable, due to intentional deception, social desirability bias, response sets, memory lapses, and wishful thinking

Matching Research Methods to Questions

Check your understanding of the uses and strengths of various research methods by figuring out which method would be optimal for investigating the following questions about behavioral processes. Choose from the following methods: (a) experiment, (b) naturalistic observation, (c) case study, and (d) survey. Indicate your choice (by letter) next to each question. You'll find the answers in Appendix A in the back of the book.

_____ **1.** Are people's attitudes about capital punishment related to their social class or education?

_____ **2.** Do people who suffer from anxiety disorders share similar early childhood experiences?

_____ **3.** Do troops of baboons display territoriality—that is, do they mark off an area as their own and defend it from intrusion?

_____ **4.** Can the presence of food-related cues (delicious-looking desserts in advertisements, for example) cause an increase in the amount of food that people eat?

> Looking for Flaws: Evaluating Research

PREVIEW QUESTIONS

● What is sampling bias?
● What are placebo effects, and how can you guard against them?
● What is the social desirability bias?
● What is experimenter bias, and how can you guard against it?

Scientific research is a more reliable source of information than casual observation or popular belief. However, it would be wrong to conclude that all published research is free of errors. Scientists are fallible human beings, and flawed studies do make their way into the body of scientific literature.

That is one of the reasons that scientists often try to replicate studies. **Replication is the repetition of a study to see whether the earlier results are duplicated.** The replication process helps science identify and purge inaccurate findings. Of course, the replication process sometimes leads to contradictory results. You'll see some examples in the upcoming chapters. Fortunately, one of the strengths of the empirical approach is that scientists work to reconcile or explain conflicting results. In fact, scientific advances often emerge out of efforts to explain contradictory findings.

Like all sources of information, scientific studies need to be examined with a critical eye. This section describes a number of common methodological problems that often spoil studies. Being aware of these pitfalls will make you more skilled in evaluating research.

Sampling Bias

A _sample_ **is the collection of subjects selected for observation in an empirical study.** In contrast, **the _population_ is the much larger collection of animals or people (from which the sample is drawn) that researchers want to generalize about.** For example, when political pollsters attempt to predict elections, all of the voters in a jurisdiction represent the population, and the voters who are actually surveyed constitute the sample. If researchers were interested in the ability of 6-year-old children to form concepts, those 6-year-olds actually studied would be the sample, and all similar 6-year-old children (perhaps those in modern, Western cultures) would be the population.

The strategy of observing a limited sample in order to generalize about a much larger population rests on the assumption that the sample is reasonably _representative_ of the population. A sample is representative if its composition (its demographic makeup in terms of age, sex, income, and so forth) is similar to the composition of the population (see **Figure 2.11**). _Sampling bias_ **exists when a sample is not representative of the population from which it was drawn.** When a sample is not representative, generalizations about the population may be inaccurate. For instance, if a political pollster were to survey only people in posh shopping areas frequented by the wealthy, the pollster's generalizations about the voting public as a whole would be off the mark.

Limits on available time and money often prevent researchers from obtaining as representative a sample as they would like. In general, when you have doubts about the results of a study, the first thing to examine is the composition of the sample.

Placebo Effects

A _placebo_ is a substance that resembles a drug but has no actual pharmacological effect. In studies that assess the effectiveness of medications, placebos are given to some participants to control for the effects of a treacherous extraneous variable: subjects' expectations. Placebos are used because researchers know that participants' expectations can influence their feelings, reactions, and behavior (Stewart-Williams, 2004). Thus, **placebo effects occur when participants' expectations lead them to experience some change even though they receive empty, fake, or ineffectual treatment.** In medicine, placebo effects are well documented (Quitkin, 1999). Many physicians tell of patients being "cured" by prescriptions of sugar pills. Similarly, psychologists have found that participants' expectations can be powerful determinants of their perceptions and behavior when they are under the microscope in an empirical study.

In describing placebo effects, I cannot help but recall a friend from my college days who would gulp one drink and start behaving in a drunken fashion before the alcohol could possibly have taken effect. In fact, this sort of placebo effect has been observed in a number of laboratory experiments on the effects of alcohol (Wilson, 1982). In these studies, some subjects are led to believe that they are drinking alcoholic beverages when in reality the drinks only seem to contain alcohol. Many of the participants act intoxicated, even though they haven't really consumed any alcohol.

Researchers should guard against placebo effects whenever participants are likely to have expectations that a treatment will affect them in a certain way. The possible role of placebo effects can be assessed by including a fake version of the experimental treatment (a placebo condition) in a study.

Distortions in Self-Report Data

Research psychologists often work with *self-report data*, made up of participants' verbal accounts of their behavior. This is the case whenever questionnaires, interviews, or personality inventories are used to measure variables. Self-report methods can be quite useful, taking advantage of the fact that people have a unique opportunity to observe themselves full-time (Baldwin, 2000). However, self-reports can be plagued by several kinds of distortion.

One of the most problematic of these distortions is **the *social desirability bias*, which is a tendency to give socially approved answers to questions about oneself.** Subjects who are influenced by this bias work overtime trying to create a favorable impression (DeMaio, 1984). For example, many survey respondents will report that they voted in an election or gave to a charity when in fact it is possible to determine that they did not (Granberg & Holmberg,

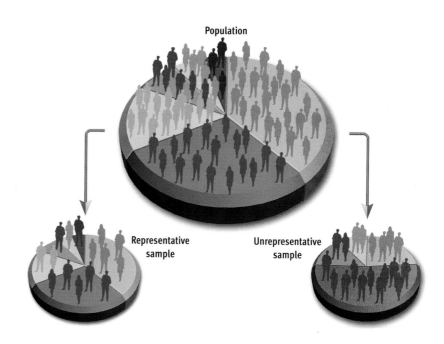

Population

Representative sample

Unrepresentative sample

1991; Hadaway, Marler, & Chaves, 1993). Interestingly, people who answer questions in socially desirable ways take slightly longer to respond to the questions, suggesting that they are carefully "editing" their responses (Holtgraves, 2004).

Other problems can also produce distortions in self-report data (Krosnick, 1999; Schuman & Kalton, 1985). Respondents misunderstand questionnaire items surprisingly often, and the way questions are worded can shape participants' responses (Schwarz, 1999). Memory errors can undermine the accuracy of verbal reports. In responding to certain kinds of scales, some people tend to agree with nearly all of the statements, while others tend to disagree with nearly everything (Krosnick & Fabrigar, 1998). Obviously, distortions like these can produce inaccurate results. Although researchers have devised ways to neutralize these problems, we should be especially cautious in drawing conclusions from self-report data (Schaeffer, 2000).

Experimenter Bias

As scientists, psychologists try to conduct their studies in an objective, unbiased way so that their own views will not influence the results. However, objectivity is a *goal* that scientists strive for, not an accomplished fact that can be taken for granted (MacCoun, 1998). In reality, most researchers have an emotional investment in the outcome of their research. Often they are testing hypotheses that they have developed themselves and that they would like to see supported by the data. It is understandable, then, that *experimenter bias* is a possible source of error in research.

Figure 2.11

The relationship between the population and the sample. The process of drawing inferences about a population based on a sample works only if the sample is reasonably representative of the population. A sample is representative if its demographic makeup is similar to that of the population, as shown on the left. If some groups in the population are overrepresented or underrepresented in the sample, as shown on the right, inferences about the population may be skewed or inaccurate.

ROBERT ROSENTHAL

"Quite unconsciously, a psychologist interacts in subtle ways with the people he is studying so that he may get the response he expects to get."

Experimenter bias **occurs when a researcher's expectations or preferences about the outcome of a study influence the results obtained.** Experimenter bias can slip through to influence studies in many subtle ways. One problem is that researchers, like others, sometimes *see what they want to see*. For instance, when experimenters make apparently honest mistakes in recording subjects' responses, the mistakes tend to be heavily slanted in favor of supporting the hypothesis (O'Leary, Kent, & Kanowitz, 1975).

Research by Robert Rosenthal (1976) suggests that experimenter bias may lead researchers to unintentionally influence the behavior of their subjects. In one study, Rosenthal and Fode (1963) recruited undergraduate psychology students to serve as the "experimenters." The students were told that they would be collecting data for a study of how participants rated the success of people portrayed in photographs. In a pilot study, photos were selected that generated (on the average) neutral ratings on a scale extending from −10 (extreme failure) to +10 (extreme success). Rosenthal and Fode then manipulated the expectations of their experimenters. Half of them were told that they would probably obtain average ratings of −5. The other half were led to expect average ratings of +5. The experimenters were forbidden from conversing with their subjects except for reading some standardized instructions. Even though the photographs were exactly the same for both groups, the experimenters who *expected* positive ratings *obtained* significantly higher ratings than those who expected negative ones.

How could the experimenters have swayed the participants' ratings? According to Rosenthal, the experimenters unintentionally influenced their subjects by sending subtle nonverbal signals as the experiment progressed. Without realizing it, they sometimes smiled, nodded, or sent other positive cues when participants made ratings that were in line with their expectations. Thus, experimenter bias may influence both researchers' observations and their subjects' behavior (Rosenthal, 1994, 2002).

The problems associated with experimenter bias can be neutralized by using a double-blind procedure. **The *double-blind procedure* is a research strategy in which neither subjects nor experimenters know which subjects are in the experimental or control groups.** It's not particularly unusual for subjects to be "blind" about their treatment condition. However, the double-blind procedure keeps the experimenter in the dark as well. Of course, a member of the research team who isn't directly involved with subjects keeps track of who is in which group.

---

concept **check** 2.4

Detecting Flaws in Research

Check your understanding of how to conduct sound research by looking for methodological flaws in the following studies. You'll find the answers in Appendix A.

Study 1. A researcher announces that he will be conducting an experiment to investigate the detrimental effects of sensory deprivation on perceptual-motor coordination. The first 40 students who sign up for the study are assigned to the experimental group, and the next 40 who sign up serve in the control group. The researcher supervises all aspects of the study's execution. Experimental subjects spend two hours in a sensory deprivation chamber, where sensory stimulation is minimal. Control subjects spend two hours in a waiting room that contains magazines and a TV. All subjects then perform ten 1-minute trials on a pursuit-rotor task that requires them to try to keep a stylus on a tiny rotating target. The dependent variable is their average score on the pursuit-rotor task.

Study 2. A researcher wants to know whether there is a relationship between age and racial prejudice. She designs a survey in which respondents are asked to rate their prejudice against six different ethnic groups. She distributes the survey to over 500 people of various ages who are approached at a shopping mall in a low-income, inner-city neighborhood.

Check the flaws that are apparent in each study.

Methodological flaw	Study 1	Study 2
Sampling bias	_____	_____
Placebo effects	_____	_____
Distortions in self-report	_____	_____
Confounding of variables	_____	_____
Experimenter bias	_____	_____

Courtesy of Robert Rosenthal

Think back to Stanley Schachter's (1959) study on anxiety and affiliation. Imagine how you would have felt if you had been one of the participants in Schachter's high-anxiety group. You show up at a research laboratory, expecting to participate in a harmless experiment. The room you are sent to is full of unusual electronic equipment. An official-looking man in a lab coat announces that this equipment will be used to give you a series of painful electric shocks. His statement that the shocks will leave "no permanent tissue damage" is hardly reassuring. Surely, you think, there must be a mistake. All of a sudden, your venture into research has turned into a nightmare! Your stomach knots up in anxiety. The researcher explains that there will be a delay while he prepares his apparatus. He asks you to fill out a short questionnaire about whether you would prefer to wait alone or with others. Still reeling in dismay at the prospect of being shocked, you fill out the questionnaire. He takes it and then announces that you won't be shocked after all—it was all a hoax! Feelings of relief wash over you, but they're mixed with feelings of anger. You feel as though the experimenter has just made a fool out of you, and you're embarrassed and resentful.

Should researchers be allowed to play with your feelings in this way? Should they be permitted to deceive participants in such a manner? Is this the cost that must be paid to advance scientific knowledge? As these questions indicate, the research enterprise sometimes presents scientists with difficult ethical dilemmas. *These dilemmas reflect concern about the possibility for inflicting harm on subjects.* In psychological research, the major ethical dilemmas center on the use of deception and the use of animals.

The Question of Deception

Elaborate deception, such as that seen in Schachter's study, has been fairly common in psychological research since the 1960s, especially in the area of social psychology (Epley & Huff, 1998; Korn, 1997). Over the years, psychologists have faked fights, thefts, muggings, faintings, epileptic seizures, rapes, and automobile breakdowns to explore a number of issues. Researchers have led subjects to believe that they (the subjects) were hurting others with electrical shocks, had homosexual tendencies, and were overhearing negative comments about themselves. Why have psychologists used so much deception in

their research? Because of the methodological problems discussed in the last section. Participants are often misled to avoid problems such as placebo effects and distortions in self-report data.

Critics argue against the use of deception on several grounds (Baumrind, 1985; Kelman, 1982; Ortmann & Hertwig, 1997). First, they assert that deception is only a nice word for lying, which they see as inherently immoral. Second, they argue that by deceiving unsuspecting participants, psychologists may undermine many individuals' trust in others. Third, they point out that many deceptive studies produce distress for participants who were not forewarned about that possibility. Specifically, participants may experience great stress during a study or be made to feel foolish when the true nature of a study is explained.

Those who defend the use of deception in research maintain that many important issues could not be investigated if experimenters were not permitted to mislead subjects (Bröder, 1998). They argue that most research deceptions involve "white lies" that are not likely to harm participants. A review of the relevant research by Larry Christensen (1988) suggests that deception studies are *not* harmful to participants. Indeed, most subjects who participate in experiments involving deception report that they enjoyed the experience and that they didn't mind being misled. Moreover, the empirical evidence does not support the notions that deceptive research undermines subjects' trust in others, or their respect for psychology or scientific research (Kimmel, 1996; Sharpe, Adair, & Roese, 1992). Curiously, the weight of the evidence suggests that researchers are more concerned about the negative effects of deception on participants than the participants themselves are (Fisher & Fyrberg, 1994; Korn, 1987). Finally, researchers who defend deception argue that the benefits—advances in knowledge that often improve human welfare—are worth the costs.

In regard to research with humans, the newest source of debate about ethics centers on social scientists' increased use of the Internet as a tool for collecting data (Keller & Lee, 2003; Pittenger, 2003). The emergence of the Internet has created a variety of new opportunities for behavioral researchers. For instance, researchers can post surveys on the web and gather data from larger and more diverse samples than ever before. Chat rooms and other types of virtual communities provide remarkable opportunities for naturalistic observation of group processes in action.

PREVIEW QUESTIONS

● What are the arguments against using deception in research?

● What are the arguments in favor of allowing deception in research?

● Why are many people opposed to animal research?

● How do animal researchers defend their work?

Web Link 2.5

Office of Research Integrity
Anyone who needs a comprehensive, up-to-date overview of ethical concerns in research from the perspective of the U.S. government should consider visiting this site. Although the Office of Research Integrity (ORI) deals with research sponsored by the U.S. Public Health Service, it also offers links to parallel offices and resources in many other agencies.

Web Link 2.6

Animal Welfare Information Center
This site, maintained by the U.S. Department of Agriculture, is an excellent jumping-off point for information relating to all aspects of how animals are (and should be) cared for in research, laboratory, and other settings.

Courtesy of Neal Miller

NEAL MILLER

"Who are the cruel and inhumane ones, the behavioral scientists whose research on animals led to the cures of the anorexic girl and the vomiting child, or the leaders of the radical animal activists who are making an exciting career of trying to stop all such research and are misinforming people by repeatedly asserting that it is without any value?"

The use of rats and other animals in scientific research is now a major ethical issue. Researchers claim that experiments on animals often yield results and knowledge beneficial to humankind. Opponents maintain that humans have no right to subject animals to harm for research purposes. What is your view?

Psychologists are moving quickly to take advantage of these opportunities, but this new venue for research sometimes raises complicated questions about how ethical guidelines should be applied. Is interaction on the Internet similar to interaction in a public location like a park or sidewalk, open to observation? Or is it more like interaction on a phone line, where one would expect some privacy? Is it acceptable for researchers to lurk in chat rooms and systematically record interactions? What if they pose as group members and provoke discussion of specific issues? If an Internet study includes deception, participants must be debriefed. But given the anonymity of the Internet, how can researchers debrief subjects who abandon their study midway and cannot be located? As you can see, the use of the Internet for research poses complex new ethical dilemmas for researchers.

The Question of Animal Research

Psychology's other major ethics controversy concerns the use of animals in research. Psychologists use animals as research subjects for several reasons. Sometimes they simply want to know more about the behavior of a specific type of animal. In other instances, they want to identify general laws of behavior that apply to both humans and animals. Finally, in some cases psychologists use animals because they can expose them to treatments that clearly would be unacceptable with human subjects. For example, most of the research on the relationship between deficient maternal nutrition during pregnancy and the incidence of birth defects has been done with animals.

It's this third reason for using animals that has generated most of the controversy. Some people maintain that it is wrong to subject animals to harm or pain for research purposes. Essentially, they argue that animals are entitled to the same rights as humans (Regan, 1997). They accuse researchers of violating these rights by subjecting animals to unnecessary cruelty in many "trivial" studies (Bowd & Shapiro, 1993; Hollands, 1989). They also argue that most animal studies are a waste of time because the results may not even apply to humans (Millstone, 1989; Ulrich, 1991). Some of the more militant animal rights activists have broken into laboratories, destroyed scientists' equipment and research records, and stolen experimental animals. The animal rights movement has enjoyed considerable success. For example, membership in People for the Ethical Treatment of Animals (PETA) grew from 8,000 in 1984 to 750,000 in 2003 (Herzog, 2005). Johnson (1990) noted that "the single issue citizens write about most often to their congresspersons and the president is not homelessness, not the drug problem, not crime. It is animal welfare" (p. 214).

In spite of the great furor, only 7%–8% of all psychological studies involve animals (mostly rodents and birds). Relatively few of these studies require subjecting the animals to painful or harmful manipulations (American Psychological Association, 1984). Psychologists who defend animal research point to the major advances attributable to psychological research on animals, which many people are unaware of (Baldwin, 1993; Compton, Dietrich, & Smith, 1995). Among them are advances in the treatment of mental disorders, neuromuscular disorders, strokes, brain injuries, visual defects, headaches, memory defects, high blood pressure, and problems with pain (Carroll & Overmier, 2001; Domjan & Purdy, 1995; Miller, 1985).

As you can see, the manner in which animals can ethically be used for research is a highly charged controversy. Psychologists are becoming increasingly sensitive to this issue. Although animals continue to be used in research, strict regulations have been imposed that regulate nearly every detail of how laboratory animals can be used for research purposes (Ator, 2005; Garnett, 2005).

The ethics issues that we have discussed in this section have led the APA to develop a set of ethical standards for researchers (American Psychological Association, 2002). Although most psychological studies are fairly benign, these ethical principles are intended to ensure that both human and animal subjects are treated with dignity. Some of the key guidelines in these ethical principles are summarized in **Figure 2.12**.

© James J. Broderick/International Stock

APA Ethical Guidelines for Research

1 A subject's participation in research should be voluntary and based on informed consent. Subjects should never be coerced into participating in research. They should be informed in advance about any aspects of the study that might be expected to influence their willingness to cooperate. Furthermore, they should be permitted to withdraw from a study at any time if they so desire.

2 Participants should not be exposed to harmful or dangerous research procedures. This guideline is intended to protect subjects from psychological as well as physical harm. Thus, even stressful procedures that might cause emotional discomfort are largely prohibited. However, procedures that carry a modest risk of moderate mental discomfort may be acceptable.

3 If an investigation requires some deception of participants (about matters that do not involve risks), the researcher is required to explain and correct any misunderstandings as soon as possible. The deception must be disclosed to subjects in "debriefing" sessions as soon as it is practical to do so without compromising the goals of the study.

4 Subjects' rights to privacy should never be violated. Information about a subject that might be acquired during a study must be treated as highly confidential and should never be made available to others without the consent of the participant.

5 Harmful or painful procedures imposed upon animals must be thoroughly justified in terms of the knowledge to be gained from the study. Furthermore, laboratory animals are entitled to decent living conditions that are spelled out in detailed rules that relate to their housing, cleaning, feeding, and so forth.

6 Prior to conducting studies, approval should be obtained from host institutions and their research review committees. Research results should be reported fully and accurately, and raw data should be promptly shared with other professionals who seek to verify substantive claims. Retractions should be made if significant errors are found in a study subsequent to its publication.

Figure 2.12

Ethics in research. Key ethical principles in psychological research, as set forth by the American Psychological Association (2002), are summarized here. These principles are meant to ensure the welfare of both human and animal subjects.

> Reflecting on the Chapter's Themes

Two of our seven unifying themes have emerged strongly in this chapter. First, the entire chapter is a testimonial to the idea that psychology is empirical. Second, the discussion of methodological flaws in research provides numerous examples of how people's experience of the world can be highly subjective. Let's examine each of these points in more detail.

As explained in Chapter 1, the empirical approach entails testing ideas, basing conclusions on systematic observation, and relying on a healthy brand of skepticism. All of those features of the empirical approach have been apparent in this chapter. As you have seen, psychologists test their ideas by formulating clear hypotheses that involve predictions about relations between variables. They then use a variety of research methods to collect data, so they can see whether their predictions are supported. The data collection methods are designed to make researchers' observations systematic and precise. The entire venture is saturated with skepticism. In planning and executing their research, scientists are constantly on the lookout for methodological flaws. They publish their findings so that other experts can subject their methods and conclusions to critical scrutiny. Collectively, these procedures represent the essence of the empirical approach.

The subjectivity of personal experience became apparent in the discussion of methodological prob-

lems, especially placebo effects and experimenter bias. When research participants report beneficial effects from a fake treatment (the placebo), it's because they expected to see these effects. The studies showing that many subjects start feeling intoxicated just because they think that they have consumed alcohol are striking demonstrations of the enormous power of people's expectations. As pointed out in Chapter 1, psychologists and other scientists are not immune to the effects of subjective experience. Although they are trained to be objective, even scientists may see what they expect to see or what they want to see. This is one reason that the empirical approach emphasizes precise measurement and a skeptical attitude. The highly subjective nature of experience is exactly what the empirical approach attempts to neutralize.

The publication of empirical studies allows us to apply our skepticism to the research enterprise. However, you cannot critically analyze studies unless you know where and how to find them. In the upcoming Personal Application, we will discuss where studies are published, how to find studies on specific topics, and how to read research reports. In the subsequent Critical Thinking Application, we'll analyze the shortcomings of anecdotal evidence, which should help you appreciate the value of empirical evidence.

 Empiricism

 Subjectivity of Experience

Answer the following "yes" or "no."

____ 1 I have read about scientific studies in newspapers and magazines and sometimes wondered, "How did they come to those conclusions?"

____ 2 When I go to the library, I often have difficulty figuring out how to find information based on research.

____ 3 I have tried to read scientific reports and found them to be too technical and difficult to understand.

If you responded "yes" to any of the above statements, you have struggled with the information explosion in the sciences. We live in a research-oriented society. The number of studies conducted in most sciences is growing at a dizzying pace. This expansion has been particularly spectacular in psychology. Moreover, psychological research increasingly commands attention from the popular press because it is often relevant to people's personal concerns.

This Personal Application is intended to help you cope with the information explosion in psychology. It assumes that there may come a time when you need to examine original psychological research. Perhaps it will be in your role as a student (working on a term paper, for instance), in another role (parent, teacher, nurse, administrator), or merely out of curiosity. In any case, this Application explains the nature of technical journals and discusses how to find and read articles in them. You can learn more about how to use library resources in psychology from an excellent little book titled *Library Use: Handbook for Psychology* (Reed & Baxter, 2003).

The Nature of Technical Journals

As you will recall from earlier in the chapter, a *journal* is a periodical that publishes technical and scholarly material, usually in a narrowly defined area of inquiry. Scholars in most fields—whether economics, chemistry, education, or psychology—publish the bulk of their work in these journals. Journal articles represent the core of intellectual activity in any academic discipline.

In general, journal articles are written for other professionals in the field. Hence, authors assume that their readers are other interested economists or chemists or psychologists. Because journal articles are written in the special language unique to a particular discipline, they are often difficult for non-professionals to understand. You will be learning a great deal of psychology's special language in this course, which will improve your ability to understand articles in psychology journals.

In psychology, most journal articles are reports that describe original empirical studies. These reports permit researchers to communicate their findings to the scientific community. Another common type of article is the review article. *Review articles* summarize and reconcile the findings of a large number of studies on a specific issue. Some psychology journals also publish comments or critiques of previously published research, book reviews, theoretical treatises, and descriptions of methodological innovations.

Finding Journal Articles

Reports of psychological research are commonly mentioned in newspapers and popular magazines. These summaries can be helpful to readers, but they often embrace the most sensational conclusions that might

be drawn from the research. They also tend to include many oversimplifications and factual errors. Hence, if a study mentioned in the press is of interest to you, you may want to track down the original article to ensure that you get accurate information.

Most discussions of research in the popular press do not mention where you can find the original technical article. However, there is a way to find out. A computerized database called PsycINFO makes it possible to locate journal articles by specific researchers or scholarly work on specific topics. This huge online database, which is updated constantly, contains brief summaries, or *abstracts,* of journal articles, books, and chapters in edited books, reporting, reviewing, or theorizing about psychological research. Over 1900 journals are checked regularly to select items for inclusion. The abstracts are concise—about 75 to 175 words. They briefly describe the hypotheses, methods, results, and conclusions of the studies. Each abstract should allow you to determine whether an article is relevant to your interests. If it is, you should be able to find the article in your library (or to order it) because a complete bibliographic reference is provided.

Although news accounts of research rarely mention where a study was published, they often mention the name of the researcher. If you have this information, the easiest way to find a specific article is to search PsycINFO for materials published by that researcher. For example, let's say you read a news report that summarized the survey study that we described earlier on the correlation between height and income (Judge & Cable, 2004; see p. 46). Let's assume that the news report mentioned the name of Timothy Judge as the lead author and indicated that the article was published in 2004. To track down the original article, you would search for journal articles published by Timothy Judge in 2004. If you conducted this search, you would turn up a list of 12 articles. The information for the first six articles in this list is shown in **Figure 2.13**. The second item in the list appears to be the article you are interested in. **Figure 2.14** on the next page shows what you would see if you clicked to obtain the Abstract and Citation for this article. As you can see, the abstract shows that the original report was published in the June 2004 issue of the *Journal of Applied Psychology.* Armed

Figure 2.13

Searching PsycINFO. If you searched PsycINFO for journal articles published by Timothy Judge during 2004, the database would return 12 listings, of which the first 6 are shown here. For each article, you can click to see its abstract or its full PsycINFO record (the abstract plus subject descriptors and other details). In some cases (depending on the version of PsycINFO that your library has ordered) you can click to see the full PsycINFO record plus references, or the *full text* of some articles.

Source: Sample search reprinted with permission of the American Psychological Association, publisher of the PsycINFO® database. Copyright © 1887–present, American Psychological Association. All rights reserved. For more information contact psycinfo.apa.org.

PsycINFO: Search Results

Your query: ((timothy judge):author) AND (2004<=Year<=2004)
Results: 12 documents (12 on this page)

1. **Intelligence and Leadership: A Quantitative Review and Test of Theoretical Propositions.**
   By Judge, Timothy A.; Colbert, Amy E.; Ilies, Remus
   Journal of Applied Psychology. 89(3), Jun 2004, 542–552.
   Citation and Abstract | Expanded Record | Expanded Record with References | View Article (HTML) | View Article (PDF)

2. **The Effect of Physical Height on Workplace Success and Income: Preliminary Test of a Theoretical Model.**
   By Judge, Timothy A.; Cable, Daniel M.
   Journal of Applied Psychology. 89(3), Jun 2004, 428–441.
   Citation and Abstract | Expanded Record | Expanded Record with References | View Article (HTML) | View Article (PDF)

3. **Organizational Justice and Stress: The Mediating Role of Work-Family Conflict.**
   By Judge, Timothy A.; Colquitt, Jason A.
   Journal of Applied Psychology. 89(3) Jun 2004, 395–404.
   Citation and Abstract | Expanded Record | Expanded Record with References | View Article (HTML) | View Article (PDF)

4. **Employee attitudes and job satisfaction.**
   By Saari, Lise M.; Judge, Timothy A.
   Human Resource Management. 43(4), Win 2004, 395–407.
   Citation and Abstract | Expanded Record | Expanded Record with References

5. **Personality and Transformational and Transactional Leadership: A Meta-Analysis.**
   By Bono, Joyce E.; Judge, Timothy A.
   Journal of Applied Psychology. 89(5) Oct 2004, 901–910.
   Citation and Abstract | Expanded Record | Expanded Record with References | View Article (HTML) | View Article (PDF)

6. **Transformational and Transactional Leadership: A Meta-Analytic Test of Their Relative Validity.**
   By Judge, Timothy A.; Piccolo, Ronald F.
   Journal of Applied Psychology. 89(5) Oct 2004, 755–768.
   Citation and Abstract | Expanded Record | Expanded Record with References | View Article (HTML) | View Article (PDF)

with this information, you could obtain the article easily.

You can also search PsycINFO for research literature on particular topics, such as achievement motivation, aggressive behavior, alcoholism, appetite disorders, or artistic ability. These computerized literature searches can be much more powerful, precise, and thorough than traditional, manual searches in a library. PsycINFO can sift through a few million articles in a matter of seconds to identify *all* the articles on a subject, such as alcoholism. Obviously,

there is no way you can match this efficiency stumbling around in the stacks at your library. Moreover, the computer allows you to pair up topics to swiftly narrow your search to exactly those issues that interest you. For example, **Figure 2.15** on the next page shows a PsycINFO search that identified all the articles on marijuana *and* memory. If you were preparing a term paper on whether marijuana affects memory, this precision would be invaluable.

The PsycINFO database can be accessed online at many libraries or via the Inter-

Figure 2.14

Example of a PsycINFO abstract. This information is what you would see if you clicked to see the abstract of item 2 in the list shown in **Figure 2.13**. It is a typical abstract from the online PsycINFO database. Each abstract in PsycINFO provides a summary of a specific journal article, book, or chapter in an edited book, and complete bibliographical information.

Source: Sample record reprinted with permission of the American Psychological Association, publisher of the PsycINFO® database. Copyright © 1887–present, American Psychological Association. All rights reserved. For more information contact psycinfo.apa.org.

PsycINFO: Citation and Abstract

Title	The Effect of Physical Height on Workplace Success and Income: Preliminary Test of a Theoretical Model.
Abstract	In this article, the authors propose a theoretical model of the relationship between physical height and career success. We then test several linkages in the model based on a meta-analysis of the literature, with results indicating that physical height is significantly related to measures of social esteem (p = .41), leader emergence (p = .24), and performance (p = .18). Height was somewhat more strongly related to success for men (p = .29) than for women (p = .21), although this difference was not significant. Finally, given that almost no research has examined the relationship between individuals' physical height and their incomes, we present four large-sample studies (total N = 8,590) showing that height is positively related to income (β = .26) after controlling for sex, age, and weight. Overall, this article presents the most comprehensive analysis of the relationship of height to workplace success to date, and the results suggest that tall individuals have advantages in several important aspects of their careers and organizational lives (PsycINFO Database Record © 2004 APA, all rights reserved)
Authors	Judge, Timothy A.; Cable, Daniel N.
Affiliations	Judge, Timothy A.: Department of Management, Warrington College of Business, University of Florida, FL, US Cable, Daniel M.: Kenan-Flagler Business School, University of North Carolina, NC, US
Source	Journal of Applied Psychology. 89(3), Jun 2004, 428–441.

Figure 2.15

Combining topics in a PsycINFO search. A computerized literature search can be a highly efficient way to locate the specific research that you need. For example, if you had set out in May of 2005 to find all the journal articles on marijuana and memory, you would have obtained the PsycINFO results summarized here. At that time, the database contained 90,610 articles related to memory and 3,156 articles related to marijuana. The search depicted on the left yielded 135 abstracts that relate to both marijuana and memory. Thus, in a matter of moments, the computer can sift through nearly 2 million abstracts to find those that are most germane to a specific question, such as: Does marijuana affect memory?

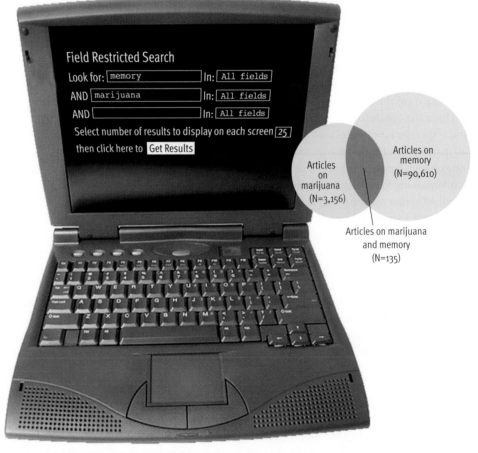

net (see Web Link 2.2 for a description of PsycINFO Direct). The database is also available at some libraries that have the information stored on CD-ROM discs. This version of the database is updated monthly. The summaries contained in PsycINFO can also be found in a monthly print journal called *Psychological Abstracts,* but fewer and fewer libraries are subscribing to this traditional publication because it cannot match the swift and efficient search capabilities of PsycINFO.

Reading Journal Articles

Once you find the journal articles you want to examine, you need to know how to decipher them. You can process the information in such articles more efficiently if you understand how they are organized. Depending on your needs and purpose, you may want to simply skim through some of the sections. Journal articles follow a fairly standard organization, which includes the following sections and features.

Abstract

Most journals print a concise summary at the beginning of each article. This abstract allows readers scanning the journal to quickly decide whether articles are relevant to their interests.

Introduction

The introduction presents an overview of the problem studied in the research. It mentions relevant theories and quickly reviews previous research that bears on the problem, usually citing shortcomings in previous research that necessitate the current study. This review of the state of knowledge on the topic usually progresses to a specific and precise statement regarding the hypotheses under investigation.

Method

The next section provides a thorough description of the research methods used in the study. Information is provided on the subjects used, the procedures followed, and the data collection techniques employed. This description is made detailed enough to permit another researcher to attempt to replicate the study.

Results

The data obtained in the study are reported in the results section. This section often creates problems for novice readers because it includes complex statistical analyses, figures, tables, and graphs. This section does not include any inferences based on the data, as such conclusions are supposed to follow in the next section. Instead, it simply contains a concise summary of the raw data and the statistical analyses.

Discussion

In the discussion section you will find the conclusions drawn by the author(s). In contrast to the results section, which is a straightforward summary of empirical observations, the discussion section allows for interpretation and evaluation of the data. Implications for theory and factual knowledge in the discipline are discussed. Conclusions are usually qualified carefully, and any limitations in the study may be acknowledged. This section may also include suggestions for future research on the issue.

References

At the end of each article is a list of bibliographic references for any studies cited. This list permits the reader to examine firsthand other relevant studies mentioned in the article. The references list is often a rich source of leads about other articles that are germane to the topic that you are looking into.

The Perils of Anecdotal Evidence: "I Have a Friend Who . . ."

Here's a tough problem. Suppose you are the judge in a family law court. As you look over the cases that will come before you today, you see that one divorcing couple have managed to settle almost all of the important decisions with minimal conflict—such as who gets the house, who gets the car and the dog, and who pays which bills. However, there is one crucial issue left: Each parent wants custody of the children, and because they could not reach an agreement on their own, the case is now in your court. You will need the wisdom of the legendary King Solomon for this decision. How can you determine what is in the best interests of the children?

Child custody decisions have major consequences for all of the parties involved. As you review the case records, you see that both parents are loving and competent, so there are no obvious reasons for selecting one parent over the other as the primary caretaker. In considering various alternatives, you mull over the possibility of awarding *joint custody,* an arrangement in which the children spend half their time with each parent, instead of the more usual arrangement where one parent has primary custody and the other has visitation rights. Joint custody seems to have some obvious benefits, but you are not sure how well these arrangements actually work. Will the children feel more attached to both parents if the parents share custody equally? Or will the children feel hassled by always moving around, perhaps spending half the week at one parent's home and half at the other parent's home? Can parents who are already feuding over child custody issues make these complicated arrangements work? Or is joint custody just too disruptive to everyone's life? You really don't know the answer to any of these vexing questions.

One of the lawyers involved in the case knows that you are thinking about the possibility of joint custody. She also understands that you want more information about how well joint custody tends to work before you render a decision. To help you make up your mind, she tells you about a divorced couple who have had a joint custody arrangement for many years and offers to have them appear in court to describe their experiences "firsthand." They and their children can answer any questions you might have about the pros and cons of joint custody. They should be in the best position to know how well joint custody works because they are living it. Sounds like a reasonable plan. What do you think?

Hopefully, you said, "No, No, No!" What's wrong with asking someone who's been there how well joint custody works? The crux of the problem is that the evidence a single family brings to the question of joint custody is *anecdotal evidence,* **which consists of personal stories about specific incidents and experiences.** Anecdotal evidence can be seductive. For example, one study found that psychology majors' choices of future courses to enroll in were influenced more by a couple of students' brief anecdotes than by extensive statistics on many other students' ratings of the courses from the previous term (Borgida & Nisbett, 1977). Anecdotes readily sway people because they often are concrete, vivid, and memorable. Indeed, people tend to be influenced by anecdotal information even when they are explicitly forewarned that the information is *not* representative (Hammill, Wilson, & Nisbett, 1980). Many politicians are keenly aware of the power of anecdotes and they frequently rely on a single vivid story rather than on solid data to sway voters' views. However, anecdotal evidence is fundamentally flawed (Ruscio, 2002; Stanovich, 2004).

What, exactly, is wrong with anecdotal evidence? Let's use some of the concepts introduced in the main body of the chapter to analyze the shortcomings of anecdotal evidence. First, in the language of research designs, the anecdotal experiences of one family resemble a single *case study*. The story they tell about their experiences with joint custody may be quite interesting, but their experiences—good or bad—cannot be used to generalize to other couples. Why not? Because they are only one family, and they may be unusual in some way that affects how well they manage joint custody. To draw general conclusions based on the case study approach, you need a systematic series of case studies, so you can look for threads of consistency. A single family is a sample size of one, which surely is not large enough to derive broad principles that would apply to other families.

Second, anecdotal evidence is similar to *self-report data,* which can be distorted for a variety of reasons, such as people's tendency to give socially approved information about

DILBERT

DILBERT: © 2002 Scott Adams/Distributed by United Feature Syndicate, Inc.

The reports linking electric power lines to cancer have been based on anecdotal evidence, which often sounds impressive and compelling. However, as the text explains, anecdotal evidence is flawed in many ways.

© Mark Bolster

themselves (the *social desirability bias*). When researchers use tests and surveys to gather self-report data, they can take steps to reduce or assess the impact of distortions in their data, but there are no comparable safeguards with anecdotal evidence. Thus, the family that appears in your courtroom may be eager to make a good impression and unknowingly slant their story accordingly.

Anecdotes are often inaccurate and riddled with embellishments. We will see in Chapter 7 that memories of personal experiences are far less accurate and reliable than widely assumed (Loftus, 2004; Schacter, 2001). And, although it would not be an issue in this case, in other situations *anecdotal evidence often consists of stories that people have heard about others' experiences.* Hearsay evidence is not accepted in courtrooms for

good reason. As stories are passed on from one person to another, they often become increasingly distorted and inaccurate.

Can you think of any other reasons for being wary of anecdotal evidence? After reading the chapter, perhaps you thought about the possibility of *sampling bias.* Do you think that the lawyer will pick a couple at random from all those who have been awarded joint custody? It seems highly unlikely. If she wants you to award joint custody, she will find a couple for whom this arrangement has worked very well; and if she wants you to award sole custody to her client, she will find a couple whose inability to make joint custody work had dire consequences for their children. One reason people love to work with anecdotal evidence is that it is so readily manipulated;

they can usually find an anecdote or two to support their position, whether or not these anecdotes are representative of most people's experiences.

If the testimony of one family cannot be used in making this critical custody decision, what sort of evidence should you be looking for? One goal of effective critical thinking is to make decisions based on solid evidence. This process is called *evidence-based decision making.* In this case, you would need to consider the overall experiences of a large sample of families who have tried joint custody arrangements. In general, across many different families, did the children in joint custody develop well? Was there an exceptionally high rate of emotional problems or other signs of stress for the children or the parents? Was the percentage of families who returned to court at a later date to change their joint custody arrangements higher than for other types of custody arrangements? You can probably think of additional information that you would want to collect regarding the outcomes of various custody arrangements.

In examining research reports, many people recognize the need to evaluate the evidence by looking for the types of flaws described in the main body of the chapter (sampling bias, experimenter bias, and so forth). Curiously, though, many of the same people then fail to apply the same principles of good evidence to their personal decisions in everyday life. The tendency to rely on the anecdotal experiences of a small number of people is sometimes called the *"I have a friend who . . ." syndrome,* because no matter what the topic is, it seems that someone will provide a personal story about a friend as evidence for his or her particular point of view. In short, when you hear people support their assertions with personal stories, a little skepticism is in order.

Table 2.2 Critical Thinking Skills Discussed in This Application

Skill	Description
Recognizing the limitations of anecdotal evidence	The critical thinker is wary of anecdotal evidence, which consists of personal stories used to support one's assertions. Anecdotal evidence tends to be unrepresentative, inaccurate, and unreliable.
Using evidence-based decision making	The critical thinker understands the need to seek sound evidence to guide decisions in everyday life.

CHAPTER 2 *Review*

Key Ideas

Looking for Laws: The Scientific Approach to Behavior

● The scientific approach assumes that there are laws of behavior that can be discovered through empirical research. The goals of the science of psychology include (1) the measurement and description of behavior, (2) the understanding and prediction of behavior, and (3) the application of this knowledge to the task of controlling behavior. By integrating apparently unrelated facts into a coherent whole, theories permit psychologists to make the leap from the description of behavior to understanding behavior.

● A scientific investigation follows a systematic pattern that includes five steps: (1) formulate a testable hypothesis, (2) select the research method and design the study, (3) collect the data, (4) analyze the data and draw conclusions, and (5) report the findings. The two major advantages of the scientific approach are its clarity in communication and its relative intolerance of error.

Looking for Causes: Experimental Research

● Experimental research involves the manipulation of an independent variable to ascertain its effect on a dependent variable. This research is usually done by comparing experimental and control groups, which must be alike in regard to important extraneous variables. Any differences between the groups in the dependent variable are presumably due to the manipulation of the independent variable.

● Experimental designs may vary. Sometimes an experimental group serves as its own control group. And many experiments have more than one independent variable or more than one dependent variable.

● The experiment is a powerful research method that permits conclusions about cause-and-effect relationships between variables. However, the experimental method is often not usable for a specific problem, and many experiments tend to be artificial.

Looking for Links: Descriptive/Correlational Research

● When psychologists are unable to manipulate the variables they want to study, they use descriptive/correlational research methods that seek to discover correlations between variables.

● Correlations may be either positive (the variables covary in the same direction) or negative (the variables covary in the opposite direction). The closer a correlation is to either +1.00 or −1.00, the stronger the association is. Higher correlations yield greater predictability. However, a high correlation is no assurance of causation.

● Key descriptive methods include naturalistic observation, case studies, and surveys. Descriptive/correlational research methods allow psychologists to explore issues that might not be open to experimental investigation. They are also less artificial than experiments. However, these research methods cannot demonstrate cause-effect relationships.

Looking for Flaws: Evaluating Research

● Scientists often try to replicate research findings to double-check their validity. Although this process leads to some contradictory findings, science works toward reconciling and explaining inconsistent results.

● Sampling bias occurs when a sample is not representative of the population of interest. Placebo effects occur when subjects' expectations cause them to experience experimental effects in response to a fake treatment. Distortions in self-reports are a source of concern whenever questionnaires and personality inventories are used to collect data. Experimenter bias occurs when researchers' expectations and desires sway their observations.

Looking at Ethics: Do the Ends Justify the Means?

● Research sometimes raises complex ethical issues. In psychology, the key questions concern the use of deception with human subjects and the use of harmful or painful manipulations with animal subjects. The APA has formulated ethical principles to serve as guidelines for researchers.

Reflecting on the Chapter's Themes

● Two of the book's unifying themes are apparent in this chapter's discussion of the research enterprise in psychology: psychology is empirical, and people's experience of the world can be highly subjective.

PERSONAL APPLICATION • Finding and Reading Journal Articles

● Journals publish technical and scholarly material, usually in a narrow area of inquiry. PsycINFO is an online database that summarizes and indexes scholarly literature related to psychology. It contains brief summaries of journal articles, books, and chapters in edited books. You can search PsycINFO for publications by specific authors or for materials on specific topics.

● Journal articles are easier to understand if one is familiar with the standard format. Most articles include six elements: abstract, introduction, method, results, discussion, and references.

CRITICAL THINKING APPLICATION • The Perils of Anecdotal Evidence: "I Have a Friend Who . . ."

● Anecdotal evidence consists of personal stories about specific incidents and experiences. Anecdotes often influence people because they tend to be concrete, vivid, and memorable.

● However, anecdotal evidence is usually based on the equivalent of a single case study, which is not an adequate sample, and there are no safeguards to reduce the distortions often found in self-report data. Many anecdotes are inaccurate, second-hand reports of others' experiences. Effective critical thinking depends on evidence-based decision making.

Key Terms

Anecdotal evidence (p. 58)
Case study (p. 45)
Confounding of variables (p. 39)
Control group (p. 38)
Correlation (p. 42)
Correlation coefficient (p. 42)
Data collection techniques (p. 36)
Dependent variable (p. 38)
Double-blind procedure (p. 50)
Experiment (p. 38)
Experimental group (p. 38)
Experimenter bias (p. 50)
Extraneous variables (p. 39)
Hypothesis (p. 33)
Independent variable (p. 38)
Journal (p. 37)
Naturalistic observation (p. 44)
Operational definition (p. 35)

Participants (p. 35)
Placebo effects (p. 49)
Population (p. 48)
Random assignment (p. 39)
Replication (p. 48)
Research methods (p. 37)
Sample (p. 48)
Sampling bias (p. 48)
Social desirability bias (p. 49)
Subjects (p. 35)
Survey (p. 46)
Theory (p. 34)
Variables (p. 33)

Key People

Neal Miller (p. 52)
Robert Rosenthal (p. 50)
Stanley Schachter (pp. 38–39)

1. Theories permit researchers to move from:
A. understanding to application.
B. concept to description.
C. application to control.
D. description to understanding.

2. Researchers must describe the actions that will be taken to measure or control each variable in their studies. In other words, they must:
A. provide operational definitions of their variables.
B. decide whether their studies will be experimental or correlational.
C. use statistics to summarize their findings.
D. decide how many subjects should participate in their studies.

3. A researcher found that clients who were randomly assigned to same-sex groups participated more in group therapy sessions than clients who were randomly assigned to coed groups. In this experiment, the independent variable was:
A. the amount of participation in the group therapy sessions.
B. whether or not the group was same-sex or coed.
C. the clients' attitudes toward group therapy.
D. how much the clients' mental health improved.

4. A researcher wants to see whether a protein-enriched diet will enhance the maze-running performance of rats. One group of rats is fed the high-protein diet for the duration of the study; the other group continues to receive ordinary rat chow. In this experiment, the diet fed to the two groups of rats is the _____ variable.
A. correlated
B. control
C. dependent
D. independent

5. In a study of the effect of a new teaching technique on students' achievement test scores, an important extraneous variable would be the students':
A. hair color.
B. athletic skills.
C. IQ scores.
D. sociability.

6. Whenever you have a cold, you rest in bed, take aspirin, and drink plenty of fluids. You can't determine which remedy is most effective because of which of the following problems?
A. Sampling bias
B. Distorted self-report data
C. Confounding of variables
D. Experimenter bias

7. A psychologist monitors a group of nursery school children during the school day, recording each instance of helping behavior as it occurs, without any intervention. The psychologist is using:
A. the experimental method.
B. naturalistic observation.
C. case studies.
D. the survey method.

8. Among the advantages of descriptive/correlational research is (are):
A. it can often be used in circumstances in which an experiment would be unethical.
B. it permits researchers to examine subjects' behavior in natural, real-world circumstances.
C. it can demonstrate conclusively that two variables are causally related.
D. both a and b.

9. Which of the following correlation coefficients would indicate the strongest relationship between two variables?
A. .58   C. −.97
B. .19   D. −.05

10. As interest rates increase, house sales decline, indicating a(n) _____ between the two variables.
A. direct correlation   C. positive correlation
B. negative correlation   D. indirect correlation

11. Sampling bias exists when:
A. the sample is representative of the population.
B. the sample is not representative of the population.
C. two variables are confounded.
D. the effect of the independent variable can't be isolated.

12. The problem of experimenter bias can be avoided by:
A. not informing subjects of the hypothesis of the experiment.
B. telling the subjects that there are no "right" or "wrong" answers.
C. using a research strategy in which neither subjects nor experimenter know which subjects are in the experimental and control groups.
D. having the experimenter use only nonverbal signals when communicating with the subjects.

13. Critics of deception in research have assumed that deceptive studies are harmful to subjects. The empirical data on this issue suggest that:
A. many deceptive studies do have significant negative effects on subjects.
B. most participants in deceptive studies report that they enjoyed the experience and didn't mind being misled.
C. deceptive research seriously undermines subjects' trust in others.
D. Both a and c.

14. Which of the following would not be included in the results section of a journal article?
A. Descriptive statistics summarizing the data
B. Statistical analysis of the data
C. Graphs and/or tables presenting the data pictorially
D. Interpretation, evaluation, and implications of the data

15. Anecdotal evidence:
A. is often concrete, vivid, and memorable.
B. tends to influence people.
C. is fundamentally flawed and unreliable.
D. is all of the above.

Answers

1 D p. 34
2 A p. 35
3 B p. 38
4 D p. 38
5 C p. 39
6 C p. 39
7 B p. 44
8 D pp. 46–47
9 C pp. 42–43
10 B p. 42
11 B pp. 48–49
12 C p. 50
13 B p. 51
14 D p. 57
15 D pp. 58–59

PsykTrek
Go to the PsykTrek website or CD-ROM for further study of the concepts in this chapter. Both online and on the CD-ROM, PsykTrek includes dozens of learning modules with videos, animations, and quizzes, as well as simulations of psychological phenomena and a multimedia glossary that includes word pronunciations.

ThomsonNOW™
www.thomsonedu.com/ThomsonNOW
Go to this site for the link to ThomsonNOW, your one-stop study shop. Take a Pre-Test for this chapter, and ThomsonNOW will generate a Personalized Study Plan based on your test results. The Study Plan will identify the topics you need to review and direct you to online resources to help you master those topics. You can then take a Post-Test to help you determine the concepts you have mastered and what you still need to work on.

Companion Website
www.thomsonedu.com/psychology/weiten
Go to this site to find online resources directly linked to your book, including a glossary, flash cards, drag-and-drop exercises, quizzes, and more!

CHAPTER 3

The Biological Bases of Behavior

© Royalty-Free/Corbis

If you have ever visited an aquarium, you may have encountered one of nature's more captivating animals: the octopus. Although this jellylike mass of arms and head appears to be a relatively simple creature, it is capable of a number of interesting behaviors. The octopus has highly developed eyes that enable it to respond to stimuli in the darkness of the ocean. When threatened, it can release an inky cloud to ward off enemies while it makes its escape by a kind of rocket propulsion. If that doesn't work, it can camouflage itself by changing color and texture to blend into its surroundings. Furthermore, the animal is surprisingly intelligent. In captivity, an octopus can learn, for example, to twist the lid off a jar with one of its tentacles to get at a treat that is inside.

Despite its talents, there are many things an octopus cannot do. An octopus cannot study psychology, plan a weekend, dream about its future, or discover the Pythagorean theorem. Yet the biological processes that underlie these uniquely human behaviors are much the same as the biological processes that enable an octopus to escape from a predator or forage for food. Indeed, some of science's most important insights about how the nervous system works came from studies of a relative of the octopus, the squid.

Organisms as diverse as humans and squid share many biological processes. However, their unique behavioral capacities depend on the differences in their physiological makeup. You and I have a larger repertoire of behaviors than the octopus because we come equipped with a more complex brain and nervous system. The activity of the human brain is so complex that no computer has ever come close to duplicating it. Your nervous system contains as many cells busily integrating and relaying information as there are stars in our galaxy. Whether you are scratching your nose or composing an essay, the activity of those cells underlies what you do. It is little wonder, then, that many psychologists have dedicated themselves to exploring the biological bases of behavior.

How do mood-altering drugs work? Are the two halves of the brain specialized to perform different functions? What happens inside the body when you feel a strong emotion? Are some mental illnesses the result of chemical imbalances in the brain? To what extent is intelligence determined by biological inheritance? These questions only begin to suggest the countless ways in which biology is fundamental to the study of behavior.

> Communication in the Nervous System

Imagine that you are watching a scary movie. As the tension mounts, your palms sweat and your heart beats faster. You begin shoveling popcorn into your mouth, carelessly spilling some in your lap. If someone were to ask you what you are doing at this moment, you would probably say, "Nothing—just watching the movie." Yet some highly complex processes are occurring without your thinking about them. A stimulus (the light from the screen) is striking your eye. Almost instantaneously, your brain is interpreting the light stimulus, and signals are flashing to other parts of your body, leading to a flurry of activity. Your sweat glands are releasing perspiration, your heartbeat is quickening, and muscular movements are enabling your hand to find the popcorn and, more or less successfully, lift it to your mouth.

Even in this simple example, you can see that behavior depends on rapid information processing. Information travels almost instantaneously from your eye to your brain, from your brain to the muscles of your arm and hand, and from your palms back to your brain. In essence, your nervous system is a complex communication network in which signals are constantly being received, integrated, and transmitted. The nervous system handles information, just as the circulatory system handles blood. In this section, we take a close look at communication in the nervous system.

Nervous Tissue: The Basic Hardware

Your nervous system is living tissue composed of cells. The cells in the nervous system fall into two major categories: *glia* and *neurons*. Let's look at neurons first.

Neurons

Neurons are individual cells in the nervous system that receive, integrate, and transmit information. They are the basic links that permit communication within the nervous system. The vast majority of them communicate only with other neurons. However, a small minority receive signals from outside

PREVIEW QUESTIONS

● What are the key parts of the neuron, and what are their functions?

● How do glial cells contribute to the functioning of the nervous system?

● What is an action potential?

● How does synaptic transmission take place?

● Which neurotransmitters regulate which aspects of behavior?

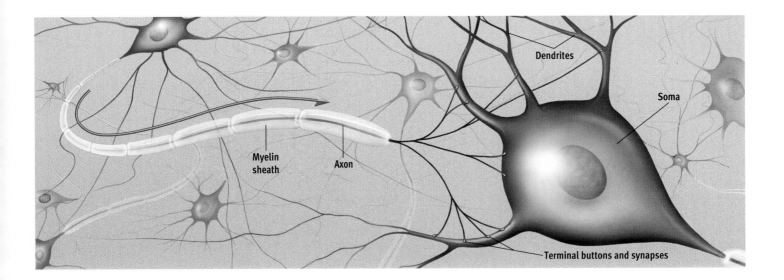

Figure 3.1

Structure of the neuron. Neurons are the communication links of the nervous system. This diagram highlights the key parts of a neuron, including specialized receptor areas (dendrites), the cell body (soma), the axon fiber along which impulses are transmitted, and the terminal buttons, which release chemical messengers that carry signals to other neurons. Neurons vary considerably in size and shape and are usually densely interconnected.

the nervous system (from sensory organs) or carry messages from the nervous system to the muscles that move the body.

A highly simplified drawing of two "typical" neurons is shown in **Figure 3.1**. Actually, neurons come in such a tremendous variety of types and shapes that no single drawing can adequately represent them. Trying to draw the "typical" neuron is like trying to draw the "typical" tree. Despite this diversity, the drawing in **Figure 3.1** highlights some common features of neurons.

The *soma,* **or cell body, contains the cell nucleus and much of the chemical machinery common to most cells** (*soma* is Greek for "body"). The rest of the neuron is devoted exclusively to handling information. The neurons in **Figure 3.1** have a number of branched, feelerlike structures called *dendritic trees* (*dendrite* is a Greek word for "tree"). Each individual branch is a *dendrite.* **Dendrites are the parts of a neuron that are specialized to receive information.** Most neurons receive information from many other cells—sometimes thousands of others—and so have extensive dendritic trees.

From the many dendrites, information flows into the cell body and then travels away from the soma along the *axon* (from the Greek for "axle"). **The *axon* is a long, thin fiber that transmits signals away from the soma to other neurons or to muscles or glands.** Axons may be quite long (sometimes several feet), and they may branch off to communicate with a number of other cells.

In humans, many axons are wrapped in cells with a high concentration of a white, fatty substance called *myelin.* **The *myelin sheath* is insulating material that encases some axons.** The myelin sheath speeds up the transmission of signals that move along axons. If an axon's myelin sheath deteriorates,

its signals may not be transmitted effectively. The loss of muscle control seen with the disease *multiple sclerosis* is due to a degeneration of myelin sheaths (Schwartz & Westbrook, 2000).

The axon ends in a cluster of *terminal buttons,* **which are small knobs that secrete chemicals called neurotransmitters.** These chemicals serve as messengers that may activate neighboring neurons. The points at which neurons interconnect are called *synapses.* **A *synapse* is a junction where information is transmitted from one neuron to another** (*synapse* is from the Greek for "junction").

To summarize, information is received at the dendrites, is passed through the soma and along the axon, and is transmitted to the dendrites of other cells at meeting points called synapses. Unfortunately, this nice, simple picture has more exceptions than the U.S. Tax Code. For example, some neurons do not have an axon, while others have multiple axons. Also, although neurons typically synapse on the dendrites of other cells, they may also synapse on a soma or an axon.

Glia

Glia **are cells found throughout the nervous system that provide various types of support for neurons.** Glia (literally "glue") tend to be much smaller than neurons, but they outnumber neurons by about 10 to 1, so glial cells appear to account for over 50% of the brain's volume. Among other things, glial cells supply nourishment to neurons, help remove neurons' waste products, and provide insulation around many axons. The myelin sheaths that encase some axons are derived from special types of glial cells. Glia also play a complicated role in orchestrating the development of the nervous system in the human embryo.

These functions, which have been known for many years, made glial cells the unsung heroes of the nervous system. Until recently, it was thought that the "glamorous" work in the nervous system—the transmission and integration of informational signals—was the exclusive province of the neurons. New research, however, suggests that glia may also send and receive chemical signals (Fields, 2004; Fields & Stevens-Graham, 2002). Some types of glia can detect neural impulses and send signals to other glial cells. Surprised by this discovery, neuroscientists are now trying to figure out how this signalling system interfaces with the neural communication system.

Although glia may contribute to information processing in the nervous system, the bulk of this crucial work is handled by the neurons. Hence, we need to examine the process of neural activity in more detail.

The Neural Impulse: Using Energy to Send Information

What happens when a neuron is stimulated? What is the nature of the signal—the *neural impulse*—that moves through the neuron? These were the questions that Alan Hodgkin and Andrew Huxley set out to answer in their groundbreaking experiments with axons removed from squid. Why did they choose to work with squid axons? Because squid have a pair of "giant" axons that are about a hundred times larger than those in humans (which still makes them only about as thick as a human hair). Their large size permitted Hodgkin and Huxley to insert fine wires called *microelectrodes* into them. By using the microelectrodes to record the electrical activity in individual neurons, Hodgkin and Huxley unraveled the mystery of the neural impulse.

The Neuron at Rest: A Tiny Battery

Hodgkin and Huxley (1952) learned that the neural impulse is a complex electrochemical reaction. Both inside and outside the neuron are fluids containing electrically charged atoms and molecules called *ions*. Positively charged sodium and potassium ions and negatively charged chloride ions flow back and forth across the cell membrane, but they do not cross at the same rate. The difference in flow rates leads to a slightly higher concentration of negatively charged ions inside the cell. The resulting voltage means that the neuron at rest is a tiny battery, a store of potential energy. **The *resting potential* of a neuron is its stable, negative charge when the cell is inactive.** As shown in **Figure 3.2(a)**, this charge is about −70

millivolts, roughly one-twentieth of the voltage of a flashlight battery.

The Action Potential

As long as the voltage of a neuron remains constant, the cell is quiet, and no messages are being sent. When the neuron is stimulated, channels in its cell membrane open, briefly allowing positively charged sodium ions to rush in. For an instant, the neuron's charge is less negative and eventually positive, creating an action potential (Koester & Siegelbaum, 2000). **An *action potential* is a very brief shift in a neuron's electrical charge that travels along an axon.** The firing of an action potential is reflected in the voltage spike shown in **Figure 3.2(b)**. Like a spark traveling along a trail of gunpowder, the voltage change races down the axon.

After the firing of an action potential, the channels in the cell membrane that opened to let in sodium close up. Some time is needed before they are ready to open again, and until that time the neuron cannot fire. **The *absolute refractory period* is the minimum length of time after an action potential during which another action potential cannot begin.** This "down time" isn't very long, only 1 or 2 milliseconds.

Figure 3.2

The neural impulse. The electrochemical properties of the neuron allow it to transmit signals. The electric charge of a neuron can be measured with a pair of electrodes connected to an oscilloscope, as Hodgkin and Huxley showed with a squid axon. Because of its exceptionally thick axons, the squid has frequently been used by scientists studying the neural impulse. **(a)** At rest, the neuron's voltage hovers around −70 millivolts. **(b)** When the axon is stimulated, there is a brief jump in a neuron's voltage, resulting in a spike on the oscilloscope recording of the neuron's electrical activity. This change in voltage, called an action potential, travels along the axon like a spark traveling along a trail of gunpowder.

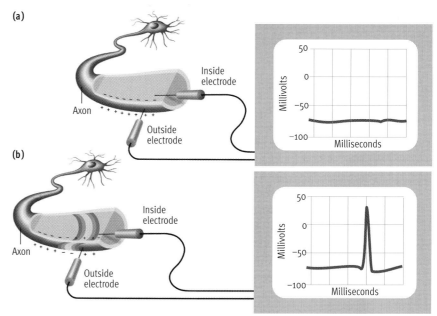

Web Link 3.1

Neuropsychology Central
This content-rich site, maintained by Professor Jeffrey Browndyke of Louisiana State University, is dedicated to all aspects of human neuropsychology from the perspectives of the experimental research laboratory as well as the applied clinical setting of the hospital and professional office.

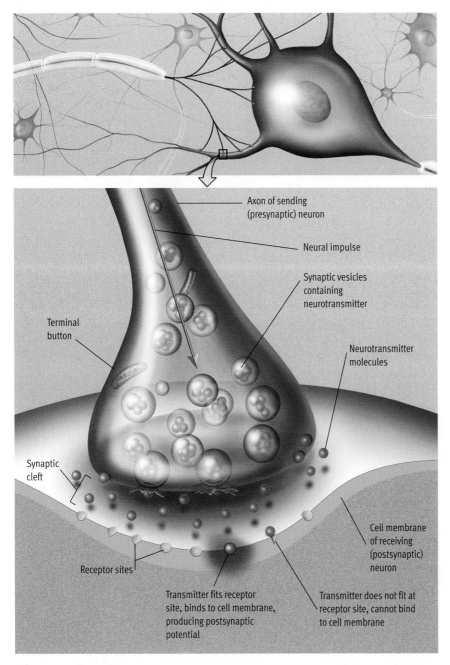

Axon of sending
(presynaptic) neuron

Neural impulse

Synaptic vesicles
containing
neurotransmitter

Terminal
button

Neurotransmitter
molecules

Synaptic
cleft

Cell membrane
of receiving
(postsynaptic)
neuron

Receptor sites

Transmitter fits receptor
site, binds to cell membrane,
producing postsynaptic
potential

Transmitter does not fit at
receptor site, cannot bind
to cell membrane

Figure 3.3

The synapse. When a neural impulse reaches an axon's terminal buttons, it triggers the release of chemical messengers called neurotransmitters. The neurotransmitter molecules diffuse across the synaptic cleft and bind to receptor sites on the postsynaptic neuron. A specific neurotransmitter can bind only to receptor sites that its molecular structure will fit into, much like a key must fit a lock.

The All-or-None Law

The neural impulse is an all-or-none proposition, like firing a gun. You can't half-fire a gun. The same is true of the neuron's firing of action potentials. Either the neuron fires or it doesn't, and its action potentials are all the same size (Kandel, 2000). That is, weaker stimuli do not produce smaller action potentials and stronger stimuli do not evoke larger action potentials.

Even though the action potential is an all-or-nothing event, neurons *can* convey information about the strength of a stimulus. They do so by varying the *rate* at which they fire action potentials. In

general, a stronger stimulus will cause a cell to fire a more rapid volley of neural impulses than a weaker stimulus will.

Various neurons transmit neural impulses at different speeds. For example, thicker axons transmit neural impulses more rapidly than thinner ones do. Although neural impulses do not travel as fast as electricity along a wire, they *are* very fast, moving at up to 100 meters per second, which is equivalent to more than 200 miles per hour. The entire complicated process of neural transmission takes only a few thousandths of a second. In the time it has taken you to read this description of the neural impulse, billions of such impulses have been transmitted in your nervous system!

The Synapse: Where Neurons Meet

In the nervous system, the neural impulse functions as a signal. For that signal to have any meaning for the system as a whole, it must be transmitted from the neuron to other cells. As noted earlier, this transmission takes place at special junctions called *synapses*, which depend on *chemical* messengers.

Sending Signals: Chemicals as Couriers

A "typical" synapse is shown in **Figure 3.3**. The first thing that you should notice is that the two neurons don't actually touch. They are separated by the *synaptic cleft*, **a microscopic gap between the terminal button of one neuron and the cell membrane of another neuron.** Signals have to cross this gap to permit neurons to communicate. In this situation, the neuron that sends a signal across the gap is called the *presynaptic neuron*, and the neuron that receives the signal is called the *postsynaptic neuron*.

How do messages travel across the gaps between neurons? The arrival of an action potential at an axon's terminal buttons triggers the release of *neurotransmitters*—**chemicals that transmit information from one neuron to another.** Within the buttons, most of these chemicals are stored in small sacs, called *synaptic vesicles*. The neurotransmitters are released when a vesicle fuses with the membrane of the presynaptic cell and its contents spill into the synaptic cleft. After their release, neurotransmitters diffuse across the synaptic cleft to the membrane of the receiving cell. There they may bind with special molecules in the postsynaptic cell membrane at various *receptor sites*. These sites are specifically "tuned" to recognize and respond to some neurotransmitters but not to others.

Receiving Signals: Postsynaptic Potentials

When a neurotransmitter and a receptor molecule combine, reactions in the cell membrane cause a *postsynaptic potential (PSP)*, a voltage change at a receptor site on a postsynaptic cell membrane. Postsynaptic potentials do *not* follow the all-or-none law like action potentials do. Instead, postsynaptic potentials are *graded*. That is, they vary in size and they increase or decrease the *probability* of a neural impulse in the receiving cell in proportion to the amount of voltage change.

Two types of messages can be sent from cell to cell: excitatory and inhibitory. An *excitatory PSP* is a positive voltage shift that *increases* the likelihood that the postsynaptic neuron will fire action potentials. An *inhibitory PSP* is a negative voltage shift that *decreases* the likelihood that the postsynaptic neuron will fire action potentials. The direction of the voltage shift, and thus the nature of the PSP (excitatory or inhibitory), depends on which receptor sites are activated in the postsynaptic neuron (Kandel, 2000).

The excitatory or inhibitory effects produced at a synapse last only a fraction of a second. Then neurotransmitters drift away from receptor sites or are inactivated by enzymes that metabolize (convert) them into inactive forms. Most are reabsorbed into

the presynaptic neuron through *reuptake,* a process in which neurotransmitters are sponged up from the synaptic cleft by the presynaptic membrane. Reuptake allows synapses to recycle their materials. Reuptake and the other key processes in synaptic transmission are summarized in **Figure 3.4**.

Integrating Signals: A Balancing Act

Most neurons are interlinked in complex, dense networks. In fact, a neuron may receive a symphony of signals from *thousands* of other neurons. The same neuron may pass its messages along to thousands of neurons as well. Thus, a neuron must do a great deal more than simply relay messages it receives. It must *integrate* excitatory and inhibitory signals arriving at many synapses before it "decides" whether to fire a neural impulse.

As Rita Carter (1998) has pointed out in *Mapping the Mind,* "The firing of a single neuron is not enough to create the twitch of an eyelid in sleep, let alone a conscious impression . . . Millions of neurons must fire in unison to produce the most trifling thought" (p. 19). Most neurons are interlinked in complex chains, pathways, circuits, and networks. Our perceptions, thoughts, and actions depend on *patterns* of neural activity in elaborate neural networks. These

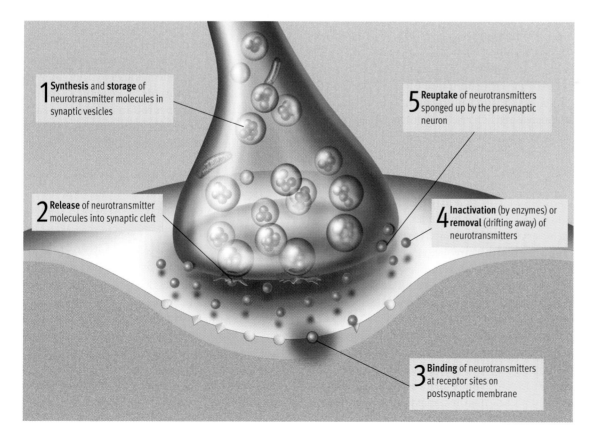

1 **Synthesis** and **storage** of neurotransmitter molecules in synaptic vesicles

2 **Release** of neurotransmitter molecules into synaptic cleft

5 **Reuptake** of neurotransmitters sponged up by the presynaptic neuron

4 **Inactivation** (by enzymes) or **removal** (drifting away) of neurotransmitters

3 **Binding** of neurotransmitters at receptor sites on postsynaptic membrane

Figure 3.4

Overview of synaptic transmission. The main elements in synaptic transmission are summarized here, superimposed on a blowup of the synapse seen in **Figure 3.3**. The five key processes involved in communication at synapses are (1) synthesis and storage, (2) release, (3) binding, (4) inactivation or removal, and (5) reuptake of neurotransmitters. As you'll see in this chapter and the remainder of the book, the effects of many phenomena—such as pain, drug use, and some diseases—can be explained in terms of how they alter one or more of these processes (usually at synapses releasing a specific neurotransmitter).

networks consist of interconnected neurons that frequently fire together or sequentially to perform certain functions (Song et al., 2005). The links in these neural networks are fluid, as new synaptic connections may be made while some old synaptic connections whither away (Hua & Smith, 2004).

Ironically, the *elimination of old synapses* appears to play a larger role in the sculpting of neural networks than the *creation of new synapses*. The nervous system normally forms more synapses than needed and then gradually eliminates the less active synapses. For example, the number of synapses in the human visual cortex peaks at around age one and then declines (Huttenlocher, 1994). Thus, *synaptic pruning* is a key process in the formation of the neural networks that are crucial to communication in the nervous system.

Neurotransmitters and Behavior

As we have seen, the nervous system relies on chemical couriers to communicate information between neurons. These *neurotransmitters* are fundamental to behavior, playing a key role in everything from muscle movements to moods and mental health.

You might guess that the nervous system would require only two neurotransmitters—one for excitatory potentials and one for inhibitory potentials. In reality, there are nine well-established, classic (small-molecule) transmitters, about 40 additional (neuropeptide) chemicals that function, at least part-time, as neurotransmitters, and a handful of recently recognized "novel" neurotransmitters (Schwartz, 2000; Snyder, 2002). As scientists continue to discover new and increasingly diverse transmitter substances, they are being forced to reevaluate their criteria regarding what qualifies as a neurotransmitter (Snyder & Ferris, 2000).

Specific neurotransmitters function at specific kinds of synapses. You may recall that transmitters deliver their messages by binding to receptor sites on the postsynaptic membrane. However, a transmitter cannot bind to just any site. The binding process operates much like a lock and key, as was shown in **Figure 3.3**. Just as a key has to fit a lock to work, a transmitter has to fit into a receptor site for binding to occur. Hence, specific transmitters can deliver signals only at certain locations on cell membranes.

Why are there many different neurotransmitters, each of which works only at certain synapses? This variety and specificity reduces crosstalk between densely packed neurons, making the nervous system's communication more precise. Let's look at

SOLOMON SNYDER

"Brain research of the past decade, especially the study of neurotransmitters, has proceeded at a furious pace, achieving progress equal in scope to all the accomplishments of the preceding fifty years—and the pace of discovery continues to accelerate."

some of the most interesting findings about how neurotransmitters regulate behavior, which are summarized in **Table 3.1**.

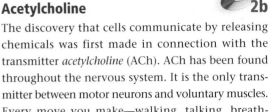

Acetylcholine

The discovery that cells communicate by releasing chemicals was first made in connection with the transmitter *acetylcholine* (ACh). ACh has been found throughout the nervous system. It is the only transmitter between motor neurons and voluntary muscles. Every move you make—walking, talking, breathing—depends on ACh released to your muscles by motor neurons (Kandel & Siegelbaum, 2000). ACh also appears to contribute to attention, arousal, and perhaps memory.

The activity of ACh (and other neurotransmitters) may be influenced by other chemicals in the brain. Although synaptic receptor sites are sensitive to specific neurotransmitters, sometimes they can be "fooled" by other chemical substances. For example, if you smoke tobacco, some of your ACh synapses will be stimulated by the nicotine that arrives in your brain. At these synapses, the nicotine acts like ACh itself. It binds to receptor sites for ACh, causing postsynaptic potentials (PSPs). In technical language, nicotine is an ACh agonist. An *agonist* is a chemical that mimics the action of a neurotransmitter.

Not all chemicals that fool synaptic receptors are agonists. Some chemicals bind to receptors but fail to produce a PSP (the key slides into the lock, but it doesn't work). In effect, they temporarily *block* the action of the natural transmitter by occupying its receptor sites, rendering them unusable. Thus, they act as antagonists. An *antagonist* is a chemical that opposes the action of a neurotransmitter. For example, the drug *curare* is an ACh antagonist. It blocks action at the same ACh synapses that are fooled by nicotine. As a result, muscles are unable to move. Some South American natives use a form of curare on arrows. If they wound an animal, the curare blocks the synapses from nerve to muscle, paralyzing the animal.

Monoamines

The *monoamines* include three neurotransmitters: dopamine, norepinephrine, and serotonin. Neurons using these transmitters regulate many aspects of everyday behavior. Dopamine (DA), for example, is used by neurons that control voluntary movements. The degeneration of such neurons apparently causes *Parkinson's disease,* a neurological illness marked by tremors, muscular rigidity, and reduced control over voluntary movements (DeLong, 2000).

Muhammed Ali and Michael J. Fox are two well-known victims of Parkinson's disease. Roughly one million Americans suffer from Parkinson's disease, which is caused by a decline in the synthesis of the neurotransmitter dopamine. The reduction in dopamine synthesis occurs because of the deterioration of a structure located in the midbrain.

Table 3.1 Common Neurotransmitters and Some of Their Functions

Neurotransmitter	Functions and Characteristics
Acetylcholine (ACh)	Activates motor neurons controlling skeletal muscles Contributes to the regulation of attention, arousal, and memory Some ACh receptors stimulated by nicotine
Dopamine (DA)	Contributes to control of voluntary movement, pleasurable emotions Decreased levels associated with Parkinson's disease Overactivity at DA synapses associated with schizophrenia Cocaine and amphetamines elevate activity at DA synapses
Norepinephrine (NE)	Contributes to modulation of mood and arousal Cocaine and amphetamines elevate activity at NE synapses
Serotonin	Involved in regulation of sleep and wakefulness, eating, aggression Abnormal levels may contribute to depression and obsessive-compulsive disorder Prozac and similar antidepressant drugs affect serotonin circuits
Endorphins	Resemble opiate drugs in structure and effects Contribute to pain relief and perhaps to some pleasurable emotions

Although other neurotransmitters are also involved, serotonin-releasing neurons appear to play a prominent role in the regulation of sleep and wakefulness (Vodelholzer et al., 1998) and eating behavior (Blundell & Halford, 1998). There also is considerable evidence that neural circuits using serotonin regulate aggressive behavior in animals (Bernhardt, 1997) and some preliminary evidence relating serotonin activity to aggression and impulsive behavior in humans (Dolan, Anderson, & Deakin, 2001; Douzenis et al., 2004).

Abnormal levels of monoamines in the brain have been related to the development of certain psychological disorders. For example, people who suffer from depression appear to have lowered levels of activation at norepinephrine (NE) and serotonin synapses. Although numerous other biochemical changes may also contribute to depression, abnormalities at NE and serotonin synapses appear to play a central role, as most antidepressant drugs exert their main effects at these synapses (Sher & Mann, 2003; Thase, Jindal, & Howland, 2002).

In a similar fashion, abnormalities in activity at dopamine synapses have been implicated in the development of *schizophrenia*. This severe mental illness is marked by irrational thought, hallucinations, poor contact with reality, and deterioration of routine adaptive behavior. Afflicting roughly 1% of the population, schizophrenia requires hospitalization more often than any other psychological disorder (see Chapter 13). Studies suggest, albeit with many complications, that overactivity at DA synapses is the neurochemical basis for schizophrenia. Why? Primarily because the therapeutic drugs that tame schizophrenic symptoms are known to be DA antagonists that reduce the neurotransmitter's activity (Tamminga & Carlsson, 2003).

Temporary alterations at monoamine synapses also appear to account for the powerful effects of some widely abused drugs, including amphetamines and cocaine. These stimulant drugs seem to exert most of their effects by creating a storm of increased activity at dopamine and norepinephrine synapses (King & Ellinwood, 2005; Repetto & Gold, 2005).

***Web Link* 3.2**

Molecular Neurobiology: A Gallery of Animations Site editor and physician Neil Busis brings together a set of QuickTime animations demonstrating activities at the molecular level of the synapse, such as the fusion of synaptic vesicles with the presynaptic membrane.

concept **check** 3.1

Understanding Nervous System Hardware Using Metaphors

A useful way to learn about the structures and functions of parts of the nervous system is through metaphors. Check your understanding of the basic components of the nervous system by matching the metaphorical descriptions below with the correct terms in the following list: (a) glia, (b) neuron, (c) soma, (d) dendrite, (e) axon, (f) myelin, (g) terminal button, (h) synapse. You'll find the answers in Appendix A.

_____ **1.** Like a tree. Also, each branch is a telephone wire that carries incoming messages to you.

_____ **2.** Like the insulation that covers electrical wires.

_____ **3.** Like a silicon chip in a computer that receives and transmits information between input and output devices as well as between other chips.

_____ **4.** Like an electrical cable that carries information.

_____ **5.** Like the maintenance personnel who keep things clean and in working order so the operations of the enterprise can proceed.

_____ **6.** Like the nozzle at the end of a hose, from which water is squirted.

_____ **7.** Like a railroad junction, where two trains may meet.

CANDACE PERT

"When human beings engage in various activities, it seems that neurojuices are released that are associated with either pain or pleasure. And the endorphins are very pleasurable."

Endorphins

PsykTrek 2b, 4d

In 1970, after a horseback-riding accident, Candace Pert, a graduate student working with scientist Solomon Snyder, lay in a hospital bed receiving frequent shots of *morphine,* a painkilling drug derived from the opium plant. This experience left her with a driving curiosity about how morphine works. A few years later, she and Snyder rocked the scientific world by showing that *morphine exerts its effects by binding to specialized receptors in the brain* (Pert & Snyder, 1973).

This discovery raised a perplexing question: Why would the brain be equipped with receptors for morphine, a powerful, addictive opiate drug not normally found in the body? It occurred to Pert and others that the nervous system must have its own, endogenous (internally produced) morphinelike substances. Investigators dubbed these as-yet undiscovered substances *endorphins—***internally produced chemicals that resemble opiates in structure and effects.** A search for the body's natural opiate ensued. In short order, a number of endogenous, opiatelike substances were identified (Hughes et al., 1975). Subsequent studies revealed that endorphins and their receptors are widely distributed in the human body and that they clearly contribute to the modulation of pain, as well as a variety of other phenomena (Basbaum & Jessell, 2000).

In this section we have highlighted just a few of the more interesting connections between neurotransmitters and behavior. These highlights barely begin to convey the rich complexity of biochemical processes in the nervous system. Most aspects of behavior are probably regulated by several types of transmitters. To further complicate matters, researchers are finding fascinating *interactions* between various neurotransmitter systems, such as serotonin and dopamine circuits (Frazer et al., 2003). Although scientists have learned a great deal about neurotransmitters and behavior, much still remains to be discovered.

concept check 3.2

Linking Brain Chemistry to Behavior

Check your understanding of relations between brain chemistry and behavior by indicating which neurotransmitters or other biological chemicals have been linked to the phenomena listed below. Choose your answers from the following list: (a) acetylcholine, (b) norepinephrine, (c) dopamine, (d) serotonin, (e) endorphins. Indicate your choice (by letter) in the spaces on the left. You'll find the answers in Appendix A.

_____ **1.** A transmitter involved in the regulation of sleep, eating, and aggression.

_____ **2.** The two monoamines that have been linked to depression.

_____ **3.** Chemicals that resemble opiate drugs in structure and that are involved in pain relief.

_____ **4.** A neurotransmitter for which abnormal levels have been implicated in schizophrenia.

_____ **5.** The only neurotransmitter between motor neurons and voluntary muscles.

> Organization of the Nervous System

PREVIEW QUESTIONS

- What are the subdivisions of the peripheral nervous system?
- What is the difference between afferent and efferent nerves?
- What does the autonomic nervous system regulate, and what are its subdivisions?
- What is the central nervous system made up of?

Clearly, communication in the nervous system is fundamental to behavior. So far we have looked at how individual cells communicate with one another. In this section, we examine the organization of the nervous system as a whole.

Experts believe that there are roughly *100 billion* neurons in the human brain (Kandel, 2000). Obviously, this is only an *estimate.* If you counted them nonstop at the rate of one per second, you'd be counting for over 3000 years! And, remember, most neurons have synaptic connections to many other neurons, so there may be *100 trillion* synapses in a human brain!

The fact that our neurons are so abundant as to be uncountable is probably why it is widely believed that "we only use 10% of our brains." This curious tidbit of folk wisdom is utter nonsense (McBurney,

1996). There is no way to quantify the percentage of the brain that is "in use" at any specific time. And think about it, if 90% of the human brain consists of unused "excess baggage," localized brain damage would not be a problem much of the time. In reality, damage in even very tiny areas of brain usually has severe disruptive effects (Zillmer & Spiers, 2001). The 10% myth appeals to people because it suggests that they have a huge reservoir of untapped potential. Hucksters selling self-improvement programs often disseminate the 10% myth because it makes their claims and promises seem more plausible ("Unleash your potential!").

In any event, the multitudes of neurons in your nervous system have to work together to keep information flowing effectively. To see how the nervous

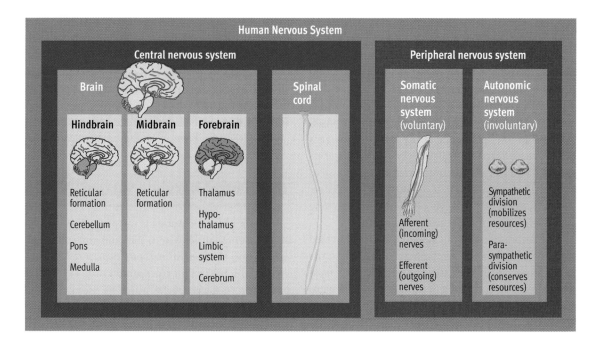

Human Nervous System

Central nervous system

Brain

Hindbrain | **Midbrain** | **Forebrain**

Hindbrain:
Reticular formation
Cerebellum
Pons
Medulla

Midbrain:
Reticular formation

Forebrain:
Thalamus
Hypothalamus
Limbic system
Cerebrum

Spinal cord

Peripheral nervous system

Somatic nervous system (voluntary)
Afferent (incoming) nerves
Efferent (outgoing) nerves

Autonomic nervous system (involuntary)
Sympathetic division (mobilizes resources)
Parasympathetic division (conserves resources)

Figure 3.5
Organization of the human nervous system. This overview of the human nervous system shows the relationships of its various parts and systems. The brain is traditionally divided into three regions: the hindbrain, the midbrain, and the forebrain. The reticular formation runs through both the midbrain and the hindbrain on its way up and down the brainstem. These and other parts of the brain are discussed in detail later in the chapter. The peripheral nervous system is made up of the somatic nervous system, which controls voluntary muscles and sensory receptors, and the autonomic nervous system, which controls the involuntary activities of smooth muscles, blood vessels, and glands.

system is organized to accomplish this end we will divide it into parts. In many instances, the parts will be divided once again. **Figure 3.5** presents an organizational chart that shows the relationships of the major parts of the nervous system.

The Peripheral Nervous System

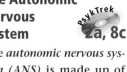
PsykTrek 2a, 8c

The first and most important division separates the *central nervous system* (the brain and spinal cord) from the *peripheral nervous system* (see **Figure 3.6**). **The *peripheral nervous system* is made up of all those nerves that lie outside the brain and spinal cord.** *Nerves* are bundles of neuron fibers (axons) that are routed together in the peripheral nervous system. This portion of the nervous system is just what it sounds like, the part that extends to the periphery (the outside) of the body. The peripheral nervous system can be subdivided into the somatic nervous system and the autonomic nervous system.

The Somatic Nervous System

PsykTrek 2a

The *somatic nervous system* is made up of nerves that connect to voluntary skeletal muscles and to sensory receptors. These nerves are the cables that carry information from receptors in the skin, muscles, and joints to the central nervous system and that carry commands from the central nervous system to the muscles. These functions require two kinds of nerve fibers. *Afferent nerve fibers* are axons that carry information inward to the central nervous system from the periphery of the body. *Efferent nerve fibers* are axons that carry information outward from the central nervous system to the periphery of the body. Each body nerve contains many axons of each type. Thus, somatic nerves are "two-way streets" with incoming (afferent) and outgoing (efferent) lanes. The somatic nervous system lets you feel the world and move around in it.

The Autonomic Nervous System

PsykTrek 2a, 8c

The *autonomic nervous system (ANS)* is made up of nerves that connect to the heart, blood vessels, smooth muscles, and glands. As its name hints, the autonomic system is a separate (autonomous) system, although it is ultimately controlled by the central nervous system. The autonomic nervous system controls automatic, involuntary, visceral functions that people don't normally think about, such as heart rate, digestion, and perspiration.

The autonomic nervous system mediates much of the physiological arousal that occurs when people experience emotions. For example,

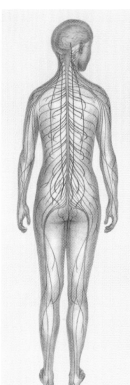

Figure 3.6
The central and peripheral nervous systems. The central nervous system consists of the brain and the spinal cord. The peripheral nervous system consists of the remaining nerves that fan out throughout the body. The peripheral nervous system is divided into the somatic nervous system, which is shown in blue, and the autonomic nervous system, which is shown in green.

Web Link 3.3

Neurosciences on the Internet
Dr. Neil Busis has gathered together what appears to be the largest collection of neuroscience links currently on the web and provides a search engine to help visitors.

Figure 3.7

The autonomic nervous system (ANS). The ANS is composed of the nerves that connect to the heart, blood vessels, smooth muscles, and glands. The ANS is divided into the *sympathetic division,* which mobilizes bodily resources in times of need, and the *parasympathetic division,* which conserves bodily resources. Some of the key functions controlled by each division of the ANS are summarized in the diagram.

imagine that you are walking home alone one night when a seedy-looking character falls in behind you and begins to follow you. If you feel threatened, your heart rate and breathing will speed up. Your blood pressure may surge, you may get goose bumps, and your palms may begin to sweat. These difficult-to-control reactions are aspects of autonomic arousal. Walter Cannon (1932), one of the first psychologists to study this reaction, called it the *fight-or-flight response.* Cannon carefully monitored this response in animals. He concluded that organisms generally respond to threat by preparing physically for attacking (fight) or fleeing (flight) the enemy.

The autonomic nervous system can be subdivided into two branches: the sympathetic division and the parasympathetic division (see **Figure 3.7**). The *sympathetic division* is the branch of the autonomic nervous system that mobilizes the body's resources for emergencies. It creates the fight-or-flight response. Activation of the sympathetic division slows digestive processes and drains blood from the periphery, lessening bleeding in the case of an injury. Key sympathetic nerves send signals to the adrenal glands, triggering the release of hormones that ready the body for exertion. In contrast, the *parasympathetic division* is the branch of the autonomic nervous system that generally conserves bodily resources. It activates processes that allow the body to save and store energy. For example, actions by parasympathetic nerves slow heart rate, reduce blood pressure, and promote digestion.

The Central Nervous System 2a

The central nervous system is the portion of the nervous system that lies within the skull and spinal column. Thus, **the *central nervous system (CNS)* consists of the brain and the spinal cord.** The CNS is bathed in its own special nutritive "soup," called *cerebrospinal fluid* (CSF). This fluid nourishes the brain and provides a protective cushion for it. Although derived from the blood, the CSF is carefully filtered. To enter the CSF, substances in the blood have to cross the *blood-brain barrier,* a semipermeable membrane that stops some chemicals from passing between the bloodstream and the brain. This barrier prevents some drugs from entering the CSF and affecting the brain.

The Spinal Cord

The *spinal cord* connects the brain to the rest of the body through the peripheral nervous system. Although the spinal cord looks like a cable from which the somatic nerves branch, it is part of the central nervous system. The spinal cord runs from the base of the brain to just below the level of the waist. It houses bundles of axons that carry the brain's commands to peripheral nerves and that relay sensations from the periphery of the body to the brain. Many forms of paralysis result from spinal cord damage, a fact that underscores the critical role it plays in transmitting signals from the brain to the neurons that move the body's muscles.

The Brain

The crowning glory of the central nervous system is, of course, the *brain.* Anatomically, the *brain* is the part of the central nervous system that fills the upper portion of the skull. Although it weighs only about three pounds and could be held in one hand, the brain contains billions of interacting cells that integrate information from inside and outside the body, coordinate the body's actions, and enable us to talk, think, remember, plan, create, and dream. Because of its central importance for behavior, the brain is the subject of the next two sections of the chapter.

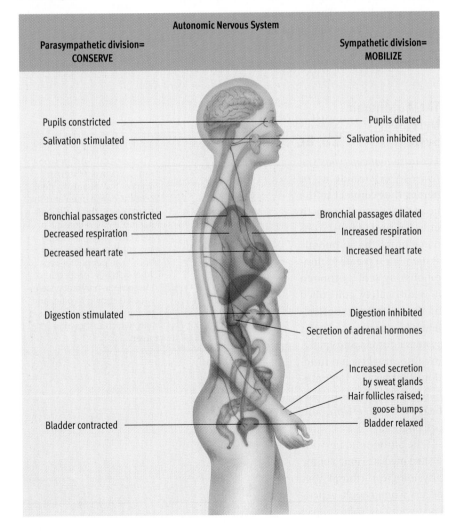

Autonomic Nervous System

Parasympathetic division= CONSERVE

Sympathetic division= MOBILIZE

Pupils constricted — — Pupils dilated

Salivation stimulated — — Salivation inhibited

Bronchial passages constricted — — Bronchial passages dilated

Decreased respiration — — Increased respiration

Decreased heart rate — — Increased heart rate

Digestion stimulated — — Digestion inhibited

— Secretion of adrenal hormones

Increased secretion by sweat glands

Hair follicles raised; goose bumps

Bladder contracted — — Bladder relaxed

Scientists who want to find out how parts of the brain are related to behavior are faced with a formidable task, because mapping out brain *function* requires a working brain. These scientists use a variety of specialized techniques to investigate brain-behavior relations. We will briefly discuss some of the innovative methods that permit scientists to look inside the brain and then outline the major findings of this research.

Looking Inside the Brain: Research Methods

Researchers sometimes observe what happens when specific brain structures in animals are purposely disabled. *Lesioning* **involves destroying a piece of the brain.** This procedure involves inserting an electrode into a brain structure and passing a high-frequency electric current through it to burn the tissue and disable the structure. Another valuable technique is *electrical stimulation of the brain (ESB),* **which involves sending a weak electric current into a brain structure to stimulate (activate) it.** As with lesioning, the current is delivered through an implanted electrode, but the current is different. This sort of electrical stimulation does not exactly duplicate normal electrical signals in the brain. However, it is usually a close enough approximation to activate the brain structures in which the electrodes are lodged. Obviously, these invasive procedures are largely limited to animal research, although ESB is occasionally used on humans in the context of brain surgery required for medical purposes.

Fortunately, in recent decades, the invention of new brain-imaging devices has led to dramatic advances in scientists' ability to look inside the human brain (Dougherty & Rauch, 2003). The *CT (computerized tomography) scan* is a computer-enhanced X ray of brain structure. Multiple X rays are shot from many angles, and the computer combines the readings to create a vivid image of a horizontal slice of the brain (see **Figure 3.8**). The more recently developed *MRI (magnetic resonance imaging) scan* uses magnetic fields, radio waves, and computerized enhancement to map out brain structure. MRI scans provide much better images of brain structure than CT scans, producing three-dimensional pictures of the brain that have remarkably high resolution (see **Figure 3.9** on the next page). Using CT and MRI scans, researchers have found abnormalities in brain structure among people suffering from specific types of mental ill-ness, especially schizophrenia (Andreasen, 2001; see Chapter 13).

In research on how brain and behavior are related, *PET (positron emission tomography) scans* have been especially valuable. PET scans use radioactive markers to map chemical activity in the brain over time. Thus, a PET scan can provide a color-coded map indicating which areas of the brain become active when subjects clench their fist, sing, or contemplate the mysteries of the universe (see **Figure 3.10**). In efforts to pinpoint the brain areas that handle various types of mental tasks, neuroscientists are increasingly using *functional magnetic resonance imaging (fMRI),* which consists of several new variations on MRI technology that monitor blood and oxygen flow in the brain to identify areas of high activity

PREVIEW QUESTIONS

- What types of research methods are used to study brain-behavior relations?
- What are some functions of the medulla, pons, and cerebellum?
- What are some functions of the midbrain, and which structure is the brain's relay center?
- What are some functions of the hypothalamus and the limbic system?
- What is each lobe in the brain known for?
- What does it mean to say that the brain is characterized by "plasticity"?

Figure 3.8

CT technology. CT scans are used to examine aspects of brain structure. They provide computer-enhanced X rays of horizontal slices of the brain.

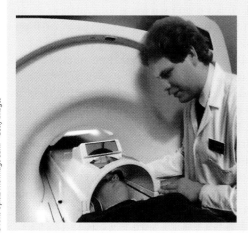

(a) The patient's head is positioned in a large cylinder, as shown here.

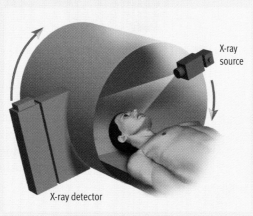

(b) An X-ray beam and X-ray detector rotate around the patient's head, taking multiple X rays of a horizontal slice of the patient's brain.

X-ray source

X-ray detector

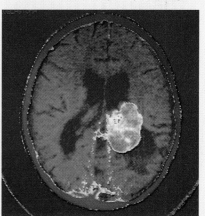

(c) A computer combines X rays to create an image of a horizontal slice of the brain. This scan shows a tumor (in red) on the right.

© Alvis Upitis/The Image Bank—Getty Images

© Dan McCoy/Rainbow

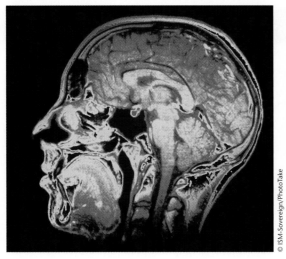

Figure 3.9

MRI scans. MRI scans can be used to produce remarkably high-resolution pictures of brain structure. A vertical view of a brain from the left side is shown here.

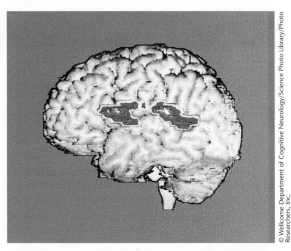

Figure 3.10

PET scans. PET scans are used to map brain activity rather than brain structure. They provide color-coded maps that show areas of high activity in the brain over time. The PET scan shown here pinpointed two areas of high activity (indicated by the red and green colors) when a research participant worked on a verbal short-term memory task.

(Dougherty & Rauch, 2003). This technology is exciting because it can provide both *functional* and *structural* information in the same image and moni-

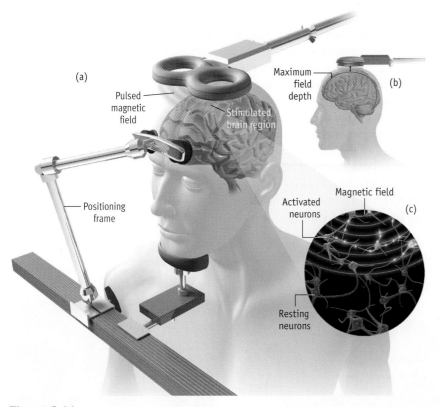

Figure 3.11

Transcranial magnetic stimulation (TMS). In TMS, magnetic pulses are delivered to a localized area of the brain from a magnet mounted on a small paddle **(a)**. The magnetic field only penetrates to a depth of two centimeters **(b)**. This technique can be used to either increase or decrease the excitability of the affected neurons. The inset at bottom right depicts neurons near the surface of the brain being temporarily activated by TMS **(c)**.

Source: Bremner, J. D. (2005). *Brain imaging handbook*, New York: W. W. Norton, p. 34. Illustration © by Bryan Christie Design

tor changes in brain activity in real time. For example, using fMRI scans, researchers have identified patterns of brain activity associated with cocaine craving in cocaine addicts (Wexler et al., 2001).

Another new research tool in neuroscience is *transcranial magnetic stimulation (TMS)*, a technique that permits scientists to temporarily enhance or depress activity in a specific area of the brain. With TMS, a magnetic coil mounted on a small paddle is held over a specific area of a subject's head (see **Figure 3.11**). By varying the timing and duration of magnetic pulses, a researcher can either increase or decrease the excitability of neurons in the local tissue (Sack & Linden, 2003). Thus far, researchers have mostly been interested in temporarily deactivating discrete areas of the brain to learn more about their functions. In essence, this technology allows scientists to create "virtual lesions" in human subjects for short periods of time, using a painless, noninvasive method. This approach has been used to explore whether specific areas of the brain are involved in visuospatial processing (Sack et al., 2002), memory for objects (Oliveri et al., 2001), and language (Knecht et al., 2002).

Now that we have discussed a few approaches to brain research, let's look at what scientists have discovered about the functions of various parts of the brain. The brain is divided into three major regions: the hindbrain, the midbrain, and the forebrain. The principal structures found in each of these regions are listed in the organizational chart of the nervous system in **Figure 3.5**. You can see where these regions are located in the brain by looking at **Figure 3.12**.

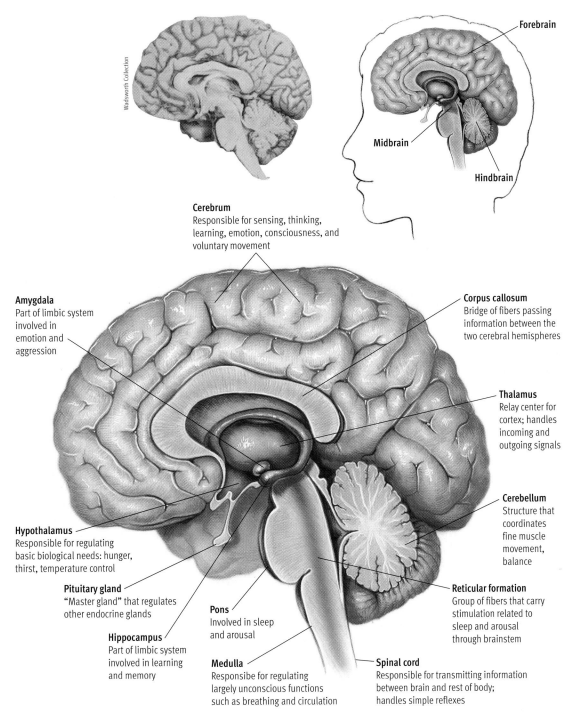

Forebrain

Midbrain

Hindbrain

Figure 3.12
Structures and areas in the human brain. **(Top left)** This photo of a human brain shows many of the structures discussed in this chapter. **(Top right)** The brain is divided into three major areas: the hindbrain, midbrain, and forebrain. These subdivisions actually make more sense for the brains of other animals than of humans. In humans, the forebrain has become so large it makes the other two divisions look trivial. However, the hindbrain and midbrain aren't trivial; they control such vital functions as breathing, waking, and maintaining balance. **(Bottom)** This cross section of the brain highlights key structures and some of their principal functions. As you read about the functions of a brain structure, such as the corpus callosum, you may find it helpful to visualize it.

Cerebrum
Responsible for sensing, thinking, learning, emotion, consciousness, and voluntary movement

Amygdala
Part of limbic system involved in emotion and aggression

Corpus callosum
Bridge of fibers passing information between the two cerebral hemispheres

Thalamus
Relay center for cortex; handles incoming and outgoing signals

Hypothalamus
Responsible for regulating basic biological needs: hunger, thirst, temperature control

Cerebellum
Structure that coordinates fine muscle movement, balance

Pituitary gland
"Master gland" that regulates other endocrine glands

Pons
Involved in sleep and arousal

Reticular formation
Group of fibers that carry stimulation related to sleep and arousal through brainstem

Hippocampus
Part of limbic system involved in learning and memory

Medulla
Responsibe for regulating largely unconscious functions such as breathing and circulation

Spinal cord
Responsible for transmitting information between brain and rest of body; handles simple reflexes

Wadsworth Collection

They can be found easily in relation to the *brainstem.* The brainstem looks like its name—it appears to be a stem from which the rest of the brain "flowers," like a head of cauliflower. At its lower end the stem is contiguous with the spinal cord. At its higher end it lies deep within the brain. We'll begin at the brain's lower end, where the spinal cord joins the brainstem. As we proceed upward, notice how the functions of brain structures go from the regulation of basic bodily processes to the control of "higher" mental processes.

The Hindbrain

The *hindbrain* includes the cerebellum and two structures found in the lower part of the brainstem: the medulla and the pons. The *medulla,*

Web Link 3.4

The Visible Human Project
This site from the National Library of Medicine provides a rich collection of online resources related to the highly detailed visual analysis of two human cadavers—a male and female—that has been carried out during the last decade. This site is a good place to explore advanced techniques in the imaging of the human body, including the central nervous system.

which attaches to the spinal cord, has charge of largely unconscious but essential functions, such as breathing, maintaining muscle tone, and regulating circulation. The *pons* (literally "bridge") includes a bridge of fibers that connects the brainstem with the cerebellum. The pons also contains several clusters of cell bodies involved with sleep and arousal.

The *cerebellum* ("little brain") is a relatively large and deeply folded structure located adjacent to the back surface of the brainstem. The cerebellum is involved in the coordination of movement and is critical to the sense of equilibrium, or physical balance (Ghez & Thach, 2000). Although the actual commands for muscular movements come from higher brain centers, the cerebellum plays a key role in the execution of these commands. It is your cerebellum that allows you to hold your hand out to the side and then smoothly bring your finger to a stop on your nose. This action is a useful roadside test for drunken driving because the cerebellum is one of the structures first depressed by alcohol. Damage to the cerebellum disrupts fine motor skills, such as those involved in writing, typing, or playing a musical instrument.

The Midbrain

The *midbrain* is the segment of the brainstem that lies between the hindbrain and the forebrain. The midbrain contains an area that is concerned with integrating sensory processes, such as vision and hearing (Stein, Wallace, & Stanford, 2000). An important system of dopamine-releasing neurons that projects into various higher brain centers originates in the midbrain. Among other things, this dopamine system is involved in the performance of voluntary movements. The decline in dopamine synthesis that causes Parkinson's disease is due to degeneration of a structure located in the midbrain (DeLong, 2000).

Running through both the hindbrain and the midbrain is the *reticular formation*. Lying at the central core of the brainstem, the reticular formation contributes to the modulation of muscle reflexes, breathing, and pain perception (Saper, 2000). It is best known, however, for its role in the regulation of sleep and wakefulness. Activity in the ascending fibers of the reticular formation contributes to arousal (Coenen, 1998).

The Forebrain

The *forebrain* is the largest and most complex region of the brain, encompassing a variety of struc- tures, including the thalamus, hypothalamus, limbic system, and cerebrum. This list is not exhaustive, and some of these structures have their own subdivisions, as you can see in the organizational chart of the nervous system (Figure 3.5). The thalamus, hypothalamus, and limbic system form the core of the forebrain. All three structures are located near the top of the brainstem. Above them is the *cerebrum*—the seat of complex thought. The wrinkled surface of the cerebrum is the *cerebral cortex*—the outer layer of the brain, the part that looks like a cauliflower.

The Thalamus: A Way Station

The *thalamus* is a structure in the forebrain through which all sensory information (except smell) must pass to get to the cerebral cortex. This way station is made up of a number of clusters of cell bodies, or somas. Each cluster is concerned with relaying sensory information to a particular part of the cortex. However, it would be a mistake to characterize the thalamus as nothing more than a passive relay station. The thalamus also appears to play an active role in integrating information from various senses.

The Hypothalamus: A Regulator of Biological Needs

The *hypothalamus* is a structure found near the base of the forebrain that is involved in the regulation of basic biological needs. The hypothalamus lies beneath the thalamus (*hypo* means "under," making the hypothalamus the area under the thalamus). Although no larger than a kidney bean, the hypothalamus contains various clusters of cells that have many key functions. One such function is to control the autonomic nervous system (Iversen, Iversen, & Saper, 2000).

The hypothalamus plays a major role in the regulation of basic biological drives related to survival, including the so-called "four F's": fighting, fleeing, feeding, and mating. For example, when researchers lesion the lateral areas (the sides) of the hypothalamus, animals lose interest in eating. The animals must be fed intravenously or they starve, even in the presence of abundant food. In contrast, when electrical stimulation (ESB) is used to *activate* the lateral hypothalamus, animals eat constantly and gain weight rapidly (Grossman et al., 1978; Keesey & Powley, 1975). Does this mean that the lateral hypothalamus is the "hunger center" in the brain? No. The regulation of hunger turns out to be complex and multifaceted, as you'll see in Chapter 9. Nonetheless, the hypothalamus clearly contributes to the control of hunger and other basic biological processes, including thirst, sex drive, and temperature regulation (Kupfermann, Kandel, & Iversen, 2000).

The Limbic System: The Seat of Emotion

The *limbic system* is a loosely connected network of structures located roughly along the border between the cerebral cortex and deeper subcortical areas (hence the term *limbic,* which means "edge"). First described by Paul MacLean (1954), the limbic system is not a well-defined anatomical system with clear boundaries. Indeed, scientists disagree about which structures should be included in the limbic system. Broadly defined, the limbic system includes parts of the thalamus and hypothalamus, the *hippocampus,* the *amygdala,* and other nearby structures.

The *hippocampal area* clearly plays a role in memory processes, although the exact nature of that role is the subject of debate (Squire & Knowlton, 2000). Similarly, there is ample evidence linking the limbic system to the experience of emotion, but the exact mechanisms of control are not yet well understood (Mega et al., 1997; Paradiso et al., 1997). Recent evidence suggests that the *amygdala* may play a central role in the learning of fear responses (Armony & LeDoux, 2000; Hamann et al., 2002).

The limbic system also appears to contain emotion-tinged "pleasure centers." This intriguing possibility first surfaced, quite by chance, in brain stimulation research with rats. James Olds and Peter Milner (1954) accidentally discovered that a rat would press a lever repeatedly to send brief bursts of electrical stimulation to a specific spot in its brain where an electrode was implanted (see **Figure 3.13**). They thought that they had inserted the electrode in the rat's reticular formation. However, they learned later that the electrode had been bent during implantation and ended up elsewhere (probably in the hypothalamus). Much to their surprise, the rat kept coming back for more self-stimulation in this area. Subsequent studies showed that rats and monkeys would press a lever *thousands of times* per hour to stimulate certain brain sites. Although the experimenters obviously couldn't ask the animals about it, they *inferred* that the animals were experiencing some sort of pleasure.

Where are the pleasure centers located in the brain? Many self-stimulation sites have been found in the limbic system (Olds & Fobe, 1981). The heaviest concentration appears to be where the *medial forebrain bundle* (a bundle of axons) passes through the hypothalamus. The medial forebrain bundle is rich in dopamine-releasing neurons. The rewarding effects of ESB at self-stimulation sites may be largely mediated by the activation of these dopamine circuits (Nakajima & Patterson, 1997). The rewarding, pleasurable effects of opiates and stimulant drugs (cocaine and amphetamines) may also depend on excitation of this dopamine system (Gratton, 1996; Wise, 1999).

The Cerebrum: The Seat of Complex Thought

The *cerebrum* is the largest and most complex part of the human brain. It includes the brain areas that are responsible for our most complex mental activities, including learning, remembering, thinking, and consciousness itself. **The *cerebral cortex* is the convoluted outer layer of the cerebrum.** The cortex is folded and bent, so that its large surface area—about 1.5 square feet—can be packed into the limited volume of the skull (Hubel & Wiesel, 1979).

The cerebrum is divided into two halves called hemispheres. Hence, **the *cerebral hemispheres* are**

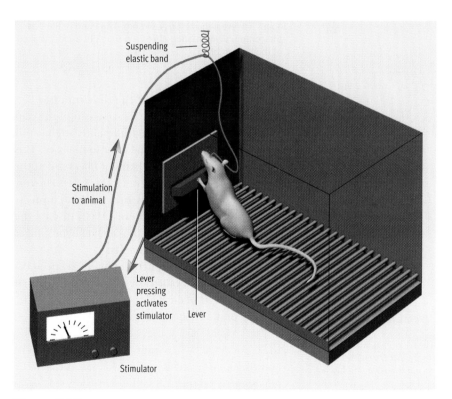

Figure 3.13

Electrical stimulation of the brain (ESB) in the rat. Olds and Milner (1954) were using an apparatus like that depicted here when they discovered self-stimulation centers, or "pleasure centers," in the brain of a rat. In this setup, the wire delivering electrical stimulation is suspended from above so the rat can move freely about the box. When the rat presses the lever, it earns brief electrical stimulation that is sent to a specific spot in the rat's brain where an electrode has been implanted.

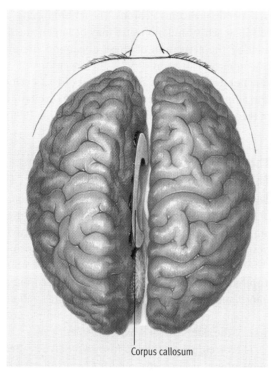

Corpus callosum

Figure 3.14

The cerebral hemispheres and the corpus callosum. In this drawing the cerebral hemispheres have been "pulled apart" to reveal the corpus callosum. This band of fibers is the communication bridge between the right and left halves of the human brain.

Web Link 3.5

The Whole Brain Atlas Here visitors will find a comprehensive and fascinating set of images of the brains of both normal individuals and those impaired by various types of neuropsychological disorders. Modern techniques of brain research and diagnosis are well illustrated and explained.

the right and left halves of the cerebrum (see Figure 3.14). The hemispheres are separated in the center of the brain by the longitudinal fissure (a split or crevice) that runs from the front to the back. This fissure descends to a thick band of fibers called the *corpus callosum* (also shown in Figure 3.14). **The *corpus callosum* is the major structure that connects the two cerebral hemispheres.** We'll discuss the functional specialization of the cerebral hemispheres in the next section of this chapter.

Each cerebral hemisphere is divided by deep fissures into four parts called *lobes*. To some extent, each of these lobes is dedicated to specific purposes. The location of these lobes can be seen in Figure 3.15.

The *occipital lobe,* at the back of the head, includes the cortical area where most visual signals are sent and visual processing is begun. This area is called the *primary visual cortex.* We will discuss how it is organized in Chapter 4.

The *parietal lobe* is forward of the occipital lobe. It includes the area that registers the sense of touch, called the *primary somatosensory cortex.* Various sections of this area receive signals from different regions of the body. When electrical stimulation is delivered in these parietal lobe areas, people report physical sensations—as if someone actually touched them on the arm or cheek, for example. The parietal lobe is also involved in integrating visual input and in monitoring the body's position in space.

The *temporal lobe* (meaning "near the temples") lies below the parietal lobe. Near its top, the temporal lobe contains an area devoted to auditory processing, the *primary auditory cortex.* As we will see momentarily, damage to an area in the temporal lobe on the left side of the brain can impair the ability to comprehend speech and language.

Continuing forward, we find the *frontal lobe,* the largest lobe in the human brain. It contains the principal areas that control the movement of muscles, the *primary motor cortex.* Electrical stimulation applied in these areas can cause actual muscle contractions. The amount of motor cortex allocated to the control of a body part depends not on the part's size but on the diversity and precision of its movements. Thus, more of the cortex is given to parts we have fine control over, such as the fingers, lips, and tongue. Less of the cortex is devoted to larger parts that make crude movements, such as the thighs and shoulders.

The portion of the frontal lobe to the front of the motor cortex, which is called the *prefrontal cortex* (see Figure 3.15), is something of a mystery. This area is disproportionately large in humans. Its apparent contributions to reasoning about relations between objects and events (Huettel, Mack, & McCarthy, 2002) and to certain types of decision making (Walton, Devlin, & Rushworth, 2004) have led some theorists to suggest that the prefrontal cortex houses some sort of "executive control system," which is thought to monitor, organize, and direct thought processes (Kane & Engle, 2002; Shimamura, 1995). Consistent with this hypothesis, people who suffer damage in the prefrontal cortex often show deficits in planning, paying attention, and getting organized (Fuster, 1996).

The Plasticity of the Brain

It was once believed that significant changes in the anatomy and organization of the brain were limited to early periods of development in both humans and animals. However, research has gradually demonstrated that the anatomical structure and functional organization of the brain is more flexible or "plastic" than widely assumed (Kolb, Gibb, & Robinson, 2003; Recanzone, 2000). This conclusion is based on several lines of research.

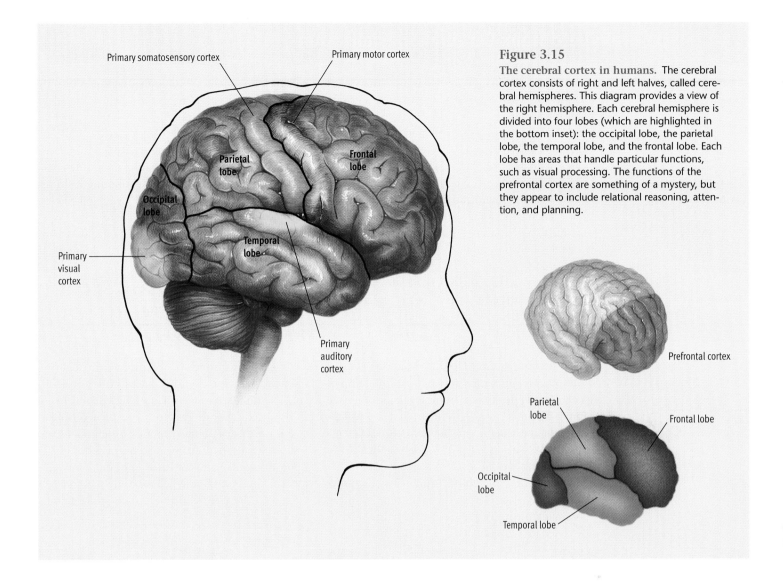

Figure 3.15

The cerebral cortex in humans. The cerebral cortex consists of right and left halves, called cerebral hemispheres. This diagram provides a view of the right hemisphere. Each cerebral hemisphere is divided into four lobes (which are highlighted in the bottom inset): the occipital lobe, the parietal lobe, the temporal lobe, and the frontal lobe. Each lobe has areas that handle particular functions, such as visual processing. The functions of the prefrontal cortex are something of a mystery, but they appear to include relational reasoning, attention, and planning.

First, studies have shown that aspects of experience can sculpt features of brain structure. For example, neuroimaging studies have shown that an area in the somatosensory cortex that receives input from the fingers of the left hand is enlarged in string musicians who constantly use the left hand to finger the strings of their instruments (Elbert et al., 1995). *Second, research has shown that damage to incoming sensory pathways or the destruction of brain tissue can lead to neural reorganization.* For example, when scientists amputated the third finger in an owl monkey, the part of its cortex that formerly responded to the third finger gradually became responsive to the second and fourth fingers (Kaas, 2000). *Third, studies now indicate that the adult brain can generate new neurons* (Gage, 2002). Until recently it was believed that the brain formed all its neurons by infancy at the latest. However, new evidence suggests that adult humans and monkeys can form new neurons in the hippocampus and other subcortical areas (Eriksson et al., 1998; Gould & Gross, 2002).

In sum, research suggests that the brain is not "hard wired" the way a computer is. It appears that the neural wiring of the brain is flexible and constantly evolving. That said, this plasticity is not unlimited. Rehabilitation efforts with people who have suffered severe brain damage clearly demonstrate that there are limits on the extent to which the brain can rewire itself (Zillmer & Spiers, 2001). And the evidence suggests that the brain's plasticity declines with increasing age (Rains, 2002). Younger brains are more flexible than older brains. Still, the neural circuits of the brain show substantial plasticity, which certainly helps organisms to adapt to their environments.

PREVIEW QUESTIONS

● How was the left hemisphere originally implicated in the control of language?

● How are sensory and motor information routed to the two hemispheres?

● What did split-brain research reveal about the right and left hemispheres of the brain?

● How do scientists study hemispheric specialization in normal subjects, and what have they learned?

As noted a moment ago, the cerebrum—the seat of complex thought—is divided into two separate hemispheres (see Figure 3.14). Recent decades have seen an exciting flurry of research on the specialized abilities of the right and left cerebral hemispheres. Some theorists have gone so far as to suggest that people really have two brains in one!

Hints of this hemispheric specialization have been available for many years, from cases in which one side of a person's brain has been damaged. The left hemisphere was implicated in the control of language as early as 1861, by Paul Broca, a French surgeon. Broca was treating a patient who had been unable to speak for 30 years. After the patient died, Broca showed that the probable cause of his speech deficit was a small lesion on the left side of the frontal lobe. Since then, many similar cases have shown that this area of the brain—known as *Broca's area*—plays an important role in the production of speech (see Figure 3.16). Another major language center—*Wernicke's area*—was identified in the temporal lobe of the left hemisphere in 1874. Damage in Wernicke's area (see Figure 3.16) usually leads to problems with the *comprehension* of language.

Evidence that the left hemisphere usually processes language led scientists to characterize it as the "dominant" hemisphere. Because thoughts are usually coded in terms of language, the left hemisphere was given the lion's share of credit for handling the "higher" mental processes, such as reasoning, remembering, planning, and problem solving. Meanwhile, the right hemisphere came to be viewed as the "nondominant," or "dumb," hemisphere, lacking any special functions or abilities.

This characterization of the left and right hemispheres as major and minor partners in the brain's work began to change in the 1960s. It all started with landmark research by Roger Sperry, Michael Gazzaniga, and their colleagues who studied "split-brain" patients: individuals whose cerebral hemispheres had been surgically disconnected (Gazzaniga, 1970; Gazzaniga, Bogen, & Sperry, 1965; Levy, Trevarthen, & Sperry, 1972; Sperry, 1982). In 1981 Sperry received a Nobel prize in physiology/medicine for this work.

Bisecting the Brain: Split-Brain Research

PsykTrek
SIM2, 2f

In *split-brain surgery* the bundle of fibers that connects the cerebral hemispheres (the corpus callosum) is cut to reduce the severity of epileptic

seizures. It is a radical procedure that is chosen only in exceptional cases that have not responded to other forms of treatment. But the surgery provides scientists with an unusual opportunity to study people who have had their brain literally split in two.

To appreciate the logic of split-brain research, you need to understand how sensory and motor information is routed to and from the two hemispheres. *Each hemisphere's primary connections are to the opposite side of the body.* Thus, the left hemisphere controls, and communicates with, the right hand, right arm, right leg, right eyebrow, and so on. In contrast, the right hemisphere controls, and communicates with, the left side of the body.

Vision and hearing are more complex. Both eyes deliver information to both hemispheres, but input is still separated. Stimuli in the right half of the visual field are registered by receptors on the left side of each eye, which send signals to the left hemisphere. Stimuli in the left half of the visual field are transmitted by both eyes to the right hemisphere (see Figure 3.17). Auditory inputs to each ear also go to both hemispheres. However, connections to the opposite hemisphere are stronger or more immediate. That is, sounds presented to the right ear are registered in the left hemisphere first, while sounds

ROGER SPERRY

"Both the left and right hemispheres of the brain have been found to have their own specialized forms of intellect."

Photo by Bob Paz/Caltech, Courtesy of Roger Sperry

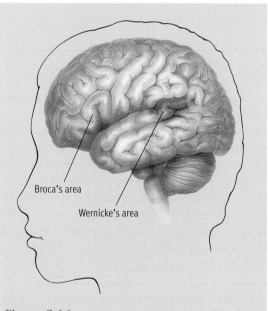

Broca's area

Wernicke's area

Figure 3.16
Language processing in the brain. This view of the left hemisphere highlights the location of two centers for language processing in the brain: Broca's area, which is involved in speech production, and Wernicke's area, which is involved in language comprehension.

presented to the left ear are registered more quickly in the right hemisphere.

For the most part, people don't notice this asymmetric, "crisscrossed" organization because the two hemispheres are in close communication with each other. Information received by one hemisphere is readily shared with the other via the corpus callosum. However, when the two hemispheres are surgically disconnected, the functional specialization of the brain becomes apparent.

In their classic study of split-brain patients, Gazzaniga, Bogen, and Sperry (1965) presented visual stimuli such as pictures, symbols, and words in a single visual field (the left or the right), so that the stimuli would be sent to only one hemisphere. The stimuli were projected onto a screen in front of the subjects, who stared at a fixation point (a spot) in the center of the screen. The images were flashed to the right or the left of the fixation point for only a split second. Thus, the subjects did not have a chance to move their eyes, and the stimuli were glimpsed in only one visual field.

When pictures were flashed in the right visual field and thus sent to the left hemisphere, the split-brain subjects were able to name and describe the objects depicted (such as a cup or spoon). However, the subjects were *not* able to name and describe the same objects when they were flashed in the left visual field and sent to the right hemisphere. In a similar fashion, an object placed out of view in the right hand (communicating with the left hemisphere) could be named. However, the same object placed in the left hand (right hemisphere) could not be. These findings supported the notion that language is housed in the left hemisphere.

Although the split-brain subjects' right hemisphere was not able to speak up for itself, further tests revealed that it was processing the information presented. If subjects were given an opportunity to *point out a picture* of an object they had held in their left hand, they were able to do so. They were also

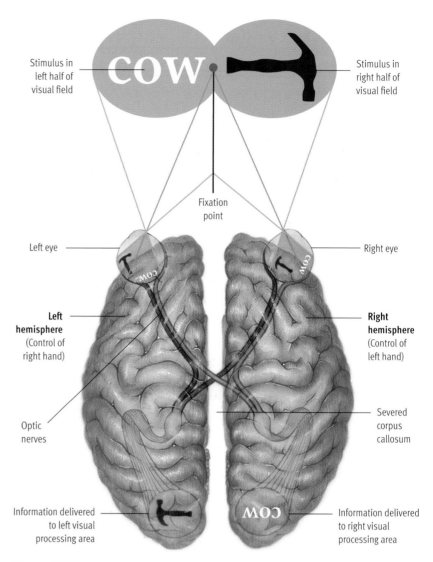

Figure 3.17

Visual input in the split brain. If a participant stares at a fixation point, the point divides the subject's visual field into right and left halves. Input from the right visual field (a picture of a hammer in this example) strikes the left side of each eye and is transmitted to the left hemisphere. Input from the left visual field strikes the right side of each eye and is transmitted to the right hemisphere. Normally, the hemispheres share the information from the two halves of the visual field, but in split-brain patients, the corpus callosum is severed, and the two hemispheres cannot communicate. Hence, the experimenter can present a visual stimulus to just one hemisphere at a time.

Relating Disorders to the Nervous System

Imagine that you are working as a neuropsychologist at a clinic. You are involved in the diagnosis of the cases described below. You are asked to identify the probable cause(s) of the disorders in terms of nervous system malfunctions. Based on the information in this chapter, indicate the probable location of any brain damage or the probable disturbance of neurotransmitter activity. The answers can be found in the back of the book in Appendix A.

Case 1. Miriam is exhibiting language deficits. In particular, she does not seem to comprehend the meaning of words.

Case 2. Camille displays tremors and muscular rigidity and is diagnosed as having Parkinson's disease.

Case 3. Ricardo, a 28-year-old computer executive, has gradually seen his strength and motor coordination deteriorate badly. He is diagnosed as having multiple sclerosis.

Case 4. Wendy is highly irrational, has poor contact with reality, and reports hallucinations. She is given a diagnosis of schizophrenic disorder.

Web Link 3.6

The Society for Neuroscience
The largest scientific association devoted solely to the study of the nervous system and its functioning has gathered a host of materials that will introduce visitors to the latest research on a full spectrum of brain-related topics.

able to point out pictures that had been flashed to the left visual field. Furthermore, the right hemisphere (left hand) turned out to be *superior* to the left hemisphere (right hand) in assembling little puzzles and copying drawings, even though the subjects were right-handed. These findings provided the first compelling demonstration that the right hemisphere has its own special talents. Subsequent studies of additional split-brain patients showed the right hemisphere to be better than the left on a variety of visual-spatial tasks, including discriminating colors, arranging blocks, and recognizing faces.

Hemispheric Specialization in the Intact Brain

The problem with the split-brain operation, of course, is that it creates a highly abnormal situation. Moreover, the surgery is done only with people who suffer from prolonged, severe cases of epilepsy. These people may have had somewhat atypical brain organization even before the operation. Thus, theorists couldn't help wondering whether it was safe to generalize broadly from the split-brain studies. For this reason, researchers developed methods that allowed them to study cerebral specialization in the intact brain.

One method involves looking at left-right imbalances in visual or auditory processing, called *perceptual asymmetries*. As we have seen, it is possible to present visual stimuli to just one visual field at a time. In normal individuals, the input sent to one hemisphere is quickly shared with the other. However, subtle differences in the "abilities" of the two hemispheres can be detected by precisely measuring how long it takes subjects to recognize different types of stimuli. For instance, when verbal stimuli are presented to the right visual field (and thus sent to the *left hemisphere* first), they are identified more quickly and more accurately than when they are presented to the left visual field (and sent to the right hemisphere first). The faster reactions in the left hemisphere presumably occur because it can recognize verbal stimuli on its own, while the right hemisphere has to take extra time to "consult" the left hemisphere. In contrast, the *right hemisphere* is faster than the left on *visual-spatial* tasks, such as locating a dot or recognizing a face (Bradshaw, 1989; Bryden, 1982).

Researchers have used a variety of other approaches to explore hemispheric specialization in normal people. For the most part, their findings have converged nicely with the results of the split-brain studies (Reuter-Lorenz & Miller, 1998). Overall, the findings suggest that the two hemispheres are specialized, with each handling certain types of cognitive tasks better than the other (Corballis, 2003; Gazzaniga, 2000; Springer & Deutsch, 1998). *The left hemisphere usually is better on tasks involving verbal processing, such as language, speech, reading, and writing. The right hemisphere exhibits superiority on many tasks involving nonverbal processing, such as most spatial, musical, and visual recognition tasks.*

Some hemispheric specialization has also been found in regard to the processing and expression of emotions. The right hemisphere appears to play a larger role than the left in the *perception* of others' emotions (Narumoto et al., 2001). For example, a right-hemisphere advantage is seen when subjects attempt to judge others' emotions based on nonverbal signals (Adolphs, Damasio, & Tranel, 2002; Everhart & Harrison, 2000). Lateralization in the *experience and expression* of emotion appears to be more complex. Negative emotions are associated with greater activation of the right hemisphere, but positive emotions tend to produce greater activation in the left hemisphere (Canli et al., 1998; Davidson, Shackman, & Maxwell, 2004).

Obviously, the specialization of the right and left halves of the brain is a burgeoning area of research that has broad implications, which we will discuss further in the Personal Application. For now, however, let's leave the brain and turn our attention to the endocrine system.

> The Endocrine System: Another Way to Communicate

The major way the brain communicates with the rest of the body is through the nervous system. However, the body has a second communication system that is also important to behavior. **The *endocrine system* consists of glands that secrete chemicals into the bloodstream that help control bodily functioning.** The messengers in this communication network are called hormones. ***Hormones* are the chemical substances released by the endocrine glands.** The endocrine system tends to be involved in the long-term regulation of basic bodily processes, as its actions can't match the high speed of neural transmission. The major endocrine glands and their functions are shown in Figure 3.18.

Much of the endocrine system is controlled by the nervous system through the *hypothalamus*. This structure at the base of the forebrain has intimate connections with the pea-sized *pituitary gland,* to which it is adjacent. **The *pituitary gland* releases a great variety of hormones that fan out within the body, stimulating actions in the other endocrine glands.** In this sense, the pituitary is the "master gland" of the endocrine system, although the hypothalamus is the real power behind the throne.

The intermeshing of the nervous system and the endocrine system can be seen in the fight-or-flight response described earlier. In times of stress, the hypothalamus sends signals along two pathways—through the autonomic nervous system and through the pituitary gland—to the adrenal glands (Clow, 2001). In response, the adrenal glands secrete hormones that radiate throughout the body, preparing it to cope with an emergency.

Hormones also play important roles in human physiological development. For example, among the more interesting hormones released by the pituitary are the *gonadotropins,* which affect the *gonads,* or sexual glands. Prior to birth, these hormones direct the formation of the external sexual organs in the developing fetus (Gorski, 2000). Thus, your sexual identity as a male or female was shaped during prenatal development by the actions of hormones. At puberty, increased levels of sexual hormones are responsible for the emergence of secondary sexual characteristics, such as male facial hair and female breasts (Susman, Dorn, & Schiefelbein, 2003). The

actions of other hormones are responsible for the spurt in physical growth that occurs around puberty.

These developmental effects of hormones illustrate how genetic programming has a hand in behavior. Obviously, the hormonal actions that launched your adolescent growth spurt and sparked your interest in sexuality were preprogrammed over a decade earlier by your genetic inheritance, which brings us to the role of heredity in shaping behavior.

PREVIEW QUESTIONS

- What are hormones?
- What is the master gland of the endocrine system?
- What are some aspects of behavior regulated by hormones?

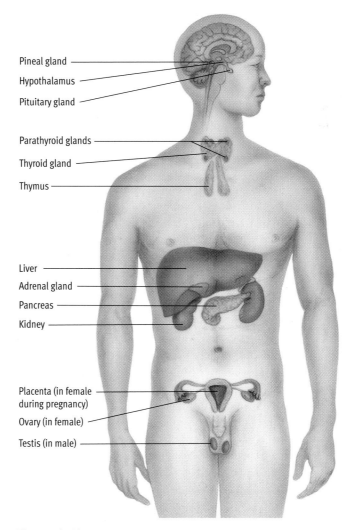

Pineal gland
Hypothalamus
Pituitary gland
Parathyroid glands
Thyroid gland
Thymus
Liver
Adrenal gland
Pancreas
Kidney
Placenta (in female during pregnancy)
Ovary (in female)
Testis (in male)

Figure 3.18
The endocrine system. This graphic depicts most of the major endocrine glands. The endocrine glands secrete hormones into the bloodstream. These hormones regulate a variety of physical functions and affect many aspects of behavior.

PREVIEW QUESTIONS

- What are the basic mechanisms of hereditary transmission?
- How are family studies conducted, and what can they reveal?
- How are twin studies conducted, and what have they revealed about intelligence and personality?
- How do adoption studies assess the role of genetics and environment?

Most people realize that physical characteristics such as height, hair color, blood type, and eye color are largely shaped by heredity. But what about psychological characteristics, such as intelligence, moodiness, impulsiveness, and shyness? To what extent are people's behavioral qualities molded by their genes? As we saw in Chapter 1, questions about the relative importance of heredity versus environment are very old ones in psychology. The nature versus nurture debate will continue to surface in many of the upcoming chapters. To help you appreciate the complexities of this debate, we will outline some basic principles of genetics and describe the methods that investigators use to assess the effects of heredity.

Basic Principles of Genetics

Every cell in your body contains enduring messages from your mother and father. These messages are found on the *chromosomes* that lie within the nucleus of each cell. *Chromosomes* **are threadlike strands of DNA (deoxyribonucleic acid) molecules that carry genetic information.** With the exception of sex cells (sperm and eggs), every cell in humans contains 46 chromosomes. These chromosomes operate in 23 pairs, with one chromosome of each pair coming from each parent. Each chromosome, in turn, contains thousands of biochemical messengers called genes. *Genes* **are DNA segments that serve as the key functional units in hereditary transmission.**

If all offspring are formed by a union of the parents' sex cells, why aren't family members identical clones? The reason is that a single pair of parents can produce an extraordinary variety of combinations of chromosomes. Each parent's 23 chromosome pairs can be scrambled in over 8 million (2^{23}) different ways, yielding roughly 70 trillion possible configurations when sperm and egg unite. Thus, genetic transmission is a complicated process, and everything is a matter of probability. Except for identical twins, each person ends up with a unique genetic blueprint.

Although different combinations of genes explain why family members aren't all alike, the overlap among these combinations explains why family members do tend to resemble one another. Members of a family share more of the same genes than nonmembers. Ultimately, each person shares half of her or his genes with each parent. On the average, full siblings (except identical twins) also share half their

genes. More distant relatives share smaller proportions of genes. **Figure 3.19** shows the amount of genetic overlap for various kinship relations.

Like chromosomes, genes operate in pairs, with one gene of each pair coming from each parent. In the simplest scenario, a single pair of genes determines a trait. However, most human characteristics appear to be *polygenic traits,* **or characteristics that are influenced by more than one pair of genes.** For example, three to five gene pairs are thought to interactively determine skin color. Complex physical abilities, such as motor coordination, may be influenced by tangled interactions among a great many pairs of genes. Most psychological characteristics that appear to be affected by heredity seem to involve complex polygenic inheritance (Plomin et al., 2001).

Detecting Hereditary Influence: Research Methods

How do scientists disentangle the effects of genetics and experience to determine how heredity affects human behavior? Researchers have designed special types of studies to assess the impact of heredity. The three most important methods are family studies, twin studies, and adoption studies.

Family Studies

In *family studies* **researchers assess hereditary influence by examining blood relatives to see how much they resemble one another on a specific trait.** If heredity affects the trait under scrutiny, researchers should find trait similarity among relatives. Furthermore, they should find more similarity among relatives who share more genes. For instance, siblings should exhibit more similarity than cousins.

Illustrative of this method are the numerous family studies conducted to assess the contribution of heredity to the development of schizophrenic disorders. These disorders strike approximately 1% of the population, yet 9% of the siblings of schizophrenic patients exhibit schizophrenia themselves (Gottesman, 1991). Thus, these first-degree relatives of schizophrenic patients show a risk for the disorder that is nine times higher than normal. This risk is greater than that observed for second-degree relatives, such as nieces and nephews (4%), which is greater than that found for third-degree relatives, such as first cousins (2%), and so on. This pattern of results is consistent with the hypothesis that genetic inheritance influences the development of schizophrenic disorders (Gottesman & Moldin, 1998; Ho, Black, & Andreasen, 2003).

Family studies can indicate whether a trait runs in families. However, this correlation does not provide conclusive evidence that the trait is influenced by heredity. Why not? Because family members generally share not only genes but also similar environments. Furthermore, closer relatives are more likely to live together than more distant relatives. Thus, genetic similarity and environmental similarity both tend to be greater for closer relatives. Either of these confounded variables could be responsible when greater trait similarity is found in closer relatives. Family studies can offer useful insights about the possible impact of heredity, but they cannot provide definitive evidence.

Twin Studies

7d

Twin studies can yield better evidence about the possible role of genetic factors. **In *twin studies* researchers assess hereditary influence by comparing**

Twin studies, which compare sets of identical twins and fraternal twins in regard to how similar the twin pairs are on a specific trait, have proven invaluable in exploring genetic influences on behavior.

© Barbara Penoyer/Photodisc Green/Getty Images

Relationship	Degree of relatedness	Genetic overlap
Identical twins		100%
Fraternal twins Brother or sister Parent or child	First-degree relatives	50%
Grandparent or grandchild Uncle, aunt, nephew, or niece Half-brother or half-sister	Second-degree relatives	25%
First cousin	Third-degree relatives	12.5%
Second cousin	Fourth-degree relatives	6.25%
Unrelated		0%

Figure 3.19

Genetic relatedness. Research on the genetic bases of behavior takes advantage of the different degrees of genetic relatedness between various types of relatives. If heredity influences a trait, relatives who share more genes should be more similar with regard to that trait than are more distant relatives, who share fewer genes. Comparisons involving various degrees of biological relationships will come up frequently in later chapters.

the resemblance of identical twins and fraternal twins with respect to a trait. *Identical (monozygotic) twins* emerge when a single fertilized egg splits for unknown reasons. Thus, they have exactly the same genetic blueprint; their genetic overlap is 100%. *Fraternal (dizygotic) twins* result when two separate eggs are fertilized simultaneously. Fraternal twins are no more alike in genetic makeup than any two siblings born to a pair of parents at different times. Their genetic overlap averages 50%.

Fraternal twins provide a useful comparison to identical twins because in both cases the twins usually grow up in the same home, at the same time, exposed to the same configuration of relatives, neighbors, peers, teachers, events, and so forth. Thus, both kinds of twins normally develop under equally similar environmental conditions. However, identical twins share more genetic kinship than fraternal twins. Consequently, if sets of identical twins tend to exhibit more similarity on a trait than sets of fraternal twins do, it is reasonable to infer that this greater similarity is probably due to heredity.

Twin studies have been conducted to assess the impact of heredity on a variety of traits; some representative results are summarized in **Figure 3.20** on the next page. The higher correlations found for identical twins indicate that they tend to be more

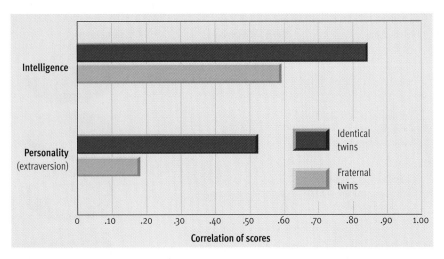

© 2003 Leo Cullum from the cartoonbank.com. All rights reserved.

Figure 3.20

Twin studies of intelligence and personality. Identical twins tend to be more similar than fraternal twins (as reflected in higher correlations) with regard to intelligence and specific personality traits, such as extraversion. These findings suggest that intelligence and personality are influenced by heredity. (Intelligence data from McGue et al., 1993; extraversion data based on Loehlin, 1992)

similar to each other than fraternal twins on measures of general intelligence (McGue et al., 1993) and measures of specific personality traits, such as extraversion (Loehlin, 1992). These results support the notion that these traits are influenced to some degree by genetic makeup.

Adoption Studies

 7d

Adoption studies **assess hereditary influence by examining the resemblance between adopted children and both their biological and their adoptive parents.** If adopted children resemble their biological parents on a trait, even though they were not raised by them, genetic factors probably influence that trait. In contrast, if adopted children resemble their adoptive parents, even though they inherited no genes from them, environmental factors probably influence the trait.

In recent years, adoption studies have contributed to science's understanding of how genetics and the environment influence intelligence. The research shows modest similarity between adopted children and their biological parents, as indicated by an average correlation of .24 (McGue et al., 1993). Interestingly, adopted children resemble their adoptive parents just as much (also an average correlation of .24). These findings suggest that both heredity and environment have an influence on intelligence.

The Interplay of Heredity and Environment

We began this section by asking, is it all in the genes? When it comes to behavioral traits, the answer clearly is no. According to Robert Plomin (1993, 2004), perhaps the leading behavioral genetics researcher in the last decade, what scientists find again and again is that heredity and experience *jointly* influence most aspects of behavior. Moreover, their

ROBERT PLOMIN

"The transformation of the social and behavioral sciences from environmentalism to biological determinism is happening so fast that I find I more often have to say, 'Yes, genetic influences are substantial, but environmental influences are important, too.'"

effects are interactive—they play off each other (Gottesman & Hanson, 2005; Rutter & Silberg, 2002).

For example, consider what researchers have learned about the development of schizophrenic disorders. Although the evidence indicates that genetic factors influence the development of schizophrenia, it does not appear that anyone directly inherits the disorder itself. Rather, what people appear to inherit is a certain degree of *vulnerability* to the disorder (McDonald & Murphy, 2003). Whether this vulnerability is ever converted into an actual disorder depends on each person's experiences in life. Thus, as Danielle Dick and Richard Rose (2002) put it in a review of behavioral genetics research, "Genes confer dispositions, not destinies" (p 73).

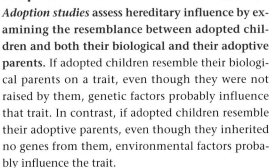

concept check 3.4

Recognizing Hereditary Influence

Check your understanding of the methods scientists use to explore hereditary influences on specific behavioral traits by filling in the blanks in the descriptive statements below. The answers can be found in the back of the book in Appendix A.

1. The findings from family studies indicate that heredity may influence a trait if _____ show more trait similarity than _____.

2. The findings from twin studies suggest that heredity influences a trait if _____ show more trait similarity than _____.

3. The findings from adoption studies suggest that heredity influences a trait if children adopted at a young age share more trait similarity with their _____ than their _____.

4. The findings from family studies, twin studies, and adoption studies suggest that heredity does not influence a trait when _____ is not related to _____.

Courtesy of Tara McKearney

To round out our look at the biological bases of behavior, we need to discuss how evolutionary forces have shaped many aspects of human and animal behavior. As you may recall from Chapter 1, *evolutionary psychology* is a major new theoretical perspective in the field that analyzes behavioral processes in terms of their adaptive significance. In this section, we will outline some basic principles of evolutionary theory and relate them to animal behavior. These ideas will create a foundation for forthcoming chapters, where we'll see how these principles can enhance our understanding of many aspects of human behavior.

Darwin's Insights

Charles Darwin, the legendary British naturalist, was *not* the first person to describe the process of evolution. Well before Darwin's time, other biologists who had studied the earth's fossil record noted that various species appeared to have undergone gradual changes over the course of a great many generations. What Darwin (1859) contributed in his landmark book, *The Origin of Species,* was a creative, new explanation for *how and why* evolutionary changes unfold over time. He identified *natural selection* as the mechanism that orchestrates the process of evolution.

The mystery that Darwin set out to solve was complicated. He wanted to explain how the characteristics of a species might change over generations and why these changes tended to be surprisingly adaptive. In other words, he wanted to shed light on why organisms tend to have characteristics that serve them well in the context of their environments. How did giraffes acquire their long necks that allow them to reach high into acacia trees to secure their main source of food? How did woodpeckers develop their sharp, chisel-shaped beaks that permit them to probe trees for insects so effectively? Darwin's explanation for the seemingly purposive nature of evolution centered on four crucial insights.

First, he noted that organisms vary in endless ways, such as size, speed, strength, aspects of appearance, visual abilities, hearing capacities, digestive processes, cell structure, and so forth. Second, he noted that some of these characteristics are heritable—that is, they are passed down from one generation to the next. Although genes and chromosomes had not yet been discovered, the concept of heredity was well established. Third, borrowing from the work of Thomas Malthus, he noted that organisms tend to produce offspring at a pace that outstrips the local

availability of food supplies, living space, and other crucial resources. As a population increases and resources dwindle, the competition for precious resources intensifies. Thus, it occurred to Darwin—and this was his grand insight—that variations in hereditary traits might affect organisms' ability to obtain the resources necessary for survival and reproduction. Fourth, building on this insight, Darwin argued that if a specific heritable trait contributes to an organism's survival or reproductive success, organisms with that trait should produce more offspring than those without the trait (or those with less of the trait), and the prevalence of that trait should gradually increase over generations—resulting in evolutionary change.

Although evolution is widely characterized as a matter of "survival of the fittest," Darwin recognized from the beginning that survival is important only insofar as it relates to reproductive success. Indeed, in evolutionary theory, **fitness refers to the reproductive success (number of descendants) of an individual organism relative to the average reproductive success in the population.** *Variations in reproductive success are what really fuels evolutionary change.* But survival is crucial because organisms typically need to mature and thrive before they can reproduce. So, Darwin theorized that there ought to be two ways in which traits might contribute to evolution: by providing either a survival advantage or a reproductive advantage. For example, a turtle's shell has great protective value that provides a survival advantage. In contrast, a firefly's emission of light is a courtship overture that provides a reproductive advantage.

To summarize, the principle of **natural selection posits that heritable characteristics that provide a survival or reproductive advantage are more likely than alternative characteristics to be passed on to subsequent generations and thus they come to be "selected" over time.** Please note, the process of natural selection works on *populations* rather than *individual organisms.* Evolution occurs when the gene pool in a population changes gradually as a result of selection pressures. Although there are occasional exceptions (Gould & Eldredge, 1977), this process tends to be extremely gradual—it generally takes thousands to millions of generations for one trait to be selected over another.

Darwin's theory was highly controversial for at least two reasons: (a) it suggested that the awe-inspiring diversity of life is the result of an unplanned, natural process rather than divine creation, and (b) it implied that humans are not unique and that they share a common ancestry with other species. Nonetheless,

PREVIEW QUESTIONS

- What were Darwin's four key insights?
- Does evolution really reflect survival of the fittest?
- What is an adaptation?
- Can adaptations linger in a population even if they are no longer adaptive?
- How can behaviors be adaptive?

Bettmann/Corbis

CHARLES DARWIN

"Can we doubt (remembering that many more individuals are born than can possibly survive) that individuals having any advantage, however slight, over others, would have the best chance of surviving and procreating their kind? . . . This preservation of favourable variations and the rejection of injurious variations, I call Natural Selection."

Web Link 3.7

Human Behavior and Evolution Society
The HBES is an interdisciplinary organization devoted to the exploration of human behavior from the perspective of evolutionary theory. This site provides a particularly rich set of links to published and online materials and organizations dealing with the evolutionary perspective on behavior.

Darwin's theory eventually gained considerable acceptance because it provided a compelling explanation for how the characteristics of various species gradually changed over many generations and for the functional, adaptive direction of these changes.

Subsequent Refinements to Evolutionary Theory

Although Darwin's evolutionary theory quickly acquired many articulate advocates, it also remained controversial for decades. Eventually, advances in the understanding of heredity were sufficient to permit Theodore Dobzhansky (1937) to write a fairly comprehensive account of the evolutionary process in genetic terms. Dobzhansky's synthesis of Darwin's ideas and modern genetics was enormously influential, and by the 1950s the core tenets of evolutionary theory enjoyed widespread acceptance among scientists.

Contemporary models of evolution recognize that natural selection operates on the gene pool of a population. *Adaptations* are the key product of this process. **An *adaptation* is an inherited characteristic that increased in a population (through natural selection) because it helped solve a problem of survival or reproduction during the time it emerged.** Because of the slow, gradual nature of evolution, adaptations sometimes linger in a population even though they no longer provide a survival or reproductive advantage. For example, humans show a taste preference for fatty substances that was adaptive in an era of hunting and gathering, when dietary fat was a scarce source of important calories. However, in our modern world, where dietary fat is typically available in abundance, this taste preference leads many people to consume too much fat, resulting in obesity, heart disease, and other health problems. Thus, the preference for fatty foods has become a liability for human survival (although its impact on reproductive success is more difficult to gauge). As you will see, evolutionary psychologists have found that many aspects of human nature reflect the adaptive demands faced by our ancient ancestors rather than contemporary demands. Of course, as natural selection continues to work, these formerly adaptive traits should gradually be eliminated, but the process is extremely slow.

Behaviors as Adaptive Traits

Scholarly analyses of evolution have focused primarily on the evolution of *physical characteristics* in the animal kingdom, but from the very beginning, Darwin recognized that natural selection was applicable to *behavioral traits* as well. Modern evolutionary psychology is based on the well-documented assumption that a species' typical patterns of behavior often reflect evolutionary solutions to adaptive problems.

Consider, for instance, the eating behavior of rats, who show remarkable caution when they encounter new foods. Rats are versatile animals that are found in an enormous range of habitats and can live off quite a variety of foods, but this diet variety can present risks, as they need to be wary of consuming toxic substances. When rats encounter unfamiliar foods, they consume only small amounts and won't eat two new foods together. If the consumption of a new food is followed by illness, they avoid that food in the future (Logue, 1991). These precautions allow rats to learn what makes them sick while reducing the likelihood of consuming a lethal amount of something poisonous. These patterns of eating behavior are highly adaptive solutions to the food selection problems faced by rats.

Let's look at some additional examples of how evolution has shaped organisms' behavior. Avoiding predators is a nearly universal problem for organisms. Because of natural selection, many species, such as the grasshopper shown in the photo on the next page, have developed physical characteristics that allow them to blend in with their environments, making detection by predators more difficult. Many organisms also engage in elaborate *behavioral maneuvers* to hide themselves. For example, the pictured grasshopper has dug itself a small trench in which to hide and has used its midlegs to pull pebbles over its back (Alcock, 1998). This clever hiding behavior is just as much a product of evolution as the grasshopper's remarkable camouflage.

Many behavioral adaptations are designed to improve organisms' chances of reproductive success. Consider, for instance, the wide variety of species in which females actively choose which male to mate with. In many such species, females demand material goods and services from males in return for copulation opportunities. For example, in one type of moth, males have to spend hours extracting sodium from mud puddles, which they then transfer to prospective mates, who use it to supply their larvae with an important nutritional element (Smedley & Eisner, 1996). In the black-tipped hangingfly, females insist on a gift of food before they mate. They reject suitors bringing unpalatable food and tie the length of subsequent copulation to the size of the gift (Thornhill, 1976).

The adaptive value of trading sex for material goods that can aid the survival of an organism and its offspring is obvious, but the evolutionary significance of other mating strategies is more perplexing. In some species characterized by female choice, the choices hinge on males' appearance and courtship behavior. Females usually prefer males sporting larger or more brightly colored ornaments, or those capable of more extreme acoustical displays. For example, female house finches are swayed by redder feathers, whereas female wild turkeys are enticed by larger beak ornaments (see Table 3.2 for additional examples). What do females gain by selecting males with redder feathers, larger beaks, and other arbitrary characteristics? It appears that favored attributes generally seem to be indicators of males' relatively good genes, sound health, or superior ability to provide future services, such as protection or food gathering, all of which may serve to make their offspring more viable (Alcock, 2005). For example, the quality of peacocks' plumage appears to be an indicator of their parasite load (Hamilton & Zuk, 1982) and their genetic quality (as indexed by their subsequent survival) (Petrie, 1994). So, even mating preferences for seemingly nonadaptive aspects of appearance may often have adaptive significance.

Table 3.2 Female Mate Choices Based on Differences in Males' Morphological and Behavioral Attributes

Species	Favored attribute
Scorpionfly	More symmetrical wings
Barn swallow	More symmetrical and larger tail ornaments
Wild turkey	Larger beak ornaments
House finch	Redder feathers
Satin bowerbird	Bowers with more ornaments
Cichlid fish	Taller display "bower"
Field cricket	Longer calling bouts
Woodhouse's toad	More frequent calls

Source: Adapted from Alcock, J. (1998). *Animal behavior* (p. 463). Sunderland, MA: Sinauer Associates. Copyright © 1998 John Alcock. Reprinted by permission of Sinauer Associates and the author.

The behavior that helps the grasshopper hide from predators is a product of evolution, just like the physical characteristics that help it to blend in with its surroundings.

Courtesy of John Alcock

> Reflecting on the Chapter's Themes

Three of our seven themes stood out in this chapter: (1) heredity and environment jointly influence behavior, (2) behavior is determined by multiple causes, and (3) psychology is empirical. Let's look at each of these points.

In Chapter 1, when it was first emphasized that heredity and environment jointly shape behavior, you may have been a little perplexed about how your genes could be responsible for your sarcastic wit or your interest in art. In fact, there are no genes for behavior per se. Experts do not expect to find genes for sarcasm or artistic interest, for example. Insofar as your hereditary endowment plays a role in your behavior, it does so *indirectly,* by molding the physiological machine that you work with. Thus, your genes influence your physiological makeup, which in turn influences your personality, temperament, intelligence, interests, and other traits. Bear in mind, however, that genetic factors do not operate in a vacuum. Genes exert their effects in an environmental context. The impact of genetic makeup depends on environment, and the impact of environment depends on genetic makeup.

It was evident throughout the chapter that behavior is determined by multiple causes, but this theme was particularly apparent in the discussions of schizophrenia. At different points in the chapter we saw that schizophrenia may be a function of (1) abnormalities in neurotransmitter activity (especially dopa-

mine), (2) structural abnormalities in the brain identified with CT and MRI scans, and (3) genetic vulnerability to the illness. These findings do not contradict one another. Rather, they demonstrate that a complex array of biological factors are involved in the development of schizophrenia. In Chapter 13, we'll see that a host of environmental factors also play a role in the multifactorial causation of schizophrenia.

The empirical nature of psychology was apparent in the numerous discussions of the specialized research methods used to study the physiological bases of behavior. As you know, the empirical approach depends on precise observation. Throughout this chapter, you've seen how investigators have come up with innovative methods to observe and measure elusive phenomena such as neural impulses, brain function, cerebral specialization, and the impact of heredity on behavior. The point is that empirical methods are the lifeblood of the scientific enterprise. When researchers figure out how to better observe something, their findings usually facilitate major advances in our scientific knowledge. That is why the new brain-imaging techniques hold exciting promise for neuroscientists.

The importance of empiricism will also be apparent in the upcoming Personal Application and in the Critical Thinking Application that follows. In both applications you'll see the importance of learning to distinguish between scientific findings and conjecture based on those findings.

 Heredity and Environment

 Multifactorial Causation

 Empiricism

Evaluating the Concept of "Two Minds in One"

Answer the following "true" or "false."

_____ **1** Each half of the brain has its own special mode of thinking.

_____ **2** Some people are left-brained while others are right-brained.

_____ **3** Our schools should devote more effort to teaching the overlooked right side of the brain.

Do we have two minds in one that think differently? Do some of us depend on one side of the brain more than the other? Is the right side of the brain neglected? These questions are too complex to resolve with a simple "true" or "false," but in this Application we'll take a closer look at the issues involved in these proposed extensions of the findings on cerebral specialization. You'll learn that some of these ideas are plausible, but in many cases the hype has outstripped the evidence.

Cerebral Specialization and Cognitive Processes

 SIM2, 2f

Using a variety of methods, scientists have compiled mountains of data on the specialized abilities of the right and left hemispheres. These findings have led to extensive theorizing about how the right and left brains might be related to cognitive processes. Some of the more intriguing ideas include the following:

1. *The two hemispheres are specialized to process different types of cognitive tasks* (Corballis, 1991; Ornstein, 1977). Research findings have been widely interpreted as showing that the left hemisphere handles verbal tasks, including language, speech, writing, math, and logic, while the right hemisphere handles nonverbal tasks, including spatial problems, music, art, fantasy, and creativity. These conclusions have attracted a great deal of public interest and media attention. For example, **Figure 3.21** shows a *Newsweek* artist's depiction of how the brain supposedly divides its work.

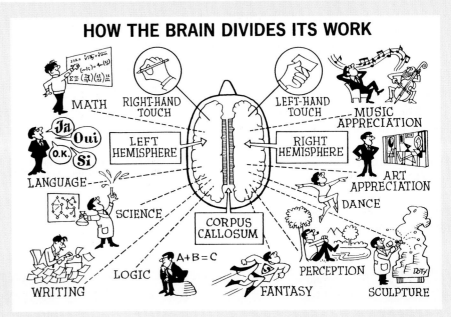

Figure 3.21

Popular conceptions of hemispheric specialization. As this *Newsweek* diagram illustrates, depictions of hemispheric specialization in the popular press have often been oversimplified.

Source: Cartoon courtesy of Roy Doty.

2. *The two hemispheres have different modes of thinking* (Banich & Heller, 1998, Joseph, 1992). According to this notion, the documented differences between the hemispheres in dealing with verbal and nonverbal materials are due to more basic differences in how the hemispheres process information. This theory holds that the reason the left hemisphere handles verbal material well is that it is analytic, abstract, rational, logical, and linear. In contrast, the right hemisphere is thought to be better equipped to handle spatial and musical material because it is synthetic, concrete, nonrational, intuitive, and holistic.

3. *People vary in their reliance on one hemisphere as opposed to the other* (Bakan, 1971; Zenhausen, 1978). Allegedly, some people are "left-brained." Their greater dependence on their left hemisphere supposedly makes them analytic, rational, and logical. Other people are "right-brained." Their greater use of their right hemisphere supposedly makes them intuitive, holistic, and irrational. Being right-brained or left-brained is thought to explain many personal characteristics, such as whether an individual likes to read, is good with maps, or enjoys music. This notion of "brainedness" has even been used to explain occupational choice. Supposedly, right-brained people are more likely to become artists or musicians, while left-brained people are more likely to become writers or scientists.

4. *Schools should place more emphasis on teaching the right side of the brain* (Blakeslee, 1980; Kitchens, 1991). Some educational experts have argued that American schools overemphasize logical, analytical left-hemisphere thinking (required by English, math, and science) while shortchanging intuitive, holistic right-hemisphere thinking (required by art and music). These educators have concluded that modern schools turn out an excess of left-brained graduates. They advocate curriculum reform to strengthen the right side of the brain in their students.

Complexities and Qualifications

The ideas just outlined are intriguing and have clearly captured the imagination of the general public. However, the research on cerebral specialization is complex, and these ideas have to be qualified very carefully (Efron, 1990; Springer & Deutsch, 1998). Let's examine each point.

1. There *is* ample evidence that the right and left hemispheres are specialized to handle different types of cognitive tasks, *but only to a degree* (Brown & Kosslyn, 1993; Corballis, 2003). Doreen Kimura (1973) compared the abilities of the right and left hemispheres to quickly recognize letters, words, faces, and melodies in a series of perceptual asymmetry studies. She found that the superiority of one hemisphere over the other on specific types of tasks was usually quite modest (see **Figure 3.22**). Most tasks probably engage both hemispheres, albeit to different degrees (Beeman & Chiarello, 1998).

Furthermore, people differ in their patterns of cerebral specialization (Springer & Deutsch, 1998). Some people display little specialization—that is, their hemispheres seem to have equal abilities on various types of tasks. Others even reverse the usual specialization, so that verbal processing might

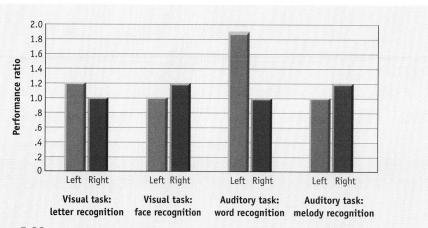

Figure 3.22

Relative superiority of one brain hemisphere over the other in studies of perceptual asymmetry. These performance ratios from a study by Doreen Kimura (1973) show the degree to which one hemisphere was "superior" to the other on each type of task in one study of normal participants. For example, the right hemisphere was 20% better than the left hemisphere in quickly recognizing melodic patterns (ratio 1.2 to 1). Most differences in the performance of the two hemispheres are quite small. (Data from Kimura, 1973)

Does artistic ability depend on being "right-brained"? The popular press has certainly suggested that this is the case, but as your text explains, there is no solid empirical evidence to support this assertion.

be housed in the right hemisphere. These unusual patterns are especially common among left-handed people (Josse & Tzourio-Mazoyer, 2004). These variations are not well understood yet. However, they clearly indicate that the special abilities of the cerebral hemispheres are not set in concrete.

2. Little direct evidence has been found to support the notion that each hemisphere has its own mode of thinking, or cognitive style (Bradshaw, 1989). This notion is plausible, and there *is* some supportive evidence, but that evidence is inconsistent and more research is needed (Gordon, 1990; Reuter-Lorenz & Miller, 1998). One key problem with this idea is that aspects of cognitive style have proven difficult to define and measure (Brownell & Gardner, 1981). For instance, there is debate about the meaning of analytic versus synthetic thinking, or linear versus holistic thinking.

3. The evidence on the assertion that some people are left-brained while others are right-brained is inconclusive at best (Hellige, 1990). This notion has some plausibility—if it means only that some people consistently display more activation of one hemisphere than the other. However, the practical significance of any such "preferences" remains to be determined. At present, researchers do not have convincing data linking brainedness to musical ability, occupational choice, or the like (Knecht et al., 2001; Springer & Deutsch, 1998).

4. The idea that schools should be reformed to better exercise the right side of the brain borders on nonsense. In neurologically intact people it is impossible to teach just one hemisphere at a time, and there is no evidence that it is beneficial to "exercise" a hemisphere of the brain (Levy, 1985). There are many sound arguments for reforming American schools to encourage more holistic, intuitive thinking, but these arguments have nothing to do with cerebral specialization.

In summary, the theories linking cerebral specialization to cognitive processes are highly speculative. There's nothing wrong with theoretical speculation. Unfortunately, the tentative, conjectural nature of these ideas about hemispheric specialization has gotten lost in the popular magazine descriptions of research on right and left brains (Coren, 1992). Commenting on this popularization, Hooper and Teresi (1986) note: "A widespread cult of the right brain ensued, and the duplex house that Sperry built grew into the K mart of brain science. Today our hairdresser lectures us about the Two Hemispheres of the Brain" (p. 223). Cerebral specialization is an important and intriguing area of research. However, it is unrealistic to expect that the hemispheric divisions in the brain will provide a biological explanation for every dichotomy or polarity in modes of thinking.

Building Better Brains: The Perils of Extrapolation

Summarizing the implications of certain widely discussed findings in brain research, science writer Ronald Kotulak (1996) concluded, "The first three years of a child's life are critically important to brain development" (pp. ix–x). Echoing this sentiment, the president of a U.S. educational commission asserted that "research in brain development suggests it is time to rethink many educational policies" (Bruer, 1999, p. 16). Based on research in the neurosciences (the various scientific disciplines that study the brain and the nervous system), many states launched expensive programs intended to foster better neural development in infants in the 1990s. For example, the Governor of Georgia at the time, Zell Miller, sought state funding to distribute classical music tapes for the state's infants, saying, "No one doubts that listening to music, especially at a very early age, affects the spatial-temporal reasoning that underlies math, engineering, and chess" (Bruer, 1999, p. 62). Well-intended educational groups and even some Hollywood celebrities have argued for the creation of schools for infants on the grounds that because the first three years of life are especially critical to brain development, enriched educational experiences during infancy will lead to smarter adults.

What are these practical, new discoveries about the brain that will permit parents and educators to optimize infants' brain development? Well, we will discuss the pertinent research momentarily, but it is not as new or as practical as suggested in many quarters. Unfortunately, as we saw in our discussion of research on hemispheric specialization, the hype in the media has greatly outstripped the realities of what scientists have learned in the laboratory (Chance, 2001).

In recent years, many childcare advocates and educational reformers have used research in neuroscience as the rationale for the policies they have sought to promote. This strategy has led to the publication of a host of books on "brain-based learning" (see E. Jensen, 2000; Sousa, 2000; Sprenger,

2001). The people advocating these ideas have good intentions, but the neuroscience rationale has been stretched to the breaking point. The result? An enlightening case study in the perils of overextrapolation.

The Key Findings on Neural Development

The education and childcare reformers who have used brain science as the basis for their campaigns have primarily cited two key findings: the discovery of critical periods in neural development and the demonstration that rats raised in "enriched environments" have more synapses than rats raised in "impoverished environments." Let's look at each of these findings.

A *critical period* is a limited time span in the development of an organism when it is optimal for certain capacities to emerge because the organism is especially responsive to certain experiences. The groundbreaking research on critical periods in neural development was conducted by David Hubel and Torsten Wiesel (1963, 1965) in the 1960s. They showed that if an eye of a newborn kitten is sewn shut early in its development (typically the first four to six weeks), the kitten will become permanently blind in that eye, but if the eye is covered for the same amount of time at later ages (after four months) blindness does not result. Such studies show that certain types of visual input are necessary during a critical period of development or neural pathways between the eye and brain will not form properly. Basically, what happens is that the inactive synapses from the closed eye are displaced by the active synapses from the open eye. Critical periods have been found for other aspects of neural development and in other species, but a great deal remains to be learned. Based on this type of research, some educational and childcare reformers have argued that the first three years of life are a critical period for human neural development.

The pioneering work on environment and brain development was begun in the 1960s by Mark Rosenzweig and his colleagues (1961, 1962). They raised some rats in an impoverished environment (housed individually in small, barren cages) and other rats in an enriched environment (housed in groups in larger cages, with a variety of objects available for exploration), as shown in Figure 3.23. They found that the rats raised in the enriched environment performed better on problem-solving tasks than the impoverished rats and had slightly heavier brains and a thicker cerebral cortex in some areas of the brain. Subsequent research by William Greenough demonstrated that enriched environments resulted in heavier and thicker cortical areas by virtue of producing denser dendritic branching, more synapses, and richer neural networks (Greenough, 1975; Greenough & Volkmar, 1973). Based on this type of research, some childcare reformers have argued that human infants need to be brought up in enriched environments during the critical period before age 3, to promote synapse formation and to enhance the development of their emerging neural circuits.

The findings on critical periods and the effects of enriched environments were genuine breakthroughs in neuroscience, but they certainly aren't *new* findings, as suggested by various political action groups. Moreover, one can raise many doubts about whether this research can serve as a meaningful guide for decisions about parenting practices, day-care programs, educational policies, and welfare reform (Thompson & Nelson, 2001).

The Tendency to Overextrapolate

Extrapolation occurs when an effect is estimated by extending beyond some known values or conditions. Extrapolation is a normal process, but some extrapolations are

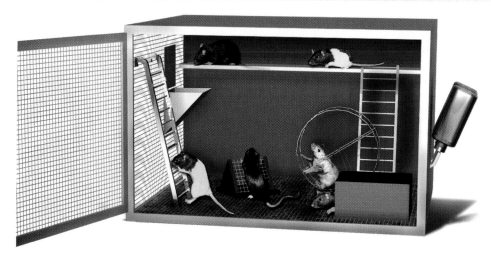

Figure 3.23

Enriched environments in the study of rats' neural development. In the studies by Rosenzweig and colleagues (1961, 1962), rats raised in an impoverished environment were housed alone in small cages, whereas rats raised in enriched environments were housed in groups and were given playthings that were changed daily. Although the enriched conditions provided more stimulating environments than what laboratory rats normally experience, they may not be any more stimulating than rats' natural habitats. Thus, the "enriched" condition may reveal more about the importance of normal stimulation than about the benefits of extra stimulation (Gopnik, Meltzoff, & Kuhl, 1999).

conservative, plausible projections drawn from directly relevant data, whereas others are wild leaps of speculation based on loosely related data. The extrapolations made regarding the educational implications of critical periods and environmental effects on synapse formation are highly conjectural *overextrapolations*. The studies that highlighted the possible importance of early experience in animals have all used extreme conditions to make their comparisons, such as depriving an animal of all visual input or raising it in stark isolation. In light of the findings, it seems plausible to speculate that children probably need normal stimulation to experience normal brain development. However, great difficulty arises when these findings are extended to conclude that adding *more* stimulation to a normal environment will be beneficial to brain development (Shatz, 1992).

The ease with which people fall into the trap of overextrapolating has been particularly apparent in recent recommendations that infants listen to classical music to enhance their brain development. These recommendations have been derived from two studies that showed that college students' performance on spatial reasoning tasks was enhanced slightly for about 10–15 minutes after listening to a brief Mozart recording (Rauscher, Shaw, & Ky, 1993, 1995). This peculiar finding, dubbed the "Mozart effect," has proven difficult to replicate (McKelvie & Low, 2002; Steele, 2003), but the pertinent point here is that there was no research on how classical music affects *infants*, no re-

search relating classical music to *brain development,* and no research on anyone showing *lasting effects.* Nonetheless, many people (including the Governor of Georgia) were quick to extrapolate the shaky findings on the Mozart effect to infants' brain development.

As discussed in Chapter 1, thinking critically about issues often involves asking questions such as: What is missing from this debate? Is there any contradictory evidence? In this case, there is some contradictory evidence that is worthy of consideration. The basis for advocating infant educational programs is the belief that brain development is more rapid and malleable during the hypothesized critical period of birth to age 3 than at later ages. However, Greenough's work on synaptic formation and other lines of research suggest that the brain remains malleable throughout life (Thompson & Nelson, 2001). Thus, advocates for the aged could just as readily argue for new educational initiatives for the elderly to help them maximize their intellectual potential. Another problem is the implicit assumption

that greater synaptic density is associated with greater intelligence. There is quite a bit of evidence that infant animals and humans begin life with an overabundance of synaptic connections and that learning involves selective *pruning* of inactive synapses, which gradually give way to heavily used neural pathways (Huttenlocher, 2002; Rakic, Bourgeois, & Goldman-Rakic, 1994). Thus, in the realm of synapses, more may *not* be better.

In conclusion, there may be many valid reasons for increasing educational programs for infants, but research in neuroscience does not appear to provide a clear rationale for much in the way of specific infant care policies (Bruer, 2002) One problem in evaluating these proposals is that few people want to argue against high-quality child care or education. But modern societies need to allocate their limited resources to the programs that appear most likely to have beneficial effects, so even intuitively appealing ideas need to be subjected to critical scrutiny.

Table 3.3 **Critical Thinking Skills Discussed in This Application**

Skill	Description
Understanding the limits of extrapolation	The critical thinker appreciates that extrapolations are based on certain assumptions, vary in plausibility, and ultimately involve speculation.
Looking for contradictory evidence	In evaluating the evidence presented on an issue, the critical thinker attempts to look for contradictory evidence that may have been left out of the debate.

CHAPTER 3 *Review*

Key Ideas

Communication in the Nervous System

● Cells in the nervous system receive, integrate, and transmit information. Neurons are the basic communication links. They normally transmit a neural impulse (a change in electrical charge, called an action potential) along an axon to a synapse with another neuron.

● Action potentials trigger the release of chemicals called neurotransmitters that diffuse across a synapse to communicate with other neurons. Most neurons are linked in neural pathways, circuits, and networks. A variety of neurotransmitters function by binding at specific receptor sites according to a lock-and-key model.

Organization of the Nervous System

● The nervous system can be divided into two main subdivisions, the central nervous system and the peripheral nervous system. The central nervous system consists of the brain and spinal cord. The brain plays a crucial role in virtually all aspects of behavior.

● The peripheral nervous system consists of the nerves that lie outside the brain and spinal cord. It can be subdivided into the somatic nervous system, which connects to muscles and sensory receptors, and the autonomic nervous system, which connects to blood vessels, smooth muscles, and glands.

The Brain and Behavior

● Neuroscientists use a variety of invasive and noninvasive techniques to study the living brain. These methods include lesioning, electrical stimulation, CT scans, MRI scans, PET scans, fMRI scans, and transcranial magnetic stimulation. The brain has three major regions: the hindbrain, midbrain, and forebrain. Structures in the hindbrain and midbrain handle essential functions such as breathing, circulation, and coordination of movement.

● The forebrain includes many structures that handle higher functions. The thalamus is primarily a relay station. The hypothalamus is involved in the regulation of basic biological drives such as hunger and sex. The limbic system is a network of loosely connected structures involved in emotion, motivation, and memory.

● The cerebrum is the brain area implicated in most complex mental activities. The cortex is the cerebrum's convoluted outer layer, which is subdivided into four areas. These areas and their primary known functions are the occipital lobe (vision), the parietal lobe (touch), the temporal lobe (hearing), and the frontal lobe (movement of the body). The organization of the brain is more plastic than widely appreciated.

Right Brain/Left Brain: Cerebral Specialization

● The cerebrum is divided into right and left hemispheres connected by the corpus callosum. Studies have revealed that the right and left halves of the brain each have unique talents, with the right hemisphere being specialized to handle visual-spatial functions, while the left hemisphere handles verbal processing.

The Endocrine System: Another Way to Communicate

● The endocrine system consists of the glands that secrete hormones, which are chemicals involved in the regulation of basic bodily processes. The control centers for the endocrine system are the hypothalamus and the pituitary gland.

Heredity and Behavior: Is It All in the Genes?

● The basic units of genetic transmission are genes housed on chromosomes. Most behavioral qualities appear to involve polygenic inheritance. Researchers assess hereditary influence through family studies, twin studies, and adoption studies. These studies indicate that most behavioral traits are influenced by a complex interaction between heredity and environment.

The Evolutionary Bases of Behavior

● Darwin argued that if a heritable trait contributes to an organism's survival or reproductive success, organisms with that trait should produce more offspring than those without the trait and that the prevalence of the trait should gradually increase over generations—thanks to natural selection.

● Adaptations sometimes linger in a population even though they no longer provide a survival or reproductive advantage. Darwin recognized from the beginning that natural selection was applicable to behavioral traits, as well as physical traits.

Reflecting on the Chapter's Themes

● Three of the book's unifying themes stand out in this chapter. First, we saw how heredity interacts with experience to govern behavior. Second, the discussions of biological factors underlying schizophrenia highlighted the multifactorial causation of behavior. Third, we saw how innovations in research methods often lead to advances in knowledge, underscoring the empirical nature of psychology.

PERSONAL APPLICATION • Thinking Critically About the Concept of "Two Minds in One"

● The cerebral hemispheres are specialized for handling different cognitive tasks, but only to a degree, and people vary in their patterns of specialization. Evidence on whether people vary in brainedness and whether the two hemispheres vary in cognitive style is inconclusive. There is no evidence that exercising a hemisphere of the brain is useful.

CRITICAL THINKING APPLICATION • Building Better Brains: The Perils of Extrapolation

● Although some education and childcare reformers have used neuroscience as the basis for their campaigns, research has not demonstrated that birth to 3 is a critical period for human neural development or that specific enrichment programs can enhance brain development. These assertions are highly conjectural overextrapolations from existing data.

Key Terms

Absolute refractory period (p. 65)
Action potential (p. 65)
Adaptation (p. 88)
Adoption studies (p. 86)
Afferent nerve fibers (p. 71)
Agonist (p. 68)
Antagonist (p. 68)
Autonomic nervous system (ANS) (p. 71)
Axon (p. 64)
Central nervous system (CNS) (p. 72)
Cerebellum (p. 76)
Cerebral cortex (p. 77)
Cerebral hemispheres (pp. 77–78)
Chromosomes (p. 84)
Corpus callosum (p. 78)
Critical period (p. 92)
Dendrites (p. 64)
Efferent nerve fibers (p. 71)
Electrical stimulation of the brain (ESB) (p. 73)
Endocrine system (p. 83)
Endorphins (p. 70)
Family studies (p. 84)
Fitness (p. 87)
Forebrain (p. 76)
Genes (p. 84)
Glia (p. 64)
Hindbrain (p. 75)
Hormones (p. 83)
Hypothalamus (p. 76)

Lesioning (p. 73)
Limbic system (p. 77)
Midbrain (p. 76)
Myelin sheath (p. 64)
Natural selection (p. 87)
Neurons (p. 63)
Neurotransmitters (p. 66)
Peripheral nervous system (p. 71)
Pituitary gland (p. 83)
Polygenic traits (p. 84)
Postsynaptic potential (PSP) (p. 67)
Resting potential (p. 65)
Reuptake (p. 67)
Soma (p. 64)
Somatic nervous system (p. 71)
Split-brain surgery (p. 80)
Synapse (p. 64)
Synaptic cleft (p. 66)
Terminal buttons (p. 64)
Thalamus (p. 76)
Twin studies (p. 85)

Key People

Alan Hodgkin and Andrew Huxley (p. 65)
James Olds and Peter Milner (p. 77)
Candace Pert and Solomon Snyder (pp. 68, 70)
Robert Plomin (p. 86)
Roger Sperry and Michael Gazzaniga (pp. 80–81)

1. A neural impulse is initiated when a neuron's charge momentarily becomes less negative, or even positive. This event is called:
   A. an action potential.
   B. a resting potential.
   C. impulse facilitation.
   D. neuromodulation.

2. Neurons convey information about the strength of stimuli by varying:
   A. the size of their action potentials.
   B. the speed of their action potentials.
   C. the rate at which they fire action potentials.
   D. all of the above.

3. Alterations in activity at dopamine synapses have been implicated in the development of:
   A. anxiety.
   B. schizophrenia.
   C. Alzheimer's disease.
   D. nicotine addiction.

4. Jim has just barely avoided a head-on collision on a narrow road. With heart pounding, hands shaking, and body perspiring, Jim recognizes that these are signs of the body's fight-or-flight response, which is controlled by the:
   A. empathetic division of the peripheral nervous system.
   B. parasympathetic division of the autonomic nervous system.
   C. somatic division of the peripheral nervous system.
   D. sympathetic division of the autonomic nervous system.

5. The hindbrain consists of the:
   A. endocrine system and the limbic system.
   B. reticular formation.
   C. thalamus, hypothalamus, and cerebrum.
   D. cerebellum, medulla, and pons.

6. The thalamus can be characterized as:
   A. a regulatory mechanism.
   B. the consciousness switch of the brain.
   C. a relay system.
   D. a bridge between the two cerebral hemispheres.

7. The _____ lobe is to hearing as the occipital lobe is to vision.
   A. frontal
   B. temporal
   C. parietal
   D. cerebellar

8. The scientist who won a Nobel prize for his work with split-brain patients is:
   A. Walter Cannon.
   B. Paul Broca.
   C. Roger Sperry.
   D. James Olds.

9. Sounds presented to the right ear are registered:
   A. only in the right hemisphere.
   B. only in the left hemisphere.
   C. more quickly in the right hemisphere.
   D. more quickly in the left hemisphere.

10. In people whose corpus callosums have not been severed, verbal stimuli are identified more quickly and more accurately:
    A. when sent to the right hemisphere first.
    B. when sent to the left hemisphere first.
    C. when presented to the left visual field.
    D. when presented auditorally rather than visually.

11. Hormones are to the endocrine system as _____ are to the nervous system.
    A. nerves
    B. synapses
    C. neurotransmitters
    D. action potentials

12. Adopted children's similarity to their biological parents is generally attributed to _____; adopted children's similarity to their adoptive parents is generally attributed to _____.
    A. heredity; the environment
    B. the environment; heredity
    C. the environment; the environment
    D. heredity; heredity

13. Which of the following statements represents the most logical resolution of the nature-nurture controversy?
    A. Environment is most important, at least for those individuals who have a normal genotype.
    B. Heredity and environment interact to affect an individual's development.
    C. Heredity is most important, but a high-quality environment can make up for genetic defects.
    D. The environment is like a rubber band that stretches to meet the needs of an individual's genotype.

14. In evolutionary theory, *fitness* refers to:
    A. the ability to survive.
    B. the ability to adapt to environmental demands.
    C. reproductive success.
    D. the physical skills necessary for survival.

15. For which of the following assertions is the empirical evidence strongest?
    A. The two cerebral hemispheres are specialized to handle different types of cognitive tasks.
    B. Schools should be reformed to better educate the right hemisphere.
    C. Each hemisphere has its own cognitive style.
    D. Some people are right-brained, while others are left-brained.

Answers

1 A p. 65	6 C p. 76	11 C p. 83
2 C p. 66	7 B p. 78	12 A p. 86
3 B p. 69	8 C p. 80	13 B p. 86
4 D p. 72	9 D pp. 80–81	14 C p. 87
5 D p. 75	10 B p. 82	15 A p. 91

PsykTrek

Go to the PsykTrek website or CD-ROM for further study of the concepts in this chapter. Both online and on the CD-ROM, PsykTrek includes dozens of learning modules with videos, animations, and quizzes, as well as simulations of psychological phenomena and a multimedia glossary that includes word pronunciations.

ThomsonNOW

www.thomsonedu.com/ThomsonNOW
Go to this site for the link to ThomsonNOW, your one-stop study shop. Take a Pre-Test for this chapter, and ThomsonNOW will generate a Personalized Study Plan based on your test results. The Study Plan will identify the topics you need to review and direct you to online resources to help you master those topics. You can then take a Post-Test to help you determine the concepts you have mastered and what you still need to work on.

Companion Website

www.thomsonedu.com/psychology/weiten
Go to this site to find online resources directly linked to your book, including a glossary, flash cards, drag-and-drop exercises, quizzes, and more!

CHAPTER (4)

Sensation and Perception

© Michael Freeman/Digital Vision/Getty Images

© Steve Cole/Photodisc Green/Getty Images

Take a look at the photo in the margin on the right. What do you see? You probably answered, "a rose" or "a flower." But is that what you really see? No, this isn't a trick question. Let's examine the odd case of "Dr. P." It shows that there's more to seeing than meets the eye.

Dr. P was an intelligent and distinguished music professor who began to exhibit some worrisome behaviors that seemed to be related to his vision. Sometimes he failed to recognize familiar students by sight, though he knew them instantly by the sound of their voices. Sometimes he acted as if he saw faces in inanimate objects, cordially greeting fire hydrants and parking meters as if they were children. On one occasion, reaching for what he thought was his hat, he took hold of his wife's head and tried to put it on! Except for these kinds of visual mistakes, Dr. P was a normal, talented man.

Ultimately Dr. P was referred to Oliver Sacks, a neurologist, for an examination. During one visit, Sacks handed Dr. P a fresh red rose to see whether he would recognize it. Dr. P took the rose as if he were being given a model of a geometric solid rather than a flower. "About six inches in length," Dr. P observed, "a convoluted red form with a linear green attachment."

"Yes," Sacks persisted, "and what do you think it is, Dr. P?"

"Not easy to say," the patient replied. "It lacks the simple symmetry of the Platonic solids . . ."

"Smell it," the neurologist suggested. Dr. P looked perplexed, as if being asked to smell symmetry, but he complied and brought the flower to his nose. Suddenly, his confusion cleared up. "Beautiful. An early rose. What a heavenly smell" (Sacks, 1987, pp. 13–14).

What accounted for Dr. P's strange inability to recognize faces and familiar objects by sight? There was nothing wrong with his eyes. He could readily spot a pin on the floor. If you're thinking that he *must* have had something wrong with his vision, look again at the photo of the rose. What you see *is* "a convoluted red form with a linear green attachment." It doesn't occur to you to describe it that way only because, without thinking about it, you instantly perceive that combination of form and color as a flower. This is precisely what Dr. P was unable to do. He could see perfectly well, but he was losing the ability to assemble what he saw into a meaningful picture of the world. Technically, he suffered from a

condition called *visual agnosia,* an inability to recognize objects through sight. As Sacks (1987) put it, "Visually, he was lost in a world of lifeless abstractions" (p. 15).

As Dr. P's case illustrates, without effective processing of sensory input, our familiar world can become a chaos of confusing sensations. To acknowledge the needs to both take in and process sensory information, psychologists distinguish between sensation and perception. *Sensation* **is the stimulation of sense organs.** *Perception* **is the selection, organization, and interpretation of sensory input.** Sensation involves the absorption of energy, such as light or sound waves, by sensory organs, such as the eyes and ears. Perception involves organizing and translating sensory input into something meaningful. For example, when you look at the photo of the rose, your eyes are sensing the light reflected from the page, including areas of low reflection where ink has been deposited in an irregular shape. What you *perceive,* however, is a picture of a rose.

The distinction between sensation and perception stands out in Dr. P's case of visual agnosia. His eyes were doing their job of registering sensory input and transmitting signals to the brain. However, damage in his brain interfered with his ability to put these signals together into organized wholes. Thus, Dr. P's process of visual *sensation* was intact, but his process of visual *perception* was severely impaired.

Dr. P's case is unusual, of course. Normally, the processes of sensation and perception are difficult to separate because people automatically start organizing incoming sensory stimulation the moment it arrives. The distinction between sensation and perception has been useful in organizing theory and research, but in actual operation the two processes merge.

We'll begin our discussion of sensation and perception with a long look at vision, then take a briefer look at the other senses. As we examine each of the sensory systems, we'll see repeatedly that people's experience of the world depends on both the physical stimuli they encounter (sensation) and their active processing of stimulus inputs (perception). The chapter's Personal Application explores how principles of visual perception come into play in art and illusion. The Critical Thinking Application discusses how perceptual contrasts can be manipulated in persuasive efforts.

PREVIEW QUESTIONS

- What are the three properties of light?
- What do the lens and pupil contribute to visual functioning?
- What are the functions of rods and cones?
- How do visual receptive fields typically function?
- How are visual signals routed from the eye to the primary visual cortex?
- What are feature detectors?

"Seeing is believing." Good students are "bright," and a good explanation is "illuminating." This section is an "overview." Do you see the point? As these common expressions show, humans are visual animals. People rely heavily on their sense of sight, and they virtually equate it with what is trustworthy (seeing is believing). Although it is taken for granted, you'll see (there it is again) that the human visual system is amazingly complex. Furthermore, as in all sensory domains, what people "sense" and what they "perceive" may be quite different.

The Stimulus: Light

3a

For people to see, there must be light. *Light* is a form of electromagnetic radiation that travels as a wave, moving, naturally enough, at the speed of light. As **Figure 4.1(a)** shows, light waves vary in *amplitude* (height) and in *wavelength* (the distance between peaks). Amplitude affects mainly the perception of brightness, while wavelength affects mainly the per-

ception of color. The lights humans normally see are mixtures of different wavelengths. Hence, light can also vary in its *purity* (how varied the mix is). Purity influences perception of the saturation, or richness, of colors. Saturation is difficult to describe, but if you glance ahead to **Figure 4.10**, you'll find it clearly illustrated. Of course, most objects do not emit light, they reflect it (the sun, lamps, and fireflies being some exceptions).

What most people call light includes only the wavelengths that humans can see. But as **Figure 4.1(c)** shows, the visible spectrum is only a slim portion of the total range of wavelengths. Vision is a filter that permits people to sense only a fraction of the real world. Other animals have different capabilities and so live in a quite different visual world. For example, many insects can see shorter wavelengths than humans can see, in the *ultraviolet* spectrum, whereas many fish and reptiles can see longer wavelengths, in the *infrared* spectrum.

Although the sense of sight depends on light waves, for people to see, incoming visual input must

Figure 4.1

Light, the physical stimulus for vision.
(a) Light waves vary in amplitude and wavelength. **(b)** Within the spectrum of visible light, amplitude (corresponding to physical intensity) affects mainly the experience of brightness. Wavelength affects mainly the experience of color, and purity is the key determinant of saturation. **(c)** If white light (such as sunlight) passes through a prism, the prism separates the light into its component wavelengths, creating a rainbow of colors. However, visible light is only the narrow band of wavelengths to which human eyes happen to be sensitive.

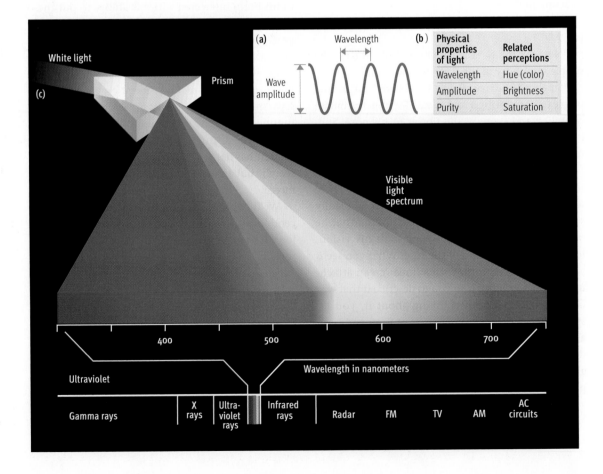

be converted into neural impulses that are sent to the brain. Let's investigate how this transformation is accomplished.

The Eye: A Living Optical Instrument

3a

The eyes serve two main purposes: they channel light to the neural tissue that receives it, called the *retina,* and they house that tissue. The structure of the eye is shown in **Figure 4.2**. Each eye is a living optical instrument that creates an image of the visual world on the light-sensitive retina that lines its inside back surface.

Light enters the eye through a transparent "window" at the front, the *cornea.* The cornea and the crystalline *lens,* located behind it, form an upside down image of objects on the retina and adjust the focus of the image. It might seem disturbing that the image is upside down, but the arrangement works. It doesn't matter how the image sits on the retina, as long as the brain knows the rule for relating positions on the retina to the corresponding positions in the world. **The *lens* is a transparent eye structure that focuses the light rays falling on the retina.** The lens is made up of relatively soft tissue, capable of adjustments that facilitate a process called accommodation. *Accommodation* occurs when the curvature of the lens adjusts to alter visual focus. When you focus on a close object, the lens of your eye gets fatter (rounder) in order to give you a clear image. When you focus on distant objects, the lens flattens out to give you a better image of them.

A number of common visual problems are caused by focusing problems or defects in the lens (Guyton, 1991). For example, **in *nearsightedness,* close objects are seen clearly but distant objects appear blurry** because the focus of light from distant objects falls a little short of the retina (see **Figure 4.3** on the next page). This focusing problem occurs when the cornea or lens bends light too much, or when the eyeball is too long. **In *farsightedness,* distant objects are seen clearly but close objects appear blurry**

Web Link 4.1

Vision Science: An Internet Resource for Research in Human and Animal Vision
Numerous online sites are devoted to the sense of sight and visual processes. Vision Science provides a convenient guide to the best of these sites, especially for online demonstrations and tutorials.

Figure 4.2

The human eye. Light passes through the cornea, pupil, and lens and falls on the light-sensitive surface of the retina, where images of objects are reflected upside down. The lens adjusts its curvature to focus the images falling on the retina. The pupil regulates the amount of light passing into the rear chamber of the eye.

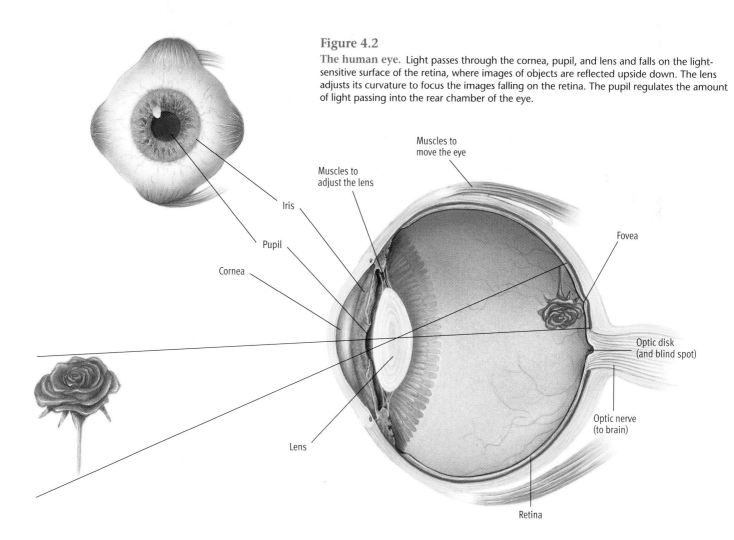

Iris
Pupil
Cornea
Lens
Muscles to adjust the lens
Muscles to move the eye
Fovea
Optic disk (and blind spot)
Optic nerve (to brain)
Retina

Nearsightedness

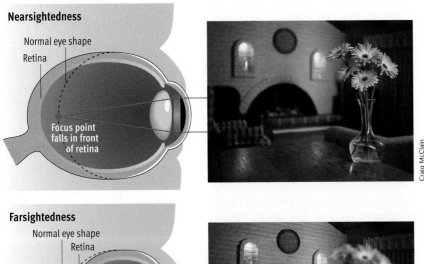

Normal eye shape

Retina

Focus point falls in front of retina

Farsightedness

Normal eye shape

Retina

Focus point falls behind retina

Craig McClain

Figure 4.3

Nearsightedness and farsightedness. The pictures on the right simulate how a scene might look to nearsighted and farsighted people. Nearsightedness occurs because light from distant objects focuses in front of the retina. Farsightedness results from the opposite situation—light from close objects focuses behind the retina.

because the focus of light from close objects falls behind the retina (again, see Figure 4.3). This focusing problem typically occurs when the eyeball is too short. A *cataract* is a lens that is clouded. This defect occurs mainly in older persons, affecting three out of four people over the age of 65.

The eye also makes adjustments to alter the amount of light reaching the retina. The *iris* is the colored ring of muscle surrounding the *pupil,* or black center of the eye. **The *pupil* is the opening in the center of the iris that helps regulate the amount of light passing into the rear chamber of the eye.** When the pupil constricts, it lets less light into the eye, but it sharpens the image falling on the retina. When the pupil dilates (opens), it lets more light in, but the image is less sharp. In bright light, the pupils constrict to take advantage of the sharpened image. But in dim light, the pupils dilate. Image sharpness is sacrificed to allow more light to fall on the retina so that more remains visible.

The Retina: The Brain's Envoy in the Eye

3b

The *retina* is the neural tissue lining the inside back surface of the eye; it absorbs light, processes images, and sends visual information to the brain.

You may be surprised to learn that the retina *processes* images. But it's a piece of the central nervous system that happens to be located in the eyeball. Much as the spinal cord is a complicated extension of the brain, the retina is the brain's envoy in the eye. Although the retina is only a paper-thin sheet of neural tissue, it contains a complex network of specialized cells arranged in layers, as shown in **Figure 4.4.**

The axons that run from the retina to the brain converge at a single spot where they exit the eye. At that point, all the fibers dive through a hole in the retina called the *optic disk.* Since the optic disk is a *hole* in the retina, you cannot see the part of an image that falls on it. It is therefore known as the *blind spot.* Most people are not aware that they have a blind spot in each eye. Why? Because each eye compensates for the blind spot of the other and because the brain somehow "fills in" the missing part of the image (Churchland & Ramachandran, 1996).

Visual Receptors: Rods and Cones

3b

The retina contains millions of receptor cells that are sensitive to light. Surprisingly, these receptors are located in the innermost layer of the retina (see Figure 4.4). Hence, light must pass through several layers of cells before it gets to the receptors that actually detect it. Only about 10% of the light arriving at the cornea reaches these receptors (Leibovic, 1990). The retina contains two types of receptors, *rods* and *cones.* Their names are based on their shapes, as rods are elongated and cones are stubbier. Rods outnumber cones by a huge margin, as humans have 100–125 million rods, but only 5–6.4 million cones (Frishman, 2001).

Cones **are specialized visual receptors that play a key role in daylight vision and color vision.** The cones handle most of our daytime vision, because bright lights dazzle the rods. The special sensitivities of cones also allow them to play a major role in the perception of color. However, cones do not respond well to dim light, which is why you don't see color very well in low illumination. Nonetheless, cones provide better *visual acuity*—that is, sharpness and precise detail—than rods. Cones are concentrated most heavily in the center of the retina and quickly fall off in density toward its sides. **The *fovea* is a tiny spot in the center of the retina that contains only cones; visual acuity is greatest at this spot** (consult Figure 4.2 again). When you want to see something in sharp focus, you usually move your eyes to center the object in the fovea.

Rods **are specialized visual receptors that play a key role in night vision and peripheral vision.**

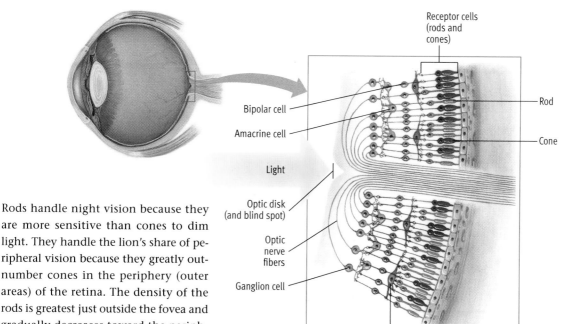

Receptor cells
(rods and cones)

Bipolar cell

Amacrine cell

Light

Rod

Cone

Optic disk
(and blind spot)

Optic
nerve
fibers

Ganglion cell

Horizontal cell

Figure 4.4

The retina. The closeup shows the several layers of cells in the retina. The cells closest to the back of the eye (the rods and cones) are the receptor cells that actually detect light. The intervening layers of cells receive signals from the rods and cones and form circuits that begin the process of analyzing incoming information before it is sent to the brain. These cells feed into many optic fibers, all of which head toward the "hole" in the retina where the optic nerve leaves the eye—the point known as the optic disk (which corresponds to the blind spot).

Rods handle night vision because they are more sensitive than cones to dim light. They handle the lion's share of peripheral vision because they greatly outnumber cones in the periphery (outer areas) of the retina. The density of the rods is greatest just outside the fovea and gradually decreases toward the periphery of the retina. Because of the distribution of rods, when you want to see a faintly illuminated object in the dark, it's best to look slightly above or below the place it should be. Averting your gaze this way moves the image from the cone-filled fovea, which requires more light, to the rod-dominated area just outside the fovea, which requires less light. This trick of averted vision is well known to astronomers, who use it to study dim objects viewed through the eyepiece of a telescope.

Dark and Light Adaptation   PsykTrek 3b

You've probably noticed that when you enter a dark theater on a bright day, you stumble about almost blindly. But within minutes you can make your way about quite well in the dim light. This adjustment is called *dark adaptation—the process in which the eyes become more sensitive to light in low illumination.* **Figure 4.5** maps out the course of this process. It shows how, as time passes, you require less and less light to see. Dark adaptation is virtually complete in about 30 minutes, with considerable progress occurring in the first 10 minutes. The curve in **Figure 4.5** that charts this progress consists of two segments because cones adapt more rapidly than rods (Walraven et al., 1990).

When you emerge from a dark theater on a sunny day, you need to squint to ward off the overwhelming brightness, and the reverse of dark adaptation occurs. *Light adaptation is the process in which the eyes become less sensitive to light in high illumination.* As with dark adaptation, light adaptation improves your visual acuity under the prevailing circumstances.

Information Processing in the Retina   PsykTrek 3b

In processing visual input, the retina transforms a pattern of light falling onto it into a very different representation of the visual scene. Light striking the

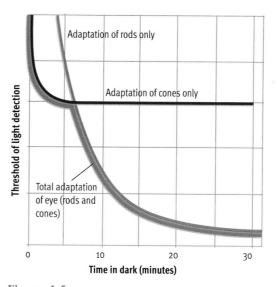

Adaptation of rods only

Adaptation of cones only

Total adaptation of eye (rods and cones)

Threshold of light detection

Time in dark (minutes)

0   10   20   30

Figure 4.5

The process of dark adaptation. The declining thresholds over time indicate that your visual sensitivity is improving, as less and less light is required to see. Visual sensitivity improves markedly during the first 5 to 10 minutes after entering a dark room, as the eye's bright-light receptors (the cones) rapidly adapt to low light levels. However, the cones' adaptation, which is plotted in purple, soon reaches its limit, and further improvement comes from the rods' adaptation, which is plotted in red. The rods adapt more slowly than the cones, but they are capable of far greater visual sensitivity in low levels of light.

Understanding Sensory Processes in the Retina

Check your understanding of sensory receptors in the retina by completing the following exercises. Consult Appendix A for the answers.

The receptors for vision are rods and cones in the retina. These two types of receptors have many important differences, which are compared systematically in the chart below. Fill in the missing information to finish the chart.

Dimension	Rods	Cones
1. Physical shape	*Elongated*	
2. Number in the retina		*5–6.4 million*
3. Area of the retina in which they are dominant receptor	*Periphery*	
4. Critical to color vision		
5. Critical to peripheral vision		*No*
6. Sensitivity to dim light	*Strong*	
7. Speed of dark adaptation		*Rapid*

retina's receptors (rods and cones) triggers neural signals that pass into the intricate network of cells in the retina. Signals move from receptors to bipolar cells to ganglion cells, which in turn send impulses along the *optic nerve*—a collection of axons that connect the eye with the brain (see **Figure 4.4**). These axons, which depart the eye through the optic disk, carry visual information, encoded as a stream of neural impulses, to the brain.

A great deal of complex information processing goes on in the retina itself before visual signals are sent to the brain. Ultimately, the information from as many as 130 million rods and cones converges to travel along "only" 1 million axons in the optic nerve (Slaughter, 1990). This means that the bipolar and ganglion cells in the intermediate layers of the retina integrate and compress signals from many receptors. The collection of rod and cone receptors that funnel signals to a particular visual cell in the retina (or ultimately in the brain) make up that cell's *receptive field*. Thus, **the *receptive field of a visual cell* is the retinal area that, when stimulated, affects the firing of that cell.**

Receptive fields in the retina come in a variety of shapes and sizes. Particularly common are circular fields with a center-surround arrangement (Tessier-Lavigne, 2000). In these receptive fields, light falling in the center has the opposite effect of light falling in the surrounding area (see **Figure 4.6**). For example, the rate of firing of a visual cell might be *in-*

Figure 4.6

Receptive fields in the retina. Visual cells' receptive fields in the retina are often circular with a center-surround arrangement, so that light striking the center of the field produces the opposite result of light striking the surround. In the receptive field depicted here, light in the center produces increased firing in the visual cell (symbolized by green at the synapse), whereas light in the surround produces decreased firing (symbolized by red at the synapse). The arrangement in other receptive fields may be just the opposite.

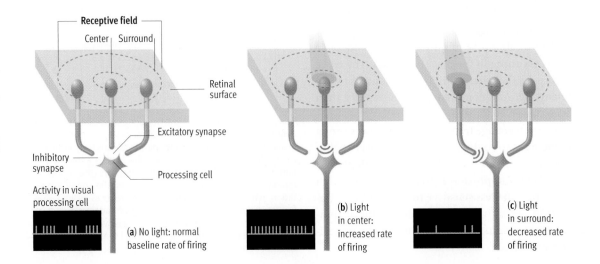

creased by light in the center of its receptive field and *decreased* by light in the surrounding area. Other visual cells may work in just the opposite way. Either way, when receptive fields are stimulated, retinal cells send signals toward the brain.

Vision and the Brain

Light falls on the eye, but you see with your brain. Although the retina does a lot of information processing for a sensory organ, visual input is meaningless until it is processed in the brain.

Visual Pathways to the Brain

How does visual information get to the brain? Axons leaving the back of each eye form the optic nerves, which travel to the *optic chiasm*. At the optic chiasm, the axons from the inside half of each eye cross over and then project to the opposite half of the brain (as we first discussed in Chapter 3—refer to **Figure 3.17**). This arrangement ensures that signals from both eyes go to both hemispheres of the brain. Thus, as **Figure 4.7** shows, axons from the left half of each retina carry signals to the left side of the brain, and axons from the right half of each retina carry information to the right side of the brain.

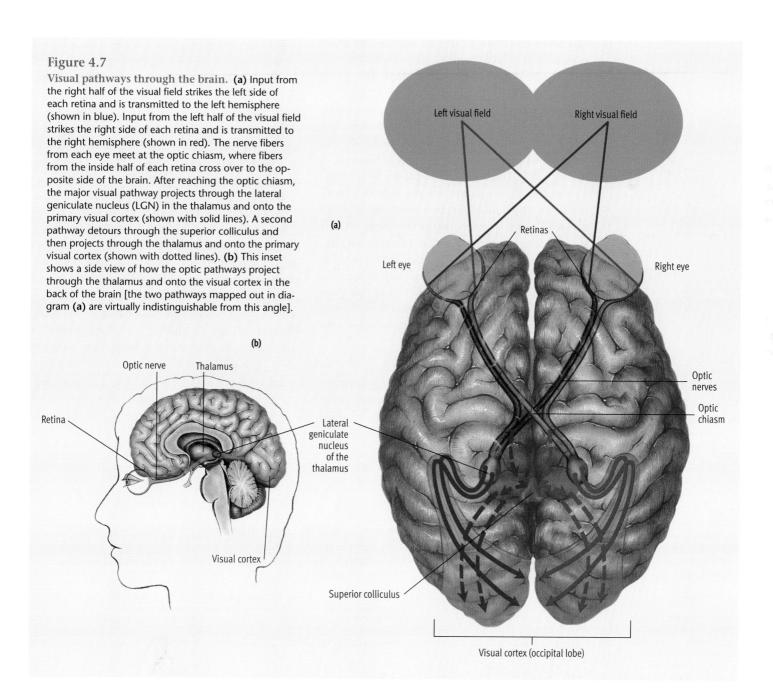

Figure 4.7
Visual pathways through the brain. (a) Input from the right half of the visual field strikes the left side of each retina and is transmitted to the left hemisphere (shown in blue). Input from the left half of the visual field strikes the right side of each retina and is transmitted to the right hemisphere (shown in red). The nerve fibers from each eye meet at the optic chiasm, where fibers from the inside half of each retina cross over to the opposite side of the brain. After reaching the optic chiasm, the major visual pathway projects through the lateral geniculate nucleus (LGN) in the thalamus and onto the primary visual cortex (shown with solid lines). A second pathway detours through the superior colliculus and then projects through the thalamus and onto the primary visual cortex (shown with dotted lines). **(b)** This inset shows a side view of how the optic pathways project through the thalamus and onto the visual cortex in the back of the brain [the two pathways mapped out in diagram **(a)** are virtually indistinguishable from this angle].

DAVID HUBEL

"One can now begin to grasp the significance of the great number of cells in the visual cortex. Each cell seems to have its own specific duties."

After reaching the optic chiasm, the optic nerve fibers split along two pathways. The main pathway projects into the lateral geniculate nucleus (LGN) of the thalamus, where visual signals are processed and then distributed to areas in the occipital lobe that make up the *primary visual cortex*. After the initial cortical processing of visual input takes place here, signals are typically shuttled on to the temporal and parietal lobes for additional processing. The second visual pathway leaving the optic chiasm branches off to an area in the midbrain (the *superior colliculus*) before traveling through the thalamus and on to the occipital lobe. However, the second pathway projects into different areas of the thalamus and the occipital lobe than the main visual pathway does. The principal function of the second pathway appears to be the coordination of visual input with other sensory input (Casanova et al., 2001; Stein & Meredith, 1993).

Researchers have found rather sizable differences among people in the sheer amount of neural resources devoted to vision. A study of 15 normal brains obtained at autopsy found two- to three-fold variations in the size of their optic nerve, their LGN, and their primary visual cortex (Andrews, Halpern, & Purves, 1997). These are huge disparities in comparison to the 30% variation usually seen in overall brain size. These differences in the architecture of individuals' visual systems could be the neural basis for variations among people in visual ability (Halpern, Andrews, & Purves, 1999). According to this fascinating line of thinking, someone like baseball star Alex Rodriguez, who obviously can see 95-mile-per-hour pitches exceptionally well, probably has an overdeveloped visual system (a larger than average optic nerve, LGN, and visual cortex).

Information Processing in the Visual Cortex

Visual input ultimately arrives in the primary visual cortex located in the occipital lobe. How these cortical cells respond to light once posed a perplexing problem. Researchers investigating the question placed microelectrodes in the visual cortex of animals to record action potentials from individual cells. They would flash spots of light in the retinal receptive fields that the cells were thought to monitor, but the cells rarely responded.

According to David Hubel and Torsten Wiesel (1962, 1963), they discovered the solution to this mystery quite by accident. One of the projector slides they used to present a spot to a cat had a crack in it. The spot elicited no response, but when they removed the slide, the crack moved through the cell's receptive field, and the cell fired like crazy in response to the moving dark line. It turns out that cortical cells don't really respond much to little spots—they are much more sensitive to lines, edges, and other more complicated stimuli. Armed with new slides, Hubel and Wiesel embarked on years of painstaking study of the visual cortex. Their work eventually earned them a Nobel prize in 1981.

Hubel and Wiesel (1979, 1998) identified three major types of visual cells in the cortex, which they called simple cells, complex cells, and hypercomplex cells. *Simple cells* are quite specific about which stimuli will make them fire. A simple cell responds best to a line of the correct width, oriented at the correct angle, and located in the correct position in its receptive field (see **Figure 4.8**). *Complex cells* also care about width and orientation, but they respond to any position in their receptive fields. Some complex

Figure 4.8

Hubel and Wiesel's procedure for studying the activity of neurons in the visual cortex. As the cat is shown various stimuli, a microelectrode records the firing of a neuron in the cat's visual cortex. The figure shows the electrical responses of a visual cell apparently "programmed" to respond to lines oriented vertically.

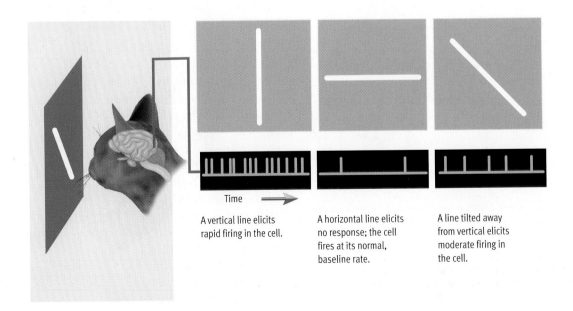

Time

A vertical line elicits rapid firing in the cell.

A horizontal line elicits no response; the cell fires at its normal, baseline rate.

A line tilted away from vertical elicits moderate firing in the cell.

cells are most responsive if a line sweeps across their receptive field—but only if it's moving in the "right" direction. *Hypercomplex* cells are cells that are particularly fussy about the length of a stimulus line.

The key point of all this is that the cells in the visual cortex seem to be highly specialized. They have been characterized as *feature detectors,* **neurons that respond selectively to very specific features of more complex stimuli.** Ultimately, most visual stimuli could be represented by combinations of lines such as those registered by these feature detectors. Some theorists believe that feature detectors are registering the basic building blocks of visual perception and that the brain somehow assembles the blocks into a coherent picture of complex stimuli (Maguire, Weisstein, & Klymenko, 1990).

After visual input is processed in the primary visual cortex, it is often routed to other cortical areas for additional processing. These signals travel through two streams that have sometimes been characterized as the *what and where pathways* (see **Figure 4.9**). The *ventral stream* processes the details of *what* objects are out there (the perception of form and color), while the *dorsal stream* processes *where* the objects are (the perception of motion and depth) (Kandel & Wurtz, 2000; Ungerleider & Haxby, 1994).

As signals move further along in the visual processing system, neurons become even more special-ized in what turns them on, and the stimuli that activate them become more and more complex. For example, researchers have identified cells in the temporal lobe (along the *what* pathway) of monkeys and humans that respond best to pictures of *faces* (Levine, 2001; Rolls & Tovee, 1995). This incredible specificity has led researchers to joke that they may eventually find a cell that only recognizes one's grandmother (Cowey, 1994). The discovery of neurons that respond to facial stimuli raises an obvious question: Why does the cortex have face detectors? Theorists are far from sure, but one line of thinking is that the ability to quickly recognize faces—such as those of friends or foes—probably has had adaptive significance over the course of evolution (Desimone, 1991). Thus, natural selection *may* have wired the brains of some species to quickly respond to faces.

Viewing the World in Color

So far, we've considered only how the visual system deals with light and dark. Let's journey now into the world of color. Of course, you can see perfectly well without seeing in color. Many animals get by with little or no color vision, and no one seemed to suffer back when photographs, movies, or TV shows were all in black and white. However, color adds not only spectacle but information to perceptions of the world. The ability to identify objects against a complex background is enhanced by the addition of color. Quickly identifying objects probably has had adaptive value in terms of finding food and detecting predators. Indeed, some theorists have suggested that color vision evolved in humans and monkeys because it improved their ability to find fruit in the forest (Mollon, 1989). Although the purpose of color vision remains elusive, scientists have learned a great deal about the mechanisms underlying the perception of color.

The Stimulus for Color

As noted earlier, the lights people see are mixtures of different wavelengths. Perceived color is primarily a function of the dominant wavelength in these mixtures. In the visible spectrum, lights with the longest wavelengths appear red, whereas those with the shortest appear violet. Notice the word *appear.* Color is a psychological interpretation. It's not a physical property of light itself.

Although wavelength wields the greatest influence, perception of color depends on complex blends of all three properties of light. Wavelength is most closely related to hue, amplitude to brightness, and purity to saturation. These three dimensions of color are illustrated in the *color solid* shown in **Figure 4.10**.

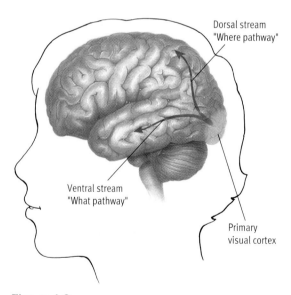

Figure 4.9

The what and where pathways from the primary visual cortex. Cortical processing of visual input is begun in the primary visual cortex. From there, signals are shuttled onward to a variety of other areas in the cortex along a number of pathways. Two prominent pathways are highlighted here. The dorsal stream, or *where* pathway, which processes information about motion and depth, moves on to areas of the parietal lobe. The ventral stream, or *what* pathway, which processes information about color and form, moves on to areas of the temporal lobe.

PREVIEW QUESTIONS

- How are additive and subtractive color mixing different?
- How have the trichromatic and opponent process theories been reconciled to explain color vision?
- What is feature analysis, and what is the difference between top-down and bottom-up processing?
- What are the Gestalt principles of form perception?
- How do perceptual hypotheses contribute to form perception?

Web Link 4.2

The Joy of Visual Perception: A Web Book Peter Kaiser of York University has crafted a comprehensive guide to human color vision, supplying plenty of graphics and demonstrations to help visitors understand what laboratory research in psychology has learned about visual perception.

Figure 4.10

The color solid. The color solid shows how color varies along three perceptual dimensions: brightness (increasing from the bottom to the top of the solid), hue (changing around the solid's perimeter), and saturation (increasing toward the periphery of the solid).

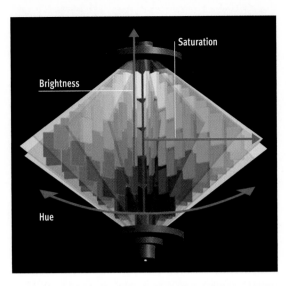

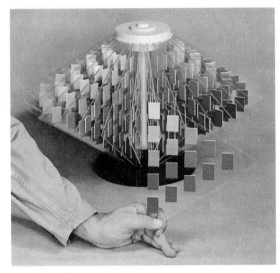

Courtesy of BASF

As a color solid demonstrates systematically, people can perceive many different colors. Indeed, experts estimate that humans can discriminate among roughly a million colors (Boynton, 1990). Most of these diverse variations are the result of mixing a few basic colors. There are two kinds of color mixture: subtractive and additive. *Subtractive color mixing works by removing some wavelengths of light, leaving less light than was originally there.* You probably became familiar with subtractive mixing as a child when you mixed yellow and blue paints to make green. Paints yield subtractive mixing because pigments *absorb* most wavelengths, selectively reflecting back specific wavelengths that give rise to particular colors. Subtractive color mixing can also be demonstrated by stacking color filters. If you look through a sandwich of yellow and blue cellophane filters, they will block out certain wavelengths. The middle wavelengths that are left will look green.

Additive color mixing works by superimposing lights, putting more light in the mixture than ex- ists in any one light by itself. If you shine red, green, and blue spotlights on a white surface, you'll have an additive mixture. As **Figure 4.11** shows, additive and subtractive mixtures of the same colors produce different results.

White light actually includes the entire visible spectrum, as you can demonstrate by allowing white light to pass through a prism (consult **Figure 4.1** once again). Accordingly, when all wavelengths are mixed additively, they yield natural white light. Human processes of color perception parallel additive color mixing much more closely than subtractive mixing, as you'll see in the following discussion of theories of color vision.

Trichromatic Theory of Color Vision

The trichromatic theory of color vision (*tri* for "three," *chroma* for "color") was first stated by Thomas Young and modified later by Hermann von Helmholtz

Figure 4.11

Additive versus subtractive color mixing. Lights mix additively because all the wavelengths contained in each light reach the eye. If red, blue, and green lights are projected onto a white screen, they produce the colors shown on the left, with white at the intersection of all three lights. If paints of the same three colors were combined in the same way, the subtractive mixture would produce the colors shown on the right, with black at the intersection of all three colors.

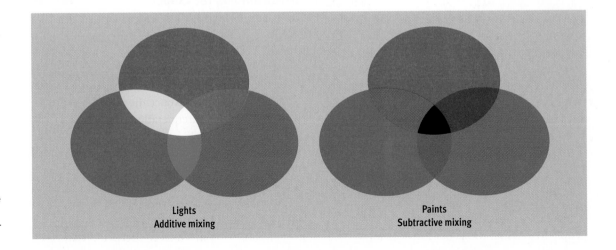

Lights
Additive mixing

Paints
Subtractive mixing

(1852). The *trichromatic theory holds that the human eye has three types of receptors with differing sensitivities to different light wavelengths.* Helmholtz believed that the eye contains specialized receptors sensitive to the wavelengths associated with red, green, or blue. According to this model, people can see all the colors of the rainbow because the eye does its own "color mixing" by varying the ratio of neural activity among these three types of receptors.

The impetus for the trichromatic theory was the demonstration that a light of any color can be matched by the additive mixture of three *primary colors.* (Any three colors that are appropriately spaced out in the visible spectrum can serve as primary colors, although red, green, and blue are usually used.) Does it sound implausible that three colors should be adequate for creating all other colors? If so, consider that this phenomenon is exactly what happens on your color TV screen. Additive mixtures of red, green, and blue fool you into seeing all the colors of a natural scene.

Most of the known facts about color blindness also meshed well with trichromatic theory. **Color blindness encompasses a variety of deficiencies in the ability to distinguish among colors.** Color blindness occurs much more frequently in males than in females. Actually, the term color *blindness* is somewhat misleading, as complete blindness to differences in colors is quite rare. Most people who are color blind are *dichromats;* that is, they make do with only two color channels. There are three types of dichromats, and each type is insensitive to a different color (red, green, or blue, although the latter is rare) (Gouras, 1991). The three deficiencies seen among dichromats support the notion that there are three channels for color vision, as proposed by trichromatic theory.

Opponent Process Theory of Color Vision

Although trichromatic theory explained some facets of color vision well, it ran aground in other areas. Consider complementary afterimages, for instance. **Complementary colors are pairs of colors that produce gray tones when mixed together.** The various pairs of complementary colors can be arranged in a *color circle,* such as the one in **Figure 4.12**. If you stare at a strong color and then look at a white background, you'll see an *afterimage*—**a visual image that persists after a stimulus is removed.** The color of the afterimage will be the *complement* of the color you originally stared at. Trichromatic theory cannot account for the appearance of complementary afterimages.

Here's another peculiarity to consider. If you ask people to describe colors but restrict them to using

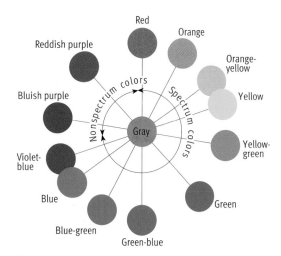

Figure 4.12

The color circle and complementary colors. Colors opposite each other on this color circle are complements, or "opposites." Additively, mixing complementary colors produces gray. Opponent process principles help explain this effect as well as the other peculiarities of complementary colors noted in the text.

three names, they run into difficulty. For example, using only red, green, and blue, they simply don't feel comfortable describing yellow as "reddish green." However, if you let them have just one more name, they usually choose yellow. Then they can describe any color quite well (Gordon & Abramov, 2001). If colors are reduced to three channels, why are four color names required to describe the full range of possible colors?

In an effort to answer questions such as these, Ewald Hering proposed the *opponent process theory* of color vision in 1878. *The opponent process theory holds that color perception depends on receptors that make antagonistic responses to three pairs of colors.* The three pairs of opponent colors hypothesized by Hering were red versus green, yellow versus blue, and black versus white. The antagonistic processes in this theory provide plausible explanations for complementary afterimages and the need for four names (red, green, blue, and yellow) to describe colors. Opponent process theory also explains some aspects of color blindness. For instance, it can explain why dichromats typically find it hard to distinguish either green from red or yellow from blue.

Reconciling Theories of Color Vision

Advocates of trichromatic theory and opponent process theory argued about the relative merits of the two models for almost a century. Most researchers assumed that one theory must be wrong and the other must be right. In recent decades, however, it

Figure 4.13

Three types of cones. Research has identified three types of cones that show varied sensitivity to different wavelengths of light. As the graph shows, these three types of cones correspond only roughly to the red, green, and blue receptors predicted by trichromatic theory, so it is more accurate to refer to them as cones sensitive to short, medium, and long wavelengths.

Source: Wald, G., & Brown, P. K. (1965). Human color vision and color blindness. *Symposium Cold Spring Harbor Laboratory of Quantitative Biology, 30,* 345–359 (p. 351). Copyright (c) 1965. Reprinted by permission of the author.

has become clear that *it takes both theories to explain color vision.* Eventually a physiological basis for both theories was found. Research that earned George Wald a Nobel prize demonstrated that *the eye has three types of cones,* with each type being most sensitive to a different band of wavelengths, as shown in **Figure 4.13** (Lennie, 2000; Wald, 1964). The three types of cones represent the three different color receptors predicted by trichromatic theory.

Researchers also discovered a biological basis for opponent processes. They found cells in the retina, the thalamus, and the visual cortex *that respond in opposite ways to red versus green and blue versus yellow* (DeValois & Jacobs, 1984; Zrenner et al., 1990). For example, some ganglion cells in the retina are excited by green and inhibited by red. Other ganglion cells in the retina work in just the opposite way, as predicted by opponent process theory.

In summary, the perception of color appears to involve stages of information processing (Hurvich, 1981). The receptors that do the first stage of processing (the cones) seem to follow the principles outlined in trichromatic theory. In later stages of processing, cells in the retina and the brain seem to follow the principles outlined in opponent process theory. As you can see, vigorous theoretical debate about color vision produced a solution that went beyond the contributions of either theory alone.

Recently, theorists have floated an interesting new explanation for why the human brain evolved to organize color experience into four basic categories. The inspiration for this explanation centers on the fact that mapmakers have long known that a minimum of four different colors are needed to create maps that avoid adjacent countries of the same color. Purves, Lotto, and Polger (2000) argue that the human visual system evolved to solve a similar problem—ensuring that no two areas separated by a common boundary will look the same if they are really different. According to Purves et al. (2000), four color categories are required to facilitate the human visual system achieving its chief purpose—reliably distinguishing one object from another.

Perceiving Forms, Patterns, and Objects

The drawing in **Figure 4.14** is a poster for a circus act involving a trained seal. What do you see?

No doubt you see a seal balancing a ball on its nose and a trainer holding a fish and a whip. But suppose you had been told that the drawing is actually a poster for a costume ball. Would you have perceived it differently?

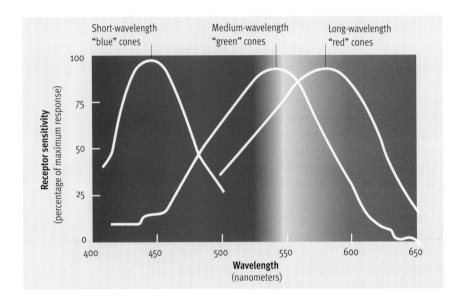

concept **check** 4.2

Comparing Theories of Color Vision

Check your understanding of the differences between the trichromatic and opponent process theories of color vision by filling in the blanks below. The answers are in Appendix A.

	Trichromatic theory	**Opponent process theory**
1. Theory proposed by	_____	_____
2. Can/can't account for complementary afterimages	_____	_____
3. Explains first/later stage of color processing	_____	_____
4. Does/doesn't account for need for four terms to describe colors	_____	_____

Figure 4.14

A poster for a trained seal act. Or is it? The picture is an ambiguous figure, which can be interpreted as either of two scenes, as explained in the text.

If you focus on the idea of a costume ball (stay with it a minute if you still see the seal and trainer), you will probably see a costumed man and woman in **Figure 4.14**. She's handing him a hat, and he has a sword in his right hand. This tricky little sketch was made ambiguous quite intentionally. It's a ***reversible figure,*** **a drawing that is compatible with two different interpretations that can shift back and forth.** Another classic reversible figure is shown in **Figure 4.15**. What do you see? A rabbit or a duck? It all depends on how you look at the drawing.

The key point is simply this: *The same visual input can result in radically different perceptions.* There is no one-to-one correspondence between sensory input and what you perceive. *This is a principal reason that people's experience of the world is subjective.* Perception involves much more than passively receiving signals from the outside world. It involves the *interpretation* of sensory input.

In this case, your interpretations result in two different "realities" because your *expectations* have been manipulated. Information given to you about the drawing has created **a *perceptual set*—a readiness to perceive a stimulus in a particular way.** A perceptual set creates a certain slant in how you interpret sensory input.

Form perception also depends on the *selection* of sensory input—that is, what people focus their attention on (Chun & Wolfe, 2001). A visual scene

may include many objects and forms. Some of these may capture viewers' attention while others may not. This fact has been demonstrated in dramatic fashion in studies of *inattentional blindness,* which involves the failure to see fully visible objects or events in a visual display. In one such study (Simons & Chabris, 1999), participants watched a video of a group of people in white shirts passing a basketball laid over another video of people in black shirts passing a basketball (the two videos were partially transparent). The observers were instructed to focus on one of the two teams and press a key whenever that team passed the ball. Thirty seconds into the task, a woman carrying an umbrella clearly walked through the scene for four seconds. You might guess that this bizarre development would be noticed by virtually all the observers, but 44% of the participants failed to see the woman. Moreover, when someone in a gorilla suit strolled through the same scene even more subjects (73%) missed the unexpected event!

Additional studies using other types of stimulus materials have demonstrated that people routinely overlook obvious forms that are unexpected (Mack & Rock, 1998). Inattentional blindness has been attributed to subjects having a perceptual set that leads them to focus most of their attention on a specific feature in a scene (such as the basketball passes) while neglecting other facets of the scene (Most et al., 2001). Inattentional blindness may account for many automobile accidents, as accident reports frequently include the statement "I looked right there, but never saw them" (Shermer, 2004). The idea that we see much less of the world than we think we do surprises many people, but there is an auditory parallel that people take for granted (Mack, 2003). Think of how often you have had someone clearly say something to you, but you did not hear a word of what was said because you were "not listening." Inattentional blindness is essentially the same thing in the visual domain.

An understanding of how people perceive forms, patterns, and objects also requires knowledge of how people *organize and interpret* visual input. Several influential approaches to this question emphasize *feature analysis.*

Feature Analysis: Assembling Forms

3c

The information received by your eyes would do you little good if you couldn't recognize objects and forms—ranging from words on a page to mice in your cellar and friends in the distance. According to some theories, perceptions of form and pattern entail *feature analysis* (Lindsay & Norman, 1977; Maguire et al.,

Figure 4.15

Another ambiguous figure. What animal do you see here? As the text explains, two very different perceptions are possible. This ambiguous figure was devised around 1900 by Joseph Jastrow, a prominent psychologist at the turn of the 20th century (Block & Yuker, 1992).

Figure 4.16

Feature analysis in form perception. One vigorously debated theory of form perception is that the brain has cells that respond to specific aspects or features of stimuli, such as lines and angles. Neurons functioning as higher-level analyzers then respond to input from these "feature detectors." The more input each analyzer receives, the more active it becomes. Finally, other neurons weigh signals from these analyzers and make a "decision" about the stimulus. In this way perception of a form is arrived at by assembling elements from the bottom up.

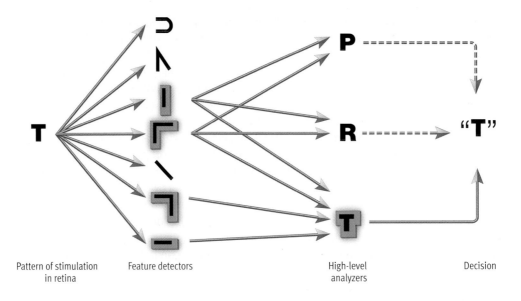

Pattern of stimulation in retina   Feature detectors   High-level analyzers   Decision

1990). *Feature analysis* **is the process of detecting specific elements in visual input and assembling them into a more complex form.** In other words, you start with the components of a form, such as lines, edges, and corners, and build them into perceptions of squares, triangles, stop signs, bicycles, ice cream cones, and telephones. An application of this model of form perception is diagrammed in **Figure 4.16**.

Feature analysis assumes that form perception involves *bottom-up processing,* **a progression from individual elements to the whole** (see **Figure 4.17**). The plausibility of this model was bolstered greatly when Hubel and Wiesel showed that cells in the visual cortex operate as highly specialized feature detectors. Indeed, their findings strongly suggested that at least some aspects of form perception involve feature analysis.

Can feature analysis provide a complete account of how people perceive forms? Clearly not. A crucial problem for the theory is that form perception often does not involve bottom-up processing. In fact, there is ample evidence that perceptions of form frequently involve *top-down processing,* **a progression from the whole to the elements** (see **Figure 4.17**). For example, there is evidence that people can perceive a word before its individual letters, a phenomenon that has to reflect top-down processing (Johnston & McClelland, 1974). If readers depended exclusively on bottom-up processing, they would have to analyze the features of letters in words to recognize them and then assemble the letters into words. This task would be time-consuming and would slow down reading speed to a snail's pace.

Looking at the Whole Picture: Gestalt Principles

Sometimes a whole, as we perceive it, may have qualities that don't exist in any of the parts. This insight became the basic assumption of *Gestalt psychology,* an influential school of thought that emerged out of Germany during the first half of the 20th century. (*Gestalt* is a German word for "form" or "shape.")

A simple example of this principle, which you have experienced countless times, is the *phi phenomenon,* first described by Max Wertheimer in 1912. **The *phi phenomenon* is the illusion of movement created by presenting visual stimuli in rapid succession.** You encounter examples of the phi phenomenon nearly every day. For example, movies and

Figure 4.17

Bottom-up versus top-down processing. As explained in these diagrams, bottom-up processing progresses from individual elements to whole elements, whereas top-down processing progresses from the whole to the individual elements.

Bottom-up processing:
- Recognize stimulus
- Combine specific features into more complex forms
- Detect specific features of stimulus

Top-down processing
- Formulate perceptual hypothesis about the nature of the stimulus as a whole
- Select and examine features to check hypothesis
- Recognize stimulus

TV consist of separate still pictures projected rapidly one after the other. You *see* smooth motion, but in reality the "moving" objects merely take slightly different positions in successive frames. Viewed as a whole, a movie has a property (motion) that isn't evident in any of its parts (the individual frames).

The Gestalt psychologists formulated a series of principles that describe how the visual system organizes a scene into discrete forms. Let's explore some of these principles.

Figure and Ground Take a look at **Figure 4.18**. Do you see the figure as two silhouetted faces against a white background, or as a white vase against a black background? This reversible figure illustrates the Gestalt principle of *figure and ground*. Dividing visual displays into figure and ground is a fundamental way in which people organize visual perceptions (Baylis & Driver, 1995). The figure is the thing being looked at, and the ground is the background against which it stands. The figure seems to have substance and appears to stand out in front of the ground. Other things being equal, an object is more likely to be viewed as a figure when it is smaller in size, higher in contrast, or greater in symmetry (Palmer, 2003), and especially when it is lower in one's frame of view (Vecera, Vogel, & Woodman, 2002). More often than not, your visual field may contain many figures sharing a background. The following Gestalt principles relate to how these elements are grouped into higher-order figures.

Proximity Things that are near one another seem to belong together. The black dots in **Figure 4.19(a)** on the next page could be grouped into vertical columns or horizontal rows. However, people tend to perceive rows because of the effect of proximity (the dots are closer together horizontally).

Closure People often group elements to create a sense of *closure*, or completeness. Thus, you may "complete" figures that actually have gaps in them. This principle is demonstrated in **Figure 4.19(b)**.

Similarity People also tend to group stimuli that are similar. This principle is apparent in **Figure 4.19(c)**, where elements of similar darkness are grouped into the number 2.

Simplicity The Gestaltists' most general principle was the law of *Pragnanz*, which translates from German as "good form." The idea is that people tend to group elements that combine to form a good figure. This principle is somewhat vague in that it's often difficult to spell out what makes a figure "good" (Biederman, Hilton, & Hummel, 1991). Some theorists maintain that goodness is largely a matter of simplicity, asserting that people tend to organize forms in the simplest way possible (see **Figure 4.19(d)**).

Continuity The principle of continuity reflects people's tendency to follow in whatever direction they've been led. Thus, people tend to connect points that result in straight or gently curved lines that create "smooth" paths, as shown in **Figure 4.19(e)**.

Although Gestalt psychology is no longer an active theoretical orientation in modern psychology, its influence is still felt in the study of perception (Banks & Krajicek, 1991). The Gestalt psychologists raised many important questions that still occupy

Figure 4.18
The principle of figure and ground. Whether you see two faces or a vase depends on which part of this drawing you see as figure and which as background. Although this reversible drawing allows you to switch back and forth between two ways of organizing your perception, you can't perceive the drawing both ways at once.

Archives of the History of American Psychology, University of Akron.

MAX WERTHEIMER
"The fundamental 'formula' of Gestalt theory might be expressed in this way: There are wholes, the behaviour of which is not determined by that of their individual elements."

Web Link 4.3

Sensation and Perception Tutorials
John Krantz of Hanover College has assembled a collection of quality tutorials on sensation and perception. Topics covered include receptive fields, depth perception, Gestalt laws, and the use of perceptual principles in art.

The illusion of movement in a highway construction sign is an instance of the phi phenomenon, which is also at work in motion pictures and television. The phenomenon illustrates the Gestalt principle that the whole can have properties that are not found in any of its parts.

Figure 4.19

Gestalt principles of perceptual organization. Gestalt principles help explain some of the factors that influence form perception. **(a) Proximity:** These dots might well be organized in vertical columns rather than horizontal rows, but because of proximity (the dots are closer together horizontally), they tend to be perceived in rows. **(b) Closure:** Even though the figures are incomplete, you fill in the blanks and see a circle and a dog. **(c) Similarity:** Because of similarity of color, you see dots organized into the number 2 instead of a random array. If you did not group similar elements, you wouldn't see the number 2 here. **(d) Simplicity:** You could view this as a complicated 11-sided figure, but given the preference for simplicity, you are more likely to see it as an overlapping rectangle and triangle. **(e) Continuity:** You tend to group these dots in a way that produces a smooth path rather than an abrupt shift in direction.

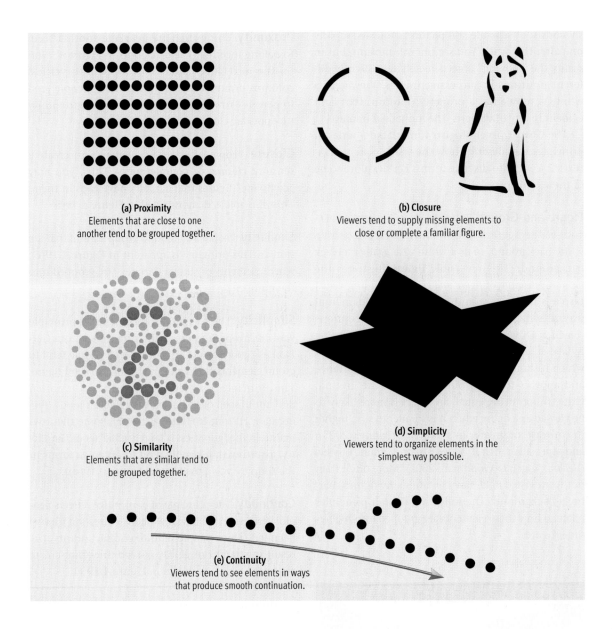

(a) Proximity
Elements that are close to one another tend to be grouped together.

(b) Closure
Viewers tend to supply missing elements to close or complete a familiar figure.

(c) Similarity
Elements that are similar tend to be grouped together.

(d) Simplicity
Viewers tend to organize elements in the simplest way possible.

(e) Continuity
Viewers tend to see elements in ways that produce smooth continuation.

researchers, and they left a legacy of many useful insights about form perception that have stood the test of time (Sharps & Wertheimer, 2000).

Formulating Perceptual Hypotheses

The Gestalt principles provide some indications of how people organize visual input. However, scientists are still one step away from understanding how these organized perceptions result in a representation of the real world. In visual perception, the images projected on the retina are distorted, two-dimensional versions of their actual, three-dimensional counterparts. For example, consider the stimulus of a square such as the one in **Figure 4.20**. If the square is lying on a desk in front of you, it is actually projecting a trapezoid on your retinas, because the top of the square is farther from your eyes than the bottom. Obviously, the trapezoid is a distorted representation of the square. If what people have to work with is so distorted, how do they get an accurate view of the world out there?

One explanation is that people are constantly making and testing *hypotheses* about what's out there in the real world (Gregory, 1973). Thus, a *perceptual hypothesis* is an inference about what form could be responsible for a pattern of sensory stimulation. The square in **Figure 4.20** may project a trapezoidal image on your retinas, but your perceptual system "guesses" correctly that it's a square—and that's what you see.

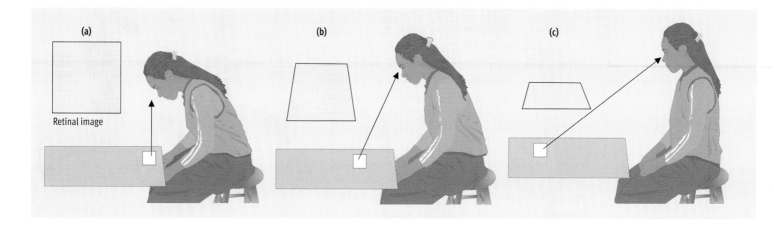

(a) Retinal image (b) (c)

Let's look at another ambiguous drawing to further demonstrate the process of making a perceptual hypothesis. **Figure 4.21** is a famous reversible figure, first published as a cartoon in a humor magazine. Perhaps you see a drawing of a young woman looking back over her right shoulder. Alternatively, you might see an old woman with her chin down on her chest. The ambiguity exists because there isn't enough information to force your perceptual system to accept only one of these hypotheses. Incidentally, studies show that people who are led to *expect* the young woman or the old woman generally see the one they expect (Leeper, 1935). This is another example of how perceptual sets influence what people see.

Psychologists have used a variety of reversible figures to study how people formulate perceptual hypotheses. Another example can be seen in **Figure 4.22**, which shows the *Necker cube*. The shaded surface can appear as either the front or the rear of the transparent cube. If you look at the cube for a while, your perception will alternate between these possibilities.

The *context* in which something appears often guides our perceptual hypotheses. To illustrate, take a look at **Figure 4.23**. What do you see? You probably

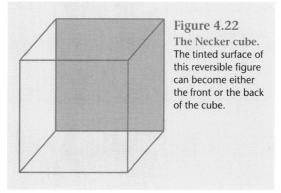

Figure 4.22
The Necker cube. The tinted surface of this reversible figure can become either the front or the back of the cube.

Figure 4.21
A famous reversible figure. What do you see? Consult the text to learn what the two possible interpretations of this figure are.

THE CHT

Figure 4.23
Context effects. The context in which a stimulus is seen can affect your perceptual hypotheses. The middle character in the word on the left is assumed to be an "H," whereas in the word on the right the same character is assumed to be an "A." In addition to showing the potential influence of context, this example shows the power of expectations and top-down processing.

Figure 4.20
Perceptual hypotheses. The images projected on the retina are often distorted, shifting representations of stimuli in the real world, requiring ongoing perceptual hypotheses about what form could be responsible for a particular pattern of sensory stimulation. For example, if you look directly down at a small, square piece of paper on a desk **(a)**, the stimulus (the paper) and the image projected on your retina will both be square. As you move the paper away on the desktop, as shown in **(b)** and **(c)**, the square stimulus projects an increasingly trapezoidal image on your retina, but you still see a square.

saw the words "THE CAT." But look again; the middle characters in both words are identical. You identified an "H" in the first word and an "A" in the second because of the surrounding letters, which shaped your expectations. The power of expectations explains why typographical errors like those in this sentence often pass unoberved (Lachman, 1996).

Our perceptual hypotheses clearly are guided by our experience-based expectations. For example, subjects recognize everyday objects more quickly when they are presented from familiar viewpoints as opposed to unfamiliar viewpoints (Enns, 2004; see **Figure 4.24**). We also realize that certain objects and settings generally go together. We expect to see a sofa sitting in a living room, but not on a beach. When subjects are given very brief glimpses of objects in typical versus unusual settings, the objects that appear in typical settings are identified more accurately (Davenport & Potter, 2004; see **Figure 4.25**). This finding illustrates the importance of both context and experience.

Figure 4.24

Effect of viewpoint on form perception. Research on object recognition shows that the time needed to recognize an object depends on the perspective from which it is viewed (Enns, 2004). Subjects recognize familiar, proto-typical views of everyday objects (such as the tricycle on the left) more quickly than atypical views of the same objects (such as the tricycle on the right) (Palmer, Rosch, & Chase, 1981). This finding shows that our perceptual hypotheses are guided by our experience.

Source: Enns, J. T. (2004). *The thinking eye, the seeing brain: Explorations in visual cognition.* New York: W. W. Norton. Copyright © 2004 by W. W. Norton & Company. Available at www.amazon.com. Used by permission.

Figure 4.25

Effect of object and background consistency on object recognition. In a study by Davenport and Potter (2004), participants were given brief glimpses of objects that were presented in a typical setting consistent with expectations, such as a football player on a football field or a priest in a church (top), or in an unusual, unexpected setting, as seen in the bottom photos, where the priest is on a football field and the football player is in a church. The findings showed that when objects are consistent with their background, they are recognized more accurately. Thus, context and experience affect form perception.

Source: Davenport, J. L., & Potter, M. C. (2004). Scene consistency in object and background perception. *Psychological Science, 15,* 559-564. Reprinted by permission of Blackwell Publishers and the author.

PREVIEW QUESTIONS

- What are some binocular and monocular depth cues?
- Are there cultural differences in depth perception?
- What are perceptual constancies?
- What do visual illusions reveal about perceptual processes?

Perceiving Depth or Distance

More often than not, forms and figures are objects in space. Spatial considerations add a third dimension to visual perception. *Depth perception involves interpretation of visual cues that indicate how near or far away objects are.* To make judgments of distance, people rely on quite a variety of clues, which can be classified into two types: binocular cues and monocular cues (Hochberg, 1988; Proffitt & Caudek, 2003).

Binocular Cues

Because the eyes are set apart, each eye has a slightly different view of the world. *Binocular depth cues are clues about distance based on the differing views of the two eyes.* "Stereo" viewers like the Viewmaster toy you may have had as a child make use of this principle by presenting slightly different flat images of the same scene to each eye. The brain then supplies the "depth," and you perceive a three-dimensional scene.

The principal binocular depth cue is *retinal disparity,* which refers to the fact that objects within

25 feet project images to slightly different locations on the right and left retinas, so the right and left eyes see slightly different views of the object. The closer an object gets, the greater the disparity between the images seen by each eye. Thus, retinal disparity increases as objects come closer, providing information about distance.

Monocular Cues

PsykTrek
3f

Monocular depth cues **are clues about distance based on the image in either eye alone.** There are two kinds of monocular cues to depth. One kind is the result of active use of the eye in viewing the world. For example, as an object comes closer, you may sense the accommodation (the change in the curvature of the lens) that must occur for the eye to adjust its focus.

The other kind of monocular cues are *pictorial depth cues*—**cues about distance that can be given in a flat picture.** There are many pictorial cues to depth, which is why paintings and photographs can seem so realistic that you feel you can climb right into them. Six prominent pictorial depth cues are described and illustrated in **Figure 4.26.** The first of these, *linear perspective*, is a depth cue reflecting the fact that lines converge in the distance. Because details are too small to see when they are far away, *texture gradients* can also provide information about depth. If an object comes between you and another object, it must be closer to you, a cue called *interposition*. *Relative size* is a cue because closer objects appear larger. *Height in plane* reflects the fact that distant objects appear higher in a picture. Finally, the familiar effects of shadowing make *light* and *shadow* useful in judging distance.

Figure 4.26
Pictorial cues to depth. Six pictorial depth cues are explained and illustrated here. Although one cue stands out in each photo, in most visual scenes several pictorial cues are present. Try looking at the light-and-shadow picture upside down. The change in shadowing reverses what you see.

© Royalty Free/Corbis

Linear perspective Parallel lines that run away from the viewer seem to get closer together.

© Jean-Marc Truchet/Getty Imagees

Texture gradient As distance increases, a texture gradually becomes denser and less distinct.

© Ron Fehling/Masterfile

Interposition The shapes of near objects overlap or mask those of more distant ones.

© Jose Fuste Raga/zeta/Corbis

Relative size If separate objects are expected to be of the same size, the larger ones are seen as closer.

© Chris George/Alamy

Height in plane Near objects are low in the visual field; more distant ones are higher up.

U.S. Department of Energy

Light and shadow Patterns of light and dark suggest shadows that can create an impression of three-dimensional forms.

BIZARRO

Bizarro © 1991 Dan Piraro. Reprinted by special permission of King Features Syndicate.

Figure 4.27

Testing understanding of pictorial depth cues. In his cross-cultural research, Hudson (1960) asked subjects to indicate whether the hunter is trying to spear the antelope or the elephant. He found cultural disparities in subjects' ability to make effective use of the pictorial depth cues, which place the elephant in the distance and make it an unlikely target.

Source: Adapted by permission from an illustration by Ilil Arbel in Deregowski, J. B. (1972, November). Pictorial perception and culture. *Scientific American, 227* (5), p. 83. Copyright © 1972 by Scientific American, Inc. All rights reserved.

Some cultural differences appear to exist in the ability to take advantage of pictorial depth cues in two-dimensional drawings. These differences were first investigated by Hudson (1960, 1967), who presented pictures like the one in **Figure 4.27** to various cultural groups in South Africa. Hudson's approach was based on the assumption that subjects who indi-cate that the hunter is trying to spear the elephant instead of the antelope don't understand the depth cues (interposition, relative size, height in plane) in the picture, which place the elephant in the dis-

concept **check** 4.3

Recognizing Pictorial Depth Cues

Painters routinely attempt to create the perception of depth on a flat canvas by using pictorial depth cues. **Figure 4.26** describes and illustrates six pictorial depth cues, most of which are apparent in Vincent van Gogh's colorful piece, titled *Corridor in the Asylum* (1889). Check your understanding of depth perception by trying to spot the depth cues in the painting.

In the list below, check off the depth cues used by van Gogh. The answers can be found in Appendix A. You can learn more about how artists use the principles of visual perception in the Personal Application at the end of this chapter.

_____ **1.** Interposition _____ **4.** Relative size

_____ **2.** Height in plane _____ **5.** Light and shadow

_____ **3.** Texture gradient _____ **6.** Linear perspective

van Gogh, Vincent, *Corridor in the Asylum (1889)*, gouche and watercolor, 24 3/8 × 18 1/2 inches (61.5 × 47 cm). Metropolitan Museum of Art. Bequest of Abby Aldrich Rockefeller, 1948. (48.190.2) Photograph © 1998 The Metropolitan Museum of Art.

tance. Hudson found that subjects from a rural South African tribe (the Bantu), who had little exposure at that time to pictures and photos, frequently misinterpreted the depth cues in his pictures. Similar difficulties with depth cues in pictures have been documented for other cultural groups who have little experience with two-dimensional representations of three-dimensional space (Berry et al., 1992). Based on this evidence, Deregowski (1989) concludes that the application of pictorial depth cues to pictures is partly an acquired skill that depends on experience.

Perceptual Constancies in Vision

When a person approaches you from the distance, his or her image on your retinas gradually changes in size. Do you perceive that person as growing right before your eyes? Of course not. Your perceptual system constantly makes allowances for this variation in visual input. In doing so, it relies in part on perceptual constancies. **A *perceptual constancy* is a tendency to experience a stable perception in the face of continually changing sensory input.** Among other things, people tend to view objects as having a stable size, shape, brightness, hue (color), and location in space. Perceptual constancies such as these help impose some order on the surrounding world.

The Power of Misleading Cues: Visual Illusions

In general, perceptual constancies, depth cues, and principles of visual organization (such as the Gestalt laws) help people perceive the world accurately. Sometimes, however, perceptions are based on inappropriate assumptions, and *visual illusions* can result. **A *visual illusion* involves an apparently inexplicable discrepancy between the appearance of a visual stimulus and its physical reality.**

One famous visual illusion is the *Müller-Lyer illusion,* shown in **Figure 4.28**. The two vertical lines in this figure are equally long, but they certainly don't look that way. Why not? Several mechanisms probably play a role (Day, 1965; Gregory, 1978). The figure on the left looks like the outside of a building, thrust toward the viewer, while the one on the right looks like an inside corner, thrust away (see **Figure 4.29**). The vertical line in the left figure therefore seems closer. If two lines cast equally long retinal images but one seems closer, the closer one is assumed to be

shorter. Thus, the Müller-Lyer illusion may be due largely to a combination of size constancy processes and misperception of depth.

The *Ponzo illusion,* shown in **Figure 4.30**, appears to result from the same factors (Coren & Girgus, 1978). The upper and lower horizontal lines are the same length, but the upper one appears longer. This

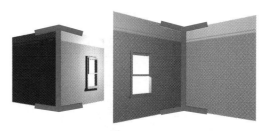

Figure 4.29
Explaining the Müller-Lyer illusion. The figure on the left seems to be closer, since it looks like an outside corner, thrust toward you, whereas the figure on the right looks like an inside corner thrust away from you. Given retinal images of the same length, you assume that the "closer" line is shorter.

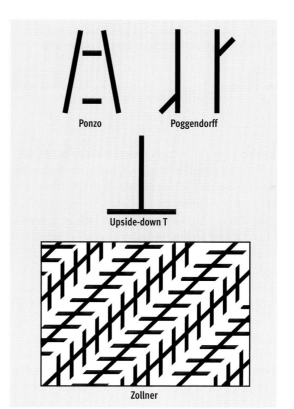

Ponzo

Poggendorff

Upside-down T

Zollner

Figure 4.30
Four geometric illusions. Ponzo: The horizontal lines are the same length. **Poggendorff:** The two diagonal segments lie on the same straight line. **Upside-down T:** The vertical and horizontal lines are the same length. **Zollner:** The long diagonals are all parallel (try covering up some of the short lines if you don't believe it).

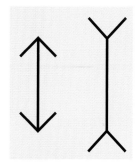

Figure 4.28
The Müller-Lyer illusion. Go ahead, measure them: The two vertical lines are of equal length.

Web Link 4.4

IllusionWorks
IllusionWorks bills itself as "the most comprehensive collection of optical and sensory illusions on the World Wide Web." At both introductory and advanced levels of explanation, this is an excellent resource for experiencing some of the strangest and most thought-provoking illusions ever created.

Figure 4.31

A monster of an illusion. The principles underlying the Ponzo illusion also explain the striking illusion seen here, in which two identical monsters appear to be quite different in size.

Source: Shepard, R. N. (1990). *Mind sights.* New York: W. H. Freeman. Copyright © 1990 by Roger N. Shepard. Reprinted by permission of Henry Holt & Co., LLC.

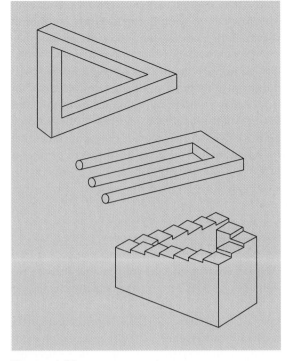

Figure 4.32

Three classic impossible figures. The figures are impossible, yet they clearly exist—on the page. What makes them impossible is that they appear to be three-dimensional representations yet are drawn in a way that frustrates mental attempts to "assemble" their features into possible objects. It's difficult to see the drawings simply as lines lying in a plane—even though this perceptual hypothesis is the only one that resolves the contradiction.

Web Link 4.5

The Moon Illusion Explained
Don McCready, professor emeritus at the University of Wisconsin (Whitewater), addresses the age-old puzzle of why the moon appears much larger at the horizon than overhead. He uses a helpful collection of illustrations in a comprehensive review of alternative theories.

illusion probably occurs because the converging lines convey linear perspective, a key depth cue suggesting that the upper line lies farther in the distance. **Figure 4.31** is a drawing by Stanford University psychologist Roger Shepard (1990) that creates a similar illusion. The second monster appears much larger than the first, even though they are really identical in size. This variation on the Ponzo illusion and the other geometric illusions shown in **Figure 4.30** demonstrate that visual stimuli can be highly deceptive.

Impossible figures create another form of illusion. **Impossible figures are objects that can be represented in two-dimensional pictures but cannot exist in three-dimensional space.** These figures may look fine at first glance, but a closer look reveals that they are geometrically inconsistent or impossible. Three classic impossible figures are shown in **Figure 4.32.** Notice that you perceive specific features of the figure as acceptable but are baffled when they are built into a whole. Your perceptual hypothesis about one portion of the figure turns out to be inconsistent with your hypothesis about another portion.

Obviously, impossible figures involve a conspiracy of cues intended to deceive the viewer. Many visual illusions, however, occur quite naturally and are part of everyday life. A well-known example is the *moon illusion.* The full moon appears to be much smaller when overhead than when looming over the horizon. As with many of the other illusions we have discussed, the moon illusion appears to result mainly from size constancy effects coupled with the misperception of distance (Coren & Aks, 1990; Kaufman & Rock, 1962).

Cross-cultural studies have uncovered some interesting differences among cultural groups in their tendency to see certain illusions. For example, Segall, Campbell, and Herskovits (1966) found that people from Western cultures are more susceptible to the Müller-Lyer illusion than people from some non-Western cultures. The most plausible explanation is that in the West, we live in a "carpentered world" dominated by straight lines, right angles, and rectangular rooms, buildings, and furniture. Thus, our experience prepares us to readily view the Müller-

Lyer figures as inside and outside corners of buildings, inferences that help foster the illusion (Segall et al., 1990).

What do illusions reveal about visual perception? They drive home the point that people go through life formulating perceptual hypotheses about what lies out there in the real world. The fact that these are only hypotheses becomes especially striking when the hypotheses are wrong, as they are with illusions. Visual illusions also show how context factors such as depth cues shape perceptual hypotheses. Finally, like ambiguous figures, illusions clearly demonstrate that human perceptions are not simple reflections of objective reality. Once again, we see that perception of the world is subjective.

These insights do not apply to visual perception only. We will encounter these lessons again as we examine other sensory systems, such as hearing, which we turn to next.

Unlike people in Western nations, the Zulus live in a culture where straight lines and right angles are scarce. Thus, they are not affected by such phenomena as the Müller-Lyer illusion nearly as much as people raised in environments that abound with rectangular structures.

> Our Sense of Hearing: The Auditory System

Stop reading for a moment, close your eyes, and listen carefully. What do you hear?

Chances are, you'll discover that you're immersed in sounds: street noises, a dog barking, the hum of a fluorescent lamp, perhaps some background music you put on a while ago but forgot about. As this little demonstration shows, physical stimuli producing sound are present almost constantly, but you're not necessarily aware of these sounds.

Like vision, the auditory (hearing) system provides input about the world "out there," but not until incoming information is processed by the brain. An auditory stimulus—a screech of tires, someone laughing, the hum of the refrigerator—produces sensory input in the form of sound waves reaching the ears. The perceptual system must somehow transform this stimulation into the psychological experience of hearing. We'll begin our discussion of hearing by looking at the stimulus for auditory experience: sound.

The Stimulus: Sound

Sound waves are vibrations of molecules, which means that they must travel through some physical medium, such as air. They move at a fraction of the speed of light. Sound waves are usually generated by vibrating objects, such as a guitar string, a loudspeaker cone, or your vocal cords. However, sound waves can

also be generated by forcing air past a chamber (as in a pipe organ), or by suddenly releasing a burst of air (as when you clap).

Like light waves, sound waves are characterized by their *amplitude,* their *wavelength,* and their *purity* (see **Figure 4.33** on the next page). The physical properties of amplitude, wavelength, and purity affect mainly the perceived (psychological) qualities of loudness, pitch, and timbre, respectively. However, the physical properties of sound interact in complex ways to produce perceptions of these sound qualities (Hirsh & Watson, 1996).

Human Hearing Capacities

Wavelengths of sound are described in terms of their *frequency,* which is measured in cycles per second, or *hertz* (Hz). For the most part, higher frequencies are perceived as having higher pitch. That is, if you strike the key for high C on a piano, it will produce higher-frequency sound waves than the key for low C. Although the perception of pitch depends mainly on frequency, the amplitude of the sound waves also influences it.

Just as the visible spectrum is only a portion of the total spectrum of light, so, too, what people can hear is only a portion of the available range of sounds. Humans can hear sounds ranging in frequency from

PREVIEW QUESTIONS

● What are the three key properties of sound?

● How are these properties related to auditory perceptions?

● What are the key structures in the ear involved in the processing of sound?

● What were the central ideas of place theory and frequency theory?

● How were the two theories reconciled?

Web Link 4.6

American Speech-Language-Hearing Association
The site for this national organization of audiologists and speech pathologists has a useful section intended for the public that provides information on the dangerous effects of loud noise, detection of hearing loss, the utility of hearing aids, and other topics related to hearing.

a low of 20 Hz up to a high of about 20,000 Hz. Sounds at either end of this range are harder to hear, and sensitivity to high-frequency tones declines as adults grow older. Other organisms have different capabilities. Low-frequency sounds under 10 Hz are au-

dible to homing pigeons, for example. At the other extreme, bats and porpoises can hear frequencies well above 20,000 Hz.

In general, the greater the amplitude of sound waves, the louder the sound perceived. Whereas frequency is measured in hertz, amplitude is measured in *decibels* (dB). The relationship between decibels (which measure a physical property of sound) and loudness (a psychological quality) is complex. A rough rule of thumb is that perceived loudness doubles about every 10 decibels (Stevens, 1955). Very loud sounds can have negative effects on the quality of your hearing. Even brief exposure to sounds over 120 decibels can be painful and may cause damage to your auditory system (Henry, 1984). As shown in **Figure 4.34**, the weakest sound a person can hear depends on its frequency. The human ear is most sensitive to sounds at frequencies near 2000–4000 Hz. Thus, loudness ultimately depends on an interaction between amplitude and frequency.

People are also sensitive to variations in the purity of sounds. The purest sound is one that has only a single frequency of vibration, such as that produced by a tuning fork. Most everyday sounds are complex mixtures of many frequencies. The purity or complexity of a sound influences how *timbre* is perceived. To understand timbre, think of a note with precisely the same loudness and pitch played on a piano and then on a violin. The difference you perceive in the sounds is a difference in timbre.

Sensory Processing in the Ear

Like your eyes, your ears channel energy to the neural tissue that receives it. **Figure 4.35** shows that the human ear can be divided into three sections: the external ear, the middle ear, and the inner ear. Sound is conducted differently in each section. The external ear depends on the *vibration of air molecules*. The middle ear depends on the *vibration of movable bones*. And the inner ear depends on *waves in a fluid*, which are finally converted into a stream of neural signals sent to the brain (Moore, 2001).

The *external ear* consists mainly of the *pinna*, a sound-collecting cone. When you cup your hand behind your ear to try to hear better, you are augmenting that cone. Many animals have large external ears that they can aim directly toward a sound source. However, humans can adjust their aim only crudely, by turning their heads. Sound waves collected by the pinna are funneled along the auditory canal toward the *eardrum*, a taut membrane that vibrates in response.

Figure 4.33

Sound, the physical stimulus for hearing. (a) Like light, sound travels in waves—in this case, waves of air pressure. A smooth curve would represent a pure tone, such as that produced by a tuning fork. Most sounds, however, are complex. For example, the wave shown here is for middle C played on a piano. The sound wave for the same note played on a violin would have the same wavelength (or frequency) as this one, but the "wrinkles" in the wave would be different, corresponding to the differences in timbre between the two sounds. **(b)** The table shows the main relations between objective aspects of sound and subjective perceptions.

Physical properties of sound	Related perceptions
Amplitude	Loudness
Frequency	Pitch
Purity	Timbre

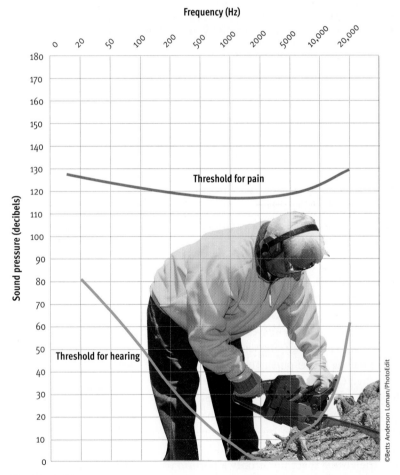

Figure 4.34

Sound pressure and auditory experience. The threshold for human hearing (graphed in green) is a function of both sound pressure (decibel level) and frequency. Human hearing is keenest for sounds at a frequency of about 2000–4000 Hz; at other frequencies, higher decibel levels are needed to produce sounds people can detect. On the other hand, the human threshold for pain (graphed in red) is almost purely a function of decibel level.

In the *middle ear,* the vibrations of the eardrum are transmitted inward by a mechanical chain made up of the three tiniest bones in your body (the hammer, anvil, and stirrup), known collectively as the *ossicles*. The ossicles form a three-stage lever system that converts relatively large movements with little force into smaller motions with greater force. The ossicles serve to amplify tiny changes in air pressure.

The *inner ear* consists largely of **the cochlea, a fluid-filled, coiled tunnel that contains the receptors for hearing.** The term *cochlea* comes from the Greek word for a spiral-shelled snail, which this chamber resembles (see **Figure 4.35**). Sound enters the cochlea through the *oval window,* which is vibrated by the ossicles. The ear's neural tissue, which is functionally similar to the retina in the eye, lies within the cochlea. This tissue sits on the basilar membrane that divides the cochlea into upper and lower chambers. **The *basilar membrane,* which runs the length of the spiraled cochlea, holds the auditory receptors, called hair cells.** Waves in the fluid of the inner ear stimulate the hair cells. Like the rods and cones in the eye, the hair cells convert this physical stimulation into neural impulses that are sent to the brain (Hudspeth, 2000). These signals are routed through the thalamus to the auditory cortex, which is located mostly in the temporal lobes of the brain.

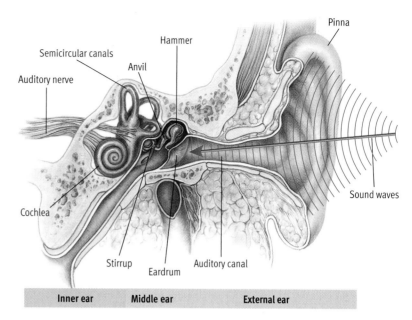

Figure 4.35

The human ear. Converting sound pressure to information processed by the nervous system involves a complex relay of stimuli. Waves of air pressure create vibrations in the eardrum, which in turn cause oscillations in the tiny bones in the inner ear (the hammer, anvil, and stirrup). As they are relayed from one bone to the next, the oscillations are magnified and then transformed into pressure waves moving through a liquid medium in the cochlea. These waves cause the basilar membrane to oscillate, stimulating the hair cells that are the actual auditory receptors (see **Figure 4.36**).

Auditory Perception: Theories of Hearing

Theories of hearing need to account for how sound waves are physiologically translated into perceptions of pitch, loudness, and timbre. To date, most of the theorizing about hearing has focused on the perception of pitch, which is reasonably well understood. Researchers' understanding of loudness and timbre perception is primitive by comparison. Hence, we'll limit our coverage to theories of pitch perception.

Place Theory

There have been two influential theories of pitch perception: *place theory* and *frequency theory.* You'll be able to follow the development of these theories more easily if you can imagine the spiraled cochlea unraveled, so that the basilar membrane becomes a long, thin sheet, lined with about 25,000 individual hair cells (see **Figure 4.36**). Long ago, Hermann von Helmholtz (1863) proposed that specific sound frequencies vibrate specific portions of the basilar membrane, producing distinct pitches, just as plucking specific strings on a harp produces sounds of varied pitch. *Thus, place theory holds that perception of pitch corresponds to the vibration of different portions, or places,*

Figure 4.36

The basilar membrane. This graphic shows how the cochlea might look if it were unwound and cut open to reveal the basilar membrane, which is covered with thousands of hair cells (the auditory receptors). Pressure waves in the fluid filling the cochlea cause oscillations to travel in waves down the basilar membrane, stimulating the hair cells to fire. Although the entire membrane vibrates, as predicted by frequency theory, the point along the membrane where the wave peaks depends on the frequency of the sound stimulus, as suggested by place theory.

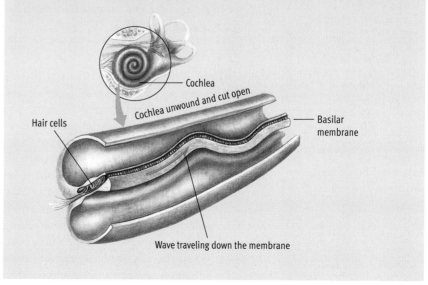

Web Link 4.7

The Cochlea: Graphic Tour of the Inner Ear's Machinery
The dynamics of hearing and the workings of the inner ear are graphically demonstrated at this site maintained by the Laboratory of Biophysics at the International School of Advanced Studies (Trieste, Italy). The collection of links to other laboratories studying hearing make this a fine jumping-off point.

along the basilar membrane. Place theory assumes that hair cells at various locations respond independently and that different sets of hair cells are vibrated by different sound frequencies. The brain then detects the frequency of a tone according to which area along the basilar membrane is most active.

Frequency Theory

Other theorists in the 19th century proposed an alternative theory of pitch perception, called frequency theory (Rutherford, 1886). *Frequency theory holds that perception of pitch corresponds to the rate, or frequency, at which the entire basilar membrane vibrates.* This theory views the basilar membrane as more like a drumhead than a harp. According to frequency theory, the whole membrane vibrates in response to sounds. However, a particular sound frequency, say 3000 Hz, causes the basilar membrane to vibrate at a corresponding rate of 3000 times per second. The brain detects the frequency of a tone by the rate at which the auditory nerve fibers fire.

Reconciling Place and Frequency Theories

The competition between these two theories is similar to the dispute between the trichromatic and op-ponent process theories of color vision. Like that argument, the debate between place and frequency theories generated roughly a century of research. Although both theories proved to have some flaws, *both turned out to be valid in part.*

Helmholtz's place theory was basically on the mark except for one detail. The hair cells along the basilar membrane are not independent. They vibrate together, as suggested by frequency theory. The actual pattern of vibration, described in Nobel prize–winning research by Georg von Békésy (1947), is a traveling wave that moves along the basilar membrane. Place theory is correct, however, in that the wave peaks at a particular place, depending on the frequency of the sound wave.

Although the original theories had to be revised, the current thinking is that pitch perception depends on both place and frequency coding of vibrations along the basilar membrane (Goldstein, 1996). Sounds under 1000 Hz appear to be translated into pitch through frequency coding. For sounds between 1000 and 5000 Hz, pitch perception seems to depend on a combination of frequency and place coding. Sounds over 5000 Hz seem to be handled through place coding only. Again we find that theories that were pitted against each other for decades are complementary rather than contradictory.

> Our Other Senses: Taste, Smell, and Touch

PREVIEW QUESTIONS

- Where are the receptors for taste and how many basic tastes are there?
- How do people vary in taste sensitivity?
- Where are the receptors for smell?
- How well do people perform when asked to name odors?
- How are tactile data routed to the brain?
- How are the two pathways for pain different?
- What is the gate-control theory of pain?

Psychologists have devoted most of their attention to the visual and auditory systems. Although less is known about other senses, taste, smell, and touch also play a critical role in people's experience of the world. Let's start by taking a brief look at what psychologists have learned about the *gustatory system— the sensory system for taste.*

Taste: The Gustatory System

True wine lovers go through an elaborate series of steps when they are served a good bottle of wine. Typically, they begin by drinking a little water to cleanse their palate. Then they sniff the cork from the wine bottle, swirl a small amount of the wine around in a glass, and sniff the odor emerging from the glass. Finally, they take a sip of the wine, rolling it around in their mouth for a short time before swallowing it. At last they are ready to indicate their approval or disapproval. Is all this activity really a meaningful way to put the wine to a sensitive test? Or is it just a harmless ritual passed on through tradition? You'll find out in this section.

The physical stimuli for the sense of taste are chemical substances that are soluble (dissolvable in water). The gustatory receptors are clusters of taste cells found in the *taste buds* that line the trenches around tiny bumps on the tongue. When these cells absorb chemicals dissolved in saliva, neural impulses are triggered that are routed through the thalamus to the cortex. Interestingly, taste cells have a short life, spanning only about 10 days, and they are constantly being replaced (Pfaffmann, 1978). New cells are born at the edge of the taste bud and migrate inward to die at the center.

It's generally (but not universally) agreed that there are four *primary tastes:* sweet, sour, bitter, and salty (Buck, 2000). Sensitivity to these tastes is distributed somewhat unevenly across the tongue. However, Linda Bartoshuk (1993b), a leading authority on taste research, emphasizes that these variations in sensitivity are quite small and very complicated (see

Comparing Vision and Hearing

Check your understanding of both vision and audition by comparing key aspects of sensation and perception in these senses. The dimensions of comparison are listed in the first column below. The second column lists the answers for the sense of vision. Fill in the answers for the sense of hearing in the third column. The answers can be found in Appendix A in the back of the book.

Dimension	Vision	Hearing
1. Stimulus	*Light waves*	
2. Elements of stimulus and related perceptions	*Wavelength/hue*	
	Amplitude/brightness	
	Purity/saturation	
3. Receptors	*Rods and cones*	
4. Location of receptors	*Retina*	
5. Main location of processing in brain	*Occipital lobe, Visual cortex*	
6. Spatial aspect of perception	*Depth perception*	

Figure 4.37). Although most taste cells respond to more than one of the primary tastes, they typically respond best to a specific taste (Di Lorenzo & Youngentob, 2003).

Some basic aspects of taste perception may be inborn, but taste preferences are largely learned and are heavily influenced by social processes (Rozin, 1990). Most parents are aware of this reality and intentionally try—with varied success—to mold their children's taste preferences early in life (Patrick et al., 2005). This strong social influence contributes greatly to the striking ethnic and cultural disparities found in taste preferences (Kittler & Sucher, 1998). Foods that are a source of disgust in Western cultures—such as worms, fish eyes, and blood—may be delicacies in other cultures. Indeed, Rozin (1990) asserts that feces may be the only universal source of taste-related

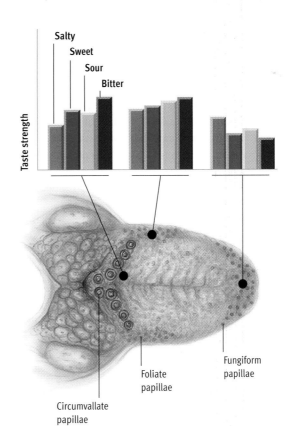

Are the elaborate wine-tasting rituals of wine lovers just a pretentious tradition, or do they make sense in light of what science has revealed about the gustatory system? Your text answers this question in this section.

© Michael Mahovlich/Masterfile

Figure 4.37

The tongue and taste. Taste buds are clustered around tiny bumps on the tongue called papillae. There are three types of papillae, which are distributed as shown here. The taste buds found in each type of papilla show slightly different sensitivities to the four basic tastes, as mapped out in the graph at the top. Thus, sensitivity to the primary tastes varies across the tongue, but these variations are small and all four primary tastes can be detected wherever there are taste receptors. (Data adapted from Bartoshuk, 1993a)

LINDA BARTOSHUK

"Good and bad are so intimately associated with taste and smell that we have special words for the experiences (e.g., repugnant, foul). The immediacy of the pleasure makes it seem absolute and thus inborn. This turns out to be true for taste but not for smell."

Courtesy of Linda Bartoshuk

Web Link 4.8

Seeing, Hearing, and Smelling the World
Hosted by the Howard Hughes Medical Institute, this site provides a graphically attractive review of what scientific research has discovered about human sensory systems, with suggestions about where research will be moving in the future.

disgust in humans. To a large degree, variations in taste preferences depend on what one has been exposed to (Capaldi & VandenBos, 1991). Exposure to various foods varies along ethnic lines because different cultures have different traditions in food preparation, different agricultural resources, different climates to work with, and so forth.

People vary considerably in their sensitivity to certain tastes. These differences depend in part on the density of taste buds on the tongue, which appears to be a matter of genetic inheritance (Bartoshuk, 1993a). People characterized as *nontasters,* as determined by their insensitivity to PTC (phenythiocarbamide), tend to have about one-quarter as many taste buds per square centimeter as people at the other end of the spectrum, who are called *supertasters* (Miller & Reedy, 1990). In the United States, roughly 25% of people are nontasters, another 25% are supertasters, and the remaining 50% fall between these extremes and are characterized as *medium tasters* (Di Lorenzo & Youngentob, 2003). Women are more likely to be supertasters than men (Bartoshuk, Duffy, & Miller, 1994).

Supertasters and nontasters respond similarly to many foods, but supertasters are much more sensitive to certain sweet and bitter substances. For example, supertasters react far more strongly to the chemical (capsaicin) in hot peppers (Tepper & Nurse, 1997). Supertasters also respond more intensely to many fatty substances (Bartoshuk, 2000). Some psychologists speculate that the gender gap in this trait may have evolutionary significance. Over the course of evolution, women have generally been more involved than men in feeding children. Increased reactivity to sweet and bitter tastes would have been adaptive in that it would have made women more sensitive to the relatively scarce high-caloric foods (which often taste sweet) needed for survival and to the toxic substances (which often taste bitter) that hunters and gatherers needed to avoid.

Scientists are currently making progress in pinning down the genetic bases for these individual differences in taste sensitivity (Bufe et al., 2005). Recent research suggests that specific genes have a dramatic impact on children's food preferences. For example, one study found that children who carry a particular bitter-sensitive gene are less fond of milk and water and more fond of carbonated beverages and high-sugar cereals than children who do not carry this gene (Menella, Pepino, & Reed, 2005). Unfortunately, this research implies that there may be a molecular basis for some youngsters' resistance to healthy foods. Although we have a long, long way to go, figuring out the genetic bases for children's food likes and dislikes could have profound implications for efforts to prevent obesity and other diet-influenced diseases.

When you eat, you are constantly mixing food and saliva and moving it about in your mouth, so the stimulus is constantly changing. However, if you place a flavored substance in a single spot on your tongue, the taste will fade until it vanishes (Krakauer & Dallenbach, 1937). This fading effect is an example of *sensory adaptation—***a gradual decline in sensitivity to prolonged stimulation.** Sensory adaptation is not unique to taste. This phenomenon occurs in other senses as well. In the taste system, sensory adaptation can leave aftereffects (Bartoshuk, 1988). For example, adaptation to a sour solution makes water taste sweet, whereas adaptation to a sweet solution makes water taste bitter.

So far, we've been discussing taste, but what we are really interested in is the *perception of flavor.* You probably won't be surprised to learn that odor contributes greatly to flavor (Lawless, 2001). The ability to identify flavors declines noticeably when odor cues are absent (Mozell et al., 1969). Although taste and smell are distinct sensory systems, they interact extensively. You might have noticed this interaction when you ate a favorite meal while enduring a severe head cold. The food probably tasted bland, because your stuffy nose impaired your sense of smell—and taste.

Now that we've explored the dynamics of taste, we can return to our question about the value of the wine-tasting ritual. This elaborate ritual is indeed an authentic way to put wine to a sensitive test. The aftereffects associated with sensory adaptation make it wise to cleanse one's palate before tasting the wine. Sniffing the cork, and the wine in the glass, is important because odor is a major determinant of flavor. Swirling the wine in the glass helps release the wine's odor inside the glass. Rolling the wine around in your mouth is especially critical because it distributes the wine over the full range of taste cells. It also forces the wine's odor up into the nasal passages. Thus, each action in this age-old ritual makes a meaningful contribution to the tasting.

Smell: The Olfactory System

The *olfactory system—***the sensory system for smell,** resembles the sense of taste in many ways. The physical stimuli are chemical substances—volatile ones that can evaporate and be carried in the air. These chemical stimuli are dissolved in fluid—specifically, the mucus in the nose. The receptors for smell are *olfactory cilia,* hairlike structures located in the upper portion of the nasal passages (Getchell & Getchell, 1991) (see **Figure 4.38**). They resemble taste cells in that they have a short life and are constantly being

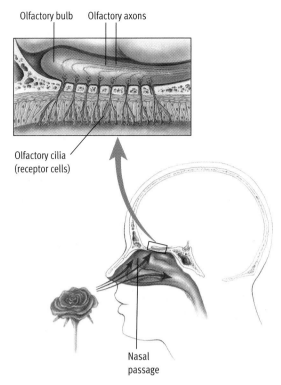

Figure 4.38

The olfactory system. Odor molecules travel through the nasal passages and stimulate olfactory cilia. An enlargement of these hairlike olfactory receptors is shown in the inset. The olfactory axons transmit neural impulses through the olfactory bulb to the brain.

replaced (Buck, 2000). The olfactory receptors have axons that synapse directly with cells in the olfactory bulb at the base of the brain. This arrangement is unique. *Smell is the only sensory system that is not routed through the thalamus before it projects onto the cortex.*

Odors cannot be classified as neatly as tastes, since efforts to identify primary odors have proven unsatisfactory (Doty, 1991). If primary odors exist, there must be a fairly large number of them. Most olfactory receptors respond to a wide range of odors (Doty, 2001). Hence, the perception of various odors probably depends on a great many types of receptors that are uniquely responsive to specific chemical structures (Bartoshuk & Beauchamp, 1994). Like the other senses, the sense of smell shows sensory adaptation. The perceived strength of an odor usually fades to less than half its original strength within about 4 minutes (Cain, 1988). For example, let's say you walk into your kitchen and find that the garbage has started to smell. If you stay in the kitchen without removing the garbage, the stench will soon start to fade.

Humans can distinguish among about 10,000 odors (Axel, 1995). However, when people are asked to identify the sources of specific odors (such as smoke or soap), their performance is rather mediocre (Engen, 1987). For some unknown reason, people have a hard time attaching names to odors (Cowart & Rawson, 2001). Gender differences have been found in the ability to identify odors, with females tending to be somewhat more accurate than males on odor recognition tasks (de Wijk, Schab, & Cain, 1995).

Touch: Sensory Systems in the Skin

The physical stimuli for touch consist of mechanical, thermal, and chemical energy that comes into contact with the skin. These stimuli can produce perceptions of tactile stimulation (the pressure of touch against the skin), warmth, cold, and pain. The human skin is saturated with at least six types of sensory receptors (Gardner, 1975). To some degree, these different types of receptors are specialized for different functions, such as the registration of pressure, heat, cold, and so forth. However, these distinctions are not as clear as researchers had originally thought (Sinclair, 1981).

If you've been to a mosquito-infested picnic lately, you'll appreciate the need to quickly know where tactile stimulation is coming from. The sense of touch is set up to meet this need for tactile localization with admirable efficiency. Cells in the nervous system that respond to touch are sensitive to specific patches of skin. These skin patches, which vary considerably in size, are the functional equivalents of *receptive fields* in vision. Like visual receptive fields, they often involve a center-surround arrangement, as shown in **Figure 4.39** (Kandel & Jessell, 1991). If a stimulus is applied continuously to a specific spot on the skin, the perception of pressure gradually fades. Thus, *sensory adaptation* occurs in the perception of touch as it does in other sensory systems.

The nerve fibers that carry incoming information about tactile stimulation are routed through the spinal cord to the brainstem. The tactile pathway then projects through the thalamus and onto the *somatosensory cortex* in the brain's parietal lobes. The entire body is sensitive to touch. However, in humans the bulk of the somatosensory cortex is devoted to processing signals coming from the fingers, lips, and tongue. Some cells in the somatosensory cortex function like the *feature detectors* discovered in vision (Gardner & Kandel, 2000). They respond to specific features of touch, such as a movement across the skin in a particular direction.

The receptors for pain are mostly free nerve endings in the skin. Pain messages are transmitted to the brain via two pathways that pass through different areas in the thalamus (Willis, 1985) (see **Figure 4.40**). One is a *fast pathway* that registers localized pain and relays it to the cortex in a fraction of a second. This

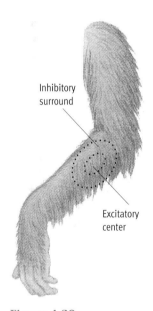

Figure 4.39

Receptive field for touch. A receptive field for touch is an area on the skin surface that, when stimulated, affects the firing of a cell that responds to pressure on the skin. Shown here is a center-surround receptive field for a cell in the thalamus of a monkey, originally described by Mountcastle and Powell (1959). Receptive fields for touch come in a variety of sizes and functional arrangements.

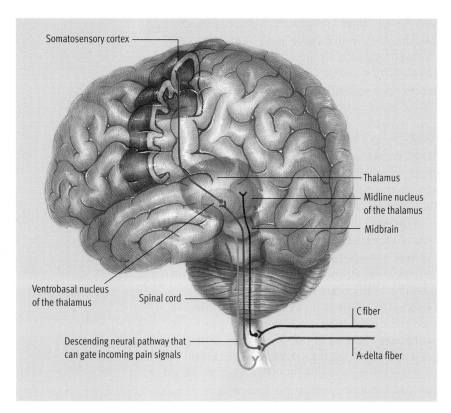

Somatosensory cortex

Thalamus

Midline nucleus
of the thalamus

Midbrain

Ventrobasal nucleus
of the thalamus

Spinal cord

C fiber

Descending neural pathway that
can gate incoming pain signals

A-delta fiber

Figure 4.40

Pathways for pain signals. Pain signals are sent inward from receptors to the brain along the two ascending pathways depicted here in red and black. The fast pathway, shown in red, and the slow pathway, shown in black, depend on different types of nerve fibers and are routed through different parts of the thalamus. The gate control mechanism hypothesized by Melzack and Wall (1965) apparently depends on signals in a descending pathway (shown in green) that originates in an area of the midbrain.

is the system that hits you with sharp pain when you first cut your finger. The second system uses a *slow pathway,* routed through the limbic system, that lags a second or two behind the fast system. This pathway (which also carries information about temperature) conveys the less localized, longer-lasting aching or burning pain that comes after the initial injury.

As with other perceptions, pain is not an automatic result of certain types of stimulation. Some people with severe injuries report little pain, whereas other people with much more modest injuries report agonizing pain (Coderre, Mogil, & Bushnell, 2003). The perception of pain can be influenced greatly by beliefs, expectations, personality, mood, and other

factors involving higher mental processes (Turk & Okifuji, 2003). The subjective nature of pain is illustrated by placebo effects. As we saw in Chapter 2, many people suffering from pain report relief when given a placebo—such as an inert "sugar pill" that is presented to them as if it were a painkilling drug (Stewart-Williams, 2004; Vase, Riley, & Price, 2002).

Cultural variations in the experience of pain provide further evidence for the subjective quality of pain. Melzack and Wall (1982) have described a number of anecdotal examples of remarkable pain tolerance in non-Western cultures. Moreover, systematic empirical comparisons have found ethnic and cultural differences in the experience of chronic pain (Bates, Edwards, & Anderson, 1993) and the pain associated with childbirth (Jordan, 1983). It appears that culture doesn't affect the process of pain perception so much as the willingness to tolerate certain types of pain (Zatzick & Dimsdale, 1990).

As you can see, then, tissue damage that sends pain impulses on their way to the brain doesn't necessarily result in the experience of pain. Cognitive and emotional processes that unfold in higher brain centers can sometimes block pain signals coming from peripheral receptors.

How are incoming pain signals blocked? In an influential effort to answer this question, Ronald Melzack and Patrick Wall (1965) devised the gate-control theory of pain. *Gate-control theory holds that incoming pain sensations must pass through a "gate" in the spinal cord that can be closed, thus blocking ascending pain signals.* The gate in this model is not an anatomical structure but a pattern of neural activity that inhibits incoming pain signals. Melzack and Wall suggested that this imaginary gate can be closed by signals from peripheral receptors or by signals from the brain. They theorized that the latter mechanism can help explain how factors such as attention and expectations can shut off pain signals. As a whole, research

concept **check** 4.5

Comparing Taste, Smell, and Touch

Check your understanding of taste, smell, and touch by comparing these sensory systems on the dimensions listed in the first column below. A few answers are supplied; see whether you can fill in the rest. The answers can be found in Appendix A.

Dimension	Taste	Smell	Touch
1. Stimulus	_____	*Volatile chemicals in the air*	_____
2. Receptors	_____	_____	*Many (at least six) types*
3. Location of receptors	_____	*Upper area of nasal passage*	_____
4. Basic elements of perception	*Sweet, sour, salty, bitter*	_____	_____

suggests that the concept of a gating mechanism for pain has merit (Craig & Rollman, 1999). However, relatively little support has been found for the neural circuitry originally hypothesized by Melzack and Wall. Other neural mechanisms, discovered after gate-control theory was proposed, appear to be responsible for blocking the perception of pain.

One of these discoveries was the identification of endorphins. As discussed in Chapter 3, *endorphins* are the body's own natural morphinelike painkillers, which are widely distributed in the central nervous system. The other discovery involved the identification of a descending neural pathway that mediates the suppression of pain (Basbaum & Jessell, 2000). This pathway appears to originate in an area of the midbrain (see **Figure 4.40**). Neural activity in this pathway is probably initiated by endorphins. The circuits in this pathway synapse in the spinal cord, where they inhibit the activity of neurons that would normally transmit incoming pain impulses to the brain. The painkilling effects of morphine appear to be at least partly attributable to activity in this descending pathway, as cutting the fibers in this pathway reduces the analgesic effects of morphine (Jessell & Kelly, 1991). Clearly, this pathway plays a central role in gating incoming pain signals.

Our understanding of the experience of pain continues to evolve. The newest discovery is that certain types of *glial cells* may contribute to the modulation of pain. As noted in Chapter 3, it has only been recently that neuroscientists have realized that glial cells contribute to signal transmission in the nervous system (Fields, 2004). Two types of glia in the spinal cord appear to play an important role in *chronic pain* (Watkins & Maier, 2002). These glia are activated by immune system responses to infection or by signals from neurons in pain pathways. Once activated, these glial cells appear to "egg on neurons in the pain pathway," thus amplifying the experience of chronic pain (Watkins & Maier, 2003). The discovery that glia play a role in the human pain system may eventually open up new avenues for treating chronic pain.

> Reflecting on the Chapter's Themes

In this chapter, three of our unifying themes were highlighted: (1) psychology is theoretically diverse, (2) people's experience of the world is highly subjective, and (3) our behavior is shaped by our cultural heritage. Let's discuss the value of theoretical diversity first.

Contradictory theories about behavior can be disconcerting and frustrating for theorists, researchers, teachers, and students alike. Yet this chapter provides two dramatic demonstrations of how theoretical diversity can lead to progress in the long run. For decades, the trichromatic and opponent process theories of color vision and the place and frequency theories of pitch perception were viewed as fundamentally incompatible. These competing theories generated and guided the research that now provides a fairly solid understanding of how people perceive color and pitch. As you know, in each case the evidence eventually revealed that the opposing theories were not really incompatible. Both were needed to fully explain the sensory processes that each sought to explain individually. If it hadn't been for these theoretical debates, our current understanding of color vision and pitch perception might be far more primitive.

This chapter should have also enhanced your appreciation of why human experience of the world is highly subjective. As ambiguous figures and visual illusions clearly show, there is no one-to-one correspondence between sensory input and perceived experience of the world. Perception is an active process in which people organize and interpret the information received by the senses. Small wonder, then, that people often perceive the same event in very different ways. Thus, individuals' experience of the world is subjective because the process of perception is inherently subjective.

Finally, this chapter provided numerous examples of how cultural factors can shape behavior—in an area of research where one might expect to find little cultural influence. Most people are not surprised to learn that there are cultural differences in attitudes, values, social behavior, and development. But perception is widely viewed as a basic, universal process that should be invariant across cultures. In most respects it is, as the similarities among cultural groups in perception far outweigh the differences. Nonetheless, we saw cultural variations in depth perception, susceptibility to illusions, taste preferences, and pain tolerance. Thus, even a fundamental, heavily physiological process such as perception can be modified to some degree by one's cultural background.

The following Personal Application highlights the subjectivity of perception once again. It focuses on how painters have learned to use the principles of visual perception to achieve a variety of artistic goals.

 Theoretical Diversity

 Subjectivity of Experience

 Cultural Heritage

Appreciating Art and Illusion

Answer the following multiple-choice question: Artistic works such as paintings:

____ 1 render an accurate picture of reality
____ 2 create an illusion of reality
____ 3 provide an interpretation of reality
____ 4 make us think about the nature of reality
____ 5 do all of the above.

The answer to this question is (5), "all of the above." Historically, artists have had many and varied purposes, including each of those listed in the question (Goldstein, 2001). To realize their goals, artists have had to use a number of principles of perception—sometimes quite deliberately, and sometimes not. Here we'll use the example of painting to explore the role of perceptual principles in art and illusion.

The goal of most early painters was to produce a believable picture of reality. This goal immediately created a problem familiar to most of us who have attempted to draw realistic pictures: The real world is three-dimensional, but a canvas or a sheet of paper is flat. Paradoxically, then, painters who set out to re-create reality had to do so by creating an *illusion* of three-dimensional reality.

Prior to the Renaissance, these efforts to create a convincing illusion of reality were awkward by modern standards. Why? Because artists did not understand how to use depth cues. This fact is apparent in **Figure 4.41**, a religious scene painted around 1300. The painting clearly lacks a sense of depth. The people seem paper-thin. They have no real position in space.

Although earlier artists made *some* use of depth cues, Renaissance artists manipulated the full range of pictorial depth cues and really harnessed the crucial cue of linear perspective (Solso, 1994). **Figure 4.42** dramatizes the resulting transition in art. This scene, painted by Italian Renaissance artists Gentile and Giovanni Bellini, seems much more realistic and lifelike than the painting in **Figure 4.41** because it uses a number of

pictorial depth cues. Notice how the buildings on the sides converge to make use of linear perspective. Additionally, distant objects are smaller than nearby ones, an application of relative size. This painting also uses height in plane, as well as interposition. By taking advantage of pictorial depth cues, an artist can enhance a painting's illusion of reality.

In the centuries since the Renaissance, painters have adopted a number of viewpoints about the portrayal of reality. For instance, the French Impressionists of the 19th century did not want to re-create the photographic "reality" of a scene. They set out to interpret a viewer's fleeting perception or impression of reality. To accomplish this end, they worked with color in unprecedented ways.

Consider, for instance, the work of Georges Seurat, a French artist who used a technique

Scala/Art Resource, New York

Figure 4.41

Master of the Arrest of Christ (detail, central part) by S. Francesco, Assisi, Italy (circa 1300). Notice how the absence of depth cues makes the painting seem flat and unrealistic.

Figure 4.42

A painting by the Italian Renaissance artists Gentile and Giovanni Bellini (circa 1480). In this painting a number of depth cues—including linear perspective, relative size, height in plane, and interposition—enhance the illusion of three-dimensional reality.

Scala/Art Resource, New York

Figure 4.43

Georges Seurat's *Sunday Afternoon on the Island of La Grande Jatte* (without artist's border) (1884–1886). Seurat used thousands of tiny dots of color and the principles of color mixing (see detail); the eye and brain combine the points into the colors the viewer actually sees.

Georges Seurat, French, 1859–1891, *Sunday Afternoon on the Island of La Grande Jatte* (and detail), oil on canvas, 1884–1886, 207.6 X 308 cm, Helen Birch Bartlett Memorial Collection, 1926.224, © 1990 The Art Institute of Chicago. All rights reserved.

called pointillism. Seurat carefully studied what scientists knew about the composition of color in the 1880s, then applied this knowledge in a calculated, laboratory-like manner. Indeed, critics in his era dubbed him the "little chemist." Seurat constructed his paintings out of tiny dots of pure, intense colors. He used additive color mixing, a departure from the norm in painting, which usually depends on subtractive mixing of pigments. A famous result of Seurat's "scientific" approach to painting was *Sunday Afternoon on the Island of La Grande Jatte* (see **Figure 4.43**). As the work of Seurat illustrates, modernist painters were moving away from attempts to recreate the world as it is literally seen.

If 19th-century painters liberated color, their successors at the turn of the 20th century liberated form. This was particularly true of the Cubists. Cubism was begun in 1909 by Pablo Picasso, a Spanish artist who went on to experiment with other styles in his prolific career. The Cubists didn't try to portray reality so much as to reassemble it. They attempted to reduce everything to combinations of geometric forms (lines, circles, triangles, rectangles, and such) laid out in a flat space, lacking depth. In a sense, they applied the theory of feature analysis to canvas, as they built their figures out of simple features.

The resulting paintings were decidedly unrealistic, but the painters would leave realistic fragments that provided clues about the subject. Picasso liked to challenge his viewers to decipher the subject of his paintings. Take a look at the painting in **Figure 4.44** and see whether you can figure out what Picasso was portraying.

Figure 4.44

Violin and Grapes by Pablo Picasso (1912). This painting makes use of Gestalt principles of perceptual organization.

Pablo Picasso, *Violin and Grapes, Céret and Sorgues* (spring-early fall 1912), oil on canvas, 20 × 24 inches (50.6 × 61 cm). Collection, The Museum of Modern Art, New York, Mrs. David M. Levy Bequest. © The Museum of Modern Art. Licensed by Scala/Art Resource, NY. © 2006 Estate of Pablo Picasso / Artists Rights Society (ARS), New York.

The work in **Figure 4.44** is titled *Violin and Grapes.* Note how Gestalt principles of perceptual organization are at work to create these forms. Proximity and similarity serve to bring the grapes together in the bottom right corner. Closure accounts for your being able to see the essence of the violin.

The Surrealists toyed with reality in a different way. Influenced by Sigmund Freud's writings on the unconscious, the Surrealists explored the world of dreams and fantasy. Specific elements in their paintings are often depicted realistically, but the strange combination of elements yields a disconcerting irrationality reminiscent of dreams. A prominent example of this style is Salvador Dali's *Slave Market with the Disappearing Bust of Voltaire,* shown in **Figure 4.45**. Notice the reversible figure near the center of the painting. The "bust of Voltaire" is made up of human figures in the distance, standing in front of an arch. Dali often used reversible figures to enhance the ambiguity of his bizarre visions.

Perhaps no one has been more creative in manipulating perceptual ambiguity than M. C. Escher, a modern Dutch artist. Escher closely followed the work of the Gestalt psychologists, and he readily acknowledged his debt to psychology as a source of inspiration (Teuber, 1974). *Waterfall,* a 1961 lithograph by Escher, is an impossible figure that appears to defy the law of gravity (see **Figure 4.46**). The puzzling problem here is that a level channel of water terminates in a waterfall that "falls" into the same channel two levels "below." This drawing is made up of two of the impossible triangles shown earlier, in **Figure 4.32**. In case you need help seeing them, the waterfall itself forms one side of each triangle.

The Necker cube, a reversible figure mentioned earlier in the chapter, was the inspiration for Escher's 1958 lithograph *Belvedere,* shown in **Figure 4.47**. You have to look carefully to realize that this is another impossible figure. Note that the top story runs at a right angle from the first story. Note also how the pillars are twisted around. The

pillars that start on one side of the building end up supporting the second story on the other side! Escher's debt to the Necker cube is manifested in several places. Notice, for instance, the drawing of a Necker cube on the floor next to the seated boy (on the lower left).

Like Escher, Hungarian artist Victor Vasarely, who pioneered Kinetic Art, challenged viewers to think about the process of perception. His paintings are based on illusions, as squares seem to advance and recede, or spheres seem to inflate and deflate. For example, note how Vasareley used the depth cues of texture gradient and linear perspective to convey the look of great

depth in his painting *Tukoer-Ter-Ur,* shown in **Figure 4.48**.

While Escher and Vasarely challenged viewers to think about perception, Belgian artist René Magritte challenged people to think about the conventions of painting. Many of his works depict paintings on an easel, with the "real" scene continuing unbroken at the edges. The painting in **Figure 4.49** is such a picture within a picture. Ultimately, Magritte's painting blurs the line between the real world and the illusory world created by the artist, suggesting that there is no line—that everything is an illusion. In this way, Magritte "framed" the ageless, unanswerable question: What is reality?

Figure 4.45
Salvador Dali's ***Slave Market with the Disappearing Bust of Voltaire*** (1940). This painting playfully includes a reversible figure (in the center of the painting, two nuns form the bust of Voltaire, a philosopher known for his stringent criticisms of the Catholic church).

Salvador Dali, *The Slave Market with the Disappearing Bust of Voltaire,* (1940), oil on canvas, 18-1/4 × 25-3/8 inches. Collection of The Salvador Dali Museum, Inc. © 2006 Kingdom of Spain, Gala-Salvador Dali Foundation/Artists Rights Society (ARS), New York.

Figure 4.46

Escher's lithograph *Waterfall* (1961). Escher's use of depth cues and impossible triangles deceives the brain into seeing water flow uphill.

M. C. Escher's *Waterval* 1961. © 2006 The M.C. Escher Company-Holland. All rights reserved. www.mcescher.com

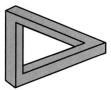

Figure 4.47

Escher's *Belvedere* (1958). This lithograph depicts an impossible figure inspired by the Necker cube. The cube appears in the architecture of the building, in the model held by the boy on the bench, and in the drawing lying at his feet.

M.C. Escher's *Belvedere*, 1958. © 2006 The M.C. Escher Company-Holland. All rights reserved. www.mcescher.com

Figure 4.49

René Magritte's *Les Promenades d'Euclide* (1955). Notice how the pair of nearly identical triangles look quite different in different contexts.

Magritte, René, *Les Promenades d'Euclide,* The Minneapolis Institute of Arts, The William Hood Dunwoody Fund. Copyright © 2006 Charly Herscovic, Brussels/Artists Rights Society (ARS) New York.

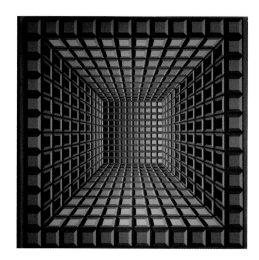

Figure 4.48

Victor Vasarely's *Tukoer-Ter-Ur* (1989). In this painting, Vasarely manipulates texture gradients and linear perspective to create a remarkable illusion of depth.

Vasarely, Victor (1908–1997) *Tukoer-Ter-Ur,* 1989. Acrylic on canvas, 220 × 220 cm. Private Collection, Monaco. © Erich Lessing / Art Resource, NY. Copyright © 2006 Artists Rights Society (ARS), New York/ADAGP, Paris.

Recognizing Contrast Effects: It's All Relative

You're sitting at home one night, when the phone rings. It's Simone, an acquaintance from school who needs help with a recreational program for youngsters that she runs for the local park district. She tries to persuade you to volunteer four hours of your time every Friday night throughout the school year to supervise the volleyball program. The thought of giving up your Friday nights and adding this sizable obligation to your already busy schedule makes you cringe with horror. You politely explain to Simone that you can't possibly afford to give up that much time and you won't be able to help her. She accepts your rebuff graciously, but the next night she calls again. This time she wants to know whether you would be willing to supervise volleyball every third Friday. You still feel like it's a big obligation that you really don't want to take on, but the new request seems much more reasonable than the original one. So, with a sigh of resignation, you agree to Simone's request.

What's wrong with this picture? Well, there's nothing wrong with volunteering your time for a good cause, but you just succumbed to a social influence strategy called the *door-in-the face technique*. The ***door-in-the-face technique* involves making a large request that is likely to be turned down as a way to increase the chances that people will agree to a smaller request later** (see Figure 4.50). The name for this strategy is derived from the expectation that the initial request will be quickly rejected (hence, the door is slammed in the salesperson's face). Although they may not be familiar with the strategy's name, many people use this manipulative tactic. For example, a husband who wants to coax his frugal wife into agreeing to buy a $30,000 sports car might begin by proposing that they purchase a $50,000 sports car. By the time the wife talks her husband out of the $50,000 car, the $30,000 price tag may look quite reasonable to her—which is what the husband wanted all along.

Research has demonstrated that the door-in-the-face technique is a highly effective persuasive strategy (Cialdini, 2001). One of the reasons it works so well is that it depends on a simple and pervasive perceptual principle: When it comes to perceptual experience, *everything is relative*. This relativity means that people are easily swayed by *contrast effects*. For example, lighting a match or a small candle in a dark room will produce a burst of light that seems quite bright, but if you light the same match or candle in a well-lit room, you may not even detect the additional illumination. The relativity of perception is apparent in the painting by Josef Albers shown in Figure 4.51. The two Xs are exactly the same color, but the X in the top half looks yellow, whereas the X in the bottom half looks brown. These varied perceptions occur because of contrast effects—the two X's are contrasted against different background colors.

The same principles of relativity and contrast that operate when people make judgments about the intensity or color of visual stimuli also affect the way they make judgments in a wide variety of areas. For example, a 6'3" basketball player, who is really quite tall, can look downright small when surrounded by teammates who are all over 6'8". And a salary of $30,000 per year for your first full-time job may seem like a princely sum, until a close friend gets an offer of $55,000 a year. The assertion that everything is relative raises the issue of *relative to what*? ***Comparitors* are people, objects, events, and other standards that are used as a baseline for comparison in making judgments.** It is fairly easy to manipulate many types of judgments by selecting *extreme* comparitors that may be unrepresentative.

The influence of extreme comparitors was demonstrated in a couple of interesting

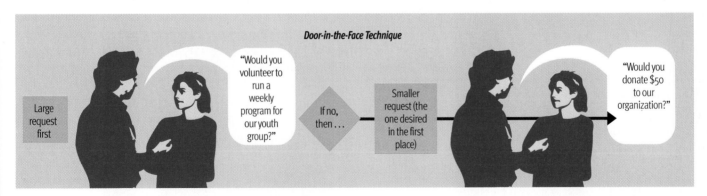

Door-in-the-Face Technique

Large request first

"Would you volunteer to run a weekly program for our youth group?"

If no, then . . .

Smaller request (the one desired in the first place)

"Would you donate $50 to our organization?"

Figure 4.50
The door-in-the-face technique. The door-in-the-face technique is a frequently used compliance strategy in which you begin with a large request and work down to the smaller request you are really after. It depends in part on contrast effects.

Figure 4.51

Contrast effects in visual perception. This composition by Joseph Albers shows how one color can be perceived differently when contrasted against different backgrounds. The top X looks yellow and the bottom X looks brown, but they're really the same color.

Source: Albers, Joseph. *Interaction of Color.* Copyright © 1963 and reprinted by permission of the publisher, Yale University Press.

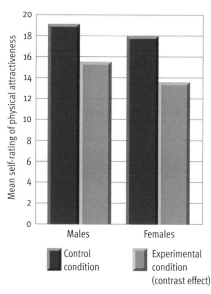

Figure 4.52

Contrast effects in judgments of physical attractiveness. Participants rated their own physical attractiveness under two conditions. In the experimental condition, the ratings occurred after subjects were exposed to a series of photos depicting very attractive models. The resulting contrast effects led to lower self-ratings in this condition. (Data based on Thornton & Moore, 1993

studies of judgments of physical attractiveness. In one study, undergraduate males were asked to rate the attractiveness of an average-looking female (who was described as a potential date for another male in the dorm) presented in a photo either just before or just after the participants watched a TV show dominated by strikingly beautiful women (Kenrick & Gutierres, 1980). The female was viewed as less attractive when the ratings were obtained just after the men had seen gorgeous women on TV as opposed to when they hadn't. In another investigation by Thornton and Moore (1993), both male and female participants rated *themselves* as less attractive after being exposed to many pictures of extremely attractive models (see **Figure 4.52**). Thus, contrast effects can influence important social judgments that are likely to affect how people feel about themselves and others.

Anyone who understands how easily judgments can be manipulated by a careful choice of comparitors could influence your thinking. For example, a politician who is

caught in some illegal or immoral act could sway public opinion by bringing to mind (perhaps subtly) the fact that many other politicians have committed acts that were much worse. When considered against a backdrop of more extreme comparitors, the politician's transgression will probably seem less offensive. A defense attorney could use a similar strategy in an attempt to obtain a lighter sentence for a client by comparing the client's offense to much more serious crimes. And a realtor who wants to sell you an expensive house that will require huge mortgage payments will be quick to men-

tion other homeowners who have taken on even larger mortgages.

In summary, critical thinking is facilitated by conscious awareness of the way comparitors can influence and perhaps distort a wide range of judgments. In particular, it pays to be vigilant about the possibility that others may manipulate contrast effects in their persuasive efforts. One way to reduce the influence of contrast effects is to consciously consider comparitors that are both worse and better than the event you are judging, as a way of balancing the effects of the two extremes.

Table 4.1   Critical Thinking Skills Discussed in This Application

Skill	Description
Understanding how contrast effects can influence judgments and decisions	The critical thinker appreciates how striking contrasts can be manipulated to influence many types of judgments.
Recognizing when extreme comparitors are being used	The critical thinker is on the lookout for extreme comparitors that distort judgments.

Key Ideas

Our Sense of Sight: The Visual System

● Light varies in terms of wavelength, amplitude, and purity. Light enters the eye through the cornea and pupil and is focused on the retina by the lens. Rods and cones are the visual receptors found in the retina. Cones play a key role in daylight vision and color perception, while rods are critical to night vision and peripheral vision. Dark adaptation and light adaptation both involve changes in the retina's sensitivity to light.

● The retina transforms light into neural impulses that are sent to the brain via the optic nerve. Receptive fields are areas in the retina that affect the firing of visual cells. They vary in shape and size, but center-surround arrangements are common.

● Two visual pathways send signals through the thalamus to the primary visual cortex. From there, visual signals are shuttled along pathways that have been characterized as the *what* and *where* pathways. The visual cortex contains cells that appear to function as feature detectors.

● Perceptions of color (hue) are primarily a function of light wavelength, while amplitude affects brightness and purity affects saturation. Perceptions of colors depend on processes that resemble additive color mixing. The accumulated evidence suggests that both the trichromatic and opponent process theories of color perception are partly correct.

● According to feature analysis theories, people detect specific elements in stimuli and build them into recognizable forms. Gestalt psychology emphasized that the whole may be greater than the sum of its parts (features). Other approaches to form perception emphasize that people develop perceptual hypotheses about the stimuli that could be responsible for sensory inputs. These perceptual hypotheses are guided by experience-based expectations.

● Depth perception depends primarily on monocular cues such as linear perspective, texture gradient, interposition, relative size, height in plane, and light and shadow. Binocular cues such as retinal disparity can also contribute to depth perception. Cultures may vary in their use of pictorial depth cues.

● Perceptual constancies in vision help viewers deal with the ever-shifting nature of proximal stimuli. Visual illusions demonstrate that perceptual hypotheses can be inaccurate and that perceptions are not simple reflections of objective reality. Researchers have found some interesting cultural variations in the susceptibility to certain illusions.

Our Sense of Hearing: The Auditory System

● Sound varies in terms of wavelength (frequency), amplitude, and purity. These properties affect mainly perceptions of pitch, loudness, and timbre, respectively.

● Sound is transmitted through the external ear via air conduction to the middle ear. In the inner ear, fluid conduction vibrates hair cells along the basilar membrane in the cochlea. These hair cells are the receptors for hearing. Modern evidence suggests that the place and frequency theories of pitch perception are complementary rather than incompatible.

Our Other Senses: Taste, Smell, and Touch

● The taste buds are sensitive to four basic tastes: sweet, sour, bitter, and salty. Sensitivity to these tastes is distributed somewhat unevenly across the tongue, but the variations in sensitivity are quite small. Taste preferences are shaped by experience and culture. Supertasters are more sensitive to bitter and sweet tastes than other people are.

● Like taste, smell is a chemical sense. Chemical stimuli activate olfactory receptors lining the nasal passages. Most of these receptors respond to more than one odor.

● Sensory receptors in the skin respond to pressure, temperature, and pain. Pain signals are sent to the brain along two pathways that are characterized as fast and slow. The perception of pain is highly subjective. Gate-control theory holds that incoming pain signals can be blocked in the spinal cord. Endorphins and a descending neural pathway appear responsible for the suppression of pain.

Reflecting on the Chapter's Themes

● This chapter underscored three of our unifying themes: the value of theoretical diversity, the subjective nature of experience, and the importance of one's cultural heritage.

PERSONAL APPLICATION • Appreciating Art and Illusion

● The principles of visual perception are often applied to artistic endeavors. Painters routinely use pictorial depth cues to make their scenes more lifelike. Color mixing, feature analysis, Gestalt principles, reversible figures, and impossible figures have also been used in influential paintings.

CRITICAL THINKING APPLICATION • Recognizing Contrast Effects: It's All Relative

● The study of perception often highlights the relativity of experience. This relativity can be manipulated by carefully arranging for contrast effects. Critical thinking is enhanced by an awareness of how comparitors can distort many types of judgments.

Key Terms

Additive color mixing (p. 106)
Afterimage (p. 107)
Basilar membrane (p. 121)
Binocular depth cues (p. 114)
Bottom-up processing (p. 110)
Cochlea (p. 121)
Color blindness (p. 107)
Comparitors (p. 132)
Complementary colors (p. 107)
Cones (p. 100)
Dark adaptation (p. 101)
Depth perception (p. 114)
Door-in-the-face technique (p. 132)
Farsightedness (p. 99)
Feature analysis (p. 110)
Feature detectors (p. 105)
Fovea (p. 100)
Gustatory system (p. 122)
Impossible figures (p. 118)
Lens (p. 99)
Light adaptation (p. 101)
Monocular depth cues (p. 115)
Nearsightedness (p. 99)
Olfactory system (p. 124)
Perception (p. 97)
Perceptual constancy (p. 117)
Perceptual set (p. 109)
Phi phenomenon (p. 110)
Pictorial depth cues (p. 115)
Pupil (p. 100)
Receptive field of a visual cell (p. 102)
Retina (p. 100)
Retinal disparity (pp. 114–115)
Reversible figure (p. 109)
Rods (p. 100)
Sensation (p. 97)
Sensory adaptation (p. 124)
Subtractive color mixing (p. 106)
Top-down processing (p. 110)
Visual illusion (p. 117)

Key People

Linda Bartoshuk (pp. 122, 124)
Hermann von Helmholtz (pp. 106, 121)
David Hubel and Torsten Wiesel (p. 104)
Ronald Melzack and Patrick Wall (p. 126)
Max Wertheimer (pp. 110–111)

1. The term used to refer to the stimulation of the sense organs is:
A. sensation.
B. perception.
C. transduction.
D. adaptation.

2. Perception of the brightness of a color is affected mainly by:
A. the wavelength of light waves.
B. the amplitude of light waves.
C. the purity of light waves.
D. the saturation of light waves.

3. The structure that controls the amount of light passing into the rear chamber of the eye is the:
A. lens.
B. pupil.
C. ciliary muscle.
D. vitreous humor.

4. In farsightedness:
A. close objects are seen clearly but distant objects appear blurry.
B. the focus of light from close objects falls behind the retina.
C. the focus of light from distant objects falls a little short of the retina.
D. both A and B occur.
E. both A and C occur.

5. The collection of rod and cone receptors that funnel signals to a particular visual cell in the retina make up that cell's:
A. blind spot.
B. optic disk.
C. opponent process field.
D. receptive field.

6. The primary visual cortex is located in the:
A. occipital lobe.
B. temporal lobe.
C. parietal lobe.
D. frontal lobe.

7. Which theory would predict that the American flag would have a green, black, and yellow afterimage?
A. Subtractive color mixing
B. Opponent process theory
C. Additive color mixing
D. Trichromatic theory

8. A readiness to perceive a stimulus in a particular way is referred to as (a):
A. Gestalt.
B. feature analysis.
C. perceptual set.
D. congruence.

9. In a painting, train tracks may look as if they go off into the distance because the artist draws the tracks as converging lines, a monocular cue to depth known as:
A. interposition.
B. texture gradient.
C. relative size.
D. linear perspective.

10. The fact that cultural groups with little exposure to carpentered buildings are less susceptible to the Müller-Lyer illusion suggests that:
A. not all cultures test perceptual hypotheses.
B. people in technologically advanced cultures are more gullible.
C. visual illusions can be experienced only by cultures that have been exposed to the concept of visual illusions.
D. perceptual inferences can be shaped by experience.

11. Perception of pitch can best be explained by:
A. place theory.
B. frequency theory.
C. both place theory and frequency theory.
D. neither theory.

12. In what way(s) is the sense of taste like the sense of smell?
A. There are four primary stimulus groups for both senses.
B. Both systems are routed through the thalamus on the way to the cortex.
C. The physical stimuli for both senses are chemical substances dissolved in fluid.
D. All of the above.
E. None of the above.

13. The fact that theories originally seen as being incompatible, such as the trichromatic and opponent process theories of color vision, are now seen as both being necessary to explain sensory processes illustrates:
A. that psychology evolves in a sociohistorical context.
B. the subjectivity of experience.
C. the value of psychology's theoretical diversity.
D. the nature-nurture controversy.

14. Which school of painting applied the theory of feature analysis to canvas by building figures out of simple features?
A. Pointillism
B. Impressionism
C. Surrealism
D. Cubism

15. In the study by Kenrick and Gutierres (1980), exposing male subjects to a TV show dominated by extremely beautiful women:
A. had no effect on their ratings of the attractiveness of a prospective date.
B. increased their ratings of the attractiveness of a prospective date.
C. decreased their ratings of the attractiveness of a prospective date.
D. decreased their ratings of their own attractiveness.

Answers
1 A p. 97
2 B p. 98
3 B p. 100
4 B pp. 99–100
5 D p. 102
6 A pp. 103–104
7 B p. 107
8 C p. 109
9 D p. 115
10 D pp. 118–119
11 C p. 122
12 C pp. 122–124
13 C p. 127
14 D p. 129
15 C p. 133

PsykTrek

Go to the PsykTrek website or CD-ROM for further study of the concepts in this chapter. Both online and on the CD-ROM, PsykTrek includes dozens of learning modules with videos, animations, and quizzes, as well as simulations of psychological phenomena and a multimedia glossary that includes word pronunciations.

ThomsonNOW
www.thomsonedu.com/ThomsonNOW
Go to this site for the link to ThomsonNOW, your one-stop study shop. Take a Pre-Test for this chapter, and ThomsonNOW will generate a Personalized Study Plan based on your test results. The Study Plan will identify the topics you need to review and direct you to online resources to help you master those topics. You can then take a Post-Test to help you determine the concepts you have mastered and what you still need to work on.

Companion Website
www.thomsonedu.com/psychology/weiten
Go to this site to find online resources directly linked to your book, including a glossary, flash cards, drag-and-drop exercises, quizzes, and more!

CHAPTER 5

Variations in Consciousness

© Nevada Wier/Corbis

Nathaniel Kleitman and Eugene Aserinsky couldn't believe their eyes—or their subject's eyes, either. It was the spring of 1952, and Kleitman, a physiologist and prominent sleep researcher, was investigating the slow, rolling eye movements displayed by subjects at the onset of sleep. Kleitman had begun to wonder whether these slow eye movements would show up during later phases of sleep. The trouble was that watching a participant's closed eyelids all night long was a surefire way to put the *researcher* to sleep. Cleverly, Kleitman and Aserinsky, a graduate student, came up with a better way to document eye movements. They hooked subjects up to an apparatus that was connected to electrodes pasted near the eyes. The electrodes picked up the small electrical signals generated by moving eyeballs. In turn, these signals moved a pen on a chart recorder, much like an electroencephalograph (EEG) traces brain waves (see Chapter 3). The result was an objective record of participants' eye movements during sleep that could be studied at leisure (Dement, 1992).

One night, while one of their subjects was asleep, the researchers were astonished to see a tracing in the recording that suggested a different, much more rapid eye movement. This result was so unexpected that they suspected the recording device was on the blink. "It was a rickety old thing, anyway," a technician in Kleitman's lab recalled (Coren, 1996, p. 21). Only when they decided to walk in and personally observe sleeping subjects were they convinced that the eye movements were real. The subjects were deeply asleep, yet the bulges in their closed eyelids showed that their eyeballs were moving laterally in sharp jerks, first in one direction and then in the other. It was almost as if the sleeping participants were watching a chaotic movie. The researchers wondered—what in the world was going on?

In retrospect, it's amazing that no one had discovered these rapid eye movements before. It turns out that periods of rapid eye movement are a routine characteristic of sleep in humans and many animals.

In fact, you can observe them for yourself in your pet dog or cat. The phenomenon had been there for everyone to see for eons, but anyone who noticed must not have attached any significance to it.

Kleitman and Aserinsky's discovery might have remained something of an oddity, but then they had a brainstorm. Could the rapid eye movements perhaps be related to dreaming? With the help of William Dement, a graduate student who was interested in dreams, they soon found the answer. When Dement woke up subjects during periods of rapid eye movement, about 80% reported that they had just been having a vivid dream. By contrast, only a small minority of participants awakened from other phases of sleep reported that they had been dreaming. Dement knew that he was on to something. "I was overwhelmed with excitement," he wrote later (1992, pp. 24–25). Subsequently, EEG recordings showed that periods of rapid eye movement were also associated with marked changes in brain-wave patterns. What Kleitman and his graduate students had stumbled on was considerably more than an oddity. It was a window into the most private aspect of consciousness imaginable—the experience of dreaming. As you will learn in this chapter, the discovery of rapid eye movement (REM) sleep blossomed into a number of other fascinating insights about what goes on in the brain during sleep. This is just one example of how modern psychologists have tried to come to grips with the slippery topic of consciousness.

We'll begin our tour of variations in consciousness with a few general points about the nature of consciousness. After that, much of the chapter will be a "bedtime story," as we take a long look at sleep and dreaming. We'll continue our discussion of consciousness by examining hypnosis, meditation, and the effects of mind-altering drugs. The Personal Application will address a number of practical questions about sleep and dreams. Finally, the Critical Thinking Application returns to the topic of drugs and looks at the concept of alcoholism to highlight the power of definitions.

PREVIEW QUESTIONS

- What is consciousness?
- What did Freud have to say about levels of awareness?
- Is there any awareness during sleep?
- How are variations in consciousness associated with EEG activity?
- How might consciousness be adaptive?

What is consciousness? *Consciousness* **is the awareness of internal and external stimuli.** Your consciousness includes (1) your awareness of external events ("The professor just asked me a difficult question about medieval history"), (2) your awareness of your internal sensations ("My heart is racing and I'm beginning to sweat"), (3) your awareness of your *self* as the unique being having these experiences ("Why me?"), and (4) your awareness of your thoughts about these experiences ("I'm going to make a fool of myself!"). To put it more concisely, consciousness is personal awareness.

The contents of your consciousness are continually changing. Rarely does consciousness come to a standstill. It moves, it flows, it fluctuates, it wanders (Wegner, 1997). Recognizing this situation, William James (1902) christened this continuous flow the *stream of consciousness*. If you could tape-record your thoughts, you would find an endless flow of ideas that zigzag all over the place. As you will soon learn, even when you sleep your consciousness moves through a series of transitions. To be constantly shifting and changing seems to be part of the essential nature of consciousness.

Variations in Levels of Awareness

While William James emphasized the stream of consciousness, Sigmund Freud (1900) wanted to examine what went on beneath the surface of this stream. As explained in Chapter 1, Freud argued that people's feelings and behavior are influenced by *unconscious* needs, wishes, and conflicts that lie below the surface of conscious awareness. According to Freud, the stream of consciousness has depth. Conscious and unconscious processes are different *levels of awareness*. Thus, Freud was one of the first theorists to recognize that consciousness is not an all-or none phenomenon.

Since Freud's time, research has shown that people continue to maintain some awareness during sleep and even when they are put under anesthesia for surgery. How do we know? Because some stimuli can still penetrate awareness. For example, people under surgical anesthesia occasionally hear comments made during their surgery, which they later repeat to their surprised surgeons (Bennett, 1993; Merikle & Daneman, 1996). Research also indicates that while asleep some people remain aware of external events to some degree (K. B. Campbell, 2000; Evans, 1990). A good example is the new parent who can sleep through a loud thunderstorm or a buzzing alarm clock but who immediately hears the muffled sound of the baby crying down the hall. The parent's selective sensitivity to sounds means that some mental processing must be going on even during sleep.

Consciousness and Brain Activity

Consciousness does not arise from any distinct structure in the brain, but rather is the result of activity in distributed networks of neural pathways (Kinsbourne, 1997). Thus, one of the best physiological indicators of variations in consciousness is the EEG, which records activity from broad swaths of the cortex. **The *electroencephalograph (EEG)* is a device that monitors the electrical activity of the brain over time by means of recording electrodes attached to the surface of the scalp** (see Chapter 3). Ultimately, the EEG summarizes the rhythm of cortical activity in the brain in terms of line tracings called *brain waves*. These brain-wave tracings vary in *amplitude* (height) and *frequency* (cycles per second, abbreviated *cps*). You can see what brain waves look like if you glance ahead to **Figure 5.2**. Human brain-wave activity is usually divided into four principal bands based on the frequency of the brain waves. These bands, named after letters in the Greek alphabet, are *beta* (13–24 cps), *alpha* (8–12 cps), *theta* (4–7 cps), and *delta* (under 4 cps).

Different patterns of EEG activity are associated with different states of consciousness, as is summarized in **Table 5.1**. For instance, when you are alertly engaged in problem solving, beta waves tend to dominate. When you are relaxed and resting, alpha waves increase. When you slip into deep, dreamless sleep, delta waves become more prevalent. Although these correlations are far from perfect, changes in

Table 5.1 EEG Patterns Associated with States of Consciousness

EEG Pattern	Frequency (cps)	Typical States of Consciousness
Beta (β)	13–24	Normal waking thought, alert problem solving
Alpha (α)	8–12	Deep relaxation, blank mind, meditation
Theta (θ)	4–7	Light sleep
Delta (Δ)	less than 4	Deep sleep

brain activity are closely related to variations in consciousness (Wallace & Fisher, 1999).

The Evolutionary Roots of Consciousness

Why do humans experience consciousness? Like other aspects of human nature, consciousness must have evolved because it helped our ancient ancestors survive and reproduce (Ornstein & Dewan, 1991). That said, there is plenty of debate about exactly how consciousness proved adaptive (Güzeldere, Flanagan, & Hardcastle, 2000). One line of thinking is that consciousness allowed our ancestors to think through courses of action and their consequences—and choose the best course—without actually executing ill-advised actions (by trial and error) that may have led to disastrous consequences (Plotkin, 1998). In other words, a little forethought and planning may have proved valuable in efforts to obtain food, avoid predators, and find mates. Although this analysis seems plausible, theorists have put forth a number of alternative explanations that focus on other adaptive benefits of personal awareness, and relatively little empirical evidence is available to judge the merits of any of these explanations. Hence, the evolutionary bases of consciousness remain elusive.

> Biological Rhythms and Sleep

Variations in consciousness are shaped in part by biological rhythms. Rhythms pervade the world around us. The daily alternation of light and darkness, the annual pattern of the seasons, and the phases of the moon all reflect this rhythmic quality of repeating cycles. Humans and many other animals display biological rhythms that are tied to these planetary rhythms (Foster, 2004). **Biological rhythms are periodic fluctuations in physiological functioning.** The existence of these rhythms means that organisms have internal "biological clocks" that somehow monitor the passage of time.

The Role of Circadian Rhythms

4a

Circadian rhythms are the 24-hour biological cycles found in humans and many other species. In humans, circadian rhythms are particularly influential in the regulation of sleep (Lavie, 2001). However, daily cycles also produce rhythmic variations in blood pressure, urine production, hormonal secretions, and other physical functions (see **Figure 5.1** on the next page), as well as in alertness, short-term memory, and other aspects of cognitive performance (Czeisler, Buxton, & Khalsa, 2005; Van Dongen & Dinges, 2005). For instance, body temperature varies rhythmically in a daily cycle, usually peaking in the afternoon and reaching its low point in the depths of the night.

Research indicates that people generally fall asleep as their body temperature begins to drop and awaken as it begins to ascend once again (Kumar, 2004). Investigators have concluded that circadian rhythms can leave individuals physiologically primed to fall asleep most easily at a particular time of day (Richardson, 1993). This optimal time varies from person to person, depending on their schedules, but each individual may have an "ideal" time for going to bed. This ideal bedtime may also promote better quality sleep during the night (Akerstedt et al., 1997), which is interesting in light of evidence that sleep *quality* may be more strongly correlated with health and well-being than the sheer quantity of sleep (Pilcher, Ginter, & Sadowsky, 1997).

Researchers have a pretty good idea of how the day-night cycle resets human biological clocks. When exposed to light, some receptors in the retina send direct inputs to a small structure in the hypothalamus called the *suprachiasmatic nucleus* (SCN) (Gooley & Saper, 2005). The SCN sends signals to the nearby *pineal gland,* whose secretion of the hormone *melatonin* plays a key role in adjusting biological clocks (Harrington & Mistlberger, 2000). Circadian rhythms in humans actually appear to be regulated by *several* internal clocks, but the central pacemaker clearly is located in the SCN (Foster, 2004).

Ignoring Circadian Rhythms

4a

What happens when you ignore your biological clock and go to sleep at an unusual time? Typically, the quality of your sleep suffers. Getting out of sync with your circadian rhythms also causes *jet lag.* When you fly across several time zones, your biological clock keeps time as usual, even though official clock time changes. You then go to sleep at the "wrong" time and are likely to experience difficulty falling asleep and poor-quality sleep. This inferior sleep, which can continue to occur for several days, can make you feel fatigued, sluggish, and irritable during the daytime

- What are biological rhythms?
- How are circadian rhythms related to falling asleep?
- Which physiological structures control our biological clocks?
- How do jet lag and rotating work shifts tend to affect circadian rhythms?
- What can be done to help people realign circadian rhythms that are out of sync?

Figure 5.1

Examples of circadian rhythms. These graphs show how alertness, core body temperature, and the secretion of growth hormone typically fluctuate in a 24-hour rhythm. Circadian rhythms are also seen for many other physiological functions.

Source: Adapted from Coleman, R. (1986). *Wide awake at 3:00 A.M.* New York: W. H. Freeman. Copyright © 1986 by Richard M. Coleman. Used with the permission of Henry Holt & Co., LLC.

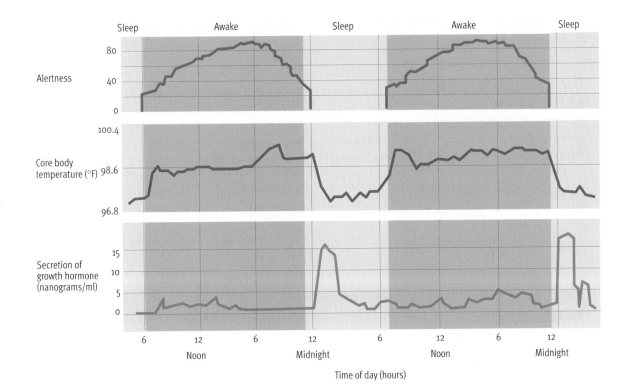

(Arendt, Stone, & Skene, 2005). Moreover, chronic jet lag appears to be associated with measurable deficits in cognitive performance (Cho et al., 2000).

People differ in how quickly they can reset their biological clocks to compensate for jet lag, but a rough rule of thumb is that the readjustment process takes about a day for each time zone crossed (Moline, 1993). In addition, the speed of readjustment depends on the direction traveled. Generally, it's easier to fly westward and lengthen your day than it is to fly eastward and shorten it (Arendt et al., 2005). This east-west disparity in jet lag is sizable enough to have an impact on the performance of sports teams. Studies have found that teams flying westward perform significantly better than teams flying eastward in professional baseball (Recht, Lew, & Schwartz, 1995) and college football (Worthen & Wade, 1999).

Of course, you don't have to hop on a jet to get out of sync with your biological clock. Just going to bed a couple of hours later than usual can affect how you sleep. Rotating work shifts that force many nurses, firefighters, and other workers to keep changing their sleep schedule play havoc with biological rhythms. Shift rotation, which affects about 20% of the United States workforce, tends to be even harder to adjust to than jet lag (Monk, 2000). Studies show that workers get less total sleep and poorer quality sleep when they go on rotating shifts. Shift rotation can also have a negative impact on employees' productivity and accident proneness at work, the quality of their social relations at home, and their physical

and mental health (Costa, 1996; Cruz, della Rocco, & Hackworth, 2000; Hossain & Shapiro, 1999). Other studies have found that shiftwork in females is associated with irregular menstrual cycles, reduced fertility, and an increased risk of premature births (Rogers & Dinges, 2002).

Realigning Circadian Rhythms

As scientists have come to appreciate the importance of circadian rhythms, they have begun to look for new ways to help people realign their daily rhythms. One promising line of research has focused on giving people small doses of the hormone melatonin, which appears to regulate the human biological clock. The evidence from a number of studies suggests that melatonin *can* reduce the effects of jet lag by helping travelers resynchronize their biological clocks, but the research results are inconsistent (Arendt & Skeen, 2005; Takahashi et al., 2002). One reason for the inconsistent findings is that when melatonin is used to ameliorate jet lag, the timing of the dose is crucial; because calculating the optimal timing is rather complicated, it is easy to get it wrong (Czeisler, Cajochen, & Turek, 2000).

Researchers have also tried carefully timed exposure to bright light as a treatment to realign circadian rhythms in rotating shift workers in industrial settings. Positive effects have been seen in some studies (Lowden, Akerstedt, & Wibom, 2004). This treatment can accelerate workers' adaptation to a new sleep-wake schedule, leading to improvements in sleep quality and alertness during work hours. However, the effects of bright-light administration have been modest and somewhat inconsistent (Rogers & Dinges, 2002), and it isn't a realistic option in many work settings. Another strategy to help shift workers involves carefully planning their rotation schedules to reduce the severity of their circadian disruption. The negative effects of shift rotation can be reduced if workers move through progressively later starting times (instead of progressively earlier starting times) and if they have longer periods between shift changes (Kostreva, McNelis, & Clemens, 2002). Although enlightened scheduling practices can help, the unfortunate reality is that most people find rotating shift work very difficult.

> The Sleep and Waking Cycle

Although it is a familiar state of consciousness, sleep is widely misunderstood. Historically, people have thought of sleep as a single, uniform state of physical and mental inactivity, during which the brain is "shut down" (Dement, 2003). In reality, sleepers experience quite a bit of physical and mental activity throughout the night. Scientists have learned a great deal about sleep since the landmark discovery of REM sleep in the 1950s.

The advances in our understanding of sleep have been the result of hard work by researchers who have spent countless nighttime hours watching other people sleep. This work is done in sleep laboratories, where volunteer participants come to spend the night. Sleep labs have one or more "bedrooms" in which the subjects retire, usually after being hooked up to a variety of physiological recording devices. In addition to an EEG, these devices typically include an *electromyograph (EMG)*, **which records muscular activity and tension; an** *electrooculograph (EOG)*, **which records eye movements; and an** *electrocardiograph (EKG)*, **which records the contractions of the heart** (Carskadon & Rechtschaffen, 2005).

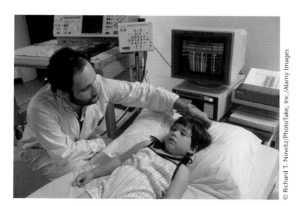

Researchers in a sleep laboratory can observe subjects while using elaborate equipment to record physiological changes during sleep. This kind of research has disclosed that sleep is a complex series of physical and mental states.

Other instruments monitor breathing, pulse rate, and body temperature. The researchers observe the sleeping subject through a window (or with a video camera) from an adjacent room, where they also monitor their elaborate physiological recording equipment. It takes most people a night to adapt to the strange bedroom and the recording devices and to return to their normal mode of sleeping (Carskadon & Dement, 2005).

Cycling Through the Stages of Sleep

 4b

Not only does sleep occur in a context of daily rhythms, but subtler rhythms are evident within the experience of sleep itself. During sleep, people cycle through a series of five distinct stages. Let's take a look at what researchers have learned about the many types of changes that occur during these sleep stages (Anch et al., 1988; Carskadon & Dement, 2005).

Stages 1–4

 4b

Although it may only take a few minutes, the onset of sleep is gradual and no obvious transition point occurs between wakefulness and sleep (Rechtschaffen, 1994). The length of time it takes people to fall asleep varies considerably, but the *average* in a recent study of over 35,000 people from 10 countries was 25 minutes (Soldatos et al., 2005). Sleep latency depends on quite an array of factors, including how long it has been since the person has slept, where the person is in his or her circadian cycle, the amount of noise or light in the sleep environment, and the person's age, desire to fall asleep, boredom level, recent caffeine or drug intake, and stress level, among other things (Broughton, 1994). In any event, stage 1 is a brief transitional stage of light sleep that usually lasts only a few (1–7) minutes. Your breathing and heart rate slow as your muscle tension and body

PREVIEW QUESTIONS

● What happens when people fall asleep?
● How is REM sleep different from non-REM sleep?
● How do sleep stages evolve over the course of a night's sleep?
● How does age affect patterns of sleeping?
● Which aspects of sleep are influenced by culture?
● What is the evolutionary significance of sleep?

Web Link 5.1

SleepNet
This extensive website offers a wealth of information on sleep disorders, sleep labs, sleep aids, and sleep research. It also includes links to other sites dedicated to the topic of sleep.

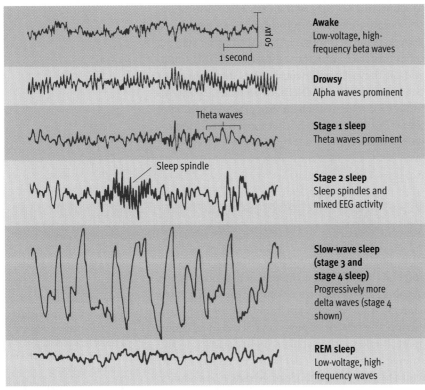

Awake
Low-voltage, high-frequency beta waves

50 µV

1 second

Drowsy
Alpha waves prominent

Theta waves

Stage 1 sleep
Theta waves prominent

Sleep spindle

Stage 2 sleep
Sleep spindles and mixed EEG activity

Slow-wave sleep (stage 3 and stage 4 sleep)
Progressively more delta waves (stage 4 shown)

REM sleep
Low-voltage, high-frequency waves

Figure 5.2

EEG patterns in sleep and wakefulness. Characteristic brain waves vary depending on one's state of consciousness. Generally, as people move from an awake state through deeper stages of sleep, their brain waves decrease in frequency (cycles per second) and increase in amplitude (height). However, brain waves during REM sleep resemble "wide awake" brain waves.

Source: Adapted from Hauri, P. (1982). *Current concepts: The sleep disorders.* Kalamazoo, MI: The Upjohn Company. Reprinted by permission.

temperature decline. The alpha waves that probably dominated your EEG activity just before you fell asleep give way to lower-frequency EEG activity in which theta waves are prominent (see **Figure 5.2**).

As you descend through stages 2, 3, and 4 of the sleep cycle, your respiration rate, heart rate, muscle tension, and body temperature continue to decline. Gradually, your brain waves become higher in amplitude and slower in frequency, as you move into a deeper form of sleep, called slow-wave sleep (see **Figure 5.2**). *Slow-wave sleep* **consists of sleep stages 3 and 4, during which low-frequency delta waves become prominent in EEG recordings.** Typically you reach slow-wave sleep in less than an hour and stay there for roughly a half-hour. Then the sleep cycle reverses itself and you gradually move upward through lighter stages of sleep. That's when things start to get interesting.

REM Sleep

PsykTrek
4b

When you reach what should be stage 1 once again, you usually go into the fifth stage of sleep, which is

most widely known as *REM sleep*. REM is the abbreviation for rapid eye movements, which are prominent during this stage of sleep. In a sleep lab, researchers use an electrooculograph to monitor these lateral movements that occur beneath the sleeping person's closed eyelids. However, they can be seen with the naked eye if you closely watch someone in the REM stage of sleep (little ripples move back and forth across his or her closed eyelids).

As we discussed at the beginning of the chapter, the discovery of REM sleep was made accidentally in the 1950s in Nathaniel Kleitman's lab at the University of Chicago (Aserinsky & Kleitman, 1953; Dement, 2005). The term *REM sleep* was coined by William Dement, a student in Kleitman's lab, who went on to become one of the world's foremost sleep researchers. The REM stage tends to be a "deep" stage of sleep in the conventional sense that it is relatively hard to awaken a person from it (although arousal thresholds vary during REM). The REM stage is also marked by irregular breathing and pulse rate. Muscle tone is extremely relaxed—so much so that bodily movements are minimal and the sleeper is virtually paralyzed. Although REM is a relatively deep sleep stage, EEG activity is dominated by high-frequency beta waves that resemble those observed when people are alert and awake (see **Figure 5.2** again).

This paradox is probably related to the association between REM sleep and dreaming. When researchers systematically awaken subjects from various stages of sleep to ask them whether they were dreaming, most dream reports come from awakenings during the REM stage (Dement, 1978; McCarley, 1994). Although decades of research have revealed that some

© Steve Bloom Images/Alamy

REM sleep is not unique to humans. Nearly all mammals and birds exhibit REM sleep. The only known exceptions among warm-blooded vertebrates are dolphins and some whales (Morrison, 2003). Dolphins are particularly interesting, as they sleep while swimming, resting one hemisphere of the brain while the other hemisphere remains alert.

dreaming occurs in the non-REM stages, dreaming is most frequent, vivid, and memorable during REM sleep (Pace-Schott, 2005).

To summarize, **REM sleep** *is a deep stage of sleep marked by rapid eye movements, high-frequency brain waves, and dreaming.* It is such a special stage of sleep that the other four stages are often characterized simply as "non-REM sleep." ***Non-REM (NREM) sleep*** *consists of sleep stages 1 through 4, which are marked by an absence of rapid eye movements, relatively little dreaming, and varied EEG activity.*

Repeating the Cycle

During the course of a night, people usually repeat the sleep cycle about four times. As the night wears on, the cycle changes gradually. The first REM period is relatively short, lasting only a few minutes. Subsequent REM periods get progressively longer, peaking at around 40–60 minutes. Additionally, NREM intervals tend to get shorter, and descents into NREM stages usually become more shallow. These trends can be seen in **Figure 5.3** on the next page, which provides an overview of a typical night's sleep cycle. These trends mean that most slow-wave sleep occurs early in the sleep cycle and that REM sleep tends to pile up in the second half of the sleep cycle. Summing across the entire cycle, young adults typically spend about 20% of their sleep time in slow-wave sleep and another 20% in REM sleep.

Age, Culture, and Sleep

Now that we have described the basic architecture of sleep, let's take a look at a couple of factors that contribute to variations in patterns of sleeping: age and culture.

Age Trends

Age alters the sleep cycle. What we have described so far is the typical pattern for young to middle-aged adults. Children, however, display different patterns (Bootzin et al., 2001; Roffwarg, Muzio, & Dement, 1966). Newborns will sleep six to eight times in a 24-hour period, often exceeding a total of 16 hours of sleep (see **Figure 5.4**). Fortunately for parents, during the first several months much of this sleep begins to get unified into one particularly long nighttime sleep period (Webb, 1992a). Interestingly, infants spend much more of their sleep time than adults do in the REM stage. In the first few months, REM accounts for about 50% of babies' sleep, as compared to 20% of

adults' sleep. During the remainder of the first year, the REM portion of infants' sleep declines to roughly 30% (Ohayon et al., 2004). The REM portion of sleep continues to decrease gradually until it levels off at about 20% during adolescence (see **Figure 5.4**).

During adulthood, gradual, age-related changes in sleep continue. Although the proportion of REM sleep remains fairly stable, the percentage of slow-wave sleep declines and the percentage of time spent in stage 1 increases slightly, with these trends stronger in men than women (Bliwise, 2005). These shifts toward lighter sleep *may* contribute to the increased frequency of nighttime awakenings seen among the elderly (Klerman et al., 2004). As **Figure 5.4** shows, the average amount of total sleep time also declines with advancing age. However, these averages mask important variability, as total sleep *increases* with age in a substantial portion of older people (Webb, 1992a).

Cultural Variations

Although age clearly affects the nature and structure of sleep itself, the psychological and physiological experience of sleep does not appear to vary much across cultures. For example, a recent cross-cultural survey (Soldatos et al., 2004) found relatively modest

Web Link 5.2

SleepQuest
Leading sleep researcher William Dement of Stanford University— the founder of sleep medicine—is the chief scientific advisor for this site. Visitors can access an archive of "columns" written by Dr. Dement and a diverse array of resources on sleep disorders.

concept **check** 5.1

Comparing REM and NREM Sleep

A table here could have provided you with a systematic comparison of REM sleep and NREM sleep, but that would have deprived you of the opportunity to check your understanding of these sleep phases by creating your own table. Try to fill in each of the blanks below with a word or phrase highlighting the differences between REM and NREM sleep with regard to the various characteristics specified. As usual, you can find the answers at the back of the book in Appendix A.

Characteristic	REM sleep	NREM sleep
1. Type of EEG activity	_____	_____
2. Eye movements	_____	_____
3. Dreaming	_____	_____
4. Depth (difficulty in awakening)	_____	_____
5. Percentage of total sleep (in adults)	_____	_____
6. Increases or decreases (as percentage of sleep during childhood)	_____	_____
7. Timing in sleep cycle (dominates early or late)	_____	_____

Figure 5.3

An overview of the cycle of sleep. The white line charts how a typical, healthy, young adult moves through the various stages of sleep during the course of a night. This diagram also shows how dreams and rapid eye movements tend to coincide with REM sleep, whereas posture changes occur in between REM periods (because the body is nearly paralyzed during REM sleep). Notice how the person cycles into REM four times, as descents into NREM sleep get shallower and REM periods get longer. Thus, slow-wave sleep is prominent early in the night, while REM sleep dominates the second half of a night's sleep. Although these patterns are typical, keep in mind that sleep patterns vary from one person to another and that they change with age.

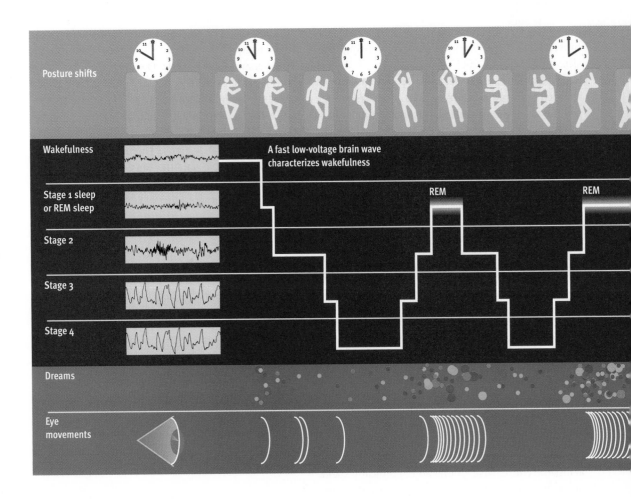

Figure 5.4

Changes in sleep patterns over the life span. Both the total amount of sleep per night and the portion of sleep that is REM sleep change with age. Sleep patterns change most dramatically during infancy, with total sleep time and amount of REM sleep declining sharply in the first two years of life. After a noticeable drop in the average amount of sleep in adolescence, sleep patterns remain relatively stable, although total sleep and slow-wave sleep continue to decline gradually with age.

Source: Adapted from an updated revision of a figure in Roffwarg, H. P., Muzio, J. N., & Dement, W. C. (1966). Ontogenetic development of human sleep dream cycle. *Science, 152,* 604–609. Adapted and revised by permission of the authors.

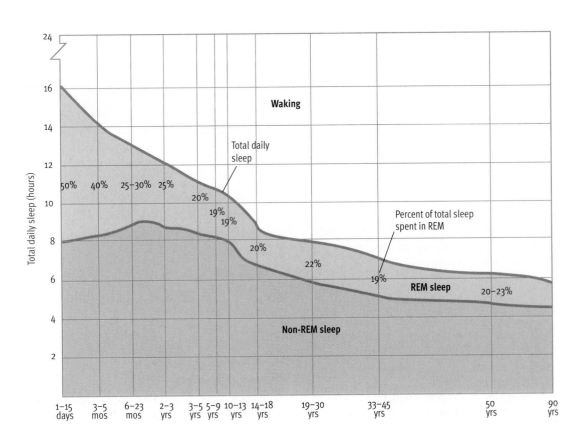

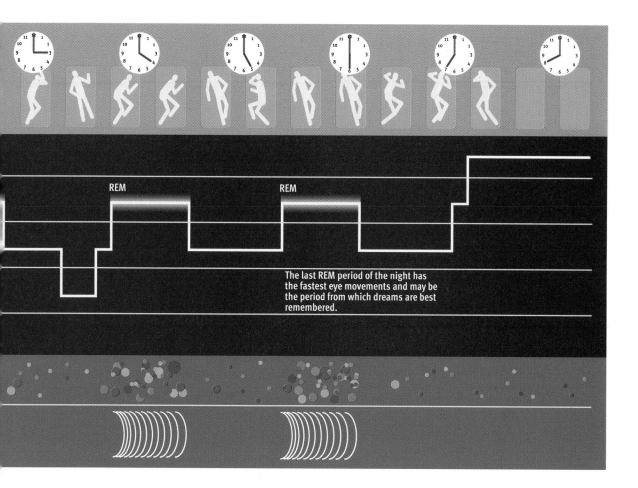

The last REM period of the night has the fastest eye movements and may be the period from which dreams are best remembered.

differences in the average amount of time that people sleep, or the time that it takes for them to fall asleep (see **Figure 5.5**). Cultural disparities in sleep are limited to more peripheral matters, such as sleeping arrangements and napping customs. For instance, there are cultural differences in *co-sleeping,* the practice of children and parents sleeping together (McKenna, 1993). In modern Western societies, co-sleeping is actively discouraged. As part of their effort to foster self-reliance, American parents teach their children to sleep alone. In contrast, co-sleeping is more widely accepted in Japanese culture, which emphasizes interdependence and group harmony (Latz, Wolf, & Lozoff, 1999). Around the world as a whole, co-sleeping is normative (Ball, Hooker, & Kelly, 2000). Strong pressure against co-sleeping appears to be largely an urban, Western phenomenon. Interestingly, a recent 18-year study of youngsters in California found no association between co-sleeping and any problematic consequences (Okami, Weisner, & Olmstead, 2002).

Napping practices also vary along cultural lines. In many societies, shops close and activities are curtailed in the afternoon to permit people to enjoy

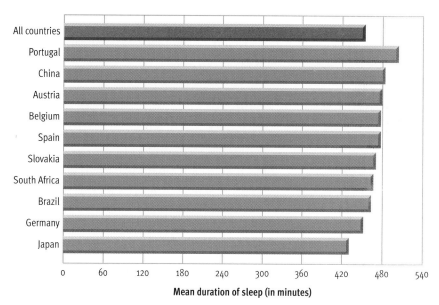

Figure 5.5

Cultural variations in how long people tend to sleep. A recent study (Soldatos et al., 2005) surveyed over 35,000 people in 10 countries about various aspects of their sleep habits. This graph shows the average duration of nighttime sleep reported by the respondents in each country. Although Japan was a bit of an "outlier," the cultural differences are rather modest. Cultural variability in the average time required to fall asleep was also modest. Consistent with previous findings, the results of this study suggest that the basic architecture of sleep does not vary much across cultures. (Data from Soldatos et al., 2005)

a 1- to 2-hour midday nap. These "siesta cultures" are found mostly in tropical regions of the world (Webb & Dinges, 1989). There, this practice is adaptive in that it allows people to avoid working during the hottest part of the day. As a rule, the siesta tradition is not found in industrialized societies, where it conflicts with the emphasis on productivity and the philosophy that "time is money."

The Evolutionary Bases of Sleep

What is the evolutionary significance of sleep? The fact that sleep is seen in a highly diverse array of organisms and that it appears to have evolved independently in birds and mammals suggests that sleep has considerable adaptive value (Zepelin, 1993). But theorists disagree about *how* exactly sleep is adaptive. One hypothesis is that sleep evolved to conserve organisms' energy. According to this notion, sleep evolved millions of years ago in service of warm-bloodedness, which requires the maintenance of a constant, high body temperature by metabolic means. An alternative hypothesis is that the immobilization associated with sleep is adaptive because it reduces exposure to predators and other sources of danger. A third hypothesis is that sleep is adaptive because it helps animals restore energy and other bodily resources depleted by waking activities. Overall, the evidence seems strongest for the energy conservation hypothesis, but there is room for extensive debate about the evolutionary bases of sleep (Zepelin, Siegel, & Tobler, 2005).

PREVIEW QUESTIONS

- What are the effects of sleep restriction?
- What are the effects of REM and slow-wave sleep deprivation?
- How common is insomnia?
- What is the role of sedative drugs in the treatment of insomnia?
- What are the symptoms of narcolepsy? Sleep apnea? Somnambulism?

Doing Without: Sleep Deprivation

Scientific research on sleep deprivation presents something of a paradox. On the one hand, some studies suggest that sleep deprivation is not as detrimental as most people subjectively feel it to be. On the other hand, evidence suggests that sleep deprivation may be a major social problem, undermining efficiency at work and contributing to countless accidents.

Research has mostly focused on partial sleep deprivation, or *sleep restriction,* which occurs when people make do with substantially less sleep than normal over a period of time. Many sleep experts believe that much of American society chronically suffers from partial sleep deprivation (Walsh, Dement, & Dinges, 2005). It appears that more and more people are trying to squeeze additional waking hours out of their days as they attempt to juggle conflicting work, family, household, and school responsibilities, leading William Dement to comment that "Most Americans no longer know what it feels like to be fully alert" (Toufexis, 1990, p. 79).

How serious are the effects of partial sleep deprivation? Studies indicate that sleep restriction can impair individuals' attention, reaction time, motor coordination, and decision making and may also have negative effects on endocrine and immune system functioning (Dinges, Rogers, & Baynard, 2005). Negative effects are most likely when subjects are asked to work on long-lasting, difficult, or monotonous tasks, or when subjects are asked to restrict their sleep to 6 hours or fewer for many nights (Gillberg & Akerstedt, 1998; Van Dongen et al., 2003). Recent research has also found variablility among individuals in how sensitive they are to sleep restriction. Over a series of three carefully controlled sleep-deprivation episodes, Van Dongen et al. (2004) found that some subjects were more vulnerable to the negative effects of sleep deprivation than others. Interestingly, people often do not appreciate the degree to which sleep deprivation has a negative impact on their functioning (Pilcher & Walters, 1997).

Evidence suggests that sleep deprivation contributes to a large proportion of transportation accidents and mishaps in the workplace (Walsh et al., 2005). Studies reveal that nighttime workers in many industries frequently fall asleep on the job (Roehrs et al., 2005). Obviously, if a person is running a punch press, driving a bus, or working as an air traffic controller, a momentary lapse in attention could be very, very costly. In recent years, a number of major ecological disasters, such as the nuclear accidents at

A large number of traffic accidents occur because drivers get drowsy or fall asleep at the wheel. Although the effects of sleep deprivation seem innocuous, sleep loss can be deadly.

© Associated Press/AP

Three Mile Island and Chernobyl and the running aground of the Exxon *Valdez* oil tanker, have been blamed in part on lapses in judgment and attention resulting from sleep deprivation (Doghramji, 2001). Experts have *estimated* that accidents attributable to drowsiness induced by sleep deprivation cost the U.S. economy over $56 billion annually, lead to the loss of over 52 million work days each year, and result in over 24,000 deaths per year (Coren, 1996).

The unique quality of REM sleep led researchers to look into the effects of a special type of partial sleep deprivation—*selective deprivation*. In a number of laboratory studies, participants were awakened over a period of nights whenever they began to go into the REM stage. These subjects usually got a decent amount of sleep in NREM stages, but they were selectively deprived of REM sleep.

What are the effects of REM deprivation? The evidence indicates that it has little impact on daytime functioning and task performance, but it *does* have some interesting effects on subjects' patterns of sleeping (Bonnet, 2005). As the nights go by in REM deprivation studies, it becomes necessary to awaken the participants more and more often to deprive them of their REM sleep, because they spontaneously shift into REM more and more frequently. Whereas most subjects normally go into REM about four times a night, REM-deprived participants start slipping into REM every time the researchers turn around. Furthermore, when a REM-deprivation experiment comes to an end and participants are allowed to sleep without interruption, they experience a "rebound effect." That is, they spend extra time in REM periods for one to three nights to make up for their REM deprivation (Bonnet, 2005).

Similar results have been observed when subjects have been selectively deprived of slow-wave sleep (Borbely & Achermann, 2005). What do theorists make of these spontaneous pursuits of REM and slow-wave sleep? They conclude that people must have specific *needs* for REM and slow-wave sleep—and rather strong needs, at that.

Why do we need REM and slow-wave sleep? Some recent studies suggest that REM and slow-wave sleep contribute to firming up learning that takes place during the day—a process called *memory consolidation* (Gais & Born, 2004; Stickgold, 2001). Efforts to explore this hypothesis have led to some interesting findings in recent years. For example, in one study participants were given training on a perceptual-motor task and then retested 12 hours later. Subjects who slept during the 12-hour interval showed substantial *improvement* in performance that was not apparent in subjects who did not sleep (Walker et al.,

2002). A host of similar studies have shown that sleep seems to enhance subjects' memory of specific learning activities that occurred during the day (Walker & Stickgold, 2004). Some studies even suggest that sleep may foster creative insights the next morning related to the previous day's learning (Stickgold & Walker, 2004; Wagner et al., 2004). The theoretical meaning of these findings is still being debated, but the most widely accepted explanations center on how time spent in specific stages of sleep may stabilize or solidify memories formed during the day (Stickgold, 2005). The practical meaning of these results, however, should be rather obvious: Sound sleep habits should facilitate learning.

Problems in the Night: Sleep Disorders

Not everyone is able to consistently enjoy the luxury of a good night's sleep. In this section we will briefly discuss what is known about a variety of sleep disorders.

Insomnia

Insomnia is the most common sleep disorder. **Insomnia refers to chronic problems in getting adequate sleep.** It occurs in three basic patterns: (1) difficulty in falling asleep initially, (2) difficulty in remaining asleep, and (3) persistent early-morning awakening. Insomnia may sound like a minor problem to those who haven't struggled with it, but it can be a very unpleasant malady. Moreover, insomnia is associated with daytime fatigue, impaired functioning, an elevated risk for accidents, reduced productivity, absenteeism at work, depression, and increased health problems (Benca, 2001; Edinger & Means, 2005).

How common is insomnia? Nearly everyone suffers occasional sleep difficulties because of stress, disruptions of biological rhythms, or other temporary circumstances. Fortunately, these problems clear up spontaneously for most people. However, studies suggest that about 34%–35% of adults report chronic problems with insomnia, and about half of these people (15%–17%) suffer from severe insomnia (Zorick & Walsh, 2000). The prevalence of insomnia increases with age and is about 50% more common in women than in men (Partinen & Hublin, 2005).

The most common approach to the treatment of insomnia is the prescription of several classes of sedative drugs. *Benzodiazepine medications,* which were originally designed to relieve anxiety, have become the most widely prescribed class of sedatives (Roehers & Roth, 2004). The various types of sedative medications

Web Link 5.3

National Sleep Foundation
This attractive, well-organized website houses a great deal of information on sleep. Highlights include an interactive test to assess your sleep habits; electronic pamphlets on practical sleep topics, such as strategies for shift workers, the dangers of drowsy driving, and reducing jet lag; and extensive coverage of the full range of sleep disorders.

Courtesy of William Dement

WILLIAM DEMENT
"Sleep deprivation is a major epidemic in our society. . . . Americans spend so much time and energy chasing the American dream, that they don't have much time left for actual dreaming."

Web Link 5.4

Sleep Medicine Homepage
This site, assembled by sleep-wake specialist Michael J. Thorpy (Montefiore Medical Center), brings together a broad range of Internet links regarding sleep in all its aspects, as well as information on clinical problems associated with disruptions in normal sleep and waking patterns.

are fairly effective in helping people fall asleep more quickly, and they reduce nighttime awakenings and increase total sleep (Mendelson, 2005).

Nonetheless, sedatives are a poor long-range solution for insomnia, for a number of reasons (Roehrs & Roth, 2000; Wesson et al., 2005). Besides the danger of overdose, some people become dependent on sedatives to fall asleep. Sedatives also have carryover effects that can make people drowsy and sluggish the next day and impair their functioning (Vermeeren, 2004). Moreover, with continued use sedatives gradually become less effective, so people need to increase their dose to more dangerous levels, creating a vicious circle of escalating dependency (Lader, 2002; see **Figure 5.6**). Ironically, sedatives also interfere with the normal cycle of sleep. Although they promote sleep, they reduce the proportion of time spent in REM and slow-wave sleep (Nishino, Mignot, & Dement, 1995).

Fortunately, the newer generation of sedatives, such as zolpidem (trade name: Ambien), reduce some of the problems associated with traditional sleeping pills (Sanger, 2004). People suffering from insomnia can also turn to melatonin, the hormone that has been used to treat jet lag (see p. 140), which is available over the counter in the United States. Research indicates that melatonin can function as a mild sedative and that it has some value in the treatment of insomnia (Turek & Gillete, 2004).

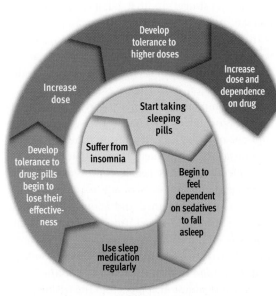

Figure 5.6
The vicious circle of dependence on sleeping pills. Because of the body's ability to develop tolerance to drugs, using sedatives routinely to "cure" insomnia can lead to a vicious circle of escalating dependency as larger and larger doses of the sedative are needed to produce the same effect.

Other Sleep Problems

Although insomnia is the most common difficulty associated with sleep, people are plagued by many other types of sleep problems as well. Let's briefly look at the symptoms, causes, and prevalence of three additional sleep problems, as described by Kryger, Roth, and Dement (2005) and Bootzin et al. (2001).

Narcolepsy **is a disease marked by sudden and irresistible onsets of sleep during normal waking periods.** A person suffering from narcolepsy goes directly from wakefulness into REM sleep, usually for a short period (10–20 minutes). This is a potentially dangerous condition, as some victims fall asleep instantly, even while driving a car or operating machinery. Narcolepsy is relatively infrequent, seen in only about 0.05% of the population (Partinen & Hublin, 2005). Its causes are not well understood, but some individuals appear to be genetically predisposed to the disease (Mignot, 2005). Stimulant drugs have been used to treat this condition with modest success (Guilleminault & Fromherz, 2005). But as you will see in our upcoming discussion of drugs, stimulants carry many problems of their own.

Sleep apnea **involves frequent, reflexive gasping for air that awakens a person and disrupts sleep.** Some victims are awakened from their sleep hundreds of times a night. Apnea occurs when a person literally stops breathing for a minimum of 10 seconds. This disorder, which is usually accompanied by loud snoring, is seen in about 2% of women and about 4% of men between the ages of 30 and 60 (Bassiri & Guilleminault, 2000). As you might expect, sleep apnea often leads to insomnia as a side effect. Apnea may be treated with surgery or drug therapy.

Somnambulism, **or sleepwalking, occurs when a person arises and wanders about while remaining asleep.** Sleepwalking tends to occur during the first two hours of sleep, when individuals are in slow-wave sleep. Episodes may last from 15 seconds to 30 minutes (Aldrich, 2000). Sleepwalkers may awaken

"Wait! Don't! It can be dangerous to wake them!"

© 2003 Joe Dator from cartoonbank.com. All rights reserved.

during their journey, or they may return to bed without any recollection of their excursion. The causes of this unusual disorder are unknown, although it may have a genetic predisposition (Keefauver & Guilleminault, 1994). Sleepwalking does not appear to be a manifestation of underlying emotional or psychological problems (Mahowald, 1993). However, sleepwalkers *are* prone to accidents. In light of this fact, it is important to note that, contrary to popular myth, it is safe to awaken people (gently) from a sleepwalking episode—much safer than letting them wander about.

> The World of Dreams

For the most part, dreams are not taken very seriously in Western societies. Paradoxically, though, Robert Van de Castle (1994) points out that dreams have sometimes changed the world. For example, Van de Castle describes how René Descartes's philosophy of dualism, Frederick Banting's discovery of insulin, Elias Howe's refinement of the sewing machine, Mohandas Gandhi's strategy of nonviolent protest, and Lyndon Johnson's withdrawal from the 1968 U.S. presidential race were all inspired by dreams. He also explains how Mary Shelley's *Frankenstein* and Robert Louis Stevenson's *The Strange Case of Dr. Jekyll and Mr. Hyde* emerged out of their dream experiences. In his wide-ranging discussion, Van de Castle also relates how the Surrealist painter Salvador Dali characterized his work as "dream photographs" and how legendary filmmakers Ingmar Bergman, Orson Welles, and Federico Fellini all drew on their dreams in making their films. Thus, Van de Castle concludes that "dreams have had a dramatic influence on almost every important aspect of our culture and history" (p. 10).

The Nature and Contents of Dreams

What do people dream about? Overall, dreams are not as exciting as advertised. Perhaps dreams are seen as exotic because people are more likely to remember their more bizarre nighttime dramas (De Koninck, 2000). After analyzing the contents of more than 10,000 dreams, Calvin Hall (1966) concluded that most dreams are relatively mundane. They tend to unfold in familiar settings with a cast of characters dominated by family, friends, and colleagues.

Certain themes tend to be more common than others in dreams. **Figure 5.7** on the next page lists the most common dream themes reported by 1181 college students in a recent study of typical dream content (Nielsen et al., 2003). If you glance through this list, you will see that people dream quite a bit about sex, aggression, and misfortune. According to Hall, dreams tend to center on classic sources of internal conflict, such as the conflict between taking chances and playing it safe. Hall was struck by how little people dream about public affairs and current events. Typically, dreams are self-centered; people dream mostly about themselves.

Though dreams seem to belong in a world of their own, what people dream about is affected by what is going on in their lives (Kramer, 1994). If you're struggling with financial problems, worried about an upcoming exam, or sexually attracted to a classmate, these themes may very well show up in your dreams. Freud noticed long ago that the contents of waking life tend to spill into dreams. He labeled this spillover the *day residue.*

A recent study suggests that people may often dream about aversive matters that they would just as soon forget (Wegner, Wenzlaff, & Kozak, 2004). In this study, participants who were instructed to *avoid thinking about a certain person* just before falling asleep ended up dreaming about that person more than subjects who were instructed to deliberately think about the target person. This finding suggests that thoughts that we try to suppress during the day (about say, trouble at work or health concerns) may be especially likely to show up in our dreams. Not

PREVIEW QUESTIONS

- What is known about the contents of people's dreams?
- Can external events affect the content of dreams?
- How does culture affect dream recall and dream content?
- How do the Freudian, cognitive, and activation-synthesis models view dreams?

Web Link 5.5

DreamResearch
If you are interested in what people dream about, this is probably the best source of information on the web. Maintained by veteran dream researcher Bill Domhoff (University of California, Santa Cruz) and his colleague Adam Schneider, this site provides access to a searchable database of thousands of dream reports. Visitors can also check out many seminal research articles on dreams.

SLEEP DISORDER RESEARCH

Rank	Dream content	Total prevalence
1	Chased or pursued, not physically injured	81.5
2	Sexual experiences	76.5
3	Falling	73.8
4	School, teachers, studying	67.1
5	Arriving too late, e.g., missing a train	59.5
6	Being on the verge of falling	57.7
7	Trying again and again to do something	53.5
8	A person now alive as dead	54.1
9	Flying or soaring through the air	48.3
10	Vividly sensing . . . a presence in the room	48.3
11	Failing an examination	45.0
12	Physically attacked (beaten, stabbed, raped)	42.4
13	Being frozen with fright	40.7
14	A person now dead as alive	38.4
15	Being a child again	36.7
16	Being killed	34.5
17	Insects or spiders	33.8
18	Swimming	34.3
19	Being nude	32.6
20	Being inappropriately dressed	32.5
21	Discovering a new room at home	32.3
22	Losing control of a vehicle	32.0
23	Eating delicious foods	30.7
24	Being half awake and paralyzed in bed	27.2
25	Finding money	25.7

Figure 5.7

Common themes in dreams. Studies of dream content find that certain themes are particularly common. The data shown here are from a recent study of 1181 college students in Canada (Nielsen et al., 2003). This list shows the 25 dreams most frequently reported by the students. Total prevalence refers to the percentage of students reporting each dream.

Source: Nielsen, T. A., Zadra, A. L., Simard, V., Saucier, S., Stenstrom, P., Smith, C., & Kuiken, D. (2003). The typical dreams of Canadian university students. *Dreaming, 13,* 211–235. Copyright © 2003 Association for the Study of Dreams. [from Table 1, p. 217]

that this finding makes dreaming any different from waking thought. Studies show that topics people try to suppress during the day also tend to intrude on their consciousness while awake (Wenzlaff & Wegner, 2000).

On occasion, the contents of dreams can also be affected by external stimuli experienced while one is dreaming (De Koninck, 2000). For example, William

Dement sprayed water on one hand of sleeping subjects while they were in the REM stage (Dement & Wolpert, 1958). Subjects who weren't awakened by the water were awakened by the experimenter a short time later and asked what they had been dreaming about. Dement found that 42% of the participants had incorporated the water into their dreams. They said that they had dreamt that they were in rainfalls, floods, baths, swimming pools, and the like. Some people report that they occasionally experience the same phenomenon at home when the sound of their alarm clock fails to awaken them. The alarm is incorporated into their dream as a loud engine or a siren, for instance.

Culture and Dreams

Striking cross-cultural variations occur in beliefs about the nature of dreams and the importance attributed to them. In modern Western society, we typically make a distinction between the "real" world we experience while awake and the "imaginary" world we experience while dreaming. Some people realize that events in the real world can affect their dreams, but few believe that events in their dreams hold any significance for their waking life. Although a small minority of individuals take their dreams seriously, in Western cultures dreams are largely written off as insignificant and meaningless (Tart, 1988).

In many non-Western cultures, however, dreams are viewed as important sources of information about oneself, about the future, or about the spiritual world (Kracke, 1991). Although no culture confuses dreams with waking reality, many view events in dreams as another type of reality that may be just as important as, or perhaps even more important than, events experienced while awake. In some instances, people are even held responsible for their dream actions. Among the New Guinea Arapesh, for example, an erotic dream about someone may be viewed as the equivalent of an adulterous act. In many cultures, dreams are seen as a window into the spiritual world, permitting communication with ancestors or supernatural beings (Bourguignon, 1972). People in some cultures believe that dreams provide information about the future—good or bad omens about upcoming battles, hunts, births, and so forth (Tedlock, 1992).

The tendency to remember one's dreams varies across cultures. In modern Western societies where little significance is attributed to dreams, dream recall tends to be mediocre. Many people remember their dreams only infrequently. In contrast, dream recall tends to be much better in cultures that take dreams seriously (Kracke, 1992). In regard to dream content, both similarities and differences occur across cultures in the types of dreams that people report (Domhoff, 2005b; Hunt, 1989). Some basic dream themes appear to be nearly universal (falling, being pursued, having sex). However, the contents of dreams vary some from one culture to another because people in different societies deal with different worlds while awake.

Theories of Dreaming

Many theories have been proposed to explain the purposes of dreaming. Sigmund Freud (1900), who analyzed clients' dreams in therapy, believed that the principal purpose of dreams is *wish fulfillment*. He thought that people fulfill ungratified needs from waking hours through wishful thinking in dreams. For example, someone who is sexually frustrated would tend to have highly erotic dreams, while an unsuccessful person would dream about great accomplishments. Freud's influential theory sounded plausible when it was proposed over 100 years ago, but research has not provided much support for Freud's conception of dreaming (Fisher & Greenberg, 1996). That said, efforts are under way to modernize and rehabilitate the Freudian view of dreams (Solms, 2002, 2004). Whether these efforts will prove to be influential remains to be seen.

Other theorists, such as Rosalind Cartwright, have proposed that dreams provide an opportunity to work through everyday problems (Cartwright, 1977; Cartwright & Lamberg, 1992). According to her cognitive, *problem-solving view,* there is considerable continuity between waking and sleeping thought. Proponents of this view believe that dreams allow people to engage in creative thinking about problems because dreams are not restrained by logic or realism. Recent research showing that sleep can enhance learning (Walker & Stickgold, 2004) adds new credibility to the problem-solving view of dreams (Cartwright, 2004).

J. Allan Hobson and Robert McCarley have argued that dreams are simply the by-product of bursts of activity emanating from subcortical areas in the brain (Hobson, 1988, 2002; Hobson & McCarley, 1977; McCarley, 1994). Their *activation-synthesis* model proposes that dreams are side effects of the neural activation that produces "wide awake" brain waves during REM sleep. According to this model, neurons firing periodically in lower brain centers send random signals to the cortex (the seat of complex thought). The cortex supposedly constructs a dream to make sense out of these signals. In contrast to the theories of Freud and Cartwright, this theory obviously downplays the role of emotional factors as determinants of dreams. Like other theories of dreams, the activation-synthesis model has its share of critics.

SIGMUND FREUD

"[Dreams are] the royal road to the unconscious."

ROSALIND CARTWRIGHT

"One function of dreams may be to restore our sense of competence. . . . It is also probable that in times of stress, dreams have more work to do in resolving our problems and are thus more salient and memorable."

J. ALLEN HOBSON

"Activation-synthesis ascribes dreaming to brain activation in sleep. The principal engine of this activation is the reticular formation of the brainstem."

Figure 5.8

Three theories of dreaming. Dreams can be explained in a variety of ways. Freud stressed the wish-fulfilling function of dreams. Cartwright emphasizes the problem-solving function of dreams. Hobson and McCarley assert that dreams are merely a by-product of periodic neural activation. All three theories are speculative and have their critics.

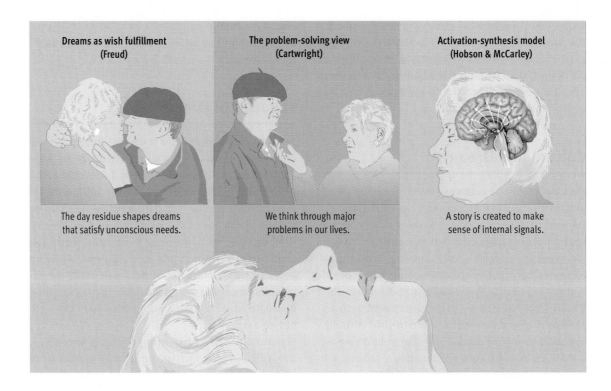

| Dreams as wish fulfillment (Freud) | The problem-solving view (Cartwright) | Activation-synthesis model (Hobson & McCarley) |

The day residue shapes dreams that satisfy unconscious needs.

We think through major problems in our lives.

A story is created to make sense of internal signals.

They point out that the model has a hard time accommodating the fact that dreaming occurs outside of REM sleep and that the contents of dreams are considerably more meaningful than the model would predict (Domhoff, 2005a; Foulkes, 1996b).

These theories, which are summarized in **Figure 5.8**, are only three of numerous ideas about the functions of dreams. All of these theories are based more on conjecture than research. In part, this is because the private, subjective nature of dreams makes it difficult to put the theories to an empirical test. Thus, the purpose of dreaming remains a mystery.

We'll encounter more unsolved mysteries in the next two sections of this chapter as we discuss hypnosis and meditation. Whereas sleep and dreams are familiar to everyone, most people have little familiarity with hypnosis and meditation, which both involve deliberate efforts to temporarily alter consciousness.

> Hypnosis: Altered Consciousness or Role Playing?

PREVIEW QUESTIONS

- What is the history of hypnosis?
- What are some prominent hypnotic phenomena?
- What lines of evidence support the role-playing theory of hypnosis?
- Does hypnosis produce an altered state of consciousness?

Hypnosis has a long and checkered history. It all began with a flamboyant 18th-century Austrian by the name of Franz Anton Mesmer. Working in Paris, Mesmer claimed to cure people of illnesses through an elaborate routine involving a "laying on of hands." Mesmer had some complicated theories about how he had harnessed "animal magnetism." However, we know today that he had simply stumbled onto the power of suggestion. Eventually he was dismissed as a charlatan and run out of town by the local authorities. Although officially discredited, Mesmer inspired followers—practitioners of "mesmerism"—who continued to ply their trade. To this day, our language preserves the memory of Franz Mesmer: When we are under the spell of an event or a story, we are "mesmerized."

Eventually, a Scottish physician, James Braid, became interested in the trancelike state that could be induced by the mesmerists. It was Braid who popularized the term *hypnotism* in 1843, borrowing it from the Greek word for sleep. Braid thought that hypnotism could be used to produce anesthesia for surgeries. However, just as hypnosis was catching on as a general anesthetic, more powerful and reliable chemical anesthetics were discovered, and interest in hypnotism dwindled.

Since then, hypnotism has led a curious dual existence. On the one hand, it has been the subject of numerous scientific studies. Furthermore, it has enjoyed considerable use as a clinical tool by physicians, dentists, and psychologists for over a century and has empirically supported value in the treatment of a variety of psychological and physical maladies (Lynn et al., 2000; Spiegel, Greenleaf, & Spiegel, 2000). On the other hand, an assortment of entertainers and quacks have continued in the less respectable tradition of mesmerism, using hypnotism for parlor tricks and chicanery. It is little wonder, then, that many myths about hypnosis have come to be widely accepted (see **Figure 5.9**).

Hypnotic Induction and Phenomena

Hypnosis **is a systematic procedure that typically produces a heightened state of suggestibility.** It may also lead to passive relaxation, narrowed attention, and enhanced fantasy. If only in popular films, virtually everyone has seen a *hypnotic induction* enacted with a swinging pendulum. Actually, many techniques can be used (Meyer, 1992). Usually, the hypnotist will suggest to the subject that he or she is relaxing. Repetitively, softly, subjects are told that they are getting tired, drowsy, or sleepy. Often, the hypnotist vividly describes bodily sensations that should be occurring. Subjects are told that their arms are going limp, that their feet are getting warm, that their eyelids are getting heavy. Gradually, most subjects succumb and become hypnotized.

People differ in how well they respond to hypnotic induction. Not everyone can be hypnotized. About 10% of the population do not respond well at all, while at the other end of the continuum, about 10% of people are exceptionally good hypnotic subjects (Hilgard, 1965). Among people who are susceptible to hypnosis, many interesting effects can be produced. Some of the more prominent hypnotic phenomena include:

1. *Anesthesia.* Although drugs are more reliable, hypnosis can be surprisingly effective in the treatment of both acute and chronic pain (Patterson & Jensen, 2003). Although the practice is not widespread, some physicians and dentists use hypnosis as a substitute for anesthetic drugs.

2. *Sensory distortions and hallucinations.* Hypnotized subjects may be led to experience auditory or visual hallucinations (Spiegel, 2003b). They may hear sounds or see things that are not there, or fail to hear or see stimuli that are present (Spiegel et al., 1985). Subjects may also have their sensations dis-

Hypnosis: Myth and Reality	
If you think . . .	**The reality is . . .**
Relaxation is an important feature of hypnosis.	It's not. Hypnosis has been induced during vigorous exercise.
It's mostly just compliance.	Many highly motivated subjects fail to experience hypnosis.
It's a matter of willful faking.	Physiological responses indicate that hypnotized subjects generally are not lying.
It has something to do with a sleeplike state.	It does not. Hypnotized subjects are fully awake.
Responding to hypnosis is like responding to a placebo.	Placebo responsiveness and hypnotizability are not correlated.
People who are hypnotized lose control of themselves.	Subjects are perfectly capable of saying no or terminating hypnosis.
Hypnosis can enable people to "relive" the past.	Age-regressed adults behave like adults play-acting as children.
When hypnotized, people can remember more accurately.	Hypnosis may actually muddle the distinction between memory and fantasy and may artificially inflate confidence.
Hypnotized people do not remember what happened during the session.	Posthypnotic amnesia does not occur spontaneously.
Hypnosis can enable people to perform otherwise impossible feats of strength, endurance, learning, and sensory acuity.	Performance following hypnotic suggestions for increased muscle strength, learning and sensory acuity does not exceed what can be accomplished by motivated subjects outside hypnosis.

Figure 5.9

Misconceptions regarding hypnosis. Mistaken ideas about the nature of hypnosis are common. Some widely believed myths about hypnosis are summarized here, along with more accurate information on each point, based on an article by Michael Nash (2001), a prominent hypnosis researcher. Many of these myths and realities are discussed in more detail in the text.

Source: Adapted from Nash, M. R. (2001, July). The truth and the hype of hypnosis. *Scientific American, 285,* 36–43. Copyright © 2001 by Scientific American, Inc. All rights reserved. Reproduced with permission.

torted so that something sweet tastes sour or an unpleasant odor smells fragrant.

3. *Disinhibition.* Hypnosis can sometimes reduce inhibitions that would normally prevent subjects from acting in ways that they would see as immoral or unacceptable. In experiments, hypnotized subjects have been induced to throw what they believed to be nitric acid into the face of a research assistant. Similarly, stage hypnotists are sometimes successful in getting people to disrobe in public. This disinhibition effect may occur simply because hypnotized people feel that they cannot be held responsible for their actions while they are hypnotized.

4. *Posthypnotic suggestions and amnesia.* Suggestions made during hypnosis may influence a subject's later behavior (Barnier, 2002). The most common posthypnotic suggestion is the creation of posthypnotic amnesia. That is, subjects are told that they will

Web Link 5.6

States of Consciousness
PsychWeb, Russ Dewey's (Georgia Southern University) superb resource page, hosts this fine collection of scientifically grounded guides to three topics that too often provoke nonsensical claims: hypnosis, out-of-body experiences, and dreaming.

remember nothing that happened while they were hypnotized. Such subjects usually remember nothing, as ordered.

Theories of Hypnosis

Although a number of theories have been developed to explain hypnosis, it is still not well understood. Most theories attribute hypnotic effects either to dramatic role playing or to a special, altered state of consciousness (a trance).

Hypnosis as Role Playing

Hypnotized subjects may feel as though they are in an altered state, but their patterns of EEG activity cannot be distinguished from their EEG patterns in normal waking states (Dixon & Laurence, 1992; Orne & Dinges, 1989). The failure to find any special physiological changes associated with hypnosis has led theorists such as Theodore Barber (1979) and Nicholas Spanos (1986; Spanos & Coe, 1992) to conclude that hypnosis produces a normal state of consciousness in which suggestible people act out the role of a hypnotized subject and behave as they think hypnotized people are supposed to. According to this notion, it is subjects' role expectations that produce hypnotic effects, rather than a special trance-like state of consciousness.

Two lines of evidence support the role-playing view. First, many of the seemingly amazing effects of hypnosis have been duplicated by nonhypnotized subjects or have been shown to be exaggerated (Kirsch, 1997). For example, much has been made of the fact that hypnotized subjects can be used as "human planks" (see the photo below), but it turns out that nonhypnotized subjects can easily match this and other hypnotic feats (Barber, 1986). This finding suggests that no special state of consciousness is required to explain hypnotic feats.

The second line of evidence involves demonstrations that hypnotized participants are often acting out a role. For example, Martin Orne (1951) regressed hypnotized subjects back to their sixth birthday and asked them to describe it. They responded with detailed descriptions that appeared to represent great feats of hypnosis-enhanced memory. However, instead of accepting this information at face value, Orne compared it with information that he had obtained from the participants' parents. It turned out that many of the subjects' memories were inaccurate and invented! Many other studies have also found that age-regressed subjects' recall of the distant past tends to be more fanciful than factual (Green, 1999). Thus, the role-playing explanation of hypnosis suggests that situational factors lead suggestible subjects to act out a certain role in a highly cooperative manner.

Hypnosis as an Altered State of Consciousness

Despite the doubts raised by role-playing explanations, many prominent theorists still maintain that hypnotic effects are attributable to a special, altered state of consciousness (Beahrs, 1983; Fromm, 1979, 1992; Hilgard, 1986; Spiegel, 1995, 2003a). These theorists argue that it is doubtful that role playing can explain all hypnotic phenomena. For instance, they assert that even the most cooperative subjects are unlikely to endure surgery without a drug anesthetic just to please their physician and live up to their expected role. They also cite studies in which hypnotized participants have continued to display hypnotic responses when they thought they were alone and not being observed (Perugini et al., 1998). If hypnotized participants were merely acting, they would drop the act when alone. The most impressive research undermining the role-playing view has come from recent brain-imaging studies, which suggest that hypnotized participants experience changes in brain activity that appear consistent with their reports of hypnosis-induced hallucinations (Spiegel, 2003b) or pain suppression (Hofbauer et al., 2001).

The most influential explanation of hypnosis as an altered state of awareness has been offered by Ernest Hilgard (1986, 1992). According to Hilgard, hypnosis creates a *dissociation* in consciousness. *Dis-*

Courtesy of X. Ted Barber

THEODORE BARBER

"Thousands of books, movies and professional articles have woven the concept of 'hypnotic trance' into the common knowledge. And yet there is almost no scientific support for it."

ERNEST HILGARD

"Many psychologists argue that the hypnotic trance is a mirage. It would be unfortunate if this skeptical view were to gain such popularity that the benefits of hypnosis are denied to the numbers of those who could be helped."

Chuck Painter/Stanford News Service

© Associated Press/AP

Some feats performed under hypnosis can be performed equally well by nonhypnotized subjects. Here "the Amazing Kreskin" demonstrates that proper positioning is the only requirement for the famous human plank feat.

sociation is a splitting off of mental processes into two separate, simultaneous streams of awareness. In other words, Hilgard theorizes that hypnosis splits consciousness into two streams. One stream is in communication with the hypnotist and the external world, while the other is a difficult-to-detect "hidden observer." Hilgard believes that many hypnotic effects are a product of this divided consciousness. For instance, he suggests that a hypnotized subject might appear unresponsive to pain because the pain isn't registered in the portion of consciousness that communicates with other people.

One appealing aspect of Hilgard's theory is that *divided consciousness* is a common, normal experience. For example, people will often drive a car a great distance, responding to traffic signals and other cars, with no recollection of having consciously done so. In such cases, consciousness is clearly divided between driving and the person's thoughts about other matters. Interestingly, this common experience has long been known as *highway hypnosis*. In summary, Hilgard presents hypnosis as a plausible variation in consciousness that has continuity with everyday experience.

The debate about whether hypnosis involves an altered or a normal state of consciousness appears likely to continue for the foreseeable future (Kihlstrom, 1998a; Kirsch & Lynn, 1998). As you will see momentarily, a similar debate has dominated the scientific discussion of meditation.

> Meditation: Pure Consciousness or Relaxation?

Recent years have seen growing interest in the ancient discipline of meditation. *Meditation* refers to a family of practices that train attention to heighten awareness and bring mental processes under greater voluntary control. In North America, the most widely practiced approaches to meditation are those associated with yoga, Zen, and transcendental meditation (TM). All three are rooted in Eastern religions (Hinduism, Buddhism, and Taoism). However, meditation has been practiced throughout history as an element of all religious and spiritual traditions, including Judaism and Christianity. Moreover, the practice of meditation can be largely divorced from religious beliefs. In fact, most Americans who meditate have only vague ideas regarding its religious significance. Of interest to psychology is the fact that meditation involves a deliberate effort to alter consciousness.

Most meditative techniques are deceptively simple. For example, in TM a person is supposed to sit in a comfortable position with eyes closed and silently focus attention on a *mantra*. A mantra is a specially assigned Sanskrit word that is personalized for each meditator. This exercise in mental self-discipline is to be practiced twice daily for about 20 minutes. The technique has been described as "diving from the active surface of the mind to its quiet depths" (Bloomfield & Kory, 1976, p. 49). Most proponents of TM believe that it involves an altered state of "pure consciousness." Many skeptics counter that meditation is simply an effective relaxation technique. Let's look at the evidence.

What happens when an experienced meditator goes into the meditative state? One intriguing finding is that alpha and theta waves become more prominent in EEG recordings. Many studies also find that subjects' heart rate, skin conductance, respiration rate, oxygen consumption, and carbon dioxide elimination decline (see **Figure 5.10**; Dillbeck & Orme-Johnson, 1987; Fenwick, 1987; Travis, 2001). Taken together, these changes suggest that meditation leads to a potentially beneficial physiological state characterized by suppression of bodily arousal. However, some researchers have argued that a variety of systematic relaxation training procedures can produce similar results (Holmes, 1987; Shapiro, 1984). Mere relaxation hardly seems like an adequate explanation for the transcendant experiences reported by many meditators. Hence, debate continues about whether

PREVIEW QUESTIONS

- What is meditation, and how is it practiced?
- How does meditation affect physiological responding?
- What's the evidence on the long-term benefits of meditation?

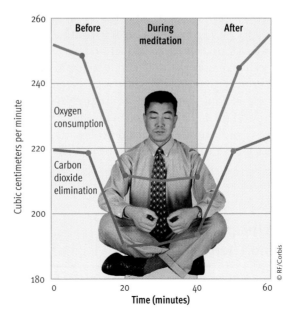

Figure 5.10

The suppression of physiological arousal during transcendental meditation. The physiological changes shown in the graph are evidence of physical relaxation during the meditative state. However, critics argue that similar changes may also be produced by systematic relaxation procedures.

Source: Adapted from Wallace, R. K., & Benson, H. (1972, February). The physiology of meditation. *Scientific American, 226*, 85–90. Graphic redrawn from illustration on p. 86 by Lorelle A. Raboni. Copyright © 1972 by Scientific American, Inc. Redrawn by permission of L. A. Raboni.

Relating EEG Activity to Variations in Consciousness

Early in the chapter we emphasized the intimate relationship between brain activity and variations in consciousness. Check your understanding of this relationship by indicating the kind of EEG activity (alpha, beta, theta, or delta) that would probably be dominant in each of the following situations. The answers are in Appendix A.

_____ **1.** You are playing a video game.

_____ **2.** You are deep in meditation.

_____ **3.** You have just fallen asleep.

_____ **4.** You are in the midst of a pleasant dream.

_____ **5.** You are a novice typist, practicing your typing.

there are physiological changes associated with meditation that are unique to a special state of consciousness (Shear & Jevning, 1999; Travis & Pearson, 2000).

What about the long-term benefits that have been claimed for meditation? Research suggests that meditation may have some value in reducing the effects of stress (Anderson et al., 1999; Winzelberg & Luskin, 1999). In particular, regular meditation is associated with lower levels of some "stress hormones" (Infante et al., 2001) and enhanced immune response (Davidson et al., 2003a). Research also suggests that meditation can improve mental health

while reducing anxiety and drug abuse (Alexander et al., 1994). Other studies report that meditation may have beneficial effects on blood pressure (Barnes, Treiber, & Davis, 2001), self-esteem (Emavardhana & Tori, 1997), mood and one's sense of control (Easterlin & Cardena, 1999), and overall physical health and well-being (Reibel et al., 2001). At first glance these results are impressive, but they need to be viewed with some caution. At least some of these effects may be just as attainable through systematic relaxation or other mental focusing procedures (Shapiro, 1984; Smith, 1975). Critics also wonder whether placebo effects, sampling bias, and other methodological problems may contribute to some of the reported benefits of meditation (Bishop, 2002; Canter, 2003; Caspi & Burleson, 2005). In a recent and relatively enthusiastic review of meditation research, the authors acknowledge that many meditation studies "do not use rigorous research design (including lack of randomization, lack of followup, and imprecise measurement of constructs) and sometimes are based on small samples" (Shapiro, Schwartz, & Santerre, 2002, p. 634).

In summary, it seems safe to conclude that meditation is a potentially worthwhile relaxation strategy. And it's possible that meditation involves more than mere relaxation, as TM advocates insist. At present, however, there is little evidence that meditation produces a unique state of "pure consciousness."

> Altering Consciousness with Drugs

PREVIEW QUESTIONS

● What are the principal categories of abused drugs, and what are their main effects?

● What kinds of factors influence drug experiences?

● Where do drugs exert their effects in the brain?

● What is the difference between physical and psychological dependence?

● What are the three ways in which abused drugs can harm health?

● What are the health risks associated with the use of marijuana and MDMA?

Like hypnosis and meditation, drugs are commonly used in deliberate efforts to alter consciousness. In this section, we focus on the use of drugs for nonmedical purposes, commonly referred to as "recreational drug use." Recreational drug use involves personal, moral, political, and legal issues that are not matters for science to resolve. However, the more knowledgeable you are about drugs, the more informed your decisions and opinions about them will be. Accordingly, this section describes the types of drugs that are most commonly used for recreational purposes and summarizes their effects on consciousness, behavior, and health.

Principal Abused Drugs and Their Effects

The drugs that people use recreationally are termed *psychoactive*. **Psychoactive drugs** are chemical sub-

stances that modify mental, emotional, or behavioral functioning. Not all psychoactive drugs produce effects that lead to recreational use. Generally, users prefer drugs that elevate their mood or produce other pleasurable alterations in consciousness. The principal types of recreational drugs are described in **Table 5.2**. The table lists representative drugs in each of six categories. It also summarizes how the drugs are taken, their medical uses, their effects on consciousness, and their common side effects (based on Julien, 2001; Levinthal, 2002; Lowinson et al., 2005). The six categories of psychoactive drugs that we will focus on are narcotics, sedatives, stimulants, hallucinogens, cannabis, and alcohol. We will also discuss "ecstasy," which has surged in popularity in recent years.

Narcotics, or **opiates**, are drugs derived from opium that are capable of relieving pain. The main drugs in this category are heroin and morphine, although less potent opiates such as codeine, Demerol, and methadone are also abused. In sufficient dosages

Table 5.2 Psychoactive Drugs: Methods of Ingestion, Medical Uses, and Effects

Drugs	Methods of Ingestion	Principal Medical Uses	Desired Effects	Potential Short-Term Side Effects
Narcotics (opiates) Morphine Heroin	Injected, smoked, oral	Pain relief	Euphoria, relaxation, anxiety reduction, pain relief	Lethargy, drowsiness, nausea, impaired coordination, impaired mental functioning, constipation
Sedatives Barbiturates (e.g., Seconal) Nonbarbiturates (e.g., Quaalude)	Oral, injected	Sleeping pill, anticonvulsant	Euphoria, relaxation, anxiety reduction, reduced inhibitions	Lethargy, drowsiness, severely impaired coordination, impaired mental functioning, emotional swings, dejection
Stimulants Amphetamines Cocaine	Oral, sniffed, injected, freebased, smoked	Treatment of hyperactivity and narcolepsy, local anesthetic (cocaine only)	Elation, excitement, increased alertness, increased energy, reduced fatigue	Increased blood pressure and heart rate, increased talkativeness, restlessness, irritability, insomnia, reduced appetite, increased sweating and urination, anxiety, paranoia, increased aggressiveness, panic
Hallucinogens LSD Mescaline Psilocybin	Oral	None	Increased sensory awareness, euphoria, altered perceptions, hallucinations, insightful experiences	Dilated pupils, nausea, emotional swings, paranoia, jumbled thought processes, impaired judgment, anxiety, panic reaction
Cannabis Marijuana Hashish THC	Smoked, oral	Treatment of glaucoma and chemotherapy—induced nausea and vomiting; other uses under study	Mild euphoria, relaxation, altered perceptions, enhanced awareness	Elevated heart rate, bloodshot eyes, dry mouth, reduced short-term memory, sluggish motor coordination, sluggish mental functioning, anxiety
Alcohol	Drinking	None	Mild euphoria, relaxation, anxiety reduction, reduced inhibitions	Severely impaired coordination, impaired mental functioning, increased urination, emotional swings, depression, quarrelsomeness, hangover

these drugs can produce an overwhelming sense of euphoria or well-being. This euphoric effect has a relaxing, "Who cares?" quality that makes the high an attractive escape from reality.

Sedatives **are sleep-inducing drugs that tend to decrease central nervous system activation and behavioral activity.** Over the years, the most widely abused sedatives have been the *barbiturates,* which are compounds derived from barbituric acid. People abusing sedatives, or "downers," generally consume larger doses than are prescribed for medical purposes. The desired effect is a euphoria similar to that produced by drinking large amounts of alcohol. Feelings of tension or dejection are replaced by a relaxed, pleasant state of intoxication, accompanied by loosened inhibitions.

Stimulants **are drugs that tend to increase central nervous system activation and behavioral activity.** Stimulants range from mild, widely available drugs, such as caffeine and nicotine, to stronger, carefully regulated ones, such as cocaine. We will focus on cocaine and amphetamines. Cocaine is a natural substance that comes from the coca shrub. In contrast, amphetamines ("speed") are synthesized in a pharmaceutical laboratory. Cocaine and amphetamines have fairly similar effects, except that cocaine produces a briefer high. Stimulants produce a euphoria very different from that created by narcotics or

sedatives. They produce a buoyant, elated, energetic, "I can conquer the world!" feeling accompanied by increased alertness. In recent years, cocaine and amphetamines have become available in much more potent (and dangerous) forms than before. "Crack" consists of relatively pure chips of cocaine that are

Web Link 5.7

Web of Addictions
From the earliest days of the World Wide Web, this page at The Well has been regularly recognized as a primary source for accurate and responsible information about alcohol and other drugs.

"JUST TELL ME WHERE YOU KIDS GET THE IDEA TO TAKE SO MANY DRUGS."

ScienceCartoonsPlus.com

usually smoked. Amphetamines are increasingly sold as a crystalline powder, called "crank," or "crystal meth" (short for methamphetamine), that may be snorted or injected intravenously.

Hallucinogens **are a diverse group of drugs that have powerful effects on mental and emotional functioning, marked most prominently by distortions in sensory and perceptual experience.** The principal hallucinogens are LSD, mescaline, and psilocybin. These drugs have similar effects, although they vary in potency. Hallucinogens produce euphoria, increased sensory awareness, and a distorted sense of time. In some users, they lead to profound, dreamlike, "mystical" feelings that are difficult to describe. The latter effect is why they have been used in religious ceremonies for centuries in some cultures. Unfortunately, at the other end of the emotional spectrum hallucinogens can also produce nightmarish feelings of anxiety and paranoia, commonly called a "bad trip."

Cannabis **is the hemp plant from which marijuana, hashish, and THC are derived.** Marijuana is a mixture of dried leaves, flowers, stems, and seeds taken from the plant. Hashish comes from the plant's resin. Smoking is the usual route of ingestion for both marijuana and hashish. THC, the active chemical ingredient in cannabis, can be synthesized for research purposes (for example, to give to animals, which can't very well smoke marijuana). When smoked, cannabis has an immediate impact that may last several hours. The desired effects of the drug are a mild, relaxed euphoria and enhanced sensory awareness.

Alcohol **encompasses a variety of beverages containing ethyl alcohol,** such as beers, wines, and distilled spirits. The concentration of ethyl alcohol varies from about 4% in most beers to 40% in 80-proof liquor—and occasionally more in higher-proof liquors. When people drink heavily, the central effect is a relaxed euphoria that temporarily boosts self-esteem, as problems seem to melt away and inhibitions diminish. Common side effects include severe impairments in mental and motor functioning, mood swings, and quarrelsomeness. Alcohol is the most widely used recreational drug in our society. Because alcohol is legal, many people use it casually without even thinking of it as a drug.

Excessive drinking is a particularly prevalent problem on college campuses. Researchers from the Harvard School of Public Health (Wechsler et al., 2002) surveyed nearly 11,000 undergraduates at 119 schools and found that 81% of the students drank. Moreover, 49% of the men and 41% of the women reported that they engage in binge drinking with the intention of getting drunk. With their inhibitions

released, some drinkers become argumentative and prone to aggression. In the Harvard survey, 29% of the students who did *not* engage in binge drinking reported that they had been insulted or humiliated by a drunken student; 19% had experienced serious arguments; 9% had been pushed, hit, or assaulted; and 19.5% had been the target of unwanted sexual advances (Wechsler et al., 2002). Worse yet, alcohol appears to contribute to about 90% of student rapes and 95% of violent crime on campus. Alcohol can also contribute to reckless sexual behavior. In the Harvard survey, 21% of students who drank reported that they had unplanned sex as a result of drinking, and 10% indicated that their drinking had led to unprotected sex.

MDMA, **or "ecstasy," is a compound drug that is related to both amphetamines and hallucinogens, especially mescaline.** MDMA was originally formulated in 1912 but was not widely used in the United States until the 1990s, when ecstasy became popular in the context of "raves" and dance clubs. MDMA produces a short-lived high that typically lasts a few hours or more. Users report that they feel warm, friendly, euphoric, sensual, insightful, and empathetic, but alert and energetic. Problematic side effects include increased blood pressure, muscle tension, and sweating, blurred vision, insomnia, and transient anxiety.

Factors Influencing Drug Effects

The drug effects summarized in **Table 5.2** are the *typical* ones. Drug effects can vary from person to person and even for the same person in different situations. The impact of any drug depends in part on the user's age, mood, motivation, personality, previous experience with the drug, body weight, and physiology. The dose and potency of a drug, the method of administration, and the setting in which a drug is taken also are likely to influence its effects (Leavitt, 1995). Our theme of *multifactorial causation* clearly applies to the effects of drugs.

So, too, does our theme emphasizing the *subjectivity of experience.* Expectations are potentially powerful factors that can influence the user's perceptions of a drug's effects. You may recall from our discussion of placebo effects in Chapter 2 that some people who are misled to *think* that they are drinking alcohol show signs of intoxication (Wilson, 1982). If people expect a drug to make them feel giddy, serene, or profound, their expectation may contribute to the feelings they experience.

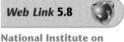

Web Link 5.8

National Institute on Alcohol Abuse and Alcoholism (NIAAA)
Just two of the many research sources here include the entire collection of the bulletin *Alcohol Alert,* issued since 1988 on specific topics related to alcoholism, and the ETOH Database, a searchable repository of more than 100,000 records on alcoholism and alcohol abuse.

A drug's effects can also change as the person's body develops a *tolerance* to the chemical. **Tolerance refers to a progressive decrease in a person's responsiveness to a drug as a result of continued use.** Tolerance usually leads people to consume larger and larger doses of a drug to attain the effects they desire. Most drugs produce tolerance, but some do so more rapidly than others. For example, tolerance to alcohol usually builds slowly, while tolerance to heroin increases much more quickly. **Table 5.3** indicates whether various categories of drugs tend to produce tolerance rapidly or gradually.

Mechanisms of Drug Action 4d

Most drugs have effects that reverberate throughout the body. However, psychoactive drugs work primarily by altering neurotransmitter activity in the brain. As we discussed in Chapter 3, *neurotransmitters* are chemicals that transmit signals between neurons at junctions called synapses.

The actions of amphetamines illustrate how drugs have selective, multiple effects on neurotransmitter activity. Amphetamines exert their main effects on two neurotransmitter systems: norepinephrine (NE) and dopamine (DA). Amphetamines appear to have two key effects at DA and NE synapses (Cami & Farre, 2003). First, they increase the release of dopamine and norepinephrine by presynaptic neurons. Second, they interfere with the reuptake of DA and NE from synaptic clefts. These actions serve to increase the levels of dopamine and norepinephrine at the affected synapses. Cocaine shares some of these actions, which is why cocaine and amphetamines produce similar stimulant effects.

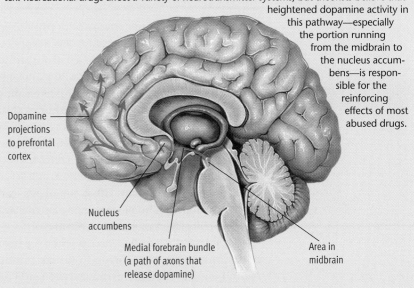

Figure 5.11

The "reward pathway" in the brain. The neural circuits shown here in blue make up the *mesolimbic dopamine pathway.* Axons in this pathway run from an area in the midbrain through the medial forebrain bundle to the *nucleus accumbens* and on to the prefrontal cortex. Recreational drugs affect a variety of neurotransmitter systems, but theorists believe that heightened dopamine activity in this pathway—especially the portion running from the midbrain to the nucleus accumbens—is responsible for the reinforcing effects of most abused drugs.

Dopamine projections to prefrontal cortex

Nucleus accumbens

Medial forebrain bundle (a path of axons that release dopamine)

Area in midbrain

Although specific drugs exert their initial effects in the brain on a wide variety of neurotransmitter systems, many theorists believe that virtually all abused drugs eventually increase activity in a particular neural pathway, called the *mesolimbic dopamine pathway* (Nestler & Malenka, 2004). This neural circuit, which runs from an area in the midbrain, through the *nucleus accumbens,* and on to the prefrontal cortex (see **Figure 5.11**), has been characterized as a "reward pathway." Large and rapid increases in the release of dopamine along this pathway are thought to

Table 5.3 Psychoactive Drugs: Tolerance, Dependence, Potential for Fatal Overdose, and Health Risks

Drugs	Tolerance	Risk of Physical Dependence	Risk of Psychological Dependence	Fatal Overdose Potential	Health Risks
Narcotics (opiates)	Rapid	High	High	High	Infectious diseases, accidents, immune suppression
Sedatives	Rapid	High	High	High	Accidents
Stimulants	Rapid	Moderate	High	Moderate to high	Sleep problems, malnutrition, nasal damage, hypertension, respiratory disease, stroke, liver disease, heart attack
Hallucinogens	Gradual	None	Very low	Very low	Accidents
Cannabis	Gradual	None	Low to moderate	Very low	Accidents, lung cancer, respiratory disease, pulmonary disease, perhaps head and neck cancer
Alcohol	Gradual	Moderate	Moderate	Low to high	Accidents, liver disease, malnutrition, brain damage, neurological disorders, heart disease, stroke, hypertension, ulcers, cancer, birth defects

be the neural basis of the reinforcing effects of most abused drugs (Volkow, Fowler, & Wang, 2004).

Drug Dependence

People can become either physically or psychologically dependent on a drug. Physical dependence is a common problem with narcotics, sedatives, and alcohol and is an occasional problem with stimulants. *Physical dependence* **exists when a person must continue to take a drug to avoid withdrawal illness.** The symptoms of withdrawal illness depend on the specific drug. Withdrawal from heroin, barbiturates, and alcohol can produce fever, chills, tremors, convulsions, vomiting, cramps, diarrhea, and severe aches and pains. Withdrawal from stimulants leads to a more subtle syndrome, marked by fatigue, apathy, irritability, depression, and disorientation.

Psychological dependence **exists when a person must continue to take a drug to satisfy intense mental and emotional craving.** Psychological dependence is more subtle than physical dependence, but the need it creates can be powerful. Cocaine, for instance, can produce an overwhelming psychological need for continued use. Psychological dependence is possible with all recreational drugs, although it seems rare for hallucinogens.

Both types of dependence are established gradually with repeated use of a drug. Drugs vary in their potential for creating either physical or psychological dependence. Table 5.3 provides estimates of the risk of each kind of dependence for the six categories of recreational drugs covered in our discussion.

Drugs and Health

Recreational drug use can affect physical health in a variety of ways. The three principal risks are overdose, tissue damage (direct effects), and health-impairing behavior that results from drug abuse (indirect effects).

Overdose

Any drug can be fatal if a person takes enough of it, but some drugs are much more dangerous than others. Table 5.3 shows estimates of the risk of accidentally consuming a *lethal* overdose of each listed drug. Drugs that are CNS depressants—sedatives, narcotics, and alcohol—carry the greatest risk of overdose. It's important to remember that these drugs are synergistic with each other, so many overdoses involve lethal *combinations* of CNS depressants. What happens when a person overdoses on these drugs? The respira-

tory system usually grinds to a halt, producing coma, brain damage, and death within a brief period. Fatal overdoses with CNS stimulants usually involve a heart attack, stroke, or cortical seizure. Years ago, deaths due to overdoses of stimulant drugs used to be relatively infrequent. However, cocaine overdoses have increased sharply as more people have experimented with freebasing, smoking crack, and other more dangerous modes of ingestion (Repetto & Gold, 2005).

Direct Effects

In some cases, drugs cause tissue damage directly. For example, chronic snorting of cocaine can damage nasal membranes. Cocaine use can also foster cardiovascular disease and crack smoking is associated with a number of respiratory problems (Gourevitch & Arnsten, 2005; Weaver & Schnoll, 1999). Long-term, excessive alcohol consumption is associated with an elevated risk for a wide range of serious health problems, including liver damage, ulcers, hypertension, stroke, heart disease, neurological disorders, and some types of cancer (Mack, Franklin, & Frances, 2003; Moak & Anton, 1999).

The health risks of marijuana have generated considerable debate in recent years. The evidence suggests that heavy use of marijuana increases the chances for respiratory and pulmonary diseases, including lung cancer (Tashkin et al., 2002), and some preliminary evidence suggests a possible link to head and neck cancers (Hashibe, Ford, & Zhang, 2002). However, many reported dangers appear to have been exaggerated in the popular press. Contrary to popular reports, it appears that cannabis does *not* produce meaningful reductions in immune system responding (Bredt et al., 2002; Klein, Friedman, & Specter, 1998) or any significant effects on male smokers' fertility or sexual functioning (Grinspoon, Bakalar, & Russo, 2005). A spate of recent studies *have* found an association between chronic, heavy marijuana use and measurable impairments in attention and memory that show up when users are not high (Ehrenreich et al., 1999; Solowij et al., 2002). However, the cognitive deficits that have been observed are modest and one study found that the deficits vanished after a month of marijuana abstinence (Pope, Gruber, & Yurgelun-Todd, 2001; Pope et al., 2001).

Indirect Effects

The negative effects of drugs on physical health are often indirect results of the drugs' impact on behavior. For instance, people using stimulants often do not eat or sleep properly. Sedatives increase the risk of accidental injuries because they severely impair motor coordination. People who abuse downers

Web Link 5.9

National Institute on Drug Abuse (NIDA) This government-sponsored site houses a great deal of information on the medical consequences of abusing various drugs. It also is an excellent resource for statistics on trends in drug abuse.

often trip down stairs, fall off stools, and suffer other mishaps. Many drugs impair driving ability, increasing the risk of automobile accidents. Alcohol, for instance, may contribute to roughly 30% of all automobile fatalities (Yi et al., 1999). Intravenous drug users risk contracting infectious diseases that can be spread by unsterilized needles. In recent years, acquired immune deficiency syndrome (AIDS) has been transmitted at an alarming rate through the population of intravenous drug users (Des Jarlais, Hagan, & Friedman, 2005).

The major health risks (other than overdose) of various recreational drugs are listed in the sixth column of Table 5.3. As you can see, alcohol appears to have the most diverse negative effects on physical health. The irony, of course, is that alcohol is the only recreational drug listed that is legal.

New Findings Regarding Ecstasy

Ecstasy is not included in Table 5.3 because research on MDMA is in its infancy and relatively little is known. However, the preliminary research is beginning to alter the common perception that ecstasy is relatively harmless. MDMA has been implicated in cases of stroke and heart attack, seizures, heat stroke, and liver damage, but gauging its exact contribution is difficult, given all the other drugs that MDMA users typically consume (Grob & Poland, 2005; Scholey et al., 2004). Chronic, heavy use of ecstasy appears to be associated with sleep disorders, depression, and elevated anxiety and hostility (Morgan, 2000). Moreover, studies of former MDMA users suggest that ecstasy may have subtle, long-term effects on cognitive

concept **check** 5.3

Recognizing the Unique Characteristics of Commonly Abused Drugs

From our discussion of the principal psychoactive drugs, it is clear that considerable overlap exists among the categories of drugs in terms of their methods of ingestion, medical uses, desired effects, and short-term side effects. Each type of drug, however, has at least one or two characteristics that make it different from the other types. Check your understanding of the unique characteristics of each type of drug by indicating which of them has the characteristics listed below. Choose from the following: (a) narcotics, (b) sedatives, (c) stimulants, (d) hallucinogens, (e) cannabis, and (f) alcohol. You'll find the answers in Appendix A.

_____ **1.** Increases alertness and energy, reduces fatigue.

_____ **2.** No recognized medical use. May lead to insightful or "mystical" experiences.

_____ **3.** Used as a "sleeping pill" because it reduces CNS activity.

_____ **4.** Contributes to 30% of all traffic fatalities.

_____ **5.** Derived from opium; used for pain relief.

_____ **6.** Most likely health risk is respiratory and pulmonary disease.

functioning (Parrott, 2000). Quite a few studies have found memory deficits in former users (Bhattachary & Powell, 2001; Rodgers et al., 2003). Other studies have found decreased performance on laboratory tasks requiring attention and learning (Gouzoulis-Mayfrank et al., 2000). Thus, although a great deal of additional research is needed, the preliminary evidence suggests that MDMA may be more harmful than widely assumed.

> Reflecting on the Chapter's Themes

This chapter highlights four of our unifying themes. First, we can see how psychology evolves in a sociohistorical context. Research on consciousness dwindled to almost nothing after John B. Watson (1913, 1919) and others redefined psychology as the science of behavior. However, in the 1960s, people began to turn inward, showing a new interest in altering consciousness through drug use, meditation, hypnosis, and biofeedback. Psychologists responded to these social trends by beginning to study variations in consciousness in earnest. This shift shows how social forces can have an impact on psychology's evolution.

A second theme that surfaced in this chapter is the idea that people's experience of the world is highly subjective. We encountered this theme toward the end of the chapter when we discussed the subjective nature of drug effects, noting that the alterations of consciousness produced by drugs depend significantly on personal expectations.

Third, we saw once again how culture molds some aspects of behavior. Although the basic physiological process of sleep appears largely invariant from one society to another, culture influences certain aspects of sleep habits and has a dramatic impact on whether people remember their dreams and how they interpret and feel about their dreams. If not for space constraints, we might also have discussed cross-cultural differences in patterns of recreational drug use, which vary considerably from one society to the next.

Finally, the chapter illustrates psychology's theoretical diversity. We discussed conflicting theories about dreams, hypnosis, meditation, and the evolutionary

 Sociohistorical Context

 Subjectivity of Experience

 Cultural Heritage

 Theoretical Diversity

bases of sleep and consciousness. For the most part, we did not see these opposing theories converging toward reconciliation, as we did in the previous chapter. However, it's important to emphasize that rival theories do not always merge neatly into tidy models of behavior. While it's always nice to resolve a theoretical debate, the debate itself can advance knowledge by stimulating and guiding empirical research.

Indeed, our upcoming Personal Application demonstrates that theoretical debates need not be resolved in order to advance knowledge. Many theoretical controversies and enduring mysteries remain in the study of sleep and dreams. Nonetheless, researchers have accumulated a great deal of practical information on these topics, which we'll discuss next.

PERSONAL *Application*

Addressing Practical Questions About Sleep and Dreams

Indicate whether the following statements are "true" or "false."

_____ 1 Naps rarely have a refreshing effect.

_____ 2 Some people never dream.

_____ 3 When people cannot recall their dreams, it's because they are trying to repress them.

These assertions were drawn from the Sleep and Dreams Information Questionnaire (Palladino & Carducci, 1984), which measures practical knowledge about sleep and dreams. Are they true or false? You'll see in this Application.

Common Questions About Sleep

How much sleep do people need? The average amount of daily sleep for young adults is 7.5 hours. However, people vary considerably in how long they sleep. Based on a synthesis of data from many studies, Webb (1992b) estimates that sleep time is distributed as shown in **Figure 5.12**. As the diagram shows, sleep needs vary from person to person. That said, many sleep experts believe that most people would function more effectively if they increased their amount of sleep (Maas, 1998).

Can short naps be refreshing? Some naps are beneficial and some are not. The effectiveness of napping varies from person to person. Also, the benefits of any specific nap depend on the time of day and the amount of sleep one has had recently (Dinges, 1993). In general, naps are not a very efficient way to sleep because you're often just

getting into the deeper stages of sleep when your nap time is up. Napping can also disrupt nighttime sleep (Thorpy & Yager, 2001). Nonetheless, most naps enhance subsequent alertness and reduce sleepiness (Gillberg et al., 1996; Takahashi et al., 2004). Many highly productive people, including Thomas Edison, Winston Churchill, and John F. Kennedy, have made effective use of naps. In conclusion, naps can be refreshing for many people, so the first statement opening this Application is false.

What is the significance of snoring? Snoring is a common phenomenon that is seen in roughly 30%–40% of adults (Hoffstein, 2005). Snoring increases after age 35, occurs in men more than women, and is more frequent among people who are overweight (Kryger, 1993; Stoohs et al., 1998). Many factors, including obesity, colds, allergies, smoking, and some drugs, can contribute to snoring, mainly by forcing people to breathe through their mouths while sleeping. Some people who snore loudly disrupt their own sleep as well as that of their bed partners. It can be difficult to prevent snoring in some people, whereas other people can reduce their snoring by losing weight or sleeping on their side instead of their back (Lugaresi et al., 1994). Snoring may seem like a trivial problem, but it is associated with sleep apnea and cardiovascular disease, and it may have more medical significance than most people realize (Dement & Vaughn, 1999).

What can be done to avoid sleep problems? There are many ways to improve your chances of getting satisfactory sleep (see **Figure 5.13**). Most of them involve devel-

oping sensible daytime habits that won't interfere with sleep (Maas, 1998; Stepanski & Wyatt, 2003; Thorpy & Yager, 2001; Zarcone, 2000). For example, if you've been having trouble sleeping at night, it's wise to avoid daytime naps, so that you'll be tired when bedtime arrives. Some people find that daytime exercise helps them fall asleep more readily at bedtime (King et al., 1997).

It's wise to minimize consumption of stimulants such as caffeine and nicotine. Because coffee and cigarettes aren't prescription drugs, people don't appreciate how much the stimulants they contain can heighten physical arousal. Many foods (such as chocolate) and beverages (such as cola drinks) contain more caffeine than people realize. Also, bear in mind that ill-advised eating habits can interfere with sleep. Try to avoid going to bed hungry, uncomfortably stuffed, or soon after eating foods that disagree with you. It's also a good idea to try to establish a reasonably regular bedtime. This habit will allow you to take advantage of your circadian rhythm, so you'll be trying to fall asleep when your body is primed to cooperate.

What can be done about insomnia? First, don't panic if you run into a little trouble sleeping. An overreaction to sleep difficulties can begin a vicious circle of escalating problems. If you jump to the conclusion that you are becoming an insomniac, you may approach sleep with anxiety that will aggravate the problem. The harder you work at falling asleep, the less success you're likely to have. As noted earlier, temporary sleep problems are common and generally clear up on their own.

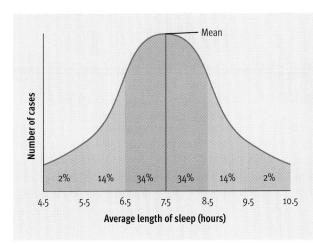

Figure 5.12

Variation in sleep needs. Based on data from a variety of sources, Webb (1992b) estimates that average sleep length among young adults is distributed normally, as shown here. Although most young adults sleep an average of 6.5 to 8.5 hours per night, some people need less and some people need more sleep.

Source: Adapted from Webb, W. B. (1992). *Sleep, the gentle tyrant* (2nd Ed.). Bolton, MA: Anker Publishing Co. Copyright © 1992 by Anker Publishing Co. Adapted by permission.

One sleep expert, Dianne Hales (1987), lists 101 suggestions for combating insomnia in her book *How to Sleep Like a Baby*. Many involve "boring yourself to sleep" by playing alphabet games, reciting poems, or listening to your clock. Another recommended strategy is to engage in some not-so-engaging activity. For instance, you might try reading your dullest textbook. It could turn out to be a superb sedative.

It's often a good idea to simply launch yourself into a pleasant daydream. This normal presleep process can take your mind off your difficulties. Whatever you think about, try to avoid ruminating about the current stresses and problems in your life. Research has shown that the tendency to ruminate is one of the key factors contributing to insomnia (Kales et al., 1984). Anything that relaxes you—whether it's music, meditation, prayer, a warm bath, or a systematic relaxation procedure—can aid you in falling asleep.

Common Questions About Dreams

Does everyone dream? Yes. Some people just don't *remember* their dreams. However, when these people are brought into a sleep lab and awakened from REM sleep, they report having been dreaming—much to their surprise (statement 2 at the start of this Application is false). Scientists have studied a small number of people who have sustained brain damage in an area of the *pons* that has wiped out their REM sleep, but even these people report dreams (Klosch & Kraft, 2005).

Why don't some people remember their dreams? The evaporation of dreams appears to be quite normal. Given the lowered level of awareness during sleep, it's understandable that memory of dreams is mediocre. Dream recall is best when people are awakened during or soon after a dream (Goodenough, 1991). Most of the time, people who *do* recall dreams upon waking are remembering either their *last* dream from their final REM period or a dream that awakened them earlier in the night. Hobson's (1989) educated guess is that people probably forget 95%–99% of their dreams. This forget-

ting is natural and is not due to repression (statement 3 is also false). People who never remember their dreams probably have a sleep pattern that puts too much time between their last REM/dream period and awakening, so even their last dream is forgotten.

Do dreams require interpretation? Yes, but interpretation may not be as difficult as generally assumed. People have long believed that dreams are symbolic and that it is necessary to interpret the symbols to understand the meaning of dreams. Freud, for instance, made a distinction between the *manifest content* and the *latent content* of a dream. **The *manifest content* consists of the plot of a dream at a surface level. The *latent content* refers to the hidden or disguised meaning of the events in the plot.** Thus, a Freudian therapist might equate such dream events as walking into a tunnel, mounting a horse, or riding a roller coaster with sexual intercourse. Freudian theorists assert that dream interpretation is a complicated task requiring considerable knowledge of symbolism.

However, many dream theorists argue that symbolism in dreams is less deceptive and mysterious than Freud thought (Faraday, 1974; Foulkes, 1985; Hall, 1979). Calvin Hall makes the point that dreams require some interpretation simply because they are more visual than verbal. That is, pictures need to be translated into ideas. According to Hall, dream symbolism is highly personal and the dreamer may be the person best equipped to decipher a dream. Unfortunately, you'll never know whether you're "correct," because there is no definitive way to judge the validity of different dream interpretations.

Could a shocking dream be fatal? According to folklore, if you fall from a height in a dream, you'd better wake up on the plunge downward, because if you hit the bottom the shock to your system will be so great that you will actually die in your sleep. Think about this one for a moment. *If* it were a genuine problem, who would have reported it? You can be sure that no one has ever testified to experiencing a fatal dream. This myth presumably exists because many people do awaken during the downward plunge, thinking they've averted a close call. A study by Barrett (1988–1989) suggests that dreams of one's own death are relatively infrequent. However, people do have such dreams—and live to tell about them.

1. Reduce stress as much as possible.
2. Exercise to stay fit.
3. Keep mentally stimulated during the day.
4. Eat a proper diet.
5. Stop smoking.
6. Reduce caffeine intake.
7. Avoid alcohol near bedtime.
8. Take a warm bath before bed.
9. Maintain a relaxing atmosphere in the bedroom.
10. Establish a bedtime ritual.
11. Have pleasurable sexual activity.
12. Clear your mind at bedtime.
13. Try some bedtime relaxation techniques.
14. Avoid trying too hard to get to sleep.
15. Learn to value sleep.

Figure 5.13

Suggestions for better sleep. In his book *Power Sleep,* James Maas (1998) offers this advice for people concerned about enhancing their sleep. Maas argues convincingly that good daytime habits can make all the difference in the world to the quality of one's sleep.

Source: Adapted from Maas, J. B. (1998). *Power sleep.* New York: Random House. Copyright © 1998 by James B. Maas, Ph.D. Reprinted by permission of Villard Books, a division of Random House, Inc.

Is Alcoholism a Disease? The Power of Definitions

Alcoholism is a major problem in most—perhaps all—societies. It destroys countless lives, tears families apart, and is associated with an elevated risk for a variety of physical maladies (Johnson & Ait-Daoud, 2005). With roughly 15 million problem drinkers in the United States (Mack et al., 2003), it seems likely that alcoholism has touched the lives of a majority of Americans.

In almost every discussion about alcoholism someone will ask, "Is alcoholism a disease?" If alcoholism is a disease, it is a strange one, because the alcoholic is the most direct cause of his or her own sickness. If alcoholism is *not* a disease, what else might it be? Over the course of history, alcoholism has been categorized under many labels, from a personal weakness to a crime, a sin, a mental disorder, and a physical illness (Meyer, 1996). Each of these definitions carries important personal, social, political, and economic implications.

Consider, for instance, the consequences of characterizing alcoholism as a disease. If that is the case, alcoholics should be treated like diabetics, heart patients, or victims of other physical illnesses. That is, they should be viewed with sympathy and should be given appropriate medical and therapeutic interventions to foster recovery from their illness. These treatments should be covered by medical insurance and delivered by health care professionals. Just as important, if alcoholism is defined as a disease, it should lose much of its stigma. After all, we don't blame people with diabetes or heart disease for their illnesses. Yes, alcoholics admittedly contribute to their own disease (by drinking too much), but so do many victims of diabetes and heart disease who eat all the wrong foods, fail to control their weight, and so forth (McLellan et al., 2000). And, as is the case with many physical illnesses, one can inherit a genetic vulnerability to alcoholism (Lin & Anthenelli, 2005), so it is difficult to argue that alcoholism is caused solely by one's behavior.

Alternatively, if alcoholism is defined as a personal failure or a moral weakness, alcoholics are less likely to be viewed with sympathy and compassion. They might be admonished to quit drinking, put in prison, or punished in some other way. These responses to their alcoholism would be administered primarily by the legal system rather than the health care system, as medical interventions are not designed to remedy moral failings. Obviously, the interventions that would be available would not be covered by health insurance, which would have enormous financial repercussions (for both health care providers and alcoholics).

The key point here is that definitions lie at the center of many complex debates, and they can have profound and far-reaching implications. People tend to think of definitions as insignificant, arbitrary sets of words found buried in the obscurity of thick dictionaries compiled by ivory tower intellectuals. Well, much of this characterization may be accurate, but definitions are not insignificant. They are vested with enormous power to shape how people think about important issues. And an endless array of issues boil down to matters of definition. For example, the next time you hear people arguing over whether a particular movie is pornographic, whether the death penalty is cruel and unusual punishment, or whether spanking is child abuse, you'll find it helps to focus the debate on clarifying the definitions of the crucial concepts.

The Power to Make Definitions

So, how can we resolve the debate about whether alcoholism is a disease? Scientists generally try to resolve their debates by conducting research to achieve a better understanding of the phenomena under study. You may have noticed already that the assertion "We need more research on this issue . . ." is a frequent refrain in this text. Is more research the answer in this case? For once, the answer is "no." There is no conclusive way to determine whether alcoholism is a disease. It is not as though there is a "right" answer to this question that we can discover through more and better research.

The question of whether alcoholism is a disease is a *matter of definition:* Does alcoholism fit the currently accepted definition of what constitutes a disease? If you consult medical texts or dictionaries, you will find that disease is typically defined as *an impairment in the normal functioning of an organism that alters its vital functions.* Given that alcoholism clearly impairs people's normal functioning and disrupts a variety of vital functions (see Figure 5.14), it seems reasonable to characterize it as a disease, and this view has been the dominant one in the United States since the middle of the 20th century (Maltzman, 1994; Meyer, 1996). This view has only been strengthened by recent evidence that addiction to alcohol (and other drugs) is the result of dysregulation in key neural circuits in the brain (Cami & Farre, 2003). Still, many critics express vigorous doubts about the wisdom of defining alcoholism as a disease (Peele, 1989, 2000). They often raise a question that comes up frequently in arguments about definitions: Who should have the power to make the definition? In this case, the power lies in the hands of the medical community, which seems sensible, given that disease is a medical concept. But some critics argue that the medical community has a strong bias in favor of defining conditions as diseases because doing so creates new markets and fuels economic growth for the health industry (Nikelly, 1994). Thus, debate about whether alcoholism is a disease seems likely to continue for the indefinite future.

To summarize, definitions generally do not emerge out of research. They are typically crafted by experts or authorities in a specific field who try to reach a consensus about how to best define a particular concept. Thus, in analyzing the validity of a definition, you need to look not only at the definition itself but at where it came from. Who decided what the definition should be? Does the source of the definition seem legitimate and appropriate? Did the authorities who formulated the definition have any biases that should be considered?

Definitions, Labels, and Circular Reasoning

One additional point about definitions is worth discussing. Perhaps because definitions are imbued with so much power, people have an interesting tendency to incorrectly use them as *explanations* for the phenomena they describe. This logical error, which equates *naming* something with *explaining* it, is sometimes called the *nominal fallacy.* Names and labels that are used as explanations often sound quite reasonable at first. *But definitions do not really have any explanatory value; they simply specify what certain terms mean.* Consider an example. Let's say your friend, Frank, has a severe drinking problem. You are sitting around with some other friends discussing why Frank drinks so much. Rest assured, at least one of these friends will assert that "Frank drinks too much because he is an alcoholic." This is *circular reasoning,* which is just as useless as explaining that Frank is an alcoholic because he drinks too much. It tells us nothing about *why* Frank has a drinking problem.

The diagnostic labels that are used in the classification of mental disorders—labels such as schizophrenia, depression, autism, and obsessive-compulsive disorder (see Chapter 13)—also seem to invite this type of circular reasoning. For example, people often say things like "That person is delusional because she is schizophrenic," or "He is afraid of small, enclosed places because he is claustrophobic." These statements may sound plausible, but they are no more logical or insightful than saying "She is a redhead because she has red hair." The logical fallacy of mistaking a label for an explanation will get us as far in our understanding as a dog gets in chasing its own tail.

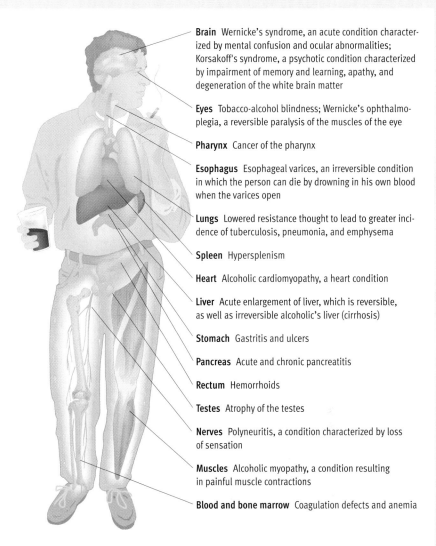

Brain Wernicke's syndrome, an acute condition characterized by mental confusion and ocular abnormalities; Korsakoff's syndrome, a psychotic condition characterized by impairment of memory and learning, apathy, and degeneration of the white brain matter

Eyes Tobacco-alcohol blindness; Wernicke's ophthalmoplegia, a reversible paralysis of the muscles of the eye

Pharynx Cancer of the pharynx

Esophagus Esophageal varices, an irreversible condition in which the person can die by drowning in his own blood when the varices open

Lungs Lowered resistance thought to lead to greater incidence of tuberculosis, pneumonia, and emphysema

Spleen Hypersplenism

Heart Alcoholic cardiomyopathy, a heart condition

Liver Acute enlargement of liver, which is reversible, as well as irreversible alcoholic's liver (cirrhosis)

Stomach Gastritis and ulcers

Pancreas Acute and chronic pancreatitis

Rectum Hemorrhoids

Testes Atrophy of the testes

Nerves Polyneuritis, a condition characterized by loss of sensation

Muscles Alcoholic myopathy, a condition resulting in painful muscle contractions

Blood and bone marrow Coagulation defects and anemia

Figure 5.14

Physiological malfunctions associated with alcoholism. This chart amply demonstrates that alcoholism is associated with a diverse array of physiological maladies. In and of itself, however, this information does not settle the argument about whether alcoholism should be regarded as a disease. It all depends on one's definition of what constitutes a disease.

Source: Edlin, G., & Golanty, E. (1992). *Health and wellness: A holistic approach.* Boston: Jones & Bartlett. Copyright © 1992 by Jones & Bartlett Publishers, Inc. www.jbpub.com. Reprinted by permission.

Table 5.4 **Critical Thinking Skills Discussed in This Application**

Skill	Description
Understanding the way definitions shape how people think about issues	The critical thinker appreciates the enormous power of definitions and the need to clarify definitions in efforts to resolve disagreements.
Identifying the source of definitions	The critical thinker recognizes the need to determine who has the power to make specific definitions and to evaluate their credibility.
Avoiding the nominal fallacy in working with definitions and labels	The critical thinker understands that labels do not have explanatory value.

Key Ideas

On the Nature of Consciousness

● Consciousness is the continually changing stream of mental activity. Variations in consciousness are related to brain activity, as measured by the EEG. Consciousness clearly is adaptive, but the question of exactly why it evolved is open to debate.

Biological Rhythms and Sleep

● Sleep is influenced by biological rhythms, especially 24-hour circadian rhythms. Exposure to light resets biological clocks by affecting the activity of the suprachiasmatic nucleus and the pineal gland, which secretes melatonin.

● Being out of sync with circadian rhythms is one reason for jet lag and for the unpleasant nature of rotating shift work. Melatonin may have some value in treating jet lag. The negative effects of rotating shifts may be reduced by bright light administration or circadian-friendly scheduling.

The Sleep and Waking Cycle

● When you fall asleep, you pass through a series of stages in cycles of approximately 90 minutes. During the REM stage you experience rapid eye movements, a brain wave that is characteristic of waking thought, and the bulk of your dreaming. The sleep cycle tends to be repeated about four times in a night, as REM sleep gradually becomes more predominant and NREM sleep dwindles.

● The REM portion of sleep declines during childhood, leveling off at around 20% during adolescence. During adulthood, slow-wave sleep declines. Culture appears to have little impact on the architecture of sleep, but it does influence sleeping arrangements and napping patterns. Hypotheses about the evolutionary bases of sleep focus on energy conservation, reduced exposure to predators, and restoration of depleted resources.

● The only consistent effect of sleep deprivation is sleepiness. However, increased sleepiness can contribute to work accidents and other mishaps. REM and slow-wave sleep may contribute to memory consolidation. Insomnia involves three distinct patterns of sleep difficulty. Sleeping pills generally are a poor solution for insomnia. Other common sleep disorders include narcolepsy, sleep apnea, and somnambulism.

The World of Dreams

● Research on dream content indicates that dreams are not as exotic as widely believed, although certain themes are particularly common. The content of one's dreams may be affected by events in one's life and by external stimuli that are experienced during the dream.

● Dramatic variations occur across cultures in beliefs about the nature of dreams and their importance, dream recall, dream content, and dream interpretation. The Freudian, cognitive, and activation-synthesis theories of dreaming are all very interesting, but scientists do not really know why people dream.

Hypnosis: Altered Consciousness or Role Playing?

● People vary in their susceptibility to hypnosis. Among other things, hypnosis can produce anesthesia, sensory distortions, disinhibition, and posthypnotic amnesia. Theories of hypnosis view it either as an altered state of consciousness or as a normal state in which subjects assume a hypnotic role.

Meditation: Pure Consciousness or Relaxation?

● Evidence suggests that meditation can lead to a potentially beneficial state characterized by suppression of bodily arousal. Research also suggests that meditation may have a variety of long-term benefits. However, some critics suggest that the observed benefits are not unique to meditation and are a product of any effective relaxation procedure.

Altering Consciousness with Drugs

● The principal types of psychoactive drugs are narcotics, sedatives, stimulants, hallucinogens, cannabis, alcohol, and MDMA. Although it's possible to describe the typical effects of various drugs, the actual effect on any individual depends on a host of factors, including subjective expectations and tolerance to the drug.

● Psychoactive drugs exert their main effects in the brain, where they alter neurotransmitter activity. The mesolimbic dopamine pathway may mediate the reinforcing effects of most abused drugs. Drugs vary in their potential for psychological and physical dependence. Recreational drug use can prove harmful to health by producing an overdose, by causing tissue damage, or by increasing health-impairing behavior.

Reflecting on the Chapter's Themes

● Four of our unifying themes were highlighted in this chapter. First, we saw how psychology's study of consciousness reflects concurrent social trends, showing that psychology evolves in a sociohistorical context. Second, we saw how states of consciousness are highly subjective. Third, we saw how culture molds some aspects of sleep and dreaming. Fourth, we saw extensive theoretical diversity that continues to generate vigorous debate about many issues in this area.

PERSONAL APPLICATION • Addressing Practical Questions About Sleep and Dreams

● Sleep needs vary, and the value of short naps depends on many factors. People can do many things to avoid or reduce sleep problems. People troubled by transient insomnia should avoid panic, pursue effective relaxation, and try distracting themselves.

● Everyone dreams, but some people cannot remember their dreams, probably because of the nature of their sleep cycle. Most theorists believe that dreams require some interpretation, but this may not be as complicated as once assumed.

CRITICAL THINKING APPLICATION • Is Alcoholism a Disease? The Power of Definitions

● Like many questions, the issue of whether alcoholism should be regarded as a disease is a matter of definition. In evaluating the validity of a definition, one should look not only at the definition but also at where it came from. People have a tendency to use definitions as explanations for the phenomena they describe, but doing so involves circular reasoning.

Key Terms

Alcohol (p. 158)
Biological rhythms (p. 139)
Cannabis (p. 158)
Circadian rhythms (p. 139)
Consciousness (p. 138)
Dissociation (pp. 154–155)
Electrocardiograph (EKG) (p. 141)
Electroencephalograph (EEG) (p. 138)
Electromyograph (EMG) (p. 141)
Electrooculograph (EOG) (p. 141)
Hallucinogens (p. 158)
Hypnosis (p. 153)
Insomnia (p. 147)
Latent content (p. 163)
Manifest content (p. 163)
MDMA (p. 158)
Meditation (p. 155)
Narcolepsy (p. 148)
Narcotics (p. 156)
Non-REM (NREM) sleep (p. 143)
Opiates (p. 156)
Physical dependence (p. 160)
Psychoactive drugs (p. 156)
Psychological dependence (p. 160)
REM sleep (p. 143)
Sedatives (p. 157)
Sleep apnea (p. 148)
Slow-wave sleep (p. 142)
Somnambulism (p. 148)
Stimulants (p. 157)
Tolerance (p. 159)

Key People

Rosalind Cartwright (p. 151)
William Dement (pp. 137, 142, 146)
Sigmund Freud (p. 151)
Ernest Hilgard (pp. 154–155)
J. Alan Hobson (p. 151)
William James (p. 138)

1. An EEG would indicate primarily _____ activity while you take this test.
   A. alpha
   B. beta
   C. delta
   D. theta

2. Readjusting your biological clock would be most difficult under which of the following circumstances?
   A. Flying west from Los Angeles to Hawaii
   B. Flying north from Miami to New York
   C. Flying east from Hawaii to Los Angeles
   D. Flying south from New York to Miami

3. As the sleep cycle evolves through the night, people tend to:
   A. spend more time in REM sleep and less time in NREM sleep.
   B. spend more time in NREM sleep and less time in REM sleep.
   C. spend a more or less equal amount of time in REM sleep and NREM sleep.
   D. spend more time in stage 4 sleep and less time in REM sleep.

4. Newborn infants spend about _____ % of their sleep time in REM, and adults spend about _____ % of their sleep time in REM.
   A. 20; 50
   B. 50; 20
   C. 20; 20
   D. 50; 50

5. After being selectively deprived of REM sleep, people typically experience:
   A. hypochondriasis.
   B. non-REM dysfunction.
   C. emotional breakdowns.
   D. a REM rebound effect.

6. Which of the following is *not* true of sleeping pills?
   A. Sleeping pills are an excellent long-range solution for all types of insomnia.
   B. There is some danger of overdose.
   C. Sleeping pills reduce the proportion of time spent in REM sleep.
   D. Sleeping pills gradually become less effective with continued use.

7. Which of the following is *not* true of cultural influences on dream experiences?
   A. The ability to recall dreams is fairly consistent across cultures.
   B. In some cultures, people are held responsible for their dream actions.
   C. In many cultures, dreams are seen as a window into the spiritual world.
   D. People in some cultures believe that dreams provide information about the future.

8. The activation-synthesis theory of dreaming contends that:
   A. dreams are simply the by-product of bursts of activity in the brain.
   B. dreams provide an outlet for energy invested in socially undesirable impulses.
   C. dreams represent the brain's attempt to process information taken in during waking hours.
   D. dreams are an attempt to restore a neurotransmitter balance within the brain.

9. A common driving experience is "highway hypnosis," in which one's consciousness seems to be divided between the driving itself and one's conscious train of thought. This phenomenon has been cited to support the idea that hypnosis is:
   A. an exercise in role playing.
   B. a dissociated state of consciousness.
   C. a goal-directed fantasy.
   D. not an altered state of consciousness.

10. Stimulant is to depressant as:
   A. cocaine is to sedative.
   B. mescaline is to crack cocaine.
   C. caffeine is to amphetamine.
   D. alcohol is to barbiturate.

11. Amphetamines work by increasing activity at _____ synapses in a variety of ways.
   A. GABA and glycine
   B. serotonin and dopamine
   C. acetylcholine
   D. norepinephrine and dopamine

12. Which of the following drugs would be most likely to result in a fatal overdose?
   A. LSD
   B. Mescaline
   C. Marijuana
   D. Barbiturates

13. Which of the following is a true statement about naps?
   A. Daytime naps invariably lead to insomnia.
   B. Daytime naps are invariably refreshing and an efficient way to rest.
   C. Daytime naps are not very efficient ways to sleep, but their effects are variable and can be beneficial.
   D. Taking many naps during the day can substitute for a full night's sleep.

14. Peter rarely remembers his dreams. What can we say about Peter?
   A. Peter must be psychologically repressed.
   B. Peter obviously does not dream very much.
   C. Peter's dreams are probably not very memorable.
   D. Peter dreams but simply does not remember his dreams.

15. Definitions:
   A. generally emerge out of research.
   B. often have great explanatory value.
   C. generally exert little influence over how people think.
   D. are usually constructed by experts or authorities in a specific field.

Answers
1 B p. 138
2 C p. 140
3 A pp. 143–144
4 B pp. 143–144
5 D p. 147
6 A p. 148
7 A p. 151
8 A pp. 151–152
9 B p. 155
10 A pp. 156–158
11 D p. 159
12 D pp. 159–160
13 C p. 162
14 D p. 163
15 D pp. 164–165

PsykTrek

Go to the PsykTrek website or CD-ROM for further study of the concepts in this chapter. Both online and on the CD-ROM, PsykTrek includes dozens of learning modules with videos, animations, and quizzes, as well as simulations of psychological phenomena and a multimedia glossary that includes word pronunciations.

ThomsonNOW™

www.thomsonedu.com/ThomsonNOW
Go to this site for the link to ThomsonNOW, your one-stop study shop. Take a Pre-Test for this chapter, and ThomsonNOW will generate a Personalized Study Plan based on your test results. The Study Plan will identify the topics you need to review and direct you to online resources to help you master those topics. You can then take a Post-Test to help you determine the concepts you have mastered and what you still need to work on.

Companion Website

www.thomsonedu.com/psychology/weiten
Go to this site to find online resources directly linked to your book, including a glossary, flash cards, drag-and-drop exercises, quizzes, and more!

CHAPTER 6

Learning

© David H. Wells/Corbis

Let's see if you can guess the answer to a riddle. What do the following scenarios have in common?

- In 1953 a Japanese researcher observed a young macaque (a type of monkey) on the island of Koshima washing a sweet potato in a stream before eating it. No one had ever seen a macaque do this before. Soon other members of the monkey's troop were showing the same behavior. Several generations later, macaques on Koshima still wash their potatoes before eating them (De Waal, 2001).

- In 2005 Wade Boggs was elected to baseball's Hall of Fame. Boggs was as renowned for his superstitions as he was for his great hitting. For 20 years Boggs ate chicken every day of the year. Before games he followed a rigorous set of rituals that included stepping on the bases in reverse order, running wind sprints at precisely 17 minutes past the hour, and tossing exactly three pebbles off the field. Every time he stepped up to hit during a game, he drew the Hebrew letter *chai* in the dirt with his bat. For Boggs, the slightest deviation in this routine was profoundly upsetting (Gaddis, 1999; Vyse, 2000).

- Barn swallows in Minnesota have built nests inside a Home Depot warehouse store, safe from the weather and from predators. So how do they get in and out to bring food to their babies when the doors are closed? They flutter around the motion sensors that operate the doors until they open!

- A firefighter in Georgia routinely braves life-threatening situations to rescue people in distress. Yet the firefighter is paralyzed with fear whenever he sees someone dressed as a clown. He has been terrified of clowns ever since the third grade (Ryckeley, 2005).

What common thread runs through these diverse situations? What connects a superstitious ballplayer or a firefighter with a morbid fear of clowns to potato-washing monkeys and door-opening swallows?

The answer is *learning*. This may surprise you. When most people think of learning, they picture students reading textbooks or novices gaining proficiency in a skill, such as skiing or playing the guitar. To a psychologist, however, **learning is any relatively durable change in behavior or knowledge that is due to experience.** Macaques aren't born with the habit of washing their sweet potatoes, nor do swallows begin life knowing how to operate motion sensors. Wade Boggs adopted his superstitious

rituals because they seemed to be associated with success in hitting a baseball. The firefighter in Georgia wasn't born with a fear of clowns, since he only began to be frightened of them in the third grade. In short, all these behaviors are the product of experience—that is, they represent learning.

When you think about it, it would be hard to name a lasting change in behavior that *isn't* due to experience. That is why learning is one of the most fundamental concepts in all of psychology. Learning shapes our personal habits, such as nailbiting; personality traits, such as shyness; personal preferences, such as a distaste for formal clothes; and emotional responses, such as reactions to favorite songs. If all your learned responses could somehow be stripped away, there would be little of your behavior left. You would not be able to talk, read a book, or cook yourself a hamburger. You would be about as complex and interesting as a turnip.

As the examples at the start of this discussion show, learning is not an exclusively human process. Learning is pervasive in the animal world as well, a fact that won't amaze anyone who has ever owned a dog or seen a trained seal in action. Another insight, however, is considerably more startling: *The principles that explain learned responses in animals explain much of human learning, too.* Thus, the same mechanisms that explain how barn swallows learn to operate an automated door can account for a professional athlete's bizarre superstitions. Indeed, many of the most fascinating discoveries in the study of learning originated in studies of animals.

In this chapter, you will see how fruitful the research into learning has been and how wide ranging its applications are. We will focus most of our attention on a specific kind of learning: conditioning. *Conditioning* involves learning associations between events that occur in an organism's environment (eating chicken and having success hitting a baseball is one example). In investigating conditioning, psychologists study learning at a fundamental level. This strategy has paid off with insights that have laid the foundation for the study of more complex forms of learning, such as learning by observation (the kind of learning that may account for the Koshima macaques picking up one monkey's habit of washing her sweet potatoes). In the Personal Application, you'll see how you can harness the principles of conditioning to improve your self-control. The Critical Thinking Application shows how conditioning procedures can be used to manipulate emotions.

PREVIEW QUESTIONS

● What happens in classical conditioning?

● What are the key elements in this type of learning?

● What types of emotional responses are modulated by classical conditioning?

● What are some physiological processes governed by classical conditioning?

● How are conditioned responses acquired and weakened?

● What is higher-order conditioning?

Do you go weak in the knees at the thought of standing on the roof of a tall building? Does your heart race when you imagine encountering a harmless garter snake? If so, you can understand, at least to some degree, what it's like to have a phobia. *Phobias* are irrational fears of specific objects or situations. Mild phobias are commonplace. Over the years, students in my classes have described their phobic responses to a diverse array of stimuli, including bridges, elevators, tunnels, heights, dogs, cats, bugs, snakes, professors, doctors, strangers, thunderstorms, and germs. If you have a phobia, you may have wondered how you managed to acquire such a foolish fear. Chances are, it was through classical conditioning (Antony & McCabe, 2003). ***Classical conditioning* is a type of learning in which a stimulus acquires the capacity to evoke a response that was originally evoked by another stimulus.** The process was first described in 1903 by Ivan Pavlov, and it is sometimes called *Pavlovian conditioning* in tribute to him.

Pavlov's Demonstration: "Psychic Reflexes"

Pavlov was a prominent Russian physiologist who did Nobel prize–winning research on digestion. Something of a "classic" himself, he was an absent-minded but brilliant professor obsessed with his research. Legend has it that Pavlov once reprimanded an assistant who arrived late for an experiment because of trying to avoid street fighting in the midst of the Russian Revolution. The assistant defended his tardiness by saying, "But Professor, there's a revolution going on with shooting in the streets!" Pavlov supposedly replied, "What the hell difference does a revolution make when you've work to do in the laboratory? Next time there's a revolution, get up earlier!" Apparently, dodging bullets wasn't an adequate excuse for delaying the march of scientific progress (Fancher, 1979; Gantt, 1975).

Pavlov was studying the role of saliva in the digestive processes of dogs when he stumbled onto what he called "psychic reflexes" (Pavlov, 1906). Like many great discoveries, Pavlov's was partly accidental, although he had the insight to recognize its significance. His subjects were dogs restrained in harnesses in an experimental chamber (see **Figure 6.1**). Their saliva was collected by means of a surgically implanted tube in the salivary gland. Pavlov would present meat powder to a dog and then collect the resulting saliva. As his research progressed, he no-

Surrounded by his research staff, the great Russian physiologist Ivan Pavlov (center, white beard) demonstrates his famous classical conditioning experiment with dogs.

ticed that dogs accustomed to the procedure would start salivating *before* the meat powder was presented. For instance, they would salivate in response to a clicking sound made by the device that was used to present the meat powder.

Intrigued by this unexpected finding, Pavlov decided to investigate further. To clarify what was happening, he paired the presentation of the meat powder with various stimuli that would stand out in the laboratory situation. For instance, he used a simple, auditory stimulus—the presentation of a tone. After the tone and the meat powder had been presented together a number of times, the tone was presented alone. What happened? The dogs responded by salivating to the sound of the tone alone.

What was so significant about a dog salivating when a tone was sounded? The key is that the tone had started out as a *neutral* stimulus. That is, it did not originally produce the response of salivation. However, Pavlov managed to change that by pairing the tone with a stimulus (meat powder) that *did* produce the salivation response. Through this process, the tone acquired the capacity to trigger the response of salivation. What Pavlov had demonstrated was how stimulus-response associations—the basic building blocks of learning—are formed by events in an organism's environment. Based on this insight, he built a broad theory of learning that attempted to explain aspects of emotion, temperament, neuroses, and language (Windholz, 1997).

Terminology and Procedures

There is a special vocabulary associated with classical conditioning. It often looks intimidating, but it's really not all that mysterious. The bond Pavlov noted

IVAN PAVLOV
"Next time there's a revolution, get up earlier!"

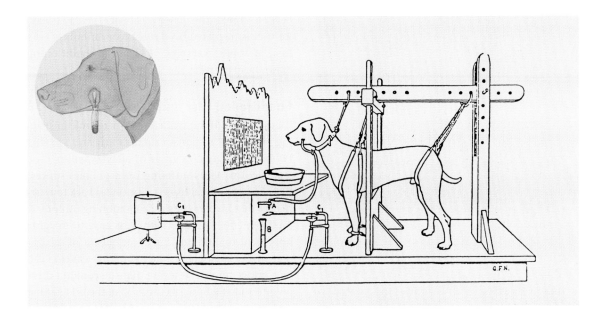

Figure 6.1

Classical conditioning apparatus. An experimental arrangement similar to the one depicted here (taken from Yerkes & Morgulis, 1909) has typically been used in demonstrations of classical conditioning, although Pavlov's original setup (see inset) was quite a bit simpler. The dog is restrained in a harness. A tone is used as the conditioned stimulus (CS), and the presentation of meat powder is used as the unconditioned stimulus (UCS). The tube inserted into the dog's salivary gland allows precise measurement of its salivation response. The pen and rotating drum of paper on the left are used to maintain a continuous record of salivary flow. (Inset) The less elaborate setup that Pavlov originally used to collect saliva on each trial is shown here (Goodwin, 1991).

between the meat powder and salivation was a natural, unlearned association. It did not have to be created through conditioning. It is therefore called an *unconditioned* association. In unconditioned bonds, **the *unconditioned stimulus (UCS)* is a stimulus that evokes an unconditioned response without previous conditioning. The *unconditioned response (UCR)* is an unlearned reaction to an unconditioned stimulus that occurs without previous conditioning.**

In contrast, the link between the tone and salivation was established through conditioning. It is therefore called a *conditioned* association. In conditioned bonds, **the *conditioned stimulus (CS)* is a previously neutral stimulus that has, through conditioning, acquired the capacity to evoke a conditioned response. The *conditioned response (CR)* is a learned reaction to a conditioned stimulus that occurs because of previous conditioning.**

To avoid possible confusion, it is worth noting that the unconditioned response and conditioned response are virtually the same behavior, although there may be subtle differences between them. In Pavlov's initial demonstration, the unconditioned response and conditioned response were both salivation. When evoked by the UCS (meat powder), salivation was an unconditioned response. When evoked by the CS (the tone), salivation was a conditioned response. The procedures involved in classical conditioning are outlined in **Figure 6.2** on the next page.

Pavlov's "psychic reflex" came to be called the *conditioned reflex*. Classically conditioned responses have traditionally been characterized as reflexes and are said to be ***elicited*** (**drawn forth**) because most of them are relatively automatic or involuntary. However, research in recent decades has demonstrated that classical conditioning is involved in a wider range of human and animal behavior than previously appreciated, including some types of nonreflexive responding (Allan, 1998; Turkkan, 1989). Finally, **a *trial* in classical conditioning consists of any presentation of a stimulus or pair of stimuli.** Psychologists are interested in how many trials are required to establish a particular conditioned bond. The number needed to form an association varies considerably. Although classical conditioning generally proceeds gradually, it can occur quite rapidly,

"HE SALIVATES."

ScienceCartoonsPlus.com

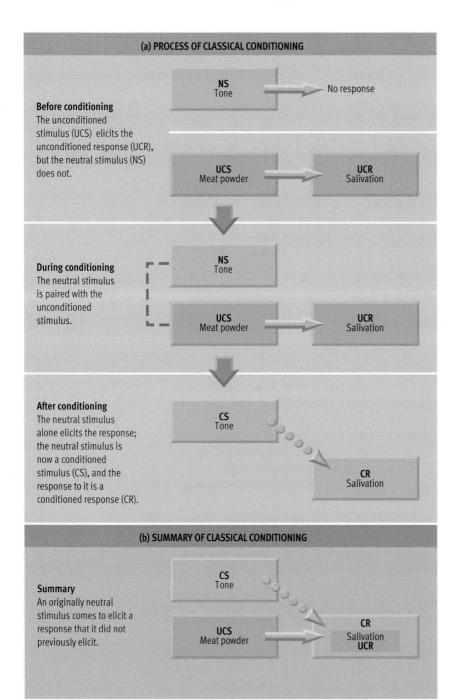

(a) PROCESS OF CLASSICAL CONDITIONING

Before conditioning
The unconditioned stimulus (UCS) elicits the unconditioned response (UCR), but the neutral stimulus (NS) does not.

NS
Tone → No response

UCS
Meat powder → UCR
Salivation

During conditioning
The neutral stimulus is paired with the unconditioned stimulus.

NS
Tone

UCS
Meat powder → UCR
Salivation

After conditioning
The neutral stimulus alone elicits the response; the neutral stimulus is now a conditioned stimulus (CS), and the response to it is a conditioned response (CR).

CS
Tone

CR
Salivation

(b) SUMMARY OF CLASSICAL CONDITIONING

Summary
An originally neutral stimulus comes to elicit a response that it did not previously elicit.

CS
Tone

UCS
Meat powder → CR
Salivation
UCR

Figure 6.2
The sequence of events in classical conditioning. **(a)** Moving downward, this series of three panels outlines the sequence of events in classical conditioning, using Pavlov's original demonstration as an example. **(b)** As we encounter other examples of classical conditioning throughout the book, we will see many diagrams like the one in this panel, which will provide snapshots of specific instances of classical conditioning.

sometimes in just one pairing of the conditioned stimulus and unconditioned stimulus.

Classical Conditioning in Everyday Life

In laboratory experiments on classical conditioning, researchers have generally worked with extremely simple responses. Besides salivation, commonly studied favorites include eyelid closure, knee jerks, the flexing of various limbs, and fear responses. The study of such simple responses has proven both practical and productive. However, these responses do not even

begin to convey the rich diversity of everyday behavior that is regulated by classical conditioning. Let's look at some examples of classical conditioning drawn from everyday life.

Conditioned Fear and Anxiety

Classical conditioning often plays a key role in shaping emotional responses such as fear and anxiety. Phobias are a good example of such responses. Case studies of patients suffering from phobias suggest that many irrational fears can be traced back to experiences that involve classical conditioning (Antony & McCabe, 2003; Ayres, 1998). It is easy to imagine how such conditioning can occur outside of the laboratory. For example, a student of mine was troubled by a bridge phobia so severe that she couldn't drive on interstate highways because of all the bridges that had to be crossed. She was able to pinpoint the source of her phobia as something that had happened during her childhood. Whenever her family drove to visit her grandmother, they had to cross an old, little-used, rickety, run-down bridge out in the countryside. Her father, in a misguided attempt at humor, made a major production out of these crossings. He would stop short of the bridge and carry on about the enormous danger. Obviously, he thought the bridge was safe or he wouldn't have driven across it. However, the naive young girl was terrified by her father's scare tactics. Hence, the bridge became a conditioned stimulus eliciting great fear (see **Figure 6.3**). Unfortunately, the fear spilled over to all bridges. Forty years later she was still carrying the burden of this phobia.

Everyday anxiety responses that are less severe than phobias may also be products of classical conditioning. For instance, if you cringe when you hear the sound of a dentist's drill, this response is due to classical conditioning. In this case, the pain you have experienced from dental drilling is the UCS. This pain has been paired with the sound of the drill, which became a CS eliciting your cringing behavior.

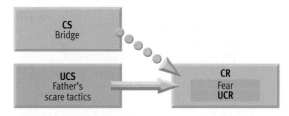

Figure 6.3
Classical conditioning of a fear response. Many emotional responses that would otherwise be puzzling can be explained by classical conditioning. In the case of one woman's bridge phobia, the fear originally elicited by her father's scare tactics became a conditioned response to the stimulus of bridges.

Other Conditioned Responses

 5a

Classical conditioning is not limited to producing unpleasant emotions such as fear and anxiety. Many pleasant emotional responses are also acquired through classical conditioning. Consider the following example, described by a 53-year-old woman who wrote a letter to newspaper columnist Bob Greene about the news that a company was bringing back a discontinued product—Beemans gum. She wrote:

That was the year (1949) I met Charlie. I guess first love is always the same. . . . Charlie and I went out a lot. He chewed Beemans gum and he smoked. . . . We would go to all the passion pits—the drive-in movies and the places to park. We did a lot of necking, but we always stopped at a certain point. Charlie wanted to get married when we got out of high school . . . [but] Charlie and I drifted apart. We both ended up getting married to different people.

And the funny thing is . . . for years the combined smell of cigarette smoke and Beemans gum made my knees weak. Those two smells were Charlie to me. When I would smell the Beemans and the cigarette smoke, I could feel the butterflies dancing all over my stomach.

The writer clearly had a unique and long-lasting emotional response to the smell of Beemans gum and cigarettes. The credit for this pleasant response goes to classical conditioning (see **Figure 6.4**).

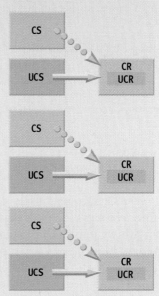

Craig McClain

Figure 6.4

Classical conditioning and romance. Pleasant emotional responses can be acquired through classical conditioning, as illustrated by one woman's unusual conditioned response to the aroma of Beemans gum and cigarette smoke.

Classical conditioning affects not only overt behaviors but *physiological processes* as well. For example, studies have shown that the functioning of the immune system can be influenced by conditioning (Ader, 2001). Robert Ader and Nicholas Cohen (1984, 1993) have shown that classical conditioning procedures can lead to *immune suppression*—a decrease in the production of antibodies. In a typical study, animals are injected with a drug (the UCS) that *chemically* causes immune suppression while they are simultaneously given an unusual-tasting liquid to drink (the CS). Days later, after the chemically induced immune suppression has ended, some of the animals are reexposed to the CS by giving them the

---

concept **check** 6.1

Identifying Elements in Classical Conditioning

Check your understanding of classical conditioning by trying to identify the unconditioned stimulus (UCS), unconditioned response (UCR), conditioned stimulus (CS), and conditioned response (CR) in each of the examples below. Fill in the diagram accompanying each example. You'll find the answers in Appendix A.

1. Sam is 3 years old. One night his parents build a roaring fire in the family room fireplace. The fire spits out a large ember that hits Sam in the arm, giving him a nasty burn that hurts a great deal for several hours. A week later, when Sam's parents light another fire in the fireplace, Sam becomes upset and fearful, crying and running from the room.

2. Melanie is driving to work on a rainy highway when she notices that the brake lights of all the cars just ahead of her have come on. She hits her brakes but watches in horror as her car glides into a four-car pileup. She's badly shaken up in the accident. A month later she's driving in the rain again and notices that she tenses up every time she sees brake lights come on ahead of her.

3. At the age of 24, Tyrone has recently developed an allergy to cats. When he's in the same room with a cat for more than 30 minutes, he starts wheezing. After a few such allergic reactions, he starts wheezing as soon as he sees a cat in a room.

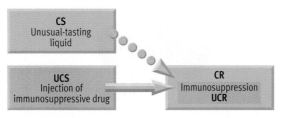

Figure 6.5
Classical conditioning of immune suppression. When a neutral stimulus is paired with a drug that chemically causes suppression of the immune response, it can become a CS that elicits immune suppression on its own. Thus, even the immune response can be influenced by classical conditioning.

unusual tasting solution. Measurements of antibody production indicate that animals exposed to the CS show a reduced immune response (see **Figure 6.5**).

Studies have also demonstrated that classical conditioning can influence *sexual arousal* (Pfaus, Kippin, & Centeno, 2001). For example, research has shown that quail can be conditioned to become sexually aroused by a neutral, nonsexual stimulus—such as a red light—that has been paired with opportunities to copulate (Domjan, 1992, 1994). Conditioned stimuli can even elicit increased sperm release in male quail (Domjan, Blesbois, & Williams, 1998). Psychologists have long suspected that stimuli routinely paired with human sexual interactions, such as seductive nightgowns, mood music, lit candles, and the like, probably become conditioned stimuli that elicit arousal, but this hypothesis is difficult to investigate with human subjects. Classical conditioning may also underlie the development of *fetishes* for inanimate objects. If quail can be conditioned to find a red light arousing, it seems likely that humans may be conditioned to be aroused by objects such as shoes, boots, leather, and undergarments.

Basic Processes in Classical Conditioning

Classical conditioning is often portrayed as a mechanical process that inevitably leads to a certain result. This view reflects the fact that most conditioned responses are reflexive and difficult to control. Pavlov's dogs would have been hard pressed to withhold their salivation. Similarly, most people with phobias have great difficulty suppressing their fear. However, this vision of classical conditioning as an "irresistible force" is misleading because it fails to consider the many factors involved in classical conditioning (Kehoe & Macrae, 1998). In this section, we'll look at basic processes in classical conditioning to expand on the rich complexity of this form of learning.

Web Link 6.1

Behaviour Analysis and Learning
A multitude of annotated links, all focusing on learning through conditioning, can be found at the excellent Psychology Centre site at Athabasca University (Alberta, Canada).

Acquisition: Forming New Responses

We have already discussed *acquisition* without attaching a formal name to the process. **Acquisition refers to the initial stage of learning something.** Pavlov theorized that the acquisition of a conditioned response depends on *stimulus contiguity*. Stimuli are contiguous if they occur together in time and space.

Stimulus contiguity is important, but learning theorists now realize that contiguity alone doesn't automatically produce conditioning (Miller & Grace, 2003). People are bombarded daily by countless stimuli that could be perceived as being paired, yet only some of these pairings produce classical conditioning. Consider the woman who developed a conditioned emotional reaction to the smell of Beemans gum and cigarettes. There were no doubt other stimuli that shared contiguity with her boyfriend, Charlie. He smoked, so ashtrays were probably present, but she doesn't get weak in the knees at the sight of an ashtray.

If conditioning does not occur to all the stimuli present in a situation, what determines its occurrence? Evidence suggests that stimuli that are novel, unusual, or especially intense have more potential to become CSs than routine stimuli, probably because they are more likely to stand out among other stimuli (Hearst, 1988).

Extinction: Weakening Conditioned Responses

Fortunately, a newly formed stimulus-response bond does not necessarily last indefinitely. If it did, learning would be inflexible, and organisms would have difficulty adapting to new situations. Instead, the right circumstances produce **extinction, the gradual weakening and disappearance of a conditioned response tendency.**

What leads to extinction in classical conditioning? The consistent presentation of the conditioned stimulus *alone,* without the unconditioned stimulus. For example, when Pavlov consistently presented only the tone to a previously conditioned dog, the tone gradually lost its capacity to elicit the response of salivation. Such a sequence of events is depicted in the left portion of **Figure 6.6**, which graphs the amount of salivation by a dog over a series of conditioning trials. Note how the salivation response declines during extinction.

For an example of extinction from outside the laboratory, let's assume that you cringe at the sound of a dentist's drill, which has been paired with pain in the past. You take a job as a dental assistant and you start hearing the drill (the CS) day in and day out without experiencing any pain (the UCS). Your cringing response will gradually diminish and extinguish altogether.

How long does it take to extinguish a conditioned response? That depends on many factors, but particularly important is the strength of the conditioned bond when extinction begins. Some conditioned responses extinguish quickly, while others are difficult to weaken.

Spontaneous Recovery: Resurrecting Responses

 5b

Some conditioned responses display the ultimate in tenacity by "reappearing from the dead" after having been extinguished. Learning theorists use the term *spontaneous recovery* to describe such a resurrection from the graveyard of conditioned associations. *Spontaneous recovery* **is the reappearance of an extinguished response after a period of nonexposure to the conditioned stimulus.**

Pavlov (1927) observed this phenomenon in some of his pioneering studies. He fully extinguished a dog's CR of salivation to a tone and then returned the dog to its home cage for a "rest interval" (a period of nonexposure to the CS). On a subsequent day, when the dog was brought back to the experimental chamber for retesting, the tone was sounded and the salivation response reappeared. However, the recovered response was weak: There was less salivation than when the response had been at its peak strength. If Pavlov consistently presented the CS by itself again, the response reextinguished quickly. Interestingly, in some of the dogs the response made still another spontaneous recovery (typically even weaker than the first) after they had spent another period in their cages (consult **Figure 6.6** once again).

The theoretical meaning of spontaneous recovery is complex and the subject of some debate. However, its practical meaning is quite simple: Even if you manage to rid yourself of an unwanted conditioned response (such as cringing when you hear a dental drill), there is a chance it will make a surprise reappearance later. This reality may also help explain why people who manage to give up cigarettes, drugs, or poor eating habits for a while often experience a relapse and return to their unhealthy habits (Bouton, 2000).

Stimulus Generalization and the Case of Little Albert

 5b

After conditioning has occurred, organisms often show a tendency to respond not only to the exact CS used but also to other, similar stimuli. For example, Pavlov's dogs might have salivated in response to a different tone, or you might cringe at the sound of a

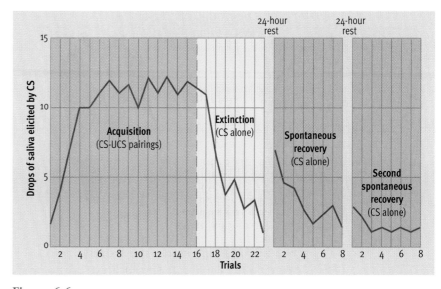

Figure 6.6

Acquisition, extinction, and spontaneous recovery. During acquisition, the strength of the dog's conditioned response (measured by the amount of salivation) increases rapidly and then levels off near its maximum. During extinction, the CR declines erratically until it's extinguished. After a "rest" period in which the dog is not exposed to the CS, a spontaneous recovery occurs, and the CS once again elicits a (weakened) CR. Repeated presentations of the CS alone reextinguish the CR, but after another "rest" interval, a weaker spontaneous recovery occurs.

jeweler's as well as a dentist's drill. These are examples of stimulus generalization. *Stimulus generalization* **occurs when an organism that has learned a response to a specific stimulus responds in the same way to new stimuli that are similar to the original stimulus.**

Generalization is adaptive given that organisms rarely encounter the exact same stimulus more than once (Thomas, 1992). Stimulus generalization is also commonplace. We have already discussed a real-life example: the woman who acquired a bridge phobia during her childhood because her father scared her whenever they went over a particular old bridge. The original CS for her fear was that specific bridge, but her fear was ultimately *generalized* to all bridges.

John B. Watson, the founder of behaviorism (see Chapter 1), conducted an influential early study of generalization. Watson and a colleague, Rosalie Rayner, examined the generalization of conditioned fear in an 11-month-old boy, known in the annals of psychology as "Little Albert." Like many babies, Albert was initially unafraid of a live white rat. Then Watson and Rayner (1920) paired the presentation of the rat with a loud, startling sound (made by striking a steel bar with a hammer). Albert *did* show fear in response to the loud noise. After seven pairings of the rat and the gong, the rat was established as a CS eliciting a fear response (see **Figure 6.7** on the next page).

Five days later, Watson and Rayner exposed the youngster to other stimuli that resembled the rat in

Archives of the History of American Psychology— The University of Akron

JOHN B. WATSON

"Surely this proof of the conditioned origin of a fear response puts us on natural science grounds in our study of emotional behavior."

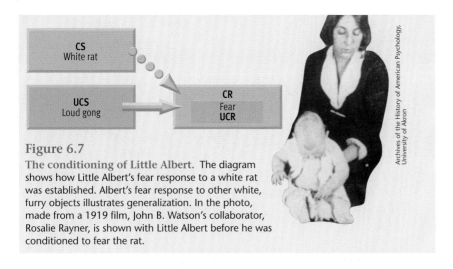

Figure 6.7

The conditioning of Little Albert. The diagram shows how Little Albert's fear response to a white rat was established. Albert's fear response to other white, furry objects illustrates generalization. In the photo, made from a 1919 film, John B. Watson's collaborator, Rosalie Rayner, is shown with Little Albert before he was conditioned to fear the rat.

being white and furry. They found that Albert's fear response generalized to a variety of stimuli, including a rabbit, a dog, a fur coat, a Santa Claus mask, and Watson's hair.

Like conditioning itself, stimulus generalization does not occur in just any set of circumstances (Balsam, 1988). Generalization depends on the similarity between the new stimulus and the original CS. The basic law governing generalization is this: *The more similar new stimuli are to the original CS, the greater the likelihood of generalization.*

Stimulus Discrimination

Stimulus discrimination is just the opposite of stimulus generalization. **Stimulus discrimination occurs when an organism that has learned a response to a specific stimulus does not respond in the same way to new stimuli that are similar to the original stimulus.** Like generalization, discrimination is adaptive in that an animal's survival may hinge on its being able to distinguish friend from foe, or edible from poisonous food (Thomas, 1992). Organisms can gradually learn to discriminate between the original CS and similar stimuli if they have adequate experience with both. For instance, let's say your dog runs around, excitedly wagging its tail, whenever

it hears your car pull up in the driveway. Initially it will probably respond to *all* cars that pull into the driveway (stimulus generalization). However, if there is anything distinctive about the sound of your car, your dog may gradually respond with excitement only to your car and not to other cars (stimulus discrimination).

The development of stimulus discrimination usually requires that the original CS (your car) continues to be paired with the UCS (your arrival), while similar stimuli (the other cars) are not paired with the UCS. As with generalization, a basic law governs discrimination: *The less similar new stimuli are to the original CS, the greater the likelihood (and ease) of discrimination.* Conversely, if a new stimulus is quite similar to the original CS, discrimination will be relatively difficult to learn.

Higher-Order Conditioning

Imagine that you were to conduct the following experiment. First, you condition a dog to salivate in response to the sound of a tone by pairing the tone with meat powder. Once the tone is firmly established as a CS, you pair the tone with a new stimulus, let's say a red light, for 15 trials. You then present the red light alone, without the tone. Will the dog salivate in response to the red light?

The answer is "yes." Even though the red light has never been paired with the meat powder, it will acquire the capacity to elicit salivation by virtue of being paired with the tone (see **Figure 6.8**). This is a demonstration of **higher-order conditioning, in which a conditioned stimulus functions as if it were an unconditioned stimulus.** Higher-order conditioning shows that classical conditioning does not depend on the presence of a genuine, natural UCS. An already established CS will do just fine. In higher-order conditioning, new conditioned responses are built on the foundation of already established conditioned responses. Many human conditioned responses are the product of higher-order conditioning. This process greatly extends the reach of classical conditioning.

Figure 6.8

Higher-order conditioning. Higher-order conditioning involves a two-phase process. In the first phase, a neutral stimulus (such as a tone) is paired with an unconditioned stimulus (such as meat powder) until it becomes a conditioned stimulus that elicits the response originally evoked by the UCS (such as salivation). In the second phase, another neutral stimulus (such as a red light) is paired with the previously established CS, so that it also acquires the capacity to elicit the response originally evoked by the UCS.

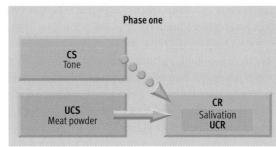

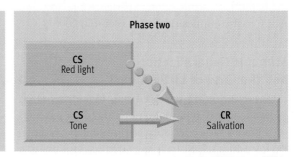

Recognizing Basic Processes in Classical Conditioning

Check your understanding of basic processes in classical conditioning by reading each of the following vignettes and identifying the process at work. Choose from the following: (a) acquisition, (b) extinction, (c) spontaneous recovery, (d) stimulus generalization, (e) stimulus discrimination, (f) higher-order conditioning. The answers can be found in Appendix A.

_____ **1.** Lucy has flunked algebra twice. Now whenever she sees any kind of math book, she begins to get that same old sick feeling in the pit of her stomach.

_____ **2.** Little Suzy is experiencing her first thunderstorm. A bolt of lightning flashes across the sky, but this doesn't bother her; she thinks it's pretty. A second later, however, she just about jumps out of her skin when a tremendous crash of thunder shakes the room.

_____ **3.** Alonzo has gotten A's on all of his quizzes in history, so he likes Professor Olden quite a bit. But he's not too crazy about Professor Datum, because he's received nothing but C's and D's in his research methods class.

_____ **4.** Glenda tried sushi for the first time when she visited her cousin in San Francisco, and she loved it. Back home in Kansas City she eagerly searched until she found a restaurant that served sushi, but the fish wasn't fresh, so she didn't like it much. On a visit to St. Louis she tried again, but she was disappointed once more. Glenda no longer gets excited by the prospect of eating sushi, unless it's San Francisco sushi, which still makes her mouth water.

_____ **5.** On his first day at work at the Joy Ice Cream Shop, Arnold helped himself and overdid it. He got sick and swore he'd never eat ice cream again. True to his word, he stayed off the stuff for the rest of the summer, though he continued working at the shop. For a while it was hard, because the sight and smell of the ice cream made him nauseous, but eventually those feelings faded. The following summer Arnold decided to visit his old employer, but as soon as he walked in the door, he felt so sick he had to turn around and leave immediately.

_____ **6.** Little Carlos used to get excited whenever Grandpa would come to visit, because Grandpa always brought Carlos some neat new toy. As Carlos got older, however, grandpa gradually stopped bringing toys. Now Grandpa's visits don't excite Carlos as much.

> Operant Conditioning

Even Pavlov recognized that classical conditioning is not the only form of conditioning. Classical conditioning best explains reflexive responding that is largely controlled by stimuli that _precede_ the response. However, humans and other animals make a great many responses that don't fit this description. Consider the response that you are engaging in right now: studying. It is definitely not a reflex (life might be easier if it were). The stimuli that govern it (exams and grades) do not precede it. Instead, your studying is mainly influenced by stimulus events that _follow_ the response—specifically, its _consequences_.

In the 1930s, this kind of learning was christened _operant conditioning_ by B. F. Skinner (1938, 1953, 1969). The term was derived from his belief that in this type of responding, an organism "operates" on the environment instead of simply reacting to stimuli. Learning occurs because responses come to be influenced by the consequences that follow them. Thus, **_operant conditioning_ is a form of learning in which voluntary responses come to be controlled by their consequences.** Learning theorists originally distinguished between classical and operant conditioning on the grounds that the former regulated reflexive, involuntary responses, whereas the latter governed voluntary responses. This distinction holds up much of the time, but it is not absolute. Research in recent decades has shown that classical conditioning sometimes contributes to the regulation of voluntary behavior; that operant conditioning can influence involuntary, visceral responses; and that the two types of conditioning jointly and interactively govern some aspects of behavior (Allan, 1998; Turkkan, 1989). Indeed, some theorists have argued

PREVIEW QUESTIONS

- What are the key elements in operant conditioning?
- How do organisms acquire new responses through operant conditioning?
- What is resistance to extinction, and why does it matter?
- How does stimulus control fit into operant responding?
- How do primary and secondary reinforcers differ?

B. F. SKINNER

"Operant conditioning shapes behavior as a sculptor shapes a lump of clay."

Web Link 6.2

The B. F. Skinner Foundation
This site is a fine place to become better acquainted with the psychologist who pioneered the study of operant conditioning. The site features Skinner's short autobiography, a complete bibliography of his publications, and annotated introductions to all of his books.

that classical and operant conditioning should be viewed as just two different aspects of a single learning process (Donahoe & Vegas, 2004).

Skinner's Demonstration: It's All a Matter of Consequences

B. F. Skinner had great admiration for Pavlov's work (Catania & Laties, 1999) and used it as the foundation for his own theory, even borrowing some of Pavlov's terminology (Dinsmoor, 2004). And, like Pavlov, Skinner (1953, 1969, 1984) conducted some deceptively simple research that became enormously influential (Lattal, 1992). The fundamental principle of operant conditioning is uncommonly elementary: *Skinner demonstrated that organisms tend to repeat those responses that are followed by favorable consequences.* This fundamental principle is embodied in Skinner's concept of reinforcement. **Reinforcement** occurs **when an event following a response increases an organism's tendency to make that response.** In other words, a response is strengthened because it leads to rewarding consequences (see **Figure 6.9**).

The principle of reinforcement may be simple, but it is immensely powerful. Skinner and his followers have shown that much of people's everyday behavior is regulated by reinforcement. For example, you study hard because good grades are likely to fol-

low as a result. You go to work because this behavior leads to your receiving paychecks. Perhaps you work extra hard because promotions and raises tend to follow such behavior. You tell jokes, and your friends laugh—so you tell some more. The principle of reinforcement clearly governs complex aspects of human behavior. Paradoxically, though, this principle emerged out of Skinner's research on the behavior of rats and pigeons in exceptionally simple situations. Let's look at that research.

Terminology and Procedures

Like Pavlov, Skinner created a prototype experimental procedure that has been repeated (with variations) thousands of times. In this procedure, an animal, typically a rat or a pigeon, is placed in an *operant chamber* that has come to be better known as a "Skinner box." A **Skinner box** is a small enclosure **in which an animal can make a specific response that is systematically recorded while the consequences of the response are controlled.** In the boxes designed for rats, the main response made available is pressing a small lever mounted on one side wall (see **Figure 6.10**). In the boxes made for pigeons, the designated response is pecking a small disk mounted on a side wall.

Operant responses such as lever pressing and disk pecking are said to be *emitted* rather than *elicited*. **To emit** means to send forth. This word was chosen because, as already noted, operant conditioning mainly governs *voluntary* responses instead of reflex responses.

The Skinner box permits the experimenter to control the reinforcement contingencies that are in effect for the animal. **Reinforcement contingencies are the circumstances or rules that determine whether responses lead to the presentation of reinforcers.** Typically, the experimenter manipulates whether positive consequences occur when the animal makes the designated response. The main positive consequence is usually delivery of a small bit of food into a cup mounted in the chamber. Because the animals are deprived of food for a while prior to the experimental session, their hunger virtually ensures that the food serves as a reinforcer.

The key dependent variable in most research on operant conditioning is the subjects' *response rate* over time. An animal's rate of lever pressing or disk pecking in the Skinner box is monitored continuously by a device known as a cumulative recorder (see **Figure 6.10**). **The cumulative recorder creates a graphic record of responding and reinforcement**

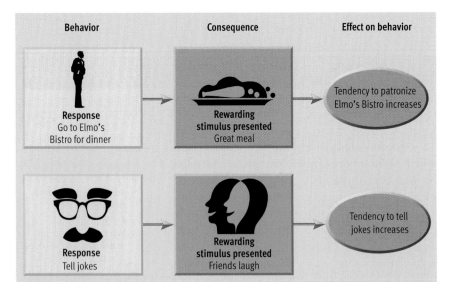

Figure 6.9

Reinforcement in operant conditioning. According to Skinner, reinforcement occurs when a response is followed by rewarding consequences and the organism's tendency to make the response increases. The two examples diagrammed here illustrate the basic premise of operant conditioning—that voluntary behavior is controlled by its consequences. These examples involve positive reinforcement (for a comparison of positive and negative reinforcement, see **Figure 6.14**).

Figure 6.10

Skinner box and cumulative recorder. **(a)** This diagram highlights some of the key features of an operant chamber, or Skinner box. In this apparatus designed for rats, the response under study is lever pressing. Food pellets, which may serve as reinforcers, are delivered into the food cup on the right. The speaker and light permit manipulations of visual and auditory stimuli, and the electric grid gives the experimenter control over aversive consequences (shock) in the box. **(b)** A cumulative recorder connected to the box keeps a continuous record of responses and reinforcements. A small segment of a cumulative record is shown here. The entire process is automatic as the paper moves with the passage of time; each lever press moves the pen up a step, and each reinforcement is marked with a slash. **(c)** This photo shows the real thing—a rat being conditioned in a Skinner box. Note the food dispenser on the left, which was omitted from the diagram.

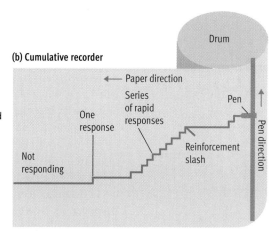

(b) Cumulative recorder

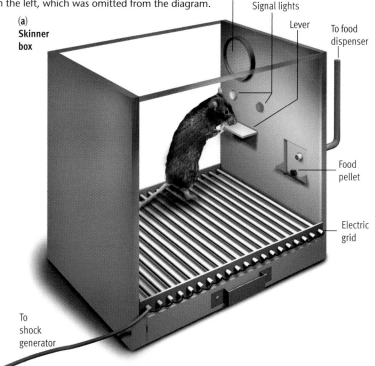

(a) Skinner box

Speaker
Signal lights
Lever
To food dispenser
Food pellet
Electric grid
To shock generator

© Richard Wood/Index Stock Imagery

in a Skinner box as a function of time. The recorder works by means of a roll of paper that moves at a steady rate underneath a movable pen. When there is no responding, the pen stays still and draws a straight horizontal line, reflecting the passage of time. Whenever the designated response occurs, however, the pen moves upward a notch. The pen's movements produce a graphic summary of the animal's responding over time. The pen also makes slash marks to record the delivery of each reinforcer. The results of operant conditioning studies are usually portrayed in graphs. In these graphs, the horizontal axis is used to mark the passage of time, while the vertical axis is used to plot the accumulation of responses (consult the four graphs in **Figure 6.13** for examples). In interpreting these graphs, the key consideration is the *slope* of the line that represents the record of responding. *A rapid response rate produces a steep slope, whereas a slow response rate produces a shallow slope.*

Basic Processes in Operant Conditioning

Although the principle of reinforcement is strikingly simple, many other processes involved in operant conditioning make this form of learning just as complex as classical conditioning. In fact, some of the same processes are involved in both types of conditioning. In this section, we'll discuss how the processes of acquisition, extinction, generalization, and discrimination occur in operant conditioning.

Acquisition and Shaping

As in classical conditioning, *acquisition* in operant conditioning is the formation of a new response tendency. However, the procedures used to establish a tendency to emit a voluntary operant response are different from those used to create a reflexive conditioned response. Operant responses are typically

Web Link 6.3

Animal Training at Sea World
The practical applications of shaping and other principles of operant conditioning are demonstrated at this interesting site, which explains how training is accomplished at this famous marine park.

established through a gradual process called **shaping: the reinforcement of closer and closer approximations of a desired response.**

Shaping is necessary when an organism does not, on its own, emit the desired response. For example, when a rat is first placed in a Skinner box, it may not press the lever at all. In this case an experimenter begins shaping by releasing food pellets whenever the rat moves toward the lever. As this response becomes more frequent, the experimenter starts requiring a closer approximation of the desired response, possibly releasing food only when the rat actually touches the lever. As reinforcement increases the rat's tendency to touch the lever, the rat will spontaneously press the lever on occasion, finally providing the experimenter with an opportunity to reinforce the designated response. These reinforcements will gradually increase the rate of lever pressing.

Shaping molds many aspects of both human and animal behavior. For instance, it is the key to training animals to perform impressive tricks. When you go to a zoo, circus, or marine park and see bears riding bicycles, monkeys playing the piano, and whales leaping through hoops, you are witnessing the results of shaping. To demonstrate the power of shaping techniques, Skinner once trained some pigeons so that they appeared to play Ping-Pong! They would run about on opposite ends of a Ping-Pong table and peck the ball back and forth. Keller and Marian Breland, a couple of psychologists influenced by Skinner, applied shaping in their business of training animals for advertising and entertainment purposes.

One of their better-known feats was shaping "Priscilla, the Fastidious Pig," to turn on a radio, eat at a kitchen table, put dirty clothes in a hamper, run a vacuum, and then "go shopping" with a shopping cart (see photo). Of course, Priscilla picked the sponsor's product off the shelf in her shopping expedition (Breland & Breland, 1961).

Extinction

In operant conditioning, *extinction* refers to the gradual weakening and disappearance of a response tendency because the response is no longer followed by reinforcement. Extinction begins in operant conditioning whenever previously available reinforcement is stopped. In laboratory studies with rats, this situation usually occurs when the experimenter stops delivering food as reinforcement for lever pressing. When the extinction process is begun, a brief surge often occurs in the rat's responding, followed by a gradual decline in response rate until it approaches zero. The same effects are generally seen in the extinction of human behavior.

A key issue in operant conditioning is how much *resistance to extinction* an organism will display when reinforcement is halted. **Resistance to extinction occurs when an organism continues to make a response after delivery of the reinforcer for it has been terminated.** The greater the resistance to extinction, the longer the responding will continue. Thus, if a researcher stops giving reinforcement for lever pressing and the response tapers off slowly, the

Shaping—an operant technique in which an organism is rewarded for closer and closer approximations of the desired response—is used in teaching both animals and humans. It is the main means of training animals to perform unnatural tricks. Breland and Breland's (1961) famous subject, "Priscilla, the Fastidious Pig," is shown on the left.

© Courtesy of Animal Behavior Enterprises, Inc.

© Gerald Davis by permission of Karen Davis

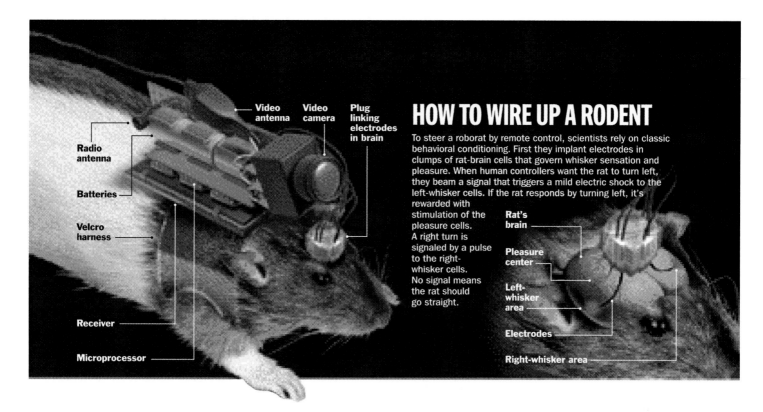

HOW TO WIRE UP A RODENT

To steer a roborat by remote control, scientists rely on classic behavioral conditioning. First they implant electrodes in clumps of rat-brain cells that govern whisker sensation and pleasure. When human controllers want the rat to turn left, they beam a signal that triggers a mild electric shock to the left-whisker cells. If the rat responds by turning left, it's rewarded with stimulation of the pleasure cells. A right turn is signaled by a pulse to the right-whisker cells. No signal means the rat should go straight.

Labels: Video antenna, Video camera, Plug linking electrodes in brain, Radio antenna, Batteries, Velcro harness, Receiver, Microprocessor, Rat's brain, Pleasure center, Left-whisker area, Electrodes, Right-whisker area

response shows high resistance to extinction. However, if the response tapers off quickly, it shows relatively little resistance to extinction.

Resistance to extinction may sound like a matter of purely theoretical interest, but actually it's quite practical. People often want to strengthen a response in such a way that it will be relatively resistant to extinction. For instance, most parents want to see their child's studying response survive even if the child hits a rocky stretch when studying doesn't lead to reinforcement (good grades). In a similar fashion, a casino wants to see patrons continue to gamble even if they encounter a lengthy losing streak.

Stimulus Control: Generalization and Discrimination

Operant responding is ultimately controlled by its consequences, as organisms learn response-outcome (R-O) associations (Colwill, 1993). However, stimuli that *precede* a response can also influence operant behavior. When a response is consistently followed by a reinforcer in the presence of a particular stimulus, that stimulus comes to serve as a "signal" indicating that the response is likely to lead to a reinforcer. Once an organism learns the signal, it tends to respond accordingly (Honig & Alsop, 1992). For example, a pigeon's disk pecking may be reinforced only when a small light behind the disk is lit. When the light is out, pecking does not lead to the reward. Pigeons quickly learn to peck the disk only when it is lit. The

light that signals the availability of reinforcement is called a discriminative stimulus. ***Discriminative stimuli* are cues that influence operant behavior by indicating the probable consequences (reinforcement or nonreinforcement) of a response.**

Discriminative stimuli play a key role in the regulation of operant behavior. For example, birds learn that hunting for worms is likely to be reinforced after a rain. Children learn to ask for sweets when their parents are in a good mood. Drivers learn to slow down when the highway is wet. Human social behavior is also regulated extensively by discriminative stimuli. Consider the behavior of asking someone out for a date. Many people emit this response cautiously, only after receiving many signals—such as eye contact, smiles, and encouraging conversational exchanges (the discriminative stimuli)—that a favorable answer (reinforcement) is fairly likely. The potential power of discriminative stimuli to govern behavior has been dramatically demonstrated by research (Talwar et al., 2002) showing that it is possible to use operant procedures to train what *Time* magazine called "roborats," radio-controlled rodents that can be precisely directed through complex environments (see **Figure 6.11**).

Reactions to a discriminative stimulus are governed by the processes of *stimulus generalization* and *stimulus discrimination,* just like reactions to a CS in classical conditioning. For instance, envision a cat that gets excited whenever it hears the sound of a can opener because that sound has become a

Figure 6.11

Remote-controlled rodents: An example of operant conditioning in action. In a study that almost reads like science fiction, Sanjiv Talwar and colleagues (2002) used operant conditioning procedures to train radio-controlled "roborats" that could have a variety of valuable applications, such as searching for survivors in a collapsed building. As this *Time* magazine graphic explains, radio signals can be used to direct the rat to go forward or turn right or left, while a video feed is sent back to a control center. The *reinforcer* in this setup is brief electrical stimulation of a pleasure center in the rat's brain (see Chapter 3), which can be delivered by remote control. The brief shocks sent to the right or left whiskers are *discriminative stimuli* that indicate which types of responses will be reinforced. The entire procedure depended on extensive *shaping.*

Source: Graphic from Lemonick, M. D. (2002, May 13). Send in the roborats. *Time, 159* (19), p. 61. © 2002 Time, Inc. Reprinted by permission.

Table 6.1 Comparison of Basic Processes in Classical and Operant Conditioning

Process and Definition	Description in Classical Conditioning	Description in Operant Conditioning
Acquisition: The initial stage of learning	CS and UCS are paired, gradually resulting in CR.	Responding gradually increases because of reinforcement, possibly through shaping.
Extinction: The gradual weakening and disappearance of a conditioned response tendency	CS is presented alone until it no longer elicits CR.	Responding gradually slows and stops after reinforcement is terminated.
Stimulus generalization: An organism's responding to stimuli other than the original stimulus used in conditioning	CR is elicited by new stimulus that resembles original CS.	Responding increases in the presence of new stimulus that resembles original discriminative stimulus.
Stimulus discrimination: An organism's lack of response to stimuli that are similar to the original stimulus used in conditioning	CR is not elicited by new stimulus that resembles original CS.	Responding does not increase in the presence of new stimulus that resembles original discriminative stimulus.

discriminative stimulus signaling a good chance of its getting fed. If the cat also responded to the sound of a new kitchen appliance (say a blender), this response would represent *generalization*—responding to a new stimulus as if it were the original. *Discrimination* would occur if the cat learned to respond only to the can opener and not to the blender.

As you have learned in this section, the processes of acquisition, extinction, generalization, and discrimination in operant conditioning parallel these same processes in classical conditioning. Table 6.1 compares these processes in the two kinds of conditioning.

Reinforcement: Consequences That Strengthen Responses

Although it is convenient to equate reinforcement with reward and the experience of pleasure, strict behaviorists object to this practice. Why? Because the experience of pleasure is an unobservable event that takes place within an organism. As explained in Chapter 1, most behaviorists believe that scientific assertions must be limited to what can be observed.

In keeping with this orientation, Skinner said that reinforcement occurs whenever an outcome strengthens a response, as measured by an increase in the rate of responding. This definition avoids the issue of what the organism is feeling and focuses on observable events. Thus, the central process in reinforcement is the *strengthening of a response tendency*.

Reinforcement is therefore defined *after the fact*, in terms of its *effect* on behavior. Something that is clearly reinforcing for an organism at one time may not function as a reinforcer later (Catania, 1992). Food will reinforce lever pressing by a rat only if the rat is hungry. Similarly, something that serves as a reinforcer for one person may not function as a reinforcer for another person. For example, parental ap-

proval is a potent reinforcer for most children, but not all.

Operant theorists make a distinction between unlearned, or primary, reinforcers as opposed to conditioned, or secondary, reinforcers. **Primary reinforcers are events that are inherently reinforcing because they satisfy biological needs.** A given species has a limited number of primary reinforcers because these reinforcers are closely tied to physiological needs. In humans, primary reinforcers include food, water, warmth, sex, and perhaps affection expressed through hugging and close bodily contact. **Secondary, or conditioned reinforcers are events that acquire reinforcing qualities by being associated with primary reinforcers.** The events that function as secondary reinforcers vary among members of a species because they depend on learning. Examples of common secondary reinforcers in humans include money, good grades, attention, flattery, praise, and applause. Most of the material things that people work hard to earn are secondary reinforcers. For example, people learn to find stylish clothes, sports cars, fine jewelry, elegant china, and state-of-the-art audio systems reinforcing.

"Mommy, we keep saying 'go home, kitty-cat' -- but she just keeps hanging around here!"

© The Family Circus-BILL KEANE, Inc. King Features Syndicate

Schedules of Reinforcement 5d

Organisms make innumerable responses that do *not* lead to favorable consequences. It would be nice if people were reinforced every time they took an exam, watched a movie, hit a golf shot, asked for a date, or made a sales call. However, in the real world most responses are reinforced only some of the time.

How does this situation affect the potency of reinforcers? To find out, operant psychologists have devoted an enormous amount of attention to how *schedules of reinforcement* influence operant behavior (Ferster & Skinner, 1957; Skinner, 1938, 1953).

A *schedule of reinforcement* **is a specific pattern of presentation of reinforcers over time.** The simplest pattern is continuous reinforcement. *Continuous reinforcement* **occurs when every instance of a designated response is reinforced.** In the laboratory, experimenters often use continuous reinforcement to shape and establish a new response before moving on to more realistic schedules involving intermittent, or partial, reinforcement. *Intermittent reinforcement* **occurs when a designated response is reinforced only some of the time.**

Which do you suppose leads to longer-lasting effects—being reinforced every time you emit a response, or being reinforced only some of the time? Studies show that, given an equal number of reinforcements, *intermittent* reinforcement makes a response more resistant to extinction than continuous reinforcement does (Falls, 1998; Schwartz & Robbins, 1995). This reality explains why behaviors that are reinforced only occasionally—such as temper tantrums in children—can be very durable and difficult to eliminate.

Reinforcement schedules come in many varieties, but four particular types of intermittent schedules have attracted the most interest. These schedules are described here along with examples drawn from the laboratory and everyday life (see **Figure 6.12** on the next page for additional examples).

Ratio schedules require the organism to make the designated response a certain number of times to gain each reinforcer. **In a *fixed-ratio (FR) schedule*, the reinforcer is given after a fixed number of nonreinforced responses.** *Examples:* (1) A rat is reinforced for every tenth lever press. (2) A salesperson receives a bonus for every fourth set of golf clubs sold. **In a *variable-ratio (VR) schedule*, the reinforcer is given after a variable number of nonreinforced responses.** The number of nonreinforced responses varies around a predetermined average. *Examples:* (1) A rat is reinforced for every tenth lever press on the average. The exact number of responses required for reinforcement varies from one time to the next. (2) A slot machine in a casino pays off once every six tries on the average. The number of nonwinning responses between payoffs varies greatly from one time to the next.

Interval schedules require a time period to pass between the presentation of reinforcers. **In a *fixed-interval (FI) schedule*, the reinforcer is given for the first response that occurs after a fixed time interval has elapsed.** *Examples:* (1) A rat is reinforced for the first lever press after a 2-minute interval has elapsed and then must wait 2 minutes before receiving the next reinforcement. (2) Students can earn grades (let's assume the grades are reinforcing) by taking exams every three weeks. **In a *variable-interval (VI) schedule*, the reinforcer is given for the first response after a variable time interval has elapsed. The interval length varies around a predetermined average.** *Examples:* (1) A rat is reinforced for the first lever press after a 1-minute interval has elapsed, but the following intervals are 3 minutes, 2 minutes, 4 minutes, and so on—with an average length of 2 minutes. (2) A person repeatedly dials a busy phone number (getting through is the reinforcer).

More than 40 years of research has yielded an enormous volume of data on how these schedules of reinforcement are related to patterns of responding (Williams, 1988; Zeiler, 1977). Some of the more prominent findings are summarized in **Figure 6.13**, which depicts typical response patterns generated by each schedule. For example, with fixed-interval schedules, a pause in responding usually occurs after each reinforcer is delivered, and then responding gradually increases to a rapid rate at the end of the interval. This pattern of behavior yields a "scalloped" response curve. In general, *ratio schedules tend to produce more rapid responding than interval schedules.* Why? Because faster responding leads to quicker reinforcement when a ratio schedule is in effect. *Variable schedules tend to generate steadier response rates and greater resistance to extinction than their fixed counterparts.*

Most of the research on reinforcement schedules was conducted on rats and pigeons in Skinner boxes. However, psychologists have found that humans react to schedules of reinforcement in much the same way as lower animals (de Villiers, 1977; Perone, Galizio, & Baron, 1988). For example, when animals are placed on ratio schedules, shifting to a higher ratio (that is, requiring more responses per reinforcement) tends to generate faster responding. Managers who run factories that pay on a piecework basis (a fixed ratio schedule) have seen the same reaction in humans. In a similar vein, most gambling is reinforced according to variable-ratio schedules, which tend to produce rapid, steady responding and great resistance to extinction—exactly what casino operators want.

PREVIEW QUESTIONS

- What are the typical effects of various schedules of reinforcement?
- How do positive and negative reinforcement differ?
- What happens in escape learning and avoidance learning?
- What is the difference between negative reinforcement and punishment?
- What does research reveal about the side effects of physical punishment?

Web Link 6.4

Cambridge Center for Behavioral Studies
A team of behavioral analysts and researchers affiliated with this non-profit organization have crafted a rich site devoted to scientific applications of the behavioral approach. Some of the practical topics covered here include behavioral approaches to parenting, education, organizational management, and pet training.

Figure 6.12

Reinforcement schedules in everyday life. Complex human behaviors are regulated by schedules of reinforcement. Piecework is reinforced on a fixed-ratio schedule. Playing slot machines is based on variable-ratio reinforcement. Watching the clock at work is rewarded on a fixed-interval basis (the arrival of quitting time is the reinforcer). Surfers waiting for a big wave are rewarded on a variable-interval basis.

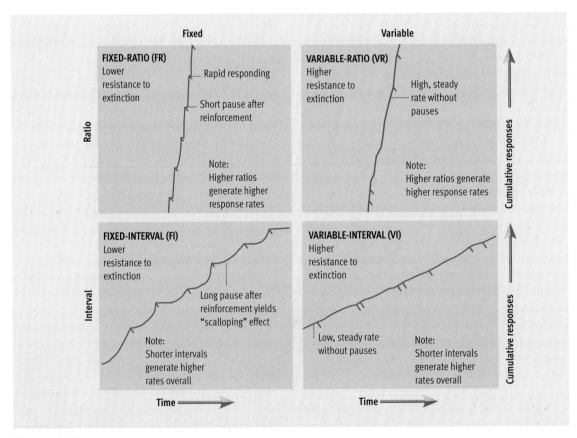

Figure 6.13

Schedules of reinforcement and patterns of response. In graphs of operant responding such as these, a steeper slope indicates a faster rate of response and the slash marks reflect the delivery of reinforcers. Each type of reinforcement schedule tends to generate a characteristic pattern of responding. In general, ratio schedules tend to produce more rapid responding than interval schedules (note the steep slopes of the FR and VR curves). In comparison to fixed schedules, variable schedules tend to yield steadier responding (note the smoother lines for the VR and VI schedules on the right).

Positive Reinforcement Versus Negative Reinforcement

According to Skinner, reinforcement can take two forms, which he called *positive reinforcement* and *negative reinforcement* (see **Figure 6.14**). ***Positive reinforcement*** **occurs when a response is strengthened because it is followed by the presentation of a rewarding stimulus.** Thus far, for purposes of simplicity, our examples of reinforcement have involved positive reinforcement. Good grades, tasty meals, paychecks, scholarships, promotions, nice clothes, nifty cars, attention, and flattery are all positive reinforcers.

In contrast, ***negative reinforcement*** **occurs when a response is strengthened because it is followed by the removal of an aversive (unpleasant) stimulus.** Don't let the word "negative" confuse you. Negative reinforcement is reinforcement. Like all reinforcement, it involves a favorable outcome that strengthens a response tendency. However, this strengthening takes place because a response leads to the removal of an aversive stimulus rather than the arrival of a pleasant stimulus (see **Figure 6.14**).

In laboratory studies, negative reinforcement is usually accomplished as follows: While a rat is in a Skinner box, a moderate electric shock is delivered to the animal through the floor of the box. When the rat presses the lever, the shock is turned off for a period of time. Thus, lever pressing leads to removal of an aversive stimulus (shock). Although this sequence of events is different from those for positive reinforcement, it reliably strengthens the rat's lever pressing response.

concept check 6.3

Recognizing Schedules of Reinforcement

Check your understanding of schedules of reinforcement in operant conditioning by indicating the type of schedule that would be in effect in each of the examples below. In the spaces on the left, fill in CR for continuous reinforcement, FR for fixed-ratio, VR for variable-ratio, FI for fixed-interval, and VI for variable-interval. The answers can be found in Appendix A.

_____ **1.** Sarah is paid on a commission basis for selling computer systems. She gets a bonus for every third sale.

_____ **2.** Juan's parents let him earn some pocket money by doing yard work *approximately* once a week.

_____ **3.** Martha is fly-fishing. Think of each time that she casts her line as the response that may be rewarded.

_____ **4.** Jamal, who is in the fourth grade, gets a gold star from his teacher for every book he reads.

_____ **5.** Skip, a professional baseball player, signs an agreement that his salary increases will be renegotiated every third year.

Everyday human behavior is regulated extensively by negative reinforcement. Consider a handful of examples. You rush home in the winter to get out of the cold. You clean house to get rid of a mess. You give in to your child's begging to halt the whining. You give in to a roommate or spouse to bring an unpleasant argument to an end.

Negative reinforcement plays a key role in both escape learning and avoidance learning. **In *escape learning,* an organism acquires a response that decreases or ends some aversive stimulation.** Psychologists often study escape learning in the laboratory

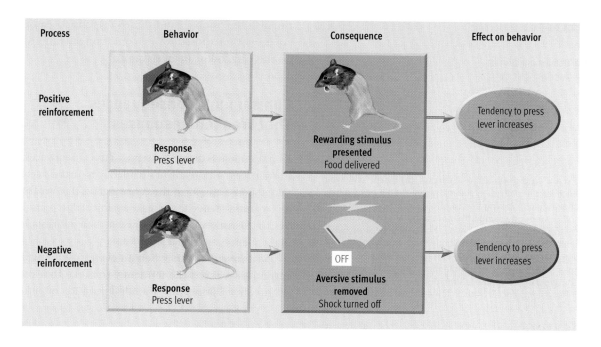

Process	Behavior	Consequence	Effect on behavior

Positive reinforcement — Response: Press lever → Rewarding stimulus presented: Food delivered → Tendency to press lever increases

Negative reinforcement — Response: Press lever → Aversive stimulus removed: Shock turned off (OFF) → Tendency to press lever increases

Figure 6.14

Positive reinforcement versus negative reinforcement. In positive reinforcement, a response leads to the presentation of a rewarding stimulus. In negative reinforcement, a response leads to the removal of an aversive stimulus. Both types of reinforcement involve favorable consequences and both have the same effect on behavior: The organism's tendency to emit the reinforced response is strengthened.

Web Link 6.5

Resources About Animal Cognition, Learning, and Behavior
This site provides extensive links to other sites focused on issues related to animal learning. In particular, there are links to most of the leading journals that publish research in this area, including the *Journal of the Experimental Analysis of Behavior.*

with dogs or rats that are conditioned in a *shuttle box.* The shuttle box has two compartments connected by a doorway, which can be opened and closed by the experimenter, as depicted in **Figure 6.15a**. In a typical study, an animal is placed in one compartment and the shock in the floor of that chamber is turned on, with the doorway open. The animal learns to escape the shock by running to the other compartment. This escape response leads to the removal of an aversive stimulus (shock), so it is strengthened through negative reinforcement. If you were to leave a party where you were getting picked on by peers, you would be engaging in an escape response.

Escape learning often leads to avoidance learning. **In *avoidance learning* an organism acquires a response that prevents some aversive stimulation from occurring.** In shuttle box studies of avoidance learning, the experimenter simply gives the animal a signal that shock is forthcoming. The typical signal is a light that goes on a few seconds prior to the shock. At first the dog or rat runs only when shocked (escape learning). Gradually, however, the animal learns to run to the safe compartment as soon as the light comes on, showing avoidance learning. Similarly, if you were to quit going to parties because of your concern about being picked on by peers, you would be demonstrating avoidance learning.

Avoidance learning presents an interesting example of how classical conditioning and operant conditioning can work together to regulate behavior (Levis, 1989; Mowrer, 1947). In avoidance learning, the warning light that goes on before the shock becomes a CS (through classical conditioning) eliciting reflexive, conditioned fear in the animal. However, the response of fleeing to the other side of the box is operant behavior. This response is strengthened through *negative reinforcement* because it reduces the animal's conditioned fear (see **Figure 6.15b**).

The principles of avoidance learning shed some light on why phobias are so resistant to extinction (Levis, 1989). For example, suppose you have a phobia of elevators, so you always take the stairs instead. Taking the stairs is an avoidance response that should lead to consistent negative reinforcement by relieving your conditioned fear—so your avoidance behavior is strengthened and continues. Moreover, your avoidance behavior prevents any opportunity to extinguish the phobic conditioned response because you're never exposed to the conditioned stimulus (in this case, riding in an elevator).

(a)

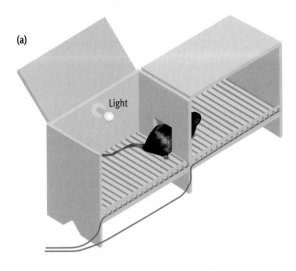

(b)

1. Classical conditioning

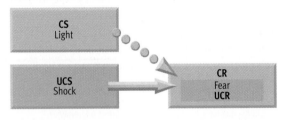

2. Operant conditioning
(negative reinforcement)

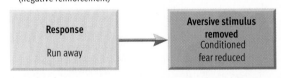

Figure 6.15

Escape and avoidance learning. **(a)** Escape and avoidance learning are often studied with a shuttle box like that shown here. Warning signals, shock, and the animal's ability to flee from one compartment to another can be controlled by the experimenter. **(b)** Avoidance begins because classical conditioning creates a conditioned fear that is elicited by the warning signal **(panel 1)**. Avoidance continues because it is maintained by operant conditioning **(panel 2)**. Specifically, the avoidance response is strengthened through negative reinforcement, since it leads to removal of the conditioned fear.

Punishment: Consequences That Weaken Responses

Reinforcement is defined in terms of its consequences. It *strengthens* an organism's tendency to make a certain response. Are there also consequences that *weaken* an organism's tendency to make a particular response? Yes. In Skinner's model of operant behavior, such consequences are called *punishment.*

Punishment occurs when an event following a response weakens the tendency to make that response. In a Skinner box, the administration of pun-

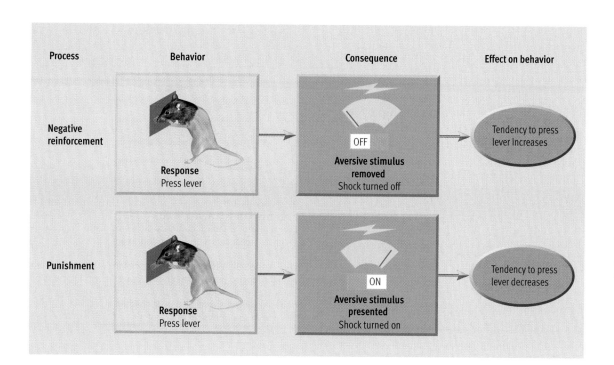

Process	Behavior	Consequence	Effect on behavior

Negative reinforcement

Response
Press lever

OFF
Aversive stimulus removed
Shock turned off

Tendency to press lever increases

Punishment

Response
Press lever

ON
Aversive stimulus presented
Shock turned on

Tendency to press lever decreases

Figure 6.16

Comparison of negative reinforcement and punishment. Although punishment can occur when a response leads to the removal of a rewarding stimulus, it more typically involves the presentation of an aversive stimulus. Students often confuse punishment with negative reinforcement because they associate both with aversive stimuli. However, as this diagram shows, punishment and negative reinforcement represent opposite procedures that have opposite effects on behavior.

ishment is very simple. When a rat presses the lever or a pigeon pecks the disk, it receives a brief shock. This procedure usually leads to a rapid decline in the animal's response rate (Dinsmoor, 1998). Punishment typically involves presentation of an aversive stimulus (for instance, spanking a child). However, punishment may also involve the removal of a rewarding stimulus (for instance, taking away a child's TV-watching privileges).

The concept of punishment in operant conditioning is confusing to many students on two counts. First, they often confuse it with negative reinforcement, which is entirely different. Negative reinforcement involves the *removal* of an aversive stimulus, thereby *strengthening* a response. Punishment, on the other hand, involves the *presentation* of an aversive stimulus, thereby *weakening* a response. Thus, punishment and negative reinforcement are *opposite procedures* that *yield opposite effects* on behavior (see Figure 6.16).

The second source of confusion involves the tendency to equate punishment with *disciplinary procedures* used by parents, teachers, and other authority figures. In the operant model, punishment occurs any time undesirable consequences weaken a response tendency. Defined in this way, the concept of punishment goes far beyond things like parents spanking children and teachers handing out detentions. For example, if you wear a new outfit and your schoolmates make fun of it, your behavior will have been punished and your tendency to emit this re-

sponse (wear the same clothing) will probably decline. Similarly, if you go to a restaurant and have a horrible meal, your response will have been punished, and your tendency to go to that restaurant will probably decline.

Although punishment in operant conditioning encompasses far more than disciplinary acts, it is used frequently for disciplinary purposes. In light of this situation, it is worth looking at the research on

---

concept check 6.4

Recognizing Outcomes in Operant Conditioning

Check your understanding of the various types of consequences that can occur in operant conditioning by indicating whether the examples below involve positive reinforcement (PR), negative reinforcement (NR), punishment (P), or extinction (E). The answers can be found in Appendix A.

_____ **1.** Antonio gets a speeding ticket.

_____ **2.** Diane's supervisor compliments her on her hard work.

_____ **3.** Leon goes to the health club for a rare workout and pushes himself so hard that his entire body aches and he throws up.

_____ **4.** Audrey lets her dog out so she won't have to listen to its whimpering.

_____ **5.** Richard shoots up heroin to ward off tremors and chills associated with heroin withdrawal.

_____ **6.** Sharma constantly complains about minor aches and pains to obtain sympathy from colleagues at work. Three co-workers who share an office with her decide to ignore her complaints instead of responding with sympathy.

punishment as a disciplinary measure. About three-quarters of parents report that they sometimes spank their children (Straus & Stewart, 1999), but quite a bit of controversy exists about the wisdom of using physical punishment. Opponents of corporal punishment argue that it produces many unintended and undesirable side effects (Hyman, 1996; Lytton, 1997; Straus, 2000). For example, they worry that physical punishment may trigger *strong emotional responses,* including anxiety, anger, and resentment, and that it can generate hostility toward the source of the punishment, such as a parent. Some theorists also argue that children who are subjected to a lot of physical punishment tend to become more aggressive than average. These views were bolstered by a recent, comprehensive review of the empirical research on physical punishment with children. Summarizing the results of 88 studies, Elizabeth Thompson Gershoff (2002) concluded that physical punishment is associated with poor quality parent-child relations, elevated aggression, delinquency, and behavioral problems in youngsters, and an increased likelihood of children being abused. Moreover, she concluded that these effects can carry over into adulthood, as studies find

Figure 6.17

The correlation between physical punishment and aggressiveness. As discussed in earlier chapters, a correlation does not establish causation. It seems plausible that extensive reliance on physical punishment causes children to be more aggressive, as many experts suspect. However, it is also possible that highly aggressive children cause their parents to depend heavily on physical punishment. Or, perhaps parents with an aggressive, hostile temperament pass on genes for aggressiveness to their children and prefer to rely on heavy use of physical punishment.

increased aggression, criminal behavior, mental health problems, and child abuse among adults who were physically punished as children.

Gershoff's (2002) review was a stinging indictment of physical punishment, but critics have raised some doubts about her conclusions. They argue that her review failed to distinguish between the effects of frequent, harsh, heavy-handed physical punishment and the effects of occasional, mild spankings, used as a backup when other disciplinary strategies fail (Baumrind, Larzelere, & Cowan, 2002). Critics also point out that the evidence linking spanking to negative effects is correlational and correlation is no assurance of causation (Kazdin & Benjet, 2003). Perhaps spanking causes children to be more aggressive, but it is also plausible that aggressive children cause their parents to rely more on physical punishment (see **Figure 6.17**). Based on objections such as these, Baumrind et al. (2002) assert that the empirical evidence "does not justify a blanket injunction against mild to moderate disciplinary spanking" (p. 586).

So, what can we conclude about the corporal punishment controversy? It is important to note that the critics of Gershoff's conclusions are not exactly *advocates* of physical punishment. As Holden (2002, p. 590) notes, "there is unanimous accord among experts that harsh, abusive punishment is detrimental for children." The critics merely think that it is premature to condemn the judicious use of mild spankings, especially when children are too young to understand a verbal reprimand or the withdrawal of privileges. But even the critics would mostly agree that parents should minimize their dependence on physical punishment.

concept **check** 6.5

Distinguishing Between Classical Conditioning and Operant Conditioning

Check your understanding of the usual differences between classical conditioning and operant conditioning by indicating the type of conditioning process involved in each of the following examples. In the space on the left, place a C if the example involves classical conditioning, an O if it involves operant conditioning, or a B if it involves both. The answers can be found in Appendix A.

_____ **1.** Whenever Midori takes her dog out for a walk, she wears the same old blue windbreaker. Eventually, she notices that her dog becomes excited whenever she puts on this windbreaker.

_____ **2.** The Wailing Creatures are a successful rock band with three hit albums to their credit. They begin their U.S. tour featuring many new, unreleased songs, all of which draw silence from their concert fans. The same fans cheer wildly when the Wailing Creatures play any of their old hits. Gradually, the band reduces the number of new songs it plays and starts playing more of the old standbys.

_____ **3.** When Cindy and Mel first fell in love, they listened constantly to the Wailing Creatures' hit song "Transatlantic Obsession." Although several years have passed, whenever they hear this song, they experience a warm, romantic feeling.

_____ **4.** For nearly 20 years Ralph has worked as a machinist in the same factory. His new foreman is never satisfied with his work and criticizes him constantly. After a few weeks of heavy criticism, Ralph experiences anxiety whenever he arrives at work. He starts calling in sick more and more frequently to evade this anxiety.

As you learned in Chapter 1, science is constantly evolving and changing in response to new research and new thinking. Such change certainly has occurred in the study of conditioning (Domjan, 1998). In this section, we will examine two major changes in thinking about conditioning that have emerged in recent decades. First, we'll consider the growing recognition that an organism's biological heritage can limit or channel conditioning. Second, we'll discuss the increased appreciation of the role of cognitive processes in conditioning.

Recognizing Biological Constraints on Conditioning

Learning theorists have traditionally assumed that the fundamental laws of conditioning have great generality—that they apply to a wide range of species. Although no one ever suggested that hamsters could learn physics, until the 1960s most psychologists assumed that associations could be conditioned between any stimulus an organism could register and any response it could make. However, findings in recent decades have demonstrated that there are limits to the generality of conditioning principles—limits imposed by an organism's biological heritage.

Instinctive Drift

One biological constraint on learning is instinctive drift. *Instinctive drift* occurs when an animal's innate response tendencies interfere with conditioning processes. Instinctive drift was first described by the Brelands, the operant psychologists who went into the business of training animals for commercial purposes (Breland & Breland, 1966). They have described many amusing examples of their "failures" to control behavior through conditioning. For instance, they once were training some raccoons to deposit coins in a piggy bank. They were successful in shaping the raccoons to pick up a coin and put it into a small box, using food as the reinforcer. However, when they gave the raccoons a couple of coins, an unexpected problem arose: The raccoons wouldn't give the coins up! In spite of the reinforcers available for depositing the coins, they would sit and rub the coins together like so many little misers.

What had happened to disrupt the conditioning program? Apparently, associating the coins with food had brought out the raccoons' innate food-washing behavior. Raccoons often rub things together to clean them. The Brelands report that they have run into this sort of instinct-related interference on many occasions with a wide variety of species.

Conditioned Taste Aversion

A number of years ago, a prominent psychologist, Martin Seligman, dined out with his wife and enjoyed a steak with sauce béarnaise. About six hours afterward, he developed a wicked case of stomach flu and endured severe nausea. Subsequently, when he ordered sauce béarnaise, he was chagrined to discover that its aroma alone nearly made him throw up. Seligman's experience was not unique. Many people develop aversions to food that has been followed by nausea from illness, alcohol intoxication, or food poisoning. However, Seligman was puzzled by what he called his "sauce béarnaise syndrome" (Seligman & Hager, 1972). On the one hand, it appeared to be the straightforward result of classical conditioning. A neutral stimulus (the sauce) had been paired with an unconditioned stimulus (the flu), which caused an unconditioned response (the nausea). Hence, the sauce béarnaise became a conditioned stimulus eliciting nausea (see **Figure 6.18**).

On the other hand, Seligman recognized that his aversion to béarnaise sauce seemed to violate certain basic principles of conditioning. First, the lengthy delay of six hours between the CS (the sauce) and the UCS (the flu) should have prevented conditioning from occurring. In laboratory studies, a delay of more than *30 seconds* between the CS and UCS makes it difficult to establish a conditioned response, yet this conditioning occurred in just one pairing. Second, why was it that *only* the béarnaise sauce became a CS eliciting nausea? Why not other stimuli that were present in the restaurant? Shouldn't plates, knives,

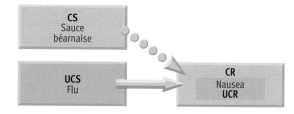

Figure 6.18

Conditioned taste aversion. Taste aversions can be established through classical conditioning, as in the "sauce béarnaise syndrome." However, as the text explains, taste aversions can be acquired in ways that *seem* to violate basic principles of classical conditioning.

PREVIEW QUESTIONS

● What is instinctive drift?

● Why are conditioned taste aversions so easy to acquire?

● To what degree are the laws of learning universal across species?

● What is latent learning, and what was its theoretical significance?

● How does the predictive value of a CS affect conditioning?

● Are responses that are followed by favorable consequences always strengthened?

JOHN GARCIA

"Taste aversions do not fit comfortably within the present framework of classical or instrumental conditioning: These aversions selectively seek flavors to the exclusion of other stimuli. Interstimulus intervals are a thousandfold too long."

tablecloths, or his wife, for example, also trigger Seligman's nausea?

The riddle of Seligman's sauce béarnaise syndrome was solved by John Garcia (1989) and his colleagues. They conducted a series of studies on *conditioned taste aversion* (Garcia, Clarke, & Hankins, 1973; Garcia & Koelling, 1966; Garcia & Rusiniak, 1980). In these studies, they manipulated the kinds of stimuli preceding the onset of nausea and other noxious experiences in rats, using radiation to artificially induce the nausea. They found that when taste cues were followed by nausea, rats quickly acquired conditioned taste aversions. However, when taste cues were followed by other types of noxious stimuli (such as shock), rats did *not* develop conditioned taste aversions. Furthermore, visual and auditory stimuli followed by nausea also failed to produce conditioned aversions. In short, Garcia and his co-workers found that it was almost impossible to create certain associations, whereas taste-nausea associations (and odor-nausea associations) were almost impossible to prevent.

What is the theoretical significance of this unique readiness to make connections between taste and nausea? Garcia argues that it is a by-product of the evolutionary history of mammals. Animals that consume poisonous foods and survive must learn not to repeat their mistakes. Natural selection will favor organisms that quickly learn what *not* to eat. Thus, evolution may have biologically programmed some organisms to learn certain types of associations more easily than others.

Arbitrary Versus Ecological Conditioned Stimuli

Michael Domjan (2005) argues that the rapid conditioning seen in taste-aversion learning is not all that unique—it is just one example of what happens when *ecologically relevant conditioned stimuli* are studied, as opposed to *arbitrary, neutral stimuli*. Domjan points out that laboratory studies of classical conditioning have traditionally paired a UCS with a neutral stimulus that is unrelated to the UCS (such as a bell, tone, or light). This strategy ensured that the association created through conditioning was a newly acquired association rather than the product of previous learning. This approach yielded decades of useful insights about the laws governing classical conditioning, but Domjan argues that there is a gap between this paradigm and the way learning takes place in the real world.

According to Domjan (2005), in natural settings conditioned stimuli generally are not arbitrary cues that are unrelated to the UCS. In the real world, con-

ditioned stimuli tend to have natural relations to the unconditioned stimuli that they predict. For example, a rattlesnake bite is typically preceded by the snake's distinctive rattling sound; copulation among animals is typically preceded by specific mating signals; the consumption of toxic food is normally preceded by a specific taste. If taste-aversion learning appears to "violate" the normal laws of conditioning, it's because these laws have been compiled in unrealistic situations that are not representative of how conditioning unfolds in natural settings.

According to Domjan (2005), over the course of evolution, organisms have developed distinct response systems to deal with crucial tasks, such as finding food and avoiding predators. When a learning task in the laboratory happens to mesh with an animal's evolutionary history, learning is likely to proceed more quickly and easily than when arbitrary stimuli are used (Domjan, Cusato, & Krause, 2004). Thus, biological constraints on learning are not really "constraints" on the general laws of learning. These *species-specific predispositions* are the norm—an insight that eluded researchers for decades because they mostly worked with neutral conditioned stimuli.

So, what is the current thinking on the idea that the laws of learning are *universal* across various species? The predominant view among learning theorists seems to be that the basic mechanisms of learning are *similar* across species but that these mechanisms have sometimes been modified in the course of evolution as species have adapted to the specialized demands of their environments (Shettleworth, 1998). According to this view, learning is a very general process because the neural substrates of learning and the basic problems confronted by various organisms are much the same across species. For example, it is probably adaptive for virtually any organism to develop the ability to recognize stimuli that signal important events. However, given that different organisms confront different adaptive problems to survive and reproduce, it makes sense that learning has evolved along somewhat different paths in different species (Hollis, 1997; Sherry, 1992).

Recognizing Cognitive Processes in Conditioning

Pavlov, Skinner, and their followers traditionally viewed conditioning as a mechanical process in which stimulus-response associations are "stamped in" by experience. Learning theorists asserted that if creatures such as snails can be conditioned, conditioning can't depend on higher mental processes. This viewpoint did not go entirely unchallenged, as we will discuss momentarily, but mainstream theories of conditioning did not allocate any role to cognitive processes. In recent decades, however, research findings have led theorists to shift toward more cognitive explanations of conditioning. Let's review how this transition gradually occurred.

Latent Learning and Cognitive Maps

The first major "renegade" to chip away at the conventional view of learning was Edward C. Tolman (1932, 1938), an American psychologist who was something of a gadfly for the behaviorist movement in the 1930s and 1940s. Tolman and his colleagues conducted a series of studies that posed some difficult questions for the prevailing views of conditioning. In one landmark study (Tolman & Honzik, 1930), three groups of food-deprived rats learned to run a complicated maze over a series of once-a-day trials (see **Figure 6.19a**). The rats in Group A received a food reward when they got to the end of the maze each day. Because of this reinforcement, their performance in running the maze (measured by how many "wrong turns" they made) gradually improved over the course of 17 days (see **Figure 6.19b**). The rats in Group B did not receive any food reward. Lacking reinforcement for getting to the goal box swiftly, this group made many "errors" and showed only modest improvement in performance. Group C was the critical group; they did not get any reward for their first 10 trials in the maze, but they were rewarded from the 11th trial onward. The rats in this group showed little improvement in performance over the first 10 trials (just like Group B), but after finding food in the goal box on the 11th trial, they showed sharp improvement on subsequent trials. In fact, their performance was even a little better than that of the Group A rats who had been rewarded after every trial (see **Figure 6.19b**).

Tolman concluded that the rats in Group C had been learning about the maze all along, just as much as the rats in group A, but they had no motivation to demonstrate this learning until a reward was introduced. Tolman called this phenomenon *latent learning*—learning that is not apparent from behavior when it first occurs. *Why did these findings present a challenge for the prevailing view of learning?* First, they suggested that learning can take place in the absence of reinforcement—at a time when learned responses were thought to be stamped in by reinforcement. Second, they suggested that the rats who displayed latent learning had formed a *cognitive map* of the maze (a mental representation of the spatial layout) at a time when cognitive processes were thought to be irrelevant to understanding conditioning even in humans.

Tolman (1948) went on to conduct other studies which suggested that cognitive processes play a role in conditioning. But his ideas were ahead of their time and mostly attracted rebuttals and criticism from the influential learning theorists of his era (Hilgard, 1987). In the long run, however, Tolman's ideas prevailed, as models of conditioning were eventually forced to incorporate cognitive factors.

Signal Relations

One theorist who was especially influential in demonstrating the importance of cognitive factors in conditioning was Robert Rescorla (1978, 1980; Rescorla & Wagner, 1972). Rescorla asserts that environmental

Archives of the History of American Psychology—The University of Akron

EDWARD CHACE TOLMAN

"Learning consists not in stimulus-response connections but in the building up in the nervous system of sets which function like cognitive maps."

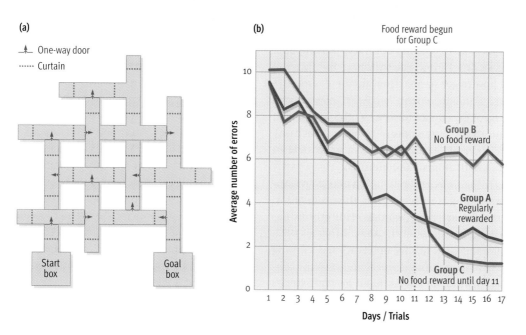

(a)

⊥ One-way door
····· Curtain

Start box

Goal box

(b)

Food reward begun for Group C

Average number of errors

Group B
No food reward

Group A
Regularly rewarded

Group C
No food reward until day 11

Days / Trials

Figure 6.19

Latent learning. **(a)** In the study by Tolman and Honzik (1930), rats learned to run the complicated maze shown here. **(b)** The results obtained by Tolman and Honzik (1930) are summarized in this graph. The rats in Group C showed a sudden improvement in performance when a food reward was introduced on Trial 11. Tolman concluded that the rats in this group were learning about the maze all along, but their learning remained "latent" until reinforcement was made available.

Source: Adapted from Tolman, E. C., & Honzik, C. H. (1930). Introduction and removal of reward and maze performance in rats. *University of California Publications in Psychology, 4,* 257-275.

ROBERT RESCORLA

"I encourage students to think of animals as behaving like little statisticians. . . . They really are very finely attuned to small changes in the likelihood of events."

stimuli serve as signals and that some stimuli are better, or more dependable, signals than others. A "good" signal is one that allows accurate prediction of the UCS. Hence, he has manipulated the *predictive value* of a conditioned stimulus by varying the proportion of trials in which the CS and UCS are paired. For example, in one study a CS (tone) and UCS (shock) were paired 100% of the time for one group of rats and only 50% of the time for another group.

What did Rescorla find when he tested the two groups of rats for conditioned fear? He found that the CS elicited a much stronger fear response in the group that had been exposed to the more dependable signal. Many other studies of signal relations have also shown that the predictive value of a CS is an influential factor governing classical conditioning (Rescorla, 1978). These studies suggest that classical conditioning may involve information processing rather than reflexive responding.

Response-Outcome Relations and Reinforcement

Studies of response-outcome relations and reinforcement also highlight the role of cognitive processes in conditioning. Imagine that on the night before an important exam you study hard while repeatedly playing a Norah Jones song. The next morning you earn an A on your exam. Does this result strengthen your tendency to play Norah Jones songs before exams? Probably not. Chances are, you will recognize the logical relation between the response of studying hard and the reinforcement of a good grade, and only the response of studying will be strengthened (Killeen, 1981). Thus, reinforcement is *not* automatic when favorable consequences follow a response. Organisms actively reason out the relations between responses and the outcomes that follow. When a response is followed by a desirable outcome, the response is more likely to be strengthened if it seems likely that the response *caused* the outcome.

In sum, modern, reformulated models of conditioning view it as a matter of detecting the *contingencies* among environmental events (Matute & Miller, 1998). According to these theories, organisms actively try to figure out what leads to what (the contingencies) in the world around them. The new, cognitively oriented theories of conditioning are quite a departure from older theories that depicted conditioning as a mindless, mechanical process. We can also see this new emphasis on cognitive processes in our next subject, observational learning.

> Observational Learning

PREVIEW QUESTIONS

● How can conditioning occur indirectly?

● What are the key processes in observational learning?

● How did research by Bandura and colleagues contribute to the dialogue regarding the effects of media violence?

● What have contemporary investigators concluded about the effects of media violence?

Can classical and operant condition account for all human learning? Absolutely not. Consider how people learn a fairly basic skill such as driving a car. They do not hop naively into an automobile and start emitting random responses until one leads to favorable consequences. On the contrary, most people learning to drive know exactly where to place the key and how to get started. How are these responses acquired? Through *observation*. Most new drivers have years of experience observing others drive and they put those observations to work. Learning through observation accounts for a great deal of learning in both animals and humans.

Observational learning **occurs when an organism's responding is influenced by the observation of others, who are called models.** This process has been investigated extensively by Albert Bandura (1977, 1986). Bandura does not see observational learning as entirely separate from classical and operant conditioning. Instead, he asserts that it greatly extends the reach of these conditioning processes. Whereas previous conditioning theorists emphasized the organism's direct experience, Bandura has demonstrated that both classical and operant conditioning can take place vicariously through observational learning.

Basic Processes

Essentially, observational learning involves being conditioned indirectly by virtue of observing another's conditioning (see **Figure 6.20**). To illustrate, suppose you observe a friend behaving assertively with a car salesperson. You see your friend's assertive behavior reinforced by the exceptionally good buy she gets on the car. Your own tendency to behave assertively with salespeople might well be strengthened as a result. Notice that the reinforcement is experienced by your friend, not you. The good buy should strengthen your friend's tendency to bargain assertively, but your tendency to do so may also be strengthened indirectly.

Bandura has identified four key processes that are crucial in observational learning. The first two—

Courtesy of Robert Rescorla

Observational learning occurs in both humans and animals. For example, the English titmouse has learned how to break into containers to swipe cream from its human neighbors and this behavior has been passed across generations through observational learning. In a similar vein, children acquire a diverse array of responses from role models.

attention and retention—highlight the importance of cognition in this type of learning:

- *Attention.* To learn through observation, you must pay attention to another person's behavior and its consequences.

- *Retention.* You may not have occasion to use an observed response for weeks, months, or even years. Hence, you must store a mental representation of what you have witnessed in your memory.

- *Reproduction.* Enacting a modeled response depends on your ability to reproduce the response by converting your stored mental images into overt behavior.

- *Motivation.* Finally, you are unlikely to reproduce an observed response unless you are motivated to do so. Your motivation depends on whether you encounter a situation in which you believe that the response is likely to pay off for you.

Observational Learning and the Media Violence Controversy

The power of observational learning has been at the center of a long-running controversy about the effects of media violence. Ever since television became popular in the 1950s social critics have expressed concern about the amount of violence on TV. In the 1960s, Albert Bandura and his colleagues conducted landmark research on the issue that remains widely cited and influential.

In one classic study, Bandura, Ross, and Ross (1963a) showed how the observation of filmed models can influence the learning of aggressive behavior in children. They manipulated whether or not nursery-school children saw an aggressive model on film and whether the aggressive model experienced

ALBERT BANDURA

"Most human behavior is learned by observation through modeling."

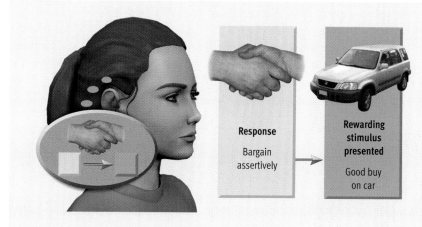

Figure 6.20
Observational learning. In observational learning, an observer attends to and stores a mental representation of a model's behavior (example: assertive bargaining) and its consequences (example: a good buy on a car). If the observer sees the modeled response lead to a favorable outcome, the observer's tendency to emit the modeled response will be strengthened.

Response

Bargain assertively

Rewarding stimulus presented

Good buy on car

TYPE OF LEARNING	PROCEDURE	DIAGRAM	RESULT

CLASSICAL CONDITIONING

Ivan Pavlov

A neutral stimulus (for example, a tone) is paired with an unconditioned stimulus (such as food) that elicits an unconditioned response (salivation).

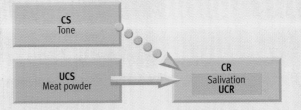

CS Tone

UCS Meat powder

CR Salivation **UCR**

The neutral stimulus becomes a conditioned stimulus that elicits the conditioned response (for example, a tone triggers salivation).

OPERANT CONDITIONING

B. F. Skinner

In a stimulus situation, a response is followed by favorable consequences (reinforcement) or unfavorable consequences (punishment).

Response Press lever

Rewarding or aversive stimulus presented or removed Food delivery or shock

If reinforced, the response is strengthened (emitted more frequently); if punished, the response is weakened (emitted less frequently).

OBSERVATIONAL LEARNING

Albert Bandura

An observer attends to a model's behavior (for example, aggressive bargaining) and its consequences (for example, a good buy on a car).

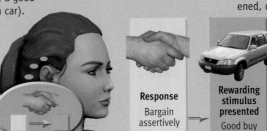

Response Bargain assertively

Rewarding stimulus presented Good buy on car

The observer stores a mental representation of the modeled response; the observer's tendency to emit the response may be strengthened or weakened, depending on the consequences observed.

TYPICAL KINDS OF RESPONSES	EXAMPLES IN ANIMALS	EXAMPLES IN HUMANS
Mostly (but not always) involuntary reflexes and visceral responses	Dogs learn to salivate to the sound of a tone that has been paired with meat powder.  © Bettmann/Corbis	Little Albert learns to fear a white rat and other white, furry objects through classical conditioning. 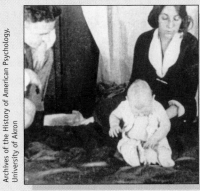 Archives of the History of American Psychology, University of Akron
Mostly (but not always) voluntary, spontaneous responses	Trained animals perform remarkable feats because they have been reinforced for gradually learning closer and closer approximations of responses they do not normally emit. Courtesy of Animal Behavior Enterprises, Inc.	Casino patrons tend to exhibit high, steady rates of gambling, as most games of chance involve complex variable-ratio schedules of reinforcement.  © David Falconer/Folio, Inc.
Mostly voluntary responses, often consisting of novel and complex sequences	An English titmouse learns to break into milk bottles by observing the thievery of other titmice.  © J. Markham/Bruce Coleman, Inc.	A young boy performs a response that he has acquired through observational learning. 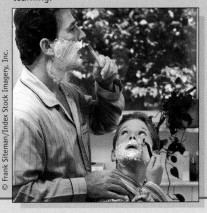 © Frank Siteman/Index Stock Imagery, Inc.

Web Link 6.6

Media Violence
Maintained by a Canadian nonprofit organization called the Media Awareness Network, which develops media literacy programs, this site permits visitors to access a great deal of background information and dialogue on the debate about the effects of violence in the media.

positive or negative consequences. Soon after the manipulations, the children were taken to a room where their play was observed through a one-way mirror. Among the toys available in the room were two "Bobo dolls" that served as convenient targets for kicks, punches, and other aggressive responses. Children who had seen the aggressive model rewarded engaged in more aggression toward the toys than children in the other conditions did. This study was one of the earliest experimental demonstrations of a cause-and-effect relationship between exposure to TV depictions of aggression and increased aggressive behavior.

Subsequent research demonstrated that youngsters are exposed to an astonishing amount of violence when they watch TV. The National Television Violence Study, a large-scale study of the content of network and cable television shows conducted in 1994–1997, revealed that 61% of programs contained violence; 44% of violent actors were enticing role models (i.e., the "good guys"); 75% of violent actions occurred without punishment or condemnation; and 51% of violent actions were "sanitized," as they featured no apparent pain (Anderson et al., 2003).

Does this steady diet of media violence foster increased aggression? Decades of research since Bandura's pioneering work indicate that the answer is "yes" (Bushman & Huesmann, 2001). The short-term effects of media violence have been investigated in hundreds of experimental studies. These studies consistently demonstrate that exposure to TV and movie violence increases the likelihood of physical aggression, verbal aggression, aggressive thoughts, and aggressive emotions in both children and adults (Anderson et al., 2003). Exposure to aggressive content in video games produces similar results (Anderson, 2004).

The real-world and long-term effects of media violence have been investigated through correlational research. The findings of these studies show that the more violence children watch on TV, the more aggressive the children tend to be at home and at school (Huesmann & Miller, 1994). Of course, critics point out that this correlation could reflect a variety of causal relationships (see **Figure 6.21**). Perhaps high aggressiveness in children causes an increased interest in violent television shows. However, there are a handful of long-term studies that have followed the same subjects since the 1960s and 1970s that have clarified the causal relations underlying the link between media violence and elevated aggression. These studies show that the extent of youngsters' exposure to media violence in childhood predicts their aggressiveness in adolescence and early adulthood, but not vice versa (Huesman, 1986; Huesman et al., 2003). In other words, high exposure to media violence precedes, and presumably contributes to the causation of, high aggressiveness.

The heated debate about media violence shows that observational learning plays an important role in regulating behavior. It represents a third major type of learning that builds on the first two types—classical conditioning and operant conditioning. These three basic types of learning are summarized and compared in the Illustrated Overview on pages 194–195.

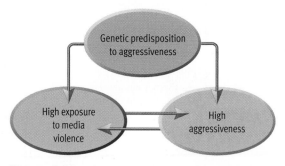

Figure 6.21

The correlation between exposure to media violence and aggression. The more violence children watch on TV, the more aggressive they tend to be, but this correlation could reflect a variety of underlying causal relationships. Although watching violent shows probably causes increased aggressiveness, it is also possible that aggressive children are drawn to violent shows. Or perhaps a third variable (such as a genetic predisposition to aggressiveness) leads to both a preference for violent shows and high aggressiveness.

CALVIN AND HOBBES

© 1995 Watterson/Dist. by Universal Press Syndicate

CALVIN AND HOBBES © 1995 by Bill Watterson. Distributed by Universal Press Syndicate. Reprinted with permission. All rights reserved.

Two of our unifying themes stand out in this chapter: (1) nature and nurture interactively govern behavior, and (2) dense interconnections exist between psychology and events in the world at large. Let's examine each of these points in more detail.

In regard to nature versus nurture, research on learning has clearly and repeatedly demonstrated the enormous power of the environment and experience in shaping behavior. Indeed, many learning theorists once believed that *all* aspects of behavior could be explained in terms of environmental determinants. In recent decades, however, evidence on instinctive drift and conditioned taste aversion has shown that there are biological constraints on conditioning. Thus, even in explanations of learning—an area once dominated by nurture theories—we see again that heredity and environment jointly influence behavior.

The history of research on conditioning also shows how progress in psychology can seep into every corner of society. For example, Skinner's ideas on the power of positive reinforcement have influenced patterns of discipline in American society. Research on operant conditioning has also affected management styles in the business world, leading to an increased emphasis on positive reinforcement. The fact that the principles of conditioning are routinely applied in homes, businesses, child-care facilities, schools, and factories clearly shows that psychology is not an ivory tower endeavor.

In the upcoming Personal Application, you will see how you can apply the principles of conditioning to improve your self-control, as we discuss the technology of behavior modification.

Heredity and Environment

Sociohistorical Context

PERSONAL *Application*

Achieving Self-Control Through Behavior Modification

Answer the following "yes" or "no."

_____ 1 Do you have a hard time passing up food, even when you're not hungry?

_____ 2 Do you wish you studied more often?

_____ 3 Would you like to cut down on your smoking or drinking?

_____ 4 Do you experience difficulty in getting yourself to exercise regularly?

If you answered "yes" to any of these questions, you have struggled with the challenge of self-control. This Application discusses how you can use the principles and techniques of behavior modification to improve your self-control. *Behavior modification* is a systematic approach to changing behavior through the application of the principles of conditioning. Advocates of behavior modification assume that behavior is mainly a product of learning, conditioning, and environmental control. They further assume that *what is learned can be unlearned.* Thus, they set out to "recondition" people to produce more desirable and effective patterns of behavior.

The technology of behavior modification has been applied with great success in schools, businesses, hospitals, factories, child-care facilities, prisons, and mental health centers (Kazdin, 2001; O'Donohue, 1998; Rachman, 1992). Moreover, behavior modification techniques have proven particularly valuable in efforts to improve self-control. Our discussion will borrow liberally from an excellent book on self-modification by David Watson and Roland Tharp (2007). We will discuss four steps in the process of self-modification, which are outlined in **Figure 6.22** on the next page.

Specifying Your Target Behavior

The first step in a self-modification program is to specify the target behavior(s) that you want to change. Behavior modification can only be applied to a clearly defined, overt response, yet many people have difficulty pinpointing the behavior they hope to alter. They tend to describe their problems in terms of unobservable personality *traits* rather than overt *behaviors.* For example, asked what behavior he would like to change, a man might say, "I'm too irritable." That statement may be true, but it is of little help in designing a self-modification program. To use a behavioral approach, vague statements about

Smoking is just one of the many types of maladaptive habits that can be reduced or eliminated through self-modification techniques.

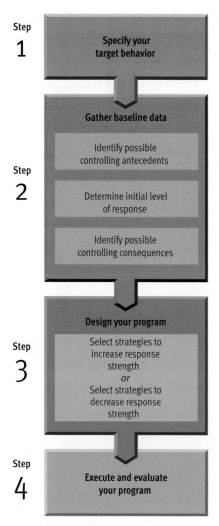

Figure 6.22
Steps in a self-modification program. This flowchart provides an overview of the four steps necessary to execute a self-modification program.

traits need to be translated into precise descriptions of specific target behaviors.

To identify target responses, you need to ponder past behavior or closely observe future behavior and list specific *examples* of responses that lead to the trait description. For instance, the man who regards himself as "too irritable" might identify two overly frequent responses, such as arguing with his wife and snapping at his children. These are specific behaviors for which he could design a self-modification program.

Gathering Baseline Data

The second step in behavior modification is to gather baseline data. You need to system-atically observe your target behavior for a period of time (usually a week or two) before you work out the details of your program. In gathering your baseline data, you need to monitor three things.

First, you need to determine the initial response level of your target behavior. After all, you can't tell whether your program is working effectively unless you have a baseline for comparison. In most cases, you would simply keep track of how often the target response occurs in a certain time interval. Thus, you might count the daily frequency of snapping at your children, smoking cigarettes, or biting your fingernails. *It is crucial to gather accurate data.* You should keep permanent written records, and it is usually best to portray these records graphically (see **Figure 6.23**).

Second, you need to monitor the *antecedents* of your target behavior. Antecedents are events that typically precede the target response. Often these events play a major role in evoking your target behavior. For example, if your target is overeating, you might discover that the bulk of your overeating occurs late in the evening while you watch TV. If you can pinpoint this kind of antecedent-response connection, you may be able to design your program to circumvent or break the link.

Third, you need to monitor the typical consequences of your target behavior. Try to identify the reinforcers that are maintaining an undesirable target behavior or the unfavorable outcomes that are suppressing a desirable target behavior. In trying to identify reinforcers, remember that avoidance behavior is usually maintained by negative reinforcement. That is, the payoff for avoidance is usually the removal of something aversive, such as anxiety or a threat to self-esteem. You should also take into account the fact that a response may not be reinforced every time, as most behavior is maintained by intermittent reinforcement.

Designing Your Program

Once you have selected a target behavior and gathered adequate baseline data, it is time to plan your intervention program. Generally speaking, your program will be

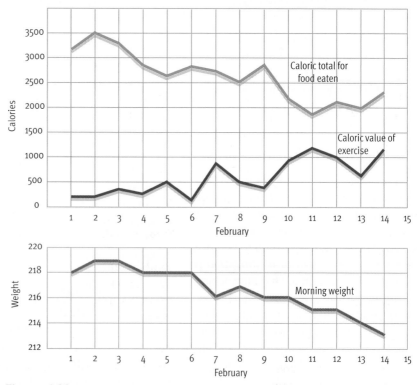

Figure 6.23
Example of record keeping in a self-modification program. Graphic records are ideal for tracking progress in behavior modification efforts. The records shown here illustrate what someone would be likely to track in a behavior modification program for weight loss.

designed either to increase or to decrease the frequency of a target response.

Increasing Response Strength

Efforts to increase the frequency of a target response depend largely on the use of positive reinforcement. In other words, you reward yourself for behaving properly. Although the basic strategy is quite simple, doing it skillfully involves a number of considerations, including selecting the right reinforcer and arranging contingencies.

Selecting a Reinforcer
To use positive reinforcement, you need to find a reward that will be effective for you. Reinforcement is subjective. What is reinforcing for one person may not be reinforcing for another. To determine your personal reinforcers you need to ask yourself questions such as: What do I like to do for fun? What makes me feel good? What would be a nice present? What would I hate to lose?

You don't have to come up with spectacular new reinforcers that you've never experienced before. *You can use reinforcers that you are already getting.* However, you have to restructure the contingencies so that you get them only if you behave appropriately. For example, if you normally buy two compact discs per week, you might make these purchases contingent on studying a certain number of hours during the week.

Arranging the Contingencies
Once you have chosen your reinforcer, you have to set up reinforcement contingencies. These contingencies will describe the exact behavioral goals that must be met and the reinforcement that may then be awarded. For example, in a program to increase exercise, you might make spending $40 on clothes (the reinforcer) contingent on having jogged 15 miles during the week (the target behavior).

Try to set behavioral goals that are both challenging and realistic. You want your goals to be challenging so that they lead to improvement in your behavior. However, setting unrealistically high goals—a common mistake in self-modification—often leads to unnecessary discouragement.

Decreasing Response Strength

Let's turn now to the challenge of reducing the frequency of an undesirable response. You can go about this task in a number of ways. Your principal options include reinforcement, control of antecedents, and punishment.

Reinforcement
Reinforcers can be used in an indirect way to decrease the frequency of a response. This may sound paradoxical, since you have learned that reinforcement strengthens a response. The trick lies in how you define the target behavior. For example, in the case of overeating you might define your target behavior as eating more than 1600 calories a day (an excess response that you want to decrease) or eating less than 1600 calories a day (a deficit response that you want to increase). You can choose the latter definition and reinforce yourself whenever you eat less than 1600 calories in a day. Thus, you can reinforce yourself for not emitting a response, or for emitting it less, and thereby decrease a response through reinforcement.

Control of Antecedents
A worthwhile strategy for decreasing the occurrence of an undesirable response may be to identify its antecedents and avoid exposure to them. This strategy is especially useful when you are trying to decrease the frequency of a consummatory response, such as smoking or eating. In the case of overeating, for instance, the easiest way to resist temptation is to avoid having to face it. Thus, you might stay away from favorite restaurants, minimize time spent in your kitchen, shop for groceries just after eating (when willpower is higher), and avoid purchasing favorite foods.

Punishment
The strategy of decreasing unwanted behavior by punishing yourself for that behavior is an obvious option that people tend to overuse. The biggest problem with punishment in a self-modification effort is that it is difficult to follow through and punish yourself. Nonetheless, there may be situations in which your manipulations of reinforcers need to be bolstered by the threat of punishment.

If you're going to use punishment, keep two guidelines in mind. First, do not use punishment alone. Use it in conjunction with positive reinforcement. If you set up a program in which you can earn only negative consequences, you probably won't stick to it. Second, use a relatively mild punishment so that you will actually be able to administer it to yourself.

Executing and Evaluating Your Program

Once you have designed your program, the next step is to put it to work by enforcing the contingencies that you have carefully planned. During this period, you need to continue to accurately record the frequency of your target behavior so you can evaluate your progress. The success of your program depends on your not "cheating." The most common form of cheating is to reward yourself when you have not actually earned it.

You can do two things to increase the likelihood that you will comply with your program. One is to make up a *behavioral contract*—**a written agreement outlining a promise to adhere to the contingencies of a behavior modification program.** The formality of signing such a contract in front of friends or family seems to make people take their program more seriously. You can further reduce the likelihood of cheating by having someone other than yourself dole out the reinforcers and punishments.

Generally, when you design your program you should spell out the conditions under which you will bring it to an end. Doing so involves setting terminal goals such as reaching a certain weight, studying with a certain regularity, or going without cigarettes for a certain length of time. Often, it is a good idea to phase out your program by planning a gradual reduction in the frequency or potency of your reinforcement for appropriate behavior.

Manipulating Emotions: Pavlov and Persuasion

With all due respect to the great Ivan Pavlov, when we focus on his demonstration that dogs can be trained to slobber in response to a tone, it is easy to lose sight of the importance of classical conditioning. At first glance, most people do not see a relationship between Pavlov's slobbering dogs and anything that they are even remotely interested in. However, in the main body of the chapter, we saw that classical conditioning actually contributes to the regulation of many important aspects of behavior, including fears, phobias, and other emotional reactions; immune function and other physiological processes; food preferences; and even sexual arousal. In this Application you will learn that classical conditioning is routinely used to manipulate emotions in persuasive efforts. If you watch TV, you have been subjected to Pavlovian techniques. An understanding of these techniques can help you recognize when your emotions are being manipulated by advertisers, politicians, and the media.

Manipulation efforts harnessing Pavlovian conditioning generally involve a special subtype of classical conditioning that theorists have recently christened *evaluative conditioning*. **Evaluative conditioning consists of efforts to transfer the emotion attached to a UCS to a new CS.** In other words, evaluative conditioning involves the acquisition of emotion-laden likes and dislikes, or preferences, through classical conditioning. Of interest here, is that research shows that attitudes can be shaped through evaluative conditioning without participants' conscious awareness (Olson & Fazio, 2001) and that evaluative conditioning is remarkably resistant to extinction (Walther, Nagengast, & Trasselli, 2005). Thus, an especially interesting aspect of evaluative conditioning is that people often are unaware of the origin of their attitudes, or even that they feel the way they do. The key to this process is simply to manipulate the automatic, subconscious associations that people make in response to various stimuli. Let's look at how this manipulation is done

in advertising, business negotiations, and the world of politics.

Classical Conditioning in Advertising

The art of manipulating people's associations has been perfected by the advertising industry, leading Till and Priluck (2000) to comment, "conditioning of attitudes towards products and brands has become generally accepted and has developed into a unique research stream" (p. 57). Advertisers consistently endeavor to pair the products they are peddling with stimuli that seem likely to elicit positive emotional responses (see **Figure 6.24**). An extensive variety of stimuli are used for this purpose. Products are paired with well-liked celebrity spokespersons; depictions of warm, loving families; beautiful pastoral scenery; cute, cuddly pets; enchanting, rosy-cheeked children; upbeat, pleasant music; and opulent surroundings that reek of wealth. Advertisers also like to pair their products with exciting

events, such as the NBA Finals, and cherished symbols, such as flags and the Olympic rings insignia. But, above all else, advertisers like to link their products with sexual imagery and extremely attractive models—especially, glamorous, alluring women (Reichert, 2003; Reichert & Lambiase, 2003).

Advertisers mostly seek to associate their products with stimuli that evoke pleasurable feelings of a general sort, but in some cases they try to create more specific associations. For example, cigarette brands sold mainly to men are frequently paired with tough-looking men in rugged settings to create an association between the cigarettes and masculinity. In contrast, cigarette brands that are mainly marketed to women are paired with images that evoke feelings of femininity. In a similar vein, manufacturers of designer jeans typically seek to forge associations between their products and things that are young, urban, and hip. Advertisers marketing expensive automobiles or platinum credit cards pair their products with symbols of affluence, luxury, and privilege, such as mansions, butlers, and dazzling jewelry.

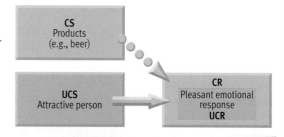

Figure 6.24

Classical conditioning in advertising. Many advertisers attempt to make their products conditioned stimuli that elicit pleasant emotional responses by pairing their products with attractive or popular people or sexual imagery.

Classical Conditioning in Business Negotiations

In the world of business interactions, two standard practices are designed to get a company's customers to make an association between the company and pleasurable feelings. The first is to take customers out to dinner at fine restaurants. The provision of delicious food and fine wine in a luxurious environment is a powerful unconditioned stimulus that reliably elicits pleasant feelings that are likely to be associated with the host. The second practice is the strategy of entertaining customers at major events, such as concerts and football games. Over the last couple decades, America's sports arenas have largely been rebuilt with vastly more "luxury skyboxes" to accommodate this business tactic. It reaches its zenith every year at the Super Bowl, where most of the seats go to the guests of Fortune 500 corporations. This practice pairs the host with both pleasant feelings and the excitement of a big event.

It is worth noting that these strategies take advantage of other processes besides classical conditioning. They also make use of the *reciprocity norm*—the social rule that one should pay back in kind what one receives from others (Cialdini, 2001). Thus, wining and dining clients creates a sense of obligation that they should reciprocate their hosts' generosity—presumably in their business dealings.

Classical Conditioning in the World of Politics

Like advertisers, candidates running for election need to influence the attitudes of many people quickly, subtly, and effectively—and they depend on evaluative conditioning to help them do so. For example, have you noticed how politicians show up at an endless variety of pleasant public events (such as the opening of a new mall) that often have nothing to do with their public service? When a sports team wins some sort of championship, local politicians are drawn like flies to the subsequent celebrations. They want to pair themselves with these positive events, so that they are associated with pleasant emotions.

Election campaign ads use the same techniques as commercial ads (except they don't rely much on sexual appeals). Candidates are paired with popular celebrities, wholesome families, pleasant music, and symbols of patriotism. Cognizant of the power of classical conditioning, politicians also exercise great care to ensure that they are not paired with people or events that might trigger negative feelings. For example, in 1999, when the U.S. government finally turned control of the Panama Canal over to Panama, President Clinton and Vice-President Gore chose to not attend the ceremonies because this event was viewed negatively in some quarters.

The ultimate political perversion of the principles of classical conditioning probably occurred in Nazi Germany. The Nazis used many propaganda techniques to create prejudice toward Jews and members of other targeted groups (such as Gypsies). One such strategy was the repeated pairing of disgusting, repulsive images with stereotypical pictures of Jews. For example, the Nazis would show alternating pictures of rats or roaches crawling over filthy garbage and stereotypical Jewish faces, so that the two images would become associated in the minds of the viewers. Thus, the German population was conditioned to have negative emotional reactions to Jews and to associate them with vermin subject to extermination. The Nazis reasoned that if people would not hesitate to exterminate rats and roaches, then why not human beings associated with these vermin?

Becoming More Aware of Classical Conditioning Processes

How effective are the efforts to manipulate people's emotions through classical conditioning? It's hard to say. In the real world, these strategies are always used in combination with other persuasive tactics, which creates multiple confounds that make it difficult to assess the impact of the Pavlovian techniques (Walther et al., 2005). Laboratory research can eliminate these confounds, but surprisingly little research on these strategies has been published, and virtually all of it has dealt with advertising. The advertising studies suggest that classical conditioning can be effective and leave enduring imprints on consumers' attitudes (Grossman & Till, 1998; Shimp, Stuart, & Engle, 1991; Walther & Grigoriadis, 2003). And research indicates that sexual appeals in advertising are attention getting, likable, and persuasive (Reichert, Heckler, & Jackson, 2001). But a great deal of additional research is needed. Given the monumental sums that advertisers spend using these techniques, it seems reasonable to speculate that individual companies have data on their specific practices to demonstrate their efficacy, but these data are not made available to the public.

What can you do to reduce the extent to which your emotions are manipulated through Pavlovian procedures? Well, you could turn off your radio and TV, close up your magazines, stop your newspaper, disconnect your modem, and withdraw into a media-shielded shell, but that hardly seems realistic for most people. Realistically, the best defense is to make a conscious effort to become more aware of the pervasive attempts to condition your emotions and attitudes. Some research on persuasion suggests that *to be forewarned is to be forearmed* (Pfau et al., 1990). In other words, if you know how media sources try to manipulate you, you should be more resistant to their strategies.

Table 6.2 Critical Thinking Skills Discussed in This Application

Skill	Description
Understanding how Pavlovian conditioning can be used to manipulate emotions	The critical thinker understands how stimuli can be paired together to create automatic associations that people may not be aware of.
Developing the ability to detect conditioning procedures used in the media	The critical thinker can recognize Pavlovian conditioning tactics in commercial and political advertisements.

Key Ideas

Classical Conditioning

● Classical conditioning explains how a neutral stimulus can acquire the capacity to elicit a response originally evoked by another stimulus. This kind of conditioning was originally described by Ivan Pavlov, who conditioned dogs to salivate when a tone was presented. Many kinds of everyday responses are regulated through classical conditioning, including phobias, anxiety responses, pleasant emotional responses, and physiological responses.

● Stimulus contiguity plays a key role in the acquisition of new conditioned responses. A conditioned response may be weakened and extinguished entirely when the CS is no longer paired with the UCS. In some cases, spontaneous recovery occurs, and an extinguished response reappears after a period of nonexposure to the CS.

● Conditioning may generalize to additional stimuli that are similar to the original CS. The opposite of generalization is discrimination, which involves not responding to stimuli that resemble the original CS. Higher order conditioning occurs when a CS functions as if it were a UCS, to establish new conditioning.

Operant Conditioning

● Operant conditioning, which was pioneered by B. F. Skinner, involves largely voluntary responses that are governed by their consequences. The key dependent variable in operant conditioning is the rate of response over time. New operant responses can be shaped by gradually reinforcing closer and closer approximations of the desired response.

● In operant conditioning, when reinforcement is terminated, the response rate usually declines and extinction may occur. Operant responses are regulated by discriminative stimuli that are cues for the likelihood of obtaining reinforcers.

● The central process in reinforcement is the strengthening of a response. Primary reinforcers are unlearned. In contrast, secondary reinforcers acquire their reinforcing quality through conditioning.

● Schedules of reinforcement influence patterns of operant responding. Intermittent schedules produce greater resistance to extinction than similar continuous schedules. Ratio schedules tend to yield higher rates of response than interval schedules. Shorter intervals and higher ratios are associated with faster responding.

● Responses can be strengthened through either the presentation of positive reinforcers or the removal of negative reinforcers. Negative reinforcement regulates escape and avoidance learning. Punishment involves unfavorable consequences that lead to a decline in response strength. Evidence suggests that physical punishment is associated with a variety of undesirable side effects, including increased aggression, but there is some debate about the issue.

Changing Directions in the Study of Conditioning

● The findings on instinctive drift and conditioned taste aversion have led to the recognition that there are species-specific biological constraints on conditioning. Domjan argues that researchers' focus on arbitrary conditioned stimuli has led to a distorted picture of the principles of conditioning. Some evolutionary psychologists argue that learning processes vary considerably across species.

● Tolman's studies of latent learning suggested that cognitive processes contribute to conditioning, but his work was not influential at the time. Studies of signal relations in classical conditioning and response-outcome relations in operant conditioning demonstrated that cognitive processes play a larger role in conditioning than originally believed.

Observational Learning

● In observational learning, an organism is conditioned by watching a model's conditioning. Both classical and operant conditioning can occur through observational learning, which depends on the processes of attention, retention, reproduction, and motivation.

● Research on observational learning has played a central role in the debate about the effects of media violence for many decades. This research suggests that media violence contributes to increased aggression among children and adults.

Reflecting on the Chapter's Themes

● Two of our key themes were especially apparent in our coverage of learning and conditioning. One theme involves the interaction of heredity and the environment in governing behavior. The other involves the way progress in psychology affects society at large.

PERSONAL APPLICATION • Achieving Self-Control Through Behavior Modification

● The first step in self-modification is to specify the overt target behavior to be increased or decreased. The second step involves gathering baseline data about the initial rate of the target response and identifying any typical antecedents and consequences associated with the behavior.

● The third step is to design a program. If you are trying to increase the strength of a response, you'll depend on positive reinforcement. A number of strategies can be used to decrease the strength of a response, including reinforcement, control of antecedents, and punishment. The fourth step involves executing and evaluating your program, and determining when you will phase it out.

CRITICAL THINKING APPLICATION • Manipulating Emotions: Pavlov and Persuasion

● Advertisers routinely pair their products with stimuli that seem likely to elicit positive emotional responses or other specific feelings. The practice of taking customers out to dinner or to major events also takes advantage of Pavlovian conditioning. Politicians also work to pair themselves with positive events. The best defense is to become more aware of efforts to manipulate your emotions.

Key Terms

Acquisition (p. 174)
Avoidance learning (p. 186)
Behavior modification (p. 197)
Behavioral contract (p. 199)
Classical conditioning (p. 170)
Conditioned reinforcers (p. 182)
Conditioned response (CR) (p. 171)
Conditioned stimulus (CS) (p. 171)
Continuous reinforcement (p. 183)
Cumulative recorder (pp. 178–179)
Discriminative stimuli (p. 181)
Elicit (p. 171)
Emit (p. 178)
Escape learning (p. 185)
Evaluative conditioning (p. 200)
Extinction (p. 174)
Fixed-interval (FI) schedule (p. 183)
Fixed-ratio (FR) schedule (p. 183)
Higher-order conditioning (p. 176)
Intermittent reinforcement (p. 183)
Latent learning (p. 191)
Learning (p. 169)
Negative reinforcement (p. 185)
Observational learning (p. 192)
Operant conditioning (p. 177)
Pavlovian conditioning (p. 170)
Positive reinforcement (p. 185)

Primary reinforcers (p. 182)
Punishment (p. 186)
Reinforcement (p. 178)
Reinforcement contingencies (p. 178)
Resistance to extinction (p. 180)
Schedule of reinforcement (p. 183)
Secondary reinforcers (p. 182)
Shaping (p. 180)
Skinner box (p. 178)
Spontaneous recovery (p. 175)
Stimulus discrimination (p. 176)
Stimulus generalization (p. 175)
Trial (p. 171)
Unconditioned response (UCR) (p. 171)
Unconditioned stimulus (UCS) (p. 171)
Variable-interval (VI) schedule (p. 183)
Variable-ratio (VR) schedule (p. 183)

Key People

Albert Bandura (pp. 192–193)
John Garcia (p. 190)
Ivan Pavlov (pp. 170–171)
Robert Rescorla (pp. 191–192)
B. F. Skinner (pp. 177–178)
Edward C. Tolman (p. 191)
John B. Watson (pp. 175–176)

1. After repeated pairings of a tone with meat powder, Pavlov found that a dog will salivate when the tone is presented. Salivation to the tone is a(n):
   A. unconditioned stimulus.
   B. unconditioned response.
   C. conditioned stimulus.
   D. conditioned response.

2. Sam's wife always wears the same black nightgown whenever she is "in the mood" for sexual relations. Sam becomes sexually aroused as soon as he sees his wife in the nightgown. For Sam, the nightgown is a(n):
   A. unconditioned stimulus.
   B. unconditioned response.
   C. conditioned stimulus.
   D. conditioned response.

3. Watson and Rayner (1920) conditioned "Little Albert" to fear white rats by banging a hammer on a steel bar as he played with a white rat. Later, it was discovered that Albert feared not only white rats but white stuffed toys and Santa's beard as well. Albert's fear of these other objects can be attributed to:
   A. shaping.
   B. stimulus generalization.
   C. stimulus discrimination.
   D. an overactive imagination.

4. The phenomenon of higher-order conditioning shows that:
   A. only a genuine, natural UCS can be used to establish a CR.
   B. auditory stimuli are easier to condition than visual stimuli.
   C. visual stimuli are easier to condition than auditory stimuli.
   D. an already established CS can be used in the place of a natural UCS.

5. Which of the following statements is (are) true?
   A. Classical conditioning regulates reflexive, involuntary responses exclusively.
   B. Operant conditioning regulates voluntary responses exclusively.
   C. The distinction between the two types of conditioning is not absolute, with both types jointly and interactively governing some aspects of behavior.
   D. A and B.

6. In a Skinner box, the dependent variable usually is:
   A. the force with which the lever is pressed or the disk is pecked.
   B. the schedule of reinforcement used.
   C. the rate of responding.
   D. the speed of the cumulative recorder.

7. A primary reinforcer has _____ reinforcing properties; a secondary reinforcer has _____ reinforcing properties.
   A. biological; acquired
   B. conditioned; unconditioned
   C. weak; potent
   D. immediate; delayed

8. The steady, rapid responding of a person playing a slot machine is an example of the pattern of responding typically generated on a _____ schedule of reinforcement.
   A. fixed-ratio
   B. variable-ratio
   C. fixed-interval
   D. variable-interval

9. Positive reinforcement _____ the rate of responding; negative reinforcement _____ the rate of responding.
   A. increases; decreases
   B. decreases; increases
   C. increases; increases
   D. decreases; decreases

10. Research on avoidance learning suggests that conditioned fear acquired through _____ conditioning plays a key role.
    A. classical
    B. operant
    C. reinforcement
    D. intermittent

11. The studies by Garcia and his colleagues demonstrate that rats easily learn to associate a taste CS with a(n) _____ UCS.
    A. shock
    B. visual
    C. auditory
    D. nausea-inducing

12. According to Rescorla, the strength of a conditioned response depends on:
    A. the number of trials in which the CS and UCS are paired.
    B. the number of trials in which the CS is presented alone.
    C. the predictive value of the CS.
    D. the schedule of reinforcement employed.

13. The current thinking on evolution and whether there are universal laws of learning is that:
    A. only mammals respond to operant conditioning.
    B. species-specific learning tendencies are a myth.
    C. due to differences in the adaptive challenges faced by various species, learning has evolved along somewhat different paths in different species.
    D. only mammals respond to classical conditioning.

14. Albert Bandura:
    A. was the first to describe species-specific learning tendencies.
    B. was the founder of behaviorism.
    C. pioneered the study of classical conditioning.
    D. pioneered the study of observational learning.

15. In designing a self-modification program, control of antecedents should be used:
    A. by people who are in poor physical condition.
    B. only when your usual reinforcers are unavailable.
    C. when you want to decrease the frequency of a response.
    D. when you are initially not capable of making the target response.

Answers

1 D pp. 171–172
2 C pp. 171–174
3 B pp. 175–176
4 D p. 176
5 C pp. 177–178
6 C pp. 178–179
7 A p. 182
8 B pp. 183–184
9 C p. 185
10 A p. 186
11 D pp. 189–190
12 C pp. 191–192
13 C p. 190
14 D p. 192
15 C p. 199

PsykTrek

Go to the PsykTrek website or CD-ROM for further study of the concepts in this chapter. Both online and on the CD-ROM, PsykTrek includes dozens of learning modules with videos, animations, and quizzes, as well as simulations of psychological phenomena and a multimedia glossary that includes word pronunciations.

ThomsonNOW™

www.thomsonedu.com/ThomsonNOW

Go to this site for the link to ThomsonNOW, your one-stop study shop. Take a Pre-Test for this chapter, and ThomsonNOW will generate a Personalized Study Plan based on your test results. The Study Plan will identify the topics you need to review and direct you to online resources to help you master those topics. You can then take a Post-Test to help you determine the concepts you have mastered and what you still need to work on.

Companion Website

www.thomsonedu.com/psychology/weiten

Go to this site to find online resources directly linked to your book, including a glossary, flash cards, drag-and-drop exercises, quizzes, and more!

CHAPTER (7)

Human Memory

© C. Lyttle/zefa/Corbis

I f you live in the United States, you've undoubtedly handled thousands upon thousands of American pennies. Surely, then, you remember what a penny looks like—or do you? Take a look at **Figure 7.1**. Which drawing corresponds to a real penny?

Did you have a hard time selecting the real one? If so, you're not alone. Nickerson and Adams (1979) found that most people can't recognize the real penny in this collection of drawings. And their surprising finding was not a fluke. Undergraduates in England showed even worse memory for British coins (Jones, 1990). How can that be? Why do most of us have so poor a memory for an object we see every day?

Let's try another exercise. A definition of a word follows. It's not a particularly common word, but there's a good chance that you're familiar with it. Try to think of the word.

Definition: Favoritism shown or patronage granted by persons in high office to relatives or close friends.

If you can't think of the word, perhaps you can remember what letter of the alphabet it begins with, or what it sounds like. If so, you're experiencing the *tip-of-the-tongue phenomenon,* in which forgotten information feels like it's just out of reach. In this case, the word you may be reaching for is *nepotism.* You've probably endured the tip-of-the-tongue phenomenon while taking exams. You blank out on a term that you're sure you know. You may feel as if you're on the verge of remembering the term, but you can't quite come up with it. Later, perhaps while you're driving home, the term suddenly comes to you. "Of course," you may say to yourself, "how could I forget that?" That's an interesting question. Clearly, the term was stored in your memory.

As these examples suggest, memory involves more than taking in information and storing it in some mental compartment. In fact, psychologists probing the workings of memory have had to grapple with three enduring questions: (1) How does information get *into* memory? (2) How is information *maintained* in memory? (3) How is information *pulled back out* of memory? These three questions correspond to the three key processes involved in memory (see **Figure 7.2**): *encoding* (getting information in), *storage* (maintaining it), and *retrieval* (getting it out).

Figure 7.1

A simple memory test. Nickerson and Adams (1979) presented these 15 versions of an object most people have seen hundreds or thousands of times and asked, "Which one is correct?" Can you identify the real penny?

Source: Nickerson, R. S., & Adams, M. J. (1979). Long-term memory for a common object. *Cognitive Psychology, 11,* 287–307. Copyright © 1979 by Elsevier Science USA. Reproduced with permission from the publisher.

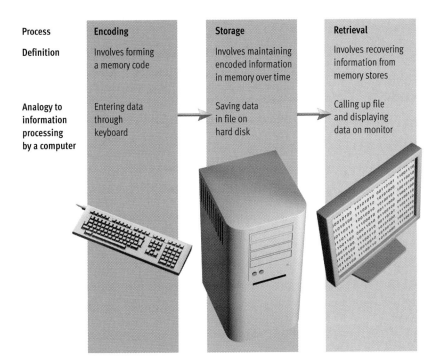

Process	Encoding	Storage	Retrieval
Definition	Involves forming a memory code	Involves maintaining encoded information in memory over time	Involves recovering information from memory stores
Analogy to information processing by a computer	Entering data through keyboard	Saving data in file on hard disk	Calling up file and displaying data on monitor

Figure 7.2

Three key processes in memory. Memory depends on three sequential processes: encoding, storage, and retrieval. Some theorists have drawn an analogy between these processes and elements of information processing by computers, as depicted here. The analogies for encoding and retrieval work pretty well, but the storage analogy is somewhat misleading. When information is stored on a hard drive, it remains unchanged indefinitely, and you can retrieve an exact copy. As you will learn in this chapter, memory storage is a much more dynamic process. Memories change over time and are rough reconstructions rather than exact copies of past events.

Encoding involves forming a memory code. For example, when you form a memory code for a word, you might emphasize how it looks, how it sounds, or what it means. Encoding usually requires attention, which is why you may not be able to recall exactly what a penny looks like—most people don't pay much attention to the appearance of a penny. As you'll see throughout this chapter, memory is largely an active process. For the most part, you're unlikely to remember something unless you make a conscious effort to do so. *Storage* **involves maintaining encoded information in memory over time.** Psychologists have focused much of their memory research on trying to identify just what factors help or hinder memory storage. But, as the tip-of-the-tongue phenomenon shows, information storage isn't enough to guarantee that you'll remember something. You need to be able to get information out of storage. *Retrieval* **involves recovering information from memory stores.** Research issues concerned with retrieval include the study of how people search memory and why some retrieval strategies are more effective than others.

Most of this chapter is devoted to an examination of memory encoding, storage, and retrieval. As you'll see, these basic processes help explain the ultimate puzzle in the study of memory: why people forget. After our discussion of forgetting, we will take a brief look at the physiological bases of memory. Finally, we will discuss the theoretical controversy about whether there are separate memory systems for different types of information. The chapter's Personal Application provides some practical advice on how to improve your memory. The Critical Thinking Application discusses some reasons that memory is less reliable than people assume it to be.

> Encoding: Getting Information into Memory

PREVIEW QUESTIONS

- What does attention have to do with memory?
- What types of encoding produce deeper processing?
- How do levels of processing relate to retention?
- How does elaboration enhance encoding?
- How does the use of visual imagery improve memory?

Have you ever been embarrassed because you couldn't remember someone's name? Perhaps you realized only 30 seconds after meeting someone that you had already "forgotten" his or her name. More often than not, this familiar kind of forgetting results from a failure to form a memory code for the name. When you're introduced to people, you're often busy sizing them up and thinking about what you're going to say. With your attention diverted in this way, names go in one ear and out the other. You don't remember them because they are never encoded for storage into memory.

This problem illustrates that encoding is an important process in memory. In this section, we discuss the role of attention in encoding, types of encoding, and ways to enrich the encoding process.

The Role of Attention

Although there are some fascinating exceptions, you generally need to pay attention to information if you intend to remember it (Lachter, Forster, & Ruthruff, 2004; Mulligan, 1998). For example, if you sit through a class lecture but pay little attention to it, you're unlikely to remember much of what the professor had to say.

Attention **involves focusing awareness on a narrowed range of stimuli or events.** Psychologists routinely refer to "selective attention," but the words are really redundant. Attention *is* selection of input. If you pause to devote a little attention to the matter, you'll realize that selective attention is critical to everyday functioning. If your attention were distributed equally among all stimulus inputs, life would be utter chaos. If you weren't able to filter out most of the potential stimulation around you, you wouldn't be able to read a book, converse with a friend, or even carry on a coherent train of thought.

The importance of attention to memory is apparent when participants are asked to focus their attention on two or more inputs simultaneously. Studies indicate that when participants are forced to divide their attention between memory encoding and some other task, large reductions in memory performance are seen (Craik, 2001; Craik & Kester, 2000). Actually, the negative effects of divided attention are not limited to memory. Divided attention can have a negative impact on the performance of quite a variety of tasks, especially when the tasks are complex or unfamiliar (Pashler, Johnston, & Ruthruff, 2001). This principle appears to apply to the controversy about driving while talking on a cell phone. One study of a simulated driving task suggested that cellular conversations double the chances of missing traffic signals and of having slow reactions to signals that *are* detected (Strayer & Johnston, 2001).

Levels of Processing
SIM5, 6a

Attention is critical to the encoding of memories, but attention comes in many forms. You can attend to things in different ways, focusing on different aspects of the stimulus input. According to some theorists, these qualitative differences in *how* people attend to information are the main factors influencing how much they remember. For example, Fergus Craik and Robert Lockhart (1972) argue that different rates of forgetting occur because some methods of encoding create more durable memory codes than others.

Craik and Lockhart propose that incoming information can be processed at different levels. For instance, they maintain that in dealing with verbal information, people engage in three progressively deeper levels of processing: structural, phonemic, and semantic encoding (see **Figure 7.3**). *Structural encoding* is relatively shallow processing that emphasizes the physical structure of the stimulus. For example, if words are flashed on a screen, structural encoding registers such things as how they are printed (capital, lowercase, and so on) or the length of the words (how many letters). Further analysis may result in *phonemic encoding,* which emphasizes what a word sounds like. Phonemic encoding involves naming or saying (perhaps silently) the words. Finally, *semantic encoding* emphasizes the meaning of verbal input. Semantic encoding involves thinking about the objects and actions the words represent. **Levels-of-processing theory proposes that deeper levels of processing result in longer-lasting memory codes.**

In one experimental test of levels-of-processing theory, Craik and Tulving (1975) compared the durability of structural, phonemic, and semantic encoding. They directed subjects' attention to particular aspects of briefly presented stimulus words by asking them questions about various characteristics of the words (examples are in **Figure 7.3**). The questions were designed to engage the participants in different levels of processing. The key hypothesis was that retention of the stimulus words would increase as subjects moved from structural to phonemic to semantic encoding. After responding to 60 words, the participants received an unexpected test of their memory for the words. As predicted, the subjects' recall was low after structural encoding, notably better after phonemic encoding, and highest after semantic encoding. The hypothesis that deeper processing leads to enhanced memory has been replicated in many studies (Craik, 2002; Lockhart & Craik, 1990). Levels-

Level of processing	Type of encoding	Example of questions used to elicit appropriate encoding
Shallow processing	*Structural encoding:* emphasizes the physical structure of the stimulus	Is the word written in capital letters?
Intermediate processing	*Phonemic encoding:* emphasizes what a word sounds like	Does the word rhyme with weight?
Deep processing	*Semantic encoding:* emphasizes the meaning of verbal input	Would the word fit in the sentence: "He met a _____ on the street"?

Depth of processing

Figure 7.3
Levels-of-processing theory. According to Craik and Lockhart (1972), structural, phonemic, and semantic encoding—which can be elicited by questions such as those shown on the right—involve progressively deeper levels of processing.

of-processing theory has been enormously influential; it has shown that memory involves more than just storage and has inspired a great deal of research on how processing considerations affect memory (Roediger, Gallo, & Geraci, 2002).

Enriching Encoding
6a

Structural, phonemic, and semantic encoding are not the only processes involved in forming memory codes. Other dimensions that can enrich the encoding process and thereby improve memory include elaboration and visual imagery.

Elaboration

Semantic encoding can often be enhanced through a process called elaboration. **Elaboration is linking a stimulus to other information at the time of encoding.** For example, let's say you read that phobias are often caused by classical conditioning, and you apply this idea to your own fear of spiders. In doing so, you are engaging in elaboration. The additional associations created by elaboration usually help people remember information. Differences in elaboration can help explain why different approaches to semantic processing result in varied amounts of retention (Craik & Tulving, 1975; Willoughby, Motz, & Wood, 1997).

Elaboration often consists of thinking of examples that illustrate an idea. The value of examples was demonstrated in a study in which participants read information about a fictitious African country (Palmere et al., 1983). Each paragraph communicated one main idea, which was followed by no example, one example, two examples, or three examples. The effect of examples on memory was dramatic. As you can see in **Figure 7.4**, additional examples led to better memory. In this study, the examples were provided to the students, but self-generated examples created through elaboration would probably be even more valuable in enhancing memory.

Visual Imagery

Imagery—the creation of visual images to represent the words to be remembered—can also be used to enrich encoding. Of course, some words are easier to create images for than others. If you were asked to remember the word *juggler,* you could readily form an image of someone juggling balls. However, if you were asked to remember the word *truth,* you would probably have more difficulty forming a suitable image. The difference is that *juggler* refers to a concrete object whereas *truth* refers to an abstract concept. Allan Paivio (1969) points out that it is easier to form images of concrete objects than of abstract concepts. He believes that this ease of image formation affects memory. For example, in one study he

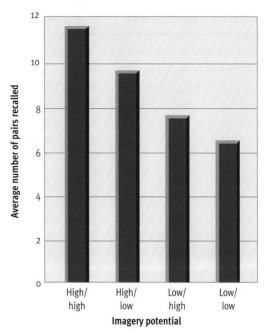

Figure 7.5

The effect of visual imagery on retention. Paivio, Smythe, and Yuille (1968) asked subjects to learn a list of 16 pairs of words. They manipulated whether the words were concrete, high-imagery words or abstract, low-imagery words. In terms of imagery potential, the list contained four types of pairings: high-high (*juggler-dress*), high-low (*letter-effort*), low-high (*duty-hotel*), and low-low (*quality-necessity*). The impact of imagery was quite evident. The best recall was of high-high pairings, and the worst recall was of low-low pairings. (Data from Paivio, Smythe, & Yuille, 1968)

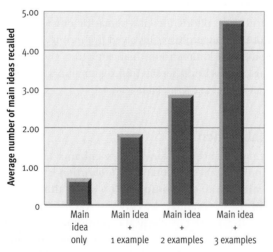

Figure 7.4

Effects of examples on retention of ideas. Palmere et al. (1983) manipulated the number of examples provided to illustrate the main idea of various paragraphs. As the number of examples increased from none to three, so did participants' retention of the main ideas. These results are consistent with the notion that elaboration enhances retention. (Data from Palmere et al., 1983)

found that subjects given pairs of words to remember showed better recall for high-imagery than low-imagery pairings (see **Figure 7.5**), demonstrating that visual imagery enriches encoding (Paivio, Smythe, & Yuille, 1968). Similar results were observed in a more recent study that controlled for additional confounding factors (Paivio, Khan, & Begg, 2000).

According to Paivio (1986), imagery facilitates memory because it provides a second kind of memory code, and two codes are better than one. His **dual-coding theory holds that memory is enhanced by forming both semantic and visual codes, since either can lead to recall.** Although some aspects of his theory have been questioned, it's clear that the use of mental imagery can enhance memory in many situations (McCauley, Eskes, & Moscovitch, 1996). The value of visual imagery demonstrates once again that encoding plays a critical role in memory. But encoding is only one of the three key processes in memory. We turn next to the process of storage, which for many people is virtually synonymous with memory.

In their efforts to understand memory storage, theorists have historically related it to the technologies of their age (Roediger, 1980). One of the earliest models used to explain memory storage was the wax tablet. Both Aristotle and Plato compared memory to a block of wax that differed in size and hardness for various individuals. Remembering, according to this analogy, was like stamping an impression into the wax. As long as the image remained in the wax, the memory would remain intact.

Modern theories of memory reflect the technological advances of the 20th century. For example, many theories formulated at the dawn of the computer age drew an analogy between information storage by computers and information storage in human memory (Atkinson & Shiffrin, 1968, 1971; Broadbent, 1958; Waugh & Norman, 1965). The main contribution of these *information-processing theories* was to subdivide memory into three separate memory stores (Estes, 1999). The names for these stores and their exact characteristics varied some from one theory to the next. For purposes of simplicity, we'll organize our discussion around the model devised by Richard Atkinson and Richard Shiffrin, which has proved to be the most influential of the information-processing theories. According to their model, incoming information passes through two temporary storage buffers—the sensory store and short-term store—before it is transferred into a long-term store (see **Figure 7.6**). Like the wax tablet before it, the information-processing model of memory is a metaphor; the three memory stores are not viewed as anatomical structures in the brain but rather as functionally distinct types of memory.

Sensory Memory

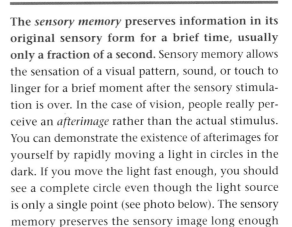
PsykTrek
6b

The *sensory memory* preserves information in its original sensory form for a brief time, usually only a fraction of a second. Sensory memory allows the sensation of a visual pattern, sound, or touch to linger for a brief moment after the sensory stimulation is over. In the case of vision, people really perceive an *afterimage* rather than the actual stimulus. You can demonstrate the existence of afterimages for yourself by rapidly moving a light in circles in the dark. If you move the light fast enough, you should see a complete circle even though the light source is only a single point (see photo below). The sensory memory preserves the sensory image long enough

© Wayne Weiten

Because the image of the sparkler persists briefly in sensory memory, when the sparkler is moved fast enough, the blending of afterimages causes people to see a continuous stream of light instead of a succession of individual points.

PREVIEW QUESTIONS

- What is sensory memory?
- What is the duration and capacity of the short-term store?
- What are the components of working memory?
- Is long-term storage permanent?
- How is information organized and represented in memory?

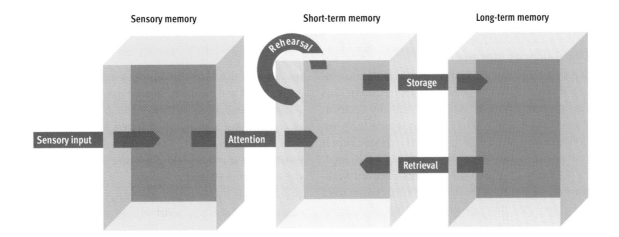

Sensory memory   Short-term memory   Long-term memory

Rehearsal

Sensory input   Attention   Storage   Retrieval

Figure 7.6

The Atkinson and Shiffrin model of memory storage. Atkinson and Shiffrin (1971) proposed that memory is made up of three information stores. *Sensory memory* can hold a large amount of information just long enough (a fraction of a second) for a small portion of it to be selected for longer storage. *Short-term memory* has a limited capacity, and unless aided by rehearsal, its storage duration is brief. *Long-term memory* can store an apparently unlimited amount of information for indeterminate periods.

for you to perceive a continuous circle rather than separate points of light.

The brief preservation of sensations in sensory memory gives you additional time to try to recognize stimuli. However, you'd better take advantage of sensory storage immediately, because it doesn't last long. In a classic experiment, George Sperling (1960) demonstrated that the memory trace in the visual sensory store decays in about one-quarter of a second. Memory traces in the auditory sensory store also appear to last approximately one-fourth of a second (Massaro & Loftus, 1996). There is some debate about whether stimulus persistence really involves *memory storage* (Nairne, 2003). Some theorists view it as an artifact of the perceptual processing of incoming stimuli that is attributable to excitatory feedback in specific neural circuits (Francis, 1999). In other words, stimulus persistence may be more like an echo than a memory.

Short-Term Memory

Short-term memory (STM) is a limited-capacity store that can maintain unrehearsed information for up to about 20 seconds. In contrast, information stored in long-term memory may last weeks, months, or years. Actually, you can maintain information in your short-term store for longer than 20 seconds. How? Primarily, by engaging in *rehearsal—the process of repetitively verbalizing or thinking about information.* You surely have used the rehearsal process on many occasions. For instance, when you obtain a phone number from the information operator, you probably recite it over and over until you can dial the number. Rehearsal keeps recycling the information through your short-term memory. In theory, this recycling could go on indefinitely, but in reality something eventually distracts you and breaks the rehearsal loop.

Durability of Storage

Without rehearsal, information in short-term memory is lost in 10 to 20 seconds (Nairne, 2003). This rapid loss was demonstrated in a study by Peterson and Peterson (1959). They measured how long undergraduates could remember three consonants if they couldn't rehearse them. To prevent rehearsal, the Petersons required the students to count backward by threes from the time the consonants were presented until they saw a light that signaled the recall test. Participants' recall accuracy was pretty dismal after only 15 seconds. Other approaches to the issue have suggested that the typical duration of STM

storage may even be shorter (Baddely, 1986). Theorists originally believed that the loss of information from short-term memory was attributable purely to time-related *decay* of memory traces, but follow-up research showed that *interference* from competing material also contributes (Lewandowsky, Duncan, & Brown, 2004; Nairne, 2002).

Capacity of Storage

Short-term memory is also limited in the number of items it can hold. The small capacity of STM was pointed out by George Miller (1956) in a famous paper titled "The Magical Number Seven, Plus or Minus Two: Some Limits on Our Capacity for Processing Information." Miller noticed that people could recall only about seven items on tasks that required them to remember unfamiliar material. The common thread in these tasks, Miller argued, was that they required the use of STM.

When short-term memory is filled to capacity, the insertion of new information often *displaces* some of the information currently in STM. For example, if you're memorizing a ten-item list of basic chemical elements, the eighth, ninth, and tenth items in the list will begin to "bump out" earlier items. Similarly, if you're reciting the phone number of a pizza parlor you're about to call when someone asks, "How much is this pizza going to cost?" your retrieval of the cost information into STM may knock part of the phone number out of STM. The limited capacity of STM constrains people's ability to perform tasks in which they need to mentally juggle various pieces of information (Baddeley & Hitch, 1974).

You can increase the capacity of your short-term memory by combining stimuli into larger, possibly higher-order, units called *chunks* (Simon, 1974). A *chunk is a group of familiar stimuli stored as a single unit.* You can demonstrate the effect of chunking by asking someone to recall a sequence of 12 letters grouped in the following way:

FB - INB - CC - IAIB - M

As you read the letters aloud, pause at the hyphens. Your subject will probably attempt to remember each letter separately because there are no obvious groups or chunks. But a string of 12 letters is too long for STM, so errors are likely. Now present the same string of letters to another person, but place the pauses in the following locations:

FBI - NBC - CIA - IBM

The letters now form four familiar chunks that should occupy only four slots in short-term memory, resulting in successful recall (Bower & Springston, 1970).

GEORGE MILLER
"The Magical Number Seven, Plus or Minus Two."

Web Link 7.1

The Magical Number Seven, Plus or Minus Two
In 1956, Princeton psychology professor George A. Miller published one of the most famous papers in the history of psychology: "The Magical Number Seven, Plus or Minus Two: Some Limits on Our Capacity for Processing Information." At this site, you'll find a copy of the original text with tables so you can see why this paper is such an important research milestone in psychology.

To successfully chunk the letters I B M, a subject must first recognize these letters as a familiar unit. This familiarity has to be stored somewhere in long-term memory. Hence, in this case information was transferred from long-term into short-term memory. This type of transfer is not unusual. People routinely draw information out of their long-term memory banks to evaluate and understand information that they are working with in short-term memory.

Short-Term Memory as "Working Memory"

Twenty years of research eventually uncovered a number of problems with the original model of short-term memory (Bower, 2000). Among other things, studies showed that short-term memory is *not* limited to phonemic encoding and that decay and displacement are not the only processes responsible for the loss of information from STM. These and other findings suggest that short-term memory involves more than a simple rehearsal buffer, as originally believed. To make sense of such findings, Alan Baddeley (1989, 1992, 2001) has proposed a more complex model of short-term memory that characterizes it as "working memory."

Baddeley's model of working memory consists of four components (see **Figure 7.7**). The first component is the *phonological loop* that represented all of STM in earlier models. This component is at work when you use recitation to temporarily hold onto a phone number. Baddeley (2003) believes that the phonological loop evolved to facilitate the acquisi-

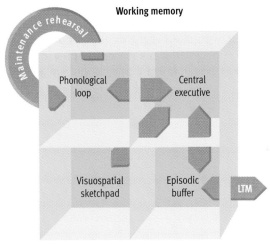

Figure 7.7

Short-term memory as working memory. This diagram depicts the revised model of the short-term store proposed by Alan Baddeley. According to Baddeley (2001), working memory includes four components: a phonological loop, a visuospatial sketchpad, a central executive system, and an episodic buffer.

tion of language. The second component in working memory is a *visuospatial sketchpad* that permits people to temporarily hold and manipulate visual images. This component is at work when you try to mentally rearrange the furniture in your bedroom. The third component is the *central executive* system. It controls the deployment of attention, switching the focus of attention and dividing attention as needed. The fourth component is the *episodic buffer,* a temporary, limited capacity store that allows the various components of working memory to integrate information and serves as an interface between working memory and long-term memory. The two key characteristics that originally defined short-term memory—small capacity and short storage duration—are still present in the concept of working memory. However, Baddeley's model accounts for evidence that STM handles a greater variety of functions and depends on more complicated processes than previously thought.

Baddeley's model of working memory has generated an enormous volume of research. Much of the early research demonstrated that the separate modules work independently, as hypothesized (Logie, Zucco, & Baddeley, 1990). Another line of research has shown that there are variations among people in how well they can juggle information in their working memory while fending off distractions (Engle, 2001). Interestingly, these variations in *working memory capacity* correlate positively with measures of high-level cognitive abilities, such as reading comprehension, complex reasoning, and even intelligence (Engle et al., 1999). This finding has led some theorists to conclude that working memory capacity plays a fundamental role in complex cognitive processes (Lepine, Barrouillet, & Camos, 2005).

Long-Term Memory

Long-term memory (LTM) is an unlimited capacity store that can hold information over lengthy periods of time. Unlike sensory and short-term memory, which decay rapidly, LTM can store information indefinitely. Long-term memories are durable. Some information may remain in LTM across an entire lifetime.

One point of view is that all information stored in long-term memory is stored there *permanently.* According to this view, forgetting occurs only because people sometimes cannot retrieve needed information from LTM. To draw an analogy, imagine that memories are stored in LTM like marbles in a barrel. According to this view, none of the marbles ever leak out. When you forget, you just aren't able to dig out

Courtesy of Alan Baddeley

ALAN BADDELEY

"The concept of working memory proposes that a dedicated system maintains and stores information in the short term, and that this system underlies human thought processes."

© The New Yorker Collection 1983 by Ed Fisher from cartoonbank.com. All rights reserved.

"The matters about which I'm being questioned, Your Honor, are all things I should have included in my long-term memory but which I mistakenly inserted in my short-term memory."

the right marble, but it's there—somewhere. An alternative point of view assumes that some memories stored in LTM do vanish forever. According to this view, the barrel is leaky and some of the marbles roll out, never to return.

The existence of *flashbulb memories* is one piece of evidence that has been cited to support the notion that LTM storage may be permanent. At first glance, **flashbulb memories, which are unusually vivid and detailed recollections of momentous events,** provide striking examples of seemingly permanent storage (Brown & Kulik, 1977). Many American adults, for instance, can remember exactly where they were, what they were doing, and how they felt when they learned that President John F. Kennedy had been shot. You may have a similar recollection related to the 1997 death of Princess Diana or the terrorist attacks that took place in New York and Washington, DC on September 11, 2001.

© Associated Press/AP

Flashbulb memories are vivid and detailed recollections of momentous events. For example, many people will long remember exactly where they were and how they felt when they learned about the terrorist attacks on the World Trade Center.

Does the evidence on flashbulb memories provide adequate support for the idea that LTM storage is permanent? No. Although flashbulb memories are remarkably durable, research eventually showed that they are neither as accurate nor as special as once believed (Neisser & Harsch, 1992). Like other memories, they become less detailed and less accurate with time (Pezdek, 2003; Weaver & Krug, 2004). Thus, although psychologists can't absolutely rule out the possibility, there is no convincing evidence that LTM storage is permanent (Payne & Blackwell, 1998).

How Is Knowledge Represented and Organized in Memory?

PsykTrek 6b

Over the years memory researchers have wrestled endlessly with another major question relating to memory storage: How is knowledge represented and organized in memory? In other words, what forms do mental representations of information take? Most theorists seem to agree that mental representations

---

concept **check** 7.1

Comparing the Memory Stores

Check your understanding of the three memory stores by filling in the blanks in the table below. The column on the left lists three features of the memory stores that can be compared. The answers can be found in the back of the book in Appendix A.

Feature	Sensory memory	Short-term memory	Long-term memory
Main encoding format	*copy of input*		*largely semantic*
Storage capacity	*limited*		
Storage duration		*up to 20 seconds*	

probably take a variety of forms, depending on the nature of the material that needs to be tucked away in memory. For example, memories of visual scenes, of how to perform actions (such as typing or hitting a backhand stroke in tennis), and of factual information (such as definitions or dates in history) are probably represented and organized in very different ways. Most of the theorizing to date has focused on how factual knowledge may be represented in memory. In this section, we'll look at a small sample of the organizational structures that have been proposed for semantic information.

Schemas

Imagine that you've just visited Professor Smith's office, which is shown in the adjacent photo. Take a brief look at the photo and then cover it up. Now pretend that you want to describe Professor Smith's office to a friend. Write down what you saw in the office (the picture).

After you finish, compare your description with the picture. Chances are, your description will include elements—filing cabinets, for instance—that were *not* in the office. This common phenomenon demonstrates how *schemas* can influence memory.

A *schema* **is an organized cluster of knowledge about a particular object or event abstracted from previous experience with the object or event.** For example, college students have schemas for what professors' offices are like. When Brewer and Treyens (1981) tested the recall of 30 subjects who had briefly visited the office shown in the photo, most subjects recalled the desks and chairs, but few recalled the wine bottle or the picnic basket, which aren't part of a typical office schema. Moreover, 9 subjects in the Brewer and Treyens study falsely recalled that the office contained books. Perhaps you made the same mistake.

These results suggest that *people are more likely to remember things that are consistent with their schemas than things that are not.* Although this principle seems applicable much of the time, the inverse is also true: *People sometimes exhibit better recall of things that violate their schema-based expectations* (Rojahn & Pettigrew, 1992). If information really clashes with a schema, it may attract extra attention and deeper processing, and become very memorable. Thus, the impact of schemas on memory can be difficult to predict, but either way it is apparent that information stored in memory is often organized around schemas.

Semantic Networks

Much of people's knowledge seems to be organized into semantic networks (Collins & Loftus, 1975). A *se-*

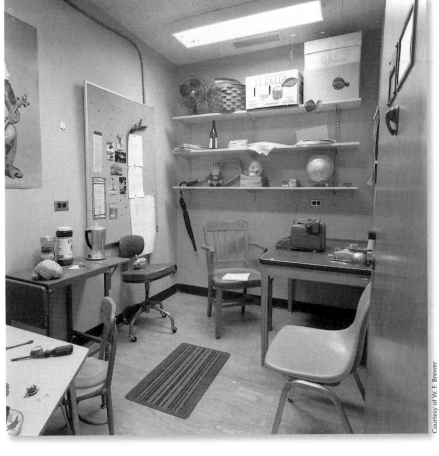

Courtesy of W. F. Brewer

Professor Smith's office is shown in this photo. Follow the instructions in the text to learn how Brewer and Treyens (1981) used it in a study of memory.

mantic network **consists of nodes representing concepts, joined together by pathways that link related concepts. Figure 7.8** (on the next page) shows a small semantic network. The ovals are the nodes, and the words inside the ovals are the interlinked concepts. The lines connecting the nodes are the pathways. A more detailed figure would label the pathways to show how the concepts are related to one another. However, in this instance the relations should be fairly clear. For example, *fire engine* is linked to *red* because of its color, to *vehicle* because it's a vehicle, and to *house* because fires often occur in houses. The length of each pathway represents the degree of association between two concepts. Shorter pathways imply stronger associations.

Semantic networks have proven useful in explaining why thinking about one word (such as *butter*) can make a closely related word (such as *bread*) easier to remember (Meyer & Schvaneveldt, 1976). According to Collins and Loftus (1975), when people think about a word, their thoughts naturally go to related words. These theorists call this process *spreading activation within a semantic network*. They assume that activation spreads out along the pathways of the semantic network surrounding the word. They also theorize that the strength of this activation decreases as it travels outward, much as ripples decrease in size as they

Web Link 7.2

Memory Principles
This brief overview of practical guidelines for improving recall of academic material is maintained by Carolyn Hopper at Middle Tennessee State University. The site succinctly outlines ten basic principles. You'll also find other worthwhile materials to help improve study techniques.

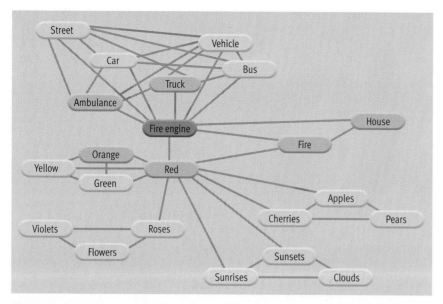

Figure 7.8

A semantic network. Much of the organization of long-term memory depends on networks of associations among concepts. In this highly simplified depiction of a fragment of a semantic network, the shorter the line linking any two concepts, the stronger the association between them. The coloring of the concept boxes represents activation of the concepts. This is how the network might look just after a person hears the words *fire engine.*

Source: Adapted from Collins, A. M., & Loftus, E. F. (1975). A spreading activation theory of semantic processing. *Psychological Review, 82,* 407–428. Copyright © 1975 by the American Psychological Association. Adapted by permission of the publisher and authors.

formation. As we noted in our discussion of visual pathways in Chapter 4, the human brain appears to depend extensively on *parallel distributed processing*—that is, simultaneous processing of the same information that is spread across networks of neurons. Based on this insight and basic findings about how neurons operate, **connectionist, or *parallel distributed processing (PDP)*, models assume that cognitive processes depend on patterns of activation in highly interconnected computational networks that resemble neural networks** (McClelland, 2000; McClelland & Rogers, 2003; McClelland & Rumelhart, 1985). A PDP system consists of a large network of interconnected computing units, or *nodes,* that operate much like neurons. These nodes may be inactive or they may send either excitatory or inhibitory signals to other units. Like an individual neuron, a specific node's level of activation reflects the weighted balance of excitatory and inhibitory inputs from many other units.

Given this framework, *PDP models assert that specific memories correspond to particular patterns of activation in these networks* (McClelland, 1992). Connectionist networks bear some superficial resemblance to semantic networks, but there is a crucial difference. In semantic networks, specific nodes represent specific concepts or pieces of knowledge. In connectionist networks, on the other hand, a piece of knowledge is represented by a particular *pattern* of activation across an entire network. Thus, the information lies in the strengths of the *connections,* which is why the PDP approach is called "connectionism."

In summary, memory storage is a complex matter, involving several memory stores and a variety of organizational devices. Let's now turn to the process of memory retrieval.

radiate outward from a rock tossed into a pond. Consider again the semantic network shown in **Figure 7.8.** If subjects see the word *red,* words that are closely linked to it (such as *orange*) should be easier to recall than words that have longer links (such as *sunrises*).

Connectionist Networks

Connectionist models of memory take their inspiration from how neural networks appear to handle in-

> Retrieval: Getting Information Out of Memory

PREVIEW QUESTIONS

● What does the tip-of-the-tongue phenomenon reveal about memory?

● Why does reinstating the context of an event aid in its recall?

● What are the misinformation effect and imagination inflation?

● How can source-monitoring errors shed light on eyewitness suggestibility?

Entering information into long-term memory is a worthy goal, but it is an insufficient one if you can't get the information back out again when you need it. Fortunately, recall often occurs without much effort. But occasionally a planned search of LTM is necessary. For instance, imagine that you were asked to recall the names of all 50 states in the United States. You would probably conduct your memory search systematically, recalling states in alphabetical order or by geographical location. Although this example is rather simple, retrieval is a complex process, as you'll see in this section.

Using Cues to Aid Retrieval

At the beginning of this chapter we discussed the *tip-of-the-tongue phenomenon*—the temporary inability to remember something you know, accompanied by a feeling that it's just out of reach. The tip-of-the-tongue phenomenon is a common experience that occurs about once a week, although its occurrence increases with age (A. Brown, 1991; Burke & Shafto, 2004). It clearly represents a failure in retrieval. However, the exact mechanisms underlying this failure are the subject of debate, as a number of explanations have been proposed for the tip-of-the-tongue phenomenon (Schwartz, 1999).

Fortunately, memories can often be jogged with *retrieval cues*—stimuli that help gain access to memories—such as hints, related information, or partial recollections. This was apparent when Roger Brown and David McNeill (1966) studied the tip-of-the-tongue phenomenon. They gave participants definitions of obscure words and asked them to think of the words. Our example at the beginning of the chapter (the definition for *nepotism*) was taken from their study. Brown and McNeill found that subjects groping for obscure words were correct in guessing the first letter of the missing word 57% of the time. This figure far exceeds chance and shows that partial recollections are often headed in the right direction.

Reinstating the Context of an Event

Let's test your memory: What did you have for breakfast two days ago? If you can't immediately answer, you might begin by imagining yourself sitting at the breakfast table (or wherever you usually have breakfast). Trying to recall an event by putting yourself back in the context in which it occurred involves working with context cues to aid retrieval.

Context cues often facilitate the retrieval of information (Smith, 1988). Most people have experienced the effects of context cues on many occasions. For instance, when people return after a number of years to a place where they used to live, they typically are flooded with long-forgotten memories. Or consider how often you have gone from one room to another to get something (scissors, perhaps), only to discover that you can't remember what you were after. However, when you return to the first room (the original context), you suddenly recall what it was ("Of course, the scissors!"). These examples illustrate the potentially powerful effects of context cues on memory. The technique of reinstating the context of an event has been used effectively in legal investigations to enhance eyewitness recall (Chandler & Fisher, 1996). The eyewitness may be encouraged to retrieve information about a crime by replaying the sequence of events.

Reconstructing Memories

When you retrieve information from long-term memory, you're not able to pull up a "mental video-tape" that provides an exact replay of the past. To some extent, your memories are sketchy *reconstructions* of the past that may be distorted and may include details that did not actually occur (Roediger, Wheeler, & Rajaram, 1993).

Research by Elizabeth Loftus (1979, 1992) and others on the *misinformation effect* has shown that reconstructive distortions show up frequently in eyewitness testimony. **The *misinformation effect* occurs when participants' recall of an event they witnessed is altered by introducing misleading postevent information.** For example, in one study Loftus and Palmer (1974) showed participants a videotape of an automobile accident. Participants were then "grilled" as if they were providing eyewitness testimony, and biasing information was introduced. Some subjects were asked, "How fast were the cars going when they *hit* each other?" Other subjects were asked, "How fast were the cars going when they *smashed into* each other?" A week later, participants' recall of the accident was tested and they were asked whether they remembered seeing any broken glass in the accident (there was none). Subjects who had earlier been asked about the cars *smashing into* each other were more likely to "recall" broken glass. Why would they add this detail to their reconstructions of the accident? Probably because broken glass is consistent with their schemas for cars *smashing* together (see **Figure 7.9**). The misinformation effect has been replicated in numerous studies by Loftus and other researchers (Ayers & Reder, 1998; Loftus, 2003). Indeed, the effect is difficult to escape, as even subjects who have been forewarned can be swayed by postevent misinformation (Koriat, Goldsmith, & Pansky, 2000).

Courtesy of Elizabeth Loftus

ELIZABETH LOFTUS

"One reason most of us, as jurors, place so much faith in eyewitness testimony is that we are unaware of how many factors influence its accuracy."

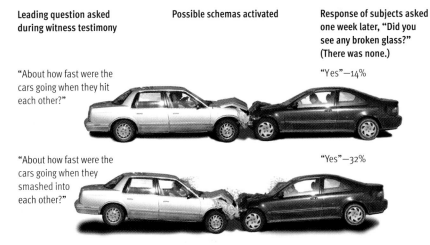

Leading question asked during witness testimony	Possible schemas activated	Response of subjects asked one week later, "Did you see any broken glass?" (There was none.)
"About how fast were the cars going when they hit each other?"		"Yes"—14%
"About how fast were the cars going when they smashed into each other?"		"Yes"—32%

Figure 7.9

The misinformation effect. In an experiment by Loftus and Palmer (1974), participants who were asked leading questions in which cars were described as *hitting* or *smashing* each other were prone to recall the same accident differently one week later, demonstrating the reconstructive nature of memory.

MARCIA K. JOHNSON

"Our long-term goal is to develop ways of determining which aspects of mental experience create one's sense of a personal past and one's conviction (accurate or not) that memories, knowledge, beliefs, attitudes, and feelings are tied to reality in a veridical fashion."

Presenting misinformation is only one way to produce memory distortions. Another method simply involves asking people to vividly imagine experiencing a childhood event (one that they previously indicated they had *not* experienced), such as breaking a window with their hand, or getting in trouble for calling 911. A few moments of imagination can significantly increase many subjects' belief that they actually had an experience similar to the imagined event (Garry & Polaschek, 2000). The surprising impact of imagining an experience on memory has been called *imagination inflation*. Studies show that even imagining *another person* experiencing an event can inflate your confidence that the same event happened to you (Garry, Frame, & Loftus, 1999).

Source Monitoring

The misinformation effect appears to be due, *in part,* to the unreliability of source monitoring (Mitchell & Johnson, 2000). *Source monitoring* **is the process of making inferences about the origins of memories.** Marcia Johnson and her colleagues maintain that source monitoring is a crucial facet of memory retrieval that contributes to many of the mistakes that people make in reconstructing their experiences (Johnson, 1996; Johnson, Hashtroudi, & Lindsay, 1993). According to Johnson, memories are not tagged with labels that specify their sources. Hence, when

people pull up specific memory records, they have to make decisions *at the time of retrieval* about where the memories came from (example: "Did I read that in the *New York Times* or *Rolling Stone*?"). Much of the time, these decisions are so easy and automatic, people make them without being consciously aware of the source-monitoring process. In other instances, however, they may consciously struggle to pinpoint the source of a memory. A *source-monitoring error* **occurs when a memory derived from one source is misattributed to another source.** For example, you might attribute something that your roommate said to your psychology professor, or something you heard on *Oprah* to your psychology textbook. Inaccurate memories that reflect source-monitoring errors may seem quite compelling, and people often feel quite confident about their authenticity even though the recollections really are inaccurate (Lampinen, Neuschatz, & Payne, 1999).

Source-monitoring errors appear to be commonplace and may shed light on many interesting memory phenomena. For instance, in studies of eyewitness suggestibility, some subjects have gone so far as to insist that they "remember" seeing something that was only verbally suggested to them. Most theories have a hard time explaining how people can have memories of events that they never actually saw or experienced, but this paradox doesn't seem all that perplexing when it is explained as a source-monitoring error (Lindsay et al., 2004).

> Forgetting: When Memory Lapses

PREVIEW QUESTIONS

● What did Ebbinghaus discover about how quickly people forget?

● What are the three methods for measuring retention?

● What is the difference between the decay and interference explanations of forgetting?

● When are retrieval failures likely to occur?

● Why do some experts believe that recovered memories of childhood sexual abuse are mostly genuine, while other experts are skeptical?

Why do people forget information—even information they would like very much to remember? Many theorists believe that there isn't one simple answer to this perplexing question. They point to the complex, multifaceted nature of memory and assert that forgetting can be caused by deficiencies in encoding, storage, or retrieval or by some combination of these processes.

How Quickly We Forget: Ebbinghaus's Forgetting Curve

The first person to conduct scientific studies of forgetting was Hermann Ebbinghaus. He published a series of insightful memory studies way back in 1885. Ebbinghaus studied only one subject—himself. To give himself lots of new material to memorize, he invented *nonsense syllables*—**consonant-vowel-consonant**

arrangements that do not correspond to words (such as BAF, XOF, VIR, and MEQ). He wanted to work with meaningless materials that would be uncontaminated by his previous learning.

Ebbinghaus was a remarkably dedicated researcher. For instance, in one study he went through over 14,000 practice repetitions, as he tirelessly memorized 420 lists of nonsense syllables (Slamecka, 1985). He tested his memory of these lists after various time intervals. **Figure 7.10** shows what he found. This diagram, called a *forgetting curve,* **graphs retention and forgetting over time.** Ebbinghaus's forgetting curve shows a sharp drop in retention during the first few hours after the nonsense syllables were memorized. He forgot more than 60% of the syllables in less than 9 hours! Thus, he concluded that most forgetting occurs very rapidly after learning something.

That's a depressing conclusion. What is the point of memorizing information if you're going to forget

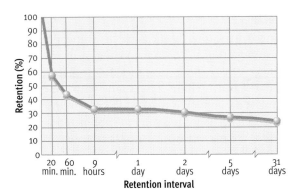

© Bettmann/Corbis

Figure 7.10

Ebbinghaus's forgetting curve for nonsense syllables. From his experiments on himself, Ebbinghaus (1985) concluded that forgetting is extremely rapid immediately after the original learning and then levels off. Although this generalization remains true, subsequent research has shown that forgetting curves for nonsense syllables are unusually steep.

HERMANN EBBINGHAUS

"Left to itself every mental content gradually loses its capacity for being revived. . . . Facts crammed at examination time soon vanish."

it all right away? Fortunately, subsequent research showed that Ebbinghaus's forgetting curve was unusually steep (Postman, 1985). Forgetting usually isn't as swift or as extensive as Ebbinghaus thought. One problem was that he was working with such meaningless material. When participants memorize more meaningful material, such as prose or poetry, forgetting curves aren't nearly as steep. Studies of how well people recall their high school classmates suggest that forgetting curves for autobiographical information are much shallower (Bahrick, 2000). Also, different methods of measuring forgetting yield varied estimates of how quickly people forget. This variation underscores the importance of the methods used to measure forgetting, the matter we turn to next.

Measures of Forgetting SIMs, 6, 6d

To study forgetting empirically, psychologists need to be able to measure it precisely. Measures of forgetting inevitably measure retention as well. **Retention refers to the proportion of material retained (remembered).** In studies of forgetting, the results may be reported in terms of the amount forgotten or the amount retained. In these studies, the *retention interval* is the length of time between the presentation of materials to be remembered and the measurement of forgetting. Psychologists use three methods to measure forgetting/retention: recall, recognition, and relearning (Lockhart, 1992).

Who is the current U.S. secretary of state? What movie won the Academy Award for best picture last year? These questions involve recall measures of retention. **A *recall measure* requires participants to reproduce information on their own without any**

cues. If you were to take a recall test on a list of 25 words you had memorized, you would simply be told to write down on a blank sheet of paper as many of the words as you could remember.

In contrast, in a recognition test you might be shown a list of 100 words and asked to choose the 25 words that you had memorized. **A *recognition measure* of retention requires participants to select previously learned information from an array of options.** Subjects not only have cues to work with, they have the answers right in front of them. In educational testing, multiple-choice, true-false, and matching questions are recognition measures; essay questions and fill-in-the-blanks questions are recall measures.

If you're like most students, you probably prefer multiple-choice tests over essay tests. This preference is understandable, because evidence shows that recognition measures tend to yield higher scores than recall measures of memory for the same information (Lockhart, 2000). This tendency was demonstrated many years ago in a study by Luh (1922), who measured subjects' retention of nonsense syllables with both a recognition test and a recall test. He found that participants' performance on the recognition measure was far superior to their performance on the recall measure. There are two ways of looking at this disparity between recall and recognition tests. One view is that recognition tests are especially *sensitive* measures of retention. The other view is that recognition tests are excessively easy measures of retention.

Actually, there is no guarantee that a recognition test will be easier than a recall test. Although this tends to be the case, the difficulty of recognition tests can vary greatly, depending on the number, similarity, and plausibility of the options provided as possible answers. To illustrate, see whether you know the answer to the following multiple-choice question:

The capital of Washington is:
a. Seattle   c. Tacoma
b. Spokane   d. Olympia

Most students who aren't from Washington find this a fairly difficult question. The answer is Olympia. Now take a look at the next question:

The capital of Washington is:
a. London   c. Tokyo
b. New York   d. Olympia

Virtually anyone can answer this question because the incorrect options are readily dismissed. Although this illustration is a bit extreme, it shows that

Web Link 7.3

Mind Tools—Tools for Improving Your Memory The Mind Tools site details practical techniques to help people improve their cognitive efficiency in many areas. The subpage dedicated to memory functioning offers an excellent collection of suggestions for ways to enhance memory.

two recognition measures of the same information can vary dramatically in difficulty.

The third method of measuring forgetting is relearning. A *relearning measure* of retention requires a participant to memorize information a second time to determine how much time or effort is saved by having learned it before. To use this method, a researcher measures how much time (or how many practice trials) a person needs in order to memorize something. At a later date, the participant is asked to relearn the information. The researcher measures how much more quickly the material is memorized the second time. Participants' *savings scores* provide an estimate of their retention. For example, if it takes you 20 minutes to memorize a list the first time and only 5 minutes to memorize it a week later, you've saved 15 minutes. Your savings score of 75% (15/20 = 3/4 = 75%) suggests that you have retained 75% and forgotten the remaining 25% of the information. Relearning measures can detect retention that is overlooked by recognition tests (Crowder & Greene, 2000).

Why We Forget

Measuring forgetting is only the first step in the long journey toward explaining why forgetting occurs. In this section, we explore the possible causes of forgetting, looking at factors that may affect encoding, storage, and retrieval processes.

Ineffective Encoding

A great deal of forgetting may only *appear* to be forgetting. The information in question may never have been inserted into memory in the first place. Since you can't really forget something you never learned, this phenomenon is sometimes called *pseudoforgetting*. We opened the chapter with an example of pseudoforgetting. People usually assume that they know what a penny looks like, but most have actually failed to encode this information. Pseudoforgetting is usually due to *lack of attention*.

Even when memory codes are formed for new information, subsequent forgetting may be the result of ineffective or inappropriate encoding (Brown & Craik, 2000). The research on levels of processing shows that some approaches to encoding lead to more forgetting than others (Craik & Tulving, 1975). For example, if you're distracted while you read your textbooks, you may be doing little more than saying the words to yourself. This is an example of *phonemic encoding*, which is inferior to *semantic encoding* for retention of verbal material.

Decay

Instead of focusing on encoding, decay theory attributes forgetting to the impermanence of memory storage. *Decay theory* proposes that forgetting occurs because memory traces fade with time. The implicit assumption is that decay occurs in the physiological mechanisms responsible for memories. According to decay theory, the mere passage of time produces forgetting. This notion meshes nicely with commonsense views of forgetting.

As we saw earlier, decay *does* appear to contribute to the loss of information from the sensory and short-term memory stores. However, the critical task for theories of forgetting is to explain the loss of information from long-term memory. Researchers have *not* been able to demonstrate that decay causes LTM forgetting (Slamecka, 1992).

If decay theory is correct, the principal cause of forgetting should be the passage of time. In studies of long-term memory, however, researchers have repeatedly found that time passage is not as influential as what happens during the time interval. Research has shown that forgetting depends not on the amount of time that has passed since learning but on the amount, complexity, and type of information that subjects have had to absorb *during* the retention interval. The negative impact of competing information on retention is called *interference*. Although theorists have not given up entirely on the intuitively plausible principle of decay (Altmann & Gray, 2002), research on LTM forgetting has been dominated by the concept of interference.

Interference

Interference theory proposes that people forget information because of competition from other material. Although demonstrations of decay in long-term memory have remained elusive, hundreds of studies have shown that interference influences forgetting (Anderson & Neely, 1996; Bjork, 1992). In many of these studies, researchers have controlled interference by varying the similarity between the original material given to subjects (the test material) and the material studied in the intervening period. Interference is assumed to be greatest when intervening material is most similar to the test material. Decreasing the similarity should reduce interference and cause less forgetting. This is exactly what McGeoch and McDonald (1931) found in an influential study (see **Figure 7.11**). They had participants memorize test material that consisted of a list of two-syllable adjectives. They varied the similarity of intervening learning by having subjects then memorize one of five lists. In order of decreasing similarity to the test material, they were synonyms of the test words, antonyms of the test words, unrelated adjectives, nonsense syllables, and numbers. Later, subjects' recall of the test material was measured. **Figure 7.11** shows that as the similarity of the intervening material decreased, the amount of forgetting also decreased—because of reduced interference.

There are two kinds of interference: *retroactive* and *proactive* (Jacoby, Hessels, & Bopp, 2001). ***Retroactive interference* occurs when new information impairs the retention of previously learned information.** Retroactive interference occurs between the original learning and the retest on that learning (see **Figure 7.12**). For example, the interference manipulated by McGeoch and McDonald (1931) was retroactive interference. In contrast, ***proactive interference* occurs when previously learned information interferes with the retention of new information.** Proactive interference is rooted in learning that comes before exposure to the test material. For example, when you get a new phone number, your old number (previous learning) may create proactive interference that hampers your recall of your new number. The evidence indicates that both types of interference can have powerful effects on how much you forget.

Retrieval Failure

6d

People often remember things that they were unable to recall at an earlier time. This phenomenon may be obvious only during struggles with the tip-of-the-tongue phenomenon, but it happens frequently. In fact, a great deal of forgetting may be due to breakdowns in the process of retrieval.

Why does an effort to retrieve something fail on one occasion and succeed on another? That's a tough question. One theory is that retrieval failures may be more likely when a mismatch exists between retrieval cues and the encoding of the information you're searching for. According to Tulving and Thomson (1973), a good retrieval cue is consistent with the original encoding of the information to be recalled. If the sound of a word—its phonemic quality—was emphasized during encoding, an effective retrieval cue should emphasize the sound of the word. If the meaning of the word was emphasized during encoding, semantic cues should be best. A general statement of the principle at work here was formulated by Tulving and Thomson (1973). **The *encoding specificity principle* states that the value of a retrieval cue depends on how well it corresponds to the memory code.** This

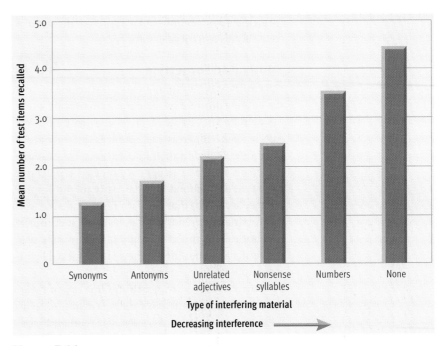

Figure 7.11

Effects of interference. According to interference theory, more interference from competing information should produce more forgetting. McGeoch and McDonald (1931) controlled the amount of interference with a learning task by varying the similarity of an intervening task. The results were consistent with interference theory. The amount of interference is greatest at the left of the graph, as is the amount of forgetting. As interference decreases (moving to the right on the graph), retention improves.

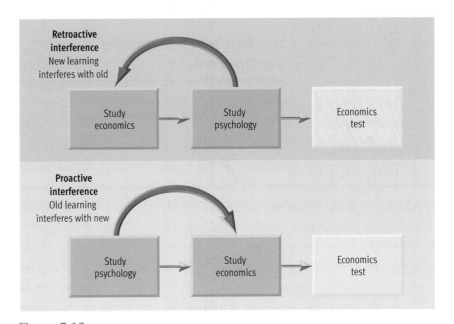

Figure 7.12

Retroactive and proactive interference. Retroactive interference occurs when learning produces a "backward" effect, reducing recall of previously learned material. Proactive interference occurs when learning produces a "forward" effect, reducing recall of subsequently learned material. For example, if you were to prepare for an economics test and then study psychology, the interference from the psychology study would be retroactive interference. However, if you studied psychology first and then economics, the interference from the psychology study would be proactive interference.

principle provides one explanation for the inconsistent success of retrieval efforts.

Motivated Forgetting

6d

A century ago, Sigmund Freud (1901) came up with an entirely different explanation for retrieval failures. As we noted in Chapter 1, Freud asserted that people often keep embarrassing, unpleasant, or painful memories buried in their unconscious. For example, a person who was deeply wounded by perceived slights at a childhood birthday party might suppress all recollection of that party. In his therapeutic work with patients, Freud recovered many such buried memories. He theorized that the memories were there all along, but their retrieval was blocked by unconscious avoidance tendencies.

The tendency to forget things one doesn't want to think about is called *motivated forgetting*, or to use Freud's terminology, *repression*. In Freudian theory, **repression refers to keeping distressing thoughts and feelings buried in the unconscious** (see Chapter 11). A number of experiments suggest that people don't remember anxiety-laden material as readily as emotionally neutral material, just as Freud proposed (Guenther, 1988; Reisner, 1998). Thus, when you forget unpleasant things such as a dental appointment, a promise to help a friend move, or a term paper deadline, motivated forgetting may be at work.

The Repressed Memories Controversy

SIM6

Although the concept of repression has been around for a century, interest in this phenomenon has surged

in recent years, thanks to a spate of prominent reports involving the return of long-lost memories of sexual abuse and other traumas during childhood. The media have been flooded with reports of adults accusing their parents, teachers, and neighbors of horrible child abuse decades earlier, based on previously repressed memories of these travesties. For the most part, these parents, teachers, and neighbors have denied the allegations. Many of the accused have seemed genuinely baffled by the charges, which have torn some previously happy families apart (Gudjonsson, 2001; Loftus & Ketcham, 1994; Wylie, 1998). In an effort to make sense of the charges, some accused parents have argued that their children's recollections are false memories created inadvertently by well-intentioned therapists through the power of suggestion. What do psychologists and psychiatrists have to say about the authenticity of repressed memories? They are sharply divided on the issue.

Support for Repressed Memories

Many psychologists and psychiatrists, especially clinicians involved in the treatment of psychological disorders, accept recovered memories of abuse at face value (Banyard & Williams, 1999; Briere & Conte, 1993; Herman, 1994; Skinner, 2001; Terr, 1994; Whitfield, 1995). They assert that sexual abuse in childhood is far more widespread than most people realize. For example, one large-scale survey (MacMillan et al., 1997), using a random sample of 9953 residents of Ontario, found that 12.8% of the females and 4.3% of the males reported that they had been victims of sexual abuse during childhood. They further assert that there is ample evidence that it is common for people to bury traumatic incidents in their unconscious (Del Monte, 2000; Wilsnack et al., 2002). For instance, in a recent study of psychiatric patients hospitalized for posttraumatic or dissociative disorders (see Chapter 13), one-third of those who reported childhood sexual abuse said that they had experienced complete amnesia for the abuse at some point in their lives (Chu et al., 1999).

Skepticism of Repressed Memories

In contrast, many other psychologists, especially memory researchers, have expressed skepticism about the recent upsurge of recovered memories of abuse (Kihlstrom, 2004; Loftus, 1998, 2003; Lynn & Nash, 1994; McNally, 2003). The skeptics do *not* argue that people are lying about their previously repressed memories. Rather, they maintain that some suggestible people wrestling with emotional problems have been convinced by persuasive therapists that their emo-

---

concept **check** 7.2

Figuring Out Forgetting

Check your understanding of why people forget by identifying the probable causes of forgetting in each of the following scenarios. Choose from (a) motivated forgetting (repression), (b) decay, (c) ineffective encoding, (d) proactive interference, (e) retroactive interference, or (f) retrieval failure. You will find the answers in Appendix A.

_____ **1.** Ellen can't recall the reasons for the Webster-Ashburton Treaty because she was daydreaming when it was discussed in history class.

_____ **2.** Rufus hates his job at Taco Heaven and is always forgetting when he is scheduled to work.

_____ **3.** Ray's new assistant in the shipping department is named John Cocker. Ray keeps calling him Joe, mixing him up with the rock singer Joe Cocker.

_____ **4.** Tania studied history on Sunday morning and sociology on Sunday evening. It's Monday, and she's struggling with her history test because she keeps mixing up prominent historians with influential sociologists.

tional difficulties must be the result of abuse that occurred years before. Critics blame a small minority of therapists who presumably have good intentions, but who operate under the questionable assumption that most or even all psychological problems are attributable to childhood sexual abuse (Lindsay & Read, 1994; Spanos, 1994). Using hypnosis, dream interpretation, and leading questions, they supposedly prod and probe patients until they inadvertently create the memories of abuse that they are searching for.

Psychologists who doubt the authenticity of repressed memories support their analysis by pointing to discredited cases of recovered memories (Brown, Goldstein, & Bjorklund, 2000). For example, with the help of a church counselor, one woman recovered memories of how her minister father had repeatedly raped her, got her pregnant, and then aborted the pregnancy with a coat-hanger, but subsequent evidence revealed that the woman was still a virgin and that her father had had a vasectomy years before (Loftus, 1997; Testa, 1996). The skeptics also point to published case histories that clearly involved suggestive questioning and to cases in which patients have recanted recovered memories of sexual abuse (see **Figure 7.13**) after realizing that these memories were implanted by their therapists (Loftus, 1994; Shobe & Schooler, 2001). Another problem for memory researchers is that some recovered memories have described incidents of abuse that occurred before the victim reached age 3. However, when adults are asked to recall their earliest memories, their oldest recollections typically don't go back that far (Bruce, Dolan, & Phillips-Grant, 2000; Eacott & Crawley, 1998).

Those who question the accuracy of repressed memories also point to findings on the misinformation effect, imagination inflation, research on source-monitoring errors, and a host of other studies that demonstrate the relative ease of creating "memories" of events that never happened (Lindsay et al., 2004; Loftus, 2003). For example, working with college students, Ira Hyman and his colleagues have managed to implant recollections of fairly substantial events (such as spilling a punch bowl at a wedding, being in a grocery store when the fire sprinkler system went off, being hospitalized for an earache) in about 25% of their subjects, just by asking them to elaborate on events supposedly reported by their parents (Hyman, Husband, & Billings, 1995; Hyman & Kleinknecht, 1999). Other studies have succeeded in implanting false memories of nearly drowning (Heaps & Nash, 2001) and of being attacked by a vicious animal (Porter, Yuille, & Lehman, 1999) in many participants. Moreover, subjects in these studies often

A Case History of Recovered Memories Recanted

Suffering from a prolonged bout of depression and desperate for help, Melody Gavigan, 39, a computer specialist from Long Beach, California, checked herself into a local psychiatric hospital. As Gavigan recalls the experience, her problems were just beginning. During five weeks of treatment there, a family and marriage counselor repeatedly suggested that her depression stemmed from incest during her childhood. While at first Gavigan had no recollection of any abuse, the therapist kept prodding. "I was so distressed and needed help so desperately, I latched on to what he was offering me," she says. "I accepted his answers."

When asked for details, she wrote page after page of what she believed were emerging repressed memories. She told about running into the yard after being raped in the bathroom. She incorporated into another lurid rape scene an actual girlhood incident, in which she had dislocated a shoulder. She went on to recall being molested by her father when she was only a year old—as her diapers were being changed—and sodomized by him at five. Following what she says was the therapist's advice, Gavigan confronted her father with her accusations, severed her relationship with him, moved away, and formed an incest survivors' group.

But she remained uneasy. Signing up for a college psychology course, she examined her newfound memories more carefully and concluded that they were false. Now Gavigan has begged her father's forgiveness and filed a lawsuit against the psychiatric hospital for the pain that she and her family suffered.

Figure 7.13

A case of recovered memories recanted. Revelations of repressed memories of sexual abuse are viewed with skepticism in some quarters. One reason is that some people who have recovered previously repressed recollections of child abuse have subsequently realized that their "memories" were the product of suggestion. A number of case histories, such as the one summarized here (from Jaroff, 1993), have demonstrated that therapists who relentlessly search for memories of child abuse in their patients sometimes instill the memories they are seeking.

Source: Jaroff, L. (1993, November 29). Lies of the mind. *Time*, pp. 52–59. Copyright © 1993 Time Inc. Reprinted by permission.

feel very confident about their false memories, which frequently generate strong emotional reactions and richly detailed "recollections" (Loftus & Bernstein, 2005).

In a similar vein, Roediger and McDermott (1995, 2000) have devised a simple laboratory paradigm involving the learning of word lists that is remarkably reliable in producing memory illusions. In this paradigm, a series of lists of 15 words are presented to participants, who are asked to recall the words immediately after each list is presented and are given a recognition measure of their retention at the end of the session. The trick is that each list consists of a set of words (such as *bed, rest, awake, tired*) that are

Web Link 7.4

False Memory Syndrome Foundation (FMSF) Online
This site marshals evidence that recovered memories of childhood abuse are often false, therapist induced, and grounded in shoddy and nonobjective scientific claims. Dealing with perhaps the most bitterly contested topic in current psychology, the FMSF has elicited fierce opposition.

Tom Rutherford (shown here with his wife, Joyce) received a $1 million settlement in a suit against a church therapist and a Springfield, Missouri, church in a false memory case. Under the church counselor's guidance, the Rutherfords' daughter, Beth, had "recalled" childhood memories of having been raped repeatedly by her minister father, gotten pregnant, and undergone a painful coat-hanger abortion. Her father lost his job and was ostracized. After he later revealed he'd had a vasectomy when Beth was age 4, and a physical exam revealed that at age 23 she was still a virgin, the memories were shown to be false.

© Associated Press/AP

Figure 7.14

The prevalence of false memories observed by Roediger and McDermott (1995). The graph shown here summarizes the recognition test results in Study 1 conducted by Roediger and McDermott (1995). Participants correctly identified words that had been on the lists that they had studied 86% of the time and only misidentified unrelated words that had not been on the lists 2% of the time, indicating that they were paying careful attention to the task. Nonetheless, they mistakenly reported that they "remembered" related target words that were not on the lists 84% of the time—a remarkably high prevalence of false memories.

Words that were on the lists that were previously studied

Unrelated words

Related (target) words

Words that were not on the lists that were previously studied

Web Link 7.5

The Recovered Memory Project

Directed by Professor Russ Cheit (Brown University), this site takes issue with the point of view that most recovered memories of abuse are false memories. It provides descriptions of "corroborated" cases of recovered memories.

strongly associated with another target word that is not on the list (in this case, *sleep*). When subjects *recall* the words on each list, they remember the non-presented target word over 50% of the time and when they are given the final *recognition* test, they typically indicate that about 80% of the nonstudied target words were presented in the lists (see **Figure 7.14**).

The trivial memory illusions created in this experiment may seem a far cry from the vivid, detailed recollections of previously forgotten sexual abuse that have generated the repressed memories controversy. But these false memories can be reliably created in normal, healthy participants in a matter of minutes, with little effort and no pressure or misleading information. Thus, the Roediger and McDermott paradigm provides a dramatic demonstration of how easy it is to get people to remember that they saw something they really didn't see.

Rebuttals to the Skeptics

Of course, psychologists who believe in recovered memories have mounted rebuttals to the arguments raised by the skeptics. For example, Kluft (1999) argues that a recantation of a recovered memory of abuse does not prove that the memory was false. Gleaves (1994) points out that individuals with a history of sexual abuse often vacillate between denying and accepting that the abuse occurred. Harvey (1999) argues that laboratory demonstrations showing that it is easy to create false memories have involved trivial memory distortions that are a far cry from the emotionally wrenching recollections of sexual abuse that have generated the recovered memories controversy. Moreover, even if one accepts the assertion that therapists *can* create false memories of abuse in their patients, some critics have noted that there is virtually no direct evidence on how often this situation occurs and no empirical basis for the claim that there has been an *epidemic* of such cases (Berliner & Briere, 1999; Leavitt, 2001; Wilsnack et al., 2002). Finally, many critics argue that contrived, artificial laboratory studies of memory and hypnosis may have limited relevance to the complexities of recovered memories in the real world (Brown, Scheflin, & Hammond, 1998; Gleaves et al., 2004).

Conclusions

Although both sides seem genuinely concerned about the welfare of the people involved, the debate about recovered memories of sexual abuse has grown increasingly bitter and emotionally charged. So, what can we conclude about the recovered memories controversy? It seems pretty clear that therapists can unknowingly create false memories in their patients and that a significant portion of recovered memories of abuse are the product of suggestion. But it also seems likely that some cases of recovered memories are authentic. At this point, we don't have adequate data to estimate what proportion of recovered memories of abuse fall in each category (Lindsay & Read, 2001). Thus, the matter needs to be addressed with great caution. On the one hand, people should be extremely careful about accepting recovered memories of abuse in the absence of convincing corroboration. On the other hand, recovered memories of abuse cannot be summarily dismissed, and

DOONESBURY

Doonesbury © 1994 by Gary Trudeau. Reprinted with permission of Universal Press Syndicate. All rights reserved.

it would be tragic if the repressed memories controversy made people overly skeptical about the all-too-real problem of childhood sexual abuse.

The repressed memories controversy deserves one last comment regarding its impact on memory research and scientific conceptions of memory. The controversy has helped inspire a great deal of research that has increased our understanding of just how fragile, fallible, malleable, and subjective human memory can be. Indeed, the implicit dichotomy underlying the repressed memories debate—that some memories are true, whereas others are false—is misleading and oversimplified. Research demonstrates that all human memories are imperfect reconstructions of the past that are subject to many types of distortion.

> In Search of the Memory Trace: The Physiology of Memory

For decades, neuroscientists have ventured forth in search of the physiological basis for memory. On several occasions scientists have been excited by new leads, only to be led down blind alleys. For example, in the 1960s James McConnell rocked the world of science when he reported that he had chemically transferred a specific memory from one flatworm to another. McConnell (1962) created a conditioned reflex (contraction in response to light) in flatworms and then transferred RNA (a basic molecular constituent of all living cells) from trained worms to untrained worms. The untrained worms showed evidence of "remembering" the conditioned reflex. McConnell boldly speculated that in the future, chemists might be able to formulate pills containing the information for Physics 201 or History 101! Unfortunately, the RNA transfer studies proved difficult to replicate (Rilling, 1996). Today, 45 years after McConnell's "breakthrough," we are still a long way from breaking the chemical code for memory.

Investigators continue to explore a variety of leads about the physiological bases for memory. In light of past failures, these lines of research should probably be viewed with guarded optimism. Nonetheless, in this section we'll look at some of the more promising research.

The Anatomy of Memory

6c

Cases of amnesia (extensive memory loss) resulting from head injury are a useful source of clues about the anatomical bases of memory. There are two basic types of amnesia: retrograde and anterograde (see **Figure 7.15**). In *retrograde amnesia* a person loses **memories for events that occurred prior to the injury.** For example, a 25-year-old gymnast who sustains a head trauma might find three years, seven years, or perhaps her entire lifetime erased. In *anterograde amnesia* **a person loses memories for events that occur after the injury.** For instance, after her accident, the injured gymnast might suffer impaired

ability to remember people she meets, where she has parked her car, and so on.

Because victims' current memory functioning is impaired, cases of anterograde amnesia have been especially rich sources of information about the brain and memory. One well-known case, that of a man referred to as H.M., has been followed by Brenda Milner and her colleagues since 1953 (Corkin, 1984, 2002; Scoville & Milner, 1957). H.M. had surgery to relieve debilitating epileptic seizures. Unfortunately, the surgery inadvertently wiped out most of his ability to form long-term memories. H.M.'s short-term memory is fine, but he has no recollection of anything that has happened since 1953 (other than about the most recent 20 seconds of his life). He doesn't recognize the doctors treating him, he can't remember routes to and from places, and he doesn't know his age. He can't remember what he did yesterday, let alone what he has done for the last 50 years. He doesn't even recognize a current photo of himself, as aging has changed his appearance considerably.

H.M.'s memory losses were originally attributed to the removal of his *hippocampus* (see **Figure 7.16** on the next page), although theorists now understand that other nearby structures that were removed also contributed to H.M.'s dramatic memory deficits (Delis & Lucas, 1996). Based on decades of additional research, scientists now believe that the entire

PREVIEW QUESTIONS

- Which brain structures appear to be involved in memory?
- How can memory be explained in terms of localized neural circuits?
- What does synaptic transmission have to do with memory?

The Montreal Neurological Institute, McGill University

BRENDA MILNER

"Some effects of temporal lobe lesions in man are hard to reconcile with any unitary-process theory of memory."

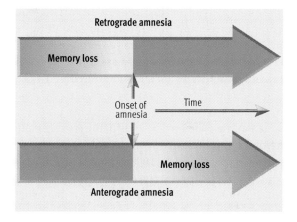

Figure 7.15

Retrograde versus anterograde amnesia. In retrograde amnesia, memory for events that occurred prior to the onset of amnesia is lost. In anterograde amnesia, memory for events that occur subsequent to the onset of amnesia suffers.

Retrograde amnesia

Memory loss

Onset of amnesia

Time

Memory loss

Anterograde amnesia

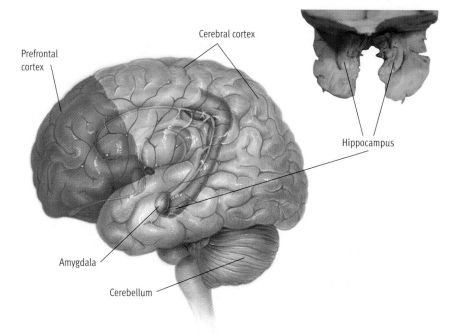

Prefrontal cortex

Cerebral cortex

Hippocampus

Amygdala

Cerebellum

Figure 7.16

The anatomy of memory. All the brain structures identified here have been implicated in efforts to discover the anatomical structures involved in memory. Although its exact contribution to memory remains the subject of debate, the hippocampus is thought to play an especially central role in memory.

ERIC KANDEL

"Learning results from changes in the strength of the synaptic connections between precisely interconnected cells."

hippocampal region plus the adjacent *parahippocampal region* are critical for many types of long-term memory (Zola & Squire, 2000). Many scientists now refer to this broader memory complex as the *medial temporal lobe memory system* (Broadbent et al., 2002). Given its apparent role in long-term memory, it is interesting to note that the hippocampal region is one of the first areas of the brain to sustain significant damage in the course of Alzheimer's disease, which produces severe memory impairment in many people, typically after age 65 (Albert & Moss, 2002).

Do these findings mean that memories are stored in the hippocampal region and adjacent areas? Probably not. Many theorists believe that the medial temporal lobe memory system plays a key role in the *consolidation* of memories (Dudai, 2004). **Consolidation is a hypothetical process involving the gradual conversion of information into durable memory codes stored in long-term memory.** According to this view, memories are consolidated in the hippocampal region and then stored in diverse and widely distributed areas of the cortex (Markowitsch, 2000). Which areas? Memories are probably stored in the same cortical areas that were originally involved in processing the sensory input that led to the memories (Gabrieli, 1998; Squire, Knowlton, & Musen, 1993). For instance, memories of visual information may be stored in areas of the visual cortex.

The Neural Circuitry and Biochemistry of Memory

6c

Richard F. Thompson (1989, 1992, 2005) and his colleagues have shown that specific memories may depend on *localized neural circuits* in the brain. In other words, memories may create unique, reusable pathways in the brain along which signals flow. Thompson has traced the pathway that accounts for a rabbit's memory of a conditioned eyeblink response. The key link in this circuit is a microscopic spot in the *cerebellum,* a structure in the hindbrain (see **Figure 7.16**). When this spot is destroyed, the conditioned stimulus no longer elicits the eyeblink response, even though the unconditioned stimulus still does (Steinmetz, 1998). This finding does *not* mean that the cerebellum is the key to all memory. Thompson theorizes that other memories probably create entirely different pathways in other areas of the brain. The key implication of Thompson's work is that it may be possible to map out specific neural circuits that correspond to specific memories.

Various other lines of research have implicated biochemical processes in the operation of memory. Among other things, studies have related memory functioning to (1) hormonal fluctuations that can facilitate or impair memory (McGaugh, 1995, 2002, 2004), and (2) protein synthesis in the brain that may be necessary for the formation of memories (Dudai, 2004; Luft et al., 2005). Another line of research suggests that memory formation results in *alterations in synaptic transmission* at specific sites. Eric Kandel (2001) and his colleagues have studied conditioned reflexes in a simple organism—a sea slug. In research that earned a Nobel prize for Kandel, they showed that reflex learning in the sea slug produces changes in the strength of specific synaptic connections by enhancing the availability and release of neurotransmitters at these synapses (Kandel & Schwartz, 1982; Kennedy, Hawkins, & Kandel, 1992). Kandel believes that durable changes in synaptic transmission may be the neural building blocks of more complex memories as well.

In summary, a host of anatomical structures, neural circuits, and biochemical processes appear to play a role in memory. Does all this sound confusing? It should, because it is. The bottom line is that neuroscientists are still assembling the pieces of the puzzle that will explain the physiological basis of memory. Although they have identified many of the puzzle pieces, they're not sure how the pieces fit together. Their difficulty is probably due to the complex, multifaceted nature of memory. Looking for the physiological basis for memory is only slightly less daunting than looking for the physiological basis for thought itself.

Courtesy of Eric Kandel

Some theorists believe that evidence on the physiology of memory is confusing because investigators are unwittingly probing into several distinct memory systems that may have different physiological bases. The various memory systems are distinguished primarily by the types of information they handle.

Declarative Versus Procedural Memory

The most basic division of memory into distinct systems contrasts *declarative memory* with *nondeclarative* or *procedural memory* (Squire, 2004; see **Figure 7.17**). **The *declarative memory system* handles factual information.** It contains recollections of words, definitions, names, dates, faces, events, concepts, and ideas. **The *procedural memory system* houses memory for actions, skills, conditioned responses, and emotional memories.** It contains memories of how to execute such actions as riding a bike, typing, and tying one's shoes. To illustrate the distinction, if you know the rules of tennis (the number of games in a set, scoring, and such), this factual information is stored in declarative memory. If you remember how to hit a serve and swing through a backhand, these perceptual-motor skills are stored in procedural memory.

Support for the distinction between declarative and procedural memory comes from evidence that the two systems seem to operate somewhat differently (Squire, Knowlton, & Musen, 1993). For example, the recall of factual information generally depends on conscious, effortful processes, whereas memory for conditioned reflexes is largely automatic and memories for skills often require little effort and attention (Johnson, 2003). People execute perceptual-motor tasks such as playing the piano or typing with little conscious awareness of what they're doing. In fact, performance on such tasks sometimes deteriorates if people think too much about what they're doing. Another disparity is that the memory for skills (such as typing and bike riding) doesn't decline much over long retention intervals, while declarative memory appears more vulnerable to forgetting.

Although much remains to be learned, researchers have made some progress toward identifying the neural bases of declarative versus procedural memory. Declarative memory appears to be handled by the *medial temporal lobe* memory system and the far-flung areas of the cortex with which it communicates (Eichenbaum, 2003). It has proven more difficult to pinpoint the neural bases of procedural memory

because it consists of more of a hodgepodge of memory functions; however, structures such as the cerebellum and amygdala appear to contribute (Delis & Lucas, 1996; Squire, 2004).

Semantic Versus Episodic Memory

Endel Tulving (1986, 1993, 2002) has further subdivided declarative memory into semantic and episodic memory (see **Figure 7.17**). Both contain factual information, but episodic memory contains *personal facts* and semantic memory contains *general facts*. **The *episodic memory system* is made up of chronological, or temporally dated, recollections of personal experiences.** Episodic memory is a record of things you've done, seen, and heard. It includes information about *when* you did these things, saw them, or heard them. It contains recollections about being in a ninth-grade play, visiting the Grand Canyon, attending a Rolling Stones concert, or going to a movie last weekend. Tulving (2001) emphasizes that the function of episodic memory is "time travel"—that is, to allow one to reexperience the past. He also speculates that episodic memory may be unique to humans.

The *semantic memory system* contains general knowledge that is not tied to the time when the information was learned. Semantic memory contains information such as Christmas is December

PREVIEW QUESTIONS

- What is the difference between declarative and procedural memory?
- Which type of memory is like an encyclopedia and which is like an autobiography?
- What is prospective memory?

Figure 7.17
Theories of independent memory systems. Theorists have distinguished between declarative memory, which handles facts and information, and non-declarative or procedural memory, which handles motor skills, conditioned responses, and emotional memories. Declarative memory is further subdivided into semantic memory (general knowledge) and episodic memory (dated recollections of personal experiences). The extent to which nondeclarative memory can be usefully subdivided remains the subject of debate.

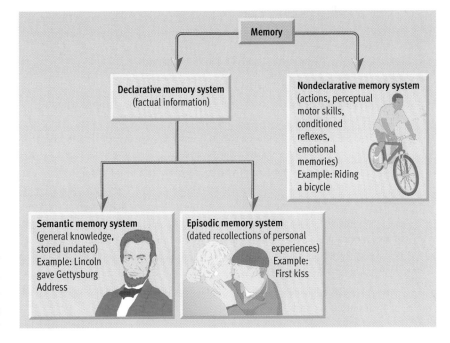

Figure 7.18

Retrospective versus prospective memory. Most memory research has explored the dynamics of *retrospective memory,* which focuses on recollections from the past. However, *prospective memory,* which requires people to remember to perform actions in the future, also plays an important role in everyday life.

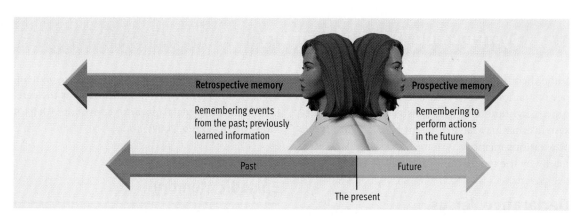

Retrospective memory — Remembering events from the past; previously learned information

Prospective memory — Remembering to perform actions in the future

Past | Future

The present

ENDEL TULVING

"Memory systems constitute the major subdivisions of the overall organization of the memory complex. . . . An operating component of a system consists of a neural substrate and its behavioral or cognitive correlates."

25th, dogs have four legs, the U.S. Supreme Court has nine justices, and Phoenix is located in Arizona. You probably don't remember when you learned these facts. Information like this is usually stored undated. The distinction between episodic and semantic memory can be better appreciated by drawing an analogy to books: Episodic memory is like an autobiography, while semantic memory is like an encyclopedia. The memory deficits seen in some cases of amnesia suggest that episodic and semantic memory are separate systems. For instance, some amnesiacs forget most personal facts, while their recall of general facts is largely unaffected (Wood, Ebert, & Kinsbourne, 1982). However, debate continues about whether episodic and semantic memory have distinct neural bases.

Prospective Versus Retrospective Memory

A 1984 paper with a clever title, "Remembering to Do Things: A Forgotten Topic" (Harris, 1984), introduced yet another distinction between types of memory: *prospective memory* versus *retrospective memory* (see **Figure 7.18**). This distinction does not refer to independent *memory systems* but rather to fundamentally different types of *memory tasks.* **Prospective memory involves remembering to perform actions in the future.** Examples of prospective memory tasks include remembering to walk the dog, to call someone, to grab the tickets for the big game, and to turn off your lawn sprinkler. In contrast, **retrospective memory involves remembering events from the past or previously learned information.** Retrospective memory is at work when you try to recall who won the Super Bowl last year, when you reminisce about your high school days, or when you try to remember what your professor said in a lecture last week. Prospective memory has been a "forgotten" topic in that it has been the subject of relatively little study. But that has begun to change, as research on prospective memory has increased in recent years.

Researchers interested in prospective memory argue that the topic merits far more study because it plays such a pervasive role in everyday life (Graf & Uttl, 2001). Think about it—a brief trip to attend class at school can be saturated with prospective memory tasks. You may need to remember to pack your notebook, take your umbrella, turn off your coffeemaker, and grab your parking card before you even get out the door. Unfortunately, experiments demonstrate that it is easy to forget such intentions, especially when you are confronted by interruptions and distractions (Einstein et al., 2003). People vary considerably in their ability to successfully carry out prospective memory tasks (Searleman, 1996). Individuals who appear deficient in prospective memory are often characterized as "absent-minded."

concept **check** 7.3

Recognizing Various Types of Memory

Check your understanding of the various types of memory discussed in this chapter by matching the definitions below with the following: (a) sensory memory, (b) short-term memory, (c) long-term memory, (d) declarative memory, (e) procedural memory, (f) episodic memory, (g) semantic memory, (h) retrospective memory, and (i) prospective memory. The answers can be found in Appendix A.

_____ **1.** Memory for factual information.

_____ **2.** An unlimited capacity store that can hold information over lengthy periods of time.

_____ **3.** The preservation of information in its original sensory form for a brief time, usually only a fraction of a second.

_____ **4.** Chronological, or temporally dated, recollections of personal experiences.

_____ **5.** The repository of memories for actions, skills, operations, and conditioned responses.

_____ **6.** General knowledge that is not tied to the time when the information was learned.

_____ **7.** Remembering to perform future actions.

_____ **8.** A limited-capacity store that can maintain unrehearsed information for about 20 seconds.

Courtesy of Endel Tulving

One of our integrative themes—the idea that people's experience of the world is subjective—stood head and shoulders above the rest in this chapter. Let's briefly review how the study of memory has illuminated this idea.

First, our discussion of attention as inherently selective should have shed light on why people's experience of the world is subjective. To a great degree, what you see in the world around you depends on where you focus your attention. This is one of the main reasons why two people can be exposed to the "same" events and walk away with entirely different perceptions. Second, the reconstructive nature of memory should further explain people's tendency to view the world with a subjective slant. When you observe an event, you don't store an exact copy of the event in your memory. Instead, you store a rough,

"bare bones" approximation of the event that may be reshaped as time goes by.

A second theme that was apparent in our discussion of memory was psychology's theoretical diversity. We saw illuminating theoretical debates about the nature of memory storage, the causes of forgetting, and the existence of multiple memory systems. Finally, the multifaceted nature of memory demonstrated once again that behavior is governed by multiple causes. For instance, your memory of a specific event may be influenced by your attention to it, your level of processing, your elaboration, how you search your memory store, how you reconstruct the event, and so forth. Given the multifaceted nature of memory, it should come as no surprise that there are many ways to improve memory. We discuss a variety of strategies in the Personal Application section.

 Subjectivity of Experience

 Theoretical Diversity

 Multifactorial Causation

PERSONAL *Application*

Improving Everyday Memory

Answer the following "true" or "false."
____ 1 Memory strategies were recently invented by psychologists.
____ 2 Overlearning of information leads to poor retention.
____ 3 Outlining what you read is not likely to affect retention.
____ 4 Massing practice in one long study session is better than distributing practice across several shorter sessions.

Mnemonic devices are strategies for enhancing memory. They have a long and honorable history. In fact, one of the mnemonic devices covered in this Application—the method of loci—was described in Greece as early as 86–82 B.C. (Yates, 1966). Actually, mnemonic devices were even more crucial in ancient times than they are today. In ancient Greece and Rome, for instance, paper and pencils were not readily available for people to write down things they needed to remember, so they had to depend heavily on mnemonic devices.

Are mnemonic devices the key to improving one's everyday memory? No. Mne-

monic devices clearly can be helpful in some situations (Wilding & Valentine, 1996), but they are not a cure-all. They can be hard to use and hard to apply to many everyday situations. Most books and training programs designed to improve memory probably overemphasize mnemonic techniques (Searleman & Herrmann, 1994). Although less exotic strategies such as increasing rehearsal, engaging in deeper processing, and organizing material are more crucial to everyday memory, we will discuss some popular mnemonics as we proceed through this Application. Along the way, you'll learn that all of our opening true-false statements are false.

Engage in Adequate Rehearsal

Practice makes perfect, or so you've heard. In reality, practice is not likely to guarantee perfection, but it usually leads to improved retention. Studies show that retention improves with increased rehearsal (Greene,

1992a). This improvement presumably occurs because rehearsal helps transfer information into long-term memory. Although the benefits of practice are well known, people have a curious tendency to overestimate their knowledge of a topic and how well they will perform on a subsequent memory test of this knowledge (Koriat & Bjork, 2005). That's why it is a good idea to informally test yourself on information that you think you have mastered before confronting a real test (for example, by taking the Practice Tests in this text or additional tests available on the website for the book).

Another possible remedy for overconfidence is trying to overlearn material (Driskell, Willis, & Copper, 1992). *Overlearning refers to continued rehearsal of material after you first appear to have mastered it.* In one study, after subjects had mastered a list of nouns (they recited the list without error), Krueger (1929) required them to continue rehearsing for 50% or 100% more trials. Measuring retention at intervals up to 28 days, Krueger found that greater overlearning was related to better recall of the list. Modern studies have also shown that overlearning can enhance performance on an exam that occurs within a week, although the evidence on its long-term benefits (months later) is inconsistent (Peladeau, Forget, & Gagne, 2003; Rohrer et al., 2005).

One other point related to rehearsal is also worth mentioning. If you are memorizing some type of list, be aware of the serial-position effect, which is often observed when subjects are tested on their memory of lists (Murdock, 2001). **The *serial-position effect* occurs when subjects show better recall for items at the beginning and end of a list than for items in the middle** (see **Figure 7.19**). The reasons for the serial-position effect are complex and need not concern us, but its pragmatic implications are clear: If you need to memorize a list of, say, cranial nerves or past presidents, allocate extra practice trials to items in the middle of the list and check your memorization of those items very carefully.

Schedule Distributed Practice and Minimize Interference

Let's assume that you need to study 9 hours for an exam. Should you "cram" all your studying into one 9-hour period (massed practice)? Or is it better to distribute your study among, say, three 3-hour periods on successive days (distributed practice)? The evidence indicates that retention tends to be greater after distributed practice than after massed practice (Payne & Wenger, 1996; Seabrook, Brown, & Solity, 2005). This advantage is especially apparent if the intervals between practice periods are fairly long, such as 24 hours (Zechmeister & Nyberg, 1982). For instance, Underwood (1970) studied children (ages 9 to 14) who practiced a list of words four times, either in one long session or in four separate sessions. He found that distributed practice led to better recall than a similar amount of massed practice (see **Figure 7.20**). The superiority of distributed practice suggests that cramming is an ill-advised approach to studying for exams (Dempster, 1996).

Because interference is a major cause of forgetting, you'll probably want to think about how you can minimize it. This issue is especially important for students, because memorizing information for one course can interfere with the retention of information for another course. Thus, the day before an exam in a course, you should study for that course only—if possible. If demands in other courses make that plan impossible, you should study the test material last.

Engage in Deep Processing and Organize Information

Research on levels of processing suggests that how *often* you go over material is less critical than the *depth* of processing that you engage in (Craik & Tulving, 1975). If you expect to remember what you read, you have to fully comprehend its meaning (Einstein & McDaniel, 2004). Many students could probably benefit if they spent less time on rote repetition and devoted more effort to actually paying attention to and analyzing the meaning of their reading assignments. In particular, it is useful to make material *personally* meaningful. When you read your textbooks, try to relate information to your own life and experience. For example, when you read about classical conditioning, try to think of your own responses that are attributable to classical conditioning.

It is also important to understand that retention tends to be greater when information is well organized (Einstein & McDaniel, 2004) Gordon Bower (1970) has shown that hierarchical organization is particularly helpful when it is applicable. Thus, it may be a good idea to *outline* reading assignments for school, since outlining forces you to organize material hierarchically. Consistent with this reasoning, there is some empirical evidence that outlining material from textbooks can enhance retention of the material (McDaniel, Waddill, & Shakesby, 1996).

Enrich Encoding with Verbal Mnemonics

Although it's often helpful to make information personally meaningful, it's not always easy to do so. For instance, when you study chemistry you may have a hard time relating to polymers at a personal level. Thus, many mnemonic devices—such as acrostics, acronyms, and narrative methods—are designed to make abstract material more meaningful.

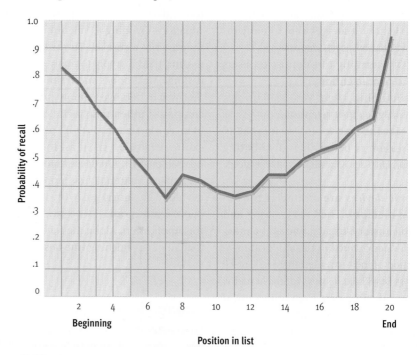

Figure 7.19

The serial-position effect. After learning a list of items to remember, people tend to recall more of the items from the beginning and the end of the list than from the middle, producing the characteristic U-shaped curve shown here. This phenomenon is called the serial-position effect.

Source: Adapted from Rundus, D. (1971). Analysis of rehearsal processes in free recall. *Journal of Experimental Psychology, 89,* 63–77. Copyright © 1971 by the American Psychological Association. Adapted by permission of the publisher and author.

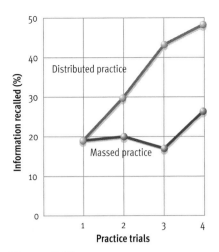

Figure 7.20

Effects of massed versus distributed practice on retention. Children in the Underwood (1970) study showed better recall of information when practice sessions were distributed over time as opposed to being massed together in one session.

Source: Adapted from Underwood, B. J. (1970). A breakdown of the total time law in free-recall learning. *Journal of Verbal Learning and Verbal Behavior, 9,* 573–580. Copyright © 1970 by Elsevier Science USA. Reproduced with permission from the publisher.

Acrostics and Acronyms

Acrostics are phrases (or poems) in which the first letter of each word (or line) functions as a cue to help you recall information to be remembered. For instance, you may remember the order of musical notes with the saying "Every good boy does fine." A slight variation on acrostics is the *acronym*—a word formed out of the first letters of a series of words. Students memorizing the order of colors in the light spectrum often store the name "Roy G. Biv" to remember red, orange, yellow, green, blue, indigo, and vio-

let. Notice that this acronym takes advantage of the principle of chunking. Acrostics and acronyms that individuals create for themselves can be effective memory tools (Hermann, Raybeck, & Gruneberg, 2002).

Narrative Methods

Another useful way to remember a list of words is to create a story that includes the words in the appropriate order. The narrative both increases the meaningfulness of the words and links them in a specific order. Bower and Clark (1969) found that this procedure greatly enhanced subjects' recall of lists of unrelated words.

Rhymes

Another verbal mnemonic that people often rely on is rhyming. You've probably repeated, "I before E except after C . . ." thousands of times. Perhaps you also remember the number of days in each month with the old standby, "Thirty days hath September . . ." Rhyming something to remember it is an old and useful trick.

Enrich Encoding with Visual Imagery

Memory can be enhanced by the use of visual imagery. As you may recall, Allan Paivio (1986) believes that visual images create a second memory code and that two codes are better than one. Many popular mnemonic devices depend on visual imagery, including the link method and the method of loci.

Link Method

The *link method* involves forming a mental image of items to be remembered in a way that links them together. For instance, suppose that you need to remember some items to pick up at the drugstore: a news magazine, shaving cream, film, and pens. To remember these items, you might visualize a public figure on the magazine cover shaving with a pen while being photographed. The more bizarre you make your image, the more helpful it is likely to be (McDaniel & Einstein, 1986).

Method of Loci

The *method of loci* involves taking an imaginary walk along a familiar path where images of items to be remembered are associated with certain locations. The first step is to commit to memory a series of loci, or places along a path. Usually these loci are specific locations in your home or neighborhood. Then envision each thing you want to remember in one of these locations. Try to form distinctive, vivid images. When you need to remember the items, imagine yourself walking along the path. The various loci on your path should serve as cues for the retrieval of the images that you formed (see Figure 7.21). Evidence suggests that the method of loci can be effective in increasing retention (Moe & De Beni, 2004). Moreover, this method ensures that items are remembered in their *correct order* because the order is determined by the sequence of locations along the pathway.

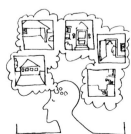

Figure 7.21

The method of loci. In this example from Bower (1970), a person about to go shopping pairs items to remember with familiar places (loci) arranged in a natural sequence: (1) hot dogs/driveway; (2) cat food/garage interior; (3) tomatoes/front door; (4) bananas/coat closet shelf; (5) whiskey/kitchen sink. The shopper then uses imagery to associate the items on the shopping list with the loci, as shown in the drawing: (1) giant hot dog rolls down a driveway; (2) a cat noisily devours cat food in the garage; (3) ripe tomatoes are splattered on the front door; (4) bunches of bananas are hung from the closet shelf; (5) the contents of a bottle of whiskey gurgle down the kitchen sink. As the last panel shows, the shopper recalls the items by mentally touring the loci associated with them.

Source: From Bower, G. H. (1970). Analysis of a mnemonic device. *American Scientist, 58,* 496–499. Copyright © 1970 by Scientific Research Society. Reprinted by permission.

Understanding the Fallibility of Eyewitness Accounts

A number of years ago, the Wilmington, Delaware, area was plagued by a series of armed robberies committed by a perpetrator who was dubbed the "gentleman bandit" by the press because he was an unusually polite and well-groomed thief. The local media published a sketch of the gentleman bandit and eventually an alert resident turned in a suspect who resembled the sketch. Much to everyone's surprise, the accused thief was a Catholic priest named Father Bernard Pagano—who vigorously denied the charges. Unfortunately for Father Pagano, his denials and alibis were unconvincing and he was charged with the crimes. At the trial, *seven* eyewitnesses confidently identified Father Pagano as the gentleman bandit. The prosecution was well on its way to a conviction when there was a stunning turn of events— another man, Ronald Clouser, confessed to the police that he was the gentleman bandit. The authorities dropped the charges against Father Pagano and the relieved priest was able to return to his normal existence (Rodgers, 1982).

This bizarre tale of mistaken identity— which sounds like it was lifted from a movie script—raises some interesting questions about memory. How could seven people "remember" seeing Father Pagnano commit armed robberies that he had nothing to do with? How could they mistake him for Ronald Clouser, when the two really didn't look very similar (see the adjacent photos)? How could they be so confident when they were so wrong? Perhaps you're thinking that this is just one case and it must be unrepresentative (which would be sound critical thinking). Well, yes, it is a rather extreme example of eyewitness fallibility, but researchers have compiled mountains of evidence that eyewitness testimony is not nearly as reliable or as accurate as widely assumed (Kassin et al., 2001; Wells & Olson, 2003). This finding is ironic in that people are most confident about their assertions when they can say "I saw it with my own eyes." Television news shows like to use the

title "Eyewitness News" to create the impression that they chronicle events with great clarity and accuracy. And our legal system accords special status to eyewitness testimony because it is considered much more dependable than hearsay or circumstantial evidence.

So, why are eyewitness accounts surprisingly inaccurate? Well, a variety of factors and processes contribute to this inaccuracy. Let's briefly review some of the relevant processes that were introduced in the main body of the chapter; then we'll focus on two common errors in thinking that also contribute.

Can you think of any memory phenomena described in the chapter that seem likely to undermine eyewitness accuracy? You could point to the fact that *memory is a reconstructive process*, and eyewitness recall is likely to be distorted by the schemas that people have for various events. A second consideration is that *witnesses sometimes make source-monitoring errors* and get confused about where they saw a face. For example, one rape victim mixed up her assailant with a guest on a TV show that she was watching when she was attacked. Fortunately, the falsely accused suspect had an

airtight alibi, as he could demonstrate that he was on live television when the rape occurred (Schacter, 1996). Perhaps the most pervasive factor is the misinformation effect (Loftus, 1993). *Witnesses' recall of events is routinely distorted by information introduced after the event* by police officers, attorneys, news reports, and so forth. In addition to these factors, eyewitness inaccuracy is fueled by *hindsight bias* and *overconfidence effects*.

The Contribution of Hindsight Bias

Hindsight bias **is the tendency to mold one's interpretation of the past to fit how events actually turned out.** When you know the outcome of an event, this knowledge slants your recall of how the event unfolded and what your thinking was at the time. With the luxury of hindsight, people have a curious tendency to say, "I knew it all along" when explaining events that objectively would have been difficult to foresee. The tendency to exhibit the hindsight bias is normal, pervasive, and surprisingly strong (Guilbault et al., 2004). With regard to eyewitnesses, their recollections may

 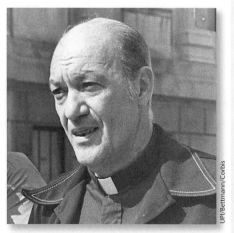

Although he doesn't look that much like the real "gentleman bandit," who is shown on the left, seven eyewitnesses identified Father Pagnano (right) as the gentleman bandit, showing just how unreliable eyewitness accounts can be.

often be distorted by knowing that a particular person has been arrested and accused of the crime in question. For example, Wells and Bradfield (1998) had simulated eyewitnesses select a perpetrator from a photo lineup. Their confidence in their identifications tended to be quite modest, which made sense given that the actual perpetrator was not even in the lineup. But when some subjects were told, "Good, you identified the actual suspect," they became highly confident about their identifications, which obviously were incorrect. In another study, participants read identical scenarios about a couple's first date that either had no ending or ended in a rape (described in one additional sentence). The subjects who received the rape ending reconstructed the story to be more consistent with their stereotypes of how rapes occur (Carli, 1999).

The Contribution of Overconfidence

Another flaw in thinking that contributes to inaccuracy in eyewitness accounts is people's tendency to be overconfident about the reliability of their memories. When tested for their memory of general information, people tend to overestimate their accuracy (Koriat & Bjork, 2005; Lichtenstein, Fischhoff, & Phillips, 1982). In studies of eyewitness recall, participants also tend to be overconfident about their recollections. Although jurors tend to be more convinced by eyewitnesses who appear confident, the evidence indicates that there is only a modest correlation between eyewitness confidence and eyewitness accuracy (Bornstein & Zickafoose, 1999). Hence, many convictions of innocent people have been attributed to the impact of testimony from highly confident, but mistaken eyewitnesses (Wells, Olson, & Charman, 2002).

Strategies to Reduce Overconfidence

Can you learn to make better judgments of the accuracy of your recall of everyday events? Yes, with effort you can get better at making accurate estimates of how likely you are to be correct in the recall of some fact or

Although courts give special credence to eyewitness testimony, scientific evidence indicates that eyewitness accounts are less reliable than widely assumed.

© Bill Fritsch/Brand X Pictures/Alamy

event. One reason that people tend to be overconfident is that if they can't think of any reasons they might be wrong, they assume they must be right. Thus, overconfidence is fueled by yet another common error in thinking—*the failure to seek disconfirming evidence*. Even veteran scientists fall prey to this weakness, as most people don't seriously consider why they might be wrong about something (Mynatt, Doherty, & Tweney, 1978).

Thus, to make more accurate assessments of what you know and don't know, it helps to engage in a deliberate process of considering why you might be wrong. Here is an example. Based on your reading of Chapter 1, write down the schools of thought associated with the following major theorists: William James, John B. Watson, and Carl Rogers. After you provide your answers, rate your confidence that the information you just provided is correct. Now, write three reasons that your answers might be wrong and three reasons that they might be correct. Most people will balk at this exercise, arguing that they cannot think of any reasons they might be wrong, but after some resistance, they can come up with several. Such reasons might include "I was half asleep when I read that part of the chapter" or "I might be confusing Watson and James." Reasons for thinking you're right could include "I distinctly recall discussing this with my friend" or "I really worked on those names in Chapter 1." After listing reasons that you might be right and might be wrong, rate your confidence in your accuracy once again. Guess what? Most people are less confident after going through such an exercise than they were before (depending, of course, on the nature of the topic).

The new confidence ratings tend to be more realistic than the original ratings (Koriat, Lichtenstein, & Fischhoff, 1980). Why? Because this exercise forces you to think more deeply about your answers and to search your memory for related information. Most people stop searching their memory as soon as they generate an answer they believe to be correct. Thus, the process of considering reasons you might be wrong about something—a process that people rarely engage in—is a useful critical thinking skill that can reduce overconfidence effects. Better assessment of what you know and don't know can be an important determinant of the quality of the decisions you make and the way you solve problems and reason from evidence.

Table 7.1   Critical Thinking Skills Discussed in This Application

Skill	Description
Understanding the limitations and fallibility of human memory	The critical thinker appreciates that memory is reconstructive and that even eyewitness accounts may be distorted or inaccurate.
Recognizing the bias in hindsight analysis	The critical thinker understands that knowing the outcome of events biases our recall and interpretation of the events.
Recognizing overconfidence in human cognition	The critical thinker understands that people are frequently overconfident about the accuracy of their projections for the future and their recollections of the past.
Understanding the need to seek disconfirming evidence	The critical thinker understands the value of thinking about how or why one might be wrong about something.

Key Ideas

Encoding: Getting Information into Memory

● The multifaceted process of memory begins with encoding. Attention, which facilitates encoding, is inherently selective. Divided attention undermines memory.

● According to levels-of-processing theory, deeper processing results in better recall of information. Structural, phonemic, and semantic encoding represent progressively deeper and more effective levels of processing.

● Elaboration enriches encoding by linking a stimulus to other information. Visual imagery may work in much the same way, creating two memory codes rather than just one.

Storage: Maintaining Information in Memory

● Information-processing theories of memory assert that people have three kinds of memory stores: a sensory memory, a short-term memory, and a long-term memory.

● Short-term memory has a limited capacity (capable of holding about seven chunks of information) and can maintain unrehearsed information for up to about 20 seconds. Working memory is a more elaborate and multifaceted model of short-term memory, which involves more than a simple rehearsal loop.

● Long-term memory is an unlimited capacity store that may hold information indefinitely. Reports of flashbulb memories suggest that LTM storage may be permanent, but the evidence is not convincing.

● Information in LTM can be organized in a variety of ways. A schema is an organized cluster of knowledge about a particular object or sequence of events. Semantic networks consist of concepts joined together by pathways. Parallel distributed processing (PDP) models of memory assert that specific memories correspond to particular patterns of activation in connectionist networks.

Retrieval: Getting Information Out of Memory

● Recall is often guided by partial information. Reinstating the context of an event can facilitate recall. Memory is highly reconstructive, and information learned after an event can alter one's memory of it, as illustrated by the misinformation effect.

● Source monitoring is the process of making attributions about the origins of memories. Source-monitoring errors may explain why people sometimes "recall" something that was only suggested to them.

Forgetting: When Memory Lapses

● Ebbinghaus's early studies of nonsense syllables suggested that we forget very rapidly. Subsequent research showed that Ebbinghaus's forgetting curve was exceptionally steep. Forgetting can be measured by asking people to recall, recognize, or relearn information.

● Some forgetting, including pseudoforgetting, is due to ineffective encoding of information. Decay theory proposes that forgetting occurs spontaneously with the passage of time. It has proven difficult to show that decay occurs in long-term memory.

● Interference theory proposes that people forget information because of competition from other material. Evidence that either prior (proactive interference) or subsequent (retroactive interference) material can cause forgetting supports interference theory.

● Forgetting is often due to retrieval failure, which may sometimes involve repression. Recent years have seen a surge of reports of recovered memories of sexual abuse in childhood. The authenticity of these recovered memories is the subject of controversy because empirical studies have demonstrated that it is not all that difficult to create inaccurate memories.

In Search of the Memory Trace: The Physiology of Memory

● The study of amnesia and other research has implicated the hippocampal region as a key player in memory processes, possibly handling the consolidation of memories.

● Thompson's research suggests that memory traces may consist of localized neural circuits. Other lines of research indicate that biochemical processes may contribute to the formation of memories.

Systems and Types of Memory

● Declarative memory is memory for facts, while procedural memory is memory for actions and skills. Declarative memory can be subdivided into episodic memory (for personal facts) and semantic memory (for general facts). Retrospective memory involves remembering things from the past, whereas prospective memory involves remembering to do things in the future.

Reflecting on the Chapter's Themes

● Our discussion of attention and memory enhances our understanding of why people's experience of the world is highly subjective. Work in this area also shows that behavior is governed by multiple factors and that psychology is marked by theoretical diversity.

PERSONAL APPLICATION • Improving Everyday Memory

● Rehearsal, even when it involves overlearning, facilitates retention, although one should be wary of the serial-position effect. Distributed practice tends to be more efficient than massed practice. It is wise to plan study sessions so as to minimize interference. Deep processing during rehearsal and good organization enhance recall.

● Meaningfulness can be enhanced through the use of verbal mnemonics such as acrostics and narrative methods. The link method and the method of loci are mnemonic devices that depend on the value of visual imagery.

CRITICAL THINKING APPLICATION • Understanding the Fallibility of Eyewitness Accounts

● Research indicates that eyewitness memory is not nearly as reliable or as accurate as widely believed. Two common errors in thinking that contribute to this phenomenon are hindsight bias and overconfidence effects.

Key Terms

Anterograde amnesia (p. 223)
Attention (p. 206)
Chunk (p. 210)
Connectionist models (p. 214)
Consolidation (p. 224)
Decay theory (p. 218)
Declarative memory system
 (p. 225)
Dual-coding theory (p. 208)
Elaboration (p. 207)
Encoding (p. 206)
Encoding specificity principle
 (p. 219)
Episodic memory system (p. 225)
Flashbulb memories (p. 212)
Forgetting curve (p. 216)
Hindsight bias (p. 230)
Interference theory (p. 218)
Levels-of-processing theory
 (p. 207)
Link method (p. 229)
Long-term memory (LTM) (p. 211)
Method of loci (p. 229)
Misinformation effect (p. 215)
Mnemonic devices (p. 227)
Nonsense syllables (p. 216)
Overlearning (p. 227)
Parallel distributed processing
 (PDP) models (p. 214)
Proactive interference (p. 219)
Procedural memory system
 (p. 225)
Prospective memory (p. 226)

Recall measure (p. 217)
Recognition measure (p. 217)
Rehearsal (p. 210)
Relearning measure (p. 218)
Repression (p. 220)
Retention (p. 217)
Retrieval (p. 206)
Retroactive interference (p. 219)
Retrograde amnesia (p. 223)
Retrospective memory (p. 226)
Schema (p. 213)
Semantic memory system (p. 225)
Semantic network (p. 213)
Sensory memory (p. 209)
Serial-position effect (p. 228)
Short-term memory (STM)
 (p. 210)
Source monitoring (p. 216)
Source-monitoring error (p. 216)
Storage (p. 206)

Key People

Richard Atkinson and Richard
 Shiffrin (p. 209)
Alan Baddeley (p. 211)
Fergus Craik and Robert Lockhart
 (p. 207)
Hermann Ebbinghaus
 (pp. 216–217)
Elizabeth Loftus (p. 215)
Marcia Johnson (p. 216)
Eric Kandel (p. 224)
George Miller (p. 210)
Endel Tulving (p. 225)

1. Getting information into memory is called _____; getting information out of memory is called _____.
   A. storage; retrieval
   B. encoding; storage
   C. encoding; retrieval
   D. storage; encoding

2. The word *big* is flashed on a screen. A mental picture of the word big represents a _____ code; the definition "large in size" represents a _____ code; "sounds like pig" represents a _____ code.
   A. structural; phonemic; semantic
   B. phonemic; semantic; structural
   C. structural; semantic; phonemic
   D. phonemic; structural; semantic

3. The capacity of short-term memory is:
   A. about 50,000 words.
   B. unlimited.
   C. about 25 stimuli.
   D. about 7 "chunks" of information.

4. Which statement best represents current evidence on the durability of long-term storage?
   A. All forgetting involves breakdowns in retrieval.
   B. LTM is like a barrel of marbles in which none of the marbles ever leaks out.
   C. There is no convincing evidence that all one's memories are stored away permanently.
   D. All long-term memories gradually decay at a constant rate.

5. An organized cluster of knowledge about a particular object or sequence of events is called a:
   A. semantic network.
   B. conceptual hierarchy.
   C. schema.
   D. retrieval cue.

6. The tip-of-the-tongue phenomenon:
   A. is a temporary inability to remember something you know, accompanied by a feeling that it's just out of reach.
   B. is clearly due to a failure in retrieval.
   C. reflects a permanent loss of information from LTM.
   D. is both A and B.

7. Loftus's work on eyewitness testimony has clearly demonstrated that:
   A. Memory errors are surprisingly infrequent.
   B. Memory errors are mainly due to repression.
   C. Information given after an event can alter a person's memory of the event.
   D. Information given after an event cannot alter a person's memory of the event.

8. If decay theory is correct:
   A. information can never be permanently lost from long-term memory.
   B. forgetting is simply a case of retrieval failure.
   C. the principal cause of forgetting should be the passage of time.
   D. all of the above.

9. Pseudoforgetting is information loss due to ineffective:
   A. encoding.
   B. storage.
   C. retrieval.
   D. all of the above.

10. Amnesia in which people lose memories for events that occurred prior to their injury is called _____ amnesia.
    A. anterograde
    B. retrospective
    C. retrograde
    D. episodic

11. Your memory of how to brush your teeth is contained in your _____ memory.
    A. declarative
    B. procedural
    C. structural
    D. episodic

12. Your knowledge that birds fly, that the sun rises in the east, and that 2 + 2 = 4 is contained in your _____ memory.
    A. structural
    B. procedural
    C. implicit
    D. semantic

13. Dorothy memorized her shopping list. When she got to the store, however, she found she had forgotten many of the items from the middle of the list. This is an example of:
    A. inappropriate encoding.
    B. retrograde amnesia.
    C. proactive interference.
    D. the serial-position effect.

14. The method of loci involves:
    A. taking an imaginary walk along a familiar path where you have associated images of items you want to remember with certain locations.
    B. forming a mental image of items to be remembered in a way that links them together.
    C. creating a phrase in which the first letter of each word functions as a cue to help you recall more abstract words that begin with the same letter.
    D. creating a story that includes each of the words to be remembered in the appropriate order.

15. The tendency to mold one's interpretation of the past to fit how events actually turned out is called:
    A. the overconfidence effect.
    B. selective amnesia.
    C. retroactive interference.
    D. the hindsight bias.

Answers

1 C pp. 205–206 6 D pp. 214–215 11 B p. 225
2 C p. 207 7 C p. 215 12 D pp. 225–226
3 D p. 210 8 C p. 218 13 D p. 228
4 C pp. 211–212 9 A p. 218 14 A p. 229
5 C p. 213 10 C p. 223 15 D p. 230

PsykTrek

Go to the PsykTrek website or CD-ROM for further study of the concepts in this chapter. Both online and on the CD-ROM, PsykTrek includes dozens of learning modules with videos, animations, and quizzes, as well as simulations of psychological phenomena and a multimedia glossary that includes word pronunciations.

ThomsonNOW

www.thomsonedu.com/ThomsonNOW
Go to this site for the link to ThomsonNOW, your one-stop study shop. Take a Pre-Test for this chapter, and ThomsonNOW will generate a Personalized Study Plan based on your test results. The Study Plan will identify the topics you need to review and direct you to online resources to help you master those topics. You can then take a Post-Test to help you determine the concepts you have mastered and what you still need to work on.

Companion Website

www.thomsonedu.com/psychology/weiten
Go to this site to find online resources directly linked to your book, including a glossary, flash cards, drag-and-drop exercises, quizzes, and more!

CHAPTER 8

Cognition and Intelligence

UNLAWFUL TO PASS WHEN RED LIGHTS FLASH

© Andersen Ross/Blend Images/Alamy

Mr. Watson—Mr. Sherlock Holmes," said Stamford, introducing us. "How are you?" he said, cordially, gripping my hand with a strength for which I should hardly have given him credit. "You have been in Afghanistan, I perceive."

"How on earth did you know that?" I asked, in astonishment. (From A Study in Scarlet by Arthur Conan Doyle)

If you've ever read any Sherlock Holmes stories, you know that the great detective continually astonished his loyal companion, Dr. Watson, with his extraordinary deductions. Obviously, Holmes could not arrive at his conclusions without a chain of reasoning. Yet to him even an elaborate reasoning process was a simple, everyday act. Consider his feat of knowing at once, upon first meeting Watson, that the doctor had been in Afghanistan. When asked, Holmes explained his reasoning as follows:

"I knew you came from Afghanistan. From long habit the train of thought ran so swiftly through my mind that I arrived at the conclusion without being conscious of the intermediate steps. There were such steps, however. The train of reasoning ran: 'Here is a gentleman of a medical type, but with the air of a military man. Clearly an army doctor, then. He has just come from the tropics, for his face is dark, and that is not the natural tint of his skin, for his wrists are fair. He has undergone hardship and sickness, as his haggard face says clearly. His left arm has been injured. He holds it in a stiff and unnatural manner. Where in the tropics could an English army doctor have seen much hardship and got his arm wounded? Clearly in Afghanistan.' The whole train of thought did not occupy a second."

Admittedly, Sherlock Holmes's deductive feats are fictional. But even to read about them appreciatively—let alone imagine them, as Sir Arthur Conan Doyle did—is a remarkably complex mental act. Our everyday thought processes seem ordinary to us only because we take them for granted, just as Holmes saw nothing extraordinary in what to him was a simple deduction.

In reality, everyone is a Sherlock Holmes, continually performing magical feats of thought. Even elementary perception—for instance, watching a football game or a ballet—involves elaborate cognitive processes. People must sort through distorted, constantly shifting perceptual inputs and deduce what they see out there in the real world. Imagine, then, the complexity of thought required to read a book, fix an automobile, or balance a checkbook. Of course, all this is not to say that human thought processes are flawless or unequaled. You probably own a $10 calculator that can run circles around you when it comes to computing square roots. As we'll see, some of the most interesting research in this chapter focuses on ways in which people's thinking can be limited, simplistic, or outright illogical.

Our topics in this chapter center on *thinking*. In the first half of the chapter, we will summarize research on cognition, or *how people think,* as we look at the subjects of problem solving and decision making. In the second half of the chapter, we will focus on *how well people think,* as measured by tests of intelligence. Thus, the first half of the chapter examines the intricacies of *thinking processes* (cognition), whereas the second half focuses on variations among people in *thinking ability* (intelligence).

The topics of cognition and intelligence have very different histories. As we will discuss later, the first useful tests of general mental ability were created between 1904 and 1916, and intelligence testing flourished throughout the 20th century. In contrast, during the first half of the 20th century, the study of cognition was actively discouraged by the theoretical dominance of behaviorism. Herbert Simon, a pioneer of cognitive psychology, recalls that "you couldn't use a word like *mind* in a psychology journal—you'd get your mouth washed out with soap" (Holden, 1986). Although it wasn't fully recognized until much later, the 1950s brought a "cognitive revolution" in psychology (Baars, 1986). Renegade theorists, such as Simon, began to argue that behaviorists' exclusive focus on overt responses was doomed to yield an incomplete understanding of human functioning. More important, creative new approaches to research on problem solving, decision making, and reasoning led to exciting progress. Thus, it was only in the second half of the 20th century that the study of cognition grew into a robust, influential area of research. We will begin our discussion of cognitive processes by examining the topic of problem solving.

HERBERT SIMON
"You couldn't use a word like mind *in a psychology journal—you'd get your mouth washed out with soap."*

PREVIEW QUESTIONS

● What types of problems have psychologists studied?

● What are some common mistakes that thwart problem-solving efforts?

● What are heuristics in problem solving?

● What are some useful problem-solving strategies?

● What is field dependence-independence?

● How is culture related to cognitive style?

Look at the two problems below. Can you solve them?

In the Thompson family there are five brothers, and each brother has one sister. If you count Mrs. Thompson, how many females are there in the Thompson family?

Fifteen percent of the people in Topeka have unlisted telephone numbers. You select 200 names at random from the Topeka phone book. How many of these people can be expected to have unlisted phone numbers?

These problems, borrowed from Sternberg (1986, p. 214), are exceptionally simple, but many people fail to solve them. The answer to the first problem is two. The only females in the family are Mrs. Thompson and her one daughter, who is a sister to each of her brothers. The answer to the second problem is none. You won't find any people with unlisted phone numbers in the phone book.

Why do many people fail to solve these simple problems? You'll learn why in a moment, when we discuss barriers to effective problem solving. But first, let's examine a scheme for classifying problems into a few basic types.

Types of Problems SIM7, 7e

Problem solving refers to active efforts to discover what must be done to achieve a goal that is not readily attainable. Obviously, if a goal is readily attainable, there isn't a problem. But in problem-solving situations, one must go beyond the given information to overcome obstacles and reach a goal. Jim Greeno (1978) has proposed that problems can be categorized into three basic classes:

1. *Problems of inducing structure.* The person must discover the relations among the parts of the prob-

lem. The *series completion problems* and the *analogy problems* in **Figure 8.1** are examples of problems of inducing structure.

2. *Problems of arrangement.* The person must arrange the parts in a way that satisfies some criterion. The parts can usually be arranged in many ways, but only one or a few of the arrangements form a solution. The *string problem* and the *anagrams* in **Figure 8.1** fit in this category.

3. *Problems of transformation.* The person must carry out a sequence of transformations in order to reach a specific goal. The *hobbits and orcs problem* and the *water jar problem* in **Figure 8.1** are examples of transformation problems. Transformation problems can be challenging. Even though you know exactly what the goal is, it's often not obvious how the goal can be achieved.

Greeno's list is not an exhaustive scheme for classifying problems, but it provides a useful system for understanding some of the variety seen in everyday problems.

Barriers to Effective Problem Solving 7e

On the basis of their studies of problem solving, psychologists have identified a number of barriers that frequently impede people's efforts to arrive at solutions. Common obstacles to effective problem solving include a focus on irrelevant information, functional fixedness, mental set, and imposition of unnecessary constraints.

Irrelevant Information 7e

We began our discussion of problem solving with two simple problems that people routinely fail to solve. The catch is that these problems contain *irrele-*

DILBERT

A. Analogy

What word completes the analogy?

Merchant : Sell : : Customer : _____

Lawyer : Client : : Doctor : _____

B. String problem

Two strings hang from the ceiling but are too far apart to allow a person to hold one and walk to the other. On the table are a book of matches, a screwdriver, and a few pieces of cotton. How could the strings be tied together?

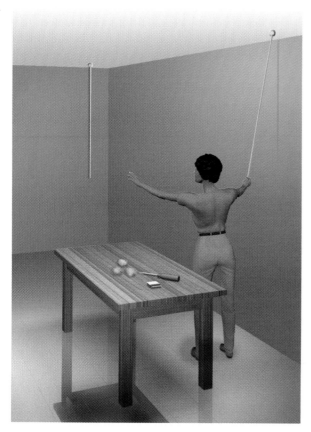

C. Hobbits and orcs problem

Three hobbits and three orcs arrive at a river bank, and they all wish to cross onto the other side. Fortunately, there is a boat, but unfortunately, the boat can hold only two creatures at one time. Also, there is another problem. Orcs are vicious creatures, and whenever there are more orcs than hobbits on one side of the river, the orcs will immediately attack the hobbits and eat them up. Consequently, you should be certain that you never leave more orcs than hobbits on either river bank. How should the problem be solved? It must be added that the orcs, though vicious, can be trusted to bring the boat back! (From Matlin, 1989, p. 319)

D. Water jar problem

Suppose that you have a 21-cup jar, a 127-cup jar, and a 3-cup jar. Drawing and discarding as much water as you like, you need to measure out exactly 100 cups of water. How can this be done?

E. Anagram

Rearrange the letters in each row to make an English word.

RWAET

KEROJ

F. Series completion

What number or letter completes each series?

1 2 8 3 4 6 5 6 _____

A B M C D M _____

vant information that leads people astray. In the first problem, the number of brothers is irrelevant in determining the number of females in the Thompson family. In the second problem, participants tend to focus on the figures of 15% and 200 names. But this numerical information is irrelevant, since all the names came out of the phone book.

Sternberg (1986) points out that people often incorrectly assume that all the numerical information in a problem is necessary to solve it. They therefore try to figure out how to use this information before they even consider whether it's relevant. Focusing on irrelevant information can have adverse effects on reasoning and problem solving (Gaeth & Shanteau, 2000). Hence, effective problem solving requires that you attempt to figure out what information is relevant and what is irrelevant before proceeding.

Figure 8.1

Six standard problems used in studies of problem solving. Try solving the problems and identifying which class each belongs to before reading further. The problems can be classified as follows. The *analogy problems* and *series completion problems* are problems of inducing structure. The solutions for the analogy problems are *Buy* and *Patient*. The solutions for the series completion problems are *4* and *E*. The *string problem* and the *anagram problems* are problems of arrangement. To solve the string problem, attach the screwdriver to one string and set it swinging as a pendulum. Hold the other string and catch the swinging screwdriver. Then you need only untie the screwdriver and tie the strings together. The solutions for the anagram problems are *WATER* and *JOKER*. The *hobbits and orcs problem* and the *water jar problem* are problems of transformation. The solutions for these two problems are outlined in **Figures 8.2** and **8.3**.

Functional Fixedness

Another common barrier to successful problem solving is *functional fixedness*—**the tendency to perceive an item only in terms of its most common use.** Functional fixedness has been seen in the difficulties that people have with the string problem

(Maier, 1931). Solving this problem requires finding a novel use for one of the objects: the screwdriver. Participants tend to think of the screwdriver in terms of its usual functions—turning screws and perhaps prying things open. They have a hard time viewing the screwdriver as a weight. Their rigid way of thinking about the screwdriver illustrates functional fixedness (Dominowski & Bourne, 1994). Ironically, young children appear to be less vulnerable to functional fixedness than older children or adults because they have less knowledge about the conventional uses of various objects (Defeyter & German, 2003).

Mental Set

Rigid thinking is also at work when a mental set interferes with effective problem solving. A *mental set exists when people persist in using problem-solving strategies that have worked in the past.* The effects of mental set were seen in a classic study by Abraham Luchins (1942). Luchins asked subjects to work a series of water jar problems, like the one introduced earlier. Six such problems are outlined in **Figure 8.4**, which shows the capacities of the three jars and the amounts of water to be measured out. Try solving these problems.

Were you able to develop a formula for solving these problems? The first four all require the same strategy, which is described in **Figure 8.3**. You have to fill jar B, draw off the amount that jar A holds once, and draw off the amount that jar C holds twice. Thus, the formula for your solution is B – A – 2C. Although there is an obvious and much simpler solution (A – C) for the fifth problem (see **Figure 8.8** on page 241), Luchins found that most participants stuck with the more cumbersome strategy that they had used in problems 1–4. Moreover, most subjects couldn't solve the sixth problem in the allotted time, because they kept trying to use their proven strategy, which does not work for this problem. The participants' reliance on their "tried and true" strategy is an illustration of mental set in problem solving. This tendency to let one's thinking get into a rut is a common barrier to successful problem solving (Smith, 1995). Mental set may explain why having expertise

Figure 8.2
Solution to the hobbits and orcs problem. This problem is difficult because it is necessary to temporarily work "away" from the goal.

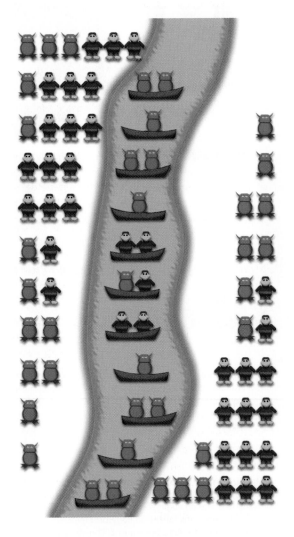

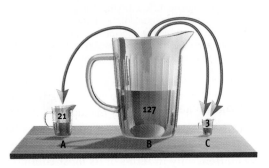

Figure 8.3
The method for solving the water jar problem. As explained in the text, the correct formula is B – A – 2C.

	Capacity of empty jars			Desired amount of water
Problem	A	B	C	
1	14	163	25	99
2	18	43	10	5
3	9	42	6	21
4	20	59	4	31
5	23	49	3	20
6	28	76	3	25

Figure 8.4
Additional water jar problems. Using jars A, B, and C, with the capacities indicated in each row, figure out how to measure out the desired amount of water specified on the far right. The solutions are shown in **Figure 8.8**. (Based on Luchins, 1942)

in an area sometimes backfires and hampers problem solving efforts (Leighton & Sternberg, 2003).

Unnecessary Constraints

Effective problem solving requires specifying all the constraints governing a problem *without assuming any constraints that don't exist.* An example of a problem in which people place an unnecessary constraint on the solution is shown in **Figure 8.5** (Adams, 1980). Without lifting your pencil from the paper, try to draw four straight lines that will cross through all nine dots. Most people will not draw lines outside the imaginary boundary that surrounds the dots. Notice that this constraint is not part of the problem statement. It's imposed only by the problem solver. Correct solutions, two of which are shown in **Figure 8.9** on page 241, extend outside the imaginary boundary. People often make assumptions that impose unnecessary constraints on problem-solving efforts.

The nine-dot problem is often solved with a burst of insight. **Insight occurs when people suddenly discover the correct solution to a problem after struggling with it for a while.** Although insight feels like a sudden, "aha" experience to problem solvers, some researchers have questioned whether insight solutions emerge full blown or are preceded by incremental movement toward a solution. Recent studies suggest the latter—that insight breakthroughs often are preceded by gradual movement toward a solution that occurs outside of the problem solver's awareness (Novick & Bassok, 2005).

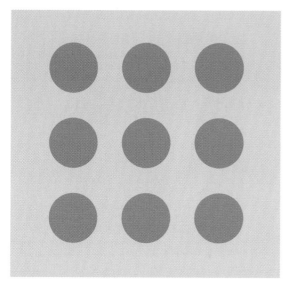

Figure 8.5
The nine-dot problem. Without lifting your pencil from the paper, draw no more than four lines that will cross through all nine dots. For possible solutions, see **Figure 8.9**.

Source: Adams, J. L. (1980). *Conceptual blockbusting: A guide to better ideas.* New York: W. H. Freeman. Copyright © 1980 by James L. Adams. Reprinted by permission of W. H. Freeman & Co.

Approaches to Problem Solving

People use a variety of strategies in attempting to solve problems. In this section, we'll examine some general strategies.

Trial and Error and Heuristics

Trial and error is a common, albeit primitive, approach to solving problems. **Trial and error involves trying possible solutions sequentially and discarding those that are in error until one works.** Trial and error can be effective when there are relatively few possible solutions to be tried out. However, this method becomes impractical when the number of possible maneuvers is large. Consider, for instance, the problem shown in **Figure 8.6**. The challenge is to move just two matches to create a pattern containing four equal squares. Sure, you could use a trial-and-error approach in moving pairs of matches. But you'd better allocate plenty of time to this effort, as there are over 60,000 possible rearrangements to check out (see **Figure 8.10** for the solution).

Because trial and error is inefficient, people often use shortcuts called *heuristics* in problem solving. A **heuristic is a guiding principle or "rule of thumb" used in solving problems or making decisions.** Heuristics are often useful, but they don't guarantee success. Helpful heuristics in problem solving include forming subgoals, searching for analogies, and changing the representation of the problem.

Forming Subgoals

It is often useful to tackle problems by formulating *subgoals,* intermediate steps toward a solution (Catrambone, 1998). When you reach a subgoal, you've solved part of the problem. Some problems have fairly obvious subgoals, and research has shown that people take advantage of them. For instance, in analogy problems, the first subgoal usually is to figure out the possible relations between the first two parts of the analogy.

The wisdom of formulating subgoals can be seen in the *tower of Hanoi problem,* depicted in **Figure 8.7** on the next page. The terminal goal for this problem is to move all three rings on peg A to peg C, while abiding by two restrictions: only the top ring on a peg can be moved and a ring must never be placed above a smaller ring. See whether you can solve the problem before continuing.

Dividing this problem into subgoals facilitates a solution (Kotovsky, Hayes, & Simon, 1985). If you think in terms of subgoals, your first task is to get

Figure 8.6
The matchstick problem. Move two matches to form four equal squares. You can find the solution in **Figure 8.10**.

Source: Kendler, H. H. (1974). *Basic psychology.* Menlo Park, CA: Benjamin-Cummings. Copyright © 1974 The Benjamin-Cummings Publishing Co. Adapted by permission of Howard H. Kendler.

Figure 8.7

The tower of Hanoi problem. Your mission is to move the rings from peg A to peg C. You can move only the top ring on a peg and can't place a larger ring above a smaller one. The solution is explained in the text.

Calvin & Hobbes © by Bill Watterson. Reprinted with permission of Universal Press Syndicate. All rights reserved.

CALVIN & HOBBES

ring 3 to the bottom of peg C. Breaking this task into sub-subgoals, subjects can figure out that they should move ring 1 to peg C, ring 2 to peg B, and ring 1 from peg C to peg B. These maneuvers allow you to place ring 3 at the bottom of peg C, thus meeting your first subgoal. Your next subgoal—getting ring 2 over to peg C—can be accomplished in just two steps: move ring 1 to peg A and ring 2 to peg C. It should then be obvious how to achieve your final subgoal—getting ring 1 over to peg C.

Searching for Analogies

Searching for analogies is another of the major heuristics for solving problems (Holyoak, 2005). If you can spot an analogy between problems, you may be able to use the solution to a previous problem to solve a current one. Of course, using this strategy depends on recognizing the similarity between two problems, which may itself be a challenging problem. People often are unable to recognize that two problems are similar (Gilhooly, 1996). One prominent reason that

---

concept **check** 8.1

Thinking About Problem Solving

Check your understanding of problem solving by answering some questions about the following problem. Begin by trying to solve the problem.

The candle problem. Using the objects shown—candles, a box of matches, string, and some tacks—figure out how you could mount a candle on a wall so that it could be used as a light. Work on the problem for a while, then turn to page 242 to see the solution. After you've seen the solution, respond to the following questions. The answers are in Appendix A.

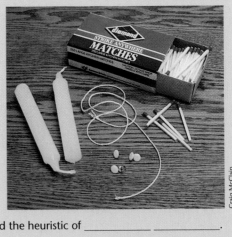

Craig McClain

1. If it didn't occur to you that the matchbox could be converted from a container to a platform, this illustrates _____ _____.

2. While working on the problem, if you thought to yourself, "How can I create a platform attached to the wall?" you used the heuristic of _____ _____.

3. If it occurred to you suddenly that the matchbox could be used as a platform, this realization would be an example of _____.

4. If you had a hunch that there might be some similarity between this problem and the string problem in **Figure 8.1** (the similarity is the novel use of an object), your hunch would illustrate the heuristic of _____ ___ _____.

5. In terms of Greeno's three types of problems, the candle problem is a(n) _____ problem.

Figure 8.8

Solutions to the additional water jar problems. The solution for problems 1–4 is the same (B – A – 2C) as the solution shown in **Figure 8.3**. This method will work for problem 5, but there also is a simpler solution (A – C), which is the only solution for problem 6. Many subjects exhibit a mental set on these problems, as they fail to notice the simpler solution for problem 5.

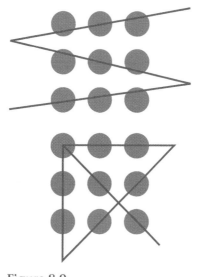

Figure 8.9

Two solutions to the nine-dot problem. The key to solving the problem is to recognize that nothing in the problem statement forbids going outside the imaginary boundary surrounding the dots.

Source: Adams, J. L. (1980). *Conceptual blockbusting: A guide to better ideas.* New York: W. H. Freeman. Copyright © 1980 by James L. Adams. Reprinted by permission of W. H. Freeman & Co.

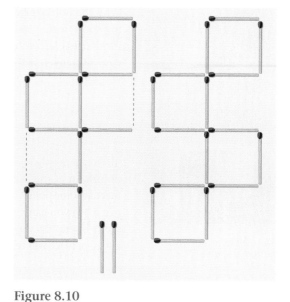

Figure 8.10

Solution to the matchstick problem. The key to solving this problem is to "open up" the figure, something many subjects are reluctant to do because they impose unnecessary constraints on the problem.

Source: Kendler, H. H. (1974). *Basic psychology.* Menlo Park, CA: Benjamin-Cummings. Copyright © 1974 The Benjamin-Cummings Publishing Co. Adapted by permission of Howard H. Kendler.

people often have difficulty recognizing analogies between problems is that they tend to focus on superficial, surface features of problems rather than their underlying structure (Bassok, 2003). Nonetheless, analogies can be a powerful tool in efforts to solve problems. Try to make use of analogies to solve the following two problems:

A teacher had 23 pupils in his class. All but 7 of them went on a museum trip and thus were away for the day. How many students remained in class that day?

Susan gets in her car in Boston and drives toward New York City, averaging 50 miles per hour. Twenty minutes later, Ellen gets in her car in New York City and starts driving toward Boston, averaging 60 miles per hour. Both women take the same route, which extends a total of 220 miles between the two cities. Which car is nearer to Boston when they meet?

These problems, taken from Sternberg (1986, pp. 213 and 215), resemble the ones that opened our discussion of problem solving. Each has an obvious solution that's hidden in irrelevant numerical information. If you recognized this similarity, you probably solved the problems easily. If not, take another look now that you know what the analogy is. Neither problem requires any calculation whatsoever. The answer to the first problem is 7. As for the sec-

ond problem, when the two cars meet they're in the same place. Obviously, they have to be the same distance from Boston.

Changing the Representation of the Problem

Whether you solve a problem often hinges on how you envision it—your *representation of the problem.* Many problems can be represented in a variety of ways, such as verbally, mathematically, or spatially. You might represent a problem with a list, a table, an equation, a graph, a matrix of facts or numbers, a hierarchical tree diagram, or a sequential flowchart (Halpern, 2003). When you fail to make progress with your initial representation of a problem, changing your representation is often a good strategy (Novick & Bassok, 2005). As an illustration, see whether you can solve the *Buddhist monk problem:*

At sunrise, a Buddhist monk sets out to climb a tall mountain. He follows a narrow path that winds around the mountain and up to a temple. He stops frequently to rest and climbs at varying speeds, arriving around sunset. After staying a few days, he begins his return journey. As before, he starts at sunrise, rests often, walks at varying speeds, and arrives around sunset. Prove that there must be a spot along the path that the monk will pass on both trips at precisely the same time of day.

The solution to the candle problem in Concept Check 8.1.

Why should there be such a spot? The monk's walking speed varies. Shouldn't it all be a matter of coincidence if he reaches a spot at the same time each day? Moreover, if there is such a spot, how would you prove it? Participants who represent this problem in terms of verbal, mathematical, or spatial information struggle. Subjects who work with a graphic representation fare much better. The best way to represent the problem is to envision the monk (or two different monks) ascending and descending the mountain at the same time. The two monks must meet at some point. If you construct a graph (see **Figure 8.11**) you can vary the speed of the monks' descent in endless ways, but you can see that there's always a place where they meet.

Culture, Cognitive Style, and Problem Solving

Do the varied experiences of people from different cultures lead to cross-cultural variations in problem solving? Yes, researchers have found cultural differences in the cognitive style that people exhibit in solving problems. Back in the 1940s, Herman Witkin was intrigued by the observation that some airplane pilots would fly into a cloud bank upright but exit it upside down without realizing that they had turned over. Witkin's efforts to explain this aviation problem led to the discovery of an interesting dimension of cognitive style (Witkin, 1950; Witkin et al., 1962). *Field dependence-independence* **refers to individuals' tendency to rely primarily on external versus internal frames of reference when orienting themselves in space.** People who are *field dependent* rely on external frames of reference and tend to accept the physical environment as a given instead of trying to analyze or restructure it. People who are *field independent* rely on internal frames of reference and tend to analyze and try to restructure the physical environment rather than accepting it as is.

An extensive body of research suggests that some cultures encourage a field-dependent cognitive style, whereas others foster a field-independent style (Berry, 1990; Mishra, 2001). The educational practices in modern Western societies seem to nourish field independence. A field-independent style is also more likely to be predominant in nomadic societies that depend on hunting and gathering for subsistence and in societies with lenient childrearing practices that encourage personal autonomy. In contrast, a field-dependent style is found more in sedentary agricultural societies and in societies that stress strict childrearing practices and conformity.

In a related line of research, Richard Nisbett and his colleagues (2001) have argued that people from Eastern Asian cultures (such as China, Japan, and Korea) display a *holistic cognitive style* that focuses on context and relationships among elements in a field, whereas people from Western cultures (America and Europe) exhibit an *analytic cognitive style* that focuses on objects and their properties rather than context. To put it simply, Easterners see wholes where Westerners see parts.

To demonstrate this disparity, Masuda and Nisbett (2001) presented computer-animated scenes of fish and other underwater objects to Japanese and American participants and asked them to report what they had seen. The initial comments of American subjects typically referred to the focal fish, whereas the initial comments of Japanese subjects usually referred to background elements (see **Figure 8.12**). Furthermore, the Japanese participants made about 70% more statements about context or background and about twice as many statements about relationships between elements in the scenes. Research also suggests that people from Eastern cultures tend to be more field-dependent than their Western counterparts (Ji, Peng, & Nisbett, 2000), but Nisbett and his colleagues view field dependence-independence as just one facet of a broader preference for holistic versus analytic thinking. Based on these and many other findings, Nisbett et al. (2001) conclude that cultural differences in cognitive style are substantial and that "literally different cognitive processes are often invoked by East Asians and Westerners dealing with the same problem" (p. 305).

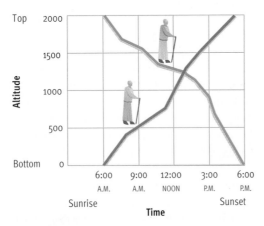

Figure 8.11

Solution to the Buddhist monk problem. If you represent this problem graphically and think in terms of two monks, it is readily apparent that the monk does pass a single spot at the same time each day.

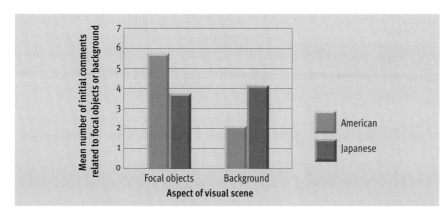

Figure 8.12

Cultural disparities in cognitive style. In one of the studies conducted by Masuda and Nisbett (2001), the participants were asked to describe computer-animated visual scenes. As you can see, the initial comments made by American subjects referred more to focal objects in the scenes, whereas the initial comments made by Japanese subjects referred more to background elements in the scenes. These findings are consistent with the hypothesis that Easterners see wholes (a holistic cognitive style) where Westerners see parts (an analytic cognitive style). (Data from Masuda & Nisbett, 2001)

Problems are not the only kind of cognitive challenge that people grapple with on a regular basis. Life also seems to constantly demand decisions. As you might expect, cognitive psychologists have shown great interest in the process of decision making, which is our next subject.

> Decision Making: Choices and Chances

Decisions, decisions. Life is full of them. You decided to read this book today. Earlier today you decided when to get up, whether to eat breakfast, and if so, what to eat. Usually you make routine decisions like these with little effort. But on occasion you need to make important decisions that require more thought. Big decisions—such as selecting a car, a home, or a job—tend to be difficult. The alternatives usually have a number of facets that need to be weighed. For instance, in choosing among several cars, you may want to compare their costs, roominess, fuel economy, handling, acceleration, stylishness, reliability, safety features, and warranties.

Decision making involves evaluating alternatives and making choices among them. Most people try to be systematic and rational in their decision making. However, the work that earned Herbert Simon the 1978 Nobel prize in economics showed that people don't always live up to these goals. Before Simon's work, most traditional theories in economics assumed that people made rational choices to maximize their economic gains. Simon (1957) noted that people have a limited ability to process and evaluate information on numerous facets of possible alternatives. He demonstrated that people tend to use simple strategies in decision making that focus on only a few facets of the available options. According to Simon's theory of *bounded rationality,* people use sensible decision strategies, given their cognitive limitations, but these limitations often result in "irrational" decisions that are less than optimal.

Spurred by Simon's analysis, psychologists have devoted several decades to the study of how cognitive biases distort people's decision making. The results of this research have sometimes been disturbing, leading some theorists to conclude that people "do a singularly bad job at the business of reasoning, even when they are calm, clearheaded, and under no pressure to perform quickly" (Stich, 1990, pp. 173–174). Let's look at this research—and recent criticism that it has inspired.

Making Choices: Selecting an Alternative

Many decisions involve choices about *preferences,* which can be made using a variety of strategies. For instance, imagine that Boris has found two reasonably attractive apartments and is trying to decide between them. How should he go about selecting between his alternatives? Let's look at some strategies Boris might use in trying to make his decision.

If Boris wanted to use an *additive strategy,* he would list the attributes that influence his decision. Then he would rate the desirability of each apartment on each attribute. For example, let's say that Boris wants to consider four attributes: rent, noise level, distance to campus, and cleanliness. He might make ratings from –3 to +3, like those shown in Table 8.1, add up the ratings for each alternative, and select the one with the largest total. Given the ratings in Table 8.1,

- How do people make choices about preferences?
- What factors are important in risky decision making?
- What shortcuts do people use in judging probabilities, and what are their effects?
- What are some common mistakes in reasoning about decisions?
- What do evolutionary psychologists have to say about error and bias in human decision making?

Table 8.1 Application of the Additive Model to Choosing an Apartment

Attribute	Apartment A	B
Rent	+1	+2
Noise level	−2	+3
Distance to campus	+3	−1
Cleanliness	+2	+2
Total	**+4**	**+6**

Web Link 8.1

Online Decision Research Center Experiments
Michael Birnbaum (California State University, Fullerton) presents a range of continuing and completed experiments conducted online that illustrate how people make decisions.

People often have to decide between alternative products, such as computers, cars, refrigerators, and so forth, that are not all that different. Hence, they often struggle with their abundant choices.

Boris should select apartment B. To make an additive strategy more useful, you can *weight* attributes differently, based on their importance (Goldstein, 1990). For example, if Boris considers distance to campus to be twice as important as the other considerations, he could multiply his ratings of this attribute by 2. The distance rating would then be +6 for apartment A and −2 for apartment B, and apartment A would become the preferred choice.

People also make choices by gradually eliminating less-attractive alternatives (Slovic, 1990; Tversky, 1972). This strategy is called *elimination by aspects* because it assumes that alternatives are eliminated by evaluating them on each attribute or aspect in turn. Whenever any alternative fails to satisfy some minimum criterion for an attribute, it is eliminated from further consideration.

To illustrate, suppose Juanita is looking for a new car. She may begin by eliminating all cars that cost over $24,000. Then she may eliminate cars that don't average at least 20 miles per gallon of gas. By continuing to reject choices that don't satisfy some minimum

criterion on selected attributes, she can gradually eliminate alternatives until only a single car remains. The final choice in elimination by aspects depends on the order in which attributes are evaluated, so it's best to evaluate attributes in the order of their importance.

Both the additive and the elimination-by-aspects strategies have advantages, but which strategy do people actually tend to use? Research suggests that when decisions involve relatively few options that need to be evaluated on only a few attributes, people tend to use additive strategies. However, as more options and factors are added to a decision task, people tend to shift to elimination by aspects (Payne & Bettman, 2004).

Beyond the basics just discussed, research has turned up a host of enlightening findings about the nuances of how people make decisions about preferences. Some of the more interesting findings include the following:

- When people decide between various options (let's say two job opportunities), their evaluations of the options' specific attributes (such as salary, commute, and work hours) fluctuate more than most models of decision making anticipated (Shafir & LeBoeuf, 2004). Models of "rational" choice assumed that people know what they like and don't like and that these evaluations would be stable, but research suggests otherwise. One reason these judgments tend to be unstable is that they are swayed by incidental emotional fluctuations (Lerner, Small, & Loewenstein, 2004).

- Another reason these evaluations tend to be inconsistent is that comparative evaluations of options tend to yield different results than separate evaluations (assessing an option on its own, in isolation) (Hsee, Zhang, & Chen, 2004). For example, when subjects directly compare a job with an $80,000 salary at a firm where one's co-workers tend to earn $100,000 against a job with a $70,000 salary at a company where peers earn only $50,000, they rate the $80,000 job as more desirable. However, when two sets of subjects evaluate the same job options in isolation, the $70,000 job is rated as more desirable (LeBoeuf & Shafir, 2005). The dynamics and implications of comparative and separate evaluations can be quite different.

- A chronic problem faced by decision makers is that they frequently make choices based on comparative evaluations, but the chosen product, activity, or event is actually experienced in isolation (Hsee & Zhang, 2004). This mismatch can lead to decisions that people regret. For example, a shopper may make precise head-to-head comparisons

© Boris Roessler/DPA/epa/Corbis

of several speaker systems at an audio store and decide to spend an extra $1500 on the best speakers, but at home the selected speakers will be experienced in isolation. This person may have been delighted with a much less expensive set of speakers if they had been brought to his or her home and evaluated in isolation.

Taking Chances: Factors Weighed in Risky Decisions

Suppose you have the chance to play a dice game in which you might win some money. You must decide whether it would be to your advantage to play. You're going to roll a fair die. If the number 6 appears, you win $5. If one of the other five numbers appears, you win nothing. It costs you $1 every time you play. Should you participate?

This problem calls for a type of decision making that is somewhat different from making choices about preferences. In selecting alternatives that reflect preferences, people generally weigh known outcomes (apartment A will require a long commute to campus, car B will get 30 miles per gallon, and so forth). In contrast, *risky decision making* involves **making choices under conditions of uncertainty.** Uncertainty exists when people don't know what will happen. At best, they know, or can estimate, the probability that a particular event will occur.

One way to decide whether to play the dice game would be to figure out the *expected value* of participation in the game. To do so, you would need to calculate the average amount of money you could expect to win or lose each time you play. The value of a win is $4 ($5 minus the $1 entry fee). The value of a loss is –$1. To calculate expected value, you also need to know the probability of a win or loss. Since a die has six faces, the probability of a win is 1 out of 6, and the probability of a loss is 5 out of 6. Thus, on five out of every six trials, you lose $1. On one out of six, you win $4. The game is beginning to sound unattractive, isn't it? We can figure out the precise expected value as follows:

Expected value = $(\frac{1}{6} \times 4) + (\frac{5}{6} \times -1)$
$= \frac{4}{6} + (-\frac{5}{6}) = -\frac{1}{6}$

The expected value of this game is $-\frac{1}{6}$ of a dollar, which means that you lose an average of about 17 cents per turn. Now that you know the expected value, surely you won't agree to play. Or will you?

If we want to understand why people make the decisions they do, the concept of expected value is not enough. People frequently behave in ways that are inconsistent with expected value (Slovic, Lichtenstein, & Fischoff, 1988). Any time the expected value is negative, a gambler should expect to lose money. Yet a great many people gamble at racetracks and casinos and buy lottery tickets. Although they realize that the odds are against them, they continue to gamble. Even people who don't gamble buy homeowner's insurance, which has a negative expected value. After all, when you buy insurance, your expectation (and hope!) is that you will lose money on the deal.

To explain decisions that violate expected value, some theories replace the objective value of an outcome with its subjective utility (Fischoff, 1988). Subjective utility represents what an outcome is personally worth to an individual. For example, buying a few lottery tickets may allow you to dream about becoming wealthy. Buying insurance may give you a sense of security. Subjective utilities like these vary from one person to another. If we know an individual's subjective utilities, we can better understand that person's risky decision making.

Heuristics in Judging Probabilities

 7f

- What are your chances of passing your next psychology test if you study only 3 hours?
- How likely is a major downturn in the stock market during the upcoming year?
- What are the odds of your getting into graduate school in the field of your choice?

These questions ask you to make probability estimates. Amos Tversky and Daniel Kahneman (1982; Kahneman & Tversky, 2000) have conducted extensive research on the *heuristics,* or mental shortcuts, that people use in grappling with probabilities. This research on heuristics earned Kahneman the Nobel Prize in Economics in 2002 (unfortunately, his collaborator, Amos Tversky, died in 1996).

Availability is one such heuristic. **The *availability heuristic* involves basing the estimated probability of an event on the ease with which relevant instances come to mind.** For example, you may estimate the divorce rate by recalling the number of divorces among your friends' parents. Recalling specific instances of an event is a reasonable strategy to use in estimating the event's probability. However, if instances occur frequently but you have difficulty retrieving them from memory, your estimate will be biased. For instance, it's easier to think of words that begin with a certain letter than words that contain that letter at some other position. Hence, people should tend to respond that there are more words starting with the letter *K* than words having a *K* in

DANIEL KAHNEMAN

"The human mind suppresses uncertainty. We're not only convinced that we know more about our politics, our businesses, and our spouses than we really do, but also that what we don't know must be unimportant."

AMOS TVERSKY

"People treat their own cases as if they were unique, rather than part of a huge lottery. You hear this silly argument that 'The odds don't apply to me.' Why should God, or whoever runs this lottery, give you special treatment?"

Courtesy of Daniel Kahneman

Courtesy of Barbara Tversky

the third position. To test this hypothesis, Tversky and Kahneman (1973) selected five consonants (*K, L, N, R, V*) that occur more frequently in the third position of a word than in the first. Subjects were asked whether each of the letters appears more often in the first or third position. Most of the subjects erroneously believed that all five letters were much more frequent in the first than in the third position, confirming the hypothesis.

Representativeness is another guide in estimating probabilities identified by Kahneman and Tversky (1982). **The *representativeness heuristic* involves basing the estimated probability of an event on how similar it is to the typical prototype of that event.** To illustrate, imagine that you flip a coin six times and keep track of how often the result is heads (H) or tails (T). Which of the following sequences is more likely?

1. T T T T T T
2. H T T H T H

People generally believe that the second sequence is more likely. After all, coin tossing is a random affair, and the second sequence looks much more representative of a random process than the first. In reality, the probability of each exact sequence is precisely the same ($\frac{1}{2} \times \frac{1}{2} \times \frac{1}{2} \times \frac{1}{2} \times \frac{1}{2} \times \frac{1}{2} = \frac{1}{64}$). Overdependence on the representativeness heuristic has been used to explain quite a variety of decision making tendencies (Teigen, 2004), as you will see in the upcoming pages.

Ignoring Base Rates and the Conjunction Fallacy

PsykTrek
7f

Steve is very shy and withdrawn, invariably helpful, but with little interest in people or in the world of reality. A meek and tidy soul, he has a need for order and structure and a passion for detail. Do you think Steve is a salesperson or a librarian? (Adapted from Tversky & Kahneman, 1974, p. 1124)

Using the *representativeness heuristic,* participants tend to guess that Steve is a librarian because he resembles their prototype of a librarian (Tversky & Kahneman, 1982). In reality, this is not a very wise guess, because *it ignores the base rates* of librarians and salespeople in the population. Virtually everyone knows that salespeople outnumber librarians by a wide margin (roughly 75 to 1 in the United States). This fact makes it much more likely that Steve is in sales. But in estimating probabilities, people often ignore information on base rates.

Researchers are still debating how common it is for people to neglect base rate information (Birnbaum, 2004; Koehler, 1996), but it does not appear to be a rare event. Moreover, people are particularly bad about applying base rates to themselves. For example, people starting new companies ignore the high failure rate for new businesses, and burglars underestimate the likelihood that they will end up in jail. Thus, in risky decision making, people often think that they can beat the odds. As Amos Tversky put it, "People treat their own cases as if they were unique, rather than part of a huge lottery. You hear this silly argument that 'The odds don't apply to me.' Why should God, or whoever runs this lottery, give you special treatment?" (McKean, 1985, p. 27).

Let's look at another common mistake in decision-related reasoning. Imagine that you're going to meet a man who is an articulate, ambitious, power-hungry wheeler-dealer. Do you think it's more likely that he's a college teacher or a college teacher who's also a politician?

People tend to guess that the man is a "college teacher who's a politician" because the description fits with the typical prototype of politicians. But stop and think for a moment. The broader category of college teachers completely includes the smaller subcategory of college teachers who are politicians (see **Figure 8.13**). The probability of being in the subcategory cannot be higher than the probability of being in the broader category. It's a logical impossibility!

© Steve Kelley, *The Times Picayune.* Reprinted with permission.

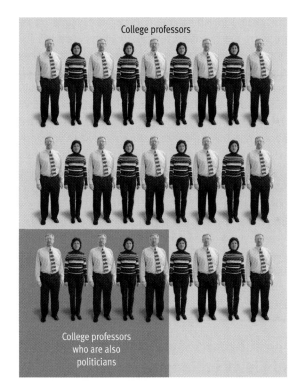

College professors

College professors who are also politicians

Figure 8.13
The conjunction fallacy. People routinely fall victim to the conjunction fallacy, but as this diagram makes obvious, the probability of being in a subcategory (college teachers who are politicians) cannot be higher than the probability of being in the broader category (college teachers). As this case illustrates, it often helps to represent a problem in a diagram.

Tversky and Kahneman (1983) call this error the *conjunction fallacy.* The *conjunction fallacy* occurs when people estimate that the odds of two uncertain events happening together are greater than the odds of either event happening alone. The conjunction fallacy has been observed in a number of studies and has generally been attributed to the powerful influence of the representativeness heuristic (Epstein, Donovan, & Denes-Raj, 1999).

The Gambler's Fallacy

Let's look at two more problems that often crop up when people work with probabilities. Consider the following scenario:

Laura is in a casino watching people play roulette. The 38 slots in the roulette wheel include 18 black numbers, 18 red numbers, and 2 green numbers. Hence, on any one spin, the probability of red or black is slightly less than 50–50 (.474 to be exact). Although Laura hasn't been betting, she has been following the pattern of results in the game very carefully. The ball has landed in red seven

times in a row. Laura concludes that black is long overdue and she jumps into the game, betting heavily on black.

Has Laura made a good bet? Do you agree with Laura's reasoning? Or do you think that Laura misunderstands the laws of probability? As you may have guessed by now, Laura's reasoning is flawed. A great many people tend to believe that Laura has made a good bet (Stanovich, 2003). However, they're wrong. Laura's behavior illustrates the *gambler's fallacy*—**the belief that the odds of a chance event increase if the event hasn't occurred recently.** People believe that the laws of probability should yield fair results and that a random process must be self-correcting (Burns & Corpus, 2004). These aren't bad assumptions in the long run. However, they don't apply to individual, independent events.

The roulette wheel does not remember its recent results and make adjustments for them. Each spin of the wheel is an independent event. The probability of black on each spin remains at .474, even if red comes up 100 times in a row! The gambler's fallacy reflects the pervasive influence of the *representativeness heuristic*. In betting on black, Laura is predicting that future results will be more representative of a random process. This logic can be used to estimate the probability of black across a *string of spins*. But it doesn't apply to a *specific spin* of the roulette wheel.

Overestimating the Improbable

Various causes of death are paired up below. In each pairing, which is the more likely cause of death?

Asthma or tornadoes?
Accidental falls or gun accidents?
Tuberculosis or floods?
Suicide or murder?

Table 8.2 shows the actual mortality rates for each of the causes of death just listed. As you can see, the first choice in each pair is the more common cause of death. If you guessed wrong for several pairings,

Table 8.2 Actual Mortality Rates for Selected Causes of Death

Cause of Death	Rate	Cause of Death	Rate
Asthma	2,000	Tornadoes	25
Accidental falls	6,021	Firearms accidents	320
Tuberculosis	400	Floods	44
Suicide	11,300	Homicide	6,800

Note: Mortality rates are per 100 million people and are based on the *Statistical Abstract of the United States, 2001.*

© Associated Press/AP

are readily available in memory because people are exposed to a great deal of publicity about such events.

As a general rule, people's beliefs about what they should fear tend to be surprisingly inconsistent with actual probabilities (Glassner, 1999). This propensity has been especially prominent in the aftermath of 9/11, which left countless people extremely worried about the possibility of being harmed in a terrorist attack (as the terrorists intended). To date, one's chances of being hurt in a terrorist attack are utterly microscopic in comparison to one's chances of perishing in an automobile accident, yet people worry about the former and not the latter (Myers, 2001). People tend to overestimate the likelihood of rare events when their estimates are based on descriptive information (such as media coverage) as opposed to when their estimates are based on personal experiences (Hertwig et al., 2004).

Evolutionary Analyses of Flaws in Human Decision Making

A central conclusion of the last 25 years of research on decision making has been that human decision-making strategies are riddled with errors and biases that yield surprisingly irrational results (Goldstein & Hogarth, 1997; Shafir & LeBoeuf, 2002). Theorists have discovered that people have "mental limitations" and have concluded that people are not as bright and rational as they think they are. Conversely, over the same period of time, researchers studying the foraging of animals in their natural en-

The availability heuristic can be dramatized by juxtaposing the unrelated phenomena of floods and tuberculosis (TB). Many people are killed by floods, but far more die from tuberculosis (see Table 8.2). However, since the news media report flood fatalities frequently and prominently, but rarely focus on deaths from tuberculosis, people tend to assume that flood-related deaths are more common.

don't feel bad. Like many other people, you may be a victim of the tendency to *overestimate the improbable.* People tend to greatly overestimate the likelihood of dramatic, vivid—but infrequent—events that receive heavy media coverage. Thus, the number of fatalities resulting from tornadoes, floods, firearms accidents, and murders is usually overestimated (Slovic, Fischoff, & Lichtenstein, 1982). Fatalities due to asthma and other common diseases, which receive less media coverage, tend to be underestimated. This tendency to exaggerate the improbable has generally been attributed to the operation of the *availability heuristic* (Reber, 2004). Instances of floods, tornadoes, and such

---

concept **check 8.2**

Recognizing Heuristics in Decision Making

Check your understanding of heuristics in decision making by trying to identify the heuristics used in the following example. Each numbered element in the anecdote below illustrates a problem-solving heuristic. Write the relevant heuristic in the space on the left. You can find the answers in Appendix A.

_____ **1.** Marsha can't decide on a college major. She evaluates all the majors available at her college on the attributes of how much she would enjoy them (likability), how challenging they are (difficulty), and how good the job opportunities are in the field (employability). She drops from consideration any major that she regards as "poor" on any of these three attributes.

_____ **2.** When she considers history as a major, she thinks to herself, "Gee, I know four history graduates who are still looking for work," and concludes that the probability of getting a job using a history degree is very low.

_____ **3.** She finds that every major gets a "poor" rating on at least one attribute, so she eliminates everything. Because this is unacceptable, she decides she has to switch to another strategy. Marsha finally focuses her consideration on five majors that received just one "poor" rating. She uses a 4-point scale to rate each of these majors on each of the three attributes she values. She totals the ratings and selects the major with the largest sum as her leading candidate.

vironments have been increasingly impressed by how the animals tend to make sound choices that approximate optimal decision making (Real, 1991; Shettleworth, 1998). So, we have quite a paradox: How can humans appear so dumb, when animals appear so bright? This paradox has led some evolutionary psychologists to reconsider the work on human decision making, and their take on the matter is quite interesting. First, they argue that traditional decision research has imposed an unrealistic standard of rationality, which assumes that people should be flawless in applying the laws of deductive logic and statistical probability while objectively and precisely weighing multiple factors in arriving at decisions (Gigerenzer, 2000). Second, they argue that humans only *seem* irrational because cognitive psychologists have presented subjects with contrived, artificial problems that have nothing to do with the real-world adaptive problems that the human mind has evolved to solve (Cosmides & Tooby, 1996).

For example, evolutionary psychologists argue that the human mind is wired to think in terms of *raw frequencies* rather than *base rates and probabilities* (Gigerenzer, 1997, 2000). Asking about the probability of a single event is routine in today's world, where we are flooded with statistical data ranging from batting averages to weather predictions. But our ancient ancestors had access to little data other than their own observations, which were accumulating counts of natural frequencies, such as "we had a good hunt three out of the last five times we went to the north plains." Thus, evolutionary theorists assert that many errors in human reasoning, such as neglect of base rates and the conjunction fallacy, should vanish if classic laboratory problems are reformulated in terms of raw frequencies rather than probabilities and base rates. Consistent with this analysis, evolutionary psychologists have shown that some errors in reasoning that are seen in laboratory studies disappear or are decreased when problems are presented in ways that resemble the type of input humans would have processed in ancestral times (Brase, Cosmides, & Tooby, 1998; Gigerenzer & Hoffrage, 1999).

Fast and Frugal Heuristics

To further expand on the evolutionary point of view, Gerd Gigerenzer has argued that humans' reasoning largely depends on "fast and frugal heuristics" that are quite a bit simpler than the complicated mental processes studied in traditional cognitive research (Gigerenzer, 2000, 2004; Goldstein & Gigerenzer, 1999; Todd & Gigerenzer, 2000). According to Gigerenzer, organisms from toads to stockbrokers have to

make fast decisions under demanding circumstances with limited information. In most instances organisms (including humans) do not have the time, resources, or cognitive capacities to gather all the relevant information, consider all the possible options, calculate all the probabilities and risks, and then make the statistically optimal decision. Instead, they use quick and dirty heuristics that are less than perfect but that work well enough most of the time to be adaptive in the real world.

To explore these fast and frugal heuristics, Gigerenzer and his colleagues have typically studied inferences from *memory,* which challenge participants to search some portion of their general knowledge, rather than inferences from *givens,* which challenge participants to draw logical conclusions from information provided by the experimenter. What has this research revealed? It has demonstrated that fast and frugal heuristics can be surprisingly effective. One heuristic that is often used in selecting between alternatives based on some quantitative dimension is the *recognition heuristic,* which works as follows: If one of two alternatives is recognized and the other is not, infer that the recognized alternative has the higher value. Consider the following questions— Which city has more inhabitants: San Diego or San Antonio? Hamburg or Munich? In choosing between U.S. cities, American college students weighed a lifetime of facts useful for inferring population and made the correct choice 71% of the time; in choosing between German cities about which they knew very little, the same students depended on the recognition heuristic and chose correctly 73% of the time (Goldstein & Gigerenzer, 2002). Thus, the recognition heuristic allowed students to perform just as well with very limited knowledge as they did with extensive knowledge.

Gigerenzer and his colleagues have studied a variety of other quick, one-reason decision-making strategies and demonstrated that they can yield inferences that are just as accurate as much more elaborate and time-consuming strategies that carefully weigh many factors. And they have demonstrated that people actually use these fast and frugal heuristics in a diverse array of situations (Gigerenzer & Todd, 1999; Rieskamp & Hoffrage, 1999). Thus, the study of fast and frugal heuristics promises to be an intriguing new line of research in the study of human decision making.

How have traditional decision making theorists responded to the challenge presented by Gigerenzer and other evolutionary theorists? They acknowledge that people often rely on fast and frugal heuristics, but they argue that this reality does not make decades of research on carefully reasoned approaches to decision making meaningless. Rather, they propose

Web Link 8.2

Has Natural Selection Shaped How Humans Reason?
This link will take you to a recorded talk by Leda Cosmides and John Tooby (University of California, Santa Barbara) in which they discuss their evolutionary perspective on human decision making.

Web Link 8.3

Simple Minds—Smart Choices
This link leads to an article from *Science News* on Gerd Gigerenzer's research, which suggests that decisions can be made quickly and accurately with remarkably simple strategies.

dual-process theories which posit that people depend on two very different modes or systems of thinking when making decisions (Kahneman, 2003; Kahneman & Frederick, 2005; Sloman, 2002; Stanovich & West, 2002). One system consists of quick, simple, effortless, automatic judgments, like Gigerenzer's fast and frugal heuristics, which traditional theorists prefer to characterize as "intuitive thinking." The second system consists of slower, more elaborate, effortful, controlled judgments, like those studied in traditional decision research. According to this view, the second system monitors and corrects the intuitive system as needed and takes over when complicated or important decisions loom. Thus, traditional theorists maintain that fast and frugal heuristics and

reasoned, rule-governed decision strategies exist side by side and that both need to be studied to fully understand decision making.

Although sound decision making and effective problem solving obviously are key aspects of intelligence, there has been relatively little overlap between research on cognition and research on intelligence. As you have seen, cognitive research investigates how people use their intelligence; the focus is on *process*. In contrast, the study of intelligence has usually been approached from a testing perspective, which emphasizes measuring the *amount* of intelligence people have and figuring out why some have more than others. Let's look at how these measurements are made.

> Measuring Intelligence

PREVIEW QUESTIONS

- When and how did intelligence testing begin?
- What types of items are found on IQ tests?
- What role does the normal distribution play in the scoring system for modern IQ tests?
- Are IQ tests reliable and valid?
- How well do IQ tests predict occupational attainment and job success?
- Do non-Western cultures make much use of IQ tests?

Web Link 8.4

Human Intelligence
A graphic approach to the history of intelligence testing is taken at this site, which uses colored arrows to show academic lineage and connections among various theorists. Maintained by Jonathan Plucker of Indiana University, this site covers all the major intelligence theorists and includes excellent discussions of such topics as the Flynn effect, *The Bell Curve* controversy, and Gardner's theory of multiple intelligences.

We'll begin our discussion with a brief overview of the history of intelligence testing and then we will address some practical questions about how intelligence tests work.

A Brief History

Intelligence tests were invented a little over a hundred years ago. The key breakthrough came in 1904, when a commission on education in France asked Alfred Binet to devise a test to identify mentally subnormal children. The commission wanted to single out youngsters in need of special training. It also wanted to avoid complete reliance on teachers' evaluations, which might often be subjective and biased. In response to this need, Binet and a colleague, Theodore Simon, created the first useful test of general mental ability in 1905. Their scale was a success because it was inexpensive, easy to administer, objective, and capable of predicting children's performance in school fairly well (Siegler, 1992). Thanks to these qualities, its use spread across Europe and America.

The Binet-Simon scale expressed a child's score in terms of "mental level" or "mental age." A child's *mental age* indicated that he or she displayed the mental ability typical of a child of that chronological (actual) age. Thus, a child with a mental age of 6 performed like the average 6-year-old on the test. Binet realized that his scale was a somewhat crude initial effort at measuring mental ability. He revised it in 1908 and again in 1911. Unfortunately, his revising came to an abrupt end with his death in

1911. However, other psychologists continued to build on Binet's work.

In America, Lewis Terman and his colleagues at Stanford University soon went to work on a major expansion and revision of Binet's test. Their work led to the 1916 publication of the Stanford-Binet Intelligence Scale (Terman, 1916). Although this revision was quite loyal to Binet's original conceptions, it incorporated a new scoring scheme based on the "intelligence quotient" suggested by William Stern (1914). **An *intelligence quotient (IQ)* is a child's mental age divided by chronological age, multiplied by 100.** IQ scores originally involved actual quotients, calculated as follows:

$$IQ = \frac{\text{Mental age}}{\text{Chronological age}} \times 100$$

The IQ ratio placed all children (regardless of age) on the same scale, which was centered at 100 if their mental age corresponded to their chronological age (see Table 8.3 for examples of IQ calculations).

Terman's technical and theoretical contributions to psychological testing were modest, but he made a convincing case for the educational benefits of testing and became the key force behind American schools' widespread adoption of IQ tests (Chapman, 1988). As a result of his efforts, the Stanford-Binet quickly became the world's foremost intelligence test and the standard of comparison for virtually all intelligence tests that followed (White, 2000). Today, it remains one of the world's most widely used psychological tests.

Table 8.3 Calculating the Intelligence Quotient

Measure	Child 1	Child 2	Child 3	Child 4
Mental age (MA)	6 years	6 years	9 years	12 years
Chronological age (CA)	6 years	9 years	12 years	9 years
$IQ = \dfrac{MA}{CA} \times 100$	$\dfrac{6}{6} \times 100 = 100$	$\dfrac{6}{9} \times 100 = 67$	$\dfrac{9}{12} \times 100 = 75$	$\dfrac{12}{9} \times 100 = 133$

Further advances in intelligence testing came from the work of David Wechsler (1939), who published the first high-quality IQ test designed specifically for *adults* in 1939. His test, the Wechsler Adult Intelligence Scale (WAIS), introduced two major innovations (Prifitera, 1994). First, Wechsler made his test less dependent on subjects' verbal ability than the Stanford-Binet. He included many items that required nonverbal reasoning. To highlight the distinction between verbal and nonverbal ability, he formalized the computation of separate scores for verbal IQ, performance (nonverbal) IQ, and full-scale (total) IQ. Examples of test items similar to those on the Wechsler scales are presented in **Figure 8.14** on the next page. Second, Wechsler discarded the intelligence quotient in favor of a new scoring scheme based on the *normal distribution.* This scoring system has since been adopted by most other IQ tests, including the Stanford-Binet. Although the term *intelligence quotient* lingers on in our vocabulary, scores on intelligence tests are no longer based on an actual quotient, as you will see momentarily.

Today, psychologists and educators have many IQ tests available for their use. Most IQ testing is conducted by school districts, which are largely free to formulate their own unique testing programs. There is little federal or state policy regarding ideal patterns of testing. Some districts administer group intelligence tests to all students at regular intervals. Others administer individual intelligence tests only on an occasional basis, as needed. Schools use intelligence tests to screen for mental retardation, to group students according to their academic ability ("tracking"), to identify gifted children, and to evaluate educational programs.

What Kinds of Questions Are on Intelligence Tests?

The nature of the questions found on IQ tests varies somewhat from test to test. These variations depend on whether the test is intended for children or adults (or both) and whether the test is designed for individuals or groups. Overall, the questions are fairly diverse in format. The Wechsler scales, with their numerous subtests, provide a representative example of the kinds of items that appear on most IQ tests. As you can see in **Figure 8.14**, the items in the Wechsler subtests require respondents to furnish information, recognize vocabulary, and demonstrate basic memory. Generally speaking, examinees are required to manipulate words, numbers, and images through abstract reasoning.

What Do Modern IQ Scores Mean?

7c

As we discussed, scores on intelligence tests once represented a ratio of mental age to chronological age. However, this system has given way to one based on the normal distribution and the *standard deviation,* a statistical index of variability in a data distribution, which is explained in Appendix B. **The *normal distribution* is a symmetrical, bell-shaped curve that represents the pattern in which many characteristics are dispersed in the population.** When a trait is normally distributed, most cases fall near the center of the distribution, and the number of cases gradually declines as one moves away from the center in either direction. The normal distribution provides a precise way to measure how people stack up in comparison to one another. The scores under the normal curve are dispersed in a fixed pattern, with the standard deviation serving as the unit of measurement (see **Figure 8.15** on page 253). About 68% of the scores in the distribution fall within one standard deviation of the mean, whereas 95% of the scores fall within two standard deviations of the mean. Given this fixed pattern, if you know the mean and standard deviation of a normally distributed trait, you can tell where any score falls in the distribution for the trait. The normal distribution was first discovered by 18th-century astronomers. They found that their measurement errors were distributed in a predictable way that resembled a bell-shaped curve. Since then, research has shown that many human

ALFRED BINET

"The intelligence of anyone is susceptible of development. With practice, enthusiasm, and especially with method one can succeed in increasing one's attention, memory, judgment, and in becoming literally more intelligent than one was before."

LEWIS TERMAN

"It is the method of tests that has brought psychology down from the clouds and made it useful to men; that has transformed the 'science of trivialities' into the 'science of human engineering.'"

© Bettmann/Corbis

Archives of the History of American Psychology, University of Akron

Wechsler Adult Intelligence Scale (WAIS)		
Test	**Description**	**Example**
Verbal scale		
Information	Taps general range of information	On what continent is France?
Comprehension	Tests understanding of social conventions and ability to evaluate past experience	Why are children required to go to school?
Arithmetic	Tests arithmetic reasoning through verbal problems	How many hours will it take to drive 150 miles at 50 miles per hour?
Similarities	Asks in what way certain objects or concepts are similar; measures abstract thinking	How are a calculator and a typewriter alike?
Digit span	Tests attention and rote memory by orally presenting series of digits to be repeated forward or backward	Repeat the following numbers backward: 2 4 3 5 1 8 6
Vocabulary	Tests ability to define increasingly difficult words	What does audacity mean?
Performance scale		
Digit symbol	Tests speed of learning through timed coding tasks in which numbers must be associated with marks of various shapes	Shown: Fill in: 
Picture completion	Tests visual alertness and visual memory through presentation of an incompletely drawn figure; the missing part must be discovered and named	Tell me what is missing: 
Block design	Tests ability to perceive and analyze patterns by presenting designs that must be copied with blocks	Assemble blocks to match this design: 
Picture arrangement	Tests understanding of social situations through a series of comic-strip-type pictures that must be arranged in the right sequence to tell a story	Put the pictures in the right order: 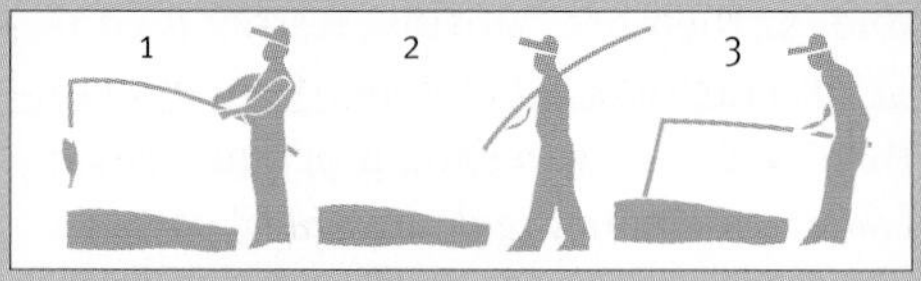
Object assembly	Tests ability to deal with part/whole relationships by presenting puzzle pieces that must be assembled to form a complete object	Assemble the pieces into a complete object: 

Figure 8.14

Subtests on the Wechsler Adult Intelligence Scale (WAIS). The WAIS is divided into scales that yield separate verbal and performance (nonverbal) IQ scores. The verbal scale consists of six subtests and the performance scale is made up of five subtests. Examples of low-level (easy) test items that closely resemble those on the WAIS are shown on the right.

traits, ranging from height to running speed to spatial ability, follow a normal distribution.

Psychologists eventually recognized that intelligence scores also fall into a normal distribution. This insight permitted David Wechsler to devise a more sophisticated scoring system for his tests that has been adopted by virtually all subsequent IQ tests. In this system, raw scores are translated into *deviation IQ scores* **that locate respondents precisely within the normal distribution.** For most IQ tests, the mean of the distribution is set at 100 and the standard deviation (SD) is set at 15. These choices were made to provide continuity with the original IQ ratio (mental age to chronological age) that was centered at

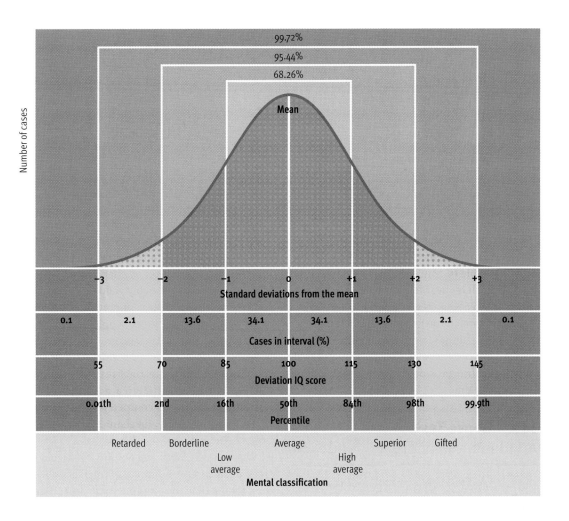

Figure 8.15

The normal distribution. Many characteristics are distributed in a pattern represented by this bell-shaped curve. The horizontal axis shows how far above or below the mean a score is (measured in plus or minus standard deviations). The vertical axis is used to graph the number of cases obtaining each score. In a normal distribution, the cases are distributed in a fixed pattern. For instance, 68.26% of the cases fall between –1 and +1 standard deviation. Modern IQ scores indicate where a person's measured intelligence falls in the normal distribution. On most IQ tests, the mean is set at an IQ of 100 and the standard deviation at 15. Any deviation IQ score can be converted into a percentile score. The mental classifications at the bottom of the figure are descriptive labels that roughly correspond to ranges of IQ scores.

100. In this system, which is depicted in **Figure 8.15**, a score of 115 means that a person scored exactly one SD (15 points) above the mean. A score of 85 means that a person scored one SD below the mean. A score of 100 means that a person showed average performance. *The key point is that modern IQ scores indicate exactly where you fall in the normal distribution of intelligence.* Thus, a score of 120 does not indicate that you answered 120 questions correctly. Nor does it mean that you have 120 "units" of intelligence. A deviation IQ score places you at a specific point in the normal distribution of intelligence (based on the norms for your age group). Deviation IQ scores can be converted into *percentile scores,* as shown in **Figure 8.15**. A *percentile score* indicates the percentage of people who score at or below the score one has obtained.

Do Intelligence Tests Have Adequate Reliability?

In the jargon of psychological testing, *reliability* refers to the measurement consistency of a test. A reliable test is one that yields similar results on repetition. Like other types of measuring devices, such as a stopwatch or a tire gauge, psychological tests need to be reasonably reliable. Estimates of reliability require the computation of correlation coefficients, which we introduced in Chapter 2. As you may recall, a *correlation coefficient* is a numerical index of the degree of relationship between two variables (see **Figure 8.16** on the next page). In gauging a test's reliability, the two variables that are correlated typically are two sets of scores from two administrations of the test. Do IQ tests produce consistent results when people are retested? Yes. Most IQ tests report commendable reliability estimates. The correlations generally range into the .90s (Kaufman, 2000), which is very high. In comparison to most other types of psychological tests, IQ tests are exceptionally reliable.

However, like other tests, they *sample* behavior, and a specific testing may yield an unrepresentative score. Variations in examinees' motivation to take an IQ test or in their anxiety about the test can sometimes produce misleading scores (Hopko et al., 2005; Zimmerman & Woo-Sam, 1984). The most common problem is that low motivation or high anxiety

Archives of the History of American Psychology, University of Akron

DAVID WECHSLER
"The subtests [of the WAIS] are different measures of intelligence, not measures of different kinds of intelligence."

Figure 8.16

Correlation and reliability. As explained in Chapter 2, a positive correlation means that two variables co-vary in the *same* direction; a negative correlation means that two variables co-vary in the *opposite* direction. The closer the correlation coefficient gets to either –1.00 or +1.00, the stronger the relationship. At a minimum, reliability estimates for psychological tests must be moderately high positive correlations. Most reliability coefficients fall between .70 and .95.

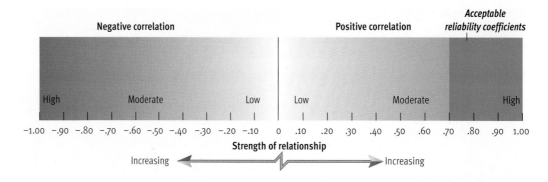

may drag a person's score down on a particular occasion. For instance, a fourth-grader who is made to feel that the test is extremely important may get jittery and be unable to concentrate. The same child might score much higher on a subsequent testing by another examiner who creates a more comfortable atmosphere. Although the reliability of IQ tests is excellent, caution is always in order in interpreting test scores. IQ scores should be viewed as estimates that are accurate within plus or minus 5 points about two-thirds of the time.

Do Intelligence Tests Have Adequate Validity?

SIM8, 7b

Even if a test is quite reliable, we still need to be concerned about its validity. *Validity* **refers to the ability of a test to measure what it was designed to measure.** Validity can be estimated in several ways, depending on the nature of the test (Golden, Sawicki, & Franzen, 1990). In measuring an abstract personal quality such as intelligence, one needs to be concerned about the test's *construct validity*. Do intelligence tests measure what they're supposed to measure? Yes, but this answer has to be qualified very carefully. IQ tests are valid measures of the kind of intelligence that's necessary to do well in academic work. But if the purpose is to assess intelligence in a broader sense, the validity of IQ tests is questionable.

As you may recall, intelligence tests were originally designed with a relatively limited purpose in mind: to predict school performance. This has continued to be the principal purpose of IQ testing. Efforts to document the validity of IQ tests have usually concentrated on their relationship to grades in school. Typically, positive correlations in the .50s are found between IQ scores and school grades (Kline, 1991). Even higher correlations (between .60 and .80) are found between IQ scores and the number of years of school that people complete (Ceci, 1991).

These correlations are about as high as one could expect, given that many factors besides a person's

intelligence are likely to affect grades and school progress. For example, school grades may be influenced by a student's motivation, diligence, or personality, not to mention teachers' subjective biases. Thus, IQ tests are reasonably valid indexes of school-related intellectual ability, or academic intelligence.

However, over the years people have mistakenly come to believe that IQ tests measure mental ability in a truly general sense. In reality, IQ tests have always focused on the abstract reasoning and verbal fluency that are essential to academic success. The tests do not tap social competence, practical problem solving, creativity, mechanical ingenuity, or artistic talent.

When Robert Sternberg and his colleagues (1981) asked people to list examples of intelligent behavior, they found that the examples fell into three categories: (1) *verbal intelligence,* (2) *practical intelligence,* and (3) *social intelligence* (see **Figure 8.17**). Thus, people generally recognize three basic types of intelligence. For the most part, IQ tests assess only the first of these three types. Although IQ tests are billed as measures of *general* mental ability, they actually focus somewhat narrowly on a specific type of intelligence: academic/verbal intelligence (Sternberg, 1998; 2003b).

Do Intelligence Tests Predict Vocational Success?

Vocational success is a vague, value-laden concept that's difficult to quantify. Nonetheless, researchers have attacked this question by examining correlations between IQ scores and specific indicators of vocational success, such as the prestige of subjects' occupations or ratings of subjects' job performance. The data relating IQ to occupational attainment are pretty clear. People who score high on IQ tests are more likely than those who score low to end up in high-status jobs (Gottfredson, 2003b; Herrnstein & Murray, 1994; Schmidt & Hunter, 2004). Because IQ tests measure school ability fairly well and school

Web Link 8.5

Educational Psychology Interactive: Intelligence
This site, maintained by Bill Huitt of Valdosta State University, leads to a helpful review of psychological approaches to intelligence and is an excellent resource for other topics in educational psychology.

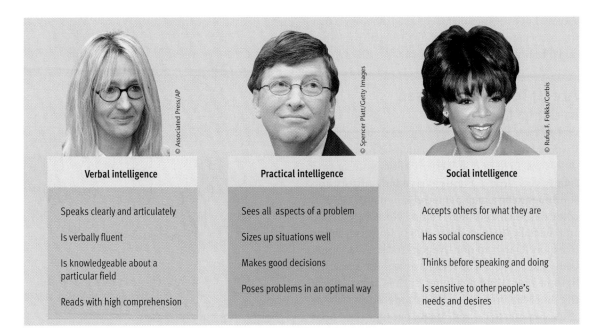

Verbal intelligence	Practical intelligence	Social intelligence
Speaks clearly and articulately	Sees all aspects of a problem	Accepts others for what they are
Is verbally fluent	Sizes up situations well	Has social conscience
Is knowledgeable about a particular field	Makes good decisions	Thinks before speaking and doing
Reads with high comprehension	Poses problems in an optimal way	Is sensitive to other people's needs and desires

Figure 8.17

Laypersons' conceptions of intelligence. Robert Sternberg and his colleagues (1981) asked participants to list examples of behaviors characteristic of intelligence. The examples tended to sort into three groups that represent the three types of intelligence recognized by the average person: verbal intelligence, practical intelligence, and social intelligence. The three well-known individuals shown here are prototype examples of verbal intelligence (J. K. Rowling), practical intelligence (Bill Gates), and social intelligence (Oprah Winfrey).

Source: Adapted from Sternberg, R. J., Conway, B. E., Keton, J. L., & Bernstein, M. (1981). People's conceptions of intelligence. *Journal of Personality and Social Psychology, 41* (1), 37–55. Copyright © 1981 by the American Psychological Association. Adapted by permission of the publisher and authors.

performance is important in attaining certain occupations, this link between IQ scores and job status makes sense. Of course, the correlation between IQ and occupational attainment is moderate, and there are plenty of exceptions to the general trend. Some people plow through the educational system with bulldog determination and hard work, in spite of limited ability as measured by IQ tests. Such people may go on to prestigious jobs, while people who are brighter (according to their test results), but less motivated, settle for lower-status jobs.

There is considerable debate, however, about whether IQ scores are effective predictors of performance within a particular occupation. On the one hand, research suggests that (a) there is a substantial correlation (about .50) between IQ scores and job performance, (b) this correlation varies somewhat depending on the complexity of a job's requirements but does not disappear even for low-level jobs (see **Figure 8.18**), (c) this association holds up even when workers have more experience at their jobs, and (d) measures of specific mental abilities and personality traits are much less predictive of job performance than measures of intelligence (Gottfredson, 2002; Ones, Viswesvaran, Dilchert, 2005; Schmidt, 2002). On the other hand, critics argue that the reported correlations have usually been corrected for statistical artifacts and that the raw, uncorrected correlations are lower (.30s) (Outtz, 2002), and they note that even a correlation of .50 would provide only modest accuracy in prediction (accounting for about 25% of the variation in job performance) (Goldstein, Zedeck, & Goldstein, 2002; Sternberg & Hedlund,

2002). Critics have also questioned the validity of the supervisory ratings that have typically been used as an index of job performance (Tenopyr, 2002). Concerns have also been raised that when IQ tests are used for job selection they can have an adverse impact on employment opportunities for those in many minority groups who tend to score somewhat lower (on average) on such tests (Murphy, 2002; Outtz, 2002). In the final analysis, there is no question that intelligence is associated with vocational

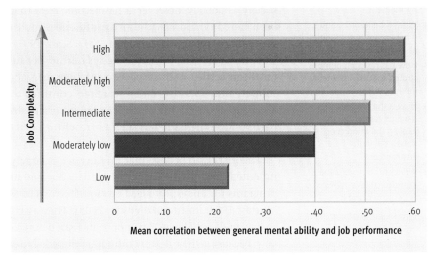

Figure 8.18

Intelligence as a predictor of job performance. Based on a review of 425 studies, Schmidt and Hunter (2004) report that the correlation between general mental ability and job performance depends on the complexity of the job. As jobs become more complicated, intelligence becomes a better predictor of performance. Schmidt and Hunter conclude that these correlations show that IQ tests can be valuable in hiring decisions. However, as the text explains, some other experts have reservations about using intelligence tests in employee selection. (Based on data from Schmidt & Hunter, 2004)

success, but there is room for argument about whether this association is strong enough to justify reliance on IQ testing in hiring employees.

Are IQ Tests Widely Used in Other Cultures?

In other Western cultures with European roots the answer is yes. In most non-Western cultures, the answer is only very little. IQ testing has a long history and continues to be a major enterprise in many Western countries, such as Britain, France, Norway, Canada, and Australia (Irvine & Berry, 1988). However, efforts to export IQ tests to non-Western societies have met with mixed results. The tests have been well received in some non-Western cultures, such as Japan, where the Binet-Simon scales were introduced as early as 1908 (Iwawaki & Vernon, 1988), but they have been met with indifference or resistance in other cultures, such as China and India (Chan & Vernon, 1988; Sinha, 1983). One reason is that some cultures have different conceptions of what intelligence is and value different mental skills (Das, 1994; Sternberg &

"YOU CAN'T BUILD A HUT, YOU DON'T KNOW HOW TO FIND EDIBLE ROOTS AND YOU KNOW NOTHING ABOUT PREDICTING THE WEATHER. IN OTHER WORDS, YOU DO TERRIBLY ON OUR I.Q. TEST."

Kaufman, 1998). Thus, the bottom line is that Western IQ tests do not translate well into the language and cognitive frameworks of many non-Western cultures (Berry, 1994; Sternberg, 2004).

> Heredity and Environment as Determinants of Intelligence

PREVIEW QUESTIONS

- What types of evidence suggest that intelligence is inherited?
- What is heritability, and what are some limitations of heritability estimates?
- How has research demonstrated that environment influences IQ?
- How is the concept of reaction range used to explain the interaction of heredity and environment?
- What are some explanations for cultural differences in average IQ scores?

Most early pioneers of intelligence testing maintained that intelligence is inherited (Cravens, 1992). Small wonder, then, that this view lingers on in our society. Gradually, however, it has become clear that both heredity and environment influence intelligence (Bartels et al., 2002; Plomin, 2003; Scarr, 1997). Does this mean that the nature versus nurture debate has been settled with respect to intelligence? Absolutely not. Theorists and researchers continue to argue vigorously about which is more important, in part because the issue has such far-reaching social and political implications.

Theorists who believe that intelligence is largely inherited downplay the value of special educational programs for underprivileged groups (Herrnstein & Murray, 1994; Rushton & Jensen, 2005). They assert that a child's intelligence cannot be increased noticeably, because genetic destiny cannot be altered. Other theorists take issue with this argument, pointing out that traits with a strong genetic component are not necessarily unchangeable (Sternberg, Grigorenko, & Kidd, 2005; Wahlsten, 1997). The people in this camp maintain that even more funds should be devoted to remedial education programs, improved schooling in lower-class neighborhoods, and college financial aid for the underprivileged. Because the debate over

the role of heredity in intelligence has direct relevance to important social issues and political decisions, we'll take a detailed look at this complex controversy.

Evidence for Hereditary Influence

Researchers have long been aware that intelligence runs in families. However, *family studies* can determine only whether genetic influence on a trait is *plausible*, not whether it is certain. Family members share not just genes, but similar environments. If high intelligence (or low intelligence) appears in a family over several generations, this consistency could reflect the influence of either shared genes or shared environment. Because of this problem, researchers must turn to *twin studies* and *adoption studies* to obtain more definitive evidence on whether heredity affects intelligence.

Twin Studies

The best evidence regarding the role of genetic factors in intelligence comes from studies that compare identical and fraternal twins. The rationale for twin studies is that both identical and fraternal twins normally develop under similar environmental conditions. However, identical twins share more genetic kinship than fraternal twins. Hence, if pairs of identical twins are more similar in intelligence than pairs of fraternal twins, it's presumably because of their greater genetic similarity. (See Chapter 3 for a more detailed explanation of the logic underlying twin studies.)

What are the findings of twin studies regarding intelligence? McGue and colleagues (1993) reviewed the results of over 100 studies of intellectual similarity for various kinds of kinship relations and child-rearing arrangements. The key findings from their review are highlighted in **Figure 8.19**. This figure plots the average correlation observed for various types of relationships. As you can see, the average correlation reported for identical twins (.86) is very high, indicating that identical twins tend to be quite similar in intelligence. The average correlation for fraternal twins (.60) is significantly lower. This correlation indicates that fraternal twins also tend to be similar in intelligence, but noticeably less similar than identical twins. These results support the notion that intelligence is inherited to a considerable degree (Bouchard, 1998; Plomin & Spinath, 2004).

Of course, critics have tried to poke holes in this line of reasoning. They argue that identical twins are more alike in IQ because parents and others treat them more similarly than they treat fraternal twins. This environmental explanation of the findings has

some merit. After all, identical twins are always the same sex, and gender influences how a child is raised. However, this explanation seems unlikely in light of the evidence on identical twins reared apart as a result of family breakups or adoption (Bouchard, 1997; Bouchard et al., 1990). *Although reared in different environments,* these identical twins still display greater similarity in IQ (average correlation: .72) than fraternal twins reared together (average correlation: .60).

Adoption Studies

Research comparing adopted children to their biological parents also provides evidence about the effects of heredity (and of environment, as we shall see). If adopted children resemble their biological parents in intelligence even though they were not reared by these parents, this finding supports the genetic hypothesis. The relevant studies indicate that there is indeed some measurable similarity between adopted children and their biological parents (Turkheimer, 1991) (refer again to **Figure 8.19**).

Heritability Estimates

Various experts have sifted through mountains of correlational evidence to estimate the *heritability* of intelligence. A *heritability ratio* is an estimate of the proportion of trait variability in a population that is determined by variations in genetic inheritance. Heritability can be estimated for any trait. For

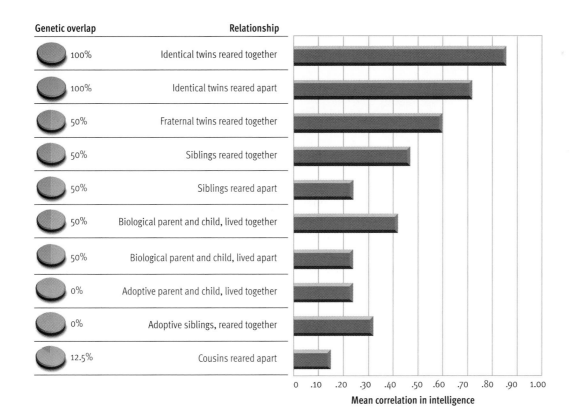

Genetic overlap	Relationship
100%	Identical twins reared together
100%	Identical twins reared apart
50%	Fraternal twins reared together
50%	Siblings reared together
50%	Siblings reared apart
50%	Biological parent and child, lived together
50%	Biological parent and child, lived apart
0%	Adoptive parent and child, lived together
0%	Adoptive siblings, reared together
12.5%	Cousins reared apart

Mean correlation in intelligence

Figure 8.19

Studies of IQ similarity. The graph shows the mean correlations of IQ scores for people of various types of relationships, as obtained in studies of IQ similarity. Higher correlations indicate greater similarity. The results show that greater genetic similarity is associated with greater similarity in IQ, suggesting that intelligence is partly inherited (compare, for example, the correlations for identical and fraternal twins). However, the results also show that living together is associated with greater IQ similarity, suggesting that intelligence is partly governed by environment (compare, for example, the scores of siblings reared together and reared apart). (Data from McGue et al., 1993)

example, the heritability of height is estimated to be around 90% (Plomin, 1994). Heritability estimates for intelligence vary (see **Figure 8.20**). At the high end, some theorists estimate that the heritability of IQ ranges as high as 80% (Bouchard, 2004; Jensen, 1980, 1998). That is, they believe that only about 20% of the variation in intelligence is attributable to environmental factors. Estimates at the low end of the spectrum suggest that the heritability of intelligence is around 40% (Plomin, 2003). In recent years, the consensus estimates of the experts tend to hover around 50% (Petrill, 2005; Plomin & Spinath, 2004).

However, it's important to understand that heritability estimates have certain limitations (Ceci et al., 1997; Grigorenko, 2000; Reeve & Hakel, 2002). First, a heritability estimate is a *group statistic* based on studies of trait variability within a specific group. A heritability estimate cannot be applied meaningfully to *individuals*. In other words, even if the heritability of intelligence truly is 60%, this does not mean that each individual's intelligence is 60% inherited. Second, the heritability of a specific trait may vary from one group to another depending on a variety of factors. To date, heritability estimates for intelligence have been based largely on research with white, middle-class subjects. Hence, they should be applied only to such groups.

Evidence for Environmental Influence

Heredity unquestionably influences intelligence, but a great deal of evidence indicates that upbringing also affects mental ability. We'll examine three lines of research—concerning adoption, environmental deprivation or enrichment, and generational changes in IQ—that show how life experiences shape intelligence.

Adoption Studies

Research with adopted children provides useful evidence about the impact of experience as well as heredity (Locurto, 1990; Loehlin, Horn, & Willerman, 1997). Many of the correlations in **Figure 8.19** reflect the influence of the environment. For example, adopted children show some resemblance to their foster parents in IQ. This similarity is usually attributed to the fact that their foster parents shape their environment. Adoption studies also indicate that siblings reared together are more similar in IQ than siblings reared apart. This is true even for identical twins. Moreover, entirely unrelated children who are raised in the same home also show a significant resemblance in IQ. All of these findings indicate that environment influences intelligence.

Environmental Deprivation and Enrichment

If environment affects intelligence, then children who are raised in substandard circumstances should experience a gradual decrease in IQ as they grow older (since other children will be progressing more rapidly). This *cumulative deprivation hypothesis* was tested decades ago. Researchers studied children consigned to understaffed orphanages and children raised in the poverty and isolation of the back hills of Appalachia (Sherman & Key, 1932; Stoddard, 1943). Generally, investigators *did* find that environmental deprivation led to the predicted decline in IQ scores. Conversely, children who are removed from a deprived environment and placed in circumstances

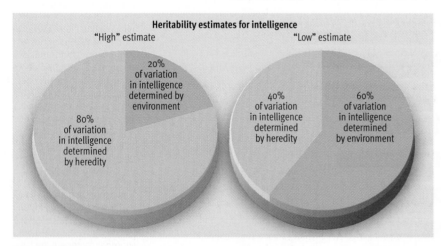

Figure 8.20

The concept of heritability. A heritability ratio is an estimate of the portion of variation in a trait determined by heredity—with the remainder presumably determined by environment—as these pie charts illustrate. Heritability estimates for intelligence range between a high of 80% and a low of 40%. The consensus estimate tends to hover around 50%. Bear in mind that heritability ratios are *estimates* and have certain limitations that are discussed in the text.

"I don't know anything about the bell curve, but I say heredity is everything."

© The New York Collection 1994 Charles Barsotti from cartoonbank.com. All rights reserved

more conducive to learning tend to benefit from their environmental enrichment (Scarr & Weinberg, 1977, 1983; Schiff & Lewontin, 1986). These findings show that environment influences IQ.

Generational Changes: The Flynn Effect

The most interesting, albeit perplexing, evidence showcasing the importance of the environment is the finding that performance on IQ tests has steadily increased over generations. This trend was not widely appreciated until recently because the tests are revised periodically with new samples and scoring adjustments so that the mean IQ always remains at 100. However, in a study of the IQ tests used by the U.S. military, James Flynn noticed that the level of performance required to earn a score of 100 jumped upward every time the scoring was adjusted. Curious about this unexpected finding, he eventually gathered extensive data from 20 nations and demonstrated that IQ performance has been rising steadily all over the industrialized world since the 1930s (Flynn, 1987, 1994, 1999, 2003). Researchers who study intelligence are now scrambling to explain this trend, which has been dubbed the "Flynn effect." About the only thing they mostly agree on is that the Flynn effect has to be attributed to environmental factors, as the modern world's gene pool could not have changed overnight (in evolutionary terms, 70 years is more like a fraction of a second) (Dickens & Flynn, 2001; Neisser, 1998; Sternberg et al., 2005).

At this point, the proposed explanations for the Flynn effect are conjectural, but it is worth reviewing some of them, as they highlight the diversity of environmental factors that may shape IQ performance. Some theorists attribute generational gains in IQ test performance to reductions in the prevalence of severe malnutrition among children (Colom, Lluis-Font, & Andres-Pueyo, 2005; Sigman & Whaley, 1998). Others attribute the Flynn effect to increased access to schooling and more demanding curricula in schools over the course of the last century (Blair et al., 2005). Patricia Greenfield (1998) argues that advances in technology, including much maligned media such as television and video games, have enhanced visuospatial skills and other specific cognitive skills that contribute to performance on IQ tests. Wendy Williams (1998) discusses the importance of a constellation of factors, including improved schools, smaller families, better-educated parents, and higher-quality parenting. All of these speculations have some plausibility and are not mutually exclusive. Thus, the causes of the Flynn effect remain under investigation.

concept check 8.3

Understanding Correlational Evidence on the Heredity-Environment Question

Check your understanding of how correlational findings relate to the nature versus nurture issue by indicating how you would interpret the meaning of each "piece" of evidence described below. The figures inside the parentheses are the median IQ correlations observed for the relationships described (based on McGue et al., 1993), which are shown in **Figure 8.19**.

In the spaces on the left, enter the letter H if the findings suggest that intelligence is shaped by heredity, enter the letter E if the findings suggest that intelligence is shaped by the environment, and enter the letter B if the findings suggest that intelligence is shaped by both (or either) heredity and environment. The answers can be found in Appendix A.

_____ 1. Identical twins reared apart are more similar (.72) than fraternal twins reared together (.60).

_____ 2. Identical twins reared together are more similar (.86) than identical twins reared apart (.72).

_____ 3. Siblings reared together are more similar (.47) than siblings reared apart (.24).

_____ 4. Biological parents and the children they rear are more similar (.42) than unrelated persons who are reared apart (no correlation if sampled randomly).

_____ 5. Adopted children show similarity to their biological parents (.24) and to their adoptive parents (.24).

The Interaction of Heredity and Environment

Clearly, heredity and environment both influence intelligence to a significant degree (Dickens & Flynn, 2001; Petrill, 2005). Indeed, many theorists now assert that the question of which is more important ought to take a backseat to the question of *how they interact* to govern IQ.

The current thinking is that heredity may set certain limits on intelligence and that environmental factors determine where individuals fall within these limits (Bouchard, 1997; Weinberg, 1989). According to Sandra Scarr, a prominent advocate of this position, genetic makeup places an upper limit on a person's IQ that can't be exceeded even when environment is ideal. Heredity is also thought to place a lower limit on an individual's IQ, although extreme circumstances (for example, being locked in an attic for years) could drag a person's IQ beneath this boundary. Theorists use the term *reaction range* to **refer to these genetically determined limits on IQ (or other traits).**

According to the reaction-range model, children reared in high-quality environments that promote

SANDRA SCARR

"My research has been aimed at asking in what kind of environments genetic differences shine through and when do they remain hidden."

ARTHUR JENSEN

"Despite more than half a century of repeated efforts by psychologists to improve the intelligence of children, particularly those in the lower quarter of the IQ distribution relative to those in the upper half of the distribution, strong evidence is still lacking as to whether or not it can be done."

the development of intelligence should score near the top of their potential IQ range. Children reared under less ideal circumstances should score lower in their reaction range. The reaction range for most people is *estimated* to be around 20–25 points on the IQ scale (Weinberg, 1989). The concept of a reaction range can explain why high-IQ children sometimes come from poor environments. It can also explain why low-IQ children sometimes come from very good environments (see **Figure 8.21**). Moreover, it can explain these apparent paradoxes without discounting the role that environment undeniably plays.

Cultural Differences in IQ Scores

Although the full range of IQ scores is seen in all ethnic groups, the average IQ for many of the larger minority groups in the United States (such as blacks, Native Americans, and Hispanics) is somewhat lower than the average for whites. The disparity ranges from 3 to 15 points, depending on the group tested and the IQ scale used (Loehlin, 2000; Nisbett, 2005; Perlman & Kaufman, 1990; Suzuki & Vraniak, 1994). There is little argument about the existence of these group differences, variously referred to as racial, ethnic, or cultural differences in intelligence. The controversy concerns *why* the differences are found. A vigorous debate continues as to whether cultural differences in intelligence are due to the influence of heredity or of environment.

Jensen's Heritability Explanation

In 1969 Arthur Jensen sparked a heated war of words by arguing that racial differences in average IQ are largely due to heredity. The cornerstone for Jensen's argument was his analysis suggesting that the heritability of intelligence is about 80%. Essentially, he asserted that (1) intelligence is largely genetic in origin, and (2) therefore, genetic factors are "strongly implicated" as the cause of ethnic differences in intelligence. Jensen's article triggered outrage and bitter criticism in many quarters, as well as a great deal of additional research on the determinants of intelligence. Twenty-five years later, Richard Herrnstein and Charles Murray (1994) reignited the same controversy with the publication of their widely discussed book *The Bell Curve*. They argued that ethnic differences in average intelligence are substantial, not easily reduced, and at least partly genetic in origin. The implicit message throughout *The Bell Curve* was that disadvantaged groups cannot avoid their fate because it is their genetic destiny. And as recently as 2005, based on an extensive review of statistical evidence, J. Phillipe Rushton and Arthur Jensen argued that genetic factors account for about half of the gap between races in average IQ, a conclusion that was echoed by Linda Gottfredson (2005).

As you might guess, these analyses and conclusions have elicited many lengthy and elaborate rebuttals. Critics argue that heritability explanations for ethnic differences in IQ have a variety of flaws and weaknesses (Brody, 2003; Devlin et al., 2002; Horn, 2002; Nisbett, 2005; Sternberg, 2003b, 2005). For example, recent research suggests that the heritability of intelligence may be notably lower in samples drawn from the lower socioeconomic classes as opposed to higher socioeconomic classes (Turkheimer et al., 2003). However, heritability estimates for intelligence have largely been based on samples drawn from white, middle-class, North American and Euro-

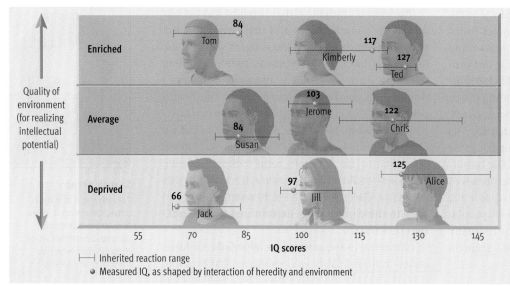

Figure 8.21

Reaction range. The concept of reaction range posits that heredity sets limits on one's intellectual potential (represented by the horizontal bars), while the quality of one's environment influences where one scores within this range (represented by the dots on the bars). People raised in enriched environments should score near the top of their reaction range, whereas people raised in poor-quality environments should score near the bottom of their range. Genetic limits on IQ can be inferred only indirectly, so theorists aren't sure whether reaction ranges are narrow (like Ted's) or wide (like Chris's). The concept of reaction range can explain how two people with similar genetic potential can be quite different in intelligence (compare Tom and Jack) and how two people reared in environments of similar quality can score quite differently (compare Alice and Jack).

pean populations (Grigerenko, 2000). Hence, there is doubt about the validity of applying these heritability estimates to other cultural groups.

Moreover, even if one accepts the assumption that the heritability of IQ is very high, it does not follow logically that differences in group averages must be due largely to heredity. Leon Kamin has presented a compelling analogy that highlights the logical fallacy in this reasoning (see **Figure 8.22**):

We fill a white sack and a black sack with a mixture of different genetic varieties of corn seed. We make certain that the proportions of each variety of seed are identical in each sack. We then plant the seed from the white sack in fertile Field A, while that from the black sack is planted in barren Field B. We will observe that within Field A, as within Field B, there is considerable variation in the height of individual corn plants. This variation will be due largely to genetic factors (seed differences). We will also observe, however, that the average height of plants in Field A is greater than that in Field B. That difference will be entirely due to environmental factors (the soil). The same is true of IQs: differences in the average IQ of various human populations could be entirely due to environmental differences, even if within each population all variation were due to genetic differences! (Eysenck & Kamin, 1981, p. 97)

Kamin's analogy shows that even if the heritability of intelligence is high, group differences in average IQ *could* still be caused entirely (or in part) by environmental factors (Block, 2002). For decades, critics

of Jensen's thesis have relied on this analogy rather than actual data to make the point that between-groups differences in IQ do not necessarily reflect genetic differences. They depended on the analogy because there were no relevant data available. However, the recent discovery of the Flynn effect has provided compelling new data that are directly relevant (Dickens & Flynn, 2001; Flynn, 2003). Generational gains in IQ scores show that a between-groups disparity in average IQ (in this case the gap is between generations rather than ethnic groups) can be environmental in origin, even though intelligence is highly heritable.

Socioeconomic Disadvantage as an Explanation

Many social scientists argue that minority students' IQ scores are depressed because these children tend to grow up in deprived environments that create a disadvantage—both in school and on IQ tests. There is no question that, on the average, whites and minorities tend to be raised in very different circumstances. Most minority groups have endured a long history of economic discrimination and are greatly overrepresented in the lower social classes. A lower-class upbringing tends to carry a number of disadvantages that work against the development of a youngster's full intellectual potential (Evans, 2004; Lareau, 2003; Lott, 2002; McLoyd, 1998; Seifer, 2001). In comparison to children from the middle and upper classes, lower-class children tend to be exposed to fewer books, to have fewer learning supplies, to have less privacy for concentrated study, and to get less parental assistance in learning. Typically, they also have poorer role models for language development, experience less pressure to work hard on intellectual pursuits, and attend poorer-quality schools.

In light of these disadvantages, it's not surprising that average IQ scores among children from lower social classes tend to run about 15 points below the average scores obtained by children from middle- and upper-class homes (Seifer, 2001; Williams & Ceci, 1997). This is the case even if race is factored out of the picture by studying whites exclusively. Admittedly, there is room for argument about the direction of the causal relationships underlying this association between social class and intelligence. Nonetheless, given the overrepresentation of minorities in the lower classes, many researchers argue that ethnic differences in intelligence are really social class differences in disguise.

The debate about cultural differences in intelligence illustrates how IQ tests have often become entangled in thorny social conflicts. This situation is

Web Link 8.6

Upstream—Issues: *The Bell Curve*
The editors of *Upstream*, champions of "politically incorrect" conversation, have assembled perhaps the broadest collection of commentaries on the net regarding Herrnstein and Murray's *The Bell Curve.* In spite of the marked political conservatism of this site, it contains a full range of opinion and analyses of the book.

Individual variation in corn plant heights within each group (cause: genetic variation in the seeds)

SEED

Field A:
More fertile soil

Field B:
Less fertile soil

Differences in average corn plant height between groups (cause: the soils in which the plants were grown)

Figure 8.22
Genetics and between-group differences on a trait. Leon Kamin's analogy (see text) shows how between-group differences on a trait (the average height of corn plants) could be due to environment, even if the trait is largely inherited. The same reasoning presumably applies to ethnic group differences in average intelligence.

unfortunate, because it brings politics to the testing enterprise. Intelligence testing has many legitimate and valuable uses. However, the controversy associated with intelligence tests has undermined their value, leading to some of the new trends that we discuss in the next section.

PREVIEW QUESTIONS

- Do measures of mental speed correlate with intelligence?
- Does IQ correlate with brain size or longevity?
- What are the key features of Sternberg's theory of successful intelligence?
- What is Gardner's thesis about the nature of intelligence?

Intelligence testing has been through a period of turmoil, and changes are on the horizon. In fact, many changes have occurred already. Let's discuss some of the major new trends and projections for the future.

Exploring Biological Indexes of Intelligence

The controversy about cultural disparities in intelligence has led to increased interest in biological indexes of intelligence. Arthur Jensen (1987, 1993b, 1998), Hans Eysenck (1988, 1989), and other researchers have attempted to find raw physiological indicators of general intelligence. Their search for a "culture-free" measure of intelligence has led them to focus on sensory processes.

Jensen's (1982, 1987, 1992) studies of mental speed are representative of this line of inquiry. In his studies, Jensen uses a panel of buttons and lights to measure participants' *reaction times* (RTs) to specific stimuli, which are typically averaged over a number of trials. Modest correlations (.20s to .30s) have been found between faster RTs and higher scores on conventional IQ tests (Deary, 2003). These correlations are theoretically interesting, but too weak to give RTs any practical value as an index of intelligence.

However, another approach to measuring mental speed may have more practical potential. Measures of *inspection time* assess how long it takes participants to make simple perceptual discriminations that meet a certain criterion of accuracy (Deary & Stough, 1996). A person's inspection time is the exposure duration required for that person to achieve a specific level of accuracy, such as 85% correct judgments. Correlations in the .40s have been found between participants' inspection time scores and their IQ scores (Deary, 2000). These correlations are high enough to have some practical potential, although a great deal of work remains to be done to standardize inspection time measures.

Some researchers have also begun to explore the relations between intelligence and brain size. The early studies in this area used various measures of

head size as an indicator of brain size. These studies generally found positive but small correlations (average = .15) between head size and IQ (Vernon et al., 2000), leading researchers to speculate that head size is probably a very crude index of brain size. This line of research might have languished, but the invention of sophisticated brain-imaging technologies gave it a huge shot in the arm. Since the 1990s, quite a few studies have examined the correlation between IQ scores and measures of brain volume based on MRI scans (see Chapter 3), yielding an average correlation of about .35 (Anderson, 2003; McDaniel, 2005). One obvious implication of these findings, eagerly embraced by those who tout the influence of heredity on intelligence, is that genetic inheritance gives some people larger brains than others and that larger brain size promotes greater intelligence (Rushton, 2003). However, as always, we must be cautious about interpreting correlational data. As discussed in Chapter 3, research has demonstrated that an enriched environment can produce denser neural networks and heavier brains in laboratory rats (Rosenzweig & Bennett, 1996). Hence, it is also possible that causation runs in the opposite direction—that developing greater intelligence promotes larger brain size, much like weight lifting can promote larger muscles.

Investigating Cognitive Processes in Intelligent Behavior

Investigators interested in intelligence and scholars who have studied cognition traditionally have pursued separate lines of research that only rarely have intersected. However, since the mid-1980s Robert Sternberg (1985, 1988b, 1991) has spearheaded an effort to apply a cognitive perspective to the study of intelligence. His *triarchic theory of human intelligence* consists of three parts: the contextual, experiential, and componential subtheories (see **Figure 8.23**). In his *contextual subtheory*, Sternberg argues that intelligence is a culturally defined concept. He asserts that

Courtesy of Robert Sternberg

ROBERT STERNBERG

"To understand intelligent behavior, we need to move beyond the fairly restrictive tasks that have been used both in experimental laboratories and in psychometric tests of intelligence."

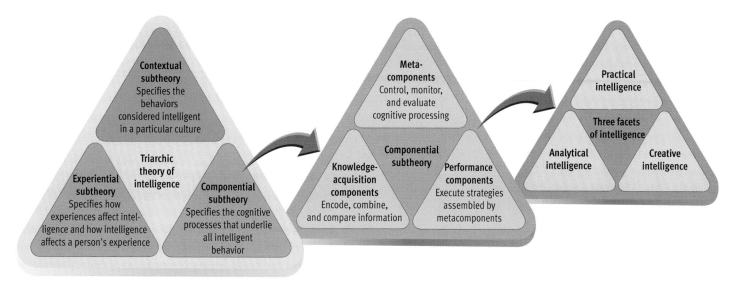

Figure 8.23

Sternberg's triarchic theory of intelligence. Sternberg's model of intelligence consists of three parts: the contextual subtheory, the experiential subtheory, and the componential subtheory. Much of Sternberg's research has been devoted to the componential subtheory, as he has attempted to identify the cognitive processes that contribute to intelligence. He believes that these processes fall into three groups: metacomponents, performance components, and knowledge-acquisition components. All three component processes contribute to each of three aspects or types of intelligence: analytical intelligence, practical intelligence, and creative intelligence.

different manifestations of intelligent behavior are valued in different contexts. In his *experiential subtheory,* Sternberg explores the relationships between experience and intelligence. He emphasizes two factors as the hallmarks of intelligent behavior. The first is the ability to deal effectively with novelty—new tasks, demands, and situations. The second factor is the ability to learn how to handle familiar tasks automatically and effortlessly. Sternberg's *componential subtheory* describes the types of mental processes that intelligent thought depends on (see **Figure 8.23**). This part of the theory has guided extensive research on the specific thinking strategies that contribute to intelligent problem solving.

In more recent extensions of his theory, Sternberg (1999, 2000b, 2003a) has asserted that there are three aspects or facets of intelligence: analytical intelligence, creative intelligence, and practical intelligence. *Analytical intelligence* involves abstract reasoning, evaluation, and judgment. It is the type of intelligence that is crucial to most school work and that is assessed by conventional IQ tests. *Creative intelligence* involves the ability to generate new ideas and to be inventive in dealing with novel problems. *Practical intelligence* involves the ability to deal effectively with the kinds of problems that people encounter in everyday life, such as on the job or at home. A big part of practical intelligence involves learning what one needs to know to work efficiently in an environ-

ment that is not explicitly taught and that often is not even verbalized.

In a series of studies, Sternberg and his colleagues have gathered data which suggest that (1) all three facets of intelligence can be measured reliably, (2) the three facets of intelligence are relatively independent (uncorrelated), and (3) the assessment of all three aspects of intelligence can improve the prediction of intelligent behavior in the real world (Grigorenko & Sternberg, 2001; Henry, Sternberg, & Grigorenko, 2005). Some critics doubt that Sternberg's measures will facilitate better prediction of meaningful outcomes than traditional IQ tests (Gottfredson, 2003a), but that is an empirical question that should be resolved by future research. In any event, Sternberg certainly has been an articulate voice arguing for a broader, expanded concept of intelligence, which is a theme that has been echoed by others.

Expanding the Concept of Intelligence

In recent years, many theorists have concluded that traditional IQ tests are too narrow in focus. This view has been articulated particularly well by Howard Gardner (1983, 1993, 1999, 2004). According to Gardner, IQ tests have generally emphasized verbal and mathematical skills, to the exclusion of other important

HOWARD GARDNER

"It is high time that the view of intelligence be widened to incorporate a range of human computational capacities. . . . But where is it written that intelligence needs to be determined on the basis of tests?"

Table 8.4 Gardner's Eight Intelligences

Intelligence	End-States	Core Components
Logical-mathematical	Scientist Mathematician	Sensitivity to, and capacity to discern, logical or numerical patterns; ability to handle long chains of reasoning
Linguistic	Poet Journalist	Sensitivity to the sounds, rhythms, and meanings of words; sensitivity to the different functions of language
Musical	Composer Violinist	Abilities to produce and appreciate rhythm, pitch, and timbre; appreciation of the forms of musical expressiveness
Spatial	Navigator Sculptor	Capacities to perceive the visual-spatial world accurately and to perform transformations on one's initial perceptions
Bodily-kinesthetic	Dancer Athlete	Abilities to control one's body movements and to handle objects skillfully
Interpersonal	Therapist Salesperson	Capacities to discern and respond appropriately to the moods, temperaments, motivations, and desires of other people
Intrapersonal	Person with detailed, accurate self-knowledge	Access to one's own feelings and the ability to discriminate among them and draw upon them to guide behavior; knowledge of one's own strengths, weaknesses, desires, and intelligences
Naturalist	Biologist Naturalist	Abilities to recognize and categorize objects and processes in nature

Source: Adapted from Gardner, H., & Hatch, T. (1989). Multiple intelligences go to school: Educational implications of the theory of multiple intelligences. *Educational Researcher, 18* (8), 4–10. American Educational Research Association. Additional information from Gardner (1998).

Should outstanding motor coordination be considered a form of intelligence? Howard Gardner argues for the recognition of eight intelligences, including bodily-kinesthetic intelligence. However, some critics assert that Gardner's view broadens the concept of intelligence to such a degree that it borders on meaningless.

© Associated Press/AP

skills. He suggests the existence of a number of relatively independent *human intelligences,* which are listed in **Table 8.4.** To build his list of separate intelligences, Gardner reviewed the evidence on cognitive capacities in normal individuals, people suffering from brain damage, and special populations, such as prodigies and idiot savants. He concluded that humans exhibit eight largely independent intelligences: logical-mathematical, linguistic, musical, spatial, bodily-kinesthetic, interpersonal, intrapersonal, and naturalist. These intelligences obviously include a variety of talents that are not assessed by conventional IQ tests.

Gardner's books have been very popular and his theory clearly resonates with many people (Shearer, 2004). His ideas have had an enormous impact on educators' attitudes and beliefs around the world (Cuban, 2004; Kornhaber, 2004). He has raised thought-provoking questions about what abilities should be included under the rubric of intelligence (Eisner, 2004). However, he has his critics (Hunt, 2001; Klein, 1997; Morgan, 1996). Some argue that his use of the term intelligence is so broad, encompassing virtually any valued human ability, it makes the term almost meaningless. These critics wonder whether there is any advantage to relabeling talents such as musical ability and motor coordination as forms of intelligence. Critics also note that Gardner's theory has not generated much research on the predictive value of measuring individual differences in the eight intelligences he has described. This research would require the development of tests to measure the eight intelligences, but Gardner is not particularly interested in the matter of assessment and he loathes conventional testing. This situation makes it difficult to predict where Gardner's theory will lead, as research is crucial to the evolution of a theory.

Recognizing Theories of Intelligence

Check your understanding of various theories on the nature of intelligence by matching the names of their originators with the brief descriptions of the theories' main themes that appear below. Choose from the following theorists: (a) Lewis Terman, (b) Howard Gardner, (c) Arthur Jensen, (d) Sandra Scarr, and (e) Robert Sternberg. The answers are in Appendix A.

_____ **1.** This theorist posited eight human intelligences.

_____ **2.** This theorist stated that the heritability of intelligence is about 80% and that IQ differences between ethnic groups are mainly due to genetics.

_____ **3.** This theorist stated that heredity sets certain limits on intelligence and that environmental factors determine where one falls within those limits.

_____ **4.** This person's theory of intelligence is divided into three parts: the contextual, experiential, and componential subtheories and proposes three facets of intelligence: analytical, practical, and creative intelligence.

Web Link 8.7

HowardGardner.com
A wealth of resources on Gardner's theory of multiple intelligences can be found at this site, including biographical information on Gardner, seminal and recent papers on his multiple intelligence perspective, and links to other relevant sites.

> Reflecting on the Chapter's Themes

Five of our unifying themes surfaced in this chapter. The first is the empirical nature of psychology. For many decades, psychologists paid little attention to cognitive processes, because most of them assumed that thinking is too private to be studied scientifically. During the 1950s and 1960s, however, psychologists began to devise creative new ways to measure mental processes. These innovations, which fueled the cognitive revolution, show that empirical methods are the lifeblood of the scientific enterprise.

Second, our review of cognition and intelligence demonstrated the importance of cultural factors. For example, we learned that there are striking cultural variations in cognitive style. We also saw that intelligence testing is largely a Western phenomenon and that ethnic differences in average intelligence may be largely cultural in origin. Thus, we see once again that if we hope to achieve a sound understanding of behavior, we need to appreciate the cultural contexts in which behavior unfolds.

Third, our coverage showed that intelligence is shaped by a complex interaction of hereditary and environmental factors. We've drawn a similar conclusion before in other chapters where we examined other topics. However, this chapter should have enhanced your appreciation of this idea by illustrating in detail how scientists arrive at this conclusion.

Fourth, we saw more evidence that psychology evolves in a sociohistorical context. Prevailing social attitudes have always exerted some influence on testing practices and the interpretation of test results. In the first half of the 20th century, a strong current of racial and class prejudice was apparent in the United States and Britain. This prejudice supported the idea that IQ tests measured innate ability and that "undesirable" groups scored poorly because of their genetic inferiority. Although these beliefs did not go unchallenged within psychology, their widespread acceptance in the field reflected the social values of the time. Today, the continuing, ferocious debate about the roots of cultural differences in intelligence shows that issues in psychology often have far-reaching social and political implications.

The final theme apparent in this chapter was the subjective nature of human experience, which was prominent in our discussion of peculiarities in human decision making.

 Empiricism

 Cultural Heritage

 Heredity and Environment

 Sociohistorical Context

 Subjectivity of Experience

Measuring and Understanding Creativity

Answer the following "true" or "false":

____ 1 Creative ideas often come out of nowhere.

____ 2 Creativity usually occurs in a burst of insight.

____ 3 Creativity and intelligence are unrelated.

Intelligence is not the only type of mental ability that psychologists have studied. They have devised tests to explore a variety of mental abilities. Among these, creativity is certainly one of the most interesting. People tend to view creativity as an essential trait for artists, musicians, and writers, but it is important in *many* walks of life. In this Application, we'll discuss psychologists' efforts to measure and understand creativity. As we progress, you'll learn that all the statements above are false.

The Nature of Creativity

What makes thought creative? *Creativity* **involves the generation of ideas that are original, novel, and useful.** Creative thinking is fresh, innovative, and inventive. But novelty by itself is not enough. In addition to being unusual, creative thinking must be adaptive. It must be appropriate to the situation and problem.

Does Creativity Occur in a Burst of Insight?

It is widely believed that creativity usually involves sudden flashes of insight and great leaps of imagination. Robert Weisberg (1986) calls this belief the "Aha! myth." Undeniably, creative bursts of insight do occur (Feldman, 1988). However, the evidence suggests that major creative achievements generally are logical extensions of existing ideas, involving long, hard work and many small, faltering steps forward (Weisberg, 1993). Creative ideas do not come out of nowhere. They come from a deep well of experience and training in a specific area, whether it's music,

painting, business, or science (Weisberg, 1999). As Snow (1986) puts it, "Creativity is not a light bulb in the mind, as most cartoons depict it. It is an accomplishment born of intensive study, long reflection, persistence, and interest" (p. 1033).

Does Creativity Depend on Divergent Thinking?

According to many theorists, the key to creativity lies in *divergent thinking*—thinking "that goes off in different directions," as J. P. Guilford (1959) put it. Guilford distinguished between convergent thinking and divergent thinking. **In convergent thinking one tries to narrow down a list of alternatives to converge on a single correct answer.** For example, when you take a multiple-choice exam, you try to eliminate incorrect options until you hit on the correct response. Most training in school encourages convergent thinking. **In divergent thinking one tries to expand the range of alternatives by generating many possible solutions.** Imagine that you work for an advertising agency. To come up with as many slogans as possible for a client's product, you must use divergent thinking. Some of your slogans may be clear losers, and eventually you will have to engage in convergent thinking to pick the best, but coming up with the range of new possibilities depends on divergent thinking.

Thirty years of research on divergent thinking has yielded mixed results. As a whole, the evidence suggests that divergent thinking contributes to creativity, but it clearly does not represent the essence of creativity, as originally proposed (Brown, 1989; Plucker & Renzulli, 1999). In retrospect, it was unrealistic to expect creativity to depend on a single cognitive skill.

Measuring Creativity

Although its nature may be elusive, creativity clearly is important in today's world.

Creative masterpieces in the arts and literature enrich human existence. Creative inventions fuel technological progress. Thus, it is understandable that psychologists have been interested in measuring creativity with psychological tests.

How Do Psychological Tests Assess Creativity?

A diverse array of psychological tests have been devised to measure individuals' creativity (Cooper, 1991). Usually, the items on creativity tests give respondents a specific starting point and then require them to generate as many possibilities as they can in a short period of time. Typical items on a creativity test might include the following: (1) List as many uses as you can for a newspaper. (2) Think of as many fluids that burn as you can. (3) Imagine that people no longer need sleep and think of as many consequences as you can. Participants' scores on these tests depend on the *number* of alternatives they generate and on the *originality* and *usefulness* of the alternatives.

How Well Do Tests Predict Creative Productivity?

In general, studies indicate that creativity tests are mediocre predictors of creative achievement in the real world (Hocevar & Bachelor, 1989; Plucker & Renzulli, 1999). Why? One reason is that these tests measure creativity in the abstract, as a *general trait*. However, the accumulation of evidence suggests that *creativity is specific to particular domains* (Amabile, 1996; Feist, 2004; Kaufman & Baer, 2002, 2004). Despite some rare exceptions, creative people usually excel in a single field, in which they typically have considerable training and expertise (Policastro & Gardner, 1999). An innovative physicist might have no potential to be a creative poet. Measuring this person's creativity outside of physics may be meaningless.

Even if better tests of creativity were devised, predicting creative achievement would probably still prove difficult. Why? Because creative achievement depends on many factors besides creativity. Creative productivity over the course of an individual's career will depend on his or her motivation, personality, and intelligence, as well as on situational factors, including training, mentoring, and good fortune (Amabile, 1983; Feldman, 1999).

Correlates of Creativity

What are creative people like? Are they brighter or less well adjusted than average? A great deal of research has been conducted on the correlates of creativity.

Is There a Creative Personality?

Creative people exhibit the full range of personality traits, but investigators have found modest correlations between certain personality characteristics and creativity (Ochse, 1990). Based on a meta-analysis of over 80 studies, Feist (1998) concludes that highly creative people "are more autonomous, introverted, open to new experiences, norm-doubting, self-confident, self-accepting, driven, ambitious, dominant, hostile, and

impulsive" (p. 299). At the core of this set of personality characteristics are the related traits of independence and nonconformity. Creative people tend to think for themselves and are less easily influenced by the opinions of others than the average person is. Sternberg and Lubart (1992) also suggest that creative people are willing to grow and change and willing to take risks.

Are Creativity and Intelligence Related?

Are creative people exceptionally smart? Conceptually, creativity and intelligence represent different types of mental ability. Thus, it's not surprising that measures of creativity and measures of intelligence are only weakly related (Sternberg & O'Hara, 1999). They're not entirely unrelated, however, as creativity in most fields requires a minimum level of intelligence. Hence, most highly creative people are probably above average in intelligence (Simonton, 1999a).

Is There a Connection Between Creativity and Mental Illness?

There may be a connection between truly exceptional creativity and mental illness—

in particular, mood disorders such as depression. When Andreasen (1987) studied 30 accomplished writers who had been invited as visiting faculty to the prestigious Iowa Writers Workshop, she found that 80% of her sample had suffered a mood disorder at some point in their lives. In a similar study of 59 female writers from another writers' conference, Ludwig (1994) found that 56% had experienced depression. These figures are far above the base rate (roughly 15%) for mood disorders in the general population. Other studies have also found an association between creativity and the prevalence of psychological disorders (Frantom & Sherman, 1999; Jamison, 1988; Ludwig, 1998; Post, 1996; Schildkraut, Hirshfeld, & Murphy, 1994). Perhaps the most ambitious examination of the issue has been Arnold Ludwig's (1995) analyses of the biographies of 1,004 people who achieved eminence in 18 fields. He found greatly elevated rates of depression and other disorders among eminent writers, artists, and composers (see Figure 8.24). Thus, accumulating empirical data tentatively suggest that there may be a correlation between major creative achievement and vulnerability to mental disorders.

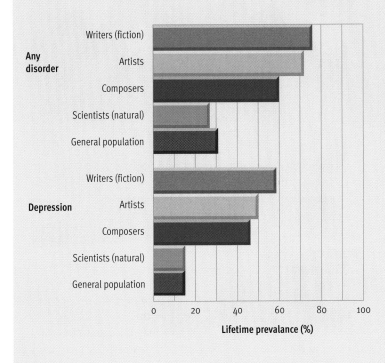

Figure 8.24

Estimated prevalence of psychological disorders among people who achieved creative eminence. Ludwig (1995) studied biographies of 1,004 people who had clearly achieved eminence in one of 18 fields and tried to determine whether each person suffered from any specific mental disorders in their lifetimes. The data summarized here show the prevalence rates for depression and for a mental disorder of any kind for four fields where creativity is often the key to achieving eminence. As you can see, the estimated prevalence of mental illness was extremely elevated among eminent writers, artists, and composers (but not natural scientists) in comparison to the general population, with depression accounting for much of this elevation.

The Intelligence Debate, Appeals to Ignorance, and Reification

A *fallacy* is a mistake or error in the process of reasoning. Cognitive scientists who study how people think have long lists of common errors that people make in their reasoning processes. One of these fallacies has a curious name, which is the *appeal to ignorance*. It involves misusing the general lack of knowledge or information on an issue (a lack of knowledge is a kind of ignorance) to support an argument. This fallacy often surfaces in the debate about the relative influence of heredity and environment on intelligence. Before we tackle the more difficult issue of how this fallacy shows up in the debate about intelligence, let's start with a simpler example.

Do ghosts exist? This is probably not the kind of question you expected to find in your psychology textbook, but it can clarify the appeal to ignorance. Those who assert that ghosts *do* exist will often support their conclusion by arguing that no one can prove that ghosts do *not* exist; therefore, ghosts must exist. The lack of evidence or inability to show that ghosts do not exist is used to conclude the opposite. Conversely, those who assert that ghosts *do not* exist often rely on the same logic. They argue that no one can prove that ghosts exist; therefore, they must not exist. Can you see what is wrong with these appeals to ignorance? The lack of information on an issue cannot be used to support any conclusion—other than the conclusion that we are too ignorant to draw a conclusion.

One interesting aspect of the appeal to ignorance is that the same appeal can be used to support two conclusions that are diametrically opposed to each other. This paradox is a telltale clue that appeals to ignorance involve flawed reasoning. It is easy to see what is wrong with appeals to ignorance when the opposite arguments (ghosts exist—ghosts do not exist) are presented together and the lack of evidence on the issue under discussion is obvious. However, when the same fallacy surfaces in more complex debates and the appeal to ignorance is not as blatant, the strategy can be more difficult to recognize. Let's look at how the appeal to ignorance has been used in the debate about intelligence.

As you saw in the main body of the chapter, the debate about the relative contributions of nature and nurture to intelligence is one of psychology's longest-running controversies. This complex debate is exceptionally bitter because it has far-reaching social and political repercussions. In this debate, one argument that has frequently been made is that we have little or no evidence that intelligence can be increased by environmental (educational) interventions; therefore, intelligence must be mostly inherited. In other words, the argument runs: No one has demonstrated that intelligence is largely shaped by environment, so it must be largely inherited. This argument was part of Jensen's (1969) landmark treatise that greatly intensified the debate about intelligence, and it was one of the arguments made by Herrnstein and Murray (1994) in their controversial book, *The Bell Curve*. What the argument refers to is the evidence that educational enrichment programs such as Head Start, which have been designed to enhance the intellectual development of underprivileged children, generally have not produced substantial, long-term gains in IQ (Neisser et al.,

Do ghosts exist? Littledean Hall, shown below, is said to be the home of 11 ghosts and is reputed to be the most haunted house in Great Britain. Those who believe in ghosts often support their view by arguing that no one can prove that ghosts do not exist. But as your text explains, this appeal to ignorance is logically flawed. This fallacy has also surfaced in some of the debates about the nature of intelligence.

© Simon Marsden/marsdenarchive.com

1996). The programs produce other benefits, including enduring improvements in school achievement, but short-term gains in IQ scores typically have faded by the middle grades (Barnett. 2004). These findings may have some important implications for government policy in the educational arena, but the way in which they have been applied to the nature-nurture debate regarding intelligence has resulted in an appeal to ignorance. In its simplest form, the absence of evidence showing that environmental changes can increase intelligence is used to support the conclusion that intelligence is mostly determined by genetic inheritance. But the absence of evidence (ignorance) cannot be used to argue for or against a position.

By the way, if you have assimilated some of the critical thinking skills discussed in earlier chapters you may be thinking, "Wait a minute. Aren't there alternative explanations for the failure of educational enrichment programs to increase IQ scores?" Yes, one could argue that the programs failed to yield the expected increments in IQ scores because they were poorly planned, poorly executed, too brief, or underfunded (Ramey, 1999; Sigel, 2004). The inability of the enrichment programs to produce enduring increases in IQ does not necessarily imply that intelligence is unchangeable because it is largely a product of heredity. You may also be wondering, "Aren't there contradictory data?" Once again, the answer is yes. Some lesser-known educational enrichment programs attempted with smaller groups of children *have* yielded durable gains in IQ scores or other measures of academic achievement (Ramey & Ramey, 2004; Reynolds et al., 2001; Woodhead, 2004).

The dialogue on intelligence has also been marred by the tendency to engage in reification. *Reification* **occurs when a hypothetical, abstract concept is given a name and then treated as though it were a concrete, tangible object.** Some hypothetical constructs just become so familiar and so taken for granted that we begin to think about them as if they were real. People often fall into this trap with the Freudian personality concepts of id, ego, and superego (see Chapter 11). They begin to think of the *ego,* for instance, as a genuine entity that can be strengthened or controlled, when the ego is really nothing more than a hypothetical abstraction. The concept of intelligence has also been reified in many quarters. Like the ego, intelligence is nothing more than a useful abstraction—a hypothetical construct that is estimated, rather arbitrarily, by a collection of paper-and-pencil measures called IQ tests. Yet people routinely act as if intelligence is a tangible commodity, fighting vitriolic battles over whether it can be measured precisely, whether it can be changed, and whether it can ensure job success. This reification clearly contributes to the tendency for people to attribute excessive importance to the concept of intelligence. It would be wise to remember that intelligence is no more real than the concept of "environment" or "cyberspace" or "the American dream."

Reification has also occurred in the debate about the degree to which intelligence is inherited. Arguments about the heritability coefficient for intelligence often imply that there is a single, true number lurking somewhere "out there" waiting to be discovered. In reality, heritability is a hypothetical construct that can be legitimately estimated in several ways that can lead to somewhat different results. Moreover, heritability ratios will vary from one population to the next, depending on the amount of genetic variability and the extent of environmental variability in the populations.

Reification occurs when we think of hypothetical constructs as if they were real. Like intelligence, the concept of cyberspace has been subject to reification. The fact that cyberspace is merely an abstraction becomes readily apparent when artists are asked to "draw" cyberspace for conference posters or book covers.

No exactly accurate number that corresponds to "true heritability" awaits discovery. Thus, it is important to understand that hypothetical constructs have great heuristic value in the study of complex phenomena such as human thought and behavior, but they do not actually exist in the world—at least not in the same way that a table or a person exists.

Table 8.5 **Critical Thinking Skills Discussed in This Application**

Skill	Description
Recognizing and avoiding appeals to ignorance	The critical thinker understands that the lack of information on an issue cannot be used to support an argument.
Recognizing and avoiding reification	The critical thinker is vigilant about the tendency to treat hypothetical constructs as if they were concrete things.
Looking for alternative explanations for findings and events	In evaluating explanations, the critical thinker explores whether there are other explanations that could also account for the findings or events under scrutiny.
Looking for contradictory evidence	In evaluating the evidence presented on an issue, the critical thinker attempts to look for contradictory evidence that may have been left out of the debate.

Key Ideas

Problem Solving: In Search of Solutions

● Psychologists have differentiated among several types of problems, including problems of inducing structure, problems of transformation, and problems of arrangement. Common barriers to problem solving include functional fixedness, mental set, getting bogged down in irrelevant information, and placing unnecessary constraints on one's solutions.

● Besides trial and error, a variety of heuristics are used for solving problems, including forming subgoals, searching for analogies, and changing the representation of a problem. Some cultures encourage a field-dependent cognitive style, whereas others foster more field independence. Research suggests that Eastern cultures exhibit a more holistic cognitive style, whereas Western cultures display a more analytic cognitive style.

Decision Making: Choices and Chances

● Simon's theory of bounded rationality suggests that human decision strategies are simplistic and often yield irrational results. In their decisions about preferences, people use additive models and elimination by aspects, and their evaluations of options tend to be less stable than assumed. In making decisions, comparative evaluations of options often yield different results than separate evaluations.

● People use the representativeness and availability heuristics in estimating probabilities. These heuristics can lead people to ignore base rates and to fall for the conjunction fallacy. The use of the representativeness heuristic contributes to the gambler's fallacy. The availability heuristic underlies the tendency to overestimate the improbable.

● Evolutionary psychologists maintain that many errors and biases in human reasoning are greatly reduced when problems are presented in ways that resemble the type of input humans would have processed in ancestral times. Gigerenzer argues that people largely depend on fast and frugal decision heuristics that are adaptive in the real world.

Measuring Intelligence

● Modern intelligence testing began with the work of Alfred Binet, who devised a scale to measure a child's mental age. Lewis Terman revised the original Binet scale to produce the Stanford-Binet, which became the standard of comparison for subsequent intelligence tests. David Wechsler devised an improved measure of intelligence for adults and a new scoring system based on the normal distribution.

● Intelligence tests contain a diverse mixture of questions. In the modern scoring system, deviation IQ scores indicate where people fall in the normal distribution of intelligence for their age group. IQ tests are exceptionally reliable. They are reasonably valid measures of academic intelligence, but they do not tap social or practical intelligence.

● IQ scores are correlated with occupational attainment, but doubts have been raised about how well they predict performance within an occupation. IQ tests are not widely used in most non-Western cultures.

Heredity and Environment as Determinants of Intelligence

● The empirical evidence clearly shows that intelligence is influenced by both heredity and environment. Estimates of the heritability of intelligence range from 40% to 80%, but heritability ratios have certain limitations. The concept of reaction range posits that heredity places limits on one's intellectual potential and the environment determines where one falls within these limits.

● Genetic explanations for cultural differences in IQ have been challenged on a variety of grounds. Ethnicity varies with social class, so socioeconomic disadvantage may account for low IQ scores among minority students.

New Directions in the Assessment and Study of Intelligence

● Biological indexes of intelligence are being explored, but they seem to have little practical utility thus far. Recent studies suggest that there may be a correlation between intelligence and brain size.

● Research on intelligence increasingly takes a cognitive perspective, which emphasizes the need to understand how people use their intelligence. Sternberg argues that there are three facets of successful intelligence: analytical, creative, and practical intelligence. Many modern theorists, most notably Howard Gardner, argue that the concept of intelligence should be expanded to encompass a greater variety of skills.

Reflecting on the Chapter's Themes

● Five of our unifying themes surfaced in the chapter: the empirical nature of psychology, the importance of cultural factors, the interaction of heredity and environment, the way psychology evolves in a sociohistorical context, and the subjectivity of human experience.

PERSONAL APPLICATION • Measuring and Understanding Creativity

● Creativity involves the generation of original, novel, and useful ideas. Creativity does not usually involve sudden insight. Divergent thinking can foster creativity, but it does not represent the essence of creativity.

● Psychologists have developed some clever and useful measures of creativity, but these tests are mediocre predictors of creative productivity in the real world. Creativity is only weakly related to intelligence. Recent evidence suggests that creative geniuses may exhibit heightened vulnerability to psychological disorders.

CRITICAL THINKING APPLICATION • The Intelligence Debate, Appeals to Ignorance, and Reification

● The appeal to ignorance involves misusing the lack of knowledge or information on an issue to support an argument. Reification occurs when a hypothetical construct is treated as though it were a tangible object. The concepts of intelligence and heritability have both been subject to reification.

Key Terms

Availability heuristic (p. 245)
Conjunction fallacy (p. 247)
Convergent thinking (p. 266)
Correlation coefficient (p. 253)
Creativity (p. 266)
Decision making (p. 243)
Deviation IQ scores (p. 252)
Divergent thinking (p. 266)
Field dependence-independence
  (p. 242)
Functional fixedness (p. 237)
Gambler's fallacy (p. 247)
Heritability ratio (p. 257)
Heuristic (p. 239)
Insight (p. 239)
Intelligence quotient (IQ) (p. 250)
Mental age (p. 250)
Mental set (p. 238)
Normal distribution (p. 251)
Percentile score (p. 253)
Problem solving (p. 236)

Reaction range (p. 259)
Reification (p. 269)
Reliability (p. 253)
Representativeness heuristic
  (p. 246)
Risky decision making (p. 245)
Trial and error (p. 239)
Validity (p. 254)

Key People

Alfred Binet (pp. 250–251)
Howard Gardner (pp. 263–264)
Arthur Jensen (pp. 260, 262)
Daniel Kahneman (pp. 245–246)
Sandra Scarr (pp. 259–260)
Herbert Simon (pp. 235, 243)
Robert Sternberg (pp. 262–263)
Lewis Terman (pp. 250–251)
Amos Tversky (pp. 245–246)
David Wechsler (pp. 251–253)

1. Problems that require a common object to be used in an unusual way may be difficult to solve because of:
   A. mental set.
   B. irrelevant information.
   C. unnecessary constraints.
   D. functional fixedness.

2. The nine-dot problem:
   A. is often solved suddenly with a burst of insight.
   B. is difficult because people assume constraints that are not part of the problem.
   C. is solved through fast mapping.
   D. is both a and b.

3. A heuristic is:
   A. a flash of insight.
   B. a guiding principle or "rule of thumb" used in problem solving or decision making.
   C. a methodical procedure for trying all possible solutions to a problem.
   D. a way of making a compensatory decision.

4. According to Nisbett, Eastern cultures tend to favor a(n) _____ cognitive style, whereas Western cultures tend to display a(n) _____ cognitive style.
   A. analytic; holistic
   B. holistic; analytic
   C. holistic; field dependent
   D. field independent; field dependent

5. The work of Herbert Simon on decision making showed that:
   A. people generally make rational choices that maximize their gains.
   B. people can evaluate an unlimited number of alternatives effectively.
   C. people tend to focus on only a few aspects of their available options and often make "irrational" decisions as a result.
   D. the more options people consider, the better their decisions tend to be.

6. When you estimate the probability of an event by judging the ease with which relevant instances come to mind, you are relying on:
   A. an additive decision-making model.
   B. the representativeness heuristic.
   C. the availability heuristic.
   D. a noncompensatory model.

7. The belief that the probability of heads is higher after a long string of tails:
   A. is rational and accurate.
   B. is an example of the "gambler's fallacy."
   C. reflects the influence of the representativeness heuristic.
   D. is both B and C.

8. On most modern IQ tests, a score of 115 would be:
   A. about average.
   B. about 15% higher than the average of one's agemates.
   C. an indication of genius.
   D. one standard deviation above the mean.

9. IQ tests have proven to be good predictors of:
   A. social intelligence.
   B. practical problem-solving intelligence.
   C. school performance.
   D. all of the above.

10. The correlation between IQ and occupational attainment appears to be:
    A. positive and moderate.
    B. positive but extremely low.
    C. nonexistent.
    D. negative or inverse.

11. Saying that the heritability of intelligence is 60% would mean that:
    A. 60% of a person's intelligence is due to heredity.
    B. 60% of the variability in intelligence scores in a group is estimated to be due to genetic variations.
    C. intelligence is 40% inherited.
    D. heredity affects intelligence in 60% of the members of the group.

12. In which of the following cases would you expect to find the greatest similarity in IQ?
    A. Between fraternal twins
    B. Between identical twins
    C. Between nontwin siblings
    D. Between parent and child

13. Evidence indicating that upbringing affects one's mental ability is provided by which of the following findings?
    A. Identical twins are more similar in IQ than fraternal twins.
    B. There is more than a chance similarity between adopted children and their biological parents.
    C. Siblings reared together are more similar in IQ than siblings reared apart.
    D. Identical twins reared apart are more similar in IQ than siblings reared together.

14. According to theories that use the concept of reaction range, the upper limits of an individual's intellectual potential are:
    A. determined during the first year of life.
    B. largely set by heredity.
    C. determined by a person's unique experiences.
    D. determined by one's heritability quotient.

15. Which of the following is a current trend in the assessment and study of intelligence?
    A. More dependence on the classic intelligence quotient instead of deviation IQ scores
    B. More reliance on IQ tests in the world of work
    C. More emphasis on reducing the convergent heritability of deviation IQ scores
    D. More interest in exploring biological indexes of intelligence

Answers

1 D pp. 237–238
2 D p. 239
3 B p. 239
4 B pp. 242–243
5 C p. 243
6 C p. 245
7 D p. 247
8 D pp. 251–253
9 C pp. 254–255
10 A pp. 254–255
11 B pp. 257–258
12 B p. 257
13 C pp. 257–258
14 B pp. 259–260
15 D pp. 262–263

PsykTrek

Go to the PsykTrek website or CD-ROM for further study of the concepts in this chapter. Both online and on the CD-ROM, PsykTrek includes dozens of learning modules with videos, animations, and quizzes, as well as simulations of psychological phenomena and a multimedia glossary that includes word pronunciations.

ThomsonNOW

www.thomsonedu.com/ThomsonNOW

Go to this site for the link to ThomsonNOW, your one-stop study shop. Take a Pre-Test for this chapter, and ThomsonNOW will generate a Personalized Study Plan based on your test results. The Study Plan will identify the topics you need to review and direct you to online resources to help you master those topics. You can then take a Post-Test to help you determine the concepts you have mastered and what you still need to work on.

Companion Website

www.thomsonedu.com/psychology/weiten

Go to this site to find online resources directly linked to your book, including a glossary, flash cards, drag-and-drop exercises, quizzes, and more!

CHAPTER 9

Motivation and Emotion

G ER Production/Corbis

It was a bright afternoon in May 1996, and 41-year-old Jon Krakauer was on top of the world—literally. Krakauer had just fulfilled a boyhood dream by climbing Mount Everest, the tallest peak on earth. Clearing the ice from his oxygen mask, he looked down on a sweeping vista of ice, snow, and majestic mountains. His triumph should have brought him intense joy, but he felt strangely detached. "I'd been fantasizing about this moment, and the release of emotion that would accompany it, for many years," he wrote later. "But now that I was finally here, standing on the summit of Mount Everest, I just couldn't summon the energy to care" (Krakauer, 1998, p. 6).

Why were Krakauer's emotions so subdued? A major reason was that he was physically spent. Climbing Mount Everest is an incredibly grueling experience. At just over 29,000 feet, the mountain's peak is at the altitude flown by jumbo jets. Because such high altitudes wreak havoc on the human body, Krakauer and his fellow climbers couldn't even approach the summit until they had spent six weeks acclimating at Base Camp, 17,600 feet above sea level. Even getting that far would test the limits of most people's endurance. At Base Camp, Krakauer found that ordinary bodily functions became painfully difficult. On most nights, he awoke three or four times, gasping for breath and feeling like he was suffocating. His appetite vanished, and his oxygen-starved digestive system failed to metabolize food normally. "My body began consuming itself for sustenance. My arms and legs gradually began to wither to sticklike proportions" (Krakauer, 1998, p. 87).

At this point you may be wondering why anyone would willingly undergo such extreme discomfort, but Base Camp was just the beginning. From Base Camp it is another 2 vertical miles through the aptly named Death Zone to the summit. Even for a fully acclimated climber, the final leg of the ascent is agonizing. By the time Krakauer reached the summit, every step was labored, every gasping breath hurt. He hadn't slept in 57 hours, and he had two separated ribs from weeks of violent coughing. He was bitterly cold and utterly exhausted. Instead of elation, he felt only apprehension. Even though his oxygen-starved brain was barely functioning, he understood that getting down from the summit would be fully as dangerous as getting up.

Tragically, events proved just how dangerous an assault on Everest can be. During Krakauer's descent, a sudden, howling storm hit the mountain. Winds exceeding 100 miles per hour whipped the snow into a blinding white blur and sent the temperature plummeting. While Krakauer barely escaped with his life, 12 men and women died on the mountain, in-cluding several in Krakauer's own party. Some of them perished needlessly because they had fallen victim to "summit fever." Once they got close to the top, they refused to turn back in spite of extreme exhaustion and the obvious threat posed by the storm.

The saga of Jon Krakauer and the other climbers is packed with motivation riddles. Why would people push on toward a goal even at the risk of their lives? Why would they choose to endure such a punishing and hazardous ordeal in the first place? In the case of Mount Everest, perhaps the most obvious motive is simply the satisfaction of conquering the world's tallest peak. When British climber George Leigh Mallory was asked why he wanted to climb Everest in the 1920s, his famous reply was, "Because it is there." Some people seem to have an intense desire to take on the toughest challenges imaginable, to achieve something incredibly difficult. Yet—as is usually the case with human behavior—things are not quite so simple. Krakauer observed that a wide variety of motives drove the climbers and professional expedition leaders he met on Everest, including desires for "minor celebrity, career advancement, ego massage, ordinary bragging rights, filthy lucre," and even a quest for "a state of grace" (Krakauer, 1998, p. 177).

Krakauer's story is also filled with strong emotions. He anticipated that he would experience a transcendent emotional high when he reached the summit of Mount Everest. As it turned out, his triumph was accompanied more by anxiety than by ecstasy. And though the harrowing events that followed initially left him emotionally numb, he was soon flooded

Jon Krakauer (the third person) and other climbers are seen here during their ascent of Mount Everest at an elevation of about 28,200 feet.

Copyright © Klev Schoening

with intense feelings of despair, grief, and guilt over the deaths of his companions. His tale illustrates the intimate connection between motivation and emotion—the topics we examine in this chapter.

> Motivational Theories and Concepts

PREVIEW QUESTIONS

- What is the distinction between drive and incentive theories of motivation?

- How do evolutionary theories explain various motives?

- What are the two major categories of human motives?

Motives are the needs, wants, interests, and desires that propel people in certain directions. In short, **motivation involves goal-directed behavior**. Psychologists have devised a number of theoretical approaches to motivation. Let's look at some of these theories and the concepts they've come up with.

Drive Theories

Many theories view motivational forces in terms of *drives*. The drive concept appears in a diverse array of theories that otherwise have little in common, such as psychoanalytic and behaviorist theories. The concept of drive was derived from Walter Cannon's (1932) observation that organisms seek to maintain *homeostasis,* **a state of physiological equilibrium or stability**. The body maintains homeostasis in various ways. For example, human body temperature nor-

mally fluctuates around 98.6 degrees Fahrenheit (see **Figure 9.1**). If your body temperature rises or drops noticeably, automatic responses occur: If your temperature goes up, you'll perspire; if your temperature goes down, you'll shiver. These reactions are designed to move your temperature back toward 98.6 degrees. Thus, your body reacts to many disturbances in physiological stability by trying to restore equilibrium.

Drive theories apply the concept of homeostasis to behavior. A *drive* is a hypothetical, **internal state of tension that motivates an organism to engage in activities that should reduce this tension**. These unpleasant states of tension are viewed as disruptions of the preferred equilibrium. According to drive theories, when individuals experience a drive, they're motivated to pursue actions that will lead to *drive reduction*. For example, the hunger motive has usually been viewed as a drive system. If you go without food for a while, you begin to experience some discomfort. This internal tension (the drive) motivates you to obtain food. Eating reduces the drive and restores physiological equilibrium.

Drive theories have been very influential, and the drive concept continues to be widely used in modern psychology. *However, drive theories cannot explain all motivation* (Berridge, 2004). Homeostasis appears irrelevant to some human motives, such as a "thirst for knowledge." Also, motivation may exist without drive arousal. This point is easy to illustrate. Think of all the times that you've eaten when you weren't the least bit hungry. You're driving or walking home from class, amply filled by a solid lunch, when an ice cream parlor beckons seductively. You stop in and have a couple of scoops of your favorite flavor. Not only are you motivated to eat in the absence of internal tension, you may actually cause yourself some internal tension—from overeating. Because drive theories assume that people always try to reduce internal tension, they can't explain this behavior very well. Incentive theories, which represent a different approach to motivation, can account for this behavior more readily.

Incentive Theories

Incentive theories propose that external stimuli regulate motivational states (Bolles, 1975; McClelland,

Figure 9.1

Temperature regulation as an example of homeostasis. The regulation of body temperature provides a simple example of how organisms often seek to maintain homeostasis, or a state of physiological equilibrium. When your temperature moves out of an acceptable range, automatic bodily reactions (such as sweating or shivering) occur that help restore equilibrium. Of course, these automatic reactions may not be sufficient by themselves, so you may have to take other actions (such as turning a furnace up or down) to bring your body temperature back into its comfort zone.

Blood vessels in skin dilate to remove heat
Person sweats

Turn down furnace
Remove sweater

Restore equilibrium

Temperature too high

Comfortable range for body temperature centered on 98.6°F

Temperature too low

Restore equilibrium

Blood vessels in skin constrict to conserve heat
Person shivers

Turn up furnace
Put on sweater

1975; Skinner, 1953). **An *incentive* is an external goal that has the capacity to motivate behavior.** Ice cream, a juicy steak, a monetary prize, approval from friends, an A on an exam, and a promotion at work are all incentives. Some of these incentives may reduce drives, but others may not.

Drive and incentive models of motivation are often contrasted as *push versus pull* theories. Drive theories emphasize how *internal* states of tension *push* people in certain directions. Incentive theories emphasize how *external* stimuli *pull* people in certain directions. According to drive theories, the source of motivation lies *within* the organism. According to incentive theories, the source of motivation lies *outside* the organism, in the environment. Thus, incentive models don't operate according to the principle of homeostasis, which hinges on internal changes in the organism. In comparison to drive theories, incentive theories emphasize environmental factors and downplay the biological bases of human motivation.

Evolutionary Theories

Psychologists who take an evolutionary perspective assert that the motives of humans and of other species are the products of evolution, just as anatomical characteristics are. They argue that natural selection favors behaviors that maximize reproductive success—that is, passing on genes to the next generation. Thus, they explain motives such as affiliation, achievement, dominance, aggression, and sex drive in terms of their adaptive value. If dominance is a crucial motive for a species, they say, it's because dominance provides a reproductive or survival advantage.

Evolutionary analyses of motivation are based on the premise that motives can best be understood in terms of the adaptive problems they have solved over the course of human history. For example, the need for dominance is thought to be greater in men than in women because it could facilitate males' reproductive success in a variety of ways, including (1) females may prefer mating with dominant males, (2) dominant males may poach females from subordinate males, (3) dominant males may intimidate male rivals in competition for sexual access, and (4) dominant males may acquire more material resources which may increase mating opportunities (Buss, 1999). Consider, also, the *affiliation motive,* or need for belongingness. The adaptive benefits of affiliation for our ancestors probably included help with offspring, collaboration in hunting and gathering, mutual defense, opportunities for sexual interaction, and so forth (Baumeister & Leary, 1995). David Buss (1995) points out that it is not by accident that

achievement, power (dominance), and intimacy are among the most heavily studied motives, as the satisfaction of each of these motives is likely to affect one's reproductive success.

The Range and Diversity of Human Motives

Motivational theorists of all persuasions agree on one point: Humans display an enormous diversity of motives. Most theories (evolutionary theories being a notable exception) distinguish between *biological motives* that originate in bodily needs, such as hunger, and *social motives* that originate in social experiences, such as the need for achievement.

People have a limited number of biological needs. According to K. B. Madsen (1968, 1973), most theories identify 10 to 15 such needs, some of which are listed on the left side of **Figure 9.2**. As you can see, most biological motives reflect needs that are essential to survival, such as the needs for food, water, and maintenance of body temperature within an acceptable range.

People all share the same biological motives, but their social motives vary depending on their experiences. For example, we all need to eat, but not everyone has a need for orderliness. Although people have a limited number of biological motives, they can acquire an unlimited number of social motives through learning and socialization. Some examples of social motives—from an influential list compiled by Henry Murray (1938)—are shown on the right side of **Figure 9.2**. He theorized that most people have needs for achievement, autonomy, affiliation, dominance, exhibition, and order, among other things. Of course, the strength of these motives varies from person to person, depending on personal history.

Given the range and diversity of human motives, we can only examine a handful in depth. To a large

Figure 9.2

The diversity of human motives. People are motivated by a wide range of needs, which can be divided into two broad classes: biological motives and social motives. The list on the left (adapted from Madsen, 1973) shows some important biological motives in humans. The list on the right (adapted from Murray, 1938) provides examples of prominent social motives in humans. The distinction between biological and social motives is not absolute.

Examples of Biological Motives in Humans	Examples of Social Motives in Humans
Hunger motive	Achievement motive (need to excel)
Thirst motive	Affiliation motive (need for social bonds)
Sex motive	Autonomy motive (need for independence)
Temperature motive (need for appropriate body temperature)	Nurturance motive (need to nourish and protect others)
Excretory motive (need to eliminate bodily wastes)	Dominance motive (need to influence or control others)
Sleep and rest motive	Exhibition motive (need to make an impression on others)
Activity motive (need for optimal level of stimulation and arousal)	Order motive (need for orderliness, tidiness, organization)
Aggression motive	Play motive (need for fun, relaxation, amusement)

degree, our choices reflect the motives psychologists have studied the most: hunger, sex, and achievement. After our discussion of these motivational systems, we will explore the elements of emotional experience and discuss various theories of emotion.

> The Motivation of Hunger and Eating

PREVIEW QUESTIONS

- Which brain centers appear to control the experience of hunger?
- How do fluctuations in blood glucose and hormones contribute to hunger?
- How is eating influenced by the availability and palatability of food?
- How is eating influenced by learned habits and stress?

Why do people eat? Because they're hungry. What makes them hungry? A lack of food. Any grade-school child can explain these basic facts. So hunger is a simple motivational system, right? Wrong! Hunger is deceptive. It only looks simple. Actually, it's a puzzling and complex motivational system. Despite extensive studies of hunger, scientists are still struggling to understand the factors that regulate eating behavior. Let's examine a few of these factors.

Biological Factors in the Regulation of Hunger

You have probably had embarrassing occasions when your stomach growled loudly at an untimely moment. Someone may have commented, "You must be starving!" Most people equate a rumbling stomach with hunger, and in fact, the first scientific theories of hunger were based on this simple equation. In an elaborate 1912 study, Walter Cannon and A. L. Washburn verified what most people have noticed based on casual observation: There is an association between stomach contractions and the experience of hunger.

Based on this correlation, Cannon theorized that stomach contractions *cause* hunger. However, as we've seen before, correlation is no assurance of causation, and his theory was eventually discredited. Stomach contractions often accompany hunger, but they don't cause it. How do we know? Because later research showed that people continue to experience hunger even after their stomachs have been removed out of medical necessity (Wangensteen & Carlson, 1931). If hunger can occur without a stomach, then stomach contractions can't be the cause of hunger. This realization led to more elaborate theories of hunger that focus on (1) the role of the brain, (2) blood sugar level and digestive factors, and (3) hormones.

Brain Regulation

Research with laboratory animals eventually suggested that the experience of hunger is controlled in the brain—specifically, in two centers located in the hypothalamus. As we have noted before, the *hypothalamus* is a tiny structure involved in the regulation of a variety of biological needs related to survival (see

Figure 9.3). Investigators found that when they surgically destroyed animals' *lateral hypothalamus* (*LH*), the animals showed little or no interest in eating, as if their hunger center had been wiped out (Anand & Brobeck, 1951). In contrast, when researchers destroyed animals' *ventromedial nucleus of the hypothalamus* (*VMH*), the animals ate excessively and gained weight rapidly, as if their ability to recognize satiety (fullness) had been neutralized (Brobeck, Tepperman, & Long, 1943). Given these results, investigators concluded that the LH and VMH were the brain's on-off switches for the control of hunger (Stellar, 1954). However, over the course of several decades, a number of findings complicated this simple picture and undermined the dual-centers model of hunger (Valenstein, 1973; Winn, 1995). The current thinking is that the lateral and ventromedial areas of the hypothalamus are elements in the neural circuitry that regulates hunger but not the key elements—and not simple on-off centers. Today, scientists believe that another area of the hypothalamus—the *paraventricular nucleus* (*PVN*)—plays a larger role in the modulation of hunger (Woods et al., 2000) (see **Figure 9.3**).

Contemporary theories of hunger focus more on *neural circuits* that pass through the hypothalamus rather than on *anatomical centers* in the brain. These circuits depend on a variety of neurotransmitters, with neuropeptide Y and serotonin playing particularly prominent roles (Halford & Blundell, 2000; Seeley & Schwartz, 1997). Accumulating evidence suggests that the hypothalamus contains a convergence of interacting systems that regulate eating by monitoring a diverse array of physiological processes. Let's look at some other physiological processes that appear to provide input to these systems.

The rat on the left has had its ventromedial hypothalamus lesioned, resulting in a dramatic increase in weight.

Glucose and Digestive Regulation

Much of the food taken into the body is converted into *glucose,* which circulates in the blood. **Glucose is a simple sugar that is an important source of energy.** Manipulations that decrease blood glucose level can increase hunger. Manipulations that increase glucose level can make people feel full. Based on these findings, Jean Mayer (1955, 1968) proposed that hunger is regulated by the rise and fall of blood glucose levels. His theory proposed that fluctuations in blood glucose level are monitored in the brain by *glucostats*—**neurons sensitive to glucose in the surrounding fluid.** Like the dual-centers theory, Mayer's theory of hunger gradually ran into several complications, not the least of which was that glucose levels in the blood don't fluctuate all that much (LeMagnen, 1981). Still, it appears likely that hunger is regulated, in part, through glucose mechanisms (Smith & Campfield, 1993).

The digestive system also includes a variety of other mechanisms that influence hunger (Ritter, 2004). It turns out that Walter Cannon was not entirely wrong in hypothesizing that the stomach regulates hunger. After you have consumed food, the stomach can send two types of signals to the brain that inhibit further eating (Deutsch, 1990). The vagus nerve carries information about the stretching of the stomach walls that indicates when the stomach is full. Other nerves carry satiety messages that depend on how rich in nutrients the contents of the stomach are.

Hormonal Regulation

A variety of hormones circulating in the bloodstream also appear to contribute to the regulation of hunger. *Insulin* is a hormone secreted by the pancreas. It must be present for cells to extract glucose from the blood. Indeed, an inadequate supply of insulin is what causes diabetes. Many diabetics are unable to use the glucose in their blood unless they are given insulin injections. In nondiabetic individuals, insulin injections stimulate hunger. Normal secretion of insulin by the pancreas is also associated with increased hunger. And, in landmark research, Judith Rodin (1985) demonstrated that the mere sight and smell of enticing food can stimulate the secretion of insulin. Moreover, insulin levels appear to be sensitive to fluctuations in the body's fat stores (Schwartz et al., 2000). These findings suggest that insulin secretions play a role in the modulation of hunger.

Finally, the recent discovery of a previously undetected hormone, since named *leptin,* has shed new light on the hormonal regulation of hunger, as well as on the regulation of numerous other bodily func-

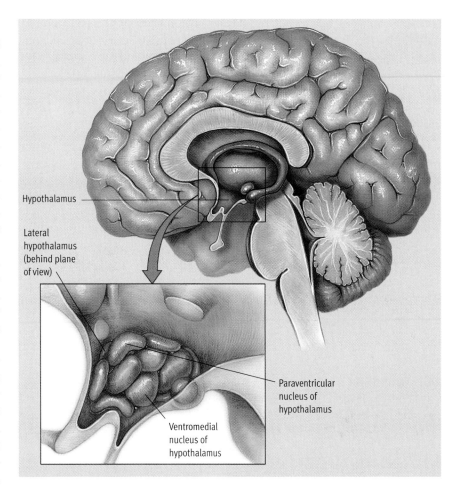

tions (Ahima & Osei, 2004). Leptin is produced by fat cells throughout the body and released into the bloodstream. Higher levels of fat generate higher levels of leptin (Schwartz et al., 1996). Leptin circulates through the bloodstream and ultimately provides the hypothalamus with information about the body's fat stores (Campfield, 2002). When leptin levels are high, the propensity to feel hungry diminishes. Researchers are currently exploring whether leptin itself, or drugs that affect leptin levels, might be helpful to people trying to lose weight (Heshka & Heymsfield, 2002).

If all this sounds confusing, it is, and I haven't even mentioned *all* the physiological processes involved in the regulation of hunger and eating. Frankly, researchers are still struggling to figure out exactly how all these processes work together, as hunger depends on complex interactions among neural circuits, neurotransmitter systems, digestive processes, and hormonal fluctuations.

Environmental Factors in the Regulation of Hunger

Hunger clearly is a biological need, but eating is not regulated by biological factors alone. Studies show

Figure 9.3

The hypothalamus. This small structure at the base of the forebrain plays a role in regulating a variety of human biological needs, including hunger. The detailed blowup on the left shows that the hypothalamus is composed of a variety of discrete areas. Scientists used to believe that the lateral and ventromedial areas were the brain's on-off centers for eating. However, more recent research suggests that the paraventricular nucleus may be more crucial to the regulation of hunger and that it makes more sense to think in terms of neural circuits than anatomical centers.

Web Link 9.1

American Obesity Association

This nonprofit organization's mission is to change public policy and make obesity a public health priority. It has an incredibly rich and well-organized website. In-depth information is available on the causes, consequences, and treatments of obesity.

that social and environmental factors govern eating to a considerable extent. Three key environmental factors are (1) the availability and palatability of food, (2) learned preferences and habits, and (3) stress.

Food Availability and Related Cues

Most of the research on the physiological regulation of hunger has been based on the assumption that hunger operates as a drive system in which homeostatic mechanisms are at work. However, some theorists emphasize the incentive value of food and argue that humans and other animals are often motivated to eat not by the need to compensate for energy deficits but by the anticipated pleasure of eating (Hetherington & Rolls, 1996; Ramsay et al., 1996). This perspective has been bolstered by evidence that three main variables exert significant influence over food consumption:

- *Palatability*. As you might expect, the better food tastes, the more people consume (de Castro et al., 2000; Pliner & Mann, 2004). This principle is not limited to humans, as the eating behavior of rats and other animals is also influenced by palatability.
- *Quantity available*. A powerful determinant of the amount eaten is the amount available. People tend to consume what is put in front of them. The more people are served, the more they eat (Mrdjenovic & Levitsky, 2005; Rozin et al., 2003). Obviously, the large portions served in modern American restaurants foster increased consumption.
- *Variety*. Humans and animals increase their consumption when there is a greater variety of foods available (Raynor & Epstein, 2001). As you eat a specific food, its incentive value declines (Vandewater & Vickers, 1996). This phenomenon is called *sensory-specific satiety*. If only a few foods are available, the appeal of all of them can decline quickly. But if many foods are available, people can keep shifting to new foods and they end up eating more overall. This principle explains why people are especially likely to overeat at buffets.

According to incentive models of hunger, the availability and palatability of food are key factors regulating hunger. An abundance of diverse foods tends to lead to increased eating.

© James Marshall/The Image Works

Eating can also be triggered by exposure to environmental cues that have been associated with food. You have no doubt had your hunger aroused by television commercials for delicious-looking food or by seductive odors coming from the kitchen. Consistent with this observation, studies have shown that hunger can be increased by exposure to pictures, written descriptions, and video depictions of attractive foods (Halford et al., 2004; Marcelino et al., 2001; Oakes & Slotterback, 2000). Thus, it's clear that hunger and eating are governed in part by the incentive qualities of food.

Learned Preferences and Habits

Are you fond of eating calves' brains? How about eels or snakes? Could I interest you in a grasshopper or some dog meat? Probably not, but these are delicacies in some regions of the world. Arctic Eskimos like to eat maggots! You probably prefer chicken, apples, eggs, lettuce, potato chips, pizza, cornflakes, or ice cream. These preferences are acquired through learning. People from different cultures display very different patterns of food consumption (Kittler & Sucher, 1998). If you doubt this fact, just visit an ethnic grocery store.

Humans do have some innate taste preferences of a general sort. For example, a preference for sweet tastes is present at birth (Mennella & Beauchamp, 1996), and humans' preference for high-fat foods appears to be at least partly genetic in origin (Schiffman et al., 1998). Nonetheless, learning wields a great deal of influence over what people prefer to eat (Booth, 1994). Taste preferences are partly a function of learned associations formed through *classical conditioning* (Capaldi, 1996). For instance, youngsters can be conditioned to prefer flavors paired with high caloric intake or other pleasant events. Of course, as we learned in Chapter 6, taste aversions can also be acquired through conditioning when foods are followed by nausea (Schafe & Bernstein, 1996).

Eating habits are also shaped by *observational learning* (see Chapter 6). To a large degree, food preferences are a matter of exposure (Rozin, 1990). People generally prefer familiar foods. But geographical, cultural, religious, and ethnic factors limit people's exposure to various foods. Repeated exposures to a new food usually lead to increased liking. However, as many parents have learned the hard way, forcing a child to eat a specific food can backfire and have a negative effect on the youngster's preference for the required food (Birch & Fisher, 1996). Learned habits and social considerations also influence *when* and *how much* people eat. For example, a key determinant of when you eat is your memory of how much time has passed since you ate your last meal and

Food preferences are influenced greatly by culture. For example, the fried tarantula shown here would not be a popular treat for most Americans, but it is a delicacy in some cultures.

what you consumed (Rozin et al., 1998). These expectations about how often and how much you should eat are the product of years of learning.

Stress and Eating

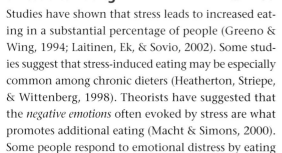

PsykTrek
8a

Studies have shown that stress leads to increased eating in a substantial percentage of people (Greeno & Wing, 1994; Laitinen, Ek, & Sovio, 2002). Some studies suggest that stress-induced eating may be especially common among chronic dieters (Heatherton, Striepe, & Wittenberg, 1998). Theorists have suggested that the *negative emotions* often evoked by stress are what promotes additional eating (Macht & Simons, 2000). Some people respond to emotional distress by eating

tasty foods because they expect the enjoyable treats to make them feel better (Tice, Bratslavsky, & Baumeister, 2001). Unfortunately, this strategy of emotional regulation does not appear to be very effective, as eating does not usually lead to lasting mood changes (Thayer, 1996). In any event, stress is another environmental factor that can influence hunger, although it's not clear whether the effects are direct or indirect.

concept **check** 9.1

Understanding Factors in the Regulation of Hunger

Check your understanding of the effects of the various factors that influence hunger by indicating whether hunger would tend to increase or decrease in each of the situations described below. Indicate your choice by marking an *I* (increase), a *D* (decrease), or a *?* (can't be determined without more information) next to each situation. You'll find the answers in Appendix A at the back of the book.

_____ **1.** The ventromedial nucleus of a rat's brain is destroyed.

_____ **2.** The glucose level in Marlene's bloodstream decreases.

_____ **3.** Norman just ate, but his roommate just brought home his favorite food—a pizza that smells great.

_____ **4.** You're offered an exotic, strange-looking food from another culture.

_____ **5.** You are eating at a huge buffet where an enormous variety of foods are available.

_____ **6.** Elton has been going crazy all day. It seems like everything's happening at once, and he feels totally stressed out. Finally he's been able to break away for a few minutes so he can catch a bite to eat.

> Sexual Motivation and Behavior

How does sex resemble food? Sometimes it seems that people are obsessed with both. People joke and gossip about sex constantly. Magazines, novels, movies, and television shows are saturated with sexual activity and innuendo. The advertising industry uses sex to sell everything from mouthwash to designer jeans to automobiles. This intense interest in sex reflects the importance of sexual motivation. In this portion of the chapter, we will examine the physiology of the human sexual response, review evolutionary analyses of human sexual motivation, and discuss the roots of sexual orientation.

The Human Sexual Response

Assuming people are motivated to engage in sexual activity, exactly what happens to them physically?

This may sound like a simple question. But scientists really knew very little about the physiology of the human sexual response before William Masters and Virginia Johnson did groundbreaking research in the 1960s. Masters and Johnson used physiological recording devices to monitor the bodily changes of volunteers engaging in sexual activities. Their observations and interviews with their subjects yielded a detailed description of the human sexual response and won them widespread acclaim. Masters and Johnson (1966, 1970) divide the sexual response cycle into four stages: excitement, plateau, orgasm, and resolution. **Figure 9.4** on the next page shows how the intensity of sexual arousal changes as women and men progress through these stages.

During the *excitement phase,* the level of physical arousal usually escalates rapidly. In both sexes, muscle tension, respiration rate, heart rate, and blood pressure increase quickly. *Vasocongestion*—engorgement

PREVIEW QUESTIONS

● What are the four phases of the human sexual response?

● What has evolutionary-oriented research revealed about gender differences in sexual activity?

● How do males and females differ in terms of mating preferences?

● Is sexual orientation an either-or distinction?

● How common is homosexuality?

● How have theorists explained the development of homosexuality?

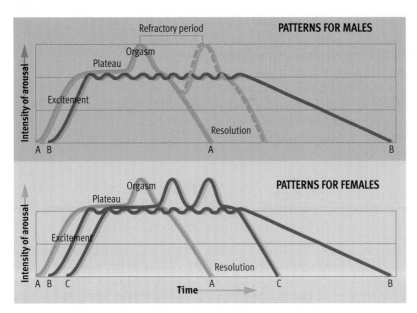

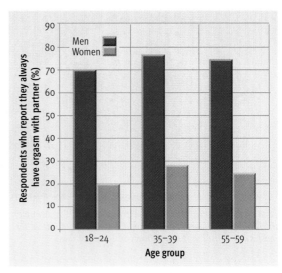

Figure 9.4

The human sexual response cycle. There are similarities and differences between men and women in patterns of sexual arousal. Pattern A, which culminates in orgasm and resolution, is the modal sequence for both sexes, but not something one can count on. Pattern B, which involves sexual arousal without orgasm followed by a slow resolution, is seen in both sexes but is more common among women (see **Figure 9.5**). Pattern C, which involves multiple orgasms, is seen almost exclusively in women, as men go through a refractory period before they are capable of another orgasm.

Source: Based on Masters, W. H., & Johnson, V. E. (1966). *Human Sexual Response.* Boston: Little, Brown. Copyright © 1966 Little, Brown and Company.

Figure 9.5

The gender gap in orgasm consistency. In their sexual interactions, men seem to reach orgasm more reliably than women. The data shown here suggest that the gender gap in orgasmic consistency is pretty sizable. Both biological and sociocultural factors may contribute to this gender gap. (Data from Laumann et al., 1994)

WILLIAM MASTERS AND VIRGINIA JOHNSON

"The conviction has grown that the most effective treatment of sexual incompatibility involves the technique of working with both members of the family unit."

of blood vessels—produces penile erection and swollen testes in males. In females, vasocongestion leads to a swelling and hardening of the clitoris, expansion of the vaginal lips, and vaginal lubrication. During the *plateau phase,* physiological arousal usually continues to build, but at a much slower pace. When foreplay is lengthy, it's normal for arousal to fluctuate in both sexes.

Orgasm occurs when sexual arousal reaches its peak intensity and is discharged in a series of muscular contractions that pulsate through the pelvic area. The subjective experience of orgasm is very similar for men and women, but women are more likely than men to experience more than one orgasm in a brief time period (pattern C in **Figure 9.4**). That said, women are also more likely than men to engage in intercourse without experiencing an orgasm (see **Figure 9.5**; Laumann et al., 1994). Whether these differences reflect attitudes and sexual practices versus physiological processes is open to debate. Evolutionary theorists argue that males' greater orgasmic consistency must be a product of evolution, as it would have obvious adaptive significance for men's reproductive fitness. But over the years other theorists have come up with a variety of plausible environmental explanations for this disparity, such as gender differences in the socialization of guilt feel-

ings about sex, and sexual scripts and practices that are unfavorable to women (Lott, 1987).

During the *resolution phase,* the physiological changes produced by sexual arousal gradually subside. If orgasm has not occurred, the reduction in sexual tension may be relatively slow. After orgasm, men experience a *refractory period,* a time following orgasm during which males are largely unresponsive to further stimulation. The length of the refractory period varies from a few minutes to a few hours and increases with age.

Evolutionary Analyses of Human Sexual Motivation

The task of explaining sexual behavior is obviously crucial to evolutionary psychologists, given their fundamental thesis that natural selection is fueled by variations in reproductive success. The thinking in this area has been guided by Robert Trivers's (1972) *parental investment theory.* **Parental investment refers to what each sex has to invest—in terms of time, energy, survival risk, and forgone opportunities (to pursue other goals)—to produce and nurture offspring.** For example, the efforts required to guard eggs, build nests, and nourish offspring represent parental investments. In most species, striking disparities exist between males and females in their parental investment, and these discrepancies shape mating strategies. So how does this theory apply to humans?

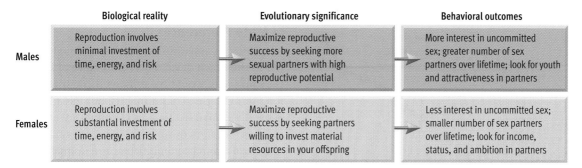

	Biological reality	Evolutionary significance	Behavioral outcomes
Males	Reproduction involves minimal investment of time, energy, and risk	Maximize reproductive success by seeking more sexual partners with high reproductive potential	More interest in uncommitted sex; greater number of sex partners over lifetime; look for youth and attractiveness in partners
Females	Reproduction involves substantial investment of time, energy, and risk	Maximize reproductive success by seeking partners willing to invest material resources in your offspring	Less interest in uncommitted sex; smaller number of sex partners over lifetime; look for income, status, and ambition in partners

Figure 9.6

Parental investment theory and mating preferences. Parental investment theory suggests that basic differences between males and females in parental investment have great adaptive significance and lead to gender differences in mating tendencies and preferences, as outlined here.

Web Link 9.2

Go Ask Alice!
One of the longest-standing and most popular sources of frank information on the Net has been *Alice!* from Columbia University's Health Education Program. Geared especially to the needs of undergraduate students, the site offers direct answers to questions about relationships, sexuality and sexual health, alcohol and drug consumption, emotional health, and general health.

As with many mammalian species, human males are *required* to invest little in the production of offspring beyond the act of copulation, so their reproductive potential is maximized by mating with as many females as possible. The situation for females is quite different. Females have to invest nine months in pregnancy, and our female ancestors typically had to devote at least several additional years to nourishing offspring through breastfeeding. These realities place a ceiling on the number of offspring women can produce, regardless of how many males they mate with. Hence, females have little or no incentive for mating with many males. Instead, females can optimize their reproductive potential by being selective in mating. Thus, in humans, males are thought to compete with other males for the relatively scarce and valuable "commodity" of reproductive opportunities.

Parental investment theory predicts that in comparison to women, men will show more interest in sexual activity, more desire for variety in sexual partners, and more willingness to engage in uncommitted sex (see **Figure 9.6**). In contrast, females are thought to be the conservative, discriminating sex that is highly selective in choosing partners. This selectivity supposedly involves seeking partners who have the greatest ability to contribute toward feeding and caring for offspring. Why? Because in the world of our ancient ancestors, males' greater strength and agility would have been crucial assets in the never-ending struggle to find food and shelter and defend territory. A female who chose a mate who was lazy or unreliable or who had no hunting, fighting, building, farming, or other useful economic skills would have suffered a substantial disadvantage in her efforts to raise her children and pass on her genes.

Gender Differences in Patterns of Sexual Activity

Consistent with evolutionary theory, males generally show a greater interest in sex than females do

(Peplau, 2003). Men think about sex more often than women (see **Figure 9.7**), and they initiate sex more frequently (Morokoff et al., 1997). Males have more frequent and varied sexual fantasies (Okami & Shackelford, 2001), and their subjective ratings of their sex drive tend to be higher than females' (Ostovich & Sabini, 2004). When heterosexual couples are asked about their sex lives, male partners are more likely than their female counterparts to report that they would like to have sex more often, and men spend vastly more money than women on sexual entertainment (Baumeister, Catanese, & Vohs, 2001).

Men also are more motivated than women to pursue sex with a greater variety of partners. Buss and Schmitt (1993) found that college men indicate that they would ideally like to have 18 sex partners across their lives, whereas college women report that they

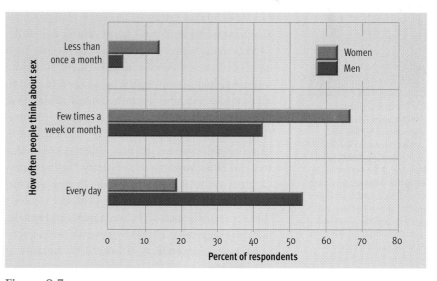

Figure 9.7

The gender gap in how much people think about sex. This graph summarizes data on how often males and females think about sex, based on a large-scale survey by Laumann, Gagnon, and Michaels (1994). As evolutionary theorists would predict, based on parental investment theory, males seem to manifest more interest in sexual activity than their female counterparts.

Figure 9.8

The gender gap in desire for a variety of sexual partners. Buss and Schmitt (1993) asked college students about how many sexual partners they ideally would like to have for various time intervals ranging up to one's entire lifetime. As evolutionary theorists would predict, males reported that they would like to have considerably more sexual partners than females.

Source: Buss, D. M., & Schmitt, D. P. (1993). Sexual strategies theory: An evolutionary perspective on human mating. *Psychological Review, 100,* 204–232. Copyright © 1993 by the American Psychological Association. Reprinted by permission of the publisher and author.

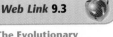

Web Link 9.3

The Evolutionary Psychology FAQ
Maintained by Edward Hagen (Institute for Theoretical Biology, Humboldt University, Berlin), this site provides answers to a host of controversial questions on the subject of evolutionary psychology. Covered questions include: What is an adaptation? How can we identify psychological adaptations? Is evolutionary psychology sexist? If my genes made me do it, am I still responsible? Why do some people hate evolutionary psychology?

would prefer only 5 partners (see **Figure 9.8**). Clear gender disparities are also seen in regard to people's willingness to engage in casual or uncommitted sex. For example, Buss and Schmitt (1993) found that men were much more likely than women to have sex with someone they had known for only a brief period. Moreover, a compelling field study, with no concerns about self-report issues, yielded similar results. Clark and Hatfield (1989) had average-looking men approach female (college-age) strangers and ask if they would go back to the man's apartment to have sex with him. None of the women agreed to this proposition. But when Clark and Hatfield had average-looking women approach males with the same proposition 75% of the men eagerly agreed!

In a definitive review of the empirical evidence, Roy Baumeister and colleagues (2001) conclude: "Across many different studies and measures, men have been shown to have more frequent and more intense sexual desires than women, as reflected in spontaneous thoughts about sex, frequency and variety of sexual fantasies, desired frequency of intercourse, desired number of partners, masturbation, liking for various sexual practices, willingness to forego sex, and other measures. No contrary findings (indicating stronger sexual motivation among women) were found" (p. 242). That said, evidence suggests that the sexual disparities between males and females may be exaggerated a little by reliance on subjects' self-reports (Alexander & Fisher, 2003). Because of the "double standard" regarding sexuality, women worry more than men about being viewed as sexually permissive, which may lead them to underestimate or downplay their sexual motivation (Crawford & Popp, 2003).

Gender Differences in Mate Preferences

According to evolutionary theorists, if males were left to their own devices over the course of history, they probably would have shown little interest in long-term mating commitments, but females have generally demanded long-term commitments from males before consenting to sex (Buss, 1994a). Hence, long-term mating commitments are a normal part of the social landscape in human societies. However, parental investment theory suggests that there should be some glaring disparities between men and women in what they look for in a long-term mate (see **Figure 9.6**).

The adaptive problem for our male ancestors was to find a female with good reproductive potential who would be sexually faithful and effective in nurturing children. Given these needs, evolutionary theory predicts that men should place more emphasis than women on such partner characteristics as youthfulness (which allows for more reproductive years) and attractiveness (which is assumed to be correlated with health and fertility). In contrast, the adaptive problem for our female ancestors was to find a male who could provide material resources and protect his family and who was dependable and willing to invest his resources in his family. Given these needs, evolutionary theory predicts that women should place more emphasis than men on such partner characteristics as intelligence, ambition, education, income, and social status (which are associated with the abil-

BIZARRO

ity to provide more material resources). If these evolutionary analyses of sexual motivation are on the mark, gender differences in mating preferences should be virtually universal and thus transcend culture.

To test this hypothesis, David Buss (1989) and 50 scientists from around the world surveyed more than 10,000 people from 37 cultures about what they looked for in a mate. As predicted by parental investment theory, they found that women placed a higher value than men on potential partners' status, ambition, and financial prospects. These priorities were not limited to industrialized or capitalist countries; they were apparent in third-world cultures, socialist countries, and all varieties of economic systems. In contrast, men around the world consistently showed more interest than women in potential partners' youthfulness and physical attractiveness. A number of studies, using diverse samples and a variety of research methods, have replicated the disparities between males and females in mating priorities and preferences (Okami & Shackelford, 2001; Schmitt, 2005).

Criticism and Alternative Explanations

So, the findings on gender differences in sexual motivation mesh very nicely with predictions derived from evolutionary theory. But, in the world of science, everyone is a critic—so you may be wondering: What type of criticism has this line of research generated? One set of concerns centers on the fact that the findings do not paint a very flattering picture of human nature. Men end up looking like sordid sexual predators; women come across as cynical, greedy materialists; and evolutionary theory appears to endorse these realities as the inevitable outcome of natural selection. As Buss (1998) acknowledges, "Much of what I discovered about human mating is not nice" (p. 408). This controversy demonstrates once again that psychological theories can have far-reaching social and political implications, but the sociopolitical fallout has no bearing on evolutionary theory's scientific validity.

However, some critics *have* expressed doubts about the validity of evolutionary explanations of gender differences in sexual motivation. They note that one can easily come up with alternative explanations for the findings. For example, women's emphasis on males' material resources could be a by-product of cultural and economic forces rather than biological forces (Wallen, 1989). Women may have learned to value males' economic clout because their own economic potential has been severely limited in virtually all cultures by a long history of discrimination

(Hrdy, 1997; Kasser & Sharma, 1999). In a similar vein, Roy Baumeister, who has convincingly documented that men have stronger sexual motivation than women (Baumeister et al., 2001), has argued that this disparity may be largely the result of extensive cultural processes that serve to suppress female sexuality (Baumeister & Twenge, 2002). Evolutionary theorists counter these arguments by pointing out that the cultural and economic processes at work may themselves be products of evolution. This interesting debate is likely to continue for some time.

The Mystery of Sexual Orientation

Sex must be a contentious topic, as the controversy swirling around evolutionary explanations of gender differences in sexuality is easily equaled by the controversy surrounding the determinants of *sexual orientation*. **Sexual orientation** refers to a person's preference for emotional and sexual relationships with individuals of the same sex, the other sex, or either sex. *Heterosexuals* seek emotional-sexual relationships with members of the other sex, *bisexuals* with members of either sex, and *homosexuals* with members of the same sex. In recent years, the terms *gay* and *straight* have become widely used to refer to homosexuals and heterosexuals, respectively. Although *gay* can refer to homosexuals of either sex, most homosexual women prefer to call themselves *lesbians*.

People tend to view heterosexuality and homosexuality as an all-or-none distinction. However, in a large-scale survey of sexual behavior, Alfred Kinsey and his colleagues (1948, 1953) discovered that many people who define themselves as heterosexuals have had homosexual experiences—and vice versa. Thus, Kinsey and others have concluded that it is more accurate to view heterosexuality and homosexuality as end points on a continuum (Haslam, 1997). Indeed, Kinsey devised a seven-point scale, shown in **Figure 9.9** on the next page, that can be used to characterize individuals' sexual orientation.

How common is homosexuality? No one knows for sure. Part of the problem is that this question is vastly more complex than it appears at first glance (LeVay, 1996). Given that sexual orientation is best represented as a continuum, where do you draw the lines between heterosexuality, bisexuality, and homosexuality? And how do you handle the distinction between overt behavior and desire? Where, for instance, do you put a person who is married and has never engaged in homosexual behavior but who

Courtesy of David M. Buss

DAVID BUSS

"Evolutionary psychologists develop hypotheses about the psychological mechanisms that have evolved in humans to solve particular adaptive problems that humans have faced under ancestral conditions."

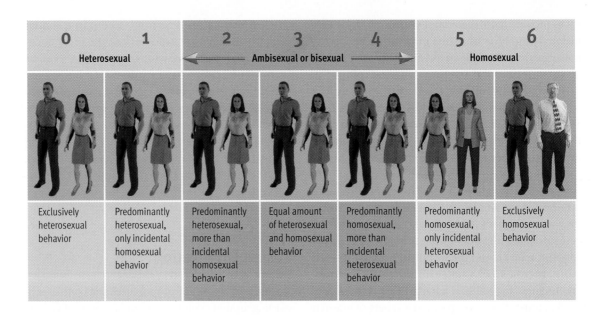

Figure 9.9

Homosexuality and heterosexuality as endpoints on a continuum. Sex researchers view heterosexuality and homosexuality as falling on a continuum rather than make an all-or-none distinction. Kinsey and his associates (1948, 1953) created this seven-point scale (from 0 to 6) to describe people's sexual orientation. They used the term *ambisexual* to describe those who fall in the middle of the scale, but such people are commonly called *bisexual* today.

0	1	2	3	4	5	6
Heterosexual		Ambisexual or bisexual			Homosexual	
Exclusively heterosexual behavior	Predominantly heterosexual, only incidental homosexual behavior	Predominantly heterosexual, more than incidental homosexual behavior	Equal amount of heterosexual and homosexual behavior	Predominantly homosexual, more than incidental heterosexual behavior	Predominantly homosexual, only incidental heterosexual behavior	Exclusively homosexual behavior

reports homosexual fantasies and acknowledges being strongly drawn to members of the same sex? The other part of the problem is that many people have extremely prejudicial attitudes about homosexuality, which makes gays cautious and reluctant to give candid information about their sexuality (Herek, 1996, 2000). Small wonder then that estimates of the portion of the population that is homosexual vary widely. A frequently cited estimate of the number of people who are gay is 10%, but recent surveys suggest that this percentage may be an overestimate. Michaels (1996) has combined data from two of the better large-scale surveys to arrive at the estimates seen in **Figure 9.10**. As you can see, the numbers are open to varying interpretations, but as a whole they suggest that about 5%–8% of the population could reasonably be characterized as homosexual.

Environmental Theories of Homosexuality

Over the years many environmental theories have been floated to explain the origins of homosexuality, but when tested empirically, these theories have received remarkably little support. For example, psychoanalytic and behavioral theorists, who usually agree on very little, both proposed environmental explanations for the development of homosexuality. The Freudian theorists argued that a male is likely to become gay when raised by a weak, detached, ineffectual father who is a poor heterosexual role model and by an overprotective, overly attached mother, with whom the boy identifies. Behavioral theorists argued that homosexuality is a learned preference acquired when same-sex stimuli have been paired with sexual arousal, perhaps through chance seductions by adult homosexuals. Extensive research on homosexuals' upbringing and childhood experiences have failed to support either of these theories (Bell, Weinberg, & Hammersmith, 1981).

However, efforts to research homosexuals' personal histories have yielded a number of interesting insights. Extremely feminine behavior in young boys or masculine behavior in young girls does predict the subsequent development of homosexuality (Bailey & Zucker, 1995). For example, 75%–90% of highly

Figure 9.10

How common is homosexuality? The answer to this question is both complex and controversial. Michaels (1996) brought together data from two large-scale surveys to arrive at the estimates shown here. If you look at how many people have actually had a same-sex partner in the last five years, the figures are relatively low, but if you count those who have had a same-sex partner since puberty the figures more than double. Still another way to look at it is to ask people whether they are attracted to people of the same sex (regardless of their actual behavior). This approach suggests that about 8% of the population could be characterized as homosexual. (Data from Michaels, 1996)

feminine young boys eventually turn out to be gay (Blanchard et al., 1995). Consistent with this finding, most gay men and women report that they can trace their homosexual leanings back to their early childhood, even before they understood what sex was really about (Bailey, 2003). Most also report that because of negative parental and societal attitudes about homosexuality, they initially struggled to deny their sexual orientation. Hence, they felt that their homosexuality was not a matter of choice and not something that they could readily change (Breedlove, 1994). Although people's subjective recollections of the past need to be interpreted with caution, these findings suggest that the roots of homosexuality are more biological than environmental.

Biological Theories of Homosexuality

Nonetheless, initial efforts to find a biological basis for homosexuality met with little success. Most theorists originally assumed that hormonal differences between heterosexuals and homosexuals must underlie a person's sexual orientation (Doerr et al., 1976; Dorner, 1988). However, studies comparing circulating hormone levels in gays and straights found only small, inconsistent differences that could not be linked to sexual orientation in any convincing way (Bailey, 2003; Banks & Gartrell, 1995).

Thus, like environmental theorists, biological theorists were frustrated for quite a while in their efforts to explain the roots of homosexuality. However, that picture changed dramatically in the 1990s (Gladue, 1994). For example, in one landmark investigation, Bailey and Pillard (1991) studied gay men who had either a twin brother or an adopted brother. They found that 52% of the participants' identical twins were gay, that 22% of their fraternal twins were gay, and that 11% of their adoptive brothers were gay. A companion study (Bailey et al., 1993) of lesbians yielded a similar pattern of results (see **Figure 9.11**). Given that identical twins share more genetic overlap than fraternal twins, who share more genes than unrelated adoptive siblings, these results suggest that there is a genetic predisposition to homosexuality (see Chapter 3 for an explanation of the logic underlying twin and adoption studies). More recent twin studies, with larger and more representative samples, have provided further support for the conclusion that heredity influences sexual orientation, although these studies have yielded smaller estimates of genetic influence (Bailey, Dunne, & Martin, 2000; Kendler et al., 2000).

Many theorists suspect that the roots of homosexuality may lie in the organizing effects of prenatal hormones on neurological development. Several

lines of research suggest that hormonal secretions during critical periods of prenatal development may shape sexual development, organize the brain in a lasting manner, and influence subsequent sexual orientation (Berenbaum & Snyder, 1995). For example, researchers have found elevated rates of homosexuality among women exposed to abnormally high androgen levels during prenatal development (because their mothers had an adrenal disorder or were given a synthetic hormone to reduce the risk of miscarriage) (Breedlove, 1994; Meyer-Bahlburg et al., 1995). Several other independent lines of research suggest that abnormalities in prenatal hormonal secretions may foster a predisposition to homosexuality (Mustanski, Chivers, & Bailey, 2002).

Despite the recent breakthroughs, much remains to be learned about the determinants of sexual orientation. The fact that identical twins of gay subjects turn out to be gay only about half the time suggests that the genetic predisposition to homosexuality is not overpowering. Environmental influences probably contribute to the development of homosexuality (Bem, 1996, 1998), but the nature of these environmental factors remains a matter of speculation.

Another complication is that the pathways to homosexuality may be somewhat different for males as opposed to females (Gladue, 1994). Females' sexuality appears to be characterized by more *plasticity* than males' sexuality (Baumeister, 2000). In other words, women's sexual behavior may be more easily shaped and modified by sociocultural factors. For example, although sexual orientation is assumed to be a stable characteristic, research shows that lesbian and bisexual women often change their sexual orientation over the course of their adult years (Diamond, 2003). And, in comparison to gay males, lesbians are less likely to trace their homosexuality back to their

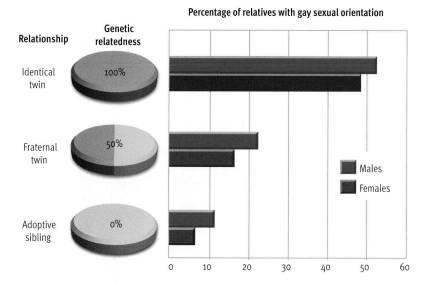

Percentage of relatives with gay sexual orientation

Figure 9.11

Genetics and sexual orientation. If relatives who share more genetic relatedness show greater similarity on a trait than relatives who share less genetic overlap, this evidence suggests a genetic predisposition to the characteristic. Recent studies of both gay men and lesbian women have found a higher prevalence of homosexuality among their identical twins than their fraternal twins, who, in turn, are more likely to be homosexual than their adoptive siblings. These findings suggest that genetic factors influence sexual orientation. (Data from Bailey & Pillard, 1991; Bailey et. al., 1993)

Web Link **9.4**

Queer Resources Directory (QRD)
In its 1994 mission statement, the Queer Resources Directory described itself as "an electronic research library specifically dedicated to sexual minorities—groups that have traditionally been labeled as 'queer' and systematically discriminated against." Composed of more than 22,000 files and still growing, QRD offers a rich array of resources.

Some people are befuddled by the fact that actress Anne Heche (left) had a lengthy intimate relationship with comedian Ellen DeGeneres (right), but now has settled into a conventional hetero-sexual marriage. Although shifts in sexual orientation like this are uncommon among males, research has shown that females' sexual orientation tends to be characterized by more plasticity than that of males. These findings suggest that males' and females' pathways into homosexuality may be some-what different.

© John Lazar/Los Angeles Daily News/Corbis Sygma

childhood and more likely to indicate that their attraction to the same sex emerged during adulthood (Tolman & Diamond, 2001). These findings suggest that sexual orientation may be more fluid and malleable in women than in men.

Once again, though, we can see that the nature versus nurture debate can have far-reaching social and political implications. Homosexuals have long been victims of extensive—and in many instances legal—discrimination. Gays cannot legally formalize their unions in marriage (in most jurisdictions), they are not allowed to openly join the United States military forces, and they are barred from some jobs (for example, many school districts will not hire gays as classroom teachers). However, if research were to show that being gay is largely a matter of biological destiny, much like being black or female or short, many of the arguments against equal rights for gays would disintegrate. Why ban gays from teaching, for instance, if their sexual preference cannot "rub off" on their students? Many individuals' opinions about gay rights may be swayed by the outcome of the nature-nurture debate on the roots of homosexuality.

> Achievement: In Search of Excellence

PREVIEW QUESTIONS

- What is the achievement motive, and how is it measured?
- How do those who score high in the need for achievement behave?
- What are some situational factors that can influence achievement strivings?

At the beginning of this chapter, we discussed Jon Krakauer's laborious, grueling effort to reach the summit of Mount Everest. He and the other climbers confronted incredible perils and endured extraordinary hardships to achieve their goal. What motivates people to push themselves so hard? In all likelihood, it's a strong need for achievement. **The *achievement motive* is the need to master difficult challenges, to outperform others, and to meet high standards of excellence.** Above all else, the need for achievement involves the desire to excel, especially in competition with others.

Research on achievement motivation was pioneered by David McClelland and his colleagues (McClelland, 1985; McClelland et al., 1953). McClelland argued that achievement motivation is of the utmost importance. He viewed the need for achievement as the spark that ignites economic growth, scientific progress, inspirational leadership, and masterpieces in the creative arts.

Individual Differences in the Need for Achievement

PsykTrek 8b

The need for achievement is a fairly stable aspect of personality. Thus, research in this area has focused

mostly on individual differences in achievement motivation. In this research, investigators usually measure participants' need for achievement with some variant of the Thematic Apperception Test (TAT) (Smith, 1992; Spangler, 1992). The TAT is a *projective* test, a test that requires subjects to respond to vague, ambiguous stimuli in ways that may reveal personal motives and traits (see Chapter 11). The stimulus materials for the TAT are pictures of people in ambiguous scenes open to interpretation. Examples include a man working at a desk and a woman seated in a chair staring off into space. Participants are asked to write or tell stories about what's happening in the scenes and what the characters are feeling. The themes of these stories are then scored to measure the strength of various needs. **Figure 9.12** shows examples of stories dominated by themes of achievement and, as another example, affiliation needs.

The research on individual differences in achievement motivation has yielded interesting findings on the characteristics of people who score high in the need for achievement. For instance, they tend to work harder and more persistently on tasks than people low in the need for achievement (Brown, 1974), and they handle negative feedback about task performance more effectively than others (Fodor & Carver, 2000). They are also more likely than others

Affiliation arousal

George is an engineer who is working late. He is *worried that his wife will be annoyed* with him for neglecting her. She has been *objecting* that he cares more about his work than his wife and family. He seems *unable to satisfy* both his boss and his wife, but he *loves her* very much and will do his best to *finish up* fast and get home to her.

Achievement arousal

George is an engineer who *wants to win* a competition in which the man with the *most practicable drawing* will be awarded the contract to build a bridge. He is taking a moment to think *how happy he will be* if he wins. He has been *baffled by how to make such a long span strong*, but he remembers to *specify a new steel alloy* of great strength, submits his entry, but does not win, and is *very unhappy*.

Figure 9.12

Measuring motives with the Thematic Apperception Test (TAT). Subjects taking the TAT tell or write stories about what is happening in a scene, such as this one showing a man at work. The two stories shown here illustrate strong affiliation motivation and strong achievement motivation. The italicized parts of the stories are thematic ideas that would be identified by a TAT scorer.

Source: Stories reprinted by permission of Dr. David McClelland.

to delay gratification in order to pursue long-term goals (Mischel, 1961; Raynor & Entin, 1982). In terms of careers, they typically go into competitive occupations that provide them with an opportunity to excel (McClelland, 1987). Apparently, their persistence and hard work often pay off: High achievement motivation correlates positively with measures of career success and with upward social mobility among lower-class men (Crockett, 1962; McClelland & Boyatzis, 1982).

Do people high in achievement need always tackle the biggest challenges available? Not necessarily. A curious finding has emerged in laboratory studies in which subjects have been asked to choose the difficulty level of a task to work on. Participants high in the need for achievement tend to select tasks of intermediate difficulty (McClelland & Koestner, 1992). For instance, in a study in which subjects playing a ring-tossing game were allowed to stand as close to or as far away from the target peg as they wanted, high achievers tended to prefer a moderate degree of challenge (Atkinson & Litwin, 1960). Research on the situational determinants of achievement behavior has suggested a reason.

Situational Determinants of Achievement Behavior

 8b

Your achievement drive is not the only determinant of how hard you work. Situational factors can also influence achievement strivings. John Atkinson (1974, 1981, 1992) has elaborated extensively on McClelland's original theory of achievement motivation and has identified some important situational determinants of achievement behavior. Atkinson theorizes that the tendency to pursue achievement in a particular situation depends on the following factors:

- The strength of one's *motivation* to *achieve* success, which is viewed as a stable aspect of personality.
- One's estimate of the *probability of success* for the task at hand. Such estimates vary from task to task.
- The *incentive value* of success, which depends on the tangible and intangible rewards for success on the specific task.

The last two variables are situational determinants of achievement behavior. That is, they vary from one situation to another. According to Atkinson, the pursuit of achievement increases as the probability of success and incentive value of success go up.

Let's apply Atkinson's model to a simple example. According to his theory, your tendency to pursue a good grade in calculus should depend on your general motivation to achieve success, your estimate of the probability of getting a good grade in the class, and the value you place on getting a good grade in calculus. Thus, given a certain motivation to achieve success, you will pursue a good grade in calculus less vigorously if your professor gives impossible exams (thus lowering your expectancy of success) or if a good grade in calculus is not required for your major (lowering the incentive value of success).

The joint influence of these situational factors may explain why people with a high need for achievement prefer tasks of intermediate difficulty. Atkinson notes that the probability of success and the incentive value of success on tasks are interdependent to some degree. As tasks get easier, success becomes less satisfying. As tasks get harder, success becomes more satisfying but becomes less likely. When the probability and incentive value of success are weighed together, moderately challenging tasks seem to offer the best overall value.

We turn next to the study of emotion. Motivation and emotion are often intertwined (Zurbriggen & Sturman, 2002). On the one hand, *emotion can cause*

DAVID McCLELLAND

"People with a high need for achievement are not gamblers; they are challenged to win by personal effort, not by luck."

Boston University Photo Services, courtesy of David McClelland

Understanding the Determinants of Achievement Behavior

According to John Atkinson, one's pursuit of achievement in a particular situation depends on several factors. Check your understanding of these factors by identifying each of the following vignettes as an example of one of the following determinants of achievement behavior: (a) need for achievement; (b) perceived probability of success; (c) incentive value of success. The answers can be found in Appendix A.

_____ **1.** Belinda is nervously awaiting the start of the finals of the 200-meter dash in the last meet of her high school career. "I've gotta win this race! This is the most important race of my life!"

_____ **2.** Corey grins as he contemplates the political science course that he is taking next semester. "I am just about sure I will get an A in the course. I hear it is pretty easy."

_____ **3.** Diana's gotten the highest grade on every test throughout the semester, yet she's still up all night studying for the final. "I know I've got an A in the bag, but I want to be the best student Dr. McClelland's ever had!"

motivation. For example, *anger* about your work schedule may motivate you to look for a new job. *Jealousy* of an ex-girlfriend may motivate you to ask out her roommate. On the other hand, *motivation can cause emotion.* For example, your motivation to win a pho-tography contest may lead to great *anxiety* during the judging and either *elation* if you win or *gloom* if you don't. Although motivation and emotion are closely related, they're *not* the same thing. We'll analyze the nature of emotion in the next section.

> The Elements of Emotional Experience

PREVIEW QUESTIONS

● How do emotions affect autonomic activity?

● How does a lie detector work?

● Which brain centers contribute to the experience of emotions?

● What is the connection between emotion and body language?

● Are there cultural differences in how people recognize, describe, or express their emotions?

The most profound and important experiences in life are saturated with emotion. Think of the *joy* that people feel at weddings, the *grief* they feel at funerals, the *ecstasy* they feel when they fall in love. Emotions also color everyday experiences. For instance, you might experience *anger* when a professor treats you rudely, *dismay* when you learn that your car needs expensive repairs, and *happiness* when you see that you aced your economics exam. In some respects, emotions lie at the core of mental health. The two most common complaints that lead people to seek psychotherapy are *depression* and *anxiety.* Clearly, emotions play an important role in people's lives. Reflecting this reality, modern psychologists have increased their research on emotion in recent decades (Cacioppo & Gardner, 1999).

Exactly what is an emotion? Everyone has plenty of personal experience with emotion, but it's an elusive concept to define (LeDoux, 1995). Emotion includes cognitive, physiological, and behavioral components, which are summarized in the following definition: **Emotion involves (1) a subjective conscious experience (the cognitive component) accompanied by (2) bodily arousal (the physiolog-**ical component) and (3) characteristic overt expressions (the behavioral component). That's a pretty complex definition. Let's take a closer look at each of these three components of emotion.

The Cognitive Component: Subjective Feelings

More than 550 words in the English language refer to emotions (Averill, 1980). Ironically, however, people often have difficulty describing their emotions (Zajonc, 1980). Emotion is a highly personal, subjective experience. In studying the cognitive component of emotions, psychologists generally rely on subjects' verbal reports of what they're experiencing. Their reports indicate that emotions are potentially intense internal feelings that sometimes seem to have a life of their own. People can't switch their emotions on and off like a bedroom light. If it were that simple, you could choose to be happy whenever you wanted. As Joseph LeDoux puts it, "Emotions are things that happen to us rather than things we will to occur" (1996, p. 19). Although some degree of emotional control is actually possible (Thayer, 1996), emotions tend to involve automatic reactions that are difficult to regulate (Ohman & Wiens, 2003).

People's cognitive appraisals of events in their lives are key determinants of the emotions they experience (Ellsworth & Scherer, 2003; Lazarus, 1995). A specific event, such as giving a speech, may be a highly threatening and thus anxiety-arousing occasion for one person but a "ho-hum," routine matter for another. The conscious experience of emotion includes an *evaluative* aspect. People characterize their emotions as pleasant or unpleasant (Lang, 1995; Schlosberg, 1954). These evaluative reactions can be automatic and subconscious (Ferguson & Bargh, 2004). Of course, individuals often experience "mixed emotions" that include both pleasant and unpleasant qualities (Cacioppo & Berntson, 1999). For example, an executive just given a promotion with challenging new responsibilities may experience both happiness and anxiety. The landscape of mixed emotions was explored in a recent study of people's reactions to good outcomes that could have been better and bad outcomes that could have been worse (Larsen et al., 2004). As predicted, these events elicited mixtures of positive and negative emotions. These contrasting emotions tended to occur *simultaneously* rather than alternating back and forth sequentially.

For the most part, researchers have paid more attention to negative emotions than positive ones (Fredrickson, 1998). Why have positive emotions been neglected? Fredrickson and Branigan (2001) note that there appear to be fewer positive than negative emotions and that positive emotions are less clearly differentiated from each other than negative emotions. Another consideration is that negative emotions appear to have more powerful effects than positive ones (Baumeister et al., 2001). Although these factors probably have contributed, the neglect of positive emotions is symptomatic of a broad and deeply rooted bias in the field of psychology, which has historically focused on pathology, weaknesses, and suffering (and how to heal these conditions) rather than on health, strengths, and resilience (Fredrickson, 2002). In recent years, the architects of the "positive psychology movement" have set out to shift the field's focus away from negative experiences (Seligman, 2002; Seligman & Csikszentmihalyi, 2000). The advocates of *positive psychology* argue for increased research on contentment, well-being, human strengths, and positive emotions. One outgrowth of this movement has been increased interest in the dynamics of happiness. We will discuss this research in the upcoming Personal Application.

© LWA-Dann Tardiff//Corbis

Emotions involve automatic reactions that can be difficult to control.

The Physiological Component: Diffuse and Multifaceted

Emotional processes are closely tied to physiological processes, but the interconnections are enormously complex. The biological bases of emotions are diffuse and multifaceted, involving many areas in the brain and many neurotransmitter systems, as well as the autonomic nervous system and the endocrine system.

Autonomic Arousal

Imagine your reaction as your car spins out of control on an icy highway. Your fear is accompanied by a variety of physiological changes. Your heart rate and breathing accelerate. Your blood pressure surges, and your pupils dilate. The hairs on your skin stand erect, giving you "goose bumps," and you start to perspire. Although your reactions may not always be as obvious as in this scenario, *emotions are accompanied by physical arousal* (Cacioppo et al., 1993). Surely you've experienced a "knot in your stomach" or a "lump in your throat" thanks to anxiety.

Much of the physiological arousal associated with emotion occurs through the actions of the *autonomic nervous system* (Janig, 2003), which regulates the activity of glands, smooth muscles, and blood vessels (see **Figure 9.13** on the next page). As you may recall from Chapter 3, the autonomic nervous system is responsible for the highly emotional *fight-or-flight response,* which is largely modulated by the release of

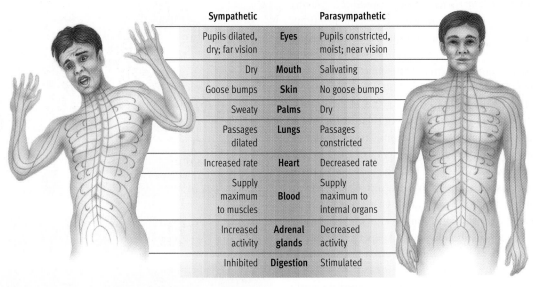

Sympathetic		Parasympathetic
Pupils dilated, dry; far vision	**Eyes**	Pupils constricted, moist; near vision
Dry	**Mouth**	Salivating
Goose bumps	**Skin**	No goose bumps
Sweaty	**Palms**	Dry
Passages dilated	**Lungs**	Passages constricted
Increased rate	**Heart**	Decreased rate
Supply maximum to muscles	**Blood**	Supply maximum to internal organs
Increased activity	**Adrenal glands**	Decreased activity
Inhibited	**Digestion**	Stimulated

Figure 9.13

Emotion and autonomic arousal. The autonomic nervous system (ANS) is composed of the nerves that connect to the heart, blood vessels, smooth muscles, and glands (consult Chapter 3 for more information). The ANS is divided into the *sympathetic division,* which mobilizes bodily resources in response to stress, and the *parasympathetic division,* which conserves bodily resources. Emotions are frequently accompanied by sympathetic ANS activation, which leads to goose bumps, sweaty palms, and the other physical responses listed on the left side of the diagram.

Figure 9.14

Emotion and the polygraph. A lie detector measures the autonomic arousal that most people experience when they tell a lie. After using nonthreatening questions to establish a baseline, a polygraph examiner looks for signs of arousal (such as the sharp change in GSR shown here) on incriminating questions. Unfortunately, as your text explains, the polygraph is not a very dependable index of whether people are lying.

adrenal *hormones* that radiate throughout the body. Hormonal changes clearly play a crucial role in emotional responses to stress and may contribute to many other emotions as well (Baum, Grunberg, & Singer, 1992).

The connection between emotion and autonomic arousal provides the basis for the *polygraph,* or *lie detector,* **a device that records autonomic fluctuations while a subject is questioned.** The polygraph was invented in 1915 by psychologist William Marston—who also dreamed up the comic book superhero Wonder Woman (Knight, 2004). A polygraph can't actually detect lies. It's really an emotion detector. It monitors key indicators of autonomic arousal, typically heart rate, blood pressure, respiration rate, and *galvanic skin response (GSR),* **an increase in the electrical conductivity of the skin that occurs when sweat glands increase their activity.** The assumption is that when people lie, they experience emotion (presumably anxiety) that produces noticeable changes in these physiological indicators (see **Figure 9.14**). The polygraph examiner asks a subject a number of nonthreatening questions to establish the person's baseline on these autonomic indicators.

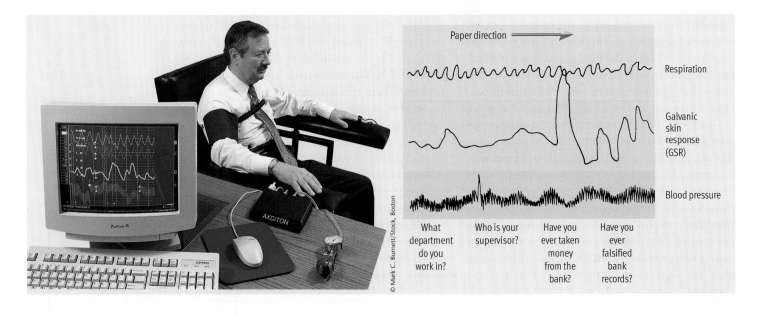

Paper direction →

Respiration

Galvanic skin response (GSR)

Blood pressure

What department do you work in?   Who is your supervisor?   Have you ever taken money from the bank?   Have you ever falsified bank records?

© Mark C. Burnett/Stock, Boston

Then the examiner asks the critical questions (for example, "Were you at home on the night of the burglary?") and observes whether the subject's autonomic arousal changes.

The polygraph has been controversial since its invention (Grubin & Madsen, 2005). Polygraph advocates claim that lie detector tests are about 85%–90% accurate and that the validity of polygraph testing has been demonstrated in empirical studies, but these claims clearly are not supported by the evidence (Iacono & Lykken, 1997; Iacono & Patrick, 1999). Methodologically sound research on the validity of polygraph testing is surprisingly sparse (largely because it is difficult research to do), and the limited evidence available is not very impressive (Branaman & Gallagher, 2005; Lykken, 1998; Saxe & Ben-Shakhar, 1999). Part of the problem is that people who are telling the truth may experience emotional arousal when they respond to incriminating questions. Thus, polygraph tests sometimes lead to accusations against people who are innocent. Another problem is that some people can lie without experiencing anxiety or autonomic arousal. The heart of the problem, as Leonard Saxe (1994) notes, is that "there is no evidence of a unique physiological reaction to deceit" (p. 71). The polygraph *is* a potentially useful tool that can help police check out leads and alibis. However, polygraph results are not reliable enough to be submitted as evidence in most types of courtrooms.

Neural Circuits

The autonomic responses that accompany emotions are ultimately controlled in the brain. The hypothalamus, amygdala, and adjacent structures in the *limbic system* have long been viewed as the seat of emotions in the brain (Izard & Saxton, 1988; MacLean, 1993). Although these structures do contribute to emotion, the limbic system is not a clearly defined anatomical system (see Chapter 3), and research has shown that a variety of brain structures that lie outside the limbic system play a variety of roles in the regulation of emotion (Berridge, 2003).

Recent evidence suggests that the *amygdala* plays a particularly central role in the acquisition of conditioned fears (LaBar & LeDoux, 2003). According to Joseph LeDoux (1996, 2000), sensory inputs capable of eliciting emotions arrive in the thalamus, which simultaneously routes the information along two separate pathways: to the nearby amygdala and to areas in the cortex (see **Figure 9.15**). The amygdala processes the information quickly, and if it detects a threat it almost instantly triggers activity in the hypothalamus that leads to autonomic arousal and

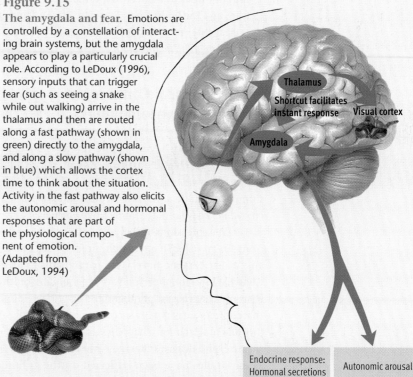

Figure 9.15

The amygdala and fear. Emotions are controlled by a constellation of interacting brain systems, but the amygdala appears to play a particularly crucial role. According to LeDoux (1996), sensory inputs that can trigger fear (such as seeing a snake while out walking) arrive in the thalamus and then are routed along a fast pathway (shown in green) directly to the amygdala, and along a slow pathway (shown in blue) which allows the cortex time to think about the situation. Activity in the fast pathway also elicits the autonomic arousal and hormonal responses that are part of the physiological component of emotion. (Adapted from LeDoux, 1994)

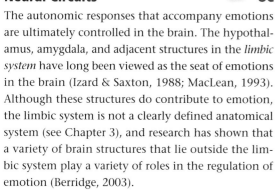

Thalamus
Shortcut facilitates instant response
Visual cortex
Amygdala

Endocrine response: Hormonal secretions

Autonomic arousal

hormonal responses. The processing in this pathway is extremely fast, so that emotions may be triggered even before the cortex has had a chance to really "think" about the input. LeDoux believes that this rapid-response pathway evolved because it is a highly adaptive warning system that can "be the difference between life and death."

What other areas of the brain are involved in the modulation of emotion? The list is extensive. Much like we saw with sleep and memory (see Chapters 5 and 7), the neural bases of emotion are widely distributed throughout the brain. Some of the more intriguing findings include the following:

- The *prefrontal cortex,* known for its role in planning and executive control, appears to contribute to efforts to voluntarily control emotional reactions (Davidson, Jackson, & Kalin, 2000). The prefrontal cortex also seems to modulate emotions associated with the pursuit of goals (Davidson et al., 2003b).

- As noted in Chapters 3 and 5, a neural circuit called the *mesolimbic dopamine pathway* plays a major role in the experience of pleasureable emotions associated with rewarding events (Berridge, 2003). In particular, this circuit is activated by cocaine and other abused drugs (Nestler & Malenka, 2004).

- Quite a variety of other brain structures have been linked to specific facets of emotion, including the

Courtesy of Joseph LeDoux, New York University

JOSEPH LEDOUX

"In situations of danger, it is very useful to be able to respond quickly. The time saved by the amygdala in acting on the thalamic information, rather than waiting for the cortical input, may be the difference between life and death."

hippocampus, the lateral hypothalamus, the septum, and the brain stem (Berridge, 2003). Thus, it is clear that emotion depends on activity in a *constellation of interacting brain centers.*

The Behavioral Component: Nonverbal Expressiveness

At the behavioral level, people reveal their emotions through characteristic overt expressions such as smiles, frowns, furrowed brows, clenched fists, and slumped shoulders. In other words, *emotions are expressed in "body language," or nonverbal behavior.*

Facial expressions reveal a variety of basic emotions. In an extensive research project, Paul Ekman and Wallace Friesen have asked participants to identify what emotion a person was experiencing on the basis of facial cues in photographs. They have found that subjects are generally successful in identifying six fundamental emotions: happiness, sadness, anger, fear, surprise, and disgust (Ekman & Friesen, 1975, 1984). These studies have been criticized on the grounds that they have used a rather small set of artificial, highly posed photographs that don't do justice to the variety of facial expressions that can accompany specific emotions (Carroll & Russell, 1997). Still, the overall evidence indicates that people are reasonably skilled at identifying emotions from others' facial expressions (Galati, Scherer, & Ricci-Bitti, 1997).

Some theorists believe that muscular feedback from one's own facial expressions contributes to one's conscious experience of emotions (Izard, 1990; Tomkins, 1991). Proponents of the *facial-feedback hypothesis* assert that facial muscles send signals to the brain and that these signals help the brain recognize the emotion that one is experiencing. According to this view, smiles, frowns, and furrowed brows help create the experience of various emotions. Consistent with this idea, studies show that if subjects are instructed to contract their facial muscles to mimic facial expressions associated with certain emotions, they tend to report that they actually experience these emotions to some degree (Kleinke, Peterson, & Rutledge, 1998; Levenson, 1992).

Culture and the Elements of Emotion

Are emotions innate reactions that are universal across cultures? Or are they socially learned reactions that are culturally variable? The research on this lingering question has not yielded a simple answer. Investigators have found both remarkable similarities and dramatic differences among cultures in the experience of emotion.

Cross-Cultural Similarities in Emotional Experience

After demonstrating that Western subjects could discern specific emotions from facial expressions, Ekman and Friesen (1975) took their facial-cue photographs on the road to other societies to see whether nonverbal expressions of emotion transcend cultural boundaries. Testing participants in Argentina, Spain, Japan, and other countries, they found considerable cross-cultural agreement in the identification of happiness, sadness, anger, fear, surprise, and disgust based on facial expressions (see **Figure 9.16**). Still, Ekman and Friesen wondered whether this agreement might be the result of learning rather than biology, given that people in different cultures often share considerable exposure to Western mass media (magazines, newspapers, television, and so forth), which provide many visual depictions of people's emotional reactions. To rule out this possibility, they took their photos to a remote area in New Guinea and showed them to a group of natives (the Fore) who had had virtually no contact with Western culture. Even the people from this preliterate culture did a fair job of identifying the emotions portrayed in the pictures (see **Figure 9.16**). Subsequent comparisons of many other societies have also shown considerable cross-cultural agreement in the judgment of facial expressions (Biehl et al., 1997; Ekman, 1992, 1993; Izard, 1994). Cross-cultural similarities have also been found in the cognitive appraisals that lead to emotions (Frijda, 1999; Scherer, 1997) and in the physiological arousal that accompanies emotional experience (Scherer & Wallbott, 1994).

Cross-Cultural Differences in Emotional Experience

The cross-cultural similarities in emotional experience are impressive, but researchers have also found many cultural disparities in how people think about and express their emotions (Mesquita, 2001, 2003). Foremost among these disparities are the fascinating variations in how cultures categorize emotions. Some basic categories of emotion that are universally understood in Western cultures appear to go unrecognized—or at least unnamed—in some non-Western cultures. James Russell (1991) has compiled numerous examples of English words for emotions that have no equivalent in other languages. For example, Tahitians have no word that corresponds to *sadness.* Many non-Western groups, including the Yoruba of Nigeria, the Kaluli of New Guinea, and the Chinese, lack

Web Link 9.5

UCSC Perceptual Science Laboratory
Perceptions of other people, especially speech perception and facial expression, serve as a primary focus for research at this laboratory at the University of California, Santa Cruz. The site offers a broad set of resources, including a comprehensive guide to nonverbal facial analysis research being conducted in laboratories worldwide.

Figure 9.16

Cross-cultural comparisons of people's ability to recognize emotions from facial expressions. Ekman and Friesen (1975) found that people in highly disparate cultures showed fair agreement on the emotions portrayed in these photos. This consensus across cultures suggests that facial expressions of emotions may be universal and that they have a strong biological basis.

Source: Data from Ekman, P., & Friesen, W. V. (1975). *Unmasking the Face.* Englewood Cliffs, NJ: Prentice-Hall. © 1975 by Paul Ekman, photographs courtesy of Paul Ekman.

	Fear	Disgust	Happiness	Anger
Country		**Agreement in judging photos (%)**		
United States	85	92	97	67
Brazil	67	97	95	90
Chile	68	92	95	94
Argentina	54	92	98	90
Japan	66	90	100	90
New Guinea	54	44	82	50

a word for *depression.* The concept of *anxiety* seems to go unrecognized among Eskimos and the Yoruba, and the Quichua of Ecuador lack a word for *remorse.*

Cultural disparities have also been found in regard to nonverbal expressions of emotion. Although the natural facial expressions associated with basic emotions appear to be universal, people can and do learn to control and modify these expressions. *Display rules* **are norms that regulate the appropriate expression of emotions.** They prescribe when, how, and to whom people can show various emotions. These norms vary from one culture to another

(Ekman, 1992), as do attitudes about specific emotions (Eid & Diener, 2001). The Ifaluk of Micronesia, for instance, severely restrict expressions of happiness because they believe that this emotion often leads people to neglect their duties (Lutz, 1987). Japanese culture emphasizes the suppression of negative emotions in public. More so than in other cultures, the Japanese are socialized to mask emotions such as anger, sadness, and disgust with stoic facial expressions or polite smiling. Thus, nonverbal expressions of emotions vary somewhat across cultures because of culture-specific attitudes and display rules.

> Theories of Emotion

How do psychologists explain the experience of emotion? A variety of theories and conflicting models exist. Some have been vigorously debated for over a century. As we describe these theories, you'll recognize a familiar bone of contention. Like theories of motivation, theories of emotion differ in their emphasis on the innate biological basis of emotion versus the social, environmental basis.

James-Lange Theory

8d

As we noted in Chapter 1, William James was an early theorist who urged psychologists to explore the functions of consciousness. James (1884) developed a theory of emotion over 100 years ago that remains influential today. At about the same time, he and Carl Lange (1885) independently proposed that the *conscious experience of emotion results from one's per-*

ception of autonomic arousal. Their theory stood common sense on its head. Everyday logic suggests that when you stumble onto a rattlesnake in the woods, the conscious experience of fear leads to autonomic arousal (the fight-or-flight response). The James-Lange theory of emotion asserts the opposite: that the perception of autonomic arousal leads to the conscious experience of fear (see **Figure 9.17** on the next page). In other words, while you might assume that your pulse is racing because you're fearful, James and Lange argue that you're fearful because your pulse is racing.

The James-Lange theory emphasizes the physiological determinants of emotion. According to this view, *different patterns of autonomic activation lead to the experience of different emotions.* Hence, people supposedly distinguish emotions such as fear, joy, and anger on the basis of the exact configuration of physical reactions they experience. Decades of research

PREVIEW QUESTIONS

• What are the differences between the James-Lange and Cannon-Bard theories of emotion?

• How did the two-factor theory of emotion try to reconcile these differences?

• How do evolutionary theorists explain emotions?

Figure 9.17

Theories of emotion. Three influential theories of emotion are contrasted with one another and with the commonsense view. The James-Lange theory was the first to suggest that feelings of arousal cause emotion, rather than vice versa. Schachter built on this idea by adding a second factor—interpretation (appraisal and labeling) of arousal.

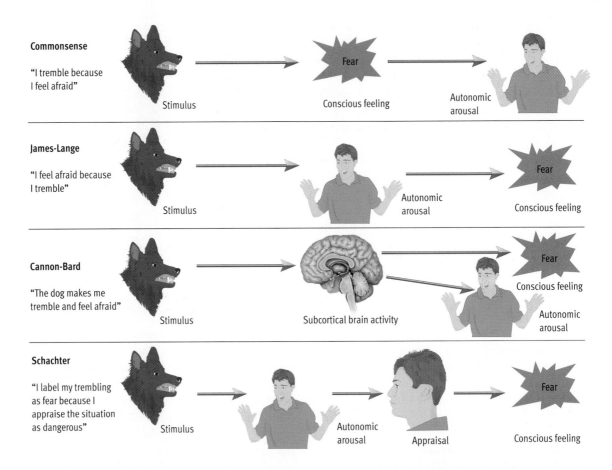

Commonsense

"I tremble because I feel afraid"

Stimulus → Conscious feeling (Fear) → Autonomic arousal

James-Lange

"I feel afraid because I tremble"

Stimulus → Autonomic arousal → Conscious feeling (Fear)

Cannon-Bard

"The dog makes me tremble and feel afraid"

Stimulus → Subcortical brain activity → Conscious feeling (Fear) / Autonomic arousal

Schachter

"I label my trembling as fear because I appraise the situation as dangerous"

Stimulus → Autonomic arousal → Appraisal → Conscious feeling (Fear)

have supported the concept of *autonomic specificity*—that different emotions are accompanied by different patterns of autonomic activation (Janig, 2003; Levenson, 2003). However, the question of whether people identify their emotions from these varied patterns of autonomic activation remains unresolved.

Cannon-Bard Theory 8d

Walter Cannon (1927) found the James-Lange theory unconvincing. Cannon pointed out that physiological arousal may occur without the experience of emotion (if one exercises vigorously, for instance). He also argued that visceral changes are too slow to precede the conscious experience of emotion. Finally, he argued that people experiencing very different emotions, such as fear, joy, and anger, exhibit almost identical patterns of autonomic arousal.

Thus, Cannon espoused a different explanation of emotion. Later, Philip Bard (1934) elaborated on it. The resulting Cannon-Bard theory argues that emotion occurs when the *thalamus* sends signals *simultaneously* to the cortex (creating the conscious experience of emotion) and to the autonomic nervous system (creating visceral arousal). The Cannon-Bard model is compared to the James-Lange model in **Figure 9.17**. Cannon and Bard were off the mark a bit in

pinpointing the thalamus as the neural center for emotion. However, many modern theorists agree with the Cannon-Bard view that emotions originate in subcortical brain structures (LeDoux, 1996; Panksepp, 1991; Rolls, 1990) and with the assertion that people do *not* infer their emotions from different patterns of autonomic activation (Frijda, 1999; Wagner, 1989).

Schachter's Two-Factor Theory 8d

In another influential analysis, Stanley Schachter asserted that people look at situational cues to differentiate between alternative emotions. According to Schachter (1964; Schachter & Singer, 1962, 1979), the experience of emotion depends on two factors: (1) autonomic arousal and (2) cognitive interpretation of that arousal. Schachter proposed that when you experience physiological arousal, you search your environment for an explanation (see **Figure 9.17** again). If you're stuck in a traffic jam, you'll probably label your arousal as anger. If you're taking an important exam, you'll probably label it as anxiety. If you're celebrating your birthday, you'll probably label it as happiness.

Schachter agrees with the James-Lange view that emotion is inferred from arousal. However, he also

STANLEY SCHACHTER

"Cognitive factors play a major role in determining how a subject interprets his bodily feelings."

Courtesy of Stanley Schachter, © Bill Apple

agrees with the Cannon-Bard position that different emotions yield indistinguishable patterns of arousal. He reconciles these views by arguing that people look to external rather than internal cues to differentiate and label their specific emotions. In essence, Schachter suggests that people think along the following lines: "If I'm aroused and you're obnoxious, I must be angry."

Although the two-factor theory has received support, studies have revealed some limitations as well (Leventhal & Tomarken, 1986). Situations can't mold emotions in just any way at any time. And in searching to explain arousal, subjects don't limit themselves to the immediate situation (Sinclair et al., 1994). Thus, emotions are not as pliable as the two-factor theory initially suggested.

Evolutionary Theories of Emotion

8d

In recent years, some theorists interested in emotion have returned to ideas espoused by Charles Darwin over a century ago. Darwin (1872) believed that emotions developed because of their adaptive value. Fear, for instance, would help an organism avoid danger and thus would aid in survival. Hence, Darwin viewed human emotions as a product of evolution. This premise serves as the foundation for several modern theories of emotion developed independently by S. S. Tomkins (1980, 1991), Carroll Izard (1984, 1991), and Robert Plutchik (1984, 1993).

These *evolutionary theories* consider emotions to be largely innate reactions to certain stimuli. As such, emotions should be immediately recognizable under most conditions without much thought. After all, primitive animals that are incapable of complex thought seem to have little difficulty in recognizing their emotions. Evolutionary theorists believe that emotion evolved before thought. They assert that thought plays a relatively small role in emotion, although they admit that learning and cognition may have some influence on human emotions. Evolutionary theories generally assume that emotions originate in subcortical brain structures (such as the hypothalamus and most of the limbic system) that evolved before the higher brain areas (in the cortex) associated with complex thought.

Evolutionary theories also assume that evolution has equipped humans with a small number of innate emotions with proven adaptive value. Thus, the principal question that evolutionary theories of emotion wrestle with is, *What are the fundamental emotions?* Evolutionary theorists attempt to identify these primary emotions by searching for universals—emotions

Silvan Tomkins	Carroll Izard	Robert Plutchik
Fear	Fear	Fear
Anger	Anger	Anger
Enjoyment	Joy	Joy
Disgust	Disgust	Disgust
Interest	Interest	Anticipation
Surprise	Surprise	Surprise
Contempt	Contempt	
Shame	Shame	
	Sadness	Sadness
Distress		
	Guilt	
		Acceptance

Figure 9.18

Primary emotions. Evolutionary theories of emotion attempt to identify primary emotions. Three leading theorists—Silvan Tomkins, Carroll Izard, and Robert Plutchik—have compiled different lists of primary emotions, but this chart shows great overlap among the basic emotions identified by these theorists. (Based on Mandler, 1984)

that are expressed and recognized in the same way in widely disparate cultures. **Figure 9.18** summarizes the conclusions of the leading theorists in this area. As you can see, Tomkins, Izard, and Plutchik have not come up with identical lists, but they show considerable agreement. All three conclude that people exhibit eight to ten primary emotions. Moreover, six of these emotions appear on all three lists: fear, anger, joy, disgust, interest, and surprise.

Web Link 9.6

The Emotion Home Page Maintained by Jean-Marc Fellous and Eva Hudlicka of Duke University, this site provides links to a wealth of information on many aspects of emotion. Visitors can learn about emotion research in psychology, neuroscience, and cognitive science. Links to journals, books, conferences, and forums are also available.

concept check 9.3

Understanding Theories of Emotion

Check your understanding of theories of emotion by matching the theories we discussed with the statements below. Let's borrow William James's classic example: Assume that you just stumbled onto a bear in the woods. The first statement expresses the commonsense explanation of your fear. Each of the remaining statements expresses the essence of a different theory; indicate which theory in the spaces provided. The answers are provided in Appendix A.

1. You tremble because you're afraid.
Common sense

2. You're afraid because you're trembling.
_____

3. You're afraid because situational cues (the bear) suggest that's why you're trembling.
_____

4. You're afraid because the bear has elicited an innate primary emotion.
_____

Cultural
Heritage

Sociohistorical
Context

Theoretical
Diversity

Heredity and
Environment

Multifactorial
Causation

Five of our organizing themes were particularly prominent in this chapter: the influence of cultural contexts, the dense connections between psychology and society at large, psychology's theoretical diversity, the interplay of heredity and environment, and the multiple causes of behavior.

Our discussion of motivation and emotion demonstrated once again that there are both similarities and differences across cultures in behavior. The neural, biochemical, genetic, and hormonal processes underlying hunger and eating, for instance, are universal. However, cultural factors influence what people prefer to eat and how much they eat. In a similar vein, researchers have found a great deal of cross-cultural similarity in the cognitive, physiological, and expressive elements of emotional experience, but they have also found cultural variations in how people think about and express their emotions. Thus, as we have seen in previous chapters, psychological processes are characterized by both cultural variance and invariance.

Our discussion of the controversies surrounding evolutionary theory and the determinants of sexual orientation show once again that psychology is not an ivory tower enterprise. It evolves in a sociohistorical context that helps shape the debates in the field, and these debates often have far-reaching social and political ramifications for society at large. We ended the chapter with a discussion of various theories of emotion, which showed once again that psychology is characterized by great theoretical diversity.

Finally, we repeatedly saw that biological and environmental factors jointly govern behavior. For example, we learned that eating behavior, sexual desire, and the experience of emotion all depend on complicated interactions between biological and environmental determinants. Indeed, complicated interactions were seen throughout the entire chapter, demonstrating that if we want to fully understand behavior, we have to take multiple causes into account. We will see more of this complexity in the upcoming Personal Application, where we will continue our discussion of emotion, looking at recent research on the correlates of happiness. In the Critical Thinking Application that follows, we discuss how to carefully analyze the types of arguments found in this chapter—and everyday life.

PERSONAL *Application*

Exploring the Ingredients of Happiness

Answer the following "true" or "false."

_____ 1 The empirical evidence indicates that most people are relatively unhappy.

_____ 2 Although wealth doesn't *guarantee* happiness, wealthy people are much more likely to be happy than the rest of the population.

_____ 3 People who have children are happier than people without children.

_____ 4 Good health is an essential requirement for happiness.

The answer to all these questions is "false." These assertions are all reasonable and widely believed hypotheses about the correlates of happiness, but they have *not* been supported by empirical research. Due in part to a new emphasis on positive psychology, recent years have brought a surge of interest in the correlates of *subjective well-being*—**individuals' personal perceptions of their overall happiness and life satisfaction.** The findings of this research are quite interesting. As you have already seen from our true-false questions, many commonsense notions about happiness appear to be inaccurate.

How Happy Are People?

One of these inaccuracies is the apparently widespread assumption that most people are relatively unhappy. Writers, social scientists, and the general public seem to believe that people around the world are predominantly dissatisfied and unhappy, yet empirical surveys consistently find that the vast majority of respondents—even those who are poor or disabled—characterize themselves as fairly happy (Diener & Diener, 1996; Myers & Diener, 1995). When people are asked to rate their happiness, only a small minority place themselves below the neutral point on the various scales used (see **Figure 9.19**). When the average subjective well-being of entire nations is computed, based on almost 1000 surveys, the means cluster toward the positive end of the scale (Veenhoven, 1993). That's not to say that everyone is equally happy. Researchers find substan-

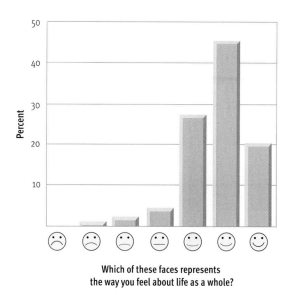

Which of these faces represents the way you feel about life as a whole?

Figure 9.19

Measuring happiness with a nonverbal scale. Researchers have employed a variety of methods to estimate the distribution of happiness. For example, in one study in the United States, respondents were asked to examine the seven facial expressions shown and select the one that "comes closest to expressing how you feel about your life as a whole." As you can see, the vast majority of participants chose happy faces. (Data adapted from Myers, 1992)

tial and thought-provoking disparities among people in subjective well-being, which we will analyze momentarily, but the overall picture seems rosier than anticipated.

Factors That Do Not Predict Happiness

Let us begin our discussion of individual differences in happiness by highlighting those things that turn out to be relatively unimportant determinants of subjective well-being. Quite a number of factors that you might expect to be influential appear to bear little or no relationship to general happiness.

Money. There *is* a positive correlation between income and subjective feelings of happiness, but in modern, affluent cultures the association is surprisingly weak (Diener & Seligman, 2004). For example, one study found a correlation of just .12 between income and happiness in the United States (Diener et al., 1993). On the average, even wealthy people are only marginally happier than those in the middle classes. The prob-

lem with money is that in this era of voracious consumption, pervasive advertising and rising income fuel escalating material desires (Frey & Stutzer, 2002; Kasser et al., 2004). When these growing desires outstrip what people can afford, dissatisfaction is likely (Solberg et al., 2002). Interestingly, there is some evidence that people who place an especially strong emphasis on the pursuit of wealth and materialistic goals tend to be somewhat less happy than others (Kasser, 2002; Ryan & Deci, 2001), perhaps in large part because they are so focused on financial success that they don't derive much satisfaction from their family life (Nickerson et al., 2003).

Age. Age and happiness are consistently found to be unrelated. Age accounts for less than 1% of the variation in people's happiness (Inglehart, 1990; Myers & Diener, 1997). The key factors influencing subjective well-being may shift some as people grow older—work becomes less important, health more so—but people's average level of happiness tends to remain remarkably stable over the life span.

Parenthood. Children can be a tremendous source of joy and fulfillment, but they can also be a tremendous source of headaches and hassles. Compared to childless couples, parents worry more and experience more marital problems (Argyle, 1987). Apparently, the good and bad aspects of parenthood balance each other out, because the evidence indicates that people who have children are neither more nor less happy than people without children (Argyle, 2001).

Intelligence and attractiveness. Intelligence and physical attractiveness are highly valued traits in modern society, but researchers have not found an association between either characteristic and happiness (Diener, 1984; Diener, Wolsic, & Fujita, 1995).

Moderately Good Predictors of Happiness

Research has identified some facets of life that appear to have a *moderate* association with subjective well-being: health, social activity, and religious belief.

Health. Good physical health would seem to be an essential requirement for happiness,

"Who can say? I suppose I'm as happy as my portfolio will allow me to be."

© The New Yorker Collection 1987 Mischa Richter from cartoonbank.com. All rights reserved.

but people adapt to health problems. Research reveals that individuals who develop serious, disabling health conditions aren't as unhappy as one might guess (Myers, 1992; Riis et al., 2005). Furthermore, Freedman (1978) argues that good health does not, by itself, produce happiness, because people tend to take good health for granted. Considerations such as these may help to explain why researchers find only a moderate positive correlation (average = .32) between health status and subjective well-being (Argyle, 1999).

Social Activity. Humans are social animals, and interpersonal relations do appear to contribute to people's happiness. Those who are satisfied with their social support and friendship networks and those who are socially active report above-average levels of happiness (Diener & Seligman, 2004; Myers, 1999). And people who are exceptionally happy tend to report greater satisfaction with their social relations than those who are average or low in subjective well-being (Diener & Seligman, 2002).

Religion. The link between religiosity and subjective well-being is modest, but a number of large-scale surveys suggest that people with heartfelt religious convictions are more likely to be happy than people who characterize themselves as nonreligious (Argyle, 1999; Ferriss, 2002).

Strong Predictors of Happiness

The list of factors that turn out to have fairly strong associations with happiness is surprisingly short. The key ingredients of happiness appear to involve love, work, and personality.

Love and Marriage. Romantic relationships can be stressful, but people consistently rate being in love as one of the critical ingredients of happiness (Myers, 1999). Furthermore, although people complain a lot about their marriages, the evidence indicates that marital status is a key correlate of happiness. Among both men and women,

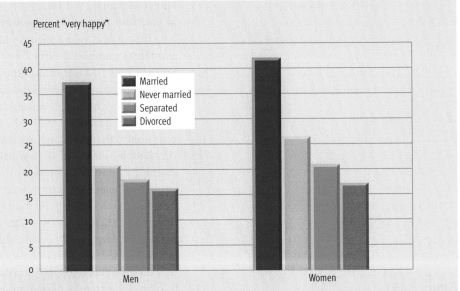

Percent "very happy"

Figure 9.20

Happiness and marital status. This graph shows the percentage of adults characterizing themselves as "Very happy" as a function of marital status (Myers, 1999). Among both women and men, happiness shows up more in those who are married, as opposed to those who are separated, who are divorced, or who have never married. These data and many others suggest that marital satisfaction is a key ingredient of happiness.

Source: Myers, D. G. (1999). Close relationships and quality of life. In D. Kahneman, E. Diener, & N. Schwarz (Eds.), *Well-being: The foundations of hedonic psychology*. New York: Russell Sage Foundation. Copyright © 1999. Reprinted by permission of the Russell Sage Foundation.

married people are happier than people who are single or divorced (see **Figure 9.20**; Myers & Diener, 1995), and this relationship holds around the world in widely different cultures (Diener et al., 2000). However, the causal relations underlying this correlation are unclear. It may be that happiness causes marital satisfaction more than marital satisfaction promotes happiness.

Work. Given the way people often complain about their jobs, one might not expect work to be a key source of happiness, but it is. Although less critical than love and marriage, job satisfaction has a substantial association with general happiness (Warr, 1999). Studies also show that unemployment has strong negative effects on subjective well-being (Lucas et al., 2004). It is difficult to sort out whether job satisfaction causes happiness or vice versa, but evidence suggests that causation flows both ways (Argyle, 2001).

Personality. The best predictor of individuals' future happiness is their past happiness (Diener & Lucas, 1999). Some people seem destined to be happy and others unhappy, regardless of their triumphs or setbacks. Evidence suggests that happiness does not depend on external circumstances—buying a nice house, getting promoted—as much as internal factors, such as one's outlook on life (Lykken & Tellegen, 1996). With this fact in mind, researchers have begun to look for links between personality and subjective well-being, and they have found some relatively strong correlations. Personality correlates of happiness include extraversion, self-esteem, and optimism (Fleeson, Malanos, & Achille, 2002; Lucas, Diener, & Suh, 1996).

Conclusions About Subjective Well-Being

We must be cautious in drawing inferences about the *causes* of happiness, because the available data are correlational (see **Figure 9.21**). Nonetheless, the empirical findings suggest a number of worthwhile insights about the roots of happiness.

First, research on happiness demonstrates that the determinants of subjective well-being are precisely that: subjective. *Objective realities are not as important as subjective feelings.* In other words, your health, your wealth, your job, and your age are not as influential as how you *feel* about your health, wealth, job, and age (Schwarz & Strack, 1999). Second, *when it comes to happiness, everything is relative* (Argyle, 1999; Hagerty, 2000). In other words, you evaluate what you have relative to what the people around you have and relative to what you expected to have. Generally, we compare ourselves with others who are similar to us. Thus, people who are wealthy assess what they have by comparing themselves with their wealthy friends and neighbors. This is one reason that there is little correlation between wealth and happiness.

Third, *research on subjective well-being indicates that people often adapt to their circumstances.* This adaptation effect is one reason that increases in income don't necessarily bring increases in happiness. **Hedonic adaptation occurs when the mental scale that people use to judge the pleasantness-unpleasantness of their experiences shifts so that their neutral point, or baseline for comparison, changes.** Unfortunately, when people's experiences improve, hedonic adaptation may *sometimes* put them on a *hedonic treadmill*—their neutral point moves upward, so that the improvements yield no real benefits (Kahneman, 1999). However, when people have to grapple with major

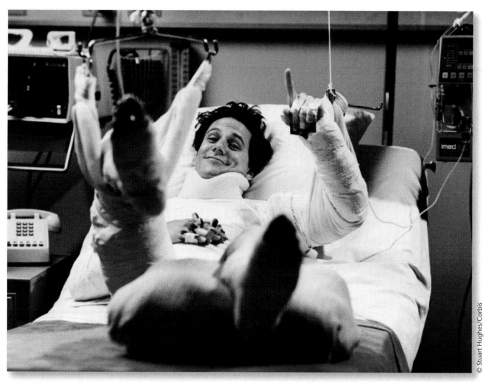

Research shows that happiness does not depend on people's positive and negative experiences as much as one would expect. Some people, presumably because of their personality, seem destined to be happy in spite of major setbacks, and others seem destined to cling to unhappiness even though their lives seem reasonably pleasant.

© Stuart Hughes/Corbis

setbacks, hedonic adaptation probably helps protect their mental and physical health. For example, people who are sent to prison and people who develop debilitating diseases are not as unhappy as one might assume, because they adapt to their changed situations and evaluate events from a new perspective (Frederick & Loewenstein, 1999).

That's not to say that hedonic adaptation in the face of life's difficulties is inevitable or complete (Lucas et al., 2003). People who suffer major setbacks, such as the death of a spouse or serious illness, often are not as happy as they were before the setback, but generally they are not nearly as unhappy as they or others would have predicted.

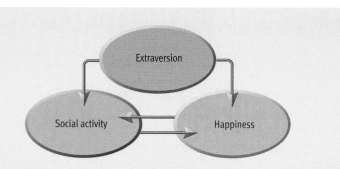

Figure 9.21

Possible causal relations among the correlates of happiness. Although we have considerable data on the correlates of happiness, it is difficult to untangle the possible causal relationships. For example, we know that there is a moderate positive correlation between social activity and happiness, but we can't say for sure whether high social activity causes happiness or whether happiness causes people to be more socially active. Moreover, in light of the research showing that a third variable—extraversion—correlates with both variables, we have to consider the possibility that extraversion causes both greater social activity and greater happiness.

Analyzing Arguments: Making Sense out of Controversy

Consider the following argument: "Dieting is harmful to your health because the tendency to be obese is largely inherited." What is your reaction to this reasoning? Do you find it convincing? We hope not, as this argument is seriously flawed. Can you see what's wrong? There is no relationship between the conclusion that "dieting is harmful to your health" and the reason given that "the tendency to be obese is largely inherited." The argument is initially seductive because most people know that obesity *is* largely inherited, so the reason provided represents a true statement. But the reason is unrelated to the conclusion advocated. This scenario may strike you as odd, but if you start listening carefully to discussions about controversial issues, you will probably notice that people often cite irrelevant considerations in support of their favored conclusions.

This chapter was loaded with controversial issues that sincere, well-meaning people could argue about for weeks. Are gender differences in mating preferences a product of evolution or of modern economic realities? Is there a biological basis for homosexuality? Unfortunately, arguments about issues such as these typically are unproductive in terms of moving toward resolution or agreement because most people know little about the rules of argumentation. In this application, we will explore what makes arguments sound or unsound in the hope of improving your ability to analyze and think critically about arguments.

The Anatomy of an Argument

In everyday usage, the word *argument* is used to refer to a dispute or disagreement between two or more people, but in the technical language of rhetoric, an *argument* consists of one or more premises that are used to provide support for a conclusion. *Premises* are the reasons that are presented to persuade someone that a conclusion is true or probably true. *Assumptions* are premises for which no proof or evidence is offered. Assumptions are often left unstated. For example, suppose that your doctor tells you that you should exercise regularly because regular exercise is good for your heart. In this simple argument, the conclusion is "You should exercise regularly." The premise that leads to this conclusion is the idea that "exercise is good for your heart." An unstated assumption is that everyone wants a healthy heart.

In the language of argument analysis, premises are said to support (or not support) conclusions. A conclusion may be supported by one reason or by many reasons. One way to visualize these possibilities is to draw an analogy between the reasons that support a conclusion and the legs that support a table (Halpern, 2003). As shown in **Figure 9.22**, a table top (conclusion) could be supported by one strong leg (a single strong reason) or many thin legs (lots of weaker reasons). Of course, the reasons provided for a conclusion may fail to support the conclusion. Returning to our table analogy, the table top might not be supported because the legs are too thin (very weak reasons) or because the legs are not attached (irrelevant reasons).

Arguments can get pretty complicated, as they usually have more parts than just premises and conclusions. In addition, there often are *counterarguments*, which are reasons that take support away from a conclusion. And sometimes the most important part of an argument is something that is not there—reasons that have been omitted, either deliberately or not, that would lead

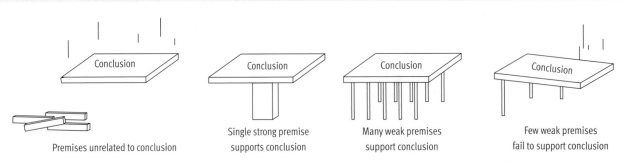

Premises unrelated to conclusion

Single strong premise supports conclusion

Many weak premises support conclusion

Few weak premises fail to support conclusion

Figure 9.22

An analogy for understanding the strength of arguments. Halpern (2003) draws an analogy between the premises that support a conclusion and the legs that support a table. She points out that a conclusion may be supported effectively by one strong premise or many weak premises. Of course, the reasons provided for a conclusion may also *fail* to provide adequate support.

Source: Halpern, D. F. (2003). *Thought & knowledge: An introduction to critical thinking.* Mahwah, NJ: Erlbaum. Copyright © 2003 Lawrence Erlbaum Associates. Reprinted by permission.

to a different conclusion if they were supplied. Given all the complex variations that are possible in arguments, it is impossible to give you simple rules for judging arguments, but we can highlight some common fallacies and then provide some criteria you can apply in thinking critically about arguments.

Common Fallacies

As noted previously, cognitive scientists have compiled lengthy lists of fallacies that people frequently display in their arguments. This section describes five common fallacies. To illustrate each one, we will assume the role of someone arguing that pornographic material on the Internet (cyberporn) should be banned or heavily regulated.

Irrelevant Reasons. Reasons cannot provide support for an argument unless they are relevant to the conclusion. Arguments that depend on irrelevant reasons—either intentionally or inadvertently—are quite common. You already saw one example at the beginning of this application. The Latin term for this fallacy is *non sequitur,* which literally translates to "it doesn't follow." In other words, the conclusion does not follow from the premise. For example, in the debate about Internet pornography, you might hear the following *non sequitur:* "We need to regulate cyberporn because research has shown that most date rapes go unreported."

Circular Reasoning. In *circular reasoning* the premise and conclusion are simply restatements of each other. People vary their wording a little so it isn't obvious, but when you look closely, the conclusion is the premise. For example, in arguments about Internet pornography you might hear someone assert, "We need to control cyberporn because it currently is unregulated."

Slippery Slope. The concept of *slippery slope* argumentation takes its name from the notion that if you are on a slippery slope and you don't dig your heels in, you will slide and slide until you reach bottom. A slippery slope argument typically asserts that if you allow X to happen, things will spin out of control and far worse events will follow. The trick is that no inherent connection exists between X and the events that are predicted to follow. For example, in the debate about medical marijuana, opponents have argued, "If you legalize medical marijuana, the next thing you know cocaine and heroin will be legal." In the debate about cyberporn, a slippery slope argument might go, "If we don't ban cyberporn, the next thing you know, grade school children will be watching smut in their school libraries."

Weak Analogies. An *analogy* asserts that two concepts or events are similar in some way. Hence, you can draw conclusions about event B because of its similarity to event A. Analogies are useful in thinking about complex issues, but some analogies are weak or inappropriate because the similarity between A and B is superficial, minimal, or irrelevant to the issue at hand. For example, in the debate about Internet erotica, someone might argue, "Cyberporn is morally offensive, just like child molestation. We wouldn't tolerate child molestation, so we shouldn't permit cyberporn."

False Dichotomy. A *false dichotomy* creates an either-or choice between two outcomes: the outcome advocated and some obviously horrible outcome that any sensible person would want to avoid. These outcomes are presented as the only possible ones, when in reality many other outcomes are possible, including some that lie between the extremes depicted in the false dichotomy. In the debate about Internet pornography, someone might argue, "We can ban cyberporn, or we can hasten the moral decay of modern society."

Evaluating the Strength of Arguments

In everyday life, you frequently need to assess the strength of arguments made by friends, family, co-workers, politicians, media pundits, and so forth. You may also want to evaluate your own arguments when you write papers or speeches for school or prepare presentations for your work. The following questions can help you to make systematic evaluations of arguments (adapted from Halpern, 2003):

- What is the conclusion?
- What are the premises provided to support the conclusion? Are the premises valid?
- Does the conclusion follow from the premises? Are there any fallacies in the chain of reasoning?
- What assumptions have been made? Are they valid assumptions? Should they be stated explicitly?
- What are the counterarguments? Do they weaken the argument?
- Is there anything that has been omitted from the argument?

Table 9.1 Critical Thinking Skills Discussed in This Application

Skill	Description
Understanding the elements of an argument	The critical thinker understands that an argument consists of premises and assumptions that are used to support a conclusion.
Recognizing and avoiding common fallacies, such as irrelevant reasons, circular reasoning, slippery slope reasoning, weak analogies, and false dichotomies	The critical thinker is vigilant about conclusions based on unrelated premises, conclusions that are rewordings of premises, unwarranted predictions that things will spin out of control, superficial analogies, and contrived dichotomies.
Evaluating arguments systematically	The critical thinker carefully assesses the validity of the premises, assumptions, and conclusions in an argument, and considers counterarguments and missing elements.

Key Ideas

Motivational Theories and Concepts

● Drive theories apply a homeostatic model to motivation. They assume that organisms seek to reduce unpleasant states of tension called drives. In contrast, incentive theories emphasize how external goals energize behavior.

● Evolutionary theorists explain motives in terms of their adaptive value. Madsen's list of biological needs and Murray's list of social needs illustrate that a diverse array of motives govern human behavior.

The Motivation of Hunger and Eating

● Eating is regulated by a complex interaction of biological and environmental factors. In the brain, the lateral, ventromedial, and paraventricular areas of the hypothalamus appear to be involved in the control of hunger, but their exact role is unclear.

● Fluctuations in blood glucose also seem to influence hunger. The stomach can send two types of satiety signals to the brain. Hormonal regulation of hunger depends primarily on insulin and leptin secretions.

● Incentive-oriented models assert that eating is regulated by the palatability, quantity, and variety of available foods. Learning processes, such as classical conditioning and observational learning, exert a great deal of influence over both what people eat and how much they eat. Cultural traditions also shape food preferences. Stress can stimulate eating.

Sexual Motivation and Behavior

● The human sexual response cycle can be divided into four stages: excitement, plateau, orgasm, and resolution. Consistent with evolutionary theory, males tend to think about and initiate sex more than females and to have more sexual partners and more interest in casual sex than females.

● Gender differences in mating preferences largely transcend cultural boundaries. Males emphasize potential partners' youthfulness and attractiveness, whereas females emphasize potential partners' material resources and financial prospects.

● The determinants of sexual orientation are not well understood. Recent studies suggest that there may be a genetic predisposition to homosexuality and that idiosyncrasies in prenatal hormonal secretions may contribute, but much remains to be learned. Females' sexual orientation may be characterized by greater plasticity than that of males.

Achievement: In Search of Excellence

● McClelland pioneered the use of the TAT to measure achievement motivation. People who are relatively high in the need for achievement work harder and more persistently than others, although they often choose to tackle challenges of intermediate difficulty. The pursuit of achievement tends to increase when both the probability of success and the incentive value of success are high.

The Elements of Emotional Experience

● Emotion is made up of cognitive, physiological, and behavioral components. The cognitive component involves subjective feelings that have an evaluative aspect. In the peripheral nervous system, the physiological component is dominated by autonomic arousal. In the brain, the amygdala seems to be the hub of the neural circuits that process conditioned fears, but a constellation of brain centers contribute to the experience of emotions. At the behavioral level, emotions are expressed through body language, with facial expressions being particularly prominent.

● Ekman and Friesen have found considerable cross-cultural agreement in the identification of emotions based on facial expressions. Cross-cultural similarities have also been found in the cognitive and physiological components of emotion. However, there are some striking cultural variations in how people categorize and display their emotions.

Theories of Emotion

● The James-Lange theory asserts that emotion results from one's perception of autonomic arousal. The Cannon-Bard theory counters with the proposal that emotions originate in subcortical areas of the brain.

● According to Schachter's two-factor theory, people infer emotion from arousal and then label it in accordance with their cognitive explanation for the arousal. Evolutionary theories of emotion maintain that emotions are innate reactions that require little cognitive interpretation.

Reflecting on the Chapter's Themes

● Our look at motivation and emotion showed once again that psychology is characterized by theoretical diversity, that biology and environment shape behavior interactively, that behavior is governed by multiple causes, that psychological processes are characterized by both cultural variance and invariance, and that psychology evolves in a sociohistorical context.

PERSONAL APPLICATION • Exploring the Ingredients of Happiness

● Factors such as income, age, parenthood, intelligence, and attractiveness are largely uncorrelated with subjective well-being. Physical health, good social relationships, and religious faith appear to have a modest association with feelings of happiness. Strong predictors of happiness include love and marriage, work satisfaction, and personality.

● Research on happiness indicates that objective realities are not as important as subjective perceptions, that happiness is relative, and that people adapt to their circumstances.

CRITICAL THINKING APPLICATION • Analyzing Arguments: Making Sense out of Controversy

● An argument consists of one or more premises used to provide support for a conclusion. Arguments are often marred by fallacies in reasoning, such as irrelevant reasons, circular reasoning, slippery slope scenarios, weak analogies, and false dichotomies. Arguments can be evaluated more effectively by applying systematic criteria.

Key Terms

Achievement motive (p. 286)
Argument (p. 300)
Assumptions (p. 300)
Bisexuals (p. 283)
Display rules (p. 293)
Drive (p. 274)
Emotion (p. 288)
Galvanic skin response (GSR) (p. 290)
Glucose (p. 277)
Glucostats (p. 277)
Hedonic adaptation (p. 299)
Heterosexuals (p. 283)
Homeostasis (p. 274)
Homosexuals (p. 283)
Incentive (p. 275)
Lie detector (p. 290)
Motivation (p. 274)
Parental investment (p. 280)
Polygraph (p. 290)
Premises (p. 300)
Sexual orientation (p. 283)
Subjective well-being (p. 296)

Key People

David Buss (p. 283)
Walter Cannon (p. 294)
Paul Ekman and Wallace Friesen (pp. 292–293)
William James (pp. 293–294)
Joseph LeDoux (p. 291)
William Masters and Virginia Johnson (pp. 279–280)
David McClelland (pp. 286–287)
Stanley Schachter (pp. 294–295)

CHAPTER 9 *Practice Test*

1. Although Jackson had a huge breakfast and felt stuffed, he ate three of the donuts that a colleague brought to a morning meeting. His behavior is consistent with:
   A. incentive theories of motivation.
   B. drive theories of motivation.
   C. evolutionary theories of motivation.
   D. the Cannon-Bard theory of motivation.

2. Results of the early studies of hypothalamic manipulations in animals implied that the lateral hypothalamus and the ventromedial nucleus of the hypothalamus may be on-off centers for the control of:
   A. emotion
   B. hunger
   C. thirst
   D. sex drive

3. Which of the following statements is false?
   A. Insulin is a hormone secreted by the pancreas.
   B. Insulin must be present for cells to utilize glucose.
   C. Leptin levels correlate with levels of the body's fat stores.
   D. Diabetics have too much insulin.

4. Which of the following has *not* been found in research on gender differences in sexual interest?
   A. Men think about sex more than women.
   B. Men initiate sex more frequently than women.
   C. Women are more interested in having many partners than men are.
   D. Men are more interested in uncommitted/casual sex than women.

5. Kinsey maintained that sexual orientation:
   A. depends on early classical conditioning experiences.
   B. should be viewed as a continuum.
   C. depends on normalities and abnormalities in the amygdala.
   D. should be viewed as an either-or distinction.

6. Which of the following approaches to explaining the origins of homosexuality has received the most empirical support overall?
   A. Behavioral
   B. Biological
   C. Psychoanalytic
   D. All of these approaches equally

7. One's need for achievement is usually assessed using the:
   A. McClelland Achievement Inventory.
   B. MMPI.
   C. Thematic Apperception Test.
   D. Atkinson Manifest Needs Scale.

8. Which of the following determinants of achievement behavior is (are) situational?
   A. The strength of one's motive to achieve success, as measured by the TAT
   B. One's estimate of the probability of success on the task at hand
   C. The incentive value of success on the task at hand
   D. Both b and c

9. A polygraph (lie detector) works by:
   A. monitoring physiological indexes of autonomic arousal.
   B. directly assessing the truthfulness of a person's statements.
   C. monitoring the person's facial expressions.
   D. doing all of the above.

10. Which of the following statements about cross-cultural comparisons of emotional experience is true?
    A. The facial expressions associated with various emotions vary widely across cultures.
    B. Some basic emotions go unnamed in some cultures.
    C. People of different cultures categorize emotions in very similar ways.
    D. People of different cultures learn to control their emotional expressions in similar ways.

11. According to the James-Lange theory of emotion:
    A. the experience of emotion depends on autonomic arousal and on one's cognitive interpretation of that arousal.
    B. different patterns of autonomic activation lead to the experience of different emotions.
    C. emotion occurs when the thalamus sends signals simultaneously to the cortex and to the autonomic nervous system.
    D. emotions develop because of their adaptive value.

12. Which theory of emotion implies that people can change their emotions simply by changing the way they label their arousal?
    A. The James-Lange theory
    B. The Cannon-Bard theory
    C. Schachter's two-factor theory
    D. Opponent process theory

13. The fact that eating behavior, sexual behavior, and the experience of emotion all depend on interactions between biological and environmental determinants lends evidence to which of your text's organizing themes?
    A. Psychology's theoretical diversity
    B. Psychology's empiricism
    C. People's experience of the world is subjective
    D. The joint influence of biology and environment

14. Which of the following statements is (are) true?
    A. For the most part, people are pretty happy.
    B. Age is largely unrelated to happiness.
    C. Income is largely unrelated to happiness.
    D. All of the above.

15. The sales pitch "We're the best dealership in town because the other dealerships just don't stack up against us" is an example of:
    A. a false dichotomy.
    B. semantic slanting.
    C. circular reasoning.
    D. slippery slope.

Answers

1 A pp. 274–275
2 B p. 276
3 D p. 277
4 C pp. 281–282
5 B pp. 283–284
6 B pp. 284–285
7 C p. 286
8 D p. 287
9 A pp. 290–291
10 B pp. 292–293
11 B pp. 293–294
12 C pp. 294–295
13 D p. 296
14 D pp. 296–297
15 C p. 301

PsykTrek

Go to the PsykTrek website or CD-ROM for further study of the concepts in this chapter. Both online and on the CD-ROM, PsykTrek includes dozens of learning modules with videos, animations, and quizzes, as well as simulations of psychological phenomena and a multimedia glossary that includes word pronunciations.

ThomsonNOW™

www.thomsonedu.com/ThomsonNOW
Go to this site for the link to ThomsonNOW, your one-stop study shop. Take a Pre-Test for this chapter, and ThomsonNOW will generate a Personalized Study Plan based on your test results. The Study Plan will identify the topics you need to review and direct you to online resources to help you master those topics. You can then take a Post-Test to help you determine the concepts you have mastered and what you still need to work on.

Companion Website

www.thomsonedu.com/psychology/weiten
Go to this site to find online resources directly linked to your book, including a glossary, flash cards, drag-and-drop exercises, quizzes, and more!

CHAPTER 10

Human Development Across the Life Span

© Reza/Webistan/Corbis

On July 29, 1981, 20-year-old Diana Spencer stood before more than 2,000 guests at St. Paul's Cathedral in London and fumbled through an exchange of wedding vows, nervously transposing two of her husband's middle names. Diana could hardly believe what was happening. Just a few months before, she had been a giggly teenager with a playful sign on her bedroom door that read "Chief Chick." Dubbed "Shy Di" by the hordes of photographers who followed her every move, she had never even had a boyfriend (Morton, 1998). Now she was getting married to Charles, Prince of Wales, the heir to the British throne, in a spectacular wedding ceremony that was televised around the world.

Marriage—let alone to a future king—is a major transition for most people, but for Diana it was only the beginning of an extraordinary series of changes. When Diana became engaged, she was a pretty if slightly pudgy 19-year-old who was just on the threshold of adulthood. A high school dropout, she had few serious interests or ambitions. Her most obvious talent was her rapport with young children, who adored her. Far from a fashion plate, she owned "one long dress, one silk skirt, one smart pair of shoes, and that was it" (Morton, 1998, p. 66).

Yet, like Cinderella, the "fairy tale princess" soon blossomed. "It happened before our very eyes," said one photographer, "the transformation from this shy teenager who hid beneath big hats, and hung her head, into the self-assured woman and mother, confident in her beauty" (Clayton & Craig, 2001, p. 113). The Shy Di who sometimes burst into tears at the sight of crowds became Disco Di, a slender beauty celebrated for her stylish clothes and hairstyles. Then came Dynasty Di, the doting mother of Princes William and Harry. Finally, as her marriage to Charles crumbled and she sought a new and more fulfilling role for herself, still another Diana emerged. Now she was Dedicated Di, a poised and effective spokesperson for important causes, such as the fight against AIDS and the removal of land mines from war-torn areas. No longer a frightened young princess or her husband's beautiful accessory, by her 30s Diana was a seemingly confident and independent woman who could publicly rebuke the royal family for their treatment of her and declare that she would rather be the "Queen of people's hearts" than the Queen of England (Edwards, 1999, p. 342).

Diana's transformations were startling, yet there was also a strong element of continuity in her life. As an adult, Diana continued to display qualities she had shown as a child, including her mischievous sense of humor, her love of swimming and dancing, and even her attachment to stuffed animals (S. B. Smith, 2000). Her childhood feeling of destiny ultimately blossomed into a deep sense of mission that took her to homeless shelters, clinics for lepers, and the bedsides of AIDS patients. Although cynics doubted the genuineness of her empathy for society's "outcasts," she had displayed a similar caring and naturalness as a young teenager dancing with patients in wheelchairs at a hospital for the mentally and physically handicapped (Clayton & Craig, 2001).

Other, more troubling, continuities also marked Diana's turbulent passage through life. Despite her growing mastery of her public roles, privately she remained vulnerable, moody, and insecure. Diana's parents had divorced when she was 6, and fears of abandonment never left her. As a young girl being taken to boarding school, she had begged her father, "If you love me, don't leave me here"—a plea she later echoed in tearful arguments with Prince Charles (Smith, 2000, p. 53). Her childhood feelings of intellectual inferiority continued to plague her as an adult. "A brain the size of a pea I've got," she would say (Clayton & Craig, 2001, p. 22). Throughout her marriage, she suffered bouts of bulimia (an eating disorder) and depression. While she projected a new confidence and maturity after her separation from Prince Charles, some observers felt that she was as needy and insecure as ever. A succession of relationships with men, before and after her divorce, seemed to bring her no closer to the love and security she craved. One biographer argues that in fundamental ways she had changed little, if at all (Smith, 2000). Others, however, believed that a new chapter in her life was just beginning, and that many more changes were undoubtedly in store, when Diana was tragically killed in an auto accident at the age of 36.

What does Princess Diana have to do with developmental psychology? Although her story is obviously unique in many ways, it provides an interesting illustration of the two themes that permeate the study of human development: *transition* and *continuity*. In investigating human development, psychologists study how people evolve through transitions over time. In looking at these transitions, developmental psychologists inevitably find continuity with the past. This continuity may be the most fascinating element in Diana's story. The metamorphosis of the shy, awkward teenager into an elegant, self-assured public figure was a more radical transformation than

The story of Princess Diana's metamorphosis from an awkward teenager into an elegant, self-assured public figure provides a dramatic demonstration of how human development is marked by both continuity and transition.

© Tim Graham/Corbis

most people go through. Nonetheless, the threads of continuity connecting Diana's childhood to her adult personality were quite obvious.

Development **is the sequence of age-related changes that occur as a person progresses from conception to death.** It is a reasonably orderly, cumulative process that includes both the biological and behavioral changes that take place as people grow older. An infant's newfound ability to grasp objects, a child's gradual mastery of grammar, an adolescent's spurt in physical growth, a young adult's increasing commitment to a vocation, and an older adult's transition into the role of grandparent all rep-

resent development. These transitions are predictable changes that are related to age.

Traditionally, psychologists have been most interested in development during childhood. Our coverage reflects this emphasis. However, decades of research have clearly demonstrated that development is a lifelong process. We'll divide the life span into four broad periods: (1) the prenatal period, between conception and birth, (2) childhood, (3) adolescence, and (4) adulthood. We'll examine aspects of development that are especially dynamic during each period. Let's begin by looking at events that occur before birth, during prenatal development.

> Progress Before Birth: Prenatal Development

PREVIEW QUESTIONS

- What are the three stages of prenatal development, and what happens in each stage?
- Can maternal nutrition affect the fetus?
- What effect does maternal drug use have?
- Which maternal illnesses can be dangerous to the fetus?

Development begins with conception. Conception occurs when fertilization creates **a** *zygote,* **a one-celled organism formed by the union of a sperm and an egg.** All the other cells in your body developed from this single cell. Each of your cells contains enduring messages from your parents carried on the *chromosomes* that lie within its nucleus. Each chromosome houses many *genes,* the functional units in hereditary transmission. Genes carry the details of your hereditary blueprints, which are revealed gradually throughout life (see Chapter 3 for more information on genetic transmission).

The *prenatal period* **extends from conception to birth, usually encompassing nine months of pregnancy.** Significant development occurs before birth. In fact, development during the prenatal period is remarkably rapid. If you were an average-sized newborn and your physical growth had continued during the first year of your life at a prenatal pace, by your first birthday you would have weighed 200 pounds! Fortunately, you didn't grow at that rate—and no human does—because in the final weeks before birth the frenzied pace of prenatal development tapers off dramatically.

In this section, we'll examine the usual course of prenatal development and discuss how environmental events can leave their mark on development even before birth exposes the newborn to the outside world.

The Course of Prenatal Development

The prenatal period is divided into three phases: (1) the germinal stage (the first two weeks), (2) the

embryonic stage (two weeks to two months), and (3) the fetal stage (two months to birth). Some key developments in these phases are outlined here.

Germinal Stage

The *germinal stage* **is the first phase of prenatal development, encompassing the first two weeks after conception.** This brief stage begins when a zygote is created through fertilization. Within 36 hours, rapid cell division begins, and the zygote becomes a microscopic mass of multiplying cells. This mass slowly migrates along the mother's fallopian tube to the uterine cavity. On about the seventh day, the cell mass begins to implant itself in the uterine wall. This process takes about a week and is far from automatic. Many zygotes are rejected at this point. As many as one in five pregnancies end with the woman never being aware that conception has occurred (Simpson, 2002).

During the implantation process, the placenta begins to form (Buster & Carson, 2002). **The** *placenta* **is a structure that allows oxygen and nutrients to pass into the fetus from the mother's bloodstream and bodily wastes to pass out to the mother.** This critical exchange takes place across thin membranes that block the passage of blood cells, keeping the fetal and maternal bloodstreams separate.

Embryonic Stage

The *embryonic stage* **is the second stage of prenatal development, lasting from two weeks until the end of the second month.** During this stage, most of the vital organs and bodily systems begin to form in the developing organism, which is now called an *embryo*. Structures such as the heart, spine, and brain emerge gradually as cell division becomes more specialized. Although the embryo is typically only about an inch long at the end of this stage, it's already beginning to look human. Arms, legs, hands, feet, fingers, toes, eyes, and ears are already discernible.

The embryonic stage is a period of great vulnerability because virtually all the basic physiological structures are being formed. If anything interferes with normal development during the embryonic phase, the effects can be devastating. Most miscarriages occur during this period (Simpson, 2002). Most major structural birth defects also result from problems that occur during the embryonic stage (Simpson & Niebyl, 2002).

Fetal Stage

PsykTrek **9a**

The *fetal stage* is the third stage of prenatal development, lasting from two months through birth. Some highlights of fetal development are summarized in **Figure 10.1**. The first two months of the fetal stage bring rapid bodily growth, as muscles and bones begin to form (Moore & Persaud, 2003). The developing organism, now called a *fetus,* becomes capable of physical movements as skeletal structures harden. Organs formed in the embryonic stage continue to grow and gradually begin to function. The sense of hearing, for example, is functional by around 20–24 weeks (Hepper, 2003).

During the final three months of the prenatal period, brain cells multiply at a brisk pace. A layer of fat is deposited under the skin to provide insulation, and the respiratory and digestive systems mature. All of these changes ready the fetus for life outside the

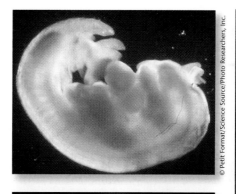
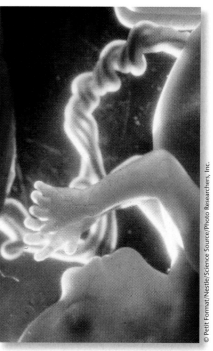
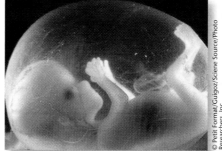

Prenatal development is remarkably rapid. Top left: This 30-day-old embryo is just 6 millimeters in length. Bottom left: At 14 weeks, the fetus is approximately 2 inches long. Note the well-developed fingers. The fetus can already move its legs, feet, hands, and head and displays a variety of basic reflexes. Right: After 4 months of prenatal development, facial features are beginning to emerge.

cozy, supportive environment of its mother's womb. Sometime between 22 weeks and 26 weeks the fetus reaches the *age of viability*—the age at which a baby can survive in the event of a premature birth. Thanks to advances in medical technology, the age of viability has declined in recent decades in modern societies. At 22–23 weeks the probability of survival is still pretty slim (14%–26%), but it climbs steadily over the next month to an 80%–83% survival rate at 26 weeks (Iams, 2002).

Figure 10.1

Overview of fetal development. This chart outlines some of the highlights of development during the fetal stage.

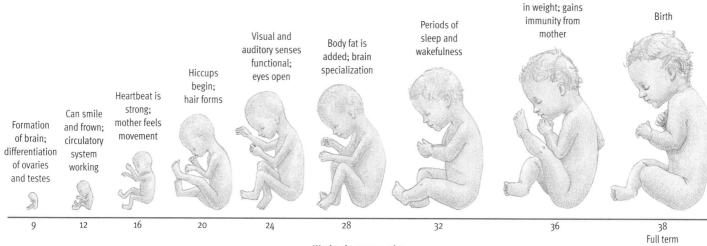

Formation of brain; differentiation of ovaries and testes

Can smile and frown; circulatory system working

Heartbeat is strong; mother feels movement

Hiccups begin; hair forms

Visual and auditory senses functional; eyes open

Body fat is added; brain specialization

Periods of sleep and wakefulness

Rapid increase in weight; gains immunity from mother

Birth

9   12   16   20   24   28   32   36   38 Full term

Weeks since conception

Understanding the Stages of Prenatal Development

Check your understanding of the stages of prenatal development by filling in the blanks in the chart below. The first column contains descriptions of a main event from each of the three stages. In the second column, write the name of the stage; in the third column, write the term used to refer to the developing organism during that stage; and in the fourth column, write the time span (in terms of weeks or months) covered by the stage. The answers are in Appendix A at the back of the book.

Event	Stage	Term for organism	Time span
1. Uterine implantation	_____	_____	_____
2. Muscle and bone begin to form	_____	_____	_____
3. Vital organs and body systems begin to form	_____	_____	_____

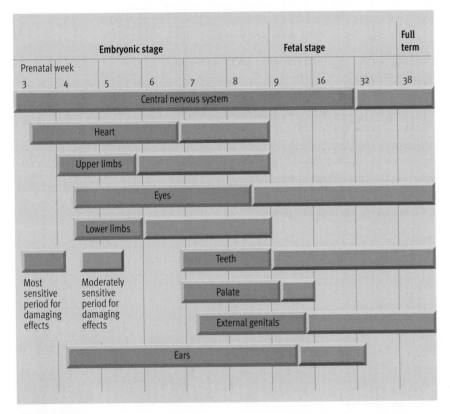

Figure 10.2

Periods of vulnerability in prenatal development. Generally, structures are most susceptible to damage when they are undergoing rapid development. The red regions of the bars indicate the most sensitive periods for various organs and structures, while the purple regions indicate periods of continued, but lessened, vulnerability. As a whole, sensitivity is greatest in the embryonic stage, but some structures remain vulnerable throughout prenatal development.

Source: Adapted from Moore, K. L., & Persaud, T. V. N. (1998). *Before we are born: Essentials of embryology and birth defects.* Philadelphia: W. B. Saunders. Copyright © 1998 Elsevier Science (USA). Reprinted by permission.

Environmental Factors and Prenatal Development

Although the fetus develops in the protective buffer of the womb, events in the external environment can affect it indirectly through the mother because the developing organism and its mother are linked via the placenta. **Figure 10.2** shows the periods of prenatal development during which various structures are most vulnerable to damage.

Maternal nutrition is very important, as the developing fetus needs a variety of essential nutrients. Severe maternal malnutrition increases the risk of birth complications and neurological deficits for the newborn (Coutts, 2000; Fifer, Monk, & Grose-Fifer, 2001). The impact of moderate malnutrition is more difficult to gauge. However, recent research suggests that moderate malnutrition can have negative effects decades after a child's birth. For example, prenatal malnutrition has been linked to vulnerability to schizophrenia and other psychiatric disorders in adolescence and early adulthood (Susser, Brown, & Matte, 1999).

Another major source of concern is the mother's consumption of drugs. Unfortunately, most drugs consumed by a pregnant woman can slip through the membranes of the placenta. Virtually all "recreational" drugs can be harmful, with sedatives, narcotics, cocaine, and methamphetamine being particularly dangerous (Finnegan & Kandall, 2005; Singer et al., 2002). Problems can even be caused by drugs prescribed for legitimate medical reasons and by some over-the-counter drugs (Niebyl, 2002). Tobacco use during pregnancy is also problematic, as pregnant women who smoke have an increased risk for miscarriage, stillbirth, and other birth complications (Andres & Day, 2000). Maternal smoking may also increase a child's risk for sudden infant death syndrome (SIDS) (Fullilove & Dieudonne, 1997), slower than average cognitive development (Trasti, Jacobson, & Bakketeig, 1999), and attention deficit disorder (Linnet et al., 2003).

Alcohol consumption during pregnancy also carries serious risks. It has long been clear that *heavy* drinking by a mother can be hazardous to a fetus. **Fetal alcohol syndrome is a collection of congenital (inborn) problems associated with excessive alcohol use during pregnancy.** Typical problems manifested in childhood include microcephaly (a small head), heart defects, irritability, hyperactivity, and retarded mental and motor development (Hannigan & Armant, 2000). Previously, the available evidence suggested that it was safe for women to drink in moderation during pregnancy. However, an ongoing series of studies suggest that normal social drinking during pregnancy can have enduring negative effects on children, including deficits in IQ, reaction time, motor skills, attention span, and math skills, as well as increased impulsive, antisocial, and delinquent behavior (Hunt et al., 1995; Streissguth et al., 1999). There appears to be a correlation between the amount of alcohol that pregnant women consume and the severity of the damage inflicted on their offspring (Ott, Tarter, & Ammerman, 1999).

The placenta screens out quite a number of infectious agents, but not all. Thus, many maternal illnesses can interfere with prenatal development. Diseases such as measles, rubella (German measles), syphilis, and chicken pox can be hazardous to the fetus (Duff, 2002). The nature of any damage depends, in part, on when the mother contracts the illness. The HIV virus that causes AIDS can also be transmitted by pregnant women to their offspring. The trans-

mission of AIDS may occur prenatally through the placenta, during delivery, or through breastfeeding (Eldred & Chaisson, 1996). Yet another risk is that a variety of genital infections, such as gonorrhea, chlamydia, and herpes, can be transmitted to newborns during delivery (Duff, 2002). These common diseases can be very dangerous. Herpes, for instance, can cause microcephaly, paralysis, deafness, blindness, and brain damage, and can be fatal for many newborns (Ismail, 1993).

Science has a long way to go before it uncovers all the factors that shape development before birth. For example, the effects of fluctuations in maternal emotions are not well understood. Nonetheless, it's clear that critical developments unfold quickly during the prenatal period. In the next section, you'll learn that development continues at a brisk pace during the early years of childhood.

> The Wondrous Years of Childhood

A certain magic is associated with childhood. Young children have an extraordinary ability to captivate adults' attention. Legions of parents apologize repeatedly to friends and strangers alike as they talk on and on about the cute things their kids do. Most wondrous of all are the rapid and momentous developmental changes of the childhood years. Helpless infants become curious toddlers almost overnight. Before parents can catch their breath, these toddlers are schoolchildren engaged in spirited play with young friends. Then, suddenly, they're insecure adolescents, worrying about dates, part-time jobs, cars, and college. The whirlwind transitions of childhood often seem miraculous.

Of course, the transformations that occur in childhood only *seem* magical. In reality, they reflect an orderly, predictable, gradual progression. In this section you'll see what psychologists have learned about this progression. We'll examine various aspects of development that are especially dynamic during childhood. Let's begin by looking at motor development.

Exploring the World: Motor Development

Motor development **refers to the progression of muscular coordination required for physical activities.** Basic motor skills include grasping and reaching for objects, manipulating objects, sitting up, crawling, walking, running, and so forth.

Basic Principles

A number of principles are apparent in motor development. One is the *cephalocaudal trend*—**the head-to-foot direction of motor development.** Children tend to gain control over the upper part of their bodies before the lower part. You've seen this trend in action if you've seen an infant learn to crawl. Infants gradually shift from using their arms for propelling themselves to using their legs. **The *proximodistal trend* is the center-outward direction of motor development.** Children gain control over their torso before their extremities. Thus, infants initially reach for things by twisting their entire body, but gradually they learn to extend just their arms.

Early progress in motor skills has traditionally been attributed almost entirely to the process of maturation. *Maturation* **is development that reflects the gradual unfolding of one's genetic blueprint.** It is a product of genetically programmed physical changes that come with age—as opposed to experience and learning. However, recent research that has taken a closer look at the *process* of motor development suggests that infants are active agents rather than passive organisms waiting for their brain and limbs to mature (Thelen, 1995). According to the new view, the driving force behind motor development is infants' ongoing exploration of their world and their need to master specific tasks (such as grasping a larger toy or looking out a window). Progress in motor development is attributed to infants' experimentation and their learning and remembering the

PREVIEW QUESTIONS

- How important are maturation and culture to motor development?
- How did Harlow and Bowlby change thinking about attachment?
- What patterns of attachment are seen in infants?
- What do stage theories have in common?
- How did Erikson explain personality development?
- What are Piaget's four major stages of cognitive development?
- How does Vygotsky's theory of cognitive development compare to Piaget's theory?
- What are Kohlberg's stages of moral development?

Web Link 10.1

PBS: The Whole Child
Coordinated with the videotape series of the same name, this Public Broadcasting System site assembles a broad collection of information for parents, caregivers, and others about the developing child from birth through age 5. Presented in English and Spanish, the resources here include an interactive timeline of developmental milestones, reading lists, and a guide to other online sites dealing with child development.

consequences of their activities. Although modern researchers acknowledge that maturation facilitates motor development, they argue that its contribution has been overestimated (Bertenthal & Clifton, 1998).

Understanding Developmental Norms

Parents often pay close attention to early motor development, comparing their child's progress with developmental norms. *Developmental norms* indicate the typical (median) age at which individuals display various behaviors and abilities. Developmental norms are useful benchmarks as long as parents don't expect their children to progress exactly at the pace specified in the norms. Some parents get unnecessarily alarmed when their children fall behind developmental norms. What these parents overlook is that developmental norms are group *averages*. Variations from the average are entirely normal. This normal variation stands out in **Figure 10.3**, which indicates the age at which 25%, 50%, and 90% of youngsters can demonstrate various motor skills. As **Figure 10.3** shows, a substantial portion of children often don't achieve a particular milestone until long after the average time cited in norms.

Cultural Variations and Their Significance

Cross-cultural research has highlighted the dynamic interplay between experience and maturation in motor development. Relatively rapid motor development has been observed in some cultures that provide special practice in basic motor skills. For example, soon after birth the Kipsigis people of Kenya begin active efforts to train their infants to sit up, stand, and walk. Thanks to this training, Kipsigis children achieve these developmental milestones (but not others) about a month earlier than babies in the United States (Super, 1976). In contrast, relatively slow motor development has been found in some cultures that discourage motor exploration. For example, among the Ache, a nomadic people living in the rain forests of Paraguay, safety concerns dictate that children under age 3 rarely venture more than 3 feet from their mothers, who carry them virtually everywhere. As a result of these constraints, Ache children are delayed in acquiring a variety of motor skills and typically begin walking about a year later than other children (Kaplan & Dove, 1987). Cultural variations in the emergence of basic motor skills demonstrate that environmental factors can accelerate or slow early motor development.

Early Emotional Development: Attachment

Attachment refers to the close, emotional bonds of affection that develop between infants and their caregivers. Researchers have shown a keen interest in how infant-mother attachments are formed early

Figure 10.3

Milestones in motor development. The left edge, interior mark, and right edge of each bar indicate the age at which 25%, 50%, and 90% of infants have mastered each motor skill shown. Developmental norms typically report only the median age of mastery (the interior mark), which can be misleading in light of the variability in age of mastery apparent in this chart.

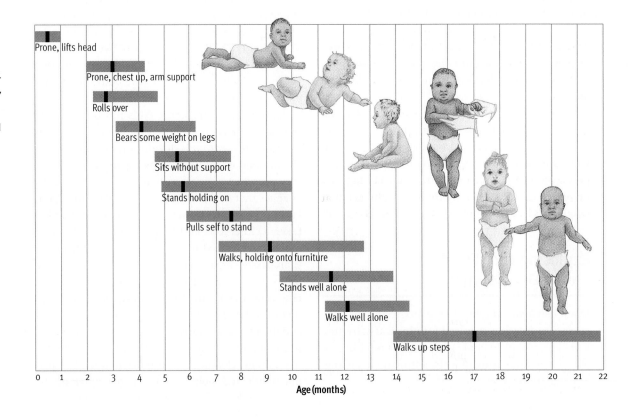

Prone, lifts head
Prone, chest up, arm support
Rolls over
Bears some weight on legs
Sits without support
Stands holding on
Pulls self to stand
Walks, holding onto furniture
Stands well alone
Walks well alone
Walks up steps

0 1 2 3 4 5 6 7 8 9 10 11 12 13 14 15 16 17 18 19 20 21 22
Age (months)

Tribes across the world use a variety of methods to foster rapid development of motor abilities in their children. The Kung San of the Kalahari, Botswana, teach their young to dance quite early, using poles to develop the kinesthetic sense of balance.

in life. Children eventually form attachments to many people, including their fathers, siblings, grandparents, and others (Cassidy, 1999). However, a child's first important attachment usually occurs with his or her mother because she is typically the principal caregiver in the early months of life (Lamb et al., 1999).

Contrary to popular belief, infants' attachment to their mothers is *not* instantaneous. Initially, babies show relatively little in the way of a special preference for their mother. At 2–3 months of age, infants may smile and laugh more when they interact with their mother, but they can be handed over to strangers such as babysitters with relatively little difficulty. This situation gradually changes, and by about 6–8 months of age, infants begin to show a pronounced preference for their mother's company and often protest when separated from her (Lamb, Ketterlinus, & Fracasso, 1992). This is the first manifestation of *separation anxiety*—**emotional distress seen in many infants when they are separated from people with whom they have formed an attachment.** Separation anxiety, which may occur with other familiar caregivers as well as the mother, typically peaks at around 14–18 months and then begins to decline.

Theories of Attachment

 9e

Why do children gradually develop a special attachment to their mothers? This question sounds simple enough, but it has been the subject of a lively theoretical dialogue. Behaviorists have argued that the infant-mother attachment develops because mothers are associated with the powerful, reinforcing event of being fed. Thus, the mother becomes a conditioned reinforcer. However, this reinforcement the-

ory of attachment came into question as a result of Harry Harlow's famous studies of attachment in infant rhesus monkeys (Harlow, 1958, 1959).

Harlow removed monkeys from their mothers at birth and raised them in the laboratory with two types of artificial "substitute mothers." One type of artificial mother was made of terrycloth and could provide "contact comfort" (see the photo below). The other type of artificial mother was made of wire. Half of the monkeys were fed from a bottle attached to a wire mother and the other half were fed by a cloth mother. The young monkeys' attachment to their substitute mothers was tested by introducing a frightening stimulus, such as a strange toy. If reinforcement through feeding were the key to attachment, the frightened monkeys should have scampered off to the mother that had fed them. This was not the case. The young monkeys scrambled for their cloth mothers, even if they were *not* fed by them.

Harlow's work made a simple reinforcement explanation of attachment unrealistic for animals, let alone for more complex human beings. Attention then turned to an alternative explanation of attachment proposed by John Bowlby (1969, 1973, 1980). Bowlby was impressed by the importance of contact comfort to Harlow's monkeys and by the apparently unlearned nature of this preference. Influenced by evolutionary theories, Bowlby argued that there must be a biological basis for attachment. According to his view, infants are biologically programmed to emit behavior (smiling, cooing, clinging, and so on)

HARRY HARLOW
"The little we know about love does not transcend simple observation, and the little we write about it has been written better by poets and novelists."

JOHN BOWLBY
"The only relevant criterion by which to consider the natural adaptedness of any particular part of present-day man's behavioural equipment is the degree to which and the way in which it might contribute to population survival in man's primeval environment."

Even if fed by a wire surrogate mother, Harlow's infant monkeys cuddled up with a terry cloth surrogate that provided contact comfort. When threatened by a frightening toy, the monkeys sought security from their terry cloth mothers.

MARY SALTER AINSWORTH

"Where familial security is lacking, the individual is handicapped by the lack of what might be called a secure base from which to work."

that triggers an affectionate, protective response from adults. Bowlby also asserted that adults are programmed by evolutionary forces to be captivated by this behavior and to respond with warmth, love, and protection. Obviously, these characteristics would be adaptive in terms of promoting children's survival. Bowlby's theory has guided most of the research on attachment over the last several decades, including Mary Ainsworth's influential work on patterns of attachment.

Patterns of Attachment

Infant-mother attachments vary in quality. Mary Ainsworth and her colleagues (1978) found that these attachments fall into three categories. Fortunately, most infants develop a *secure attachment*. They play and explore comfortably with their mother present, become visibly upset when she leaves, and are quickly calmed by her return. However, some children display a pattern called *anxious-ambivalent attachment* (also called *resistant attachment*). They appear anxious even when their mothers are near and protest excessively when she leaves, but they are not particularly comforted when she returns. Children in the third category seek little contact with their mothers and often are not distressed when she leaves, a condition labeled *avoidant attachment.*

Maternal behaviors appear to have considerable influence over the type of attachment that emerges between an infant and mother (Ainsworth et al., 1978). Mothers who are sensitive and responsive to their children's needs are more likely to promote secure attachments than mothers who are relatively insensitive or inconsistent in their responding (Isabella, 1995; van den Boom, 1994). However, infants are not passive bystanders as this process unfolds. They are active participants who influence the process with their crying, smiling, fussing, and babbling. Difficult infants who spit up most of their food, make bathing a major battle, and rarely smile may sometimes slow the process of attachment (Mangelsdorf et al., 1990). Thus, the type of attachment that emerges between an infant and mother may depend on the nature of the infant's temperament as well as the mother's sensitivity (Seifer et al., 1996; Vaughn & Bost, 1999).

Evidence suggests that the quality of the attachment relationship can have important consequences for children's subsequent development. Based on their attachment experiences, children develop *internal working models* of the dynamics of close relationships, that influence their future interactions with a wide range of people (Bretherton & Munholland, 1999). Infants with a relatively secure attachment tend to become resilient, competent toddlers with

high self-esteem (Goldsmith & Harman, 1994). In their preschool years, they display more persistence, curiosity, self-reliance, and leadership and have better peer relations (Weinfield et al., 1999), while experiencing fewer negative emotions and more positive emotions (Kochanska, 2001). Studies have also found a relationship between secure attachment and more advanced cognitive development during childhood and adolescence (Jacobsen, Edelstein, & Hofmann, 1994), as well as healthier intimate relations during adulthood (Feeney, 1999; Kirkpatrick, 1999).

Culture and Attachment

Separation anxiety emerges in children at about 6–8 months and peaks at about 14–18 months in cultures around the world (Grossmann & Grossmann, 1990). These findings, which have been replicated in quite a variety of non-Western cultures, suggest that attachment is a universal feature of human development. However, studies have found some modest cultural variations in the proportion of infants who fall into the three attachment categories described by Ainsworth. Working mostly with white, middle-class subjects in the United States, researchers have found that 67% of infants display a secure attachment, 21% an avoidant attachment, and 12% an anxious-ambivalent attachment (van IJzendoorn & Sagi, 1999). Interestingly, studies in Japan and Germany have yielded somewhat different estimates of the prevalence of various types of attachment, as shown in **Figure 10.4**. That said, the differences are small, and secure attachment appears to be the predominant type of attachment around the world.

Becoming Unique: Personality Development

How do individuals develop their unique sets of personality traits over time? Many theories have addressed this question. The first major theory of personality development was put together by Sigmund Freud back around the turn of the 20th century. As we'll discuss in Chapter 11, he claimed that the basic foundation of an individual's personality is firmly laid down by age 5. Half a century later, Erik Erikson (1963) proposed a sweeping revision of Freud's theory that has proven influential. Like Freud, Erikson concluded that events in early childhood leave a permanent stamp on adult personality. However, unlike Freud, Erikson theorized that personality continues to evolve over the entire life span.

Building on Freud's earlier work, Erikson devised a stage theory of personality development. As you'll see in this chapter, many theories describe develop-

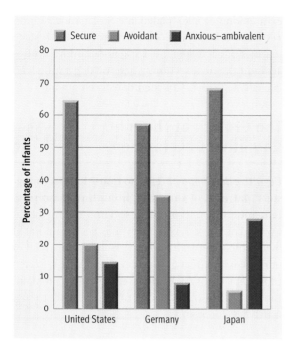

Figure 10.4

Cultural variations in attachment patterns. This graph shows the prevalence of secure, avoidant, and anxious-ambivalent attachment patterns found in specific studies in Germany, Japan, and the United States. As you can see, secure attachment is the most common pattern in all three societies, as it is around the world. However, there are some modest cultural differences in the prevalence of each pattern of attachment, which are probably attributable to cultural variations in childrearing practices. (Data from van IJzendoorn & Kroonenberg, 1988)

ment in terms of stages. **A *stage* is a developmental period during which characteristic patterns of behavior are exhibited and certain capacities become established.** Stage theories assume that (1) individuals must progress through specified stages in a particular order because each stage builds on the previous

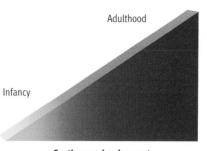

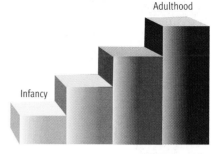

Figure 10.5

Stage theories of development. Some theories view development as a relatively continuous process, albeit not as smooth and perfectly linear as shown on the left. In contrast, stage theories assume that development is marked by major discontinuities, as shown on the right, that bring fundamental, qualitative changes in capabilities or characteristic behavior.

stage, (2) progress through these stages is strongly related to age, and (3) development is marked by major discontinuities that usher in dramatic transitions in behavior (see **Figure 10.5**).

Erikson's Stage Theory

Erikson partitioned the life span into eight stages, each characterized by a *psychosocial crisis* involving transitions in important social relationships. According to Erikson, personality is shaped by how individuals deal with these psychosocial crises. Each crisis is a potential turning point that can yield different outcomes. Erikson described the stages in terms of these alternative outcomes, which represent personality traits that people display over the remainder of their lives. All eight stages in Erikson's theory are charted in **Figure 10.6**. We describe the first four childhood stages here and discuss the remaining stages in the upcoming sections on adolescence and adulthood.

Web Link 10.2

Early Childhood Care and Development
This site's subtitle, International Resources for Early Childhood Development, emphasizes the focus of resources provided: the worldwide (not just North American) challenge of caring for children from birth through age 6 and fulfilling the needs of their families.

Figure 10.6

Erikson's stage theory. Erikson's theory of personality development asserts that people evolve through eight stages over the life span. Each stage is marked by a *psychosocial crisis* that involves confronting a fundamental question, such as "Who am I and where am I going?" The stages are described in terms of alternative traits that are potential outcomes from the crises. Development is enhanced when a crisis is resolved in favor of the healthier alternative (which is listed first for each stage).

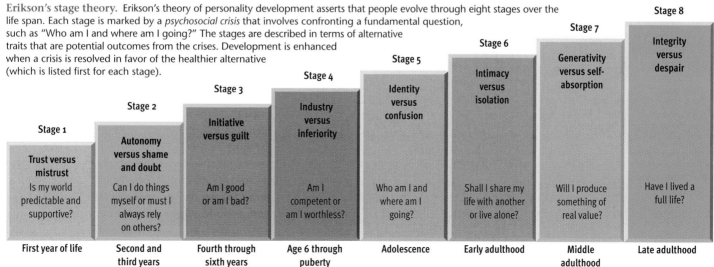

ERIK ERIKSON

"Human personality in principle develops according to steps predetermined in the growing person's readiness to be driven toward, to be aware of, and to interact with a widening social radius."

JEAN PIAGET

"It is virtually impossible to draw a clear line between innate and acquired behavior patterns."

Trust Versus Mistrust. Erikson's first stage encompasses the first year of life, when an infant has to depend completely on adults to take care of its basic needs for such necessities as food, a warm blanket, and changed diapers. If an infant's basic biological needs are adequately met by its caregivers and sound attachments are formed, the child should develop an optimistic, trusting attitude toward the world. However, if the infant's basic needs are taken care of poorly, a more distrusting, insecure personality may result.

Autonomy Versus Shame and Doubt. Erikson's second stage unfolds during the second and third years of life, when parents begin toilet training and other efforts to regulate the child. The child must begin to take some personal responsibility for feeding, dressing, and bathing. If all goes well, he or she acquires a sense of self-sufficiency. But if parents are never satisfied with the child's efforts and if parent-child conflicts are constant, the child may develop a sense of personal shame and self-doubt.

Initiative Versus Guilt. In Erikson's third stage, roughly from ages 3 to 6, the challenge facing children is to function socially within their families. If children think only of their own needs and desires, family members may begin to instill feelings of guilt, and self-esteem may suffer. But if children learn to get along well with siblings and parents, a sense of self-confidence should begin to grow.

Industry Versus Inferiority. In the fourth stage (age 6 through puberty), the challenge of learning to function socially is extended beyond the family to the broader social realm of the neighborhood and school. Children who are able to function effectively in this less nurturant social sphere where productivity is highly valued should develop a sense of competence.

Evaluating Erikson's Theory

The strength of Erikson's theory is that it accounts for both continuity and transition in personality development. It accounts for transition by showing how new challenges in social relations stimulate personality development throughout life. It accounts for continuity by drawing connections between early childhood experiences and aspects of adult personality. One measure of a theory's value is how much research it generates, and Erikson's theory continues to guide a fair amount of research (Thomas, 2005).

On the negative side of the ledger, Erikson's theory provides an "idealized" description of "typical" developmental patterns. Thus, it's not well suited for explaining the enormous personality differences that

exist among people. Inadequate explanation of individual differences is a common problem with stage theories of development. This shortcoming surfaces again in the next section, where we'll examine Jean Piaget's stage theory of cognitive development.

The Growth of Thought: Cognitive Development

Cognitive development refers to transitions in youngsters' patterns of thinking, including reasoning, remembering, and problem solving. The investigation of cognitive development has been dominated by the theory of Jean Piaget (Kessen, 1996). Much of our discussion of cognitive development is devoted to Piaget's theory and the research it generated, although we'll also delve into other approaches to cognitive development.

Overview of Piaget's Stage Theory

Jean Piaget (1929, 1952, 1983) was a Swiss scholar whose own cognitive development was exceptionally rapid. In his early 20s, after he had earned a doctorate in natural science and published a novel, Piaget turned to psychology. He met Theodore Simon, who had collaborated with Alfred Binet in devising the first useful intelligence tests. Working in Simon's Paris laboratory, Piaget administered intelligence tests to many children to develop better test norms. In doing this testing, Piaget was intrigued by the reasoning underlying the children's *wrong* answers. He decided that measuring children's intelligence was less interesting than studying how children *use* their intelligence. In 1921 he moved to Geneva, where he spent the remainder of his life studying cognitive development. Many of his ideas were based on insights gleaned from careful observations of his own three children during their infancy.

Noting that children actively explore the world around them, Piaget asserted that interaction with the environment and maturation gradually alter the way children think. Like Erikson's theory, Piaget's model is a *stage theory* of development. Piaget proposed that children's thought processes go through a series of four major stages: (1) the *sensorimotor period* (birth to age 2), (2) the *preoperational period* (ages 2 to 7), (3) the *concrete operational period* (ages 7 to 11), and (4) the *formal operational period* (age 11 onward). **Figure 10.7** provides an overview of each of these periods. Piaget regarded his age norms as approximations and acknowledged that transitional ages may vary from one child to another.

Sensorimotor Period.

One of Piaget's foremost contributions was to greatly enhance our understanding of mental development in the earliest months of life. The first stage in his theory is the *sensorimotor period,* which lasts from birth to about age 2. Piaget called this stage *sensorimotor* because infants are developing the ability to coordinate their sensory input with their motor actions.

The major development during the sensorimotor stage is the gradual appearance of symbolic thought. At the beginning of this stage, a child's behavior is dominated by innate reflexes; infants aren't "thinking" as much as they are simply responding to stimuli. But by the end of the stage, the child can use mental symbols to represent objects (for example, a mental image of a favorite toy). The key to this transition is the acquisition of the concept of object permanence.

Object permanence develops when a child recognizes that objects continue to exist even when they are no longer visible. Although you surely take the permanence of objects for granted, infants aren't aware of this permanence at first. If you show a 4-month-old child an eye-catching toy and then cover the toy with a pillow, the child will not attempt to search for the toy. Piaget inferred from this observation that the child does not understand that the toy continues to exist under the pillow. The notion of object permanence does not dawn on children overnight. The first signs of this insight usually appear between 4 and 8 months of age, when children will often pursue an object that is *partially* covered in their presence. Progress is gradual, and Piaget believed that children typically don't master the concept of object permanence until they're about 18 months old.

Preoperational Period.

During the *preoperational period,* which extends roughly from age 2 to age 7, children gradually improve in their use of mental images. Although progress in symbolic thought continues, Piaget emphasized the *shortcomings* in preoperational thought.

Consider a simple problem that Piaget presented to youngsters. He would take two identical beakers and fill each with the same amount of water. After a child had agreed that the two beakers contained the same amount of water, he would pour the water from one of the beakers into a much taller and thinner beaker (see **Figure 10.8**). He would then ask the child whether the two differently shaped beakers still contained the same amount of water. Confronted with a problem like this, children in the preoperational period generally said "no." They typically focused on

the higher water line in the taller beaker and insisted that there was more water in the slender beaker. They had not yet mastered the principle of conservation. **Conservation is Piaget's term for the awareness that physical quantities remain constant in spite of changes in their shape or appearance.**

Why are preoperational children unable to solve conservation problems? According to Piaget, their inability to understand conservation is the result of some basic flaws in preoperational thinking. These flaws include centration, irreversibility, and egocentrism.

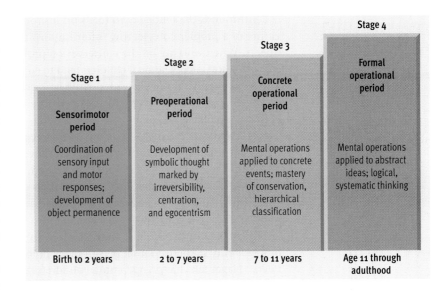

Figure 10.7

Piaget's stage theory. Piaget's theory of cognitive development identifies four stages marked by fundamentally different modes of thinking through which youngsters evolve. The approximate age norms and some key characteristics of thought at each stage are summarized here.

Figure 10.8

Piaget's conservation task. After watching the transformation shown, a preoperational child will usually answer that the taller beaker contains more water. In contrast, the child in the concrete operations period tends to respond correctly, recognizing that the amount of water in beaker C remains the same as the amount in beaker A.

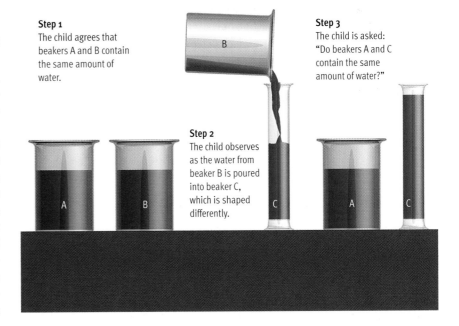

Step 1
The child agrees that beakers A and B contain the same amount of water.

Step 2
The child observes as the water from beaker B is poured into beaker C, which is shaped differently.

Step 3
The child is asked: "Do beakers A and C contain the same amount of water?"

Centration is the tendency to focus on just one feature of a problem, neglecting other important aspects. When working on the conservation problem with water, preoperational children tend to concentrate on the height of the water while ignoring the width. They have difficulty focusing on several aspects of a problem at once.

Irreversibility is the inability to envision reversing an action. Preoperational children can't mentally "undo" something. For instance, in grappling with the conservation of water, they don't think about what would happen if the water were poured back from the tall beaker into the original beaker.

Egocentrism in thinking is characterized by a limited ability to share another person's viewpoint. Indeed, Piaget felt that preoperational children fail to appreciate that there are points of view other than their own. For instance, if you ask a preoperational girl whether her sister has a sister, she'll probably say "no" if they are the only two girls in the family. She's unable to view sisterhood from her sister's perspective (this example also shows irreversibility).

A notable feature of egocentrism is *animism*—the belief that all things are living, just like oneself. Thus, youngsters attribute lifelike, human qualities to inanimate objects, asking questions such as, "When does the ocean stop to rest?" or "Why does the wind get so mad?"

As you can see, Piaget emphasized the weaknesses apparent in *pre*operational thought. Indeed, that is why he called this stage preoperational. The ability to perform *operations*—internal transformations, manipulations, and reorganizations of mental structures—emerges in the next stage.

Concrete Operational Period.

The development of mental operations marks the beginning of the *concrete operational period,* which usually lasts from about age 7 to age 11. Piaget called this stage *concrete* operations because children can perform operations only on images of tangible objects and actual events.

Among the operations that children master during this stage are reversibility and decentration. *Reversibility* permits a child to mentally undo an action. *Decentration* allows the child to focus on more than one feature of a problem simultaneously. The newfound ability to coordinate several aspects of a problem helps the child appreciate that there are several ways to look at things. This ability in turn leads to a *decline in egocentrism and gradual mastery of conservation* as it applies to liquid, mass, number, volume, area, and length.

As children master concrete operations, they develop a variety of new problem-solving capacities.

Let's examine another problem studied by Piaget. Give a preoperational child seven carnations and three daisies. Tell the child the names for the two types of flowers and ask the child to sort them into carnations and daisies. That should be no problem. Now ask the child whether there are more carnations or more daisies. Most children will correctly respond that there are more carnations. Now ask the child whether there are more carnations or more flowers. At this point, most preoperational children will stumble and respond incorrectly that there are more carnations than flowers. Generally, preoperational children can't handle *hierarchical classification* problems that require them to focus simultaneously on two levels of classification. However, the child who has advanced to the concrete operational stage is not as limited by centration and can work successfully with hierarchical classification problems.

Formal Operational Period.

The final stage in Piaget's theory is the *formal operational period,* which typically begins at around 11 years of age. In this stage, children begin to apply their operations to *abstract* concepts in addition to concrete objects. Indeed, during this stage, youngsters come to *enjoy* the contemplation of abstract concepts. Many adolescents spend hours mulling over hypothetical possibilities related to abstractions such as justice, love, and free will.

According to Piaget, youngsters graduate to relatively adult modes of thinking in the formal operations stage. He did *not* mean to suggest that no further cognitive development occurs once children reach this stage. However, he believed that after children achieve formal operations, further developments in thinking are changes in *degree* rather than fundamental changes in the *nature* of thinking.

Adolescents in the formal operational period become more *systematic* in their problem-solving efforts. Children in earlier developmental stages tend to attack problems quickly, with a trial-and-error approach. In contrast, children who have achieved formal operations are more likely to think things through. They envision possible courses of action and try to use logic to reason out the likely consequences of each possible solution before they act. Thus, thought processes in the formal operational period can be characterized as increasingly abstract, systematic, logical, and reflective.

Evaluating Piaget's Theory

Jean Piaget made a landmark contribution to psychology's understanding of children in general and their

Web Link 10.3

Theories of Development
Maintained by the Psychology Department at George Mason University, this site is an excellent resource, providing links to many other sites that focus on influential theories of human development. Starting here, a visitor can learn a great deal about the ideas of Erik Erikson, Jean Piaget, Lev Vygotsky, and Lawrence Kohlberg.

cognitive development in particular (Beilin, 1992). He founded the field of cognitive development and fostered a new view of children that saw them as active agents constructing their own worlds (Fischer & Hencke, 1996). Above all else, he sought answers to new questions. As he acknowledged in a 1970 interview, "It's just that no adult ever had the idea of asking children about conservation. It was so obvious that if you change the shape of an object, the quantity will be conserved. Why ask a child? The novelty lay in asking the question" (Hall, 1987, p. 56). Piaget's theory guided an enormous volume of productive research that continues through today (Brainerd, 1996; Feldman, 2003). This research has supported many of Piaget's central propositions (Flavell, 1996). In such a far-reaching theory, however, there are bound to be some weak spots. Here are some criticisms of Piaget's theory:

1. In many areas, Piaget appears to have underestimated young children's cognitive development (Lutz & Sternberg, 1999). For example, researchers have found evidence that children understand object permanence much earlier than Piaget thought, perhaps as early as 3 to 4 months of age (Baillargeon, 1987, 1994). Others have marshaled evidence that preoperational children exhibit less egocentrism and animism than Piaget believed (Newcombe & Huttenlocher, 1992).

2. Piaget's model suffers from problems that plague most stage theories. Like Erikson, Piaget had little to say about the variability among children in development (Siegler, 1994). Also, individuals often simultaneously display patterns of thinking that are characteristic of several stages. This "mixing" of stages calls into question the value of organizing development in terms of stages (Courage & Howe, 2002; Bjorklund, 2005).

3. Piaget believed that his theory described universal processes that should lead children everywhere to progress through uniform stages of thinking at roughly the same ages. Subsequent research has shown that the *sequence* of stages is largely invariant, but the *timetable* that children follow in passing through these stages varies considerably across cultures (Dasen, 1994; Rogoff, 1990). Thus, Piaget underestimated the influence of cultural factors on cognitive development.

Vygotsky's Sociocultural Theory

In recent decades, as the limitations and weaknesses of Piaget's ideas have become more apparent, some developmental researchers have looked elsewhere for theoretical guidance. Ironically, the theory that

concept **check** 10.2

Recognizing Piaget's Stages

Check your understanding of Piaget's theory by indicating the stage of cognitive development illustrated by each of the examples below. For each scenario, fill in the letter for the appropriate stage in the space on the left. The answers are in Appendix A.

    a. Sensorimotor period   **c.** Concrete operational period

    b. Preoperational period   **d.** Formal operational period

_____ **1.** Upon seeing a glass lying on its side, Sammy says, "Look, the glass is tired. It's taking a nap."

_____ **2.** Maria is told that a farmer has nine cows and six horses. The teacher asks, "Does the farmer have more cows or more animals?" Maria answers, "More animals."

_____ **3.** Alice is playing in the living room with a small red ball. The ball rolls under the sofa. She stares for a moment at the place where the ball vanished and then turns her attention to a toy truck sitting in front of her.

has recently inspired the greatest interest—Lev Vygotsky's *sociocultural theory*—dates back to around the same time that Piaget began formulating his theory (1920s–1930s). Vygotsky was a prominent Russian psychologist whose research ended prematurely in 1934 when he died of tuberculosis at the age of 37. Western scientists had little exposure to his ideas until the 1960s, and it was only in 1986 that a complete version of his principal book (Vygotsky, 1934) was published in English. Working in a perilous political climate in the postrevolution Soviet Union, Vygotsky had to devise a theory that would not be incompatible with the Marxist social philosophy that ruled communist thinking (Thomas, 2005). Given the constraints placed on his theorizing one might expect that 70 years later his ideas would not resonate with contemporary psychologists in capitalist societies, but the reality is just the opposite, as his theory has become quite influential (Feldman, 2003).

Vygotsky's and Piaget's perspectives on cognitive development have much in common, but they also differ in several important respects (DeVries, 2000; Matusov & Hayes, 2000; Rowe & Wertsch, 2002). First, in Piaget's theory, cognitive development is primarily fueled by individual children's active exploration of the world around them. The child is viewed as the agent of change. In contrast, Vygotsky places enormous emphasis on how children's cognitive development is fueled by social interactions with parents, teachers, and older children who can

LEV VYGOTSKY

"In the process of development the child not only masters the items of cultural experience but the habits and forms of cultural behaviour, the cultural methods of reasoning."

Archives of the History of American Psychology—University of Akron.

provide invaluable guidance. Second, Piaget viewed cognitive development as a universal process that should unfold in largely the same way across widely disparate cultures. Vygotsky, on the other hand, asserted that culture exerts great influence over how cognitive growth unfolds. For example, the cognitive skills acquired in literate cultures that rely on schools for training will differ from those acquired in tribal societies with no formal schooling. Third, Piaget viewed children's gradual mastery of language as just another aspect of cognitive development, whereas Vygotsky argued that language acquisition plays a crucial, central role in fostering cognitive development.

According to Vygotsky, children acquire most of their culture's cognitive skills and problem-solving strategies through collaborative dialogues with more experienced members of their society. He sees cognitive development as more like an *apprenticeship* than a journey of individual discovery. Vygotsky's emphasis on the primacy of language is reflected in his discussion of *private speech*. Preschool children talk aloud to themselves a lot as they go about their activities. Piaget viewed this speech as egocentric and insignificant. Vygotsky argued that children use this private speech to plan their strategies, regulate their actions, and accomplish their goals. As children grow older, this private speech is internalized and becomes the normal verbal dialogue that people have with themselves as they go about their business. Thus, language increasingly serves as the *foundation* for youngsters' cognitive processes.

Vygotsky's sociocultural theory is guiding a great deal of contemporary research on cognitive development (Feldman, 2003). This research has provided empirical support for many of Vygotsky's ideas (Rogoff, 1998; Winsler, 2003). Like Piaget's theory, Vygotsky's perspective promises to enrich our understanding of how children's thinking develops and matures.

Are Some Cognitive Abilities Innate?

The frequent finding that Piaget underestimated infants' cognitive abilities has led to a rash of research suggesting that infants have a surprising grasp of many complex concepts. Studies have demonstrated that infants understand basic properties of objects and some of the rules that govern them (Baillargeon, 2002, 2004). At 3 to 4 months of age, infants understand that objects are distinct entities with boundaries, that objects move in continuous paths, that one solid object cannot pass through another, that an object cannot pass through an opening that is smaller than the object, and that objects on slopes roll down rather than up (Kim & Spelke, 1992; Spelke & Newport, 1998).

In this line of research, perhaps the most stunning discovery has been the finding that *infants seem to be able to add and subtract small numbers* (Bremner, 2001). If 5-month-old infants are shown a sequence of events in which one object is added to another behind a screen, they expect to see two objects when the screen is removed, and they exhibit surprise when their expectation is violated (see **Figure 10.9**). This expectation suggests that they understand that 1 + 1 = 2 (Wynn, 1992, 1996). Similar manipulations suggest that infants also understand that 2 – 1 = 1, that 2 + 1 = 3, that 3 – 1 = 2, and other, more complicated calculations (Hauser & Carey, 1998; McCrink & Wynn, 2004; Wynn, 1998).

Again and again in recent years, research has shown that infants appear to understand surprisingly complex concepts that they have had virtually no opportunity to learn about. These findings have led some theorists to conclude that certain basic cognitive abilities are biologically built into humans' neural architecture. The theorists who have reached this conclusion tend to fall into two camps: nativists and evolutionary theorists. The *nativists* simply assert that humans are prewired to readily understand certain concepts without making any assumptions about *why* humans are prewired in these ways (Spelke, 1994; Spelke & Newport, 1998). Their principal in-

Figure 10.9

The procedure used to test infants' understanding of number. To see whether 5-month-old infants have some appreciation of addition and subtraction, Wynn (1992, 1996) showed them sequences of events like those depicted here. If children express surprise (primarily assessed by time spent looking) when the screen drops and they see only one object, this result suggests that they understand that 1 + 1 = 2. Wynn and others have found that infants seem to have some primitive grasp of simple addition and subtraction.

Source: Adapted from Wynn, K. (1992). Addition and subtraction by human infants. *Nature, 358,* 749–750. Copyright © 1992 Macmillan Magazines, Ltd. Reprinted with permission.

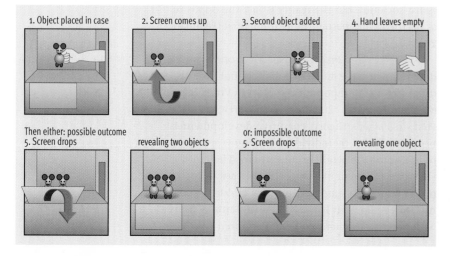

terest is to sort out the complex matter of what is prewired and what isn't. Evolutionary theorists agree with the nativists that humans are prewired for certain cognitive abilities, but they are keenly interested in *why*. As you might anticipate, they maintain that this wiring is a product of natural selection, and they strive to understand its adaptive significance (Hauser & Carey, 1998; Wynn, 1998). For example, evolutionary theorists are interested in how basic addition-subtraction abilities may have enhanced our ancient ancestors' success in hunting, foraging, and social bargaining.

The Development of Moral Reasoning

In Europe, a woman was near death from cancer. One drug might save her, a form of radium that a druggist in the same town had recently discovered. The druggist was charging $2,000, ten times what the drug cost him to make. The sick woman's husband, Heinz, went to everyone he knew to borrow the money, but he could only get together about half of what it cost. He told the druggist that his wife was dying and asked him to sell it cheaper or let him pay later. But the druggist said, "No." The husband got desperate and broke into the man's store to steal the drug for his wife. Should the husband have done that? Why? (Kohlberg, 1969, p. 379)

What's your answer to Heinz's dilemma? Would you have answered the same way three years ago? Can you guess what you might have said at age 6? By presenting similar dilemmas to participants and studying their responses, Lawrence Kohlberg (1976, 1984; Colby & Kohlberg, 1987) developed a model of *moral development.* What is morality? That's a complicated question that philosophers have debated for centuries. For our purposes, it will suffice to say that

morality involves the ability to distinguish right from wrong and to behave accordingly.

Kohlberg's Stage Theory

Kohlberg's model is the most influential of a number of competing theories that attempt to explain how youngsters develop a sense of right and wrong. His work was derived from much earlier work by Piaget (1932). Piaget theorized that moral development is determined by cognitive development. By this he meant that the way individuals think out moral issues depends on their level of cognitive development. This assumption provided the springboard for Kohlberg's research.

Kohlberg's theory focuses on moral *reasoning* rather than overt *behavior.* This point is best illustrated by describing Kohlberg's method of investigation. He presented his participants with thorny moral questions such as Heinz's dilemma, then asked the subjects what the actor in the dilemma should do, and more important, why. It was the *why* that interested Kohlberg. He examined the nature and progression of subjects' moral reasoning.

The result of this work is the stage theory of moral reasoning outlined in **Figure 10.10**. Kohlberg found that individuals progress through a series of three levels of moral development, each of which can be broken into two sublevels, yielding a total of six stages. Each stage represents a different approach to thinking about right and wrong.

Younger children at the *preconventional level* think in terms of external authority. Acts are wrong because they are punished, or right because they lead to positive consequences. Older children who have reached the *conventional level* of moral reasoning see rules as necessary for maintaining social order. They therefore accept these rules as their own. They "internalize" these rules not to avoid punishment but

Harvard University Archives, Call #UAV 605.295.8p Kohlberg

LAWRENCE KOHLBERG

"Children are almost as likely to reject moral reasoning beneath their level as to fail to assimilate reasoning too far above their level."

Web Link 10.4

National Parent Information Network (NPIN)
Parents are faced with all sorts of questions about development; the NPIN site describes many guides to online and other resources for answering those questions.

Figure 10.10
Kohlberg's stage theory. Kohlberg's model describes three levels of moral reasoning, each of which can be divided into two stages. This chart summarizes some of the key facets in how individuals think about right and wrong at each stage.

Stage 1	Stage 2	Stage 3	Stage 4	Stage 5	Stage 6
Punishment orientation	**Naive reward orientation**	**Good boy/good girl orientation**	**Authority orientation**	**Social contract orientation**	**Individual principles and conscience orientation**
Right and wrong is determined by what is punished.	Right and wrong is determined by what is rewarded.	Right and wrong is determined by close others' approval or disapproval.	Right and wrong is determined by society's rules, and laws, which should be obeyed rigidly.	Right and wrong is determined by society's rules, which are viewed as fallible rather than absolute.	Right and wrong is determined by abstract ethical principles that emphasize equity and justice.
Preconventional level		**Conventional level**		**Postconventional level**	

to be virtuous and win approval from others. Moral thinking at this stage is relatively inflexible. Rules are viewed as absolute guidelines that should be enforced rigidly.

During adolescence, some youngsters move on to the *postconventional level,* which involves working out a personal code of ethics. Acceptance of rules is less rigid, and moral thinking shows some flexibility. Subjects at the postconventional level allow for the possibility that someone might not comply with some of society's rules if they conflict with personal ethics. For example, participants at this level might applaud a newspaper reporter who goes to jail rather than reveal a source of information who was promised anonymity.

Evaluating Kohlberg's Theory

How has Kohlberg's theory fared in research? The central ideas have received reasonable support. Progress in moral reasoning is indeed closely tied to cognitive development (Walker, 1988). Studies also show that youngsters generally do progress through Kohlberg's stages of moral reasoning in the order that he proposed (Walker, 1989). Furthermore, relations between age and level of moral reasoning are in the predicted directions (Rest, 1986). Representative age trends are

Figure 10.11

Age and moral reasoning. The percentages of different types of moral judgments made by subjects at various ages are graphed here (based on Kohlberg, 1963, 1969). As predicted, preconventional reasoning declines as children mature, conventional reasoning increases during middle childhood, and postconventional reasoning begins to emerge during adolescence. But at each age, children display a mixture of various levels of moral reasoning.

shown in **Figure 10.11**: As children get older, stage 1 and stage 2 reasoning declines, while stage 3 and stage 4 reasoning increases. Finally, evidence suggests that moral *reasoning* is predictive of moral *behavior,* although the association is modest (Bruggerman & Hart, 1996). That is, youngsters who are at higher stages of moral development are somewhat more likely to be altruistic, conscientious, and honest than youngsters at lower stages (Fabes et al., 1999; Taylor & Walker, 1997). Although these findings support the utility of Kohlberg's model, like all influential theorists, he has his critics. They have raised the following issues:

1. It's not unusual to find that a person shows signs of several adjacent levels of moral reasoning at a particular point in development (Walker & Taylor, 1991). As we noted in the critique of Piaget, this mixing of stages is a problem for virtually all stage theories.
2. Evidence is mounting that Kohlberg's dilemmas may not be valid indicators of moral development in some cultures (Nucci, 2002). Some critics believe that the value judgments built into Kohlberg's theory reflect a liberal, individualistic ideology characteristic of modern Western nations that is much more culture-specific than Kohlberg appreciated (Miller, 2001).

concept **check** 10.3 ✓

Analyzing Moral Reasoning

Check your understanding of Kohlberg's theory of moral development by analyzing hypothetical responses to the following moral dilemma.

A midwest biologist has conducted numerous studies demonstrating that simple organisms such as worms and paramecia can learn through conditioning. It occurs to her that perhaps she could condition fertilized human ova, to provide a dramatic demonstration that abortions destroy adaptable, living human organisms. This possibility appeals to her, as she is ardently opposed to abortion. However, there is no way to conduct the necessary research on human ova without sacrificing the lives of potential human beings. She desperately wants to conduct the research, but obviously, the sacrifice of human ova is fundamentally incompatible with her belief in the sanctity of human life. What should she do? Why? [Submitted by a student (age 13) to Professor Barbara Banas at Rochester Community College]

In the spaces on the left of each numbered response, indicate the level of moral reasoning shown, choosing from the following: (a) preconventional level, (b) conventional level, or (c) postconventional level. The answers are in Appendix A.

_____ **1.** She should do the research. Although it's wrong to kill, there's a greater good that can be realized through the research.

_____ **2.** She shouldn't do the research because people will think that she's a hypocrite and condemn her.

_____ **3.** She should do the research because she may become rich and famous as a result.

Adolescence is a bridge between childhood and adulthood. During this time, individuals continue to experience significant changes in cognitive, moral, and social development. However, the most dynamic areas of development during adolescence are physical changes and related transitions in emotional and personality development.

Physiological and Neural Changes

Recall for a moment your junior high school days. Didn't it seem that your body grew so fast about this time that your clothes just couldn't "keep up"? This phase of rapid growth in height and weight is called the *adolescent growth spurt.* Brought on by hormonal changes, it typically starts at about age 10 in girls and at about 12 in boys (Archibald, Graber, & Brooks-Dunn, 2003). Scientists are not sure about what triggers the hormonal changes that underlie the adolescent growth spurt, but recent evidence suggests that rising levels of *leptin,* the recently discovered hormone that reflects the body's fat cell storage (see Chapter 9), may provide the crucial signals (Spear, 2000).

In addition to growing taller and heavier, children begin to develop the physical features that characterize adults of their respective sexes. These features are termed *secondary sex characteristics—***physical features that distinguish one sex from the other but that are not essential for reproduc-**

tion. For example, males go through a voice change, develop facial hair, and experience greater skeletal and muscle growth in the upper torso, leading to broader shoulders (see **Figure 10.12**). Females experience breast growth and a widening of the pelvic bones plus increased fat deposits in this area, resulting in wider hips (Susman & Rogol, 2004).

Soon, youngsters reach *puberty—***the stage during which sexual functions reach maturity, which marks the beginning of adolescence.** It is during puberty that the *primary sex characteristics—***the structures necessary for reproduction—**develop fully. In the male, these include the testes, penis, and related internal structures. Primary sex characteristics in the female include the ovaries, vagina, uterus, and other internal structures.

In females, puberty is typically signaled by *menarche—***the first occurrence of menstruation,** which reflects the culmination of a series of hormonal changes (Dorn et al., 1999). American girls typically reach menarche at ages 12–13, with further sexual maturation continuing until approximately age 16 (Susman, Dorn, & Schiefelbein, 2003). American boys typically experience *spermarche—***the first occurrence of ejaculation—**at ages 13–14, with further sexual maturation continuing until approximately age 18 (Archibald et al., 2003). Interestingly, *generational* changes have occurred in the timing of puberty for females. Today's adolescent girls begin puberty at a younger age, and complete it more rapidly, than their counterparts in earlier generations

PREVIEW QUESTIONS

● When do children reach pubescence and puberty?

● What changes do these landmarks bring?

● What have neuroscientists learned about the adolescent brain?

● Does the empirical evidence support the notion that adolescence is a time of great turmoil?

● What is the chief challenge of adolescence, according to Erikson?

● What are Marcia's four identity statuses?

Web Link **10.5**

Adolescence Directory OnLine
Browsers visiting this site hosted by the University of Indiana will find guides to resources about adolescence that cover many of the health, mental health, safety, personal, and parenting issues important to this phase of development.

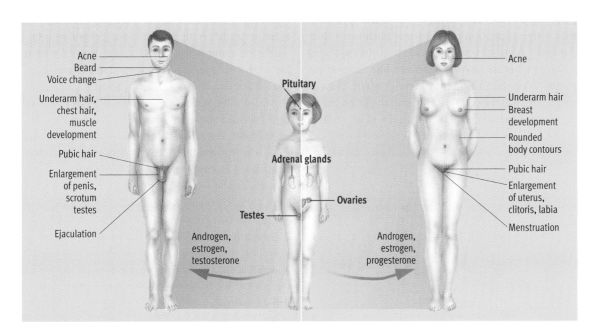

Figure 10.12

Physical development at puberty. Hormonal changes during puberty lead not only to a growth spurt but also to the development of secondary sex characteristics. The pituitary gland sends signals to the adrenal glands and gonads (ovaries and testes), which secrete hormones responsible for various physical changes that differentiate males and females.

*The timing of sexual matur-
ation can have important
implications for adolescents.
Youngsters who mature un-
usually early or unusually
late often feel uneasy about
this transition.*

© Kevin Cooley/Taxi/Getty Images

Figure 10.13

The prefrontal cortex.
Recent research suggests
that neural development
continues throughout ado-
lescence. Moreover, the
chief site for much of this
development is the pre-
frontal cortex, which ap-
pears to be the last area of
the brain to mature fully.
This discovery may have
fascinating implications for
understanding the adoles-
cent brain, as the prefrontal
cortex appears to play a key
role in emotional regulation
and self-control.

did (Anderson, Dallal, & Must, 2003; Fredriks et al.,
2000). The factors underlying this trend and the reasons it has only been seen in females have scientists
perplexed (Archibald et al., 2003), as the most obvious potential causes—improvements in nutrition
and medical care—should apply equally to males
and females.

The timing of puberty varies from one adolescent
to the next over a range of about 5 years (10–15 for
girls, 11–16 for boys). Generally, *girls who mature early
and boys who mature late seem to experience more subjective distress and emotional difficulty with the transition
to adolescence* (Susman et al., 2003). However, in both
males and females, early maturation is associated
with greater use of alcohol and drugs, more high-risk
behavior, and more trouble with the law (Steinberg
& Morris, 2001). Among females, early maturation is
also correlated with earlier experience of intercourse,
more unwanted pregnancies, a greater risk for eating
problems, and a variety of psychological disorders
(Archibald et al., 2003). Thus, we might speculate
that early maturation often thrusts both sexes (but
especially females) toward the adult world too soon.

Recent studies have uncovered some interesting
trends in adolescents' neural development. For example, the volume of white matter in the brain grows
throughout adolescence (Schmithorst et al., 2002).

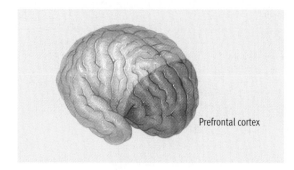

Prefrontal cortex

This means that *neurons are becoming more myelinated*
(see Chapter 3), which presumably leads to enhanced
conductivity and connectivity in the brain. In contrast, gray matter decreases in volume (Sowell et al.,
2002). This finding is thought to reflect the process
of *synaptic pruning*—the elimination of less-active
synapses—which plays a key role in the formation
of neural networks (see Chapter 3).

Perhaps the most interesting discovery about the
adolescent brain has been that increased myeliniza-
tion and synaptic pruning are most pronounced in the
prefrontal cortex (Keating, 2004). Thus, *the prefrontal
cortex appears to be the last area of the brain to fully mature,* and this maturation is not complete until late
adolescence or early adulthood (see **Figure 10.13**).
Much has been made of this finding because the
prefrontal cortex has been characterized as an "executive control center" that is crucial to high-level cognitive functions, such as planning, organization,
emotional regulation, and response inhibition (Nelson et al., 2002). Theorists have suggested that the
immaturity of the prefrontal cortex may explain why
risky behavior (such as reckless driving, experimentation with drugs, dangerous stunts, unprotected
sex, and so forth) peaks during adolescence (Compas, 2004; Dahl, 2003). This conclusion is rather
speculative at this juncture, but it has become clear
that the brain continues to mature during the adolescent years.

Time of Turmoil?

Back around the turn of the 20th century, G. Stanley
Hall (1904), one of psychology's great pioneers, proposed that the adolescent years are characterized by
instability and turmoil. Hall attributed this turmoil
to adolescents' erratic physical changes and resultant
confusion about self-image. Over the decades, a number of theorists have agreed with Hall's characterization of adolescence as a stormy period.

Statistics on *adolescent suicide* would seem to support the idea that adolescence is a time marked by
turmoil, but the figures can be interpreted in various
ways. On the one hand, suicide rates among adolescents have risen alarmingly in recent decades. On
the other hand, even with this steep increase, suicide
rates for adolescents are lower than those for older
age groups (see **Figure 10.14**).

Actually, the suicide crisis among teenagers involves *attempted* suicide more than *completed* suicide.
It is difficult to compile accurate data on suicide attempts (which are often covered up), but experts estimate that when all age groups are lumped together,

suicide attempts outnumber actual suicidal deaths by a ratio of at least 8 to 1 and perhaps as high as 25 to 1. However, this ratio of attempted to completed suicides is much higher for adolescents. It is estimated to range anywhere from 100:1 to 200:1 (Maris, Berman, & Silverman, 2000). Thus, attempted suicide is a major problem during adolescence. About 2% of adolescent males and about 5% of adolescent females attempt suicide each year in the United States (Blum & Rinehart, 2000).

Returning to our original question, does the weight of evidence support the idea that adolescence is usually a period of turmoil and turbulence? Overall, the consensus of the experts has been that adolescence is not an exceptionally difficult period (Petersen et al., 1993; Steinberg & Levine, 1997). However, in a reanalysis of the evidence, Jeffrey Arnett (1999) has argued convincingly that "not all adolescents experience storm and stress, but storm and stress is more likely during adolescence than at other ages" (p. 317). Although turbulence and turmoil are not *universal* in adolescence, challenging adaptations *do* have to be made during this period. In particular, most adolescents struggle to some extent in their effort to achieve a comfortable sense of identity.

The Search for Identity

Erik Erikson was especially interested in personality development during adolescence, which is the fifth of the eight major life stages he described. The psychosocial crisis during this stage pits *identity* against *confusion* as potential outcomes. According to Erikson (1968), the main challenge of adolescence is the struggle to form a clear sense of identity. This struggle involves working out a stable concept of oneself as a unique individual and embracing an ideology or system of values that provides a sense of direction. In Erikson's view, adolescents grapple with questions such as "Who am I?" and "Where am I going in life?"

Although the struggle for a sense of identity is a lifelong process (Waterman & Archer, 1990), it does tend to be especially intense during adolescence. Adolescents deal with identity formation in a variety of ways. According to James Marcia (1966, 1980, 1994), the presence or absence of a sense of commitment (to life goals and values) and a sense of crisis (active questioning and exploration) can combine to produce four different *identity statuses* (see **Figure 10.15**). These are not stages that people pass through, but orientations that may occur at a particular time. In order of increasing maturity, Marcia's four identity statuses are as follows (Meeus, 1996):

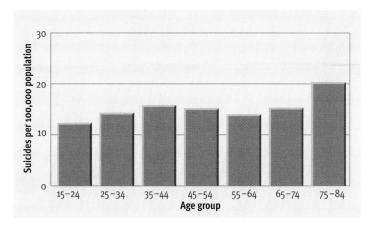

Figure 10.14

Suicide rates by age. Although suicide rates for adolescents have increased dramatically in recent decades, the suicide rates for this youthful age group remain lower than suicide rates for older age groups. (Source: Centers for Disease Control and Prevention)

- *Identity diffusion* is a state of rudderless apathy. Some people simply refuse to confront the challenge of charting a life course and committing to an ideology. Although this stance allows them to evade the crisis of identity, the lack of direction can become problematic, as people in this status exhibit more social and psychological problems than others (Adams, Gullotta, & Montemayor, 1992).
- *Identity foreclosure* is a premature commitment to visions, values, and roles—typically those prescribed by one's parents. This path allows a person to circumvent much of the struggle for an identity. However, foreclosure is associated with attachment-related anxiety, conformity, and not being very open to new experiences (Kroger, 2003).

Web Link 10.6

Adolescent Health and Mental Health
This site devoted to issues related to adolescence is edited by Michael Fenichel, a prominent psychologist interested in using the Internet to distribute quality professional information to the public.

Figure 10.15

Marcia's four identity statuses. According to Marcia (1980), the occurrence of identity crisis and exploration and the development of personal commitments can combine into four possible identity statuses, as shown in this diagram. The progressively darker shades of blue signify progressively more mature identity statuses.

Source: Adapted from Marcia, J. E. (1980). Identity in adolescence. In J. Adelson (Ed.), *Handbook of adolescent psychology* (pp. 159–210). New York: John Wiley. Copyright © 1980 by John Wiley. Adapted by permission.

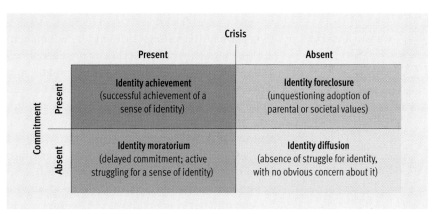

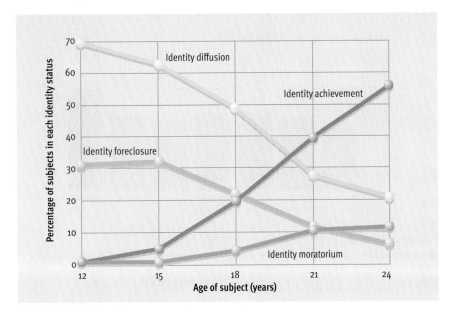

Figure 10.16

Age and identity status. These data from Meilman (1979) summarize the relationship between age and Marcia's (1980) identity statuses. The less mature statuses (diffusion and foreclosure) become less common as people move into young adulthood, and the more mature statuses (moratorium and identity achievement) become more common. As you can see, at age 18 relatively few people have reached identity achievement.

Source: Adapted from Meilman, P. W. (1979). Cross-sectional age changes in ego identity status during adolescence. *Developmental Psychology,* 15, 230–231. Copyright © 1979 by the American Psychological Association. Reprinted by permission of the publishers and author.

- An *identity moratorium* involves delaying commitment for a while to experiment with alternative ideologies and careers. Such experimentation can be valuable. Unfortunately, some people remain indefinitely in what should be a temporary phase. Identity moratorium is associated with self-doubt and confusion (Flum, 1994).

- *Identity achievement* involves arriving at a sense of self and direction after some consideration of alternative possibilities. Commitments have the strength of some conviction, although they're not absolutely irrevocable. Identity achievement is associated with higher self-esteem, conscientiousness, security, achievement motivation, and capacity for intimacy (Kroger, 2003).

Age trends in identity status are depicted in **Figure 10.16**. Consistent with Marcia's theory, identity moratorium and achievement increase with age, while identity diffusion and foreclosure decline in prevalence (Meeus et al., 1999). Although the age trends seen in **Figure 10.16** make sense, they mask the extent to which a sizable majority of adolescents shift back and forth among the four identity statuses (Berzonsky & Adams, 1999). Moreover, young people tend to reach identity achievement at later ages than originally envisioned by Marcia. By late adolescence, only a small minority of individuals have reached identity achievement, so the struggle for a sense of identity routinely extends into young adulthood. Actually, even after people reach identity achievement, their sense of identity can continue to evolve (Kroger, 1996).

Erikson, Marcia, and many other theorists believe that adequate identity formation is a cornerstone of sound psychological health. Identity confusion can interfere with important developmental transitions that should unfold during the adult years, as you'll see in the next section, which takes a look at developmental trends during adulthood.

> The Expanse of Adulthood

PREVIEW QUESTIONS

- How stable is personality over the life span?
- How did Erikson describe adult development?
- How difficult are the transitions to parenthood and the empty nest?
- What kinds of physical changes occur in middle and late adulthood?
- What is dementia, and what is its chief cause in old age?
- How well do intelligence and memory hold up in middle and late adulthood?

The concept of development was once associated almost exclusively with childhood and adolescence, but today development is widely recognized as a lifelong journey. Interestingly, patterns of development during the adult years are becoming increasingly diverse. The boundaries between young, middle, and late adulthood are becoming blurred as more and more people have children later than one is "supposed" to, retire earlier than one is "supposed" to, and so forth. In the upcoming pages we will look at some of the major developmental transitions in adult life, but you should bear in mind that in adulthood (even more so than childhood or adolescence) there are many divergent pathways and timetables.

Personality Development 9b

Research on adult personality development has been dominated by one key question: How stable is personality over the life span? We'll look at this issue, the question of the midlife crisis, and Erikson's view of adulthood in our discussion of personality development in the adult years.

The Question of Stability

How common are significant personality changes in adulthood? Is a grouchy 20-year-old going to be a grouchy 40-year-old and a grouchy 65-year-old? Or can the grouchy young adult become a mellow senior citizen? After tracking subjects through adulthood, many researchers have been impressed by the amount of change observed. Roger Gould (1975) studied two samples of men and women and concluded that "the evolution of a personality continues through the fifth decade of life." After tracking development between the ages of 20 and 42, Whitbourne and her colleagues (1992) found "consistent patterns of personality change." In a long-running study that has followed participants from their 20s through their 70s, Helson, Jones, and Kwan (2002) found "evidence that personality changes in general ways over time."

In contrast, many other researchers have been struck by the stability and durability they have found in personality. The general conclusion that emerged from several studies using objective assessments of personality traits was that personality tends to be quite stable over periods of 20 to 40 years (Block, 1981; Caspi & Herbener, 1990; Costa & McCrae, 1994, 1997). Moreover, a recent review of 150 relevant studies, involving almost 50,000 participants, concluded that personality in early adulthood was a good predictor of personality in late adulthood and that the stability of personality increases with age up to about age 50 (Roberts & DelVecchio, 2000). Moreover, correlations computed between personality measures administered many years apart often yield figures in the .70s, which are regarded as remarkably high (McCrae & Costa, 2003).

Clearly, researchers assessing the stability of personality in adulthood have reached very different conclusions. How can these contradictory conclusions be reconciled? It appears that *both* conclusions are accurate, they just reflect different ways of looking at the data (Bertrand & Lachman, 2003). As noted in Chapter 8, psychological test scores are *relative* measures—they show how one scores *relative to other people*. Raw scores are converted into *percentile scores* that indicate the precise degree to which one is above or below average on a particular trait. The data indicate that these percentile scores tend to be remarkably stable over lengthy spans of time—people's relative standing on personality traits doesn't tend to change much. However, if you examine participants' raw scores, there are some meaningful developmental trends. For example, adults' average scores on extraversion, neuroticism, and openness to experience tend to decline moderately with increasing age, while measures of agreeableness and conscientiousness tend to increase (Bertrand & Lachman, 2003; Caspi, Roberts, & Shiner, 2005). In sum, it appears that personality in adulthood is characterized by *both* stability and change.

The Question of the Midlife Crisis

Debate also has been spirited about whether most people go through a *midlife crisis—a difficult, turbulent period of doubts and reappraisal of one's life.* The two most influential studies of adult development in the 1970s (Gould, 1978; Levinson et al., 1978) both concluded that a midlife crisis is a normal transition experienced by a majority of people. However, numerous subsequent studies have failed to detect an increase in emotional turbulence at midlife (Eisler & Ragsdale, 1992; Roberts & Newton, 1987; Rosenberg, Rosenberg, & Farrell, 1999). These studies, which have used more objective measures of emotional stability, have found signs of midlife crises in only a tiny minority (2%–5%) of participants (McCrae & Costa, 1990). Midlife may bring a period of increased reflection as people contemplate the remainder of their lives, but it's clear that the fabled midlife *crisis* is not typical (Lemme, 1999).

Erikson's View of Adulthood

Insofar as personality changes during the adult years, Erik Erikson's (1963) theory offers some clues about the kinds of changes people can expect. In his eight-stage model of development over the life span, Erikson divided adulthood into three stages (see again **Figure 10.6**):

Intimacy Versus Isolation. In early adulthood, the key concern is whether one can develop the capacity to share intimacy with others. Successful resolution of the challenges in this stage should promote empathy and openness, rather than shrewdness and manipulativeness.

Generativity Versus Self-Absorption. In middle adulthood, the key challenge is to acquire a genuine concern for the welfare of future generations, which results in providing unselfish guidance to younger people. Self-absorption is characterized by self-indulgent concerns with meeting one's own needs and desires.

Integrity Versus Despair. During the retirement years, the challenge is to avoid the tendency to dwell on the mistakes of the past and on one's imminent death. People need to find meaning and satisfaction in their lives, rather than wallow in bitterness and resentment.

Transitions in Family Life

Many of the important transitions in adulthood involve changes in family responsibilities and relation-

Web Link 10.7

Adult Development and Aging (APA Division 20) Psychological researchers interested in adulthood and aging form a distinct division within the American Psychological Association, Division 20. The division's homepage contains a wide range of educational, instructional, and clinical resources and references for this area of concern.

ships. Everyone emerges from a family, and most people go on to form their own families. However, the transitional period during which young adults are "between families" until they form a new family is being prolonged by more and more people. The percentage of young adults who are postponing marriage until their late twenties or early thirties has risen dramatically (Teachman, Polonko, & Scanzoni, 1999; see **Figure 10.17**). This trend is probably the result of a number of factors. Chief among them are the availability of new career options for women, increased educational requirements in the world of work, and increased emphasis on personal autonomy. Remaining single is a much more acceptable option today than it was a few decades ago (DeFrain & Olson, 1999). Nonetheless, over 90% of adults eventually marry.

Adjusting to Marriage

The newly married couple usually settle into their roles as husband and wife gradually. Difficulties with this transition are more likely when spouses come into a marriage with different expectations about marital roles (Lye & Biblarz, 1993). Unfortunately, substantial differences in role expectations seem particularly likely in this era of transition in gender roles (Brewster & Padavic, 2000).

Women may be especially vulnerable to ambivalence about shifting marital roles. More and more women are aspiring to demanding careers. Yet research shows that husbands' careers continue to take priority over their wives' vocational ambitions (Haas, 1999). Moreover, many husbands maintain traditional role expectations about housework, child care, and decision making. Men's contribution to housework has increased noticeably since the 1960s, as you can see in **Figure 10.18**. However, studies indi-

cate that wives are still doing the bulk of the household chores in America, even when they work outside the home (Bianchi et al., 2000). Although married women perform about two-thirds of all housework, only about one-third of wives characterize their division of labor as unfair, because most women don't expect a 50-50 split (Coltrane, 2001).

The prechildren phase of the family life cycle used to be rather short for most newly married couples. Traditionally, couples just *assumed* that they would proceed to have children. In recent decades, however, ambivalence about the prospect of having children clearly has increased (T. W. Smith, 1999), and the percentage of childless couples has doubled since 1960 (Bulcroft & Teachman, 2004). Hence, more and more couples are finding themselves struggling to decide *whether* to have children.

Adjusting to Parenthood

Although an increasing number of people are choosing to remain childless, the vast majority of married couples continue to have children. Most parents are happy with their decision to have children, but the arrival of the first child represents a major transition, and the disruption of routines can be emotionally draining (Bost et al., 2002; Carter, 1999). The transition to parenthood tends to have more impact on mothers than fathers (Nomaguchi & Milkie, 2003). The new mother, already physically exhausted by the birth process, is particularly prone to postpartum distress, and about 10% of new moms experience de-

Figure 10.17

Median age at first marriage. The median age at which people in the United States marry for the first time has been creeping up for both males and females since the mid-1960s. This trend indicates that more people are postponing marriage. (Data from the U. S. Bureau of the Census)

Figure 10.18

Housework trends since the 1960s. As these data show, the housework gap between husbands and wives has narrowed since the 1960s. Married men have more than doubled their housework, but it is the large reduction in wives' housework that has really shrunk the housework gap. (Data from Bianchi et al., 2000)

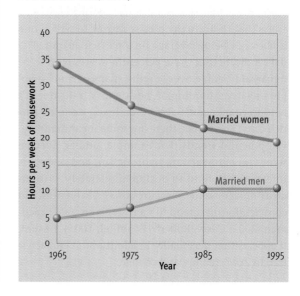

pression (Formicelli, 2001). The transition is more difficult when a wife's expectations regarding how much the father will be involved in child care are not met (Fox, Bruce, & Combs-Orme, 2000). A review of decades of research on parenthood and marital satisfaction, found that: (1) parents exhibit lower marital satisfaction than comparable nonparents, (2) mothers of infants report the steepest decline in marital satisfaction, and (3) the more children couples have, the lower their marital satisfaction tends to be (Twenge, Campbell, & Foster, 2003).

Crisis during the transition to first parenthood is far from universal, however (Cox et al., 1999). Couples who have high levels of affection and commitment prior to the first child's birth are likely to maintain a stable level of satisfaction after the child's birth (Shapiro, Gottman, & Carrere, 2000). The key to making this transition less stressful may be to have *realistic expectations* about parental responsibilities. Studies find that stress is greatest in new parents who have overestimated the benefits and underestimated the costs of their new role (Belsky & Kelly, 1994).

As children grow up, parental influence over them tends to decline, and the early years of parenting—that once seemed so difficult—are often recalled with fondness. When youngsters reach adolescence and seek to establish their own identities, gradual realignments occur in parent-child relationships. On the one hand, parent-adolescent relations generally are not as bitter or contentious as widely assumed (Laursen, Coy, & Collins, 1998). On the other hand, adolescents do spend less time in family activities (Larson et al., 1996), and their closeness to their parents declines while conflicts become more frequent (Grotevant, 1997). The conflicts tend to involve everyday matters (chores and appearance) more than substantive issues (sex and drugs) (Barber, 1994). When conflicts occur, they seem to have more adverse effects on the parents than the children (Steinberg & Steinberg, 1994). Ironically, although research has shown that adolescence is not as turbulent or difficult for youngsters as once believed, their parents *are* stressed out (Steinberg, 2001).

Adjusting to the Empty Nest

When parents do manage to get all their children launched into the adult world, they find themselves faced with an "empty nest." This period was formerly thought to be a difficult transition for many parents, especially mothers who were familiar only with the maternal role. In recent decades, however, more women have experience with other roles outside the home. Hence, recent evidence suggests that most parents adjust effectively to the empty nest transition and are more likely to have problems if their

SALLY FORTH

children *return* to the once-empty nest (Blacker, 1999; Dennerstein, Dudley, & Guthrie, 2002).

Aging and Physical Changes

People obviously experience many physical changes as they progress through adulthood. In both sexes, hair tends to thin out and become gray, and many males confront receding hairlines and baldness. To the dismay of many, the proportion of body fat tends to increase with age. Overall, weight tends to increase in most adults through the mid-50s, when a gradual decline may begin. These changes have little functional significance, but in our youth-oriented society, they often lead people to view themselves as unattractive (Whitbourne, 1999).

In the sensory domain, the key developmental changes occur in vision and hearing. The proportion of people with 20/20 visual acuity declines with age. Farsightedness, difficulty adapting to darkness, and poor recovery from glare are common among older people (Fozard, 1990). Sensitivity to color and contrast also decline (Fozard & Gordon-Salant, 2001). A decline in hearing sensitivity begins gradually in early adulthood but usually isn't noticeable until after age 50. Hearing loss tends to be greater in men than in women and for high-frequency sounds more than low-frequency sounds (Yost, 2000). These sensory losses could be problematic, but in modern society they can usually be compensated for with eyeglasses, contact lenses, and hearing aids.

Age-related changes also occur in hormonal functioning during adulthood. Among women, these changes lead to *menopause*. This ending of menstrual periods, accompanied by a loss of fertility, typically occurs around age 50 (Avis, 1999). Not long ago, menopause was thought to be almost universally accompanied by severe emotional strain. However, it is now clear that reactions vary and that most women experience relatively modest psychological distress (George, 2002; Walter, 2000). Although people sometimes talk about "male menopause," men don't really go through an equivalent experience. Starting in middle age, testosterone levels *do* decline substantially (Morley, 2001), but these decreases are gradual and are not associated with a collection of symptoms comparable to what women experience (Jacobs, 2001).

The amount of brain tissue and brain weight decline gradually after age 60 (Vinters, 2001). These trends appear to reflect both a decrease in the number of active neurons in some areas of the brain and shrinkage of still-active neurons, with neuron loss perhaps being less important than once believed (Albert & Killiany, 2001). Although this gradual loss of brain tissue sounds alarming, it is a normal part of the aging process. Its functional significance is the subject of some debate, but it doesn't appear to be a key factor in any of the age-related dementias. **A *dementia* is an abnormal condition marked by multiple cognitive deficits that include memory impairment.** Dementia can be caused by quite a variety of diseases, such as Alzheimer's disease, Parkinson's disease, Huntington's disease, and AIDS, to name just a few (Caine & Lyness, 2000). Because many of these diseases are more prevalent in older adults, dementia is seen in about 15%–20% of people over age 75 (Wise, Gray, & Seltzer, 1999). However, it is important to emphasize that dementia and "senility" are not part of the normal aging process. As Cavanaugh (1993) notes, "The term *senility* has no valid medical or psychological meaning, and its continued use simply perpetuates the myth that drastic mental decline is a product of normal aging" (p. 85).

Alzheimer's disease accounts for roughly two-thirds of all cases of dementia (Cummings & Cole, 2002). Alzheimer's disease is accompanied by major structural deterioration in the brain (Vinters, 2001). It is a vicious affliction that can strike during middle age but usually emerges after age 65. The hallmark early symptom is the forgetting of newly learned information after surprisingly brief periods of time (Albert & Killiany, 2001). The course of the disease is one of progressive deterioration, typically over a period of 8 to 10 years, ending in death (Rabins, Lykestone, & Steele, 1999). In the beginning, victims simply lose the thread of conversations or forget to follow through on tasks they have started. Gradually, much more obvious problems begin to emerge, including difficulties in speaking, comprehending, and performing complicated tasks, as well as depression and sleep disturbance. Job performance deteriorates noticeably as victims forget important appointments and suffer indignities such as getting lost while driving and paying the same bill several times. From this point, profound memory loss develops. For example, patients may fail to recognize familiar people, something particularly devastating to family and friends. Many patients become very restless and experience hallucinations, delusions, and paranoid thoughts. Eventually, victims become completely disoriented and are unable to care for themselves. There are some encouraging leads for treatments that might slow the progression of this horrible disease, but a cure does not appear to be on the horizon.

The causes that launch this debilitating neural meltdown are not well understood. Genetic factors clearly contribute, but their exact role remains unclear (Ashford & Mortimer, 2002). Some "protective" factors that reduce vulnerability to Alzheimer's disease have been identified, including regular exercise (Schuit et al., 2001) and frequent participation in stimulating cognitive activities (Wilson & Bennett, 2003). The importance of the latter factor emerged in a widely discussed longitudinal investigation called the Nun Study, which followed a group of elderly Catholic Nuns who agreed to donate their brains upon death. The findings of the Nun study suggest that a high prevalence of positive emotions and strong engagement in mentally challenging work and recreation reduce one's risk for Alzheimer's disease (Danner, Snowdon, & Friesen, 2001; Snowdon, 2001).

Aging and Cognitive Changes

The evidence indicates that general intelligence is fairly stable throughout most of adulthood, with a small decline in *average* test scores often seen after age 60 (Schaie, 1990, 1994, 1996). However, this seemingly simple assertion masks many complexities and needs to be qualified carefully. Group averages can be deceptive in that mean scores can be dragged down by a small minority of people who show a decline. For example, when Schaie (1990) calculated the percentage of people who maintain stable performance on various abilities, he found that about 80% showed no decline by age 60 and that about two-thirds were still stable through age 81.

What about memory? Numerous studies report decreases in older adults' memory capabilities (Bäckman et al., 1999). Most researchers maintain that the memory losses associated with normal aging tend to be moderate and are *not* experienced by everyone (Dixon & Cohen, 2003; Shimamura et al., 1995). However, Salthouse (2003, 2004) takes a much more pessimistic view, arguing that age-related decreases in memory are substantial in magnitude, that they begin in early adulthood, and that they affect everyone. One reason for these varied conclusions may be that a variety of types of memory can be assessed (see Chapter 7 for a review of various systems of memory). The most reliable decrements are usually seen

Web Link **10.8**

USDHHS: Administration on Aging
The U.S. Department of Health and Human Services provides a content-rich site devoted to all aspects of aging; it includes one of the best available guides to online information about older Americans.

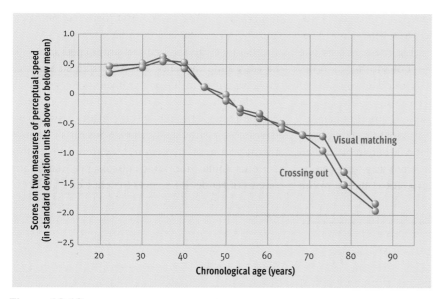

Figure 10.19

Age and mental speed. Many studies have found that mental speed decreases with age. The data shown here, from Salthouse (2000), are based on two perceptual speed tasks. The data points are means for large groups of subjects expressed in terms of how many standard deviations (see Appendix B) they are above or below the mean for all ages (which is set at 0). Similar age-related declines are seen on many tasks that depend on mental speed.

Source: Adapted from Salthouse, T. A. (2000). Aging and measures of processing speed. *Biological Psychology, 54,* 35-54. Reproduced by permission of Elsevier Science.

Courtesy of Wayne Weiten

in *episodic memory* and *working memory,* with less consistent losses observed on tasks involving *procedural memory* and *semantic memory* (Bäckman, Small, & Wahlin, 2001; Dixon & Cohen, 2003).

In the cognitive domain, aging does seem to take its toll on *speed* first. Many studies indicate that speed in learning, solving problems, and processing information tends to decline with age (Salthouse, 1996). The evidence suggests that the erosion of processing speed may be a gradual, lengthy trend beginning in middle adulthood (see **Figure 10.19**). The general nature of this trend (across differing tasks) suggests that it may be the result of age-related changes in neurological functioning (Salthouse, 2000), although doubts have been raised about this conclusion (Bashore,

Ridderinkhof, & van der Molen, 1997). Although mental speed declines with age, problem-solving ability remains largely unimpaired if older people are given adequate time to compensate for their reduced speed.

It should be emphasized that many people remain capable of great intellectual accomplishments well into their later years (Simonton, 1990, 1997). This fact was verified in a study of scholarly, scientific, and artistic productivity that examined lifelong patterns of work among 738 men who lived at least through the age of 79. Dennis (1966) found that the 40s decade was the most productive in most professions. However, productivity was remarkably stable through the 60s and even the 70s in many areas.

Contrary to widespread stereotypes, many people remain active and productive in their 70s, 80s, and even beyond. Pictured here is the author's Auntie Mildred, at age 99, having a little fun at a child's birthday party held at a rock-climbing facility. Now 106, Mildred still composes poetry and you can't pull her away from her personal computer.

> Reflecting on the Chapter's Themes

Five of our seven integrative themes surfaced to some degree in our coverage of human development. We saw theoretical diversity in our discussions of cognitive development and personality development. We saw that psychology evolves in a sociohistorical context, investigating complex, real-world issues—such as the controversy surrounding adolescent suicide—that emerge as our society changes. We encountered multifactorial causation of behavior in the development of attachment, among other things. We saw

cultural invariance and cultural diversity in our examination of attachment, motor development, cognitive development, and moral development.

But above all else, we saw how heredity and environment jointly mold behavior. We've encountered the dual influence of heredity and environment before, but this theme is rich in complexity, and each chapter draws out different aspects and implications. Our discussion of development amplified the point that genetics and experience work *interactively* to

 Theoretical Diversity

 Sociohistorical Context

 Multifactorial Causation

 Cultural Heritage

 Heredity and Environment

shape behavior. What does it mean to say that heredity and environment interact? In the language of science, an interaction means that the effects of one variable depend on the effects of another. In other words, heredity and environment do not operate independently. Children with "difficult" temperaments will elicit different reactions from different parents, depending on the parents' personalities and expectations. Likewise, a particular pair of parents will affect different children in different ways, depending on the inborn characteristics of the children. An interplay, or feedback loop, exists between biological and environmental factors.

All aspects of development are shaped jointly by heredity and experience. We often estimate their relative weight or influence, as if we could cleanly divide behavior into genetic and environmental components. Although we can't really carve up behavior that neatly, such comparisons can be of great theoretical interest, as you'll see in our upcoming Personal Application, which discusses the nature and origins of gender differences in behavior.

PERSONAL *Application*

Understanding Gender Differences

Answer the following "true" or "false."

____ 1 Females are more socially oriented than males.

____ 2 Males outperform females on most spatial tasks.

____ 3 Females are more irrational than males.

____ 4 Males are less sensitive to nonverbal cues than females.

____ 5 Females are more emotional than males.

Are there genuine behavioral differences between the sexes similar to those mentioned above? If so, why do these differences exist? How do they develop? These are the complex and controversial questions that we'll explore in this Personal Application.

Before proceeding further, we need to clarify how some key terms are used, as terminology in this area of research has been evolving and remains a source of confusion (Deaux, 1993; Unger & Crawford, 1993). *Sex* refers to the biologically based categories of female and male. In contrast, *gender* refers to culturally constructed distinctions between femininity and masculinity. Individuals are born female or male. However, they become feminine or masculine through complex developmental processes that take years to unfold.

The statements at the beginning of this Application reflect popular gender stereotypes in our society. *Gender stereotypes* are widely held beliefs about females' and males' abilities, personality traits, and so-

cial behavior. Table 10.1 lists some characteristics that are part of the masculine and feminine stereotypes in North American so-

Table 10.1 Elements of Traditional Gender Stereotypes

Masculine	Feminine
Active	Aware of other's feelings
Adventurous	Considerate
Aggressive	Creative
Ambitious	Cries easily
Competitive	Devotes self to others
Dominant	Emotional
Independent	Enjoys art and music
Leadership qualities	Excitable in a crisis
Likes math and science	Expresses tender feelings
Makes decisions easily	Feelings hurt easily
Mechanical aptitude	Gentle
Not easily influenced	Home oriented
Outspoken	Kind
Persistent	Likes children
Self-confident	Neat
Skilled in business	Needs approval
Stands up under pressure	Tactful
Takes a stand	Understanding

Source: Adapted from Ruble, T. L. (1983). Sex stereotypes: Issues of change in the 70s. *Sex Roles, 9,* 397–402. Copyright © 1983 Plenum Publishing Group. Adapted with kind permission of Springer Science and Business Media.

ciety. The table shows something you may have already noticed on your own. The male stereotype is much more flattering, suggesting that men have virtually cornered the market on competence and rationality. After all, everyone knows that females are more dependent, emotional, irrational, submissive, and talkative than males. Right? Or is that not the case? Let's look at the research.

How Do the Sexes Differ in Behavior?

Gender differences are actual disparities between the sexes in typical behavior or average ability. Mountains of research, literally thousands of studies, exist on gender differences. What does this research show? Are the stereotypes of males and females accurate? Well, the findings are a mixed bag. The research indicates that genuine behavioral differences *do* exist between the sexes and that people's stereotypes are not entirely inaccurate (Eagly, 1995; Swim, 1994). But the differences are fewer in number, smaller in size, and far more complex than stereotypes suggest. As you'll see, only two of the differences mentioned in our opening true-false questions (the even-numbered items) have been largely supported by the research.

Cognitive Abilities

In the cognitive domain, it appears that there are three genuine—albeit very small—

gender differences. First, on the average, females tend to exhibit slightly better *verbal skills* than males (Halpern, 2000). In particular, females seem stronger on tasks that require rapid access to semantic and other information in long-term memory (Halpern, 1997, 2004). Second, starting during high school, males show a slight advantage on tests of *mathematical ability.* When all students are compared, males' advantage is quite small (Hyde, Fennema, & Lamon, 1990). However, at the high end of the ability distribution, the gender gap is larger, as far more males than females are found to have exceptional math skills (Stumpf & Stanley, 1996). Third, starting in the grade-school years, males tend to score higher than females on most measures of *visual-spatial ability* (Voyer, Voyer, & Bryden, 1995). The size of these gender differences varies from moderate to small depending on the exact nature of the spatial task. Males appear to be strongest on tasks that require visual transformations in working memory (Halpern, 2004).

Social Behavior

In regard to social behavior, research findings support the existence of some additional gender differences. First, studies indicate that males tend to be much more *physically aggressive* than females (Archer, 2005). This disparity shows up early in childhood. Its continuation into adulthood is supported by the fact that men account for a grossly disproportionate number of the violent crimes in our society (Halpern, 2000). The findings on *verbal aggression* are more complex, as females appear to exhibit more relational aggression (snide remarks and so forth) (Archer, 2005). Second, there are gen-

CATHY

CATHY © Cathy Guisewite. Reprinted with permission of UNIVERSAL PRESS SYNDICATE. All rights reserved.

der differences in *nonverbal communication.* The evidence indicates that females are more sensitive than males to subtle nonverbal cues (Hall, Carter, & Horgan, 2000; McClure, 2000). Third, males are more sexually active than females in a variety of ways, and they have more permissive attitudes about casual, premarital, and extramarital sex (Baumeister et al., 2001; see Chapter 9).

Some Qualifications

Although research has identified some genuine gender differences in behavior, bear in mind that these are group differences that indicate nothing about individuals. Essentially, research results compare the "average man" with the "average woman." However, you are—and every individual is—unique. The average female and male are ultimately figments of our imagination. Furthermore, the genuine group differences noted are relatively small. **Figure 10.20** shows how scores on a trait, perhaps verbal ability, might be distributed for men and women. Although the group averages are detectably different, you can see the great variability within each group (sex) and the huge overlap between the two group distributions.

Biological Origins of Gender Differences

What accounts for the development of gender differences? To what degree are they the product of learning or of biology? This question is yet another manifestation of the *nature versus nurture* issue. Investigations of the biological origins of gender differences have centered on the evolutionary bases of behavior, hormones, and brain organization.

Evolutionary Explanations

Evolutionary psychologists argue that gender differences in behavior reflect different natural selection pressures operating on males and females over the course of human history (Archer, 1996; Buss & Kenrick, 1998). For example, as we discussed in Chapter 9, males supposedly are more sexually active and permissive because they invest less than females in the process of procreation and can maximize their reproductive success by seeking many sexual partners (Buss, 1996; Schmitt, 2005). The gender gap in aggression is also explained in terms of reproductive fitness. Because females are more selective about mating than males, males have to engage in more competition for sexual partners than females do. Greater aggressiveness is thought to be adaptive for males in this competition for sexual access because it should foster social dominance over other males and facilitate the acquisition of the material resources emphasized by females when evaluating potential partners (Campbell, 2005; Cummins, 2005). Evolutionary theorists assert that gender differences in spatial ability reflect the division of labor in ancestral hunting-and-gathering societies in which males typically handled the hunting and females the gathering. Males'

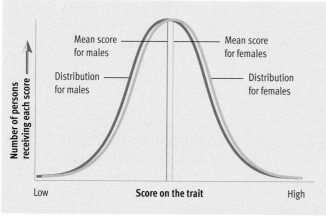

Figure 10.20

The nature of gender differences. Gender differences are group differences that indicate little about individuals because of the great overlap between the groups. For a given trait, one gender may score higher on the average, but far more variation occurs within each gender than between the genders.

superiority on most spatial tasks has been attributed to the adaptive demands of hunting (Silverman & Choi, 2005; see Chapter 1).

Evolutionary analyses of gender differences are interesting, but controversial. On the one hand, it seems eminently plausible that evolutionary forces could have led to some divergence between males and females in typical behavior. On the other hand, evolutionary hypotheses are highly speculative and difficult to test empirically (Eagly & Wood, 1999; Halpern, 1997). The crucial problem for some critics is that evolutionary analyses are so "flexible" they can be used to explain almost anything. For example, if the situation regarding spatial ability were reversed—if females scored higher than males—evolutionary theorists might attribute females' superiority to the adaptive demands of gathering food, weaving baskets, and making clothes—and it would be difficult to prove otherwise (Cornell, 1997).

The Role of Hormones

Hormones play a key role in sexual differentiation during prenatal development. The high level of androgens (the principal class of male hormones) in males and the low level of androgens in females lead to the differentiation of male and female genital organs. The critical role of prenatal hormones becomes apparent when something interferes with normal prenatal hormonal secretions. About a half-dozen endocrine disorders can cause overproduction or underproduction of specific gonadal hormones during prenatal development. Scientists have also studied children born to mothers who were given an androgenlike drug to prevent miscarriage. The general trend in this research is that females exposed prenatally to abnormally high levels of androgens exhibit more male-typical behavior than other females do and that males exposed prenatally to abnormally low levels of androgens exhibit more female-typical behavior than other males (Collaer & Hines, 1995).

These findings suggest that prenatal hormones contribute to the shaping of gender differences in humans. But there are some problems with this evidence (Basow, 1992; Fausto-Sterling, 1992). First, the evidence is much stronger for females than for males. Second, it's always dangerous to draw conclusions about the general population based on small samples of people who have abnormal conditions. Looking at the evidence as a whole, it does seem likely that hormones contribute to gender differences in behavior. However, a great deal remains to be learned.

Differences in Brain Organization

Interpretive problems have also cropped up in efforts to link gender differences to specialization of the cerebral hemispheres in the brain (see **Figure 10.21**). As you may recall from Chapter 3, in most people the left hemisphere is more actively involved in verbal processing, whereas the right hemisphere is more active in visual-spatial processing (Sperry, 1982; Springer & Deutsch, 1998). After these findings surfaced, theorists began to wonder whether this division of labor in the brain might be related to gender differences in verbal and spatial skills. Consequently, they began looking for sex-related disparities in brain organization.

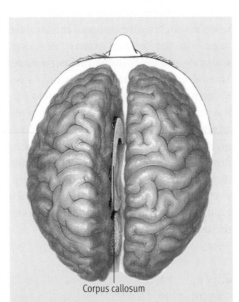

Corpus callosum

Figure 10.21

The cerebral hemispheres and the corpus callosum. In this drawing the cerebral hemispheres have been "pulled apart" to reveal the corpus callosum, the band of fibers that connects the right and left halves of the brain. Research has shown that the right and left hemispheres are specialized to handle different types of cognitive tasks (see Chapter 3), leading some theorists to speculate that patterns of hemispheric specialization might contribute to gender differences in verbal and spatial abilities.

Some thought-provoking findings *have* been reported. For instance, some studies have found that *males tend to exhibit more cerebral specialization than females* (Hellige, 1993b; Voyer, 1996). In other words, there's a trend for males to depend more heavily than females do on the left hemisphere in verbal processing and more heavily on the right in spatial processing. Differences between males and females have also been found in the size of the corpus callosum, the band of fibers that connects the two hemispheres of the brain. Some studies suggest that *females tend to have a larger corpus callosum* (Bigler et al., 1997), which might allow for better interhemispheric transfer of information, which, in turn, might underlie the less lateralized organization of females' brains (Innocenti, 1994). Thus, some theorists have concluded that differences between the sexes in brain organization are responsible for gender differences in verbal and spatial ability (Geschwind & Galaburda, 1987; Kimura & Hampson, 1993).

This idea is intriguing, but psychologists have a long way to go before they can explain gender differences in terms of right brain/left brain specialization. Studies have not been consistent in finding that males have more specialized brain organization than females (Halpern, 1992; Kinsbourne, 1980), and the finding of a larger corpus callosum in females has proven controversial (Bishop & Wahlsten, 1997; Byne & Parsons, 1993). Moreover, even if these findings were replicated consistently, no one is really sure just how they would account for the observed gender differences in cognitive abilities.

In summary, researchers have made some intriguing progress in their efforts to document the biological roots of gender differences in behavior. However, the idea that "anatomy is destiny" has proven difficult to demonstrate. Many theorists remain convinced that gender differences are largely shaped by experience. Let's examine their evidence.

Environmental Origins of Gender Differences

All societies make efforts to train children about gender roles. **Gender roles** are expectations about what is appropriate behavior for each sex. Although gender roles are in a period of transition in modern Western society, there are still many disparities in how males and females are brought up. Investigators have identified three key processes involved in the development of gender roles: operant conditioning, observational learning, and self-socialization. First we'll examine these processes. Then we'll look at the principal sources of gender-role socialization: families, schools, and the media.

Operant Conditioning

In part, gender roles are shaped by the power of reward and punishment—the key processes in *operant conditioning* (see Chapter 6). Parents, teachers, peers, and others often reinforce (usually with tacit approval) "gender-appropriate" behavior and respond negatively to "gender-inappropriate" behavior (Bussey & Bandura, 1999; Fagot, Leinbach, & O'Boyle, 1992). If you're a man, you might recall getting hurt as a young boy and being told that "big boys don't cry." If you succeeded in inhibiting your crying, you may have earned an approving smile or even something tangible like an ice cream cone. The reinforcement probably strengthened your tendency to "act like a man" and suppress emotional displays. If you're a woman, chances are your crying wasn't discouraged as gender-inappropriate. Studies suggest that fathers encourage and reward gender-appropriate behavior in their youngsters more than mothers do and that boys experience more pressure to behave in gender-appropriate ways than girls do (Levy, Taylor, & Gelman, 1995).

Observational Learning

Observational learning (see Chapter 6) by children can lead to the imitation of adults' sex-appropriate behavior. Children imitate both males and females, but most children tend to imitate same-sex role models more than opposite-sex role models (Bussey & Bandura, 1984; Frey & Ruble, 1992). Thus, imitation often leads young girls to play with dolls, dollhouses, and toy stoves, while

young boys are more likely to tinker with toy trucks, miniature gas stations, or tool kits.

Self-Socialization

Children themselves are active agents in their own gender-role socialization. Several *cognitive theories* of gender-role development emphasize self-socialization (Bem, 1985; Cross & Markus, 1993; Martin & Ruble, 2004). Self-socialization entails three steps. First, children learn to classify themselves as male or female and to recognize their sex as a permanent quality (around ages 5 to 7). Second, this self-categorization motivates them to value those characteristics and behaviors associated with their sex. Third, they strive to bring their behavior in line with what is considered gender-appropriate in their culture. In other words, children get involved in their own socialization, working diligently to discover the rules that are supposed to govern their behavior.

Sources of Gender-Role Socialization

There are three main sources of influence in gender-role socialization: families, schools, and the media. Of course, we are now in an era of transition in gender roles, so the generalizations that follow may say more about how you were socialized than about how children will be socialized in the future.

Families. A great deal of gender-role socialization takes place in the home (McHale, Crouter, & Whiteman, 2003). Fathers engage in more "rough-housing" play with their sons than with their daughters, even in infancy (McBride-Chang & Jacklin, 1993). As children grow, boys and girls are encouraged to play with different types of toys (Wood, Desmarais, & Gugula, 2002). Generally, boys have less leeway to play with "feminine" toys than girls do with "masculine" toys. When children are old enough to help with household chores, the assignments tend to depend on sex (Cunningham, 2001). For example, girls wash dishes and boys mow the lawn. And parents are more likely to explain scientific concepts to boys than to girls (Crowley et al., 2001).

Schools. Schools and teachers clearly contribute to the socialization of gender roles. The books that children use in learning to read can influence their ideas about what is suitable behavior for males and females (Diekman & Murnen, 2004). Traditionally, males have been more likely to be portrayed as clever, heroic, and adventurous in these books, while females have been more likely to be shown doing domestic chores. Preschool and grade-school teachers frequently reward gender-appropriate behavior in their pupils (Fagot et al., 1985; Ruble & Martin, 1998). Interestingly, teachers tend to pay greater attention to males, helping them, praising them, and scolding them more than females (Sadker & Sadker, 1994). As youngsters progress through the school system, they are often channeled in career directions considered appropriate for their sex (Read, 1991).

Media. Television is another source of gender-role socialization (Luecke-Aleksa et al., 1995). Although some improvement has occurred in recent years, television shows have traditionally depicted men and women in highly stereotypic ways (Galambos, 2004; Signorielli, 2001). Women are often portrayed as submissive, passive, and emotional. Men are more likely to be portrayed as independent, assertive, and competent. Even commercials contribute to the socialization of gender roles (Bretl & Cantor, 1988; Signorielli, McLeod, & Healy, 1994). Women are routinely shown worrying about trivial matters such as the whiteness of their laundry or the shine of their dishes.

Conclusion

As you can see, the findings on gender and behavior are complex and confusing. Nonetheless, the evidence does permit one very general conclusion—a conclusion that you have seen before and will see again. Taken as a whole, the research in this area suggests that biological factors and environmental factors both contribute to gender differences in behavior—as they do to all other aspects of development.

Are Fathers Essential to Children's Well-Being?

Are fathers essential for children to experience normal, healthy development? This question is currently the subject of heated debate. A number of social scientists have mounted a thought-provoking argument that father absence is the chief factor underlying a variety of modern social ills. For example, David Blankenhorn (1995) argues that "fatherlessness is the most harmful demographic trend of this generation. It is the leading cause of declining child well-being in our society" (p. 1). Expressing a similar view, David Popenoe (1996) maintains that "today's fatherlessness has led to social turmoil—damaged children, unhappy children, aimless children, children who strike back with pathological behavior and violence" (p.192).

The Basic Argument

What is the evidence for the proposition that fathers are essential to healthy development? Over the last 40 years, the proportion of children growing up without a father in the home has more than doubled. During the same time, we have seen dramatic increases in teenage pregnancy, juvenile delinquency, violent crime, drug abuse, eating disorders, teen suicide, and family dysfunction. Moreover, mountains of studies have demonstrated an association between father absence and an elevated risk for these problems. Summarizing this evidence, Popenoe (1996) asserts that "fatherless children have a risk factor two to three times that of fathered children for a wide range of negative outcomes, including dropping out of high school, giving birth as a teenager, and becoming a juvenile delinquent" (p. 192), which leads him to infer that "fathers have a unique and irreplaceable role to play in child development" (p. 197). Working from this premise, Popenoe concludes, "If present trends continue, our society could be on the verge of committing social suicide" (p. 192). Echoing this dire conclusion, Blankenhorn (1995) comments that "to tolerate the trend of fatherlessness is to accept the inevitability of continued societal recession" (p. 222).

You might be thinking, "What's all the fuss about?" Surely, proclaiming the importance of fatherhood ought to be no more controversial than advocacy for motherhood or apple pie. But the assertion that a father is *essential* to a child's well-being has some interesting political implications. It suggests that heterosexual marriage is the only appropriate context in which to raise children and that other family configurations are fundamentally deficient. Based on this line of reasoning, some people have argued for new laws that would make it more difficult to obtain a divorce and other policies and programs that would favor traditional families over families headed by single mothers, cohabiting parents, and gay and lesbian parents (Silverstein & Auerbach, 1999). Thus, the question about the importance of fathers is creating a great deal of controversy because it is really a question about alternatives to traditional family structure.

Evaluating the Argument

In light of the far-reaching implications of the view that fathers are essential to normal development, it makes sense to subject this view to critical scrutiny. How could you use critical thinking skills to evaluate this argument? At least three previously discussed ideas seem pertinent.

First, it is important to recognize that the position that fathers are essential for healthy development rests on a foundation of correlational evidence, and as we have seen repeatedly, *correlation is no assurance of causation.* Yes, there has been an increase in fatherlessness that has been paralleled by increases in teenage pregnancy, drug abuse, eating disorders, and other disturbing social problems. But think of all the other changes

Are fathers crucial to children's well-being? This seemingly simple question has sparked heated debate.

© Royalty Free/Corbis

that have occurred in American culture over the last 40 years, such as the decline of organized religion, the growth of mass media, dramatic shifts in sexual mores, and so forth. Increased fatherlessness has co-varied with a host of other cultural trends. Thus, it is highly speculative to infer that father absence is the chief cause of most modern social problems.

Second, it always pays to think about whether there are *alternative explanations* for findings that you might have doubts about. What other factors might account for the association between father absence and children's maladjustment? Think for a moment: What is the most frequent cause of father absence? Obviously, it is divorce. Divorces tend to be highly stressful events that disrupt children's entire lives. Although the evidence suggests that a majority of children seem to survive divorce without lasting, detrimental effects, it is clear that divorce elevates youngsters' risk for a wide range of negative developmental outcomes (Amato, 2001, 2003; Hetherington, 1999, 2003). Given that father absence and divorce are often intertwined, it is possible that the negative effects of divorce account for much of the association between father absence and social problems.

Are there any other alternative explanations for the correlation between fatherlessness and social maladies? Yes, critics point out that the prevalence of father absence co-varies with socioeconomic status. Father absence is much more common in low-income families (Anderson, Kohler, & Letiecq, 2002). Thus, the effects of father absence are entangled to some extent with the many powerful, malignant effects of poverty, which might account for much of the correlation between fatherlessness and negative outcomes (McLoyd, 1998).

A third possible strategy in thinking critically about the effects of father absence would be to look for some of the *fallacies in reasoning* introduced in Chapter 9 (irrelevant reasons, circular reasoning, slippery slope, weak analogies, and false dichotomy). A couple of the quotes from Popenoe and Blankenhorn were chosen to give you an opportunity to detect two of these fallacies in a new context. Take a look at the quotes once again and see whether you can spot the fallacies.

Popenoe's assertion that "if present trends continue, our society could be on the verge of social suicide" is an example of *slippery slope argumentation*, which involves predictions that if one allows X to happen, things will spin out of control and catastrophic events will follow. "Social suicide" is a little vague, but it sounds as if Popenoe is predicting that father absence will lead to the destruction of modern American culture. The other fallacy that you might have spotted was the *false dichotomy* apparent in Blankenhorn's assertion that "to tolerate the trend of fatherlessness is to accept the inevitability of continued societal recession." A false dichotomy creates an either-or choice between the position one wants to advocate (in this case, new social policies to reduce father absence) and some obviously horrible outcome that any sensible person would want to avoid (social decay), while ignoring other possible outcomes that might lie between these extremes.

In summary, we can find a number of flaws and weaknesses in the argument that fathers are *essential* to normal development. However, our critical evaluation of this argument *does not mean that fathers are unimportant.* Many types of evidence suggest that fathers generally make significant contributions to their children's development (Anderson et al., 2002; Phares, 1996; Rohner & Veneziano, 2001). We could argue with merit that fathers typically provide a substantial advantage for children that fatherless children do not have. But there is a crucial dis-tinction between arguing that fathers *promote* normal, healthy development and arguing that fathers are *necessary* for normal, healthy development. If fathers are *necessary*, children who grow up without them could not achieve the same level of well-being as those who have fathers, yet it is clear that a great many children from single-parent homes turn out just fine.

Fathers surely are important, and it seems likely that father absence *contributes* to a variety of problems in modern society. So, why do Blankenhorn (1995) and Popenoe (1996) argue for the much stronger conclusion—that fathers are *essential?* They appear to prefer the stronger conclusion because it raises much more serious questions about the viability of nontraditional family forms. Thus, they seem to want to advance a *political agenda* that champions traditional family values. They are certainly entitled to do so, but when research findings are used to advance a political agenda—whether conservative or liberal—a special caution alert should go off in your head. When a political agenda is at stake, it pays to scrutinize arguments with extra care, because research findings are more likely to be presented in a slanted fashion. The field of psychology deals with a host of complex questions that have profound implications for a wide range of social issues. The skills and habits of critical thinking can help you find your way through the maze of reasons and evidence that hold up the many sides of these complicated issues.

Table 10.2 Critical Thinking Skills Discussed in This Application

Skill	Description
Understanding the limitations of correlational evidence	The critical thinker understands that a correlation between two variables does not demonstrate that there is a causal link between the variables.
Looking for alternative explanations for findings and events	In evaluating explanations, the critical thinker explores whether there are other explanations that could also account for the findings or events under scrutiny.
Recognizing and avoiding common fallacies, such as irrelevant reasons, circular reasoning, slippery slope reasoning, weak analogies, and false dichotomies	The critical thinker is vigilant about conclusions based on unrelated premises, conclusions that are rewordings of premises, unwarranted predictions that things will spin out of control, superficial analogies, and contrived dichotomies.

Key Ideas

Progress Before Birth: Prenatal Development

● Prenatal development proceeds through the germinal, embryonic, and fetal stages as the zygote is differentiated into a human organism. During this period, development may be affected by maternal drug use, maternal malnutrition, and some maternal illnesses.

The Wondrous Years of Childhood

● Motor development follows cephalocaudal (head-to-foot) and proximodistal (center-outward) trends. Developmental norms for motor skills and other types of development are only group averages. Cross-cultural research on the pacing of motor development shows that maturation and experience both are important.

● Harlow's work with monkeys undermined the reinforcement explanation of attachment. Bowlby proposed an evolutionary explanation that has been very influential. Separation anxiety usually appears at around 6 to 8 months of age. Research shows that attachment emerges out of an interplay between infant and mother.

● Infant-mother attachments fall into three categories: secure, anxious-ambivalent, and avoidant. Cultural variations in childrearing can affect the patterns of attachment seen in a society. Attachment patterns may have lasting effects on individuals. Modest cultural variations in the prevalence of various patterns of attachment are seen, but secure attachment predominates in all cultures.

● Erik Erikson's theory of personality development proposes that individuals evolve through eight stages over the life span. Successful progress through the four childhood stages should yield a trustful, autonomous person with a sense of initiative and industry.

● According to Piaget's theory of cognitive development, the key advance during the sensorimotor period is the child's gradual recognition of the permanence of objects. The preoperational period is marked by centration, irreversibility, and egocentrism. During the concrete operations period, children develop the ability to perform operations on mental representations. Formal operations ushers in more abstract, systematic, and logical thought.

● Vygotsky's sociocultural theory maintains that cognitive development is fueled by social interactions with parents and others. Vygotsky argued that language is central to cognitive development and that culture exerts great influence over how cognitive growth unfolds. Recent research has shown that infants appear to understand surprisingly complex concepts that they have had virtually no opportunity to learn about, leading some theorists to conclude that basic cognitive abilities are innate.

● According to Kohlberg, moral reasoning progresses through three levels that are related to age and determined by cognitive development. Age-related progress in moral reasoning *has* been found in research, although there is a great deal of overlap between adjacent stages.

The Transition of Adolescence

● The growth spurt at puberty is a prominent event involving the development of reproductive maturity and secondary sexual characteristics. Neural development continues through adolescence and the prefrontal cortex appears to be the last area of the brain to fully mature.

● Recent decades have brought a surge in attempted suicide by adolescents. Evidence suggests that adolescence may be slightly more stressful than other periods of life. According to Erikson, the key challenge of adolescence is to make some progress toward a sense of identity. Marcia described four patterns of identity formation.

The Expanse of Adulthood

● During adulthood, personality is marked by both stability and change. Doubts have surfaced about whether a midlife crisis is a normal developmental transition. Many landmarks in adult development involve transitions in family relationships, including adjusting to marriage, parenthood, and the empty nest.

● In middle age, normal physical transitions include changes in appearance, sensory losses, and hormonal changes. Drastic mental decline is not a part of the normal aging process. However, 15%–20% of adults over age 75 suffer from some form of dementia. In late adulthood, mental speed declines and working memory suffers, but many people remain productive well into old age.

Reflecting on the Chapter's Themes

● Five of our seven integrative themes stood out in this chapter, including the value of theoretical diversity, the influence of cultural factors, the importance of sociohistorical context, and the inevitability of multifactorial causation. But above all else, our discussion of development showed how heredity and environment interactively shape behavior.

PERSONAL APPLICATION • Understanding Gender Differences

● Gender differences in behavior are fewer in number and smaller in magnitude than gender stereotypes suggest. Research reviews suggest that there are genuine gender differences in verbal ability, mathematical ability, spatial ability, aggression, nonverbal communication, and sexual behavior.

● Evolutionary explanations of gender differences assert that the adaptive pressures faced by males and females have fostered behavioral disparities. There is research linking gender differences in humans to hormones and brain organization, but the research is marred by interpretive problems. Operant conditioning, observational learning, and self-socialization contribute to the development of gender differences. Families, schools, and the media are among the main sources of gender-role socialization.

CRITICAL THINKING APPLICATION • Are Fathers Essential to Children's Well-Being?

● Some social scientists have argued that father absence is the chief cause of a host of social problems and that fathers are essential for normal, healthy development. Critics have argued that there are alternative explanations for the association between father absence and negative developmental outcomes.

Key Terms

Age of viability (p. 307)
Animism (p. 316)
Attachment (p. 310)
Centration (p. 316)
Cephalocaudal trend (p. 309)
Cognitive development (p. 314)
Conservation (p. 315)
Dementia (p. 328)
Development (p. 306)
Developmental norms (p. 310)
Egocentrism (p. 316)
Embryonic stage (p. 306)
Fetal alcohol syndrome (p. 308)
Fetal stage (p. 307)
Gender (p. 330)
Gender differences (p. 330)
Gender roles (pp. 332–333)
Gender stereotypes (p. 330)
Germinal stage (p. 306)
Irreversibility (p. 316)
Maturation (p. 309)
Menarche (p. 321)
Midlife crisis (p. 325)

Motor development (p. 309)
Object permanence (p. 315)
Placenta (p. 306)
Prenatal period (p. 306)
Primary sex characteristics (p. 321)
Proximodistal trend (p. 309)
Puberty (p. 321)
Secondary sex characteristics (p. 321)
Separation anxiety (p. 311)
Sex (p. 330)
Spermarche (p. 321)
Stage (p. 313)
Zygote (p. 306)

Key People

Mary Ainsworth (p. 312)
John Bowlby (pp. 311–312)
Erik Erikson (pp. 312–314, 323, 325)
Harry Harlow (p. 311)
Lawrence Kohlberg (pp. 319–320)
Jean Piaget (pp. 314–317)
Lev Vygotsky (pp. 317–318)

1. The stage of prenatal development during which the developing organism is most vulnerable to injury is the:
   A. zygotic stage.
   B. germinal stage.
   C. fetal stage.
   D. embryonic stage.

2. The cephalocaudal trend in the motor development of children can be described simply as a:
   A. head-to-foot direction.
   B. center-outward direction.
   C. foot-to-head direction.
   D. body-appendages direction.

3. Developmental norms:
   A. can be used to make extremely precise predictions about the age at which an individual child will reach various developmental milestones.
   B. indicate the maximum age at which a child can reach a particular developmental milestone and still be considered "normal."
   C. indicate the average age at which individuals reach various developmental milestones.
   D. involve both A and B.

4. The formation of an attachment between infant and caregiver seems to be:
   A. exclusively a function of the infant's temperament.
   B. exclusively a function of the caregiver's sensitivity.
   C. largely a matter of how well the child's nutritional needs are met.
   D. a function of the combined effect of the infant's temperament and the caregiver's sensitivity.

5. The behavioral, reinforcement explanation of the basis for infant-caregiver attachment was undermined by the research of:
   A. Erik Erikson.
   B. Harry Harlow.
   C. Lawrence Kohlberg.
   D. Lev Vygotsky.

6. During the second year of life, toddlers begin to take some personal responsibility for feeding, dressing, and bathing themselves in an attempt to establish what Erikson calls a sense of:
   A. superiority.
   B. industry.
   C. generativity.
   D. autonomy.

7. Five-year-old David watches as you pour water from a short, wide glass into a tall, narrow one. He says there is now more water than before. This response demonstrates that:
   A. David understands the concept of conservation.
   B. David does not understand the concept of conservation.
   C. David's cognitive development is "behind" for his age.
   D. both B and C are happening.

8. Which of the following is *not* one of the criticisms of Piaget's theory of cognitive development?
   A. Piaget may have underestimated the cognitive skills of children in some areas.
   B. Piaget may have underestimated the influence of cultural factors on cognitive development.
   C. The theory does not clearly address the issue of variability among people in cognitive development.
   D. Evidence for the theory is based on children's answers to questions.

9. If a child's primary reason for not drawing pictures on the living room wall with crayons is to avoid the punishment that would inevitably follow this behavior, she would be said to be at which level of moral development?
   A. Conventional
   B. Postconventional
   C. Preconventional
   D. Unconventional

10. The assumption of a preoperational child that a car is moving because she is in it is an example of:
    A. egocentrism.
    B. centration.
    C. conservation.
    D. preconventional reasoning.

11. Girls who mature _____ and boys who mature _____ feel more subjective distress about the transition of puberty.
    A. early; early
    B. early; late
    C. late; early
    D. late; late

12. Sixteen-year-old Foster wants to spend a few years experimenting with different lifestyles and careers before he settles on who and what he wants to be. Foster is in the adolescent phase called:
    A. moratorium.
    B. foreclosure.
    C. identity achievement.
    D. identity diffusion.

13. The recent evidence suggests that a midlife crisis:
    A. is universal around the world.
    B. occurs in the vast majority of people.
    C. occurs in the vast majority of men, but only a handful of women.
    D. is seen in only a small minority of people.

14. Two cognitive areas that may decline at around 60 years of age are:
    A. verbal and math test scores.
    B. cognitive speed and working memory.
    C. vocabulary scores and abstract reasoning.
    D. none of the above.

15. Males have been found to differ slightly from females in three well-documented areas of mental abilities. Which of the following is *not* one of these?
    A. Verbal ability
    B. Mathematical ability
    C. Intelligence
    D. Visual-spatial abilities

Answers

1 D p. 307
2 A p. 309
3 C p. 310
4 D p. 312
5 B p. 311
6 D p. 314
7 B p. 315
8 D p. 317
9 C pp. 319–320
10 A p. 316
11 B p. 322
12 A pp. 322–324
13 D p. 325
14 B pp. 328–329
15 C pp. 330–331

PsykTrek

Go to the PsykTrek website or CD-ROM for further study of the concepts in this chapter. Both online and on the CD-ROM, PsykTrek includes dozens of learning modules with videos, animations, and quizzes, as well as simulations of psychological phenomena and a multimedia glossary that includes word pronunciations.

ThomsonNOW

www.thomsonedu.com/ThomsonNOW

Go to this site for the link to ThomsonNOW, your one-stop study shop. Take a Pre-Test for this chapter, and ThomsonNOW will generate a Personalized Study Plan based on your test results. The Study Plan will identify the topics you need to review and direct you to online resources to help you master those topics. You can then take a Post-Test to help you determine the concepts you have mastered and what you still need to work on.

Companion Website

www.thomsonedu.com/psychology/weiten

Go to this site to find online resources directly linked to your book, including a glossary, flash cards, drag-and-drop exercises, quizzes, and more!

CHAPTER 11

Personality:
Theory, Research,
and Assessment

© Bryan F. Peterson/Corbis

Before his untimely death in 2006, Steve Irwin became known to millions around the world as the Crocodile Hunter. Watching the khaki-clad Irwin on television, you felt like he was about to jump right out of the set and into your living room. The Australian was famous—some would say notorious—for his frenzied energy, seeming love of danger, and enthusiastic affection for some of the world's most terrifying creatures. As one writer described it, "Like some crazed cross between Tarzan and a frat pledge, Steve Irwin flings himself on top of a thrashing crocodile. Slick with mud and blood (his), Irwin wrestles the beast into restraints, then declares to the TV camera, 'She's a beauty'!" (Lee, 2000)

You don't need to have seen Steve Irwin in action to appreciate that he had what most people would describe as an unusual *personality*. He routinely sought out situations that would give many of us nightmares—getting covered with biting green ants, swimming with killer sharks, grabbing poisonous snakes by the tail, hurling himself out of a boat at night onto the back of a twelve-foot crocodile whose powerful jaws could easily crush his legs. And he did it all with wide-eyed, boisterous enthusiasm.

Irwin's onscreen persona was not just a matter of showmanship. By all accounts, Irwin was just as wildly energetic and thrill-seeking off camera as he was on television. One less than friendly interviewer described him as "like a boy with attention deficit disorder after a very serious Hershey's binge" (White, 1997). And if Irwin seemed unusually demonstrative in his affection for deadly creatures, that, too, was genuine. When he was not filming, he devoted his time to directing Australia's largest private zoo, and he declared that educating people about conservation was his life's work. Saving a crocodile threatened by poachers could bring him to tears (Irwin & Irwin, 2001). Tragically, after surviving countless more dangerous situations, Irwin died when he was stung in the heart by a normally placid stingray. Irwin was mourned all over the world, especially in his native Australia, where he was viewed as a national icon.

The example of Steve Irwin points to the mystery of personality. While Irwin was unusual in many respects, all of us can be described in terms of characteristics that make up our personalities. But what exactly is personality? How does it develop over time? Are we born with a certain personality, or is experience critical in shaping the qualities that make us who we are? Consider that many of Steve Irwin's qualities were evident from a very early age. Irwin himself remarked, "I get called an adrenaline junkie every other minute, and I'm just fine with that. You know what though, mate? I'm doing exactly what I've done from when I was a small boy" (Simpson, 2001). His late mother agreed. She once recalled, "He's always been very, very active—on the verge of hyperactive, really, very much so. If he went missing, you could always look up a tree; there he'd be" (Stainton, 1999). On the other hand, Irwin's life story also points to the role of environment in shaping personality. Irwin clearly had an unusual upbringing. His parents were both lovers of wildlife who opened their own zoo, where Steve grew up. When he was six years old, his birthday present from his parents was a 12-foot python. If Irwin was genuinely fond of snakes, was it because that trait was "in his blood," or was it because he was exposed to them from very early in life?

Psychologists have approached questions like these from a variety of perspectives. Traditionally, the study of personality has been dominated by "grand theories" that attempt to explain a great many aspects of behavior. Our discussion will reflect this emphasis, as we'll devote most of our time to the sweeping theories of Freud, Jung, Skinner, Rogers, and several others. In the Personal Application, we'll discuss how psychological tests are used to measure various aspects of personality. In the Critical Thinking Application, you'll see how hindsight bias can taint people's analyses of personality.

The late Steve Irwin, better known as the Crocodile Hunter, clearly manifested a powerful and unusual personality. But everyone has his or her unique personality, which makes the study of personality a fascinating area of inquiry in psychology.

© Associated Press/AP

PREVIEW QUESTIONS

- What are the essential features of the concept of personality?
- What are personality traits?
- How many personality traits are necessary to describe personality adequately?

Personality is a complex hypothetical construct that has been defined in a variety of ways. Let's take a closer look at the concepts of personality and personality traits.

Defining Personality: Consistency and Distinctiveness

What does it mean to say that someone has an optimistic personality? This assertion indicates that the person has a fairly *consistent tendency* to behave in a cheerful, hopeful, enthusiastic way, looking at the bright side of things, across a wide variety of situations. Although no one is entirely consistent in behavior, this quality of *consistency across situations* lies at the core of the concept of personality.

Distinctiveness is also central to the concept of personality. Personality is used to explain why different people do not act the same in similar situations. If you were stuck in an elevator with three people, each might react differently. One might crack jokes to relieve tension. Another might make ominous predictions that "we'll never get out of here." The third person might calmly think about how to escape. These varied reactions to the same situation occur because each person has a different personality. Each person has traits that are seen in other people, but each individual has his or her own distinctive *set* of personality traits.

In summary, the concept of personality is used to explain (1) the stability in a person's behavior over time and across situations (consistency) and (2) the behavioral differences among people reacting to the same situation (distinctiveness). We can combine these ideas into the following definition: *Personality* **refers to an individual's unique collection of consistent behavioral traits.** Let's explore the concept of *traits* in more detail.

Personality Traits: Dispositions and Dimensions

Everyone makes remarks like "Jan is very *conscientious.*" Or you might assert that "Jamaal is too *timid* to succeed in that job." These descriptive statements refer to personality traits. **A *personality trait* is a durable disposition to behave in a particular way in a variety of situations.** Adjectives such as *honest, depend-* *able, moody, impulsive, suspicious, anxious, excitable, domineering,* and *friendly* describe dispositions that represent personality traits. People use an enormous number of these trait terms to describe one another's personality. One prominent personality theorist, Gordon Allport (1937, 1961), went through an unabridged dictionary and identified over 4500 personality traits!

Most approaches to personality assume that some traits are more basic than others. According to this notion, a small number of fundamental traits determine other, more superficial traits. For example, a person's tendency to be impulsive, restless, irritable, boisterous, and impatient might all be derived from a more basic tendency to be excitable.

A number of psychologists have taken on the challenge of identifying the basic traits that form the core of personality. For example, Raymond Cattell (1950, 1966, 1990) used the statistical procedure of *factor analysis* to reduce a huge list of personality traits to just 16 basic dimensions of personality. In *factor analysis,* **correlations among many variables are analyzed to identify closely related clusters of variables.** If the measurements of a number of variables (in this case, personality traits) correlate highly with one another, the assumption is that a single factor is influencing all of them. Cattell believes that psychologists can thoroughly describe an individual's personality by measuring the 16 traits that he identified in his factor analyses. In the Personal Application, we'll discuss a personality test he designed to assess these traits.

The Five-Factor Model of Personality Traits

Robert McCrae and Paul Costa (1987, 1997, 1999, 2003) have used factor analysis to arrive at an even simpler, *five-factor model of personality* (see **Figure 11.1**). McCrae and Costa maintain that most personality traits are derived from just five higher-order traits that have come to be known as the "Big Five":

- *Extraversion.* People who score high in extraversion are characterized as outgoing, sociable, upbeat, friendly, assertive, and gregarious.
- *Neuroticism.* People who score high in neuroticism tend to be anxious, hostile, self-conscious, insecure, and vulnerable.
- *Openness to experience.* Openness is associated with curiosity, flexibility, vivid fantasy, imaginativeness, artistic sensitivity, and unconventional attitudes.

- *Agreeableness.* Those who score high in agreeableness tend to be sympathetic, trusting, cooperative, modest, and straightforward.
- *Conscientiousness.* Conscientious people tend to be diligent, disciplined, well-organized, punctual, and dependable.

Research shows that the Big Five traits are predictive of specific aspects of behavior, as one would expect (Paunonen, 2003). For example, extraversion correlates positively with popularity and dating a greater variety of people. Conscientiousness correlates with greater honesty, earning a higher grade point average in college, higher job performance ratings, and relatively low alcohol consumption. Openness to experience is associated with playing a musical instrument, whereas agreeableness correlates with honesty.

Like Cattell, McCrae and Costa maintain that personality can be described adequately by measuring the basic traits that they've identified. Their bold claim has been supported in many studies by other researchers, and the Big Five model has become the dominant conception of personality structure in contemporary psychology (John & Srivastava, 1999; McCrae, 2005). However, some theorists have argued that more than five traits are necessary to account for most of the variation seen in human personality (Ashton et al., 2004; Benet & Waller, 1995).

The debate about how many dimensions are necessary to describe personality is likely to continue for

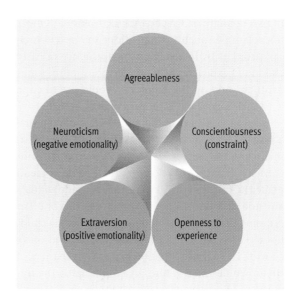

Figure 11.1

The five-factor model of personality. Trait models attempt to break personality down into its basic dimensions. McCrae and Costa (1985, 1987, 1997) maintain that personality can be described adequately with the five higher-order traits identified here, which are widely referred to as the "Big Five."

many years to come. As you'll see throughout the chapter, the study of personality is an area in psychology that has a long history of "dueling theories." We'll divide these diverse personality theories into four broad groups that share certain assumptions, emphases, and interests: (1) psychodynamic perspectives, (2) behavioral perspectives, (3) humanistic perspectives, and (4) biological perspectives. We'll begin our discussion of personality theories by examining the life and work of Sigmund Freud.

> Psychodynamic Perspectives

Psychodynamic theories **include all the diverse theories descended from the work of Sigmund Freud that focus on unconscious mental forces.** Freud inspired many scholars who followed in his intellectual footsteps. Some of these followers simply refined and updated Freud's theory. Others veered off in new directions and established independent, albeit related, schools of thought. Today, the psychodynamic umbrella covers a large collection of loosely related theories that we can only sample from in this text. In this section, we'll examine the ideas of Sigmund Freud in some detail. Then we'll take a briefer look at the psychodynamic theories of Carl Jung and Alfred Adler.

Freud's Psychoanalytic Theory

Born in 1856, Sigmund Freud grew up in a middle-class Jewish home in Vienna, Austria. He showed an

early interest in intellectual pursuits and became an intense, hardworking young man, driven to achieve fame. Freud lived in the Victorian era, which was marked by sexual repression. His life was also affected by World War I, which devastated Europe, and by the growing anti-Semitism of the times. We'll see that the sexual repression and aggressive hostilities that Freud witnessed left their mark on his view of human nature.

Freud was a physician specializing in neurology when he began his medical practice in Vienna toward the end of the 19th century. Like other neurologists in his era, he often treated people troubled by nervous problems such as irrational fears, obsessions, and anxieties. Eventually he devoted himself to the treatment of mental disorders using an innovative procedure he had developed, called *psychoanalysis,* that required lengthy verbal interactions with patients during which Freud probed deeply into their lives.

Freud's (1901, 1924, 1940) *psychoanalytic theory* grew out of his decades of interactions with his clients

PREVIEW QUESTIONS

- How did Freud view the structure of personality?
- Why did Freud think sex and aggression were such important motives?
- How do defense mechanisms work?
- How did Freud explain the development of personality?
- How was Jung's view of the unconscious different from Freud's?
- How did Adler explain inferiority feelings?
- What are the strengths and weaknesses of the psychodynamic approach?

SIGMUND FREUD

"No one who, like me, conjures up the most evil of those half-tamed demons that inhabit the human beast, and seeks to wrestle with them, can expect to come through the struggle unscathed."

National Library of Medicine

in psychoanalysis. Psychoanalytic theory attempts to explain personality, motivation, and psychological disorders by focusing on the influence of early childhood experiences, on unconscious motives and conflicts, and on the methods people use to cope with their sexual and aggressive urges.

Most of Freud's contemporaries were uncomfortable with his theory, for at least three reasons. First, in arguing that people's behavior is governed by unconscious factors of which they are unaware, Freud made the disconcerting suggestion that individuals are not masters of their own minds. Second, in claiming that adult personalities are shaped by childhood experiences and other factors beyond one's control, he suggested that people are not masters of their own destinies. Third, by emphasizing the importance of how people cope with their sexual urges, he offended those who held the conservative, Victorian values of his time. Thus, Freud endured a great deal of criticism, condemnation, and outright ridicule, even after his work began to attract favorable attention. Let's examine the ideas that generated so much controversy.

Structure of Personality 10a

Freud divided personality structure into three components: the id, the ego, and the superego. He saw a person's behavior as the outcome of interactions among these three components.

The *id* **is the primitive, instinctive component of personality that operates according to the pleasure principle.** Freud referred to the id as the reservoir of psychic energy. By this he meant that the id houses the raw biological urges (to eat, sleep, defecate, copulate, and so on) that energize human behavior. The id operates according to **the** *pleasure principle,* **which demands immediate gratification of its urges.** The id engages in *primary-process thinking,* which is primitive, illogical, irrational, and fantasy-oriented.

The *ego* **is the decision-making component of personality that operates according to the reality principle.** The ego mediates between the id, with its forceful desires for immediate satisfaction, and the external social world, with its expectations and norms regarding suitable behavior. The ego considers social realities—society's norms, etiquette, rules, and customs—in deciding how to behave. The ego is guided by **the** *reality principle,* **which seeks to delay gratification of the id's urges until appropriate outlets and situations can be found.** In short, to stay out of trouble, the ego often works to tame the unbridled desires of the id.

In the long run, the ego wants to maximize gratification, just as the id does. However, the ego engages in *secondary-process thinking,* which is relatively rational, realistic, and oriented toward problem solving. Thus, the ego strives to avoid negative consequences from society and its representatives (for example, punishment by parents or teachers) by behaving "properly." It also attempts to achieve long-range goals that sometimes require putting off gratification.

While the ego concerns itself with practical realities, **the** *superego* **is the moral component of personality that incorporates social standards about what represents right and wrong.** Throughout their lives, but especially during childhood, people receive training about what constitutes good and bad behavior. Many social norms regarding morality are eventually internalized. The superego emerges out of the ego at around 3 to 5 years of age. In some people, the superego can become irrationally demanding in its striving for moral perfection. Such people are plagued by excessive feelings of guilt.

According to Freud, the id, ego, and superego are distributed differently across three levels of awareness, which we'll describe next.

Levels of Awareness 10a

Perhaps Freud's most enduring insight was his recognition of how unconscious forces can influence behavior. He inferred the existence of the unconscious from a variety of observations that he made with his patients. For example, he noticed that "slips of the tongue" often revealed a person's true feelings (hence the expression "Freudian slip"). He also realized that his patients' dreams often expressed hidden desires. Most important, through psychoanalysis he often helped patients discover feelings and conflicts they had previously been unaware of.

Freud contrasted the unconscious with the conscious and preconscious, creating three levels of awareness. **The** *conscious* **consists of whatever one is aware of at a particular point in time.** For example, at this moment your conscious may include the train of thought in this text and a dim awareness in the back of your mind that your eyes are getting tired and you're beginning to get hungry. **The** *preconscious* **contains material just beneath the surface of awareness that can easily be retrieved.** Examples might include your middle name, what you had for supper last night, or an argument you had with a friend yesterday. **The** *unconscious* **contains thoughts, memories, and desires that are well below the surface of conscious awareness but that nonetheless exert great influence on behavior.** Examples of ma-

Web Link 11.1

The Victorian Web
Psychoanalysis initially developed within a late-19th-century context that is comprehensively portrayed in English Professor George Landow's (Brown University) important hypertext archive.

Freud's psychoanalytic theory was based on decades of clinical work. He treated a great many patients in the consulting room pictured here. The room contains numerous artifacts from other cultures—and the original psychoanalytic couch.

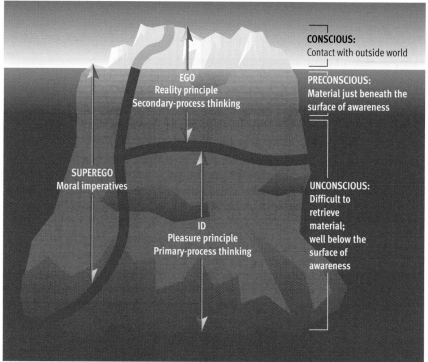

terial that might be found in your unconscious include a forgotten trauma from childhood, hidden feelings of hostility toward a parent, and repressed sexual desires.

Freud's conception of the mind is often compared to an iceberg that has most of its mass hidden beneath the water's surface (see **Figure 11.2**). He believed that the unconscious (the mass below the surface) is much larger than the conscious or preconscious. As you can see in **Figure 11.2**, he proposed that the ego and superego operate at all three levels of awareness. In contrast, the id is entirely unconscious, expressing its urges at a conscious level through the ego. Of course, the id's desires for immediate satisfaction often trigger internal conflicts with the ego and superego. These conflicts play a key role in Freud's theory.

Conflict and the Tyranny of Sex and Aggression

Freud assumed that behavior is the outcome of an ongoing series of internal conflicts. He saw internal battles between the id, ego, and superego as routine. Why? Because the id wants to gratify its urges immediately, but the norms of civilized society frequently dictate otherwise. For example, your id might feel an urge to clobber a co-worker who constantly irritates you. However, society frowns on such behavior, so your ego would try to hold this urge in check. Hence, you would find yourself in conflict. You may be experiencing conflict at this very moment. In Freudian terms, your id may be secretly urging you to abandon reading this chapter so that you can fix a snack and watch some television. Your ego may be weighing this appealing option against your society-induced need to excel in school.

Freud believed that people's lives are dominated by conflict. He asserted that individuals career from one conflict to another. The following scenario provides a concrete illustration of how the three components of personality interact to create constant conflicts:

Imagine lurching across your bed to shut off your alarm clock as it rings obnoxiously. It's 7 A.M. and time to get up for your history class. However, your id (operating according to the pleasure principle) urges you to return to the immediate gratification of additional sleep. Your ego (operating according to the reality principle) points out that you really must go to class since you haven't been able to decipher the history textbook on your own. Your id (in its typical unrealistic fashion) smugly assures you that you will get the A grade that you need and suggests lying back to dream about how impressed your roommates will be. Just as you're relaxing, your superego jumps into the fray. It tries to make you feel guilty about all the money your parents paid in tuition for the class that you're about to skip. You haven't even gotten out of bed yet, but there's already a pitched battle in your psyche.

Let's say your ego wins the battle. You pull yourself out of bed and head for class. On the way, you pass a bakery and your id clamors for cinnamon rolls. Your ego reminds you that you're supposed to be on a diet. Your id wins this time, and you have a roll. After you've attended your history lecture, your ego reminds you that you need to do some library research for a paper in philosophy. However, your id insists on returning to your apartment

Figure 11.2

Freud's model of personality structure. Freud theorized that people have three levels of awareness: the conscious, the preconscious, and the unconscious. The enormous size of the unconscious is often dramatized by comparing it to the portion of an iceberg that lies beneath the water's surface. Freud also divided personality structure into three components—id, ego, and superego—which operate according to different principles and exhibit different modes of thinking. In Freud's model, the id is entirely unconscious, but the ego and superego operate at all three levels of awareness.

to watch some sitcom reruns. As you reenter your apartment, you're overwhelmed by how messy it is. It's your roommates' mess, and your id suggests that you tell them off. As you're about to lash out, however, your ego convinces you that diplomacy will be more effective. It's only midday—and already you've been through a series of internal conflicts.

Freud believed that conflicts centering on sexual and aggressive impulses are especially likely to have far-reaching consequences. Why did he emphasize sex and aggression? Two reasons were prominent in his thinking. First, he thought that sex and aggression are subject to more complex and ambiguous social controls than other basic motives. The norms governing sexual and aggressive behavior are subtle, and people often get inconsistent messages about what's appropriate. Second, he noted that the aggressive and sexual drives are thwarted more regularly than other basic, biological urges. Think about it: If you get hungry or thirsty, you can simply head for a nearby vending machine or a drinking fountain. But if a department store clerk infuriates you, you aren't likely to reach across the counter and slug him or her. Likewise, when you see an attractive person who inspires lustful urges, you don't normally walk up and propose a tryst in a nearby broom closet. There's nothing comparable to vending machines or drinking fountains for the satisfaction of sexual and aggressive urges. Freud ascribed great importance to these needs because social norms dictate that they're routinely frustrated.

Anxiety and Defense Mechanisms

10a

Most internal conflicts are trivial and are quickly resolved. Occasionally, however, a conflict will linger for days, months, or even years, creating internal tension. More often than not, such prolonged and troublesome conflicts involve sexual and aggressive impulses that society wants to tame. These conflicts are often played out entirely in the unconscious. Although you may not be aware of these unconscious battles, they can produce *anxiety* that slips to the surface of conscious awareness.

The arousal of anxiety is a crucial event in Freud's theory of personality functioning (see **Figure 11.3**). Anxiety is distressing, so people try to rid themselves

"ALL I WANT FROM THEM IS A SIMPLE MAJORITY ON THINGS."

of this unpleasant emotion any way they can. This effort to ward off anxiety often involves the use of defense mechanisms. **Defense mechanisms are largely unconscious reactions that protect a person from unpleasant emotions such as anxiety and guilt.** Typically, they're mental maneuvers that work through self-deception (see **Table 11.1**). Consider *rationalization,* **which is creating false but plausible excuses to justify unacceptable behavior.** For example, after cheating someone in a business transaction, you might reduce your guilt by rationalizing that "everyone does it."

According to Freud, the most basic and widely used defense mechanism is repression. **Repression is keeping distressing thoughts and feelings buried in the unconscious.** People tend to repress desires that make them feel guilty, conflicts that make them anxious, and memories that are painful. As pointed out in Chapter 7, repression has been called "motivated forgetting." If you forget a dental appointment or the name of someone you don't like, repression may be at work.

Self-deception can also be seen in projection and displacement. *Projection* **is attributing one's own thoughts, feelings, or motives to another.** Usually, the thoughts one projects onto others are those that would make one feel guilty. For example, if lusting for a co-worker makes you feel guilty, you might attribute any latent sexual tension between the two of you to the *other person's* desire to seduce you. *Displacement* **is diverting emotional feelings (usually anger) from their original source to a substitute target.** If your boss gives you a hard time at work and you come home and slam the door, kick the dog, and scream at your spouse, you're displacing your anger onto irrelevant targets. Unfortunately, social constraints often force people to hold back their anger,

Figure 11.3

Freud's model of personality dynamics. According to Freud, unconscious conflicts between the id, ego, and superego sometimes lead to anxiety. This discomfort may lead to the use of defense mechanisms, which may temporarily relieve anxiety.

Intrapsychic conflict (between id, ego, and superego) → Anxiety → Reliance on defense mechanisms

and they end up lashing out at the people they love the most.

Other prominent defense mechanisms include reaction formation, regression, and identification. **Reaction formation is behaving in a way that's exactly the opposite of one's true feelings.** Guilt about sexual desires often leads to reaction formation. Freud theorized that many homophobic males who ridicule homosexuals are defending against their own latent homosexual impulses. The telltale sign of reaction formation is the exaggerated quality of the opposite behavior. **Regression is a reversion to immature patterns of behavior.** When anxious about their self-worth, some adults respond with childish boasting and bragging (as opposed to subtle efforts to impress others). For example, a fired executive having difficulty finding a new job might start making ridiculous statements about his incomparable talents and achievements. Such bragging is regressive when it's marked by massive exaggerations that virtually anyone can see through. **Identification is bolstering self-esteem by forming an imaginary or real alliance with some person or group.** Youngsters often shore up precarious feelings of self-worth by identifying with rock stars, movie stars, or famous athletes. Adults may join exclusive country clubs or civic organizations as a means of boosting their self-esteem via identification.

Development: Psychosexual Stages

 10a

Freud made the rather startling assertion that the basic foundation of an individual's personality has been laid down by the tender age of 5. To shed light on these crucial early years, Freud formulated a stage theory of development. He emphasized how young children deal with their immature but powerful sexual urges (he used the term *sexual* in a general way to refer to many urges for physical pleasure). According to Freud, these sexual urges shift in focus as children progress from one stage of development to another. Indeed, the names for the stages (oral, anal, genital, and so on) are based on where children are focusing their erotic energy during that period. Thus, *psychosexual* stages are developmental periods with a characteristic sexual focus that leave their mark on adult personality.

Freud theorized that each psychosexual stage has its own unique developmental challenges or tasks (see **Table 11.2** on the next page). The way these challenges are handled supposedly shapes personality. The notion of *fixation* plays an important role in this process. *Fixation* involves a failure to move forward from one stage to another as expected. Es-

Table 11.1 Defense Mechanisms, with Examples

Defense Mechanism	Definition	Example
Repression	Keeping distressing thoughts and feelings buried in the unconscious	A traumatized soldier has no recollection of the details of a close brush with death.
Projection	Attributing one's own thoughts, feelings, or motives to another	A woman who dislikes her boss thinks she likes her boss but feels that the boss doesn't like her.
Displacement	Diverting emotional feelings (usually anger) from their original source to a substitute target	After parental scolding, a young girl takes her anger out on her little brother.
Reaction formation	Behaving in a way that is exactly the opposite of one's true feelings	A parent who unconsciously resents a child spoils the child with outlandish gifts.
Regression	A reversion to immature patterns of behavior	An adult has a temper tantrum when he doesn't get his way.
Rationalization	Creating false but plausible excuses to justify unacceptable behavior	A student watches TV instead of studying, saying that "additional study wouldn't do any good anyway."
Identification	Bolstering self-esteem by forming an imaginary or real alliance with some person or group	An insecure young man joins a fraternity to boost his self-esteem.

sentially, the child's development stalls for a while. Fixation can be caused by excessive *gratification* of needs at a particular stage or by excessive *frustration* of those needs. Either way, fixations left over from childhood affect adult personality. Generally, fixation leads to an overemphasis on the psychosexual needs prominent during the fixated stage. Freud described a series of five psychosexual stages. Let's

concept **check** 11.1

Identifying Defense Mechanisms

Check your understanding of defense mechanisms by identifying specific defenses in the story below. Each example of a defense mechanism is underlined, with a number beneath it. Write in the defense at work in each case in the numbered spaces after the story. The answers are in Appendix A.

My boyfriend recently broke up with me after we had dated seriously for several years. At first, I cried a great deal and <u>locked myself in my room, where I pouted endlessly.</u>¹ I was sure that my former boyfriend felt as miserable as I did. <u>I told several friends that he was probably lonely and depressed.</u>² Later, I decided that I hated him. <u>I was happy about the breakup and talked about how much I was going to enjoy my newfound freedom.</u>³ I went to parties and socialized a great deal and just forgot about him. <u>It's funny—at one point I couldn't even remember his phone number!</u>⁴ Then I started pining for him again. But eventually I began to look at the situation more objectively. I realized that he had many faults and that <u>we were bound to break up sooner or later, so I was better off without him.</u>⁵

1. _____   4. _____

2. _____   5. _____

3. _____

Table 11.2 Freud's Stages of Psychosexual Development

Stage	Approximate Ages	Erotic Focus	Key Tasks and Experiences
Oral	0–1	Mouth (sucking, biting)	Weaning (from breast or bottle)
Anal	2–3	Anus (expelling or retaining feces)	Toilet training
Phallic	4–5	Genitals (masturbating)	Identifying with adult role models; coping with Oedipal crisis
Latency	6–12	None (sexually repressed)	Expanding social contacts
Genital	Puberty onward	Genitals (being sexually intimate)	Establishing intimate relationships; contributing to society through working

Web Link 11.2

Sigmund Freud Museum, Vienna, Austria
This online museum, in both English and German versions, offers a detailed chronology of Freud's life and an explanation of the most important concepts of psychoanalysis. The highlights here, though, are the rich audiovisual resources, including photos, amateur movie clips, and voice recordings of Freud.

According to Freud, early childhood experiences such as toilet training (a parental attempt to regulate a child's biological urges) can influence an individual's personality, with consequences lasting throughout adulthood.

examine some of the highlights in this sequence and how fixation might occur.

Oral Stage. The oral stage encompasses the first year of life. During this period, the main source of erotic stimulation is the mouth (in biting, sucking, chewing, and so on). In Freud's view, the handling of the child's feeding experiences is crucial to subsequent development. He attributed considerable importance to the manner in which the child is weaned from the breast or the bottle. According to Freud, fixation at the oral stage could form the basis for obsessive eating or smoking later in life (among many other things).

Anal Stage. In their second year, children get their erotic pleasure from their bowel movements, through either the expulsion or retention of feces. The crucial event at this time is toilet training, which represents society's first systematic effort to regulate the child's biological urges. Severely punitive toilet training can lead to a variety of possible outcomes. For example, excessive punishment might produce a latent feeling of hostility toward the "trainer," usually the mother. This hostility might generalize to women as a class. Another possibility is that heavy reliance on punitive measures could lead to an association between genital concerns and the anxiety that the punishment arouses. This genital anxiety derived from severe toilet training could evolve into anxiety about sexual activities later in life.

Phallic Stage. In the third through fifth years, the genitals become the focus for the child's erotic energy, largely through self-stimulation. During this pivotal stage, the *Oedipal complex* emerges. That is, little boys develop an erotically tinged preference for their mother. They also feel hostility toward their father, whom they view as a competitor for mom's affection. Similarly, little girls develop a special attachment to their father. Around the same time, they learn that little boys have very different genitals, and supposedly they develop *penis envy*. According to Freud, young girls feel hostile toward their mother because they

blame her for their anatomical "deficiency." To summarize, in the *Oedipal complex* **children manifest erotically tinged desires for their opposite-sex parent, accompanied by feelings of hostility toward their same-sex parent.** The name for this syndrome was taken from the Greek myth in which Oedipus, not knowing the identity of his real parents, inadvertently killed his father and married his mother.

According to Freud, the way parents and children deal with the sexual and aggressive conflicts inherent in the Oedipal complex is of paramount importance. The child has to resolve the Oedipal dilemma by purging the sexual longings for the opposite-sex parent and by crushing the hostility felt toward the same-sex parent. In Freud's view, healthy psychosexual development hinges on the resolution of the Oedipal conflict. Why? Because continued hostility toward the same-sex parent may prevent the child from identifying adequately with that parent. Freudian theory predicts that without such identification, many aspects of the child's development won't progress as they should.

Latency and Genital Stages. From around age 5 through puberty, the child's sexuality is largely suppressed—it becomes *latent*. Important events during this *latency stage* center on expanding social contacts beyond the immediate family. With the advent of puberty, the child progresses into the *genital stage*. Sexual urges reappear and focus on the genitals once again. At this point, sexual energy is normally channeled toward peers of the other sex, rather than toward oneself as in the phallic stage.

In arguing that the early years shape personality, Freud did not mean that personality development comes to an abrupt halt in middle childhood. However, he did believe that the foundation for adult personality is solidly entrenched by this time. He maintained that future developments are rooted in early, formative experiences and that significant conflicts in later years are replays of crises from childhood.

In fact, Freud believed that unconscious sexual conflicts rooted in childhood experiences cause most personality disturbances. His steadfast belief in the psychosexual origins of psychological disorders eventually led to bitter theoretical disputes with two of his most brilliant colleagues: Carl Jung and Alfred Adler. Jung and Adler both argued that Freud overemphasized sexuality. Freud summarily rejected their ideas, and the other two theorists felt compelled to go their own way, developing their own psychodynamic theories of personality.

Jung's Analytical Psychology

Carl Jung was born to middle-class Swiss parents in 1875. The son of a Protestant pastor, he was a deeply introverted, lonely child, but an excellent student. Jung had earned his medical degree and was an established young psychiatrist in Zurich when he began to write to Freud in 1906. When the two men had their first meeting, they were so taken by each other's insights, they talked nonstop for 13 hours! They exchanged 359 letters before their friendship and theoretical alliance were torn apart in 1913.

Jung called his new approach *analytical psychology* to differentiate it from Freud's psychoanalytic theory. Unlike Freud, Jung encouraged his followers

to develop their own theoretical views. Perhaps because of his bitter conflict with Freud, he deplored the way schools of thought often become dogmatic, discouraging creative, new ideas. Although many theorists came to characterize themselves as "Jungians," Jung himself often remarked, "I am not a Jungian" and said, "I do not want anybody to be a Jungian. I want people above all to be themselves" (van der Post, 1975).

Like Freud, Jung (1921, 1933) emphasized the unconscious determinants of personality. However, he proposed that the unconscious consists of two layers. The first layer, called the *personal unconscious,* is essentially the same as Freud's version of the unconscious. The personal unconscious houses material that is not within one's conscious awareness, because it has been repressed or forgotten. In addition, Jung theorized the existence of a deeper layer he called the collective unconscious. **The *collective unconscious* is a storehouse of latent memory traces inherited from people's ancestral past.** According to Jung, each person shares the collective unconscious with the entire human race (see **Figure 11.4**). It contains the "whole spiritual heritage of mankind's evolution, born anew in the brain structure of every individual" (Jung, quoted in Campbell, 1971, p. 45).

© Bettmann/Corbis

CARL JUNG
"I am not a Jungian . . . I do not want anybody to be a Jungian. I want people above all to be themselves."

Figure 11.4

Jung's vision of the collective unconscious. Much like Freud, Jung theorized that each person has conscious and unconscious levels of awareness. However, he also proposed that the entire human race shares a collective unconscious, which exists in the deepest reaches of everyone's awareness. He saw the collective unconscious as a storehouse of hidden ancestral memories, called archetypes. Jung believed that important cultural symbols emerge from these universal archetypes. Thus, he argued that remarkable resemblances among symbols from disparate cultures (such as the mandalas shown here) are evidence of the existence of the collective unconscious.

Source: Images from C. G. Jung Bild Und Wort, © Walter-Verlag AG, Olten, Switzerland, 1977

Mandalas from various cultures

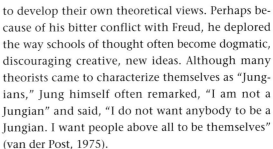

Russia

Navajo Indians

Tibet

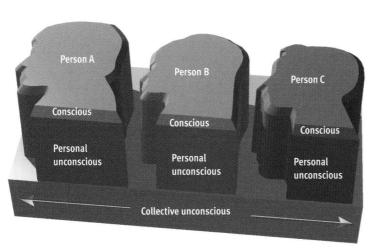

Adler's theory has been used to analyze the tragic life of the legendary actress Marilyn Monroe (Ansbacher, 1970). During her childhood, Monroe suffered from parental neglect that left her with acute feelings of inferiority. Her inferiority feelings led her to overcompensate by flaunting her beauty, marrying celebrities (Joe DiMaggio and Arthur Miller), keeping film crews waiting for hours, and seeking the adoration of her fans.

Bettmann/Corbis

Web Link 11.3

C. G. Jung, Analytical Psychology, and Culture
Synchronicity, archetypes, collective unconscious, introversion, extraversion—these and many other important concepts arising from analytical psychology and Jung's tremendously influential theorizing are examined at this comprehensive site.

Jung called these ancestral memories *archetypes*. They are not memories of actual, personal experiences. Instead, *archetypes* **are emotionally charged images and thought forms that have universal meaning.** These archetypal images and ideas show up frequently in dreams and are often manifested in a culture's use of symbols in art, literature, and religion. According to Jung, symbols from very different cultures often show striking similarities because they emerge from archetypes that are shared by the entire human race. For instance, Jung found numerous cultures in which the *mandala,* or "magic circle," has served as a symbol of the unified wholeness of the self. Jung felt that an understanding of archetypal symbols helped him make sense of his patients' dreams. Dream analysis was of great concern to him, as he thought that dreams contain important messages from the unconscious. Like Freud, he depended extensively on dream analysis in his treatment of patients.

Adler's Individual Psychology

Like Freud, Alfred Adler grew up in Vienna in a middle-class Jewish home. He was a sickly child who struggled to overcome rickets (a bone disease caused by vitamin D deficiency) and an almost fatal case of pneumonia. At home, he was overshadowed by an exceptionally bright and successful older brother. Nonetheless, he went on to earn his medical degree, and he practiced ophthalmology and general medicine before his interest turned to psychiatry. He was

a charter member of Freud's inner circle—the Vienna Psychoanalytic Society. However, he soon began to develop his own approach to personality, which he called *individual psychology.*

Like Jung, Adler (1917, 1927) argued that Freud had gone overboard in centering his theory on sexual conflicts. According to Adler, the foremost source of human motivation is a striving for superiority. In his view, this striving does not necessarily translate into the pursuit of dominance or high status. Adler saw ***striving for superiority* as a universal drive to adapt, improve oneself, and master life's challenges.** He noted that young children understandably feel weak and helpless in comparison with more competent older children and adults. These early inferiority feelings supposedly motivate them to acquire new skills and develop new talents. Thus, Adler maintained that striving for superiority is the prime goal of life, rather than physical gratification (as suggested by Freud).

Adler asserted that everyone has to work to overcome some feelings of inferiority—a process he called compensation. *Compensation* **involves efforts to overcome imagined or real inferiorities by developing one's abilities.** Adler believed that compensation is entirely normal. However, in some people inferiority feelings can become excessive, resulting in what is widely known today as an *inferiority complex*—exaggerated feelings of weakness and inadequacy. Adler thought that either parental pampering or parental neglect could cause an inferiority complex. Thus, he agreed with Freud on the importance of early childhood experiences, although he focused on different aspects of parent-child relations.

Evaluating Psychodynamic Perspectives

The psychodynamic approach has provided a number of far-reaching, truly "grand" theories of personality. These theories yielded some bold new insights when they were first presented. Although one might argue about exact details of interpretation, psychodynamic theory and research have demonstrated that (1) unconscious forces can influence behavior, (2) internal conflict often plays a key role in generating psychological distress, (3) early childhood experiences can influence adult personality, and (4) people do use defense mechanisms to reduce their experience of unpleasant emotions (Bornstein, 2003; Westen, 1998; Westen & Gabbard, 1999).

In addition to being praised, psychodynamic formulations have also been criticized on several grounds, including the following (Eysenck, 1990b; Fine, 1990; Macmillan, 1991; Torrey, 1992):

© Bettmann/Corbis

ALFRED ADLER
"The goal of the human soul is conquest, perfection, security, superiority."

1. *Poor testability.* Scientific investigations require testable hypotheses. Psychodynamic ideas have often been too vague and conjectural to permit a clear scientific test. For instance, how would you prove or disprove the assertion that the id is entirely unconscious?

2. *Inadequate evidence.* The empirical evidence on psychodynamic theories has often been characterized as "inadequate." Psychodynamic theories depend too heavily on clinical case studies in which it's much too easy for clinicians to see what they expect to see. Reexaminations of Freud's own clinical work suggest that he frequently distorted his patients' case histories to make them mesh with his theory (Esterson, 2001; Powell & Boer, 1995) and that there was a substantial disparity between Freud's writings and his actual therapeutic methods (Lynn & Vaillant, 1998). Insofar as researchers have accumulated evidence on psychodynamic theories, the evidence has provided only modest support for many of the central hypotheses (Fisher & Greenberg, 1985, 1996; Westen & Gabbard, 1999).

3. *Sexism.* Many critics have argued that psychodynamic theories are characterized by a sexist bias against women. Freud believed that females' penis envy made them feel inferior to men. He also thought that females tended to develop weaker superegos and to be more prone to neurosis than men. The sex bias in modern psychodynamic theories has been reduced considerably. Nonetheless, the psychodynamic approach has generally provided a rather male-centered point of view (Lerman, 1986; Person, 1990).

It's easy to ridicule Freud for concepts such as penis envy, and it's easy to point to Freudian ideas

concept **check** 11.2

Comparing Psychodynamic Theorists

As followers of Freud, Jung and Adler shared some ideas with their mentor. However, both eventually broke with Freud and established their own theoretical systems because of disagreements on some issues. Below are terms for seven concepts about which Freud, Jung, and Adler agreed or disagreed. Check your understanding of the theorists and their ideas by placing checkmarks in the appropriate spaces to indicate which theorists emphasized which concepts. Then check your answers in Appendix A.

	Freud	Jung	Adler
1. Archetypes	____	____	____
2. Physical gratification	____	____	____
3. Striving for superiority	____	____	____
4. Collective unconscious	____	____	____
5. Early childhood experiences	____	____	____
6. Dream analysis	____	____	____
7. Unconscious determinants	____	____	____

that have turned out to be wrong. However, you have to remember that Freud, Jung, and Adler began to fashion their theories over a century ago. It's not entirely fair to compare these theories to other models that are only a decade or two old. Freud and his colleagues deserve great credit for breaking new ground with their speculations about psychodynamics. Standing at a distance a century later, we have to be impressed by the extraordinary impact that psychodynamic theory has had on modern intellectual thought. In psychology as a whole, no other school of thought has been so influential—with the exception of behaviorism, which we turn to next.

> Behavioral Perspectives

Behaviorism is a theoretical orientation based on the premise that scientific psychology should study only observable behavior. As we saw in Chapter 1, behaviorism has been a major school of thought in psychology since 1913, when John B. Watson began campaigning for the behavioral point of view. Research in the behavioral tradition has focused largely on learning. For many decades behaviorists devoted relatively little attention to the study of personality. However, their interest in personality began to pick up after John Dollard and Neal Miller (1950) attempted to translate selected Freudian ideas into behavioral terminology. Dollard and Miller showed that behavioral concepts could provide enlightening insights about the complicated subject of personality.

In this section, we'll examine three behavioral views of personality, as we discuss the ideas of B. F. Skinner, Albert Bandura, and Walter Mischel. For the most part, you'll see that behaviorists explain personality the same way they explain everything else—in terms of learning.

Skinner's Ideas Applied to Personality

10b

As we noted in Chapters 1 and 6, modern behaviorism's most prominent theorist has been B. F. Skinner,

PREVIEW QUESTIONS

- How can Skinner's theory explain personality and its development?
- How did Bandura revise the behavioral approach to personality?
- What is self-efficacy, and how does it affect behavior?
- How did Mischel question the concept of personality?
- What are the strengths and weaknesses of the behavioral approach?

B. F. SKINNER

"The practice of looking inside the organism for an explanation of behavior has tended to obscure the variables which are immediately available for a scientific analysis. These variables lie outside the organism, in its immediate environment and in its environmental history. . . . The objection to inner states is not that they do not exist, but that they are not relevant."

Figure 11.5

A behavioral view of personality. Staunch behaviorists devote little attention to the structure of personality because it is unobservable, but they implicitly view personality as an individual's collection of response tendencies. A possible hierarchy of response tendencies for a particular person in specific stimulus situation (a large party) is shown here.

an American psychologist who lived from 1904 to 1990. After earning his doctorate in 1931, Skinner spent most of his career at Harvard University. There he achieved renown for his research on learning in lower organisms, mostly rats and pigeons. Skinner's (1953, 1957) principles of *operant conditioning* were never meant to be a theory of personality. However, his ideas have affected thinking in all areas of psychology and have been applied to the explanation of personality. Here we'll examine Skinner's views as they relate to personality structure and development.

Personality Structure: A View from the Outside

Skinner made no provision for internal personality structures similar to Freud's id, ego, and superego because such structures can't be observed. Following in the tradition of Watson, Skinner showed little interest in what goes on "inside" people. He argued that it's useless to speculate about private, unobservable cognitive processes. Instead, he focused on how the external environment molds overt behavior. Indeed, he argued for a strong brand of *determinism,* asserting that behavior is fully determined by environmental stimuli.

How can Skinner's theory explain the consistency that can be seen in individuals' behavior? According to his view, people show some consistent patterns of behavior because they have some stable *response tendencies* that they have acquired through experience. These response tendencies may change in the future, as a result of new experience, but they're enduring enough to create a certain degree of consistency in a person's behavior. Implicitly, then, Skinner viewed an individual's personality as a *collection of response tendencies that are tied to various stimulus situations.*

A specific situation may be associated with a number of response tendencies that vary in strength, depending on past conditioning (see **Figure 11.5**).

Personality Development as a Product of Conditioning

Skinner's theory accounts for personality development by explaining how various response tendencies are acquired through learning. He believed that most human responses are shaped by the type of conditioning that he described: operant conditioning. As we discussed in Chapter 6, Skinner maintained that environmental consequences—reinforcement, punishment, and extinction—determine people's patterns of responding. On the one hand, when responses are followed by favorable consequences (reinforcement), they are strengthened. For example, if your joking at a party pays off with favorable attention, your tendency to joke at parties will increase (see **Figure 11.6**). On the other hand, when responses lead to negative consequences (punishment), they are weakened. Thus, if your impulsive decisions always backfire, your tendency to be impulsive will decline.

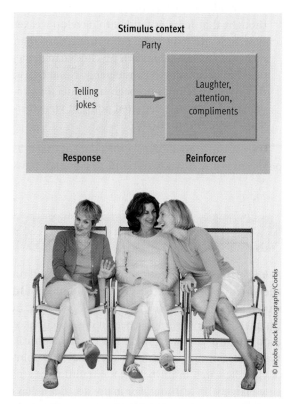

Figure 11.6

Personality development and operant conditioning. According to Skinner, people's characteristic response tendencies are shaped by reinforcers and other consequences that follow behavior. Thus, if your joking at a party leads to attention and compliments, your tendency to be witty and humorous will be strengthened.

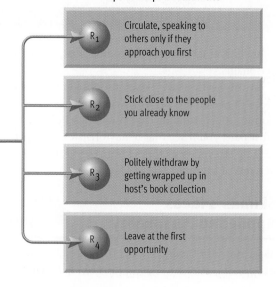

Because response tendencies are constantly being strengthened or weakened by new experiences, Skinner's theory views personality development as a continuous, lifelong journey. Unlike Freud and many other theorists, Skinner saw no reason to break the developmental process into stages. Nor did he attribute special importance to early childhood experiences.

Bandura's Social Cognitive Theory

 10b

Albert Bandura is a modern theorist who has helped reshape the theoretical landscape of behaviorism. He has spent his entire academic career at Stanford University, where he has conducted influential research on behavior therapy and the determinants of aggression.

Bandura is one of several behaviorists who have added a cognitive flavor to behaviorism since the 1960s. Bandura (1977), Walter Mischel (1973), and Julian Rotter (1982) take issue with Skinner's "pure" behaviorism. They point out that humans obviously are conscious, thinking, feeling beings. Moreover, these theorists argue that in neglecting cognitive processes, Skinner ignored the most distinctive and important feature of human behavior. Bandura and like-minded theorists originally call their modified brand of behaviorism *social learning theory*. Today, Bandura refers to his model as *social cognitive theory*.

Bandura (1982, 1986, 1999a) agrees with the fundamental thrust of behaviorism in that he believes that personality is largely shaped through learning. However, he contends that conditioning is not a mechanical process in which people are passive participants. Instead, he maintains that people actively seek out and process information about their environment to maximize favorable outcomes. In focusing on information processing, he brings unobservable cognitive events into the picture.

Observational Learning

 10b

Bandura's foremost theoretical contribution has been his description of observational learning, which we introduced in Chapter 6. *Observational learning occurs when an organism's responding is influenced by the observation of others.* According to Bandura, both classical and operant conditioning can occur indirectly when one person observes another's conditioning. For example, watching your sister get burned by a bounced check upon selling her old stereo could strengthen your tendency to be suspicious of others. Although your sister would be the one actually experiencing the negative consequences,

they might also influence you—through observational learning. Bandura maintains that people's characteristic patterns of behavior are shaped by the *models* that they're exposed to. In observational learning, **a *model* is a person whose behavior is observed by another.** At one time or another, everyone serves as a model for others. Bandura's key point is that many response tendencies are the product of imitation. According to Bandura, models have a great impact on personality development. Children learn to be assertive, conscientious, self-sufficient, dependable, easygoing, and so forth by observing parents, teachers, relatives, siblings, and peers behaving in these ways.

Self-Efficacy

 10b

Bandura discusses how a variety of personal factors (aspects of personality) govern behavior. In recent years, the factor he has emphasized the most is self-efficacy (Bandura, 1990, 1993, 1995). *Self-efficacy refers to one's belief about one's ability to perform behaviors that should lead to expected outcomes.* When self-efficacy is high, individuals feel confident that they can execute the responses necessary to earn reinforcers. When self-efficacy is low, individuals worry that the necessary responses may be beyond their abilities. Perceptions of self-efficacy are subjective and specific to certain kinds of tasks. For instance, you might feel extremely confident about your ability to handle difficult social situations but doubtful about your ability to handle academic challenges.

Perceptions of self-efficacy can influence which challenges people tackle and how well they perform. Studies have found that feelings of greater self-efficacy are associated with greater success in giving up smoking (Boudreaux et al., 1998); greater adherence to an exercise regimen (Rimal, 2001); better outcomes in substance abuse treatment (Bandura, 1999b); more success in coping with medical rehabilitation (Waldrop et al., 2001); better self-care among diabetics (Williams & Bond, 2002); greater persistence and effort in academic pursuits (Zimmerman, 1995); higher levels of academic performance (Chemers, Hu, & Garcia, 2001); enhanced performance in athletic competition (Kane et al., 1996); higher work-related performance (Stajkovic & Luthans, 1998); and greater resistance to stress (Jex et al., 2001), among many other things.

Mischel and the Person-Situation Controversy

Walter Mischel was born in Vienna, not far from Freud's home. His family immigrated to the United

ALBERT BANDURA

"Most human behavior is learned by observation through modeling."

Photo by Keeble, courtesy of Albert Bandura

***Web Link* 11.4**

Personality Theories
C. George Boeree (Shippensburg University) provides access to his electronic textbook on personality theories at this site. Behavioral theorists B. F. Skinner and Albert Bandura are discussed extensively, along with many other theorists covered in this chapter.

WALTER MISCHEL

"It seems remarkable how each of us generally manages to reconcile his seemingly diverse behavior into one self-consistent whole."

States in 1939, when he was 9. After earning his doctorate in psychology, he spent many years on the faculty at Stanford, as a colleague of Bandura's. He has since moved to Columbia University. Mischel's (1973, 1984) chief contribution to personality theory has been to focus attention on the extent to which situational factors govern behavior.

According to Mischel, people make responses that they think will lead to reinforcement in the situation at hand. For example, if you believe that hard work in your job will pay off by leading to raises and promotions, you'll probably be diligent and industrious. But if you think that hard work in your job is unlikely to be rewarded, you may behave in a lazy and irresponsible manner. Thus, Mischel's version of social learning theory predicts that people will often behave differently in different situations. Mischel (1968, 1973) reviewed decades of research and concluded that, indeed, people exhibit far less consistency across situations than had been widely assumed. For example, studies show that a person who is honest in one situation may be dishonest in another.

Thus, Mischel's provocative theories have sparked a robust debate about the relative importance of the *person* as opposed to the *situation* in determining behavior. This debate has led to a growing recognition that *both* the person and the situation are important determinants of behavior (Funder, 2001; Roberts & Pomerantz, 2004). As William Fleeson (2004) puts it, "The person-situation debate is coming to an end because both sides of the debate have turned out to be right" (p. 83). Fleeson reconciles the two opposing views by arguing that each prevails at a different level of analysis. When small chunks of behavior are examined on a moment-to-moment basis, situational factors dominate and most individuals' behavior tends to be highly variable. However, when larger chunks of typical behavior over time are examined, people tend to be reasonably consistent and personality traits prove to be more influential.

Evaluating Behavioral Perspectives

Behavioral theories are firmly rooted in extensive empirical research. Skinner's ideas have shed light on how environmental consequences and conditioning mold people's characteristic behavior. Bandura's social learning theory has expanded the horizons of behaviorism and increased its relevance to the study of personality. Mischel deserves credit for increasing psychology's awareness of how situational factors shape behavior.

Of course, each theoretical approach has its shortcomings, and the behavioral approach is no exception. Critics argue (1) that behaviorists have indiscriminately generalized from animal behavior to human behavior and (2) that in carving personality into stimulus-response bonds, behaviorists have provided a fragmented view of personality (Liebert & Liebert, 1998; Maddi, 1989). Humanistic theorists, whom we shall cover next, have been particularly vocal in criticizing this piecemeal analysis of personality.

> Humanistic Perspectives

PREVIEW QUESTIONS

- What led to the emergence of humanism, and what are its central assumptions?
- How did Rogers explain the development of the self and defensive behavior?
- How did Maslow organize motives?
- What was Maslow's view of the healthy personality?
- What are the strengths and weaknesses of the humanistic approach?

Humanistic theory emerged in the 1950s as something of a backlash against the behavioral and psychodynamic theories that we have just discussed (Cassel, 2000). The principal charge hurled at these two models was that they are dehumanizing (DeCarvalho, 1991). Freudian theory was criticized for its belief that behavior is dominated by primitive, animalistic drives. Behaviorism was criticized for its preoccupation with animal research and for its mechanistic, fragmented view of personality. Critics argued that both schools of thought are too deterministic and that both fail to recognize the unique qualities of human behavior.

Many of these critics blended into a loose alliance that came to be known as humanism, because of its exclusive focus on human behavior. *Humanism* is a theoretical orientation that emphasizes the unique qualities of humans, especially their freedom and their potential for personal growth. In contrast to most psychodynamic and behavioral theorists, humanistic theorists, such as Carl Rogers and Abraham Maslow, take an optimistic view of human nature. They assume (1) that people can rise above their primitive animal heritage and control their biological urges and (2) that people are largely conscious and rational beings who are not dominated by unconscious, irrational needs and conflicts. Humanistic theorists also maintain that a person's subjective view of the world is more important than objective reality. According to this notion, if you think that you're homely or bright or sociable, then this belief will influence your behavior more than the realities of how homely, bright, or sociable you actually are.

Rogers's Person-Centered Theory

Carl Rogers (1951, 1961, 1980) was one of the fathers of the human potential movement. This movement emphasizes self-realization through sensitivity training, encounter groups, and other exercises intended to foster personal growth. Like Freud, Rogers based his personality theory on his extensive therapeutic interactions with many clients. Because of its emphasis on a person's subjective point of view, Rogers called his approach a *person-centered theory*.

The Self

Rogers viewed personality structure in terms of just one construct. He called this construct the *self*, although it's more widely known today as the *self-concept*. A **self-concept is a collection of beliefs about one's own nature, unique qualities, and typical behavior.** Your self-concept is your own mental picture of yourself. It's a collection of self-perceptions. For example, a self-concept might include beliefs such as "I'm easygoing" or "I'm sly and crafty" or "I'm pretty" or "I'm hardworking." According to Rogers, individuals are aware of their self-concept. It's not buried in their unconscious.

Rogers stressed the subjective nature of the self-concept. Your self-concept may not be entirely consistent with your experiences. Most people tend to distort their experiences to some extent to promote a relatively favorable self-concept. For example, you may believe that you're quite bright, but your grade transcript might suggest otherwise. Rogers called the gap between self-concept and reality "incongruence". *Incongruence* **is the degree of disparity between one's self-concept and one's actual experience.** In contrast, if a person's self-concept is reasonably accurate, it's said to be *congruent* with reality (see **Figure 11.7**). Everyone experiences a certain amount of incongruence. The crucial issue is how much. As we'll see, Rogers maintained that too much incongruence undermines one's psychological well-being.

Development of the Self

In terms of personality development, Rogers was concerned with how childhood experiences promote congruence or incongruence between one's self-

Congruence
Self-concept meshes well with actual experience (some incongruence is probably unavoidable)

Incongruence
Self-concept does not mesh well with actual experience

concept and one's experience. According to Rogers, people have a strong need for affection, love, and acceptance from others. Early in life, parents provide most of this affection. Rogers maintained that some parents make their affection *conditional*. That is, it depends on the child's behaving well and living up to expectations. When parental love seems conditional, children often block out of their self-concept those experiences that make them feel unworthy of love. They do so because they're worried about parental acceptance, which appears precarious. At the other end of the spectrum, some parents make their affection *unconditional*. Their children have less need to block out unworthy experiences because they've been assured that they're worthy of affection, no matter what they do.

Rogers believed that unconditional love from parents fosters congruence and that conditional love fosters incongruence. He further theorized that if individuals grow up believing that affection from others is highly conditional, they will go on to distort more and more of their experiences in order to feel worthy of acceptance from a wider and wider array of people.

Anxiety and Defense

According to Rogers, experiences that threaten people's personal views of themselves are the principal cause of troublesome anxiety. The more inaccurate your self-concept is, the more likely you are to have experiences that clash with your self-perceptions. Thus, people with highly incongruent self-concepts are especially likely to be plagued by recurrent anxiety (see **Figure 11.8** on the next page).

To ward off this anxiety, individuals often behave defensively in an effort to reinterpret their experience

CARL ROGERS
"I have little sympathy with the rather prevalent concept that man is basically irrational, and that his impulses, if not controlled, will lead to destruction of others and self. Man's behavior is exquisitely rational, moving with subtle and ordered complexity toward the goals his organism is endeavoring to achieve."

Courtesy of Carl Rogers Memorial Library

Figure 11.7
Rogers's view of personality structure. In Rogers's model, the self-concept is the only important structural construct. However, Rogers acknowledged that one's self-concept may not be consistent with the realities of one's actual experience—a condition called incongruence.

Figure 11.8

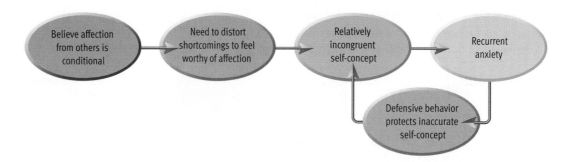

Rogers's view of personality development and dynamics. Rogers's theory of development asserts that conditional love leads to a need to distort experiences, which fosters an incongruent self-concept. Incongruence makes one prone to recurrent anxiety, which triggers defensive behavior, which fuels more incongruence.

ABRAHAM MASLOW

"It is as if Freud supplied to us the sick half of psychology and we must now fill it out with the healthy half."

so that it appears consistent with their self-concept. Thus, they ignore, deny, and twist reality to protect and perpetuate their self-concept. Consider a young lady who, like most people, considers herself a "nice person." Let's suppose that in reality she is rather conceited and selfish. She gets feedback from both boyfriends and girlfriends that she is a "self-centered, snotty brat." How might she react in order to protect her self-concept? She might ignore or block out those occasions when she behaves selfishly. She might attribute her girlfriends' negative comments to their jealousy of her good looks. Perhaps she would blame her boyfriends' negative remarks on their disappointment because she won't get more serious with them. As you can see, people will sometimes go to great lengths to defend their self-concept.

Maslow's Theory of Self-Actualization

Abraham Maslow, who grew up in Brooklyn, described his childhood as "unhappy, lonely, [and] isolated." To follow through on his interest in psychology, he had to resist parental pressures to go into law. Mas-

low spent much of his career at Brandeis University, where he created an influential theory of motivation and provided crucial leadership for the fledgling humanistic movement. Like Rogers, Maslow (1968, 1970) argued that psychology should take an optimistic view of human nature instead of dwelling on the causes of disorders. "To oversimplify the matter somewhat," he said, "it's as if Freud supplied to us the sick half of psychology and we must now fill it out with the healthy half" (1968, p. 5). Maslow's key contributions to personality theory were his analysis of how motives are organized hierarchically and his description of the healthy personality.

Hierarchy of Needs

Maslow proposed that human motives are organized into a *hierarchy of needs*—a systematic arrangement of needs, according to priority, in which basic needs must be met before less basic needs are aroused. This hierarchical arrangement is usually portrayed as a pyramid (see **Figure 11.9**). The needs toward the bottom of the pyramid, such as physiological or security needs, are the most basic. Higher levels in the pyramid consist of progressively less

Figure 11.9

Maslow's hierarchy of needs. According to Maslow, human needs are arranged in a hierarchy, and people must satisfy their basic needs before they can satisfy higher needs. In the diagram, higher levels in the pyramid represent progressively less basic needs. Individuals progress upward in the hierarchy when lower needs are satisfied reasonably well, but they may regress back to lower levels if basic needs are no longer satisfied.

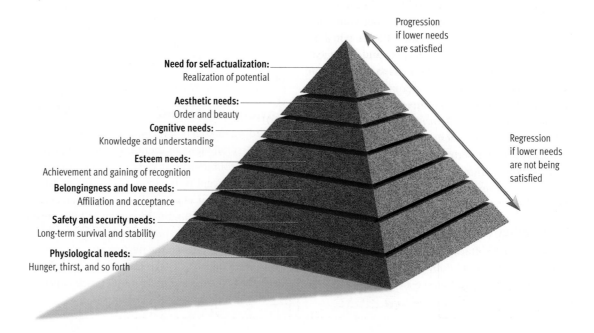

basic needs. When a person manages to satisfy a level of needs reasonably well (complete satisfaction is not necessary), *this satisfaction activates needs at the next level.*

Like Rogers, Maslow argued that humans have an innate drive toward personal growth—that is, evolution toward a higher state of being. Thus, he described the needs in the uppermost reaches of his hierarchy as *growth needs.* These include the needs for knowledge, understanding, order, and aesthetic beauty. Foremost among them is the **need for self-actualization, which is the need to fulfill one's potential.** It is the highest need in Maslow's motivational hierarchy. Maslow summarized this concept with a simple statement: "What a man *can* be, he *must* be." According to Maslow, people will be frustrated if they are unable to fully utilize their talents or pursue their true interests. For example, if you have great musical talent but must work as an accountant, or if you have scholarly interests but must work as a sales clerk, your need for self-actualization will be thwarted.

The Healthy Personality

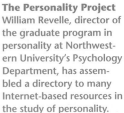

PsykTrek 10c

Because of his interest in self-actualization, Maslow set out to discover the nature of the healthy personality. Over a period of years, he conducted studies and accumulated case histories. Gradually, he sketched, in broad strokes, a picture of ideal psychological health. According to Maslow, *self-actualizing persons* **are people with exceptionally healthy personalities, marked by continued personal growth.** Maslow identified various traits characteristic of self-actualizing people. Many of these traits are listed in **Figure 11.10.** In brief, Maslow found that self-actualizers are accurately tuned in to reality and that they're at peace with themselves. He found that they're open and spontaneous and that they retain a fresh appreciation of the world around them. Socially, they're sensitive to others' needs and enjoy rewarding interpersonal relations. However, they're not dependent on others for approval or uncomfortable with solitude. They thrive on their work, and they enjoy their sense of humor. Maslow also noted that they have "peak experiences" (profound emo-

tional highs) more often than others. Finally, he found that they strike a nice balance between many polarities in personality. For instance, they can be both childlike and mature, both rational and intuitive, both conforming and rebellious.

Evaluating Humanistic Perspectives

The humanists added a refreshing new perspective to the study of personality. Their argument that a person's subjective views may be more important than objective reality has proven compelling. The humanistic approach also deserves credit for making the self-concept an important construct in psychology. Today, theorists of many persuasions use the self-concept in their analyses of personality. Finally, one could argue that the humanists' optimistic, growth- and health-oriented approach laid the foundation for the emergence of the positive psychology movement that is increasingly influential in contemporary psychology (Kennon & Kasser, 2001; Taylor, 2001).

Of course, the balance sheet has a negative side as well (Burger, 2004; Geller, 1982). Critics argue that

---

Characteristics of self-actualizing people

- Clear, efficient perception of reality and comfortable relations with it
- Spontaneity, simplicity, and naturalness
- Problem centering (having something outside themselves they "must" do as a mission)
- Detachment and need for privacy
- Autonomy, independence of culture and environment
- Continued freshness of appreciation

- Mystical and peak experiences
- Feelings of kinship and identification with the human race
- Strong friendships, but limited in number
- Democratic character structure
- Ethical discrimination between good and evil
- Philosophical, unhostile sense of humor
- Balance between polarities in personality

Figure 11.10
Maslow's view of the healthy personality. Humanistic theorists emphasize psychological health instead of maladjustment. Maslow's description of characteristics of self-actualizing people evokes a picture of the healthy personality.

Source: Adapted from Potkay, C. R., & Allen, B. P. (1986). *Personality: Theory, research and application.* Pacific Grove, CA: Brooks/Cole. Copyright © 1986 by C. R. Potkay & B. P. Allen. Adapted by permission of the publisher and author.

Web Link 11.5

The Personality Project
William Revelle, director of the graduate program in personality at Northwestern University's Psychology Department, has assembled a directory to many Internet-based resources in the study of personality.

Recognizing Key Concepts in Personality Theories

Check your understanding of psychodynamic, behavioral, and humanistic personality theories by identifying key concepts from these theories in the scenarios below. The answers can be found in Appendix A.

1. Thirteen-year-old Sarah watches a TV show in which the leading female character manipulates her boyfriend by acting helpless and purposely losing a tennis match against him. The female lead repeatedly expresses her slogan, "Never let them [men] know you can take care of yourself." Sarah becomes more passive and less competitive around boys her own age.

Concept: _____

2. Yolanda has a secure, enjoyable, reasonably well-paid job as a tenured English professor at a state university. Her friends are dumbfounded when she announces that she's going to resign and give it all up to try writing a novel. She tries to explain, "I need a new challenge, a new mountain to climb. I've had this lid on my writing talents for years, and I've got to break free. It's something I have to try. I won't be happy until I do."

Concept: _____

3. Vladimir, who is 4, seems to be emotionally distant from and inattentive to his father. He complains whenever he's left with his dad. In contrast, he cuddles up in bed with his mother frequently and tries very hard to please her by behaving properly.

Concept: _____

(1) many aspects of humanistic theory are difficult to put to a scientific test, (2) humanists have been unrealistically optimistic in their assumptions about human nature and their descriptions of the healthy personality, and (3) more experimental research is needed to catch up with the theorizing in the humanistic camp. This last complaint is precisely the opposite of what we'll encounter in the next section, on biological perspectives, where more theorizing is needed to catch up with the research.

> Biological Perspectives

PREVIEW QUESTIONS

- How did Eysenck explain variations in personality?
- To what degree is personality heritable?
- Do family environments have much impact on personality?
- What do evolutionary theorists have to say about personality?
- What are the strengths and weaknesses of the biological approach?

Like many identical twins reared apart, Jim Lewis and Jim Springer found they had been leading eerily similar lives. Separated four weeks after birth in 1940, the Jim twins grew up 45 miles apart in Ohio and were reunited in 1979. Eventually, they discovered that both drove the same model blue Chevrolet, chain-smoked Salems, chewed their fingernails, and owned dogs named Toy. Each had spent a good deal of time vacationing at the same three-block strip of beach in Florida. More important, when tested for such personality traits as flexibility, self-control, and sociability, the twins responded almost exactly alike. (Leo, 1987, p. 63)

So began a *Time* magazine summary of a major twin study conducted at the University of Minnesota Center for Twin and Adoption Research. Since 1979 the investigators at this center have been studying the personality resemblance of identical twins reared apart. Not all the twin pairs have been as similar as Jim Lewis and Jim Springer, but many of the paral-

lels have been uncanny (Lykken et al., 1992). Identical twins Oskar Stohr and Jack Yufe were separated soon after birth. Oskar was sent to a Nazi-run school in Czechoslovakia, while Jack was raised in a Jewish home on a Caribbean island. When they were reunited for the first time during middle age, they showed up wearing similar mustaches, haircuts, shirts, and wire-rimmed glasses! A pair of previously separated female twins both arrived at the Minneapolis airport wearing seven rings on their fingers. One had a son named Richard Andrew and the other had a son named Andrew Richard!

Could personality be largely inherited? These anecdotal reports of striking resemblances between identical twins reared apart certainly raise this possibility. In this section we'll discuss Hans Eysenck's theory, which emphasizes the influence of heredity, look at recent behavioral genetics research on the heritability of personality, and outline evolutionary views on personality.

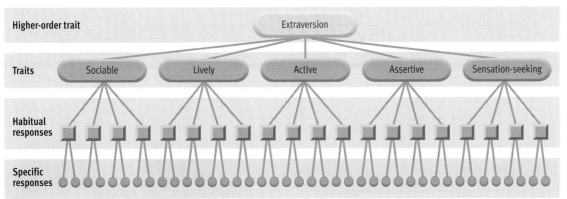

Higher-order trait			Extraversion		
Traits	Sociable	Lively	Active	Assertive	Sensation-seeking
Habitual responses					
Specific responses					

Figure 11.11

Eysenck's model of personality structure. Eysenck described personality structure as a hierarchy of traits. In this scheme, a few higher-order traits, such as extraversion, determine a host of lower-order traits, which determine a person's habitual responses.

Source: Eysenck, H. J. (1976). *The biological basis of personality.* Springfield, IL: Charles C. Thomas. Reprinted by permission of the publisher.

Eysenck's Theory

 10d

Hans Eysenck was born in Germany but fled to London during the era of Nazi rule. He went on to become one of Britain's most prominent psychologists. Eysenck (1967, 1982, 1990a) views personality structure as a hierarchy of traits, in which many superficial traits are derived from a smaller number of more basic traits, which are derived from a handful of fundamental higher-order traits, as shown in **Figure 11.11**.

According to Eysenck, "Personality is determined to a large extent by a person's genes" (1967, p. 20). How is heredity linked to personality in Eysenck's model? In part, through conditioning concepts borrowed from behavioral theory (consult Chapter 6 for an overview of classical conditioning). Eysenck theorizes that some people can be conditioned more readily than others because of differences in their physiological functioning. These variations in "conditionability" are assumed to influence the personality traits that people acquire through conditioning processes.

Eysenck has shown a special interest in explaining variations in *extraversion-introversion*. He has proposed that introverts tend to have high levels of physiological arousal, which make them more easily conditioned than extraverts. According to Eysenck, people who condition easily acquire more conditioned inhibitions than others. These inhibitions make them more bashful, tentative, and uneasy in social situations. This social discomfort leads them to turn inward. As a result, they become introverted.

Behavioral Genetics and Personality

 10d

Recent research in behavioral genetics has provided impressive support for the idea that personality is largely inherited (Livesley, Jang, & Vernon, 2003; Rowe & van den Oord, 2005). For instance, in twin studies of the Big Five personality traits, identical twins have been found to be much more similar than fraternal twins on all five traits (Loehlin, 1992; see **Figure 11.12** on the next page). These findings strongly suggest that genetic factors exert considerable influence over personality.

Some skeptics wonder whether identical twins might exhibit more trait similarity than fraternal twins because they're treated more alike. In other words, they wonder whether environmental factors (rather than heredity) could be responsible for identical twins' greater personality resemblance. This nagging question can be answered only by studying identical twins reared apart, which is why the twin study at the University of Minnesota is so important.

HANS EYSENCK

"Personality is determined to a large extent by a person's genes."

By permission from the H. J. Eysenck Memorial Fund

concept check 11.4

Understanding the Implications of Major Theories: Who Said This?

Check your understanding of the implications of the personality theories we've discussed by indicating which theorist is likely to have made the statements below. The answers are in Appendix A.

Choose from the following theorists:

Alfred Adler _____

Albert Bandura

Hans Eysenck

Sigmund Freud _____

Abraham Maslow

Walter Mischel

Quotes

1. "If you deliberately plan to be less than you are capable of being, then I warn you that you'll be deeply unhappy for the rest of your life."

2. "I feel that the major, most fundamental dimensions of personality are likely to be those on which [there is] strong genetic determination of individual differences."

_____

3. "People are in general not candid over sexual matters . . . they wear a heavy overcoat woven of a tissue of lies, as though the weather were bad in the world of sexuality."

Figure 11.12

Twin studies of personality. Loehlin (1992) has summarized the results of twin studies that have examined the Big Five personality traits. The N under each trait indicates the number of twin studies that have examined that trait. The chart plots the average correlations obtained for identical and fraternal twins in these studies. As you can see, identical twins have shown greater resemblance in personality than fraternal twins have, suggesting that personality is partly inherited. (Based on data from Loehlin, 1992)

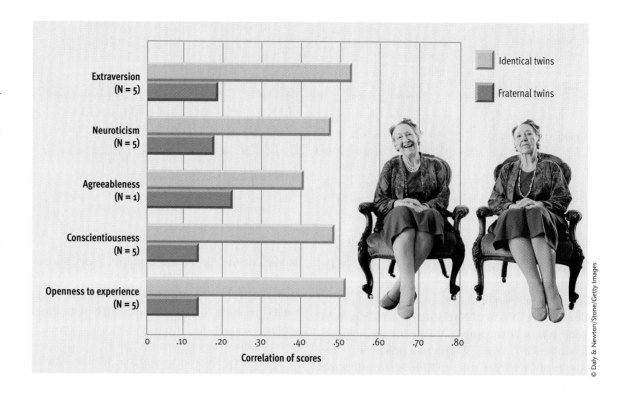

© Daly & Newton/Stone/Getty Images

The Minnesota study (Tellegen et al., 1988) was the first to administer the same personality test to identical and fraternal twins reared apart, as well as together. Most of the twins reared apart were separated quite early in life (median age of 2.5 months) and remained separated for a long time (median period of almost 34 years).

The results revealed that identical twins reared together were more similar on all three major traits examined in the study than fraternal twins reared together. More telling, though, were the results for the identical twins reared apart. On all three traits, identical twins reared apart were still substantially more similar to each other than fraternal twins reared together. The *heritability estimates* (see Chapter 8) for the three traits ranged from 40% to 58%. The investigators concluded that their results provided dramatic support for the hypothesis that genetic blueprints shape the contours of personality.

Research on the heritability of personality has inadvertently turned up a surprising finding: *shared family environment* appears to have remarkably little impact on personality. This unexpected finding has been observed quite consistently in behavioral genetics research (Beer, Arnold, & Loehlin, 1998; Rowe & van den Oord, 2005). It is surprising in that social scientists have long assumed that the family environment shared by children growing up together led to some personality resemblance among them. *These findings have led some theorists to conclude that parents don't matter—that they wield very little influence over*

how their children develop (Cohen, 1999; Harris, 1998; Rowe, 1994).

Critics have argued with merit that the methods used in behavioral genetics studies have probably underestimated the impact of shared environment on personality (Collins et al., 2000; Stoolmiller, 1999). They also note that shared experiences—such as being raised with authoritarian discipline—may often have different effects on two siblings, which obscures the impact of environment, but is not the same result as having no effect (Turkheimer & Waldron, 2000). And the critics argue that decades of research in developmental psychology have clearly demonstrated that parents have significant influence on their children (Maccoby, 2000).

Although the assertion that "parents don't matter" seems premature and overstated, the perplexing findings in behavioral genetics studies of personality have led researchers to investigate why children from the same family are often so different. Thus far, the evidence suggests that children in the same family experience home environments that are not nearly as similar as previously assumed (Hetherington, Reiss, & Plomin, 1994; Pike et al., 2000). Children in the same home may be treated quite differently, because gender and birth order can influence parents' approaches to childrearing. Temperamental differences between children may also evoke differences in parenting. Focusing on how environmental factors vary *within* families represents a promising new way to explore the determinants of personality.

The Evolutionary Approach to Personality

In the realm of biological perspectives on personality, the most recent development has been the emergence of evolutionary theory. Evolutionary theorists assert that personality has a biological basis because natural selection has favored certain traits over the course of human history (Figueredo et al., 2005). Thus, evolutionary analyses focus on how various personality traits—and the ability to recognize these traits in others—may have contributed to reproductive fitness in ancestral human populations.

For example, David Buss (1991, 1995, 1997) has argued that the Big Five personality traits stand out as important dimensions of personality across a variety of cultures because those traits have had significant adaptive implications. Buss points out that humans historically have depended heavily on groups, which afford protection from predators or enemies, opportunities for sharing food, and a diverse array of other benefits. In the context of these group interactions, people have had to make difficult but crucial judgments about the characteristics of others, asking such questions as: Who will make a good member of my coalition? Who can I depend on when in need? Who will share their resources? Thus, Buss (1995) argues, "those individuals able to accurately discern and act upon these individual differences likely enjoyed a considerable reproductive advantage" (p. 22). According to Buss, the Big Five emerge as fundamental dimensions of personality because humans have evolved special sensitivity to variations in the ability to bond with others (extraversion), the willingness to cooperate and collaborate (agreeableness), the tendency to be reliable and ethical (conscientiousness), the capacity to be an innovative problem solver (openness to experience), and the ability to handle stress (low neuroticism).

Evaluating Biological Perspectives

Researchers have compiled convincing evidence that biological factors help shape personality, and findings on the meager effects of shared family environment have launched intriguing new approaches to the investigation of personality development. Nonetheless, we must take note of some weaknesses in biological approaches to personality. Critics assert that (1) too much emphasis has been placed on heritability estimates that vary depending on sampling and statistical procedures (Funder, 2001), and (2) there's no comprehensive biological theory of personality, so additional theoretical work is needed to catch up with recent empirical findings.

Web Link 11.6

Great Ideas in Personality
Northwestern University personality psychologist G. Scott Acton demonstrates that scientific research programs in personality generate broad and compelling ideas about what it is to be a human being. He charts the contours of 12 research perspectives, including behaviorism, behavioral genetics, and sociobiology, and backs them up with extensive links to published and online resources associated with each perspective.

> A Contemporary Empirical Approach: Terror Management Theory

So far, our coverage has been largely devoted to grand, panoramic theories of personality. In this section we'll examine a new approach to understanding personality functioning that has a narrower focus than the classic theories of personality. *Terror management theory* emerged as an influential perspective in the 1990s. Although the theory borrows from Freudian and evolutionary formulations, it provides its own unique analysis of the human condition. Developed by Sheldon Solomon, Jeff Greenberg, and Tom Pyszczynski (1991, 2004b), this fresh perspective is currently generating a huge volume of research.

Essentials of Terror Management Theory

One of the chief goals of terror management theory is to explain why people need self-esteem (Solomon, Greenberg, & Pyszczynski, 1991). The theory begins with the assumption that humans share an evolutionary heritage with other animals that includes an instinctive drive for self-preservation. However, unlike other animals, humans have evolved complex cognitive abilities that permit self-awareness and contemplation of the future. These cognitive capacities make humans keenly aware of the inevitability of death—they appreciate that life can be snuffed out unpredictably at any time. The collision between humans' self-preservation instinct and their awareness of the inevitability of death create the potential for experiencing anxiety, alarm, and terror when people think about their mortality (see **Figure 11.13** on the next page).

How do humans deal with this potential for terror? According to terror management theory, "What saves us is culture. Cultures provide ways to view the world—worldviews—that 'solve' the existential crisis engendered by the awareness of death" (Pyszczynski, Solomon, & Greenberg, 2003, p. 16). Cultural worldviews diminish anxiety by providing answers to such universal questions as: Why am I here? What is the

PREVIEW QUESTIONS

- What are the chief hypotheses of terror management theory?
- How do reminders of death influence people's behavior?
- Does terror management theory have anything to say about reactions to terrorism?

Figure 11.13

Overview of terror management theory. This graphic maps out the relations among the key concepts proposed by terror management theory. The theory asserts that humans' unique awareness of the inevitability of death fosters a need to defend one's cultural worldview and one's self-esteem, which serve to protect one from mortality-related anxiety.

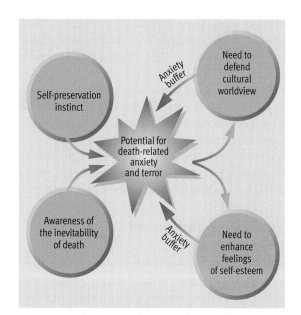

meaning of life? Cultures create stories, traditions, and institutions that give their members a sense of being part of an enduring legacy through their contributions to their families, tribes, schools, churches, professions, and so forth. Thus, faith in a cultural worldview can give people a sense of order, meaning, and context that can soothe humans' fear of death.

Where does self-esteem fit into the picture? Self-esteem is viewed as a sense of personal worth that depends on one's confidence in the validity of one's cultural worldview and the belief that one is living up to the standards prescribed by that worldview. "It is the feeling that one is a valuable contributor to a meaningful universe" (Pyszczynski et al., 2004, p. 437). Hence, self-esteem buffers people from the profound anxiety associated with the awareness that we are transient animals destined to die. In other words, self-esteem serves a *terror management* function (refer to **Figure 11.13**).

The notion that self-esteem functions as an *anxiety buffer* has been supported by numerous studies (Pyszczynski et al., 2004). In many of these experiments, researchers have manipulated what they call *mortality salience* by asking subjects to briefly think about their own death. Consistent with the anxiety buffer hypothesis, reminding people of their mortality leads subjects to engage in a variety of behaviors that are likely to bolster their self-esteem, thus reducing anxiety.

Applications of Terror Management Theory

Increasing mortality salience also leads people to work harder at defending their cultural worldview (Arndt, Cook, & Routledge, 2004). For instance, after briefly pondering their mortality, research participants (1) hand out harsher penalties to moral transgressors, (2) respond more negatively to people who criticize their country, (3) give larger rewards to people who uphold cultural standards, and (4) show more respect for cultural icons, such as a flag (Greenberg et al., 1990; Rosenblatt et al., 1989). This need to defend one's cultural worldview may even fuel prejudice and aggression. Reminding subjects of their mortality leads to (1) more negative evaluations of people from different religious or ethnic backgrounds, (2) more stereotypic thinking about minority group members, and (3) more aggressive behavior toward people with opposing political views (McGregor et al., 1998; Schimel et al., 1999).

Terror management theory yields novel hypotheses regarding many phenomena. For instance, Solomon, Greenberg, and Pyszczynski (2004a) explain excessive materialism in terms of the anxiety buffering function of self-esteem. Specifically, they argue that "conspicuous possession and consumption are thinly veiled efforts to assert that one is special and therefore more than just an animal fated to die and decay" (p. 134). One recent study even applied terror management theory to the political process. Cohen et al. (2004) found that mortality salience increases subjects' preference for "charismatic" candidates who articulate a grand vision that makes people feel like they are part of an important movement of lasting significance.

Given its focus on death anxiety, terror management theory has much to say about people's reactions to the contemporary threat of terrorism. Pyszczynski, Solomon, and Greenberg (2003) point out that terrorist attacks are intended to produce a powerful, nationwide manipulation of mortality salience. When mortality salience is elevated, terror management theory predicts that people will embrace their cultural worldviews even more strongly than before. Consistent with this prediction, in the months following 9/11, expressions of patriotism and religious faith increased dramatically. Research on terror management processes has also shown that when death anxiety is heightened, people become less tolerant of opposing views and more prejudiced against those who are different. Consistent with this analysis, in the aftermath of 9/11, individuals who questioned government policies met more hostility than usual. The theory also predicts that reminders of mortality increase the tendency to admire those who uphold cultural standards. More than ever, people need heroes who personify cultural values. This need was apparent after the September 11 terrorist attacks in the way the media made firefighters into larger-than-life heroes.

At first glance, a theory that explains everything from prejudice to compulsive shopping in terms of death anxiety may seem highly implausible. After all, most people do not appear to walk around all day obsessing about the possibility of their death. The architects of terror management theory are well aware of this reality. They explain that the defensive reactions uncovered in their research generally occur when death anxiety surfaces on the fringes of conscious awareness and that these reactions are automatic and subconscious (Pyszczynski, Greenberg, & Solomon, 1999).

Terror management theory has been applied to a remarkably diverse array of phenomena. For example, it has even been used to explain conspicuous consumption.

> Culture and Personality

Are there connections between culture and personality? For the most part, continuity has been apparent in cross-cultural comparisons of the *trait structure* of personality. When English language personality scales have been translated and administered in other cultures, the predicted dimensions of personality have emerged from the statistical analyses. For example, when scales that tap the Big Five personality traits have been administered and subjected to statistical analysis in other cultures, the usual five traits have typically emerged (Katigbak et al., 2002; McCrae et al., 2005). The cross-cultural similarities observed thus far seem impressive, but skepticism has been voiced in some quarters. Critics argue that the strategy of "exporting" Western tests to other cultures is slanted in favor of finding cross-cultural compatibility and is unlikely to uncover culture-specific traits (Church & Lonner, 1998). Thus, preliminary research suggests that the basic dimensions of personality trait structure may transcend culture, but additional research is needed.

In contrast, when researchers have compared cultural groups on specific aspects of personality, some intriguing disparities have surfaced. Perhaps the most interesting work has been that of Hazel Markus and Shinobu Kitayama (1991, 1994) comparing American and Asian conceptions of the self. According to Markus and Kitayama, American parents teach their children to be self-reliant, to feel good about themselves, and to view themselves as special individuals. Children are encouraged to excel in competitive endeavors and to strive to stand out from the crowd. They are told that "the squeaky wheel gets the grease" and that "you have to stand up for yourself." Thus, Markus and Kitayama argue that *American culture fosters an independent view of the self.* American youngsters learn to define themselves in terms of their personal attributes, abilities, accomplishments, and possessions. Their unique strengths and achievements become the basis for their sense of self-worth.

Most of us take this individualistic mentality for granted. Indeed, Markus and Kitayama maintain that "most of what psychologists currently know about human nature is based on one particular view—the so-called Western view of the individual as an independent, self-contained, autonomous entity" (1991, p. 224). However, they marshal convincing evidence that this view is *not* universal. They argue that in Asian cultures such as Japan and China, socialization practices foster a more *interdependent view of the self,* which emphasizes the fundamental connectedness of people to each other (see Figure 11.14 on page 364). In these cultures, parents teach their children that they can rely on family and friends, that they should be modest about their personal accomplishments so they don't diminish others' achievements, and that they should view themselves as part of a larger social matrix. Children are encouraged to fit in with others and to avoid standing out from the crowd. A popular adage in Japan reminds children that "the nail that stands out gets pounded down." Hence, Markus and Kitayama assert that Asian youngsters typically learn to define themselves in terms of the groups they belong to. Their harmonious relations with others and their pride in group achievements become the basis for their sense of self-worth. Thus, Asian and American conceptions of self appear to be noticeably different.

PREVIEW QUESTIONS

- Does the five-factor model have any relevance in non-Western cultures?
- How do conceptions of self vary across cultures?

HAZEL MARKUS AND SHINOBU KITAYAMA

"Most of what psychologists currently know about human nature is based on one particular view—the so-called Western view of the individual as an independent, self-contained, autonomous entity."

THEORIST AND ORIENTATION	SOURCE OF DATA AND OBSERVATIONS	KEY MOTIVATIONAL FORCES

A PSYCHODYNAMIC VIEW

Sigmund Freud

© Peter Aprahamian/Corbis

Case studies from clinical practice of psychoanalysis

Sex and aggression; need to reduce tension resulting from internal conflicts

A BEHAVIORAL VIEW

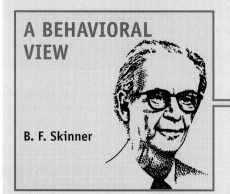

B. F. Skinner

Laboratory experiments, primarily with animals

© Richard Wood/Index Stock

Pursuit of primary (unlearned) and secondary (learned) reinforcers; priorities depend on personal history

A HUMANISTIC VIEW

Carl Rogers

Case studies from clinical practice of client-centered therapy

© Tom Stewart/Corbis

Actualizing tendency (motive to develop capacities, and experience personal growth) and self-actualizing tendency (motive to maintain self-concept and behave in ways that are consistent with self-concept)

A BIOLOGICAL VIEW

Hans Eysenck

Twin, family, and adoption studies of heritability; factor analysis studies of personality structure

© Daly & Newton/Stone/Getty Images

No specific motivational forces singled out

MODEL OF PERSONALITY STRUCTURE

Three interacting components (id, ego, superego) operating at three levels of consciousness

CONSCIOUS
PRECONSCIOUS
EGO
SUPEREGO
ID
UNCONSCIOUS

Collections of response tendencies tied to specific stimulus situations

Operant response tendencies

Stimulus situation → R₁, R₂, R₃, R₄

Self-concept, which may or may not mesh well with actual experience

Self-concept **Actual experience**

Congruence

Incongruence

Hierarchy of traits, with specific traits derived from more fundamental, general traits

Extraversion
Lively   Active   Assertive

VIEW OF PERSONALITY DEVELOPMENT

Emphasis on fixation or progress through psychosexual stages; experiences in early childhood (such as toilet training) can leave lasting mark on adult personality

© Michael Newman/PhotoEdit

Personality evolves gradually over the life span (not in stages); responses (such as extraverted joking) followed by reinforcement (such as appreciative laughter) become more frequent

© Jacobs Stock Photography/Corbis

Children who receive unconditional love have less need to be defensive; they develop more accurate, congruent self-concept; conditional love fosters incongruence

© Stephanie Rausser/Taxi/Getty Images

Emphasis on unfolding of genetic blueprint with maturation; inherited predispositions interact with learning experiences

ROOTS OF DISORDERS

Unconscious fixations and unresolved conflicts from childhood, usually centering on sex and aggression

Maladaptive behavior due to faulty learning; the "symptom" is the problem, not a sign of underlying disease

Incongruence between self and actual experience (inaccurate self-concept); overdependence on others for approval and sense of worth

Genetic vulnerability activated in part by environmental factors

Figure 11.14

Culture and conceptions of self. According to Markus and Kitayama (1991), Western cultures foster an independent view of the self as a unique individual who is separate from others, as diagrammed on the left. In contrast, Asian cultures encourage an interdependent view of the self as part of an interconnected social matrix, as diagrammed on the right. The interdependent view leads people to define themselves in terms of their social relationships (for instance, as someone's daughter, employee, colleague, or neighbor).

Source: Adapted from Markus, H. R., & Kitayama, S. (1991). Culture and the self: Implications for cognition, emotion, and motivation. *Psychological Review, 98,* 224–253. Copyright © 1991 by the American Psychological Association. Adapted by permission of the author.

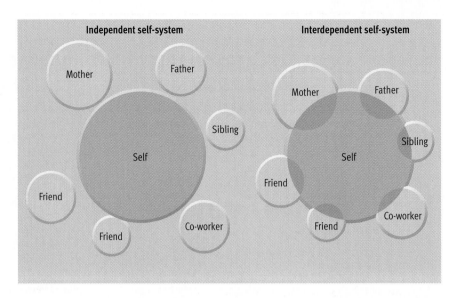

> Reflecting on the Chapter's Themes

Cultural Heritage

Theoretical Diversity

Sociohistorical Context

The preceding discussion of culture and personality obviously highlighted the text's theme that our behavior is influenced by our cultural heritage. This chapter has also been ideally suited for embellishing on two other unifying themes: psychology's theoretical diversity and the idea that psychology evolves in a sociohistorical context.

No other area of psychology is characterized by as much theoretical diversity as the study of personality, where there are literally dozens of insightful theories. Some of this diversity exists because different theories attempt to explain different facets of behavior. Of course, much of this diversity reflects genuine disagreements on basic questions about personality. These disagreements should be apparent on pages 362–363, where you'll find an Illustrated Overview of the ideas of Freud, Skinner, Rogers, and Eysenck, as representatives of the psychodynamic, behavioral, humanistic, and biological approaches to personality.

The study of personality also highlights the sociohistorical context in which psychology evolves. Personality theories have left many marks on modern culture. The theories of Freud, Adler, and Skinner have had an enormous impact on childrearing practices. The ideas of Freud and Jung have found their way into literature (influencing the portrayal of fictional characters) and the visual arts. For example, Freud's theory helped inspire surrealism's interest in the world of dreams. Maslow's hierarchy of needs and Skinner's affirmation of the value of positive re-

inforcement have given rise to new approaches to management in the world of business and industry.

Sociohistorical forces also leave their imprint on psychology. This chapter provided many examples of how personal experiences, prevailing attitudes, and historical events have contributed to the evolution of ideas in psychology. For example, Freud's pessimistic view of human nature and his emphasis on the dark forces of aggression were shaped to some extent by his exposure to the hostilities of World War I and prevailing anti-Semitic sentiments. Freud's emphasis on sexuality was surely influenced by the Victorian climate of sexual repression that existed in his youth. Adler's views also reflected the social context in which he grew up. His interest in inferiority feelings and compensation appears to have sprung from his own sickly childhood and the difficulties he had to overcome. Likewise, it's reasonable to speculate that Jung's childhood loneliness and introversion may have sparked his interest in the introversion-extraversion dimension of personality.

Progress in the study of personality has also been influenced by developments in other areas of psychology. For instance, the enterprise of psychological testing originally emerged out of efforts to measure general intelligence. Eventually, however, the principles of psychological testing were applied to the challenge of measuring personality. In the upcoming Personal Application we discuss the logic and limitations of personality tests.

PERSONAL *Application*

Understanding Personality Assessment

Answer the following "true" or "false."

_____ 1 Responses to personality tests are subject to unconscious distortion.

_____ 2 The results of personality tests are often misunderstood.

_____ 3 Personality test scores should be interpreted with caution.

_____ 4 Personality tests serve many important functions.

If you answered "true" to all four questions, you earned a perfect score. Yes, personality tests are subject to distortion. Admittedly, test results are often misunderstood, and they should be interpreted cautiously. In spite of these problems, however, psychological tests can be quite useful.

Everyone engages in efforts to size up his or her own personality as well as that of others. When you think to yourself that "Mary Ann is shrewd and poised," or when you remark to a friend that "Carlos is timid and submissive," you're making personality assessments. In a sense, then, personality assessment is an ongoing part of daily life. Given the popular interest in personality assessment, it's not surprising that psychologists have devised formal measures of personality.

Personality tests can be helpful in (1) making clinical diagnoses of psychological disorders, (2) vocational counseling, (3) personnel selection in business and industry, and (4) measuring specific personality traits for research purposes. Personality tests can be divided into two broad categories: *self-report inventories* and *projective tests*. In this Personal Application, we'll discuss some representative tests from both categories and discuss their strengths and weaknesses.

Self-Report Inventories

Self-report inventories are personality tests that ask individuals to answer a series of questions about their characteristic be-havior. The logic underlying this approach is very simple: Who knows you better? Who has known you longer? Who has more access to your private feelings? We'll look at three examples of self-report scales: the MMPI, the 16PF, and the NEO Personality Inventory.

The MMPI

The most widely used self-report inventory is the Minnesota Multiphasic Personality Inventory (MMPI). The MMPI was originally designed to aid clinicians in the diagnosis of psychological disorders. It measures 10 personality traits that, when manifested to an extreme degree, are thought to be symptoms of disorders. Examples include traits such as paranoia, depression, and hysteria.

Are the MMPI clinical scales valid? That is, do they measure what they were designed to measure? Originally, it was assumed that the 10 clinical subscales would provide direct indexes of specific types of disorders. In other words, a high score on the depression scale would be indicative of depression, a high score on the paranoia scale would be indicative of a paranoid disorder, and so forth. However, research revealed that the relations between MMPI scores and various types of mental illness are much more complex than originally anticipated. People with most types of disorders show elevated scores on *several* MMPI subscales. This means that certain score *profiles* are indicative of specific disorders (see **Figure 11.15** on the next page). Thus, the interpretation of MMPI is quite complicated. Nonetheless, the MMPI can be a helpful diagnostic tool for the clinician. The fact that the inventory has been translated into more than 115 languages is a testimonial to its usefulness (Butcher, 1990).

The 16PF and NEO Personality Inventory

Raymond Cattell (1957, 1965) set out to identify and measure the *basic dimensions* of the *normal* personality. He started with a previ-ously compiled list of 4504 personality traits. This massive list was reduced to 171 traits by weeding out terms that were virtually synonyms. Cattell then used factor analysis to identify clusters of closely related traits. Eventually, he reduced the list of 171 traits to 16 *source traits*. The Sixteen Personality Factor (16PF) Questionnaire is a 187–item scale that assesses these 16 basic dimensions of personality (Cattell, Eber, & Tatsuoka, 1970), which are listed in **Figure 11.16** on page 367.

As we noted in the main body of the chapter, some theorists believe that only five trait dimensions are required to provide a full description of personality. This view led to the creation of the NEO Personality Inventory. Developed by Paul Costa and Robert McCrae (1985, 1992), the NEO Inventory is designed to measure the Big Five traits: neuroticism, extraversion, openness to experience, agreeableness, and conscientiousness. In spite of its relatively short life span, the NEO is already widely used in research and clinical work.

Strengths and Weaknesses of Self-Report Inventories

To appreciate the strengths of self-report inventories, consider how else you might inquire about an individual's personality. For instance, if you want to know how assertive someone is, why not just ask the person? Why administer an elaborate 50–item personality inventory that measures assertiveness? The advantage of the personality inventory is that it can provide a more objective and more precise estimate of the person's assertiveness.

Of course, self-report inventories are only as accurate as the information that respondents provide. They are susceptible to several sources of error (Ben-Porath, 2003; Kline, 1995; Paulhus, 1991), including the following:

1. *Deliberate deception.* Some self-report inventories include many questions whose purpose is easy to figure out. This problem

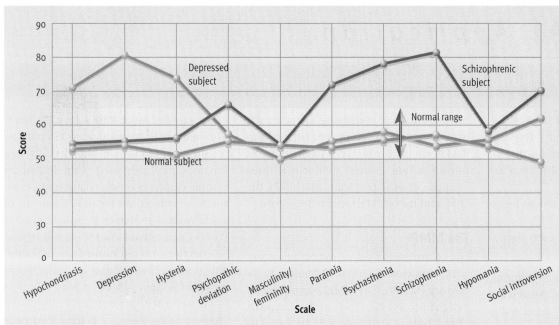

Figure 11.15

MMPI profiles. Scores on the 10 clinical scales of the MMPI are often plotted as shown here to create a profile for a client. The normal range for scores on each subscale is 50 to 65. People with disorders frequently exhibit elevated scores on several clinical scales rather than just one.

makes it possible for some respondents to intentionally fake particular personality traits (Rees & Metcalfe, 2003).

2. *Social desirability bias.* Without realizing it, some people consistently respond to questions in ways that make them look good. The social desirability bias isn't a matter of deception so much as wishful thinking.

3. *Response sets.* A response set is a systematic tendency to respond to test items in a particular way that is unrelated to the content of the items. For instance, some people, called "yea-sayers," tend to agree with virtually every statement on a test. Other people, called "nay-sayers," tend to disagree with nearly every statement.

Test developers have devised a number of strategies to reduce the impact of deliberate deception, social desirability bias, and response sets (Berry, Wetter, & Baer, 1995; Lanyon & Goodstein, 1997). For instance, it's possible to insert a "lie scale" into a test to assess the likelihood that a respondent is engaging in deception. The best way to reduce the impact of social desirability bias is to identify items that are sensitive to this bias and drop them from the test. Problems with response sets can be reduced by systematically varying the way in which test items are worded.

Projective Tests 7a

Projective tests, which all take a rather indirect approach to the assessment of personality, are used extensively in clinical work. *Projective tests* **ask participants to respond to vague, ambiguous stimuli in ways that may reveal the subjects' needs, feelings, and personality traits.** The Rorschach test, for instance, consists of a series of ten inkblots. Respondents are asked to describe what they see in the blots. In the Thematic Apperception Test (TAT), a series of pictures of simple scenes is presented to individuals who are asked to tell stories about what is happening in the scenes and what the characters are feeling. For instance, one TAT card shows a young boy contemplating a violin resting on a table in front of him (see **Figure 11.17** for another example).

The Projective Hypothesis 7a

The "projective hypothesis" is that ambiguous materials can serve as a blank screen onto which people project their characteristic concerns, conflicts, and desires (Frank, 1939). Thus, a competitive person who is shown the TAT card of the boy at the table with the violin might concoct a story about how the boy is contemplating an upcoming musical competition at which he hopes to excel. The same card shown to a person high in impulsiveness might elicit a story about how the boy is planning to sneak out the door to go dirt-bike riding with friends.

The scoring and interpretation of projective tests is very complicated. Rorschach responses may be analyzed in terms of content, originality, the feature of the inkblot that determined the response, and the amount of the inkblot used, among other criteria. In fact, five different systems exist for scoring the Rorschach (Edberg, 1990). TAT stories are examined in terms of heroes, needs, themes, and outcomes.

Strengths and Weaknesses of Projective Tests

Proponents of projective tests assert that the tests have two unique strengths. First, they are not transparent to respondents. That is, the subject doesn't know how the test provides information to the tester. Hence, it may be difficult for people to engage in intentional deception (Groth-Marnat, 1997). Second, the indirect approach used in these tests may make them especially sensitive to unconscious, latent features of personality.

Unfortunately, the scientific evidence on projective measures is unimpressive (Garb, Florio, & Grove, 1998; Hunsley, Lee, & Wood, 2003; Lanyon & Goodstein, 1997). In a thor-

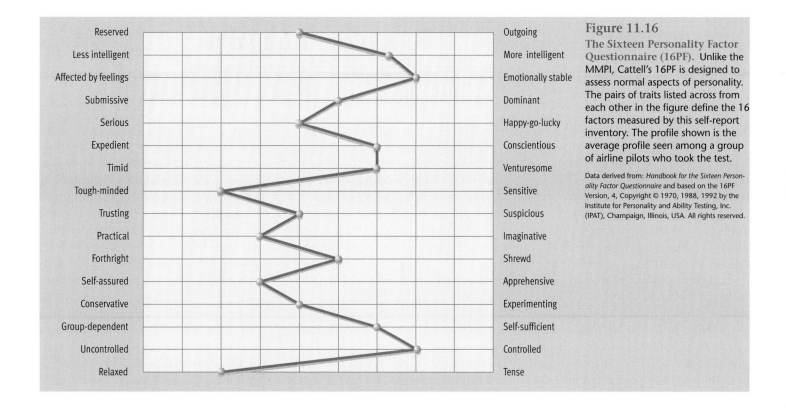

Figure 11.16

The Sixteen Personality Factor Questionnaire (16PF). Unlike the MMPI, Cattell's 16PF is designed to assess normal aspects of personality. The pairs of traits listed across from each other in the figure define the 16 factors measured by this self-report inventory. The profile shown is the average profile seen among a group of airline pilots who took the test.

Data derived from: *Handbook for the Sixteen Personality Factor Questionnaire* and based on the 16PF Version, 4, Copyright © 1970, 1988, 1992 by the Institute for Personality and Ability Testing, Inc. (IPAT), Champaign, Illinois, USA. All rights reserved.

Figure 11.17

The Thematic Apperception Test (TAT). In taking the TAT, a respondent is asked to tell stories about scenes such as this one. The themes apparent in each story can be scored to provide insight about the respondent's personality.

Source: Murray. H. A. (1971). *Thematic Apperception Test.* Cambridge, MA: Harvard University Press. Copyright © 1943 by The President and Fellows of Harvard College, Copyright © 1971 by Henry A. Murray. Reprinted by permission of the publisher.

ough review of the relevant research, Lillienfeld, Wood, and Garb (2000) conclude that projective tests tend to be plagued by inconsistent scoring, low reliability, inadequate test norms, cultural bias, and poor validity estimates. They also assert that, contrary to advocates' claims, projective tests are susceptible to some types of intentional deception (primarily, faking poor mental health). Based on their analysis, Lillienfeld and his colleagues argue that projective tests should be referred to as projective "techniques" or "instruments" rather than tests because "most of these techniques as used in daily clinical practice do not fulfill the traditional criteria for psychological tests" (p. 29). In spite of these problems, projective tests continue to be used by many clinicians. Although the questionable scientific status of these techniques is a very real problem, their continued popularity suggests that they yield subjective information that many clinicians find useful (Viglione & Rivera, 2003).

Hindsight in Everyday Analyses of Personality

Consider the case of two close sisters who grew up together: Lorena and Christina. Lorena grew into a frugal adult who is careful about spending her money, only shops when there are sales, and saves every penny she can. In contrast, Christina became an extravagant spender who lives to shop and never saves any money. How do the sisters explain their striking personality differences? Lorena attributes her thrifty habits to the fact that her family was so poor when she was a child that she learned the value of being careful with money. Christina attributes her extravagant spending to the fact that her family was so poor that she learned to really enjoy any money that she might have. Now, it *is* possible that two sisters could react to essentially the same circumstances quite differently, but the more likely explanation is that both sisters have been influenced by *hindsight bias*—the tendency to mold one's interpretation of the past to fit how events actually turned out. We saw how hindsight can distort memory in Chapter 7. Here, we will see how hindsight tends to make people feel as if they are personality experts and how it creates interpretive problems even for scientific theories of personality.

The Prevalence of Hindsight Bias

Hindsight bias is *ubiquitous,* which means that it occurs in many settings, with all sorts of people. Most of the time, people are not aware of the way their explanations are skewed by the fact that the outcome is already known. The experimental literature on hindsight bias offers a rich array of findings on how the knowledge of an outcome biases the way people think about its causes (Hawkins & Hastie, 1990). For example, when college students were told the results of hypothetical experiments, each group of students could "explain" why the studies turned out the way they did, even though different groups were given opposite results

to explain (Slovic & Fischhoff, 1977). The students believed that the results of the studies were obvious when they were told what the experimenter found, but when they were given only the information that was available before the outcome was known, it was not obvious at all. This bias is also called the "I knew it all along" effect because that is the typical refrain of people when they have the luxury of hindsight. Indeed, after the fact, people often act as if events that would have been difficult to predict had in fact been virtually *inevitable*. Looking back at the disintegration of the Soviet Union and the end of the Cold War, for instance, many people today act as though these events were bound to happen, but in reality these landmark events were predicted by almost no one.

Hindsight bias shows up in many contexts. For example, when a couple announces that they are splitting up, many people in their social circle will typically claim they "saw it coming." When a football team loses in a huge upset, you will hear many fans claim, "I knew they were overrated and vul-

nerable." When public officials make a difficult decision that leads to an unfortunate outcome—such as NASA's decision to proceed with the space shuttle *Columbia*'s return to earth, which resulted in the shuttle's disintegration—many of the pundits in the press are quick to criticize, often asserting that only incompetent fools could have failed to foresee the catastrophe. Interestingly, people are not much kinder to themselves when they make ill-fated decisions. When individuals make tough calls that lead to negative results—such as buying a car that turns out to be a lemon, or investing in a stock that plummets—they often say things like, "Why did I ignore the obvious warning signs?" or "How could I have been such an idiot?"

Hindsight and Personality

Hindsight bias appears to be pervasive in everyday analyses of personality. Think about it: If you attempt to explain why you are so

When public officials make tough decisions that backfire, critics are often quick to argue that the officials should have shown greater foresight. This type of hindsight bias has been apparent in discussions of whether NASA could have prevented the disintegration of the space shuttle Columbia. In retrospect, it is clear that NASA made some disastrous mistakes in its handling of the Columbia mission. But mistakes that look obvious with the luxury of hindsight often are far from obvious before the results of a tough decision are known.

suspicious, why your mother is so domineering, or why your best friend is so insecure, the starting point in each case will be the personality outcome. It would probably be impossible to reconstruct the past without being swayed by your knowledge of these outcomes. Thus, hindsight makes everybody an expert on personality, as we can all come up with plausible explanations for the personality traits of people we know well. Perhaps this is why Judith Harris (1998) ignited a firestorm of protest when she wrote a book arguing that parents have relatively little effect on their children's personalities beyond the genetic material that they supply.

In her book *The Nurture Assumption,* Harris summarizes behavioral genetics research (which we discussed in the main body of the chapter; see p. 358) and other evidence suggesting that family environment has surprisingly little impact on children's personality. There is room for debate on this complex issue (Kagan, 1998; Tavris, 1998), but our chief interest here is that Harris made a cogent, compelling argument that attracted extensive coverage in the press, which generated an avalanche of commentary from angry parents who argued that *parents do matter.* For example, *Newsweek* magazine received 350 letters, mostly from parents who provided examples of how they thought they had influenced their children's personalities. However, parents' retrospective analyses of their children's personality development have to be treated with great skepticism, as they are likely to be distorted by hindsight bias (not to mention the selective recall frequently seen in anecdotal reports).

Unfortunately, hindsight bias is so prevalent, it also presents a problem for scientific theories of personality. For example, the issue of hindsight bias has been raised in many critiques of psychoanalytic theory (Torrey, 1992). Freudian theory was originally built mainly on a foundation of case studies of patients in therapy. Obviously, Freudian therapists who knew what their patients' adult personalities were like probably went looking for the types of childhood experiences hypothesized by Freud (oral fixations, punitive toilet training, Oedipal conflicts, and so forth) in their efforts to explain their patients' personalities.

Another problem with hindsight bias is that once researchers know an outcome, more often than not they can fashion some plausible explanation for it. For instance, Torrey (1992) describes a study inspired by Freudian theory that examined breast-size preferences among men. The original hypothesis was that men who scored higher in dependence—thought to be a sign of oral fixation—would manifest a stronger preference for women with large breasts. When the actual results of the study showed just the opposite—that dependence was associated with a preference for smaller breasts—the finding was attributed to reaction formation (the defense mechanism that involves behaving in a way opposite of one's true feelings). Instead of failing to support Freudian theory, the unexpected findings were simply reinterpreted in a way that was consistent with Freudian theory.

The hindsight bias also presents thorny problems for evolutionary theorists, who generally work backward from known outcomes to reason out how adaptive pressures in humans' ancestral past may have led to those outcomes (Cornell, 1997). Consider, for instance, evolutionary theorists' assertion that the Big Five traits are found to be fundamental dimensions of personality around the world because those specific traits have had major adaptive implications over the course of human history (Buss, 1995; MacDonald, 1998). Their explanation makes sense, but what would have happened if some *other traits* had shown up in the Big Five? Would the evolutionary view have been weakened if dominance or paranoia had turned up in the Big Five? Probably not. With the luxury of hindsight, evolutionary theorists surely could have constructed plausible explanations for how these traits promoted reproductive success in the distant past. Thus, hindsight bias is a fundamental feature of human cognition and the

scientific enterprise is not immune to this problem.

Other Implications of "20-20 Hindsight"

Our discussion of hindsight has focused on its implications for thinking about personality, but there is ample evidence that hindsight can bias thinking in all sorts of domains. For example, consider the practice of obtaining second opinions on medical diagnoses. The doctor providing the second opinion usually is aware of the first physician's diagnosis, which creates a hindsight bias (Arkes et al., 1981). Second opinions would probably be more valuable if the doctors rendering them were not aware of previous diagnoses. Hindsight also has the potential to distort legal decisions in cases involving allegations of negligence. Jurors' natural tendency to think "How could they have failed to foresee this problem?" may exaggerate the appearance of negligence (LaBine & LaBine, 1996).

Hindsight bias is powerful. The next time you hear of an unfortunate outcome to a decision made by a public official, carefully examine the way news reporters describe the decision. You will probably find that they believe that the disastrous outcome should have been obvious, because they can clearly see what went wrong after the fact. Similarly, if you find yourself thinking, "Only a fool would have failed to anticipate this disaster" or "I would have forseen this problem," take a deep breath and try to review the decision *using only information that was known at the time the decision was being made.* Sometimes good decisions based on the best available information can have terrible outcomes. Unfortunately, the clarity of "20-20 hindsight" makes it difficult for people to learn from their own and others' mistakes.

Table 11.3 Critical Thinking Skill Discussed in This Application

Skill	Description
Recognizing the bias in hindsight analysis	The critical thinker understands that knowing the outcome of events biases our recall and interpretation of the events.

Key Ideas

The Nature of Personality

● The concept of personality explains the consistency in people's behavior over time and situations while also explaining their distinctiveness. Personality traits are dispositions to behave in certain ways.

● There is considerable debate as to how many trait dimensions are necessary to fully describe personality. Nonetheless, the five-factor model has become the dominant conception of personality structure.

Psychodynamic Perspectives

● Freud's psychoanalytic theory emphasizes the importance of the unconscious. Freud described personality structure in terms of three components—the id, ego, and superego—which are routinely involved in an ongoing series of internal conflicts.

● Freud theorized that conflicts centering on sex and aggression are especially likely to lead to significant anxiety. According to Freud, anxiety and other unpleasant emotions such as guilt are often warded off with defense mechanisms, which work primarily through self-deception.

● Freud believed that the first five years of life are extremely influential in shaping adult personality. He described a series of five psychosexual stages of development. Certain experiences during these stages can have lasting effects on adult personality.

● Jung's most innovative and controversial concept was the collective unconscious. Adler's individual psychology emphasizes how people strive for superiority to compensate for their feelings of inferiority. Psychodynamic theories have been criticized for their poor testability, their inadequate base of empirical evidence, and their male-centered views.

Behavioral Perspectives

● Behavioral theories explain how personality is shaped through learning. Behaviorists see personality as a collection of response tendencies tied to specific stimulus situations. Skinner assumed that personality development is a lifelong process in which response tendencies are shaped by learning.

● Social cognitive theory focuses on how cognitive factors regulate learned behavior. Bandura's concept of observational learning accounts for the acquisition of responses from models. The behaviorists have been criticized for their overdependence on animal research and their fragmented analysis of personality.

Humanistic Perspectives

● Humanistic theories take an optimistic view of people's conscious, rational ability to chart their own courses of action. Rogers focused on the self-concept as the critical aspect of personality. He maintained that anxiety is attributable to incongruence between one's self-concept and reality.

● Maslow theorized that needs are organized hierarchically and that psychological health depends on meeting one's need for self-actualization, which is the need to fulfill one's human potential. Humanistic theories lack a firm base of research, are difficult to put to an empirical test, and may be overly optimistic about human nature.

Biological Perspectives

● Eysenck suggests that heredity influences individual differences in physiological functioning that affect how easily people acquire conditioned responses. Twin and adoption studies provide impressive evidence that genetic factors shape personality. Behavioral genetics research also suggests that shared family environment may have surprisingly little impact on personality.

● Evolutionary analyses of personality have emphasized how the "Big Five" personality traits may have had significant adaptive value. The biological approach has been criticized because of methodological problems with heritability estimates and because it offers no systematic model of how physiology governs personality.

A Contemporary Empirical Approach: Terror Management Theory

● Terror management theory proposes that self-esteem and faith in a cultural worldview shield people from the profound anxiety associated with their mortality. Consistent with this analysis, increasing mortality salience leads people to make efforts to bolster their self-esteem and defend their worldviews. These defensive reactions are automatic and subconscious.

Culture and Personality

● Some studies suggest that the basic trait structure of personality may be much the same across cultures. However, notable differences have been found when researchers have compared cultural groups on specific aspects of personality, such as their conceptions of self.

Reflecting on the Chapter's Themes

● The study of personality illustrates how psychology is characterized by great theoretical diversity. The study of personality also demonstrates how ideas in psychology are shaped by sociohistorical forces and how cultural factors influence psychological processes.

PERSONAL APPLICATION • Understanding Personality Assessment

● Self-report inventories, such as the MMPI, 16PF, and NEO Personality Inventory, ask subjects to describe themselves. Self-report inventories are vulnerable to certain sources of error, including deception, the social desirability bias, and response sets.

● Projective tests, such as the Rorschach and TAT, assume that subjects' responses to ambiguous stimuli reveal something about their personality. While the projective hypothesis seems plausible, projective tests' reliability and validity are disturbingly low.

CRITICAL THINKING APPLICATION • Hindsight in Everyday Analyses of Personality

● Hindsight bias often leads people to assert that "I knew it all along" in discussing outcomes that they did not actually predict. Thanks to hindsight, people can almost always come up with plausible-sounding explanations for known personality traits. Problems with hindsight bias have been raised in critiques of Freudian theory and evolutionary theory.

Key Terms

Archetypes (p. 348)
Behaviorism (p. 349)
Collective unconscious (p. 347)
Compensation (p. 348)
Conscious (p. 342)
Defense mechanisms (p. 344)
Displacement (p. 344)
Ego (p. 342)
Factor analysis (p. 340)
Fixation (p. 345)
Hierarchy of needs (p. 354)
Hindsight bias (p. 368)
Humanism (p. 352)
Id (p. 342)
Identification (p. 345)
Incongruence (p. 353)
Model (p. 351)
Need for self-actualization (p. 355)
Observational learning (p. 351)
Oedipal complex (p. 346)
Personality (p. 340)
Personality trait (p. 340)
Pleasure principle (p. 342)
Preconscious (p. 342)
Projection (p. 344)
Projective tests (p. 366)

Psychodynamic theories (p. 341)
Psychosexual stages (p. 345)
Rationalization (p. 344)
Reaction formation (p. 345)
Reality principle (p. 342)
Regression (p. 345)
Repression (p. 344)
Self-actualizing persons (p. 355)
Self-concept (p. 353)
Self-efficacy (p. 351)
Self-report inventories (p. 365)
Striving for superiority (p. 348)
Superego (p. 342)
Unconscious (p. 342)

Key People

Alfred Adler (p. 348)
Albert Bandura (p. 351)
Hans Eysenck (p. 357)
Sigmund Freud (pp. 341–346)
Carl Jung (pp. 347–348)
Abraham Maslow (pp. 354–355)
Walter Mischel (pp. 351–352)
Carl Rogers (pp. 353–354)
B. F. Skinner (pp. 349–350)

1. Harvey Hedonist has devoted his life to the search for physical pleasure and immediate need gratification. Freud would say that Harvey is dominated by:
   A. his ego.
   B. his superego.
   C. his id.
   D. Bacchus.

2. Furious at her boss for what she considers to be unjust criticism, Clara turns around and takes out her anger on her subordinates. Clara may be using the defense mechanism of:
   A. displacement.
   B. reaction formation.
   C. identification.
   D. replacement.

3. Freud believed that most personality disturbances are due to:
   A. the failure of parents to reinforce healthy behavior.
   B. a poor self-concept resulting from excessive parental demands.
   C. unconscious and unresolved sexual conflicts rooted in childhood experiences.
   D. the exposure of children to unhealthy role models.

4. According to Alfred Adler, the prime motivating force in a person's life is:
   A. physical gratification.
   B. existential anxiety.
   C. striving for superiority.
   D. the need for power.

5. Which of the following learning mechanisms does B. F. Skinner see as being the major means by which behavior is learned?
   A. Classical conditioning
   B. Operant conditioning
   C. Observational learning
   D. Insight learning

6. Always having been a good student, Irving is confident that he will do well in his psychology course. According to Bandura's social cognitive theory, Irving would be said to have:
   A. strong feelings of self-efficacy.
   B. a sense of superiority.
   C. strong feelings of narcissism.
   D. strong defense mechanisms.

7. Which of the following is a criticism of the behavioral approach to personality?
   A. Behaviorists overgeneralize from animal research.
   B. Behaviorists place too much emphasis on biological factors.
   C. Behaviorists value empirical research.
   D. Behaviorists provide an overly holistic, optimistic view of personality.

8. Which of the following approaches to personality is least deterministic?
   A. The humanistic approach
   B. The psychoanalytic approach
   C. The social learning approach
   D. The behavioral approach

9. Which of the following did Carl Rogers believe fosters a congruent self-concept?
   A. Conditional love
   B. Appropriate role models
   C. Immediate need gratification
   D. Unconditional love

10. What need was Abraham Maslow expressing when he said, "What a man can be, he must be"?
    A. The need for superiority
    B. The need for unconditional love
    C. The need for self-actualization
    D. The need to achieve

11. The strongest support for the theory that personality is heavily influenced by genetics is provided by strong personality similarity between:
    A. identical twins reared together.
    B. identical twins reared apart.
    C. fraternal twins reared together.
    D. nontwins reared together.

12. In which of the following cultures is an independent view of the self most likely to be the norm?
    A. China
    B. Japan
    C. Korea
    D. United States

13. Which of the following is *not* a shortcoming of self-report personality inventories?
    A. The accuracy of the results is a function of the honesty of the respondent.
    B. Respondents may attempt to answer in a way that makes them look good.
    C. There is sometimes a problem with "yea-sayers" or "nay-sayers."
    D. They are objective measures.

14. Which of the following is a projective test?
    A. The Rorschach Inkblot Test
    B. The Minnesota Multiphasic Personality Inventory
    C. Cattell's 16 Personality Factor Questionnaire
    D. The NEO Personality Inventory

15. In *The Nurture Assumption,* Judith Harris argues that the evidence indicates that family environment has _____ on children's personalities.
    A. largely positive effects
    B. largely negative effects
    C. surprisingly little effect
    D. a powerful effect

Answers
1 C p. 342   6 A p. 351   11 B pp. 357–358
2 A pp. 344–345   7 A p. 352   12 D pp. 361, 364
3 C pp. 346–347   8 A p. 352   13 D pp. 365–366
4 C p. 348   9 D p. 353   14 A p. 366
5 B p. 350   10 C p. 355   15 C p. 369

PsykTrek
Go to the PsykTrek website or CD-ROM for further study of the concepts in this chapter. Both online and on the CD-ROM, PsykTrek includes dozens of learning modules with videos, animations, and quizzes, as well as simulations of psychological phenomena and a multimedia glossary that includes word pronunciations.

ThomsonNOW
www.thomsonedu.com/ThomsonNOW
Go to this site for the link to ThomsonNOW, your one-stop study shop. Take a Pre-Test for this chapter, and ThomsonNOW will generate a Personalized Study Plan based on your test results. The Study Plan will identify the topics you need to review and direct you to online resources to help you master those topics. You can then take a Post-Test to help you determine the concepts you have mastered and what you still need to work on.

Companion Website
www.thomsonedu.com/psychology/weiten
Go to this site to find online resources directly linked to your book, including a glossary, flash cards, drag-and-drop exercises, quizzes, and more!

CHAPTER 12

Stress, Coping, and Health

© Alan Schein Photography/Corbis

You're in your car headed home from school with a classmate. Traffic is barely moving. A radio report indicates that the traffic jam is only going to get worse. You groan as you fiddle impatiently with the radio dial. Another motorist nearly takes your fender off trying to cut into your lane. Your pulse quickens as you shout insults at the unknown driver, who can't even hear you. You think about the term paper that you have to work on tonight. Your stomach knots up as you think about all the research you still have to do. If you don't finish that paper soon, you won't be able to find any time to study for your math test, not to mention your biology quiz. Suddenly, you remember that you promised the person you're dating that the two of you would get together tonight. There's no way. Another fight looms on the horizon. Your classmate asks how you feel about the tuition increase that the college announced yesterday. You've been trying not to think about it. You're already in debt up to your ears. Your parents are bugging you about changing schools, but you don't want to leave your friends. Your heartbeat quickens as you contemplate the debate you're sure to have with your parents. You feel wired with tension as you realize that the stress in your life never seems to let up.

Many circumstances can create stress. It comes in all sorts of packages: big and small, pretty and ugly, simple and complex. All too often, the package comes as a surprise. In this chapter we'll try to sort out these packages. We'll discuss the nature of stress, how people cope with stress, and the potential effects of stress.

Our examination of the relationship between stress and physical illness will lead us into a broader discussion of the psychology of health. The way people in health professions think about physical illness has changed considerably in the past 20 to 30 years. The traditional view of physical illness as a purely biological phenomenon has given way to a biopsychosocial model of illness. **The *biopsychosocial model* holds that physical illness is caused by a complex interaction of biological, psychological, and sociocultural factors.** This model does not suggest that biological factors are unimportant. It simply asserts that these factors operate in a psychological and social context that is also influential.

What has led to this shift in thinking? In part, it's a result of changing patterns of illness. Prior to the 20th century, the principal threats to health were *contagious diseases* caused by infectious agents—diseases such as smallpox, typhoid fever, diphtheria, yellow fever, malaria, cholera, tuberculosis, and polio. Today, none of these diseases are among the leading killers in the United States. They were tamed by improvements in nutrition, public hygiene, sanitation, and medical treatment. Unfortunately, the void left by contagious diseases has been filled all too quickly by *chronic diseases* that develop gradually, such as heart disease, cancer, and stroke (see **Figure 12.1**). Psycho-

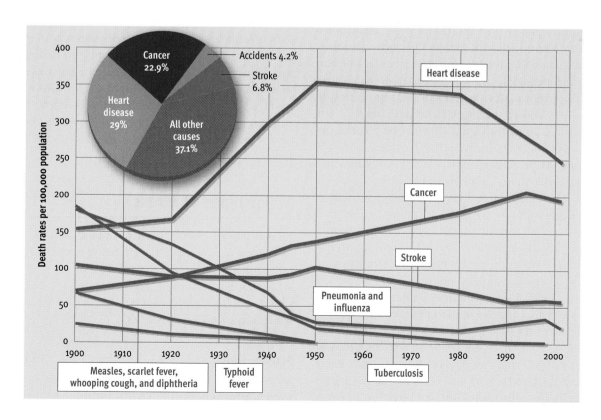

Figure 12.1

Changing patterns of illness. Trends in the death rates for various diseases during the 20th century reveal that contagious diseases (shown in blue) have declined as a threat to health. However, the death rates for stress-related chronic diseases (shown in red) have remained quite high. The pie chart (inset) shows the results of these trends: Three chronic diseases (heart disease, cancer, and stroke) account for almost 60% of all deaths. (Based on data from the U.S. National Center for Health Statistics)

social factors, such as stress and lifestyle, play a large role in the development of these chronic diseases.

The growing recognition that psychological factors influence physical health eventually led to the emergence of a new specialty in psychology. *Health psychology* **is concerned with how psychosocial factors relate to the promotion and maintenance** **of health and with the causation, prevention, and treatment of illness.** In the second half of this chapter, we'll explore this domain of psychology. In the Personal Application, we'll focus on strategies for enhancing stress management, and in the Critical Thinking Application we'll discuss strategies for improving health-related decision making.

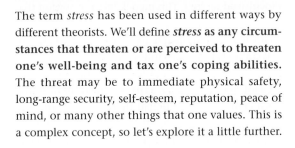

> The Nature of Stress

PREVIEW QUESTIONS

- How significant are minor, everyday stressors?
- How objective are our appraisals of stress?
- What is frustration?
- What are the three types of conflict?
- What evidence led to the conclusion that life changes are stressful?
- What is pressure?

The term *stress* has been used in different ways by different theorists. We'll define *stress* **as any circumstances that threaten or are perceived to threaten one's well-being and tax one's coping abilities.** The threat may be to immediate physical safety, long-range security, self-esteem, reputation, peace of mind, or many other things that one values. This is a complex concept, so let's explore it a little further.

Stress as an Everyday Event

The word *stress* tends to spark images of overwhelming, traumatic crises. People may think of terrorist attacks, hurricanes, military combat, and nuclear accidents. Undeniably, major disasters of this sort are extremely stressful (Brende, 2000; Raphael & Dobson, 2000). However, these unusual events are only a small part of what constitutes stress. Many everyday events such as waiting in line, having car trouble, shopping for Christmas presents, misplacing your checkbook, and staring at bills you can't pay are also stressful. Of course, major and minor stressors are not entirely independent. A major stressful event, such as going through a divorce, can trigger a cascade of minor stressors, such as looking for an attorney, taking on new household responsibilities, and so forth (Pillow, Zautra, & Sandler, 1996).

You might guess that minor stresses would produce minor effects, but that isn't necessarily true. Richard Lazarus and his colleagues, who developed a scale to measure everyday hassles, have shown that routine hassles may have significant harmful effects on mental and physical health (Delongis, Folkman, & Lazarus, 1988; Johnson & Sherman, 1997). Why would minor hassles be related to mental health? The answer isn't entirely clear yet, but it may be because of the *cumulative* nature of stress (Seta, Seta, & McElroy, 2002). Stress adds up. Routine stresses at home, at school, and at work might be fairly benign individually, but collectively they could create great strain.

RICHARD LAZARUS

"We developed the Hassle Scale because we think scales that measure major events miss the point. The constant, minor irritants may be much more important than the large, landmark changes."

Courtesy of Richard S. Lazarus

Appraisal: Stress Lies in the Eye of the Beholder

The experience of feeling stressed depends on what events one notices and how one appraises them (Lazarus, 1999; Semmer, McGrath, & Beehr, 2005). Events that are stressful for one person may be routine for another. For example, many people find flying in an airplane somewhat stressful, but frequent fliers may not be bothered at all. Some people enjoy the excitement of going out on a date with someone new; others find the uncertainty terrifying.

Often, people aren't very objective in their appraisals of potentially stressful events. A study of hospitalized patients awaiting surgery showed only a slight correlation between the objective seriousness of a person's upcoming surgery and the amount of fear experienced by the patient (Janis, 1958). Clearly, some people are more prone than others to feel threatened by life's difficulties. A number of studies have shown that anxious, neurotic people report more stress than others (Cooper & Bright, 2001; Watson, David, & Suls, 1999), as do people who are relatively unhappy (Seidlitz & Diener, 1993). Thus, stress lies in the eye (actually, the mind) of the beholder. People's appraisals of stressful events are highly subjective.

Major Types of Stress

An enormous variety of events can be stressful for one person or another. Although they're not entirely independent, the four principal types of stress are (1) frustration, (2) conflict, (3) change, and (4) pressure. As you read about each type, you'll surely recognize some familiar adversaries.

Frustration

As psychologists use the term, *frustration* **is experienced whenever the pursuit of some goal is** thwarted. In essence, you experience frustration when you want something and you can't have it. Everyone has to deal with frustration virtually every day. Traffic jams, difficult daily commutes, and annoying drivers, for instance, are a routine source of frustration that can elicit anger and aggression (Hennessy & Wiesenthal, 1999; Rasmussen, Knapp, & Garner, 2000). Fortunately, most frustrations are brief and insignificant. You may be quite upset when you go to a repair shop to pick up your ailing laptop and find that it hasn't been fixed as promised. However, a week later you'll probably have your computer back, and the frustration will be forgotten. Of course, some frustrations—such as failing to get a promotion at work or losing a boyfriend or girlfriend—can be sources of significant stress.

Conflict

Like frustration, conflict is an unavoidable feature of everyday life. The perplexing question "Should I or shouldn't I?" comes up countless times in one's life. **_Conflict_ occurs when two or more incompatible motivations or behavioral impulses compete for expression.** As we discussed in Chapter 11, Sigmund Freud proposed a century ago that internal conflicts generate considerable psychological distress. This link between conflict and distress was measured with new precision in studies by Laura King and Robert Emmons (1990, 1991). They used an elaborate questionnaire to assess the overall amount of internal conflict experienced by subjects. They found that higher levels of conflict were associated with higher levels of anxiety, depression, and physical symptoms.

Conflicts come in three types, which were originally described by Kurt Lewin (1935) and investigated extensively by Neal Miller (1944, 1959). These three basic types of conflict—approach-approach, avoidance-avoidance, and approach-avoidance—are diagrammed in **Figure 12.2**.

In an _approach-approach conflict_ a choice must be made between two attractive goals. The problem, of course, is that you can choose just one of the two goals. For example: You have a free afternoon—should you play tennis or racquetball? You can't afford both the blue sweater and the gray jacket—which should you buy? Among the three kinds of conflict, the approach-approach type tends to be the least stressful. Nonetheless, approach-approach conflicts over important issues may sometimes be troublesome. If you're torn between two appealing college majors or two attractive boyfriends, for example, you may find the decision-making process quite stressful.

In an _avoidance-avoidance conflict_ a choice must be made between two unattractive goals. Forced to choose between two repellent alternatives, you are, as they say, "caught between a rock and a hard place." For example, should you continue to collect unemployment checks, or should you take that boring job at the car wash? Or suppose you have painful backaches. Should you submit to surgery that you dread, or should you continue to live with the pain? Obviously, avoidance-avoidance conflicts are most unpleasant and highly stressful.

In an _approach-avoidance conflict_ a choice must be made about whether to pursue a single goal that has both attractive and unattractive aspects. For instance, imagine that you're offered a promotion that will mean a large increase in pay, but you'll have to move to a city that you hate. Approach-avoidance conflicts are common and can be quite stressful. Any time you have to take a risk to pursue some desirable outcome, you're likely to find yourself in an approach-avoidance conflict. Should you risk rejection by approaching that attractive person in class? Should you risk your savings by investing in a new business that could fail? Approach-avoidance conflicts often produce _vacillation_ (Miller, 1944). That is, you go back and forth, beset by indecision. You decide to go ahead, then you decide not to, and then you decide to go ahead again.

Change

Thomas Holmes and Richard Rahe have led the way in exploring the idea that life changes—including positive events, such as getting married or getting promoted—represent a key type of stress. **_Life changes_ are any noticeable alterations in one's living circumstances that require readjustment.** Based on

Web Link 12.1

The Web's Stress Management and Emotional Wellness Page
Ernesto Randolfi (Montana State University) has gathered a comprehensive set of resources dealing with stress management. Topics covered include cognitive restructuring, relaxation techniques, and stress in the workplace and in college life.

Figure 12.2

Types of conflict. Psychologists have identified three basic types of conflict. In approach-approach and avoidance-avoidance conflicts, a person is torn between two goals. In an approach-avoidance conflict, there is only one goal under consideration, but it has both positive and negative aspects.

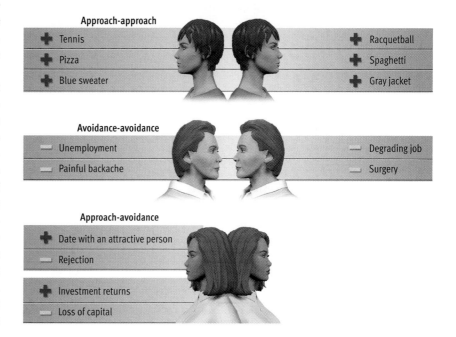

Identifying Types of Conflict

Check your understanding of the three basic types of conflict by identifying the type experienced in each of the following examples. The answers are in Appendix A.

Examples

_____ **1.** John can't decide whether to take a boring job in a car wash or to go on welfare.

_____ **2.** Desiree wants to apply to a highly selective law school, but she hates to risk the possibility of rejection.

_____ **3.** Vanessa has been shopping for a new car and is torn between a nifty little sports car and a classy sedan, both of which she really likes.

Types of conflict

a. approach-approach

b. avoidance-avoidance

c. approach-avoidance

The SRRS and similar scales based on it have been used in thousands of studies by researchers all over the world. Overall, these studies have shown that people with higher scores tend to be more vulnerable to many kinds of physical illness and to many types of psychological problems as well (Derogatis & Coons, 1993: Gruen, 1993; Scully, Tosi, & Banning, 2000). These results have attracted a great deal of attention, and the SRRS has been reprinted in many popular newspapers and magazines. The attendant publicity has led to the widespread conclusion that life change is inherently stressful.

However, experts have criticized this research, citing problems with the methods used and problems in interpreting the findings (Hobson & Delunas, 2001; Jones & Kinman, 2001; Wethington, 2000). At this point, it's a key interpretive issue that concerns us. A variety of critics have collected evidence showing that the SRRS does not measure _change_ exclusively (McLean & Link, 1994; Turner & Wheaton, 1995). In reality, it assesses a wide range of kinds of stressful experiences. Thus, we have little reason to believe that change is _inherently_ or _inevitably_ stressful. Undoubtedly, some life changes may be quite challenging, but others may be quite benign.

Pressure 11f

At one time or another, most people have remarked that they're "under pressure." What does this mean? _Pressure_ **involves expectations or demands that one behave in a certain way.** You are under pressure

their theory, Holmes and Rahe (1967) developed the Social Readjustment Rating Scale (SRRS) to measure life change as a form of stress. The scale assigns numerical values to 43 major life events. These values are supposed to reflect the magnitude of the readjustment required by each change (see Table 12.1). In using the scale, respondents are asked to indicate how often they experienced any of these 43 events during a certain time period (typically, the past year). The numbers associated with each checked event are then added. This total is an index of the amount of change-related stress the person has recently experienced.

Table 12.1 Social Readjustment Rating Scale

Life Event	Mean Value	Life Event	Mean Value
Death of a spouse	100	Change in responsibilities at work	29
Divorce	73	Son or daughter leaving home	29
Marital separation	65	Trouble with in-laws	29
Jail term	63	Outstanding personal achievement	28
Death of a close family member	63	Spouse begins or stops work	26
Personal injury or illness	53	Begin or end school	26
Marriage	50	Change in living conditions	25
Fired at work	47	Revision of personal habits	24
Marital reconciliation	45	Trouble with boss	23
Retirement	45	Change in work hours or conditions	20
Change in health of family member	44	Change in residence	20
Pregnancy	40	Change in school	20
Sex difficulties	39	Change in recreation	19
Gain of a new family member	39	Change in church activities	19
Business readjustment	39	Change in social activities	18
Change in financial state	38	Mortgage or loan for lesser purchase (car, TV, etc.)	17
Death of a close friend	37	Change in sleeping habits	16
Change to a different line of work	36	Change in number of family get-togethers	15
Change in number of arguments with spouse	35	Change in eating habits	15
Mortgage or loan for major purchase (home, etc.)	31	Vacation	13
		Christmas	12
Foreclosure of mortgage or loan	30	Minor violations of the law	11

Source: Adapted from Holmes, T. H., & Rahe, R. (1967). The Social Readjustment Rating Scale. _Journal of Psychosomatic Research, 11,_ 213–218. Copyright © 1967 by Elsevier. Reprinted by permission.

Recognizing Sources of Stress

Check your understanding of the major sources of stress by indicating which type or types of stress are at work in each of the examples below. Bear in mind that the four basic types of stress are not mutually exclusive. There's some potential for overlap, so a specific experience might include both change and pressure, for instance. The answers are in Appendix A.

Examples

_____ **1.** Marie is stuck in line at the bank.

_____ **2.** Tamika decides that she won't be satisfied unless she gets straight A's this year.

_____ **3.** Jose has just graduated from business school and has taken an exciting new job.

_____ **4.** Morris has just been fired from his job and needs to find another.

Types of stress

a. frustration

b. conflict

c. change

d. pressure

---

to *perform* when you're expected to execute tasks and responsibilities quickly, efficiently, and successfully. For example, salespeople are usually under pressure to move merchandise. Professors at research institutions are often under pressure to publish in respected journals. Stand-up comedians are under intense pressure to make people laugh. Pressures to *conform* to others' expectations are also common in our lives. Businessmen are expected to wear suits and ties. Suburban homeowners are expected to keep their yards well groomed. Teenagers are expected to respect their parents' values and rules.

Although widely discussed by the general public, the concept of pressure has received scant attention from researchers. However, Weiten (1988b, 1998) has devised a scale to measure pressure as a form of life stress. It assesses self-imposed pressure, pressure from work and school, and pressure from family relations, peer relations, and intimate relations. In research with this scale, a strong relationship has been found between pressure and a variety of psychological symptoms and problems. In fact, pressure has turned out to be more strongly related to measures of mental health than the SRRS and other established measures of stress.

> Responding to Stress

The human response to stress is complex and multidimensional. Stress affects the individual at several levels. Consider again the chapter's opening scenario, in which you're driving home in heavy traffic and thinking about overdue papers, tuition increases, and parental pressures. Let's look at some of the reactions that were mentioned. When you groan in reaction to the traffic report, you're experiencing an *emotional response* to stress, in this case annoyance and anger. When your pulse quickens and your stomach knots up, you're exhibiting *physiological responses* to stress. When you shout insults at another driver, your verbal aggression is a *behavioral response* to the stress at hand. Thus, we can analyze a person's reactions to stress at three levels: (1) emotional responses, (2) physiological responses, and (3) behavioral responses. **Figure 12.3** on the next page provides an overview of the stress process.

Emotional Responses

When people are under stress, they often react emotionally. Studies that have tracked stress and mood on a daily basis have found intimate relationships between the two (Affleck et al., 1994; van Eck, Nicolson, & Berkhof, 1998).

Emotions Commonly Elicited

No simple one-to-one connections have been found between certain types of stressful events and particular emotions. However, researchers *have* begun to uncover some strong links between *specific cognitive reactions to stress* (appraisals) and specific emotions (Smith & Lazarus, 1993). For example, self-blame tends to lead to guilt, helplessness to sadness, and so forth. Although many emotions can be evoked by

PREVIEW QUESTIONS

- What are some common emotional reactions to stress?

- How does emotional arousal affect performance?

- What are the three stages of the general adaptation syndrome?

- What tends to happen physiologically when people feel stressed?

- What are some relatively unhealthful coping responses?

- How do defense mechanisms work and can they be adaptive?

- What is constructive coping?

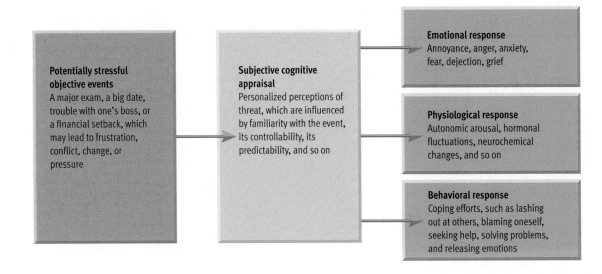

Figure 12.3
Overview of the stress process. A potentially stressful event, such as a major exam, elicits a subjective appraisal of how threatening the event is. If the event is viewed with alarm, the stress may trigger emotional, physiological, and behavioral reactions, as people's response to stress is multi-dimensional.

Web Link 12.2

Stress Management
University of Nebraska Professor Wesley E. Sime has posted outlines and notes of his lectures on the fundamentals of stress management and on other topics related to stress and its impact on health and performance.

Web Link 12.3

Centre for Stress Management
This British site houses a diverse collection of brief online articles concerned with many aspects of the stress process. It also features links to many additional sites around the world that provide information on stress.

stressful events, some are certainly more likely than others. Common emotional responses to stress include (a) annoyance, anger, and rage, (b) apprehension, anxiety, and fear, and (c) dejection, sadness, and grief (Lazarus, 1993; Woolfolk & Richardson, 1978).

Although investigators have tended to focus heavily on the connection between stress and negative emotions, research shows that positive emotions also occur during periods of stress (Folkman, 1997). Although this finding seems counterintuitive, researchers have found that people experience a diverse array of pleasant emotions even while enduring the most dire of circumstances. Consider, for example, the results of a five-year study of coping patterns in 253 caregiving partners of men with AIDS (Folkman et al., 1997). Surprisingly, over the course of the study, the caregivers reported experiencing positive emotions about as often as they experienced negative emotions—except during the time immediately surrounding the death of their partners.

Similar findings have been observed in some other studies of serious stress that made an effort to look for positive emotions. The most interesting of these was a recent study that examined subjects' emotional functioning early in 2001 and again in the weeks following the 9/11 terrorist attacks in the United States (Fredrickson et al., 2003). Like most U.S. citizens, these subjects reported many negative emotions in the aftermath of 9/11, including anger, sadness, and fear. However, within this "dense cloud of anguish" positive emotions also emerged. For example, people felt gratitude for the safety of their loved ones, many took stock and counted their blessings, and quite a few reported renewed love for their friends and family. Fredrickson et al. (2003) also found that the frequency of pleasant emotions correlated positively with a measure of subjects' resilience, whereas the frequency of unpleasant emotions

correlated negatively with resilience (see Table 12.2). Thus, contrary to common sense, positive emotions do *not* vanish during times of severe stress. Moreover, these positive emotions appear to play a key role in helping people bounce back from the difficulties associated with stress (Tugade & Fredrickson, 2004).

Effects of Emotional Arousal

Emotional responses are a natural and normal part of life. Even unpleasant emotions serve important purposes. Like physical pain, painful emotions can serve as warnings that one needs to take action. However, strong emotional arousal can also interfere with efforts to cope with stress. For example, there's evidence that high emotional arousal can interfere with attention and memory retrieval and can impair judgment and decision making (Janis, 1993; Mandler, 1993).

Table 12.2 Correlation Between Resilience and the Frequency of Selected Emotions in the Aftermath of 9/11

Specific Emotions	Correlation with Resilience
Negative Emotions	
Angry/irritated/annoyed	−.44*
Sad/downhearted/unhappy	−.29*
Scared/fearful/afraid	−.19
Disgust/distaste/revulsion	−.09
Positive Emotions	
Grateful/appreciative/thankful	.13
Glad/happy/joyful	.52*
Hopeful/optimistic/encouraged	.40*
Content/serene/peaceful	.47*

*Statistically significant

Although emotional arousal may hurt coping efforts, that isn't *necessarily* the case. The *inverted-U hypothesis* predicts that task performance should improve with increased emotional arousal—up to a point, after which further increases in arousal become disruptive and performance deteriorates (Anderson, 1990; Mandler, 1993). This idea is referred to as the inverted-U hypothesis because when performance is plotted as a function of arousal, the resulting graphs approximate an upside-down U (see **Figure 12.4**). In these graphs, the level of arousal at which performance peaks is characterized as the *optimal level of arousal* for a task.

This optimal level of arousal appears to depend in part on the complexity of the task at hand. The conventional wisdom is that *as a task becomes more complex, the optimal level of arousal (for peak performance) tends to decrease*. This relationship is depicted in **Figure 12.4**. As you can see, a fairly high level of arousal should be optimal on simple tasks (such as driving 8 hours to help a friend in a crisis). However, performance should peak at a lower level of arousal on complex tasks (such as making a major decision in which you have to weigh many factors).

The research evidence on the inverted-U hypothesis is inconsistent and subject to varied interpretations (Neiss, 1988, 1990). Nonetheless, the inverted-U hypothesis provides a plausible model of how emotional arousal could have either beneficial or disruptive effects on coping, depending on the nature of the stressful demands one encounters.

Physiological Responses

As we just discussed, stress frequently elicits strong emotional responses. Now we'll look at the important physiological changes that often accompany these emotions.

The General Adaptation Syndrome

Concern about the physical effects of stress was first voiced by Hans Selye (1936, 1956, 1982), a Canadian scientist who launched stress research many decades ago. Selye was born in Vienna but spent his entire professional career at McGill University in Montreal. Beginning in the 1930s, Selye exposed laboratory animals to a diverse array of both physical and psychological stressors (heat, cold, pain, mild shock, restraint, and so on). The patterns of physiological arousal seen in the animals were largely the same, regardless of the type of stress. Thus, Selye concluded that stress reactions are *nonspecific*. In other words, he maintained that the reactions do not vary according to the specific type of stress encountered. Initially, Selye wasn't sure what to call this nonspecific response to a variety of noxious agents. In the 1940s he decided to call it *stress*, and the word has been part of our vocabulary ever since.

Selye (1956, 1974) explained stress reactions in terms of the general adaptation syndrome. **The *general adaptation syndrome* is a model of the body's stress response, consisting of three stages: alarm, resistance, and exhaustion.** In the first stage, an *alarm reaction* occurs when an organism first recognizes the existence of a threat: physiological arousal occurs as the body musters its resources to combat the challenge. Selye's alarm reaction is essentially the fight-or-flight response described in Chapters 3 and 9.

However, Selye took his investigation of stress a few steps further by exposing laboratory animals to *prolonged stress,* similar to the chronic stress often endured by humans. As stress continues, the organism may progress to the second phase of the general adaptation syndrome, the *stage of resistance*. During this phase, physiological changes stabilize as coping efforts get under way. Typically, physiological arousal continues to be higher than normal, although it may

HANS SELYE

"There are two main types of human beings: 'racehorses,' who thrive on stress and are only happy with a vigorous, fast-paced lifestyle; and 'turtles,' who in order to be happy require peace, quiet, and a generally tranquil environment."

Figure 12.4

Arousal and performance. Graphs of the relationship between emotional arousal and task performance tend to resemble an inverted U, as increased arousal is associated with improved performance up to a point, after which higher arousal leads to poorer performance. The optimal level of arousal for a task depends on the complexity of the task. On complex tasks, a relatively low level of arousal tends to be optimal. On simple tasks, however, performance may peak at a much higher level of arousal.

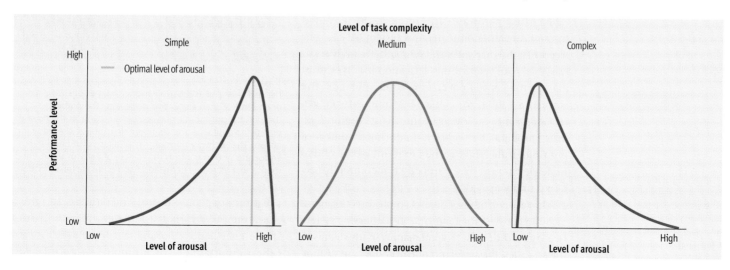

DILBERT

FREE BLOOD PRESSURE SCREENING TODAY

135 OVER 88.

YOU'RE BELOW THE COMPANY AVERAGE. HERE'S SOME MORE WORK.

HOW LONG DID YOU THINK YOU COULD GET AWAY WITH THAT?

DILBERT © Scott Adams/Distributed by United Features Syndicate, Inc.

Web Link 12.4

The American Institute of Stress
The American Institute of Stress is a nonprofit organization established in 1978 at the request of stress pioneer Hans Selye. Its Board of Trustees reads like a who's who of stress research. The resources available online are a bit limited, as you have to send for the information packets published by the institute. But there is a very interesting online tribute to Selye.

level off somewhat as the organism becomes accustomed to the threat.

If the stress continues over a substantial period of time, the organism may enter the third stage, the *stage of exhaustion.* According to Selye, the body's resources for fighting stress are limited. If the stress can't be overcome, the body's resources may be depleted, and physiological arousal will decrease. Eventually, the organism may collapse from exhaustion. During this phase, the organism's resistance declines. This reduced resistance may lead to what Selye called "diseases of adaptation."

Brain-Body Pathways

11g

Even in cases of moderate stress, you may notice that your heart has started beating faster, you've begun to breathe harder, and you're perspiring more than usual. How does all this (and much more) happen? It appears that there are two major pathways along which the brain sends signals to the endocrine system (Dallman, Bhatnagar, & Viau, 2000; Tsigos, Kyrou, & Chrousos, 2005). As we noted in Chapter 3, the *endocrine system* consists of glands located at various sites in the body that secrete chemicals called *hormones.* The hypothalamus is the part of the brain that appears to initiate action along these two pathways.

The first pathway (see **Figure 12.5**) is routed through the autonomic nervous system (ANS). Your hypothalamus activates the sympathetic division of the ANS. A key part of this activation involves stimulating the central part of the adrenal glands (the adrenal medulla) to release large amounts of *catecholamines* into the bloodstream. These hormones radiate throughout your body, producing a number of physiological changes. The net result of catecholamine elevation is that your body is mobilized for action (Lundberg, 2000).

The second pathway involves more direct communication between the brain and the endocrine system (see **Figure 12.5**). The hypothalamus sends signals to the so-called master gland of the endocrine system,

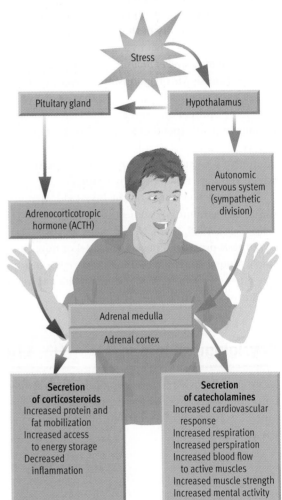

Stress

Pituitary gland

Hypothalamus

Adrenocorticotropic hormone (ACTH)

Autonomic nervous system (sympathetic division)

Adrenal medulla

Adrenal cortex

Secretion of corticosteroids
Increased protein and fat mobilization
Increased access to energy storage
Decreased inflammation

Secretion of catecholamines
Increased cardiovascular response
Increased respiration
Increased perspiration
Increased blood flow to active muscles
Increased muscle strength
Increased mental activity

Figure 12.5
Brain-body pathways in stress. In times of stress, the brain sends signals along two pathways. The pathway through the autonomic nervous system controls the release of catecholamine hormones that help mobilize the body for action. The pathway through the pituitary gland and the endocrine system controls the release of corticosteroid hormones that increase energy and ward off tissue inflammation.

the pituitary gland. In turn, the pituitary secretes a hormone (ACTH) that stimulates the outer part of the adrenal glands (the adrenal cortex) to release another important set of hormones—*corticosteroids.*

These hormones stimulate the release of chemicals that help increase your energy and help inhibit tissue inflammation in case of injury (Munck, 2000).

Thus, it's becoming clear that physiological responses to stress extend into all parts of the body. As you'll see later, these physiological reactions can affect people's health.

Behavioral Responses

 11g

Although people respond to stress at several levels, it's clear that behavior is the crucial dimension of their reactions. Most behavioral responses to stress involve coping. *Coping* **refers to efforts to master, reduce, or tolerate the demands created by stress.** Notice that this definition is neutral as to whether coping efforts are healthful or maladaptive. The popular use of the term often implies that coping is inherently healthful. When people say that someone "coped with her problems," the implication is that she handled them effectively.

In reality, however, coping responses may be adaptive or maladaptive (Moos & Schaefer, 1993; Vaillant, 2000). For example, if you were flunking a history course at midterm, you might cope with this stress by (1) increasing your study efforts, (2) seeking help from a tutor, (3) blaming your professor, or (4) giving up on the class without really trying. Clearly, the first two of these coping responses would be more adaptive than the last two.

People cope with stress in many ways, but most individuals exhibit certain styles of coping that are fairly consistent across situations (Carver & Scheier, 1994; Heszen-Niejodek, 1997). Given the immense variety in coping strategies, we can only highlight some of the more common patterns of coping. In this section we'll focus most of our attention on styles of coping that tend to be less than ideal. We'll discuss more healthful coping strategies in the Personal Application on stress management.

Giving Up and Blaming Oneself

 11g

When confronted with stress, people sometimes simply give up and withdraw from the battle. Some people routinely respond to stress with fatalism and resignation, passively accepting setbacks that might be dealt with effectively. This syndrome is referred to as *learned helplessness* (Seligman, 1974, 1992). *Learned helplessness* **is passive behavior produced by exposure to unavoidable aversive events.** Learned helplessness seems to occur when individuals come to believe that events are beyond their control. As you might guess, giving up is not a highly regarded method of coping. Carver and his colleagues (1989,

concept check 12.3

Tracing Brain-Body Pathways in Stress

Check your understanding of the two major pathways along which the brain sends signals to the endocrine system in the event of stress by separating the eight terms below into two sets of four and arranging each set in the appropriate sequence. You'll find the answers in Appendix A.

ACTH	catecholamines	pituitary
adrenal cortex	corticosteriods	sympathetic division of the ANS
adrenal medulla	hypothalamus	

Pathway 1

_____

_____

_____

_____

Pathway 2

_____

_____

_____

_____

1993) have studied this coping strategy, which they refer to as *behavioral disengagement,* and found that it is associated with increased rather than decreased distress. Furthermore, many studies suggest that learned helplessness can contribute to depression (Seligman & Isaacowitz, 2000).

Blaming oneself is another common response when people are confronted by stressful difficulties. The tendency to become highly self-critical in response to stress has been noted by a number of influential theorists. Albert Ellis (1973, 1987) calls this phenomenon "catastrophic thinking." According to Ellis, catastrophic thinking causes, aggravates, and perpetuates emotional reactions to stress that are often problematic (see the Personal Application for this chapter). In a similar vein, Aaron Beck (1976, 1987) argues that negative thinking can contribute to the development of depressive disorders (see Chapter 14). Although there is something to be said for recognizing one's weaknesses and taking responsibility for one's failures, Ellis and Beck maintain that excessive self-blame can be very unhealthy.

Striking Out at Others

 11g

People often respond to stressful events by striking out at others with aggressive behavior. *Aggression* **is any behavior that is intended to hurt someone, either physically or verbally.** Many years ago, a team of psychologists (Dollard et al., 1939) proposed the *frustration-aggression hypothesis,* which held that aggression is always caused by frustration. Decades of research have supported this idea of a causal link between frustration and aggression (Berkowitz, 1989). However, this research has also shown that there isn't an inevitable, one-to-one correspondence between the two.

ALBERT ELLIS
"People largely disturb themselves by thinking in a self-defeating, illogical, and unrealistic manner."

Courtesy, Albert Ellis Institute

© Paul Thomas/The Image Bank/Getty Images

Lashing out at others with verbal aggression tends to be an ineffective coping tactic that often backfires, creating additional stress.

Freud theorized that behaving aggressively could get pent-up emotion out of one's system and thus be adaptive. He coined the term *catharsis* **to refer to this release of emotional tension.** The Freudian notion that it is a good idea to vent anger has become widely disseminated and accepted in modern society. Books, magazines, and self-appointed experts routinely advise that it is healthy to "blow off steam" and thereby release and reduce anger. However, experimental research generally has *not* supported the catharsis hypothesis. Indeed, *most studies find just the opposite: Behaving in an aggressive manner tends to fuel more anger and aggression* (Bushman, 2002; Bushman, Baumeister, & Stack, 1999).

Indulging Oneself

Stress sometimes leads to reduced impulse control, or *self-indulgence* (Tice, Bratslavsky, & Baumeister, 2001). When troubled by stress, many people engage in excessive or unwise patterns of eating, drinking, smoking, using drugs, spending money, and so forth. It makes sense that when things are going poorly in one area of their lives, people may try to compensate by pursuing substitute forms of satisfaction. Thus, it's not surprising that studies have linked stress to increases in eating (Laitinen, Ek, & Sovio, 2002), smoking (Kassel, Stroud, & Paronis, 2003), and consumption of alcohol and drugs (Colder, 2001; Goeders, 2004).

A new manifestation of this coping strategy that has attracted much attention recently is the ten-dency to immerse oneself in the online world of the Internet. Kimberly Young (1996, 1998) has described a syndrome called *Internet addiction,* **which consists of spending an inordinate amount of time on the Internet and inability to control online use.** People who exhibit this syndrome tend to feel anxious, depressed, or empty when they are not online (Kandell, 1998). Their Internet use is so excessive, it begins to interfere with their functioning at work, at school, or at home, which leads victims to start concealing the extent of their dependence on the Internet. It is difficult to estimate the prevalence of Internet addiction, but the syndrome does *not* appear to be rare (Greenfield, 1999; Morahan-Martin & Schumacher, 2000). Research suggests that Internet addiction is not limited to shy, male computer whizzes, as one might expect (Young, 1998). Although there is active debate about the wisdom of characterizing excessive Internet surfing as an *addiction* (Griffiths, 1999), it is clear that this new coping pattern is likely to become increasingly common.

Defensive Coping

Many people exhibit consistent styles of defensive coping in response to stress (Vaillant, 1994). We noted in the previous chapter that Sigmund Freud originally developed the concept of the *defense mechanism*. Though rooted in the psychoanalytic tradition, this concept has gained widespread acceptance from psychologists of most persuasions (Cramer, 2000). Building on Freud's initial insights, modern psychologists have broadened the scope of the concept and added to Freud's list of defense mechanisms.

Defense mechanisms **are largely unconscious reactions that protect a person from unpleasant emotions such as anxiety and guilt.** Many specific defense mechanisms have been identified. For example, Laughlin (1979) lists 49 different defenses. We described 7 common defense mechanisms in our discussion of Freud's theory in the previous chapter: repression, projection, displacement, reaction forma-

CATHY

CATHY © Cathy Guisewite. Reprinted with permission of UNIVERSAL PRESS SYNDICATE. All rights reserved.

tion, regression, rationalization, and identification (consult **Table 11.1** on p. 345).

The main purpose of defense mechanisms is to shield individuals from the emotional discomfort so often elicited by stress. They accomplish this purpose through *self-deception,* distorting reality so that it doesn't appear so threatening. Defense mechanisms operate at varying levels of awareness, although they're largely unconscious (Cramer, 2001; Erdelyi, 2001).

Generally, defensive coping is less than optimal because avoidance and wishful thinking rarely solve personal problems (Bolger, 1990; Holahan & Moos, 1990). That said, Shelley Taylor and Jonathon Brown (1988, 1994) have reviewed evidence suggesting that "positive illusions" may sometimes be adaptive for mental health. Some of the personal illusions that people create through defensive coping may help them deal with life's difficulties. Roy Baumeister (1989) theorizes that it's all a matter of degree and that there is an "optimal margin of illusion." According to Baumeister, extreme distortions of reality are maladaptive, but small illusions can be beneficial.

Constructive Coping

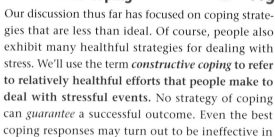 **11g**

Our discussion thus far has focused on coping strategies that are less than ideal. Of course, people also exhibit many healthful strategies for dealing with stress. We'll use the term ***constructive coping* to refer to relatively healthful efforts that people make to deal with stressful events.** No strategy of coping can *guarantee* a successful outcome. Even the best coping responses may turn out to be ineffective in

some circumstances. Thus, the concept of constructive coping is simply meant to convey a healthful, positive approach, without promising success.

What makes certain coping strategies constructive? Frankly, it's a gray area in which psychologists' opinions vary to some extent. Nonetheless, a consensus about the nature of constructive coping has emerged from the sizable literature on stress management. Key themes in this literature include the following:

1. Constructive coping involves confronting problems directly. It is task relevant and action oriented. It entails a conscious effort to rationally evaluate your options so that you can try to solve your problems.
2. Constructive coping is based on reasonably realistic appraisals of your stress and coping resources. A little self-deception may sometimes be adaptive, but excessive self-deception and highly unrealistic negative thinking are not.
3. Constructive coping involves learning to recognize, and in some cases inhibit, potentially disruptive emotional reactions to stress.
4. Constructive coping includes making efforts to ensure that your body is not especially vulnerable to the potentially damaging effects of stress.

The principles just described provide a rather general and abstract picture of constructive coping. We'll look at patterns of constructive coping in more detail in the Personal Application, which discusses various stress management strategies that people can use. We turn next to some of the possible outcomes of struggles with stress.

Courtesy of Shelley Taylor

SHELLEY TAYLOR

"Rather than perceiving themselves, the world, and the future accurately, most people regard themselves, their circumstances, and the future as considerably more positive than is objectively likely. . . . These illusions are not merely characteristic of human thought; they appear actually to be adaptive, promoting rather than undermining good mental health."

> Stress and Physical Health

People struggle with many stresses every day. Most stresses come and go without leaving any enduring imprint. However, when stress is severe or when many stressful demands pile up, one's mental or physical health may be affected. In Chapter 13 you'll learn that chronic stress contributes to many types of psychological disorders, including depression, schizophrenia, and anxiety disorders. In this section, we'll discuss the link between stress and physical illness.

Prior to the 1970s, it was thought that stress contributed to the development of only a few physical diseases, such as high blood pressure, ulcers, and asthma, which were called *psychosomatic diseases.* However, in the 1970s, research began to uncover new links between stress and a great variety of diseases previously believed to be purely physiological

in origin (Dougall & Baum, 2001; Hubbard & Workman, 1998). Let's look at some of this research.

Personality, Hostility, and Heart Disease

Heart disease accounts for nearly 30% of the deaths in the United States every year. *Coronary heart disease* involves a reduction in blood flow in the coronary arteries, which supply the heart with blood. This type of heart disease accounts for about 90% of heart-related deaths.

Atherosclerosis is the principal cause of coronary heart disease. This condition is characterized by a gradual narrowing of the coronary arteries. A buildup

PREVIEW QUESTIONS

- What is the Type A personality, and how is hostility related to heart disease?
- Can stress trigger emotional reactions that cause heart attacks?
- How is depression related to heart disease?
- How does stress affect immune functioning?
- How strong is the association between stress and illness?
- How are social support and optimism related to people's health?

Stress, Coping, and Health

of fatty deposits and other debris on the inner walls of the arteries is the usual cause of this narrowing. Atherosclerosis progresses slowly over a period of years. However, when a narrowed coronary artery is blocked completely (by a blood clot, for instance), the abrupt interruption of blood flow can produce a heart attack. Atherosclerosis is more prevalent in men than women and tends to increase with age. Other established risk factors for atherosclerosis include smoking, lack of exercise, high cholesterol levels, and high blood pressure (Greenland et al., 2003; Khot et al., 2003). Contrary to public perception, cardiovascular diseases kill women just as much as men, but these diseases tend to emerge in women abut 10 years later than in men (Stoney, 2003).

Recently, attention has shifted to the possibility that *inflammation* may contribute to atherosclerosis and elevated coronary risk (Hackam & Anand, 2003). Evidence is mounting that inflammation plays a key role in the initiation and progression of atherosclerosis, as well as the acute complications that trigger heart attacks (Albert et al., 2002; Libby, Ridker, & Maseri, 2002). Fortunately, researchers have found a marker—levels of C-reactive protein (CRP) in the blood—that may help physicians estimate individuals' coronary risk more accurately than was possible previously (Ridker et al., 2005).

Research on the relationship between *psychological* factors and heart attacks began in the 1960s and 1970s, when a pair of cardiologists, Meyer Friedman and Ray Rosenman (1974), discovered an apparent connection between coronary risk and a syndrome they called the *Type A personality,* which involves self-imposed stress and intense reactions to stress. **The *Type A personality* includes three elements: (1) a strong competitive orientation, (2) impatience and time urgency, and (3) anger and hostility.** Type A's are ambitious, hard-driving perfectionists who are exceedingly time-conscious. They routinely try to do several things at once. They fidget frantically over the briefest delays. Often they are highly competitive, achievement-oriented workaholics who drive themselves with many deadlines. They are easily irritated and are quick to anger. In contrast, **the *Type B personality* is marked by relatively relaxed, patient, easygoing, amicable behavior.** Type B's are less hurried, less competitive, and less easily angered than Type A's.

Decades of research uncovered a tantalizingly modest correlation between Type A behavior and increased coronary risk. More often than not, studies found a correlation between Type A personality and an elevated incidence of heart disease, but the findings were not as strong nor as consistent as expected (Ragland & Brand, 1988; Smith & Gallo, 2001). However, in recent years, researchers have found a stronger

People who are classified as being a Type A personality tend to be workaholics. They try to do several things at the same time, and they put themselves under constant time pressure. According to some theorists, the extra stress that such people experience may be associated with a higher risk of heart attack.

link between personality and coronary risk by focusing on a specific component of the Type A personality: *anger and hostility* (Eaker et al., 2004; Niaura et al., 2002). For example, in one study of almost 13,000 men and women who had no prior history of heart disease (Williams et al., 2000), investigators found an elevated incidence of heart attacks among participants who exhibited an angry temperament. The participants, who were followed for a median period of 4.5 years, were classified as being low (37.1% of the subjects), moderate (55.2%), or high (7.7%) in the tendency to experience anger. Among participants with normal blood pressure, the high-anger subjects experienced almost three times as many coronary events as the low-anger subjects (see **Figure 12.6**). In another study, CT scans were used to look for signs of atherosclerosis in a sample of 374 young men and women whose hostility had been assessed a decade earlier when they were 18 to 30 years old (Iribarren et al., 2000). Participants with above-average hostility scores were twice as likely to exhibit atherosclerosis as participants with below-average hostility scores. Thus, recent research suggests that hostility may be the crucial toxic element in the Type A syndrome.

Emotional Reactions, Depression, and Heart Disease

Although work on personality risk factors has dominated research on how psychological functioning

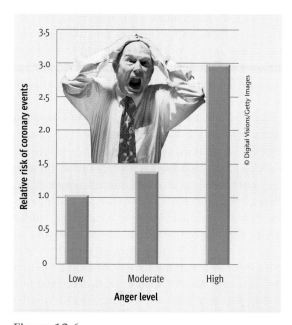

Figure 12.6

Anger and coronary risk. Working with a large sample of healthy men and women who were followed for a median of 4.5 years, Williams et al. (2000) found an association between participants' propensity to get angry and the likelihood of a coronary event. Among subjects who manifested normal blood pressure at the beginning of the study, a moderate anger level was associated with a 36% increase in coronary attacks, and a high level of anger nearly tripled participants' risk for coronary disease. (Based on data in Williams et al., 2000)

contributes to heart disease, recent studies suggest that emotional reactions may also be critical. *One line of research has supported the hypothesis that transient mental stress and the resulting emotions that people experience can tax the heart.* Based on anecdotal evidence, cardiologists and laypersons have long voiced suspicions that strong emotional reactions might trigger heart attacks in individuals with coronary disease, but it has been difficult to document this connection. However, advances in cardiac monitoring have facilitated investigation of the issue.

As suspected, laboratory experiments with cardiology patients have shown that brief periods of mental stress can trigger sudden symptoms of heart disease (Gottdiener et al., 1994). Overall, the evidence suggests that mental stress can elicit cardiac symptoms in about 30%–70% of patients with stable coronary disease (Kop, Gottdiener, & Krantz, 2001). Moreover, research indicates that these patients have a higher risk for heart attack than the cardiology patients who do not exhibit symptoms in response to mental stress (Krantz et al., 2000). In a study that approached the issue from another angle, 660 patients who experienced a nonfatal heart attack were subsequently interviewed about events that occurred in the 6 hours prior to the onset of their heart attack (Möller et al.,

1999). The interviews suggested that episodes of anger were a frequent trigger for the participants' heart attacks. Taken together, these studies suggest that emotional reactions to stressful events may precipitate heart attacks in people with coronary disease (Strike & Steptoe, 2005).

Another line of research has recently implicated depression as a risk factor for heart disease (Krantz & McCeney, 2002). *Depressive disorders,* which are characterized by persistent feelings of sadness and despair, are a fairly common form of mental illness (see Chapter 13). Elevated rates of depression have been found among patients suffering from heart disease in many studies, but most theorists explained this correlation by asserting that being diagnosed with heart disease makes people depressed. Recent evidence, however, suggests that the causal relations may be just the opposite—*that the emotional dysfunction of depression may cause heart disease* (Frasure-Smith & Lesperance, 2005; Thomas, Kalaria, & O'Brien, 2004). For example, Pratt et al. (1996) examined a large sample of people 13 years after they were screened for depression. They found that participants who were depressed at the time of the original study were four times more likely than others to experience a heart attack during the intervening 13 years. Since the participants' depressive disorders preceded their heart attacks, it can't be argued that their heart disease caused their depression. Overall, other studies have found that depression roughly doubles one's chances of developing heart disease (Lett et al., 2004; Rudisch & Nemeroff, 2003). Moreover, depression also appears to influence how heart disease *progresses,* as it is associated with a worse prognosis among cardiology patients (Glassman et al., 2003). Although the new emphasis is on how depression contributes to heart disease, experts caution that the relationship between the two conditions is surely bidirectional, and that heart disease also increases vulnerability to depression (Sayers, 2004).

Stress, Other Diseases, and Immune Functioning

The development of questionnaires to measure life stress has allowed researchers to look for correlations between stress and a variety of diseases. These researchers have uncovered many connections between stress and illness. For example, Zautra and Smith (2001) found an association between life stress and the course of rheumatoid arthritis. Another study found an association between stressful life events and the emergence of lower back pain (Lampe et al., 1998). Other studies have connected stress to the

Healthfinder
Through the Department of Health and Human Services, the U.S. government has opened an ambitious online gateway to consumer-oriented information about health in all its aspects. Annotated descriptions are available for all resources identified in no-cost searches of this database.

development of diabetes (Landel-Graham, Yount, & Rudnicki, 2003), herpes (Padgett & Sheridan, 2000), and flare-ups of irritable bowel syndrome (Blanchard & Keefer, 2003).

These are just a handful of representative examples of studies relating stress to physical diseases. Table 12.3 provides a longer list of health problems that have been linked to stress. Many of these stress-illness connections are based on tentative or inconsistent findings, but the sheer length and diversity of the list is remarkable. Why should stress increase the risk for so many kinds of illness? A partial answer may lie in the body's immune functioning.

The *immune response* is the body's defensive reaction to invasion by bacteria, viral agents, or other foreign substances. The immune response works to protect organisms from many forms of disease.

Table 12.3 Health Problems That May Be Linked to Stress

Health Problem	Representative Evidence
AIDS	Stetler et al. (2005)
Appendicitis	Creed (1989)
Asthma	Lehrer et al. (2002)
Cancer	Dalton & Johansen (2005)
Chronic back pain	Lampe et al. (1998)
Common cold	Stone et al. (1992)
Complications of pregnancy	Dunkel-Schetter et al. (2001)
Heart disease	Theorell (2005)
Diabetes	Landel-Graham, Yount, & Rudnicki (2003)
Epileptic seizures	Kelly & Schramke (2000)
Hemophilia	Buxton et al. (1981)
Herpes virus	Padgett & Sheridan (2000)
Hypertension	O'Callahan, Andrews, & Krantz (2003)
Hyperthyroidism	Yang, Liu, & Zang (2000)
Inflammatory bowel disease	Searle & Bennett (2001)
Migraine headaches	Ramadan (2000)
Multiple sclerosis	Grant et al. (1989)
Periodontal disease	Marcenes & Sheiham (1992)
Premenstrual distress	Stanton et al. (2002)
Rheumatoid arthritis	Keefe et al. (2002)
Skin disorders	Arnold (2000)
Stroke	Harmsen et al. (1990)
Ulcers	Levenstein (2002)
Vaginal infections	Williams & Deffenbacher (1983)

A wealth of studies indicate that experimentally induced stress can impair immune functioning *in animals* (Ader & Cohen, 1993; Chiappelli & Hodgson, 2000). Stressors such as crowding, shock, and restraint reduce various aspects of immune reactivity in laboratory animals.

Some studies have also related stress to suppressed immune activity *in humans* (Kiecolt-Glaser & Glaser, 1995). In one study, medical students provided researchers with blood samples so that their immune response could be assessed (Kiecolt-Glaser et al., 1984). They provided a baseline sample a month before final exams and contributed a high-stress sample on the first day of their finals. The subjects also responded to the SRRS to measure recent stress. Reduced levels of immune activity were found during the extremely stressful finals week. Reduced immune activity was also correlated with higher scores on the SRRS. In another study, investigators exposed quarantined volunteers to respiratory viruses that cause the common cold and found that those under high stress were more likely to be infected by the viruses (Cohen, Tyrell, & Smith, 1993).

In a thorough review of 30 years of research on stress and immunity, Segerstrom and Miller (2004) conclude that chronic stress can reduce both *cellular immune responses* (which attack intracellular pathogens, such as viruses) and *humoral immune responses* (which attack extracellular pathogens, such as bacteria). They also report that the *duration* of a stressful event is a key factor determining its impact on immune function. Long-lasting stressors, such as caring for a seriously ill spouse or being unemployed for months, are associated with greater immune suppression than relatively brief stressors. Underscoring the importance of the link between stress and immune function, a recent study found evidence that chronic stress may produce *premature aging of immune system cells* (Epel et al., 2004). The study revealed that women who were dealing with heavy, long-term stress (caring for a child with a serious, chronic illness, such as cerebral palsy) had immune system cells that appeared to be a decade older than their chronological age, perhaps shedding light for the first time on why people under severe stress often look old and haggard.

Sizing Up the Link Between Stress and Illness

A wealth of evidence shows that stress is related to physical health, and converging lines of evidence suggest that stress contributes to the *causation* of illness. But we have to put this intriguing finding in perspective. Virtually all of the relevant research is correlational, so it can't demonstrate conclusively that stress *causes* illness (Smith & Gallo, 2001; see Chapter 2 for a discussion of correlation and causation). Subjects' elevated levels of stress and illness could both be due to a third variable, perhaps some aspect of personality (see **Figure 12.7**). For instance, some evidence suggests that neuroticism may make people overly prone to interpret events as stressful and overly prone to interpret unpleasant sensations as symptoms of illness, thus inflating the correlation between stress and illness (Watson & Pennebaker, 1989).

In spite of methodological problems favoring inflated correlations, the research in this area consistently indicates that the *strength* of the relationship between stress and health is *modest*. The correlations typically fall in the .20s and .30s (Cohen, Kessler, & Gordon, 1995). Clearly, stress is not an irresistible force that produces inevitable effects on health. Actually, this fact should come as no surprise, as stress is but one factor operating in a complex network of biopsychosocial determinants of health. Other key factors include one's genetic endowment, exposure to infectious agents and environmental toxins, nutrition, exercise, alcohol and drug use, smoking, use of medical care, and cooperation with medical advice. Furthermore, some people handle stress better than others, which is the matter we turn to next.

Factors Moderating the Impact of Stress

Some people seem to be able to withstand the ravages of stress better than others (Holahan & Moos, 1994). Why? Because certain factors can lessen the impact of stress on physical and mental health. We'll look at two such factors—social support and optimism—to shed light on individual differences in how well people tolerate stress.

Social Support

Friends may be good for your health! This startling conclusion emerges from studies on social support as a moderator of stress. *Social support* **refers to various types of aid and comfort provided by members of one's social networks.** In one study, Jemmott and Magloire (1988) examined the effect of social support on immune functioning in a group of students going through the stress of final exams. They found that students who reported stronger social support had higher levels of an antibody that plays a key role in warding off respiratory infections. Positive correlations between high social support and

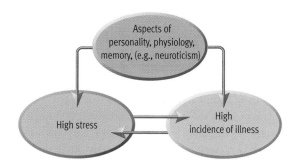

Figure 12.7

The stress-illness correlation. One or more aspects of personality, physiology, or memory could play the role of a postulated third variable in the relationship between high stress and high incidence of illness. For example, neuroticism may lead some subjects to view more events as stressful and to remember more illness, thus inflating the apparent correlation between stress and illness.

greater immune functioning have also been found in other studies (Uchino, Uno, & Holt-Lunstad, 1999).

In recent decades, a vast body of studies have found evidence that social support is favorably related to physical health (Uchino, 2004; Wills & Fegan, 2001), including all-important coronary health (Rutledge et al., 2004). Social support seems to be good medicine for the mind as well as the body, as most studies also find an association between social support and mental health (Davis, Morris, & Kraus, 1998). It appears that social support serves as a protective buffer during times of high stress, reducing the negative impact of stressful events—and that social support has its own positive effects on health, which may be apparent even when people aren't under great stress (Wills & Fegan, 2001). Interestingly, a recent study suggests that *providing* social support to others can also be beneficial (Brown et al., 2003). Another study has demonstrated that pet owners who view their pets as sources of support experience health benefits (Allen, Blascovich, & Mendes, 2002).

Optimism

Defining *optimism* **as a general tendency to expect good outcomes,** Michael Scheier and Charles Carver (1985) found a correlation between optimism and relatively good physical health in a sample of college students. Another study found optimism to be associated with more effective immune functioning (Segerstrom et al., 1998). Research suggests that optimists cope with stress in more adaptive ways than pessimists (Aspinwall, Richter, & Hoffman, 2001; Carver & Scheier, 1999). Optimists are more likely to engage in action-oriented, problem-focused coping. They are more willing than pessimists to seek social support, and they are more likely to emphasize the positive in their appraisals of stressful events. In comparison, pessimists are more likely to deal with stress by giving up or engaging in denial.

In a related line of research, Christopher Peterson and Martin Seligman have studied how people explain bad events (personal setbacks, mishaps, disappointments, and such). They identified a *pessimistic*

MARTIN SELIGMAN

"The concept of explanatory style brings hope into the laboratory, where scientists can dissect it in order to understand how it works."

explanatory style in which people tend to blame setbacks on their own personal shortcomings versus an *optimistic explanatory style* which leads people to attribute setbacks to temporary situational factors. In two retrospective studies of people born many decades ago, they found a relationship between this optimistic explanatory style and relatively good health (Peterson, Seligman, & Vaillant, 1988) and increased longevity (Peterson et al., 1998). Many other studies have linked this optimistic explanatory style to superior physical health (Peterson & Bossio, 2001), as well as higher academic achievement, increased job productivity, enhanced athletic performance, and higher marital satisfaction (Gillham et al., 2001).

Positive Effects of Stress

Our discussion of the link between stress and illness may have given you the impression that the effects of stress are entirely negative, but this most certainly is not the case. Recent years have brought increased interest in the positive aspects of the stress process, including favorable outcomes that follow in the wake of stress (Folkman & Moskowitz, 2000). To some extent, the new focus on the possible benefits of stress reflects a new emphasis on "positive psychology." As we noted in Chapter 1, the advocates of positive psychology argue for increased research on

well-being, courage, perseverance, tolerance, and other human strengths and virtues (Seligman, 2003). One of these strengths is resilience in the face of stress (Seligman & Csikszentmihalyi, 2000).

Research on resilience suggests that stress can promote personal growth or self-improvement (Tedeschi, Park, & Calhoun, 1998). For example, studies of people grappling with major health problems show that the majority of respondents report that they derived benefits from their adversity (Tennen & Affleck, 1999). Stressful events sometimes force people to develop new skills, reevaluate priorities, learn new insights, and acquire new strengths. In other words, the adaptation process initiated by stress may lead to personal changes that are changes for the better. Confronting and conquering a stressful challenge may lead to improvements in specific coping abilities and to an enhanced self-concept. Moreover, even if people do not conquer stressors, they may be able to learn from their mistakes. Thus, researchers have begun to explore the growth potential of stressful events (Calhoun & Tedeschi, 2001; Park & Fenster, 2004).

Individual differences among people in social support, optimism, and resilience explain why stress doesn't have the same impact on everyone's health. Differences in lifestyle may play an even larger role in determining health. We'll examine some critical aspects of lifestyle in the next section.

> Health-Impairing Behavior

PREVIEW QUESTIONS

● Why does smoking increase mortality?

● What are some examples of links between nutrition and health?

● What are the health benefits of exercise?

● How are behavioral factors related to the risk of HIV infection?

● What are some misconceptions about HIV transmission?

Some people seem determined to dig an early grave for themselves. They do precisely those things that are bad for their health. For example, some people drink heavily even though they know that they're damaging their liver. Others eat all the wrong foods even though they know that they're increasing their risk of a second heart attack. Behavior that's downright *self-destructive* is surprisingly common. In this section we'll discuss how health is affected by smoking, poor nutrition, and lack of exercise, and we'll look at behavioral factors in AIDS. (The health risks of alcohol and drug use are discussed in Chapter 5.)

Smoking

The smoking of tobacco is widespread in our culture. The percentage of people who smoke has declined noticeably since the mid-1960s (see **Figure 12.8**). Nonetheless, about 26% of adult men and 21% of adult

women in the United States continue to smoke regularly. Smokers face a much greater risk of premature death than nonsmokers. For example, the average smoker has an estimated life expectancy *13–14 years shorter* than that of a similar nonsmoker (Schmitz & Delaune, 2005). The overall risk is positively correlated with the number of cigarettes smoked and their tar and nicotine content.

Why are mortality rates higher for smokers? Smoking increases the likelihood of developing a surprisingly large range of diseases (Thun, Apicella, & Henley, 2000). Lung cancer and heart disease kill the largest number of smokers. However, smokers also have an elevated risk for oral, bladder, and kidney cancer, as well as cancers of the larynx, esophagus, and pancreas; for arteriosclerosis, hypertension, stroke, and other cardiovascular diseases; and for bronchitis, emphysema, and other pulmonary diseases. Most smokers know about the risks associated with tobacco use, but they tend to underestimate the

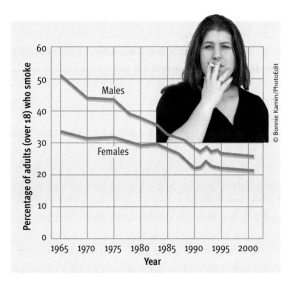

Figure 12.8

The prevalence of smoking in the United States. This graph shows how the percentage of U.S. adults who smoke has declined steadily since the mid-1960s. Although considerable progress has been made, smoking still accounts for a huge number of premature deaths in the United States each year. (Based on data from the Centers for Disease Control and Prevention)

actual risks as applied to themselves (Ayanian & Cleary, 1999).

Studies show that if people can give up smoking, their health risks decline reasonably quickly (Samet, 1992; Williams et al., 2002). Evidence suggests that most smokers would like to quit but are reluctant to give up a major source of pleasure, and they worry about craving cigarettes, gaining weight, becoming anxious and irritable, and feeling less able to cope with stress (Grunberg, Faraday, & Rahman, 2001).

Unfortunately, it's difficult to give up cigarettes. People who enroll in formal smoking cessation programs are only slightly more successful than people who try to quit on their own (Swan, Hudman, & Khroyan, 2003). Long-term success rates peak in the vicinity of only 25%, and many studies report lower figures. Nonetheless, the fact that there are nearly 40 million ex-smokers in the United States indicates that it is possible to quit smoking successfully. Interestingly, many people fail several times before they eventually succeed. Evidence suggests that the readiness to give up smoking builds gradually as people cycle through periods of abstinence and relapse (Herzog et al., 1999; Prochaska, 1994).

Poor Nutritional Habits

Evidence is accumulating that patterns of nutrition influence susceptibility to a variety of diseases and health problems. Possible connections between eating patterns and diseases include the following:

Knowing that their personal habits adversely affect their well-being, many people nonetheless persist in doing things that are self-destructive, such as over eating and not exercising.

1. Heavy consumption of foods that elevate serum cholesterol level (eggs, cheeses, butter, shellfish, sausage, and the like) appears to increase the risk of cardiovascular disease (Stamler et al., 2000; see **Figure 12.9**). Eating habits are only one of several factors that influence serum cholesterol level, but they do make an important contribution.

2. Vulnerability to cardiovascular diseases may also be influenced by other dietary factors. For example, low-fiber diets may increase the likelihood of coronary disease (Ludwig et al., 1999; Wolk et al., 1999), and high intake of red and processed meats, sweets, potatoes, and refined grains is associated with increased cardiovascular risk (Hu & Willett, 2002). Recent research indicates that the omega 3 fatty acids found in fish and fish oils offer protection against coronary disease (Din, Newby, & Flapan, 2004).

3. High salt intake is thought to be a contributing factor in the development of hypertension

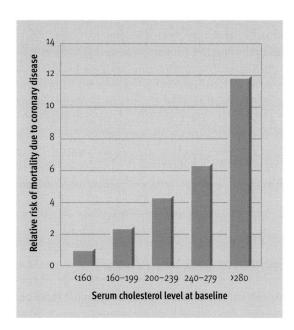

Figure 12.9

The link between cholesterol and coronary risk. In a review of several major studies, Stamler et al. (2000) summarize crucial evidence on the association between cholesterol levels and the prevalence of cardiovascular disease. This graph is based on a sample of over 11,000 men who were aged 18 to 39 at the beginning of the study (1967–1973), when their serum cholesterol level was measured. The data shown here depict participants' relative risk for coronary heart disease during the ensuing 25 years, as a function of their initial cholesterol level. (Data from Stamler et al., 2000)

(Vollmer et al., 2001), although there is still some debate about its exact role.

4. High caffeine consumption may elevate one's risk for hypertension (James, 2004) and for coronary disease (Happonen, Voutilainen, & Salonen, 2004), although the negative effects of caffeine appear relatively modest.

5. High-fat diets have been implicated as possible contributors to some forms of cancer, especially prostate cancer (Rose, 1997), colon and rectal cancer (Shike, 1999), and breast cancer (Wynder et al., 1997). Some studies also suggest that high-fiber diets may reduce one's risk for colon and rectal cancer (Reddy, 1999), but the evidence is not conclusive.

Of course, nutritional habits interact with other factors to determine whether one develops a particular disease. Nonetheless, the examples just described indicate that eating habits are relevant to physical health.

Lack of Exercise

There is considerable evidence linking lack of exercise to poor health. Research indicates that regular exercise is associated with increased longevity (Lee & Skerrett, 2001). Why would exercise help people live longer? For one thing, an appropriate exercise program can enhance cardiovascular fitness and thereby reduce susceptibility to deadly cardiovascular problems (Lee et al., 2001b; Phillips, Kiernan, & King, 2001). Second, fitness may indirectly reduce one's risk for a variety of obesity-related health problems, such as diabetes and respiratory difficulties (Corsica & Perri, 2003). Third, recent studies suggest that physical fitness is also associated with a decreased risk for colon cancer in men and for breast and reproductive cancer in women (Thune & Furberg, 2001). The apparent link between exercise and reduced cancer risk has been a pleasant surprise for scientists, who are now scrambling to figure out the physiological mechanisms underlying this association. Fourth, exercise can serve as a buffer that reduces the potentially damaging physical effects of stress (Plante, 1999b; Plante, Caputo, & Chizmar, 2000). This buffering effect may occur because people high in fitness show less physiological reactivity to stress than those who are less fit.

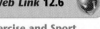

Web Link 12.6

Exercise and Sport Psychology
For anyone wondering about how psychological science deals with sports and athletics, this site, maintained by Division 47 of the American Psychological Association, is an excellent starting point, especially for those looking for career information.

Behavior and HIV/AIDS

At present, some of the most problematic links between behavior and health may be those related to AIDS. AIDS stands for *acquired immune deficiency syndrome,* **a disorder in which the immune system is gradually weakened and eventually disabled by the human immunodeficiency virus (HIV).** Being infected with the HIV virus is *not* equivalent to having AIDS; AIDS is the final stage of the HIV infection process, typically manifested about ten years after the original infection (Treisman, 1999). With the onset of AIDS, one is left virtually defenseless against numerous infectious agents. AIDS inflicts its harm indirectly by opening the door to other diseases. The symptoms of AIDS vary widely depending on the specific constellation of diseases that one develops (Cunningham & Selwyn, 2005). Unfortunately, the worldwide prevalence of this deadly disease continues to increase at an alarming rate, especially in certain regions of Africa (De Cock & Janssen, 2002).

Prior to 1996–1997, the average length of survival for people after the onset of the AIDS syndrome was about 18 to 24 months. Encouraging advances in the treatment of AIDS with drug regimens referred to as *highly active antiretroviral therapy* (*HAART*) hold out promise for *substantially* longer survival (Sande & Ronald, 2004). But these drugs have been rushed into service, and their long-term efficacy is yet to be determined. Medical experts are concerned that the general public has gotten the impression that these treatments have transformed AIDS from a fatal disease to a manageable one, which is a premature conclusion. HIV strains are evolving, and many have developed resistance to the currently available antiretroviral drugs (Trachenberg & Sande, 2002). Moreover, many patients do not respond well to the new drugs, and many patients who are responsive have difficulty sticking to their drug administration regimens, which can be complicated and often have adverse side effects (Catz & Kelly, 2001; Sorenson, Haug, Batki, 2005).

Transmission

The HIV virus is transmitted through person-to-person contact involving the exchange of bodily fluids, primarily semen and blood. The two principal modes of transmission in the United States have been sexual contact and the sharing of needles by intravenous (IV) drug users. In the United States, sexual transmission has occurred primarily among gay and bisexual men, but heterosexual transmission has increased in recent years (Rosenberg & Biggar, 1998). In the world as a whole, infection through heterosexual relations has been much more common from the beginning. In heterosexual relations, male-to-female transmission is estimated to be about eight times more likely than female-to-male transmission (Ickovics, Thayaparan, & Ethier, 2001). The HIV virus can be found in the tears and saliva of infected individuals, but the concentrations are low and there is no evidence that the infection can be spread through casual contact. Even most forms of noncasual contact, including kissing, hugging, and sharing food with infected individuals, appear safe (Kalichman, 1995).

Misconceptions

Misconceptions about AIDS are widespread. Ironically, the people who hold these misconceptions fall into two polarized camps. On the one hand, a great many people have unrealistic fears that AIDS can be readily transmitted through casual contact with infected individuals. These people worry unnecessarily about contracting AIDS from a handshake, a sneeze, or an eating utensil. They tend to be paranoid about interacting with homosexuals, thus fueling discrimination against gays in regard to housing, employment, and so forth. Some people also believe that it is dangerous to donate blood, when in fact blood *donors* are at no risk whatsoever.

On the other hand, many young heterosexuals who are sexually active with a variety of partners foolishly downplay their risk for HIV, naively assuming that they are safe as long as they avoid IV drug use and sexual relations with gay or bisexual men. They greatly underestimate the probability that their sexual partners previously may have used IV drugs or had unprotected sex with an infected individual. Also, many young people believe that prospective sexual partners who carry the HIV virus will exhibit telltale signs of illness. However, as we have already noted, having AIDS and being infected with HIV are not the same thing, and HIV carriers often remain healthy and symptom-free for many years after they are infected. In sum, many myths about AIDS persist,

in spite of extensive efforts to educate the public about this complex and controversial disease. **Figure 12.10** contains a short quiz to test your knowledge of the facts about AIDS.

So far, we've seen that physical health may be affected by stress and by aspects of lifestyle. Next, we'll look at the importance of how people react to physical symptoms, health problems, and health care efforts.

AIDS Risk Knowledge Test

Answer the following "true" or "false."

T F **1.** The AIDS virus cannot be spread through kissing.
T F **2.** A person can get the AIDS virus by sharing kitchens and bathrooms with someone who has AIDS.
T F **3.** Men can give the AIDS virus to women.
T F **4.** The AIDS virus attacks the body's ability to fight off diseases.
T F **5.** You can get the AIDS virus by someone sneezing, like a cold or the flu.
T F **6.** You can get AIDS by touching a person with AIDS.
T F **7.** Women can give the AIDS virus to men.
T F **8.** A person who got the AIDS virus from shooting up drugs cannot give the virus to someone by having sex.
T F **9.** A pregnant woman can give the AIDS virus to her unborn baby.
T F **10.** Most types of birth control also protect against getting the AIDS virus.
T F **11.** Condoms make intercourse completely safe.
T F **12.** Oral sex is safe if partners "do not swallow."
T F **13.** A person must have many different sexual partners to be at risk for AIDS.
T F **14.** It is more important to take precautions against AIDS in large cities than in small cities.
T F **15.** A positive result on the AIDS virus antibody test often occurs for people who do not even have the virus.
T F **16.** Only receptive (passive) anal intercourse transmits the AIDS virus.
T F **17.** Donating blood carries no AIDS risk for the donor.
T F **18.** Most people who have the AIDS virus look quite ill.

Answers: 1.T 2.F 3.T 4.T 5.F 6.F 7.T 8.F 9.T 10.F 11.F 12.F 13.F 14.F 15.F 16.F 17.T 18.F

Figure 12.10

A quiz on knowledge of HIV/AIDS. Because misconceptions about HIV infection and AIDS abound, it may be wise to take this brief quiz to test your knowledge of HIV/AIDS. The answers are shown at the bottom of the figure.

Source: Adapted from Kalichman, S. C. (1995). *Understanding AIDS: A guide for mental health professionals.* Washington, DC: American Psychological Association. Copyright © Reprinted by permission of the publisher and author.

> Reactions to Illness

Some people respond to physical symptoms and illnesses by ignoring warning signs of developing diseases, while others actively seek to conquer their diseases. Let's examine the decision to seek medical treatment, communication with health providers, and factors that affect adherence to medical advice.

Deciding to Seek Treatment

Have you ever experienced nausea, diarrhea, stiffness, headaches, cramps, chest pains, or sinus problems? Of course you have; everyone experiences some of these problems periodically. However, whether

someone views these sensations as *symptoms* is a matter of individual interpretation. When two persons experience the same unpleasant sensations, one may shrug them off as a nuisance while the other may rush to a physician (Martin & Leventhal, 2004). Studies suggest that people who are relatively high in anxiety and neuroticism tend to report more symptoms of illness than others do (Petrie & Pennebaker, 2004). Those who are extremely attentive to bodily sensations and health concerns also report more symptoms than the average person (Barsky, 1988).

The biggest problem in regard to treatment seeking is the tendency of many people to delay the pursuit of needed professional consultation. Delays can

PREVIEW QUESTIONS

● What is the biggest problem related to people's decisions to seek medical treatment?

● What are some barriers to effective communication between patients and their health providers?

● What can patients do to improve communication?

● How much of a problem is nonadherence to medical advice?

● What are the causes of nonadherence?

Web Link 12.7

Centers for Disease Control and Prevention (CDC)
The CDC is the federal agency charged with monitoring and responding to serious threats to the nation's health as well as taking steps to prevent illness. This site's "Health Information from A to Z" offers the public in-depth medical explanations of many health problems both common (flu, allergies, etc.) and unusual (fetal alcohol syndrome, meningitis, etc.).

ROBIN DiMATTEO

"A person will not carry out a health behavior if significant barriers stand in the way, or if the steps interfere with favorite or necessary activities."

be critical, because early diagnosis and quick intervention may facilitate more effective treatment of many health problems (Petrie & Pennebaker, 2004). Unfortunately, procrastination is the norm even when people are faced with a medical emergency, such as a heart attack (Martin & Leventhal, 2004). Why do people dawdle in the midst of a crisis? Robin DiMatteo (1991), a leading expert on patient behavior, mentions a number of reasons, noting that people delay because they often (a) misinterpret and downplay the significance of their symptoms, (b) fret about looking silly if the problem turns out to be nothing, (c) worry about "bothering" their physician, (d) are reluctant to disrupt their plans (to go out to dinner, see a movie, and so forth), and (e) waste time on trivial matters (such as taking a shower, gathering personal items, or packing clothes) before going to a hospital emergency room.

Communicating with Health Providers

A large portion of medical patients leave their doctors' offices not understanding what they have been told and what they are supposed to do (Johnson & Carlson, 2004). This situation is most unfortunate because good communication is a crucial requirement for sound medical decisions, informed choices about treatment, and appropriate follow-through by patients (Buckman, 2002; Gambone, Reiter, & DiMatteo, 1994).

There are many barriers to effective provider-patient communication (DiMatteo, 1997; Marteau & Weinman, 2004). Economic realities dictate that medical visits generally be quite brief, allowing little time for discussion. Many providers use too much medical jargon and overestimate their patients' understanding of technical terms. Patients who are upset and worried about their illness may simply forget to report some symptoms or to ask questions they meant to ask. Other patients are evasive about their real concerns because they fear a serious diagnosis. Many patients are reluctant to challenge doctors' authority and are too passive in their interactions with providers.

What can you do to improve your communication with health care providers? The key is to not be a passive consumer of medical services (Ferguson, 1993; Kane, 1991). Arrive at a medical visit on time, with your questions and concerns prepared in advance. Try to be accurate and candid in replying to your doctor's questions. If you don't understand something the doctor says, don't be embarrassed about asking for clarification. And if you have doubts about the suitability or feasibility of your doctor's recommendations, don't be afraid to voice them.

Adhering to Medical Advice

Many patients fail to follow the instructions they receive from physicians and other health care professionals. This problem, which is called *nonadherence* or *noncompliance,* is distressingly common. The evidence suggests that noncompliance with medical advice may occur 30% of the time when short-term treatments are prescribed for acute conditions and 50% of the time when long-term treatments are needed for chronic illness (Johnson & Carlson, 2004). Nonadherence takes many forms. Patients may fail to begin a treatment regimen, may stop the regimen early, may reduce or increase the levels of treatment that were prescribed, or may be inconsistent and unreliable in following treatment procedures (Dunbar-Jacob & Schlenk, 2001). Nonadherence has been linked to increased sickness, treatment failures, and higher mortality (Christensen & Johnson, 2002; DiMatteo et al., 2002). Moreover, nonadherence wastes expensive medical visits and medications and increases hospital admissions, leading to enormous economic costs. Robin DiMatteo (2004b) speculates that in the United States alone, nonadherence may be a $300 billion a year drain on the health care system.

Concern about nonadherence does not mean that patients should passively accept all professional advice from medical personnel. However, when patients have doubts about a prescribed treatment, they should speak up and ask questions. Passive resistance can backfire. For instance, if a physician sees no improvement in a patient who falsely insists that he has been taking his medicine, the physician may abandon an accurate diagnosis in favor of an inaccurate one. The inaccurate diagnosis could then lead to inappropriate treatments that might be harmful to the patient.

Why don't people comply with the advice that they've sought out from highly regarded health care professionals? Physicians tend to attribute noncompliance to patients' personal characteristics, but research indicates that personality traits and demographic factors are surprisingly unrelated to adherence rates (DiMatteo, 2004b; Marteau & Weinman, 2004). One factor that *is* related to adherence is patients' *social support.* Adherence is improved when patients have family members, friends, or co-workers who remind them and help them to comply with

Courtesy of University of California, Riverside

treatment requirements (DiMatteo, 2004a). Other considerations that influence the likelihood of adherence include the following (Dunbar-Jacob & Schlenk, 2001; Johnson & Carlson, 2004):

1. Frequently, nonadherence occurs because the patient doesn't understand the instructions as given. Highly trained professionals often forget that what seems obvious and simple to them may be obscure and complicated to many of their patients.
2. Another key factor is how aversive or difficult the instructions are. If the prescribed regimen is unpleasant, adherence will tend to decrease. And the more that following instructions interferes with routine behavior, the less probable it is that the patient will cooperate successfully.
3. If a patient has a negative attitude toward a physician, the probability of noncompliance will increase. When patients are unhappy with their interactions with the doctor, they're more likely to ignore the medical advice provided, no matter how important it may be.

In response to the noncompliance problem, researchers have investigated many methods of increasing patients' adherence to medical advice. Interventions have included simplifying instructions, providing more rationale for instructions, reducing the complexity of treatment regimens, helping pa-

Communication between health care providers and patients tends to be far from optimal, for a variety of reasons.

tients with emotional distress that undermines adherence, and training patients in the use of behavior modification strategies. All of these interventions can improve adherence, although their effects tend to be modest (Christensen & Johnson, 2002; Roter et al., 1998).

> Reflecting on the Chapter's Themes

Which of our themes were prominent in this chapter? As you probably noticed, our discussion of stress and health illustrated multifactorial causation and the subjectivity of experience.

Our discussion of the psychology of health provided a particularly complex illustration of multifactorial causation. As we noted in Chapter 1, people are likely to think simplistically, in terms of single causes. In recent years, the highly publicized research linking stress to health has led many people to point automatically to stress as an explanation for illness. In reality, stress has only a modest impact on physical health. Stress can increase the risk for illness, but health is governed by a dense network of factors. Important factors include inherited vulnerabilities, exposure to infectious agents, health-impairing habits, reactions to symptoms, treatment-seeking behavior, compliance with medical advice, optimism, and social support. In other words, stress is

but one actor on a crowded stage. This should be apparent in **Figure 12.11** on the next page, which shows the multitude of biopsychosocial factors that jointly influence physical health. It illustrates multifactorial causation in all its complexity.

The subjectivity of experience was demonstrated by the frequently repeated point that stress lies in the eye of the beholder. The same job promotion may be stressful for one person and invigorating for another. One person's pressure is another's challenge. When it comes to stress, objective reality is not nearly as important as subjective perceptions. More than anything else, the impact of stressful events seems to depend on how people view them. The critical importance of stress appraisals will continue to be apparent in our Personal Application on stress management. Many stress-management strategies depend on altering one's appraisals of events.

 Multifactorial Causation

 Subjectivity of Experience

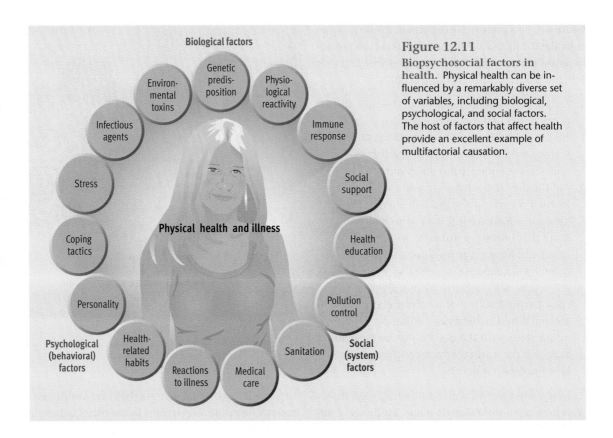

Figure 12.11
Biopsychosocial factors in health. Physical health can be influenced by a remarkably diverse set of variables, including biological, psychological, and social factors. The host of factors that affect health provide an excellent example of multifactorial causation.

Labels in figure:
Biological factors
Environmental toxins
Genetic predisposition
Physiological reactivity
Immune response
Infectious agents
Social support
Stress
Health education
Coping tactics
Pollution control
Personality
Psychological (behavioral) factors
Health-related habits
Reactions to illness
Medical care
Sanitation
Social (system) factors
Physical health and illness

PERSONAL *Application*

Improving Coping and Stress Management

Answer the following "true" or "false."

____ 1 The key to managing stress is to avoid or circumvent it.
____ 2 It's best to suppress emotional reactions to stress.
____ 3 Laughing at one's problems is immature.
____ 4 Exercise has little or no impact on stress resistance.

Courses and books on stress management have multiplied at a furious pace in recent decades. They summarize experts' advice on how to cope with stress more effectively. How do these experts feel about the four statements above? As you'll see in this Personal Application, most would agree that all four are false.

The key to managing stress does not lie in avoiding it. Stress is an inevitable element in the fabric of modern life. As Hans Selye (1973) noted, "Contrary to public opin-

ion, we must not—and indeed can't—avoid stress" (p. 693). Thus, most stress-management programs train people to use more effective coping strategies. In this Application, we'll examine a variety of constructive coping tactics, beginning with Albert Ellis's ideas about changing one's appraisals of stressful events.

Reappraisal: Ellis's Rational Thinking

Albert Ellis is a prominent theorist who believes that people can short-circuit their emotional reactions to stress by altering their appraisals of stressful events. Ellis's insights about stress appraisal are the foundation for a widely used system of therapy, called *rational emotive behavior therapy* (Ellis, 1977, 1987), and several popular books on effective coping (Ellis, 1985, 1999, 2001).

Ellis maintains that *you feel the way you think*. He argues that problematic emotional reactions are caused by negative self-talk, which he calls catastrophic thinking. *Catastrophic thinking* involves unrealistically pessimistic appraisals of stress that exaggerate the magnitude of one's problems. According to Ellis, people unwittingly believe that stressful events cause their emotional turmoil, but he maintains that emotional reactions to personal setbacks are actually caused by overly negative appraisals of stressful events (see **Figure 12.12**).

Ellis theorizes that unrealistic appraisals of stress are derived from irrational assumptions that people hold. He maintains that if you scrutinize your catastrophic thinking, you'll find that your reasoning is based on a logically indefensible premise, such as "I must have approval from everyone" or "I must perform well in all endeavors." These faulty assumptions, which people often hold

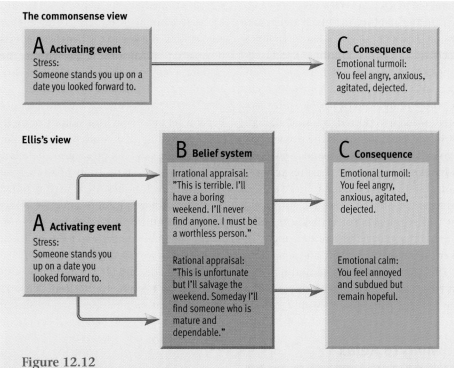

The commonsense view

A **Activating event**
Stress:
Someone stands you up on a
date you looked forward to.

C **Consequence**
Emotional turmoil:
You feel angry, anxious,
agitated, dejected.

Ellis's view

A **Activating event**
Stress:
Someone stands you
up on a date you
looked forward to.

B **Belief system**
Irrational appraisal:
"This is terrible. I'll
have a boring
weekend. I'll never
find anyone. I must be
a worthless person."

Rational appraisal:
"This is unfortunate
but I'll salvage the
weekend. Someday I'll
find someone who is
mature and
dependable."

C **Consequence**
Emotional turmoil:
You feel angry,
anxious, agitated,
dejected.

Emotional calm:
You feel annoyed
and subdued but
remain hopeful.

Figure 12.12
Albert Ellis's model of emotional reactions. Although most people attribute their nega-tive emotional reactions directly to negative events that they experience, Ellis argues that events themselves do *not* cause emotional distress; rather, distress is caused by the way people *think* about negative events. According to Ellis, the key to managing stress is to change one's appraisal of stressful events.

unconsciously, generate catastrophic think-ing and emotional turmoil. How can you re-duce your unrealistic appraisals of stress? Ellis asserts that you must learn (1) how to detect catastrophic thinking and (2) how to dis-pute the irrational assumptions that cause it.

Humor as a Stress Reducer

A number of years ago, the Chicago suburbs experienced their worst flooding in about a century. Thousands of people saw their homes wrecked when two rivers spilled over their banks. As the waters receded, the flood victims returning to their homes were sub-jected to the inevitable TV interviews. A re-markable number of victims, surrounded by the ruins of their homes, *joked* about their misfortune. When the going gets tough, it may pay to laugh about it. In a study of cop-ing styles, McCrae (1984) found that 40% of his subjects used humor to deal with stress.

Empirical evidence showing that humor moderates the impact of stress has been accumulating over the last 25 years (Abel,

1998; Lefcourt, 2001). How does humor help to reduce the effects of stress and promote wellness? Several explanations have been proposed (see **Figure 12.13**). One possibil-ity is that humor affects appraisals of stress-ful events (Abel, 2002). Jokes can help people to put a less threatening spin on their trials and tribulations. Another possibility is that humor increases the experience of positive

emotions (Martin, 2002), which can help people bounce back from stressful events (Tugade & Fredrickson, 2004). Another hy-pothesis is that a good sense of humor facil-itates rewarding social interactions, which promote social support, which is known to buffer the effects of stress (Martin, 2002). Finally, Lefcourt and colleagues (1995) ar-gue that high-humor people may benefit from not taking themselves as seriously as low-humor people do. As they put it, "If per-sons do not regard themselves too seriously and do not have an inflated sense of self-importance, then defeats, embarrassments, and even tragedies should have less pervasive emotional consequences for them" (p. 375).

Releasing Pent-Up Emotions

Try as you might to temper your stress ap-praisals, you no doubt still go through times when you feel wired with stress-induced tension. When this happens, there's merit in the commonsense notion that you should try to release the emotions welling up inside. Why? Because the physiological arousal that accompanies emotions can be-come problematic. For example, research suggests that people who inhibit the expres-sion of anger and other emotions are some-what more likely than other people to have elevated blood pressure (Jorgensen et al., 1996). Moreover, research suggests that ef-forts to actively suppress emotions result in increased autonomic arousal (Gross, 1998,

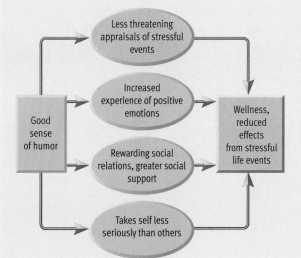

Figure 12.13
Possible explanations for the link between humor and wellness. Research suggests that a good sense of humor buffers the effects of stress and promotes wellness. Four hypoth-esized explanations for the link between humor and wellness are outlined in the middle column of this diagram. As you can see, humor may have a variety of beneficial effects.

Good sense of humor →
- Less threatening appraisals of stressful events
- Increased experience of positive emotions
- Rewarding social relations, greater social support
- Takes self less seriously than others

→ Wellness, reduced effects from stressful life events

2001) and decreased immune function (Petrie, Booth, & Pennebaker, 1998).

Although there's no guarantee of it, you can sometimes reduce your physiological arousal by expressing your emotions. For instance, evidence is accumulating that writing or talking about life's difficulites can be valuable in dealing with stress (Hemenover, 2003; Smyth & Pennebaker, 1999). In one study of college students, half of the subjects were asked to write three essays about their difficulties in adjusting to college, while the other half wrote three essays about superficial topics. The subjects who wrote about their personal problems enjoyed better health in the following months than the other subjects did (Pennebaker, Colder, & Sharp, 1990). Subsequent similar studies have replicated this finding (Francis & Pennebaker, 1992; Greenberg, Wortman, & Stone, 1996) and shown that emotional disclosure is associated with better immune functioning (Slatcher & Pennebaker, 2005; Smyth & Pennebaker, 2001). So, if you can find a good listener, you may be able to discharge problematic emotions by letting your fears, misgivings, and frustrations spill out in a candid conversation.

Managing Hostility and Forgiving Others

Scientists have compiled quite a bit of evidence that hostility is related to increased risk for heart attacks and other types of illness (Williams, 2001). In light of this fact, many experts assert that people should strive to learn how to manage their feelings of hostility more effectively (Williams & Williams, 2001). The goal of hostility management is not merely to suppress the overt expression of hostility that may continue to seethe beneath the surface but to actually reduce the frequency and intensity of one's hostile feelings.

People tend to experience hostility and other negative emotions when they feel "wronged"—that is when they believe that the actions of another person were harmful, immoral, or unjust. When people feel wronged, their natural inclination is either to seek revenge or to avoid further contact with the offender (McCullough, 2001). *Forgiving* someone involves counteracting these

natural tendencies and releasing the person from further liability for his or her transgression. Research suggests that forgiving is associated with better adjustment and well-being (McCollough & Witvliet, 2002; Worthington & Scherer, 2004). For example, in one study of divorced or permanently separated women reported by McCollough (2001), the extent to which the women had forgiven their former husbands was positively related to several measures of well-being and inversely related to measures of anxiety and depression. Research also shows that vengefulness is correlated with more rumination and negative emotion and with lower life satisfaction (McCullough et al., 2001). Taken together, these findings suggest that it may be healthful for people to learn to forgive others more readily.

Learning to Relax

Relaxation is a valuable stress-management technique that can soothe emotional turmoil and suppress problematic physiological arousal (Lehrer & Woolfolk, 1984, 1993; Smyth et al., 2001). The value of relaxation became apparent to Herbert Benson (1975; Benson & Klipper, 1988) as a result of his re-

search on meditation. Benson, a Harvard Medical School cardiologist, believes that relaxation is the key to the beneficial effects of meditation. According to Benson, the elaborate religious rituals and beliefs associated with meditation are irrelevant to its effects. After "demystifying" meditation, Benson set out to devise a simple, nonreligious procedure that could provide similar benefits. He calls his procedure the *relaxation response*. From his study of a variety of relaxation techniques, Benson concluded that four factors promote effective relaxation: (1) a quiet, distraction-free environment, (2) a mental device to focus on (such as a sound or word recited repetitively), (3) a passive attitude, and (4) a comfortable position that isn't conducive to sleep. Benson's simple relaxation procedure is described in **Figure 12.14**. For full benefit, it should be practiced daily.

Minimizing Physiological Vulnerability

Your body is intimately involved in your response to stress, and the wear and tear of stress can be injurious to your health. To

In September 1994, Reg and Maggie Green were vacationing in Italy when their seven-year-old son Nicholas was shot and killed during a highway robbery. In an act of forgiveness that stunned Europe, the Greens chose to donate their son's organs, which went to seven Italians. The Greens, shown here five years after the incident, have weathered their horrific loss better than most, perhaps in part because of their willingness to forgive.

© Acey Harper/Time Life Pictures/Getty Images

combat this potential problem, it helps to keep your body in relatively sound shape. The potential benefits of regular exercise are substantial. Regular exercise is associated with increased longevity (Lee & Skerrett, 2001). Moreover, research has shown that you don't have to be a dedicated athlete to benefit from exercise (Blair et al., 1989). Even a moderate amount of exercise reduces your risk of disease (Richardson et al., 2004; see **Figure 12.15**). Successful participation in an exercise program can also lead to improvements in your mood and ability to deal with stress (Hays, 1999; Plante, 1999b).

Embarking on an exercise program is difficult for many people. Exercise is time-consuming, and if you're out of shape, your initial attempts may be painful and discouraging. To avoid these problems, it's wise to (1) select an activity that you find enjoyable, (2) increase your participation gradually, (3) exercise regularly without overdoing it, and (4) reinforce yourself for your efforts (Greenberg, 2002). If you choose a competitive sport (such as basketball or tennis), try to avoid falling into the competition trap. If you become obsessed with winning, you'll put yourself under pressure and *add* to the stress in your life.

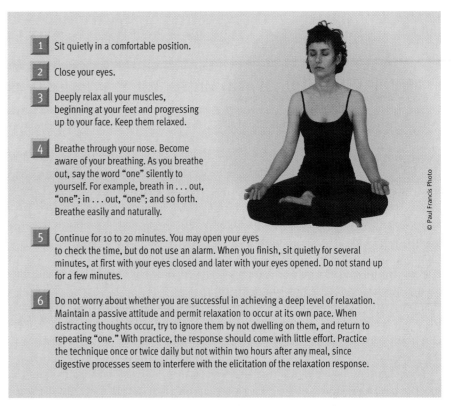

1. Sit quietly in a comfortable position.

2. Close your eyes.

3. Deeply relax all your muscles, beginning at your feet and progressing up to your face. Keep them relaxed.

4. Breathe through your nose. Become aware of your breathing. As you breathe out, say the word "one" silently to yourself. For example, breath in . . . out, "one"; in . . . out, "one"; and so forth. Breathe easily and naturally.

5. Continue for 10 to 20 minutes. You may open your eyes to check the time, but do not use an alarm. When you finish, sit quietly for several minutes, at first with your eyes closed and later with your eyes opened. Do not stand up for a few minutes.

6. Do not worry about whether you are successful in achieving a deep level of relaxation. Maintain a passive attitude and permit relaxation to occur at its own pace. When distracting thoughts occur, try to ignore them by not dwelling on them, and return to repeating "one." With practice, the response should come with little effort. Practice the technique once or twice daily but not within two hours after any meal, since digestive processes seem to interfere with the elicitation of the relaxation response.

Figure 12.14

Benson's relaxation procedure. Herbert Benson's relaxation procedure is described here. According to Benson, his simple relaxation response can yield benefits similar to meditation. To experience these benefits, you should practice the procedure daily.

Source: Benson, H., & Klipper, M. Z. (1975, 1988). *The relaxation response.* New York: Morrow. Copyright © 1975 by William Morrow & Co. Reprinted by permission of HarperCollins Publishers.

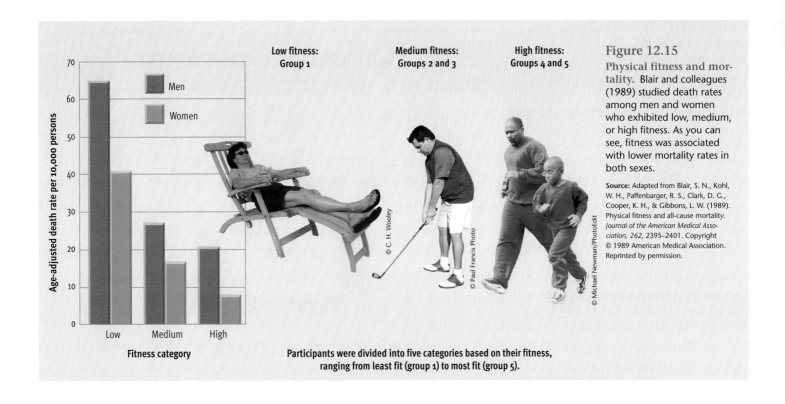

Figure 12.15

Physical fitness and mortality. Blair and colleagues (1989) studied death rates among men and women who exhibited low, medium, or high fitness. As you can see, fitness was associated with lower mortality rates in both sexes.

Source: Adapted from Blair, S. N., Kohl, W. H., Paffenbarger, R. S., Clark, D. G., Cooper, K. H., & Gibbons, L. W. (1989). Physical fitness and all-cause mortality. *Journal of the American Medical Association, 262,* 2395–2401. Copyright © 1989 American Medical Association. Reprinted by permission.

Low fitness: Group 1   Medium fitness: Groups 2 and 3   High fitness: Groups 4 and 5

Participants were divided into five categories based on their fitness, ranging from least fit (group 1) to most fit (group 5).

With so many conflicting claims about the best ways to prevent or treat diseases, how can anyone ever decide what to do? It seems that every day a report in the media claims that yesterday's health news was wrong. The inconsistency of health news is only part of the problem. We are also overwhelmed by health-related statistics. As mathematics pundit John Allen Paulos (1995, p. 133) puts it, "Health statistics may be bad for our mental health. Inundated by too many of them, we tend to ignore them completely, to accept them blithely, to disbelieve them closemindedly, or simply to misinterpret their significance."

Personal decisions about health-related issues can be extremely important, even a matter of life and death. Although not always easy, it is particularly important to try to think rationally and systematically about health issues. In this Application, we will discuss a few insights that can help you to think critically about statistics on health risks, then we'll briefly outline a systematic approach to thinking through health decisions.

Evaluating Statistics on Health Risks

News reports seem to suggest that there are links between virtually everything people do, touch, and consume and some type of physical illness. For example, media have reported that coffee consumption is related to hypertension, that sleep loss is related to mortality, and that a high-fat diet is related to heart disease. Such reports are enough to send even the most subdued person into a panic. Fortunately, your evaluation of data on health risks can become more sophisticated by considering the following factors.

Correlation Is No Assurance of Causation. It is not easy to conduct experiments on health risks, so the vast majority of stud-

ies linking lifestyle and demographic factors to diseases are correlational studies. Hence, it pays to remember that no causal link may exist between two variables that happen to be correlated. Thus, when you hear that a factor is related to some disease, try to dig a little deeper and find out *why* scientists think this factor is associated with the disease. The suspected causal factor may be something very different from what was measured.

Statistical Significance Is Not Equivalent to Practical Significance. Reports on health statistics often emphasize that the investigators uncovered "statistically significant" findings. Statistically significant findings are results that are not likely to be due to chance fluctuations. Statistical significance is a useful concept, but it can sometimes be misleading (Matthey, 1998). Medical studies are often based on rather large samples, because they tend to yield more reliable conclusions than small samples. However, when a large sample is used, weak

relationships and small differences between groups can turn out to be statistically significant, and these small differences may not have much practical importance. For example, in one study of sodium (salt) intake and cardiovascular disease, which used a sample of over 14,000 participants, He et al. (1999) found a statistically significant link between high sodium intake and the prevalence of hypertension among normal-weight subjects. However, this statistically significant difference was not particularly large. The prevalence of hypertension among subjects with the lowest sodium intake was 19.1% compared to 21.8% for subjects with the highest sodium intake—not exactly a difference worthy of panic.

Base Rates Should Be Considered in Evaluating Probabilities. In evaluating whether a possible risk factor is associated with some disease, people often fail to consider the base rates of these events and draw far-reaching conclusions based on what

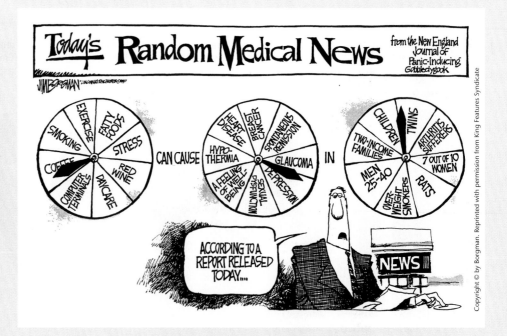

Copyright © by Borgman. Reprinted with permission from King Features Syndicate

may be a matter of sheer coincidence. For example, Paulos (1995) discusses how a handful of cases in which cellular phone users developed brain cancer led to unfounded allegations that cell phones cause brain cancer. Brain cancer is a rare disease, striking only about 6 out of 100,000 Americans per year. But given that many millions of Americans use cell phones, one would expect to find thousands upon thousands of new cases of brain cancer annually among cell phone users. Given the small number of reported cases, Paulos playfully concludes that cellular phones must prevent brain cancer.

It is also useful to consider base rates in evaluating percentage increases in diseases. If the base rate of a disease is relatively low, a small increase can sound quite large if it is reported as a percentage. For example, in the He et al. (1999) study, the prevalence of diabetes among subjects with the lowest sodium intake was 2.1% compared to 3.8% for subjects with the highest sodium intake. Based on this small but statistically significant difference, one could say (the investigators did not) that high sodium intake was associated with a 81% increase ($[3.8 - 2.1] \div 2.1$) in the prevalence of diabetes.

Thinking Systematically About Health Decisions

Health decisions are oriented toward the future, which means that there are always uncertainties. And they usually involve weighing potential risks and benefits. None of these variables is unique to health decisions—uncertainty, risks, and benefits play prominent roles in economic and political decisions as well as in personal decisions. Let's apply some basic principles of quantitative reasoning to a treatment decision involving whether to prescribe Ritalin for a boy who has been diagnosed with attention deficit disorder (ADD). Keep in mind that the general principles applied in this example can be used for a wide variety of decisions.

Seek Information to Reduce Uncertainty.
Gather information and check it carefully for accuracy, completeness, and the presence or absence of conflicting information. For example, is the diagnosis of ADD correct? Look for conflicting information that does not fit with this diagnosis. If the child can sit and read for a long period of time, maybe the problem is an undetected hearing loss that makes him appear to be hyperactive in some situations. As you consider the additional information, begin quantifying the degree of uncertainty or its "flip side," your degree of confidence that the diagnosis is correct. If you decide that you are not confident about the diagnosis, you may be trying to solve the wrong problem.

Make Risk-Benefit Assessments.
What are the risks and benefits of Ritalin? How likely is this child to benefit from Ritalin, and just how much improvement can be expected? If the child is 8 years old and unable to read and is miserable in school and at home, any treatment that could reduce his problems deserves serious consideration. As in the first step, the quantification is at an approximate level.

List Alternative Courses of Action.
What are the alternatives to Ritalin? How well do they work? What are the risks associated with the alternatives, including the risk of falling further behind in school? Consider the pros and cons of each alternative. A special diet that sometimes works might be a good first step along with the decision to start drug therapy if the child does not show improvement over some time period. What are the relative success rates for different types of treatment for children like the one being considered? In order to answer these questions, you will need to use probability estimates in your decision making.

As you can see from this example, many parts of the problem have been quantified (confidence in the diagnosis, likelihood of improvement, probability of negative outcomes, and so forth). Precise probability values were not used because often the actual numbers are not known. Some of the quantified values reflect value judgments, others reflect likelihoods, and others assess the degree of uncertainty. If you are thinking that the quantification of many unknowns in decision making is a lot of work, you are right. But, it is work worth doing. Whenever there are important decisions to be made about health, the ability to think with numbers will help you reach a better decision. And yes, that assertion is a virtual certainty.

Table 12.4 Critical Thinking Skills Discussed in This Application

Skill	Description
Understanding the limitations of correlational evidence	The critical thinker understands that a correlation between two variables does not demonstrate that there is a causal link between the variables.
Understanding the limitations of statistical significance	The critical thinker understands that weak relationships can be statistically significant when large samples are used in research.
Utilizing base rates in making predictions and evaluating probabilities	The critical thinker appreciates that the initial proportion of some group or event needs to be considered in weighing probabilities.
Seeking information to reduce uncertainty	The critical thinker understands that gathering more information can often decrease uncertainty, and reduced uncertainty can facilitate better decisions.
Making risk-benefit assessments	The critical thinker is aware that most decisions have risks and benefits that need to be weighed carefully.
Generating and evaluating alternative courses of action	In problem solving and decision making, the critical thinker knows the value of generating as many alternatives as possible and assessing their advantages and disadvantages.

Key Ideas

The Nature of Stress

● Stress involves circumstances and experiences that are perceived as threatening. Stress is a common, everyday event, and even seemingly minor stressors or hassles can be problematic. Whether one feels stressed by events depends on how one appraises them.

● Major types of stress include frustration, conflict, change, and pressure. Frustration occurs when an obstacle prevents one from attaining some goal. There are three principal types of conflict: approach-approach, avoidance-avoidance, and approach-avoidance. The third type is especially stressful. Vacillation is a common response to approach-avoidance conflict.

● A large number of studies with the SRRS suggest that change is stressful. Although this may be true, it is now clear that the SRRS is a measure of general stress rather than just change-related stress. Two kinds of pressure (to perform and conform) also appear to be stressful.

Responding to Stress

● Emotional reactions to stress typically include anger, fear, and sadness, although positive emotions may also occur. Emotional arousal may interfere with coping. According to the inverted-U hypothesis, the optimal level of arousal on a task depends on the complexity of the task.

● Selye's general adaptation syndrome describes three stages in physiological reactions to stress: alarm, resistance, and exhaustion. There are two major pathways along which the brain sends signals to the endocrine system in response to stress.

● The behavioral response to stress takes the form of coping. Some coping responses are less than optimal. Among these are giving up, blaming oneself, striking out at others with acts of aggression, and indulging oneself. Defense mechanisms protect against emotional distress through self-deception. Defensive illusions may sometimes be adaptive. Relatively healthy coping tactics are called constructive coping.

The Effects of Stress on Physical Health

● Type A personality has been implicated as a contributing cause of coronary heart disease. Hostility may be the most toxic element of the Type A syndrome. Transient emotional reactions and depression have also been identified as cardiovascular risk factors.

● Researchers have found associations between stress and the onset of a great variety of specific diseases. Stress may play a role in a host of diseases because it can temporarily suppress the effectiveness of the immune system.

● While there's little doubt that stress can contribute to the development of physical illness, the link between stress and illness is modest in strength. There are individual differences in how much stress people can tolerate. Social support and optimism appear to reduce the effects of stress. Stress may also have positive effects, stimulating personal growth and the acquisition of new strengths.

Health-Impairing Behavior

● People frequently display health-impairing lifestyles. Smokers have much higher mortality rates than nonsmokers because they are more vulnerable to a host of diseases. Poor nutritional habits have been linked to a variety of health problems. Lack of exercise elevates one's risk for cardiovascular diseases and perhaps for certain types of cancer.

● Aspects of behavior also influence the risk of HIV infection, which is transmitted through person-to-person contact involving the exchange of bodily fluids, primarily semen and blood. Misconceptions about AIDS are common, and the people who hold these misconceptions tend to fall into polarized camps, either overestimating or underestimating the risk of infection.

Reactions to Illness

● Ignoring physical symptoms may result in the delay of needed medical treatment. There are many barriers to effective communication between patients and health care providers.

● Nonadherence to medical advice is a major problem. The likelihood of noncompliance is greater when instructions are difficult to understand, when recommendations are difficult to follow, and when patients are unhappy with their doctor.

Reflecting on the Chapter's Themes

● Two of our integrative themes were prominent in this chapter. First, we saw that behavior and health are influenced by multiple causes. Second, we saw that experience is highly subjective, as stress lies in the eye of the beholder.

PERSONAL APPLICATION • Improving Coping and Stress Management

● People use a variety of coping strategies, and some are healthier than others. Ellis emphasizes the importance of reappraising stressful events to detect and dispute catastrophic thinking. Using humor to cope with stress may be beneficial in a variety of ways.

● In some cases, it may pay to release pent-up emotions by expressing them. Managing hostility and forgiving others' transgressions can also reduce stress. Relaxation techniques, such as Benson's relaxation response, can reduce the wear and tear of stress. Physical vulnerability may also be reduced through regular exercise.

CRITICAL THINKING APPLICATION • Thinking Rationally About Health Statistics and Decisions

● Evaluations of statistics on health risks can be enhanced by remembering that correlation is no assurance of causation, statistical significance is not equivalent to practical significance, and base rates need to be considered in assessing probabilities.

● In trying to think systematically about health decisions, one should seek information to reduce uncertainty, make risk-benefit assessments, and consider alternative courses of action.

Key Terms

Acquired immune deficiency
    syndrome (AIDS) (p. 390)
Aggression (p. 381)
Approach-approach conflict
    (p. 375)
Approach-avoidance conflict
    (p. 375)
Avoidance-avoidance conflict
    (p. 375)
Biopsychosocial model (p. 373)
Catastrophic thinking (p. 394)
Catharsis (p. 382)
Conflict (p. 375)
Constructive coping (p. 383)
Coping (p. 381)
Defense mechanisms (p. 382)
Frustration (pp. 374–375)
General adaptation syndrome
    (p. 379)
Health psychology (p. 374)
Immune response (p. 386)

Internet addiction (p. 382)
Learned helplessness (p. 381)
Life changes (p. 375)
Optimism (p. 387)
Pressure (p. 376)
Social support (p. 387)
Stress (p. 374)
Type A personality (p. 384)
Type B personality (p. 384)

Key People

Robin DiMatteo (p. 392)
Albert Ellis (pp. 381, 394–395)
Meyer Friedman and Ray
    Rosenman (p. 384)
Thomas Holmes and Richard Rahe
    (pp. 375–376)
Richard Lazarus (p. 374)
Martin Seligman (pp. 387–388)
Hans Selye (pp. 379–380)
Shelley Taylor (p. 383)

1. It is the weekend before a major psychology exam on Monday, and Janine is experiencing total panic even though she is thoroughly prepared and she aced the previous two psychology exams. Janine's panic illustrates that:
   A. high arousal is optimal on complex tasks.
   B. the appraisal of stress is quite objective.
   C. the appraisal of stress is highly subjective.
   D. her adrenal cortex is malfunctioning.

2. The notion that health is governed by a complex interaction of biological, psychological, and sociocultural factors is referred to as the:
   A. medical model.
   B. multifactorial model.
   C. biopsychosocial model.
   D. interactive model.

3. The four principal sources of stress are:
   A. frustration, conflict, pressure, and anxiety.
   B. frustration, anger, pressure, and change.
   C. anger, anxiety, depression, and annoyance.
   D. frustration, conflict, pressure, and change.

4. When your boss tells you that a complicated report that you have not yet begun to write must be on her desk by this afternoon, you may experience:
   A. burnout.   C. a double bind.
   B. pressure.   D. catharsis.

5. You want very badly to ask someone for a date, but you are afraid to risk rejection. You are experiencing:
   A. an approach-avoidance conflict.
   B. an avoidance-avoidance conflict.
   C. optimized arousal.
   D. conformity pressure.

6. Research suggests that a high level of arousal may be most optimal for the performance of a task when:
   A. the task is complex.
   B. the task is simple.
   C. the rewards are high.
   D. an audience is present.

7. The alarm stage of Hans Selye's general adaptation syndrome is essentially the same as:
   A. the fight-or-flight response.
   B. constructive coping.
   C. approach-avoidance conflict.
   D. secondary appraisal.

8. The brain structure responsible for initiating action along the two major pathways through which the brain sends signals to the endocrine system is the:
   A. hypothalamus.   C. corpus callosum.
   B. thalamus.   D. medulla.

9. You are way behind in your psychology class and are in danger of flunking. Which of the following qualifies as a defense mechanism in response to this situation?
   A. You seek the aid of a tutor.
   B. You decide to withdraw from the class and take it another time.
   C. You rationalize that everyone is behind in the class and convince yourself that you will somehow catch up and ace the final.
   D. You consult with the instructor to see what you can do to pass the class.

10. Which of the following is least accurate in regard to defense mechanisms?
    A. There are many different defense mechanisms.
    B. They are always unhealthy.
    C. They work through self-deception.
    D. They are used to ward off unpleasant emotions.

11. Which element of the Type A personality seems to be most strongly related to increased coronary risk?
    A. Time consciousness
    B. Perfectionism
    C. Ambitiousness
    D. Hostility

12. Research has found that optimists are more likely than pessimists to:
    A. take their time in confronting problems.
    B. identify the negatives before they identify the positives.
    C. engage in action-oriented, problem-focused coping.
    D. seek social support only after they have exhausted all individual efforts to deal with the problem.

13. Which of the following has *not* been found to be a mode of transmission for the HIV virus?
    A. Sexual contact among homosexual men
    B. The sharing of needles by intravenous drug users
    C. Heterosexual contact
    D. Sharing food

14. The fact that health is governed by a dense network of factors is an illustration of the theme of:
    A. psychology in a sociohistorical context.
    B. the phenomenology of experience.
    C. multifactorial causation.
    D. empiricism.

15. In evaluating health statistics, it is useful to:
    A. remember that statistical significance is equivalent to practical significance.
    B. remember that correlation is a reliable indicator of causation.
    C. consider base rates in thinking about probabilities.
    D. do all of the above.

Answers

1 C p. 374
2 C p. 373
3 D pp. 374–377
4 B pp. 376–377
5 A p. 375

6 B p. 379
7 A p. 379
8 A p. 380
9 C pp. 382–383
10 B p. 383

11 D p. 384
12 C p. 387
13 D pp. 390–391
14 C pp. 393–394
15 C pp. 398–399

PsykTrek

Go to the PsykTrek website or CD-ROM for further study of the concepts in this chapter. Both online and on the CD-ROM, PsykTrek includes dozens of learning modules with videos, animations, and quizzes, as well as simulations of psychological phenomena and a multimedia glossary that includes word pronunciations.

ThomsonNOW

www.thomsonedu.com/ThomsonNOW
Go to this site for the link to ThomsonNOW, your one-stop study shop. Take a Pre-Test for this chapter, and ThomsonNOW will generate a Personalized Study Plan based on your test results. The Study Plan will identify the topics you need to review and direct you to online resources to help you master those topics. You can then take a Post-Test to help you determine the concepts you have mastered and what you still need to work on.

Companion Website

www.thomsonedu.com/psychology/weiten
Go to this site to find online resources directly linked to your book, including a glossary, flash cards, drag-and-drop exercises, quizzes, and more!

CHAPTER 13

Psychological Disorders

© Klaus Hackenberg/zefa/Corbis

The government of the United States was overthrown more than a year ago! I'm the president of the United States of America and Bob Dylan is vice president!" So said Ed, the author of a prominent book on journalism, who was speaking to a college journalism class, as a guest lecturer. Ed also informed the class that he had killed both John and Robert Kennedy, as well as Charles de Gaulle, the former president of France. He went on to tell the class that all rock music songs were written about him, that he was the greatest karate expert in the universe, and that he had been fighting "space wars" for 2000 years. The students in the class were mystified by Ed's bizarre, disjointed "lecture," but they assumed that he was putting on a show that would eventually lead to a sensible conclusion. However, their perplexed but expectant calm was shattered when Ed pulled a hatchet from the props he had brought with him and hurled the hatchet at the class! Fortunately, he didn't hit anyone, as the hatchet sailed over the students' heads. At that point, the professor for the class realized that Ed's irrational behavior was not a pretense. The professor evacuated the class quickly while Ed continued to rant and rave about his presidential administration, space wars, vampires, his romances with female rock stars, and his personal harem of 38 "chicks." (Adapted from Pearce, 1974)

Clearly Ed's behavior was abnormal. Even he recognized that when he agreed later to be admitted to a mental hospital, signing himself in as the "President of the United States of America." What causes such abnormal behavior? Does Ed have a mental illness, or does he just behave strangely? What is the basis for judging behavior as normal versus abnormal? How common are psychological disorders? Are the same mental disorders seen in different cultures? These are just a few of the questions that we will address in this chapter as we discuss psychological disorders and their complex causes.

> Abnormal Behavior: Myths and Realities

Misconceptions about abnormal behavior are common. Consequently, we need to clear up some preliminary issues before we describe the various types of disorders. In this section, we will discuss (1) the medical model of abnormal behavior, (2) the criteria of abnormal behavior, and (3) the classification of psychological disorders.

The Medical Model Applied to Abnormal Behavior

In Ed's case, there's no question that his behavior was abnormal. But does it make sense to view his unusual and irrational behavior as an illness? This is a controversial question. **The *medical model* proposes that it is useful to think of abnormal behavior as a disease.** This point of view is the basis for many of the terms used to refer to abnormal behavior, including mental *illness,* psychological *disorder,* and *psychopathology* (*pathology* refers to manifestations of disease). The medical model gradually became the dominant way of thinking about abnormal behavior during the 18th and 19th centuries, and its influence remains strong today.

The medical model clearly represented progress over earlier models of abnormal behavior. Prior to the 18th century, most conceptions of abnormal behav-

ior were based on superstition. People who behaved strangely were thought to be possessed by demons, to be witches in league with the devil, or to be victims of God's punishment. Their disorders were "treated" with chants, rituals, exorcisms, and such. If individuals' behavior was seen as threatening, they were candidates for chains, dungeons, torture, and death (see **Figure 13.1** on the next page).

The rise of the medical model brought improvements in the treatment of those who exhibited abnormal behavior. As victims of an illness, they were viewed with more sympathy and less hatred and fear. Although living conditions in early asylums were often deplorable, gradual progress was made toward more humane care of the mentally ill. It took time, but ineffective approaches to treatment eventually gave way to scientific investigation of the causes and cures of psychological disorders.

However, in recent decades, some critics have suggested that the medical model may have outlived its usefulness (Kiesler, 1999). A particularly vocal critic has been Thomas Szasz (1974, 1990). He asserts that "strictly speaking, disease or illness can affect only the body; hence there can be no mental illness . . . Minds can be 'sick' only in the sense that jokes are 'sick' or economies are 'sick'" (1974, p. 267). He further argues that abnormal behavior usually involves a deviation from social norms rather than an illness.

PREVIEW QUESTIONS

- What is the medical model?
- What criteria are used to judge abnormality?
- What classification system is used to diagnose psychological disorders?

Web Link **13.1**

Mental Health Net
This is arguably the premier site on the Net to explore all aspects of mental health, including psychological disorders and treatment, professional issues, and information for consumers. It is a great starting point, with links to more than 8000 resources.

Figure 13.1

Historical conceptions of mental illness. In the Middle Ages people who behaved strangely were sometimes thought to be in league with the devil. The drawing on the right depicts some of the cruel methods used to extract confessions from suspected witches and warlocks. Some psychological disorders were also thought to be caused by demonic possession. The illustration below depicts an exorcism.

Source: (Right) Culver Pictures, Inc. (Below) *St. Catherine of Siena Exorcising a Possessed Woman,* c. 1500–1510. Girolamo Di Benvenuto. Denver Art Museum Collection, Gift of Samuel H. Kress Foundation Collection, 1967.171 © Denver Art Museum, 2006. All rights reserved.

THOMAS SZASZ

"Minds can be 'sick' only in the sense that jokes are 'sick' or economies are 'sick.'"

He contends that such deviations are "problems in living" rather than medical problems. According to Szasz, the medical model's disease analogy converts moral and social questions about what is acceptable behavior into medical questions.

Although Szasz's criticism has some merit, we'll take the position that the disease analogy continues to be useful, although one should remember that it is *only* an analogy. Medical concepts such as *diagnosis, etiology,* and *prognosis* have proven valuable in the treatment and study of abnormality. **Diagnosis involves distinguishing one illness from another. Etiology refers to the apparent causation and developmental history of an illness. A prognosis is a forecast about the probable course of an illness.** These medically based concepts have widely shared meanings that permit clinicians, researchers, and the public to communicate more effectively in their discussions of abnormal behavior.

Criteria of Abnormal Behavior

If your next-door neighbor scrubs his front porch twice every day and spends virtually all his time cleaning and recleaning his house, is he normal? If your sister-in-law goes to one physician after another seeking treatment for ailments that appear imaginary, is she psychologically healthy? How are we to judge what's normal and what's abnormal? More important, who's to do the judging?

These are complex questions. In a sense, *all* people make judgments about normality in that they all express opinions about others' (and perhaps their own) mental health. Of course, formal diagnoses of psychological disorders are made by mental health professionals. In making these diagnoses, clinicians rely on a variety of criteria, the foremost of which are the following:

1. *Deviance.* As Szasz has pointed out, people are often said to have a disorder because their behavior deviates from what their society considers acceptable. What constitutes normality varies somewhat from one culture to another, but all cultures have such norms. When people violate these standards and expectations, they may be labeled mentally ill. For example, *transvestic fetishism* is a sexual disorder in which a man achieves sexual arousal by dressing in women's clothing. This behavior is regarded as disordered because a man who wears a dress, brassiere, and nylons is deviating from our culture's norms. This example illustrates the arbitrary nature of cultural standards regarding normality, as the same overt behavior (cross-sex dressing) is acceptable for women but deviant for men.

2. *Maladaptive behavior.* In many cases, people are judged to have a psychological disorder because their everyday adaptive behavior is impaired. This is the key criterion in the diagnosis of substance use (drug) disorders. In and of itself, alcohol and drug use is not terribly unusual or deviant. However, when the use of cocaine, for instance, begins to interfere with a person's social or occupational functioning, a substance use disorder exists. In such cases, it is the maladaptive quality of the behavior that makes it disordered.

3. *Personal distress.* Frequently, the diagnosis of a psychological disorder is based on an individual's report of great personal distress. This is usually the criterion met by people who are troubled by depression or anxiety disorders. Depressed people, for instance, may or may not exhibit deviant or maladaptive behavior. Such people are usually labeled as having a disorder when they describe their

subjective pain and suffering to friends, relatives, and mental health professionals.

Although two or three criteria may apply in a particular case, people are often viewed as disordered when only one criterion is met. As you may have already noticed, diagnoses of psychological disorders involve *value judgments* about what represents normal or abnormal behavior (Widiger & Sankis, 2000). The criteria of mental illness are not nearly as value-free as the criteria of physical illness. In evaluating physical diseases, people can usually agree that a weak heart or a malfunctioning kidney is pathological, regardless of their personal values. However, judgments about mental illness reflect prevailing cultural values, social trends, and political forces, as well as scientific knowledge (Kutchins & Kirk, 1997, Mechanic, 1999).

These realities are readily apparent if you consider how psychiatric views of homosexuality have changed over time. Homosexuality used to be listed as a sexual disorder in the American Psychiatric Association's diagnostic system (which we will discuss shortly). Because homosexuality was viewed as pathological, many gays were coaxed or coerced into therapeutic treatments for their "disorder"—treatment that often proved demeaning or harmful (Smith, Bartlett, & King, 2004). However, in 1973 a committee appointed by the American Psychiatric Association voted to delete homosexuality from the official list of psychological disorders. This action occurred for several reasons (Bayer, 1987; Forstein, 2004; Rothblum, Solomon, & Albee, 1986). First, attitudes toward homosexuality in our society had become more tolerant. Second, gay rights activists became more politically active and campaigned vigorously for the change. Third, research showed that gays and heterosexuals were indistinguishable on measures of psychological health. Although this long overdue decision was informed by scientific findings, it was also influenced by political lobbying and shifts in social values.

Psychodiagnosis: The Classification of Disorders

 SIM9

Obviously, we cannot lump all psychological disorders together without giving up all hope of understanding them better. A sound classification system for mental disorders can facilitate empirical research and enhance communication among scientists and clinicians (Williams, 1999). Thus, a great deal of effort has been invested in devising an elaborate system for classifying psychological disorders. This system is outlined in detail in a book published by the American Psychiatric Association, titled the *Diagnostic and Statistical Manual of Mental Disorders*. The current,

fourth edition, known as DSM-IV, was released in 1994 and revised in 2000. DSM-IV is a "multiaxial" system that asks for judgments about individuals on five separate dimensions, or "axes." **Figure 13.2** on the next page provides an overview of the entire system and the five axes. The diagnoses of disorders are made on Axes I and II. Clinicians record most types of disorders on Axis I. They use Axis II to list long-running personality disorders or mental retardation. People may receive diagnoses on both Axes I and II. The remaining axes are used to record supplemental information. A patient's physical disorders are listed on Axis III (General Medical Conditions). On Axis IV (Psychosocial and Environmental Problems), the clinician makes notations regarding the types of stress experienced by the individual in the past year. On Axis V (Global Assessment of Functioning), estimates are made of the individual's current level of adaptive functioning (in social and occupational behavior, viewed as a whole) and of the individual's highest level of functioning in the past year.

Obviously, in this chapter we cannot cover all 200 or so disorders listed in DSM-IV. However, we will in-

Web Link 13.2

National Alliance for the Mentally Ill (NAMI) NAMI describes itself as "a grassroots, self-help support and advocacy organization of families and friends of people with serious mental illness, and those persons themselves." Its online site responds to their needs with extensive and current information about schizophrenia, bipolar disorder, and other severe disorders.

concept **check** 13.1

Applying the Criteria of Abnormal Behavior

Check your understanding of the criteria of abnormal behavior by identifying the criteria met by each of the examples below and checking them off in the table provided. Remember, a specific behavior may meet more than one criterion. The answers are in Appendix A.

Behavioral examples

1. Alan's performance at work has suffered because he has been drinking alcohol to excess. Several co-workers have suggested that he seek help for his problem, but he thinks that they're getting alarmed over nothing. "I just enjoy a good time once in a while," he says.

2. Monica has gone away to college and feels lonely, sad, and dejected. Her grades are fine, and she gets along okay with the other students in the dormitory, but inside she's choked with gloom, hopelessness, and despair.

3. Boris believes that he's Napoleon reborn. He believes that he is destined to lead the U.S. military forces into a great battle to recover California from space aliens.

4. Natasha panics with anxiety whenever she leaves her home. Her problem escalated gradually until she was absent from work so often that she was fired. She hasn't been out of her house in nine months and is deeply troubled by her problem.

Criteria met by each example

	Maladaptive behavior	Deviance	Personal distress
1. Alan	_____	_____	_____
2. Monica	_____	_____	_____
3. Boris	_____	_____	_____
4. Natasha	_____	_____	_____

Figure 13.2

Overview of the DSM diagnostic system. Published by the American Psychiatric Association, the *Diagnostic and Statistical Manual of Mental Disorders* is the formal classification system used in the diagnosis of psychological disorders. It is a *multiaxial* system, which means that information is recorded on the five axes described here. (Based on American Psychiatric Association, 1994, 2000)

Source: Adapted with permission from the *Diagnostic and Statistical Manual of Mental Disorders, 4th ed.* (DSM-TR). Copyright © 2000 American Psychiatric Association.

Axis I
Clinical Syndromes

1. **Disorders usually first diagnosed in infancy, childhood, or adolescence**
   This category includes disorders that arise before adolescence, such as attention deficit disorders, autism, enuresis, and stuttering.

2. **Organic mental disorders**
   These disorders are temporary or permanent dysfunctions of brain tissue caused by diseases or chemicals. Examples are delirium, dementia, and amnesia.

3. **Substance-related disorders**
   This category refers to the maladaptive use of drugs and alcohol. This category requires an abnormal pattern of use, as with alcohol abuse and cocaine dependence.

4. **Schizophrenia and other psychotic disorders**
   The schizophrenias are characterized by psychotic symptoms (for example, grossly disorganized behavior, delusions, and hallucinations) and by over six months of behavioral deterioration. This category also includes delusional disorder and schizoaffective disorder.

5. **Mood disorders**
   The cardinal feature is emotional disturbance. These disorders include major depression, bipolar disorder, dysthymic disorder, and cyclothymic disorder.

6. **Anxiety disorders**
   These disorders are characterized by physiological signs of anxiety (for example, palpitations) and subjective feelings of tension, apprehension, or fear. Anxiety may be acute and focused (panic disorder) or continual and diffuse (generalized anxiety disorder).

7. **Somatoform disorders**
   These disorders are dominated by somatic symptoms that resemble physical illnesses. These symptoms cannot be fully accounted for by organic damage. This category includes somatization and conversion disorders and hypochondriasis.

8. **Dissociative disorders**
   These disorders all feature a sudden, temporary alteration or dysfunction of memory, consciousness, and identity, as in dissociative amnesia and dissociative identity disorder.

9. **Sexual and gender-identity disorders**
   There are three basic types of disorders in this category: gender identity disorders (discomfort with identity as male or female), paraphilias (preference for unusual acts to achieve sexual arousal), and sexual dysfunctions (impairments in sexual functioning).

10. **Eating Disorders**
    Eating disorders are severe disturbances in eating behavior characterized by preoccupation with weight concerns and unhealthy efforts to control weight. Examples include anorexia nervosa and bulimia nervosa.

Axis II
Personality Disorders or Mental Retardation

Personality disorders are longstanding patterns of extreme, inflexible personality traits that are deviant or maladaptive and lead to impaired functioning or subjective distress. *Mental retardation* refers to subnormal general mental ability accompanied by deficiencies in adaptive skills, originating before age 18.

Axis III
General Medical Conditions

Physical disorders or conditions are recorded on this axis. Examples include diabetes, arthritis, and hemophilia.

Axis IV
Psychosocial and Environmental Problems

Axis IV is for reporting psychosocial and environmental problems that may affect the diagnosis, treatment, and prognosis of mental disorders (Axes I and II). A psychosocial or environmental problem may be a negative life event, an environmental difficulty or deficiency, a familial or other interpersonal stressor, an inadequacy of social support or personal resources, or another problem that describes the context in which a person's difficulties have developed.

Axis V
Global Assessment of Functioning (GAF) Scale

Code	Symptoms
100	Superior functioning in a wide range of activities
90	Absent or minimal symptoms, good functioning in all areas
80	Symptoms are transient and expectable reactions to psychosocial stressors
70	Some mild symptoms or some difficulty in social, occupational, or school functioning, but generally functioning pretty well
60	Moderate symptoms or difficulty in social, occupational, or school functioning
50	Serious symptoms or impairment in social, occupational, or school functioning
40	Some impairment in reality testing or communication or major impairment in family relations, judgment, thinking, or mood
30	Behavior considerably influenced by delusions or hallucinations, serious impairment in communication or judgment, or inability to function in almost all areas
20	Some danger of hurting self or others, occasional failure to maintain minimal personal hygiene, or gross impairment in communication
10	Persistent danger of severely hurting self or others
1	

troduce most of the major categories of disorders to give you an overview of the many forms abnormal behavior takes. In discussing each set of disorders, we will begin with brief descriptions of the specific subtypes that fall in the category. If data are available, we will discuss the *prevalence* of the disorders in that category (how common they are in the population). Then we'll focus on the *etiology* of that set of disorders. Although many paths can lead to specific disorders, some are more common than others. We'll highlight some of the common paths to enhance your understanding of the roots of abnormal behavior.

Everyone experiences anxiety from time to time. It is a natural and common reaction to many of life's difficulties. For some people, however, anxiety becomes a chronic problem. These people experience high levels of anxiety with disturbing regularity. *Anxiety disorders are a class of disorders marked by feelings of excessive apprehension and anxiety.* There are five principal types of anxiety disorders: generalized anxiety disorder, phobic disorder, panic disorder, obsessive-compulsive disorder, and posttraumatic stress disorder. Studies suggest that anxiety disorders are quite common. Over the course of their lives, roughly 19% of people experience an anxiety disorder (Dew, Bromet, & Switzer, 2000; Regier & Burke, 2000).

Generalized Anxiety Disorder

The *generalized anxiety disorder* **is marked by a chronic, high level of anxiety that is not tied to any specific threat.** People with this disorder worry constantly about yesterday's mistakes and tomorrow's problems. They worry about minor matters related to family, finances, work, and personal illness. In particular, they worry about how much they worry (Barlow et al., 2003). They often dread decisions and brood over them endlessly. Their anxiety is frequently accompanied by physical symptoms, such as trembling, muscle tension, diarrhea, dizziness, faintness, sweating, and heart palpitations. Generalized anxiety disorder tends to have a gradual onset and is seen more frequently in females than males (Brown, 1999). The lifetime prevalence of generalized anxiety disorder appears to be around 5% (Barlow et al., 2003).

Phobic Disorder

In a phobic disorder, an individual's troublesome anxiety has a specific focus. **A *phobic disorder* is marked by a persistent and irrational fear of an object or situation that presents no realistic danger.** The following case provides an example of a phobic disorder:

Hilda is 32 years of age and has a rather unusual fear. She is terrified of snow. She cannot go outside in the snow. She cannot even stand to see snow or hear about it on the weather report. Her phobia severely constricts her day-to-day behavior. Probing in therapy revealed that her phobia was caused by a traumatic experience at age 11. Playing at a ski lodge, she was buried briefly by a small avalanche of snow. She had no recollection of this experience until it was recovered in therapy. (Adapted from Laughlin, 1967, p. 227)

As Hilda's unusual snow phobia illustrates, people can develop phobic responses to virtually anything. Nonetheless, certain types of phobias are relatively common, including acrophobia (fear of heights), claustrophobia (fear of small, enclosed places), brontophobia (fear of storms), hydrophobia (fear of water), and various animal and insect phobias (Antony & McCabe, 2003). Many people troubled by phobias realize that their fears are irrational but still are unable to calm themselves when confronted by a phobic object.

Panic Disorder and Agoraphobia

A *panic disorder* **is characterized by recurrent attacks of overwhelming anxiety that usually occur suddenly and unexpectedly.** These paralyzing attacks are accompanied by physical symptoms of anxiety. After a number of anxiety attacks, victims often become apprehensive, wondering when their next panic will occur. Their concern about exhibiting panic in public may increase to the point where they are afraid to leave home. This fear creates a condition called agoraphobia, which is a common complication of panic disorders.

Agoraphobia **is a fear of going out to public places** (its literal meaning is "fear of the marketplace or open places"). Because of this fear, some people become prisoners confined to their homes, although many will venture out if accompanied by a trusted companion (Hollander & Simeon, 2003). As its name suggests, agoraphobia was originally viewed as a phobic disorder. However, evidence eventually showed that agoraphobia is mainly a complication of panic disorder. About two-thirds of people who suffer from panic disorder are female (Horwath & Weissman, 2000). The onset of panic disorder typically occurs during late adolescence or early adulthood (Pine, 2000).

PREVIEW QUESTIONS

● What are the five major anxiety disorders, and what are their chief symptoms?

● Which biological factors have been implicated in anxiety disorders?

● How do conditioning and learning contribute to anxiety disorders?

● How do cognitive factors and stress contribute to anxiety disorders?

Web Link 13.3

Mental Health: A Report of the Surgeon General
In late 1999, the Surgeon General issued the first comprehensive survey of the state of mental health in the United States. This report has provided a crucial foundation of statistics and other information for understanding the needs for mental health care in the first decade of the 21st century.

Obsessive-Compulsive Disorder

11a

Obsessions are *thoughts* that repeatedly intrude on one's consciousness in a distressing way. Compulsions are *actions* that one feels forced to carry out. Thus, **obsessive-compulsive disorder (OCD) is marked by persistent, uncontrollable intrusions of unwanted thoughts (obsessions) and urges to engage in senseless rituals (compulsions).** To illustrate, let's examine the bizarre behavior of a man once reputed to be the wealthiest person in the world:

The famous industrialist Howard Hughes was obsessed with the possibility of being contaminated by germs. This led him to devise extraordinary rituals to minimize the possibility of such contamination. He would spend hours methodically cleaning a single telephone. He once wrote a three-page memo instructing assistants on exactly how to open cans of fruit for him. The following is just a small portion of the instructions that Hughes provided for a driver who delivered films to his bungalow. "Get out of the car on the traffic side. Do not at any time be on the side of the car between the car and the curb. . . . Carry only one can of film at a time. Step over the gutter opposite the place where the sidewalk dead-ends into the curb from a point as far out into the center of the road as possible. Do not ever walk on the grass at all, also do not step into the gutter at all. Walk to the bungalow keeping as near to the center of the sidewalk as possible." (Adapted from Barlett & Steele, 1979, pp. 227–237)

Obsessions often center on inflicting harm on others, personal failures, suicide, or sexual acts. People troubled by obsessions may feel that they have lost control of their mind. Compulsions usually involve stereotyped rituals that may temporarily relieve the anxiety produced by one's obsessions. Common examples include constant handwashing; repetitive cleaning of things that are already clean; endless rechecking of locks, faucets, and such; and excessive arranging, counting, and hoarding of things (Pato, Eisen, & Phillips, 2003). Unusual rituals intended to bring good luck are also a common form of compulsive behavior. Although many of us can be compulsive at times, full-fledged obsessive-compulsive disorders occur in roughly 2.5% of people at some time in their lives (Turner et al., 2001). The typical age of onset for OCD is late adolescence, with most cases (75%) emerging before the age of 30 (Kessler et al., 2005a).

Posttraumatic Stress Disorder

Posttraumatic stress disorder (PTSD) involves enduring psychological disturbance attributed to the experience of a major traumatic event. PTSD is often seen after a rape or assault, a severe automobile accident, a harrowing war experience, a natural disaster, or the witnessing of someone's death (Koren, Arnon, & Klein, 1999; Stein et al., 1997b; Vernberg et al., 1996). Unfortunately, traumatic experiences such as these appear to be much more common than widely assumed. In some instances, PTSD does not surface until many months or years after a person's exposure to severe stress (Holen, 2000). Common symptoms include reexperiencing the traumatic event in the form of nightmares and flashbacks, emotional numbing, alienation, problems in social relations, an increased sense of vulnerability, and elevated arousal, anxiety, anger, and guilt (Flannery, 1999; Shalev, 2001). Research suggests that a variety of factors are predictors of individuals' risk for PTSD (McNally, 1999; Norris et al., 2001; Ursano, Fullerton, & Norwood, 2001). As you might expect, increased vulnerability is associated with greater personal injuries and losses, greater intensity of exposure to the traumatic event, and more exposure to the grotesque aftermath of the event. One key predictor of vulnerability that emerged in a recent review of the relevant research is the *intensity of one's reaction at the time of the traumatic event* (Ozer et al., 2003). Individuals who have especially intense emotional reactions during or immediately after the traumatic event go on to show elevated vulnerability to PTSD. Vulnerability seems to be greatest among people whose reactions are so intense that they report dissociative experiences (a sense that things are not real, that time is stretching out, that one is watching oneself in a movie).

As a young man (shown in the photo), Howard Hughes was a handsome, dashing daredevil pilot and movie producer who appeared to be reasonably well adjusted. However, as the years went by, his behavior gradually became more and more maladaptive, as obsessions and compulsions came to dominate his life. In his later years (shown in the drawing), he spent most of his time in darkened rooms, naked, unkempt, and dirty, following bizarre rituals to alleviate his anxieties. (The drawing was done by an NBC artist and was based on descriptions from men who had seen Hughes.)

© Bettmann/Corbis

© Associated Press/AP

Etiology of Anxiety Disorders

Like most psychological disorders, anxiety disorders develop out of complicated interactions among a variety of factors. Classical conditioning, observational learning, and cognitive and personality factors appear especially important, but biological factors may also contribute to anxiety disorders.

Biological Factors

In studies that assess the impact of heredity on psychological disorders, investigators look at *concordance rates*. **A *concordance rate* indicates the percentage of twin pairs or other pairs of relatives that exhibit the same disorder.** If relatives who share more genetic similarity show higher concordance rates than relatives who share less genetic overlap, this finding supports the genetic hypothesis. The results of both *twin studies* (see **Figure 13.3**) and *family studies* (see Chapter 3 for discussions of both methods) suggest that there is a moderate genetic predisposition to anxiety disorders (Fyer, 2000; Hettema, Neale, & Kendler, 2001).

Recent evidence suggests that a link may exist between anxiety disorders and neurochemical activity in the brain. As you learned in Chapter 3, *neurotransmitters* are chemicals that carry signals from one neuron to another. Therapeutic drugs (such as Valium) that reduce excessive anxiety appear to alter neurotransmitter activity at synapses that release a neurotransmitter called GABA. This finding and other lines of evidence suggest that disturbances in the neural circuits using GABA may play a role in some types of anxiety disorders (Skolnick, 2003). Abnormalities in other neural circuits using serotonin have recently been implicated in panic and obsessive-compulsive disorders (Sullivan & Coplan, 2000). Thus, scientists are beginning to unravel the neurochemical bases for anxiety disorders.

Conditioning and Learning

Many anxiety responses may be *acquired through classical conditioning* and *maintained through operant conditioning* (see Chapter 6). According to Mowrer (1947), an originally neutral stimulus (the snow in Hilda's case, for instance) may be paired with a frightening event (the avalanche) so that it becomes a conditioned stimulus eliciting anxiety (see **Figure 13.4**). Once a fear is acquired through classical conditioning, the person may start avoiding the anxiety-producing stimulus. The avoidance response is negatively reinforced because it is followed by a reduction in anxiety. This process involves operant conditioning (see

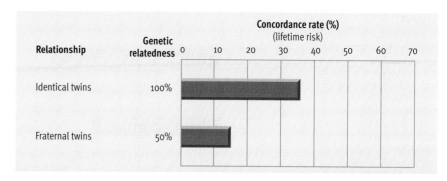

Figure 13.3
Twin studies of anxiety disorders. The concordance rate for anxiety disorders in identical twins is higher than that for fraternal twins, who share less genetic overlap. These results suggest that there is a genetic predisposition to anxiety disorders. (Data based on Noyes et al., 1987; Slater & Shields, 1969; Torgersen, 1979, 1983)

Figure 13.4). Thus, separate conditioning processes may create and then sustain specific anxiety responses (Levis, 1989). Consistent with this view, studies find that a substantial portion of people suffering from phobias can identify a traumatic conditioning experience that probably contributed to their anxiety disorder (Antony & McCabe, 2003; King, Eleonora, & Ollendick, 1998).

The tendency to develop phobias of certain types of objects and situations may be explained by Martin Seligman's (1971) concept of *preparedness*. Like many theorists, Seligman believes that classical conditioning creates most phobic responses. *However, he suggests that people are biologically prepared by their evolutionary history to acquire some fears much more easily than others.* His theory would explain why people develop phobias of ancient sources of threat (such as snakes and spiders) much more readily than modern sources of threat (such as electrical outlets or hot irons). Some laboratory studies of conditioned fears have yielded evidence that supports Seligman's theory, but the evidence is inconsistent (Ohman & Mineka, 2003; Rapee & Barlow, 2001).

Web Link 13.4

National Institute of Mental Health: For the Public
A wealth of information on psychological disorders is available at this subpage of the U.S. National Institute of Mental Health's massive website. Visitors will find detailed online booklets on generalized anxiety disorder, obsessive-compulsive disorder, panic disorder, depression, bipolar disorder, and so forth. Brief fact sheets, dense technical reports, and many other resources can also be found here.

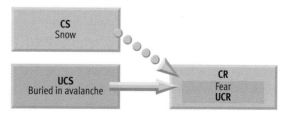
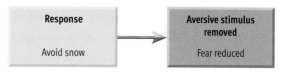

(a) Classical conditioning: Acquisition of phobic fear

(b) Operant conditioning: Maintenance of phobic fear
(negative reinforcement)

Figure 13.4
Conditioning as an explanation for phobias. **(a)** Many phobias appear to be acquired through classical conditioning when a neutral stimulus is paired with an anxiety-arousing stimulus. **(b)** Once acquired, a phobia may be maintained through operant conditioning. Avoidance of the phobic stimulus reduces anxiety, resulting in negative reinforcement.

Figure 13.5
Cognitive factors in anxiety disorders.
Eysenck and his colleagues (1991) compared how subjects with anxiety problems and nonanxious subjects tended to interpret sentences that could be viewed as threatening or nonthreatening. Consistent with cognitive models of anxiety disorders, anxious subjects were more likely to interpret the sentences in a threatening light.

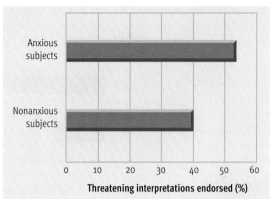

(Eysenck et al., 1991). For instance, one such sentence was "The doctor examined little Emma's growth," which could mean that the doctor checked her height or the growth of a tumor. As **Figure 13.5** shows, the anxious participants interpreted the sentences in a threatening way more often than the nonanxious participants did. Thus, consistent with our theme that human experience is highly subjective, the cognitive view holds that some people are prone to anxiety disorders because they see threat in every corner of their lives (Aikens & Craske, 2001; Riskind, 2005).

Cognitive Factors

Cognitive theorists maintain that certain styles of thinking make some people particularly vulnerable to anxiety disorders. According to these theorists, some people are more likely to suffer from anxiety problems because they tend to (a) misinterpret harmless situations as threatening, (b) focus excessive attention on perceived threats, and (c) selectively recall information that seems threatening (Beck, 1997; McNally, 1994, 1996). In one intriguing test of the cognitive view, anxious and nonanxious subjects were asked to read 32 sentences that could be interpreted in either a threatening or a nonthreatening manner

Stress

Obviously, cases of posttraumatic stress disorder are attributed to individuals' exposure to extremely stressful incidents. Research has also demonstrated that other types of anxiety disorders can be stress related (Sandin et al., 2004; Venturello et al., 2002). For instance, Faravelli and Pallanti (1989) found that patients with panic disorder had experienced a dramatic increase in stress in the month prior to the onset of their disorder. In another study, Brown and colleagues (1998) found an association between stress and the development of social phobia. Thus, there is reason to believe that high stress often helps precipitate the onset of anxiety disorders.

> Somatoform Disorders

PREVIEW QUESTIONS

- How do psychosomatic diseases and somatoform disorders differ?
- What are the three major somatoform disorders, and what are their chief symptoms?
- What factors have been implicated in the etiology of somatoform disorders?

Chances are, you have met people who always seem to be complaining about aches, pains, and physical maladies of doubtful authenticity. You may have thought to yourself, "It's all in his head" and concluded that the person exhibited a "psychosomatic" condition. However, the term *psychosomatic* is widely misused. ***Psychosomatic diseases* are genuine physical ailments caused in part by psychological factors, especially emotional distress.** These diseases, which include maladies such as ulcers, asthma, and high blood pressure, have a genuine organic basis and are not imagined ailments. They are recorded on the DSM axis for physical problems (Axis III). When physical illness appears *largely* psychological in origin, we are dealing with somatoform disorders, which are recorded on Axis I. ***Somatoform disorders* are physical ailments that cannot be fully explained by organic conditions and are largely due to psychological factors.** Although their symptoms are more imaginary than real, victims of somatoform disorders are *not* simply faking. Deliberate faking of illness for personal gain is another matter altogether, called *malingering.*

We will discuss three specific types of somatoform disorders: somatization disorder, conversion disorder, and hypochondriasis. Diagnostic difficulties make it hard to obtain sound data on the prevalence of somatoform disorders (Bouman, Eifert, & Lejuez, 1999).

Somatization Disorder

Individuals with somatization disorder are often said to "cling to ill health." A ***somatization disorder* is marked by a history of diverse physical complaints that appear to be psychological in origin.** Somatization disorder occurs mostly in women (Guggenheim, 2000) and often coexists with depression and anxiety disorders (Gureje et al., 1997). Victims report an endless succession of minor physical ailments that seem to wax and wane in response to the stress in their lives (Servan-Schreiber, Kolb, & Tabas, 1999). They usually have a long and complicated history of medical treatment from many doctors. The distinguishing feature of this disorder is the diversity of the victims' physical complaints. Over the years, they report a mixed bag of cardiovascular, gastrointestinal, pulmonary, neurological, and genitourinary symptoms. The unlikely nature of such a mixture of symptoms occurring together often alerts a physician to the possible psychological basis for the patient's problems.

Conversion Disorder

***Conversion disorder* is characterized by a significant loss of physical function (with no apparent organic basis), usually in a single organ system.** Common symptoms include partial or complete loss of vision, partial or complete loss of hearing, partial paralysis, severe laryngitis or mutism, and loss of feeling or function in limbs. People with conversion disorder are usually troubled by more severe ailments than people with somatization disorder. In some cases of conversion disorder, there are telltale clues about the psychological origins of the illness because the patient's symptoms are not consistent with medical knowledge about their apparent disease. For instance, the loss of feeling in one hand that is seen in "glove anesthesia" is inconsistent with the known facts of neurological organization (see **Figure 13.6**).

Hypochondriasis

Hypochondriacs constantly monitor their physical condition, looking for signs of illness. Any tiny alteration from their physical norm leads them to conclude that they have contracted a disease. ***Hypochondriasis* (more widely known as *hypochondria*) is characterized by excessive preoccupation with one's health and incessant worry about developing physical illnesses.** When hypochondriacs are assured by their physician that they do not have any real illness, they often are skeptical and disbelieving (Starcevic, 2001). They frequently assume that the physician must be incompetent, and they go shopping for another doctor. Hypochondriacs don't subjectively suffer from physical distress as much as they *overinterpret* every conceivable sign of illness. Hypochondria often appears alongside other psychological disorders, especially anxiety disorders and depression (Iezzi, Duckworth, & Adams, 2001). For example, Howard Hughes's obsessive-compulsive disorder was coupled with profound hypochondria.

Etiology of Somatoform Disorders

Inherited aspects of physiological functioning may predispose people to somatoform disorders (Weiner, 1992). However, available evidence suggests that these disorders are largely a function of psychological considerations.

Cognitive Factors

In recent years, theorists have devoted increased attention to how cognitive peculiarities might contribute to somatoform disorders. For example, Barsky (2001) asserts that some people focus excessive attention on their internal physiological processes and amplify normal bodily sensations into symptoms of distress, which lead them to pursue unnecessary medical treatment. Recent evidence suggests that people with somatoform disorders tend to draw catastrophic conclusions about minor bodily complaints (Salkovskis & Warwick, 2001). They also seem to apply a faulty standard of good health, equating health with a complete absence of symptoms and discomfort, which is unrealistic (Barsky et al., 1993).

Personality Factors

People with certain types of personality traits seem to develop somatoform disorders more readily than others. For example, the personality trait of *neuroticism,* one of the Big Five traits described in Chapter 11, seems to elevate individuals' susceptibility to somatoform disorders (Noyes et al., 2005). Research also suggests that the pathological care-seeking behavior seen in these disorders may be caused by *insecure attachment styles* (see the discussion of attachment in Chapter 10) that are rooted in early experiences with caregivers (Noyes et al., 2003).

The Sick Role

Another consideration is that some people grow fond of the role associated with being sick (Hotopf, 2004; Pilowsky, 1993). Their complaints of physical symptoms may be reinforced by indirect benefits derived from their illness (Schwartz, Slater, & Birchler, 1994). What kinds of benefits are commonly associated with physical illness? One payoff is that becoming ill is a superb way to avoid having to confront life's challenges. Many people with somatoform disorders are avoiding facing up to marital problems, career frustrations, family responsibilities, and the like. After all, when you're sick, others cannot place great demands on you.

Another benefit is that physical problems can provide a convenient excuse when people fail, or worry about failing, in endeavors that are critical to their self-esteem (Organista & Miranda, 1991). Attention

Figure 13.6
Glove anesthesia. In conversion disorders, the physical complaints are sometimes inconsistent with the known facts of physiology, indicating that the patient's problem is psychological in origin. For instance, in a condition known as glove anesthesia, patients complain of a loss of feeling in one of their hands. The problem with this complaint is that given the patterns of nerve distribution in the arm shown in **(a)**, it is impossible that a loss of feeling would occur in the hand exclusively, as shown in **(b)**. Loss of feeling in the hand would have to be accompanied by some loss of feeling in the nerves in the arm.

"Assuming I am a hypochondriac, couldn't that condition be brought on by a brain tumor?"

Copyright © by Patrick Hardin, www.CartoonStock.com

Distinguishing Anxiety and Somatoform Disorders

Check your understanding of the nature of anxiety and somatoform disorders by making preliminary diagnoses for the cases described below. Read each case summary and write your tentative diagnosis in the space provided. The answers are in Appendix A.

1. Malcolm religiously follows an exact schedule every day. His showering and grooming ritual takes 2 hours. He follows the same path in walking to his classes every day, and he always sits in the same seat in each class. He can't study until his apartment is arranged perfectly. Although he tries not to, he thinks constantly about flunking out of school. Both his grades and his social life are suffering from his rigid routines.

Preliminary diagnosis: _____

2. Jane has been unemployed for the last eight years because of poor health. She has suffered through a bizarre series of illnesses of mysterious origin. Troubles with devastating headaches were followed by months of chronic back pain. Then she developed respiratory problems, frequently gasping for breath. Her current problem is stomach pain. Physicians have been unable to find any physical basis for her maladies.

Preliminary diagnosis: _____

3. Nathan owns a small restaurant that's in deep financial trouble. He dreads facing the possibility that his restaurant will fail. One day, he suddenly loses all feeling in his right arm and the ability to control the arm. He's hospitalized for his condition, but physicians can't find any organic cause for his arm trouble.

Preliminary diagnosis: _____

from others is yet another payoff that may reinforce complaints of physical illness. When people become ill, they command the attention of family, friends, co-workers, neighbors, and doctors. The sympathy that illness often brings may strengthen the person's tendency to feel ill.

> Dissociative Disorders

PREVIEW QUESTIONS

● What are the principal types of dissociative disorders, and what are their chief symptoms?
● Why is the dissociative identity disorder controversial?
● What factors have been implicated in the etiology of dissociative disorders?

Dissociative disorders are among the more unusual syndromes that we will discuss. *Dissociative disorders are a class of disorders in which people lose contact with portions of their consciousness or memory, resulting in disruptions in their sense of identity.* We'll describe three dissociative syndromes—dissociative amnesia, dissociative fugue, and dissociative identity disorder—all of them relatively uncommon.

Dissociative Amnesia and Fugue

Dissociative amnesia and fugue are overlapping disorders characterized by serious memory deficits. *Dissociative amnesia is a sudden loss of memory for important personal information that is too extensive to be due to normal forgetting.* Memory losses may occur for a single traumatic event (such as an automobile accident or home fire) or for an extended period of time surrounding the event. Cases of am-

nesia have been observed after people have experienced disasters, accidents, combat stress, physical abuse, and rape, or after they have witnessed the violent death of a parent, among other things (Arrigo & Pezdek, 1997; Loewenstein, 1996). In *dissociative fugue, people lose their memory for their entire lives along with their sense of personal identity.* These people forget their name, their family, where they live, and where they work! In spite of this wholesale forgetting, they remember matters unrelated to their identity, such as how to drive a car and how to do math.

Dissociative Identity Disorder

Dissociative identity disorder (DID) involves the coexistence in one person of two or more largely complete, and usually very different, personalities. The name for this disorder used to be *multiple personality disorder,* which still enjoys informal usage.

In dissociative identity disorder, the divergences in behavior go far beyond those that people normally display in adapting to different roles in life. People with "multiple personalities" feel that they have more than one identity. Each personality has his or her own name, memories, traits, and physical mannerisms. Although rare, this "Dr. Jekyll and Mr. Hyde" syndrome is frequently portrayed in novels, movies, and television shows. In popular media portrayals, the syndrome is often mistakenly called *schizophrenia*. As you will see later, schizophrenic disorders are entirely different.

In dissociative identity disorder, the various personalities generally report that they are unaware of each other (Eich et al., 1997), although doubts have been raised about the accuracy of this assertion (Allen & Iacono, 2001). The alternate personalities commonly display traits that are quite foreign to the original personality. For instance, a shy, inhibited person might develop a flamboyant, extraverted alternate personality. Transitions between identities often occur suddenly. The disparities between identities can be bizarre, as different personalities may assert that they are different in age, race, gender, and sexual orientation (Kluft, 1996).

Starting in the 1970s, a dramatic increase was seen in the diagnosis of multiple-personality disorder (Kihlstrom, 2001). Only 79 well-documented cases had accumulated up through 1970, but by the late-1990s about 40,000 cases were estimated to have been reported (Lilienfeld & Lynn, 2003). Some theorists believe that these disorders used to be under-diagnosed—that is, they often went undetected (Maldonado & Spiegel, 2003). However, other theorists argue that a handful of clinicians have begun overdiagnosing the condition and that some clinicians even contribute to the emergence of DID (McHugh, 1995; Powell & Gee, 1999). Consistent with this view, a survey of all the psychiatrists in Switzerland found that 90% of them had never seen a case of dissociative identity disorder, whereas three of the psychiatrists had each seen more than 20 patients with dissociative identity disorder (Modestin, 1992). The data from this study suggest that 6 psychiatrists (out of 655 surveyed) accounted for two-thirds of the dissociative identity disorder diagnoses in Switzerland.

Etiology of Dissociative Disorders

Dissociative amnesia and fugue are usually attributed to excessive stress. However, relatively little is known about why this extreme reaction to stress occurs in a tiny minority of people but not in the vast majority who are subjected to similar stress.

The causes of dissociative identity disorder are particularly obscure. Some skeptical theorists, such as Nicholas Spanos (1994, 1996) and others (Gee, Allen, & Powell, 2003; Lilienfeld et al., 1999) believe that people with multiple personalities are engaging in intentional role playing to use mental illness as a face-saving excuse for their personal failings. Spanos also argues that a small minority of therapists help create DID in their patients by subtly encouraging the emergence of alternate personalities. According to Spanos, dissociative identity disorder is a creation of modern North American culture, much as demonic possession was a creation of early Christianity. To bolster his argument, he discusses how DID patients' symptom presentations seem to have been influenced by popular media. For example, the typical multiple-personality patient used to report having two or three personalities, but since the publication of *Sybil* (Schreiber, 1973) and other books describing patients with many personalities, the average number of alternate personalities has climbed to about 15. In a similar vein, there has been a dramatic upsurge in the number of DID patients reporting that they were victims of ritual satanic abuse during childhood that dates back to the publication of *Michelle Remembers* (Smith & Pazder, 1980), a book about a DID patient who purportedly was tortured by a satanic cult.

In spite of these concerns, many clinicians are convinced that dissociative identity disorder is an authentic disorder (Gleaves, May, & Cardena, 2001). They argue that there is no incentive for either patients or therapists to manufacture cases of multiple personalities, which are often greeted with skepticism and outright hostility. They maintain that most cases of dissociative identity disorder are rooted in severe emotional trauma that occurred during childhood (Draijer & Langeland, 1999). A substantial majority of people with dissociative identity disorder report a childhood history of rejection from parents and of physical and sexual abuse (Lewis et al., 1997; Scroppo et al., 1998). However, this abuse typically has not been independently verified (Lilienfeld & Lynn, 2003). Moreover, this association would not be unique to DID, as a history of child abuse elevates the likelihood of *many* disorders, especially among females (MacMillan et al., 2001). In the final analysis, little is known about the causes of dissociative identity disorder, which remains a controversial diagnosis (Barry-Walsh, 2005).

PREVIEW QUESTIONS

● What are the principal mood disorders, and what are their chief symptoms?

● Which biological factors have been implicated in mood disorders?

● How do cognitive processes contribute to depressive disorders?

● How do social skills and stress contribute to depressive disorders?

Web Link 13.5

Dr. Ivan's Depression Central
Some suggest that psychiatrist Ivan Goldberg's site would be better titled "Everything You Ever Wanted to Know About Depression . . ." He offers a great depth of resources regarding depression and mood disorders.

Mood disorders are common and have afflicted many successful, well-known people, such as Jane Pauley and Ben Stiller.

What did Abraham Lincoln, Marilyn Monroe, Kurt Cobain, Vincent van Gogh, Ernest Hemingway, Winston Churchill, Janis Joplin, and Leo Tolstoy have in common? Yes, they all achieved great prominence, albeit in different ways at different times. But, more pertinent to our interest, they all suffered from severe mood disorders. Although mood disorders can be crippling, people with mood disorders may still achieve greatness, because such disorders tend to be *episodic*. In other words, mood disturbances often come and go, interspersed among periods of normality. These episodes of disturbance can vary greatly in length, but they typically last 3 to 12 months (Akiskal, 2000).

Mood disorders **are a class of disorders marked by emotional disturbances of varied kinds that may spill over to disrupt physical, perceptual, social, and thought processes.** There are two basic types of mood disorders: bipolar and unipolar (see **Figure 13.7**). People with *bipolar disorder* experience emotional extremes at both ends of the mood continuum, going through periods of both *depression and mania* (excitement and elation). The mood swings in bipolar disorder can be patterned in many ways. People with *unipolar disorder* experience emotional extremes at just one end of the mood continuum, as they are troubled only by periodic bouts of *depression* (for the most part, patients do not exhibit manic episodes only). Let's look at the symptoms seen in major depressive disorder.

Major Depressive Disorder 11b

Everyone gets depressed once in a while. Thus, the line between normal and abnormal depression can be difficult to draw (Kendler & Gardner, 1998). Ultimately,

a subjective judgment is required. Crucial considerations in this judgment include the duration of the depression and its disruptive effects. When a depression significantly impairs everyday adaptive behavior for more than a few weeks, there is reason for concern.

In *major depressive disorder* **people show persistent feelings of sadness and despair and a loss of interest in previous sources of pleasure.** Negative emotions form the heart of the depressive syndrome, but many other symptoms may also appear. The most common symptoms of depression are summarized and compared with the symptoms of mania in **Table 13.1**. Depressed people often give up activities that they used to find enjoyable. For example, a depressed person might quit going bowling or might give up a favorite hobby like photography. Reduced appetite and insomnia are common. People with depression often lack energy. They tend to move sluggishly and talk slowly. Anxiety, irritability, and brooding are commonly observed. Self-esteem tends to sink as the depressed person begins to feel worthless. Depression plunges people into feelings of hopelessness, dejection, and boundless guilt. The severity of abnormal depression varies considerably.

The onset of depression can occur at any point in the life span, but a substantial majority of cases emerge before age 40 (Hammen, 2003). Depression occurs in children as well as adolescents and adults (Gruenberg & Goldstein, 2003). The median duration of depressive episodes is 5 months (Solomon et al., 1997). The vast majority (75%–95%) of people who suffer from depression experience more than one episode over the course of their lifetime (Dubovsky, Davies, & Dubovsky, 2003). In one longitudinal study, after recovery from one's first episode of depression, the cumulative probability of recurrence was 25% after 1 year, 42% after two years, and 60% after 5 years (Solomon et al., 2000).

How common are depressive disorders? Very common. Research suggests that about 7%–18% of Americans endure a depressive disorder at some time in their lives (Blazer, 2000; Regier & Burke, 2000). Estimates of the prevalence of depression vary quite a bit because of the previously mentioned difficulty in drawing a line between normal dejection and abnormal depression. As a result, different researchers using different assessment procedures and cutoff points obtain varied estimates. Moreover, evidence suggests that the prevalence of depression is increasing, as it is higher among age groups born in more recent decades (Rehm, Wagner, & Ivens-Tyndal, 2001). In particular, age cohorts born since World War II appear to have an elevated risk for depression (Kessler, 2002). The factors underlying this rise in depression are not readily apparent, and researchers are scrambling to collect data that might shed light on this unanticipated trend.

Researchers also find that the prevalence of depression is about twice as high in women as it is in men (Nolen-Hoeksema, 2002). This gender gap in depression opens up during mid- to late adolescence (Hankin et al., 1998). The many possible explanations for this gap are the subject of considerable debate. Susan Nolen-Hoeksema (2001) argues that women experience more depression than men because they are far more likely to be victims of sexual abuse and somewhat more likely to endure poverty, harassment, and role constraints. In other words, she attributes the higher prevalence of depression among women to their experience of greater stress and adversity. Nolen-Hoeksema also believes that women have a greater tendency than men to *ruminate* about setbacks and problems. Evidence suggests that this tendency to dwell on one's difficulties elevates vulnerability to depression, as we will discuss momentarily.

Bipolar Disorder 11b

Bipolar disorder **(formerly known as *manic-depressive disorder*) is marked by the experience of both depressed and manic periods.** The symptoms seen in manic periods generally are the opposite of those seen in depression (see **Table 13.1** for a comparison). In a manic episode, a person's mood becomes elevated to the point of euphoria. Self-esteem skyrockets as the person bubbles over with optimism, energy, and extravagant plans. He or she becomes hyperactive and may go for days without sleep. The individual talks rapidly and shifts topics wildly, as his or her mind races at breakneck speed. Judgment is often impaired. Some people in manic periods gamble impulsively, spend money frantically, or become sexually reckless. Like depressive disorder, bipolar disorder varies considerably in severity.

You may be thinking that the euphoria in manic episodes sounds appealing. If so, you are not entirely wrong. In their milder forms, manic states can seem attractive. The increases in energy, self-esteem, and optimism can be deceptively seductive (Goodwin & Jamison, 1990). However, manic periods often carry a paradoxical negative undercurrent of uneasiness and irritability (Dilsaver et al., 1999). Moreover, mild manic episodes usually escalate to higher levels that become scary and disturbing. Impaired judgment leads many victims to do things that they greatly regret later, as you'll see in the following case history:

Robert, a dentist, awoke one morning with the idea that he was the most gifted dental surgeon in his tri-state area. He decided that he should try to provide services to as many people as possible, so that more people could benefit from his talents. Thus, he decided to remodel his two-chair dental office, installing 20 booths so that he could simultaneously attend to 20 patients. That same day he drew up plans for this arrangement, telephoned a number of remodelers, and invited bids for the work. Later that day, impatient to get rolling on his remodeling, he rolled up his sleeves, got himself a sledgehammer, and began to knock down the walls in his office. Annoyed when that didn't go so well, he smashed his dental tools, washbasins and X-ray equipment. Later, Robert's wife became concerned about his behavior and summoned two of her adult daughters for assistance. The daughters responded quickly, arriving at the family home with their husbands. In the ensuing discussion, Robert—after bragging about his sexual prowess—made advances toward his daughters. He had to be subdued by their husbands. (Adapted from Kleinmuntz, 1980, p. 309)

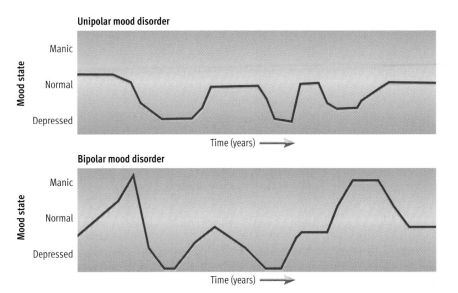

Figure 13.7

Episodic patterns in mood disorders. Time-limited episodes of emotional disturbance come and go unpredictably in mood disorders. People with unipolar disorder suffer from bouts of depression only, whereas people with bipolar disorder experience both manic and depressive episodes. The time between episodes of disturbance and the length of the episodes varies greatly.

Table 13.1 Comparisons of Common Symptoms in Manic and Depressive Episodes

Characteristics	Manic Episode	Depressive Episode
Emotional	Elated, euphoric, very sociable, impatient at any hindrance	Gloomy, hopeless, socially withdrawn, irritable
Cognitive	Characterized by racing thoughts, flight of ideas, desire for action, and impulsive behavior; talkative, self-confident; experiencing delusions of grandeur	Characterized by slowness of thought processes, obsessive worrying, inability to make decisions, negative self-image, self-blame and delusions of guilt and disease
Motor	Hyperactive, tireless, requiring less sleep than usual, showing increased sex drive and fluctuating appetite	Less active, tired, experiencing difficulty in sleeping, showing decreased sex drive and decreased appetite

Source: Sarason, I. G., & Sarason, B. G. (1987). *Abnormal psychology: The problem of maladaptive behavior.* Upper Saddle River, NJ: Prentice-Hall. © 1987 Prentice-Hall, Inc. Reprinted by permission.

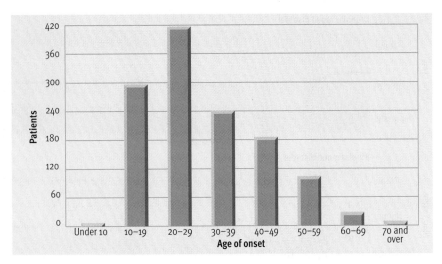

Figure 13.8

Age of onset for bipolar mood disorder. The onset of bipolar disorder typically occurs in adolescence or early adulthood. The data graphed here, which were combined from ten studies, show the distribution of age of onset for 1304 bipolar patients. As you can see, bipolar disorder emerges most frequently during the 20s decade.

Source: Goodwin, F. K., & Jamison, K. R. (1990). *Manic-depressive illness* (p. 132). New York: Oxford University Press. Copyright © 1990 Oxford University Press., Inc. Reprinted by permission.

Although not rare, bipolar disorder is much less common than unipolar disorder. Bipolar disorder affects about 1%–2.5% of the population (Dubovsky et al., 2003). Unlike depressive disorder, bipolar disorder is seen equally often in males and females (Bauer, 2003). As **Figure 13.8** shows, the onset of bipolar disorder is age related, with the peak of vulnerability occurring between the ages of 20 and 29 (Goodwin & Jamison, 1990).

Etiology of Mood Disorders 11b

Quite a bit is known about the etiology of mood disorders, although the puzzle hasn't been assembled completely. There appear to be a number of routes

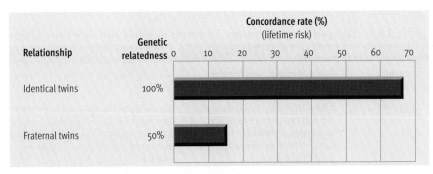

Figure 13.9

Twin studies of mood disorders. The concordance rate for mood disorders in identical twins is much higher than that for fraternal twins, who share less genetic overlap. These results suggest that there is a genetic predisposition to mood disorders. (Data from Gershon, Berrettini, & Goldin, 1989)

into these disorders, involving intricate interactions between psychological and biological factors.

Genetic Vulnerability 11b

The evidence strongly suggests that genetic factors influence the likelihood of developing major depression or bipolar disorder (Kalidindi & McGuffin, 2003; Sullivan, Neale, & Kendler, 2000). *Twin studies* have found a huge disparity between identical and fraternal twins in concordance rates for mood disorders. The concordance rate for identical twins is much higher (see **Figure 13.9**). This evidence suggests that heredity can create a *predisposition* to mood disorders. Environmental factors probably determine whether this predisposition is converted into an actual disorder. The influence of genetic factors appears to be stronger for bipolar disorder than for unipolar disorder (Kieseppa et al., 2004; Merikangas & Risch, 2003).

Neurochemical and Neuroanatomical Factors 11b

Heredity may influence susceptibility to mood disorders by creating a predisposition toward certain types of neurochemical abnormalities in the brain. Correlations have been found between mood disorders and abnormal levels of two neurotransmitters in the brain: norepinephrine and serotonin (Sher & Mann, 2003), although other neurotransmitter disturbances may also contribute (Thase, Jindal, & Howland, 2002). The details remain elusive, but low levels of serotonin appear to be a crucial factor underlying most forms of depression (Flores et al., 2004). A variety of drug therapies are fairly effective in the treatment of severe mood disorders. Most of these drugs are known to affect the availability (in the brain) of the neurotransmitters that have been related to mood disorders (Dubovsky et al., 2003). Since this effect is unlikely to be a coincidence, it bolsters the plausibility of the idea that neurochemical changes produce mood disturbances.

Studies have also found some interesting correlations between mood disorders and a variety of structural abnormalities in the brain (Flores et al., 2004). Perhaps the best documented correlation is the association between depression and *reduced hippocampal volume* (Campbell et al, 2004). The *hippocampus,* which is known to play a major role in memory consolidation (see Chapter 7), tends to be about 8%–10% smaller in depressed subjects than in normal subjects (Videbech & Ravnkilde, 2004). A fascinating new theory of the biological bases of depression may be able to account for this finding. The springboard for this theory is the recent discovery that the human brain continues to generate new neurons in adulthood, especially in the hippocampal formation (Gage, 2002; see Chapter 3). This process is called *neurogenesis*. Jacobs (2004) has theorized that depression occurs when major life stress causes neurochemical reactions that suppress neurogenesis, resulting in reduced hippocampal volume. According to this view, it is the suppression of neurogenesis that is the central cause of depression. Consistent with this view, Jacobs maintains that antidepressant drugs that elevate serotonin levels relieve depression because serotonin promotes neurogenesis. A great deal of additional research will be required to fully test this innovative new model of the biological bases of depressive disorders.

Cognitive Factors

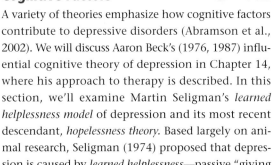 11b

A variety of theories emphasize how cognitive factors contribute to depressive disorders (Abramson et al., 2002). We will discuss Aaron Beck's (1976, 1987) influential cognitive theory of depression in Chapter 14, where his approach to therapy is described. In this section, we'll examine Martin Seligman's *learned helplessness model* of depression and its most recent descendant, *hopelessness theory.* Based largely on animal research, Seligman (1974) proposed that depression is caused by *learned helplessness*—passive "giving up" behavior produced by exposure to unavoidable aversive events (such as uncontrollable shock in the laboratory). He originally considered learned helplessness to be a product of conditioning but eventually revised his theory, giving it a cognitive slant. The reformulated theory of learned helplessness asserted that the roots of depression lie in how people explain the setbacks and other negative events that they experience (Abramson, Seligman, & Teasdale, 1978). According to Seligman (1990), people who exhibit a *pessimistic explanatory style* are especially vulnerable to depression. These people tend to attribute their setbacks to their personal flaws instead of to situational factors, and they tend to draw global, far-reaching conclusions about their personal inadequacies based on these setbacks. *Hopelessness theory* builds on these insights by proposing a sense of hopelessness as the "final pathway" leading to depression and by incorporating additional factors that may interact with explanatory style to foster this sense of hopelessness (Abramson, Alloy, & Metalsky, 1995).

In accord with this line of thinking, Susan Nolen-Hoeksema (1991, 2000) has found that depressed people who *ruminate* about their depression remain depressed longer than those who try to distract themselves. People who respond to depression with rumination repetitively focus their attention on their feelings of depression, thinking constantly about how sad, lethargic, and unmotivated they are. According to

Nolen-Hoeksema (1995), excessive rumination tends to extend and amplify individuals' episodes of depression. She believes that women are more likely to ruminate than men and that this disparity may help explain why depression is more prevalent in women.

In sum, cognitive models of depression maintain that negative thinking is what leads to depression in many people. The principal problem with cognitive theories is their difficulty in separating cause from effect (Rehm, Wagner, & Ivens-Tyndal, 2001). Does negative thinking cause depression? Or does depression cause negative thinking (see **Figure 13.10**)? A *clear* demonstration of a causal link between negative thinking and depression is not possible because it would require manipulating people's explanatory style (which is not easy to change) in sufficient degree to produce full-fledged depressive disorders (which would not be ethical). However, research has provided impressive evidence consistent with a causal link between negative thinking and vulnerability to depression. Lauren Alloy and her colleagues (1999) assessed the explanatory style of a sample of first-year college students who were not depressed at the outset of the study. The students were characterized as being at high risk or low risk for depression based on whether they exhibited a negative cognitive style. The follow-up data over the next 2.5 years on students who had no prior history of depression showed dramatic differences between the two groups in vulnerability to depression. During this relatively brief period, a major depressive disorder emerged in 17% of the high-risk students in comparison to only 1% of the low-risk students. The high-risk subjects also displayed a much greater incidence of minor depressive episodes (39% versus 6%). These findings and other data from the study suggest that negative thinking makes a causal contribution to the development of depressive disorders.

Interpersonal Roots

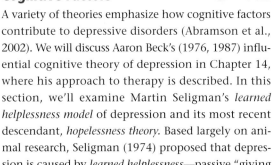 11b

Behavioral approaches to understanding depression emphasize how inadequate social skills put people on the road to depressive disorders (see **Figure 13.11** on the next page; Coyne, 1999). According to this

Courtesy of Susan Nolen-Hoeksema

SUSAN NOLEN-HOEKSEMA

"By adolescence, girls appear to be more likely than boys to respond to stress and distress with rumination—focusing inward on feelings of distress and personal concerns rather than taking action to relieve their distress."

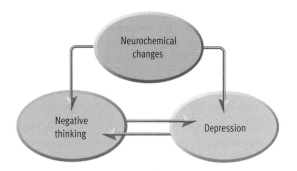

Figure 13.10
Interpreting the correlation between negative thinking and depression. Cognitive theories of depression assume that consistent patterns of negative thinking cause depression. Although these theories are highly plausible, depression could cause negative thoughts, or both could be caused by a third factor, such as neurochemical changes in the brain.

Figure 13.11

Interpersonal factors in depression. Behavioral theories about the etiology of depression emphasize how inadequate social skills may contribute to the development of the disorder through several mechanisms, as diagrammed here.

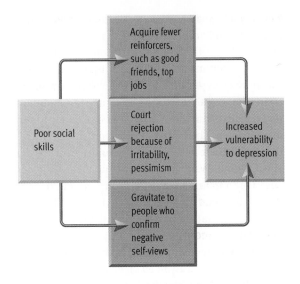

Individuals suffering from depression often are irritable and pessimistic. They complain a lot and aren't particularly enjoyable companions. As a consequence, depressed people tend to court rejection from those around them (Joiner & Metalsky, 1995). Depressed people thus have fewer sources of social support than nondepressed people. Social rejection and lack of support may in turn aggravate and deepen a person's depression (Potthoff, Holahan, & Joiner, 1995). Recent evidence suggests that lack of social support may make a larger contribution to depression in women than in men (Kendler, Myers, & Prescott, 2005).

Precipitating Stress 11b

Mood disorders sometimes appear mysteriously in people who are leading benign, nonstressful lives. For this reason, experts used to believe that stress has little influence on mood disorders. However, advances in the measurement of personal stress have altered this picture. The evidence available today suggests the existence of a moderately strong link between stress and the onset of mood disorders (Kendler, Kuhn, & Prescott, 2004; Kessler, 1997). Stress also appears to affect how people with mood disorders respond to treatment and whether they experience a relapse of their disorder (Monroe & Hadjiyannakis, 2002).

notion, depression-prone people lack the social finesse needed to acquire many important kinds of reinforcers, such as good friends, top jobs, and desirable spouses. This lack of reinforcers could understandably lead to negative emotions and depression. Consistent with this theory, researchers have found correlations between poor social skills and depression (Ingram, Scott, & Siegle, 1999).

Another interpersonal factor is that depressed people tend to be depressing (Joiner & Katz, 1999).

> Schizophrenic Disorders

PREVIEW QUESTIONS

● What are the general symptoms of schizophrenia?

● What are the subtypes of schizophrenic disorders, and what are their chief symptoms?

● What is known about the course and outcome of schizophrenia?

● Which biological factors have been implicated in schizophrenic disorders?

● What is the neurodevelopmental hypothesis of schizophrenia?

● How do family dynamics and stress contribute to schizophrenic disorders?

Literally, *schizophrenia* means "split mind." However, when Eugen Bleuler coined the term in 1911 he was referring to the fragmentation of thought processes seen in the disorder—not to a "split personality." Unfortunately, writers in the popular media often assume that the split-mind notion, and thus schizophrenia, refers to the rare syndrome in which a person manifests two or more personalities. As you have already learned, this syndrome is actually called *multiple-personality disorder* or *dissociative identity disorder.* Schizophrenia is a much more common, and altogether different, type of disorder.

Schizophrenic disorders **encompass a class of disorders marked by delusions, hallucinations, disorganized speech, and deterioration of adaptive behavior.** Prevalence estimates suggest that about 1% of the population may suffer from schizophrenic disorders (Jablensky, 1999). That may not sound like much, but it means that in the United States alone several million people may be troubled by schizophrenic disturbances. Moreover, schizophrenia is an extremely costly illness for society, because it is a se-

vere, debilitating illness that tends to have an early onset and often requires lengthy hospital care (Buchanan & Carpenter, 2000).

General Symptoms 11c

There are a number of distinct schizophrenic syndromes, but they share some general characteristics that we will examine before looking at the subtypes. Many of these characteristics are apparent in the following case history, adapted from Sheehan (1982).

Sylvia was first diagnosed as schizophrenic at age 15. She has been in and out of many types of psychiatric facilities since then. She has never been able to hold a job for any length of time. During severe flare-ups of her disorder, her personal hygiene deteriorates. She rarely washes, she wears clothes that neither fit nor match, she smears makeup on heavily but randomly, and she slops food all over herself. Sylvia occasionally hears voices talking to her. She tends to be argumentative, aggressive, and emotionally volatile. Over the years, she has been involved in innumerable fights with fellow patients, psychiatric staff members, and strangers. Her thoughts can be highly irrational, as is apparent from the following quote:

"Mick Jagger wants to marry me. If I have Mick Jagger, I don't have to covet Geraldo Rivera. Mick Jagger is St. Nicholas and the Maharishi is Santa Claus. I want to form a gospel rock group called the Thorn Oil, but Geraldo wants me to be the music critic on Eyewitness News, so what can I do? Got to listen to my boyfriend. Teddy Kennedy cured me of my ugliness. I'm pregnant with the son of God. Creedmoor (her hospital) is the headquarters of the American Nazi Party. They're eating the patients here. Archie Bunker wants me to play his niece on his TV show. I'm Joan of Arc. I'm Florence Nightingale. The door between the ward and the porch is the dividing line between New York and California. Forget about Zip Codes. I need shock treatments. The body is run by electricity. My wiring is all faulty." (Adapted from Sheehan, 1982; quotation from pp. 104–105)

Sylvia's case clearly shows that schizophrenic thinking can be bizarre and that schizophrenia can be a severe and crippling disorder. Although no single symptom is inevitably present, the following symptoms are commonly seen in schizophrenia (Cancro & Lehmann, 2000; Ho, Black, & Andreasen, 2003).

Delusions and Irrational Thought. Cognitive deficits and disturbed thought processes are the central, defining feature of schizophrenic disorders (Barch, 2003; Heinrichs, 2005). Various kinds of delusions are common. *Delusions* **are false beliefs that are maintained even though they clearly are out of touch with reality.** For example, one patient's delusion that he was a tiger (with a deformed body) persisted for 15 years (Kulick, Pope, & Keck, 1990). More typically, affected persons believe that their private thoughts are being broadcast to other people, that thoughts are being injected into their mind against their will, or that their thoughts are being controlled by some external force (Maher, 2001). In *delusions of grandeur,* people maintain that they are famous or important. Sylvia expressed an endless array of grandiose delusions, such as thinking that Mick Jagger wanted to marry her, that she had dictated the hobbit stories to J. R. R. Tolkien, and that she was going to win the Nobel prize for medicine. In addition to delusions, the schizophrenic person's train of thought deteriorates. Thinking becomes chaotic rather than logical and linear. A "loosening of associations" occurs, as the person shifts topics in disjointed ways. The quotation from Sylvia illustrates this symptom dramatically. The entire quote involves a wild flight of ideas in which the thoughts mostly have no apparent connection to each other.

Deterioration of Adaptive Behavior. Schizophrenia usually involves a noticeable deterioration in the quality of the person's routine functioning in work, social relations, and personal care. Friends will often make remarks such as "Hal just isn't himself anymore." This deterioration is readily apparent in Sylvia's inability to get along with others or to function in the work world. It's also apparent in her neglect of personal hygiene.

Distorted Perception. A variety of perceptual distortions may occur with schizophrenia, the most common being auditory hallucinations. *Hallucinations* **are sensory perceptions that occur in the absence of a real, external stimulus or are gross distortions of perceptual input.** Schizophrenics frequently report that they hear voices of nonexistent or absent people talking to them. Sylvia, for instance, said she heard messages from former Beatle Paul McCartney. These voices often provide an insulting, running commentary on the person's behavior ("You're an idiot for shaking his hand"). They may be argumentative ("You don't need a bath"), and they may issue commands ("Prepare your home for visitors from outer space").

Disturbed Emotion. Normal emotional tone can be disrupted in schizophrenia in a variety of ways. Some victims show a flattening of emotions. In other words, they show little emotional responsiveness. Others show inappropriate emotional responses that don't jell with the situation or with what they are saying. People with schizophrenia may also become emotionally volatile. This pattern was displayed by Sylvia, who often overreacted emotionally in erratic, unpredictable ways.

Subtypes and Course

11c

Four subtypes of schizophrenic disorders are recognized, including a category for people who don't fit neatly into any of the first three categories. Let's look at the major symptoms of each subtype (Ho et al., 2003).

Paranoid Type. As its name implies, *paranoid schizophrenia* **is dominated by delusions of persecution, along with delusions of grandeur.** In this common form of schizophrenia, people come to believe that they have many enemies who want to harass and oppress them. They may become suspicious of friends and relatives, or they may attribute the persecution

Web Link 13.6

Doctor's Guide to the Internet: Schizophrenia Produced by a communications and medical education consulting company, the free Doctor's Guide site is updated frequently to provide a current overview of the state of research on schizophrenic disorders. A more detailed set of resources for physicians parallels this site, which is intended primarily for patients and their families.

NANCY ANDREASEN

"Schizophrenia disfigures the emotional and cognitive faculties of its victims, and sometimes nearly destroys them."

to mysterious, unknown persons. They are convinced that they are being watched and manipulated. To make sense of this persecution, they often develop delusions of grandeur. They believe that they must be enormously important people, frequently seeing themselves as great inventors or as great religious or political leaders. For example, in the case described at the beginning of the chapter, Ed's belief that he was president of the United States was a delusion of grandeur.

Catatonic Type. *Catatonic schizophrenia* **is marked by striking motor disturbances, ranging from muscular rigidity to random motor activity.** Some patients go into an extreme form of withdrawal known as a catatonic stupor. They may remain virtually motionless and seem oblivious to the environment around them for long periods of time. Others go into a state of catatonic excitement. They become hyperactive and incoherent. Some alternate between these dramatic extremes. The catatonic subtype is not particularly common, and its prevalence seems to be declining.

Disorganized Type. In *disorganized schizophrenia,* **a particularly severe deterioration of adaptive behavior is seen.** Prominent symptoms include emotional indifference, frequent incoherence, and virtually complete social withdrawal. Aimless babbling and giggling are common. Delusions often center on bodily functions ("My brain is melting out my ears").

Undifferentiated Type. People who are clearly schizophrenic but who cannot be placed into any of the three previous categories are said to have *undifferentiated schizophrenia,* **which is marked by idiosyncratic mixtures of schizophrenic symptoms.** The undifferentiated subtype is fairly common.

Positive Versus Negative Symptoms. Many theorists have raised doubts about the value of dividing schizophrenic disorders into the four subtypes just described (Sanislow & Carson, 2001). Critics note that the catatonic subtype is disappearing and that undifferentiated cases aren't so much a subtype as a hodgepodge of "leftovers." Critics also point out that the subtypes lack meaningful differences in etiology, prognosis, and response to treatment. The absence of such differences casts doubt on the value of the current classification scheme. Because of such problems, Nancy Andreasen (1990) and others (Carpenter, 1992; McGlashan & Fenton, 1992) have proposed an alternative approach to subtyping. This scheme divides schizophrenic disorders into just two categories based on the predominance of negative versus positive symptoms. *Negative symptoms* **involve behavioral deficits, such as flattened emotions, social withdrawal, apathy, impaired attention, and poverty of speech.** *Positive symptoms* **involve behavioral excesses or peculiarities, such as hallucinations, delusions, bizarre behavior, and wild flights of ideas.**

Theorists advocating this scheme hoped to find consistent differences between the two subtypes in etiology, prognosis, and response to treatment, and some progress along these lines *has* been made. For example, a predominance of positive symptoms is associated with better adjustment prior to the onset of schizophrenia and greater responsiveness to treatment (Fenton & McGlashan, 1994; Galderisi et al., 2002). However, the assumption that patients can be placed into discrete categories based on this scheme has not been supported. Most patients exhibit both types of symptoms and vary only in the degree to which positive or negative symptoms dominate (Black & Andreasen, 1999). Although it seems fair to say that the distinction between positive and negative symptoms is enhancing our understanding of schizophre-

Courtesy of Nancy Andreasen, M.D.

concept **check 13.3**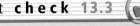

Distinguishing Schizophrenic and Mood Disorders

Check your understanding of the nature of schizophrenic and mood disorders by making preliminary diagnoses for the cases described below. Read each case summary and write your tentative diagnosis in the space provided. The answers are in Appendix A.

1. Max hasn't slept in four days. He's determined to write the "great American novel" before his class reunion, which is a few months away. He expounds eloquently on his novel to anyone who will listen, talking at such a rapid pace that no one can get a word in edgewise. He feels like he's wired with energy and is supremely confident about the novel, even though he's only written 10 to 20 pages. Last week, he charged $8000 worth of new computer equipment, which is supposed to help him write his book.

   Preliminary diagnosis: _____

2. Eduardo maintains that he invented the atomic bomb, even though he was born after its invention. He says he invented it to punish homosexuals, Nazis, and short people. It's short people that he's really afraid of. He's sure that all the short people on TV are talking about him. He thinks that short people are conspiring to make him look like a Republican. Eduardo frequently gets in arguments with people and is emotionally volatile. His grooming is poor, but he says it's okay because he's the Secretary of State.

   Preliminary diagnosis: _____

3. Margaret has hardly gotten out of bed for weeks, although she's troubled by insomnia. She doesn't feel like eating and has absolutely no energy. She feels dejected, discouraged, spiritless, and apathetic. Friends stop by to try to cheer her up, but she tells them not to waste their time on "pond scum."

   Preliminary diagnosis: _____

nia, it has not yielded a classification scheme that can replace the traditional subtypes of schizophrenia.

Course and Outcome. Schizophrenic disorders usually emerge during adolescence or early adulthood and only infrequently after age 45 (Howard et al., 1993). Those who develop schizophrenia usually have a long history of peculiar behavior and cognitive and social deficits, although most do not manifest a full-fledged psychological disorder during childhood (Walker et al., 2004). The emergence of schizophrenia may be sudden or gradual. Once it clearly emerges, the course of schizophrenia is variable (Norman & Malla, 1995), but patients tend to fall into three broad groups. Some patients, presumably those with milder disorders, are treated successfully and enjoy a full recovery. Other patients experience a partial recovery, but they have frequent relapses and are in and out of treatment facilities for much of the remainder of their lives. Finally, a third group of patients endure chronic illness that sometimes results in permanent hospitalization. Estimates of the percentage of patients falling in each category vary. Overall, it appears that about 15-20% of schizophrenic patients enjoy a full recovery, although some long-term studies have yielded higher estimates (Modestin et al., 2003; Robinson et al., 2004).

Etiology of Schizophrenia **11c**

You can probably identify, at least to some extent, with people who suffer from mood disorders, somatoform disorders, and anxiety disorders. You can probably imagine events that could unfold that might leave you struggling with depression, grappling with anxiety, or worrying about your physical health. But what could possibly have led Ed to believe that he had been fighting space wars and vampires? What could account for Sylvia's thinking that she was Joan of Arc or that she had dictated the hobbit novels to Tolkien? As mystifying as these delusions may seem, you'll see that the etiology of schizophrenic disorders is not all that different from the etiology of other psychological disorders. We'll begin our discussion by examining the matter of genetic vulnerability.

Genetic Vulnerability **11c**

Evidence is plentiful that hereditary factors play a role in the development of schizophrenic disorders (Kendler, 2000; Tsuang, Glatt, & Faraone, 2003). For instance, in twin studies, concordance rates average around 48% for identical twins, in comparison to about 17% for fraternal twins (Gottesman, 1991,

John Nash, the Nobel prize–winning mathematician whose story was told in the film A Beautiful Mind, *has struggled with paranoid schizophrenia since 1959.*

2001). Studies also indicate that a child born to two schizophrenic parents has about a 46% probability of developing a schizophrenic disorder (as compared to the probability in the general population of about 1%). These and other findings that demonstrate the genetic roots of schizophrenia are summarized in **Figure 13.12**. Overall, the picture is similar to that

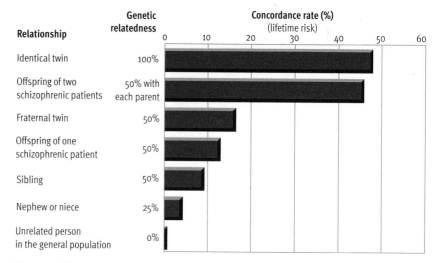

Figure 13.12

Genetic vulnerability to schizophrenic disorders. Relatives of schizophrenic patients have an elevated risk for schizophrenia. This risk is greater among closer relatives. Although environment also plays a role in the etiology of schizophrenia, the concordance rates shown here suggest that there is a genetic vulnerability to the disorder. These concordance estimates are based on pooled data from 40 studies conducted between 1920 and 1987. (Data adapted from Gottesman, 1991)

Figure 13.13

The dopamine hypothesis as an explanation for schizophrenia. Decades of research have implicated overactivity at dopamine synapses as a key cause of schizophrenic disorders. However, the evidence on the exact mechanisms underlying this overactivity, which is summarized in this graphic, is complex and open to debate. Recent hypotheses about the neurochemical bases of schizophrenia go beyond the simple assumption that dopamine activity is increased. For example, one theory posits that schizophrenia may be accompanied by decreased dopamine activity in one area of the brain (the prefrontal cortex) and increased activity or poor regulation in other areas of the brain (Egan & Hyde, 2000). Moreover, abnormalities in other neurotransmitter systems may also contribute to schizophrenia.

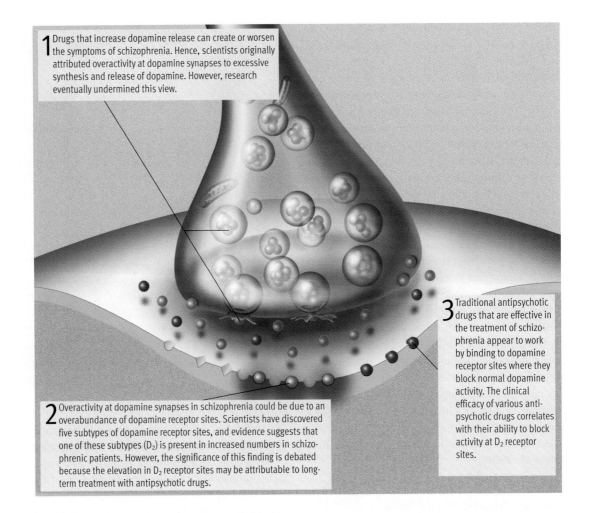

1 Drugs that increase dopamine release can create or worsen the symptoms of schizophrenia. Hence, scientists originally attributed overactivity at dopamine synapses to excessive synthesis and release of dopamine. However, research eventually undermined this view.

2 Overactivity at dopamine synapses in schizophrenia could be due to an overabundance of dopamine receptor sites. Scientists have discovered five subtypes of dopamine receptor sites, and evidence suggests that one of these subtypes (D_2) is present in increased numbers in schizophrenic patients. However, the significance of this finding is debated because the elevation in D_2 receptor sites may be attributable to long-term treatment with antipsychotic drugs.

3 Traditional antipsychotic drugs that are effective in the treatment of schizophrenia appear to work by binding to dopamine receptor sites where they block normal dopamine activity. The clinical efficacy of various antipsychotic drugs correlates with their ability to block activity at D_2 receptor sites.

seen for mood disorders. Several converging lines of evidence indicate that some people inherit a *vulnerability* to schizophrenia (Schneider & Deldin, 2001).

Neurochemical Factors 11c

Like mood disorders, schizophrenic disorders appear to be accompanied by changes in the activity of one or more neurotransmitters in the brain (Patel, Pinals, & Breier, 2003). The *dopamine hypothesis* asserts that excess dopamine activity is the neurochemical basis for schizophrenia, as discussed in **Figure 13.13**. This hypothesis makes sense because most of the drugs that are useful in the treatment of schizophrenia are known to dampen dopamine activity in the brain (Tamminga & Carlsson, 2003). However, the evidence linking schizophrenia to high dopamine levels is riddled with inconsistencies, complexities, and interpretive problems (Abi-Dargham, 2004; Egan & Hyde, 2000). Researchers are currently exploring how interactions between the dopamine and serotonin neurotransmitter systems may contribute to schizophrenia (Patel et al., 2003). Recent research has also

suggested that abnormalities in neural circuits using *glutamate* as a neurotransmitter may play a role in schizophrenic disturbance (Tibbo et al., 2004). Thus, investigators are gradually making progress in their search for the neurochemical bases of schizophrenia.

Structural Abnormalities in the Brain 11c

For decades, studies have suggested that individuals with schizophrenia exhibit a variety of deficits in attention, perception, and information processing (Bellack, Gearon, & Blanchard, 2000). These cognitive deficits suggested that schizophrenic disorders may be caused by neurological defects (Perry & Braff, 1994). Until recent decades, however, this theory was based more on speculation than on actual research. However, advances in brain imaging technology have yielded mountains of intriguing data since the mid-1980s. The most reliable finding is that CT scans and MRI scans (see Chapter 3) suggest an association between enlarged brain ventricles (the hollow, fluid-filled cavities in the brain depicted in **Figure 13.14**)

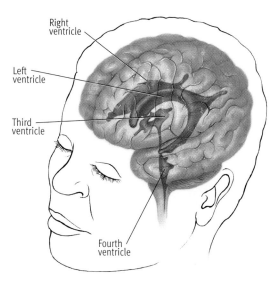

Figure 13.14

Schizophrenia and the ventricles of the brain. Cerebrospinal fluid (CSF) circulates around the brain and spinal cord. The hollow cavities in the brain filled with CSF are called ventricles. The four ventricles in the human brain are depicted here. Recent studies with CT scans and MRI scans suggest an association between enlarged ventricles in the brain and the occurrence of schizophrenic disturbance.

[Labels on figure: Right ventricle, Left ventricle, Third ventricle, Fourth ventricle]

and schizophrenic disturbance (Egan & Hyde, 2000). Enlarged ventricles are assumed to reflect the degeneration of nearby brain tissue. The significance of enlarged ventricles is hotly debated, however. This structural deterioration could be a *consequence* of schizophrenia, or it could be a contributing *cause* of the illness.

The Neurodevelopmental Hypothesis

In recent years, several new lines of evidence have led to the emergence of the *neurodevelopmental hypothesis* of schizophrenia, which asserts that schizophrenia is caused in part by various disruptions in the normal maturational processes of the brain before or at birth (Brown, 1999). According to this hypothesis, insults to the brain during sensitive phases of prenatal development or during birth can cause subtle neurological damage that elevates individuals' vulnerability to schizophrenia years later in adolescence and early adulthood (see **Figure 13.15**). What are the sources of these early insults to the brain? Thus far, research has focused on viral infections or malnutrition during prenatal development and obstetrical complications during the birth process.

The evidence on viral infections has been building since Sarnoff Mednick and his colleagues (1988)

discovered an elevated incidence of schizophrenia among individuals who had been in their second trimester of prenatal development during a 1957 influenza epidemic in Finland. Several subsequent studies in other locations have also found a link between exposure to influenza during the second trimester and increased prevalence of schizophrenia (Brown et al., 2004). Another study, which investigated the possible impact of prenatal malnutrition, found an elevated incidence of schizophrenia in a group of people who were prenatally exposed to a severe famine in 1944–45 due to a Nazi blockade of food deliveries in the Netherlands during World War II (Susser et al., 1996). Other research has shown that schizophrenic patients are more likely than control subjects to have experienced obstetrical complications when they were born (Kelly et al., 2004; Rosso et al., 2000). Finally, research suggests that minor physical anomalies (slight anatomical defects of the head, hands, feet, and face) that would be consistent with prenatal neurological damage are more common among people with schizophrenia than among others (McNeil, Canton-Graae, & Ismail, 2000; Schiffman et al., 2002).

Collectively, these diverse studies argue for a relationship between early neurological trauma and a predisposition to schizophrenia (Mednick et al., 1998). Much remains to be learned about the neurodevelopmental bases of schizophrenia, but this new line of inquiry should increase our understanding of the etiology of schizophrenic disorders.

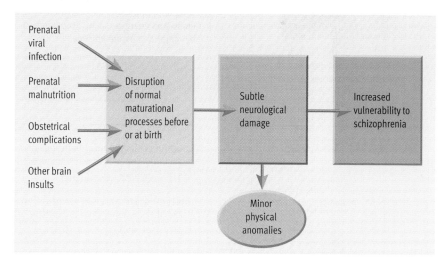

Figure 13.15

The neurodevelopmental hypothesis of schizophrenia. Recent findings have suggested that insults to the brain sustained during prenatal development or at birth may disrupt crucial maturational processes in the brain, resulting in subtle neurological damage that gradually becomes apparent as youngsters develop. This neurological damage is believed to increase both vulnerability to schizophrenia and the incidence of minor physical anomalies (slight anatomical defects of the head, face, hands, and feet).

AXIS I CATEGORY	SUBTYPES	PREVALENCE/ WELL-KNOWN VICTIM

ANXIETY DISORDERS

Edvard Munch's *The Scream* expresses overwhelming feelings of anxiety.

National Gallery, Oslo, Norway. SCALA/Art; © 2006 The Munch Museum/The Munch-Ellingsen Group/Artists Rights Society (ARS), NY.

Generalized anxiety disorder: Chronic, high level of anxiety not tied to any specific threat

Phobic disorder: Persistent, irrational fear of object or situation that presents no real danger

Panic disorder: Recurrent attacks of overwhelming anxiety that occur suddenly and unexpectedly

Obsessive-compulsive disorder: Persistent, uncontrollable intrusions of unwanted thoughts and urges to engage in senseless rituals

Posttraumatic stress disorder: Enduring psychological disturbance attributable to the experience of a major traumatic event

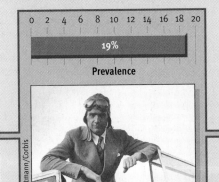

0 2 4 6 8 10 12 14 16 18 20
19%
Prevalence

© Bettmann/Corbis

The famous industrialist Howard Hughes suffered from obsessive-compulsive disorder.

MOOD DISORDERS

Musee d'Orsay, Paris. © Erich Lessing/ Art Resource, NY.

Vincent Van Gogh's *Portrait of Dr. Gachet* captures the profound dejection experienced in depressive disorders.

Major depressive disorder: Two or more major depressive episodes marked by feelings of sadness, worthlessness, despair

Bipolar disorder: One or more manic episodes marked by inflated self-esteem, grandiosity, and elevated mood and energy, usually accompanied by major depressive episodes

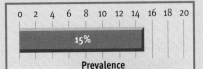

0 2 4 6 8 10 12 14 16 18 20
15%
Prevalence

Actor Ben Stiller has suffered from depression.

© Graeme Robertson/ Getty Images

SCHIZOPHRENIC DISORDERS

The perceptual distortions seen in schizophrenia probably contributed to the bizarre imagery apparent in this portrait of a cat painted by Louis Wain.

© Derek Bayes/Aspect Picture Library

Paranoid schizophrenia: Delusions of persecution and delusions of grandeur; frequent auditory hallucinations

Catatonic schizophrenia: Motor disturbances ranging from immobility to excessive, purposeless activity

Disorganized schizophrenia: Flat or inappropriate emotions; disorganized speech and adaptive behavior

Undifferentiated schizophrenia: Idiosyncratic mixtures of schizophrenic symptoms that cannot be placed into above three categories

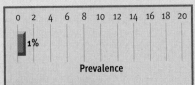

0 2 4 6 8 10 12 14 16 18 20
1%
Prevalence

© Reuters/Corbis

John Nash, the Nobel Prize-winning mathematician whose story was told in the film *A Beautiful Mind*, has struggled with schizophrenia.

ETIOLOGY: BIOLOGICAL FACTORS

Genetic vulnerability: Twin studies and other evidence suggest a mild genetic predisposition to anxiety disorders.

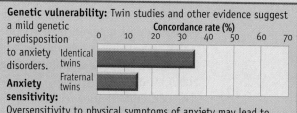

Concordance rate (%)

Anxiety sensitivity: Oversensitivity to physical symptoms of anxiety may lead to overreactions to feelings of anxiety, so anxiety breeds anxiety.

Neurochemical bases: Disturbances in neural circuits releasing GABA may contribute to some disorders; abnormalities at serotonin synapses have been implicated in panic and obsessive-compulsive disorders.

Genetic vulnerability: Twin studies and other evidence suggest a genetic predisposition to mood disorders.

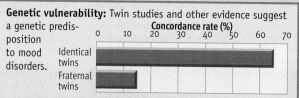

Concordance rate (%)

Sleep disturbances: Disruption of biological rhythms and sleep patterns may lead to neurochemical changes that contribute to mood disorders.

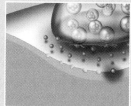

Neurochemical bases: Disturbances in neural circuits releasing norepinephrine may contribute to some mood disorders; abnormalities at serotonin synapses have also been implicated as a factor in depression.

Genetic vulnerability: Twin studies and other evidence suggest a genetic predisposition to schizophrenic disorders.

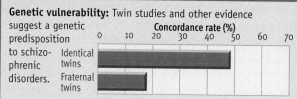

Concordance rate (%)

Neurochemical bases: Overactivity in neural circuits releasing dopamine is associated with schizophrenia; but abnormalities in other neurotransmitter systems may also contribute.

Structural abnormalities in brain: Enlarged brain ventricles are associated with schizophrenia, but they may be an effect rather than a cause of the disorder.

ETIOLOGY: PSYCHOLOGICAL FACTORS

Learning: Many anxiety responses may be acquired through classical conditioning or observational learning; phobic responses may be maintained by operant reinforcement.

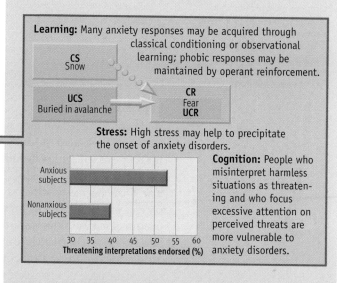

Stress: High stress may help to precipitate the onset of anxiety disorders.

Cognition: People who misinterpret harmless situations as threatening and who focus excessive attention on perceived threats are more vulnerable to anxiety disorders.

Threatening interpretations endorsed (%)

Interpersonal roots: Behavioral theories emphasize how inadequate social skills can result in a paucity of reinforcers and other effects that make people vulnerable to depression.

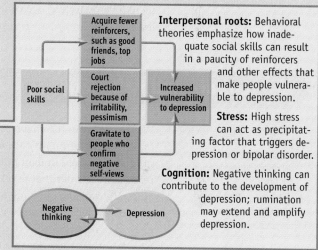

Stress: High stress can act as precipitating factor that triggers depression or bipolar disorder.

Cognition: Negative thinking can contribute to the development of depression; rumination may extend and amplify depression.

Expressed emotion: A family's expressed emotion is a good predictor of the course of a schizophrenic patient's illness.

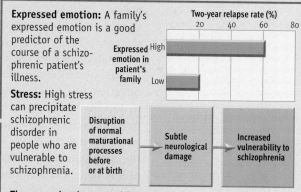

Two-year relapse rate (%)

Stress: High stress can precipitate schizophrenic disorder in people who are vulnerable to schizophrenia.

The neurodevelopmental hypothesis: Insults to the brain sustained during prenatal development or at birth may disrupt maturational processes in the brain resulting in elevated vulnerability to schizophrenia.

Figure 13.16

Figure 13.16
Expressed emotion and relapse rates in schizophrenia. Schizophrenic patients who return to a home that is high in expressed emotion have higher relapse rates than those who return to a home low in expressed emotion. Thus, unhealthy family dynamics can influence the course of schizophrenia. (Data adapted from Leff & Vaughn, 1981)

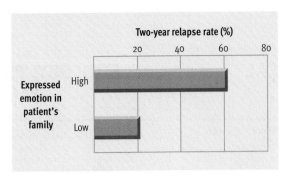

Expressed Emotion

Studies of expressed emotion have primarily focused on how this element of family dynamics influences the *course* of schizophrenic illness, after the onset of the disorder (Leff & Vaughn, 1985). *Expressed emotion* is the degree to which a relative of a schizophrenic patient displays highly critical or emotionally overinvolved attitudes toward the patient. Audiotaped interviews of relatives' communication are carefully evaluated for critical comments, resentment toward the patient, and excessive emotional involvement (overprotective, overconcerned attitudes) (Hooley, 2004).

Studies show that a family's expressed emotion is a good predictor of the course of a schizophrenic patient's illness (Hooley & Candela, 1999). After release from a hospital, schizophrenic patients who return to a family high in expressed emotion show relapse rates three times that of patients who return to a family low in expressed emotion (Hooley & Hiller, 1998; see **Figure 13.16**). Part of the problem for patients returning to homes high in expressed emotion is that their families probably are sources of stress rather than of social support (Cutting & Docherty, 2000). And as with virtually all mental disorders, schizophrenia is influenced to some extent by life stress.

Precipitating Stress

Most theories of schizophrenia assume that stress plays a key role in triggering schizophrenic disorders (Walker et al., 2004). According to this notion, various biological and psychological factors influence individuals' *vulnerability* to schizophrenia. High stress may then serve to precipitate a schizophrenic disorder in someone who is vulnerable (McGlashan & Hoffman, 2000).

> Culture and Pathology

PREVIEW QUESTIONS

● Are the same psychological disorders found in all cultures?

● What are culture-bound disorders?

We saw earlier in the chapter that judgments of normality and abnormality are influenced by cultural norms and values. In light of this reality, would it be reasonable to infer that psychological disorders are culturally variable phenomena? Social scientists are sharply divided on the answer to this question. Some embrace a *relativistic view* of psychological disorders, whereas others subscribe to a *universalistic* or *pancultural view* (Tanaka-Matsumi, 2001). Theorists who embrace the *relativistic view* argue that the criteria of mental illness vary greatly across cultures and that there are no universal standards of normality and abnormality. According to the relativists, the DSM diagnostic system reflects an ethnocentric, Western, white, urban, middle- and upper-class cultural orientation that has limited relevance in other cultural contexts. In contrast, those who subscribe to the *pancultural view* argue that the criteria of mental illness are much the same around the world and that basic standards of normality and abnormality are universal across cultures. Theorists who accept the pancultural view of psychopathology typically maintain that Western diagnostic concepts have validity and utility in other cultural contexts. The debate about culture and pathology basically boils down to this question: Are

the psychological disorders seen in Western societies found throughout the world? Let's briefly examine the evidence on this issue.

Most investigators agree that the principal categories of *serious* psychological disturbance—schizophrenia, depression, and bipolar illness—are identifiable in all cultures (Tsai et al., 2001). Most behaviors that are regarded as clearly abnormal in Western culture are also viewed as abnormal in other cultures. People who are delusional, hallucinatory, disoriented, or incoherent are thought to be disturbed in all societies, although there are cultural disparities in exactly what is considered delusional or hallucinatory.

Cultural variations are more apparent in the recognition of less severe forms of psychological disturbance (Mezzich, Lewis-Fernandez, & Ruiperez, 2003). Additional research is needed, but relatively mild types of pathology that do not disrupt behavior in obvious ways appear to go unrecognized in many societies. Thus, syndromes such as generalized anxiety disorder, hypochondriasis, and somatization disorder, which are firmly established as important diagnostic categories in the DSM, are viewed in some cultures as "run-of-the-mill" difficulties and peculiarities rather than as full-fledged disorders.

Finally, researchers have discovered a small number of *culture-bound disorders* that further illustrate the diversity of abnormal behavior around the world (Griffith, Gonzalez, & Blue, 2003; Guarnaccia & Rogler, 1999). **Culture-bound disorders are abnormal syndromes found only in a few cultural groups.** For example, *koro,* an obsessive fear that one's penis will withdraw into one's abdomen, is seen only among Chinese males in Malaya and several other regions of southern Asia. *Windigo,* which involves an intense craving for human flesh and fear that one will turn into a cannibal, is seen only among Algonquin In-

dian cultures. And until recently, *anorexia nervosa,* which involves an intense fear of becoming fat, a loss of appetite, and refusal to eat adequately, was seen almost exclusively in affluent Western cultures (see the Personal Application).

So, what can we conclude about the validity of the relativistic versus pancultural views of psychological disorders? Both views appear to have some merit. As we have seen in other areas of research, psychopathology is characterized by both cultural variance and invariance.

> Reflecting on the Chapter's Themes

Our examination of abnormal behavior and its roots has highlighted four of our organizing themes: multifactorial causation, the interplay of heredity and environment, the sociohistorical context in which psychology evolves, and the influence of culture on psychological phenomena.

We can safely assert that every disorder described in this chapter has multiple causes. The development of mental disorders involves an interplay among a variety of psychological, biological, and social factors. We also saw that most psychological disorders depend on an interaction of genetics and experience. This interaction shows up most clearly in the *stress-vulnerability models* for mood disorders and schizophrenic disorders. *Vulnerability* to these disorders seems to depend primarily on heredity, although experience contributes. Stress is largely a function of environment, although physiological factors may influence people's stress reactions. According to stress-

vulnerability theories, disorders emerge when high vulnerability intersects with high stress. Thus, the impact of heredity depends on the environment, and the effect of environment depends on heredity.

This chapter also demonstrated that psychology evolves in a sociohistorical context. We saw that modern conceptions of normality and abnormality are largely shaped by empirical research, but social trends, prevailing values, and political realities also play a role. Finally, our discussion of psychological disorders showed once again that psychological phenomena are shaped to some degree by cultural parameters. Although some standards of normality and abnormality transcend cultural boundaries, cultural norms influence what is regarded as abnormal. Indeed, the influence of culture will be apparent in our upcoming Personal Application on eating disorders. These disorders are largely a creation of modern, affluent, Western culture.

 Multifactorial Causation

 Heredity and Environment

 Sociohistorical Context

 Cultural Heritage

PERSONAL *Application*

Understanding Eating Disorders

Answer the following "true" or "false."

____ 1 Although they have only attracted attention in recent years, eating disorders have a long history and have always been fairly common.

____ 2 People with anorexia nervosa are much more likely to recognize that their eating behavior is pathological

than people suffering from bulimia nervosa.

____ 3 The prevalence of eating disorders is twice as high in women as it is in men.

____ 4 The binge-and-purge syndrome seen in bulimia nervosa is not common in anorexia nervosa.

All of the above statements are false, as you will see in this Application. The psychological disorders that we discussed in the main body of the chapter have largely been recognized for centuries and are generally found in one form or another in all cultures and societies. Eating disorders present a sharp contrast to this picture; they have only been recognized in recent decades and have largely been confined to affluent, Westernized cultures (Russell, 1995; Szmukler & Patton, 1995). In spite of these fascinating differences, eating disorders have much in common with traditional forms of pathology.

Description

Eating disorders **are severe disturbances in eating behavior characterized by preoccupation with weight concerns and unhealthy efforts to control weight.** The vast majority of cases consist of two sometimes overlapping syndromes: *anorexia nervosa* and *bulimia nervosa.* **Anorexia nervosa** **involves intense fear of gaining weight, disturbed body image, refusal to maintain normal weight, and dangerous measures to lose weight.** Two subtypes have been observed (Herzog & Delinsky, 2001). In *restricting type anorexia nervosa,* people drastically reduce their intake of food, sometimes literally starving themselves. In *binge-eating/purging type anorexia nervosa,* individuals attempt to lose weight by forcing themselves to vomit after meals, by misusing laxatives and diuretics, and by engaging in excessive exercise.

Both types suffer from disturbed body image. No matter how frail they become, they insist that they are too fat. Their morbid fear of obesity means that they are never satisfied with their weight. If they gain a pound or two, they panic. The only thing that makes them happy is to lose more weight. The frequent result is a relentless decline in body weight; people entering treatment for anorexia nervosa are typically 25%–30% below their normal weight (Hsu, 1990). Because of their disturbed body image, individuals suffering from anorexia generally do *not* appreciate the maladaptive quality of their behavior and rarely seek treatment on their own. They are typically coaxed or coerced into treatment by friends or family members who are alarmed by their appearance.

Anorexia nervosa eventually leads to a cascade of medical problems, including *amenorrhea* (a loss of menstrual cycles in women), gastrointestinal problems, low blood pressure, *osteoporosis* (a loss of bone density), and metabolic disturbances that can lead to cardiac arrest or circulatory collapse (Pomeroy & Mitchell, 2002; Walsh, 2003). Anorexia is a serious illness that leads to death

in 5%–10% of patients (Steinhausen, 2002).

Bulimia nervosa **involves habitually engaging in out-of-control overeating followed by unhealthy compensatory efforts, such as self-induced vomiting, fasting, abuse of laxatives and diuretics, and excessive exercise.** The eating binges are usually carried out in secret and are followed by intense guilt and concern about gaining weight. These feelings motivate ill-advised strategies to undo the effects of the overeating. However, vomiting prevents the absorption of only about half of recently consumed food, and laxatives and diuretics have negligible impact on caloric intake, so individuals suffering from bulimia nervosa typically maintain a reasonably normal weight (Beumont, 2002). Medical problems associated with bulimia nervosa include cardiac arrythmias, dental problems, metabolic deficiencies, and gastrointestinal problems (Halmi, 2002, 2003).

Obviously, bulimia nervosa shares many features with anorexia nervosa, such as a morbid fear of becoming obese, preoccupation with food, and rigid, maladaptive approaches to controlling weight that are grounded in naive all-or-none thinking. However, the syndromes also differ in crucial ways. First and foremost, bulimia is a much less life-threatening condition. Second, although their appearance is usually more "normal" than that seen with anorexia, people with bulimia are much more likely to recognize that their eating behavior is pathological and are more likely to cooperate with treatment (Striegel-Moore, Silberstein, & Rodin, 1993).

History and Prevalence

Historians have been able to track down descriptions of anorexia nervosa that date back centuries, so the disorder is *not* entirely new, but anorexia nervosa did not become a common affliction until the middle of the 20th century (Vandereycken, 2002). Although binging and purging have a long

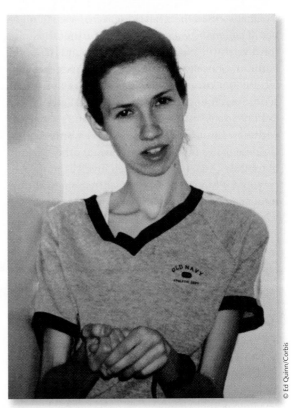

Eating disorders have become distressingly common among young women in Western cultures. No matter how frail they become, people suffering from anorexia insist that they are too fat.

© Ed Quinn/Corbis

history in some cultures, they were not part of pathological efforts to control weight, and bulimia nervosa appears to be an entirely new syndrome that emerged gradually in the middle of the 20th century and was first recognized in the 1970s (Russell, 1997; Vandereycken, 2002).

Both disorders are a product of modern, affluent Western culture, in which food is generally plentiful and the desirability of being thin is widely endorsed. Until recently, these disorders were not seen outside of Western cultures (Hoek, 2002). However, advances in communication have exported Western culture to far-flung corners of the globe, and eating disorders have started showing up in many non-Western societies, especially affluent Asian countries (Lee & Katzman, 2002).

There is a huge gender gap in the likelihood of developing eating disorders. About 90%–95% of individuals with anorexia nervosa and bulimia nervosa are female (Thompson & Kinder, 2003). This staggering discrepancy appears to be a result of cultural pressures rather than biological factors (Smolak & Murnen, 2001). Western standards of attractiveness emphasize slenderness more for females than for males, and women generally experience greater pressure to be physically attractive than men do (Sobal, 1995). Eating disorders mostly afflict *young* women. The typical age of onset for anorexia is 14 to 18; for bulimia it is 15 to 21 (see **Figure 13.17**).

How common are eating disorders in Western societies? The prevalence of these disorders has increased substantially in recent decades, although this escalation may be leveling off (Steiger & Seguin, 1999). Studies of young women suggest that about 1%–1.5% develop anorexia nervosa (Walters & Kendler, 1995) and about 2%–3% develop bulimia nervosa (Romano & Quinn, 2001). These figures may seem small, but they mean that millions of young women wrestle with serious eating problems.

Etiology of Eating Disorders

Like other types of psychological disorders, eating disorders are caused by multiple determinants that work interactively. Let's take a brief look at some of the factors that contribute to the development of anorexia nervosa and bulimia nervosa.

Genetic Vulnerability

The evidence is not nearly as strong or complete as it is for many other types of psychopathology (such as anxiety, mood, and schizophrenic disorders), but some people may inherit a genetic vulnerability to eating disorders. Studies show that relatives of patients with eating disorders have elevated rates of anorexia nervosa and bulimia nervosa (Bulik, 2004). And twin studies suggest that a genetic predisposition may be at work (Steiger, Bruce, & Israel, 2003).

Personality Factors

Certain personality traits may increase vulnerability to eating disorders. There are innumerable exceptions, but victims of anorexia nervosa tend to be obsessive, rigid, and emotionally restrained, whereas victims of bulimia nervosa tend to be impulsive, overly sensitive, and low in self-esteem (Anderluh et al., 2003; Wonderlich, 2002). Recent research also suggests that perfectionism is a risk factor for anorexia (Bulik et al., 2003).

Cultural Values

The contribution of cultural values to the increased prevalence of eating disorders can hardly be overestimated (Anderson-Fye & Becker, 2004; Stice, 2001). In Western society, young women are socialized to believe that they must be attractive, and to be attractive they must be as thin as the actresses and fashion models that dominate the media (Lavine, Sweeney, & Wagner, 1999). Thanks to this cultural milieu, many young women are dissatisfied with their weight because the societal ideals promoted by the media are unattainable for most of them (Thompson & Stice, 2001). Unfortunately, in a small portion of these women, the pressure to be thin, in combination with genetic vulnerability, family pathology, and other factors, leads to unhealthy efforts to control weight.

The Role of the Family

Quite a number of theorists emphasize how family dynamics can contribute to the development of anorexia nervosa and bulimia nervosa in young women (Haworth-Hoeppner, 2000). Some theorists suggest that parents who are overly involved in their children's lives turn the normal adolescent push for independence into an unhealthy struggle (Minuchin, Rosman, & Baker, 1978). Needing to assert their autonomy, some adolescent girls seek extreme control over their body, leading to pathological patterns of eating (Bruch, 1978). Other theorists maintain that some mothers contribute to eating disorders simply by endorsing society's message that "you can never be too thin" and by modeling unhealthy dieting behaviors of their own (Pike & Rodin, 1991).

Cognitive Factors

Many theorists emphasize the role of disturbed thinking in the etiology of eating disorders (Williamson et al., 2001). For example, anorexic patients' typical belief that they are fat when they are really wasting away is a dramatic illustration of how thinking goes awry. Patients with eating disorders display rigid, all-or-none thinking and many maladaptive beliefs, such as "I must be thin to be accepted," "If I am not in complete control, I will lose all control," "If I gain one pound, I'll go on to gain enormous weight." Additional research is needed to determine whether distorted thinking is a *cause* or merely a *symptom* of eating disorders.

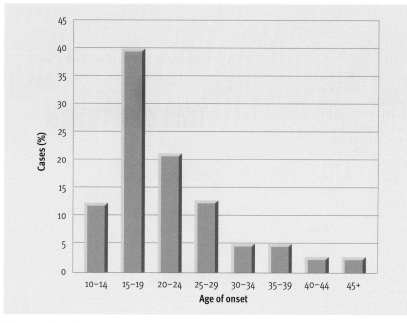

Figure 13.17

Age of onset for anorexia nervosa. Eating disorders mostly emerge during adolescence, as these data for anorexia nervosa show. This graph shows how age of onset was distributed in a sample of 166 female patients from Minnesota. As you can see, over half the patients experienced the onset of their illness before the age of 20, with vulnerability clearly peaking between the ages of 15 and 19. (Based on data from Lucas et al., 1991)

Working with Probabilities in Thinking About Mental Illness

As you read about the various types of psychological disorders, did you think to yourself that you or someone you know was being described? On the one hand, there is no reason to be alarmed. The tendency to see yourself and your friends in descriptions of pathology is a common one, sometimes called the *medical students' syndrome* because beginning medical students often erroneously believe that they or their friends have whatever diseases they are currently learning about. On the other hand, realistically speaking, it *is* quite likely that you know *many* people with psychological disorders. Recent data on the prevalence of psychological disorders—which are summarized in **Figure 13.18**—suggest that the likelihood of anyone having at least one DSM disorder is about 44%.

This estimate strikes most people as surprisingly high. Why is this so? One reason is that when people think about psychological disorders they tend to think of severe disorders, such as bipolar disorder or schizophrenia, which are relatively infrequent, rather than "ordinary" disturbances, such as anxiety and depressive disorders, which are much more common. When it comes to mental illness, people tend to think of patients in straightjackets or of obviously psychotic homeless people who do not reflect the broad and diverse population of people who suffer from psychological disorders. In other words, their *prototypes* or "best examples" of mental illness consist of severe disorders that are infrequent, so they underestimate the prevalence of mental disorders. This distortion illustrates the influence of the *representativeness heuristic,* which is **basing the estimated probability of an event on how similar it is to the typical prototype of that event** (see Chapter 8).

Do you still find it hard to believe that the overall prevalence of psychological disorders is about 44%? Another reason this number seems surprisingly high is that many people do not understand that the probability of having *at least one* disorder is much higher than the probability of having the most prevalent disorder by itself. For example, the probability of having a substance-use disorder, the single most common type of disorder, is approximately 24%, but the probability of having a substance-use disorder *or* an anxiety disorder *or* a mood disorder *or* a schizophrenic disorder jumps to 44%. These "or" relationships represent *cumulative probabilities.*

What about "and" relationships—that is, relationships in which we want to know the probability of someone having condition A *and* condition B? For example, given the lifetime prevalence estimates (from **Figure 13.18**) for each category of disorder, which are shown in the parentheses, what is the probability of someone having a substance-use disorder (24% prevalence) *and* an anxiety disorder (19%) *and* a mood disorder (15%) *and* a schizophrenic disorder (1%) during his or her lifetime? Such "and" relationships represent *conjunctive probabilities.*

Stop and think: What must be true about the probability of having all four types of disorders? Will this probability be less than 24%, between 24% and 44%, or over 44%? You may be surprised to learn that this figure is under 1%. You can't have all four disorders unless you have the least frequent disorder (schizophrenia), which has a prevalence of 1%, so the answer *must* be 1% or less. Moreover, of all of the people with schizophrenia, only a tiny subset of them are likely to have all three of the other disorders, so the answer is surely well under 1% (see **Figure 13.19**). If this type of question strikes you as contrived, think again. Epidemiologists have devoted an enormous amount of research to the estimation of *comorbidity*—**the coexistence of two or more disorders**—because it can greatly complicate treatment issues.

These are two examples of using statistical probabilities as a critical thinking tool. Let's apply this type of thinking to another problem dealing with physical health. Here

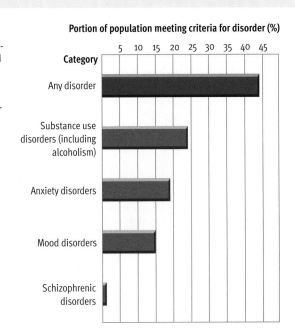

Figure 13.18

Lifetime prevalence of psychological disorders. The estimated percentage of people who have, at any time in their life, suffered from one of four types of psychological disorders or from a disorder of any kind (top bar) is shown here. Prevalence estimates vary somewhat from one study to the next, depending on the exact methods used in sampling and assessment. The estimates shown here are based on pooling data from Wave 1 and 2 of the Epidemiological Catchment Area studies and the National Comorbidity Study, as summarized by Regier and Burke (2000) and Dew, Bromet, and Switzer (2000). These studies, which collectively evaluated over 28,000 subjects, provide the best data to date on the prevalence of mental illness in the United States.

Portion of population meeting criteria for disorder (%)

Category
- Any disorder
- Substance use disorders (including alcoholism)
- Anxiety disorders
- Mood disorders
- Schizophrenic disorders

is a problem used in a study by Tversky and Kahneman (1983, p. 308) that many physicians got wrong:

A health survey was conducted in a sample of adult males in British Columbia, of all ages and occupations. Please give your best estimate of the following values:
What percentage of the men surveyed have had one or more heart attacks?_____
What percentage of the men surveyed both are over 55 years old and have had one or more heart attacks? _____

Fill in the blanks above with your best guesses. Of course, you probably have only a very general idea about the prevalence of heart attacks, but go ahead and fill in the blanks anyway.

The actual values are not as important in this example as the relative values are. Over

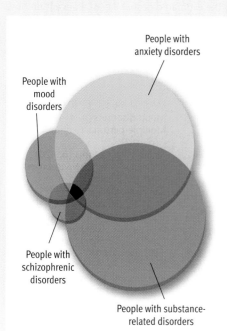

Figure 13.19

Conjunctive probabilities. The probability of someone having all four disorders depicted here cannot be greater than the probability of the least common condition by itself, which is 1% for schizophrenia. The intersection of all four disorders (shown in black) has to be a subset of schizophrenic disorders and is probably well under 1%. Efforts to think about probabilities can sometimes be facilitated by creating diagrams that show the relationships and overlap among various events.

People with anxiety disorders

People with mood disorders

People with schizophrenic disorders

People with substance-related disorders

65% of the physicians who participated in the experiment by Tversky and Kahneman gave a higher percentage value for the second question than for the first. What is wrong with their answers? The second question is asking about the conjunctive probability of two events. Hopefully, you see why this figure *must* be less than the probability of either one of these events occurring alone. Of all of the men in the survey who had had a heart attack, only some of them are also over 55, so the second number must be smaller than the first. As we saw in Chapter 8, this common error in thinking is called the *conjunction fallacy*. **The *conjunction fallacy* occurs when people estimate that the odds of two uncertain events happening together are greater than the odds of either event happening alone.**

Why did so many physicians get this problem wrong? They were vulnerable to the conjunction fallacy because they were influenced by the *representativeness heuristic*, or the power of prototypes. When physicians think "heart attack," they tend to envision a man over the age of 55. Hence, the second scenario fit so well with their prototype of a heart attack victim, they carelessly overestimated its probability.

Let's consider some additional examples of erroneous reasoning about probabilities involving how people think about psychological disorders. Many people tend to stereo-

typically assume that mentally ill people are likely to be violent. People also tend to wildly overestimate (37-fold in one study) how often the insanity defense is used in criminal trials (Silver, Cirincione, & Steadman, 1994). These mistaken beliefs reflect the influence of the *availability heuristic,* **which is basing the estimated probability of an event on the ease with which relevant instances come to mind.** Because of the availability heuristic, people tend to overestimate the probability of dramatic events that receive heavy media coverage, even when these events are rare, because examples of the events are easy to retrieve from memory. Violent acts by former psychiatric patients tend to get lots of attention in the press. And because of the *hindsight bias,* journalists tend to question why authorities couldn't foresee and prevent the violence (see the Critical Thinking Application for Chapter 11), so the mental illness angle tends to be emphasized. In a similar vein, press coverage is usually intense when a defendant in a murder trial mounts an insanity defense.

In sum, the various types of statistics that come up in thinking about psychological disorders demonstrate that we are constantly working with probabilities, even though we may not realize it. Critical thinking requires a good understanding of the laws of probability because there are very few certainties in life.

Table 13.2 Critical Thinking Skills Discussed in This Application

Skill	Description
Understanding the limitations of the representativeness heuristic	The critical thinker understands that focusing on prototypes can lead to inaccurate probability estimates.
Understanding cumulative probabilities	The critical thinker understands that the probability of at least one of several events occurring is additive, and increases with time and the number of events.
Understanding conjunctive probabilities	The critical thinker appreciates that the probability of two uncertain events happening together is less than the probability of either event happening alone.
Understanding the limitations of the availability heuristic	The critical thinker understands that the ease with which examples come to mind may not be an accurate guide to the probability of an event.

CHAPTER 13 *Review*

Key Ideas

Abnormal Behavior: Myths and Realities

● The medical model assumes that it is useful to view abnormal behavior as a disease. This view has been criticized on the grounds that it turns ethical questions about deviance into medical questions. Although there are some problems with the medical model, the concept is useful if one remembers that it is only an analogy.

● Three criteria are used in deciding whether people suffer from psychological disorders: deviance, personal distress, and maladaptive behavior. To some extent, judgments about mental illness are value judgments that reflect cultural norms and social trends, as well as scientific knowledge.

● DSM-IV is the official psychodiagnostic classification system in the United States. This system asks for information about patients on five axes or dimensions.

Anxiety Disorders

● The anxiety disorders include generalized anxiety disorder, phobic disorder, panic disorder, obsessive-compulsive disorder, and posttraumatic stress disorder. These disorders may have a genetic component. Abnormalities in neurotransmitter activity at GABA and serotonin synapses may also play a role.

● Many anxiety responses, especially phobias, may be caused by classical conditioning and maintained by operant conditioning. Cognitive theorists maintain that a tendency to overinterpret harmless situations as threatening makes some people vulnerable to anxiety disorders. Stress may also contribute to the development of anxiety disorders.

Somatoform Disorders

● Somatoform disorders include somatization disorder, conversion disorder, and hypochondriasis. People with these disorders may focus excessive attention on bodily processes. Somatoform disorders may be a learned avoidance strategy reinforced by attention and sympathy. Neuroticism and insecure attachment may also increase vulnerability to these disorders.

Dissociative Disorders

● Dissociative disorders include dissociative amnesia, fugue, and dissociative identity disorder. Dissociative identity disorder may be rooted in emotional trauma that occurred during childhood, although some theorists argue that the disorder typically involves intentional role playing.

Mood Disorders

● The principal mood disorders are unipolar depression and bipolar disorder. Mood disorders are episodic. Unipolar depression is more common than bipolar disorder.

● Evidence indicates that people vary in their genetic vulnerability to the severe mood disorders. These disorders are accompanied by changes in neurochemical activity in the brain. Depression is associated with reduced hippocampal volume and suppressed neurogenesis. Cognitive models posit that negative thinking and rumination contribute to depression. Depression is often rooted in interpersonal inadequacies and setbacks and sometimes is stress related.

Schizophrenic Disorders

● Schizophrenic disorders are characterized by deterioration of adaptive behavior, irrational thought, distorted perception, and disturbed mood. Schizophrenic disorders are classified as paranoid, catatonic, disorganized, or undifferentiated. A new classification scheme based on the predominance of positive versus negative symptoms is under study.

● Research has linked schizophrenia to genetic vulnerability, changes in neurotransmitter activity, structural abnormalities in the brain, and disruptions in the normal maturational processes of the brain before or at birth. Precipitating stress and unhealthy family dynamics (high expressed emotion) may also contribute to the development of schizophrenia.

Culture and Pathology

● The principal categories of psychological disturbance are identifiable in all cultures. However, milder disorders may go unrecognized in some societies, and culture-bound disorders further illustrate the diversity of abnormal behavior around the world.

Reflecting on the Chapter's Themes

● This chapter highlighted four of our unifying themes, showing that psychological disorders are governed by multiple causes, that heredity and environment jointly influence mental disorders, that psychology evolves in a sociohistorical context, and that pathology is characterized by both cultural variance and invariance.

PERSONAL APPLICATION • Understanding Eating Disorders

● The principal eating disorders are anorexia nervosa and bulimia nervosa. Both appear to be largely a product of modern, affluent Westernized culture. Females account for 90%–95% of eating disorders.

● There appears to be a genetic vulnerability to eating disorders, which may be mediated by heritable personality traits. Cultural pressures on young women to be thin clearly help foster eating disorders. Unhealthy family dynamics and disturbed thinking can also contribute.

CRITICAL THINKING APPLICATION • Working with Probabilities in Thinking About Mental Illness

● Probability estimates can be distorted by the representativeness heuristic, which involves basing the estimated probability of an event on how similar it is to the typical prototype of that event. Cumulative probabilities are additive, whereas conjunctive probabilities are always less than the likelihood of the least likely event happening alone. Probability estimates can be biased by the availability heuristic, which involves basing the estimated probability of an event on the ease with which relevant instances come to mind.

Key Terms

Agoraphobia (p. 407)
Anorexia nervosa (p. 428)
Anxiety disorders (p. 407)
Availability heuristic (p. 431)
Bipolar disorder (p. 415)
Bulimia nervosa (p. 428)
Catatonic schizophrenia (p. 420)
Comorbidity (p. 430)
Concordance rate (p. 409)
Conjunction fallacy (p. 431)
Conversion disorder (p. 411)
Culture-bound disorders (p. 427)
Delusions (p. 419)
Diagnosis (p. 404)
Disorganized schizophrenia (p. 420)
Dissociative amnesia (p. 412)
Dissociative disorders (p. 412)
Dissociative fugue (p. 412)
Dissociative identity disorder (DID) (p. 412)
Eating disorders (p. 428)
Etiology (p. 404)
Generalized anxiety disorder (p. 407)
Hallucinations (p. 419)
Hypochondriasis (p. 411)
Major depressive disorder (p. 414)
Manic-depressive disorder (p. 415)

Medical model (p. 403)
Mood disorders (p. 414)
Multiple-personality disorder (p. 412)
Negative symptoms (p. 420)
Obsessive-compulsive disorder (OCD) (p. 408)
Panic disorder (p. 407)
Paranoid schizophrenia (p. 419)
Phobic disorder (p. 407)
Positive symptoms (p. 420)
Posttraumatic stress disorder (PTSD) (p. 408)
Prognosis (p. 404)
Psychosomatic diseases (p. 410)
Representativeness heuristic (p. 430)
Schizophrenic disorders (p. 418)
Somatization disorder (p. 410)
Somatoform disorders (p. 410)
Undifferentiated schizophrenia (p. 420)

Key People

Nancy Andreasen (p. 420)
Susan Nolen-Hoeksema (pp. 415, 417)
Martin Seligman (p. 417)
Thomas Szasz (pp. 403–404)

1. According to Thomas Szasz, abnormal behavior usually involves:
   A. behavior that is statistically unusual.
   B. behavior that deviates from social norms.
   C. a disease of the mind.
   D. biological imbalance.

2. Although Sue always feels a high level of dread, worry, and anxiety, she still manages to meet her daily responsibilities. Sue's behavior:
   A. should not be considered abnormal, since her adaptive functioning is not impaired.
   B. should not be considered abnormal, since everyone sometimes experiences worry and anxiety.
   C. can still be considered abnormal, since she feels great personal distress.
   D. both a and b are true.

3. The observation that people acquire phobias of ancient sources of threat (such as snakes) much more readily than modern sources of threat (such as electrical outlets) can best be explained by:
   A. classical conditioning.   C. observational learning.
   B. operant conditioning.   D. preparedness.

4. Which of the following statements about dissociative identity disorder is true?
   A. The original personality is always aware of the alternate personalities.
   B. The alternate personalities are always unaware of the original personality.
   C. The personalities are typically all quite similar to one another.
   D. Starting in the 1970s, there was a dramatic increase in the diagnosis of dissociative identity disorder.

5. People with unipolar disorder experience _____; people with bipolar disorder experience _____.
   A. alternating periods of depression and mania; mania only
   B. depression only; alternating periods of depression and mania
   C. mania only; alternating periods of depression and mania
   D. alternating periods of depression and mania; depression and mania simultaneously

6. A concordance rate indicates:
   A. the percentage of twin pairs or other relatives who exhibit the same disorder.
   B. the percentage of people with a given disorder who are currently receiving treatment.
   C. the prevalence of a given disorder in the general population.
   D. the rate of cure for a given disorder.

7. People who consistently come up with _____ explanations for negative events are more prone to depression.
   A. overly optimistic   C. delusional
   B. pessimistic   D. dysthymic

8. Mary believes that while she sleeps at night, space creatures are attacking her and invading her uterus, where they will multiply until they are ready to take over the world. Mary was chosen for this task, she believes, because she is the only one with the power to help the space creatures succeed. Mary would most likely be diagnosed as _____ schizophrenic.
   A. paranoid   C. disorganized
   B. catatonic   D. undifferentiated

9. As an alternative to the current classification scheme, it has been proposed that schizophrenic disorders be divided into just two categories based on:
   A. whether the prognosis is favorable or unfavorable.
   B. whether the disorder is mild or severe.
   C. the predominance of thought disturbances versus emotional disturbances.
   D. the predominance of negative versus positive symptoms.

10. Most of the drugs that are useful in the treatment of schizophrenia are known to dampen _____ activity in the brain, suggesting that disruptions in the activity of this neurotransmitter may contribute to the development of the disorder.
    A. norepinephrine   C. acetylcholine
    B. serotonin   D. dopamine

11. Bipolar disorder occurs in _____ of the population.
    A. about 1–2.5%   C. nearly one-third
    B. about 10%   D. about 20%

12. Research suggests that there is an association between schizophrenia and:
    A. atrophied brain ventricles.   C. hippocampal degeneration.
    B. enlarged brain ventricles.   D. abnormalities in the cerebellum.

13. Those who embrace a relativistic view of psychological disorders would assert that:
    A. the criteria of mental illness vary greatly across cultures.
    B. there are universal standards of normality and abnormality.
    C. Western diagnostic concepts have validity and utility in other cultural contexts.
    D. both B and C are true.

14. About _____ of patients with eating disorders are female.
    A. 40%   C. 75%
    B. 50%–60%   D. 90%–95%

15. Victims of _____ are more likely to recognize that their eating behavior is pathological; the more life-threatening eating disorder is _____.
    A. anorexia nervosa; bulimia nervosa
    B. bulimia nervosa; anorexia nervosa
    C. anorexia nervosa; anorexia nervosa
    D. bulimia nervosa; bulimia nervosa

Answers

1 B pp. 403–404   6 A p. 409   11 A p. 416
2 C pp. 404–405   7 B p. 417   12 B pp. 422–423
3 D p. 409   8 A pp. 419–420 13 A p. 426
4 D p. 413   9 D p. 420   14 D p. 428
5 B pp. 414–415   10 D p. 422   15 B p. 428

PsykTrek

Go to the PsykTrek website or CD-ROM for further study of the concepts in this chapter. Both online and on the CD-ROM, PsykTrek includes dozens of learning modules with videos, animations, and quizzes, as well as simulations of psychological phenomena and a multimedia glossary that includes word pronunciations.

ThomsonNOW

www.thomsonedu.com/ThomsonNOW
Go to this site for the link to ThomsonNOW, your one-stop study shop. Take a Pre-Test for this chapter, and ThomsonNOW will generate a Personalized Study Plan based on your test results. The Study Plan will identify the topics you need to review and direct you to online resources to help you master those topics. You can then take a Post-Test to help you determine the concepts you have mastered and what you still need to work on.

Companion Website

www.thomsonedu.com/psychology/weiten
Go to this site to find online resources directly linked to your book, including a glossary, flash cards, drag-and-drop exercises, quizzes, and more!

CHAPTER 14

Treatment of Psychological Disorders

© Dennis Cooper/zefa/Corbis

What do you picture when you hear the term *psychotherapy*? Unless you've had some personal exposure to therapy, your image of it has likely been shaped by portrayals you've seen on television or in the movies. A good example is the 1999 film *Analyze This,* a comedy starring Billy Crystal as psychiatrist Ben Sobol and Robert De Niro as Paul Vitti, a mob boss who is suffering from "panic attacks." Complications develop when Vitti—a man no one says "no" to—demands that Dr. Sobol cure him of his problem before his rivals in crime turn his "weakness" against him.

With his glasses and beard, Billy Crystal's Dr. Sobol resembles many people's picture of a therapist. Like many movie therapists, Dr. Sobol practices "talk therapy." He listens attentively as his patients talk about what is troubling them. Occasionally he offers comments that reflect their thoughts and feelings back to them or that offer some illuminating insight into their problems. We can get a feeling for his approach from a funny scene in which the uneducated Vitti turns Dr. Sobol's techniques on him:

VITTI: *Hey, let's see how you like it. Let's talk about your father.*
SOBOL: *Let's not.*
VITTI: *What kind of work does your father do?*
SOBOL: *It's not important.*
VITTI: *You paused.*
SOBOL: *I did not.*
VITTI: *You just paused. That means you had a feeling, like a thought . . .*
SOBOL: *You know, we're running out of time. Let's not waste it talking about my problems.*
VITTI: *Your father's a problem?*
SOBOL: *No!*
VITTI: *That's what you just said.*
SOBOL: *I did not!*
VITTI: *Now you're upset.*
SOBOL: *(getting upset): I am not upset!*
VITTI: *Yes you are.*
SOBOL: *Will you stop it!*
VITTI: *You know what, I'm getting good at this.*

As in this scene, the film derives much of its humor from popular conceptions—and misconceptions—about therapy. The technique that Vitti makes fun of does resemble one type of therapeutic process. Like Vitti, many people do associate needing therapy with having a shameful weakness. Further, therapy is often of considerable benefit in helping people make significant changes in their lives—even if those

changes are not as dramatic as Vitti's giving up his life of crime at the end of the movie. On the other hand, the film's comic exaggerations also highlight some misconceptions about therapy, including the following:

- Vitti is driven to see a "shrink" because he feels like he's "falling apart." In fact, therapists help people with all kinds of problems. People need not have severe symptoms of mental illness to benefit from therapy.
- Dr. Sobol is a psychiatrist, but most therapists are not. And although Dr. Sobol quotes Freud and the film's plot turns on interpreting a dream (in this case, it's the psychiatrist's dream!), many therapists make little or no use of Freudian techniques.
- Dr. Sobol relies on "talk therapy" to produce insights that will help his patients overcome their troubles. In reality, this approach is only one of the many techniques used by therapists.
- Dr. Sobol "cures" Vitti by getting him to acknowledge a traumatic event in his childhood (the death of his father) that is at the root of his problems. But only rarely does therapy produce a single dramatic insight that results in wholesale change for the client.

In this chapter, we'll take a down-to-earth look at *psychotherapy,* using the term in its broadest sense, to refer to all the diverse approaches used in the treatment of mental disorders and psychological problems. We'll start by discussing some general questions about how treatment is provided. After considering these issues, we'll examine the goals, techniques,

The popular film Analyze This *derived much of its humor from common misconceptions about the process of psychotherapy.*

Warner Bros./Shooting Star

and effectiveness of some of the more widely used approaches to therapy and discuss recent trends and issues in treatment, including changes in institutional treatment. In the Personal Application, we'll look at practical questions related to finding and choosing a therapist. And in the Critical Thinking Application we'll address problems involved in determining whether therapy actually helps.

> The Elements of the Treatment Process

PREVIEW QUESTIONS

- What are the three major approaches to the treatment of psychological disorders?
- Are some people more likely to seek treatment than others?
- Why do only a portion of the people who need treatment receive it?
- What professions are involved in the treatment of psychological disorders?

Sigmund Freud is widely credited with launching modern psychotherapy. Ironically, the landmark case that inspired Freud was actually treated by one of his colleagues, Josef Breuer. Around 1880, Breuer began to treat a young woman known in the annals of psychiatry as Anna O (her real name, which came out years later, was Bertha Pappenheim). Anna exhibited a variety of physical maladies, including headaches, coughing, and a loss of feeling and movement in her right arm. Much to his surprise, Breuer discovered that Anna's physical symptoms cleared up when he encouraged her to talk about emotionally charged experiences from her past.

When Breuer and Freud discussed the case, they speculated that talking things through had enabled Anna to drain off bottled-up emotions that had caused her symptoms. Breuer found the intense emotional exchange in this treatment not to his liking, so he didn't follow through on his discovery. However, Freud applied Breuer's insight to other patients, and his successes led him to develop a systematic treatment procedure, which he called *psychoanalysis*. Anna O called her treatment "the talking cure." However, as you'll see, psychotherapy isn't always curative, and many modern therapies place little emphasis on talking.

Freud's breakthrough ushered in a century of progress for psychotherapy. Psychoanalysis spawned many offspring as Freud's followers developed their own systems of treatment. Since then, approaches to psychotherapy have steadily grown more numerous, more diverse, and more effective.

Treatments: How Many Types Are There?

In their efforts to help people, psychotherapists use many treatment methods. One expert (Kazdin, 1994) estimates that there may be over 400 different approaches to treatment! Fortunately, we can impose some order on this chaos. As varied as therapists' procedures are, approaches to treatment can be classified into three major categories:

1. *Insight therapies.* Insight therapy is "talk therapy" in the tradition of Freud's psychoanalysis. In insight therapies, clients engage in complex, often lengthy verbal interactions with their therapists. The goal in these discussions is to pursue increased insight regarding the nature of the client's difficulties and to sort through possible solutions.

2. *Behavior therapies.* Behavior therapies are based on the principles of learning, which were introduced in Chapter 6. Instead of emphasizing personal insights, behavior therapists make direct efforts to alter problematic responses (phobias, for instance) and maladaptive habits (drug use, for instance).

3. *Biomedical therapies.* Biomedical approaches to therapy involve interventions into a person's biological functioning. The most widely used procedures are drug therapy and electroconvulsive (shock) therapy. As the name bio*medical* therapies suggests, these treatments have traditionally been provided only by physicians with a medical degree (usually psychiatrists). This situation is changing, however, as psychologists have been campaigning for prescription privileges (Norfleet, 2002; Welsh, 2003). To date psychologists have obtained prescription authority in two states (New Mexico and Louisiana) and they have made legislative progress toward this goal in many other states (Long, 2005). Although some psychologists have argued against pursuing the right to prescribe medication (Heiby, 2002; Robiner et al., 2003), the movement is gathering momentum and seems likely to prevail.

Clients: Who Seeks Therapy?

In the therapeutic triad (therapists, treatments, clients), the greatest diversity of all is seen among the clients. According to the 1999 U.S. Surgeon General's report on mental health (U.S. Department of Health and Human Services, 1999) about 15% of the U.S. population use mental health services in a given year. These people bring to therapy the full range of human problems: anxiety, depression, unsatisfactory interpersonal relations, troublesome habits, poor self-control, low self-esteem, marital conflicts, self-doubt, a sense of emptiness, and feelings of personal stagnation.

Interestingly, people often delay for many years before finally seeking treatment for their psychological problems (Kessler, Olfson, & Berglund, 1998).

The case of Anna O, whose real name was Bertha Pappenheim, provided the inspiration for Sigmund Freud's invention of psychoanalysis.

One recent large-scale study (Wang, Berglund et al., 2005) found that the median delay in seeking treatment was 6 years for bipolar disorder and for drug dependence, 8 years for depression, 9 years for generalized anxiety disorder, and 10 years for panic disorder! A client in treatment does *not* necessarily have an identifiable psychological disorder. Some people seek professional help for everyday problems or vague feelings of discontent (Strupp, 1996). One surprising finding in recent research has been that only about half of the people who use mental health services in a given year meet the criteria for a full-fledged mental disorder (Kessler et al., 2005b).

People vary considerably in their willingness to seek psychotherapy. One study found that even when people perceive a need for professional assistance, only 59% actually seek professional help (Mojtabai, Olfson, & Mechanic, 2002). As you can see in **Figure 14.1**, women are more likely than men to receive therapy. Treatment is also more likely when people have medical insurance and when they have more education (Olfson et al., 2002; Wang, Lane et al., 2005). *Unfortunately, it appears that many people who need therapy don't receive it* (Kessler et al., 2005b). As **Figure 14.2** shows, only a portion of the people who need treatment get it. People who could benefit from therapy do not seek it for a variety of reasons. Lack of health insurance and cost concerns appear to be major barriers to obtaining needed care for many people. According to the Surgeon General's report, the biggest roadblock is the "stigma surrounding the receipt of mental health treatment." Unfortunately, many people—like Paul Vitti in *Analyze This*—equate seeking therapy with admitting personal weakness.

Therapists: Who Provides Professional Treatment?

Friends and relatives may provide you with excellent advice about your personal problems, but their assistance does not qualify as therapy. Psychotherapy refers to *professional* treatment by someone with special training. However, a common source of confusion

Figure 14.2
Psychological disorders and professional treatment. Not everyone who has a psychological disorder receives professional treatment, and not everyone who seeks treatment has a clear disorder. This graph, from the Surgeon General's report on mental health, shows that 15% of the U.S. adult population receive mental health treatment each year. Almost half of these people (7%) do not receive a psychiatric diagnosis, although some of them probably have milder disorders that are not assessed in epidemiological research. This graph also shows that over two-thirds of the people who *do* have disorders do *not* receive professional treatment. (Data from U.S. Department of Health & Human Services, 1999)

Figure 14.1
Therapy utilization rates. Olfson and colleagues (2002) gathered data on the use of nonhospital outpatient mental health services in the United States in relation to various demographic variables. In regard to marital status, utilization rates are particularly high among those who are divorced or separated. The use of therapy is greater among those who have more education, and, in terms of age, utilization peaks in the 35–44 age bracket. Females are more likely to pursue therapy than males are, but utilization rates are extremely low among ethnic minorities. (Data from Olfson et al., 2002)

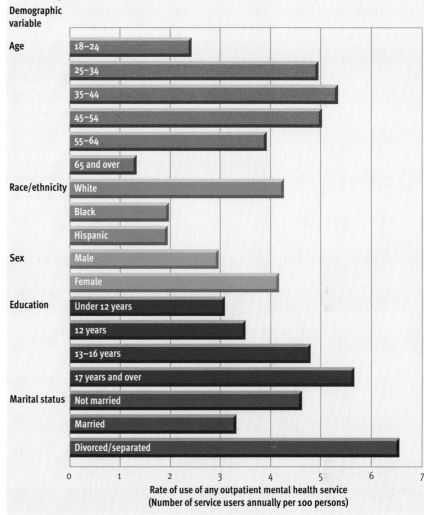

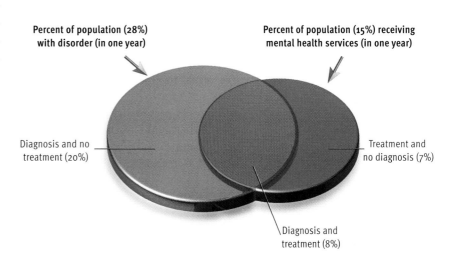

Web Link 14.1

Online Dictionary of Mental Health
This thematically arranged "dictionary" at the University of Sheffield (UK) Medical School comprises diverse links related to many forms of psychotherapy, the treatment of psychological disorders, and general issues of mental health.

about psychotherapy is the variety of "helping professions" involved (Murstein & Fontaine, 1993). Psychology and psychiatry are the principal professions involved in the delivery of psychotherapy, providing the lion's share of mental health care. However, treatment is also provided by other types of therapists. Let's look at these mental health professions.

Psychologists

Two types of psychologists may provide therapy, although the distinction between them is more theoretical than real. *Clinical psychologists* and *counseling psychologists* **specialize in the diagnosis and treatment of psychological disorders and everyday behavioral problems.** In theory, clinical psychologists' training emphasizes the treatment of full-fledged disorders. In contrast, counseling psychologists' training is supposed to be slanted toward the treatment of everyday adjustment problems in normal people. In practice, however, clinical and counseling psychologists overlap greatly in training, skills, and the clientele they serve. Both types of psychologists must earn a doctoral degree (Ph.D., Psy.D., or Ed.D.). In providing therapy, psychologists use either insight or behavioral approaches. Clinical and counseling psychologists do psychological testing as well as psychotherapy, and many also conduct research.

Psychiatrists

Psychiatrists **are physicians who specialize in the diagnosis and treatment of psychological disorders.** Many psychiatrists also treat everyday behavioral problems. However, in comparison to psychologists, psychiatrists devote more time to relatively severe disorders (schizophrenia, mood disorders) and less time to everyday marital, family, job, and school problems. Psychiatrists have an M.D. degree. In their treatment efforts, psychiatrists increasingly emphasize drug therapies (Olfson, Marcus, & Pincus, 1999), which the other, nonmedical helping professions generally have not been able to provide.

Other Mental Health Professionals

Several other mental health professions provide psychotherapy services. *Psychiatric social workers* and *psychiatric nurses* often work as part of a treatment team with a psychologist or psychiatrist. Although social workers have traditionally worked in hospitals and social service agencies, many also provide a wide range of therapeutic services as independent practitioners. Many kinds of *counselors* also provide therapeutic services. They often specialize in particular types of problems, such as vocational counseling, marital counseling, rehabilitation counseling, and drug counseling.

Although there are clear differences among the helping professions in education, training, and approach to therapy, their roles in the treatment process overlap considerably. In this chapter, we will refer to psychologists or psychiatrists as needed, but otherwise we'll use the terms *clinician, therapist,* and *mental health professional* to refer to psychotherapists of all kinds, regardless of their professional degree.

Now that we have discussed the basic elements in psychotherapy, we can examine specific approaches to treatment in terms of their goals, procedures, and effectiveness. We'll begin with some representative insight therapies.

> Insight Therapies

PREVIEW QUESTIONS

● What are the goals and techniques of psychoanalysis?

● What are resistance and transference?

● What are the goals and techniques of client-centered therapy?

● How is group therapy conducted?

● What is the evidence on the efficacy of insight therapy?

● What are common factors in insight therapy?

Many schools of thought offer ideas about how to do insight therapy. Therapists with various theoretical orientations use different methods to pursue different kinds of insights. However, what these varied approaches have in common is that **insight therapies involve verbal interactions intended to enhance clients' self-knowledge and thus promote healthful changes in personality and behavior.** In this section, we'll delve into psychoanalysis, client-centered therapy, and group therapy.

Psychoanalysis

11d

After the case of Anna O, Sigmund Freud worked as a psychotherapist for almost 50 years in Vienna. Through a painstaking process of trial and error, he developed innovative techniques for the treatment of psychological disorders and distress. His system of *psychoanalysis* came to dominate psychiatry for many decades. Although the dominance of psychoanalysis has eroded in recent years, a diverse collection of psychoanalytic approaches to therapy continue to evolve and to remain influential today (Eagle & Wolitzky, 1992; Ursano & Silberman, 1999).

Psychoanalysis **is an insight therapy that emphasizes the recovery of unconscious conflicts, motives, and defenses through techniques such as free association and transference.** To appreciate the logic of psychoanalysis, we have to look at Freud's thinking about the roots of mental disorders. Freud mostly treated anxiety-dominated disturbances, such as phobic, panic, obsessive-compulsive, and conversion disorders, which were then called *neuroses*.

Freud believed that neurotic problems are caused by unconscious conflicts left over from early childhood. As explained in Chapter 11, he thought that people depend on defense mechanisms to avoid confronting these conflicts, which remain hidden in the depths of the unconscious (see **Figure 14.3**). However, he noted that defensive maneuvers tend to be only partially successful in alleviating anxiety, guilt, and other distressing emotions. With this model in mind, let's take a look at the therapeutic procedures used in psychoanalysis.

Probing the Unconscious

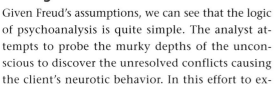

Given Freud's assumptions, we can see that the logic of psychoanalysis is quite simple. The analyst attempts to probe the murky depths of the unconscious to discover the unresolved conflicts causing the client's neurotic behavior. In this effort to explore the unconscious, the therapist relies on two techniques: free association and dream analysis.

In *free association* clients spontaneously express their thoughts and feelings exactly as they occur, with as little censorship as possible. In free associating, clients talk about anything that comes to mind, regardless of how trivial, silly, or embarrassing it might be. The analyst studies these free associations for clues about what is going on in the unconscious. In *dream analysis* the therapist interprets the symbolic meaning of the client's dreams. For Freud, dreams were the "royal road to the unconscious," the most direct means of access to patients' innermost conflicts, wishes, and impulses. Psychoanalytic clients are encouraged and trained to remember their dreams, which they describe in therapy.

To better illustrate these matters, let's look at an actual case treated through psychoanalysis (adapted from Greenson, 1967, pp. 40–41). Mr. N was troubled by an unsatisfactory marriage. He claimed to love his wife, but he preferred sexual relations with prostitutes. Mr. N reported that his parents also endured lifelong marital difficulties. His childhood conflicts about their relationship appeared to be related to his problems. Both dream analysis and free association can be seen in the following description of a session in Mr. N's treatment:

Mr. N reported a fragment of a dream. All that he could remember is that he was waiting for a red traffic light to change when he felt that someone had bumped into him from behind. . . . The associations led to Mr. N's love of cars, especially sports cars. He loved the sensation, in particular, of whizzing by those fat, old expensive cars. . . .

Figure 14.3

Freud's view of the roots of disorders. According to Freud, unconscious conflicts between the id, ego, and superego sometimes lead to anxiety. This discomfort may lead to pathological reliance on defensive behavior.

His father always hinted that he had been a great athlete, but he never substantiated it. . . . Mr. N doubted whether his father could really perform. His father would flirt with a waitress in a cafe or make sexual remarks about women passing by, but he seemed to be showing off. If he were really sexual, he wouldn't resort to that.

As is characteristic of free association, Mr. N's train of thought meandered about with little direction. Nonetheless, clues about his unconscious conflicts were apparent. What did Mr. N's therapist extract from this session? The therapist saw sexual overtones in the dream fragment, where Mr. N was bumped from behind. The therapist also inferred that Mr. N had a competitive orientation toward his father, based on the free association about whizzing by fat, old expensive cars. As you can see, analysts must *interpret* their clients' dreams and free associations. Contrary to popular belief, analysts generally don't try to dazzle clients with startling revelations. Instead, analysts move forward inch by inch, offering interpretations that should be just out of the client's own reach. Mr. N's therapist eventually offered the following interpretations to his client:

I said to Mr. N near the end of the hour that I felt he was struggling with his feelings about his father's sexual life. He seemed to be saying that his father was sexually not a very potent man. . . . He also recalls that he once found a packet of condoms under his father's pillow when he was an adolescent and he thought, "My father must be going to prostitutes." I then intervened and pointed out that the condoms under his father's pillow seemed to indicate more obviously that his father used the condoms with his mother, who slept in the same bed. However, Mr. N wanted to believe his wish-fulfilling fantasy: mother doesn't want sex with father and father is not very potent. The patient was silent and the hour ended.

As you may have already guessed, the therapist concluded that Mr. N's difficulties were rooted in an *Oedipal complex* (see Chapter 11). He had unresolved sexual feelings toward his mother and hostile feelings about his father. These unconscious conflicts,

SIGMUND FREUD

"The news that reaches your consciousness is incomplete and often not to be relied on."

National Library of Medicine

Web Link 14.2

The American Psychoanalytic Association
The site for this professional organization provides a great deal of useful information about psychoanalytic approaches to treatment. The resources include news releases, background information on psychoanalysis, an engine for literature searches, and a bookstore.

rooted in Mr. N's childhood, were distorting his intimate relations as an adult.

Resistance and Transference 11d

How would you expect Mr. N to respond to the therapist's suggestion that he was in competition with his father for the sexual attention of his mother? Obviously, most clients would have great difficulty accepting such an interpretation. Freud fully expected clients to display some resistance to therapeutic efforts. *Resistance* **refers to largely unconscious defensive maneuvers intended to hinder the progress of therapy.** Why would clients try to resist the helping process? Because they don't want to face up to the painful, disturbing conflicts that they have buried in their unconscious. Although they have sought help, they are reluctant to confront their real problems. Analysts use a variety of strategies to deal with clients' resistance. Often, a key consideration is the handling of transference.

Transference **occurs when clients start relating to their therapists in ways that mimic critical relationships in their lives.** Thus, a client might start relating to a therapist as if the therapist were an overprotective mother, a rejecting brother, or a passive spouse. In a sense, the client *transfers* conflicting feelings about important people onto the therapist. Psychoanalysts often encourage transference so that clients can reenact relations with crucial people in the context of therapy. These reenactments can help bring repressed feelings and conflicts to the surface, allowing the client to work through them.

Undergoing psychoanalysis is not easy. It can be a slow, painful process of self-examination that routinely requires three to five years of hard work. Ultimately, if resistance and transference can be handled effectively, the therapist's interpretations should lead the client to profound insights. For instance, Mr. N eventually admitted, "The old boy is probably right,

In psychoanalysis, the therapist encourages the client to reveal thoughts, feelings, dreams, and memories, which can then be interpreted in relation to the client's current problems.

it does tickle me to imagine that my mother preferred me and I could beat out my father. Later, I wondered whether this had something to do with my own screwed-up sex life with my wife." According to Freud, once clients recognize the unconscious sources of conflicts, they can resolve these conflicts and discard their neurotic defenses.

Modern Psychodynamic Treatments

Though still available, classical psychoanalysis as done by Freud is not widely practiced anymore (Kay & Kay, 2003). Freud's psychoanalytic method was geared to a particular kind of clientele that he was seeing in Vienna many years ago. As his followers fanned out across Europe and America, many found it necessary to adapt psychoanalysis to different cultures, changing times, and new kinds of patients. Thus, many variations on Freud's original approach to psychoanalysis have developed over the years. These descendants of psychoanalysis are collectively known as *psychodynamic approaches* to therapy.

Some of these adaptations, such as those by Carl Jung (1917) and Alfred Adler (1927), were sweeping revisions based on fundamental differences in theory. Other variations, such as those devised by Melanie Klein (1948) and Heinz Kohut (1971), involved more subtle changes in theory. Still other revisions (Alexander, 1954; Stekel, 1950) simply involved efforts to modernize and streamline psychoanalytic techniques. As a result, today we have a rich diversity of psychodynamic approaches to therapy.

Client-Centered Therapy 11d

You may have heard of people going into therapy to "find themselves," or to "get in touch with their real feelings." These now-popular phrases emerged out of the *human potential movement,* which was stimulated in part by the work of Carl Rogers (1951, 1986). Using a humanistic perspective, Rogers devised client-centered therapy (also known as person-centered therapy) in the 1940s and 1950s.

Client-centered therapy **is an insight therapy that emphasizes providing a supportive emotional climate for clients, who play a major role in determining the pace and direction of their therapy.** Rogers's theory about the principal causes of neurotic anxieties is quite different from the Freudian explanation. As discussed in Chapter 11, Rogers maintains that most personal distress is due to inconsistency, or "incongruence," between a person's self-concept and reality (see **Figure 14.4**). According to his theory, incongruence makes people feel threatened by realis-

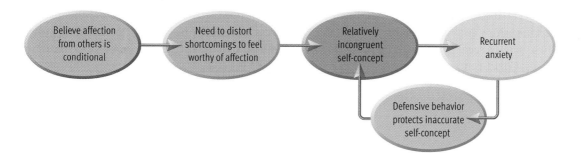

tic feedback about themselves from others. According to Rogers, anxiety about such feedback often leads to reliance on defense mechanisms, to distortions of reality, and to stifled personal growth. Excessive incongruence is thought to be rooted in clients' overdependence on others for approval and acceptance.

Given Rogers's theory, client-centered therapists stalk insights that are quite different from the repressed conflicts that psychoanalysts go after. Client-centered therapists help clients realize that they do not have to worry constantly about pleasing others and winning acceptance. They help people restructure their self-concept to correspond better to reality. Ultimately, they try to foster self-acceptance and personal growth.

Therapeutic Climate **11d**

According to Rogers, the *process* of therapy is not as important as the emotional *climate* in which the therapy takes place. He believes that it is critical for the therapist to provide a warm, supportive climate in which clients can confront their shortcomings without feeling threatened. The lack of threat should reduce clients' defensive tendencies and thus help them open up. To create this supportive atmosphere, client-centered therapists must provide three conditions: (1) *genuineness* (honest communication), (2) *unconditional positive regard* (nonjudgmental acceptance of the client), and (3) *accurate empathy* (understanding of the client's point of view).

Therapeutic Process **11d**

In client-centered therapy, the client and therapist work together as equals. The therapist provides relatively little guidance and keeps interpretation and advice to a minimum. The therapist's key task is *clarification*. Client-centered therapists try to function like a human mirror, reflecting statements back to their clients, but with enhanced clarity. They help clients become more aware of their true feelings by highlighting themes that may be obscure in the clients' rambling discourse. The reflective nature of client-centered therapy can be seen in the following exchange between a client and therapist:

CLIENT: *I really feel bad today . . . just terrible.*
THERAPIST: *You're feeling pretty bad.*
CLIENT: *Yeah, I'm angry and that's made me feel bad, especially when I can't do anything about it. I just have to live with it and shut up.*
THERAPIST: *You're very angry and feel like there's nothing you can safely do with your feelings.*
CLIENT: *Uh-huh. I mean . . . if I yell at my wife she gets hurt. If I don't say anything to her I feel tense.*
THERAPIST: *You're between a rock and a hard place— no matter what you do, you'll wind up feeling bad.*
CLIENT: *I mean she chews ice all day and all night. I feel stupid saying this. It's petty, I know. But when I sit there and try to concentrate I hear all these slurping and crunching noises. I can't stand it . . . and I yell. She feels hurt—I feel bad—like I shouldn't have said anything.*
THERAPIST: *So when you finally say something you feel bad afterward.*
CLIENT: *Yeah, I can't say anything to her without getting mad and saying more than I should. And then I cause more trouble than it's worth. (Duke & Nowicki, 1979, p. 565)*

By working with clients to clarify their feelings, client-centered therapists hope to gradually build toward more far-reaching insights. In particular, they

CARL ROGERS
"To my mind, empathy is in itself a healing agent."

Client-centered therapists emphasize the importance of a supportive emotional climate in therapy. They also work to clarify, rather than interpret, the feelings expressed by their patients.

try to help clients better understand their interpersonal relationships and become more comfortable with their genuine selves. Obviously, these are ambitious goals. Client-centered therapy resembles psychoanalysis in that both seek to achieve a major reconstruction of a client's personality.

Group Therapy

Many approaches to insight therapy, such as client-centered therapy, can be conducted on either an individual or group basis. *Group therapy* **is the simultaneous treatment of several clients in a group.** Although group therapy can be conducted in a variety of ways, we can provide a general overview of the process (see Alonso, Alonso, & Piper, 2003; Stone, 2003; Vinogradov, Cox, & Yalom, 2003).

A therapy group typically consists of 4 to 12 people, with 6 to 8 participants regarded as ideal (Vinogradov et al., 2003). The therapist usually screens the participants, excluding persons who seem likely to be disruptive. Some theorists maintain that judicious selection of participants is crucial to effective group treatment (Salvendy, 1993). In group therapy, participants essentially function as therapists for one another (Stone, 2003). Group members describe their problems, trade viewpoints, share experiences, and discuss coping strategies. Most important, they provide acceptance and emotional support for each other. In this atmosphere, group members work at peeling away the social masks that cover their insecurities. As members come to value one another's opinions, they work hard to display healthy changes. In group treatment, the therapist's responsibilities include selecting participants, setting goals for the group, initiating and maintaining the therapeutic process, and preventing interactions among group members that might be psychologically harmful (Vinogradov et al., 2003). The therapist often plays a relatively subtle role in group therapy, staying in the background and focusing mainly on promoting group cohesiveness.

Group therapies obviously save time and money, which can be critical in understaffed mental hospitals and other institutional settings. Therapists in private practice usually charge less for group than individual therapy, making therapy affordable for more people. However, group therapy is *not* just a less costly substitute for individual therapy (Alonso et al., 2003; Stone, 2003). Group therapy has unique strengths of its own, and certain kinds of problems are especially well suited to group treatment.

Whether insight therapies are conducted on a group or an individual basis, clients usually invest considerable time, effort, and money. Are these therapies worth the investment? Let's examine the evidence on their effectiveness.

How Effective Are Insight Therapies?

Evaluating the effectiveness of any approach to psychotherapy is a complex matter (Hill & Lambert, 2004; Kendall, Holmbeck, & Verduin, 2004). For one thing, psychological disorders sometimes clear up on their own, a phenomenon called *spontaneous remission.* If a client experiences a recovery after treatment, we cannot automatically assume that the recovery was due to the treatment (see the Critical Thinking Application). Evaluations of insight therapies are especially complicated given that various schools of thought pursue entirely different goals. Judgments of therapeutic outcome in insight therapy tend to be subjective, with little consensus about the best way to assess therapeutic progress. Moreover, people enter therapy with diverse problems of varied severity, so the efficacy of treatment can be evaluated meaningfully only for specific clinical problems.

Despite these difficulties, thousands of outcome studies have been conducted to evaluate the effectiveness of insight therapy. These studies have examined a broad range of clinical problems and used diverse methods to assess therapeutic outcomes, including scores on psychological tests and ratings by family members, as well as therapists' and clients' ratings. These studies consistently indicate that insight therapy *is* superior to no treatment or to placebo treatment and that the effects of therapy are reason-

Group treatments have proven particularly helpful when members share similar problems, such as alcoholism, overeating, or having been sexually abused as a child. Many approaches to insight therapy that were originally designed for individuals—such as client-centered therapy—have been adapted for treatment of groups.

© Manchan/Photodisc Red/Getty Images

ably durable (Kopta et al., 1999; Lambert & Ogles, 2004). Studies generally find the greatest improvement early in treatment (the first 13–18 weekly sessions), with further gains gradually diminishing in size over time (Lambert, Bergin, & Garfield, 2004). Overall, about 50% of patients show a clinically meaningful recovery within about 20 sessions, and another 25% of patients achieve this goal after about 45 sessions (Lambert & Ogles, 2004; see **Figure 14.5**). Of course, these broad generalizations mask considerable variability in outcome, but the general trends are encouraging.

How Do Insight Therapies Work?

Although there is considerable evidence that insight therapy tends to produce positive effects for a sizable majority of clients, there is vigorous debate about the mechanisms of action underlying these positive effects. The advocates of various therapies tend to attribute the benefits of therapy to the particular procedures used by each specific therapy (Chambless & Hollon, 1998). An alternative view is that the diverse approaches to therapy share certain *common factors* and that these common factors account for much of the improvement experienced by clients (Frank & Frank, 1991). Evidence supporting the common factors view has mounted in recent years (Ahn & Wampold, 2001; Lambert & Barley, 2001).

What are the common elements that lie at the core of diverse approaches to therapy? The models proposed to answer this question vary considerably, but there is some agreement. The most widely cited common factors include (1) the development of a therapeutic alliance with a professional helper, (2) the provision of emotional support and empathic understanding by the therapist, (3) the cultivation of hope and positive expectations in the client, (4) the provision of a rationale for the client's prob-

lems and a plausible method for resolving them, and (5) the opportunity to express feelings, confront problems, gain new insights, and learn new patterns of behavior (Grencavage & Norcross, 1990; Weinberger, 1995). How important are the common factors in therapy? Some theorists argue that common factors account for virtually *all* of the progress that clients make in therapy (Wampold, 2001). It seems more likely that the benefits of therapy represent the combined effects of common factors and specific procedures (Beutler & Harwood, 2002). Either way, it is clear that common factors play a significant role in insight therapy.

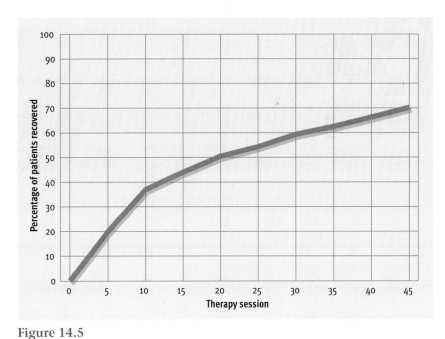

Figure 14.5

Recovery as a function of number of therapy sessions. Based on a national sample of over 6000 patients, Lambert, Hansen, and Finch (2001) mapped out the relationship between recovery and the duration of treatment. These data show that about half of the patients had experienced a clinically significant recovery after 20 weekly sessions of therapy. After 45 sessions of therapy, about 70% had recovered.

Source: Adapted from Lambert, M. J., Hansen, N. B., & Finch, A. E. (2001). Patient-focused research: Using patient outcome data to enhance treatment effects. *Journal of Consulting and Clinical Psychology, 69,* 159–172. Copyright © 2001 by the American Psychological Association. Used by permission of the publisher and authors.

PREVIEW QUESTIONS

- What assumptions are behavior therapies based on?
- How do systematic desensitization and aversion therapy work?
- What are the goals and techniques of social skills training?
- How do cognitive-behavioral techniques work?
- What is the evidence on the efficacy of behavior therapy?

JOSEPH WOLPE

"Neurotic anxiety is nothing but a conditioned response."

Behavior therapy is different from insight therapy in that behavior therapists make no attempt to help clients achieve grand insights about themselves. Why not? Because behavior therapists believe that such insights aren't necessary to produce constructive change. For example, consider a client troubled by compulsive gambling. The behavior therapist doesn't care whether this behavior is rooted in unconscious conflicts or parental rejection. What the client needs is to get rid of the maladaptive behavior. Consequently, the therapist simply designs a program to eliminate the compulsive gambling.

Behavior therapies involve the application of the principles of learning and conditioning to direct efforts to change clients' maladaptive behaviors. Behaviorists devoted little attention to clinical issues until the 1950s, when behavior therapy emerged out of three independent lines of research fostered by B. F. Skinner and his colleagues (Skinner, Solomon, & Lindsley, 1953) in the United States, Hans Eysenck (1959) and his colleagues in Britain, and Joseph Wolpe (1958) and his colleagues in South Africa (Glass & Arnkoff, 1992).

Behavior therapies are based on certain assumptions (Berkowitz, 2003). *First, it is assumed that behavior is a product of learning.* No matter how self-defeating or pathological a client's behavior might be, the behaviorist believes that it is the result of past conditioning. *Second, it is assumed that what has been learned can be unlearned.* Thus, behavior therapists attempt to change clients' behavior by applying the principles of classical conditioning, operant conditioning, and observational learning (see Chapter 6). Behavior therapy involves designing specific procedures for specific types of problems, as you'll see in our discussion of systematic desensitization.

Systematic Desensitization 11e

Devised by Joseph Wolpe (1958), systematic desensitization revolutionized psychotherapy by giving therapists their first useful alternative to traditional "talk therapy" (Fishman & Franks, 1992). *Systematic desensitization is a behavior therapy used to reduce clients' phobic responses.* The treatment assumes that most anxiety responses are acquired through classical conditioning (as discussed in Chapter 13). According to this model, a harmless stimulus (for instance, a bridge) may be paired with a fear-arousing event (lightning striking it), so that it becomes a conditioned stimulus eliciting anxiety. The goal of systematic desensitization is to weaken the association between the conditioned stimulus (the bridge) and the conditioned response of anxiety (see **Figure 14.6**). Systematic desensitization involves three steps.

First, the therapist helps the client build an anxiety hierarchy. The hierarchy is a list of anxiety-arousing stimuli related to the specific source of anxiety, such as flying, academic tests, or snakes. The client ranks the stimuli from the least anxiety arousing to the most anxiety arousing. This ordered list of stimuli is the *anxiety hierarchy.* An example of an anxiety hierarchy for one woman's fear of heights is shown in **Figure 14.7**.

The second step involves training the client in deep muscle relaxation. Various therapists use different relaxation training procedures. Whatever procedures are used, the client must learn to engage in deep, thorough relaxation on command from the therapist.

In the third step, the client tries to work through the hierarchy, learning to remain relaxed while imagining each stimulus. Starting with the least anxiety-arousing stimulus, the client imagines the situation as vividly as possible while relaxing. If the client experiences strong

concept **check 14.1**

Understanding Therapists' Goals

Check your understanding of therapists' goals by matching various therapies with the appropriate description. The answers are in Appendix A.

Principal therapeutic goals

_____ **1.** Elimination of maladaptive behaviors or symptoms

_____ **2.** Acceptance of genuine self, personal growth

_____ **3.** Recovery of unconscious conflicts, character reconstruction

Therapy

a. Psychoanalysis

b. Client-centered therapy

c. Behavior therapy

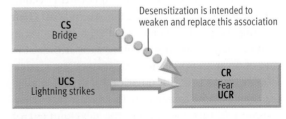

Figure 14.6

The logic underlying systematic desensitization. Behaviorists argue that many phobic responses are acquired through classical conditioning. For example, a person traumatized by a lightning strike while crossing a bridge might develop a phobia of bridges, as diagrammed here. Systematic desensitization targets the conditioned associations between phobic stimuli and fear responses.

Systematic desensitization is a behavioral treatment for phobias. Early studies of the procedure's efficacy often used people who had snake phobias as research subjects because people with snake phobias were relatively easy to find. This research showed that systematic desensitization is generally an effective treatment.

An Anxiety Hierarchy for Systematic Desensitization	
Degree of fear	
5	I'm standing on the balcony of the top floor of an apartment tower.
10	I'm standing on a stepladder in the kitchen to change a light bulb.
15	I'm walking on a ridge. The edge is hidden by shrubs and treetops.
20	I'm sitting on the slope of a mountain, looking out over the horizon.
25	I'm crossing a bridge 6 feet above a creek. The bridge consists of an 18-inch-wide board with a handrail on one side.
30	I'm riding a ski lift 8 feet above the ground.
35	I'm crossing a shallow, wide creek on an 18-inch-wide board, 3 feet above water level.
40	I'm climbing a ladder outside the house to reach a second-story window.
45	I'm pulling myself up a 30-degree wet, slippery slope on a steel cable.
50	I'm scrambling up a rock, 8 feet high.
55	I'm walking 10 feet on a resilient, 18-inch-wide board, which spans an 8-foot-deep gulch.
60	I'm walking on a wide plateau, 2 feet from the edge of a cliff.
65	I'm skiing an intermediate hill. The snow is packed.
70	I'm walking over a railway trestle.
75	I'm walking on the side of an embankment. The path slopes to the outside.
80	I'm riding a chair lift 15 feet above the ground.
85	I'm walking up a long, steep slope.
90	I'm walking up (or down) a 15-degree slope on a 3-foot-wide trail. On one side of the trail the terrain drops down sharply; on the other side is a steep upward slope.
95	I'm walking on a 3-foot-wide ridge. The slopes on both sides are long and more than 25 degrees steep.
100	I'm walking on a 3-foot-wide ridge. The trail slopes on one side. The drop on either side of the trail is more than 25 degrees.

Figure 14.7

Example of an anxiety hierarchy. Systematic desensitization requires the construction of an anxiety hierarchy like the one shown here, which was developed for a woman who had a fear of heights but wanted to go hiking in the mountains.

Source: Rudestam, K. E. (1980). *Methods of self-change: An ABC primer.* Belmont, CA: Wadsworth. Copyright © 1980 by Wadsworth Publishing. Reprinted by permission of the author.

anxiety, he or she drops the imaginary scene and concentrates on relaxation. The client keeps repeating this process until he or she can imagine a scene with little or no anxiety. Once a particular scene is conquered, the client moves on to the next stimulus situation in the anxiety hierarchy. Gradually, over a number of therapy sessions, the client progresses through the hierarchy, unlearning troublesome anxiety responses.

Desensitization to imagined stimuli can be effective by itself, but many behavior therapists advocate following it up with direct exposures to the real anxiety-arousing stimuli (Emmelkamp, 2004). The desensitization process should reduce anxiety enough so that clients will be able to confront situations they used to avoid. Although it seems deceptively simple, systematic desensitization can be quite effective in treating specific anxieties and phobic disorders (Spiegler & Guevremont, 2003).

Aversion Therapy

11e

Aversion therapy uses classical conditioning to create a negative response to a stimulus that has elicited problematic behavior. For example, alcoholics may be given an *emetic drug* (one that causes nausea and vomiting) in conjunction with their favorite drinks during therapy sessions (Landabaso et al., 1999). By pairing the drug with alcohol, the therapist hopes to create a conditioned aversion to alcohol. Aversion therapy takes advantage of the automatic, reflexive nature of responses produced through classical conditioning. Admittedly, alcoholics treated with aversion therapy know that they won't be given an emetic outside of their therapy sessions. However, their reflex response to the stimulus of alcohol may be changed so they respond to it with nausea and distaste (see **Figure 14.8**). Obviously, this response should make it much easier to resist the urge to drink.

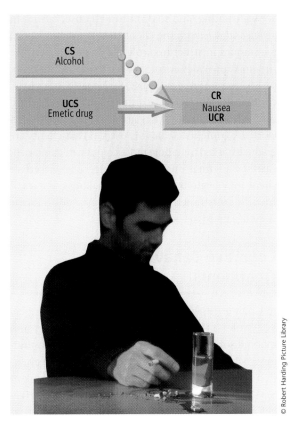

Figure 14.8

Aversion therapy. Aversion therapy uses classical conditioning to create an aversion to a stimulus that has elicited problematic behavior. For example, in the treatment of drinking problems, alcohol may be paired with a nausea-inducing drug to create an aversion to drinking.

Aversion therapy is not a widely used technique, and when used it is usually only one element in a larger treatment program. Troublesome behaviors treated successfully with aversion therapy have included drug and alcohol abuse, sexual deviance, gambling, shoplifting, stuttering, cigarette smoking, and overeating (Bordnick et al., 2004; Emmelkamp, 1994; Grossman & Ruiz, 2004; Maletzky, 2002).

Social Skills Training

Many psychological problems grow out of interpersonal difficulties. Behavior therapists point out that people are not born with social finesse—they acquire social skills through learning. Unfortunately, some people have not learned how to be friendly, how to make conversation, how to express anger appropriately, and so forth. As a result, behavior therapists are increasingly using social skills training in efforts to improve clients' social abilities. This approach to therapy has yielded promising results in the treatment of social anxiety (Shear & Beidel, 1998), autism (Kransny et al., 2003), attention deficit disorder (Antshel & Remer, 2003) and schizophrenia (Bellack et al., 2004).

Social skills training **is a behavior therapy designed to improve interpersonal skills that emphasizes modeling, behavioral rehearsal, and shaping.** With *modeling,* clients are encouraged to watch socially skilled friends and colleagues so that they can acquire appropriate responses (eye contact, active listening, and so on) through observation. In *behavioral rehearsal,* the client tries to practice social techniques in structured role-playing exercises. The therapist provides corrective feedback and uses approval to reinforce progress. Eventually, of course, clients try their newly acquired skills in real-world interactions. Usually, they are given specific homework assignments. *Shaping* is used in that clients are gradually asked to handle more complicated and delicate social situations. For example, a nonassertive client may begin by working on making requests of friends. Only much later will he be asked to tackle standing up to his boss at work.

Cognitive-Behavioral Treatments

In Chapter 13, we learned that cognitive factors play a key role in the development of many anxiety and mood disorders. Citing the importance of such findings, behavior therapists started to focus more attention on their clients' cognitions in the 1970s (Arnkoff & Glass, 1992; Hollon & Beck, 2004). *Cognitive-behavioral treatments* **use combinations of verbal**

AARON BECK

"Most people are barely aware of the automatic thoughts which precede unpleasant feelings or automatic inhibitions."

Courtesy of Aaron T. Beck

concept check 14.2

Understanding Behavior Therapies

Check your understanding of the varieties of behavior therapy discussed in your text by matching each therapy with the appropriate description. Choose from the following: (a) systematic desensitization, (b) social skills training, and (c) aversion therapy. The answers are in Appendix A.

_____ **1.** Anxiety is reduced by conditioning the client to respond positively to stimuli that previously aroused anxiety.

_____ **2.** Unwanted behaviors are eliminated by conditioning the client to have an unpleasant response to stimuli that previously triggered the behavior.

_____ **3.** Behavioral techniques are used to teach clients new behaviors aimed at enhancing the quality of their interactions with others.

interventions and behavior modification techniques to help clients change maladaptive patterns of thinking. Some of these treatments, such as Albert Ellis's (1973) *rational emotive behavior therapy* and Aaron Beck's (1976) *cognitive therapy* emerged out of an insight therapy tradition, whereas other treatments, such as the systems developed by Donald Meichenbaum (1977) and Michael Mahoney (1974) emerged from the behavioral tradition. We will focus on Beck's cognitive therapy as an example of a cognitive-behavioral treatment (see Chapter 12 for a discussion of some of Ellis's ideas).

Cognitive therapy **uses specific strategies to correct habitual thinking errors that underlie various types of disorders.** In recent years cognitive therapy has been applied fruitfully to a wide range of disorders (Rush & Beck, 2000), but it was originally devised as a treatment for depression. According to cognitive therapists, depression is caused by "errors" in thinking (see **Figure 14.9**). They assert that depression-prone people tend to (1) blame their setbacks on personal inadequacies without considering circumstantial explanations, (2) focus selectively on negative events while ignoring positive events, (3) make unduly pessimistic projections about the future, and (4) draw negative conclusions about their worth as a person based on insignificant events. For instance, imagine that you got a low grade on a minor quiz in a class. If you made the kinds of errors in thinking just described, you might blame the grade on your woeful stupidity, dismiss comments from a classmate that it was an unfair test, gloomily predict that you will surely flunk the course, and conclude that you are not genuine college material.

The goal of cognitive therapy is to change clients' negative thoughts and maladaptive beliefs. To begin, clients are taught to detect their automatic negative thoughts—the self-defeating statements that people are prone to make when analyzing problems. Examples might include "I'm just not smart enough," "No one really likes me," or "It's all my fault." Clients are then trained to subject these automatic thoughts to reality testing. The therapist helps them to see how unrealistically negative the thoughts are.

Cognitive therapy uses a variety of behavioral techniques, such as modeling, systematic monitoring of one's behavior, and behavioral rehearsal (Wright, Beck, & Thase, 2003). For example, cognitive therapists often give their clients "homework assignments" that focus on changing clients' overt behaviors. Clients may be instructed to engage in overt responses on their own, outside of the clinician's office. For example, one shy, insecure young man in cognitive therapy was told to go to a singles bar and engage three different women in conversations for up to five minutes each (Rush, 1984). He was instructed to record his thoughts before and after each of the conversations. This assignment elicited various maladaptive patterns of thought that gave the young man and his therapist plenty to work on in subsequent sessions.

How Effective Are Behavior Therapies?

How does the effectiveness of behavior therapy compare with that of insight therapy? In direct comparisons, the differences are usually small, but they tend

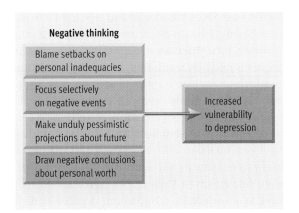

Negative thinking

Blame setbacks on personal inadequacies

Focus selectively on negative events

Make unduly pessimistic projections about future

Draw negative conclusions about personal worth

Increased vulnerability to depression

Figure 14.9

Beck's view of the roots of disorders. Beck's theory initially focused on the causes of depression, although it was gradually broadened to explain other disorders. According to Beck, depression is caused by the types of negative thinking shown here.

to favor behavioral approaches for certain types of disorders (Lambert & Bergin, 1992). However, it's fruitless to make global statements about the effectiveness of behavior therapies, because they include many procedures designed for different purposes. For example, the value of systematic desensitization for phobias has no bearing on the value of aversion therapy for sexual deviance.

For our purposes, it is sufficient to note that there is favorable evidence on the efficacy of most of the widely used behavioral interventions (Jacob & Pelham, 2000). Behavior therapies can make important contributions to the treatment of phobias, obsessive-compulsive disorders, sexual dysfunction, schizophrenia, drug-related problems, eating disorders, psychosomatic disorders, hyperactivity, autism, and mental retardation (Berkowitz, 2003; Emmelkamp, 2004).

Many of these problems could not be treated with the biomedical therapies, which we consider next. To some extent, the three major approaches to treatment have different strengths. Let's see where the strengths of the biomedical therapies lie.

Web Link 14.3

The Beck Institute of Cognitive Therapy and Research
This site offers a diverse array of materials relating to Aaron Beck's cognitive therapy. Resources found here include newsletters, a referral system, a bookstore, recommended readings for clients, and questions and answers abut cognitive therapy.

> Biomedical Therapies

Biomedical therapies **are physiological interventions intended to reduce symptoms associated with psychological disorders.** These therapies assume that psychological disorders are caused, at least in part, by biological malfunctions. As we discussed in the previous chapter, this assumption clearly has merit for many disorders, especially the more severe ones. We will discuss two biomedical treatments: drug therapy and electroconvulsive (shock) therapy.

Treatment with Drugs

 11e

Since the 1950s drug therapy has become increasingly important in the treatment of psychological dis-

orders. Therapeutic drugs fall into four major groups: antianxiety drugs, antipsychotic drugs, antidepressant drugs, and mood stabilizers.

Antianxiety Drugs

 11e

Most of us know someone who pops pills to relieve anxiety. *Antianxiety drugs,* **which reduce tension, apprehension, and nervousness,** are the drugs used in this common coping strategy. The most popular of these drugs are Valium and Xanax (trade names for the generic drugs diazepam and alprazolam, respectively).

Valium, Xanax, and other similar drugs are often called *tranquilizers.* These drugs exert their effects

PREVIEW QUESTIONS

- What are the principal types of psychiatric drugs, and what disorders are they used for?
- How effective are psychiatric drugs, and what are their disadvantages?
- What is ECT, and what is it used for?
- How effective is ECT, and what are the risks?

almost immediately, and they can be fairly effective in relieving feelings of anxiety (Ballenger, 2000). However, their effects are measured in hours, so their impact is relatively short-lived. Antianxiety drugs are routinely prescribed for people with anxiety disorders, but they are also given to millions of people who simply suffer from chronic nervous tension.

All the drugs used to treat psychological disorders have potentially troublesome side effects that show up in some patients but not others. The most common side effects of Valium and Xanax are drowsiness, lightheadedness, cottonmouth, depression, nausea, and constipation. These drugs also have potential for abuse, drug dependence, and overdose, although these risks have probably been exaggerated in the press (Ballenger, 2000; Silberman, 1998). Another drawback is that patients who have been on antianxiety drugs for a while often experience unpleasant withdrawal symptoms when their drug treatment is stopped (Raj & Sheehan, 2004).

Antipsychotic Drugs

Antipsychotic drugs are used primarily in the treatment of schizophrenia. They are also given to people with severe mood disorders who become delusional. **Antipsychotic drugs are used to gradually reduce psychotic symptoms, including hyperactivity, mental confusion, hallucinations, and delusions.** The traditional antipsychotics appear to decrease activity at dopamine synapses, although the exact relationship between their neurochemical effects and their clinical effects remains obscure (Egan & Hyde, 2000; Miyamoto et al., 2003).

Studies suggest that antipsychotic drugs reduce psychotic symptoms in about 70% of patients, albeit in varied degrees (Marder, 2000). When antipsychotic drugs are effective, they work their magic gradually, as shown in **Figure 14.10**. Patients usually begin to respond within two days to a week. Further improvement may occur for several months. Many schizophrenic patients are placed on antipsychotics indefinitely because these drugs can reduce the likelihood of a relapse into an active schizophrenic episode (Marder & van Kammen, 2000).

Antipsychotic drugs undeniably make a major contribution to the treatment of severe mental disorders, but they are not without problems. They have many unpleasant side effects (Cohen, 1997; Wilkaitis, Mulvihill, & Nasrallah, 2004). Drowsiness, constipation, and cottonmouth are common. Tremors, muscular rigidity, and impaired coordination may also occur. After being released from a hospital, many patients who have been placed on antipsychotics stop their drug regimen because of the side effects. Unfortunately, most patients eventually experience a relapse after they cease taking antipsychotic medication (Gitlin et al., 2001). In addition to their nuisance side effects, antipsychotics may cause a more severe and lasting problem called *tardive dyskinesia,* which is seen in about 20%–30% of patients who receive long-term treatment with traditional antipsychotics (Marder, 2000). **Tardive dyskinesia is a neurological disorder marked by involuntary writhing and ticlike movements of the mouth, tongue, face, hands, or feet.** Once this debilitating syndrome emerges, there is no cure, although spontaneous remission sometimes occurs after the discontinuation of antipsychotic medication (Pi & Simpson, 2000).

Psychiatrists are currently enthusiastic about a new class of antipsychotic agents called *atypical antipsychotic drugs.* These drugs are roughly as effective as traditional antipsychotics (Fleischhacker, 2002), and they can help some patients who do not respond to conventional antipsychotic medications (Volavka et al., 2002). Moreoever, the atypical antipsychotics produce fewer unpleasant side effects and carry less risk for tardive dyskinesia (Correll, Leucht, & Kane, 2004; Lieberman et al., 2003). Of course, like all powerful drugs, they are not without their risks, as they appear to increase patients' vulnerability to diabetes and cardiovascular problems (Meltzer et al., 2002).

Antidepressant Drugs

As their name suggests, *antidepressant drugs* gradually elevate mood and help bring people out of a

Figure 14.10
The time course of antipsychotic drug effects. Antipsychotic drugs reduce psychotic symptoms gradually, over a span of weeks, as graphed here. In contrast, patients given placebo medication show little improvement.

Source: Cole, J. O., Goldberg, S. C., & Davis, J. M. (1966). Drugs in the treatment of psychosis. In P. Solomon (Ed.), *Psychiatric drugs.* New York: Grune & Stratton. From data in the NIMH-PSC Collaborative Study I. Reprinted by permission of J. M. Davis.

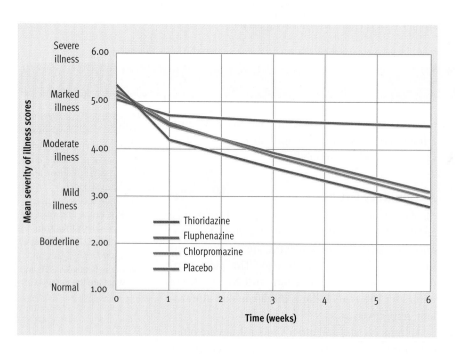

depression. Prior to 1987, there were two principal classes of antidepressants: *tricyclics* and *MAO inhibitors.* These two sets of drugs have different effects on neurotransmitter activity (see **Figure 14.11**) and tend to work with different patients. Overall, they are beneficial for about two-thirds of depressed patients (Gitlin, 2002), although only about one-third of treated patients experience a *complete resolution* of their symptoms (Shulman, 2001). The tricyclics have fewer problems with side effects and complications than the MAO inhibitors (Rush, 2000). Like antipsychotic drugs, antidepressants exert their effects gradually over a period of weeks.

Today, psychiatrists are more likely to prescribe a newer class of antidepressants, called *selective serotonin reuptake inhibitors (SSRIs),* which slow the reuptake process at serotonin synapses (see **Figure 14.11**). The drugs in this class, which include Prozac (fluoxetine), Paxil (paroxetine), and Zoloft (sertraline), seem to yield rapid therapeutic gains in the treatment of depression (Boland & Keller, 2003) while producing fewer unpleasant or dangerous side effects (Marangell et al., 2003).

However, a major concern in recent years has been evidence from a number of studies that SSRIs may increase patients' risk for suicide (Healy & Whitaker, 2003; Holden, 2004). The challenge of collecting definitive data on this issue is much more daunting than one might guess, in part because suicide rates are already elevated among people who exhibit the disorders for which SSRIs are prescribed (Rihmer, 2003; Wessely & Kerwin, 2004). Some researchers have collected data that suggest that suicide rates have *declined* slightly because of widespread prescription of SSRIs (Olfson et al., 2003), while others

have found no association between SSRIs and suicide (Lapiere, 2003; Tardiff, Marzuk, & Leon, 2002). At present, the data are too fragmentary and inconsistent to permit a firm, confident conclusion (Gunnell & Ashby, 2004). That said, the issue should be taken seriously, and patients on SSRIs should be carefully monitored by their physicians and families (Culpepper et al., 2004). Elevated suicide risk appears to be a problem mainly among a small minority of children and adolescents in the first month after starting antidepressants, especially the first nine days (Jick, Kaye, & Jick, 2004).

Mood Stabilizers

Mood stabilizers **are drugs used to control mood swings in patients with bipolar mood disorders.** For many years, *lithium* was the only effective drug in this category. Lithium has proven valuable in preventing *future* episodes of both mania and depression in patients with bipolar illness (Geddes et al., 2004). Lithium can also be used in efforts to bring patients with bipolar illness out of *current* manic or depressive episodes. However, antipsychotics and antidepressants are more frequently used for these purposes. On the negative side of the ledger, lithium does have some dangerous side effects if its use isn't managed skillfully (Jefferson & Greist, 2000). Lithium levels in the patient's blood must be monitored carefully, because high concentrations can be toxic and even fatal. Kidney and thyroid gland complications are the other major problems associated with lithium therapy.

In recent years a number of alternatives to lithium have been developed. The most popular of these

Web Link 14.4

Dr. Bob's Psychopharmacology Tips
Psychopharmacology is the use of medication to treat psychological disorders. Physician and pharmacology specialist Robert Hsiang (University of Chicago) provides both broad and specific references about the interface of drugs and the human mind, including a searchable archive of professional information.

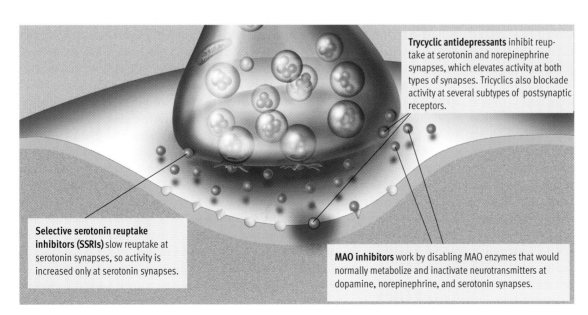

Trycyclic antidepressants inhibit reuptake at serotonin and norepinephrine synapses, which elevates activity at both types of synapses. Tricyclics also blockade activity at several subtypes of postsynaptic receptors.

Selective serotonin reuptake inhibitors (SSRIs) slow reuptake at serotonin synapses, so activity is increased only at serotonin synapses.

MAO inhibitors work by disabling MAO enzymes that would normally metabolize and inactivate neurotransmitters at dopamine, norepinephrine, and serotonin synapses.

Figure 14.11
Antidepressant drugs' mechanisms of action. The three types of antidepressant drugs all increase activity at serotonin synapses, which is probably the principal basis for their therapeutic effects. However, they increase serotonin activity in different ways, with different spillover effects (Marangell et al. 1999). Tricyclics and MAO inhibitors have effects at a much greater variety of synapses, which presumably explains why they have more side effects. The more recently developed SSRIs are much more specific in targeting serotonin synapses.

newer mood stabilizers is an anticonvulsant agent called *valproate,* which has become about as widely used as lithium in the treatment of bipolar disorders (Blanco et al., 2002). Valproate appears to be roughly as effective as lithium in efforts to treat current manic episodes and to prevent future affective disturbances (Moseman et al., 2003). The advantage provided by valproate is that it has fewer side effects than lithium and is better tolerated by patients (Bowden, 2004).

Evaluating Drug Therapies

Drug therapies can produce clear therapeutic gains for many kinds of patients. What's especially impressive is that they can be effective with severe disorders that otherwise defy therapeutic endeavors. Nonetheless, drug therapies are controversial. Critics of drug therapy have raised a number of issues (Cohen & McCubbin, 1990; Healy, 2004; Lickey & Gordon, 1991; Whitaker, 2002). First, some critics argue that drug therapies are not as effective as advertised and that they often produce superficial, short-lived curative effects. For example, Valium does not really solve problems with anxiety; it merely provides temporary relief from an unpleasant symptom. Moreover, relapse rates are substantial when drug regimens are discontinued. Second, critics charge that many drugs are overprescribed and many patients overmedicated. According to these critics, a number of physicians routinely hand out prescriptions without giving adequate consideration to more complicated and difficult interventions. Third, some critics charge that the damaging side effects of therapeutic drugs are underestimated by psychiatrists and that these side effects are often worse than the illnesses that the drugs are supposed to cure.

Critics maintain that the negative effects of psychiatric drugs are not fully appreciated because the pharmaceutical industry has managed to gain undue influence over the research enterprise as it relates to drug testing (Angell, 2000, 2004; Carpenter, 2002; Healy, 2004). Today, most researchers who investigate the benefits and risks of medications and write treatment guidelines have lucrative financial arrangements with the pharmaceutical industry (Bodenheimer, 2000; Choudhry, Stelfox, & Detsky, 2002). Their studies are funded by drug companies, and they often receive substantial consulting fees. Unfortunately, these financial ties appear to undermine the objectivity required in scientific research, as studies funded by drug companies are far less likely to report unfavorable results than nonprofit-funded studies (Bekelman, Li, & Gross, 2003; Rennie & Luft, 2000). Industry-financed drug trials also tend to be

"I medicate first and ask questions later."

© The New Yorker Collection 2000 Frank Cotham from cartoonbank.com. All rights reserved.

much too brief to detect the long-term risks associated with new drugs, and when unfavorable results emerge, the data are often withheld from publication (Antonuccio, Danton, & McClanahan, 2003). Also, research designs are often slanted in a variety of ways so as to exaggerate the positive effects and minimize the negative effects of the drugs under scrutiny (Carpenter, 2002; Chopra, 2003; Moncrieff, 2001). The conflicts of interest that appear to be pervasive in contemporary drug research raise grave concerns that require attention from researchers, universities, and federal agencies.

Electroconvulsive Therapy (ECT)

In the 1930s, a Hungarian psychiatrist named Ladislas von Meduna speculated that epilepsy and schizophrenia could not coexist in the same body. On the basis of this observation, which turned out to be inaccurate, von Meduna theorized that it might be useful to induce epileptic-like seizures in schizophrenic patients. Initially, a drug was used to trigger these seizures. However, by 1938 a pair of Italian psychiatrists (Cerletti & Bini, 1938) demonstrated that it was safer to elicit the seizures with electric shock. Thus, modern electroconvulsive therapy was born.

Electroconvulsive therapy (ECT) **is a biomedical treatment in which electric shock is used to produce a cortical seizure accompanied by convulsions.** In ECT, electrodes are attached to the skull over the temporal lobes of the brain (see the photo on the next page). A light anesthesia is administered, and the patient is given a variety of drugs to minimize the likelihood of complications, such as spinal fractures. An electric current is then applied for about a second. The current triggers a brief (5–20 seconds) convulsive seizure, during which the patient usually loses consciousness. The patient normally awakens in an hour or two. People typically receive between 6 and 20 treatments as inpatients at a hospital.

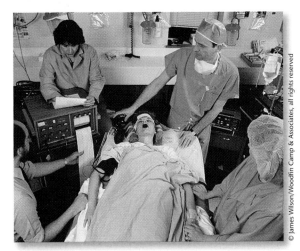

© James Wilson/Woodfin Camp & Associates, all rights reserved

This patient is being prepared for electroconvulsive therapy. The mouthpiece keeps the patient from biting her tongue during the electrically induced seizures.

The clinical use of ECT peaked in the 1940s and 1950s, before effective drug therapies were widely available. ECT has long been controversial, and its use declined in the 1960s and 1970s. Nonetheless, the use of ECT has seen a resurgence in recent decades, and it is not a rare form of therapy. Although only about 8% of psychiatrists administer ECT (Hermann et al., 1998), it is estimated that about 100,000 people receive ECT treatments yearly in the United States (Hermann et al., 1995). Some critics argue that ECT is overused because it is a lucrative procedure that boosts psychiatrists' income while consuming relatively little of their time in comparison to insight therapy (Frank, 1990). Conversely, some ECT advocates argue that ECT is underutilized because the public harbors many misconceptions about its risks and side effects (McDonald et al., 2004).

Effectiveness of ECT

The evidence on the therapeutic efficacy of ECT is open to varied interpretations. Proponents of ECT maintain that it is a remarkably effective treatment for major depression (Prudic & Sackeim, 1999; Rudorfer, Henry, & Sackeim, 2003). Moreover, they note that many patients who do not benefit from antidepressant medication improve in response to ECT (Isenberg & Zorumski, 2000). However, opponents of ECT argue that the available studies are flawed and inconclusive and that ECT is probably no more effective than a placebo (Rose et al., 2003). Overall, there does seem to be enough favorable evidence to justify *conservative* use of ECT in treating severe mood disorders in patients who have not responded to medication (Carney & Geddes, 2003; Metzger, 1999). Unfortunately, relapse rates after ECT are distressingly high. Over 50% of patients relapse within 6 to 12 months, although relapse rates can be reduced by giving ECT patients antidepressant drugs (Sackeim et al., 2001).

Risks Associated with ECT

Even ECT proponents acknowledge that memory losses are common short-term side effects of electroconvulsive therapy (Lisanby et al., 2000; Weiner, 2000). However, ECT proponents assert that these deficits are mild and usually disappear within a month or two (Glass, 2001). A recent American Psychiatric Association task force (2001) concluded that there is no objective evidence that ECT causes structural damage in the brain or that it has any lasting negative effects on the ability to learn and remember information. In contrast, ECT critics maintain that ECT-induced cognitive deficits are often significant and sometimes permanent (Breggin, 1991; Rose et al., 2003), although their evidence seems to be largely anecdotal. Given the doubts that have been raised about the efficacy and risks of electroconvulsive therapy, it appears that this treatment will remain controversial for some time to come.

---

concept **check** 14.3

Understanding Biomedical Therapies

Check your understanding of biomedical therapies by matching each treatment with its chief use. The answers are in Appendix A.

Treatment

_____ **1.** Antianxiety drugs

_____ **2.** Antipsychotic drugs

_____ **3.** Antidepressant drugs

_____ **4.** Mood stabilizers

_____ **5.** Electroconvulsive therapy (ECT)

Chief purpose

a. To reduce psychotic symptoms

b. To bring a major depression to an end

c. To suppress tension, nervousness, and apprehension

d. To prevent future episodes of mania or depression in bipolar disorders

Treatment of Psychological Disorders

THERAPY/FOUNDER

ROOTS OF DISORDERS

PSYCHOANALYSIS

National Library of Medicine

Developed by Sigmund Freud in Vienna, from the 1890s through the 1930s

Intrapsychic conflict (among id, ego, and superego) → Anxiety → Reliance on defense mechanisms

Unconscious conflict resulting from fixations in earlier development cause anxiety, which leads to defensive behavior. The repressed conflicts typically center on sex and aggression.

CLIENT-CENTERED THERAPY

Created by Carl Rogers at the University of Chicago during the 1940s and 1950s

Courtesy of Carl Rogers Memorial Library

Need to distort shortcomings to feel worthy of affection → Relatively incongruent self-concept → Recurrent anxiety

Defensive behavior protects inaccurate self-concept

Overdependence on acceptance from others fosters incongruence, which leads to anxiety and defensive behavior and thwarts personal growth.

BEHAVIOR THERAPY

Courtesy of Dr. Joseph Wolpe

Launched primarily by South African Joseph Wolpe's description of systematic desensitization in 1958

Maladaptive patterns of behavior are acquired through learning. For example, many phobias are thought to be created through classical conditioning and maintained by operant conditioning.

CS Bridge

UCS Lightning strikes

CR Fear **UCR**

COGNITIVE–BEHAVIORAL TREATMENTS

One approach devised by Aaron Beck at the University of Pennsylvania in the 1960s and 1970s

Courtesy of Aaron T. Beck

Pervasive negative thinking about events related to self fosters anxiety and depression, and other forms of pathology.

Blame setbacks on personal inadequacies

Focus selectively on negative events

Make unduly pessimistic projections about future

Draw negative conclusions about personal worth

→ Increased vulnerability to depression

BIOMEDICAL THERAPY

Many researchers contributed; key break-throughs in drug treatment made around 1950 by John Cade in Australia, Henri Laborit in France, and Jean Delay and Pierre Deniker, also in France

Most disorders are attributed to genetic predisposition and physiological malfunc-tions, such as abnormal neurotransmitter activity. For example, schizophrenia appears to be associated with overactivity at dopamine synapses.

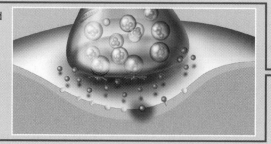

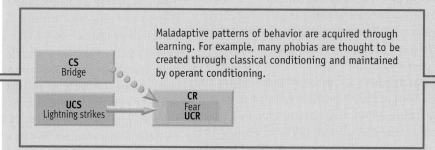

THERAPEUTIC GOALS

THERAPEUTIC TECHNIQUES

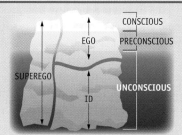

CONSCIOUS
EGO
PRECONSCIOUS
SUPEREGO
ID
UNCONSCIOUS

Insights regarding unconscious conflicts and motives; resolution of conflicts; personality reconstruction

Free association, dream analysis, interpretation, transference

© Bruce Ayres/Stone/Getty Images

Increased congruence between self-concept and experience; acceptance of genuine self; self-determination and personal growth

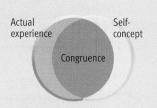

Actual experience

Self-concept

Congruence

Genuineness, empathy, unconditional positive regard, clarification, reflecting back to client

© Zigy Kaluzny/Stone/Getty Images

Elimination of maladaptive symptoms; acquisition of more adaptive responses

CS
Bridge

Desensitization is intended to weaken and replace this association

UCS
Lightning strikes

CR
Fear
UCR

Classical and operant conditioning, systematic desensitization, aversive conditioning, social skills training, reinforcement, shaping, punishment, extinction, biofeedback

© Kent News & Picture/ Corbis Sygma

Reduction of negative thinking; substitution of more realistic thinking

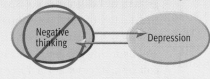

Negative thinking

Depression

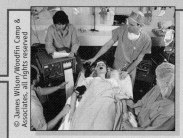

© Manchan/Photodisc Red/ Getty Images

Thought stopping, recording of automatic thoughts, refuting of negative thinking, homework assignments

Severity of illness

Placebo

Antipsychotic drugs

Time (weeks)

Elimination or reduction of symptoms; prevention of relapse

© James Wilson/Woodfin Camp & Associates, all rights reserved

PhotoDisc, Inc.

Antianxiety, antidepressant, antipsychotic, and mood-stabilizing drugs, electro-convulsive therapy

Treatment of Psychological Disorders   453

PREVIEW QUESTIONS

● How has managed care affected mental health treatment?

● Why is therapy under-utilized by some ethnic groups?

● What can be done to improve mental health services for minority groups?

The controversy about ECT is only one of many contentious issues and shifting trends in the world of mental health care. In this section, we will discuss the impact of managed care on psychotherapy and efforts to respond more effectively to increasing cultural diversity in Western societies.

Grappling with the Constraints of Managed Care

The 1990s brought a dramatic shift in how people in the United States pay for their health care. Alarmed by skyrocketing health care costs, huge numbers of employers and individuals moved from traditional fee-for-service arrangements to managed care health plans (Hogan & Morrison, 2003; Kiesler, 2000). In the *fee-for-service* system, hospitals, physicians, psychologists, and other providers charged fees for whatever health care services were needed, and most of these fees were reimbursed by private insurance or the government (through medicaid, medicare, and other programs). In *managed care systems* people enroll in prepaid plans with small co-payments for services, typically run by health maintenance organizations (HMOs), which agree to provide ongoing health care for a specific sum of money. Managed care usually involves a tradeoff: Consumers pay lower prices for their care, but they give up much of their freedom to choose their providers and to obtain whatever treatments they believe necessary. If an HMO's treatment expenses become excessive, it won't turn a profit, so HMOs have strong incentives to hold treatment costs down. The HMOs originally promised individuals and employers that they would be able to hold costs down without having a negative impact on the quality of care, by negotiating lower fees from providers, reducing inefficiency, and cracking down on medically unnecessary services. However, critics charge that managed care systems have squeezed all the savings they can out of the "fat" that existed in the old system and that they have responded to continued inflation in their costs by rationing care and limiting access to medically *necessary* services (Duckworth & Borus, 1999; Giles & Marafiote, 1998; Sanchez & Turner, 2003).

The possibility that managed care is having a negative effect on the quality of treatment is a source of concern throughout the health care professions, but the issue is especially sensitive in the domain of mental health care (Campbell, 2000). Critics maintain that mental health care has suffered particularly severe cuts in services because the question of what is "medically necessary" can be more subjective than in other treatment specialties (such as cardiology) and because patients who are denied psychotherapy services are relatively unlikely to complain (Duckworth & Borus, 1999). For example, a business executive who is trying to hide his depression or cocaine addiction from his employer will be reluctant to complain to his employer if therapeutic services are denied.

According to critics, the restriction of mental health services sometimes involves outright denial of treatment, but it often takes more subtle forms, such as underdiagnosing conditions, failing to make needed referrals to mental health specialists, and arbitrarily limiting the length of treatment (Miller, 1996). Long-term therapy is becoming a thing of the past unless patients can pay for it out of pocket, and the goal of treatment has been reduced to reestablishing a reasonable level of functioning (Zatzick, 1999). Many managed care systems hold down costs by rerouting patients from highly trained providers, such as psychiatrists and psychologists, to less-well-trained providers, such as masters-level counselors, who may not be adequately prepared to handle serious psychological disorders (Seligman & Levant, 1998). Cost containment is also achieved by requiring physicians to prescribe older antidepressant and antipsychotic drugs instead of the newer and much more expensive SSRIs and atypical antipsychotics (Docherty, 1999).

Unfortunately, there are no simple solutions to these problems on the horizon. Restraining the rapid growth of health care costs without compromising the quality of care, consumers' freedom of choice, and providers' autonomy is an enormously complex and daunting challenge. At this juncture, it is difficult to predict what the future holds. However, it is clear that economic realities have ushered in an era of transition for the treatment of psychological disorders and problems.

Increasing Multicultural Sensitivity in Treatment

Modern psychotherapy emerged during the second half of the 19th century in Europe and America, spawned in part by a cultural milieu that viewed the person as an independent, reflective, rational being,

Web Link 14.5

Psych Central
The work of John Grohol, Psych Central is a superb source for learning about all aspects of mental health, including psychological disorders and treatment, professional issues, and information for mental health care consumers. Almost 2000 annotated listings to information sources are offered here.

capable of self-improvement (Cushman, 1992). Psychological disorders were assumed to have natural causes like physical diseases do and to be susceptible to medical treatments derived from scientific research. But the individualized, medicalized institution of modern psychotherapy reflects Western cultural values that are far from universal (Sue & Sue, 1999). In many nonindustrialized societies, psychological disorders are attributed to supernatural forces (possession, witchcraft, angry gods, and so forth), and victims seek help from priests, shamans, and folk healers, rather than doctors (Wittkower & Warnes, 1984). Thus, efforts to export Western psychotherapies to non-Western cultures have met with mixed success. Indeed, the highly culture-bound origins of modern therapies have raised questions about their applicability to ethnic minorities *within* Western culture.

Research on how cultural factors influence the process and outcome of psychotherapy has increased in recent years, motivated in part by the need to improve mental health services for ethnic minority groups in American society (Lee & Ramirez, 2000; Miranda et al., 2005). The data are ambiguous for a couple of ethnic groups, but studies suggest that American minority groups generally underutilize therapeutic services (Olfson et al., 2002; Vega et al., 1999; Wells et al., 2001). Why? A variety of barriers appear to contribute to this problem (Snowden & Yamada, 2005; U.S. Department of Health and Human Services, 1999; Zane et al., 2004). One major consideration is that many members of minority groups have a history of frustrating interactions with American bureaucracies and are distrustful of large, intimidating institutions, such as hospitals and community mental health centers. Another issue is that most hospitals and mental health agencies are not adequately staffed with therapists who speak the languages used by minority groups in their service areas. Yet another problem is that the vast majority of thera-

Cultural barriers have emerged in the psychotherapy process. A number of minority groups in the United States shy away from using professional services in this field. Those who do try it also tend to quickly terminate treatment more often than white Americans.

pists have been trained almost exclusively in the treatment of white, middle-class Americans and are not familiar with the cultural backgrounds and unique characteristics of various ethnic groups. This culture gap often leads to misunderstandings and ill-advised treatment strategies.

What can be done to improve mental health services for American minority groups? Researchers in this area have offered a variety of suggestions (Hong, Garcia, & Soriano, 2000; Miranda et al., 2005; Pedersen, 1994; Yamamoto et al., 1993). Discussions of possible solutions usually begin with the need to recruit and train more ethnic minority therapists. Studies show that individuals are more likely to go to mental health facilities staffed by a higher proportion of people who share their ethnic background (Snowden & Hu, 1996; Sue, Zane, & Young, 1994). Furthermore, clients' satisfaction with therapy tends to be greater when they are treated by therapists from their own culture. Therapists can also be given special training to work more effectively with people from different cultural backgrounds. Finally, most authorities urge further investigation of how traditional approaches to therapy can be modified and tailored to be more compatible with specific cultural groups' attitudes, values, norms, and traditions.

> Institutional Treatment in Transition

Traditionally, much of the treatment of mental illness has been carried out in institutional settings, primarily in mental hospitals. **A *mental hospital* is a medical institution specializing in providing inpatient care for psychological disorders.** In the United States, a national network of state-funded mental hospitals started to emerge in the 1840s through the efforts of Dorothea Dix and other reformers (see **Figure 14.12** on the next page). Prior to

these reforms, the mentally ill who were poor were housed in jails and poorhouses or were left to wander the countryside. Today, mental hospitals continue to play an important role in the delivery of mental health services. However, since World War II, institutional care for mental illness has undergone a series of major transitions—and the dust hasn't settled yet. Let's look at how institutional care has evolved in recent decades.

PREVIEW QUESTIONS

- What led to the community mental health movement?
- What is deinstitutionalization?
- What problems has deinstitutionalization been blamed for?

Figure 14.12

Dorothea Dix and the advent of mental hospitals in America. During the 19th century, Dorothea Dix (inset) campaigned tirelessly to obtain funds for building mental hospitals. Many of these hospitals, such as the New York State Lunatic Asylum, were extremely large facilities. Although public mental hospitals improved the care of the mentally ill, they had a variety of shortcomings, which eventually prompted the deinstitutionalization movement.

Source: Culver Pictures, Inc.; (inset) Detail of painting in Harrisburg State Hospital, photo by Ken Smith/LLR Collection.

Disenchantment with Mental Hospitals

By the 1950s, it had become apparent that public mental hospitals were not fulfilling their goals very well (Mechanic, 1980). Experts began to realize that hospitalization often *contributed* to the development of pathology instead of curing it.

What were the causes of these unexpected negative effects? Part of the problem was that the facilities were usually underfunded (Bloom, 1984). The lack of adequate funding meant that the facilities were overcrowded and understaffed. Hospital personnel were undertrained and overworked, making them hardpressed to deliver minimal custodial care. Despite gallant efforts at treatment, the demoralizing conditions made most public mental hospitals decidedly nontherapeutic (Scull, 1990). These problems were aggravated by the fact that state mental hospitals served large geographic regions but were rarely placed near major population centers. As a result, most patients were uprooted from their community and isolated from their social support networks.

Disenchantment with the public mental hospital system inspired the *community mental health movement* that emerged in the 1960s (Duckworth & Borus, 1999). The community mental health movement emphasizes local, community-based care, reduced dependence on hospitalization, and the prevention of psychological disorders.

Deinstitutionalization

Mental hospitals continue to care for many people troubled by chronic mental illness, but their role in patient care has diminished. Since the 1960s, a policy of deinstitutionalization has been followed in the United States, as well as most other Western countries (Fakhoury & Priebe, 2002). *Deinstitutionalization refers to transferring the treatment of mental illness from inpatient institutions to community-based facilities that emphasize outpatient care.* This shift in responsibility was made possible by two developments: (1) the emergence of effective drug therapies for severe disorders and (2) the deployment of community mental health centers to coordinate local care (Goff & Gudeman, 1999).

The exodus of patients from mental hospitals has been dramatic. The average inpatient population in state and county mental hospitals has dropped from a peak of nearly 550,000 in the mid-1950s to around 70,000, as shown in **Figure 14.13**. This trend does not mean that hospitalization for mental illness has become a thing of the past. A great many people are

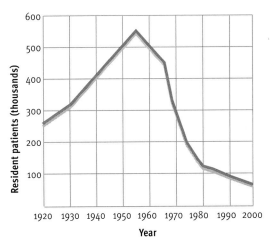

Figure 14.13

Declining inpatient population at state and county mental hospitals. The inpatient population in public mental hospitals has declined dramatically since the late 1950s, as a result of deinstitutionalization and the development of effective antipsychotic medication. (Data from the National Institute of Mental Health)

still hospitalized, but the shift has been toward placing them in local general hospitals for brief periods instead of distant psychiatric hospitals for long periods (Kiesler, 1992). In keeping with the philosophy of deinstitutionalization, these local facilities try to get patients stabilized and back into the community as swiftly as possible.

How has deinstitutionalization worked out? It gets mixed reviews. On the positive side, many people have benefited by avoiding disruptive and unnecessary hospitalization. Ample evidence suggests that alternatives to hospitalization can be as effective as and less costly than inpatient care (McGrew et al., 1999; Reinharz, Lesage, & Contandriopoulos, 2000). Moreover, follow-up studies of discharged patients reveal that a substantial majority prefer the greater freedom provided by community-based treatment (Leff, Trieman, & Gooch, 1996).

Nonetheless, some unanticipated problems have arisen (Elpers, 2000; Munk-Jorgensen, 1999; Talbott, 2004). Many patients suffering from chronic psychological disorders had nowhere to go when they were released. They had no families, friends, or homes to return to. Many had no work skills and were poorly prepared to live on their own. These people were supposed to be absorbed by "halfway houses," sheltered workshops, and other types of intermediate care facilities. Unfortunately, many communities were never able to fund and build the planned facilities (Hogan & Morrison, 2003; H. Lamb, 1998). Thus, deinstitutionalization left two major problems in its wake: a "revolving door" population of people who flow in and out of psychiatric facilities, and a sizable population of homeless mentally ill people.

Mental Illness, the Revolving Door, and Homelessness

Although the proportion of hospital days attributable to mental illness has dwindled, admission rates for psychiatric hospitals have actually climbed. What has happened? Deinstitutionalization and drug therapy have created a revolving door through which many mentally ill people pass again and again (Geller, 1992; Langdon et al., 2001).

Most of the people caught in the mental health system's revolving door suffer from chronic, severe disorders (usually schizophrenia) that frequently require hospitalization (Haywood et al., 1995). However, they respond to drug therapies in the hospital. Once they're stabilized through drug therapy, they no longer qualify for expensive hospital treatment according to the new standards created by deinstitutionalization and managed care. Thus, they're sent back out the door, into communities that often aren't prepared to provide adequate outpatient care. Because they lack appropriate care and support, their

DOONESBURY

Doonesbury © 1986 by G. B. Trudeau. Reprinted with permission of Universal Press Syndicate. All rights reserved.

Increased homelessness is a tragic and controversial problem in many urban areas. The media tend to equate homelessness with mental illness, but as your text explains, this is an oversimplification.

© Associated Press/AP

condition deteriorates, and they soon require re-admission to a hospital, where the cycle begins once again. Over two-thirds of all psychiatric inpatient admissions involve rehospitalizing a former patient.

Deinstitutionalization has also been blamed for the growing population of homeless people. Studies have consistently found elevated rates of mental illness among the homeless. Taken as a whole, the evidence suggests that roughly one-third of the homeless suffer from severe mental illness (schizophrenic and mood disorders), that another one-third or more are struggling with alcohol and drug problems, that many qualify for multiple diagnoses, and that the prevalence of mental illness among the homeless may be increasing (Bassuk et al., 1998; Folsom et al., 2005; Haugland et al., 1997; North et al., 2004; Vazquez, Munoz, & Sanz, 1997).

The popular media routinely equate homelessness with mental illness, and it is widely assumed that deinstitutionalization is largely responsible for the rapid growth of homelessness in America. Al-

though deinstitutionalization probably has *contributed* to the growth of homelessness, many experts in this area maintain that it is an oversimplification to blame the problem of homelessness chiefly on deinstitutionalization (Main, 1998; Sullivan, Burnam, & Koegel, 2000).

In light of the revolving door problem and homelessness among the mentally ill, what can we conclude about deinstitutionalization? It appears to be a worthwhile idea that has been poorly executed (H. Lamb, 1998). Overall, the policy has probably been a benefit to countless people with milder disorders but a cruel trick on many others with severe, chronic disorders. Ultimately, it's clear that our society is not providing adequate care for a sizable segment of the mentally ill population (Appelbaum, 2002; Elpers, 2000; Torrey, 1996). That's not a new development. Inadequate care for mental illness has always been the norm. Societies always struggle with the problem of what to do with the mentally ill and how to pay for their care (Duckworth & Borus, 1999).

> Reflecting on the Chapter's Themes

Theoretical Diversity

Cultural Heritage

In our discussion of psychotherapy, one of our unifying themes—the value of theoretical diversity—was particularly prominent, and one other theme—the importance of culture—surfaced briefly. Let's discuss the latter theme first. The approaches to psychotherapy described in this chapter are products of modern, white, middle-class, Western culture. Some of these therapies have proven useful in some other cultures, but many have turned out to be irrelevant

or counterproductive when used with different cultural groups. Thus, we have seen once again that Western psychology cannot assume that its theories and practices have universal applicability.

As for theoretical diversity, its value can be illustrated with a rhetorical question: Can you imagine what the state of modern psychotherapy would be if everyone in psychology and psychiatry had simply accepted Freud's theories about the nature and treatment of psychological disorders? If not for theoretical diversity, mental health treatment might still be in the dark ages. Psychoanalysis can be a useful method of therapy, but we would have a tragic state of affairs if it were the *only* treatment available to people experiencing psychological distress. Multitudes of people have benefited from alternative approaches to treatment that emerged out of tension between psychoanalytic theory and various other theoretical perspectives.

Given that people have diverse problems, rooted in varied origins, it is fortunate that they can choose from a diverse array of approaches to treatment. The graphic overview on pages 452–453 summarizes and compares the approaches that we've discussed in this chapter. This overview shows that the major approaches to therapy each have their own vision of the nature of human discontent and the ideal remedy.

Of course, diversity can be confusing. The range and variety of available treatments in modern psychotherapy leaves many people puzzled about their options. Thus, in our Personal Application we'll sort through the practical issues involved in selecting a therapist.

PERSONAL *Application*

Looking for a Therapist

Answer the following "true" or "false."

_____ 1 Psychotherapy is an art as well as a science.

_____ 2 Psychotherapy can be harmful or damaging to a client.

_____ 3 Mental health treatment does not have to be expensive.

_____ 4 The type of professional degree that a therapist holds is relatively unimportant.

All of these statements are true. Do any of them surprise you? If so, you're in good company. Many people know relatively little about the practicalities of selecting a therapist.

The task of finding an appropriate therapist is no less complex than shopping for any other major service. Should you see a psychologist or a psychiatrist? Should you opt for individual therapy or group therapy? Should you see a client-centered therapist or a behavior therapist? The unfortunate part of this complexity is that people seeking psychotherapy often feel overwhelmed by personal problems. The last thing they need is to be confronted by yet another complex problem.

Nonetheless, the importance of finding a good therapist cannot be overestimated. Therapy can sometimes have harmful rather than helpful effects. We have already discussed how drug therapies and ECT can sometimes be damaging, but problems are not limited to biological interventions. Talking about your problems with a therapist may sound pretty harmless, but studies indicate that insight therapies can also backfire (Lambert & Ogles, 2004; Singer & Lalich, 1996). Although a great many talented therapists are available, psychotherapy, like any other profession, has incompetent practitioners as well. Therefore, you should shop for a skilled therapist, just as you would for a good attorney or a good mechanic.

In this Application, we'll go over some information that should be helpful if you

Finding the right therapist is no easy task. You need to take into account the therapist's training and orientation, fees charged, and personality. An initial visit should give you a good idea of what a particular therapist is like.

ever have to look for a therapist for yourself or for a friend or family member (based on Beutler, Bongar, & Shurkin, 2001; Bruckner-Gordon, Gangi, & Wallman, 1988; Ehrenberg & Ehrenberg, 1994; Pittman, 1994).

Where Do You Find Therapeutic Services?

Psychotherapy can be found in a variety of settings. Contrary to general belief, most therapists are not in private practice. Many work in institutional settings such as community mental health centers, hospitals, and human service agencies. The principal sources of therapeutic services are described in **Table 14.1**. The exact collection of therapeutic services available will vary from one community to another. To find out what your community has to offer, it is a good idea to consult your friends, your local phone book, or your local community mental health center.

Is the Therapist's Profession or Sex Important?

Psychotherapists may be trained in psychology, psychiatry, social work, counseling, psychiatric nursing, or marriage and family therapy. Researchers have *not* found any reliable associations between therapists' professional background and therapeutic efficacy (Beutler et al., 2004), probably because many talented therapists can be found in all of these professions. Thus, the type of degree that a therapist holds doesn't need to be a crucial consideration in your selection process. It *is* true that currently only psychiatrists can prescribe drugs in most states. However, critics argue that many psychiatrists are too quick to use drugs to solve problems (Breggin, 1991). In any case, other types of therapists can refer you to a psychiatrist if they think that drug therapy would be helpful. If you have a health insurance policy that covers psychotherapy, you may want to check to see whether it carries any restrictions about the therapist's profession.

Whether a therapist's sex is important depends on your attitude. If *you* feel that the therapist's sex is important, then for you it is. The therapeutic relationship must be characterized by trust and rapport. Feeling uncomfortable with a therapist of one sex or the other could inhibit the therapeutic process. Hence, you should feel free to look for a male or female therapist if you prefer to do so.

Speaking of sex, you should be aware that sexual exploitation is an occasional problem in the context of therapy. Studies indicate that a small minority of therapists take advantage of their clients sexually (Pope, Keith-Spiegel, & Tabachnick, 1986). These incidents almost always involve a male therapist making advances to a female client. The available evidence indicates that these sexual liaisons are usually harmful to clients (Williams, 1992). There are absolutely no situations in which therapist-client sexual relations are an ethical therapeutic practice. If a therapist makes sexual advances, a client should terminate treatment.

Is Treatment Always Expensive?

Psychotherapy does not have to be prohibitively expensive. Private practitioners tend to be the most expensive, charging between $75 and $140 per (50-minute) hour. These fees may seem high, but they are in line with those of similar professionals, such as dentists and attorneys. Community mental health centers and social service agencies are usually supported by tax dollars. Consequently, they can charge lower fees than most therapists in private practice. Many of these organizations use a sliding scale, so that clients are charged according to how much they can afford to pay. Thus, most communities have inexpensive opportunities for treatment. Moreover, many health insurance plans provide at least partial reimbursement for the cost of psychotherapy.

Is the Therapist's Theoretical Approach Important?

Logically, you might expect that the diverse approaches to therapy would vary in effectiveness. For the most part, that is *not* what researchers find, however. After reviewing many studies of therapeutic efficacy, Jerome Frank (1961) and Lester Luborsky and his colleagues (1975) both quote the dodo bird who has just judged a race in *Alice in Wonderland:* "Everybody has won, and *all* must have prizes." Improvement rates for various theoretical orientations usually come out pretty close in most studies (Lambert, Bergin, & Garfield, 2004; Luborsky et al., 2002; Wampold, 2001; see **Figure 14.14**).

Table 14.1 Principal Sources of Therapeutic Services

Source	Comments
Private practitioners	Self-employed therapists are listed in the Yellow Pages under their professional category, such as psychologists or psychiatrists. Private practitioners tend to be relatively expensive, but they also tend to be highly experienced therapists.
Community mental health centers	Community mental health centers have salaried psychologists, psychiatrists, and social workers on staff. The centers provide a variety of services and often have staff available on weekends and at night to deal with emergencies.
Hospitals	Several kinds of hospitals provide therapeutic services. There are both public and private mental hospitals that specialize in the care of people with psychological disorders. Many general hospitals have a psychiatric ward, and those that do not usually have psychiatrists and psychologists on staff and on call. Although hospitals tend to concentrate on inpatient treatment, many provide outpatient therapy as well.
Human service agencies	Various social service agencies employ therapists to provide short-term counseling. Depending on your community, you may find agencies that deal with family problems, juvenile problems, drug problems, and so forth.
Schools and workplaces	Most high schools and colleges have counseling centers where students can get help with personal problems. Similarly, some large businesses offer in-house counseling to their employees.

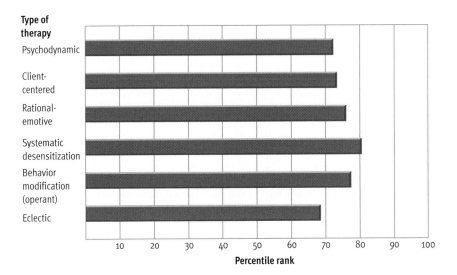

Figure 14.14

Estimates of the effectiveness of various approaches to psychotherapy. Smith and Glass (1977) reviewed nearly 400 studies in which clients who were treated with a specific type of therapy were compared with a control group made up of individuals with similar problems who went untreated. The bars indicate the percentile rank (on outcome measures) attained by the average client treated with each type of therapy when compared to control subjects. The higher the percentile, the more effective the therapy was. As you can see, the various approaches were fairly similar in their overall effectiveness.

Source: Adapted from Smith, M. L., & Glass, G. V. (1977). Meta-analysis of psychotherapy outcome series. *American Psychologist, 32,* 752–760. Copyright © 1977 by the American Psychological Association. Adapted by permission of the publisher and author.

However, these findings are a little misleading, as these estimates of overall effectiveness have been averaged across many types of patients and many types of problems. Most experts seem to think that *for certain types of problems, some approaches to therapy are more effective than others* (Beutler, 2002; Crits-Christoph, 1997; Norcross, 1995). For example, Martin Seligman (1995) asserts that panic disorders respond best to cognitive therapy, that specific phobias are most amenable to treatment with systematic desensitization, and that obsessive-compulsive disorders are best treated with behavior therapy or medication. Thus, for a specific type of problem, a therapist's theoretical approach may make a difference.

It is also important to point out that the finding that different approaches to therapy are roughly equal in overall efficacy does not mean that all *therapists* are created equal. Some therapists unquestionably are more effective than others. However, these variations in effectiveness appear to depend on individual therapists' personal skills rather than on their theoretical orientation (Beutler et al., 2004). Good, bad, and mediocre therapists are found within each school of thought.

The key point is that effective therapy requires skill and creativity. Arnold Lazarus, who devised multimodal therapy, emphasizes that therapists "straddle the fence between science and art." Therapy is scientific in that interventions are based on extensive theory and empirical research (Forsyth & Strong, 1986). Ultimately, though, each client is a unique human being, and the therapist has to creatively fashion a treatment program that will help that individual.

What Is Therapy Like?

It is important to have realistic expectations about therapy, or you may be unnecessarily disappointed. Some people expect miracles. They expect to turn their life around quickly with little effort. Others expect their therapist to run their lives for them. These are unrealistic expectations.

Therapy usually is a slow process. Your problems are not likely to melt away quickly. Moreover, therapy is hard work, and your therapist is only a facilitator. Ultimately, you have to confront the challenge of changing your behavior, your feelings, or your personality. This process may not be pleasant. You may have to face up to some painful truths about yourself. As Ehrenberg and Ehrenberg (1994) point out, "Psychotherapy takes time, effort, and courage."

From Crisis to Wellness—But Was It the Therapy?

It often happens this way. Problems seem to go from bad to worse—the trigger could be severe pressures at work, an emotional fight with your spouse, or a child's unruly behavior spiraling out of control. At some point, you recognize that it might be wise to seek professional assistance from a therapist, but where do you turn? If you are like most people, you will probably hesitate before actively seeking professional help. People hesitate because therapy carries a stigma, because the task of finding a therapist is daunting, and because they hope that their psychological problems will clear up on their own—which *does* happen with some regularity. When people finally decide to pursue mental health care, it is often because they feel like they have reached rock bottom in terms of their functioning and have no choice. Motivated by their crisis, they enter into treatment, looking for a ray of hope. Will therapy help them to feel better?

It may surprise you to learn that the answer *generally* would be "yes," even if professional treatment itself were utterly worthless and totally ineffective. People entering therapy are likely to get better, regardless of whether their treatment is effective, for two major reasons: placebo effects and regression toward the mean. *Placebo effects* occur when people's expectations lead them to experience some change even though they receive a fake treatment (such as getting a sugar pill instead of a real drug). Clients generally enter therapy with expectations that it will have positive effects, and as we have emphasized throughout this text, *people have a remarkable tendency to see what they expect to see*. Because of this factor, studies of the efficacy of medical drugs always include a placebo condition in which subjects are given fake medication (see Chapter 2). Researchers are often quite surprised by just how much the placebo subjects improve (Fisher & Greenberg, 1997; Walsh et al., 2002). Placebo effects can be powerful and should be taken into consideration whenever efforts are made to evaluate the efficacy of some approach to treatment.

The other factor at work is the main focus in this Application. It is an interesting statistical phenomenon that we have not discussed previously. *Regression toward the mean occurs when people who score extremely high or low on some trait are measured a second time and their new scores fall closer to the mean (average).* Regression effects work in both directions: On the second measurement high scorers tend to fall back toward the mean and low scorers tend to creep upward toward the mean. For example, let's say we wanted to evaluate the effectiveness of a one-day coaching program intended to improve performance on the SAT test. We reason that coaching is most likely to help students who have performed poorly on the test, so we recruit a sample of high school students who have previously scored in the bottom 20% on the SAT. Thanks to regression toward the mean, most of these students will score higher if they take the SAT a second time, so our coaching program may *look* effective even if it has no value. By the way, if we set out to see whether our coaching program could increase the performance of high scorers, regression effects would be working

against us. The processes underlying regression toward the mean are complex matters of probability, but they can be approximated by a simple principle: If you are near the bottom, you have almost nowhere to go but up, and if you are near the top, you have almost nowhere to go but down.

What does all of this have to do with the effects of professional treatment for psychological problems and disorders? Well, recall that most people enter psychotherapy during a time of severe crisis, when they are at a really low point in their lives. If you measure the mental health of a group of people entering therapy, most will get relatively low scores. If you measure their mental health again a few months later, chances are that most of them will score higher—with or without therapy—because of regression toward the mean. This is not a matter of idle speculation. In studies of therapeutic efficacy, data on *untreated (control group) subjects* demonstrate that poor scores on measures of mental health regress toward the mean when participants are assessed a second time (Flett, Vredenburg, & Krames, 1995; Hsu, 1995).

Does the fact that most people will get better even without therapy mean that there

Placebo effects and regression toward the mean are two prominent factors that make it difficult to evaluate the efficacy of various approaches to therapy.

© International Stock/Robert Harding Picture Library

is no sound evidence that psychotherapy works? No. Regression effects, along with placebo effects, do create major headaches for researchers evaluating the efficacy of various therapies, but these problems *can* be neutralized. Control groups, random assignment, placebo conditions, and statistical adjustments can be used to control for regression and placebo effects, as well as for other threats to validity. As discussed in the main body of the chapter, researchers have accumulated rigorous evidence that most approaches to therapy have demonstrated efficacy. However, our discussion of placebo and regression effects shows you some of the complexities that make this type of research far more complicated than might be anticipated.

Recognizing how regression toward the mean can occur in a variety of contexts is an important critical thinking skill, so let's look at some additional examples. Think about an outstanding young pro baseball player who has a fabulous first season and is named "Rookie of the Year." What sort of performance would you predict for this athlete the next year? Statistically speaking, our Rookie of the Year is likely to perform well above average the next year, but not as well as he did in his first year. If you are a sports fan, you may recognize this pattern as the "sophomore slump." Many sports columnists have written about the sophomore slump, which they typically blame on the athlete's personality or motivation ("He got lazy,'" "He got cocky," "The money and fame went to his head," and so forth). A simple appeal to regression toward the mean could explain this sort of outcome, with no need to criticize the personality or motivation of the athlete. Of course, sometimes the Rookie of the Year performs even better during his second year. Thus, our baseball example can be used to emphasize an important point. Regression toward the mean is not an inevitability. It is a statistical tendency that predicts what will happen far more often than not, but it is merely a matter of probability—which means it is a much more reliable principle when applied to groups (say, the top ten rookies in a specific year) rather than to individuals.

People who do not understand regression toward the mean can make some interesting mistakes in their efforts to improve task performance. For instance, Kahneman and Tversky (1973) worked with Israeli flight instructors who, logically enough, would praise students when they handled a difficult maneuver exceptionally well and criticize students when they exhibited particularly poor performance. Because of regression toward the mean, the students' performance tended to decline after they earned praise for extremely good work and to improve after they earned criticism for extremely bad work. Taking note of this trend, the flight instructors erroneously concluded that praise led to poorer performance and criticism led to improved performance— until the concept of regression toward the mean was explained to them. Many parents and coaches working to train children have probably made the same mistake and naively inferred that praise has a negative effect on subsequent performance, when what they were really witnessing was regression toward the mean.

Let's return to the world of therapy for one last thought about the significance of both regression and placebo effects. Over the years, a host of quacks, charlatans, con artists, herbalists, and faith healers have marketed an endless array of worthless treatments for both psychological problems and physical maladies. In many instances, people who have been treated with these phony therapies have expressed satisfaction or even praise and gratitude. For instance, you may have heard someone sincerely rave about some herbal remedy or psychic advice that you were pretty sure was really worthless. If so, you were probably puzzled by their glowing testimonials. Well, you now have two explanations for why people can

Placebo effects and regression toward the mean can help explain why phony, worthless treatments can have sincere supporters who really believe that the bogus interventions are effective.

honestly believe that they have derived great benefit from harebrained, bogus treatments: placebo effects and regression effects. The people who provide testimonials for worthless treatments may have experienced *genuine* improvements in their conditions, but those improvements were probably the results of placebo effects and regression toward the mean. Placebo and regression effects add to the many reasons that you should always be skeptical about anecdotal evidence. And they help explain why charlatans can be so successful and why unsound, ineffective treatments can have sincere proponents.

Table 14.2 Critical Thinking Skills Discussed in This Application

Skill	Description
Recognizing situations in which placebo effects might occur	The critical thinker understands that if people have expectations that a treatment will produce a certain effect, they may experience that effect even if the treatment was fake or ineffectual.
Recognizing situations in which regression toward the mean may occur	The critical thinker understands that when people are selected for their extremely high or low scores on some trait, their subsequent scores will probably fall closer to the mean.
Recognizing the limitations of anecdotal evidence	The critical thinker is wary of anecdotal evidence, which consists of personal stories used to support one's assertions. Anecdotal evidence tends to be unrepresentative, inaccurate, and unreliable.

Key Ideas

The Elements of the Treatment Process

● Approaches to psychotherapy are diverse, but they can be grouped into three categories: insight therapies, behavior therapies, and biomedical therapies. People vary in their willingness to seek treatment, and many people who need therapy do not receive it.

● Therapists come from a variety of professional backgrounds. Each of these professions shows different preferences for approaches to treatment. Psychologists typically practice insight or behavior therapy. Psychiatrists tend to depend on drug therapies.

Insight Therapies

● Insight therapies involve verbal interactions intended to enhance self-knowledge. In psychoanalysis, free association and dream analysis are used to explore the unconscious. When an analyst's probing hits sensitive areas, resistance can be expected. The transference relationship may be used to overcome this resistance so the client can handle interpretations that lead to insight. Classical psychoanalysis is not widely practiced anymore, but Freud's legacy lives on in a rich diversity of modern psychodynamic therapies.

● Rogers's client-centered therapy assumes that neurotic anxieties are derived from incongruence between a person's self-concept and reality. Accordingly, the client-centered therapist tries to provide a supportive climate in which clients can restructure their self-concept.

● Many theoretical approaches to insight therapy have been adapted for use with groups. Group therapists usually play a subtle role, staying in the background and working to promote group cohesiveness.

● Evaluating the effectiveness of any approach to therapy is complex and difficult. Nonetheless, the weight of the evidence suggests that insight therapies are superior to no treatment or placebo treatment. Studies suggest that common factors make a significant contribution to the benefits of various therapies.

Behavior Therapies

● Behavior therapies use the principles of learning in direct efforts to change specific aspects of behavior. Wolpe's systematic desensitization, a treatment for phobias, involves the construction of an anxiety hierarchy, relaxation training, and step-by-step movement through the hierarchy, pairing relaxation with each phobic stimulus.

● In aversion therapy, a stimulus associated with an unwanted response is paired with an unpleasant stimulus in an effort to eliminate the maladaptive response. Social skills training can improve clients' interpersonal skills through shaping, modeling, and behavioral rehearsal. Beck's cognitive therapy concentrates on changing the way clients think about events in their lives. There is ample evidence that behavior therapies are effective.

Biomedical Therapies

● Biomedical therapies are physiological interventions for psychological problems. The principal types of therapeutic drugs are antianxiety drugs, antipsychotic drugs, antidepressant drugs, and mood stabilizers. Drug therapies can be quite effective, but they have their drawbacks, such as problematic side effects and high relapse rates.

● Electroconvulsive therapy (ECT) is used to trigger a cortical seizure that is believed to have therapeutic value for mood disorders, especially depression. There is heated debate about the effectiveness of ECT and about possible risks associated with its use.

Current Trends and Issues in Treatment

● Many clinicians and their clients believe that managed care has restricted access to mental health care and undermined its quality. Unfortunately, there are no simple solutions to these problems.

● The highly culture-bound origins of Western therapies have raised doubts about their applicability to other cultures and even to ethnic groups in Western society. Because of cultural and language barriers, therapeutic services are underutilized by ethnic minorities in America.

Institutional Treatment in Transition

● Disenchantment with the negative effects of mental hospitals led to the advent of more localized community mental health centers and a pol-icy of deinstitutionalization. Unfortunately, deinstitutionalization has left some unanticipated problems in its wake, including the revolving door problem and increased homelessness.

Reflecting on the Chapter's Themes

● Our discussion of psychotherapy highlighted the value of theoretical diversity. Our coverage of therapy also showed once again that cultural factors shape psychological processes.

PERSONAL APPLICATION • Looking for a Therapist

● Therapeutic services are available in many settings, and such services do not have to be expensive. Therapists' personal skills are more important than their professional degree. In selecting a therapist, it is reasonable to insist on a therapist of one sex or the other.

● When different theoretical approaches to therapy are compared, no significant differences are found in their overall effectiveness. However, most experts believe that for specific types of problems, some approaches to therapy are more effective than others. Therapy requires time, hard work, and the courage to confront your problems.

CRITICAL THINKING APPLICATION • From Crisis to Wellness—But Was It the Therapy?

● People entering therapy are likely to get better even if their treatment is ineffective, because of placebo effects and regression toward the mean. Regression toward the mean occurs when people selected for their extremely high or low scores on some trait are measured a second time and their new scores fall closer to the mean. Regression and placebo effects may help explain why people can often be enthusiastic about phony, ineffectual treatments.

Key Terms

Antianxiety drugs (p. 447)
Antidepressant drugs
  (pp. 448–449)
Antipsychotic drugs (p. 448)
Aversion therapy (p. 445)
Behavior therapies (p. 444)
Biomedical therapies (p. 447)
Client-centered therapy (p. 440)
Clinical psychologists (p. 438)
Cognitive-behavioral treatments
  (p. 446)
Cognitive therapy (p. 446)
Counseling psychologists (p. 438)
Deinstitutionalization (p. 456)
Dream analysis (p. 439)
Electroconvulsive therapy (ECT)
  (p. 450)
Free association (p. 439)
Group therapy (p. 442)
Insight therapies (p. 438)

Mental hospital (p. 455)
Mood stabilizers (p. 449)
Placebo effects (p. 462)
Psychiatrists (p. 438)
Psychoanalysis (p. 438)
Regression toward the mean
  (p. 462)
Resistance (p. 440)
Social skills training (p. 446)
Systematic desensitization (p. 444)
Tardive dyskinesia (p. 448)
Transference (p. 440)

Key People

Aaron Beck (pp. 446–447)
Dorothea Dix (pp. 455–456)
Sigmund Freud (pp. 438–440)
Carl Rogers (pp. 440–442)
Joseph Wolpe (p. 444)

1. One key problem with the provision of psychotherapy is that:
   A. there are too many different approaches to treatment.
   B. there are too many different professions involved.
   C. there is a shortage of qualified therapists.
   D. there are many people who need therapy but do not receive treatment.

2. After undergoing psychoanalysis for several months, Karen has suddenly started "forgetting" to attend her therapy sessions. Karen's behavior is most likely a form of:
   A. resistance.   C. insight.
   B. transference.   D. catharsis.

3. Because Suzanne has an unconscious sexual attraction to her father, she behaves seductively toward her therapist. Suzanne's behavior is most likely a form of:
   A. resistance.   C. misinterpretation.
   B. transference.   D. an unconscious defense mechanism.

4. The key task of the client-centered therapist is:
   A. interpretation of the client's thoughts, feelings, memories, and behaviors.
   B. clarification of the client's feelings.
   C. confrontation of the client's irrational thoughts.
   D. modification of the client's problematic behaviors.

5. Evaluating the effectiveness of psychotherapy is complicated and difficult because:
   A. disorders sometimes clear up on their own.
   B. different approaches to treatment pursue entirely different goals.
   C. clients' problems vary in severity.
   D. all of the above are involved.

6. The goal of behavior therapy is to:
   A. identify the early childhood unconscious conflicts that are the source of the client's symptoms.
   B. pursue personality reconstruction.
   C. directly change clients' behaviors by using the principles of learning and conditioning.
   D. alter the client's brain chemistry by prescribing specific drugs.

7. Systematic desensitization is particularly effective for the treatment of _____ disorders.
   A. generalized anxiety   C. obsessive-compulsive
   B. panic   D. phobic

8. Linda's therapist has her practice active listening skills in structured role-playing exercises. Later, Linda is gradually asked to practice these skills with family members, friends, and finally, her boss. Linda is undergoing:
   A. systematic desensitization.   C. a token economy.
   B. cognitive restructuring.   D. social skills training.

9. After being released from a hospital, many schizophrenic patients stop taking their antipsychotic medication because:
   A. their mental impairment causes them to forget.
   B. of the unpleasant side effects.
   C. most schizophrenics don't believe they are ill.
   D. all of the above are involved.

10. Selective serotonin reuptake inhibitors (SSRIs) appear to have value for the treatment of _____ disorders.
    A. depressive   C. dissociative
    B. schizophrenic   D. alcoholic

11. Modern psychotherapy:
    A. was spawned by a cultural milieu that viewed the self as an independent, rational being.
    B. embraces universal cultural values.
    C. has been successfully exported to most non-Western cultures.
    D. both B and C.

12. The community mental health movement emphasizes:
    A. segregation of the mentally ill from the general population.
    B. increased dependence on long-term inpatient care.
    C. local care and the prevention of psychological disorders.
    D. all of the above.

13. Many people repeatedly go in and out of mental hospitals. Typically, such people are released because _____; they are eventually readmitted because _____.
    A. they have been stabilized through drug therapy; their condition deteriorates once again because of inadequate outpatient care
    B. they run out of funds to pay for hospitalization; they once again can afford it
    C. they have been cured of their disorder; they develop another disorder
    D. they no longer want to be hospitalized; they voluntarily recommit themselves

14. The type of professional training a therapist has:
    A. is the most important indicator of his or her competence.
    B. should be the major consideration in choosing a therapist.
    C. is not all that important, since talented therapists can be found in all of the mental health professions.
    D. both A and B are true.

15. Which of the following could be explained by regression toward the mean?
    A. You get an average bowling score in one game and a superb score in the next game.
    B. You get an average bowling score in one game and a very low score in the next game.
    C. You get an average bowling score in one game and another average score in the next game.
    D. You get a terrible bowling score in one game and an average score in the next game.

Answers

1 D p. 437	6 C p. 444	11 A pp. 454–455
2 A p. 440	7 D pp. 444–445	12 C p. 456
3 B p. 440	8 D p. 446	13 A p. 457
4 B p. 441	9 B p. 448	14 C p. 460
5 D p. 442	10 A p. 449	15 D pp. 462–463

PsykTrek

Go to the PsykTrek website or CD-ROM for further study of the concepts in this chapter. Both online and on the CD-ROM, PsykTrek includes dozens of learning modules with videos, animations, and quizzes, as well as simulations of psychological phenomena and a multimedia glossary that includes word pronunciations.

ThomsonNOW

http://www.thomsonedu.com/ThomsonNOW
Go to this site for the link to ThomsonNOW, your one-stop study shop. Take a Pre-Test for this chapter, and ThomsonNOW will generate a Personalized Study Plan based on your test results. The Study Plan will identify the topics you need to review and direct you to online resources to help you master those topics. You can then take a Post-Test to help you determine the concepts you have mastered and what you still need to work on.

Companion Website

http://www.thomsonedu.com/psychology/weiten
Go to this site to find online resources directly linked to your book, including a glossary, flash cards, drag-and-drop exercises, quizzes, and more!

CHAPTER 15

Social Behavior

© Dennis Stock/Magnum Photos

When Muffy, "the quintessential yuppie," met Jake, "the ultimate working-class stiff," her friends got very nervous.

Muffy is a 28-year-old stockbroker and a self-described "snob" with a group of about ten close women friends. Snobs all. They're graduates of fancy business schools. All consultants, investment bankers, and CPAs. All "cute, bright, fun to be with, and really intelligent," according to Muffy. They're all committed to their high-powered careers, but they all expect to marry someday, too.

Unfortunately, most of them don't date much. In fact, they spend a good deal of time "lamenting the dearth of 'good men.'" You know who the "good men" are. Those are the ones who are "committed to their work, open to the idea of marriage and family, and possessed of a good sense of humor."

Well, lucky Muffy actually met one of those "good men." Jake is a salesman. He comes from a working-class neighborhood. His clothes come from Sears.

He wasn't like the usual men Muffy dated. He treats Muffy the way she's always dreamed of being treated. He listens; he cares; he remembers. "He makes me feel safe and more cherished than any man I've ever known," she says.

So she decided to bring him to a little party of about 30 of her closest friends. . . .

Perhaps it was only Jake's nerves that caused him to commit some truly unforgivable faux pas that night. His sins were legion. Where do we start? First of all, he asked for a beer when everyone else was drinking white wine. He wore a worn turtleneck while everyone else had just removed the Polo tags from their clothing. He smoked. . . .

"The next day at least half of the people who had been at the party called to give me their impressions. They all said that they felt they just had to let me know that they thought Jake 'lacked polish' or 'seemed loud' or 'might not be a suitable match,'" Muffy says.

Now, you may think that Muffy's friends are simply very sensitive, demanding people. A group of princes and princesses who can detect a pea under the fluffiest stack of mattresses. But you'd be wrong. Actually, they've been quite accepting of some of the other men that Muffy has brought to their little parties. Or should we call them inquisitions? Winston, for example, was a great favorite.

"He got drunk, ignored me, and asked for other women's phone numbers right in front of me. But he was six-foot-four, the classic preppie, with blond hair, horn-rimmed glasses, and Ralph Lauren clothes."

And most important of all, he didn't ask for a Pabst Blue Ribbon. So now Muffy is confused. "Jake is the first guy I've been out with in a long time that I've really liked. I was excited about him and my friends knew that. I was surprised by their reaction. I'll admit there's some validity to all their comments, but it's hard to express how violent it was. It made me think about what these women really want in a man. Whatever they say, what they really want is someone they can take to a business dinner. They want someone who comes with a tux. Like a Ken doll."

Muffy may have come to a crossroads in her young life. It's clear that there's no way she can bring Jake among her friends for a while.

"I don't want their reaction to muddy my feelings until I get them sorted out," she says.

It just may be time for Muffy to choose between her man and her friends.

(Excerpt from *Tales from the Front* by Cheryl Lavin and Laura Kavesh, Copyright © 1988 by Cheryl Lavin and Laura Kavesh. Used by permission of Doubleday, a division of Random House, Inc.)

The preceding account is a real story, taken from a book about intimate relationships titled *Tales from the Front* (Lavin & Kavesh, 1988, pp. 118–121). Muffy is on the horns of a difficult dilemma. Romantic relationships are important to most people, but so are friendships, and Muffy may have to choose between the two. Muffy's story illustrates the significance of social relations in people's lives. It also foreshadows each of the topics that we'll cover in this chapter, as we look at behavior in its social context.

Social psychology is the branch of psychology concerned with the way individuals' thoughts, feelings, and behaviors are influenced by others. Our coverage of social psychology will focus on six broad topics. Let's return to Muffy's story to get a glimpse of the various facets of social behavior that we'll examine in the coming pages:

- *Person perception.* The crux of Muffy's problem is that Jake didn't make a very good impression on her friends. To what extent do people's expectations and stereotypes color their impressions of others?

- *Attribution processes.* Muffy is struggling to understand her friends' rejection of Jake. When she implies that Jake's rejection is due to their snotty elitism, she's engaging in attribution, making an inference about the causes of her friends' behavior. How do people use attributions to explain social behavior?

- *Interpersonal attraction.* Jake and Muffy are different in many important ways—is it true that opposites attract? Does similarity foster liking?

- *Attitudes.* Muffy's girlfriends have negative attitudes about working-class men. How are attitudes formed? What leads to attitude change?

- *Conformity and obedience.* Muffy's friends discourage her from dating Jake, putting her under pressure to conform to their values. What factors influence conformity? Can people be coaxed into doing things that contradict their values?
- *Behavior in groups.* Muffy belongs to a tight-knit group of friends who think along similar lines. Is people's behavior in groups similar to their behavior when alone? Why do people in groups often think alike?

Social psychologists study how people are affected by the actual, imagined, or implied presence of others. Their interest is not limited to individuals' *interactions* with others, as people can engage in social behavior even when they're alone. For instance, if you were driving by yourself on a deserted highway and tossed your trash out your car window, your littering would be a social action. It would defy social norms, reflect your socialization and attitudes, and have repercussions (albeit, small) for other people in your society. Thus, social psychologists often study *individual* behavior in a social context. This interest in understanding individual behavior should be readily apparent in our first section, on person perception.

> Person Perception: Forming Impressions of Others

PREVIEW QUESTIONS

- How do aspects of physical appearance sway impressions of others?
- What are social schemas and stereotypes?
- How do illusory correlations and other phenomena illustrate subjectivity in person perception?
- How do evolutionary psychologists explain biases in person perception?

Can you remember the first meeting of your introductory psychology class? What kind of impression did your professor make on you that day? Did your instructor appear to be confident? Easygoing? Pompous? Open-minded? Cynical? Friendly? Were your first impressions supported or undermined by subsequent observations? When you interact with people, you're constantly engaged in **person perception, the process of forming impressions of others.** In this section we consider some of the factors that influence, and often distort, people's perceptions of others.

Effects of Physical Appearance

"You shouldn't judge a book by its cover." "Beauty is only skin deep." People know better than to let physical attractiveness determine their perceptions of others' personal qualities. Or do they? Studies have shown that judgments of others' personality are often swayed by their appearance, especially their physical attractiveness. People tend to see desirable personality characteristics in those who are good looking, seeing them as more sociable, friendly, poised, warm, and well adjusted than those who are less attractive (Eagly et al., 1991; Wheeler & Kim, 1997). In reality, research findings suggest that little correlation exists between attractiveness and personality traits (Feingold, 1992). Why do we inaccurately assume that a connection exists between good looks and personality? One reason is that extremely attractive people are vastly overrepresented in the entertainment media, where they are mostly portrayed in a highly favorable light (Smith, McIntosh, & Bazzini, 1999).

You might guess that physical attractiveness would influence perceptions of competence less than perceptions of personality, but the data suggest otherwise. A recent review of the relevant research found that people have a surprisingly strong tendency to view good-looking individuals as more competent than less-attractive individuals (Langlois et al., 2000). This bias pays off for good-looking people, as they tend to secure better jobs and earn higher salaries

"*Beauty is life's E–Z Pass.*"

© The New Yorker Collection 2005 Marisa Acocella Marchetto from cartoonbank.com. All rights reserved.

than less-attractive individuals (Collins & Zebrowitz, 1995; Frieze, Olson, & Russell, 1991). For example, research on attorneys whose law school class photos were evaluated by independent raters found that physical attractiveness boosted income by 10%–12% (Engemann & Owyang, 2005).

Cognitive Schemas

Even though every individual is unique, people tend to categorize one another. For instance, in our opening story, Muffy is characterized as "the quintessential yuppie," and Jake as a "working-class stiff." Such labels reflect the use of cognitive schemas in person perception. As we discussed in the chapter on memory (Chapter 7), *schemas* are cognitive structures that guide information processing. Individuals use schemas to organize the world around them—including their social world. **Social schemas are organized clusters of ideas about categories of social events and people.** People have social schemas for events such as dates, picnics, committee meetings, and family reunions, as well as for certain categories of people, such as "dumb jocks," "social climbers," "frat rats," and "wimps" (see **Figure 15.1**). Individuals depend on social schemas because these schemas help them to efficiently process and store the wealth of information that they take in about others in their interactions. Hence, people routinely place one another in categories, and these categories influence the process of person perception (Macrae & Bodenhausen, 2000).

Stereotypes

Some of the schemas that individuals apply to people are unique products of their personal experiences,

Sophisticated professional   **Working-class stiff**

Drinks fine wine | Drinks beer
Hobby is travel | Hobby is bowling
Patron of the arts | Sports fan
Health-conscious | Smokes
Reads books often | Watches TV often

© image100/Alamy

Figure 15.1

Examples of social schemas. Everyone has social schemas for various "types" of people, such as sophisticated professionals or working-class stiffs. Social schemas are clusters of beliefs that guide information processing.

while other schemas may be part of their shared cultural background. *Stereotypes* are special types of schemas that fall into the latter category. **Stereotypes are widely held beliefs that people have certain characteristics because of their membership in a particular group.**

The most common stereotypes in our society are those based on gender and on membership in ethnic or occupational groups. People who subscribe to traditional *gender stereotypes* tend to assume that women are emotional, submissive, illogical, and passive, while men are unemotional, dominant, logical, and aggressive. Preconceived notions that Jews are mercenary, blacks have rhythm, Germans are methodical, and Italians are passionate are examples of common *ethnic stereotypes*. *Occupational stereotypes* suggest that lawyers are manipulative, computer programmers

DILBERT

DILBERT © Scott Adams/distributed by United Features Syndicate, Inc.

Web Link 15.1

Social Psychology Network
Wesleyan University social psychologist Scott Plous offers a broad collection of resources related to all aspects of social (and general) psychology as well as information about careers and graduate study in this field.

are nerdy, accountants are conforming, artists are moody, and so forth.

Stereotyping is a normal cognitive process that is frequently automatic and that saves on the time and effort required to get a handle on people individually (Devine & Monteith, 1999; Operario & Fiske, 2001). Stereotypes save energy by simplifying our social world. However, this conservation of energy often comes at some cost in terms of accuracy (Wigboldus, Dijksterhuis, & van Knippenberg, 2003). Stereotypes tend to be broad overgeneralizations that ignore the diversity within social groups and foster inaccurate perceptions of people (Hilton & von Hippel, 1996). Obviously, not all males, Jews, and lawyers behave alike. Most people who subscribe to stereotypes realize that not all members of a group are identical. For instance, they may admit that some men aren't competitive, some Jews aren't mercenary, and some lawyers aren't manipulative. However, people may still tend to assume that males, Jews, and lawyers are *more likely* than others to have these characteristics. Even if stereotypes mean only that people think in terms of slanted *probabilities,* their expectations may lead them to misperceive individuals with whom they interact. As we've noted in previous chapters, perception is subjective, and people often see what they expect to see.

Subjectivity in Person Perception

Stereotypes and other schemas create biases in person perception that frequently lead to confirmation of people's expectations about others. If any ambiguity exists in someone's behavior, people are likely to interpret what they see in a way that's consistent with their expectations (Olson, Roese, & Zanna, 1996). People not only see what they expect to see, they also tend to overestimate how often they see it (Johnson & Mullen, 1994; Shavitt et al., 1999). *Illusory correlation* **occurs when people estimate that they have encountered more confirmations of an association between social traits than they have actually seen.** People also tend to underestimate the number of disconfirmations they have encountered, as illustrated by statements like "I've never met an honest lawyer."

Memory processes can contribute to confirmatory biases in person perception in a variety of ways. Often, individuals selectively recall facts that fit with their schemas and stereotypes (Fiske, 1998; Quinn, Macrae, & Bodenhausen, 2003). Evidence for such a tendency was found in a study by Cohen (1981). In this experiment, subjects watched a videotape of a woman, described as either a waitress or a librarian, who engaged in a variety of activities, including listening to classical music, drinking beer, and watching TV. When asked to recall what the woman did during the filmed sequence, participants tended to remember activities consistent with their stereotypes of waitresses and librarians. For instance, participants who thought the woman was a waitress tended to recall her drinking beer, whereas subjects who thought she was a librarian tended to recall her listening to classical music.

An Evolutionary Perspective on Bias in Person Perception

Why is the process of person perception riddled with bias? Evolutionary psychologists argue that many of the biases seen in social perception were adaptive in humans' ancestral environment (Krebs & Denton, 1997). For example, they argue that person perception is swayed by physical attractiveness because attractiveness was associated with reproductive potential in women and with health, vigor, and the accumulation of material resources in men.

Evolutionary theorists attribute the human tendency to automatically categorize others to our distant ancestors' need to quickly separate friend from foe. They assert that humans are programmed by evolution to immediately classify people as members of an *ingroup*—**a group that one belongs to and identifies with,** or as members of an *outgroup*—**a group that one does not belong to or identify with.** This crucial categorization is thought to structure subsequent perceptions. As Krebs and Denton (1997) put it, "It is as though the act of classifying others as ingroup or outgroup members activates two quite different brain circuits" (p. 27). Ingroup members tend to be viewed in a favorable light, whereas outgroup members tend to be viewed in terms of various negative stereotypes. According to Krebs and Denton, these negative stereotypes ("They are inferior; they are all alike; they will exploit us") move outgroups out of our domain of empathy, so we feel justified in not liking them. Thus, evolutionary psychologists assert that much of the bias in person perception is due to cognitive mechanisms that have been wired into the human brain by natural selection.

It's Friday evening and you're sitting around at home feeling bored. You call a few friends to see whether they'd like to go out. They all say that they'd love to go, but they have other commitments and they can't. Their commitments sound vague, and you feel that their reasons for not going out with you are rather flimsy. How do you explain these rejections? Do your friends really have commitments? Are they worn out by school and work? Are they just lazy and apathetic about going out? These questions illustrate a process that people engage in routinely: the explanation of behavior. *Attributions* play a key role in these explanatory efforts, and they have significant effects on social relations.

What are attributions? ***Attributions* are inferences that people draw about the causes of events, others' behavior, and their own behavior.** If you conclude that a friend turned down your invitation because she's overworked, you've made an attribution about the cause of her behavior (and, implicitly, rejected other possible explanations). If you conclude that you're stuck at home with nothing to do because you failed to plan ahead, you've made an attribution about the cause of an event (being stuck at home). If you conclude that you failed to plan ahead because you're a procrastinator, you've made an attribution about the cause of your own behavior. *Why do people make attributions?* Individuals make attributions because they have a strong need to understand their experiences. They want to make sense out of their own behavior, others' actions, and the events in their lives.

Internal Versus External Attributions 12a

Fritz Heider (1958) was the first to describe how people make attributions. He asserted that people tend to locate the cause of behavior either *within a person,* attributing it to personal factors, or *outside a person,* attributing it to environmental factors.

Elaborating on Heider's insight, various theorists have agreed that explanations of behavior and events can be categorized as internal or external attributions (Jones & Davis, 1965; Kelley, 1967; Weiner, 1974). ***Internal attributions* ascribe the causes of behavior to personal dispositions, traits, abilities, and feelings.** *External attributions* **ascribe the causes of behavior to situational demands and en-**vironmental constraints. For example, if a friend's business fails, you might attribute it to your friend's lack of business acumen (an internal, personal factor) or to negative trends in the nation's economic climate (an external, situational explanation). Parents who find out that their teenage son has just banged up the car may blame it on his carelessness (an internal attribution) or on slippery road conditions (an external attribution).

Internal and external attributions can have a tremendous impact on everyday interpersonal interactions. Blaming a friend's business failure on poor business judgment as opposed to a poor economy will have a great impact on how you view your friend—not to mention on whether you'll lend him or her money in the future. Likewise, if parents attribute their son's automobile accident to slippery road conditions, they're likely to deal with the event very differently than if they attribute it to his carelessness.

Attributions for Success and Failure 12a

Some psychologists have sought to discover additional dimensions of attributional thinking besides the internal-external dimension. After studying the attributions that people make in explaining success and failure, Bernard Weiner (1980, 1986, 1994) concluded that people often focus on the *stability* of the causes underlying behavior. According to Weiner, the stable-unstable dimension in attribution cuts across the internal-external dimension, creating four types of attributions for success and failure, as shown in **Figure 15.2** on the next page.

Let's apply Weiner's model to a concrete event. Imagine that you're contemplating why you failed to get a job that you wanted. You might attribute your setback to internal factors that are stable (lack of ability) or unstable (inadequate effort to put together an eye-catching résumé). Or you might attribute your setback to external factors that are stable (too much outstanding competition) or unstable (bad luck). If you got the job, the explanations you might offer for your success would fall into the same four categories: internal-stable (your excellent ability), internal-unstable (your hard work to assemble a superb résumé), external-stable (lack of top-flight competition), and external-unstable (good luck).

PREVIEW QUESTIONS

● What are attributions, and how do internal and external attributions differ?

● What types of attributions do people make regarding success and failure?

● How do actors and observers differ in their patterns of attribution?

● What is the self-serving bias in attribution?

● How do individualism and collectivism influence attribution bias?

FRITZ HEIDER

"Often the momentary situation which, at least in part, determines the behavior of a person is disregarded and the behavior is taken as a manifestation of personal characteristics."

Bias in Attribution

Attributions are only inferences. Your attributions may not be the correct explanations for events. Paradoxical as it may seem, people often arrive at inaccurate explanations even when they contemplate the causes of *their own behavior*. Attributions ultimately represent guesswork about the causes of events, and

Figure 15.2

Weiner's model of attributions for success and failure. Weiner's model assumes that people's explanations for success and failure emphasize internal versus external causes and stable versus unstable causes. Examples of causal factors that fit into each of the four cells in Weiner's model are shown in the diagram.

Source: Weiner, B., Friese, I., Kukla, A., Reed, L., & Rosenbaum, R. M. (1972). Perceiving the causes of success and failure. In E. E. Jones, D. E. Kanouse, H. H. Kelley, R. E. Nisbett, S. Valins, & B. Weiner (Eds.) *Perceiving the causes of behavior*. Morristown, NJ: General Learning Press. Used by permission of Bernard Weiner.

concept **check** 15.1

Analyzing Attributions

Check your understanding of attribution processes by analyzing possible explanations for an athletic team's success. Imagine that the women's track team at your school has just won a regional championship that qualifies it for the national tournament. Around the campus, you hear people attribute the team's success to a variety of factors. Examine the attributions shown below and place each of them in one of the cells of Weiner's model of attribution (just record the letter inside the cell). The answers are in Appendix A.

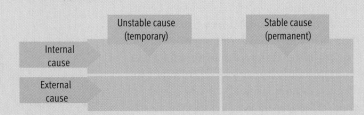

a. "They won only because the best two athletes on Central State's team were out with injuries—talk about good fortune!"

b. "They won because they have some of the best talent in the country."

c. "Anybody could win this region; the competition is far below average in comparison to the rest of the country."

d. "They won because they put in a great deal of last-minute effort and practice, and they were incredibly fired up for the regional tourney after last year's near miss."

these guesses tend to be slanted in certain directions. Let's look at the principal biases seen in attribution.

Actor-Observer Bias

Your view of your own behavior can be quite different from the view of someone else observing you. When an actor (the person exhibiting the behavior) and an observer draw inferences about the causes of the actor's behavior, they often make different attributions. **The *fundamental attribution error* refers to observers' bias in favor of internal attributions in explaining others' behavior.** Of course, in many instances, an internal attribution may not be an "error." However, observers have a curious tendency to overestimate the likelihood that an actor's behavior reflects personal qualities rather than situational factors (Krull, 2001). Why? It is not that people assume that situational factors have little impact on behavior (Gawronski, 2004). Rather, it's that attributing others' behavior to their dispositions is a relatively effortless, almost automatic process, whereas explaining people's behavior in terms of situational factors requires more thought and effort (see **Figure 15.3**; Krull & Erickson, 1995). Another factor favoring internal attributions is that many people feel that few situations are so coercive that they negate all freedom of choice (Forsyth, 2004).

To illustrate the gap that often exists between actors' and observers' attributions, imagine that you're visiting your bank and you fly into a rage over a mistake made on your account. Observers who witness your rage are likely to make an internal attribution and infer that you are surly, temperamental, and quarrelsome. They may be right, but if asked, you'd probably attribute your rage to the frustrating situation. Perhaps you're normally a calm, easygoing person, but today you've been in line for 20 minutes, you just straightened out a similar error by the same bank last week, and you're being treated rudely by the teller. Observers often are unaware of situational considerations such as these, so they tend to make internal attributions for another's behavior (Gilbert, 1998).

In contrast, the circumstances that have influenced an actor's behavior tend to be more salient to the actor. Hence, actors are more likely than observers to locate the cause of their behavior in the situation. In general, then, *actors favor external attributions for their behavior, while observers are more likely to explain the same behavior with internal attributions* (Jones & Nisbett, 1971; Krueger, Ham, & Linford, 1996).

Self-Serving Bias

The self-serving bias in attribution comes into play when people attempt to explain success and failure

(Campbell & Sedikides, 1999; Mezulis et al., 2004). The *self-serving bias* **is the tendency to attribute one's successes to personal factors and one's failures to situational factors.** In explaining *failure,* the usual actor-observer biases are apparent. But in explaining *success,* the usual actor-observer differences are reversed to some degree; actors prefer internal attributions so they can take credit for their triumphs. Interestingly, this bias grows stronger as time passes after an event, so that people tend to take progressively more credit for their successes and less blame for their failures (Burger, 1986).

Culture and Attributions

Do the patterns of attribution observed in subjects from Western societies transcend culture? More research is needed, but the preliminary evidence suggests not. Some interesting cultural disparities have emerged in research on attribution processes.

According to Harry Triandis (1989, 1994, 2001), cultural differences in *individualism* versus *collectivism* influence attributional tendencies as well as other aspects of social behavior. *Individualism* **involves putting personal goals ahead of group goals and defining one's identity in terms of personal attributes rather than group memberships.** In contrast, *collectivism* **involves putting group goals ahead of personal goals and defining one's identity in terms of the groups one belongs to** (such as one's family, tribe, work group, social class, caste, and so on). In comparison to individualistic cultures, collectivist cultures place a higher priority on shared values and resources, cooperation, mutual interdependence, and concern for how one's actions will affect other group members. Childrearing patterns in collectivist cultures emphasize the importance of

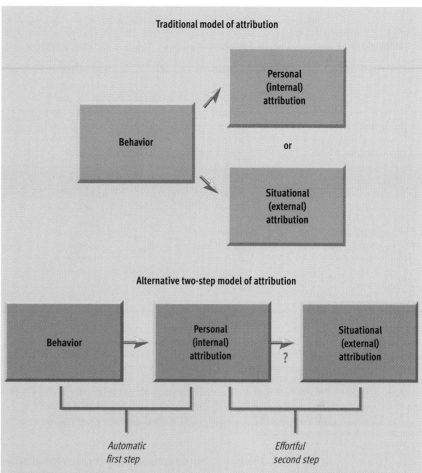

Traditional model of attribution

Alternative two-step model of attribution

Automatic first step

Effortful second step

Figure 15.3

An alternative view of the fundamental attribution error. According to Gilbert (1989) and others, the nature of attribution processes favors the *fundamental attribution error.* Traditional models of attribution assume that internal and external attributions are an either-or proposition requiring equal amounts of effort. In contrast, the two-step model of attribution posits that people tend to automatically make internal attributions with little effort, then *may* expend additional effort to adjust for the influence of situational factors, which can lead to an external attribution. Thus, external attributions for others' behavior require more thought and effort, which makes them less common than personal attributions.

Triumphant athletes from cultures high in collectivism typically exhibit different attributional biases than winning athletes from Western societies that are high in individualism. Collectivist cultures tend to promote a self-effacing bias in explaining success, rather than a self-serving bias.

obedience, reliability, and proper behavior, whereas individualistic cultures emphasize the development of independence, self-esteem, and self-reliance.

A variety of factors influence whether societies cherish individualism as opposed to collectivism. Among other things, increases in a culture's affluence, education, urbanization, and social mobility tend to foster more individualism (Triandis, 1994). Many contemporary societies are in transition, but generally speaking, North American and Western European cultures tend to be individualistic, whereas Asian, African, and Latin American cultures tend to be collectivistic (Hofstede, 1980, 1983, 2001) (see **Figure 15.4** on the next page).

How does individualism versus collectivism relate to patterns of attribution? The evidence suggests that

Web Link 15.2

Y? The National Forum on People's Differences Did you ever want to ask a sensitive question of someone who was different from you— another race or religion or sexual orientation—but were too embarrassed or shy? In a cyberforum with clear rules for courteous and respectful dialogue, newspaper writer and editor Philip J. Milano allows visitors to share differences openly and frankly and to learn about topics that are frequently kept quiet.

Hofstede's rankings of national cultures' individualism		
Individualistic cultures	**Intermediate cultures**	**Collectivist cultures**
1. United States	19. Israel	37. Hong Kong
2. Australia	20. Spain	38. Chile
3. Great Britain	21. India	40. Singapore
4. Canada	22. Argentina	40. Thailand
4. Netherlands	22. Japan	40. West Africa region
6. New Zealand	24. Iran	42. El Salvador
7. Italy	25. Jamaica	43. South Korea
8. Belgium	26. Arab region	44. Taiwan
9. Denmark	26. Brazil	45. Peru
10. France	28. Turkey	46. Costa Rica
11. Sweden	29. Uruguay	47. Indonesia
12. Ireland	30. Greece	47. Pakistan
13. Norway	31. Philippines	49. Colombia
14. Switzerland	32. Mexico	50. Venezuela
15. West Germany	34. East Africa region	51. Panama
16. South Africa	34. Portugal	52. Ecuador
17. Finland	34. Yugoslavia	53. Guatemala
18. Austria	36. Malaysia	

Figure 15.4

Individualism versus collectivism around the world. Hofstede (1980, 1983, 2001) used survey data from over 100,000 employees of a large, multinational corporation to estimate the emphasis on individualism versus collectivism in 50 nations and 3 regions. His large, diverse international sample remains unequaled to date. In the figure, cultures are ranked in terms of how strongly they embraced the values of individualism. As you can see, Hofstede's estimates suggest that North American and Western European nations tend to be relatively individualistic, whereas more collectivism is found in Asian, African, and Latin American countries.

Source: Adapted from Hofstede, G. (2001). *Culture's consequences* (2nd ed., p. 215). Thousand Oaks, CA: Sage. Copyright © 2001 Sage Publications. Adapted by permission of Dr. Geert Hofstede.

collectivist cultures may promote different attributional biases than individualistic cultures do. For example, people from collectivist societies appear to be less susceptible to the *fundamental attribution error* than those from individualistic societies (Choi, Nisbett, & Norenzayan, 1999; Triandis, 2001). And the *self-serving bias* may be particularly prevalent in individualistic, Western societies, where an emphasis on competition and high self-esteem motivates people to try to impress others, as well as themselves (Mezulis et al., 2004). In contrast, Japanese individuals exhibit a *self-effacing bias* in explaining success (Akimoto & Sanbonmatsu, 1999). That is, they tend to attribute their successes to help they receive from others or to the ease of the task, while downplaying the importance of their ability. When they fail, Japanese subjects tend to be more self-critical than subjects from individualistic cultures (Heine & Renshaw, 2002). It is not that self-enhancement motives are absent in collectivist cultures. Cultural disparities in attributional bias reflect the fact that people from individualist and collectivist cultures cherish and value different traits (Sedikides, Gaertner, & Toguchi, 2003). People from individualistic cultures exhibit attributional biases (such as the self-serving bias) that help them to feel independent, competent, and self-reliant. In contrast, people from collectivist cultures display attributional biases that help them to feel loyal, cooperative, and respectful. People from both types of cultures show distortions in attribution that are intended to enhance their feelings of self-esteem, but the distortions are different because self-esteem is derived from different virtues.

concept **check** 15.2 ✓

Recognizing Bias in Social Cognition

Check your understanding of bias in social cognition by identifying various types of errors that are common in person perception and attribution. Imagine that you're a nonvoting student member of a college committee at Southwest State University that is hiring a new political science professor. As you listen to the committee's discussion, you hear examples of (a) the illusory correlation effect, (b) stereotyping, and (c) the fundamental attribution error. Indicate which of these is at work in the excerpts from committee members' deliberations below. The answers are in Appendix A.

_____ **1.** "I absolutely won't consider the fellow who arrived 30 minutes late for his interview. Anybody who can't make a job interview on time is either irresponsible or hopelessly disorganized. I don't care what he says about the airline messing up his reservations."

_____ **2.** "You know, I was very, very impressed with the young female applicant, and I would love to hire her, but every time we add a young woman to the faculty in liberal arts, she gets pregnant within the first year." The committee chairperson, who has heard this line from this professor before replies, "You always say that, so I finally did a systematic check of what's happened in the past. Of the last 14 women hired in liberal arts, only one has become pregnant within a year."

_____ **3.** "The first one I want to rule out is the guy who's been practicing law for the last ten years. Although he has an excellent background in political science, I just don't trust lawyers. They're all ambitious, power hungry, manipulative cutthroats. He'll be a divisive force in the department."

"I just don't know what she sees in him. She could do so much better for herself. I suppose he's a nice guy, but they're just not right for each other." Can't you imagine Muffy's friends making these comments in discussing her relationship with Jake? You've probably heard similar remarks on many occasions. These comments illustrate people's interest in analyzing the dynamics of attraction. *Interpersonal attraction refers to positive feelings toward another person.* Social psychologists use this term broadly to encompass a variety of experiences, including liking, friendship, admiration, lust, and love.

Key Factors in Attraction

Many factors influence who is attracted to whom. Here we'll discuss factors that promote the development of liking, friendship, and love. Although these are different types of attraction, the interpersonal dynamics at work in each are surprisingly similar.

Physical Attractiveness

Although people often remark that "beauty is only skin deep," the empirical evidence suggests that most people don't really believe this saying (Fitness, Fletcher, & Overall, 2003). The importance of physical attractiveness was demonstrated in a study of college students in which unacquainted men and women were sent off on a "get-acquainted" date (Sprecher & Duck, 1994). The investigators were mainly interested in how communication might affect the process of attraction, but to put this factor in context they also measured participants' perceptions of their date's physical attractiveness and similarity to themselves. They found that the quality of communication during the date did have some effect on females' interest in friendship, but the key determinant of romantic attraction for both sexes was the physical attractiveness of the other person.

Many other studies have demonstrated the singular prominence of physical attractiveness in the initial stage of dating and have shown that it continues to influence the course of commitment as dating relationships evolve (Hendrick & Hendrick, 1992). In the realm of romance, being physically attractive appears to be more important for females than males (Regan, 2003). For example, in a study of college students (Speed & Gangestad, 1997), the correlation between dating popularity (assessed by peer ratings)

and physical attractiveness was higher for females (.76) than for males (.47).

Although people prefer physically attractive partners in romantic relationships, they may consider their own level of attractiveness in pursuing dates. What people want in a partner may be different from what they are willing to settle for (Regan, 1998). **The matching hypothesis proposes that males and females of approximately equal physical attractiveness are likely to select each other as partners.** The matching hypothesis is supported by evidence that married couples tend to be very similar in level of physical attractiveness (Feingold, 1988b). Interestingly, people expect that individuals who are similar in attractiveness will be more satisfied as couples and less likely to break up (Garcia & Khersonsky, 1996).

Similarity Effects

Is it true that "birds of a feather flock together," or do "opposites attract"? Research provides far more support for the former than the latter. Married and dating couples tend to be similar in age, race, religion, social class, education, intelligence, physical attractiveness, and attitudes (Kalmijn, 1998; Watson et al., 2004), although similarity in personality appears to be modest (Luo & Klohnen, 2005). Similarity

© Stockbyte Platinum/Alamy

PREVIEW QUESTIONS

- To what extent are good looks, similarity, reciprocity, and ideals important in interpersonal attraction?
- How do theorists distinguish among different types of love?
- How are attachment patterns related to intimate relations?
- How does culture influence patterns of mating?
- How have mating strategies been shaped by evolution?

According to the matching hypothesis, males and females who are similar in physical attractiveness are likely to be drawn together. This type of matching may also influence the formation of friendships.

© The New Yorker Collection 2002 Alex Gregory from cartoonbank.com. All rights reserved.

"It would never work out between us, Tom—we're from two totally different tiers of the upper middle class."

is also seen among friends. For instance, adult friends tend to be relatively similar in terms of income, education, occupational status, ethnicity, and religion (Blieszner & Adams, 1992).

The most obvious explanation for these correlations is that similarity causes attraction. Laboratory experiments on *attitude similarity*, conducted by Donn Byrne and his colleagues, suggest that similarity *does* cause liking (Byrne, 1997; Byrne, Clore, & Smeaton, 1986). However, research also suggests that attraction can foster similarity (Anderson, Keltner, & John, 2003). For example, Davis and Rusbult (2001) found that dating partners gradually modify their attitudes in ways that make them more congruent, a phenomenon they called *attitude alignment*. Moreover, people in stable, satisfying intimate relationships tend to subjectively overestimate how similar their partners are (Murray et al., 2002). Wanting to believe that they have found a kindred spirit, they tend to assume that their partners are mirrors of themselves.

Reciprocity Effects

In his widely read book *How to Win Friends and Influence People*, Dale Carnegie (1936) suggested that people can gain others' liking by showering them with praise and flattery. However, we've all heard that "flattery will get you nowhere." Which advice is right? The evidence suggests that flattery will get you somewhere, with some people, some of the time.

In interpersonal attraction, *reciprocity* **involves liking those who show that they like you.** In general, research indicates that we tend to like those who show that they like us and that we tend to see others as liking us more if we like them. Thus, it appears that liking breeds liking and loving promotes loving (Sprecher, 1998). Reciprocating attraction generally entails providing friends and intimate partners with positive feedback that results in a *self-enhancement* effect—in other words, you help them

ELLEN BERSCHEID

"The emotion of romantic love seems to be distressingly fragile. As a 16th-century sage poignantly observed, 'the history of a love affair is the drama of its fight against time.'"

Courtesy of Ellen Berscheid

ELAINE HATFIELD

"Passionate love is like any other form of excitement. By its very nature, excitement involves a continuous interplay between elation and despair, thrills and terror."

Courtesy of Elaine Hatfield

feel good about themselves (Sedikides & Strube, 1997). However, studies suggest that people are also interested in *self-verification*—that is, they seek feedback that matches and supports their self-concepts (Bosson & Swann, 2001).

Romantic Ideals

In the realm of romance, people want their partner to measure up to their ideals. These ideals spell out the personal qualities that one hopes to find in a partner, such as warmth, good looks, loyalty, high status, a sense of humor, and so forth. According to Simpson, Fletcher, and Campbell (2001), people routinely evaluate how close their intimate partners come to matching these ideal standards and these evaluations influence how relationships progress. Consistent with this theory, research shows that the more closely individuals' perceptions of their partners match their ideals, the more satisfied they tend to be with their relationship—both in the early stages of dating (Fletcher, Simpson, & Thomas, 2000) and in stable, long-term relationships (Fletcher et al., 1999). Moreover, the size of the discrepancy between ideals and perceptions predicts whether a dating relationship will continue or dissolve (Fletcher et al., 2000).

Of course, these evaluations of how a partner compares to one's ideals are subjective, leaving room for distortion. When people are highly invested in a relationship, they can reduce the discrepancy between their ideals and their perceptions either by lowering their standards or by making charitable evaluations of their partners. Research suggests that the latter strategy is more common. For example, in a study of 180 couples, Murray, Holmes, and Griffin (1996) found that most participants viewed their partners more favorably than the partners viewed themselves. Individuals' perceptions of their romantic partners seemed to reflect their ideals for a partner more than reality.

Perspectives on the Mystery of Love

People have always been interested in love and romance, but love has proven to be an elusive subject for scientific study. It's difficult to define, difficult to measure, and often difficult to understand. Nonetheless, psychologists have begun to make some progress in their study of love. Let's look at their theories and research.

Passionate and Companionate Love

Two pioneers in research on love, Elaine Hatfield and Ellen Berscheid (Berscheid, 1988; Hatfield & Rapson,

1993), proposed that romantic relationships are characterized by two kinds of love: passionate love and companionate love. **Passionate love** is a complete absorption in another that includes tender sexual feelings and the agony and ecstasy of intense emotion. **Companionate love** is warm, trusting, tolerant affection for another whose life is deeply intertwined with one's own. Passionate and companionate love *may* coexist, but they don't necessarily go hand in hand. Research suggests that, as a general rule, companionate love is more strongly related to relationship satisfaction than passionate love (Fehr, 2001).

The distinction between passionate and companionate love has been further refined by Robert Sternberg (1988c), who suggests that love has three facets rather than just two. He subdivides companionate love into intimacy and commitment. *Intimacy* refers to warmth, closeness, and sharing in a relationship. *Commitment* is an intent to maintain a relationship in spite of the difficulties and costs that may arise. Sternberg has mapped out the probable relations between the passage of time and the three components of love, as shown in **Figure 15.5**. He argues that passion reaches its peak in the early phases of love and then erodes. He believes that intimacy and commitment increase with time, although at different rates. Research suggests that commitment is a crucial element of love that is predictive of relationship stability (Sprecher, 1999).

Love as Attachment

12b

Cindy Hazan and Phillip Shaver (1987) have looked not at the types of love but at similarities between adult love and attachment relationships in infancy. We noted in Chapter 10 that infant-caretaker bonding, or *attachment,* emerges in the first year of life. Early attachments vary in quality, and infants tend to fall into three groups (Ainsworth et al., 1978). Most infants develop a *secure attachment.* However, some are very anxious when separated from their caretaker, a syndrome called *anxious-ambivalent attachment.* A third group of infants, characterized by *avoidant attachment,* never bond very well with their caretaker.

According to Hazan and Shaver, romantic love is an attachment process, and people's intimate relationships in adulthood follow the same form as their attachments in infancy. According to their theory, a person who had an anxious-ambivalent attachment in infancy will tend to have romantic relations marked by anxiety and ambivalence in adulthood. In other words, people relive their early bonding with their parents in their romantic relationships in adulthood.

Hazan and Shaver's (1987) initial survey study provided striking support for their theory. They found

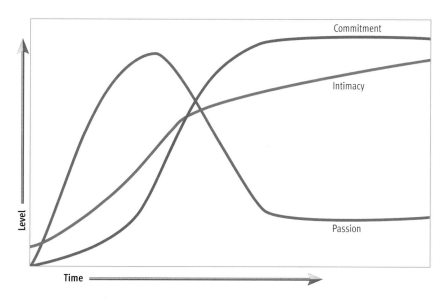

Figure 15.5

Sternberg's view of love over time. In his theory of love, Robert Sternberg (1988c) hypothesizes that the various elements of love progress in different ways over the course of time. According to Sternberg, passion peaks early in a relationship, whereas intimacy and commitment typically continue to build gradually. (Graphs adapted from Trotter, 1986)

that adults' love relationships could be sorted into groups that paralleled the three patterns of attachment seen in infants (see **Figure 15.6**). *Secure adults* found it relatively easy to get close to others and described their love relations as trusting. *Anxious-ambivalent adults* reported a preoccupation with love accompanied by expectations of rejection, and they described their love relations as volatile and marked by jealousy. *Avoidant adults* found it difficult to get close to others and described their love relations as

Adult attachment style

Secure
I find it relatively easy to get close to others and am comfortable depending on them and having them depend on me. I don't often worry about being abandoned or about someone getting too close to me.

Avoidant
I am somewhat uncomfortable being close to others; I find it difficult to trust them, difficult to allow myself to depend on them. I am nervous when anyone gets too close, and often love partners want me to be more intimate than I feel comfortable being.

Anxious/ambivalent
I find that others are reluctant to get as close as I would like. I often worry that my partner doesn't really love me or won't want to stay with me. I want to merge completely with another person, and this desire sometimes scares people away.

Figure 15.6

Attachment and romantic relationships. According to Hazan and Shaver (1987), people's romantic relationships in adulthood are similar in form to their attachment patterns in infancy, which fall into three categories. The three attachment styles seen in adult intimate relations are described here. (Based on Hazan and Shaver, 1986, 1987)

Web Link 15.3

Phillip R. Shaver's Homepage
Phillip Shaver of the University of California, Davis, has conducted pioneering and highly influential research on adult attachment style and intimate relationships. His homepage provides a link to his Adult Attachment Lab, where visitors can learn about early and current work and find links to other relevant sites.

lacking intimacy. Consistent with their theory, Hazan and Shaver (1987) found that the percentage of adults falling into each category was roughly the same as the percentage of infants in each comparable category—a finding that was subsequently replicated with a nationally representative sample of American adults (Mickelson, Kessler, & Shaver, 1997). Also, subjects' recollections of their childhood relations with their parents were consistent with the hypothesis that people relive their infant attachment experiences in adulthood.

Understandably, Hazan and Shaver's theory has attracted considerable interest and has generated a number of studies within a relatively short period of time. For example, research has shown that securely attached individuals have more committed, satisfying, well-adjusted, and longer-lasting relationships compared to people with either anxious-ambivalent or avoidant attachment styles (Feeney, 1999). Moreover, studies have shown attachment patterns are reasonably stable over time (Fraley, 2002), and that people with different attachment styles are predisposed to think, feel, and behave differently in their relationships (Collins & Allard, 2001). For example, anxious-ambivalent people tend to report more intense emotional highs and lows in their romantic relationships. They also report having more conflicts with their partners, that these conflicts are especially stressful, and that these conflicts often have a negative impact on how they feel about their relationship (Campbell et al., 2005). In a similar vein, attachment anxiety promotes *excessive reassurance seeking*—the tendency to persistently ask for assurances from partners that one is worthy of love (Shaver, Schachner, & Mikulincer, 2005). Reactions to romantic breakups also tend to vary depending on one's attachment style. People who are high in attachment anxiety have much more difficulty than others in dealing with the dissolution of romantic relationships. They report greater emotional and physical distress, greater preoccupation with the former partner, more attempts to regain the lost partner, more angry and vengeful behavior, and more maladaptive coping responses, such as using alcohol and drugs to cope with the loss (Davis, Shaver, & Vernon, 2003).

Studies have further suggested that attachment patterns may have far-reaching repercussions that extend into many aspects of people's lives besides their romantic relationships. For instance, attachment security promotes compassionate feelings and values and more helping behavior when people are in need (Mikulincer & Shaver, 2005). Researchers have also found correlations between attachment

styles and gender roles (Schwartz, Waldo, & Higgins, 2004), religious beliefs (Kirkpatrick, 2005), health habits (Huntsinger & Luecken, 2004), styles of coping with stress (Howard & Medway, 2004), and vulnerability to burnout (Pines, 2004). Thus, Hazan and Shaver's innovative ideas about the long-term effects of infant attachment experiences have triggered an avalanche of thought-provoking research.

Culture and Close Relationships

The limited evidence available suggests both similarities and differences among cultures in romantic relationships (Hendrick & Hendrick, 2000; Schmitt, 2005). For the most part, similarities have been seen when research has focused on what people look for in prospective mates—such as mutual attraction, kindness, and intelligence (Buss, 1989, 1994b). Cultures vary, however, in their emphasis on love—especially passionate love—as a prerequisite for marriage. Love as the basis for marriage is an 18th-century invention of Western culture (Stone, 1977). As Hatfield and Rapson (1993) note, "Marriage-for-love represents an ultimate expression of individualism" (p. 2). In contrast, marriages arranged by families and other go-betweens remain common in cultures high in collectivism, including India (Gupta, 1992), Japan (Iwao, 1993), and China (Xiaghe & Whyte, 1990). This practice is declining in some societies as a result of Westernization, but in collectivist societies people contemplating marriage still tend to think in terms of "What will my parents and other people say?" rather than "What does my heart say?" (Triandis, 1994). Studies show that attitudes about love in collectivist societies reflect these cultural priorities. For example, in comparison to Western participants, subjects from Eastern countries (such as India, Pakistan, and Thailand) report that romantic love is less important for marriage (Levine et al., 1995; Medora et al., 2002).

An Evolutionary Perspective on Attraction

Evolutionary psychologists have a great deal to say about heterosexual attraction. For example, they assert that physical appearance is an influential determinant of attraction because certain aspects of good looks can be indicators of sound health, good genes, and high fertility, all of which can contribute to reproductive potential (Soler et al., 2003; Sugiyama,

2005). Consistent with the evolutionary view, research has found that some standards of attractiveness are more consistent across cultures than previously believed (Sugiyama, 2005). For example, *facial symmetry* seems to be a key element of attractiveness in highly diverse cultures (Fink & Penton-Voak, 2002). Facial symmetry is thought to be valued because a variety of environmental insults and developmental abnormalities are associated with physical asymmetries, which may serve as markers of relatively poor genes or health (Jones et al., 2001).

The most thoroughly documented findings on the evolutionary bases of heterosexual attraction are those on gender differences in mating preferences. Consistent with the notion that humans are programmed by evolution to behave in ways that enhance their reproductive fitness, evidence indicates that men generally are more interested than women in seeking youthfulness and physical attractiveness in their mates because these traits should be associated with greater reproductive potential (see Chapter 9). On the other hand, research shows that women place a greater premium on prospective mates' ambition, social status, and financial potential because these traits should be associated with the ability to invest material resources in children (Li et al., 2002; Shackelford, Schmitt, & Buss, 2005). The degree to which these trends transcend history and culture was driven home by a recent study that examined the mate preferences apparent in 658 traditional folktales drawn from the ancient oral traditions of 48 different cultures (Gottschall et al., 2004). The analyses showed that the characters in these extremely old and diverse stories showed the same gender differences seen in contemporary research: Male characters tended to place a greater emphasis on potential mates' physical attractiveness, while female characters showed more interest in potential mates' wealth and social status.

Does the gender gap in mating priorities influence the tactics people actually use in pursuing romantic relationships? Yes, evidence indicates that during courtship men tend to emphasize their material resources, whereas women are more likely to work at enhancing their appearance (Buss, 1988). Interestingly, the tactics used by both sexes may include efforts at deception. One study found that many men and women would be willing to lie about their personality, income, past relationships, career skills, and intelligence to impress a prospective date who was attractive (Rowatt, Cunningham, & Druen, 1999). Consistent with evolutionary theory, women report that they are most upset when men exagger-

ate their social status, their financial resources, or the depth of their romantic commitment to the woman, whereas men are most upset when women conceal a history of "promiscuity" (Haselton et al., 2005).

Deception lies at the heart of *mate poaching,* a phenomenon that has recently attracted the interest of evolutionary psychologists. Mate poaching occurs when someone tries to attract another person who is already in a relationship. Although it presents some extra challenges and risks, mate poaching has

Marriages based on romantic love are the norm in Western cultures, whereas arranged marriages prevail in collectivist cultures.

BIZARRO

probably occurred throughout history. It is universally seen across cultures, although its prevalence varies some from one culture to another (Schmitt et al., 2004). Men are somewhat more likely than women to make poaching attempts, but the gap is modest and poaching by women is common (Schmitt et al., 2004). The tactics employed in poaching efforts overlap considerably with the normal tactics of attraction, except the tactics are more likely to be executed in a disguised and secretive manner.

> Attitudes: Making Social Judgments

PREVIEW QUESTIONS

- What are the key components and dimensions of attitudes?
- What factors influence the effectiveness of persuasive efforts?
- How do learning theory and dissonance theory explain attitude change?
- What are the two routes to persuasion?

In our chapter-opening story, Muffy's friends exhibited decidedly negative attitudes about working-class men. Their example reveals a basic feature of attitudes: they're evaluative. Social psychology's interest in attitudes has a much longer history than its interest in attraction. Indeed, in its early days social psychology was defined as the study of attitudes. In this section we'll discuss the nature of attitudes, efforts to change attitudes through persuasion, and theories of attitude change.

What are attitudes? **Attitudes are positive or negative evaluations of objects of thought.** "Objects of thought" may include social issues (capital punishment or gun control, for example), groups (liberals, farmers), institutions (the Lutheran church, the Supreme Court), consumer products (yogurt, computers), and people (the president, your next-door neighbor).

Components and Dimensions of Attitudes

Social psychologists have traditionally viewed attitudes as being made up of three components: a cognitive component, an affective component, and a behavioral component. However, in recent years it has become apparent that many attitudes do not include all three components (Fazio & Olson, 2003), so it is more accurate to say that *attitudes may include up to three components.* The *cognitive component* of an attitude is made up of the beliefs that people hold about the object of an attitude. The *affective component* consists of the *emotional feelings* stimulated by an object of thought. The *behavioral component* consists of *predispositions to act* in certain ways toward an attitude object. **Figure 15.7** provides concrete examples of how someone's attitude about gun control might be divided into its components.

Attitudes vary along several crucial dimensions, including their *strength, accessibility,* and *ambivalence* (Olson & Maio, 2003). Definitions of *attitude strength* differ, but strong attitudes are genereally viewed as ones that are firmly held (resistant to change), that are durable over time, and that have a powerful impact on behavior (Petty, Wheeler, & Tormala, 2003). The *accessibility* of an attitude refers to how often one thinks about it and how quickly it comes to mind. Highly accessible attitudes are quickly and readily available (Fabrigar, MacDonald, & Wegener,

Figure 15.7
The possible components of attitudes. Attitudes may include cognitive, affective, and behavioral components, as illustrated here for a hypothetical person's attitude about gun control.

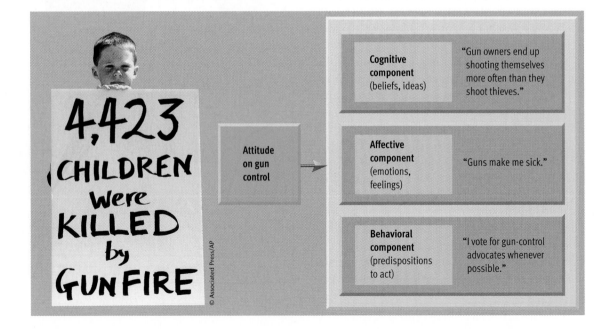

2005). Attitude accessibility is correlated with attitude strength, as highly accessible attitudes *tend* to be strong, but the concepts are distinct and there is no one-to-one correspondence. *Ambivalent attitudes* are conflicted evaluations that include both positive and negative feelings about an object of thought (Fabrigar et al., 2005). Like attitude strength, attitude ambivalence has been measured in various ways (Priester & Petty, 2001). Generally speaking, ambivalence increases as the ratio of positive to negative evaluations gets closer to being equal. When ambivalence is high, an attitude tends to be less predictive of behavior and more pliable in the face of persuasion (Armitage & Conner, 2000).

Trying to Change Attitudes: Factors in Persuasion

Every day you're bombarded by efforts to alter your attitudes. In light of this reality, let's examine some of the factors that determine whether persuasion works.

The process of persuasion includes four basic elements: the source, receiver, message, and channel (see **Figure 15.8**). **The *source* is the person who sends a communication, and the *receiver* is the person to whom the message is sent.** Thus, if you watch a presidential news conference on TV, the president is the source, and you and millions of other viewers are the receivers. **The *message* is the information transmitted by the source, and the *channel* is the medium through which the message is sent.** Although the research on communication channels is interesting, we'll confine our discussion to source, message, and receiver variables.

Source Factors

Occasional exceptions to the general rule are seen, but persuasion tends to be more successful when the source has high *credibility* (Pornpitakpan, 2004). What gives a person credibility? Either expertise or trustworthiness. *Expertise* tends to be more influential when arguments are ambiguous (Chaiken & Maheswaran, 1994). People try to convey their expertise by mentioning their degrees, their training, and their experience or by showing an impressive grasp of the issue at hand. Expertise is a plus, but *trustworthiness* can be even more important. Many people tend to accept messages from trustworthy sources with little scrutiny (Priester & Petty, 1995, 2003). Trustworthiness is undermined when a source appears to have something to gain. In contrast, trustworthiness is enhanced when people appear to argue against their own best interests (Hunt, Smith, & Kernan, 1985). *Likability* also increases the effectiveness of a persuasive source (Johnson, Maio, & Smith-McLallen, 2005).

The importance of source variables can be seen in advertising. Many companies spend a fortune to obtain an ideal spokesperson, such as Jerry Seinfeld, Michael Jordan, Bill Cosby, or Catherine Zeta-Jones, who combine trustworthiness and likability. Companies quickly abandon spokespersons when their likability declines.

Message Factors

If you were going to give a speech to a local community group advocating a reduction in state taxes on corporations, you'd probably wrestle with a number of questions about how to structure your message. Should you look at both sides of the issue, or should you just present your side? Should you deliver a low-key, logical speech? Or should you try to strike fear into the hearts of your listeners? These questions are concerned with message factors in persuasion.

In general, two-sided arguments seem to be more effective than one-sided presentations (Petty & Wegener, 1998). Just mentioning that an issue has two sides can increase your credibility with an audience. Fear appeals appear to work—if they are successful in arousing fear. Research reveals that many messages intended to induce fear fail to do so. However, studies involving a wide range of issues (nuclear policy, auto safety, dental hygiene, and so on) have

Web Link 15.4

Influence at Work
This site offers an intriguing set of materials that explore a wide variety of social influence phenomena, including persuasion, propaganda, brainwashing, and the tactics that cults use in recruiting. The site is maintained by Kelton Rhodes and Robert Cialdini, perhaps the world's leading authority on social influence strategies.

Figure 15.8

Overview of the persuasion process. The process of persuasion essentially boils down to *who* (the source) communicates *what* (the message) *by what means* (the channel) *to whom* (the receiver). Thus, four sets of variables influence the process of persuasion: source, message, channel, and receiver factors. The diagram lists some of the more important factors in each category (including some that are not discussed in the text due to space limitations). (Adapted from Lippa, 1994)

Who	What	By what means	To whom
Source factors	***Message factors***	***Channel factors***	***Receiver factors***
Credibility	Fear appeal versus logic	In person	Personality
Expertise	One-sided versus two-sided argument	On television, or radio	Expectations (e.g., forewarning)
Trustworthiness	Number of strong or weak arguments	Via audiotape	Initial attitude on issue
Likability	Repetition	Via computer	Strength of preexisting attitudes
Attractiveness			
Similarity			

shown that messages that are effective in arousing fear tend to increase persuasion (Ruiter, Abraham, & Kok, 2001). Fear appeals are most likely to work when your listeners view the dire consequences that you describe as exceedingly unpleasant, fairly probable if they don't take your advice, and avoidable if they do (Das, de Wit, & Stroebe, 2003).

Receiver Factors

What about the receiver of the persuasive message? Are some people easier to persuade than others? Undoubtedly, but transient factors such as the forewarning a receiver gets about a persuasive effort and the receiver's initial position on an issue seem to be more influential than the receiver's personality. Consider, for instance, the old adage that "to be forewarned is to be forearmed." The value of *forewarning* does apply to targets of persuasive efforts (Johnson, 1994). When you shop for a new car, you *expect* salespeople to work at persuading you, and to some extent this forewarning reduces the impact of their arguments. Considerations that stimulate counterarguing in the receiver tend to increase resistance to persuasion (Jain, Buchanan, & Maheswaran, 2000).

A receiver's resistance to persuasion also depends on the nature of the attitude or belief that the source is trying to change. Obviously, resistance is greater when you have to advocate a position that is incompatible with the receiver's existing attitudes or beliefs (Edwards & Smith, 1996). Furthermore, studies show that *stronger attitudes are more resistant to change* (Eagly & Chaiken, 1995). Strong attitudes may be tougher to alter because they tend to be anchored in networks of beliefs and values that might also require change (Erber, Hodges, & Wilson, 1995).

Our review of source, message, and receiver variables has shown that attempting to change attitudes through persuasion involves a complex interplay of factors—and we haven't even looked beneath the surface yet. How do people acquire attitudes in the first place? What dynamic processes within people produce attitude change? We turn to these theoretical issues next.

Theories of Attitude Formation and Change 12c

Many theories have been proposed to explain the mechanisms at work in attitude change, whether or not it occurs in response to persuasion. We'll look at three theoretical perspectives: learning theory, dissonance theory, and the elaboration likelihood model.

Learning Theory 12c

We've seen repeatedly that the concepts of *learning* and *conditioning* can help explain a wide range of phenomena, from conditioned fears to the acquisition of gender roles to the development of personality traits. Now we can add attitude formation and change to our list.

The affective, or emotional, component in an attitude can be created through a special subtype of *classical conditioning,* called evaluative conditioning (Olson & Fazio, 2001, 2002). As we discussed in Chapter 6, *evaluative conditioning* consists of efforts to transfer the emotion attached to a UCS to a new CS (Kruglanski & Stroebe, 2005; Schimmack & Crites, 2005). Advertisers routinely try to take advantage of evaluative conditioning by pairing their products with stimuli that elicit pleasant emotional responses, such as extremely attractive models, highly likable spokespersons, and cherished events, such as the Olympics (Till & Priluck, 2000). This conditioning process is diagrammed in **Figure 15.9**.

Operant conditioning may come into play when you openly express an attitude, such as "I believe that husbands should do more housework." Some

concept **check** 15.3

Understanding Attitudes and Persuasion

Check your understanding of the components of attitudes and the elements of persuasion by analyzing hypothetical political strategies. Imagine you're working on a political campaign and you're invited to join the candidate's inner circle in strategy sessions, as staff members prepare the candidate for upcoming campaign stops. During the meetings, you hear various strategies discussed. For each strategy below, indicate which component of voters' attitudes (cognitive, affective, or behavioral) is being targeted for change, and indicate which element in persuasion (source, message, or receiver factors) is being manipulated. The answers are in Appendix A.

1. "You need to convince this crowd that your program for regulating nursing homes is sound. Whatever you do, don't acknowledge the two weaknesses in the program that we've been playing down. I don't care if you're asked point blank. Just slide by the question and keep harping on the program's advantages."

2. "You haven't been smiling enough lately, especially when the TV cameras are rolling. Remember, you can have the best ideas in the world, but if you don't seem likable, you're not gonna get elected. By the way, I think I've lined up some photo opportunities that should help us create an image of sincerity and compassion."

3. "This crowd is already behind you. You don't have to alter their opinions on any issue. Get right to work convincing them to contribute to the campaign. I want them lining up to donate money."

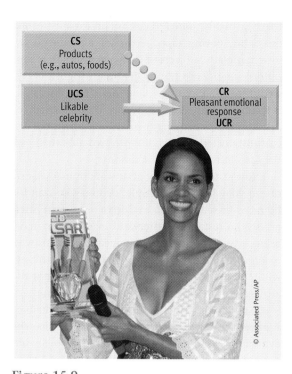

Figure 15.9

Classical conditioning of attitudes in advertising.
Advertisers routinely pair their products with likable celebrities in the hope that their products will come to elicit pleasant emotional responses. As discussed in Chapter 6, this special type of classical conditioning is called *evaluative conditioning.* See the Critical Thinking Application in Chapter 6 for a more in-depth discussion of this practice.

people may endorse your view, while others may jump down your throat. Agreement from other people generally functions as a reinforcer, strengthening your tendency to express a specific attitude (Bohner & Schwarz, 2001). Disagreement often functions as a form of punishment, which may gradually weaken your commitment to your viewpoint.

Another person's attitudes may rub off on you through *observational learning* (Oskamp, 1991). If you hear your uncle say, "Republicans are nothing but puppets of big business" and your mother heartily agrees, your exposure to your uncle's attitude and your mother's reinforcement of your uncle may influence your attitude toward the Republican party. Studies show that parents and their children tend to have similar political attitudes (Sears, 1975). Observational learning presumably accounts for much of this similarity. The opinions of teachers, coaches, co-workers, talk-show hosts, rock stars, and so forth are also likely to sway people's attitudes through observational learning.

Dissonance Theory

PsykTrek **12c**

Leon Festinger's *dissonance theory* assumes that inconsistency among attitudes propels people in the direction of attitude change. Dissonance theory burst into prominence in 1959 when Festinger and J. Merrill Carlsmith published a landmark study. Let's look at their findings and at how dissonance theory explains them.

Festinger and Carlsmith (1959) had male college students come to a laboratory and work on excruciatingly dull tasks, such as turning pegs repeatedly. When a subject's hour was over, the experimenter confided that some participants' motivation was being manipulated by telling them that the task was interesting and enjoyable before they started it. Then, after a moment's hesitation, the experimenter asked if the subject could help him out of a jam. His usual helper was delayed and he needed someone to testify to the next "subject" (really an accomplice) that the experimental task was interesting. He offered to pay the subject if he would tell the person in the adjoining waiting room that the task was enjoyable and involving.

This entire scenario was enacted to coax participants into doing something that was inconsistent with their true feelings. Some subjects received a token payment of $1 for their effort, while others received a more substantial payment of $20 (an amount equivalent to about $120 today, in light of inflation). Later, a second experimenter inquired about the participants' true feelings regarding the dull experimental task. **Figure 15.10** on the next page summarizes the design of the Festinger and Carlsmith study.

Who do you think rated the task more favorably—the subjects who were paid $1 or those who were paid $20? Both common sense and learning theory would predict that the subjects who received the greater reward ($20) should come to like the task more. In reality, however, the participants who were paid $1 exhibited more favorable attitude change—just as Festinger and Carlsmith had predicted. Why? Dissonance theory provides an explanation.

According to Festinger (1957), **cognitive dissonance exists when related attitudes or beliefs are inconsistent—that is, when they contradict each other.** Festinger's model assumes that dissonance is possible only when cognitions are relevant to each other, since unrelated cognitions ("I am hardworking" and "Fire engines are red") can't contradict each other. However, when cognitions are related, they may be consonant ("I am hardworking" and "I'm staying overtime to get an important job done") or dissonant ("I am hardworking" and "I'm playing hooky from work"). When aroused, cognitive dissonance is supposed to create an unpleasant state of tension that motivates people to reduce their dissonance—usually by altering their cognitions.

Courtesy of Professor Jerry Suls

LEON FESTINGER

"Cognitive dissonance is a motivating state of affairs. Just as hunger impels a person to eat, so does dissonance impel a person to change his opinions or his behavior."

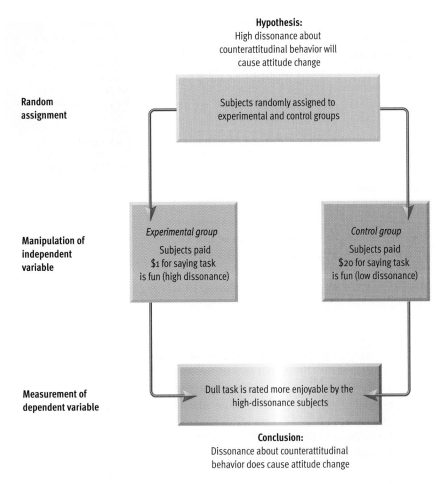

Hypothesis:
High dissonance about counterattitudinal behavior will cause attitude change

Random assignment

Subjects randomly assigned to experimental and control groups

Manipulation of independent variable

Experimental group
Subjects paid $1 for saying task is fun (high dissonance)

Control group
Subjects paid $20 for saying task is fun (low dissonance)

Measurement of dependent variable

Dull task is rated more enjoyable by the high-dissonance subjects

Conclusion:
Dissonance about counterattitudinal behavior does cause attitude change

Figure 15.10

Design of the Festinger and Carlsmith (1959) study. The manipulations of variables and the results of Festinger and Carlsmith's landmark study of attitude change are outlined here.

In the study by Festinger and Carlsmith (1959), the subjects' contradictory cognitions were "The task is boring" and "I told someone the task was enjoyable." The participants who were paid $20 for lying had an obvious reason for behaving inconsistently with their true attitudes, so these subjects experienced little dissonance. In contrast, the participants paid $1 had no readily apparent justification for their lie and experienced high dissonance. To reduce it, they tended to persuade themselves that the task was more enjoyable than they had originally thought. *Thus, dissonance theory sheds light on why people sometimes come to believe their own lies.*

Cognitive dissonance is also at work when people turn attitude somersaults to justify efforts that haven't panned out, a syndrome called *effort justification.* Aronson and Mills (1959) studied effort justification by putting college women through a "severe initiation" before they could qualify to participate in what promised to be an interesting discussion of sexuality. In the initiation, the women had to read obscene passages out loud to a male experimenter. After all

that, the highly touted discussion of sexuality turned out to be a boring, taped lecture on reproduction in lower animals. Subjects in the severe initiation condition experienced highly dissonant cognitions ("I went through a lot to get here" and "This discussion is terrible"). How did they reduce their dissonance? Apparently by changing their attitude about the discussion, since they rated it more favorably than participants in two control conditions.

Effort justification may be at work in many facets of everyday life. For example, people who wait for hours to be seated at an exclusive restaurant often praise the restaurant afterward even if they have been served a poorly prepared meal. Rock fans who pay hundreds of dollars for scalped concert tickets will tend to view the concert favorably, even if the artists show up in a stupor and play out of tune.

Dissonance theory has been tested in hundreds of studies with mixed, but largely favorable, results. The dynamics of dissonance appear to underlie many important types of attitude changes (Draycott & Dabbs, 1998; Keller & Block, 1999; Petty et al., 2003). Research has largely supported Festinger's claim that dissonance involves genuine psychological discomfort and even physiological arousal (Visser & Cooper, 2003; Devine et al., 1999). However, dissonance effects are not among the most reliable phenomena in social psychology. Researchers have had difficulty specifying the conditions under which dissonance will occur, and it has become apparent that people can reduce their dissonance in quite a variety of ways besides changing their attitudes (Olson & Stone, 2005; Visser & Cooper, 2003).

Elaboration Likelihood Model **12c**

A more recent theory of attitude change proposed by Richard Petty and John Cacioppo (1986) asserts that there are two basic "routes" to persuasion (Petty & Wegener, 1999). The *central route* is taken when people carefully ponder the content and logic of persuasive messages. The *peripheral route* is taken when persuasion depends on nonmessage factors, such as the attractiveness and credibility of the source, or on conditioned emotional responses (see **Figure 15.11**). For example, a politician who campaigns by delivering carefully researched speeches that thoughtfully analyze complex issues is following the central route to persuasion. In contrast, a politician who depends on marching bands, flag waving, celebrity endorsements, and emotional slogans is following the peripheral route.

Both routes can lead to effective persuasion and attitude change. However, according to the elaboration likelihood model, the durability of attitude

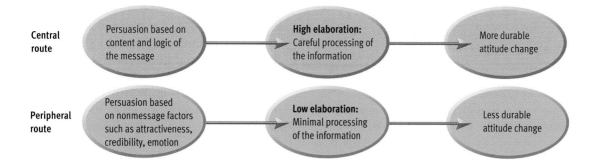

| Central route | Persuasion based on content and logic of the message | → | **High elaboration:** Careful processing of the information | → | More durable attitude change |
| Peripheral route | Persuasion based on nonmessage factors such as attractiveness, credibility, emotion | → | **Low elaboration:** Minimal processing of the information | → | Less durable attitude change |

Figure 15.11

The elaboration likelihood model. According to the elaboration likelihood model (Petty & Cacioppo, 1986), the central route to persuasion leads to more elaboration of message content and more enduring attitude change than the peripheral route to persuasion.

change depends on the extent to which people elaborate on (think about) the contents of persuasive communications. Studies suggest that the central route to persuasion leads to more enduring attitude change than the peripheral route (Petty & Wegener, 1998). Research also suggests that attitudes changed through central processes predict behavior better than attitudes changed through peripheral processes (Kruglanski & Stroebe, 2005; Petty, Wegener, & Fabrigar, 1997).

> Conformity and Obedience: Yielding to Others

A number of years ago, the area that I lived in experienced a severe spring flood that required the mobilization of the National Guard and several other emergency services. At the height of the crisis, a young man arrived at the scene of the flood, announced that he was from an obscure state agency that no one had ever heard of, and proceeded to take control of the emergency. City work crews, the fire department, local police, municipal officials, and the National Guard followed his orders with dispatch for several days, evacuating entire neighborhoods—until an official thought to check and found out that the man was just someone who had walked in off the street. The imposter, who had had small armies at his beck and call for several days, had no training in emergency services, just a history of unemployment and psychological problems.

After news of the hoax spread, people criticized red-faced local officials for their compliance with the imposter's orders. However, many of the critics probably would have cooperated in much the same way if they had been in the officials' shoes. For most people, willingness to obey an apparent authority figure is the rule, not the exception. In this section, we'll analyze the dynamics of social influence at work in conformity and obedience.

Conformity

12e

If you keep a well-manicured lawn and praise the talents of the band Green Day, are you exhibiting conformity? According to social psychologists, it depends on whether your behavior is the result of group pressure. *Conformity* occurs when people yield to real or imagined social pressure. For example, if you maintain a well-groomed lawn only to avoid complaints from your neighbors, you're yielding to social pressure. If you like Green Day because you genuinely enjoy their music, that's *not* conformity. However, if you like Green Day because it's "hip" and your friends would question your taste if you didn't, then you're conforming.

In the 1950s, Solomon Asch (1951, 1955, 1956) devised a clever procedure that minimized ambiguity about whether subjects were conforming, allowing him to investigate the variables that govern conformity. Let's re-create one of Asch's (1955) classic experiments. The participants are male undergraduates recruited for a study of visual perception. A group of seven subjects are shown a large card with a vertical line on it and then are asked to indicate which of three lines on a second card matches the original "standard line" in length (see Figure 15.12).

PREVIEW QUESTIONS

● How did Asch study conformity, and what did he learn?

● How did Milgram study obedience, and what did he learn?

● Why were Milgram's findings so controversial?

● How well do American findings on conformity and obedience generalize to other cultures?

● How did the Stanford Prison Simulation demonstrate the power of the situation?

Figure 15.12

Stimuli used in Asch's conformity studies. Subjects were asked to match a standard line (top) with one of three other lines displayed on another card (bottom). The task was easy—until experimental accomplices started responding with obviously incorrect answers, creating a situation in which Asch evaluated subjects' conformity.

Source: Adapted from Asch, S. (1955). Opinion and social pressure. *Scientific American, 193* (5), 31–35, from an illustration by Sara Love on p. 32. Copyright © 1955 by Scientific American, Inc. All rights reserved.

SOLOMON ASCH

"That we have found the tendency to conformity in our society so strong that reasonably intelligent and well-meaning young people are willing to call white black is a matter of concern."

Figure 15.13

Conformity and group size. This graph shows the percentage of trials on which participants conformed as a function of group size in Asch's research. Asch found that conformity became more frequent as group size increased up to four, peaked at seven, and then leveled off. (Data from Asch, 1955)

Source: Adapted from Asch, S. (1955). Opinion and social pressure. *Scientific American, 193* (5), 31–35 from an illustration by Sara Love on p. 35. Copyright © 1955 by Scientific American, Inc. All rights reserved.

All seven participants are given a turn at the task, and they announce their choice to the group. The subject in the sixth chair doesn't know it, but everyone else in the group is an accomplice of the experimenter, and they're about to make him wonder whether he has taken leave of his senses.

The accomplices give accurate responses on the first two trials. On the third trial, line number 2 clearly is the correct response, but the first five "subjects" all say that line number 3 matches the standard line. The genuine subject is bewildered and can't believe his ears. Over the course of the next 15 trials, the accomplices all give the same incorrect response on 11 of them. How does the real subject respond? The line judgments are easy and unambiguous. So, if the participant consistently agrees with the accomplices, he isn't making honest mistakes—he's conforming.

Averaging across all 50 subjects, Asch (1955) found that the young men conformed on 37% of the trials. The participants varied considerably in their tendency to conform, however. Of the 50 subjects, 13 never caved in to the group, while 14 conformed on more than half the trials. One could argue that the results show that people confronting a unanimous majority generally tend to *resist* the pressure to conform, but given how clear and easy the line judgments were, most social scientists viewed the findings as a dramatic demonstration of humans' propensity to conform (Levine, 1999).

In subsequent studies, *group size* and *group unanimity* turned out to be key determinants of conformity (Asch, 1956). To examine the impact of group size, Asch repeated his procedure with groups that included from 1 to 15 accomplices. Little conformity was seen when a subject was pitted against just 1 person, but conformity increased rapidly as group size

went from 2 to 4, peaked at a group size of 7, and then leveled off (see **Figure 15.13**). Thus, Asch reasoned that as groups grow larger, conformity increases—up to a point—a conclusion that has been echoed by other researchers (Cialdini & Trost, 1998).

However, group size made little difference if just one accomplice "broke" with the others, wrecking their unanimous agreement. The presence of another dissenter lowered conformity to about one-quarter of its peak, even when the dissenter made *inaccurate* judgments that happened to conflict with the majority view. Apparently, the participants just needed to hear someone else question the accuracy of the group's perplexing responses. The importance of unanimity in fostering conformity has been replicated in subsequent research (Nemeth & Chiles, 1988).

Obedience

***Obedience* is a form of compliance that occurs when people follow direct commands, usually from someone in a position of authority.** To a surprising extent, when an authority figure says, "Jump!" many people simply ask, "How high?"

Milgram's Studies

Stanley Milgram wanted to study this tendency to obey authority figures. Like many other people after World War II, he was troubled by how readily the citizens of Germany followed the orders of dictator Adolf Hitler, even when the orders required shockingly immoral actions, such as the slaughter of millions of Jews. Milgram, who had worked with Solomon Asch, set out to design a standard laboratory procedure for the study of obedience, much like Asch's procedure for studying conformity. The clever experiment that Milgram devised became one of the most famous and controversial studies in the annals of psychology.

Milgram's (1963) participants were a diverse collection of 40 men from the local community. They were told that they would be participating in a study concerned with the effects of punishment on learning. When they arrived at the lab, they drew slips of paper from a hat to get their assignments. The drawing was rigged so that the subject always became the "teacher" and an experimental accomplice (a likable 47-year-old accountant) became the "learner."

The learner was strapped into an electrified chair through which a shock could be delivered whenever he made a mistake on the task (see **Figure 15.14**). The subject was then taken to an adjoining room

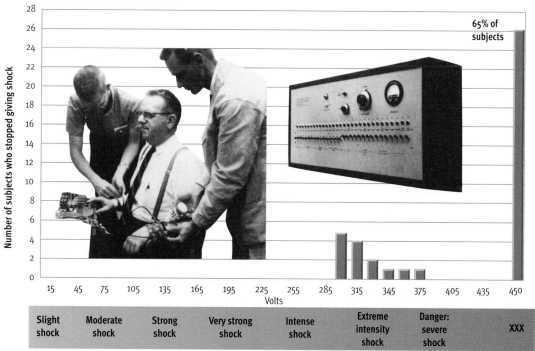

Figure 15.14

Milgram's experiment on obedience. The photo on the left shows the "learner" being connected to the shock generator during one of Milgram's experimental sessions. The photo on the right shows the fake shock generator used in the study. The surprising results of the Milgram (1963) study are summarized in the bar graph. Although subjects frequently protested, the vast majority (65%) delivered the entire series of shocks to the learner.

Source: Photos Copyright © 1965 by Stanley Milgram. From the film *Obedience*, distributed by Penn State Media Sales. Reprinted by permission of Alexandra Milgram.

STANLEY MILGRAM

"The essence of obedience is that a person comes to view himself as the instrument for carrying out another person's wishes, and he therefore no longer regards himself as responsible for his actions."

that housed the shock generator that he would control in his role as the teacher. Although the apparatus looked and sounded realistic, it was a fake and the learner was never shocked.

As the "learning experiment" proceeded, the accomplice made many mistakes that necessitated shocks. The teacher was instructed to increase the shock level after each wrong answer. At 300 volts, the learner began to pound on the wall between the two rooms in protest and soon stopped responding to the teacher's questions. From this point forward, participants frequently turned to the experimenter for guidance. Whenever they did so, the experimenter firmly indicated that the teacher should continue to give stronger and stronger shocks to the now-silent learner. The dependent variable was the maximum shock the participant was willing to administer before refusing to go on.

As **Figure 15.14** shows, 26 of the 40 subjects (65%) administered all 30 levels of shock. Although they tended to obey the experimenter, many subjects voiced and displayed considerable distress about harming the learner. The horrified participants groaned, bit their lips, stuttered, trembled, and broke into a sweat, but continued administering the shocks. Based on these results, Milgram concluded that obedience to authority was even more common than he or others anticipated. Before the study was conducted, Milgram had described it to 40 psychiatrists and had asked them to predict how much shock sub-

jects would be willing to administer to their innocent victims. Most of the psychiatrists had predicted that fewer than 1% of the subjects would continue to the end of the series of shocks!

In interpreting his results, Milgram argued that strong pressure from an authority figure can make decent people do indecent things to others. Applying this insight to Nazi war crimes and other travesties, Milgram asserted that some sinister actions may not be due to actors' evil character so much as to situational pressures that can lead normal people to engage in acts of treachery and violence. Thus, he arrived at the disturbing conclusion that given the right circumstances, any of us might obey orders to inflict harm on innocent strangers.

The Ensuing Controversy

Milgram's study evoked a controversy that continues through today. Some critics argued that Milgram's results wouldn't generalize to the real world (Orne & Holland, 1968). For example, Baumrind (1964) asserted that subjects who agree to participate in a scientific study *expect to obey* orders from an experimenter. Milgram (1964, 1968) replied by pointing out that so do soldiers and bureaucrats in the real world who are accused of villainous acts performed in obedience to authority. "I reject Baumrind's argument that the observed obedience doesn't count because it occurred where it is appropriate," said Milgram

Web Link 15.5

Stanley Milgram
This site provides a wealth of accurate information about the work of Stanley Milgram, arguably one of the most controversial and creative social psychologists in the field's history. The site is maintained by Thomas Blass, a psychology professor at the University of Maryland (Baltimore County), who has published many articles and books on the life and work of Milgram.

Courtesy of Philip Zimbardo

PHILIP ZIMBARDO

"But in the end, I called off the experiment not because of the horror I saw out \there in the prison yard, but because of the horror of realizing that I could have easily traded places with the most brutal guard or become the weakest prisoner full of hatred at being so powerless."

(1964). "That is precisely why it *does* count." Overall, the weight of evidence supports the generalizability of Milgram's results. They were consistently replicated for many years, in diverse settings, with a variety of subjects and procedural variations (Blass, 1999; Miller, 1986).

Critics also questioned the ethics of Milgram's experimental procedures (Baumrind, 1964; Kelman, 1967). They noted that without prior consent, participants were exposed to extensive deception that could undermine their trust in people and severe stress that could leave emotional scars. Milgram's defenders argued that the brief distress experienced by his subjects was a small price to pay for the insights that emerged from his obedience studies. Looking back, however, many psychologists seem to share the critics' concerns about the ethical implications of Milgram's ground-breaking work. His procedure is questionable by contemporary standards of research ethics, and no replications of his obedience study have been conducted in the United States since the mid-1970s (Blass, 1991)—a bizarre epitaph for what may be psychology's best-known experiment.

Cultural Variations in Conformity and Obedience

Are conformity and obedience unique to American culture? By no means. The Asch and Milgram experiments have been repeated in many other societies, where they have yielded results roughly similar to those seen in the United States. Thus, the phenomena of conformity and obedience seem to transcend culture.

The replications of Milgram's obedience study have largely been limited to industrialized nations similar to the United States. Many of these studies have reported even *higher* obedience rates than those seen in Milgram's American samples (Smith & Bond, 1994). Thus, the surprisingly high level of obedience observed by Milgram does not appear to be peculiar to the United States. The Asch experiment has been repeated in a more diverse range of societies than the Milgram experiment. Various theorists have hypothesized that collectivistic cultures, which emphasize respect for group norms, cooperation, and harmony, encourage more conformity than individualistic cultures, with their emphasis on independence (Kim & Markus, 1999; Matsumoto, 1994). Consistent with this analysis, replications of the Asch experiment have tended to find somewhat higher levels of conformity in collectivistic cultures than in individualistic cultures (Bond & Smith, 1996; Smith, 2001).

The Power of the Situation: The Stanford Prison Simulation

The research of Asch and Milgram provided dramatic demonstrations of the potent influence that situational factors can have on social behavior. The power of the situation was underscored once again, about a decade after Milgram's obedience research, in another landmark study conducted by Philip Zimbardo, who, ironically, was a high school classmate of Milgram's. Zimbardo and his colleagues designed the Stanford Prison Simulation to investigate why prisons tend to become abusive, degrading violent environments (Haney, Banks, & Zimbardo, 1973; Zimbardo, Haney, & Banks, 1973). Like Milgram, Zimbardo wanted to see how much the power of the situation would shape the behavior of normal, average subjects.

The participants were college students recruited for a study of prison life through a newspaper ad. After 70 volunteers were given an extensive battery of tests and interviews, the researchers chose 24 students who appeared to be physically healthy and psychologically stable to be the subjects. A coin flip determined which of them would be "guards" and which would be the "prisoners" in a simulated prison set up at Stanford University. The prisoners were "arrested" at their homes, handcuffed, and transported to a mock prison on the Stanford campus. Upon arrival, they were ordered to strip, sprayed with a delousing agent, given prison uniforms (smocks), assigned numbers as their identities, and locked up in iron-barred cells. The subjects assigned to be guards were given khaki uniforms, billy clubs, whistles, and reflective sunglasses. They were told that they could run their prison in whatever way they wanted except that they were not allowed to use physical punishment.

What happened? In short order, confrontations occurred between the guards and prisoners and the guards quickly devised a variety of sometimes cruel strategies to maintain total control over their prisoners. Meals, blankets, and bathroom privileges were selectively denied to some prisoners to achieve control. The prisoners were taunted, humiliated, called demeaning names, and forced to beg for opportunities to go to the bathroom. Pointless, petty rules were strictly enforced, and difficult prisoners were punished with hard labor (doing pushups and jumping jacks, cleaning toilets with their bare hands). And the guards creatively turned a 2-foot by 2-foot closet into a "hole" for solitary confinement of rebellious prisoners. Although there was some variation among

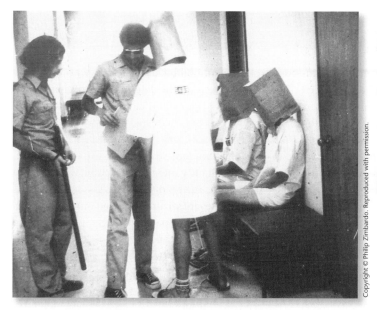

Copyright © Philip Zimbardo. Reproduced with permission.

© AFP/Getty Images

The recent Abu Ghraib prison scandal in Iraq has sparked renewed interest in the Stanford Prison Simulation. Some of the photos taken of the abuse at Abu Ghraib (right) are stunningly similar to photos from the Stanford study (left). For instance, in both cases, the guards "dehumanized" their prisoners by placing bags over their heads.

the guards, collectively they became mean, malicious, and abusive in fulfilling their responsibilities. How did the prisoners react? A few of them showed signs of emotional disturbance and had to be released early, but they mostly became listless, apathetic, and demoralized. The study was designed to run two weeks, but Zimbardo decided to end it prematurely after just six days because he was concerned about the rapidly escalating abuse and degradation of the prisoners. The subjects were debriefed, offered counseling, and sent home.

How did Zimbardo and his colleagues explain the stunning transformations of their subjects? First, they attributed the participants' behavior to the enormous influence of social roles. **Social roles are widely shared expectations about how people in certain positions are supposed to behave.** We have role expectations for salespeople, waiters, ministers, medical patients, students, bus drivers, tourists, flight attendants, and, of course, prison guards and prisoners. The participants had a rough idea of what it meant to act like a guard or a prisoner, and they were gradually consumed by their roles (Haney & Zimbardo, 1998). Second, the researchers attributed their subjects' behavior to the compelling power of situational factors. Before the study began, the tests and interviews showed no measureable differences in personality or character between those randomly assigned to be guards versus prisoners. The stark differences in their behavior had to be due to the radically different situations that they found themselves in. As Haney and Zimbardo (1998) put it, the study "demonstrated the power of situations to overwhelm

people and elicit from them unexpectedly cruel, yet 'situationally appropriate' behavior" (p. 719). As a result, Zimbardo, like Milgram before him, concluded that situational pressures can lead normal, decent people to behave in sinister, repugnant ways.

Although the Stanford Prison Simulation was conducted over 30 years ago, renewed interest in the study was sparked by the recent Abu Ghraib prison scandal in Iraq. American military personnel with little or no experience in running prisons were found to have engaged in "sadistic, blatant, and wanton criminal abuses" of their Iraqi prisoners (Hersh, 2004). Some of the photos taken of the abuse at Abu Ghraib are eerily reminiscent of photos from the Stanford simulation. The U.S. government blamed these horrific abuses on "a few bad apples" who were presumed to be pathological or morally deficient, writing off the incident as an aberration. Yet the evidence from the Stanford Prison Simulation clearly suggests otherwise. Phil Zimbardo (2004, 2005) argues, and has testified as an expert witness, that it is far more likely that situational pressures led normal, average Americans to commit morally reprehensible abuses. This explanation does *not* absolve the brutal guards of responsibility for their behavior. However, Zimbardo emphasizes that making scapegoats out of a handful of guards does not solve the real problem, which lies in the system. He maintains that abuses in prisons are more likely than not and can only be reduced if authorities provide extensive training and strong supervision for guards, enact explicit sanctions for abuses, and maintain clear accountability in the chain of command.

Web Link 15.6

Stanford Prison Experiment
The Stanford Prison Simulation is one of psychology's most renowned studies. At this site, Phil Zimbardo provides a fascinating slide show explaining the study in depth. The site also includes discussion questions, reflections on the study 30 years after it was conducted, and links to a host of related materials. The links include recent writings by Zimbardo that analyze the Abu Ghraib prison scandal.

PREVIEW QUESTIONS

- What is the bystander effect?
- What processes contribute to reduced individual productivity in larger groups?
- What is group polarization?
- What are the antecedent conditions and symptoms of groupthink?

Social psychologists study groups as well as individuals, but exactly what is a group? Are all the divorced fathers living in Baltimore a group? Are three strangers moving skyward in an elevator a group? What if the elevator gets stuck? How about four students from your psychology class who study together regularly? How about a jury working to render a verdict in a trial? The Boston Celtics? Some of these collections of people are groups and others aren't. Let's examine the concept of a group to find out which of these collections qualify.

In social psychologists' eyes, **a *group* consists of two or more individuals who interact and are interdependent.** The divorced fathers in Baltimore aren't likely to qualify on either count. Strangers sharing an elevator might interact briefly, but they're not interdependent. However, if the elevator gets stuck and they have to deal with an emergency together, they could suddenly become a group. Your psychology classmates who study together qualify as a group, since they interact and depend on each other to achieve shared goals. So do the members of a jury and a sports team such as the Celtics. Historically, most groups have interacted on a face-to-face basis, but advances in telecommunications are rapidly changing that situation. In the era of the Internet, people can interact, become interdependent, and develop a group identity without ever meeting in person (Bargh & McKenna, 2004; McKenna & Bargh, 1998).

Behavior Alone and in Groups: The Case of the Bystander Effect

Imagine that you have a precarious medical condition and that you must go through life worrying about whether someone will leap forward to provide help if the need ever arises. Wouldn't you feel more secure around larger groups? After all, there's "safety in numbers." Logically, as group size increases, the probability of having a good Samaritan on the scene increases. Or does it? We've seen before that human behavior isn't necessarily logical. When it comes to helping behavior, many studies have uncovered an apparent paradox called the ***bystander effect: People are less likely to provide needed help when they are in groups than when they are alone.***

Evidence that your probability of getting help *declines* as group size increases was first described by

John Darley and Bibb Latané (1968), who were conducting research on the determinants of helping behavior. In the Darley and Latané study, students in individual cubicles connected by an intercom participated in discussion groups of three sizes. Early in the discussion, a student who was an experimental accomplice hesitantly mentioned that he was prone to seizures. Later in the discussion, the same accomplice faked a severe seizure and cried out for help. Although a majority of participants sought assistance for the student, the tendency to seek help *declined* with increasing group size.

Similar trends have been seen in many other experiments, in which over 6000 subjects have had opportunities to respond to apparent emergencies, including fires, asthma attacks, faintings, crashes, and flat tires, as well as less pressing needs to answer a door or to pick up objects dropped by a stranger. Pooling the results of this research, Latané and Nida (1981) estimated that participants who were alone provided help 75% of the time, whereas participants in the presence of others provided help only 53% of the time.

What accounts for the bystander effect? A number of factors may be at work. For instance, the *diffusion of responsibility* that occurs in a group is important. If you're by yourself when you encounter someone in need of help, the responsibility to provide help rests squarely on your shoulders. However, if other people are present, the responsibility is divided among you, and you may all say to yourselves "Someone else will help." A reduced sense of responsibility may contribute to other aspects of behavior in groups, as we'll see in the next section.

Group Productivity and Social Loafing

Have you ever driven through a road construction project—at a snail's pace, of course—and become irritated because so many workers seem to be just standing around? Maybe the irony of the posted sign "Your tax dollars at work" made you imagine that they were all dawdling. And then again, perhaps not. Individuals' productivity often does decline in larger groups (Latané, Williams, & Harkins, 1979).

Two factors appear to contribute to reduced individual productivity in larger groups. One factor is *reduced efficiency* resulting from the *loss of coordination* among workers' efforts. As you put more people on a yearbook staff, for instance, you'll probably create more and more duplication of effort and increase how often group members end up working at cross purposes.

The second factor contributing to low productivity in groups involves *effort* rather than efficiency. **Social loafing is a reduction in effort by individuals when they work in groups as compared to when they work by themselves.** To investigate social loafing, Latané et al. (1979) measured the sound output produced by subjects who were asked to cheer or clap as loudly as they could. So they couldn't see or hear other group members, participants were told that the study concerned the importance of sensory feedback and were asked to don blindfolds and put on headphones through which loud noise was played. This maneuver permitted a simple deception: Subjects were led to *believe* that they were working alone or in a group of two or six, when in fact *individual* output was actually measured.

When subjects *thought* that they were working in larger groups, their individual output declined. Because lack of coordination could not affect individual output, the participants' decreased sound production had to be attributable to reduced effort. Latané and his colleagues also had the same subjects clap and shout in genuine groups of two and six and found an additional decrease in production that was attributed to loss of coordination. **Figure 15.15** shows how social loafing and loss of coordination combined to reduce productivity as group size increased.

Social loafing and the bystander effect appear to share a common cause: diffusion of responsibility in groups (Comer, 1995; Latané, 1981). As group size increases, the responsibility for getting a job done is divided among more people, and many group members ease up because their individual contribution is less recognizable. Thus, social loafing occurs in situations where individuals can "hide in the crowd." Consistent with this line of thinking, research shows that social loafing is more likely (a) in larger groups, (b) on tasks where individual output is hard to evaluate, and (c) in situations where group members expect their co-workers to perform well and "carry them" (Karau & Williams, 1993).

Cultural factors also influence the likelihood of social loafing. Studies with subjects from Japan, China, and Taiwan suggest that social loafing may be less prevalent in collectivistic cultures, which place a high priority on meeting group goals and contributing to one's ingroups (Karau & Williams, 1995; Smith, 2001).

concept **check** 15.4

Scrutinizing Common Sense

Check your understanding of the implications of research in social psychology by indicating whether the common sense assertions listed below have been supported by empirical findings. Do the trends in research summarized in this chapter indicate that the following statements are true or false? The answers are in Appendix A.

_____ **1.** Generally, in forming their impressions of others, people don't judge a book by its cover.

_____ **2.** When it comes to attraction, birds of a feather flock together.

_____ **3.** In the realm of love, opposites attract.

_____ **4.** If you're the target of persuasion, to be forewarned is to be forearmed.

_____ **5.** When you need help, there's safety in numbers.

Decision Making in Groups

Productivity is not the only issue that commonly concerns groups. When people join together in groups, they often have to make decisions about what the group will do and how it will use its resources. Whether it's your study group deciding what

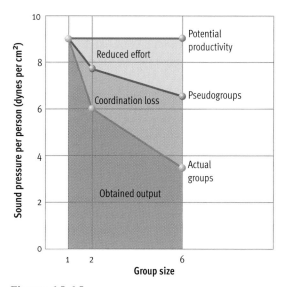

Figure 15.15

The effect of loss of coordination and social loafing on group productivity. The amount of sound produced per person declined noticeably when subjects worked in actual groups of two or six (orange line). This decrease in productivity reflects both loss of coordination and social loafing. Sound per person also declined when subjects merely thought they were working in groups of two or six (purple line). This smaller decrease in productivity is attributed to social loafing.

Source: Adapted from Latané, B., Williams, K., & Harkins, S. (1979). Many hands make light the work: The causes and consequences of social loafing. *Journal of Personality and Social Psychology, 37*, 822–832. Copyright © 1979 by the American Psychological Association. Adapted by permission of the author.

© Pictor International/ImageState/Alamy

Many types of groups have to arrive at collective decisions. The social dynamics of group decisions are complicated, and a variety of factors can undermine effective decision making.

type of pizza to order, a jury deciding on a verdict, or Congress deciding whether to pass a bill, groups make decisions. Social psychologists have discovered some interesting tendencies in group decision making. We'll take a brief look at two of these, *group polarization* and *groupthink*.

Group Polarization

Who leans toward more cautious decisions: individuals or groups? Common sense suggests that groups will work out compromises that cancel out members' extreme views. Hence, the collective wisdom of the group should yield relatively conservative choices. Is common sense correct? To investigate this question, Stoner (1961) asked individual participants to give their recommendations on tough decisions and then asked the same subjects to engage in group discussion to arrive at joint recommendations. When Stoner compared individuals' average recommendation against their group decision generated through discussion, he found that groups arrived at *riskier* decisions than individuals did. Stoner's finding was replicated in other studies (Pruitt, 1971), and the phenomenon acquired the name *risky shift*.

However, investigators eventually determined that groups can shift either way, toward risk or caution, depending on which way the group is leaning to begin with (Friedkin, 1999; Myers & Lamm, 1976). A shift toward a more extreme position, an effect called *polarization,* is often the result of group discussion (Tindale, Kameda, & Hinsz, 2003). Thus, **group polarization occurs when group discussion strengthens a group's dominant point of view and produces a shift toward a more extreme decision in that direction** (see **Figure 15.16**). Group polarization does not involve widening the gap between factions in a group, as its name might suggest. In fact, group polarization can contribute to consensus in a group, as we'll see in our discussion of groupthink.

Groupthink

In contrast to group polarization, which is a normal process in group dynamics, groupthink is more like a "disease" that can infect decision making in groups. **Groupthink occurs when members of a cohesive group emphasize concurrence at the expense of critical thinking in arriving at a decision.** As you might imagine, groupthink doesn't produce very effective decision making. Indeed, groupthink often leads to major blunders that may look incomprehensible after the fact. Irving Janis (1972) first described groupthink in his effort to explain how President John F. Kennedy and his advisers could have miscalculated so badly in deciding to invade Cuba at the Bay of Pigs in 1961. The attempted invasion failed miserably and, in retrospect, seemed remarkably ill-conceived. Applying his many years of research on group dynamics to the Bay of Pigs fiasco, Janis developed a model of groupthink, which is summarized in **Figure 15.17**.

When groups get caught up in groupthink, members suspend their critical judgment and the group starts censoring dissent as the pressure to conform

Before group discussion   **After group discussion**

Group average   Group average

Example 1

−   +   −   +

Neutral   Neutral
Views held by individual group members   Views held by individual group members

Group average   Group average

Example 2

−   +   −   +

Neutral   Neutral
Views held by individual group members   Views held by individual group members

Figure 15.16

Group polarization. Two examples of group polarization are diagrammed here. In the first example (top) a group starts out mildly opposed to an idea, but after discussion sentiment against the idea is stronger. In the second example (bottom), a group starts out with a favorable disposition toward an idea, and this disposition is strengthened by group discussion.

increases. Soon, everyone begins to think alike. More-over, "mind guards" try to shield the group from information that contradicts the group's view. If the group's view is challenged from outside, victims of groupthink tend to think in simplistic "us versus them" terms. Members begin to overestimate the ingroup's unanimity, and they begin to view the outgroup as the enemy. Groupthink also promotes incomplete gathering of information. Like individuals, groups often display a confirmation bias, as they tend to seek and focus on information that supports their initial views (Schulz-Hardt et al., 2000).

What causes groupthink? One key precondition is high group cohesiveness. *Group cohesiveness* **refers to the strength of the liking relationships linking group members to each other and to the group itself.** Members of cohesive groups are close-knit, are committed, have "team spirit," and are loyal to the group. Cohesiveness itself isn't bad. It can help groups achieve great things. But Janis maintains that the danger of groupthink is greater when groups are highly cohesive. Groupthink is also more likely when a group works in relative isolation, when its power structure is dominated by a strong, directive leader, and when it is under pressure to make a major decision quickly (see **Figure 15.17**).

Only a handful of experiments have been conducted to test Janis's theory, because the antecedent conditions thought to foster groupthink—such as high decision stress, strong group cohesiveness, and dominating leadership—are difficult to create effectively in laboratory settings (Aldag & Fuller, 1993). The evidence on groupthink consists mostly of retrospective case studies of major decision-making fiascos (Eaton, 2001). Thus, Janis's model of group-

think should probably be characterized as an innovative, sophisticated, intuitively appealing theory that needs to be subjected to much more empirical study (Esser, 1998).

Antecedent conditions
1. High cohesiveness
2. Insulation of the group
3. Lack of methodical procedures for search and appraisal
4. Directive leadership
5. High stress with low degree of hope for finding better solution than the one favored by the leader or other influential persons

Concurrence-seeking tendency

Symptoms of groupthink
1. Illusion of invulnerability
2. Collective rationalization
3. Belief in inherent morality of the group
4. Stereotypes of outgroups
5. Direct pressure on dissenters
6. Self-censorship
7. Illusion of unanimity
8. Self-appointed mind guards

Symptoms of defective decision making
1. Incomplete survey of alternatives
2. Incomplete survey of objectives
3. Failure to examine risks of preferred choice
4. Poor information search
5. Selective bias in processing information at hand
6. Failure to reappraise alternatives
7. Failure to work out contingency plans

Figure 15.17

Overview of Janis's model of groupthink. The contributing conditions, symptoms, and resultant effects of groupthink described by Janis (1972) are outlined here. Although his model of groupthink has been influential, practical difficulties have limited research on the theory.

Source: Adapted from Janis, I. L., & Mann, L. (1977). *Decision making: A psychological analysis of conflict, choice and commitment.* New York: Free Press. Adapted with permission of The Free Press, a Division of Simon & Schuster. Copyright © 1977 by The Free Press.

Web Link 15.7

Group Dynamics
Donelson Forsyth of Virginia Commonwealth University maintains this excellent site devoted to the dynamics of group interaction. Topics of interest include group structure, group cohesiveness, influence in groups, conflict in groups, and the history of research on groups. The site also houses a rich set of links to organizations that study groups.

> Reflecting on the Chapter's Themes

Our discussion of social psychology has provided a final embellishment on four of our seven unifying themes: psychology's commitment to empiricism, the importance of cultural factors, multifactorial causation, and the extent to which people's experience of the world is highly subjective. Let's consider the virtues of empiricism first.

It's easy to question the need to do scientific research on social behavior, because studies in social psychology often seem to verify common sense. While most people wouldn't presume to devise their own theory of color vision or question the significance of REM sleep, everyone has beliefs about the nature of

love, how to persuade others, and the limits of obedience. Thus, when studies demonstrate that credibility enhances persuasion or that good looks facilitate attraction, it's tempting to conclude that social psychologists go to great lengths to document the obvious, and some critics say, "Why bother?"

You saw why in this chapter. Research in social psychology has repeatedly shown that the predictions of logic and common sense are often wrong. Consider just a few examples. Even psychiatric experts failed to predict the remarkable obedience to authority uncovered in Milgram's research. The bystander effect in helping behavior violates cold-blooded

 Empiricism

 Cultural Heritage

 Multifactorial Causation

 Subjectivity of Experience

mathematical logic. Dissonance research has shown that after a severe initiation, the bigger the letdown, the more favorable people's feelings are. These findings defy common sense.

Thus, research on social behavior provides dramatic illustrations of why psychologists put their faith in empiricism. The moral of social psychology's story is this: Although scientific research often supports ideas based on common sense and logic, we can't count on this result. If psychologists want to achieve sound understanding of the principles governing behavior, they have to put their ideas to an empirical test.

Our coverage of social psychology also demonstrated once again that behavior is characterized by both cultural variance and invariance. Although basic social phenomena such as stereotyping, attraction, obedience, and conformity probably occur all over the world, cross-cultural studies of social behavior show that research findings based on American samples may not generalize precisely to other cultures. Our discussion of social behavior also demonstrated once again that behavior is determined by multiple causes. For example, we saw how a variety of factors influence the processes of person perception, interpersonal attraction, and persuasion.

Research in social psychology is also uniquely well suited for making the point that people's view of the world is highly personal and subjective. In this chapter we saw how physical appearance can color perceptions of a person's ability or personality, how social schemas can lead people to see what they expect to see in their interactions with others, how pressure to conform can make people begin to doubt their senses, and how groupthink can lead group members down a perilous path of shared illusions.

The subjectivity of social perception will surface once again in our applications for the chapter. The Personal Application focuses on prejudice, a practical problem that social psychologists have shown great interest in, whereas the Critical Thinking Application examines aspects of social influence.

PERSONAL *Application*

Understanding Prejudice

Answer the following "true" or "false."
_____ 1 Prejudice and discrimination amount to the same thing.
_____ 2 Stereotypes are always negative or unflattering.
_____ 3 Ethnic and racial groups are the only widespread targets of prejudice in modern society.

James Byrd Jr., a 49-year-old black man, was walking home from a family gathering in the summer of 1998 when he was offered a ride by three white men, one of whom he knew. Shortly thereafter, pieces of Byrd's savagely beaten body were found strewn along a rural road in Texas. Apparently, he had been beaten, then shackled by his ankles to the back of the truck and dragged to death over 2 miles of road. Police say that Byrd was targeted simply because he was black. Thankfully, such tragic events are relatively rare in the United States. Nonetheless, they remind us that prejudice and discrimination are *major* social problems.

Prejudice can harm victims' self-concepts, suppress their potential, create enormous stress in their lives, and promote tension and strife between groups (Dion, 2003). The first step toward reducing prejudice is to understand its roots. Hence, in this Application we'll strive to achieve a better understanding of why prejudice is so common. Along the way, you'll learn the answers to the true-false questions above.

Prejudice and discrimination are closely related concepts, and the terms have become nearly interchangeable in popular use. Social scientists, however, prefer to define their terms precisely, so let's clarify which is which. *Prejudice* **is a negative attitude held toward members of a group.** Like other attitudes, prejudice can include three components (see **Figure 15.18**): beliefs ("Indians are mostly alcoholics"), emotions ("I despise Jews"), and behavioral dispositions ("I wouldn't hire a Mexican"). Racial prejudice receives the lion's share of publicity, but prejudice is not limited to ethnic groups. Women, homosexuals, the aged, the disabled, and the mentally ill are also targets of widespread prejudice. Thus, many people hold prejudicial attitudes toward one group or another, and many have been victims of prejudice.

Prejudice may lead to ***discrimination***, **which involves behaving differently, usually unfairly, toward the members of a group.** Prejudice and discrimination tend to go hand in hand, but attitudes and behavior do not necessarily correspond (see **Figure 15.19**). In our discussion, we'll concentrate primarily on the attitude of prejudice. Let's begin by looking at processes in person perception that promote prejudice.

Stereotyping and Subjectivity in Person Perception

Perhaps no factor plays a larger role in prejudice than *stereotypes*. However, stereotypes

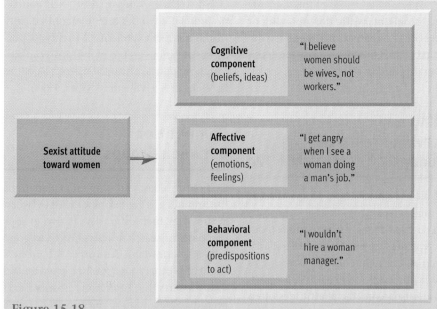

Cognitive component
(beliefs, ideas)

"I believe women should be wives, not workers."

Affective component
(emotions, feelings)

"I get angry when I see a woman doing a man's job."

Behavioral component
(predispositions to act)

"I wouldn't hire a woman manager."

Sexist attitude toward women

Figure 15.18

The three potential components of prejudice as an attitude. Attitudes can consist of up to three components. The tricomponent model of attitudes, applied to prejudice against women, would view sexism as negative beliefs about women (cognitive component) that lead to emotional reactions (affective component), and promote a readiness to discriminate against women (behavioral component).

© Associated Press/AP

Members of many types of groups are victims of prejudice. Besides racial minorities, others that have been stereotyped and discriminated against include gays and lesbians, women, the homeless, and those who are overweight.

are not inevitably negative. Although a massive overgeneralization, it's hardly insulting to assert that Americans are ambitious or that the Japanese are industrious. Unfortunately, many people *do* subscribe to derogatory stereotypes of various ethnic groups. Studies suggest that negative racial stereotypes have diminished over the last 50 years, but they're not a thing of the past (Madon et al., 2001; Mellor, 2003). According to a variety of investigators, modern racism has merely become more subtle (Devine, Plant, & Blair, 2001; Dovidio & Gaertner, 1999, 2000).

Research indicates that stereotypes are highly accessible cognitive schemas that are readily activated, even in people who truly renounce prejudice (Amodio et al., 2004; Fiske, 2000). Thus, a heterosexual man who rejects prejudice against homosexuals may still feel uncomfortable sitting next to a gay male on a bus, even though he regards his reaction as inappropriate.

Stereotypes also persist because the *subjectivity* of person perception makes it likely that people will see what they expect to see when they actually come into contact with members of groups that they view with prejudice (Dunning & Sherman, 1997). For example, Duncan (1976) had white subjects

watch and evaluate interaction on a TV monitor that was supposedly live (actually it was a videotape), and he varied the race of a person who gets into an argument and gives another person a slight shove. The shove was coded as "violent behavior" by 73% of the participants when the actor was black but by only 13% of the participants when the actor was white. As we've noted before, people's perceptions are highly subjective. Because of stereotypes, even "violence" may lie in the eye of the beholder.

Memory biases are also tilted in favor of confirming people's prejudices (Ybarra, Stephan, & Schaberg, 2000). For example, if a man believes that "women are not cut out for leadership roles," he may dwell with delight on his female supervisor's mistakes and quickly forget about her achievements. Thus, the *illusory correlation effect* can contribute to the maintenance of prejudicial stereotypes (Berndsen et al., 2002).

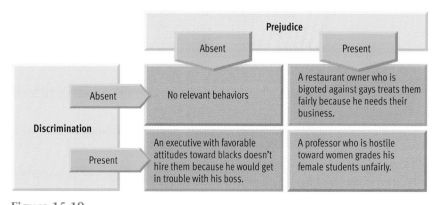

Prejudice

		Absent	Present
Discrimination	Absent	No relevant behaviors	A restaurant owner who is bigoted against gays treats them fairly because he needs their business.
	Present	An executive with favorable attitudes toward blacks doesn't hire them because he would get in trouble with his boss.	A professor who is hostile toward women grades his female students unfairly.

Figure 15.19

Relationship between prejudice and discrimination. As these examples show, prejudice can exist without discrimination and discrimination without prejudice. In the green cells, there is a disparity between attitude and behavior.

Biases in Attribution

Attribution processes can also help perpetuate stereotypes and prejudice. Research taking its cue from Weiner's (1980) model of attribution has shown that people often make *biased attributions for success and failure*. For example, men and women don't get equal credit for their successes (Swim & Sanna, 1996). Observers often discount a woman's success by attributing it to good luck, sheer effort, or the ease of the task (except on traditional feminine tasks). In comparison, a man's success is more likely to be attributed to his outstanding ability. **Figure 15.20** shows how gender bias tends to affect attributions for success and failure. These biased patterns of attribution help sustain the stereotype that men are more competent than women. Similar patterns of bias have been seen in attributional explanations of ethnic minorities' successes and failures (Jackson, Sullivan, & Hodge, 1993; Kluegel, 1990).

Recall that the *fundamental attribution error* is a slant toward explaining events by pointing to the personal characteristics of the actors as causes (internal attributions). Research suggests that people are particularly likely to make this error when evaluating targets of prejudice (Hewstone, 1990). Thus, when people take note of ethnic neighborhoods dominated by crime and poverty, they blame the personal qualities of the residents for these problems, while downplaying or ignoring other explanations emphasizing situational factors (job discrimination, poor police service, and so on).

Forming and Preserving Prejudicial Attitudes

If prejudice is an attitude, where does it come from? Many prejudices appear to be handed down as a legacy from parents (Ponterotto & Pedersen, 1993). Prejudicial attitudes can be found in children as young as ages 4 or 5 (Aboud & Amato, 2001). Research suggests that parents' racial attitudes often influence their children's racial attitudes (Sinclair, Dunn, & Lowery, 2004). This transmission of prejudice across generations presumably depends to some extent on *observational learning*. For example, if a young boy hears his father ridicule homosexuals, his exposure to his father's attitude is likely to affect his attitude about gays. If the young boy then goes to school and makes disparaging remarks about gays that are reinforced by approval from peers, his prejudice will be strengthened through *operant conditioning*. Consistent with this analysis, one study found that college students' opinions on racial issues were swayed by overhearing others voice racist or antiracist sentiments (Blanchard, Lilly, & Vaughn, 1991). Of course, prejudicial attitudes are not acquired only through direct experience. Stereotypic portrayals of various groups in the media can also foster prejudicial attitudes (Herrett-Skjellum & Allen, 1996; Williams & Giles, 1998).

Competition Between Groups

One of the oldest and simplest explanations for prejudice is that competition between groups can fuel animosity. If two groups compete for scarce resources, such as good jobs and affordable housing, one group's gain is the other's loss. *Realistic group conflict theory* asserts that intergroup hostility and prejudice are a natural outgrowth of fierce competition between groups.

A classic study at Robbers' Cave State Park in Oklahoma provided support for this theory many years ago (Sherif et al., 1961). The subjects were 11-year-old white boys attending a three-week summer camp at the park, who did not know that the camp counselors were actually researchers (their parents knew). The boys were randomly assigned to one of two groups. During the first week, the boys got to know the other members of their own group through typical camp activities and developed a group identity, choosing to call themselves the Rattlers and the Eagles. In the second week, the Rattlers and Eagles were put into a series of competitive situations, such as a football game, a treasure hunt, and a tug of war, with trophies and other prizes at stake. As predicted by realistic group conflict theory, hostile feelings quickly erupted between the two groups, as food fights broke out in the mess hall, cabins were ransacked, and group flags were burned. If competition between innocent groups of children pursuing trivial prizes can foster hostility, you can imagine what is likely to happen when adults from very different backgrounds battle for genuinely important resources. Research has repeatedly shown that conflict over scarce resources can fuel prejudice and discrimination (Bourhis & Gagnon, 2001). Even the mere *perception* of competition can breed prejudice (Zarate et al., 2004).

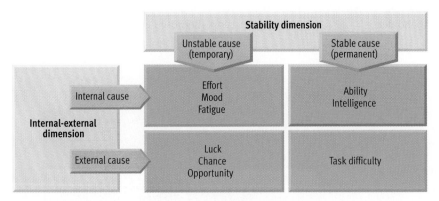

Figure 15.20

Bias in the attributions used to explain success and failure by men and women. Attributions about the two sexes often differ. For example, men's successes tend to be attributed to their ability and intelligence (blue cell), whereas women's successes tend to be attributed to hard work, good luck, or low task difficulty (green cells). These attributional biases help to perpetuate the belief that men are more competent than women.

Threats to Social Identity

According to the *social identity perspective,* self-esteem depends on both one's *personal* identity and one's *social* identity (Tajfel & Turner, 1979; Turner et al., 1987). *Social identity* refers to the pride people derive from their memberships in various groups, such as ethnic groups, religious denominations, occupational groups, neighborhoods, country clubs, and so forth. The theory further proposes that self-esteem can be undermined by either threats to personal identity (you didn't get called for that job interview) or social identity (your football team loses a big game). Threats to both personal and social identity may motivate efforts to restore self-esteem, but threats to social identity are more likely to provoke responses that foster prejudice and discrimination. When social identity is threatened, individuals may react in two key ways to bolster it (see **Figure 15.21**). One common response is to show *ingroup favoritism*—for example, tapping an ingroup member for a job opening or rating the performance of an ingroup member higher than that of an outgroup member (Capozza & Brown, 2000). A second common reaction is to engage in *outgroup derogation*—in other words, to "trash" outgroups that are perceived as threatening. Outgroup

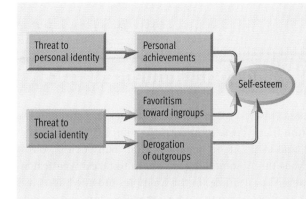

Figure 15.21

Threats to social identity and prejudice. According to Tajfel (1982) and Turner et al. (1987), individuals have both a personal identity (based on a unique sense of self) and a social identity (based on group memberships). When social identity is threatened, people are motivated to restore self-esteem by either showing favoritism to ingroup members or by derogating members of outgroups. These tactics contribute to prejudice and discrimination. (Adapted from Brehm & Kassin, 1993)

derogation is more likely when people identify especially strongly with the threatened ingroup (Levin et al, 2003; Schmitt & Maes, 2002). When people derogate an outgroup, they tend to feel superior as a result, and this feeling helps to affirm their self-worth (Fein & Spencer, 1997). These unfortunate reactions are *not* inevitable, but threats to social identity represent yet another dynamic process that can foster prejudice (Turner & Reynolds, 2001).

Our discussion has shown that a plethora of processes conspire to create and maintain personal prejudices against a diverse array of outgroups. Most of the factors at work reflect normal, routine processes in social behavior. Thus, it is understandable that most people—whether privileged or underprivileged, minority members or majority members—probably harbor some prejudicial attitudes. Our analysis of the causes of prejudice may have permitted you to identify prejudices of your own or their sources. Perhaps it's wishful thinking on my part, but an enhanced awareness of your personal prejudices may help you become a little more tolerant of the endless diversity seen in human behavior. If so, that alone would mean that my efforts in writing this book have been amply rewarded.

Analyzing Credibility and Social Influence Tactics

You can run, but you cannot hide. This statement aptly sums up the situation that exists when it comes to persuasion and social influence. There is no way to evade the constant, never-ending efforts of others to shape your attitudes and behavior. In this Application we will discuss two topics that can enhance your resistance to manipulation. First, we will outline some ideas that can be useful in evaluating the credibility of a persuasive source. Second, we will describe some widely used social influence strategies that it pays to know about.

Evaluating Credibility

The salesperson at your local health food store swears that a specific herb combination improves memory and helps people stay healthy. A popular singer touts a psychic hotline, where the operators can "really help" with the important questions in life. Speakers at a "historical society" meeting claim that the Holocaust never happened. These are just a few real-life examples of how people attempt to persuade the public to believe something. In these examples, the "something" people are expected to believe runs counter to the conventional or scientific view, but who is to say who is right? After all, people are entitled to their own opinions, aren't they?

Yes, people *are* entitled to their own opinions, but that does not mean that all opinions are equally valid. Some opinions are just plain wrong and others are highly questionable. People are not equally believable. In deciding what to believe, it is important to carefully examine the evidence presented and the logic of the argument that supports the conclusion (see the Critical Thinking Application for Chapter 9). In deciding what to believe, you also need to decide *whom* to believe, a task that requires assessing the *credibility* of the source of the information. Let's look at some questions that can provide guidance in this process.

Does the source have a vested interest in the issue at hand? If the source is likely to benefit in some way from convincing you of something, you need to take a skeptical attitude. In the examples provided here, it is easy to see how the sales clerk and popular singer will benefit if you buy the products they are selling, but what about the so-called historical society? How would members benefit by convincing large numbers of people that the Holocaust never happened? Like the sales clerk and singer, they are also selling something, in this case a particular view of history that they hope will influence future events in certain ways. Of course, the fact that these sources have a vested interest does not necessarily mean that their arguments are invalid. But a source's credibility needs to be evaluated with extra caution when the person or group has something to gain.

What are the source's credentials? Does the person have any special training, an advanced degree, or any other basis for claiming special knowledge about the topic? The usual training for a sales clerk or singer does not include how to assess research results in medical journals or to evaluate claims of psychic powers. The Holocaust deniers are more difficult to evaluate. Some of them have studied history and written books on the topic, but the books are mostly self-published, and few of these "experts" hold positions at reputable universities where scholars are subject to peer evaluation. That's *not* to say that legitimate credentials ensure a source's credibility. A number of popular diets that are widely regarded by nutritional experts as worthless, if not hazardous (Drewnowski, 1995; Dwyer, 1995), were created and marketed by genuine physicians. Of course, these physicians have a *vested interest* in the diets, as they have made millions of dollars from them.

Is the information grossly inconsistent with the conventional view on the issue? Just being different from the mainstream view certainly does *not* make a conclusion wrong. But claims that vary radically from most other information on a subject should raise a red flag that leads to careful scrutiny. Bear in mind that charlatans and hucksters are often successful because they typically try to persuade people to believe things that they want to believe. Wouldn't it be great if we could effortlessly enhance our memory, foretell the future, eat all we want and still lose weight, and earn hundreds of dollars per hour working at home? And wouldn't it be nice if the Holocaust never happened? It pays to be wary of wishful thinking.

What was the method of analysis used in reaching the conclusion? The purveyors of miracle cures and psychic advice inevitably rely on anecdotal evidence. But you have already learned about the perils and unreliability of anecdotal evidence (see the Critical Thinking Application for Chapter 2). One method frequently used by charlatans is to undermine the credibility of conventional information by focusing on trivial inconsistencies. This is one of the many strategies used by the people who argue that the Holocaust never occurred. They question the credibility of thousands of historical documents, photographs, and artifacts and the testimony of countless people by highlighting small inconsistencies among historical records relating to trivial matters, such as the number of people transported to a concentration camp in a specific week or the number of bodies that could be disposed of in a single day (Shermer, 1997). Some inconsistencies are exactly what one should expect based on piecing together multiple accounts from sources working with different portions of incomplete information. But the strategy of focusing on trivial inconsistencies is a standard method for raising doubts about credible information.

Recognizing Social Influence Strategies

It pays to understand social influence strategies because advertisers, salespeople, and fundraisers—not to mention friends and neighbors—frequently rely on them to manipulate people's behavior. Let's look at four basic strategies: the foot-in-the-door technique, misuse of the reciprocity norm, the lowball technique, and feigned scarcity.

Door-to-door salespeople have long recognized the importance of gaining a *little* cooperation from sales targets (getting a "foot in the door") before hitting them with the real sales pitch. The *foot-in-the-door technique* **involves getting people to agree to a small request to increase the chances that they will agree to a larger request later.** This technique is widely used in all walks of life. For example, groups seeking donations often ask people to simply sign a petition first.

In an early study of the foot-in-the-door technique (Freedman & Fraser, 1966), the large request involved asking homemakers whether a team of six men doing consumer research could come into their home to classify *all* their household products. Only 22% of the control subjects agreed to this outlandish request. However, when the same request was made three days after a small request (to answer a few questions about soap preferences), 53% of the participants agreed to the larger request. Why does the foot-in-the-door technique work? According to Burger (1999), quite a variety of processes contribute to its effectiveness, including people's tendency to try to behave consistently (with their initial response) and their reluctance to renege on their sense of commitment to the person who made the initial request.

Most of us have been socialized to believe in the *reciprocity norm*—**the rule that we should pay back in kind what we receive from others.** Robert Cialdini (2001) has written extensively about how the reciprocity norm is used in social influence efforts. For example, groups seeking donations routinely send address labels, key rings, and other small gifts with their pleas. Salespeople using the reciprocity principle distribute free samples to prospective customers. When they return a few days later, most of the customers feel obligated to buy some of their products. The reciprocity rule is meant to promote fair exchanges in social interactions. However, when people manipulate the reciprocity norm, they usually give some-

Advertisers often try to artificially create scarcity to make their products seem more desirable.

© Tony Freeman/PhotoEdit

thing of minimal value in the hopes of getting far more in return (Howard, 1995).

The lowball technique is even more deceptive. The name for this technique derives from a common practice in automobile sales, in which a customer is offered a terrific bargain on a car. The bargain price gets the customer to commit to buying the car. Soon after this commitment is made, however, the dealer starts revealing some hidden costs. Typically, the customer learns that options assumed to be included in the original price are actually going to cost extra or that a promised low loan rate has "fallen through." Once they have committed to buying a car, most customers are unlikely to cancel the deal. Thus, **the lowball technique involves getting someone to commit to a seemingly attractive proposition before its hidden costs are revealed.** Car dealers aren't the only ones who use this technique, which is a surprisingly effective strategy (Cialdini & Trost, 1998).

A number of years ago, Jack Brehm (1966) demonstrated that telling people they can't have something only makes them want it more. This phenomenon helps explain why companies often try to create the impression that their products are in scarce supply. Scarcity threatens your freedom to choose a product, thus creating an increased desire for the scarce commodity. Advertisers frequently feign scarcity to drive up the demand for products. Thus, we constantly see ads that scream "limited supply available," "for a limited time only," "while they last," and "time is running out." Like genuine scarcity, feigned scarcity can enhance the desirability of a commodity (Highhouse et al., 1998; Lynn, 1992).

In summary, people use quite a variety of "tricks" in their efforts to manipulate each other. The more you know about such strategies, the less likely you are to be taken in by them.

Table 15.1 Critical Thinking Skills Discussed in This Application

Skill	Description
Judging the credibility of an information source	The critical thinker understands that credibility and bias are central to determining the quality of information and looks at factors such as vested interests, credentials, and appropriate expertise.
Recognizing social influence strategies	The critical thinker is aware of manipulative tactics such as the foot-in-the-door and lowball techniques, misuse of the reciprocity norm, and feigned scarcity.

Key Ideas

Person Perception: Forming Impressions of Others

● Perceptions of others can be distorted by a variety of factors, including physical appearance. People attribute desirable personality characteristics and competence to those who are good-looking. People use social schemas to categorize others into types.

● Stereotypes may lead people to see what they expect to see and to overestimate how often they see it. Evolutionary psychologists argue that many biases in person perception were adaptive in humans' ancestral past.

Attribution Processes: Explaining Behavior

● Internal attributions ascribe behavior to personal dispositions and traits, whereas external attributions locate the cause of behavior in the environment. Weiner's model proposes that attributions for success and failure should be analyzed in terms of the stability of causes, as well as along the internal-external dimension.

● Observers favor internal attributions to explain another's behavior (the fundamental attribution error), while actors favor external attributions to explain their own behavior. The self-serving bias is the tendency to attribute one's good outcomes to personal factors and one's bad outcomes to situational factors. Cultures vary in their emphasis on individualism as opposed to collectivism, and these differences appear to influence attributional tendencies.

Interpersonal Attraction: Liking and Loving

● People tend to like and love others who are similar, who reciprocate expressions of affection, and who are physically attractive. Romantic ideals influence the progress of intimate relationships.

● Some theorists have distinguished between passionate love and companionate love, which can be subdivided into intimacy and commitment. Hazan and Shaver's theory suggests that love relationships in adulthood mimic attachment patterns in infancy. Hence, people tend to exhibit secure, anxious-ambivalent, or avoidant attachment styles in their romantic relationships.

● Cultures vary considerably in their emphasis on passionate love as a prerequisite for marriage. According to evolutionary psychologists, certain aspects of good looks influence attraction because they are indicators of reproductive fitness. Consistent with evolutionary theory, gender differences in mating preferences appear to transcend culture. Mate poaching is common and appears to be universal across cultures.

Attitudes: Making Social Judgments

● Attitudes may be made up of cognitive, affective, and behavioral components. Attitudes vary in strength, accessibility, and ambivalence. A source of persuasion who is credible, expert, trustworthy, and likable tends to be relatively effective. Two-sided arguments and fear arousal tend to be effective in persuasive efforts.

● Persuasion is more difficult when a receiver is forewarned, when the source advocates a position that is incompatible with the receiver's existing attitudes, or when the source tries to change strong attitudes.

● Attitudes may be shaped through classical conditioning, operant conditioning, and observational learning. Dissonance theory asserts that inconsistent attitudes cause tension and that people alter their attitudes to reduce dissonance. The elaboration likelihood model holds that the central route to persuasion tends to yield longer-lasting attitude change than the peripheral route.

Conformity and Obedience: Yielding to Others

● Asch found that conformity in groups becomes more likely as group size increases, up to a point. In Milgram's landmark study of obedience to authority, adult men drawn from the community showed a remarkable tendency, in spite of their misgivings, to follow orders to shock an innocent stranger. The generalizability of Milgram's findings has stood the test of time, but his work also helped to stimulate stricter ethical standards for research.

● The Stanford Prison Simulation demonstrated that social roles and other situational pressures can exert tremendous influence over social be-

havior. Like Milgram, Zimbardo showed that situational forces can lead normal people to exhibit surprisingly callous, abusive behavior.

Behavior in Groups: Joining with Others

● People who help someone in need when alone are less likely to provide help when a group is present. The bystander effect occurs primarily because a group creates diffusion of responsibility. Productivity often declines in larger groups because of loss of coordination and social loafing.

● Group polarization occurs when a group shifts toward a more extreme decision in the direction it was already leaning. In groupthink, a cohesive group suspends critical judgment in a misguided effort to promote agreement in decision making.

Reflecting on the Chapter's Themes

● Social psychology illustrates the value of empiricism because research in this area often proves that common sense is wrong. Additionally, research in social psychology demonstrates that people's experience of the world is highly subjective, that culture shapes behavior, and that multifactorial causation is common.

PERSONAL APPLICATION • Understanding Prejudice

● Prejudice is a negative attitude toward a group. Prejudice is supported by subjectivity in person perception, stereotyping, and attributional biases. Negative attitudes about groups are often acquired through observational learning and supported by operant conditioning.

● Realistic group conflict theory posits that competition between groups fosters prejudice. Threats to social identity can lead to ingroup favoritism and outgroup derogation.

CRITICAL THINKING APPLICATION • Analyzing Credibility and Social Influence Tactics

● Useful criteria in judging credibility include whether a source has vested interests or appropriate credentials. One should also consider the method of analysis used in reaching conclusions and why information might not coincide with conventional wisdom.

● To resist manipulative efforts, it helps to be aware of social influence tactics, such as the foot-in-the-door technique, misuse of the reciprocity norm, the lowball technique, and feigned scarcity.

Key Terms

Attitudes (p. 480)
Attributions (p. 471)
Bystander effect (p. 490)
Channel (p. 481)
Cognitive dissonance (p. 483)
Collectivism (p. 473)
Companionate love (p. 477)
Conformity (p. 485)
Discrimination (p. 494)
External attributions (p. 471)
Foot-in-the-door technique
  (p. 499)
Fundamental attribution error
  (p. 472)
Group (p. 490)
Group cohesiveness (p. 493)
Group polarization (p. 492)
Groupthink (p. 492)
Illusory correlation (p. 470)
Individualism (p. 473)
Ingroup (p. 470)
Internal attributions (p. 471)
Interpersonal attraction (p. 475)
Lowball technique (p. 499)
Matching hypothesis (p. 475)

Message (p. 481)
Obedience (p. 486)
Outgroup (p. 470)
Passionate love (p. 477)
Person perception (p. 468)
Prejudice (p. 494)
Receiver (p. 481)
Reciprocity (p. 476)
Reciprocity norm (p. 499)
Self-serving bias (p. 473)
Social loafing (p. 491)
Social psychology (p. 467)
Social roles (p. 489)
Social schemas (p. 469)
Source (p. 481)
Stereotypes (p. 469)

Key People

Solomon Asch (pp. 485–486)
Ellen Berscheid (pp. 476–477)
Leon Festinger (pp. 483–484)
Elaine Hatfield (pp. 476–477)
Fritz Heider (p. 471)
Irving Janis (pp. 492–493)
Stanley Milgram (pp. 486–488)
Philip Zimbardo (pp. 488–489)

1. Stereotypes are:
   A. special types of schemas that are part of people's shared cultural background.
   B. widely held beliefs that people have certain characteristics because of their membership in a particular group.
   C. equivalent to prejudice.
   D. both A and B.

2. You believe that short men have a tendency to be insecure. The concept of illusory correlation implies that you will:
   A. overestimate how often you meet short men who are insecure.
   B. underestimate how often you meet short men who are insecure.
   C. overestimate the frequency of short men in the population.
   D. falsely assume that shortness in men causes insecurity.

3. A father suggests that his son's low marks in school are due to the child's laziness. The father has made _____ attribution.
   A. an external
   B. an internal
   C. a situational
   D. a high consensus

4. Bob explains his failing grade on a term paper by saying that he really didn't work very hard at it. According to Weiner's model, Bob is making an _____ attribution about his failure.
   A. internal-stable
   B. internal-unstable
   C. external-stable
   D. external-unstable

5. The fundamental attribution error refers to the tendency of:
   A. observers to favor external attributions in explaining the behavior of others.
   B. observers to favor internal attributions in explaining the behavior of others.
   C. actors to favor external attributions in explaining the behavior of others.
   D. actors to favor internal attributions in explaining their behavior.

6. Which of the following factors is *not* one that influences interpersonal attraction?
   A. Physical attractiveness
   B. Similarity
   C. Reciprocity
   D. Latitude of acceptance

7. According to Hazan and Shaver (1987):
   A. romantic relationships in adulthood follow the same form as attachment relationships in infancy.
   B. those who had ambivalent attachments in infancy are doomed never to fall in love as adults.
   C. those who had avoidant attachments in infancy often overcompensate by becoming excessively intimate in their adult love relationships.
   D. all of the above are the case.

8. Cross-cultural disparities are most likely to be found in which of the following areas?
   A. What people look for in prospective mates
   B. The positive value of facial symmetry
   C. Passionate love as a prerequisite for marriage
   D. All of the above

9. Which of the following variables does *not* tend to facilitate persuasion?
   A. Source credibility
   B. Source trustworthiness
   C. Forewarning of the receiver
   D. A two-sided argument

10. Cognitive dissonance theory predicts that after people engage in behavior that contradicts their true feelings, they will:
    A. convince themselves they really didn't perform the behavior.
    B. change their attitude to make it more consistent with their behavior.
    C. change their attitude to make it less consistent with their behavior.
    D. do nothing.

11. The elaboration likelihood model of attitude change suggests that:
    A. the peripheral route results in more enduring attitude change.
    B. the central route results in more enduring attitude change.
    C. only the central route to persuasion can be effective.
    D. only the peripheral route to persuasion can be effective.

12. The results of Milgram's (1963) study imply that:
    A. in the real world, most people will refuse to follow orders to inflict harm on a stranger.
    B. many people will obey an authority figure even if innocent people get hurt.
    C. most people are willing to give obviously wrong answers when ordered to do so.
    D. most people stick to their own judgment, even when group members unanimously disagree.

13. According to Latané, social loafing is due to:
    A. social norms that stress the importance of positive interactions among group members.
    B. duplication of effort among group members.
    C. diffusion of responsibility in groups.
    D. a bias toward making internal attributions about the behavior of others.

14. Groupthink occurs when members of a cohesive group:
    A. are initially unanimous about an issue.
    B. stress the importance of caution in group decision making.
    C. emphasize concurrence at the expense of critical thinking in arriving at a decision.
    D. shift toward a less extreme position after group discussion.

15. The foot-in-the-door technique involves asking people to agree to a _____ request first to increase the likelihood that they will comply with a _____ request later.
    A. large; small
    B. small; large
    C. large; large
    D. large; larger

Answers

1 D p. 469	6 D pp. 475–476	11 B pp. 484–485
2 A p. 470	7 A p. 477	12 B pp. 486–487
3 B p. 471	8 C p. 478	13 C p. 491
4 B pp. 471–472	9 C p. 481	14 C pp. 492–493
5 B p. 472	10 B pp. 483–484	15 B p. 499

PsykTrek
Go to the PsykTrek website or CD-ROM for further study of the concepts in this chapter. Both online and on the CD-ROM, PsykTrek includes dozens of learning modules with videos, animations, and quizzes, as well as simulations of psychological phenomena and a multimedia glossary that includes word pronunciations.

ThomsonNOW
http://www.thomsonedu.com/ThomsonNOW
Go to this site for the link to ThomsonNOW, your one-stop study shop. Take a Pre-Test for this chapter, and ThomsonNOW will generate a Personalized Study Plan based on your test results. The Study Plan will identify the topics you need to review and direct you to online resources to help you master those topics. You can then take a Post-Test to help you determine the concepts you have mastered and what you still need to work on.

Companion Website
http://www.thomsonedu.com/psychology/weiten
Go to this site to find online resources directly linked to your book, including a glossary, flash cards, drag-and-drop exercises, quizzes, and more!

Chapter 1

Concept Check 1.1

1. c. Sigmund Freud (1905, pp. 77–78) arguing that it is possible to probe into the unconscious depths of the mind.

2. a. Wilhelm Wundt (1904 revision of an earlier text, p. v) campaigning for a new, independent science of psychology.

3. b. William James (1890) commenting negatively on the structuralists' efforts to break consciousness into its elements and his view of consciousness as a continuously flowing stream.

Concept Check 1.2

1. b. B. F. Skinner (1971, p. 17) explaining why he believes that freedom is an illusion.

2. c. Carl Rogers (1961, p. 27) commenting on others' assertion that he had an overly optimistic (Pollyannaish) view of human potential and discussing humans' basic drive toward personal growth.

3. a. John B. Watson (1930, p. 103) dismissing the importance of genetic inheritance while arguing that traits are shaped entirely by experience.

Concept Check 1.3

1. c. Thomas and Chess's (1977) well-known New York Longitudinal Study is a landmark in developmental psychology.

2. a. Olds and Milner (1954) made this discovery by accident and thereby opened up a fascinating line of inquiry in physiological psychology.

3. e. Zuckerman (1971) pioneered the study of sensation seeking as a personality trait.

Concept Check 1.4

a. 2. Psychology is theoretically diverse.

b. 6. Heredity and environment jointly influence behavior.

c. 4. Behavior is determined by multiple causes.

d. 7. People's experience of the world is highly subjective.

Chapter 2

Concept Check 2.1

1. IV: Film violence (present versus absent).
   DV: Heart rate and blood pressure (there are two DVs).

2. IV: Courtesy training (training versus no training).
   DV: Number of customer complaints.

3. IV: Stimulus complexity (high versus low) and stimulus contrast (high versus low) (there are two IVs).
   DV: Length of time spent staring at the stimuli.

4. IV: Group size (large versus small).
   DV: Conformity.

Concept Check 2.2

1. b and e. The other three conclusions all equate correlation with causation.

2. a. Negative. As age increases, more people tend to have visual problems and acuity tends to decrease.

   b. Positive. Studies show that highly educated people tend to earn higher incomes and that people with less education tend to earn lower incomes.

   c. Negative. As shyness increases, the size of one's friendship network should decrease. However, research suggests that this inverse association may be weaker than widely believed.

Concept Check 2.3

1. d. Survey. You would distribute a survey to obtain information on subjects' social class, education, and attitudes about nuclear disarmament.

2. c. Case study. Using a case study approach, you could interview people with anxiety disorders, interview their parents, and examine their school records to look for similarities in childhood experiences. As a second choice, you might have people with anxiety disorders fill out a survey about their childhood experiences.

3. b. Naturalistic observation. To answer this question properly, you would want to observe baboons in their natural environment, without interference.

4. a. Experiment. To demonstrate a causal relationship, you would have to conduct an experiment. You would manipulate the presence or absence of food-related cues in controlled circumstances where subjects had an opportunity to eat some food, and monitor the amount eaten.

Concept Check 2.4

Methodological flaw	Study 1	Study 2
Sampling bias	✓	✓
Placebo effects	✓	
Confounding of variables	✓	
Distortions in self-report data		✓
Experimenter bias	✓	

Explanations for Study 1. Sensory deprivation is an unusual kind of experience that may intrigue certain potential subjects, who may be more adventurous or more willing to take risks than the population at large. Using the first 80 students who sign up for this study may not yield a sample that is representative of the population. Assigning the first 40 subjects who sign up to the experimental group may confound these extraneous variables with the treatment (students who sign up most quickly may be the most adventurous). In announcing that he will be examining the detrimental effects of sensory deprivation, the experimenter has created expectations in the subjects. These expectations could lead to placebo effects that have not been controlled for with a placebo group. The experimenter has also revealed that he has a bias about the outcome of the study. Since he supervises the treatments, he knows which subjects are in the experimental and control groups, thus aggravating potential problems with experimenter bias. For example, he might unintentionally give the control group subjects better instructions on how to do the pursuit-rotor task and thereby slant the study in favor of finding support for his hypothesis.

Explanations for Study 2. Sampling bias is a problem because the researcher has sampled only subjects from a low-income, inner-city neighborhood. A sample obtained in this way is not likely to be representative of the population at large. People are sensitive about the issue of racial prejudice, so distortions in self-report data are also likely. Many subjects may be swayed by social desirability bias and rate themselves as less prejudiced than they really are.

Chapter 3

Concept Check 3.1

1. d. Dendrite.
2. f. Myelin.
3. b. Neuron.
4. e. Axon.
5. a. Glia.
6. g. Terminal button.
7. h. Synapse.

Concept Check 3.2

1. d. Serotonin.
2. b and d. Norepinephrine and serotonin.
3. e. Endorphins.
4. c. Dopamine.
5. a. Acetylcholine.

Concept Check 3.3

1. Left hemisphere damage, probably to Wernicke's area.
2. Deficit in dopamine synthesis in an area of the midbrain.
3. Deterioration of myelin sheaths surrounding axons.
4. Disturbance in dopamine activity.

Please note that neuropsychological assessment is not as simple as this introductory exercise may suggest. There are many possible causes of most disorders, and we discussed only a handful of leading causes for each.

Concept Check 3.4

1. Closer relatives; more distant relatives.
2. Identical twins; fraternal twins.
3. Biological parents; adoptive parents.
4. Genetic overlap or closeness; trait similarity.

Chapter 4

Concept Check 4.1

Dimension	Rods	Cones
1. Physical shape	Elongated	Stubby
2. Number in the retina	125 million	5–6.4 million
3. Area of the retina in which they are dominant receptor	Periphery	Center/fovea
4. Critical to color vision	No	Yes
5. Critical to peripheral vision	Yes	No
6. Sensitivity to dim light	Strong	Weak
7. Speed of dark adaptation	Slow	Rapid

Concept Check 4.2

	Trichromatic	Opponent process
1. Theory proposed by:	Young, Helmholtz	Hering
2. Can/can't account for complementary afterimages	can't	can
3. Explains first/later stage of color processing	first	later
4. Does/doesn't account for need for four terms to describe colors	doesn't	does

Concept Check 4.3

✓ 1. Interposition. The arches in front cut off part of the corridor behind them.

✓ 2. Height in plane. The back of the corridor is higher on the horizontal plane than the front of the corridor is.

✓ 3. Texture gradient. The more distant portions of the hallway are painted in less detail than the closer portions are.

✓ 4. Relative size. The arches in the distance are smaller than those in the foreground.

✓ 5. Light and shadow. Light shining in from the crossing corridor (it's coming from the left) contrasts with shadow elsewhere.

✓ 6. Linear perspective. The lines of the corridor converge in the distance.

Concept Check 4.4

Dimension	Vision	Hearing
1. Stimulus	Light waves	Sound waves
2. Elements of stimulus and related perceptions	Wavelength/hue Amplitude/ brightness Purity/saturation	Frequency/pitch Amplitude/ loudness Purity/timbre
3. Receptors	Rods and cones	Hair cells
4. Location of receptors	Retina	Basilar membrane
5. Main location of processing in brain	Occipital lobe, visual cortex	Temporal lobe, auditory cortex

Concept Check 4.5

Dimension	Taste	Smell	Touch
1. Stimulus	Soluble chemicals in saliva	Volatile chemicals in air	Mechanical, thermal, and chemical energy due to external contact
2. Receptors	Clusters of taste cells	Olfactory cilia (hairlike structures)	Many (at least 6) types
3. Location of receptors	Taste buds on tongue	Upper area of nasal passages	Skin
4. Basic elements of perception	Sweet, sour, salty, bitter	No satisfactory classification scheme	Pressure, hot, cold, pain

Chapter 5

Concept Check 5.1

Characteristic	REM sleep	NREM sleep
1. Type of EEG activity	"Wide awake" brain waves, mostly beta	Varied, lots of delta waves
2. Eye movements	Rapid, lateral	Slow or absent
3. Dreaming	Frequent, vivid	Less frequent
4. Depth (difficulty in awakening)	Difficult to awaken	Varied, generally easier to awaken
5. Percentage of total sleep (in adults)	About 20%	About 80%
6. Increases or decreases (as percentage of sleep) during childhood	Percent decreases	Percent increases
7. Timing in sleep (dominates early or late)	Dominates later in cycle	Dominates early in cycle

Concept Check 5.2

1. Beta. Video games require alert information processing, which is associated with beta waves.

2. Alpha. Meditation involves relaxation, which is associated with alpha waves, and studies show increased alpha in meditators.

3. Theta. In stage 1 sleep, theta waves tend to be prevalent.

4. Beta. Dreams are associated with REM sleep, which paradoxically produces "wide awake" beta waves.

5. Beta. If you're a beginner, typing will require alert, focused attention, which should generate beta waves.

Concept Check 5.3

1. c. Stimulants.

2. d. Hallucinogens.

3. b. Sedatives.

4. f. Alcohol.

5. a. Narcotics.

6. e. Cannabis.

Chapter 6

Concept Check 6.1

1. CS: Fire in fireplace
   UCS: Pain from burn   CR/UCR: Fear

2. CS: Brake lights in rain
   UCS: Car accident   CR/UCR: Tensing up

3. CS: Sight of cat
   UCS: Cat dander   CR/UCR: Wheezing

Concept Check 6.2

1. d. Stimulus generalization.

2. a. Acquisition.

3. f. Higher-order conditioning.

4. e. Stimulus discrimination.

5. c. Spontaneous recovery.

6. b. Extinction.

Concept Check 6.3

1. FR. Each sale is a response and every third response earns reinforcement.

2. VI. A varied amount of time elapses before the response of doing yard work can earn reinforcement.

3. VR. Reinforcement occurs after a varied number of unreinforced casts (time is irrelevant; the more casts Martha makes, the more reinforcers she will receive).

4. CR. The designated response (reading a book) is reinforced (with a gold star) each and every time.

5. FI. A fixed time interval (3 years) has to elapse before Skip can earn a salary increase (the reinforcer).

Concept Check 6.4

1. Punishment.

2. Positive reinforcement.

3. Punishment.

4. Negative reinforcement (for Audrey); the dog is positively reinforced for its whining.

5. Negative reinforcement.

6. Extinction. When Sharma's co-workers start to ignore her complaints, they are trying to extinguish the behavior (which had been positively reinforced when it won sympathy).

Concept Check 6.5

1. Classical conditioning. Midori's blue windbreaker is a CS eliciting excitement in her dog.

2. Operant conditioning. Playing new songs leads to negative consequences (punishment), which weaken the tendency to play new songs. Playing old songs leads to positive reinforcement, which gradually strengthens the tendency to play old songs.

3. Classical conditioning. The song was paired with the passion of new love so that it became a CS eliciting emotional, romantic feelings.

4. Both. Ralph's workplace is paired with criticism so that his workplace becomes a CS eliciting anxiety. Calling in sick is operant behavior that is strengthened through negative reinforcement (because it reduces anxiety).

Chapter 7

Concept Check 7.1

Feature	Sensory memory	Short-term memory	Long-term memory
1. Main encoding format	Copy of input	Largely phonemic	Largely semantic
2. Storage	Limited capacity	Small (7 ± 2 chunks)	No known limit
3. Storage duration	About ¼ second	Up to 20 seconds	Minutes to years

Concept Check 7.2

1. Ineffective encoding due to lack of attention.

2. Retrieval failure due to motivated forgetting.

3. Proactive interference (previous learning of Joe Cocker's name interferes with new learning).

4. Retroactive interference (new learning of sociology interferes with older learning of history).

Concept Check 7.3

1. d. Declarative memory.

2. c. Long-term memory.

3. a. Sensory memory.

4. f. Episodic memory.

5. e. Nondeclarative memory.

6. g. Semantic memory.

7. i. Prospective memory.

8. b. Short-term memory.

Chapter 8

Concept Check 8.1

1. Functional fixedness.

2. Forming subgoals.

3. Insight.

4. Searching for analogies.

5. Arrangement problem.

Concept Check 8.2

1. Elimination by aspects.

2. Availability heuristic.

3. Shift to an additive model.

Concept Check 8.3

1. H. Given that the identical twins were reared apart, their greater similarity in comparison to fraternals reared together can only be due to heredity. This comparison is probably the most important piece of evidence supporting the genetic determination of IQ.

2. E. We tend to associate identical twins with evidence supporting heredity, but in this comparison genetic similarity is held constant since both sets of twins are identical. The only logical explanation for the greater similarity in identicals reared together is the effect of their being reared together (environment).

3. E. This comparison is similar to the previous one. Genetic similarity is held constant and a shared environment produces greater similarity than being reared apart.

4. B. This is nothing more than a quantification of the observation that intelligence runs in families. Since families share both genes and environment, either or both could be responsible for the observed correlation.

5. B. The similarity of adopted children to their biological parents can only be due to shared genes, and the similarity of adopted children to their foster parents can only be due to shared environment, so these correlations show the influence of both heredity and environment.

Concept Check 8.4

1. b. Gardner.

2. c. Jensen.

3. d. Scarr.

4. e. Sternberg.

Chapter 9

Concept Check 9.1

1. I. Early studies indicated that lesioning the ventromedial nucleus of the hypothalamus leads to overeating (although it is an oversimplification to characterize the VMH as the brain's "stop eating" center).

2. I. According to Mayer, hunger increases when the amount of glucose in the blood decreases.

3. I or ?. Food cues generally trigger hunger and eating, but reactions vary among individuals.

4. D. Food preferences are mostly learned, and we tend to like what we are accustomed to eating. Most people will not be eager to eat a strange-looking food.

5. I. People tend to eat more when a variety of foods are available.

6. I. Reactions vary, but stress generally tends to increase eating.

Concept Check 9.2

1. c. Incentive value of success.

2. b. Perceived probability of success.

3. a. Need for achievement.

Concept Check 9.3

2. James-Lange theory.

3. Schachter's two-factor theory.

4. Evolutionary theories.

Chapter 10

Concept Check 10.1

	Event	Stage	Organism	Time span
1.	Uterine implantation	Germinal	Zygote	0–2 weeks
2.	Muscle and bone begin to form	Fetal	Fetus	2 months to birth
3.	Vital organs and body systems begin to form	Embryonic	Embryo	2 weeks to 2 months

Concept Check 10.2

1. b. Animism is characteristic of the preoperational period.

2. c. Mastery of hierarchical classification occurs during the concrete operational period.

3. a. Lack of object permanence is characteristic of the sensorimotor period.

Concept Check 10.3

1. c. Commitment to personal ethics is characteristic of postconventional reasoning.

2. b. Concern about approval of others is characteristic of conventional reasoning.

3. a. Emphasis on positive or negative consequences is characteristic of preconventional reasoning.

Chapter 11

Concept Check 11.1

1. Regression.

2. Projection.

3. Reaction formation.

4. Repression.

5. Rationalization.

Concept Check 11.2

		Freud	Jung	Adler
1.	Archetypes		✓	
2.	Physical gratification	✓		
3.	Striving for superiority			✓
4.	Collective unconscious		✓	
5.	Early childhood experiences	✓		✓
6.	Dream analysis	✓	✓	
7.	Unconscious determinants	✓	✓	

Concept Check 11.3

1. Bandura's observational learning. Sarah imitates a role model from television.

2. Maslow's need for self-actualization. Yolanda is striving to realize her fullest potential.

3. Freud's Oedipal complex. Vladimir shows preference for his opposite-sex parent and emotional distance from his same-sex parent.

Concept Check 11.4

1. Maslow (1971, p. 36) commenting on the need for self-actualization.

2. Eysenck (1977, pp. 407–408) commenting on the biological roots of personality.

3. Freud (in Malcolm, 1980) commenting on the repression of sexuality.

Chapter 12

Concept Check 12.1

1. b. A choice between two unattractive options.

2. c. Weighing the positive and negative aspects of a single goal.

3. a. A choice between two attractive options.

Concept Check 12.2

1. a. Frustration due to delay.

2. d. Pressure to perform.

3. c. Change associated with leaving school and taking a new job.

4. a. Frustration due to loss of job.

   c. Change in life circumstances.

   d. Pressure to perform (in quickly obtaining new job).

Concept Check 12.3

Pathway 1: hypothalamus, sympathetic division of the ANS, adrenal medulla, catecholamines.

Pathway 2: pituitary, ACTH, adrenal cortex, corticosteroids.

Chapter 13

Concept Check 13.1

	Deviance	Maladaptive behavior	Personal distress
1. Alan	_____	✓	_____
2. Monica	_____	_____	✓
3. Boris	✓	_____	_____
4. Natasha	✓	✓	✓

Concept Check 13.2

1. Obsessive-compulsive disorder (key symptoms: frequent rituals, ruminations about school).

2. Somatization disorder (key symptoms: history of physical complaints involving many different organ systems).

3. Conversion disorder (key symptom: loss of function in single organ system).

Concept Check 13.3

1. Bipolar disorder, manic episode (key symptoms: extravagant plans, hyperactivity, reckless spending).

2. Paranoid schizophrenia (key symptoms: delusions of persecution and grandeur, along with deterioration of adaptive behavior).

3. Major depression (key symptoms: feelings of despair, low self-esteem, lack of energy).

Chapter 14

Concept Check 14.1

1. c.
2. b.
3. a.

Concept Check 14.2

1. a. Systematic desensitization.
2. c. Aversion therapy.
3. b. Social skills training.

Concept Check 14.3

1. c.
2. a.
3. b.
4. d.
5. b.

Chapter 15

Concept Check 15.1

	Unstable	Stable
Internal	d	b
External	a	c

Concept Check 15.2

1. c. Fundamental attribution error (assuming that arriving late reflects personal qualities).

2. a. Illusory correlation effect (overestimating how often one has seen confirmations of the assertion that young, female professors get pregnant soon after being hired).

3. b. Stereotyping (assuming that all lawyers have certain traits).

Concept Check 15.3

1. *Target:* Cognitive component of attitudes (beliefs about program for regulating nursing homes).

   Persuasion: Message factor (advice to use one-sided instead of two-sided arguments).

2. *Target:* Affective component of attitudes (feelings about candidate).

   Persuasion: Source factor (advice on appearing likable, sincere, and compassionate).

3. *Target:* Behavioral component of attitudes (making contributions).

   Persuasion: Receiver factor (considering audience's initial position regarding the candidate).

Concept Check 15.4

1. False.
2. True.
3. False.
4. True.
5. False.

Empiricism depends on observation; precise observation depends on measurement; and measurement requires numbers. Thus, scientists routinely analyze numerical data to arrive at their conclusions. Over 2000 empirical studies are cited in this text, and all but a few of the simplest ones required a statistical analysis. *Statistics* **is the use of mathematics to organize, summarize, and interpret numerical data.** We discussed correlation briefly in Chapter 2, but in this Appendix we look at a variety of statistics.

To illustrate statistics in action, let's assume that we want to test a hypothesis that has generated quite an argument in your psychology class. The hypothesis is that college students who watch a great deal of television aren't as bright as those who watch TV infrequently. For the fun of it, your class decides to conduct a correlational study of itself, collecting survey and psychological test data. Your classmates all agree to respond to a short survey on their TV viewing habits. Because everyone at your school has had to take the SAT, the class decides to use scores on the SAT verbal subtest as an index of how bright students are. All of them agree to allow the records office at the college to furnish their SAT scores to the professor, who replaces each student's name with a subject number (to protect students' right to privacy). Let's see how we could use statistics to analyze the data collected in our pilot study (a small, preliminary investigation).

Graphing Data

After collecting our data, our next step is to organize the data to get a quick overview of our numerical results. Let's assume that there are 20 students in your class, and when they estimate how many hours they spend per day watching TV, the results are as follows:

3	2	0	3	1
3	4	0	5	1
2	3	4	5	2
4	5	3	4	6

One of the simpler things that we can do to organize data is to create a *frequency distribution*—an orderly arrangement of scores indicating the frequency of each score or group of scores. Figure B.1(a) shows a frequency distribution for our data on TV viewing. The column on the left lists the possible scores (estimated hours of TV viewing) in order, and the column on the right lists the number of subjects with each score. Graphs can provide an even better overview of the data. One approach is to portray the data in a *histogram*, which is a bar graph that presents data from a frequency distribution. Such a histogram, summarizing our TV viewing data, is presented in Figure B.1(b).

Another widely used method of portraying data graphically is the *frequency polygon*—a line figure used to present data from a frequency distribution. Figures B.1(c) and B.1(d) show how our TV viewing data can be converted from a histogram to a frequency polygon. In both the bar graph and the line figure, the horizontal axis lists the possible scores and the vertical axis is used to indicate the frequency of each score. This use of the axes is nearly universal for frequency polygons, although sometimes it is reversed in histograms (the vertical axis lists possible scores, so the bars become horizontal).

Figure B.1

Graphing data. **(a)** Our raw data are tallied into a frequency distribution. **(b)** The same data are portrayed in a bar graph called a histogram. **(c)** A frequency polygon is plotted over the histogram. **(d)** The resultant frequency polygon is shown by itself.

Score	Tallies	Frequency
6	I	1
5	III	3
4	IIII	4
3	THL	5
2	III	3
1	II	2
0	II	2

(a) Frequency distribution

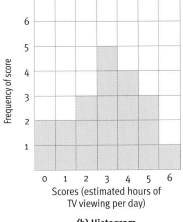

(b) Histogram

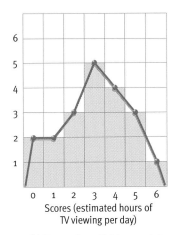

(c) Conversion of histogram into frequency polygon

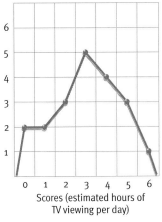

(d) Frequency polygon

Figure B.2

Measures of central tendency. The mean, median, and mode sometimes yield different results, but they usually converge, as in the case of our TV viewing data.

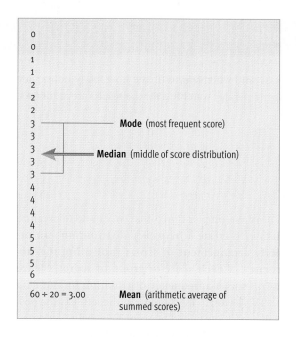

```
0
0
1
1
2
2
2
3  ┐——— Mode (most frequent score)
3  │
3  ◄——— Median (middle of score distribution)
3  │
3  ┘
4
4
4
4
5
5
5
6
60 ÷ 20 = 3.00    Mean (arithmetic average of
                 summed scores)
```

Our graphs improve on the jumbled collection of scores that we started with, but *descriptive statistics,* **which are used to organize and summarize data,** provide some additional advantages. Let's see what the three measures of central tendency tell us about our data.

Measuring Central Tendency 1c

In examining a set of data, it's routine to ask "What is a typical score in the distribution?" For instance, in this case we might compare the average amount of TV watching in our sample against national estimates to determine whether our subjects appear to be representative of the population. The three measures of central tendency, the median, the mean, and the mode, give us indications regarding the typical score in a data set. **The *median* is the score that falls in the center of a distribution, the *mean* is** the arithmetic average of the scores, and the *mode* is the score that occurs most frequently.

All three measures of central tendency are calculated for our TV viewing data in **Figure B.2.** As you can see, in this set of data, the mean, median, and mode all turn out to be the same score, which is 3. The correspondence among the three measures of central tendency seen in our TV viewing data is quite common, but there are situations in which the mean, median, and mode can yield very different estimates of central tendency. To illustrate, imagine that you're interviewing for a sales position at a company. Unbeknownst to you, the company's five salespeople earned the following incomes in the previous year: $20,000, $20,000, $25,000, $35,000, and $200,000. You ask how much the typical salesperson earns in a year. The sales director proudly announces that her five salespeople earned *a mean* income of $60,000 last year. However, before you order that expensive, new sports car, you had better inquire about the *median* and *modal* income for the sales staff. In this case, one extreme score ($200,000) has inflated the mean, making it unrepresentative of the sales staff's earnings. In this instance, the median ($25,000) and the mode ($20,000) both provide better estimates of what you are likely to earn.

In general, the mean is the most useful measure of central tendency because additional statistical manipulations can be performed on it that are not possible with the median or mode. However, the mean is sensitive to extreme scores in a distribution, which can sometimes make the mean misleading. Thus, lack of agreement among the three measures of central tendency usually occurs when a few extreme scores pull the mean away from the center of the distribution, as shown in **Figure B.3.** The curves plotted in **Figure B.3** are simply "smoothed out" frequency polygons based on data from many subjects. They show that when a distribution is symmetric, the

Figure B.3

Measures of central tendency in skewed distributions. In a symmetrical distribution (a), the three measures of central tendency converge. However, in a negatively skewed distribution (b) or in a positively skewed distribution (c), the mean, median, and mode are pulled apart as shown here. Typically, in these situations the median provides the best index of central tendency.

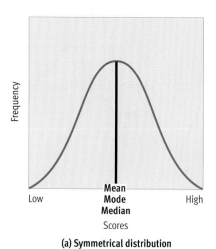

(a) Symmetrical distribution

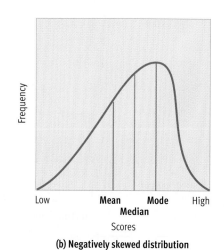

(b) Negatively skewed distribution

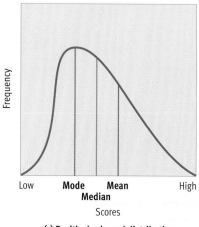

(c) Positively skewed distribution

measures of central tendency fall together, but this is not true in skewed or unbalanced distributions.

Figure B.3(b) shows a *negatively skewed distribution,* **in which most scores pile up at the high end of the scale** (the negative skew refers to the direction in which the curve's "tail" points). A *positively skewed distribution,* **in which scores pile up at the low end of the scale,** is shown in Figure B.3(c). In both types of skewed distributions, a few extreme scores at one end pull the mean, and to a lesser degree the median, away from the mode. In these situations, the mean may be misleading and the median usually provides the best index of central tendency.

In any case, the measures of central tendency for our TV viewing data are reassuring, since they all agree and they fall reasonably close to national estimates regarding how much young adults watch TV. Given the small size of our group, this agreement with national norms doesn't *prove* that our sample is representative of the population, but at least there's no obvious reason to believe that they're unrepresentative.

Figure B.4

The standard deviation and dispersion of data. Although both these distributions of golf scores have the same mean, their standard deviations will be different. In (a) the scores are bunched together and there is less variability than in (b), yielding a lower standard deviation for the data in distribution (a).

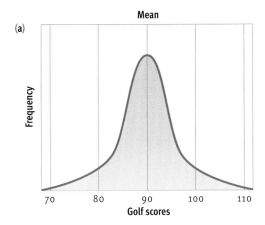

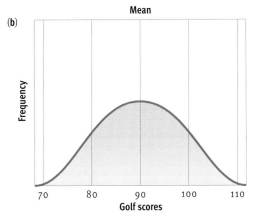

Of course, everyone in our sample did not report identical TV viewing habits. Virtually all data sets are characterized by some variability. *Variability* **refers to how much the scores tend to vary or depart from the mean score.** For example, the distribution of golf scores for a mediocre, erratic golfer would be characterized by high variability, while scores for an equally mediocre but more consistent golfer would show less variability.

The *standard deviation* **is an index of the amount of variability in a set of data.** It reflects the dispersion of scores in a distribution. This principle is portrayed graphically in Figure B.4, where the two distributions of golf scores have the same mean but the top one has less variability because the scores are bunched up in the center (for the consistent golfer). The distribution in Figure B.4(b) is characterized by more variability, as the erratic golfer's scores are more spread out. This distribution will yield a higher standard deviation than the distribution in Figure B.4(a).

The formula for calculating the standard deviation is shown in Figure B.5, where d stands for each score's deviation from the mean and Σ stands for summation.

TV viewing score (X)	Deviation from mean (d)	Deviation squared (d^2)
0	−3	9
0	−3	9
1	−2	4
1	−2	4
2	−1	1
2	−1	1
2	−1	1
3	0	0
3	0	0
3	0	0
3	0	0
3	0	0
4	+1	1
4	+1	1
4	+1	1
4	+1	1
5	+2	4
5	+2	4
5	+2	4
6	+3	9

$N = 20$

$\Sigma X = 60$ $\qquad \Sigma d^2 = 54$

$$\text{Mean} = \frac{\Sigma X}{N} = \frac{60}{20} = 3.0$$

$$\text{Standard deviation} = \sqrt{\frac{\Sigma d^2}{N}} = \sqrt{\frac{54}{20}}$$

$$= \sqrt{2.70} = 1.64$$

Figure B.5

Steps in calculating the standard deviation. (1) Add the scores (ΣX) and divide by the number of scores (N) to calculate the mean (which comes out to 3.0 in this case). (2) Calculate each score's deviation from the mean by subtracting the mean from each score (the results are shown in the second column). (3) Square these deviations from the mean and total the results to obtain (Σd^2) as shown in the third column. (4) Insert the numbers for N and Σd^2 into the formula for the standard deviation and compute the results.

A step-by-step application of this formula to our TV viewing data, shown in **Figure B.5**, reveals that the standard deviation for our TV viewing data is 1.64. The standard deviation has a variety of uses. One of these uses will surface in the next section, where we discuss the normal distribution.

The Normal Distribution

The hypothesis in our study is that brighter students watch less TV than relatively dull students. To test this hypothesis, we're going to correlate TV viewing with SAT scores. But to make effective use of the SAT data, we need to understand what SAT scores mean, which brings us to the normal distribution.

The *normal distribution* is a symmetrical, bell-shaped curve that represents the pattern in which many human characteristics are dispersed in the population. A great many physical qualities (for ex-

ample, height, nose length, and running speed) and psychological traits (intelligence, spatial reasoning ability, introversion) are distributed in a manner that closely resembles this bell-shaped curve. When a trait is normally distributed, most scores fall near the center of the distribution (the mean) and the number of scores gradually declines as one moves away from the center in either direction (see **Figure B.6**). The normal distribution is *not* a law of nature. It's a mathematical function, or theoretical curve, that approximates the way nature seems to operate.

The normal distribution is the bedrock of the scoring system for most psychological tests, including the SAT. As we discuss in Chapter 8, psychological tests are *relative measures;* they assess how people score on a trait in comparison to other people. The normal distribution gives us a precise way to measure how people stack up in comparison to each other. The scores under the normal curve are dispersed in a fixed pattern, with the standard devia-

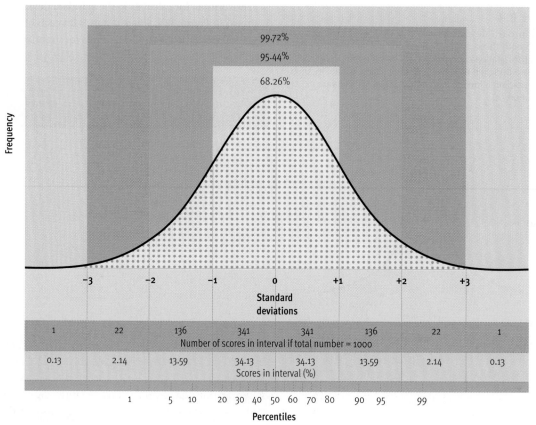

Figure B.6

The normal distribution. Many characteristics are distributed in a pattern represented by this bell-shaped curve (each dot represents a case). The horizontal axis shows how far above or below the mean a score is (measured in plus or minus standard deviations). The vertical axis shows the number of cases obtaining each score. In a normal distribution, most cases fall near the center of the distribution, so that 68.26% of the cases fall within plus or minus 1 standard deviation of the mean. The number of cases gradually declines as one moves away from the mean in either direction, so that only 13.59% of the cases fall between 1 and 2 standard deviations above or below the mean, and even fewer cases (2.14%) fall between 2 and 3 standard deviations above or below the mean.

tion serving as the unit of measurement, as shown in **Figure B.6**. About 68% of the scores in the distribution fall within plus or minus 1 standard deviation of the mean, while 95% of the scores fall within plus or minus 2 standard deviations of the mean. Given this fixed pattern, if you know the mean and standard deviation of a normally distributed trait, you can tell where any score falls in the distribution for the trait.

Although you may not have realized it, you probably have taken many tests in which the scoring system is based on the normal distribution. On the SAT, for instance, raw scores (the number of items correct on each subtest) are converted into standard scores that indicate where you fall in the normal distribution for the trait measured. In this conversion, the mean is set arbitrarily at 500 and the standard deviation at 100, as shown in **Figure B.7**. Therefore, a score of 400 on the SAT verbal subtest means that you scored 1 standard deviation below the mean, while an SAT score of 600 indicates that you scored 1 standard deviation above the mean. Thus, SAT scores tell you how many standard deviations above or below the mean your score was. This system also provides the metric for IQ scales and many other types of psychological tests (see Chapter 8).

Test scores that place examinees in the normal distribution can always be converted to percentile scores, which are a little easier to interpret. A **percentile score indicates the percentage of people who score at or below the score you obtained.** For example, if you score at the 60th percentile, 60% of the people who take the test score the same or below you, while the remaining 40% score above you. There are tables available that permit us to convert any standard deviation placement in a normal distribution into a precise percentile score. **Figure B.6** gives some percentile conversions for the normal curve.

Of course, not all distributions are normal. As we saw in **Figure B.3**, some distributions are skewed in one direction or the other. As an example, consider what would happen if a classroom exam were much too easy or much too hard. If the test were too easy, scores would be bunched up at the high end of the scale, as in **Figure B.3(b)**. If the test were too hard, scores would be bunched up at the low end, as in **Figure B.3(c)**.

Measuring Correlation 1d

To determine whether TV viewing is related to SAT scores, we have to compute a *correlation coefficient*— **a numerical index of the degree of relationship**

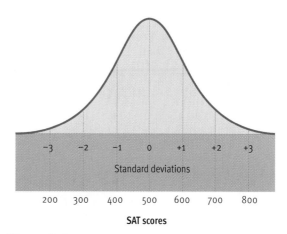

Figure B.7

The normal distribution and SAT scores. The normal distribution is the basis for the scoring system on many standardized tests. For example, on the SAT, the mean is set at 500 and the standard deviation at 100. Hence, an SAT score tells you how many standard deviations above or below the mean you scored. For example, a score of 700 means you scored 2 standard deviations above the mean.

that exists between two variables. As discussed in Chapter 2, a *positive* correlation means that the two variables—say X and Y—covary together. This means that high scores on variable X are associated with high scores on variable Y and that low scores on X are associated with low scores on Y. A *negative* correlation indicates that there is an inverse relationship between two variables. This means that people who score high on variable X tend to score low on variable Y, whereas those who score low on X tend to score high on Y. In our study, we hypothesized that as TV viewing increases, SAT scores will decrease, so we should expect a negative correlation between TV viewing and SAT scores.

The *magnitude* of a correlation coefficient indicates the *strength* of the association between two variables. This coefficient can vary between 0 and ±1.00. The coefficient is usually represented by the letter r (for example, r = .45). A coefficient near 0 tells us that there is no relationship between two variables. A coefficient of +1.00 or −1.00 indicates that there is a perfect, one-to-one correspondence between two variables. A perfect correlation is found only rarely when working with real data. The closer the coefficient is to either −1.00 or +1.00, the stronger the relationship is.

The direction and strength of correlations can be illustrated graphically in scatter diagrams. **A *scatter diagram* is a graph in which paired X and Y scores for each subject are plotted as single points.** **Figure B.8** on the next page shows scatter diagrams for positive correlations in the upper half and for

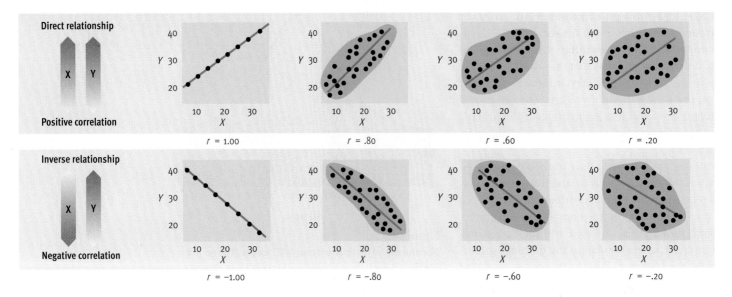

Figure B.8

Scatter diagrams of positive and negative correlations. Scatter diagrams plot paired X and Y scores as single points. Score plots slanted in the opposite direction result from positive (top row) as opposed to negative (bottom row) correlations. Moving across both rows (to the right), you can see that progressively weaker correlations result in more and more scattered plots of data points.

negative correlations in the bottom half. A perfect positive correlation and a perfect negative correlation are shown on the far left. When a correlation is perfect, the data points in the scatter diagram fall exactly in a straight line. However, positive and negative correlations yield lines slanted in the opposite direction because the lines map out opposite types of associations. Moving to the right in **Figure B.8**, you can see what happens when the magnitude of a correlation decreases. The data points scatter farther and farther from the straight line that would represent a perfect relationship.

What about our data relating TV viewing to SAT scores? **Figure B.9** shows a scatter diagram of these data. Having just learned about scatter diagrams, perhaps you can estimate the magnitude of the correlation between TV viewing and SAT scores. The scatter diagram of our data looks a lot like the one seen in the bottom right corner of **Figure B.8**, suggesting that the correlation will be in the vicinity of −.20.

The formula for computing the most widely used measure of correlation—the Pearson product-moment correlation—is shown in **Figure B.10**, along with the

calculations for our data on TV viewing and SAT scores. The data yield a correlation of $r = -.24$. This coefficient of correlation reveals that we have found a weak inverse association between TV viewing and performance on the SAT. Among our subjects, as TV viewing increases, SAT scores decrease, but the trend isn't very strong. We can get a better idea of how strong this correlation is by examining its predictive power.

Correlation and Prediction

As the magnitude of a correlation increases (gets closer to either −1.00 or +1.00), our ability to predict one variable based on knowledge of the other variable steadily increases. This relationship between the magnitude of a correlation and predictability can be quantified precisely. All we have to do is square the correlation coefficient (multiply it by itself) and this gives us the *coefficient of determination,* **the percentage of variation in one variable that can be predicted based on the other variable.** Thus, a correlation of .70 yields a coefficient of determination of .49 (.70 × .70 = .49), indicating that variable X can account for 49% of the variation in variable Y. **Figure B.11** shows how the coefficient of determination goes up as the magnitude of a correlation increases.

Unfortunately, a correlation of −.24 doesn't give us much predictive power. We can account only for a little over 6% of the variation in variable Y. So, if we tried to predict individuals' SAT scores based on how much TV they watched, our predictions wouldn't be very accurate. Although a low correlation doesn't have much practical, predictive utility, it may still have theoretical value. Just knowing that there is a relationship between two variables can be theoretically interesting. However, we haven't yet addressed the question of whether our observed correlation is

Figure B.9

Scatter diagram of the correlation between TV viewing and SAT scores. Our hypothetical data relating TV viewing to SAT scores are plotted in this scatter diagram. Compare it to the scatter diagrams seen in **Figure B.8** and see whether you can estimate the correlation between TV viewing and SAT scores in our data (see the text for the answer).

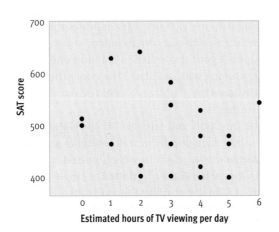

strong enough to support our hypothesis that there is a relationship between TV viewing and SAT scores. To make this judgment, we have to turn to inferential statistics and the process of hypothesis testing.

Hypothesis Testing

Inferential statistics go beyond the mere description of data. *Inferential statistics* are used to interpret data and draw conclusions. They permit researchers to decide whether their data support their hypotheses.

In our study of TV viewing we hypothesized that we would find an inverse relationship between amount of TV watched and SAT scores. Sure enough, that's what we found. However, we have to ask ourselves a critical question: Is this observed correlation large enough to support our hypothesis, or might a correlation of this size have occurred by chance?

We have to ask a similar question nearly every time we conduct a study. Why? Because we are working only with a sample. In research, we observe a limited *sample* (in this case, 20 subjects) to draw conclusions about a much larger *population* (college students in general). There's always a possibility that if we drew a different sample from the population, the results might be different. Perhaps our results are unique to our sample and not generalizable to the larger population. If we were able to collect data on the entire population, we would not have to wrestle with this problem, but our dependence on a sample necessitates the use of inferential statistics to precisely evaluate the likelihood that our results are due to chance

Subject number	TV viewing score (X)	X^2	SAT score (Y)	Y^2	XY
1	0	0	500	250,000	0
2	0	0	515	265,225	0
3	1	1	450	202,500	450
4	1	1	650	422,500	650
5	2	4	400	160,000	800
6	2	4	675	455,625	1350
7	2	4	425	180,625	850
8	3	9	400	160,000	1200
9	3	9	450	202,500	1350
10	3	9	500	250,000	1500
11	3	9	550	302,500	1650
12	3	9	600	360,000	1800
13	4	16	400	160,000	1600
14	4	16	425	180,625	1700
15	4	16	475	225,625	1900
16	4	16	525	275,625	2100
17	5	25	400	160,000	2000
18	5	25	450	202,500	2250
19	5	25	475	225,625	2375
20	6	36	550	302,500	3300
N = 20	$\Sigma X = 60$	$\Sigma X^2 = 234$	$\Sigma Y = 9815$	$\Sigma Y^2 = 4,943,975$	$\Sigma XY = 28,825$

Formula for Pearson product-moment correlation coefficient

$$r = \frac{(N)\Sigma XY - (\Sigma X)(\Sigma Y)}{\sqrt{[(N)\Sigma X^2 - (\Sigma X)^2][(N)\Sigma Y^2 - (\Sigma Y)^2]}}$$

$$= \frac{(20)(28,825) - (60)(9815)}{\sqrt{[(20)(234) - (60)^2][(20)(4,943,975) - (9815)^2]}}$$

$$= \frac{-12,400}{\sqrt{[1080][2,545,275]}}$$

$$= -.237$$

Figure B.10

Computing a correlation coefficient. The calculations required to compute the Pearson product-moment coefficient of correlation are shown here. The formula looks intimidating, but it's just a matter of filling in the figures taken from the sums of the columns shown above the formula.

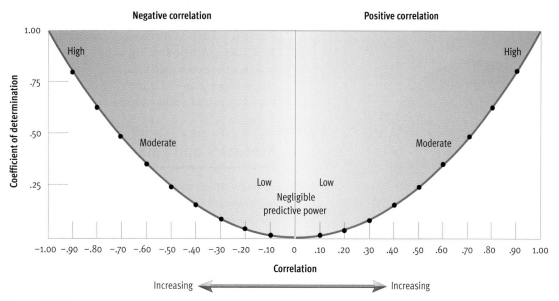

Figure B.11

Correlation and the coefficient of determination. The coefficient of determination is an index of a correlation's predictive power. As you can see, whether positive or negative, stronger correlations yield greater predictive power.

factors in sampling. Thus, inferential statistics are the key to making the inferential leap from the sample to the population (see **Figure B.12**).

Although it may seem backward, in hypothesis testing we formally test the *null* hypothesis. As applied to correlational data, the **null hypothesis is the assumption that there is no true relationship between the variables observed.** In our study, the null hypothesis is that there is no genuine association between TV viewing and SAT scores. We want to determine whether our results will permit us to *reject* the null hypothesis and thus conclude that our *research hypothesis* (that there is a relationship between the variables) has been supported. Why do we test the null hypothesis instead of the research hypothesis? Because our probability calculations depend on assumptions tied to the null hypothesis. Specifically, we compute the probability of obtaining the results that we have observed if the null hypthesis is indeed true. The calculation of this probability hinges on a number of factors. A key factor is the amount of variability in the data, which is why the standard deviation is an important statistic.

Statistical Significance

When we reject the null hypothesis, we conclude that we have found *statistically significant* results. **Statistical significance is said to exist when the probability that the observed findings are due to chance is very low, usually less than 5 chances in 100.** This means that if the null hypothesis is correct and we conduct our study 100 times, drawing a new sample from the population each time, we will get results such as those observed only 5 times out of 100. If our

calculations allow us to reject the null hypothesis, we conclude that our results support our research hypothesis. Thus, statistically significant results typically are findings that *support* a research hypothesis.

The requirement that there be less than 5 chances in 100 that research results are due to chance is the *minimum* requirement for statistical significance. When this requirement is met, we say the results are significant at the .05 level. If researchers calculate that there is less than 1 chance in 100 that their results are due to chance factors in sampling, the results are significant at the .01 level. If there is less than a 1 in 1000 chance that findings are attributable to sampling error, the results are significant at the .001 level. Thus, there are several *levels* of significance that you may see cited in scientific articles.

Because we are only dealing in matters of probability, there is always the possibility that our decision to accept or reject the null hypothesis is wrong. The various significance levels indicate the probability of erroneously rejecting the null hypothesis (and inaccurately accepting the research hypothesis). At the .05 level of significance, there are 5 chances in 100 that we have made a mistake when we conclude that our results support our hypothesis, and at the .01 level of significance the chance of an erroneous conclusion is 1 in 100. Although researchers hold the probability of this type of error quite low, the probability is never zero. This is one of the reasons that competently executed studies of the same question can yield contradictory findings. The differences may be due to chance variations in sampling that can't be prevented.

What do we find when we evaluate our data linking TV viewing to students' SAT scores? The calculations indicate that, given our sample size and the variability in our data, the probability of obtaining a correlation of −.24 by chance is greater than 20%. That's not a high probability, but it's not low enough to reject the null hypothesis. Thus, our findings are not strong enough to allow us to conclude that we have supported our hypothesis.

Statistics and Empiricism

In summary, conclusions based on empirical research are a matter of probability, and there's always a possibility that the conclusions are wrong. However, two major strengths of the empirical approach are its precision and its intolerance of error. Scientists can give you precise estimates of the likelihood that their conclusions are wrong, and because they're intolerant of error, they hold this probability extremely low. It's their reliance on statistics that allows them to accomplish these goals.

Figure B.12
The relationship between the population and the sample. In research, we are usually interested in a broad population, but we can observe only a small sample from the population. After making observations of our sample, we draw inferences about the population, based on the sample. This inferential process works well as long as the sample is reasonably representative of the population.

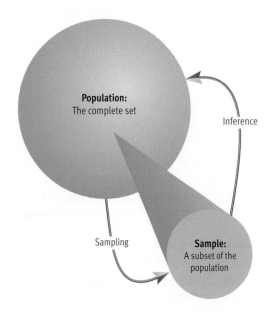

Population:
The complete set

Inference

Sampling

Sample:
A subset of the population

by Vincent W. Hevern (LeMoyne College)

Is the earth a globe or flat as a pancake? Was Copernicus right that the sun stands at the center of the solar system or does it circle the earth? Did Neil Armstrong really set foot on the lunar surface in 1969 or did NASA stage all those moon landings at a secret movie lot somewhere in the American desert? Probably 99.9999% of people know that the earth is round, Copernicus was right, and Armstrong really walked on the moon. But, type these four words—"flat earth Charles Johnson"—into Google, Yahoo, or another Internet search engine and you'll discover what the other 0.0001% believe. The late Mr. Johnson claimed that he could prove the earth was flat, Copernicus lied, and NASA has tricked us all for decades. So, who's right? After all, information supporting the "Flat Earth" hypothesis can be found on the Internet. Isn't that enough to justify you becoming a "Flat Earther" yourself?

I am starting out with this silly example to highlight a serious problem that students and teachers face in the 21st century: it is easy to find a lot of terrible as well as excellent information online. And, when students (and some teachers, too) don't critically judge their information sources, the overall quality of their research slips (Brown, Freeman, & Williamson, 2000). We live at a time when the amount and availability of information is growing exponentially. But our use of all that data is often handicapped, as it seems harder and harder to figure out where to find, and how to evaluate, research sources. So, whether you are exploring psychology as your major or just because it is an interesting subject, you need to learn how to think critically about Internet-based sources of information in psychology (and every other subject). When you finish school, you may find yourself working in business or for a governmental agency or even in another academic setting. Wherever your future takes you, your skills at finding and evaluating information online will be important and valued. I hope that some of the suggestions in this essay will help you learn to be a better researcher online.

Two Fundamental Facts about Research

No matter how large the Internet grows, *libraries* will continue to be the foundation for good research. Yet, as Jenson (2004) argues, "many students are convinced that they can and should do all of their library work in their pajamas and slippers from the relative comfort of their dorm rooms or apartments" (p. 111). If that's your belief, frankly you will not become a better researcher, whether online or off. Colleges continue to spend hundreds of thousands to millions of dollars every year on their libraries because libraries remain the principal repositories of sound, scholarly information. That money also pays for librarians who have special skills and knowledge that permit them to help students and faculty with their research. So, the most basic rule of informational literacy states that *you need to know what is in your school's library*. And, to do so, you should consult the professional reference librarians there to help you. Because the best materials for research in cyberspace are often rooted in print-based library resources, you should learn the basics of the library to enhance your sophistication online.

The second fundamental fact can be summed up by the phrase, "No pain, no gain." It takes time and real effort to develop the skills necessary to be effective in seeking scholarly information. Just as you wouldn't think of playing a varsity sport unless you had trained for it over many months or years, *your ability to conduct research requires regular practice*. In fact, studies usually find that hard work and practice—more so than talent or genius—are what distinguishes experts from other people (van Gelder, 2005). A corollary to the need for practice is the notion that *good research itself takes time*. Very few students can gather the sources needed for a important report in just a few hours or overnight. Assembling the data, weighing the arguments, synthesizing the best materials, and preparing a report in your own words requires dedicated time and attention. That said, the process of research does get easier with experience.

Criteria for Quality on the Net

So, what are the standards or criteria by which you can judge the quality of a webpage or resource? What can you do to increase the chances that the material you take from the Internet is worth your effort? In recent years, information specialists have explored how to answer these questions. Their studies have come to slightly different conclusions, but there is substantial agreement about what characteristics are

Questions to Ask in Evaluating Materials on the Internet

1. Identity and qualifications of the author(s)

- Who is the author of the material? Is the author identified or anonymous?
- What is the author's academic or professional background and experience?
- Is the author writing within or outside his/her area of expertise and skill?
- If the material is the product of a group (a committee, governmental agency, or the like), what is that group's qualifications or expertise regarding this subject?

2. Publisher or sponsor of the website

- Is the material self-published by the author or is there some recognized organization (university, medical center, government agency, nonprofit foundation, and so forth) that sponsors the website for the material?
- Does the site's sponsor or publisher have a positive reputation?

3. Balance, objectivity, and independence

- Does the material or website strive for balance and objectivity rather than use extreme, inflammatory, or highly subjective language or opinions?
- Is more than one point of view evident at the site?
- If the material takes a strong stand on one side of a controversial issue, does the author or site acknowledge there may be another side to the matter?
- Is the website sponsored by any commercial or political organization that advocates for a particular point of view?
- Does the author have any financial or commercial interest that might conflict with a fair or objective presentation of the topic?
- Is the material drawn from a site that sells a product or solicits customers for a service?

4. Quality of online presentation and other cues

- Is the site well organized or designed so that browsers can easily visit and retrieve information?
- Does the site or online material show care in its preparation, such as proper spelling and good grammar in all posted materials?
- Does the site work effectively, so that the links to subpages and external sites are accurate and helpful?
- How recently has the site been updated? Does the site show evidence that someone regularly attends to it with corrections, new materials, and so forth?
- Does the material contain clear and useful references to other scholarship from journals, professional books, and recognized research studies?
- Have supporting references in the material been published in recent years, or do they include mostly out-of-date, or possibly obsolete sources?

Figure C.1

Evaluating online resources. The questions listed here, which draw heavily on the work of Alexander and Tate (1999), can help you to evaluate the quality and reliability of resource materials found on the Internet.

associated with quality on the web. The rest of this essay synthesizes their work and my own experience from over a decade of helping students and teachers use the Net (see **Figure C.1** for an overview). If I had to reduce this advice to its simplest terms, the most important key to finding quality resources online will always be the *active exercise of judgment and critical thinking.*

Let's discuss the process of finding sources first. *It is important to understand the difference between online databases and Internet search engines.* Although it is simple and painless to type a phrase into Google or Yahoo! or another Internet search engine, these engines should *not* normally be the first or only mechanism you use to find resources. It is a better idea to go to the indexes your school's library provides. These indexes can often be accessed through a library's web-

page. By subscribing to various *online databases* (such as PsycINFO and full-text digital *journal archives* such as PsycARTICLES), your library has already pointed out the most direct path to finding quality materials. If you do use an Internet search engine, try the more specialized ones such as Google Scholar <http:// scholar.google.com/> or Scirus <www.scirus.com/>. And remember, it may be prudent to ask your school's reference librarian for suggestions as you develop your own research competence.

It is also critical that you understand the difference between print-based and web-based sources. Online databases such as PsycINFO will give you *abstracts* (brief summaries) of articles from professional journals. The articles themselves may be found in any of three places: in digital archives online, on the shelves of your school's library, or via interlibrary loan from another school. Every school has different levels of access or availability for different journals. Thus, print-based sources, particularly journal articles, may require you to recover them in person rather than online. On the other hand, Internet search engines will generally lead you to sources at different websites. The materials at these sites may appear directly on your web browser, or you may need to download the documents to your personal computer.

Once you have found such sources, how do you evaluate if they are worthwhile? The comments that follow suggest what you should think about.

Identity and Qualifications of the Authors

The Internet is a kind of worldwide democracy. Just about anyone—qualified or not—can construct a webpage and put what they want to say online. With so few restrictions on Internet publishing, the range and quality of online resources is bound to vary from invaluable to completely worthless. So, researchers who turn to the Net need to ask two related questions: *Who has written this material?* and *What are their qualifications for so doing?* These are probably the two most important guides to the quality of online resources.

Sometimes you will find no clues to the identity of the author of a particular webpage or resource— no name, no organizational affiliation, nothing that reveals the authorship of the material. If this is the case, you should be skeptical about relying on this information. It's hard to defend the quality of a work when "Anonymous" is the author.

Suppose one or more authors are listed by name. The next task is to discover the *qualifications* of these authors. Do they have some type of expertise to justify writing the online material or constructing the online site? You should look for a statement of an author's academic credentials (such as an advanced degree like a Ph.D. or an M.D.) or appropriate work experience (such as "director of personnel" at a company or "senior researcher" at a laboratory). You may be able to read through a resumé at a personal webpage showing the author's qualifications. You should also try to determine whether the author has published on a similar topic in reputable, peer-reviewed journals or belongs to professional or scholarly organizations concerned with the subject.

There are other cautions to keep in mind. Some authors may be qualified to comment on one topic but go beyond their expertise into other domains of knowledge—for example, a physician commenting on economics or a biologist on educational methods. Researchers need to be cautious with writers who move too far away from their fields of specialization. Another consideration is whether authors may have a financial stake or commercial interest in the issue that might compromise their objectivity.

Finally, suppose the "author" of a web-based publication has an institutional identity such as a professional association, a governmental agency, a research center, or a nonprofit organization. How should qualifications be weighed in such a case? Certainly the overall reputation of the institutional author should be recognized. For example, a consensus statement on a treatment approach produced by the National Institute of Mental Health or a report on the employment characteristics of psychologists issued by the American Psychological Association would both be rated positively as reference sources. You may also check whether a broad corporate board of editors or advisors is associated with an institutional voice on the Net. However, beware of fancy-sounding "Institutes" or "Commissions" or "Associations" that may be the product of a single person or handful of individuals and serve only to artificially embellish the opinions of their creators.

Publisher or Sponsor of the Website

Book authors traditionally use print publishers to promote and distribute their writings. In turn, publishers place their reputations on the line by issuing new books. Discerning readers rely on a publisher's overall standing when they consider whether to acquire new works. Especially in academic publishing, readers know that an editorial and review process precedes publication and that such efforts seek to ensure a high level of quality for the published material. Indeed, the essence of academic scholarship lies in a willingness to submit research to prepublication critiques by knowledgeable colleagues. Occasionally, though, an author circumvents the editorial and peer review process and pays to have his or her book set

in print directly. This practice is called "vanity publishing" and is usually looked down upon by other scholars.

In a practice reminiscent of vanity publishing, many web authors post materials online directly through commercial or free Internet service providers. Because these writings have not been edited or evaluated prior to their publication, you need to be cautious in judging their quality. This is not to disparage all self-published resources on the web. Clearly, experts have posted some valuable resources online without peer review. But, in the absence of a clear process of scholarly peer review, you must look for other indicators of quality. For this reason, the overall qualifications of an author as an expert may be crucial in determining whether to use a resource published without peer review.

Websites that are sponsored by academic institutions, government agencies, and nonprofit or scholarly organizations have URLs that end with the designation *.edu, .gov,* or *.org* rather than *.com* or *.net.* Such sites would be expected to offer some assurance of higher quality for data posted there. A particular clue to quality at corporate sites may be a copyright notice by a sponsoring organization rather than a single individual. Often located at the bottom of a webpage, this notice may signal that the organization is willing to put its reputation behind the resource. For example, there are many online health information centers that range in quality from dismal to superb. At one excellent site, The Virtual Hospital <www.vh.org>, it is significant to find the notice on its title page, "Copyright © 1992–2006 the Author(s) and The University of Iowa."

Balance, Objectivity, and Independence

At the checkout line in a supermarket, shoppers often face a set of tabloid newspapers with outrageous headlines and the promise of lurid stories inside. Many people pick up a copy of their favorite tabloid as entertainment, something to be read purely for relaxation and enjoyment but not as an objective or reliable source of reporting about the world. Although tabloid papers are an extreme example, other sources of information should arouse similar suspicions because of their subjective, unbalanced, and biased style of presentation. In similar fashion, Internet resources should be evaluated for their apparent balance and objectivity. Certainly, the presence of language, graphic images, or opinions that are extreme, inflammatory, or highly subjective suggests that the material should be treated with some skepticism. The more extreme, vulgar, or intemperate the manner of presentation, the less likely that the resource is reliable and trustworthy.

A more difficult case arises from material found on sites clearly advocating a particular point of view, such as those for a lobbying group, political movement, or professional advocacy or commercial trade association. Researchers should expect that resources available at these sites will support the point of view of the group. This fact does not necessarily disqualify the importance of materials found there. The sponsoring organizations may provide valuable information for visitors to their sites. Greater reliance can probably be given to resources found on a site that acknowledges there is more than one side to a controversial issue or, even, that the topic is controversial in the first place. Some sites even offer links to the opposing side of a disputed topic. This openness should inspire confidence by users of the site because it suggests a sense of fairness.

A frequent challenge to researchers of psychological topics arises from commercial sites that stand to make money or gain new customers on the basis of what they post online. These sites may be businesses (with a *.com* address) or may be allied with the professional office or practice of individuals such as psychotherapists or physicians. Sometimes these sites offer a "Resource Center" or similar area that is filled with articles relating to the product or service of the site's sponsor. These articles may include scientific-sounding titles and come from magazines, journals, or books that seem to be similarly professional. Most evaluators warn researchers to be careful when using materials from any site that has a direct financial motivation in sharing information. Finding quality in online materials is always a judgment call, and the more you know about a topic from other sources, the better you can make that call at commercial sites.

Quality of Online Presentation and Other Cues

Another important index of quality is the care with which websites and materials have been organized and maintained. You should consider how easily you can use a website. Do the hypertext links within the site work or do they point to empty or missing pages? Can visitors easily find the information they are looking for? Is there evidence that the design of the site was carefully considered and executed? Similarly, the actual text of materials retrieved from the Net should be free from gross errors. Poor grammar and improper spelling usually signal that something is amiss. Reputable scholars are fanatical about eliminating sloppiness or careless mistakes in what they write. They believe any such errors would suggest a parallel sloppiness in their thinking. Thus, the presence of mechanical and stylistic mistakes at a website or in a document should raise doubts about how reputable

the actual content of a resource may be. Finally, more credibility can be assigned to materials retrieved from sites that are frequently updated and carefully corrected. You should look for clear dates on pages containing important information. Ideally, one date will indicate when the page was first posted online and another when it was last changed or revised.

When I use the Net for research purposes, I use at least two further cues to evaluate the quality of the material or sites I find. First, in articles or papers online, I look at the references used by the author and consider whether they include scholarly materials from journals, professional books, or other recognized research sources. These sources should go well beyond the author's own previous writings. Second, I examine the dates of the supporting references. How recent are they? Do they include sources published in the last several years? Or, do they include only older and possibly out-of-date materials? The more up-to-date the references, the greater I tend to trust the source.

A Final Note of Advice

I hope the suggestions summarized here make it clear that any researcher must actively exercise judgment and critical thinking skills in evaluating online resources. Such skills are enormously enhanced when the researcher chooses a balanced overall research strategy. It is one thing to seek a quick fact or a simple definition through a website; it is another to rely on the Internet as the *sole* data source for a major paper or research project. Yet for many people, the Internet is an easily "surfable" medium, one that can quickly lead to information of varying levels of quality. The very ease of conducting research online often seduces student researchers to skip more difficult, but crucially important, steps offline.

The most important strategy a student can bring to any research project is to develop an overall perspective or a broad vantage point regarding the topic of the project. This situation is unlikely to happen unless the investigator uses sources of different types—scholarly books, journal and magazine articles, and printed research reports—*in addition to* materials retrieved from the Internet. It is both easy to understand, but embarrassing in the long run, when a student hands in a paper with only Internet-based sources and later discovers in a professor's grading that the Net provided a biased or slanted view of the topic. Without the counterbalance of non-Net sources, a student risks seriously misjudging how psychologists, physicians, and other research scientists actually approach an issue. So, my final suggestion about research is a simple rule of thumb: The longer and more important the research project or paper, the broader the kinds of references you should use to answer the research question.

For Further Reference and Reading

Students who wish to further enhance their ability to evaluate Internet materials and sites should consider these outstanding online resources:

Beck, S. (1997). Evaluation criteria. [Online] *The good, the bad, and the ugly: Or, why it's a good idea to evaluate web sources.* Available at the New Mexico State University Library website: http://lib.nmsu.edu/instruction/eval.html

Kirk, E. E. (1996). *Evaluating information found on the Internet.* [Online] Available at the Sheridan Libraries of the Johns Hopkins University website: http://www.library.jhu.edu/researchhelp/general/evaluating/

U.C. Berkeley Teaching Library Internet Workshops. (2005). *Evaluating webpages: Techniques to apply and questions to ask.* [Online] Available at the University of California at Berkeley Library website: http://www.lib.berkeley.edu/TeachingLib/Guides/Internet/Evaluate.html

A

Absolute refractory period The minimum length of time after an action potential during which another action potential cannot begin.

Achievement motive The need to master difficult challenges, to outperform others, and to meet high standards of excellence.

Acquired immune deficiency syndrome (AIDS) A disorder in which the immune system is gradually weakened and eventually disabled by the human immunodeficiency virus (HIV).

Acquisition The formation of a new conditioned response tendency.

Action potential A brief change in a neuron's electrical charge.

Adaptation An inherited characteristic that increased in a population (through natural selection) because it helped solve a problem of survival or reproduction during the time it emerged.

Additive color mixing Formation of colors by superimposing lights, putting more light in the mixture than exists in any one light by itself.

Adoption studies Research studies that assess hereditary influence by examining the resemblance between adopted children and both their biological and their adoptive parents.

Afferent nerve fibers Axons that carry information inward to the central nervous system from the periphery of the body.

Afterimage A visual image that persists after a stimulus is removed.

Age of viability The age at which a baby can survive in the event of a premature birth.

Aggression Any behavior that is intended to hurt someone, either physically or verbally.

Agonist A chemical that mimics the action of a neurotransmitter.

Agoraphobia A fear of going out to public places.

Alcohol A variety of beverages containing ethyl alcohol.

Amnesia See *Anterograde amnesia, Retrograde amnesia.*

Anecdotal evidence Personal stories about specific incidents and experiences.

Animism The belief that all things are living.

Anorexia nervosa Eating disorder characterized by intense fear of gaining weight, disturbed body image, refusal to maintain normal weight, and dangerous measures to lose weight.

Antagonist A chemical that opposes the action of a neurotransmitter.

Anterograde amnesia Loss of memories for events that occur after a head injury.

Antianxiety drugs Medications that relieve tension, apprehension, and nervousness.

Antidepressant drugs Medications that gradually elevate mood and help bring people out of a depression.

Antipsychotic drugs Medications used to gradually reduce psychotic symptoms, including hyperactivity, mental confusion, hallucinations, and delusions.

Anxiety disorders A class of disorders marked by feelings of excessive apprehension and anxiety.

Applied psychology The branch of psychology concerned with everyday, practical problems.

Approach-approach conflict A conflict situation in which a choice must be made between two attractive goals.

Approach-avoidance conflict A conflict situation in which a choice must be made about whether to pursue a single goal that has both attractive and unattractive aspects.

Archetypes According to Jung, emotionally charged images and thought forms that have universal meaning.

Argument One or more premises used to provide support for a conclusion.

Assumptions Premises for which no proof or evidence is offered.

Attachment A close, emotional bond of affection between infants and their caregivers.

Attention Focusing awareness on a narrowed range of stimuli or events.

Attitudes Orientations that locate objects of thought on dimensions of judgment.

Attributions Inferences that people draw about the causes of events, others' behavior, and their own behavior.

Autonomic nervous system (ANS) The system of nerves that connect to the heart, blood vessels, smooth muscles, and glands.

Availability heuristic Basing the estimated probability of an event on the ease with which relevant instances come to mind.

Aversion therapy A behavior therapy in which an aversive stimulus is paired with a stimulus that elicits an undesirable response.

Avoidance-avoidance conflict A conflict situation in which a choice must be made between two unattractive goals.

Avoidance learning Learning that has occurred when an organism engages in a response that prevents aversive stimulation from occurring.

Axon A long, thin fiber that transmits signals away from the neuron cell body to other neurons, or to muscles or glands.

B

Basilar membrane A structure that runs the length of the cochlea in the inner ear and holds the auditory receptors, called hair cells.

Behavior Any overt (observable) response or activity by an organism.

Behavior modification A systematic approach to changing behavior through the application of the principles of conditioning.

Behavior therapies Application of the principles of learning to direct efforts to change clients' maladaptive behaviors.

Behavioral contract A written agreement outlining a promise to adhere to the contingencies of a behavior modification program.

Behaviorism A theoretical orientation based on the premise that scientific psychology should study only observable behavior.

Binocular depth cues Clues about distance based on the differing views of the two eyes.

Biological rhythms Periodic fluctuations in physiological functioning.

Biomedical therapies Physiological interventions intended to reduce symptoms associated with psychological disorders.

Biopsychosocial model A model of illness that holds that physical illness is caused by a complex interaction of biological, psychological, and sociocultural factors.

Bipolar disorder (formerly known as manic-depressive disorder) Mood disorder marked by the experience of both depressed and manic periods.

Bisexuals Persons who seek emotional-sexual relationships with members of either sex.

Bottom-up processing In form perception, progression from individual elements to the whole.

Bulimia nervosa Eating disorder characterized by habitually engaging in out-of-control overeating followed by unhealthy compensatory efforts, such as self-induced vomiting, fasting, abuse of laxatives and diuretics, and excessive exercise.

Bystander effect A paradoxical social phenomenon in which people are less likely to provide needed help when they are in groups than when they are alone.

C

Cannabis The hemp plant from which marijuana, hashish, and THC are derived.

Case study An in-depth investigation of an individual subject.

Catastrophic thinking Unrealistically pessimistic appraisals of stress that exaggerate the magnitude of one's problems.

Catatonic schizophrenia A type of schizophrenia marked by striking motor disturbances, ranging from muscular rigidity to random motor activity.

Catharsis The release of emotional tension.

Central nervous system (CNS) The brain and the spinal cord.

Centration The tendency to focus on just one feature of a problem, neglecting other important aspects.

Cephalocaudal trend The head-to-foot direction of motor development.

Cerebellum A relatively large and deeply folded structure located adjacent to the back surface of the brainstem.

Cerebral cortex The convoluted outer layer of the cerebrum.

Cerebral hemispheres The right and left halves of the cerebrum.

Channel The medium through which a message is sent.

Chromosomes Threadlike strands of DNA (deoxyribonucleic acid) molecules that carry genetic information.

Chunk A group of familiar stimuli stored as a single unit.

Circadian rhythms The 24-hour biological cycles found in humans and many other species.

Classical conditioning A type of learning in which a neutral stimulus acquires the ability to evoke a response that was originally evoked by another stimulus.

Client-centered therapy An insight therapy that emphasizes providing a supportive emotional climate for clients, who play a major role in determining the pace and direction of their therapy.

Clinical psychologists Psychologists who specialize in the diagnosis and treatment of psychological disorders and everyday behavioral problems.

Clinical psychology The branch of psychology concerned with the diagnosis and treatment of psychological problems and disorders.

Cochlea The fluid-filled, coiled tunnel in the inner ear that contains the receptors for hearing.

Coefficient of determination The percentage of variation in one variable that can be predicted based on the other variable.

Cognition The mental processes involved in acquiring knowledge.

Cognitive-behavioral treatments A varied combination of verbal interventions and behavioral modification techniques used to help clients change maladaptive patterns of thinking.

Cognitive development Transitions in youngsters' patterns of thinking, including reasoning, remembering, and problem solving.

Cognitive dissonance A psychological state that exists when related cognitions are inconsistent.

Cognitive therapy An insight therapy that emphasizes recognizing and changing negative thoughts and maladaptive beliefs.

Collective unconscious According to Jung, a storehouse of latent memory traces inherited from people's ancestral past.

Collectivism Putting group goals ahead of personal goals and defining one's identity in terms of the groups one belongs to.

Color blindness Deficiency in the ability to distinguish among colors.

Comorbidity The coexistence of two or more disorders.

Companionate love Warm, trusting, tolerant affection for another whose life is deeply intertwined with one's own.

Comparitors People, objects, events, and other standards that are used as a baseline for comparisons in making judgments.

Compensation According to Adler, efforts to overcome imagined or real inferiorities by developing one's abilities.

Complementary colors Pairs of colors that produce gray tones when added together.

Concordance rate The percentage of twin pairs or other pairs of relatives that exhibit the same disorder.

Conditioned reinforcers. See *Secondary reinforcers.*

Conditioned response (CR) A learned reaction to a conditioned stimulus that occurs because of previous conditioning.

Conditioned stimulus (CS) A previously neutral stimulus that has, through conditioning, acquired the capacity to evoke a conditioned response.

Cones Specialized visual receptors that play a key role in daylight vision and color vision.

Conflict A state that occurs when two or more incompatible motivations or behavioral impulses compete for expression.

Conformity The tendency for people to yield to real or imagined social pressure.

Confounding of variables A condition that exists whenever two variables are linked together in a way that makes it difficult to sort out their independent effects.

Conjunction fallacy An error that occurs when people estimate that the odds of two uncertain events happening together are greater than the odds of either event happening alone.

Connectionist models See *Parallel distributed processing (PDP) models*

Conscious Whatever one is aware of at a particular point in time.

Consciousness One's awareness of internal and external stimuli.

Conservation Piaget's term for the awareness that physical quantities remain constant in spite of changes in their shape or appearance.

Consolidation A hypothetical process involving the gradual conversion of information into durable memory codes stored in long-term memory.

Constructive coping Relatively healthful efforts that people make to deal with stressful events.

Continuous reinforcement Reinforcing every instance of a designated response.

Control group Subjects in a study who do not receive the special treatment given to the experimental group.

Convergent thinking Narrowing down a list of alternatives to converge on a single correct answer.

Conversion disorder A somatoform disorder characterized by a significant loss of physical function (with no apparent organic basis), usually in a single organ system.

Coping Active efforts to master, reduce, or tolerate the demands created by stress.

Corpus callosum The structure that connects the two cerebral hemispheres.

Correlation The extent to which two variables are related to each other.

Correlation coefficient A numerical index of the degree of relationship between two variables.

Counseling psychologists Psychologists who specialize in the treatment of everyday adjustment problems.

Creativity The generation of ideas that are original, novel, and useful.

Critical period A limited time span in the development of an organism when it is optimal for certain capacities to emerge because the organism is especially responsive to certain experiences.

Critical thinking Purposeful, reasoned, goal-directed thinking that involves solving problems, formulating inferences, working with probabilities, and making carefully thought-out decisions.

Cross-sectional study A research design in which investigators compare groups of subjects of differing age who are observed at a single point in time.

Culture The widely shared customs, beliefs, values, norms, institutions, and other products of a community that are transmitted socially across generations.

Culture-bound disorders Abnormal syndromes found only in a few cultural groups.

Cumulative recorder A graphic record of reinforcement and responding in a Skinner box as a function of time.

D

Dark adaptation The process in which the eyes become more sensitive to light in low illumination.

Data collection techniques Procedures for making empirical observations and measurements.

Decay theory The idea that forgetting occurs because memory traces fade with time.

Decision making The process of evaluating alternatives and making choices among them.

Declarative memory system Memory for factual information.

Defense mechanisms Largely unconscious reactions that protect a person from unpleasant emotions such as anxiety and guilt.

Deinstitutionalization Transferring the treatment of mental illness from inpatient institutions to community-based facilities that emphasize outpatient care.

Delusions False beliefs that are maintained even though they are clearly out of touch with reality.

Dementia An abnormal condition marked by multiple cognitive defects that include memory impairment.

Dendrites Branchlike parts of a neuron that are specialized to receive information.

Dependent variable In an experiment, the variable that is thought to be affected by the manipulation of the independent variable.

Depth perception Interpretation of visual cues that indicate how near or far away objects are.

Descriptive statistics Statistics that are used to organize and summarize data.

Development The sequence of age-related changes that occur as a person progresses from conception to death.

Developmental norms The average age at which individuals display various behaviors and abilities.

Deviation IQ scores Scores that locate subjects precisely within the normal distribution, using the standard deviation as the unit of measurement.

Diagnosis Distinguishing one illness from another.

Discrimination Behaving differently, usually unfairly, toward the members of a group.

Discriminative stimuli Cues that influence operant behavior by indicating the probable consequences (reinforcement or nonreinforcement) of a response.

Disorganized schizophrenia A type of schizophrenia in which particularly severe deterioration of adaptive behavior is seen.

Displacement Diverting emotional feelings (usually anger) from their original source to a substitute target.

Display rules Cultural norms that regulate the appropriate expressions of emotions.

Dissociation A splitting off of mental processes into two separate, simultaneous streams of awareness.

Dissociative amnesia A sudden loss of memory for important personal information that is too extensive to be due to normal forgetting.

Dissociative disorders A class of disorders in which people lose contact with portions of their consciousness or memory, resulting in disruptions in their sense of identity.

Dissociative fugue A disorder in which people lose their memory for their entire lives along with their sense of personal identity.

Dissociative identity disorder A type of dissociative disorder characterized by the coexistence in one person of two or more largely complete, and usually very different, personalities. Also called multiple-personality disorder.

Divergent thinking Trying to expand the range of alternatives by generating many possible solutions.

Door-in-the-face technique Making a large request that is likely to be turned down as a way to increase the chances that people will agree to a smaller request later.

Double-blind procedure A research strategy in which neither subjects nor experimenters know which subjects are in the experimental or control groups.

Dream analysis A psychoanalytic technique in which the therapist interprets the symbolic meaning of the client's dreams.

Dual-coding theory Paivio's theory that memory is enhanced by forming semantic and visual codes, since either can lead to recall.

Drive An internal state of tension that motivates an organism to engage in activities that should reduce the tension.

E

Eating disorders Severe disturbances in eating behavior characterized by preoccupation with weight concerns and unhealthy efforts to control weight.

Efferent nerve fibers Axons that carry information outward from the central nervous system to the periphery of the body.

Ego According to Freud, the decision-making component of personality that operates according to the reality principle.

Egocentrism A limited ability to share another person's viewpoint.

Elaboration Linking a stimulus to other information at the time of encoding.

Electrical stimulation of the brain (ESB) Sending a weak electric current into a brain structure to stimulate (activate) it.

Electrocardiograph (EKG) A device that records the contractions of the heart.

Electroconvulsive therapy (ECT) A biomedical treatment in which electric shock is used to produce a cortical seizure accompanied by convulsions.

Electroencephalograph (EEG) A device that monitors the electrical activity of the brain over time by means of recording electrodes attached to the surface of the scalp.

Electromyograph (EMG) A device that records muscular activity and tension.

Electrooculograph (EOG) A device that records eye movements.

Elicit To draw out or bring forth.

Embryonic stage The second stage of prenatal development, lasting from two weeks until the end of the second month.

Emit To send forth.

Emotion A subjective conscious experience (the cognitive component) accompanied by bodily arousal (the physiological component) and by characteristic overt expression (the behavioral component).

Empiricism The premise that knowledge should be acquired through observation.

Encoding Forming a memory code.

Encoding specificity principle The idea that the value of a retrieval cue depends on how well it corresponds to the memory code.

Endocrine system A group of glands that secrete chemicals into the bloodstream that help control bodily functioning.

Endorphins The entire family of internally produced chemicals that resemble opiates in structure and effects.

Episodic memory system Chronological, or temporally dated, recollections of personal experiences.

Escape learning A type of learning in which an organism acquires a response that decreases or ends some aversive stimulation.

Etiology The apparent causation and developmental history of an illness.

Evaluative conditioning Efforts to transfer the emotion attached to a UCS to a new CS.

Evolutionary psychology Theoretical perspective that examines behavioral processes in terms of their adaptive value for a species over the course of many generations.

Experiment A research method in which the investigator manipulates a variable under carefully controlled conditions and observes whether any changes occur in a second variable as a result.

Experimental group The subjects in a study who receive some special treatment in regard to the independent variable.

Experimenter bias A phenomenon that occurs when a researcher's expectations or preferences about the outcome of a study influence the results obtained.

External attributions Ascribing the causes of behavior to situational demands and environmental constraints.

Extinction The gradual weakening and disappearance of a conditioned response tendency.

Extraneous variables Any variables other than the independent variable that seem likely to influence the dependent variable in a specific study.

F

Factor analysis Statistical analysis of correlations among many variables to identify closely related clusters of variables.

Family studies Scientific studies in which researchers assess hereditary influence by examining blood relatives to see how much they resemble each other on a specific trait.

Farsightedness A visual deficiency in which distant objects are seen clearly but close objects appear blurry.

Feature analysis The process of detecting specific elements in visual input and assembling them into a more complex form.

Feature detectors Neurons that respond selectively to very specific features of more complex stimuli.

Fetal alcohol syndrome A collection of congenital (inborn) problems associated with excessive alcohol use during pregnancy.

Fetal stage The third stage of prenatal development, lasting from two months through birth.

Field dependence-independence Individuals' tendency to rely primarily on external versus internal frames of reference when orienting themselves in space.

Fitness The reproductive success (number of descendants) of an individual organism relative to the average reproductive success of the population.

Fixation According to Freud, failure to move forward from one psychosexual stage to another as expected.

Fixed-interval (FI) schedule A reinforcement schedule in which the reinforcer is given for the first response that occurs after a fixed time interval has elapsed.

Fixed-ratio (FR) schedule A reinforcement schedule in which the reinforcer is given after a fixed number of nonreinforced responses.

Flashbulb memories Unusually vivid and detailed recollections of momentous events.

Foot-in-the-door technique Getting people to agree to a small request to increase the chances that they will agree to a larger request later.

Forebrain The largest and most complicated region of the brain, encompassing a variety of structures, including the thalamus, hypothalamus, limbic system, and cerebrum.

Forgetting curve A graph showing retention and forgetting over time.

Fovea A tiny spot in the center of the retina that contains only cones; visual acuity is greatest at this spot.

Free association A psychoanalytic technique in which clients spontaneously express their thoughts and feelings exactly as they occur, with as little censorship as possible.

Frequency distribution An orderly arrangement of scores indicating the frequency of each score or group of scores.

Frequency polygon A line figure used to present data from a frequency distribution.

Frustration The feeling that people experience in any situation in which their pursuit of some goal is thwarted.

Functional fixedness The tendency to perceive an item only in terms of its most common use.

Functionalism A school of psychology based on the belief that psychology should investigate the function or purpose of consciousness, rather than its structure.

Fundamental attribution error Observers' bias in favor of internal attributions in explaining others' behavior.

G

Galvanic skin response (GSR) An increase in the electrical conductivity of the skin that occurs when sweat glands increase their activity.

Gambler's fallacy The belief that the odds of a chance event increase if the event hasn't occurred recently.

Gender Culturally constructed distinctions between masculinity and femininity.

Gender differences Actual disparities between the sexes in typical behavior or average ability.

Gender roles Expectations about what is appropriate behavior for each sex.

Gender stereotypes Widely held beliefs about males' and females' abilities, personality traits, and behavior.

General adaptation syndrome Selye's model of the body's stress response, consisting of three stages: alarm, resistance, and exhaustion.

Generalized anxiety disorder A psychological disorder marked by a chronic, high level of anxiety that is not tied to any specific threat.

Genes DNA segments that serve as the key functional units in hereditary transmission.

Germinal stage The first phase of prenatal development, encompassing the first two weeks after conception.

Glia Cells found throughout the nervous system that provide various types of support for neurons.

Glucose A simple sugar that is an important source of energy.

Glucostats Neurons sensitive to glucose in the surrounding fluid.

Group Two or more individuals who interact and are interdependent.

Group cohesiveness The strength of the liking relationships linking group members to each other and to the group itself.

Group polarization A phenomenon that occurs when group discussion strengthens a group's dominant point of view and produces a shift toward a more extreme decision in that direction.

Group therapy The simultaneous treatment of several clients in a group.

Groupthink A process in which members of a cohesive group emphasize concurrence at the expense of critical thinking in arriving at a decision.

Gustatory system The sensory system for taste.

H

Hallucinations Sensory perceptions that occur in the absence of a real, external stimulus, or gross distortions of perceptual input.

Hallucinogens A diverse group of drugs that have powerful effects on mental and emotional functioning, marked most prominently by distortions in sensory and perceptual experience.

Health psychology The subfield of psychology concerned with how psychosocial factors relate to the promotion and maintenance of health and with the causation, prevention, and treatment of illness.

Hedonistic adaptation An effect that occurs when the mental scale that people use to judge the pleasantness-unpleasantness of their experiences shifts so that their neutral point, or baseline for comparison, changes.

Heritability ratio An estimate of the proportion of trait variability in a population that is determined by variations in genetic inheritance.

Heterosexuals Persons who seek emotional-sexual relationships with members of the other sex.

Heuristic A strategy, guiding principle, or rule of thumb used in solving problems or making decisions.

Hierarchy of needs Maslow's systematic arrangement of needs according to priority, which assumes that basic needs must be met before less basic needs are aroused.

Higher-order conditioning A type of conditioning in which a conditioned stimulus functions as if it were an unconditioned stimulus.

Hindbrain The part of the brain that includes the cerebellum and two structures found in the lower part of the brainstem: the medulla and the pons.

Hindsight bias The tendency to mold one's interpretation of the past to fit how events actually turned out.

Histogram A bar graph that presents data from a frequency distribution.

Homeostasis A state of physiological equilibrium or stability.

Homosexuals Persons who seek emotional-sexual relationships with members of the same sex.

Hormones The chemical substances released by the endocrine glands.

Humanism A theoretical orientation that emphasizes the unique qualities of humans, especially their freedom and their potential for personal growth.

Hypnosis A systematic procedure that typically produces a heightened state of suggestibility.

Hypochondriasis A somatoform disorder characterized by excessive preoccupation with health concerns and incessant worry about developing physical illnesses.

Hypothalamus A structure found near the base of the forebrain that is involved in the regulation of basic biological needs.

Hypothesis A tentative statement about the relationship between two or more variables.

I

Id According to Freud, the primitive, instinctive component of personality that operates according to the pleasure principle.

Identification Bolstering self-esteem by forming an imaginary or real alliance with some person or group.

Illusory correlation A misperception that occurs when people estimate that they have encountered more confirmations of an association between social traits than they have actually seen.

Immune response The body's defensive reaction to invasion by bacteria, viral agents, or other foreign substances.

Impossible figures Objects that can be represented in two-dimensional pictures but cannot exist in three-dimensional space.

Incentive An external goal that has the capacity to motivate behavior.

Incongruence The degree of disparity between one's self-concept and one's actual experience.

Independent variable In an experiment, a condition or event that an experimenter varies in order to see its impact on another variable.

Individualism Putting personal goals ahead of group goals and defining one's identity in terms of personal attributes rather than group memberships.

Inferential statistics Statistics that are used to interpret data and draw conclusions.

Ingroup The group that people belong to and identify with.

Insight In problem solving, the sudden discovery of the correct solution following incorrect attempts based primarily on trial and error.

Insight therapies Psychotherapy methods characterized by verbal interactions intended to enhance clients' self-knowledge and thus promote healthful changes in personality and behavior.

Insomnia Chronic problems in getting adequate sleep.

Intelligence quotient (IQ) A child's mental age divided by chronological age, multiplied by 100.

Interference theory The idea that people forget information because of competition from other material.

Intermittent reinforcement A reinforcement schedule in which a designated response is reinforced only some of the time.

Internal attributions Ascribing the causes of behavior to personal dispositions, traits, abilities, and feelings.

Internet addiction Spending an inordinate amount of time on the Internet and being unable to control online use.

Interpersonal attraction Positive feelings toward another.

Introspection Careful, systematic observation of one's own conscious experience.

Irreversibility The inability to envision reversing an action.

J

Journal A periodical that publishes technical and scholarly material, usually in a narrowly defined area of inquiry.

L

Latent content According to Freud, the hidden or disguised meaning of the events in a dream.

Latent learning Learning that is not apparent from behavior when it first occurs.

Learned helplessness Passive behavior produced by exposure to unavoidable aversive events.

Learning A relatively durable change in behavior or knowledge that is due to experience.

Lens The transparent eye structure that focuses the light rays falling on the retina.

Lesioning Destroying a piece of the brain.

Levels-of-processing theory The theory holding that deeper levels of mental processing result in longer-lasting memory codes.

Lie detector See *Polygraph.*

Life changes Any noticeable alterations in one's living circumstances that require readjustment.

Light adaptation The process whereby the eyes become less sensitive to light in high illumination.

Limbic system A densely connected network of structures roughly located along the border between the cerebral cortex and deeper subcortical areas.

Link method Forming a mental image of items to be remembered in a way that links them together.

Long-term memory (LTM) An unlimited capacity store that can hold information over lengthy periods of time.

Lowball technique Getting someone to commit to an attractive proposition before revealing the hidden costs.

M

Major depressive disorder Mood disorder characterized by persistent feelings of sadness and despair and a loss of interest in previous sources of pleasure.

Manic-depressive disorder See *Bipolar disorder.*

Manifest content According to Freud, the plot of a dream at a surface level.

Matching hypothesis The idea that males and females of approximately equal physical attractiveness are likely to select each other as partners.

Maturation Development that reflects the gradual unfolding of one's genetic blueprint.

MDMA A compound drug related to both amphetamines and hallucinogens, especially mescaline; commonly called "ecstasy."

Mean The arithmetic average of the scores in a distribution.

Median The score that falls exactly in the center of a distribution of scores.

Medical model The view that it is useful to think of abnormal behavior as a disease.

Meditation A family of mental exercises in which a conscious attempt is made to focus attention in a nonanalytical way.

Menarche The first occurrence of menstruation.

Mental age In intelligence testing, a score that indicates that a child displays the mental ability typical of a child of that chronological (actual) age.

Mental hospital A medical institution specializing in providing inpatient care for psychological disorders.

Mental set Persisting in using problem-solving strategies that have worked in the past.

Message The information transmitted by a source.

Method of loci A mnemonic device that involves taking an imaginary walk along a familiar path where images of items to be remembered are associated with certain locations.

Midbrain The segment of the brain stem that lies between the hindbrain and the forebrain.

Midlife crisis A difficult, turbulent period of doubts and reappraisal of one's life.

Misinformation effect Phenomenon that occurs when participants' recall of an event they witnessed is altered by introducing misleading post-event information.

Mnemonic devices Strategies for enhancing memory.

Mode The score that occurs most frequently in a distribution.

Model A person whose behavior is observed by another.

Monocular depth cues Clues about distance based on the image from either eye alone.

Mood disorders A class of disorders marked by emotional disturbances of varied kinds that may spill over to disrupt physical, perceptual, social, and thought processes.

Mood stabilizers Drugs used to control mood swings in patients with bipolar mood disorders.

Motivation Goal-directed behavior.

Motor development The progression of muscular coordination required for physical activities.

Multiple-personality disorder See *Dissociative identity disorder.*

Myelin sheath Insulating material, derived from glial cells, that encases some axons of neurons.

N

Narcolepsy A disease marked by sudden and irresistible onsets of sleep during normal waking periods.

Narcotics (opiates) Drugs derived from opium that are capable of relieving pain.

Natural selection Principle stating that inherited characteristics that provide a survival or reproductive advantage are more likely than alternative characteristics to be passed on to subsequent generations and thus come to be "selected" over time.

Naturalistic observation A descriptive research method in which the researcher engages in careful, usually prolonged, observation of behavior without intervening directly with the subjects.

Nearsightedness A visual deficiency in which close objects are seen clearly but distant objects appear blurry.

Need for self-actualization The need to fulfill one's potential.

Negative reinforcement The strengthening of a response because it is followed by the removal of an aversive (unpleasant) stimulus.

Negative symptoms Schizophrenic symptoms that involve behavioral deficits, such as flattened emotions, social withdrawal, apathy, impaired attention, and poverty of speech.

Negatively skewed distribution A distribution in which most scores pile up at the high end of the scale.

Neurons Individual cells in the nervous system that receive, integrate, and transmit information.

Neurotransmitters Chemicals that transmit information from one neuron to another.

Non-REM (NREM) sleep Sleep stages 1 through 4, which are marked by an absence of rapid eye movements, relatively little dreaming, and varied EEG activity.

Nonsense syllables Consonant-vowel-consonant arrangements that do not correspond to words.

Normal distribution A symmetric, bell-shaped curve that represents the pattern in which many characteristics are dispersed in the population.

Null hypothesis In inferential statistics, the assumption that there is no true relationship between the variables being observed.

O

Obedience A form of compliance that occurs when people follow direct commands, usually from someone in a position of authority.

Object permanence Recognizing that objects continue to exist even when they are no longer visible.

Observational learning A type of learning that occurs when an organism's responding is influenced by the observation of others, who are called models.

Obsessive-compulsive disorder (OCD) A type of anxiety disorder marked by persistent, uncontrollable intrusions of unwanted thoughts (obsessions) and urges to engage in senseless rituals (compulsions).

Oedipal complex According to Freud, children's manifestation of erotically tinged desires for their opposite-sex parent, accompanied by feelings of hostility toward their same-sex parent.

Olfactory system The sensory system for smell.

Operant conditioning A form of learning in which voluntary responses come to be controlled by their consequences.

Operational definition A definition that describes the actions or operations that will be used to measure or control a variable.

Opiates. See *Narcotics.*

Optimism A general tendency to expect good outcomes.

Outgroup People who are not part of the ingroup.

Overlearning Continued rehearsal of material after one first appears to have mastered it.

P

Panic disorder A type of anxiety disorder characterized by recurrent attacks of overwhelming anxiety that usually occur suddenly and unexpectedly.

Parallel distributed processing (PDP) models Models of memory that assume cognitive processes depend on patterns of activation in highly interconnected computational networks that resemble neural networks. Also called connectionist models.

Paranoid schizophrenia A type of schizophrenia that is dominated by delusions of persecution along with delusions of grandeur.

Parental investment What each sex invests—in terms of time, energy, survival risk, and forgone opportunities—to produce and nurture offspring.

Participants See *Subjects.*

Passionate love A complete absorption in another that includes tender sexual feelings and the agony and ecstasy of intense emotion.

Pavlovian conditioning. See *Classical conditioning.*

Percentile score A figure that indicates the percentage of people who score below the score one has obtained.

Perception The selection, organization, and interpretation of sensory input.

Perceptual constancy A tendency to experience a stable perception in the face of continually changing sensory input.

Perceptual set A readiness to perceive a stimulus in a particular way.

Peripheral nervous system All those nerves that lie outside the brain and spinal cord.

Person perception The process of forming impressions of others.

Personality An individual's unique constellation of consistent behavioral traits.

Personality trait A durable disposition to behave in a particular way in a variety of situations.

Phi phenomenon The illusion of movement created by presenting visual stimuli in rapid succession.

Phobic disorder A type of anxiety disorder marked by a persistent and irrational fear of an object or situation that presents no realistic danger.

Physical dependence The condition that exists when a person must continue to take a drug to avoid withdrawal illness.

Pictorial depth cues Clues about distance that can be given in a flat picture.

Pituitary gland The "master gland" of the endocrine system; it releases a great variety of hormones that fan out through the body, stimulating actions in the other endocrine glands.

Place theory The idea that perception of pitch corresponds to the vibration of different portions, or places, along the basilar membrane.

Placebo effects The fact that subjects' expectations can lead them to experience some change even though they receive an empty, fake, or ineffectual treatment.

Placenta A structure that allows oxygen and nutrients to pass into the fetus from the mother's bloodstream and bodily wastes to pass out to the mother.

Pleasure principle According to Freud, the principle upon which the id operates, demanding immediate gratification of its urges.

Polygenic traits Characteristics that are influenced by more than one pair of genes.

Polygraph A device that records autonomic fluctuations while a subject is questioned, in an effort to determine whether the subject is telling the truth.

Population The larger collection of animals or people from which a sample is drawn and that researchers want to generalize about.

Positive psychology Approach to psyychology that uses theory and research to better understand the positive, adaptive, creative, and fulfilling aspects of human existence.

Positive reinforcement Reinforcement that occurs when a response is strengthened because it is followed by the presentation of a rewarding stimulus.

Positive symptoms Schizophrenic symptoms that involve behavioral excesses or peculiarities, such as hallucinations, delusions, bizarre behavior, and wild flights of ideas.

Positively skewed distribution A distribution in which scores pile up at the low end of the scale.

Postsynaptic potential (PSP) A voltage change at the receptor site on a postsynaptic cell membrane.

Posttraumatic stress disorder Disturbed behavior that is attributed to a major stressful event but that emerges after the stress is over.

Preconscious According to Freud, the level of awareness that contains material just beneath the surface of conscious awareness that can easily be retrieved.

Prejudice A negative attitude held toward members of a group.

Premises The reasons presented to persuade someone that a conclusion is true or probably true.

Prenatal period The period from conception to birth, usually encompassing nine months of pregnancy.

Pressure Expectations or demands that one behave in a certain way.

Primary reinforcers Events that are inherently reinforcing because they satisfy biological needs.

Primary sex characteristics The sexual structures necessary for reproduction.

Proactive interference A memory problem that occurs when previously learned information interferes with the retention of new information.

Problem solving Active efforts to discover what must be done to achieve a goal that is not readily available.

Procedural memory system The repository of memories for actions, skills, and operations.

Prognosis A forecast about the probable course of an illness.

Projection Attributing one's own thoughts, feelings, or motives to another.

Projective tests Psychological tests that ask subjects to respond to vague, ambiguous stimuli in ways that may reveal the subjects' needs, feelings, and personality traits.

Prospective memory The ability to remember to perform actions in the future.

Proximodistal trend The center-outward direction of motor development.

Psychiatrists Physicians who specialize in the diagnosis and treatment of psychological disorders.

Psychoactive drugs Chemical substances that modify mental, emotional, or behavioral functioning.

Psychoanalysis An insight therapy that emphasizes the recovery of unconscious conflicts, motives, and defenses through techniques such as free association and transference.

Psychoanalytic theory A theory developed by Freud that attempts to explain personality, motivation, and mental disorders by focusing on unconscious determinants of behavior.

Psychological dependence The condition that exists when a person must continue to take a drug in order to satisfy intense mental and emotional craving for the drug.

Psychological test A standardized measure of a sample of a person's behavior.

Psychology The science that studies behavior and the physiological and cognitive processes that underlie it, and the profession that applies the accumulated knowledge of this science to practical problems.

Psychosexual stages According to Freud, developmental periods with a characteristic sexual focus that leave their mark on adult personality.

Psychosomatic diseases Physical ailments with a genuine organic basis that are caused in part by psychological factors, especially emotional distress.

Puberty The period of early adolescence marked by rapid physical growth and the development of sexual (reproductive) maturity.

Punishment An event that follows a response that weakens or suppresses the tendency to make that response.

Pupil The opening in the center of the iris that helps regulate the amount of light passing into the rear chamber of the eye.

R

Random assignment The design of a study such that all subjects have an equal chance of being assigned to any group or condition.

Rationalization Creating false but plausible excuses to justify unacceptable behavior.

Reaction formation Behaving in a way that's exactly the opposite of one's true feelings.

Reaction range Genetically determined limits on IQ or other traits.

Reality principle According to Freud, the principle on which the ego operates, which seeks to delay gratification of the id's urges until appropriate outlets and situations can be found.

Recall measure A memory test that requires subjects to reproduce information on their own without any cues.

Receiver The person to whom a message is sent.

Receptive field of a visual cell The retinal area that, when stimulated, affects the firing of that cell.

Reciprocity Liking those who show that they like you.

Reciprocity norm The rule that people should pay back in kind what they receive from others.

Recognition measure A memory test that requires subjects to select previously learned information from an array of options.

Regression A reversion to immature patterns of behavior.

Regression toward the mean Effect that occurs when people who score extremely high or low on some trait are measured a second time and their new score falls closer to the mean (average).

Rehearsal The process of repetitively verbalizing or thinking about information to be stored in memory.

Reification Giving an abstract concept a name and then treating it as though it were a concrete, tangible object.

Reinforcement An event following a response that strengthens the tendency to make that response.

Reinforcement contingencies The circumstances or rules that determine whether responses lead to the presentation of reinforcers.

Relearning measure A memory test that requires a subject to memorize information a second time to determine how much time or effort is saved by having learned it before.

Reliability The measurement consistency of a test (or of other kinds of measurement techniques).

REM sleep A deep stage of sleep marked by rapid eye movements, high-frequency brain waves, and dreaming.

Replication The repetition of a study to see whether the earlier results are duplicated.

Representativeness heuristic Basing the estimated probability of an event on how similar it is to the typical prototype of that event.

Repression Keeping distressing thoughts and feelings buried in the unconscious.

Research methods Differing approaches to the observation, measurement, and manipulation and control of variables in empirical studies.

Resistance Largely unconscious defensive maneuvers a client uses to hinder the progress of therapy.

Resistance to extinction In operant conditioning, the phenomenon that occurs when an organism continues to make a response after delivery of the reinforcer for it has been terminated.

Respondent conditioning. See *Classical conditioning*.

Resting potential The stable, negative charge of a neuron when it is inactive.

Retention The proportion of material retained (remembered).

Retina The neural tissue lining the inside back surface of the eye; it absorbs light, processes images, and sends visual information to the brain.

Retinal disparity A cue to the depth based on the fact that objects within 25 feet project images to slightly different locations on the left and right retinas, so the right and left eyes see slightly different views of the object.

Retrieval Recovering information from memory stores.

Retroactive interference A memory problem that occurs when new information impairs the retention of previously learned information.

Retrograde amnesia Loss of memories for events that occurred prior to a head injury.

Retrospective memory The ability to remember events from the past or previously learned information.

Reuptake A process in which neurotransmitters are sponged up from the synaptic cleft by the presynaptic membrane.

Reversible figure A drawing that is compatible with two different interpretations that can shift back and forth.

Risky decision making Making choices under conditions of uncertainty.

Rods Specialized visual receptors that play a key role in night vision and peripheral vision.

S

Sample The collection of subjects selected for observation in an empirical study.

Sampling bias A problem that occurs when a sample is not representative of the population from which it is drawn.

Scatter diagram A graph in which paired X and Y scores for each subject are plotted as single points.

Schedule of reinforcement A specific presentation of reinforcers over time.

Schema An organized cluster of knowledge about a particular object or sequence of events.

Schizophrenic disorders A class of psychological disorders marked by disturbances in thought that spill over to affect perceptual, social, and emotional processes.

Secondary (conditioned) reinforcers Stimulus events that acquire reinforcing qualities by being associated with primary reinforcers.

Secondary sex characteristics Physical features that are associated with gender but that are not directly involved in reproduction.

Sedatives Sleep-inducing drugs that tend to decrease central nervous system activation and behavioral activity.

Self-actualizing persons People with exceptionally healthy personalities, marked by continued personal growth.

Self-concept A collection of beliefs about one's own nature, unique qualities, and typical behavior.

Self-efficacy One's belief about one's ability to perform behaviors that should lead to expected outcomes.

Self-report inventories Personality tests that ask individuals to answer a series of questions about their characteristic behavior.

Self-serving bias The tendency to attribute one's successes to personal factors and one's failures to situational factors.

Semantic memory system General knowledge that is not tied to the time when the information was learned.

Semantic network Concepts joined together by links that show how the concepts are related.

Sensation The stimulation of sense organs.

Sensory adaptation A gradual decline in sensitivity to prolonged stimulation.

Sensory memory The preservation of information in its original sensory form for a brief time, usually only a fraction of a second.

Separation anxiety Emotional distress seen in many infants when they are separated from people with whom they have formed an attachment.

Serial-position effect In memory tests, the fact that subjects show better recall for items at the beginning and end of a list than for items in the middle.

Sex The biologically based categories of male and female.

Sexual orientation A person's preference for emotional and sexual relationships with individuals of the same sex, the other sex, or either sex.

Shaping The reinforcement of closer and closer approximations of a desired response.

Short-term memory (STM) A limited-capacity store that can maintain unrehearsed information for about 20 to 30 seconds.

Skinner box A small enclosure in which an animal can make a specific response that is systematically recorded while the consequences of the response are controlled.

Sleep apnea A sleep disorder characterized by frequent reflexive gasping for air that awakens the sleeper and disrupts sleep.

Slow-wave sleep Sleep stages 3 and 4, during which low-frequency delta waves become prominent in EEG recordings.

Social desirability bias A tendency to give socially approved answers to questions about oneself.

Social loafing A reduction in effort by individuals when they work in groups as compared to when they work by themselves.

Social psychology The branch of psychology concerned with the way individuals' thoughts, feelings, and behaviors are influenced by others.

Social roles Widely shared expectations about how people in certain positions are supposed to behave.

Social schemas Organized clusters of ideas about categories of social events and people.

Social skills training A behavior therapy designed to improve interpersonal skills that emphasizes shaping, modeling, and behavioral rehearsal.

Social support Various types of aid and succor provided by members of one's social networks.

Socialization The acquisition of the norms, roles, and behaviors expected of people in a particular society.

Soma The cell body of a neuron; it contains the nucleus and much of the chemical machinery common to most cells.

Somatic nervous system The system of nerves that connect to voluntary skeletal muscles and to sensory receptors.

Somatization disorder A type of somatoform disorder marked by a history of diverse physical complaints that appear to be psychological in origin.

Somatoform disorders A class of psychological disorders involving physical ailments with no authentic organic basis that are due to psychological factors.

Somnambulism Arising and walking about while remaining asleep; sleepwalking.

Source The person who sends a communication.

Source monitoring The process of making attributions about the origins of memories.

Source-monitoring error An error that occurs when a memory derived from one source is misattributed to another source.

Spermarche The first occurrence of ejaculation.

Split-brain surgery A procedure in which the bundle of fibers that connects the cerebral hemispheres (the corpus callosum) is cut to reduce the severity of epileptic seizures.

Spontaneous recovery In classical conditioning, the reappearance of an extinguished response after a period of nonexposure to the conditioned stimulus.

SQ3R A study system designed to promote effective reading by means of five steps: survey, question, read, recite, and review.

Stage A developmental period during which characteristic patterns of behavior are exhibited and certain capacities become established.

Standard deviation An index of the amount of variability in a set of data.

Standardization The uniform procedures used in the administration and scoring of a test.

Statistical significance The condition that exists when the probability that the observed findings are due to chance is very low.

Statistics The use of mathematics to organize, summarize, and interpret numerical data. See also *Descriptive statistics, Inferential statistics*.

Stereotypes Widely held beliefs that people have certain characteristics because of their membership in a particular group.

Stimulants Drugs that tend to increase central nervous system activation and behavioral activity.

Stimulus discrimination The phenomenon that occurs when an organism that has learned a response to a specific stimulus does not respond in the same way to stimuli that are similar to the original stimulus.

Stimulus generalization The phenomenon that occurs when an organism that has learned a response to a specific stimulus responds in the same way to new stimuli that are similar to the original stimulus.

Storage Maintaining encoded information in memory over time.

Stress Any circumstances that threaten or are perceived to threaten one's well-being and that thereby tax one's coping abilities.

Striving for superiority According to Adler, the universal drive to adapt, improve oneself, and master life's challenges.

Structuralism A school of psychology based on the notion that the task of psychology is to analyze consciousness into its basic elements and to investigate how these elements are related.

Subjective well-being Individuals' perceptions of their overall happiness and life satisfaction.

Subjects The persons or animals whose behavior is systematically observed in a study.

Subtractive color mixing Formation of colors by removing some wavelengths of light, leaving less light than was originally there.

Superego According to Freud, the moral component of personality that incorporates social standards about what represents right and wrong.

Survey A descriptive research method in which researchers use questionnaires or interviews to gather information about specific aspects of subjects' behavior.

Synapse A junction where information is transmitted from one neuron to the next.

Synaptic cleft A microscopic gap between the terminal button of a neuron and the cell membrane of another neuron.

Systematic desensitization A behavior therapy used to reduce clients' anxiety responses through counterconditioning.

T

Tardive dyskinesia A neurological disorder marked by chronic tremors and involuntary spastic movements.

Terminal buttons Small knobs at the end of axons that secrete chemicals called neurotransmitters.

Testwiseness The ability to use the characteristics and format of a cognitive test to maximize one's score.

Thalamus A structure in the forebrain through which all sensory information (except smell) must pass to get to the cerebral cortex.

Theory A system of interrelated ideas that is used to explain a set of observations.

Tolerance A progressive decrease in a person's responsiveness to a drug.

Top-down processing In form perception, a progression from the whole to the elements.

Transference In therapy, the phenomenon that occurs when clients start relating to their therapists in ways that mimic critical relationships in their lives.

Trial In classical conditioning, any presentation of a stimulus or pair of stimuli.

Trial and error Trying possible solutions sequentially and discarding those that are in error until one works.

Twin studies A research design in which hereditary influence is assessed by comparing the resemblance of identical twins and fraternal twins with respect to a trait.

Type A personality Personality characterized by (1) a strong competitive orientation, (2) impatience and time urgency, and (3) anger and hostility.

Type B personality Personality characterized by relatively relaxed, patient, easygoing, amicable behavior.

U

Unconditioned response (UCR) An unlearned reaction to an unconditioned stimulus that occurs without previous conditioning.

Unconditioned stimulus (UCS) A stimulus that evokes an unconditioned response without previous conditioning.

Unconscious According to Freud, thoughts, memories, and desires that are well below the surface of conscious awareness but that nonetheless exert great influence on behavior.

Undifferentiated schizophrenia A type of schizophrenia marked by idiosyncratic mixtures of schizophrenic symptoms.

V

Validity The ability of a test to measure what it was designed to measure.

Variability The extent to which the scores in a data set tend to vary from each other and from the mean.

Variable-interval (VI) schedule A reinforcement schedule in which the reinforcer is given for the first response after a variable time interval has elapsed.

Variable-ratio (VR) schedule A reinforcement schedule in which the reinforcer is given after a variable number of nonreinforced responses.

Variables Any measurable conditions, events, characteristics, or behaviors that are controlled or observed in a study.

Visual illusion An apparently inexplicable discrepancy between the appearance of a visual stimulus and its physical reality.

Z

Zygote A one-celled organism formed by the union of a sperm and an egg.

Abel, E. L. (1998). *Fetal alcohol abuse syndrome.* New York: Plenum.

Abel, M. H. (2002). Humor, stress, and coping strategies. *Humor: International Journal of Humor Research, 15,* 365–381.

Abi-Dargham, A. (2004). Do we still believe in the dopamine hypothesis? New data bring new evidence. *International Journal of Neuropsychopharmacology, 7*(Supplement 1), S1–S5.

Abi-Dargham, A., Gil, R., Krystal, J., Baldwin, R. M., Seibyl, J. P., Bowers, M., van Dyck, C. H., Charney, D. S., Innis, R. B., & Laruelle, M. (1998). Increased striatal dopamine transmission in schizophrenia: Confirmation in a second cohort. *American Journal of Psychiatry, 155,* 761–767.

Aboud, F. E., & Amato, M. (2001). Developmental and socialization influences on intergroup bias. In R. Brown & S. L. Gaertner (Eds.), *Blackwell handbook of social psychology: Intergroup processes.* Malden, MA: Blackwell.

Abramowitz, A. J., & O'Leary, S. G. (1990). Effectiveness of delayed punishment in an applied setting. *Behavior Therapy, 21,* 231–239.

Abramson, L. Y., Alloy, L. B., & Metalsky, J. I. (1995). Hopelessness depression. In J. N. Buchanan & M. E. P. Seligman (Eds.), *Explanatory style.* Hillsdale, NJ: Erlbaum.

Abramson, L. Y., Alloy, L. B., Hankin, B. L., Haeffel, G. J., MacCoon, D. G., & Gibb, B. E. (2002). Cognitive vulnerability-stress models of depression in a self-regulatory and psychobiological context. In I. H. Gotlib & C. L. Hammen (Eds.), *Handbook of depression.* New York: Guilford.

Abramson, L. Y., Seligman, M. E. P., & Teasdale, J. (1978). Learned helplessness in humans: Critique and reformulation. *Journal of Abnormal Psychology, 87,* 32–48.

Adamopoulos, J., & Lonner, W. J. (2001). Culture and psychology at a crossroad: Historical perspective and theoretical analysis. In D. Matsumoto (Ed.), *The handbook of culture and psychology.* New York: Oxford University Press.

Adams, G., Gullotta, T., & Montemayor, R. (1992). *Adolescent identity formation.* Newbury Park, CA: Sage.

Adams, J. L. (1980). *Conceptual blockbusting.* San Francisco: W. H. Freeman.

Ader, R. (2001). Psychoneuroimmunology. *Current Directions in Psychological Science, 10*(3), 94–98.

Ader, R., & Cohen, N. (1984). Behavior and the immune system. In W. D. Gentry (Ed.), *Handbook of behavioral medicine.* New York: Guilford.

Ader, R., & Cohen, N. (1993). Psychoneuroimmunology: Conditioning and stress. *Annual Review of Psychology, 44,* 53–85.

Adler, A. (1917). *Study of organ inferiority and its psychical compensation.* New York: Nervous and Mental Diseases Publishing Co.

Adler, A. (1927). *Practice and theory of individual psychology.* New York: Harcourt, Brace & World.

Adler, L. L. (Ed.). (1993). *International handbook on gender roles.* Westport, CT: Greenwood.

Adolphs, R., Damasio, H., & Tranel, D. (2002). Neural systems for recognition of emotional prosody: A 3-D lesion study. *Emotion, 2,* 23–51.

Affleck, G., Tennen, H., Urrows, S., & Higgins, P. (1994). Person and contextual features of daily stress reactivity: Individual differences in relations of undesirable daily events with mood disturbance and chronic pain intensity. *Journal of Personality and Social Psychology, 66,* 329–340.

Agras, W. S., & Berkowitz, R. I. (1999). Behavior therapies. In R. E. Hales, S. C. Yudofsky, & J. A. Talbott (Eds.), *American Psychiatric Press textbook of psychiatry.* Washington, DC: American Psychiatric Press.

Ahima, R. S., & Osei, S. Y. (2004). Leptin signaling. *Physiology & Behavior, 81,* 223–241.

Ahn, H., & Wampold, B. E. (2001). Where oh where are the specific ingredients? A meta-analysis of component studies in counseling and psychotherapy. *Journal of Counseling Psychology, 48,* 251–257.

Aikins, D. E., & Craske, M. G. (2001). Cognitive theories of generalized anxiety disorder. *Psychiatric Clinics of North America, 24*(1), 57–74.

Ainsworth, M. D. S., Blehar, M. C., Waters, E., & Wall, S. (1978). *Patterns of attachment: A psychological study of the strange situation.* Hillsdale, NJ: Erlbaum.

Akerstedt, T., Hume, K., Minors, D., & Waterhouse, J. (1997). Good sleep—its timing and physiological sleep characteristics. *Journal of Sleep Research, 6,* 221–229.

Akimoto, S. A., & Sanbonmatsu, D. M. (1999). Differences in self-effacing behavior between European and Japanese Americans: Effect on competence evaluations. *Journal of Cross-Cultural Psychology, 30,* 159–177.

Akiskal, H. S. (2000). Mood disorders: Clinical features. In B. J. Sadock & V. A. Sadock (Eds.), *Kaplan and Sadock's comprehensive textbook of psychiatry* (7th ed., Vol. 1, pp. 1338–1376). Philadelphia: Lippincott/Williams & Wilkins.

Albee, G. W. (1998). Fifty years of clinical psychology: Selling our soul to the devil. *Applied and Preventive Psychology, 7*(3), 189–194.

Albert, C. M., Ma, J., Rifai, N., Stampfer, M. J., & Ridker, P. M. (2002). Prospective study of C-reactive protein, homocysteine, and plasma lipid levels as predictors of sudden cardiac death. *Circulation, 105,* 2595–2599.

Albert, M. S., & Killiany, R. J. (2001). Age-related cognitive change and brain-behavior relationships. In J. E. Birren & K. W. Schaie (Eds.), *Handbook of the psychology of aging* (5th ed., pp. 160–184). San Diego, CA: Academic Press.

Albert, M. S., & Moss, M. B. (2002). Neuropsychological approaches to preclinical identification of Alzheimers disease. In L. R. Squire & D. L. Schacter (Eds.), *Neuropsychology of memory.* New York: Guilford.

Alcock, J. (1998). *Animal behavior: An evolutionary approach.* Sunderland, MA: Sinauer Associates.

Alcock, J. (2005). *Animal behavior.* Sunderland, MA: Sinauer Associates.

Aldag, R. J., & Fuller, S. R. (1993). Beyond fiasco: A reappraisal of the groupthink phenomenon and a new model of group decision processes. *Psychological Bulletin, 113,* 533–552.

Aldrich, M. S. (2000). Cardinal manifestations of sleep disorders. In M. H. Kryger, T. Roth, & W. C. Dement (Eds), *Principles and practice of sleep medicine.* Philadelphia: Saunders.

Alexander, C. N., Robinson, P., Orme-Johnson, D. W., Schneider, R. H., et al. (1994). The effects of transcendental meditation compared with other methods of relaxation and meditation in reducing risk factors, morbidity, and mortality. *Homeostasis in Health & Disease, 35,* 243–263.

Alexander, F. (1954). Psychoanalysis and psychotherapy. *Journal of the American Psychoanalytic Association, 2,* 722–733.

Alexander, J., & Tate, M. (1999). *Web wisdom: How to evaluate and create information quality on the web.* Mahwah, NJ: Erlbaum.

Alexander, M. G., & Fisher, T. D. (2003). Truth and consequences: Using the bogus pipeline to examine sex differences in self-reported sexuality. *Journal of Sex Research, 40*(1), 27–35.

Allan, R. W. (1998). Operant-respondent interactions. In W. O'Donohue (Ed.), *Learning and behavior therapy.* Boston: Allyn & Bacon.

Allen, J. J. B., & Iacono, W. G. (2001). Assessing the validity of amnesia in dissociative identity disorder: A dilemma for the DSM and the courts. *Psychology, Public Policy, and Law, 7,* 311–344.

Allen, K., Blascovich, J., & Mendes, W. B. (2002). Cardiovascular reactivity in the presence of pets, friends, and spouses: The truth about cats and dogs. *Psychosomatic Medicine, 64,* 727–739.

Alloy, L. B., Abramson, L. Y., Whitehouse, W. G., Hogan, M. E., Tashman, N. A., Steinberg, D. L., Rose, D. T., & Donovan, P. (1999). Depressogenic cognitive styles: Predictive validity, information processing and personality characteristics, and developmental origins. *Behavioral Research and Therapy, 37,* 503–531.

Allport, G. W. (1937). *Personality: A psychological interpretation.* New York: Holt.

Allport, G. W. (1961). *Pattern and growth in personality.* New York: Holt.

Alonso, A., Alonso, S., & Piper, W. (2003). Group psychotherapy. In G. Stricker & T. A. Widiger (Eds.), *Handbook of psychology, Vol. 8: Clinical psychology.* New York: Wiley.

Altman, I. (1990). Centripetal and centrifugal trends in psychology. In L. Brickman & H. Ellis (Eds.), *Preparing psychologists for the 21st century: Proceedings of the National Conference on Graduate Education in Psychology.* Hillsdale, NJ: Erlbaum.

Altmann, E. M., & Gray, W. D. (2002). Forgetting to remember: The functional relationship of decay and interference. *Psychological Science, 13*(1), 27–33.

Amabile, T. M. (1983). *The social psychology of creativity.* New York: Springer-Verlag.

Amabile, T. M. (1996). *Creativity in context.* Boulder, CO: Westview.

Amato, P. R. (2001). The consequences of divorce for adults and children. In R. M. Milardo (Ed.), *Understanding families into the new millenium: A decade in review.* Minneapolis: National Council on Family Relations.

Amato, P. R. (2003). Reconciling divergent perspectives: Judith Wallerstein, quantitative family research and children of divorce. *Family Relations: Interdisciplinary Journal of Applied Family Studies, 52,* 332–339.

American Psychiatric Association. (1994). *Diagnostic and statistical manual of mental disorders* (4th ed.). Washington, DC: Author.

American Psychiatric Association. (2000). *Diagnostic and statistical manual of mental disorders* (4th ed. Text revision). Washington, DC: Author.

American Psychiatric Association Task Force on Electroconvulsive Therapy. (2001). *The practice of electroconvulsive therapy: Recommendations for treatment* (2nd ed.). Washington, DC: American Psychiatric Association.

American Psychological Association. (1984). *Behavioral research with animals.* Washington, DC: Author.

American Psychological Association. (2002). Ethical principles of psychologists and code of conduct. *American Psychologist, 57,* 1060–1073.

Amodio, D. M., Harmon-Jones, E., Devine, P. G., Curtin, J. J., Hartley, S. L., & Covert, A. E. (2004). Neural signals for the detection of unintentional race bias. *Psychological Science, 15*(2), 88–93.

Anand, B. K., & Brobeck, J. R. (1951). Hypothalamic control of food intake in rats and cats. *Yale Journal of Biology and Medicine, 24,* 123–140.

Anch, A. M., Browman, C. P., Mitler, M. M., & Walsh, J. K. (1988). *Sleep: A scientific perspective.* Englewood Cliffs, NJ: Prentice-Hall.

Anderluh, M. B., Tchanturia, K., Rabe-Hesketh, S., & Treasure, J. (2003). Childhood obsessive-compulsive personality traits in adult women with eating disorders: Defining a broader eating disorder phenotype. *American Journal of Psychiatry, 160,* 242–247.

Anderson, B. (2003). Brain imaging and *g.* In H. Nyborg (Ed.), *The scientific study of general intelligence: Tribute to Arthur R. Jensen.* Oxford, UK: Pergamon.

Anderson, C., Keltner, D., & John, O. P. (2003). Emotional convergence between people over time. *Journal of Personality and Social Psychology, 84,* 1054–1068.

Anderson, C. A. (2004). An update on the effects of playing violent video games. *Journal of Adolescence, 27*(1), 113–122.

Anderson, C. A., Berkowitz, L., Donnerstein, E., Huesman, L. R., Johnson, J. D., Linz, D., Malamuth, N. M. , & Wartella, E. (2003). The influence of media violence on youth. *Psychological Science in the Public Interest, 4*(3), 81–110.

Anderson, E. A., Kohler, J. K., & Letiecq, B. L. (2002). Low-income fathers and "Responsible Fatherhood" programs: A qualitative investigation of participants' experiences. *Family Relations, 51,* 148–155.

Anderson, K. J. (1990). Arousal and the inverted-U hypothesis: A critique of Neiss's "reconceptualizing arousal." *Psychological Bulletin, 107,* 96–100.

Anderson, M. C., & Neely, J. H. (1996). Interference and inhibition in memory retrieval. In E. L. Bjork & R. A. Bjork (Eds.), *Memory.* San Diego: Academic Press.

Anderson, S. E., Dallal, G. E., & Must, A. (2003). Relative weight and race influence average age at menarche: Results from two nationally representative surveys of U.S. girls studied 25 years apart. *Pediatrics, 111,* 844–850.

Anderson, V. L., Levinson, E. M., Barker, W., & Kiewra, K. R. (1999). The effects of meditation on teacher-perceived occupational stress, state and trait anxiety and burnout. *School Psychology Quarterly, 14,* 3–25.

Anderson-Fye, E. P., & Becker, A. E. (2004). Sociocultural aspects of eating disorders and obesity. In J. K. Thompson (Ed.), *Handbook of eating disorders and obesity.* New York: Wiley.

Andreasen, N. C. (1987). Creativity and mental illness: Prevalence rates in writers and their first-degree relatives. *American Journal of Psychiatry, 144,* 1288–1292.

Andreasen, N. C. (1990). Positive and negative symptoms: Historical and conceptual aspects. In N. C. Andreasen (Ed.), *Modern problems of pharmacopsychiatry: Positive and negative symptoms and syndromes.* Basel: Karger.

Andreasen, N. C. (2001). *Brave new brain: Conquering mental illness in the era of the human genome.* New York: Oxford University Press.

Andres, R. L., & Day, M.-C. (2000). Perinatal complications associated with maternal tobacco use. *Seminars in Neonatology, 5,* 231–241.

Andrews, T. J., Halpern, S. D., & Purves, D. (1997). Correlated size variations in human visual cortex, lateral geniculate nucleus, and optic tract. *Journal of Neuroscience, 17*(8), 2859–2868.

Angell, M. (2000). Is academic medicine for sale? *New England Journal of Medicine, 342,* 1516–1518.

Angell, M. (2004). *The truth about the drug companies: How they deceive us and what to do about it.* New York: Random House.

Ansbacher, H. (1970, February). Alfred Adler, individual psychology. *Psychology Today,* pp. 42–44, 66.

Antonuccio, D. O., Danton, W. G., & McClanahan, T. M. (2003). Psychology in the prescription era: Building a firewall between marketing and science. *American Psychologist, 58,* 1028–1043.

Antony, M. M., & McCabe, R. E. (2003). Anxiety disorders: Social and specific phobias. In A. Tasman, J. Kay, & J. A. Lieberman (Eds.), *Psychiatry.* New York: Wiley.

Antshel, K. M., & Remer, R. (2003). Social skills training in children with attention deficit hyperactivity disorder: A randomized-controlled clinical trial. *Journal of Clinical Child & Adolescent Psychology, 32*(1), 153–165.

Appelbaum, P. S. (2002). Responses to the presidential debate—The systematic defunding of psychiatric care: A crisis at our doorstep. *American Journal of Psychiatry, 159,* 1638–1640.

Archer, J. (1996). Sex differences in social behavior: Are the social role and evolutionary explanations compatible? *American Psychologist, 51,* 909–917.

Archer, J. (2005). Are women or men the more aggressive sex? In S. Fein, G. R. Goethals, & M. J. Sansdtrom (Eds.), *Gender and aggression: Interdisciplinary perspectives.* Mahwah, NJ: Erlbaum.

Archibald, A. B., Graber, J. A., & Brooks–Gunn, J. (2003). Pubertal processes and physiological growth in adolescence. In G. R. Adams & M. D. Berzonsky (Eds.), *Blackwell handbook of adolescence.* Malden, MA: Blackwell Publishing.

Arendt, J., & Skene, D. J. (2005). Melatonin as a chronobiotic. *Sleep Medicine Review, 9*(1), 25–39.

Arendt, J., Stone, B., & Skene, D. (2000). Jet lag and sleep disruption. In M. H. Kryger, T. Roth, & W. C. Dement (Eds.), *Principles and practice of sleep medicine.* Philadelphia: Saunders.

Arendt, J., Stone, B., & Skene, D. J. (2005). Sleep disruption in jet lag and other circadian rhythm-related disorders. In M. H. Kryger, T. Roth, & W. C. Dement (Eds.). *Principles and practice of sleep medicine.* Philadelphia: Elsevier Saunders.

Argyle, M. (1987). *The psychology of happiness.* London: Metheun.

Argyle, M. (1999). Causes and correlates of happiness. In D. Kahneman, E. Diener, & N. Schwarz (Eds.), *Well-being: The foundations of hedonic psychology.* New York: Russell Sage Foundation.

Argyle, M. (2001). *The psychology of happiness.* New York: Routledge.

Arkes, H. R., Wortmann, R. L., Saville, P. D., & Harkness, A. R. (1981). Hindsight bias among physicians weighing the likelihood of diagnoses. *Journal of Applied Psychology, 66,* 252–254.

Armbruster, B. B. (2000). Taking notes from lectures. In R. F. Flippo & D. C. Caverly (Eds.), *Handbook of college reading and study strategy research.* Mahwah, NJ: Erlbaum.

Armitage, C. J., & Conner, M. (2000). Attitudinal ambivalence: A test of three key hypotheses. *Personality and Social Psychology Bulletin, 26,* 1421–1432.

Armony, J. L., & LeDoux, J. E. (2000). How danger is encoded: Toward a systems, cellular, and computational understanding of cognitive-emotional interactions in fear. In M. S. Gazzaniga (Ed.), *The new cognitive neurosciences* (2nd ed., pp. 1067–1080). Cambridge, MA: MIT Press.

Arndt, J., Cook, A., & Routledge, C. (2004). The blueprint of terror manangement: Understanding the cognitive architecture of psychological defense against the awareness of death. In J. Greenberg, S. L. Koole, & T. Pyszczynski (Eds.), *Handbook of experimental existential psychology.* New York: Guilford.

Arnett, J. J. (1999). Adolescent storm and stress, reconsidered. *American Psychologist, 54,* 317–326.

Arnkoff, D. B., & Glass, C. R. (1992). Cognitive therapy and psychotherapy. In D. K. Freedheim (Ed.), *History of psychotherapy: A century of change.* Washington, DC: American Psychological Association.

Arnold, L. M. (2000). Psychocutaneous disorders. In B. J. Sadock & V. A. Sadock (Eds.), *Kaplan and Sadock's comprehensive textbook of psychiatry* (7th ed., pp. 1818–1827). Philadelphia: Lippincott/Williams & Wilkins.

Arrigo, J. M., & Pezdek, K. (1997). Lessons from the study of psychogenic amnesia. *Current Directions in Psychological Science, 6,* 148–152.

Asch, S. E. (1951). Effects of group pressure on the modification and distortion of judgments. In H. Guetzkow (Ed.), *Groups, leadership and men.* Pittsburgh: Carnegie Press.

Asch, S. E. (1955). Opinions and social pressures. *Scientific American, 193*(5), 31–35.

Asch, S. E. (1956). Studies of independence and conformity: A minority of one against a unanimous majority. *Psychological Monographs, 70*(9, Whole No. 416).

Aserinsky, E., & Kleitman, N. (1953). Regularly occurring periods of eye mobility and concomitant phenomena during sleep. *Science, 118,* 273–274.

Ashford, J. W., & Mortimer, J. A. (2002). Non-familial Alzheimer's disease is mainly due to genetic factors. *Journal of Alzheimer's Disease, 4,* 169–177.

Ashton, M. C., Lee, K., Perugini, M. , Szarota, P., de Vries, R. E., Di Blas, L., Boies, K., & De Raad, B. (2004). A six-factor structure of personality descriptive adjectives: Solutions from psycholexical studies in seven languages. *Journal of Personality and Social Psychology, 86*(2), 356–366.

Aspinwall, L. G., Richter, L., & Hoffman R. R., III. (2001). Understanding how optimism works: An examination of optimists' adaptive moderation of belief and behavior. In E. C. Chang (Ed.), *Optimism and pessimism: Implications for theory, research, and practice* (pp. 217–238). Washington, DC: American Psychological Association.

Atkinson, J. W. (1974). The mainsprings of achievement-oriented activity. In J. W. Atkinson & J. O. Raynor (Eds.), *Motivation and achievement.* New York: Wiley.

Atkinson, J. W. (1981). Studying personality in the context of an advanced motivational psychology. *American Psychologist, 36,* 117–128.

Atkinson, J. W. (1992). Motivational determinants of thematic apperception. In C. P. Smith (Ed.), *Motivation and personality: Handbook of thematic content analysis.* New York: Cambridge University Press.

Atkinson, J. W., & Litwin, G. H. (1960). Achievement motive and test anxiety conceived as motive to approach success and to avoid failure. *Journal of Abnormal and Social Psychology, 60,* 52–63.

Atkinson, R. C., & Shiffrin, R. M. (1968). Human memory: A proposed system and its control processes. In K. W. Spence & J. T. Spence (Eds.), *The psychology of learning and motivation* (Vol. 2). New York: Academic Press.

Atkinson, R. C., & Shiffrin, R. M. (1971). The control of short-term memory. *Scientific American, 225,* 82–90.

Ator, N. A. (2005). Conducting behavioral research: Methodological and laboratory animal welfare issues. In C. K. Akins, S. Panicker & C. L. Cunningham (Eds.), *Laboratory animals in research and teaching: Ethics, care and methods.* Washington, DC: American Psychological Association.

Averill, J. A. (1980). A constructivist view of emotion. In R. Plutchik & H. Kellerman (Eds.), *Emotion: Theory, research, and experience: Vol. 1. Theories of emotion.* New York: Academic Press.

Avis, N. E. (1999). Women's health at midlife. In S. L. Willis & J. D. Reid (Eds.), *Life in the middle: Psychological and social development in middle age* (pp. 105–146). San Diego, CA: Academic Press.

Axel, R. (1995, April). The molecular logic of smell. *Scientific American, 273,* 154–159.

Ayanian, J. Z., & Cleary, P. D. (1999). Perceived risks of heart disease and cancer among cigarette smokers. *Journal of the American Medical Association, 281,* 1019–1021.

Ayers, M. S., & Reder, L. M. (1998). A theoretical review of the misinformation effect: Predictions from an activation-based memory model. *Psychonomic Bulletin & Review, 5,* 1–21.

Ayres, J. J. B. (1998). Fear conditioning and avoidance. In W. O'Donohue (Ed.), *Learning and behavior therapy.* Boston: Allyn & Bacon.

Baars, B. J. (1986). *The cognitive revolution in psychology.* New York: Guilford.

Bäckman, L., Small, B. J., & Wahlin, Å. (2001). Aging and memory: Cognitive and biological perspectives. In J. E. Birren & K. W. Schaie (Eds.), *Handbook of the psychology of aging* (5th ed., pp. 348–376). San Diego, CA: Academic Press.

Bäckman, L., Small, B. J., Wahlin, Å., & Larsson, M. (1999). Cognitive functioning in very old age. In F. I. M. Craik & T. A. Salthouse (Eds.), *Handbook of cognitive aging* (Vol. 2, pp. 499–558). Mahwah, NJ: Erlbaum.

Baddeley, A. D. (1986). *Working memory.* New York: Oxford University Press.

Baddeley, A. D. (1989). The uses of working memory. In P. R. Soloman, G. R. Goethals, C. M. Kelley, & B. R. Stephens (Eds.), *Memory: Interdisciplinary approaches.* New York: Springer-Verlag.

Baddeley, A. D. (1992). Working memory. *Science, 255,* 556–559.

Baddeley, A. D. (2001). Is working memory still working? *American Psychologist, 56,* 851–864.

Baddeley, A. D. (2003). Working memory: Looking back and looking forward. *Nature Reviews Neuroscience, 4,* 829–839.

Baddeley, A. D., & Hitch, G. (1974). Working memory. In G. H. Bower (Ed.), *The psychology of learning and motivation* (Vol. 8). New York: Academic Press.

Bahrick, H. P. (2000). Long-term maintenance of knowledge. In E. Tulving & F. I. M. Craik (Eds.), *The Oxford handbook of memory* (pp. 347–362). New York: Oxford University Press.

Bailey, J. M. (2003). Biological perspectives on sexual orientation. In L. D. Garnets & D. C. Kimmel (Eds.), *Psychological perspectives on lesbian, gay, and bisexual experiences.* New York: Columbia University Press.

Bailey, J. M., Dunne, M. P., & Martin, N. G. (2000). Genetic and environmental influences on sexual orientation and its correlates in an Australian twin sample. *Journal of Personality and Social Psychology, 78,* 524–536.

Bailey, J. M., & Pillard, R. C. (1991). A genetic study of male homosexual orientation. *Archives of General Psychology, 48,* 1089–1097.

Bailey, J. M., Pillard, R. C., Neale, M. C. I., & Agyei, Y. (1993). Heritable factors influence sexual orientation in women. *Archives of General Psychiatry, 50,* 217–223.

Bailey, J. M., & Zucker, K. J. (1995). Childhood sex-typed behavior and sexual orientation: A conceptual analysis and quantitative review. *Developmental Psychology, 31,* 43–55.

Baillargeon, R. (1987). Object permanence in 3.5- and 4.5-month-old infants. *Developmental Psychology, 23,* 655–664.

Baillargeon, R. (1994). How do infants learn about the physical world? *Current Directions in Psychological Science, 3,* 133–140.

Baillargeon, R. (2002). The acquisition of physical knowledge in infancy: A summary in eight lessons. In U. Goswami (Ed.), *Blackwell handbook of childhood cognitive development.* Malden, MA: Blackwell Publishing.

Baillargeon, R. (2004). Infants' physical world. *Current Directions in Psychological Science, 13*(3), 89–94.

Bakan, P. (1971, August). The eyes have it. *Psychology Today,* pp. 64–69.

Baldwin, E. (1993). The case for animal research in psychology. *Journal of Social Issues, 49*(1), 121–131.

Baldwin, W. (2000). Information no one else knows: The value of self-report. In A. A. Stone, J. S. Turkkan, C. A. Bachrach, J. B. Jobe, H. S. Kurtzman, & V. Cain (Eds.), *The science of self-report: Implications for research and practice.* Mahwah, NJ: Erlbaum.

Ball, H. L., Hooker, E., & Kelly, P. J. (2000). Parent-infant co-sleeping: Father's roles and perspectives. *Infant and Child Development, 9*(2), 67–74.

Ballenger, J. C. (2000). Benzodiazepine receptor agonists and antagonists. In B. J. Sadock & V. A. Sadock (Eds.), *Kaplan and Sadock's comprehensive textbook of psychiatry.* Philadelphia: Lippincott/Williams & Wilkins.

Balsam, P. D. (1988). Selection, representation, and equivalence of controlling stimuli. In R. C. Atkinson, R. J. Herrnstein, G. Lindzey, & R. D. Luce (Eds.), *Stevens' handbook of experimental psychology.* New York: Wiley.

Bandura, A. (1977). *Social learning theory.* Englewood Cliffs, NJ: Prentice-Hall.

Bandura, A. (1982). The psychology of chance encounters and life paths. *American Psychologist, 37,* 747–755.

Bandura, A. (1986). *Social foundations of thought and action: A social-cognitive theory.* Englewood Cliffs, NJ: Prentice-Hall.

Bandura, A. (1990). Perceived self-efficacy in the exercise of personal agency. *Journal of Applied Sport Psychology, 2*(2), 128–163.

Bandura, A. (1993). Perceived self-efficacy in cognitive development and functioning. *Educational Psychologist, 28*(2), 117–148.

Bandura, A. (1995). Exercise of personal and collective efficacy in changing societies. In A. Bandura (Ed.), *Self-efficacy in changing societies.* New York: Cambridge University Press.

Bandura, A. (1999a). Social cognitive theory of personality. In L. A. Pervin & O. P. John (Eds.), *Handbook of personality: Theory and research.* New York: Guilford.

Bandura, A. (1999b). A sociocognitive analysis of substance abuse: An agentic perspective. *Psychological Science, 10*(3), 214–217.

Bandura, A. (2001). Social cognitive theory: An agentic perspective. *Annual Review of Psychology, 52,* 1–26.

Bandura, A., Ross, D., & Ross, S. A. (1963a). Imitation of film-mediated aggressive models. *Journal of Abnormal and Social Psychology, 66,* 3–11.

Bandura, A., Ross, D., & Ross, S. (1963b). Vicarious reinforcement and imitative learning. *Journal of Abnormal and Social Psychology, 67* (6), 6011–607.

Banich, M. T., & Heller, W. (1998). Evolving perspectives on lateralization of function. *Current Directions in Psychological Science, 7,* 1.

Banks, A., & Gartell, N. K. (1995). Hormones and sexual orientation: A questionable link. *Journal of Homosexuality, 28,* 247–268.

Banks, W. P., & Krajicek, D. (1991). Perception. *Annual Review of Psychology, 42,* 305–331.

Banyard, V. L., & Williams, L. M. (1999). Memories for child sexual abuse and mental health functioning: Findings on a sample of women and implications for future research. In L. M. Williams & V. L. Banyard (Eds.), *Trauma & memory.* Thousand Oaks, CA: Sage Publications.

Barber, B. K. (1994). Cultural, family, and personal contexts of parent-adolescent conflict. *Journal of Marriage and the Family, 56,* 375–386.

Barber, T. X. (1979). Suggested ("hypnotic") behavior: The trance paradigm versus an alternative paradigm. In E. Fromm & R. E. Shor (Eds.), *Hypnosis: Developments in research and new perspectives.* New York: Aldine.

Barber, T. X. (1986). Realities of stage hypnosis. In B. Zilbergeld, M. G. Edelstien, & D. L. Araoz (Eds.), *Hypnosis: Questions and answers.* New York: Norton.

Barch, D. M. (2003). Cognition in schizophrenia: Does working memory work? *Current Directions in Psychological Science, 12*(4), 146–150.

Bard, P. (1934). On emotional experience after decortication with some remarks on theoretical views. *Psychological Review, 41,* 309–329.

Bargh, J. A., & McKenna, K. Y. A. (2004). The Internet and social life. *Annual Review of Psychology, 55,* 573–590.

Barlett, D. L., & Steele, J. B. (1979). *Empire: The life, legend and madness of Howard Hughes.* New York: Norton.

Barlow, D. H., Pincus, D. B., Heinrichs, N., & Choate, M. L. (2003). Anxiety disorders. In G. Stricker & T. A. Widiger (Eds.), *Handbook of psychology, Vol. 8: Clinical psychology.* New York: Wiley.

Barnes, V. A., Treiber, F., & Davis, H. (2001). The impact of Transcendental Meditation on cardiovascular function at rest and during acute stress in adolescents with high normal blood pressure. *Journal of Psychosomatic Research, 51,* 597–605.

Barnett, S. W. (2004). Does Head Start have lasting cognitive effects? The myth of fade-out. In E. Zigler & S. J. Styfco (Eds.), *The Head Start debates*. Baltimore: Paul H. Brooks Publishing.

Barnier, A. J. (2002). Posthypnotic amnesia for autobiographical episodes: A laboratory model of functional amnesia. *Psychological Science, 13,* 232–237.

Barrett, D. (1988–1989). Dreams of death. *Omega, 19*(2), 95–101.

Barry, L. J. (2004). Depression: The brain finally gets into the act. *Current Directions in Psychological Science, 13*(3), 104–106.

Barry-Walsh, J. (2005). Dissociative identity disorder. *Australian & New Zealand Journal of Psychiatry, 39*(1-2), 109–110.

Barsky, A. J. (1988). The paradox of health. *New England Journal of Medicine, 318,* 414–418.

Barsky, A. J. (2001). Somatosensory amplification and hypochondriasis. In V. Starcevic & D. R. Lipsitt (Eds.), *Hypochondriasis: Modern perspectives on an ancient malady*. New York: Oxford University Press.

Barsky, A. J., Coeytaux, R. R., Sarnie, M. K., & Cleary, P. D. (1993). Hypochondriacal patients' beliefs about good health. *American Journal of Psychiatry, 150,* 1085–1090.

Bartels, M., Rietveld, M. J. H., Van Baal, G. C. M., & Boomsma, D. I. (2002). Genetic and environmental influences on the development of intelligence. *Behavior Genetics, 32*(4), 237–249.

Bartoshuk, L. M. (1988). Taste. In R. C. Atkinson, R. J. Herrnstein, G. Lindzey, & R. D. Luce (Eds.), *Stevens' handbook of experimental psychology: Perception and motivation* (Vol. 1). New York: Wiley.

Bartoshuk, L. M. (1993a). Genetic and pathological taste variation: What can we learn from animal models and human disease? In D. Chadwick, J. Marsh, & J. Goode (Eds.), *The molecular basis of smell and taste transduction*. New York: Wiley.

Bartoshuk, L. M. (1993b). The biological basis of food perception and acceptance. *Food Quality and Preference, 4,* 21–32.

Bartoshuk, L. M. (2000). Comparing sensory experiences across individuals: Recent psychophysical advances illuminate genetic variation in taste perception. *Chemical Senses, 25,* 447–460.

Bartoshuk, L. M., & Beauchamp, G. K. (1994). Chemical senses. *Annual Review of Psychology, 45,* 419–449.

Bartoshuk, L. M., Duffy, V. B., & Miller, I. J. (1994). PTC/PROP taste: Anatomy, psychophysics, and sex effects. *Physiology & Behavior, 56,* 1165–1171.

Basbaum, A. I., & Jessel, T. M. (2000). The perception of pain. In E. R. Kandel, J. H. Schwartz, & T. M. Jessell (Eds.), *Principles of neural science*. New York: McGraw-Hill.

Bashore, T. R., Ridderinkhof, K. R., & van der Molen, M. W. (1997). The decline of cognitive processing speed in old age. *Current Directions in Psychological Science, 6,* 163–169.

Basow, S. A. (1992). *Gender: Stereotypes and roles*. Pacific Grove, CA: Brooks/Cole.

Bassiri, A. B., & Guilleminault, C. (2000). Clinical features and evaluation of obstructive sleep apnea-hypopnea syndrome. In M. H. Kryger, T. Roth, & W. C. Dement (Eds.), *Principles and practice of sleep medicine*. Philadelphia: Saunders.

Bassok, M. (2003). Analogical transfer in problem solving. In J. E. Davidson & R. J. Sternberg (Eds.), *The psychology of problem solving*. New York: Cambridge University Press.

Bassuk, E. L., Buckner, J. C., Perloff, J. N., & Bassuk, S. S. (1998). Prevalence of mental health and substance use disorders among homeless and low-income housed mothers. *American Journal of Psychiatry, 155,* 1561–1564.

Bates, M. S., Edwards, W. T., & Anderson, K. O. (1993). Ethnocultural influences on variation in chronic pain perception. *Pain, 52*(1), 101–112.

Bauer, M. S. (2003). Mood disorders: Bipolar (manic-depressive) disorders. In A. Tasman, J. Kay, & J. A. Lieberman (Eds.), *Psychiatry*. New York: Wiley.

Baum, A., Grunberg, N. E., & Singer, J. E. (1992). Biochemical measurements in the study of emotion. *Psychological Science, 3,* 56–60.

Baumeister, R. F. (1989). The optimal margin of illusion. *Journal of Social and Clinical Psychology, 8,* 176–189.

Baumeister, R. F. (2000). Gender differences in erotic plasticity: The female sex drive as socially flexible and responsive. *Psychological Bulletin, 126,* 347–374.

Baumeister, R. F., Bratslavsky, E., Finkenauer, C., & Vohs, K. D. (2001). Bad is stronger than good. *Review of General Psychology, 5,* 323–370.

Baumeister, R. F., Catanese, K. R., & Vohs, K. D. (2001). Is there a gender difference in strength of sex drive? Theoretical views, conceptual distinctions and a review of relevant evidence. *Personality and Social Psychology Review, 5,* 242–273.

Baumeister, R. F., & Leary, M. R. (1995). The need to belong: Desire for interpersonal attachments as a fundamental human motivation. *Psychological Bulletin, 117,* 497–529.

Baumeister, R. F., & Twenge, J. M. (2002). Cultural suppression of female sexuality. *Review of General Psychology, 6,* 166–203.

Baumrind, D. (1964). Some thoughts on the ethics of reading Milgram's "Behavioral study of obedience." *American Psychologist, 19,* 421–423.

Baumrind, D. (1985). Research using intentional deception: Ethical issues revisited. *American Psychologist, 40,* 165–174.

Baumrind, D., Larzelere, R. E., & Cowan, P. A. (2002). Ordinary physical punishment: Is it harmful? Comment on Gershoff. *Psychological Bulletin, 128,* 580–589.

Bayer, R. (1987). *Homosexuality and American psychiatry: The politics of diagnosis*. Princeton, NJ: Princeton University Press.

Baylis, G. C., & Driver, J. (1995). One-sided edge assignment in vision: 1. Figure-ground segmentation and attention to objects. *Current Directions in Psychological Science, 4,* 140–146.

Beahrs, J. O. (1983). Co-consciousness: A common denominator in hypnosis, multiple personality and normalcy. *American Journal of Clinical Hypnosis, 26*(2), 100–113.

Beck, A. T. (1976). *Cognitive therapy and the emotional disorders*. New York: International Universities Press.

Beck, A. T. (1987). Cognitive therapy. In J. K. Zeig (Ed.), *The evolution of psychotherapy*. New York: Brunner/Mazel.

Beck, A. T. (1991). Cognitive therapy: A 30-year retrospective. *American Psychologist, 46,* 368–375.

Beck, A. T. (1997). Cognitive therapy: Reflections. In J. K. Zeig (Ed.), *The evolution of psychotherapy: The third conference*. New York: Brunner/Mazel.

Beeman, M. J., & Chiarello, C. (1998). Complementary right and left hemisphere language comprehension. *Current Directions in Psychological Science, 7,* 2–7.

Beer, J. M., Arnold, R. D., & Loehlin, J. C. (1998). Genetic and environmental influences on MMPI Factor Scales: Joint model fitting to twin and adoption data. *Journal of Personality and Social Psychology, 74,* 818–827.

Beilin, H. (1992). Piaget's enduring contribution to developmental psychology. *Developmental Psychology, 28,* 191–204.

Bekelman, J. E., Li, Y., & Gross, C. P. (2003). Scope and impact of financial conflicts of interest in biomedical research. *Journal of the American Medical Association, 289,* 454–465.

Békésy, G. von. (1947). The variation of phase along the basilar membrane with sinusoidal vibrations. *Journal of the Acoustical Society of America, 19,* 452–460.

Bell, A. P., Weinberg, M. S., & Hammersmith, S. K. (1981). *Sexual preference: Its development in men and women*. Bloomington: Indiana University Press.

Bellack, A. S., Gearon, J. S., & Blanchard, J. J. (2000). Schizophrenia: Psychopathology. In M. Hersen & A. S. Bellack (Eds.), *Psychopathology in adulthood*. Boston: Allyn & Bacon.

Bellack, A. S., Mueser, K. T., & Gingerich, J. A. (2004). *Social skills training for schizophrenia: A step-by-step guide*. New York: Guilford.

Belsky, J., & Kelly, J. (1994). *The transition to parenthood*. New York: Dell.

Bem, D. J. (1996). Exotic becomes erotic: A developmental theory of sexual orientation. *Psychological Review, 103,* 320–335.

Bem, D. J. (1998). Is EBE theory supported by the evidence? Is it androcentric? A reply to Peplau et al. (1998). *Psychological Review, 105,* 395–398.

Bem, S. L. (1985). Androgyny and gender schema theory: A conceptual and empirical integration. In T. B. Sonderegger (Ed.), *Nebraska symposium on motivation, 1984: Psychology and gender* (Vol. 32). Lincoln: University of Nebraska Press.

Benca, R. M. (2001). Consequences of insomnia and its therapies. *Journal of Clinical Psychiatry, 62*(suppl 10), 33–38.

Benet, V., & Waller, N. G. (1995). The big seven factor model of personality description: Evidence for its cross-cultural generality in a Spanish sample. *Journal of Personality and Social Psychology, 69,* 701–718.

Benjamin, L. T., Jr. (2000). The psychology laboratory at the turn of the 20th century. *American Psychologist, 55,* 318–321.

Benjamin, L. T., Jr., Cavell, T. A., & Shallenberger, W. R., III. (1984). Staying with initial answers on objective tests: Is it a myth? *Teaching of Psychology, 11,* 133–141.

Benjamin, L. T., Jr., DeLeon, P. H., Freedheim, D. K., & VandenBos, G. R. (2003). Psychology as a profession. In D. K. Freedheim (Ed.), *Handbook of psychology, Vol. 1: History of psychology*. New York: Wiley.

Bennett, H. L. (1993). The mind during surgery: The uncertain effects of anesthesia. *Advances, 9*(1), 5–16.

Ben-Porath, Y. S. (2003). Assessing personality and psychopathology with self-report inventories. In J. R. Graham & J. A. Naglieri (Eds.), *Handbook of psychology, Volume 10: Assessment psychology*. New York: Wiley.

Benson, H. (1975). *The relaxation response*. New York: Morrow.

Benson, H., & Klipper, M. Z. (1988). *The relaxation response*. New York: Avon.

Bereczkei, T. (2000). Evolutionary psychology: A new perspective in the behavioral sciences. *European Psychologist, 5*(3), 175–190.

Berenbaum, S. A., & Snyder, E. (1995). Early hormonal influences on childhood sex-typed activity and playmate preferences: Implications for the development of sexual orientation. *Developmental Psychology, 31*, 31–42.

Berkowitz, L. (1989). Frustration-aggression hypothesis: Examination and reformulation. *Psychological Bulletin, 106*, 59–73.

Berkowitz, R. I. (2003). Behavior therapies. In R. E. Hales & S. C. Yudofsky (Eds.), *Textbook of Clinical Psychiatry*. Washington, DC: American Psychiatric Publishing.

Berliner, L., & Briere, J. (1999). Trauma, memory, and clinical practice. In L. M. Williams & V. L. Banyard (Eds.), *Trauma & memory*. Thousand Oaks, CA: Sage Publications.

Berndsen, M., Spears, R., van der Plight, J., & McGarty, C. (2002). Illusory correlation and stereotype formation: Making sense of group differences and cognitive biases. In C. McGarty, V. Y. Yzerbyt, & R. Spears (Eds.), *Stereotypes as explanations: The formation of meaningful beliefs about social groups*. New York: Cambridge University Press.

Bernhardt, P. C. (1997). Influences of serotonin and testosterone in aggression and dominance: Convergence with social psychology. *Current Directions in Psychological Science, 6*, 44–48.

Berridge, K. C. (2003). Comparing the emotional brains of humans and other animals. In R. J. Davidson, K. R. Scherer, & H. H. Goldsmith (Eds.), *Handbook of affective sciences*. New York: Oxford University Press.

Berridge, K. C. (2004). Motivation concepts in behavioral neuroscience. *Physiology and Behavior, 81*(2), 179–209.

Berry, D. T. R., Wetter, M. W., & Baer, R. A. (1995). Assessment of malingering. In J. N. Butcher (Ed.), *Clinical personality assessment: Practical approaches*. New York: Oxford University Press.

Berry, J. W. (1990). Cultural variations in cognitive style. In S. P. Wapner (Ed.), *Bio-psycho-social factors in cognitive style*. Hillsdale, NJ: Erlbaum.

Berry, J. W. (1994). Cross-cultural variations in intelligence. In R. J. Sternberg (Ed.), *Encyclopedia of human intelligence*. New York: Macmillan.

Berry, J. W., Poortinga, Y., Segall, M., & Dasen, P. (1992). *Cross-cultural psychology*. New York: Cambridge University Press.

Berscheid, E. (1988). Some comments on love's anatomy: Or, whatever happened to old-fashioned lust? In R. J. Sternberg & M. L. Barnes (Eds.), *The psychology of love*. New Haven: Yale University Press.

Bertenthal, B. I., & Clifton, R. K. (1998). Perception and action. In W. Damon (Ed.), *Handbook of child psychology, Vol. 2: Cognition, perception, and language*. New York: Wiley.

Bertrand, R. M., & Lachman, M. E. (2003). Personality development in adulthood and old age. In R. M. Lerner, M. A. Easterbrooks, & J. Mistry (Eds.), *Handbook of psychology, Vol. 6: Developmental psychology*. New York: Wiley.

Berzonsky, M., & Adams, G. (1999). Commentary: Reevaluating the identity status paradigm: Still useful after 35 years. *Developmental Review, 19*, 557–590.

Beumont, P. J. V. (2002). Clinical presentation of anorexia nervosa and bulimia nervosa. In C. G. Fairburn & K. D. Brownell (Eds.), *Eating disorders and obesity: A comprehensive handbook*. New York: Guilford.

Beutler, L. E. (2002). The dodo bird is extinct. *Clinical Psychology: Science & Practice, 9*(1), 30–34.

Beutler, L. E., Bongar, B., & Shurkin, J. N. (1998). *Am I crazy, or is it my shrink?* New York: Oxford University Press.

Beutler, L. E., Bongar, B., & Shurkin, J. N. (2001). *A consumer's guide to psychotherapy*. New York: Oxford University Press.

Beutler, L. E., & Harwood, T. M. (2002). What is and can be attributed to the therapeutic relationship? *Journal of Contemporary Psychotherapy, 32*(1), 25–33.

Beutler, L. E., Malik, M., Alimohamed, S., Harwood, T. M., Talebi, H., Noble, S., & Wong, E. (2004). Therapist variables. In M. J. Lambert (Ed.), *Bergin and Garfield's handbook of psychotherapy and behavior change*. New York: Wiley.

Bhattachary, S., & Powell, J. H. (2001). Recreational use of 3,4-methylenedioxymethamphetamine (MDMA) or "ecstasy": Evidence for cognitive impairment. *Psychological Medicine, 31*, 647–658.

Bianchi, S., Milkie, M. A., Sayer, L. C., & Robinson, J. P. (2000). Is anyone doing the housework? Trends in the gender division of household labor. *Social Forces, 79*(1), 191–228.

Biederman, I., Hilton, H. J., & Hummel, J. E. (1991). Pattern goodness and pattern recognition. In G. R. Lockhead & J. R. Pomerantz (Eds.), *The perception of structure*. Washington, DC: American Psychological Association.

Biehl, M., Matsumoto, D., Ekman, P., Hearn, V., Heider, K., Kudoh, T., & Ton, V. (1997). Matsumoto and Ekman's Japanese and Caucasian Facial Expressions of Emotion (JACFEE): Reliability data and cross-national differences. *Journal of Nonverbal Behavior, 21*, 3–21.

Bigler, E. D., Blatter, D. D., Anderson, C. V., Johnson, S. C., Gale, S. D., Hopkins, R. O., & Burnett, B. (1997). Hippocampal volume in normal aging and traumatic brain injury. *American Journal of Neuroradiology, 18*, 11–23.

Birch, L. L., & Fisher, J. A. (1996). The role of experience in the development of children's eating behavior. In E. D. Capaldi (Ed.), *Why we eat what we eat: The psychology of eating* (pp. 113–143). Washington, DC: American Psychological Association.

Birnbaum, M. H. (2004). Base rates in Bayesian inference. In F. P. Rudiger (Ed.), *Cognitive illusions*. New York: Psychology Press.

Bishop, K. M., & Wahlstein, D. (1997). Sex differences in the human corpus callosum: Myth or reality? *Neuroscience and Biobehavioral Reviews, 12*, 581–601.

Bishop, S. R. (2002). What do we really know about mindfulness-based stress reduction? *Psychosomatic Medicine, 64*(1), 71–83.

Bjork, R. A. (1992). Interference and forgetting. In L. R. Squire (Ed.), *Encyclopedia of learning and memory*. New York: Macmillan.

Bjorklund, D. F. (2005). *Children's thinking: Cognitive development and individual differences*. Belmont, CA: Wadsworth.

Black, D. W., & Andreasen, N. C. (1999). Schizophrenia, schizophreniform disorder, and delusional (paranoid) disorders. In R. E. Hales, S. C. Yudofsky, & J. A. Talbott (Eds.), *American Psychiatric Press textbook of psychiatry* (3rd ed.). Washington, DC: American Psychiatric Press.

Blacker, L. (1999). The launching phase of the life cycle. In B. Carter & M. McGoldrick (Eds.), *The expanded family life cycle: Individual, family, and social perspectives* (3rd ed., pp. 287–306). Boston: Allyn & Bacon.

Blair, C., Gamson, D., Thorne, S., & Baker, D. (2005). Rising mean IQ: Cognitive demand of mathematics education for young children, population exposure to formal schooling, and the neurobiology of the prefrontal cortex. *Intelligence, 33*, 93–106.

Blair, S. N., Kohl, H. W., Paffenbarger, R. S., Clark, D. G., Cooper, K. H., & Gibbons, L. W. (1989). Physical fitness and all-cause mortality: A prospective study of healthy men and women. *Journal of the American Medical Association, 262*, 2395–2401.

Blakeslee, T. R. (1980). *The right brain*. Garden City, NY: Doubleday/Anchor.

Blanchard, E. B., & Keefer, L. (2003). Irritable bowel syndrome. In A. M. Nezu, C. M. Nezu, & P. A. Geller (Eds.), *Handbook of psychology, Vol. 9: Health psychology*. New York: Wiley.

Blanchard, F. A., Lilly, T., & Vaughn, L. A. (1991). Reducing the expression of racial prejudice. *Psychological Science, 2*, 101–105.

Blanchard, R., Zucker, K. J., Bradley, S. J., & Hume, C. S. (1995). Birth order and siblings sex ratio in homosexual male adolescents and probably prehomosexual feminine boys. *Developmental Psychology, 31*, 22–30.

Blanco, C., Laje, G., Olfson, M., Marcus, S. C., & Pincus, H. A. (2002). Trends in the treatment of bipolar disorder by outpatient psychiatrists. *American Journal of Psychiatry, 159*, 1005–1010.

Blankenhorn, D. (1995). *Fatherless America: Confronting our most urgent social problem*. New York: Basic Books.

Blass, T. (1991). Understanding behavior in the Milgram obedience experiment: The role of personality, situations, and their interactions. *Journal of Personality and Social Psychology, 60*, 398–413.

Blass, T. (1999). The Milgram Paradigm after 35 years: Some things we now know about obedience to authority. *Journal of Applied Social Psychology, 29*, 955–978.

Blazer, D. G. (2000). Mood disorders: Epidemiology. In B. J. Sadock & V. A. Sadock (Eds.), *Kaplan and Sadock's Comprehensive textbook of psychiatry* (7th ed., Vol. 1, pp. 1298–1307). Philadelphia: Lippincott/Williams & Wilkins.

Bleuler, E. (1911). *Dementia praecox or the group F schizophrenias*. New York: International Universities Press.

Blieszner, R., & Adams, R. G. (1992). *Adult friendship*. Newbury Park, CA: Sage.

Bliwise, D. L. (2005). Normal aging. In M. H. Kryger, T. Roth, & W. C. Dement (Eds.), *Principles and practice of sleep medicine*. Philadelphia: Elsevier Saunders.

Block, J. (1981). Some enduring and consequential structures of personality. In A. I. Rabins, J. Aronoff, A. Barclay, & R. Zucker (Eds.), *Further explorations in personality*. New York: Wiley.

Block, J. R., & Yuker, H. E. (1992). *Can you believe your eyes?: Over 250 illusions and other visual oddities*. New York: Brunner/Mazel.

Block, N. (2002). How heritability misleads us about race. In J. Fish (Ed.), *Race and intelligence: Separating science from myth*. Mahwah, NJ: Erlbaum.

Bloom, B. L. (1984). *Community mental health: A general introduction*. Pacific Grove, CA: Brooks/Cole.

Bloomfield, H. H., & Kory, R. B. (1976). *Happiness: The TM program, psychiatry, and enlightenment*. New York: Simon & Schuster.

Blum, R., & Rinehart, P. (2000). *Reducing the risk: Connections that make a difference in the lives of youth*. Minneapolis: University of Minnesota, Division of General Pediatrics and Adolescent Health.

Blundell, J. E., & Halford, J. C. G. (1998). Serotonin and appetite regulation: Implications for the pharmacological treatment of obesity. *CNS Drugs, 9,* 473–495.

Bodenheimer, T. (2000). Uneasy alliance: Clinical investigators and the pharmaceutical industry. *New England Journal of Medicine, 342,* 1539–1544.

Bohner, G., & Schwarz, N. (2001). Attitudes, persuasion, and behavior. In A. Tesser & N. Schwarz (Eds.), *Blackwell handbook of social psychology: Intraindividual processes.* Malden, MA: Blackwell.

Boland, R. J., & Keller, M. B. (2003). Antidepressants. In A. Tasman, J. Kay, & J. A. Lieberman (Eds.), *Psychiatry.* New York: Wiley.

Bolger, N. (1990). Coping as a personality process: A prospective study. *Journal of Personality and Social Psychology, 59,* 525–537.

Bolles, R. C. (1975). *Theory of motivation.* New York: Harper & Row.

Bond, R., & Smith, P. B. (1996). Culture and conformity: A meta-analysis of studies using Asch's line judgment task. *Psychological Bulletin, 119,* 111–137.

Bonnet, M. H. (2000). Sleep deprivation. In M. H. Kryger, T. Roth, & W. C. Dement (Eds.), *Principles and practice of sleep medicine.* Philadelphia: Saunders.

Bonnet, M. H. (2005). Acute sleep deprivation. In M. H. Kryger, T. Roth, & W. C. Dement (Eds.), *Principles and practice of sleep medicine.* Philadelphia: Elsevier Saunders.

Booth, D. (1994). Palatability and the intake of food and drinks. In M. S. Westerterp-Plantenga, E. W. H. M. Frederix, & A. B. Steffens (Eds.), *Food intake and energy expenditure.* Boca Raton, FL: CRC Press.

Bootzin, R. R., Manber, R., Loewy, D. H., Kuo, T. F., & Franzen, P. L. (2001). Sleep disorders. In P. B. Sutker & H. E. Adams (Eds.), *Comprehensive handbook of psychopathology.* New York: Kluwer Academic/Plenum.

Borbely, A. A., & Achermann, P. (2005). Sleep homeostasis and models of sleep regulation. In M. H. Kryger, T. Roth, & W. C. Dement (Eds.), *Principles and practice of sleep medicine.* Philadelphia: Elsevier Saunders.

Bordnick, P. S., Elkins, R. L., Orr, T. E., Walters, P., & Thyer, B. A. (2004). Evaluating the relative effectiveness of three aversion therapies designed to reduce craving among cocaine abusers. *Behavioral Interventions, 19*(1), 1–24.

Boring, E. G. (1966). A note on the origin of the word *psychology. Journal of the History of the Behavioral Sciences, 2,* 167.

Bornstein, B. H., & Zickafoose, D. J. (1999). "I know I know it, I know I saw it": The stability of the confidence-accuracy relationship across domains. *Journal of Experimental Psychology: Applied, 5,* 76–88.

Bornstein, R. F. (2003). Psychodynamic models of personality. In T. Millon & M. J. Lerner (Eds.), *Handbook of psychology, Vol. 5: Personality and social psychology.* New York: Wiley.

Bosson, J. K., & Swann, W. B. (2001). The paradox of the sincere chameleon: Strategic self-verification in close relationships. In J. H. Harvey & A. Wenzel (Eds.), *Close romantic relationships: Maintenance and enhancement.* Mahwah, NJ: Erlbaum.

Bost, K. K., Cox, M. J., Burchinal, M. R., & Payne, C. (2002). Structural and supporting changes in couples' family and friendship networks across the transition to parenthood. *Journal of Marriage and the Family, 64,* 517–531.

Bouchard, T. J., Jr. (1997). IQ similarity in twins reared apart: Findings and responses to critics. In R. J. Sternberg, & E. L. Grigorenko (Eds.), *Intelligence,*

heredity, and environment. New York: Cambridge University Press.

Bouchard, T. J., Jr. (1998). Genetic and environmental influences on adult intelligence and special mental abilities. *Human Biology, 70,* 257–279.

Bouchard, T. J., Jr. (2004). Genetic influence on human psychological traits: A survey. *Current Directions in Psychological Science, 13*(4), 148–151.

Bouchard, T. J., Jr., Lykken, D. T., McGue, M., Segal, N. L., & Tellegen, A. (1990). Sources of human psychological differences: The Minnesota study of twins reared apart. *Science, 250,* 223–228.

Boudreaux, E., Carmack, C. L., Scarinci, I. C., & Brantley, P. J. (1998). Predicting smoking stage of change among a sample of low socioeconomic status, primary care outpatients: Replication and extension using decisional balance and self-efficacy theories. *International Journal of Behavioral Medicine, 5,* 148–165.

Bouman, T. K., Eifert, G. H., & Lejeuz, C. W. (1999). Somatoform disorders. In T. Millon, P. H. Blaney, & R. D. Davis (Eds.), *Oxford textbook of psychopathology* (pp. 444–465). New York: Oxford University Press.

Bourguignon, E. (1972). Dreams and altered states of consciousness in anthropological research. In F. L. K. Hsu (Ed.), *Psychological anthropology* (2nd ed.). Cambridge, MA: Schenkman.

Bourhis, R. Y., & Gagnon, A. (2001). Social orientations in the minimal group paradigm. In R. Brown & S. L. Gaertner (Eds.), *Blackwell handbook of social psychology: Intergroup processes.* Malden, MA: Blackwell Publishing.

Bouton, M. E. (2000). A learning theory perspective on lapse, relapse, and the maintenance of behavior change. *Health Psychology, 19,* 57–63.

Bowd, A. D., & Shapiro, K. J. (1993). The case against laboratory animal research in psychology. *Journal of Social Issues, 49*(1), 133–142.

Bowden, C. L. (2004). Valproate. In A. F. Schatzberg & C. B. Nemeroff (Eds.), *Textbook of psychopharmacology.* Washington, DC: American Psychiatric Publishing.

Bower, G. H. (1970). Organizational factors in memory. *Cognitive Psychology, 1,* 18–46.

Bower, G. H. (2000). A brief history of memory research. In E. Tulving & F. I. M. Craik (Eds.), *The Oxford handbook of memory* (pp. 3–32). New York: Oxford University Press.

Bower, G. H., & Clark, M. C. (1969). Narrative stories as mediators of serial learning. *Psychonomic Science, 14,* 181–182.

Bowlby, J. (1969). *Attachment and loss: Vol. 1. Attachment.* New York: Basic Books.

Bowlby, J. (1973). *Attachment and loss: Vol. 2. Separation, anxiety and anger.* New York: Basic Books.

Bowlby, J. (1980). *Attachment and loss: Vol. 3. Sadness and depression.* New York: Basic Books.

Boynton, R. M. (1990). Human color perception. In K. N. Leibovic (Ed.), *Science of vision.* New York: Springer-Verlag.

Bradshaw, J. L. (1989). *Hemispheric specialization and psychological function.* New York: Wiley.

Brainerd, C. J. (1996). Piaget: A centennial celebration. *Psychological Science, 7,* 191–195.

Branaman, T. F., & Gallagher, S. N. (2005). Polygraph testing in sex offender treatment: A review of limitations. *American Journal of Forensic Psychology, 23*(1), 45–64.

Brase, G. L., Cosmides, L., & Tooby, J. (1998). Individuation, counting, and statistical inference: The role of frequency and whole-object representations

in judgment under certainty. *Journal of Experimental Psychology: General, 127,* 3–21.

Bredt, B. M., Higuera-Alhino, D., Hebert, S. J., McCune, J. M., & Abrams, D. I. (2002). Short-term effects of cannabinoids on immune phenotype and function in HIV-1-infected patients. *Journal of Clinical Pharmacology, 42,* 90S–96S.

Breedlove, S. M. (1994). Sexual differentiation of the human nervous system. *Annual Review of Psychology, 45,* 389–418.

Breggin, P. R. (1991). *Toxic psychiatry.* New York: St. Martin's Press.

Brehm, J. W. (1966). *A theory of psychological reactance.* New York: Academic Press.

Brehm, S. S., & Kassin, S. M. (1993). *Social psychology.* Boston: Houghton Mifflin.

Breland, K., & Breland, M. (1961). The misbehavior of organisms. *American Psychologist, 16,* 681–684.

Breland, K., & Breland, M. (1966). *Animal behavior.* New York: Macmillan.

Bremner, J. G. (2001). Cognitive development: Knowledge of the physical world. In G. Bremner & A. Fogel (Eds.), *Blackwell handbook of infant development* (pp. 99–138). Malden, MA: Blackwell.

Brende, J. O. (2000). Stress effects of floods. In G. Fink (Ed.), *Encyclopedia of stress* (Vol. 2, pp. 153–157). San Diego: Academic Press.

Breslau, N., Kilbey, M. M., & Andreski, P. (1991). Nicotine dependence, major depression, and anxiety in young adults. *Archives of General Psychiatry, 48,* 1069–1074.

Breslau, N., Kilbey, M. M., & Andreski, P. (1993). Nicotine dependence and major depression: New evidence from a prospective investigation. *Archives of General Psychiatry, 50,* 31–35.

Bretherton, I., & Munholland, K. A. (1999). Internal working models in attachment relationships. In J. Cassidy & P. R. Shaver (Eds.), *Handbook of attachment: Theory, research, and clinical applications.* New York: Guilford.

Bretl, D. J., & Cantor, J. (1988). The portrayal of men and women in U.S. television commercials: A recent content analysis and trend over 15 years. *Sex Roles, 18,* 595–609.

Brewer, W. F., & Treyens, J. C. (1981). Role of schemata in memory for places. *Cognitive Psychology, 13,* 207–230.

Brewster, K. L., & Padavic, I. (2000). Change in gender-ideology, 1977–1996: The contributions of intracohort change and population turnover. *Journal of Marriage and the Family, 62,* 477–487.

Briere, J., & Conte, J. R. (1993). Self-reported amnesia for abuse in adults molested as children. *Journal of Traumatic Stress, 6*(1), 21–31.

Bringmann, W. G., & Balk, M. M. (1992). Another look at Wilhelm Wundt's publication record. *History of Psychology Newsletter, 24*(3/4), 50–66.

Brislin, R. (1993). *Understanding culture's influence on behavior.* Fort Worth: Harcourt Brace College Publishers.

Broadbent, D. E. (1958). *Perception and communication.* New York: Pergamon Press.

Broadbent, N. J., Clark, R. E., Zola, S., & Squire, L. R. (2002). The medial temporal lobe and memory. In L. R. Squire & D. L. Schacter (Eds.), *Neuropsychology of memory.* New York: Guilford.

Brobeck, J. R., Tepperman, T., & Long, C. N. (1943). Experimental hypothalamic hyperphagia in the albino rat. *Yale Journal of Biology and Medicine, 15,* 831–853.

Bröder, A. (1998). Deception can be acceptable. *American Psychologist, 53*, 805–806.

Brody, N. (2003). Jensen's genetic interpretation of racial differences in intelligence: Critical evaluation. In H. Nyborg (Ed.), *The scientific study of general intelligence: Tribute to Arthur R. Jensen*. Oxford, UK: Pergamon.

Broughton, R. (1994). Important underemphasized aspects of sleep onset. In R. D. Ogilvie & J. R. Harsh (Eds.), *Sleep onset: Normal and abnormal processes*. Washington, DC: American Psychological Association.

Brown, A. S. (1991). A review of the tip-of-the-tongue experience. *Psychological Bulletin, 109*, 204–223.

Brown, A. S. (1999). New perspectives on the neurodevelopmental hypothesis of schizophrenia. *Psychiatric Annals, 29*(3), 128–130.

Brown, A. S., Begg, M. D., Gravenstein, S., Schaefer, C. S., Wyatt, R. J., Bresnahan, M., Babulas, V. P., & Susser, E. S. (2004). Serologic evidence of prenatal influenza in the etiology of schizophrenia. *Archives of General Psychiatry, 61*, 774–780.

Brown, D., Scheflin, A. W., & Hammond, D. C. (1998). *Memory, trauma treatment, and the law*. New York: Norton.

Brown, E. J., Juster, H. R., Heimberg, R. G., & Winning, C. D. (1998). Stressful life events and personality styles: Relation to impairment and treatment outcome in patients with social phobia. *Journal of Anxiety Disorders, 12*, 233–251.

Brown, H. D., & Kosslyn, S. M. (1993). Cerebral lateralization. *Current Opinion in Neurobiology, 3*, 183–186.

Brown, M. (1974). Some determinants of persistence and initiation of achievement-related activities. In J. W. Atkinson & J. O. Raynor (Eds.), *Motivation and achievement*. Washington, DC: Halsted.

Brown, M. N., Freeman, K. E., & Williamson, C. L. (2000). The importance of critical thinking for student use of the Internet. *College Student Journal, 34*, 391–398.

Brown, R. D., Goldstein, E., & Bjorklund, D. F. (2000). The history and zeitgeist of the repressed–false-memory debate: Scientific and sociological perspectives on suggestibility and childhood memory. In D. F. Bjorklund (Ed.), *False-memory creation in children and adults* (pp. 1–30). Mahwah, NJ: Erlbaum.

Brown, R. T. (1989). Creativity: What are we to measure? In J. A. Glover, R. R. Ronning, & C. R. Reynolds (Eds.), *Handbook of creativity*. New York: Plenum.

Brown, R., & Kulik, J. (1977). Flashbulb memories. *Cognition, 5*, 73–79.

Brown, R., & McNeill, D. (1966). The "tip-of-the-tongue" phenomenon. *Journal of Verbal Learning and Verbal Behavior, 5*(4), 325–337.

Brown, S. C., & Craik, F. I. M. (2000). Encoding and retrieval of information. In E. Tulving & F. I. M. Craik (Eds.), *The Oxford handbook of memory* (pp. 93–108). New York: Oxford University Press.

Brown, S. L., Nesse, R. M., Vinokur, A. D., & Smith, D. M. (2003). Providing social support may be more beneficial than receiving it: Results from a prospective study of mortality. *Psychological Science, 14*, 320–327.

Brownell, H. H., & Gardner, H. (1981). Hemisphere specialization: Definitions not incantations. *Behavioral and Brain Sciences, 4*, 64–65.

Bruce, D., Dolan, A., & Phillips-Grant, K. (2000). On the transition from childhood amnesia to the recall of personal memories. *Psychological Science, 11*, 360–364.

Bruch, H. (1978). *The golden cage: The enigma of anorexia nervosa*. Cambridge, MA: Harvard University Press.

Bruckner-Gordon, F., Gangi, B. K., & Wallman, G. U. (1988). *Making therapy work: Your guide to choosing, using, and ending therapy*. New York: Harper & Row.

Bruer, J. T. (1999). *The myth of the first three years: A new understanding of early brain development and lifelong learning*. New York: Free Press.

Bruer, J. T. (2002). Avoiding the pediatrician's error: How neuroscientists can help educators (and themselves). *Nature Neuroscience, 5*, 1031–1033.

Bruggerman, E. L., & Hart, K. J. (1996). Cheating, lying, and moral reasoning by religious and secular high school students. *Journal of Educational Research, 89*, 340–344.

Bryden, M. P. (1982). *Laterality: Functional asymmetry in the intact brain*. New York: Academic Press.

Buchanan, R. W., & Carpenter, W. T. (2000). Schizophrenia: Introduction and overview. In B. J. Sadock & V. A. Sadock (Eds.), *Kaplan and Sadock's comprehensive textbook of psychiatry* (7th ed., Vol. 1). Philadelphia: Lippincott/Williams & Wilkins.

Buck, L. B. (2000). Smell and taste: The chemical senses. In E. R. Kandel, J. H. Schwartz, & T. M. Jessell (Eds.), *Principles of neural science*. New York: McGraw-Hill.

Buckman, R. (2002). Communications and emotions: Skills and effort are key. *British Medical Journal, 325*, 672.

Bufe, B., Breslin, P. A. S., Kuhn, C., Reed, D. R., Tharp, C. D., Slack, J. P., Kim, U., Drayna, D., & Meyerhof, W. (2005). The molecular basis of individual differences in phenylthiocarbamide and propylthiouracil bitterness perception. *Current Biology, 15*, 322–327.

Bühler, C., & Allen, M. (1972). *Introduction to humanistic psychology*. Pacific Grove, CA: Brooks/Cole.

Bulcroft, R., & Teachman, J. (2004). Ambiguous constructions: Development of a childless or childfree life course. In M. Coleman & L. H. Ganong (Eds.), *Handbook of contemporary families: Considering the past, contemplating the future*. Thousand Oaks, CA: Sage.

Bulik, C. M. (2004). Genetic and biological risk factors. In J. K. Thompson (Ed.), *Handbook of eating disorders and obesity*. New York: Wiley.

Bulik, C. M., Tozzi, F., Anderson, C., Mazzeo, S. E., Aggen, S., & Sullivan, P. F. (2003). The relation between eating disorders and components of perfectionism. *American Journal of Psychiatry, 160*, 366–368.

Burger, J. M. (1986). Temporal effects on attributions: Actor and observer differences. *Social Cognition, 4*, 377–387.

Burger, J. M. (1997). *Personality*. Pacific Grove: Brooks/Cole.

Burger, J. M. (1999). The foot-in-the-door compliance procedure: A multiple process analysis review. *Personality and Social Psychology Review, 3*, 303–325.

Burger, J. M. (2004). *Personality*. Belmont, CA: Wadsworth.

Burke, D. M., & Shafto, M. A. (2004). Aging and language production. *Current Directions in Psychological Science, 13*(1), 21–24.

Burns, B. D., & Corpus, B. (2004). Randomness and inductions from streaks: "Gambler's fallacy" versus "hot hand." *Psychonomic Bulletin & Review, 11*(1), 179–184.

Bushman, B. J. (2002). Does venting anger feed or extinguish the flame? Catharsis, rumination, distraction, anger, and aggressive responding. *Personality and Social Psychology Bulletin, 28*, 724–731.

Bushman, B. J., Baumeister, R. F., & Stack, A. D. (1999). Catharsis, aggression, and persuasive influence: Self-fulfilling or self-defeating prophecies? *Journal of Personality and Social Psychology, 76*, 367–376.

Bushman, B. J., & Huesmann, L. R. (2001). Effects of televised violence on aggression. In D. G. Singer & J. L. Singer (Eds.), *Handbook of children and the media*. Thousand Oaks, CA: Sage.

Buss, D. M. (1985). Human mate selection. *American Scientist, 73*, 47–51.

Buss, D. M. (1988). The evolution of human intrasexual competition: Tactics of mate attraction. *Journal of Personality and Social Psychology, 54*, 616–628.

Buss, D. M. (1989). Sex differences in human mate preferences: Evolutionary hypotheses tested in 37 cultures. *Behavioral and Brain Sciences, 12*, 1–49.

Buss, D. M. (1991). Evolutionary personality psychology. *Annual Review of Psychology, 42*, 459–491.

Buss, D. M. (1994a). *The evolution of desire: Strategies of human mating*. New York: Basic Books.

Buss, D. M. (1994b). Mate preferences in 37 cultures. In W. J. Lonner & R. S. Malpass (Eds.), *Psychology and culture*. Boston: Allyn & Bacon.

Buss, D. M. (1995). Evolutionary psychology: A new paradigm for psychological science. *Psychological Inquiry, 6*, 1–30.

Buss, D. M. (1996). The evolutionary psychology of human social strategies. In E. T. Higgins & A. W. Kruglanski (Eds.), *Social psychology: Handbook of basic principles*. New York: Guilford.

Buss, D. M. (1997). Evolutionary foundation of personality. In R. Hogan, J. Johnson, & S. Briggs (Eds.), *Handbook of personality psychology*. San Diego: Academic Press.

Buss, D. M. (1998). The psychology of human mate selection: Exploring the complexity of the strategic repertoire. In C. Crawford, & D. L. Krebs (Eds.), *Handbook of evolutionary psychology: Ideas, issues, and applications*. Mahwah, NJ: Erlbaum.

Buss, D. M. (1999). *Evolutionary psychology: The new science of the mind*. Boston: Allyn & Bacon.

Buss, D. M. (2001). Cognitive biases and emotional wisdom in the evolution of conflict between the sexes. *Current Directions in Psychological Science, 10*, 219–223.

Buss, D. M., & Kenrick, D. T. (1998). Evolutionary social psychology. In D. T. Gilbert, S. T. Fiske, & G. Lindzey (Eds.), *The handbook of social psychology*. New York: McGraw-Hill.

Buss, D. M., & Reeve, H. K. (2003). Evolutionary psychology and developmental dynamics: Comment on Lickliter and Honeycutt (2003). *Psychological Bulletin, 129*, 848–853.

Buss, D. M., & Schmitt, D. P. (1993). Sexual strategies theory: A contextual evolutionary analysis of human mating. *Psychological Review, 100*, 204–232.

Bussey, K., & Bandura, A. (1984). Influence of gender constancy and social power on sex-linked modeling. *Journal of Personality and Social Psychology, 47*, 1292–1302.

Bussey, K., & Bandura, A. (1999). Social cognitive theory of gender development and differentiation. *Psychological Review, 106*, 676–713.

Buster, J. E., & Carson, S. A. (2002). Endocrinology and diagnosis of pregnancy. In S. G. Gabbe, J. R. Niebyl, & J. L. Simpson (Eds.), *Obstetrics: Normal and problem pregnancies*. New York: Churchill Livingstone.

Butcher, J. N. (1990). *The MMPI-2 in psychological treatment*. New York: Oxford University Press.

Buxton, C. E. (1985). American functionalism. In C. E. Buxton (Ed.), *Points of view in the modern history of psychology*. Orlando: Academic Press.

Buxton, M. N., Arkey, Y., Lagos, J., Deposito, F., Lowenthal, F., & Simring, S. (1981). Stress and platelet aggregation in hemophiliac children and their family members. *Research Communications in Psychology, Psychiatry and Behavior, 6*(1), 21–48.

Byne, W., Kemether, E., Jones, L., Haroutunian, V., & Davis, K. L. (1999). The neurochemistry of schizophrenia. In D. S. Charney, E. J. Nestler & B. S. Bunney (Eds.), *Neurobiology of mental illness* (pp. 236–245). New York: Oxford University Press.

Byne, W., & Parsons, B. (1993). Human sexual orientation: The biological theories reappraised. *Archives of General Psychiatry, 50*, 228–239.

Byrne, D. (1997). An overview (and underview) of research and theory within the attraction paradigm. *Journal of Social and Personal Relationships, 14*, 417–431.

Byrne, D., Clore, G. L., & Smeaton, G. (1986). The attraction hypothesis: Do similar attitudes affect anything? *Journal of Personality and Social Psychology, 51*, 1167–1170.

Cacioppo, J. T., & Berntson, G. G. (1999). The affect system: Architecture and operating characteristics. *Current Directions in Psychological Science, 8*, 133–137.

Cacioppo, J. T., & Gardner, W. L. (1999). Emotion. *Annual Review of Psychology, 50*, 191–214.

Cacioppo, J. T., Klein, D. J., Berntson, G. G., & Hatfield, E. (1993). The psychophysiology of emotions. In M. Lewis & J. M. Haviland (Eds.), *Handbook of emotions*. New York: Guilford.

Cain, W. S. (1988). Olfaction. In R. C. Atkinson, R. J. Herrnstein, G. Lindzey, & R. D. Luce (Eds.), *Stevens' handbook of experimental psychology: Perception and motivation* (Vol. 1). New York: Wiley.

Caine, E. D., & Lyness, J. M. (2000). Delirium, dementia, and amnestic and other cognitive disorders. In B. J. Sadock & V. A. Sadock (Eds.), *Kaplan and Sadock's comprehensive textbook of psychiatry*. Philadelphia: Lippincott/Williams & Wilkins.

Calhoun, L. G., & Tedeschi, R. G. (2001). Posttraumatic growth: The positive lessons of loss. In R. A. Neimeyer (Ed.), *Meaning reconstruction and the experience of loss* (pp. 157–172). Washington, DC: American Psychological Association.

Cami, J., & Farre, M. (2003). Mechanisms of disease: Drug addiction. *New England Journal of Medicine, 349*, 975–986.

Campbell, A. (2005). Aggression. In D. M. Buss (Ed.), *The handbook of evolutionary psychology*. New York: Wiley.

Campbell, J. (1971). *Hero with a thousand faces*. New York: Harcourt Brace Jovanovich.

Campbell, K. B. (2000). Introduction to the special section: Information processing during sleep onset and sleep. *Canadian Journal of Experimental Psychology, 54*(4), 209–218.

Campbell, L., Simpson, J. A., Boldry, J., & Kashy, D. A. (2005). Perceptions of conflict and support in romantic relationships: The role of attachment anxiety. *Journal of Personality and Social Psychology, 88*, 510–531.

Campbell, R. J. (2000). Managed care. In B. J. Sadock & V. A. Sadock (Eds.), *Kaplan and Sadock's comprehensive textbook of psychiatry* (7th ed., Vol. 2). Philadelphia: Lippincott/Williams & Wilkins.

Campbell, S., Marriott, M., Nahmias, C., & Mac-Queen, G. M. (2004). Lower hippocampal volume in patients suffering from depression: A meta-analysis. *American Journal of Psychiatry, 161*, 598–607.

Campbell, W. K., & Sedikides, C. (1999). Self-threat magnifies the self-serving bias: A meta-analytic integration. *Review of General Psychology, 3*, 23–43.

Campfield, L. A. (2002). Leptin and body weight regulation. In C. G. Fairburn & K. D. Brownell (Eds.), *Eating disorders and obesity: A comprehensive handbook* (pp. 32–36). New York: Guilford.

Cancro, R., & Lehmann, H. E. (2000). Schizophrenia: Clinical features. In B. J. Sadock & V. A. Sadock (Eds.), *Kaplan and Sadock's comprehensive textbook of psychiatry* (7th ed., Vol. 1, pp. 1169–1198). Philadelphia: Lippincott/Williams & Wilkins.

Canli, T., Desmond, J. E., Zhao, Z., Glover, G., & Gabrieli, J. D. E. (1998). Hemispheric asymmetry for emotional stimuli detected with fMRI. *Neuroreport: An International Journal for the Rapid Communication of Research in Neuroscience, 9*, 3233–3239.

Cannon, W. B. (1927). The James-Lange theory of emotions: A critical examination and an alternate theory. *American Journal of Psychology, 39*, 106–124.

Cannon, W. B. (1932). *The wisdom of the body*. New York: Norton.

Cannon, W. B., & Washburn, A. L. (1912). An explanation of hunger. *American Journal of Physiology, 29*, 444–454.

Canter, P. H. (2003). The therapeutic effects of meditation. *British Medical Journal, 326*, 1049–1050.

Capaldi, E. D. (1996). Conditioned food preferences. In E. D. Capaldi (Ed.), *Why we eat what we eat: The psychology of eating* (pp. 53–81). Washington, DC: American Psychological Association.

Capozza, D., & Brown, R. (2000). *Social identity processes: Trends in theory and research*. London: Sage.

Carey, G., & DiLalla, D. L. (1994). Personality and psychopathology: Genetic perspectives. *Journal of Abnormal Psychology, 103*, 32–43.

Carli, L. L. (1999). Cognitive, reconstruction, hindsight, and reactions to victims and perpetrators. *Personality & Social Psychology Bulletin, 25*, 966–979.

Carnegie, D. (1936). *How to win friends and influence people*. New York: Simon & Schuster.

Carney, S., & Geddes, J. (2003). Electroconvulsive therapy. *British Medical Journal, 326*, 1343–1344.

Carpenter, W. T. (1992). The negative symptom challenge. *Archives of General Psychiatry, 49*, 236–237.

Carpenter, W. T. (2002). From clinical trial to prescription. *Archives of General Psychology, 59*, 282–285.

Carroll, J. M., & Russell, J. A. (1997). Facial expressions in Hollywood's portrayal of emotion. *Journal of Personality and Social Psychology, 72*, 164–176.

Carroll, M. E., & Overmier, J. B. (2001). *Animal research and human health*. Washington, DC: American Psychological Association.

Carskadon, M. A., & Dement, W. C. (2005). Normal human sleep: An overview. In M. H. Kryger, T. Roth, & W. C. Dement (Eds.), *Principles and practice of sleep medicine*. Philadelphia: Elsevier Saunders.

Carskadon, M. A., & Rechtschaffen, A. (2005). Monitoring and staging human sleep. In M. H. Kryger, T. Roth, & W. C. Dement (Eds.). *Principles and practice of sleep medicine*. Philadelphia: Elsevier Saunders.

Carter, B. (1999). Becoming parents: The family with young children. In B. Carter & M. McGoldrick (Eds.), *The expanded family life cycle: Individual, family, and social perspectives* (3rd ed., pp. 249–273). Boston: Allyn & Bacon.

Carter, R. (1998). *Mapping the mind*. Berkeley: University of California Press.

Cartwright, R. D. (1977). *Night life: Explorations in dreaming*. Englewood Cliffs, NJ: Prentice-Hall.

Cartwright, R. D. (1994). Dreams and their meaning. In M. H. Kryger, T. Roth, & W. C. Dement (Eds.), *Principles and practice of sleep medicine* (2nd ed.). Philadelphia: Saunders.

Cartwright, R. D. (2004). The role of sleep in changing our minds: A psychologist's discussion of papers on memory reactivation and consolidation in sleep. *Learning & Memory, 11*, 660–663.

Cartwright, R. D., & Lamberg, L. (1992). *Crisis dreaming*. New York: HarperCollins.

Carver, C. S., Pozo, C., Harris, S. D., Noriega, V., Scheier, M. F., Robinson, D. S., Ketcham, A. S., Moffat, F. L., Jr., & Clark, K. C. (1993). How coping mediates the effect of optimism on distress: A study of women with early stage breast cancer. *Journal of Personality and Social Psychology, 65*, 375–390.

Carver, C. S., & Scheier, M. F. (1994). Situational coping and coping dispositions in a stressful transaction. *Journal of Personality and Social Psychology, 66*, 184–195.

Carver, C. S., & Scheier, M. F. (1999). Optimism. In C. R. Snyder (Ed.), *Coping: The psychology of what works*. New York: Oxford University Press.

Carver, C. S., Scheier, M. F., & Weintraub, J. K. (1989). Assessing coping strategies: A theoretically based approach. *Journal of Personality and Social Psychology, 56*, 267–283.

Casanova, C., Merabet, L., Desautels, A., & Minville, K. (2001). Higher-order motion processing in the pulvinar. *Progress in Brain Research, 134*, 71–82.

Casey, R., & Rozin, P. (1989). Changing children's food preferences: Parent opinions. *Appetite, 12*, 171–182.

Caspi, A., & Herbener, E. S. (1990). Continuity and change: Assortative marriage and the consistency of personality in adulthood. *Journal of Personality and Social Psychology, 58*(2), 250–258.

Caspi, A., Roberts, B. W., & Shiner, R. L. (2005). Personality development: Stability and change. *Annual Review of Psychology, 56*, 453–484.

Caspi, O., & Burleson, K. O. (2005). Methodological challenges in meditation research. *Advances in Mind-Body Medicine, 21*(1), 4–11.

Cassel, R. N. (2000). Third force psychology and person-centered theory: From ego-status to ego-ideal. *Psychology: A Journal of Human Behavior, 37*(3), 44–48.

Cassidy, J. (1999). The nature of the child's ties. In J. Cassidy & P. R. Shaver (Eds.), *Handbook of attachment: Theory, research, and clinical applications*. New York: Guilford.

Catania, A. C. (1992). Reinforcement. In L. R. Squire (Ed.), *Encyclopedia of learning and memory*. New York: Macmillan.

Catania, A. C., & Laties, V. G. (1999). Pavlov and Skinner: Two lives in science (an introduction to B. F. Skinner's "Some responses to the stimulus 'Pavlov'"). *Journal of the Experimental Analysis of Behavior, 72*, 455–461.

Catrambone, R. (1998). The subgoal learning model: Creating better examples so that students can solve novel problems. *Journal of Experimental Psychology: General, 127*, 355–376.

Cattell, R. B. (1950). *Personality: A systematic, theoretical and factual study*. New York: McGraw-Hill.

Cattell, R. B. (1957). *Personality and motivation: Structure and measurement*. New York: Harcourt, Brace & World.

Cattell, R. B. (1965). *The scientific analysis of personality*. Baltimore: Penguin.

Cattell, R. B. (1966). *The scientific analysis of personality.* Chicago: Aldine.

Cattell, R. B. (1990). Advances in Cattellian personality theory. In L. A. Pervin (Ed.), *Handbook of personality: Theory and research.* New York: Guilford.

Cattell, R. B., Eber, H. W., & Tatsuoka, M. M. (1970). *Handbook of the Sixteen Personality Factor Questionnaire (16PF).* Champaign, IL: Institute for Personality and Ability Testing.

Catz, S. L., & Kelly, J. A. (2001). Living with HIV disease. In A. Baum, T. A. Revenson, & J. E. Singer (Eds.), *Handbook of health psychology* (pp. 841–850). Mahwah, NJ: Erlbaum.

Cavanaugh, J. C. (1993). *Adult development and aging* (2nd ed.). Pacific Grove, CA: Brooks/Cole.

Caverly, D. C., Orlando, V. P., & Mullen, J. L. (2000). Textbook study reading. In R. F. Flippo & D. C. Caverly (Eds.), *Handbook of college reading and study strategy research.* Mahwah, NJ: Erlbaum.

Ceci, S. J. (1991). How much does schooling influence general intelligence and its cognitive components? A reassessment of the evidence. *Developmental Psychology, 27,* 703–722.

Ceci, S. J., Rosenblum, T., de Bruyn, E., & Lee, D. Y. (1997). A bio-ecological model of intellectual development: Moving beyond h2. In R. J. Sternberg & E. L. Grigorenko (Eds.), *Intelligence, heredity, and environment.* New York: Cambridge University Press.

Cerletti, U., & Bini, L. (1938). Un nuevo metodo di shockterapie "L'elettro-shock." *Boll. Acad. Med. Roma, 64,* 136–138.

Chaiken, S., & Maheswaran, D. (1994). Heuristic processing can bias systematic processing: Effects of source credibility, argument ambiguity, and task importance on attitude judgment. *Journal of Personality and Social Psychology, 66,* 460–473.

Chambless, D. L., & Hollon, S. D. (1998). Defining empirically supported therapies. *Journal of Consulting & Clinical Psychology, 66,* 7–18.

Chambless, D. L., & Ollendick, T. H. (2001). Empirically supported psychological interventions: Controversies and evidence. *Annual Review of Psychology, 52,* 685–716.

Chan, J. W. C., & Vernon, P. E. (1988). Individual differences among the peoples of China. In S. H. Irvine & J. W. Berry (Eds.), *Human abilities in cultural context.* New York: Cambridge University Press.

Chance, P. (2001, September/October). The brain goes to school: Why neuroscience research is going to the head of the class. *Psychology Today,* p. 72.

Chandler, C. C., & Fisher, R. P. (1996). Retrieval processes and witness memory. In E. L. Bjork & R. A. Bjork (Eds.), *Memory.* San Diego: Academic Press.

Chapman, P. D. (1988). *Schools as sorters: Lewis M. Terman, applied psychology, and the intelligence testing movement.* New York: New York University Press.

Chemers, M. M., Hu, L., & Garcia, B. F. (2001). Academic self-efficacy and first-year college student performance and adjustment. *Journal of Educational Psychology, 93*(1), 55–64.

Chess, S., & Thomas, A. (1996). *Temperament: Theory and practice.* New York: Brunner/Mazel.

Chiappelli, F., & Hodgson, D. (2000). Immune suppression. In G. Fink (Ed.), *Encyclopedia of stress* (Vol. 2, pp. 531–535). San Diego: Academic Press.

Cho, K., Ennaceur, A., Cole, J. C., & Kook Suh, C. (2000). Chronic jet lag produces cognitive deficits. *Journal of Neuroscience, 20*(6), RC66.

Choi, I., Nisbett, R. E., & Norenzayan, A. (1999). Causal attribution across cultures: Variation and universality. *Psychological Bulletin, 125,* 47–63.

Chomsky, N. (1957). *Syntactic structures.* The Hague: Mouton.

Chopra, S. S. (2003). Industry funding of clinical trials: Benefit of bias? *Journal of the American Medical Association, 290,* 113–114.

Choudhry, N. K., Stelfox, H. T., & Detsky, A. S. (2002). Relationships between authors of clinical practice guidelines and the pharmaceutical industry. *Journal of the American Medical Association, 287*(5), 612–617.

Christensen, A. J., & Johnson, J. A. (2002). Patient adherence with medical treatment regimens: An interactive approach. *Current Directions in Psychological Science, 11*(3), 94–97.

Christensen, L. (1988). Deception in psychological research: When is its use justified? *Personality and Social Psychology Bulletin, 14,* 664–675.

Chu, J. A., Frey, L. M., Ganzel, B. L., & Matthews, J. A. (1999). Memories of childhood abuse: Dissociation, amnesia, and corroboration. *American Journal of Psychiatry, 156,* 749–755.

Chun, M. M., & Wolfe, J. M. (2001). Visual attention. In E. B. Goldstein (Ed.), *Blackwell handbook of perception.* Malden, MA: Blackwell.

Church, A. T., & Lonner, W. J. (1998). The cross-cultural perspective in the study of personality: Rationale and current research. *Journal of Cross-Cultural Psychology, 29,* 32–62.

Churchland, P. S., & Ramachandran, V. S. (1996). Filling in: Why Dennett is wrong. In K. Atkins (Ed.), *Perception.* Oxford, England: Oxford University Press.

Cialdini, R. B. (2001). *Influence: Science and practice.* Boston: Allyn & Bacon.

Cialdini, R. B., & Trost, M. R. (1998). Social influence: Social norms, conformity, and compliance. In D. T. Gilbert, S. T. Fiske, & G. Lindzey (Eds.), *The handbook of social psychology.* New York: McGraw-Hill.

Clark, R. D., & Hatfield, E. (1989). Gender differences in receptivity to sexual offers. *Journal of Psychology & Human Sexuality, 2*(1), 39–55.

Clayton, T., & Craig, P. (2001). *Diana: Story of a princess.* New York: Pocket Books.

Clow, A. (2001). The physiology of stress. In F. Jones & J. Bright (Eds.), *Stress: Myth, theory, and research.* Harlow, UK: Pearson, Education.

Coderre, T. J., Mogil, J. S., & Bushnell, M. C. (2003). The biological psychology of pain. In M. Gallagher & R. J. Nelson (Eds.), *Handbook of psychology, Vol. 3:Biological psychology.* New York: Wiley.

Coenen, A. (1998). Neuronal phenomena associated with vigilance and consciousness: From cellular mechanisms to electroencephalographic patterns. *Consciousness & Cognition: An International Journal, 7,* 42–53.

Cohen, C. E. (1981). Person categories and social perception: Testing some boundaries of the processing effects of prior knowledge. *Journal of Personality and Social Psychology, 40,* 441–452.

Cohen, D. (1997). A critique of the use of neuroleptic drugs in psychiatry. In S. Fisher & R. P. Greenberg (Eds.), *From placebo to panacea: Putting psychiatric drugs to the test.* New York: Wiley.

Cohen, D., & McCubbin, M. (1990). The political economy of tardive dyskinesia: Asymmetries in power and responsibility. *The Journal of Mind and Behavior, 11*(3/4), 465–488.

Cohen, D. B. (1999). *Stranger in the nest: Do parents really shape their child's personality, intelligence, or character?* New York: Wiley.

Cohen, F., Solomon, S., Maxfield, M., Pyszczynski, T., & Greenberg, J. (2004). Fatal attraction: The effects of mortality salience on evaluations of charismatic, task-oriented, and relationship-oriented leaders. *Psychological Science, 15,* 846–851.

Cohen, S., Kessler, R. C., & Gordon, L. U. (1995). Strategies for measuring stress in studies of psychiatric and physical disorders. In S. Cohen, R. C. Kessler, & L. U. Gordon (Eds.), *Measuring stress: A guide for health and social scientists* (pp. 3–28). New York: Oxford University Press.

Cohen, S., & Lichtenstein, E. (1990). Perceived stress, quitting smoking, and smoking relapse. *Health Psychology, 9,* 466–478.

Cohen, S., Tyrrell, D. A. J., & Smith, A. P. (1993). Negative life events, perceived stress, negative affect, and susceptibility to the common cold. *Journal of Personality and Social Psychology, 64,* 131–140.

Colby, A., & Kohlberg, L. (1987). *The measurement of moral judgment* (Vols. 1–2). New York: Cambridge University Press.

Colder, C. R. (2001). Life stress, physiological and subjective indexes of negative emotionality and coping reasons for drinking: Is there evidence for a self-medication model of alcohol use? *Psychology of Addictive Behaviors, 15,* 237–245.

Collaer, M. L., & Hines, M. (1995). Human behavioral sex differences: A role for gonadal hormones during early development? *Psychological Bulletin, 118,* 55–107.

Collins, A. M., & Loftus, E. F. (1975). A spreading activation theory of semantic processing. *Psychological Review, 82,* 407–428.

Collins, M. A., & Zebrowitz, L. A. (1995). The contributions of appearance to occupational outcomes in civilian and military settings. *Journal of Applied Social Psychology, 25,* 129–163.

Collins, N. L., & Allard, L. M. (2001). Cognitive representations of attachment: The content and function of working models. In G. J. O. Fletcher & M. S. Clark (Eds.), *Blackwell handbook of social psychology: Interpersonal processes.* Malden, MA: Blackwell.

Collins, W. A., Maccoby, E. E., Steinberg, L., Hetherington, E. M., & Bornstein, M. H. (2000). Contemporary research in parenting: The case for nature and nurture. *American Psychologist, 55,* 218–232.

Colom, R., Lluis-Font, J. M., & Andres-Pueyo, A. (2005). The generational intelligence gains are caused by decreasing variance in the lower half of the distribution: Supporting evidence for the nutrition hypothesis. *Intelligence, 33,* 83–91.

Coltrane, S. (2001). Research on household labor: Modeling and measuring the social embeddedness of routine family work. In R. M. Milardo (Ed.), *Understanding families into the new millennium: A decade in review* (pp. 427–452). Minneapolis, MN: National Council on Family Relations.

Colwill, R. M. (1993). An associative analysis of instrumental learning. *Current Directions in Psychological Science, 2*(4), 111–116.

Comer, D. R. (1995). A model of social loafing in real work groups. *Human Relations, 48,* 647–667.

Compas, B. E. (2004). Processes of risk and resilience during adolescence: Linking contexts and individuals. In R. M. Lerner & L. Steinberg (Eds.), *Handbook of adolescent psychology.* New York: Wiley.

Compton, D. M., Dietrich, K. L., & Smith, J. S. (1995). Animal rights activism and animal welfare concerns in the academic setting: Levels of activism and perceived importance of research with animals. *Psychological Reports, 76,* 23–31.

Conway, L. C., & Schaller, M. (2002). On the verifiability of evolutionary psychological theories: An analysis of the psychology of scientific persuasion. *Personality and Social Psychology Review, 6,* 152–166.

Cooper, E. (1991). A critique of six measures for assessing creativity. *Journal of Creative Behavior, 25*(3), 194–204.

Cooper, L., & Bright, J. (2001). Individual differences in reactions to stress. In F. Jones & J. Bright (Eds.), *Stress: Myth, theory and research*. Harlow, UK: Pearson Education.

Corballis, M. C. (1991). *The lopsided ape*. New York: Oxford University Press.

Corballis, P. M. (2003). Visuospatial processing and the right-hemisphere interpreter. *Brain & Cognition, 53*(2), 171–176.

Coren, S. (1992). *The left-hander syndrome: The causes and consequences of left-handedness*. New York: Free Press.

Coren, S. (1996). *Sleep thieves: An eye-opening exploration into the science and mysteries of sleep*. New York: Free Press.

Coren, S., & Aks, D. J. (1990). Moon illusion in pictures: A multimechanism approach. *Journal of Experimental Psychology: Human Perception and Performance, 16*, 365–380.

Coren, S., & Girgus, J. S. (1978). *Seeing is deceiving: The psychology of visual illusions*. Hillsdale, NJ: Erlbaum.

Corkin, S. (1984). Lasting consequences of bilateral medial temporal lobectomy: Clinical course and experimental findings in H. M. *Seminars in Neurology, 4*, 249–259.

Corkin, S. (2002). What's new with the amnesic patient H. M.? *Nature Reviews Neuroscience, 3*, 153–159.

Cornell, D. G. (1997). Post hoc explanation is not prediction. *American Psychologist, 52*, 1380.

Correll, C. U., Leucht, S., & Kane, J. M. (2004). Lower risk for tardive dyskinesia associated with second-generation antipsychotics: A systematic review of 1-year studies. *American Journal of Psychiatry, 161*, 414–425.

Corsica, J. A., & Perri, M. G. (2003). Obesity. In A. M. Nezu, C. M. Nezu, & P. A. Geller (Eds.), *Handbook of psychology, Vol. 9: Health psychology*. New York: Wiley.

Cosmides, L. L., & Tooby, J. (1989). Evolutionary psychology and the generation of culture. Part II. Case study: A computational theory of social exchange. *Ethology and Sociobiology, 10*, 51–97.

Cosmides, L., & Tooby, J. (1996). Are humans good intuitive statisticians after all? Rethinking some conclusions from the literature on judgment under uncertainty. *Cognition, 58*, 1–73.

Costa, G. (1996). The impact of shift and night work on health. *Applied Ergonomics, 27*, 9–16.

Costa, P. T., Jr., & McCrae, R. R. (1985). *NEO Personality Inventory*. Odessa, FL: Psychological Assessment Resources.

Costa, P. T., Jr., & McCrae, R. R. (1992). *Revised NEO Personality Inventory: NEO PI and NEO Five-Factor Inventory* (Professional Manual). Odessa, FL: Psychological Assessment Resources.

Costa, P. T., Jr., & McCrae, R. R. (1994). Set like plaster? Evidence for the stability of adult personality. In T. F. Heatherton & J. L. Weinberger (Eds.), *Can personality change?* Washington, DC: American Psychological Association.

Costa, P. T., Jr., & McCrae, R. R. (1997). Longitudinal stability of adult personality. In R. Hogan, J. Johnson, & S. Briggs (Eds.), *Handbook of personality psychology*. San Diego: Academic Press.

Courage, M. L., & Howe, M. L. (2002). From infant to child: The dynamics of cognitive change in the second year of life. *Psychological Bulletin, 128*(2), 250–277.

Coutts, A. (2000). Nutrition and the life cycle. 1: Maternal nutrition and pregnancy. *British Journal of Nursing, 9*, 1133–1138.

Cowart, B. J., & Rawson, N. E. (2001). Olfaction. In E. B. Goldstein (Ed.), *Blackwell handbook of perception*. Malden, MA: Blackwell.

Cowey, A. (1994). Cortical visual areas and the neurobiology of higher visual processes. In M. J. Farah & G. Ratcliff (Eds.), *The neuropsychology of high-level vision: Collected tutorial essays*. Hillsdale, NJ: Erlbaum.

Cox, M. J., Paley, B., Burchinal, M., & Payne, C. (1999). Marital perceptions and interactions across the transition to parenthood. *Journal of Marriage and the Family, 61*, 611–625.

Coyne, J. C. (1999). Thinking interactionally about depression: A radical restatement. In T. E. Joiner & J. C. Coyne (Eds.), *Interpersonal processes in depression* (pp. 369–392). Washington, DC: American Psychological Association.

Craig, J. C., & Rollman, G. B. (1999). Somesthesis. *Annual Review of Psychology, 50*, 305–331.

Craik, F. I. M. (2001). Effects of dividing attention on encoding and retrieval processes. In H. L. Roediger III, J. S. Nairne, I. Neath, & A. M. Surprenant (Eds.), *The nature of remembering: Essays in honor of Robert G. Crowder* (pp. 55–68). Washington, DC: American Psychological Association.

Craik, F. I. M. (2002). Levels of processing: Past, present . . . and future? *Memory, 10*(5–6), 305–318.

Craik, F. I. M., & Kester, J. D. (2000). Divided attention and memory: Impairment of processing or consolidation? In E. Tulving (Ed.), *Memory, consciousness, and the brain: The Tallinn conference* (pp. 38–51). Philadelphia: Psychology Press.

Craik. F. I. M., & Lockhart, R. S. (1972). Levels of processing: A framework for memory research. *Journal of Verbal Learning and Verbal Behavior, 11*, 671–684.

Craik, F. I. M., & Tulving, E. (1975). Depth of processing and the retention of words in episodic memory. *Journal of Experimental Psychology: General, 104*, 268–294.

Cramer, P. (2000). Defense mechanisms in psychology today: Further processes for adaptation. *American Psychologist, 55*(6), 637–646.

Cramer, P. (2001). The unconscious status of defense mechanisms. *American Psychologist, 56*, 762–763.

Cravens, H. (1992). A scientific project locked in time: The Terman Genetic Studies of Genius, 1920s–1950s. *American Psychologist, 47*, 183–189.

Crawford, M., & Popp, D. (2003). Sexual double standards: A review and methodological critique of two decades of research. *Journal of Sex Research, 40*(1), 13–26.

Creed, F. (1989). Appendectomy. In G. W. Brown & T. O. Harris (Eds.), *Life events and illness*. New York: Guilford.

Crits-Christoph, P. (1997). Limitations of the dodo bird verdict and the role of clinical trials in psychotherapy research: Comment on Wampold et al (1997). *Psychological Bulletin, 122*, 216–220.

Crockett, H. (1962). The achievement motive and differential occupational mobility in the United States. *American Sociological Review, 27*, 191–204.

Cross, S. E., & Markus, H. R. (1993). Gender in thought, belief, and action: A cognitive approach. In A. E. Beall & R. J. Sternberg (Eds.), *The psychology of gender*. New York: Guilford.

Crowder, R. G., & Greene, R. L. (2000). Serial learning: Cognition and behavior. In E. Tulving & F. I. M. Craik (Eds.), *The Oxford handbook of memory* (pp. 125–136). New York: Oxford University Press.

Crowley, K., Callanan, M. A., Tenenbaum, H. R., & Allen, E. (2001). Parents explain more often to boys than to girls during shared scientific thinking. *Psychological Science, 12*, 258–261.

Cruz, C., della Rocco, P., & Hackworth, C. (2000). Effects of quick rotating schedules on the health and adjustment of air traffic controllers. *Aviation, Space, & Environmental Medicine, 71*, 400–407.

Csikszentmihalyi, M. (2000). The contribution of flow to positive psychology. In J. E. Gillham (Ed.), *The science of optimism and hope: Research essays in honor of Martin E. P. Seligman*. Philadelphia: Templeton Foundation Press.

Cuban, L. (2004). Assessing the 20-year impact of multiple intelligences on schooling. *Teachers College Record, 106*(1), 140–146.

Culpepper, L., Davidson, J. R. T., Dietrich, A. J., Goodman, W. K., Kroenke, K., & Schwenk, T. L. (2004). Suicidality as a possible effect of antidepressant treatment. *Journal of Clinical Psychiatry, 65*, 742–749.

Cummings, J. L., & Cole, G. (2002). Alzheimer's disease. *Journal of the American Medical Association , 287*, 2335–2338.

Cummins, D. (2005). Dominance, status, and social hierarchies. In D. M. Buss (Ed.), *The handbook of evolutionary psychology*. New York: Wiley.

Cunningham, C. O., & Selwyn, P. A. (2005). HIV-related medical complications and treatment. In J. H. Lowinson, P. Ruiz, R. B. Millman, & J. G. Langrod (Eds.), *Substance abuse: A comprehensive textbook*. Philadelphia: Lippincott/Williams & Williams.

Cunningham, M. (2001). The influence of parental attitudes and behaviors on children's attitudes toward gender and household labor in early adulthood. *Journal of Marriage and the Family, 63*, 111–122.

Cushman, P. (1992). Psychotherapy to 1992: A historically situated interpretation. In D. K. Freedheim (Ed.), *History of psychotherapy: A century of change*. Washington, DC: American Psychological Association.

Cutting, L. P., & Docherty, N. M. (2000). Schizophrenia outpatients' perceptions of their parents: Is expressed emotion a factor? *Journal of Abnormal Psychology, 109*, 266–272.

Czeisler, C. A., Buxton, O. M., & Khalsa, S. (2005). The human circadian timing system and sleep-wake regulation. In M. H. Kryger, T. Roth, & W. C. Dement (Eds.), *Principles and practice of sleep medicine*. Philadelphia: Elsevier Saunders.

Czeisler, C. A., Cajochen, C., & Turek, F. W. (2000). Melatonin in the regulation of sleep and circadian rhythms. In M. H. Kryger, T. Roth, & W. C. Dement (Eds.), *Principles and practice of sleep medicine*. Philadelphia: Saunders.

Dahl, R. (2003). Beyond raging hormones: The tinderbox in the teenage brain. *Cerebrum, 5*(3), 7–22.

Dallman, M. F., Bhatnagar, S., & Viau, V. (2000). Hypothalamo-pituitary-adrenal axis. In G. Fink (Ed.), *Encyclopedia of stress* (Vol. 2, pp. 468–476). San Diego: Academic Press.

Daly, M., & Wilson, M. (1985). Child abuse and other risks of not living with both parents. *Ethology and Sociobiology, 6*, 197–210.

Daly, M., & Wilson, M. (1988). *Homicide*. Hawthorne, NY: Aldine.

Danner, D. D., Snowdon, D. A., & Friesen, W. V. (2001). Positive emotions in early life and longevity: Findings from the nun study. *Journal of Personality & Social Psychology, 80*, 804–813.

Danziger, K. (1990). *Constructing the subject: Historical origins of psychological research*. Cambridge, England: Cambridge University Press.

Darley, J. M., & Latané, B. (1968). Bystander intervention in emergencies: Diffusion of responsibility. *Journal of Personality and Social Psychology, 8*, 377–383.

Darwin, C. (1859). *The origin of species.* London: Murray.

Darwin, C. (1871). *Descent of man.* London: Murray.

Darwin, C. (1872). *The expression of emotions in man and animals.* New York: Philosophical Library.

Das, H. H. J., de Wit, J. B. F., & Stroebe, W. (2005). Fear appeals motivate acceptance of action recommendations: Evidence for a positive bias in the processing of persuasive messages. *Personality and Social Psychology Bulletin, 29*, 650–664.

Das, J. P. (1994). Eastern views of intelligence. In R. J. Sternberg (Ed.), *Encyclopedia of human intelligence.* New York: Macmillan.

Dasen, P. R. (1994). Culture and cognitive development from a Piagetian perspective. In W. J. Lonner & R. Malpass (Eds.), *Psychology and culture.* Boston: Allyn & Bacon.

Davenport, J. L., & Potter, M. C. (2004). Scene consistency in object and background perception. *Psychological Science, 15*, 559–564.

Davidson, R. J., Jackson, D. C., & Kalin, N. H. (2000). Emotion, plasticity, context, and regulation: Perspectives from affective neuroscience. *Psychological Bulletin, 126*, 890–909.

Davidson, R. J., Kabat-Zinn, J., Schumacher, J., Rosenkranz, M., Muller, D., Santorelli, S. F., Urbanowski, F., Harrington, A., Bonus, K., & Sheridan, J. F. (2003a). Alterations in brain and immune function produced by mindfulness meditation. *Psychosomatic Medicine, 65*, 564–570.

Davidson, R. J., Pizzagalli, D., Nitschke, J. B., & Kalin, N. H. (2003b). Parsing the subcomponents of emotion and disorders of emotion: Perspectives from affective neuroscience. In R. J. Davidson, K. R. Scherer, & H. H. Goldsmith (Eds.), *Handbook of affective sciences.* New York: Oxford University Press.

Davidson, R. J., Shackman, A. J., & Maxwell, J. S. (2004). Asymmetries in face and brain related to emotion. *Trends in Cognitive Sciences, 8*(9), 389–391.

Davis, D., Shaver, P. R., & Vernon, M. L. (2003). Physical, emotional, and behavioral reactions to breaking up: The roles of gender, age, emotional involvement, and attachment style. *Personality and Social Psychology Bulletin, 29*, 871–884.

Davis, J. L., & Rusbult, C. E. (2001). Attitude alignment in close relationships. *Journal of Personality and Social Psychology, 81*(1), 65–84.

Davis, M. H., Morris, M. M., & Kraus, L. A. (1998). Relationship-specific and global perceptions of social support: Associations with well-being and attachment. *Journal of Personality and Social Psychology, 74*, 468–481.

Day, R. H. (1965). Inappropriate constancy explanation of spatial distortions. *Nature, 207*, 891–893.

Deary, I. J. (2000). Simple information processing and intelligence. In R. J. Sternberg (Ed.), *Handbook of intelligence* (pp. 267–284). New York: Cambridge University Press.

Deary, I. J. (2003). Reaction time and psychometric intelligence: Jensen's contributions. In H. Nyborg (Ed.), *The scientific study of general intelligence: Tribute to Arthur R. Jensen.* Oxford, UK: Pergamon.

Deary, I. J., & Stough, C. (1996). Intelligence and inspection time: Achievements, prospects, and problems. *American Psychologist, 51*, 599–608.

Deaux, K. (1993). Commentary: Sorry, wrong number—A reply to Gentile's call. *Psychological Science, 4*, 125–126.

DeCarvalho, R. J. (1991). *The founders of humanistic psychology.* New York: Praeger.

de Castro, J. M., Bellisle, F., Dalix, A., & Pearcey, S. M. (2000). Palatability and intake relationships in free-living humans: Characterization and independence of influence in North Americans. *Physiology & Behavior, 70*, 343–350.

De Cock, K. M., & Janssen, R. S. (2002). An unequal epidemic in an unequal world. *Journal of the American Medical Association, 288*, 236–238.

Defeyter, M. A., & German, T. P. (2003). Acquiring an understanding of design: Evidence from children's insight problem solving. *Cognition, 89*(2), 133–155.

DeFrain, J., & Olson, D. H. (1999). Contemporary family patterns and relationships. In M. B. Sussman, S. K. Steinmetz, & G. W. Peterson (Eds.), *Handbook of marriage and the family* (pp. 309–326). New York: Plenum.

De Koninck, J. (2000). Waking experiences and dreaming. In M. H. Kryger, T. Roth, & W. C. Dement (Eds.), *Principles and practice of sleep medicine.* Philadelphia: Saunders.

Delis, D. C., & Lucas, J. A. (1996). Memory. In B. S. Fogel, R. B. Schiffer, & S. M. Rao (Eds.), *Neuropsychiatry.* Baltimore: Williams & Wilkins.

DelMonte, M. M. (2000). Retrieved memories of childhood sexual abuse. *British Journal of Medical Psychology, 73*, 1–13.

DeLong, M. R. (2000). The basal ganglia. In E. R. Kandel, J. H. Schwartz, & T. M. Jessell (Eds.), *Principles of neural science* (pp. 853–872). New York: McGraw-Hill.

DeLongis, A., Folkman, S., & Lazarus, R. S. (1988). The impact of daily stress on health and mood: Psychological and social resources as mediators. *Journal of Personality and Social Psychology, 54*, 486–495.

Delprato, D. J., & Midgley, B. D. (1992). Some fundamentals of B. F. Skinner's behaviorism. *American Psychologist, 47*, 1507–1520.

DeMaio, T. J. (1984). Social desirability and survey measurement: A review. In C. F. Turner & E. Martin (Eds.), *Surveying subjective phenomena* (Vol. 2). New York: Russell Sage Foundation.

Dement, W. C. (1978). *Some must watch while some must sleep.* New York: Norton.

Dement, W. C. (1992). *The sleepwatchers.* Stanford, CA: Stanford Alumni Association.

Dement, W. C. (2003). Knocking on Kleitman's door: The view from 50 years later. *Sleep Medicine Reviews, 7*(4), 289–292.

Dement, W. C. (2005). History of sleep psychology. In M. H. Kryger, T. Roth, & W. C. Dement (Eds.), *Principles and practice of sleep medicine.* Philadelphia: Elsevier Saunders.

Dement, W. C., & Vaughan, C. (1999). *The promise of sleep.* New York: Delacorte Press.

Dement, W. C., & Wolpert, E. (1958). The relation of eye movements, bodily motility, and external stimuli to dream content. *Journal of Experimental Psychology, 53*, 543–553.

Dempster, F. N. (1996). Distributing and managing the conditions of encoding and practice. In E. L. Bjork & R. A. Bjork (Eds.), *Memory.* San Diego: Academic Press.

Dennerstein, L. (1996). Well-being, symptoms and the menopausal transition. *Maturitas, 23*, 147–157.

Dennis, W. (1966). Age and creative productivity. *Journal of Gerontology, 21*(1), 1–8.

Deregowski, J. B. (1972, November). Pictorial perception and culture. *Scientific American, 227*(5), 83.

Derevensky, J. L., & Gupta, R. (2004). Preface. In J. L. Derevensky & R. Gupta (Eds.), *Gambling problems in youth: Theoretical and applied perspectives* (pp. xxi–xxiv). New York: Kluwer/Plenum.

Derogatis, L. R., & Coons, H. L. (1993). Self-report measures of stress. In L. Goldberger & S. Breznitz (Eds.), *Handbook of stress: Theoretical and clinical aspects* (2nd ed.). New York: Free Press.

Des Jarlais, D. C., Hagan, H., & Friedman, S. R. (2005). Epidemiology and emerging public health perspectives. In J. H. Lowinson, P. Ruiz, R. B. Millman, & J. G. Langrod (Eds.), *Substance abuse: A comprehensive textbook.* Philadelphia: Lippincott/ Williams & Wilkins.

Desimone, R. (1991). Face selective cells in the temporal cortex of monkeys. *Journal of Cognitive Neuroscience, 3*, 1–8.

Deutsch, J. A. (1990). Food intake: Gastric factors. In E. M. Stricker (Ed), *Handbook of behavioral neurobiology: Vol 10. Neurobiology of food and fluid intake.* New York: Plenum.

DeValois, R. L., & Jacobs, G. H. (1984). Neural mechanisms of color vision. In I. Darian-Smith (Ed.), *The nervous system* (Vol. 3). Baltimore: Williams & Wilkins.

De Villiers, P. (1977). Choice in concurrent schedules and a quantitative formulation of the law of effect. In W. K. Honig & J. E. R. Staddon (Eds.), *Handbook of operant behavior.* Englewood Cliffs, NJ: Prentice-Hall.

Devine, P. G., & Monteith, M. J. (1999). Automaticity and control in stereotyping. In S. Chaiken & Y. Trope (Eds.), *Dual-process theories in social psychology.* New York: Guilford.

Devine, P. G., Plant, E. A., & Blair, I. V. (2001). Classic and contemporary analysis of racial prejudice. In R. Brown & S. L. Gaertner (Eds.), *Blackwell handbook of social psychology: Intergroup processes.* Malden, MA: Blackwell.

Devine, P. G., Tauer, J. M., Barron, K. E., Elliot, A. J., & Vance, K. M. (1999). Moving beyond attitude change in the study of dissonance-related processes. In E. Harmon-Jones & J. Mills (Eds.), *Cognitive dissonance: Progress on a pivotal theory in social psychology.* Washington, DC: American Psychological Association.

Devlin, B., Fienberg, S. E., Resnick, D. P., & Roeder, K. (2002). Intelligence and success: Is it all in the genes? In J. M. Fish (Ed.), *Race and intelligence: Separating science from myth* (pp. 355–368). Mahwah, NJ: Erlbaum.

DeVries, R. (2000). Vygotsky, Piaget, and education: A reciprocal assimilation of theories and educational practices. *New Ideas in Psychology, 18*(2–3), 187–213.

Dew, M. A., Bromet, E. J., & Switzer, G. E. (2000). Epidemiology. In M. Hersen & A. S. Bellack (Eds.), *Psychopathology in adulthood.* Boston: Allyn & Bacon.

De Waal, F. (2001). *The ape and the sushi master: Cultural reflections of a primatologist.* New York: Basic Books.

de Wijk, R. A., Schab, F. R., & Cain, W. S. (1995). Odor identification. In F. R. Schab & R. G. Crowder (Eds.), *Memory for odors.* Mahwah, NJ: Erlbaum.

Di Lorenzo, P. M., & Youngentob, S. L. (2003). Olfaction and taste. In M. Gallagher & R. J. Nelson (Eds.), *Handbook of psychology, Vol. 3:Biological psychology.* New York: Wiley.

Diamond, L. M. (2003). Was it a phase? Young women's relinquishment of lesbian/bisexual identities over a 5-year period. *Journal of Personality and Social Psychology, 84*, 352–364.

Dick, D. M., & Rose, R. J. (2002). Behavior genetics: What's new? What's next? *Current Directions in Psychological Science, 11*(2), 70–74.

Dickens, W. T., & Flynn, J. R. (2001). Heritability estimates versus large environmental effects: The IQ paradox resolved. *Psychological Review, 108,* 346–369.

Diekman, A. B., & Murnen, S. K. (2004). Learning to be little women and little men: The inequitable gender equality of nonsexist children's literature. *Sex Roles, 50,* 373–385.

Diener, E. (1984). Subjective well-being. *Psychological Bulletin, 93,* 542–575.

Diener, E., & Diener, C. (1996). Most people are happy. *Psyhological Science, 7,* 181–185.

Diener, E., Gohm, C. L., Suh, E., & Oishi, S. (2000). Similarity of the relations between marital status and subjective well-being across cultures. *Journal of Cross-Cultural Psychology, 31,* 419–436.

Diener, E., & Lucas, R. E. (1999). Personality and subjective well-being. In D. Kahneman, E. Diener, & N. Schwarz (Eds.), *Well-being: The foundations of hedonic psychology.* New York: Russell Sage Foundation.

Diener, E., Sandvik, E., Seidlitz, L., & Diener, M. (1993). The relationship between income and subjective well-being. Relative or absolute? *Social Indicators Research, 28,* 195–223.

Diener, E., & Seligman, M. E. P. (2002). Very happy people. *Psychological Science, 13,* 81–84.

Diener, E., & Seligman, M. E. P. (2004). Beyond money: Toward an economy of well-being. *Psychological Science in the Public Interest, 5*(1), 1–31.

Diener, E., Wolsic, B., & Fujita, F. (1995). Physical attractiveness and subjective well-being. *Journal of Personality and Social Psychology, 69,* 120–129.

Dillbeck, M. C., & Orme-Johnson, D. W. (1987). Physiological differences between transcendental meditation and rest. *American Psychologist, 42,* 879–881.

Dilsaver, S. C., Chen, Y. R., Shoaib, A. M., & Swann, A. C. (1999). Phenomenology of mania: Evidence for distinct depressed, dysphoric, and euphoric presentations. *American Journal of Psychiatry, 156,* 426–430.

DiMatteo, M. R. (1991). *The psychology of health, illness, and medical care: An individual perspective.* Pacific Grove, CA: Brooks/Cole.

DiMatteo, M. R. (1997). Health behaviors and care decisions: An overview of professional-patient communication. In D. S. Gochman (Ed.), *Handbook of health behavior research II: Provider determinants.* New York: Plenum.

DiMatteo, M. R. (2004a). Social support and patient adherence to medical treatment: A meta analysis. *Health Psychology, 23,* 207–218.

DiMatteo, M. R. (2004b). Variations in patients' adherence to medical recommendations: A quantitative review of 50 years of research. *Medical Care, 42,* 200–209.

DiMatteo, M. R., Giordani, P. J., Lepper, H. S., & Croghan, T. W. (2002). Patient adherence and medical treatment outcomes: A meta-analysis. *Medical Care, 40,* 794–811.

Din, J. N., Newby, D. E., & Flapan, A. D. (2004). Omega 3 fatty acids and cardiovascular disease—fishing for a natural treatment. *British Medical Journal, 328,* 30–35.

Dinges, D. F. (1993). Napping. In M. A. Carskadon (Ed.), *Encyclopedia of sleep and dreaming.* New York: Macmillan.

Dinges, D. F., Rogers, N. L., & Baynard, M. D. (2005). Chronic sleep deprivation. In M. H. Kryger, T. Roth, & W. C. Dement (Eds.), *Principles and practice of sleep medicine.* Philadelphia: Elsevier Saunders.

Dinsmoor, J. A. (1998). Punishment. In W. O'Donohue (Ed.), *Learning and behavior therapy.* Boston: Allyn & Bacon.

Dinsmoor, J. A. (2004). The etymology of basic concepts in the experimental analysis of behavior. *Journal of the Experimental Analysis of Behavior, 82,* 311–316.

Dion, K. L. (2003). Prejudice, racism, and discrimination. In T. Millon & M. J. Lerner (Eds.), *Handbook of Psychology, Vol. 5: Personality and social psychology.* New York: Wiley.

Dissell, R. (2005, December 14). Student from Ohio robbed bank to feed gambling habit, lawyer says. *The Plain Dealer.* Retrieved March 11, 2006, from http://www.cleveland.com/crime/plaindealer/index.ssf?/base/iscri/113456491142670.xml&coll=2&thispage=1.

Dixon, M., & Laurence, J. R. (1992). Two hundred years of hypnosis research: Questions resolved? Questions unanswered! In E. Fromm & M. R. Nash (Eds.), *Contemporary hypnosis research.* New York: Guilford.

Dixon, R. A., & Cohen, A. (2003). Cognitive development in adulthood. In R. M. Lerner, M. A. Easterbrooks, & J. Mistry (Eds.), *Handbook of psychology, Vol. 6: Developmental psychology.* New York: Wiley.

Dobzhansky, T. (1937). *Genetics and the origin of species.* New York: Columbia University Press.

Docherty, J. P. (1999). Cost of treating mental illness from a managed care perspective. *Journal of Clinical Psychiatry, 60,* 49–53.

Doerr, P., Pirke, K. M., Kockott, G., & Dittmor, F. (1976). Further studies on sex hormones in male homosexuals. *Archives of General Psychiatry, 33,* 611–614.

Doghramji, P. P. (2001). Detection of insomnia in primary care. *Journal of Clinical Psychiatry, 62*(suppl 10), 18–26.

Dolan, M., Anderson, I. M., & Deakin, J. F. W. (2001). Relationship between 5-HT function and impulsivity and aggression in male offenders with personality disorders. *British Journal of Psychiatry, 178,* 352–359.

Dollard, J., Doob, L. W., Miller, N. E., Mowrer, O. H., & Sears, R. R. (1939). *Frustration and aggression.* New Haven: Yale University Press.

Dollard, J., & Miller, N. E. (1950). *Personality and psychotherapy: An analysis in terms of learning, thinking and culture.* New York: McGraw-Hill.

Domhoff, G. W. (2005a). The content of dreams: Methodologic and theoretical implications. In M. H. Kryger, T. Roth, & W. C. Dement (Eds.), *Principles and practice of sleep medicine.* Philadelphia: Elsevier Saunders.

Domhoff, G. W. (2005b). Refocusing the neurocognitive approach to dreams: A critique of the Hobson versus Solms debate. *Dreaming, 15*(1), 3–20.

Dominowski, R. L., & Bourne, L. E., Jr. (1994). History of research on thinking and problem solving. In R. J. Sternberg (Ed.), *Thinking and problem solving.* San Diego: Academic Press.

Domjan, M. (1992). Adult learning and mate choice: Possibilities and experimental evidence. *American Zoologist, 32,* 48–61.

Domjan, M. (1994). Formulation of a behavior system for sexual conditioning. *Psychonomic Bulletin & Review, 1,* 421–428.

Domjan, M. (1998). *The principles of learning and behavior.* Pacific Grove: Brooks/Cole.

Domjan, M. (2005). Pavlovian conditioning: A functional perspective. *Annual Review of Psychology, 56,* 179–206.

Domjan, M., & Purdy, J. E. (1995). Animal research in psychology: More than meets the eye of the general psychology student. *American Psychologist, 50,* 496–503.

Domjan, M., Blesbois, E., & Williams, J. (1998). The adaptive significance of sexual conditioning: Pavlovian control of sperm release. *Psychological Science, 9,* 411–415.

Domjan, M., Cusato, B., & Krause, M. (2004). Learning with arbitrary versus ecological conditioned stimuli: Evidence from sexual conditioning. *Psychonomic Bulletin & Review, 11,* 232–246.

Donahoe, J. W., & Vegas, R. (2004). Pavlovian conditioning: The CS-UR relation. *Journal of Experimental Psychology: Animal Behavior Processes, 30*(1), 17–33.

Dorn, L. D., Nottelmann, E. D., Susman, E. J., Inoff-Germain, G., Cutler, G. B., & Chrousos, G. P. (1999). Variability in hormone concentrations and self-reported menstrual histories in young adolescents: Menarche as an integral part of a developmental process. *Journal of Youth and Adolescence, 28,* 283–304.

Dorner, G. (1988). Neuroendocrine response to estrogen and brain differentiation. *Archives of Sexual Behavior, 17*(1), 57–75.

Doty, R. L. (1991). Olfactory system. In T. V. Getchell, R. L. Doty, L. M. Bartoshuk, & J. B. Snow, Jr. (Eds.), *Smell and taste in health and disease.* New York: Raven.

Doty, R. L. (2001). Olfaction. *Annual Review of Psychology, 52,* 423–452.

Dougall, A. L., & Baum, A. (2001). Stress, health, and illness. In A. Baum, T. A. Revenson, & J. E. Singer (Eds.), *Handbook of health psychology* (pp. 321–338). Mahwah, NJ: Erlbaum.

Dougherty, D. D., & Rauch, S. L. (2003). Brain imaging in psychiatry. In A. Tasman, J. Kay, & J. A. Lieberman (Eds.), *Psychiatry.* New York: Wiley.

Douzenis, A., Tsirka, Z., Vassilopoulou, C., & Christodoulou, G. N. (2004). The role of serotonin in neurobiology of aggression. *Psychiatriki, 15*(2), 169–179.

Dovidio, J. F., & Gaertner, S. L. (1999). Reducing prejudice: Combating intergroup biases. *Current Directions in Psychological Science, 8,* 101–105.

Dovidio, J. F., & Gaertner, S. L. (2000). Aversive racism and selection decisions: 1989 and 1999. *Psychological Science, 11,* 315–319.

Draijer, N., & Langeland, W. (1999). Childhood trauma and perceived parental dysfunction in the etiology of dissociative symptoms in psychiatric inpatients. *American Journal of Psychiatry, 156,* 379–385.

Draycott, S., & Dabbs, A. (1998). Cognitive dissonance 1: An overview of the literature and its integration into theory and practice of clinical psychology. *British Journal of Clinical Psychology, 37,* 341–353.

Drazen, J. M., & Curfman, G. D. (2002). Financial associations of authors. *New England Journal of Medicine, 346,* 1901–1902.

Drewnowski, A. (1995). Standards for the treatment of obesity. In K. D. Brownell, & C. G. Fairburn (Eds.), *Eating disorders and obesity: A comprehensive handbook.* New York: Guilford.

Driskell, J. E., Willis, R. P., & Copper, C. (1992). Effect of overlearning on retention. *Journal of Applied Psychology, 77*(5), 615–622.

Dubovsky, S. L., Davies, R., & Dubovsky, A. N. (2003). Mood disorders. In R. E. Hales & S. C. Yudofsky (Eds.), *Textbook of clinical psychiatry*. Washington, DC: American Psychiatric Publishing.

Duckworth, K., & Borus, J. F. (1999). Population-based psychiatry in the public sector and managed care. In A. M. Nicholi (Ed.), *The Harvard guide to psychiatry*. Cambridge, MA: Harvard University Press.

Dudai, Y. (2004). The neurobiology of consolidation, or, how stable is the engram? *Annual Review of Psychology, 55*, 51–86.

Duff, P. (2002). Maternal and perinatal infection. In S. G. Gabbe, J. R. Niebyl, & J. L. Simpson (Eds.), *Obstetrics: Normal and problem pregnancies*. New York: Churchill Livingstone.

Duke, M., & Nowicki, S., Jr. (1979). *Abnormal psychology: Perspectives on being different*. Pacific Grove, CA: Brooks/Cole.

Dunbar-Jacob, J., & Schlenk, E. (2001). Patient adherence to treatment regimen. In A. Baum, T. A. Revenson, & J. E. Singer (Eds.), *Handbook of health psychology* (pp. 571–580). Mahwah, NJ: Erlbaum.

Duncan, B. L. (1976). Differential social perception and attribution of intergroup violence: Testing the lower limits of stereotyping of blacks. *Journal of Personality and Social Psychology, 34*, 590–598.

Dunkel-Schetter, C., Gurung, R. A. R., Lobel, M., & Wadhwa, P. D. (2001). Stress processes in pregnancy and birth: Psychological, biological, and sociocultural influences. In A. Baum, T. A. Revenson, & J. E. Singer (Eds.), *Handbook of health psychology* (pp. 495–518). Mahwah, NJ: Erlbaum.

Dunning, D., & Sherman, D. A. (1997). Stereotypes and tacit inference. *Journal of Personality and Social Psychology, 73*, 459–471.

Dwyer, J. (1995). Popular diets. In K. D. Brownell & C. G. Fairburn (Eds.), *Eating disorders and obesity*. New York: Guilford.

Eacott, M. J., & Crawley, R. A. (1998). The offset of childhood amnesia: Memory for events that occurred before age three. *Journal of Experimental Psychology: General, 127*, 22–23.

Eagle, M. N., & Wolitzky, D. L. (1992). Psychoanalytic theories of psychotherapy. In D. K. Freedheim (Ed.), *History of psychotherapy: A century of change*. Washington, DC: American Psychological Association.

Eagly, A. H. (1995). The science and politics of comparing women and men. *American Psychologist, 50*, 145–158.

Eagly, A. H., Ashmore, R. D., Makhijani, M. G., & Longo, L. C. (1991). What is beautiful is good, but . . .: A meta-analytic review of research on the physical attractiveness stereotype. *Psychological Bulletin, 110*, 109–128.

Eagly, A. H., & Chaiken, S. (1995). Attitude strength, attitude structure, and resistance to change. In R. E. Petty & J. A. Krosnick (Eds.), *Attitude strength: Antecedents and consequences*. Mahwah, NJ: Erlbaum.

Eagly, A. H., & Wood, W. (1999). The origins of sex differences in human behavior: Evolved dispositions versus social roles. *American Psychologist, 54*, 408–423.

Eaker, E. D., Sullivan, L. M., Kelly-Hayes, M., D'Agostino, R. B., & Benjamin, E. J. (2004). Anger and hostility predict the development of atrial fibrillation in men in the Framingham Offspring Study. *Circulation, 109*, 1267–1271.

Easterlin, B. L., & Cardena, E. (1999). Cognitive and emotional differences between short- and long-term Vipassana meditators. *Imagination, Cognition and Personality, 18*(1), 68–81.

Eaton, J. (2001). Management communication: The threat of groupthink. *Corporate Communications, 6*, 183–192.

Ebbinghaus, H. (1885/1964). *Memory: A contribution to experimental psychology* (H. A. Ruger & E. R. Bussemius, Trans.). New York: Dover.

Edberg, P. (1990). Rorschach assessment. In A. Goldstein & M. Hersen (Eds.), *Handbook of psychological assessment*. New York: Pergamon Press.

Edinger, J. D., & Means, M. K. (2005). Overview of insomnia: Definitions, epidemiology, differential diagnosis, and assessment. In M. H. Kryger, T. Roth, & W. C. Dement (Eds.), *Principles and practice of sleep medicine*. Philadelphia: Elsevier Saunders.

Edwards, A. (1999). *Ever after: Diana and the life she led*. New York: St. Martin's Press.

Edwards, K., & Smith, E. E. (1996). A disconfirmation bias in the evaluation of arguments. *Journal of Personality an Social Psychology, 71*, 5–24.

Efron, R. (1990). *The decline and fall of hemispheric specialization*. Hillsdale, NJ: Erlbaum.

Egan, M. F., & Hyde, T. M. (2000). Schizophrenia: Neurobiology. In B. J. Sadock & V. A. Sadock (Eds.), *Kaplan and Sadock's comprehensive textbook of psychiatry* (7th ed., Vol. 1, pp. 1129–1146). Philadelphia: Lippincott/Williams & Wilkins.

Ehrenberg, O., & Ehrenberg, M. (1994). *The psychotherapy maze: A consumer's guide to getting in and out of therapy*. Northvale, NJ: Jason Aronson.

Ehrenreich, H., Rinn, T., Kunert, H. J., Moeller, M. R., Poser, W., Schilling, L., Gigerenzer, G., & Hoehe, M. R. (1999). Specific attentional dysfunction in adults following early start of cannabis use. *Psychopharmacology, 142*, 295–301.

Eich, E., Macaulay, D., Loewenstein, R. J., & Dihle, P. H. (1997). Memory, amnesia, and dissociative identity disorder. *Psychological Science, 8*, 417–422.

Eichenbaum, H. (2003). Memory systems. In M. Gallagher & R. J. Nelson (Eds.), *Handbook of psychology, Vol. 3: Biological psychology*. New York: Wiley.

Eid, M., & Diener, E. (2001). Norms for experiencing emotions in different cultures: Inter- and intranational differences. *Journal of Personality and Social Psychology, 81*, 869–885.

Einstein, G. O., & McDaniel, M. A. (1996). Remembering to do things: Remembering a forgotten topic. In D. J. Herrmann, C. McEvoy, C. Hertzog, P. Hertel, & M. K. Johnson (Eds.), *Basic and applied memory research: Practical applications* (Vol. 2). Mahwah, NJ: Erlbaum.

Einstein, G. O., & McDaniel, M. A. (2004). *Memory fitness: A guide for successful aging*. New Haven, CT: Yale University Press.

Einstein, G. O., McDaniel, M. A., Williford, C. L., Pagan, J. L., & Dismukes, R. K. (2003). Forgetting of intentions in demanding situations is rapid. *Journal of Experimental Psychology: Applied, 9*(3), 147–162.

Eisler, R. M., & Ragsdale, K. (1992). Masculine gender role and midlife transition in men. In V. B. Van Hasselt & M. Hersen (Eds.), *Handbook of social development: A lifespan perspective*. New York: Plenum.

Eisner, E. W. (2004). Multiple intelligences. *Teachers College Record, 106*(1), 31–39.

Ekman, P. (1992). Facial expressions of emotion: New findings, new questions. *Psychological Science, 3*, 34–38.

Ekman, P. (1993). Facial expression and emotion. *American Psychologist, 48*, 384–392.

Ekman, P., & Friesen, W. V. (1975). *Unmasking the face*. Englewood Cliffs, NJ: Prentice-Hall.

Ekman, P., & Friesen, W. V. (1984). *Unmasking the face*. Palo Alto: Consulting Psychologists Press.

Elbert, T., Pantev, C., Weinbruch, C., Rockstroh, B., & Taub, E. (1995). Increased cortical representation of the fingers of the left hand in string players. *Science, 270*, 305–307.

Eldred, L., & Chaisson, R. (1996). The clinical course of HIV infection in women. In R. R. Faden & N. E. Kass (Eds.), *HIV, AIDS, and childbearing*. New York: Oxford University Press.

Ellis, A. (1973). *Humanistic psychotherapy: The rational-emotive approach*. New York: Julian Press.

Ellis, A. (1977). *Reason and emotion in psychotherapy*. Seacaucus, NJ: Lyle Stuart.

Ellis, A. (1985). *How to live with and without anger*. New York: Citadel Press.

Ellis, A. (1987). The evolution of rational-emotive therapy (RET) and cognitive behavior therapy (CBT). In J. K. Zeig (Ed.), *The evolution of psychotherapy*. New York: Brunner/Mazel.

Ellis, A. (1999). *How to make yourself happy and remarkably less disturbable*. Atascadero, CA: Impact Publishers.

Ellis, A. (2001). *Feeling better, getting better: Profound self-help therapy for your emotions*. Atascadero, CA: Impact Publishers.

Ellsworth, P. C., & Scherer, K. R. (2003). Appraisal processes in emotion. In R. J. Davidson, K. R. Scherer, & H. H. Goldsmith (Ed.), *Handbook of affective sciences*. New York: Oxford University Press.

Elpers, J. R. (2001). Public psychiatry. In B. J. Sadock & V. A. Sadock (Eds.), *Kaplan and Sadock's comprehensive textbook of psychiatry* (7th ed., Vol. 2). Philadelphia: Lippincott/Williams & Wilkins.

Emavardhana, T., & Tori, C. D. (1997). Changes in self-concept, ego defense mechanisms, and religiosity following seven-day Vipassana meditation retreats. *Journal for the Scientific Study of Religion, 36*, 194–206.

Emmelkamp, P. M. G. (1994). Behavior therapy with adults. In A. E. Bergin & S. L. Garfield (Eds.), *Handbook of psychotherapy and behavior change* (4th ed.). New York: Wiley.

Emmelkamp, P. M. G. (2004). Behavior therapy with adults. In M. J. Lambert (Ed.), *Bergin and Garfield's handbook of psychotherapy and behavior change*. New York: Wiley.

Engemann, K. M., & Owyang, M. T. (2005, April). So much for that merit raise: The link between wages and appearance. *The Regional Economist*, pp. 10–11.

Engen, T. (1987). Remembering odors and their names. *American Scientist, 75*, 497-503.

Engle, R. W. (2001). What is working memory capacity? In H. L. Roediger III, J. S. Nairne, I. Neath, & A. M. Surprenant (Eds.), *The nature of remembering: Essays in honor of Robert G. Crowder*. Washington, DC: American Psychological Association.

Engle, R. W., Tuhulski, S. W., Laughlin, J. E., & Conway, A. R. A. (1999). Working memory, short-term memory, and general fluid intelligence: A latent variable approach. *Journal of Experimental Psychology: General, 128*, 309–331.

Enns, J. T. (2004). *The thinking eye, the seeing brain: Explorations in visual cognition*. New York: Norton.

Epel, E. S., Blackburn, E. H., Lin, J., Dhabhar, F. S., Adler, N. E., Morrow, J. D., & Cawthon, R. M. (2004). Accelerated telomere shortening in response to life stress. *Proceedings of the National Academy of Science, 101*, 17312–17315.

Epley, N., & Huff, C. (1998). Suspicion, affective response, and educational benefit as a result of deception in psychology research. *Personality and Social Psychology Bulletin, 24*, 759–768.

Epstein, S., Donovan, S., & Denes-Raj, V. (1999). The missing link in the paradox of the Linda conjunction problem: Beyond knowing and thinking of the conjunction rule, the intrinsic appeal of heuristic processing. *Personality and Social Psychology Bulletin, 25,* 204–214.

Erber, M. W., Hodges, S. D., & Wilson, T. D. (1995). Attitude strength, attitude stability, and the effects of analyzing reasons. In R. E. Petty & J. A. Krosnick (Eds.), *Attitude strength: Antecedents and consequences.* Mahwah, NJ: Erlbaum.

Erdelyi, M. H. (2001). Defense processes can be conscious or unconscious. *American Psychologist, 56,* 761–762.

Erikson, E. (1963). *Childhood and society.* New York: Norton.

Erikson, E. (1968). *Identity: Youth and crisis.* New York: Norton.

Eriksson, P. S., Perfilieva, E., Bjork-Eriksson, T., Alborn, A. M., Nordborg, C., Peterson, D. A., & Gage, F. H. (1998). Neurogenesis in the adult human hippocampus. *Nature Medicine, 4,* 1313–1317.

Esser, J. K. (1998). Alive and well after twenty-five years: A review of groupthink research. *Organizational Behavior & Human Decision Processes, 73,* 116–141.

Esterson, A. (2001). The mythologizing of psychoanalytic history: Deception and self-deception in Freud's accounts of the seduction theory episode. *History of Psychiatry, 7,* 329–352.

Estes, W. K. (1999). Models of human memory: A 30-year retrospective. In C. Izawa (Ed.), *On human memory: Evolution, progress, and reflections on the 30th anniversary of the Atkinson-Shiffrin model.* Mahwah, NJ: Erlbaum.

Evans, F. J. (1990). Behavioral responses during sleep. In R. R. Bootzin, J. F. Kihlstrom, & D. L. Schacter (Eds.), *Sleep and cognition.* Washington, DC: American Psychological Association.

Evans, G. W. (2004). The environment of childhood poverty. *American Psychologist, 59*(2), 77–92.

Everhart, D. E., & Harrison, D. W. (2000). Facial affect perception in anxious and nonanxious men without depression. *Psychobiology, 28*(1), 90–98.

Eysenck, H. J. (1959). Learning theory and behaviour therapy. *Journal of Mental Science, 195,* 61–75.

Eysenck, H. J. (1967). *The biological basis of personality.* Springfield, IL: Charles C. Thomas.

Eysenck, H. J. (1977). *Crime and personality.* London: Routledge & Kegan Paul.

Eysenck, H. J. (1982). *Personality, genetics and behavior: Selected papers.* New York: Praeger.

Eysenck, H. J. (1988). The concept of "intelligence": Useful or useless? *Intelligence, 12*(1), 1–16.

Eysenck, H. J. (1989). Discrimination reaction time and "*g*": A reply to Humphreys. *Intelligence, 13*(4), 325–326.

Eysenck, H. J. (1990a). Biological dimensions of personality. In L. A. Pervin (Ed.), *Handbook of personality: Theory and research.* New York: Guilford.

Eysenck, H. J. (1990b). *Decline and fall of the Freudian empire.* Washington, DC: Scott-Townsend.

Eysenck, H. J., & Kamin, L. (1981). *The intelligence controversy.* New York: Wiley.

Eysenck, M. W., Mogg, K., May, J., Richards, A., & Mathews, A. (1991). Bias in interpretation of ambiguous sentences related to threat in anxiety. *Journal of Abnormal Psychology, 100,* 144–150.

Fabes, R. A., Carlo, G., Kupanoff, K., & Laible, D. (1999). Early adolescence and prosocial/moral behavior I: The role of individual processes. *Journal of Early Adolescence, 19,* 5–16.

Fabrigar, L. R., MacDonald, T. K., & Wegener, D. T. (2005). The structure of attitudes. In D. Albarracin, B. T. Johnson, & M. P. Zanna (Eds.), *The handbook of attitudes.* Mahwah, NJ: Erlbaum.

Fagot, B. I., Hagan, R., Leinbach, M. D., & Kronsberg, S. (1985). Differential reactions to assertive and communicative acts of toddler boys and girls. *Child Development, 56,* 1499–1505.

Fagot, B. I., Leinbach, M. D., & O'Boyle, C. (1992). Gender labeling, gender stereotyping, and parenting behaviors. *Developmental Psychology, 28,* 225–230.

Fakhoury, W., & Priebe, S. (2002). The process of deinstitutionalization: An international overview. *Current Opinion in Psychiatry, 15*(2), 187–192.

Falls, W. A. (1998). Extinction: A review of therapy and the evidence suggesting that memories are not erased with nonreinforcement. In W. O'Donohue (Ed.), *Learning and behavior therapy.* Boston: Allyn & Bacon.

Fancher, R. E. (1979). *Pioneers of psychology.* New York: Norton.

Fancher, R. E. (2000). Snapshot of Freud in America, 1899–1999. *American Psychologist, 55,* 1025–1028.

Faraday, A. (1974). *The dream game.* New York: Harper & Row.

Farah, A. (1997). An overview of ECT. *Primary Psychiatry, 4,* 58–62.

Faravelli, C., & Pallanti, S. (1989). Recent life events and panic disorders. *American Journal of Psychiatry, 146,* 622–626.

Fausto-Sterling, A. (1992). *Myths of gender.* New York: Basic Books.

Fazio, R. H., & Olson, M. A. (2003). Attitudes: Foundations, functions, and consequences. In M. A. Hogg & J. Cooper (Eds.), *The Sage handbook of social psychology.* Thousand Oaks, CA: Sage.

Feeney, D. M. (1987). Human rights and animal welfare. *American Psychologist, 42,* 593–599.

Feeney, J. A. (1999). Adult romantic attachment and couple relationships. In J. Cassidy & P. R. Shaver (Eds.), *Handbook of attachment: Theory, research, and clinical applications.* New York: Guilford.

Fehr, B. (2001). The status of theory and research on love and commitment. In G. J. O. Fletcher & M. S. Clark (Eds.), *Blackwell handbook of social psychology: Interpersonal processes.* Malden, MA: Blackwell Publishing.

Fein, S., & Spencer, S. J. (1997). Prejudice as self-image maintenance: Affirming the self through derogating others. *Journal of Personality and Social Psychology, 73,* 31–44.

Feingold, A. (1988a). Cognitive gender differences are disappearing. *American Psychologist, 43,* 95–103.

Feingold, A. (1988b). Matching for attractiveness in romantic partners and same-sex friends: A meta-analysis and theoretical critique. *Psychological Bulletin, 104,* 226–235.

Feingold, A. (1992). Good-looking people are not what we think. *Psychological Bulletin, 111,* 304–341.

Feist, G. J. (1998). A meta-analysis of personality in scientific and artistic creativity. *Personality and Social Psychology Review, 2,* 290-309.

Feist, G. J. (2004). The evolved fluid specificity of human creativity talent. In R. J. Sternberg, E. L. Grigorenko, & J. L. Singer (Eds.), *Creativity: From potential to realization.* Washington, DC: American Psychological Association.

Feldman, D. H. (1988). Creativity: Dreams, insights, and transformations. In R. J. Sternberg (Ed.), *The nature of creativity: Contemporary psychological perspectives.* Cambridge: Cambridge University Press.

Feldman, D. H. (1999). The development of creativity. In R. J. Sternberg (Ed.), *Handbook of creativity.* New York: Cambridge University Press.

Feldman, D. H. (2003). Cognitive development in childhood. In R. M. Lerner, M. A. Easterbrooks, & J. Mistry (Eds.), *Handbook of psychology, Vol. 6: Developmental psychology.* New York: Wiley.

Fenton, W. S., & McGlashan, T. H. (1994). Antecedents, symptom progression, and long-term outcome of the deficit syndrome in schizophrenia. *American Journal of Psychiatry, 151,* 351–356.

Fenwick, P. (1987). Meditation and the EEG. In M. A. West (Ed.), *The psychology of meditation.* Oxford: Clarendon Press.

Ferguson, M. J., & Bargh, J. A. (2004). Liking is for doing: The effects of goal pursuit on automatic evaluation. *Journal of Personality and Social Psychology, 87,* 557–572.

Ferguson, T. (1993). Working with your doctor. In D. Goleman & J. Gurin (Eds.), *Mind-body medicine: How to use your mind for better health.* Yonkers, NY: Consumer Reports Books.

Ferris, A. L. (2002). Religion and the quality of life. *Journal of Happiness Studies, 3,* 199–215.

Ferster, C. S., & Skinner, B. F. (1957). *Schedules of reinforcement.* New York: Appleton-Century-Crofts.

Festinger, L. (1957). *A theory of cognitive dissonance.* Stanford, CA: Stanford University Press.

Festinger, L., & Carlsmith, J. M. (1959). Cognitive consequences of forced compliance. *Journal of Abnormal and Social Psychology, 58,* 203–210.

Fields, R. D. (2004). The other half of the brain. *Scientific American, 290*(4), 54–61.

Fields, R. D., & Stevens-Graham, B. (2002). New insights into neuron-glia communication. *Science, 298,* 556–562.

Fifer, W. P., Monk, C. E., & Grose-Fifer, J. (2001). Prenatal development and risk. In G. Bremner & A. Fogel (Eds.), *Blackwell handbook of infant development* (pp. 505–542). Malden, MA: Blackwell.

Figueredo, A. J., Sefcek, J. A., Vasquez, G., Brumbach, B. H., King, J. E., & Jacobs, W. J. (2005). Evolutionary personality psychology. In D. M. Buss (Ed.), *The handbook of evolutionary psychology.* New York: Wiley.

Fine, R. (1990). *The history of psychoanalysis.* New York: Continuum.

Fink, B., & Penton-Voak, I. (2002). Evolutionary psychology of facial attractiveness. *Current Directions in Psychological Science, 11*(5), 154–158.

Finnegan, L. P., & Kandall, S. R. (2005). Maternal and neonatal effects of alcohol and drugs. In J. H. Lowinson, P. Ruiz, R. B. Millman, & J. G. Langrod (Eds.), *Substance abuse: A comprehensive textbook.* Baltimore: Williams & Wilkins.

Fischer, K. W., & Hencke, R. W. (1996). Infants' construction of actions in context: Piaget's contribution to research on early development. *Psychological Science, 7,* 204–210.

Fischhoff, B. (1988). Judgment and decision making. In R. J. Sternberg & E. E. Smith (Eds.), *The psychology of human thought.* Cambridge: Cambridge University Press.

Fisher, C., & Fyrberg, D. (1994). College students weigh the costs and benefits of deceptive research. *American Psychologist, 49,* 417–427.

Fisher, S., & Greenberg, R. P. (1985). *The scientific credibility of Freud's theories and therapy.* New York: Columbia University Press.

Fisher, S., & Greenberg, R. P. (1996). *Freud scientifically reappraised: Testing the theories and therapy.* New York: Wiley.

Fisher, S., & Greenberg, R. P. (1997). The curse of the placebo: Fanciful pursuit of a pure biological therapy. In S. Fisher & R. P. Greenberg (Eds.), *From placebo to panacea: Putting psychiatric drugs to the test.* New York: Wiley.

Fishman, D. B., & Franks, C. M. (1992). Evolution and differentiation within behavior therapy: A theoretical epistemological review. In D. K. Freedheim (Ed.), *History of psychotherapy: A century of change.* Washington, DC: American Psychological Association.

Fiske, S. T. (1998). Stereotyping, prejudice, and discrimination. In D. T. Gilbert, S. T. Fiske, & G. Lindzey (Eds.), *The handbook of social psychology.* New York: McGraw-Hill.

Fiske, S. T. (2000). Stereotyping, prejudice, and discrimination at the seam between the centuries: Evolution, culture, mind and brain. *European Journal of Social Psychology, 30,* 299–322.

Fiske, S. T. (2004). Mind the gap: In praise of informal sources of formal theory. *Personality and Social Psychology Review, 8*(2), 132–137.

Fitness, J., Fletcher, G., & Overall, N. (2003). Interpersonal attraction and intimate relationships. In M. A. Hogg & J. Cooper (Eds.), *The Sage handbook of social psychology.* Thousand Oaks, CA: Sage.

Flannery, R. B., Jr. (1999). Psychological trauma and posttraumatic stress disorder: A review. *International Journal of Mental Health, 1,* 135–140.

Flavell, J. H. (1996). Piaget's legacy. *Psychological Science, 7,* 200–203.

Fleeson, W. (2004). Moving personality beyond the person-situation debate: The challenge and the opportunity of within-person variability. *Current Directions in Psychological Science, 13*(2), 83–87.

Fleeson, W., Malanos, A. B., & Achille, N. M. (2002). An intraindividual process approach to the relationship between extraversion and positive affect: Is acting extraverted as "good" as being extraverted? *Journal of Personality and Social Psychology, 83,* 1409–1422.

Fleischhacker, W. W. (2002). Second-generation antipsychotics. *Psychopharmacology, 162*(1), 90–91.

Fletcher, G. J. O., Simpson, J. A., & Thomas, G. (2000). Ideals, perceptions, and evaluations in early relationship development. *Journal of Personality and Social Psychology, 79,* 933–940.

Fletcher, G. J. O., Simpson, J. A., Thomas, G., & Giles, L. (1999). Ideals in intimate relationships. *Journal of Personality and Social Psychology, 76,* 72–89.

Flett, G. L., Vredenburg, K., & Krames, L. (1995). The stability of depressive symptoms in college students: An empirical demonstration of regression to the mean. *Journal of Psychopathology & Behavioral Assessment, 17,* 403–415.

Flippo, R. F. (2000). *Testwise: Strategies for success in taking tests.* Torrance, CA: Good Apple.

Flippo, R. F., Becker, M. J., & Wark, D. M. (2000). Preparing for and taking tests. In R. F. Flippo & D. C. Caverly (Eds.), *Handbook of college reading and study strategy research.* Mahwah, NJ: Erlbaum.

Flores, B. H., Musselman, D. L., DeBattista, C., Garlow, S. J., Schatzberg, A. F., & Nemeroff, C. B. (2004). Biology of mood disorders. In A. F. Schatzberg & C. B. Nemeroff (Eds.), *Textbook of psychopharmacology.* Washington, DC: American Psychiatric Publishing.

Flum, H. (1994). Styles of identity formation in early and middle adolescence. *Genetic, Social, and General Psychology Monographs, 120,* 435–467.

Flynn, J. R. (1987). Massive IQ gains in 14 nations: What IQ tests really measure. *Psychological Bulletin, 101,* 171–191.

Flynn, J. R. (1994). IQ gains over time. In R. J. Sternberg (Ed.), *The encyclopedia of human intelligence.* New York: Macmillan.

Flynn, J. R. (1999). Searching for justice: The discovery of IQ gains over time. *American Psychologist, 54,* 5–20.

Flynn, J. R. (2003). Movies about intelligence: The limitations of g. *Current Directions in Psychological Science, 12*(3), 95–99.

Fodor, E. M., & Carver, R. A. (2000). Achievement and power motives, performance feedback, and creativity. *Journal of Research in Personality, 34,* 380–396.

Folkman, S. (1997). Positive psychological states and coping with severe stress. *Social Science and Medicine, 45,* 1207–1221.

Folkman, S., & Moskowitz, J. T. (2000). Positive affect and the other side of coping. *American Psychologist, 55,* 647–654.

Folkman, S., Moskowitz, J. T., Ozer, E. M., & Park, C. L. (1997). Positive meaningful events and coping in the context of HIV/AIDS. In B. H. Gottlieb (Ed.), *Coping with chronic stress* (pp. 293–314). New York: Plenum.

Folsom, D. P., Hawthorne, W., Lindamer, L., Gilmer, T., Bailey, A., Golsham, S., Garcia, P., Unutzer, J., Hough, R., & Jeste, D. V. (2005). Prevalence and risk factors for homelessness and utilization of mental health services among 10,340 patients with serious mental illness in a large public mental health system. *American Journal Psychiatry, 162,* 370–376.

Formicelli, L. (2001, March-April). Baby blues. *Psychology Today,* p. 24.

Forstein, M. (2004). The pseudoscience of sexual orientation change therapy. *British Medical Journal USA, 4,* 143–144.

Forsyth, D. R. (2004). Inferences about actions performed in constraining contexts: Correspondence bias or correspondent inference? *Current Psychology: Developmental, Learning, Personality, Social , 23*(1), 41–51.

Foster, R. G. (2004). Are we trying to banish biological time? *Cerebrum, 6,* 7–26.

Foulkes, D. (1985). *Dreaming: A cognitive-psychological analysis.* Hillsdale, NJ: Erlbaum.

Fox, G. L., Bruce, C., & Combs-Orme, T. (2000). Parenting expectations and concerns of fathers and mothers of newborn infants. *Family Relations, 49*(2), 123–131.

Fozard, J. L. (1990). Vision and hearing in aging. In J. E. Birren & K.W. Schaie (Eds.), *Handbook of the psychology of aging* (3rd ed.). San Diego: Academic Press.

Fozard, J. L., & Gordon-Salant, S. (2001). Changes in vision and hearing with aging. In J. E. Birren & K. W. Schaie (Eds.), *Handbook of the psychology of aging* (5th ed., pp. 240–265). San Diego, CA: Academic Press.

Fraley, R. C. (2002). Attachment stability from infancy to adulthood: Meta-analysis and dynamic modeling of developmental mechanisms. *Personality and Social Psychology Review, 6,* 123–151.

Francis, G. (1999). Spatial frequency and visual persistence: Cortical reset. *Spatial Vision, 12,* 31–50.

Francis, M. E., & Pennebaker, J. W. (1992). Putting stress into words: The impact of writing on psychological, absentee and self-reported emotional well-being measures. *American Journal of Health Promotion, 6,* 280–287.

Frank, J. D. (1961). *Persuasion and healing.* Baltimore: Johns Hopkins University Press.

Frank, J. D., & Frank, J. B. (1991). *Persuasion and healing: A comparison study of psychotherapy.* Baltimore: Johns Hopkins University Press.

Frank, L. K. (1939). Projective methods for the study of personality. *Journal of Psychology, 8,* 343–389.

Frank, L. R. (1990). Electroshock: Death, brain damage, memory loss, and brainwashing. *The Journal of Mind and Behavior, 11*(3/4), 489–512.

Frantom, C., & Sherman, M. F. (1999). At what price art? Affective instability within a visual art population. *Creativity Research Journal, 12,* 15–23.

Frasure-Smith, N., & Lesperance, F. (2005). Depression and coronary heart disease: Complex synergism of mind, body, and environment. *Current Directions in Psychological Science, 14*(1), 39–43.

Frazer, A., Daws, L. C., Duncan, G. E., & Morilak, D. A. (2003). Basic mechanisms of neurotransmitter action. In A. Tasman, J. Kay, & J. A. Lieberman (Eds.), *Psychiatry.* New York: Wiley.

Frederick, S., & Loewenstein, G. (1999). Hedonic adaptation. In D. Kahneman, E. Diener, & N. Schwarz (Eds.), *Well-being: The foundations of hedonic psychology.* New York: Russell Sage Foundation.

Frederickson, B. L. (1998). What good are positive emotions? *Review of General Psychology, 2,* 300–319.

Fredrickson, B. L. (2002). Positive emotions. In C. R. Snyder & S. J. Lopez (Eds.), *Handbook of positive psychology* (pp. 120–134). New York: Oxford University Press.

Fredrickson, B. L., & Branigan, C. (2001). Positive emotions. In T. J. Mayne & G. A. Bonanno (Eds.), *Emotions: Current issues and future directions* (pp. 123–151). New York: Guilford.

Fredrickson, B. L., Tugade, M. M., Waugh, C. E., & Larkin, G. R. (2003). What good are positive emotions in crises? A prospective study of resilience and emotions following the terrorist attacks on the United States on September 11, 2001. *Journal of Personality and Social Psychology, 84,* 365–376.

Fredriks, A. M., Van Buren, S., Burgmeijer, R. J. F., Muelmeester, J. F., Roelien, J., Brugman, E., Roede, M. J., Verloove-Vanhorick, S. P., & Wit, J. M. (2000). Continuing positive secular growth change in the Netherlands 1955-1997. *Pediatric Research, 47,* 316–323.

Freedman, J. L. (1978). *Happy people.* New York: Harcourt Brace Jovanovich.

Freedman, J. L., & Fraser, S. C. (1966). Compliance without pressure: The foot-in-the-door technique. *Journal of Personality and Social Psychology, 4,* 195–202.

Freud, S. (1900/1953). *The interpretation of dreams.* In J. Strachey (Ed.), *The standard edition of the complete psychological works of Sigmund Freud* (Vols. 4 and 5). London: Hogarth.

Freud, S. (1901/1960). *The psychopathology of everyday life.* In J. Strachey (Ed.), *The standard edition of the complete psychological works of Sigmund Freud* (Vol. 6). London: Hogarth.

Freud, S. (1905/1953). *Fragment of an analysis of a case of hysteria.* In J. Strachey (Ed.), *The standard edition of the complete psychological works of Sigmund Freud* (Vol. 7). London: Hogarth.

Freud, S. (1924). *A general introduction to psychoanalysis.* New York: Boni & Liveright.

Freud, S. (1933/1964). *New introductory lectures on psychoanalysis.* In J. Strachey (Ed.), *The standard edition of the complete psychological works of Sigmund Freud* (Vol. 22). London: Hogarth.

Freud, S. (1940). An outline of psychoanalysis. *International Journal of Psychoanalysis, 21,* 27–84.

Frey, B. S., & Stutzer, A. (2002). What can economists learn from happiness research? *Journal of Economic Literature, 40,* 402–435.

Frey, K. S., & Ruble, D. N. (1992). Gender constancy and the cost of sex-typed behavior: A test of the conflict hypothesis. *Developmental Psychology, 28,* 714–721.

Friedkin, N. E. (1999). Choice shift and group polarization. *American Sociological Review, 64,* 856–875.

Friedman, M., & Rosenman, R. F. (1974). *Type A behavior and your heart.* New York: Knopf.

Frieze, I. H., Olson, J. E., & Russell, J. (1991). Attractiveness and income for men and women in management. *Journal of Applied Social Psychology, 21,* 1039–1057.

Frijda, N. H. (1999). Emotions and hedonic experience. In D. Kahneman, E. Diener, & N. Schwarz (Eds.), *Well-being: The foundations of hedonic psychology.* New York: Russell Sage Foundation.

Frishman, L. J. (2001). Basic visual processes. In E. B. Goldstein (Ed.), *Blackwell handbook of perception.* Malden, MA: Blackwell.

Fromm, E. (1979). The nature of hypnosis and other altered states of consciousness: An ego-psychological theory. In E. Fromm & R. E. Shor (Eds.), *Hypnosis: Developments in research and new perspectives.* New York: Aldine.

Fuchs, A. H., & Milar, K. S. (2003). Psychology as a science. In D. K. Freedheim (Ed.), *Handbook of psychology, Vol. 1: History of psychology.* New York: Wiley.

Fullilove, M., & Dieudonne, I. (1996). Substance abuse in pregnancy. In *The Hatherleigh guide to treating substance abuse* (pp. 93–117). New York: Hatherleigh Press.

Funder, D. C. (2001). Personality. *Annual Review of Psychology, 52,* 197–221.

Furumoto, L., & Scarborough, E. (1986). Placing women in the history of psychology: The first American women psychologists. *American Psychologist, 41,* 35–42.

Fuster, J. M. (1996). Frontal lobe lesions. In B. S. Fogel, R. B. Schiffer, & S. M. Rao (Eds), *Neuropsychiatry.* Baltimore: Williams & Wilkins.

Fyer, A. J. (2000). Anxiety disorders: Genetics. In B. J. Sadock & V. A. Sadock (Eds.), *Kaplan and Sadock's comprehensive textbook of psychiatry* (7th ed., Vol. 1, pp. 1457–1463). Philadelphia: Lippincott/Williams & Wilkins.

Gabrieli, J. D. E. (1998). Cognitive neuroscience of human memory. *Annual Review of Psychology, 49,* 87–115.

Gaddis, C. (1999, August 8). A Boggs life. *Tampa Tribune.* Retrieved at http://rays.tbo.com/rays/MGBWZ4RSL3E.html.

Gaeth, G. J., & Shanteau, J. (2000). Reducing the influence of irrelevant information on experienced decision makers. In T. Connolly, H. R. Arkes, & K. R. Hammond (Eds.), *Judgment and decision making: An interdisciplinary reader* (2nd ed., pp. 305–323). New York: Cambridge University Press.

Gage, F. H. (2002). Neurogenesis in the adult brain. *Journal of Neuroscience, 22,* 612–613.

Gais, S., & Born, J. (2004). Declarative memory consolidation: Mechanisms acting during human sleep. *Learning & Memory, 11,* 679–685.

Galambos, N. L. (2004). Gender and gender role development in adolescence. In R. M. Lerner & L. Steinberg (Eds.), *Handbook of adolescent psychology.* New York: Wiley.

Galati, D., Scherer, K. R., & Ricci-Bitti, P. E. (1997). Voluntary facial expression of emotion: Comparing congenitally blind with normally sighted en-

coders. *Journal of Personality and Social Psychology, 73,* 1363–1379.

Galderisi, S., Maj, M., Mucci, A., Cassano, G. B., Invernizzi, G., Rossi, A., Vita, A., Dell'Osso, L., Daneluzzo, E., & Pini, S. (2002). Historical, psychopathological, neurological, and neuropsychological aspects of deficit schizophrenia: A multicenter study. *American Journal of Psychiatry, 159,* 983–990.

Gambone, J. C., Reiter, R. C., & DiMatteo, M. R. (1994). *The PREPARED provider: A guide for improved patient communication.* Beaverton, OR: Mosybl Great Performance.

Gantt, W. H. (1975, April 25). Unpublished lecture, Ohio State University. Cited in D. Hothersall, (1984), *History of psychology.* New York: Random House.

Garb, H. N., Florio, C. M., & Grove, W. M. (1998). The validity of the Rorschach and the Minnesota Multiphasic Personality Inventory: Results form meta-analysis. *Psychological Science, 9,* 402–404.

Garcia, J. (1989). Food for Tolman: Cognition and cathexis in concert. In T. Archer & L. G. Nilsson (Eds.), *Aversion, avoidance, and anxiety: Perspectives on aversively motivated behavior.* Hillsdale, NJ: Erlbaum.

Garcia, J., Clarke, J. C., & Hankins, W. G. (1973). Natural responses to scheduled rewards. In P. P. G. Bateson & P. Klopfer (Eds.), *Perspectives in ethology.* New York: Plenum.

Garcia, J., & Koelling, R. A. (1966). Learning with prolonged delay of reinforcement. *Psychonomic Science, 5,* 121–122.

Garcia, J., & Rusiniak, K. W. (1980). What the nose learns from the mouth. In D. Muller-Schwarze & R. M. Silverstein (Eds.), *Chemical signals.* New York: Plenum.

Garcia, S. D., & Khersonsky, D. (1996). "They make a lovely couple": Perceptions of couple attractiveness. *Journal of Social Behavior and Personality, 11,* 667–682.

Gardner, E. (1975). *Fundamentals of neurology.* Philadelphia: Saunders.

Gardner, E. P., & Kandel, E. R. (2000). Touch. In E. R. Kandel, J. H. Schwartz, & T. M. Jessell (Eds.), *Principles of neural science.* New York: McGraw-Hill.

Gardner, H. (1983). *Frames of mind: The theory of multiple intelligences.* New York: Basic Books.

Gardner, H. (1985). *The mind's new science: A history of the cognitive revolution.* New York: Basic Books.

Gardner, H. (1993). *Multiple intelligences: The theory in practice.* New York: Basic Books.

Gardner, H. (1999). *Intelligence reframed: Multiple intelligences for the 21st century.* New York: Basic Books.

Gardner, H. (2004). Audiences for the theory of multiple intelligences. *Teachers College Record, 106*(1), 212–220.

Garnett, N. (2005). Laws, regulations, and guidelines. In C. K. Akins, S. Panicker, & C. L. Cunningham (Eds.), *Laboratory animals in research and teaching: Ethics, care and methods.* Washington, DC: American Psychological Association.

Garry, M., Frame, S., & Loftus, E. F. (1999). Lie down and let me tell you about your childhood. In S. D. Sala (Ed.), *Mind myths: Exploring popular assumptions about mind and brain.* New York: Wiley.

Garry, M., & Polaschek, D. L. L. (2000). Imagination and memory. *Current Directions in Psychological Science, 9,* 6–10.

Garvey, C. R. (1929). List of American psychology laboratories. *Psychological Bulletin, 26,* 652–660.

Gatchel, R. J., & Maddrey, A. M. (2004). The biopsychosocial perspective of pain. In J. M. Raczynski &

L. C. Leviton (Eds.), *Handbook of clinical health psychology Vol. 2: Disorders of behavior and health.* Washington, DC: American Psychological Association.

Gawronski, B. (2004). Theory-based bias correction in dispositional inference: The fundamental attribution error is dead, long live the correspondence bias. In W. Stroebe & M. Hewstone (Eds.). *European review of social psychology* (Vol. 15). Hove, England: Psychology Press/Taylor & Francis.

Gazzaniga, M. S. (1970). *The bisected brain.* New York: Appleton-Century-Crofts.

Gazzaniga, M. S. (2000). Cerebral specialization and interhemispheric communication. *Brain, 123,* 1293–1326.

Gazzaniga, M. S., Bogen, J. E., & Sperry, R. W. (1965). Observations on visual perception after disconnection of the cerebral hemispheres in man. *Brain, 88,* 221–236.

Geddes, J. R., & Lawrie, S. M. (1995). Obstetrical complications and schizophrenia: A meta-analysis. *British Journal of Psychiatry, 167,* 786–793.

Gee, T., Allen, K., & Powell, R. A. (2003). Questioning premorbid dissociative symptomatology in dissociative identity disorder. *Professional Psychology: Research & Practice, 34*(1), 114–116.

Geiger, M. A. (1997). An examination of the relationship between answer changing, testwiseness and examination performance. *Journal of Experimental Education, 66,* 49–60.

Geller, J. L. (1992). A historical perspective on the role of state hospitals viewed from the era of the "revolving door." *American Journal of Psychiatry, 149,* 1526–1533.

Geller, L. (1982). The failure of self-actualization theory: A critique of Carl Rogers and Abraham Maslow. *Journal of Humanistic Psychology, 22,* 56–73.

George, S. A. (2002). The menopause experience: A woman's perspective. *Journal of Obstetric, Gynecologic, and Neonatal Nursing, 31,* 71–85.

Gershoff, E. T. (2002). Parental corporal punishment and associated child behaviors and experiences: A meta-analytic and theoretical review. *Psychological Bulletin, 128,* 539–579.

Gershon, E. S., Berrettini, W. H., & Goldin, L. R. (1989). Mood disorders: Genetic aspects. In H. I. Kaplan & B. J. Sadock (Eds.), *Comprehensive textbook of psychiatry* (Vol. 5). Baltimore: Williams & Wilkins.

Geschwind, N., & Galaburda, A. M. (1987). *Cerebral lateralization: Biological mechanisms, associations, and pathology.* Cambridge, MA: MIT Press.

Getchell, T. Y., & Getchell, M. L. (1991). Physiology of olfactory reception and transduction: General principles. In D. G. Laing, R. L. Doty, & W. Breipohl (Eds.), *The human sense of smell.* Berlin: Springer-Verlag.

Ghez, C., & Thach, W. T. (2000). The cerebellum. In E. R. Kandel, J. H. Schwartz & T. M. Jessell (Eds.), *Principles of neural science* (pp. 832–852). New York: McGraw-Hill.

Gigerenzer, G. (1997). Ecological intelligence: An adaption for frequencies. *Psychologische Beitraege, 39,* 107–125.

Gigerenzer, G. (2000). *Adaptive thinking: Rationality in the real world.* New York: Oxford University Press.

Gigerenzer, G. (2004). Fast and frugal heuristics: The tools of bounded rationality. In D. J. Koehler & N. Harvey (Eds.), *Blackwell handbook of judgment and decision making.* Malden, MA: Blackwell Publishing.

Gigerenzer, G., & Hoffrage, U. (1999). Overcoming difficulties in Bayesian reasoning: A reply to Lewis and Keren (1999) and Mellers and McGraw (1999). *Psychological Review, 106,* 425–430.

Gigerenzer, G., & Todd, P. M. (1999). Fast and frugal heuristics: The adaptive toolbox. In G. Gigerenzer, P. M. Todd, & ABC Research Group (Eds.), *Simple heuristics that make us smart* (pp. 3–36). New York: Oxford University Press.

Gilbert, D. T. (1998). Speeding with Ned: A personal view of the correspondence bias. In J. M. Darley & J. Cooper (Ed.), *Attribution and social interaction: The legacy of Edward E. Jones.* Washington, DC: American Psychological Association.

Giles, T. R., & Marafiote, R. A. (1998). Managed care and the practitioner: A call for unity. *Clinical Psychology: Science & Practice, 5,* 41–50.

Gilgen, A. R. (1982). *American psychology since World War II: A profile of the discipline.* Westport, CT: Greenwood Press.

Gilhooly, K. J. (1996). *Thinking: Directed, undirected and creative.* London: Academic Press.

Gillberg, M., & Akerstedt, T. (1998). Sleep loss and performance: No "safe" duration of a monotonous task. *Physiology & Behavior, 64,* 599–604.

Gillberg, M., Kecklund, G., Axelsson, J., & Akerstedt, T. (1996). The effects of a short daytime nap after restricted night sleep. *Sleep, 19,* 570–575.

Gillham, J. E., Shatté, A. J., Reivich, K. J., & Seligman, M. E. P. (2001). Optimism, pessimism, and explanatory style. In E. C. Chang (Ed.), *Optimism & pessimism: Implications for theory, research, and practice* (pp. 53–76). Washington, DC: American Psychological Association.

Gitlin, M. (2002). Pharmacological treatment of depression. In I. H. Gotlib & C. L. Hammen (Eds.), *Handbook of depression.* New York: Guilford.

Gitlin, M., Nuechterlein, K., Subotnik, K. L., Ventura, J., Mintz, J., Fogelson, D. L., Bartzokis, G., & Aravagiri, M. (2001). Clinical outcome following neuroleptic discontinuation in patients with remitted recent-onset schizophrenia. *American Journal of Psychiatry, 158,* 1835–1842.

Gladue, B. A. (1994). The biopsychology of sexual orientation. *Current Directions in Psychological Science, 3,* 150–154.

Glass, C. R., & Arnkoff, D. B. (1992). Behavior therapy. In D. K. Freedheim (Ed.), *History of psychotherapy: A century of change.* Washington, DC: American Psychological Association.

Glass, R. M. (2001). Electroconvulsive therapy. *Journal of the American Medical Association, 285,* 1346–1348.

Glassman, A., Shapiro, P. A., Ford, D. E., Culpepper, L., Finkel, M. S., Swenson, J. R., Bigger, J. T., Rollman, B. L., & Wise, T. N. (2003). Cardiovascular health and depression. *Journal of Psychiatric Practice, 9,* 409–421.

Glassner, B. (1999). *The culture of fear: Why Americans are afraid of the wrong things.* New York: Perseus Books Group.

Gleaves, D. H. (1994). On "The reality of repressed memories." *American Psychologist, 49,* 440–441.

Gleaves, D. H., May, M. C., & Cardena, E. (2001). An examination of the diagnostic validity of dissociative identity disorders. *Clinical Psychology Review, 21,* 577–608.

Gleaves, D. H., Smith, S. M., Butler, L. D., & Spiegel, D. (2004). False and recovered memories in the laboratory and clinic: A review of experimental and clinical evidence. *Clinical Psychology: Science & Practice, 11*(1), 3–28.

Goeders, N. E. (2004). Stress, motivation, and drug addiction. *Current Directions in Psychological Science, 13*(1), 33–35.

Goff, D. C., & Gudeman, J. E. (1999). The person with chronic mental illness. In A. M. Nicholi (Ed.),

The Harvard guide to psychiatry. Cambridge, MA: Harvard University Press.

Golden, C. J., Sawicki, R. F., & Franzen, M. D. (1990). Test construction. In G. Goldstein & M. Hersen (Eds.), *Handbook of psychological assessment.* New York: Pergamon Press.

Goldenberg, H. (1983). *Contemporary clinical psychology.* Pacific Grove, CA: Brooks/Cole.

Goldsmith, H. H., & Harman, C. (1994). Temperament and attachment; individuals and relationships. *Current Directions in Psychological Science, 3,* 53–57.

Goldstein, D. G., & Gigerenzer, G. (1999). The recognition heuristic: How ignorance makes us smart. In G. Gigerenzer, P. M. Todd, & ABC Research Group (Eds.), *Simple heuristics that make us smart* (pp. 37–58). New York: Oxford University Press.

Goldstein, D. G., & Gigerenzer, G. (2002). Models of ecological rationality: The recognition heuristic. *Psychological Review, 109,* 75–90.

Goldstein, E. B. (1996). *Sensation and perception* (4th ed.). Pacific Grove, CA: Brooks/Cole.

Goldstein, E. B. (2001). Pictorial perception and art. In E. B. Goldstein (Ed.), *Blackwell handbook of perception.* Malden, MA: Blackwell.

Goldstein, H. W., Zedeck, S., & Goldstein, I. L. (2002). *g:* Is this your final answer. *Human Performance, 15,* 123–142.

Goldstein, W. M. (1990). Judgments of relative importance in decision making: Global vs. local interpretations of subjective weight. *Organizational Behavior and Human Decision Processes, 47,* 313–336.

Goldstein, W. M., & Hogarth, R. M. (1997). Judgment and decision research: Some historical context. In W. M. Goldstein, & R. M. Hogarth (Eds.), *Research on judgment and decision making.* New York: Cambridge University Press.

Goodenough, D. R. (1991). Dream recall: History and current status of the field. In S. J. Ellman & J. S. Antrobus (Eds.), *The mind in sleep: Psychology and psychophysiology* (2nd ed.). New York: Wiley.

Goodwin, C. J. (1991). Misportraying Pavlov's apparatus. *American Journal of Psychology, 104*(1), 135–141.

Goodwin, F. K., & Jamison, K. R. (1990). *Manic-depressive illness.* New York: Oxford University Press.

Gooley, J. J., & Saper, C. B. (2005). Anatomy of the mammalian circadian system. In M. H. Kryger, T. Roth, & W. C. Dement (Eds.), *Principles and practice of sleep medicine.* Philadelphia: Elsevier Saunders.

Gopnik, A., Meltzoff, A. N., & Kuhl, P. K. (1999). *The scientist in the crib: Minds, brains, and how children learn.* New York: Morrow.

Gordon, H. W. (1990). The neurobiological basis of hemisphericity. In C. Trevarthen (Ed.), *Brain circuits and functions of the mind. Essays in honor of Roger W. Sperry.* Cambridge, MA: Cambridge University Press.

Gordon, J., & Abramov, I. (2001). Color vision. In E. B. Goldstein (Ed.), *Blackwell handbook of perception.* Malden, MA: Blackwell.

Gorski, R. A. (2000). Sexual differentiation of the nervous system. In E. R. Kandel, J. H. Schwartz, & T. M. Jessell (Eds.), *Principles of Neural Science.* New York: McGraw-Hill.

Gottdiener, J. S., Krantz, D. S., Howell, R. H., Hecht, G. M., Klein, J., Falconer, J. J., & Rozanski, A. (1994). Induction of silent myocardial ischemia with mental stress testing: Relationship to the triggers of ischemia during daily life activities and to ischemic functional severity. *Journal of the American College of Cardiology, 24,* 1645–1651.

Gottesman, I. I. (1991). *Schizophrenia genesis: The origins of madness.* New York: W. H. Freeman.

Gottesman, I. I. (2001). Psychopathology through a life span–genetic prism. *American Psychologist, 56,* 867–878.

Gottesman, I. I., & Hanson, D. R. (2005). Human development: Biological and genetic processes. *Annual Review of Psychology, 56,* 263–86.

Gottesman, I. I., & Moldin, S. O. (1998). Genotypes, genes, genesis, and pathogenesis in schizophrenia. In M. F. Lenzenweger & R. H. Dworkin (Eds.), *Origins and development of schizophrenia: Advances in experimental psychopathology.* Washington, DC: American Psychological Association.

Gottfredson, L. S. (2002). Where and why *g* matters: Not a mystery. *Human Performance, 15,* 25–46.

Gottfredson, L. S. (2003a). Dissecting practical intelligence theory: Its claims and evidence. *Intelligence, 31,* 343–397.

Gottfredson, L. S. (2003b). *G,* jobs and life. In H. Nyborg (Ed.), *The scientific study of general intelligence: Tribute to Arthur R. Jensen.* Oxford, UK: Pergamon.

Gottfredson, L. S. (2005). What if the hereditarian hypothesis is true? *Psychology, Public Policy, and the Law, 11*(2), 311–319.

Gottschall, J., Martin, J., Quish, H., & Rea, J. (2004). Sex differences in mate choice criteria are reflected in folktales from around the world and in historical European literature. *Evolution and Human Behavior, 25,* 102–112.

Gould, E., & Gross, C. G. (2002). Neurogenesis in adult mammals: Some progress and problems. *Journal of Neuroscience, 22,* 619–623.

Gould, R. L. (1975, February). Adult life stages: Growth toward self-tolerance. *Psychology Today,* pp. 74–78.

Gould, R. L. (1978). *Transformations: Growth and change in adult life.* New York: Simon & Schuster.

Gould, S. J. (1993). The sexual politics of classification. *Natural History,* 20–29.

Gould, S. J., & Eldredge, N. (1977). Punctuated equilibria: The tempo and mode of evolution reconsidered. *Paleobiology, 3,* 115–151.

Goulven, J., & Tzourio-Mazoyer, N. (2004). Hemispheric specialization for language. *Brain Research Reviews, 44*(1), 1–12.

Gouras, P. (1991). Color vision. In E. R. Kandel, J. H. Schwartz, & T. M. Jessell (Eds.), *Principles of neural science* (3rd ed.). New York: Elsevier.

Gourevitch, M. N., & Arnsten, J. H. (2005). Medical complications of drug use. In J. H. Lowinson, P. Ruiz, R. B. Millman, & J. G. Langrod (Eds.), *Substance abuse: A comprehensive textbook.* Philadelphia: Lippincott/Williams & Wilkins.

Gouzoulis-Mayfrank, E., Daumann, J., Tuchtenhagen, F., Pelz, S., Becker, S., Kunert, H. J., Fimm, B., & Sass, H. (2000). Impaired cognition in drug free users of recreational ecstasy (MDMA). *Journal of Neurology, Neurosurgery, & Psychiatry, 68,* 719–725.

Graf, P., & Uttl, B. (2001). Prospective memory: A new focus for research. *Consciousness & Cognition: An International Journal, 10,* 437–450.

Granberg, G., & Holmberg, S. (1991). Self-reported turnout and voter validation. *American Journal of Political Science, 35,* 448–459.

Grant, I., McDonald, W. I., Patterson, T., & Trimble, M. R. (1989). Multiple sclerosis. In G. W. Brown & T. O. Harris (Eds.), *Life events and illness.* New York: Guilford.

Gratton, A. (1996). In vivo analysis of the role of dopamine in stimulant and opiate self-administration. *Journal of Psychiatry & Neuroscience, 21,* 264–279.

Graziano, W. G. (1995). Evolutionary psychology: Old music, but now on CDs? *Psychological Inquiry, 6,* 41–44.

Green, J. P. (1999). Hypnosis, context effects, and recall of early autobiographical memories. *International Journal of Clinical & Experimental Hypnosis, 47,* 284–300.

Greenberg, J., Pyszczynski, T., Solomon, S., Rosenblatt, A., Veeder, M., & Kirkland, S. (1990). Evidence for terror management theory II: The effects of mortality salience on reactions to those who threaten or bolster the cultural worldview. *Journal of Personality and Social Psychology, 58,* 308–318.

Greenberg, J. S. (2002). *Comprehensive stress management: Health and human performance.* New York: McGraw-Hill.

Greenberg, M. A., Wortman, C. B., & Stone, A. A. (1996). Emotional expression and physical health: Revising traumatic memories or fostering self-regulation? *Journal of Personality and Social Psychology, 71,* 588–602.

Greene, R. L. (1992a). *Human memory: Paradigms and paradoxes.* Hillsdale, NJ: Erlbaum.

Greene, R. L. (1992b). Repetition and learning. In L. R. Squire (Ed.), *Encyclopedia of learning and memory.* New York: Macmillian.

Greenfield, D. N. (1999). Psychological characteristics of compulsive Internet use: A preliminary analysis. *CyberPsychology and Behavior, 2,* 403–412.

Greenfield, P. M. (1998). The cultural evolution of IQ. In U. Neisser (Ed.), *The rising curve: Long-term gains in IQ and related measures.* Washington, DC: American Psychological Association.

Greenland, P., Knoll, M. D., Stamler, J., Neaton, J. D., Dyer, A. R., Garside, D. B., & Wilson, P. W. (2003). Major risk factors as antecedents of fatal and nonfatal coronary heart disease events. *Journal of the American Medical Association, 290,* 891–897.

Greeno, C. G., & Wing, R. R. (1994). Stress-induced eating. *Psychological Bulletin, 115,* 444–464.

Greeno, J. G. (1978). Nature of problem-solving abilities. In W. K. Estes (Ed.), *Handbook of learning and cognitive processes* (Vol. 5). Hillsdale, NJ: Erlbaum.

Greenough, W. T. (1975). Experiential modification of the developing brain. *American Scientist, 63,* 37–46.

Greenough, W. T., & Volkmar, F. R. (1973). Pattern of dendritic branching in occipital cortex of rats reared in complex environments. *Experimental Neurology, 40,* 491–504.

Greenson, R. R. (1967). *The technique and practice of psychoanalysis* (Vol. 1). New York: International Universities Press.

Gregory, R. J. (1996). *Psychological testing: History, principles, and applications* (2nd ed.). Boston: Allyn & Bacon.

Gregory, R. L. (1973). *Eye and brain.* New York: McGraw-Hill.

Gregory, R. L. (1978). *Eye and brain* (2nd ed.). New York: McGraw-Hill.

Grencavage, L. M., & Norcross, J. C. (1990). Where are the commonalities among the therapeutic factors? *Professional Psychology: Research and Practice, 21,* 372–378.

Griffith, E. E., Gonzales, C. A., & Blue, H. C. (2003). Introduction to cultural psychiatry. In R. E. Hales & S. C. Yudofsky (Eds.), *Textbook of clinical psychiatry.* Washington, DC: American Psychiatric Publishing.

Griffiths, M. (1999). Internet addiction: Fact or fiction? *Psychologist, 12,* 246–250.

Grigorenko, E. L. (2000). Heritability and intelligence. In R. J. Sternberg (Ed.), *Handbook of intelligence* (pp. 53–91). New York: Cambridge University Press.

Grigorenko, E. L., & Sternberg, R. J. (2001). Analytical, creative, and practical intelligence as predictors of self-reported adaptive functioning: A case study in Russia. *Intelligence, 29,* 57–73.

Grigorenko, E. L., & Sternberg, R. J. (2003). The nature-nurture issue. In A. Slater & G. Bremner (Eds.), *An introduction to development psychology.* Malden, MA: Blackwell Publishers.

Grinspoon, L., Bakalar, J. B., & Russo, E. (2005). Marihuana: Clinical aspects. In J. H. Lowinson, P. Ruiz, R. B. Millman, & J. G. Langrod (Eds.), *Substance abuse: A comprehensive textbook.* Philadelphia: Lippincott/Williams & Wilkins.

Grob, C. S., & Poland, R. E. (2005). MDMA. In J. H. Lowinson, P. Ruiz, R. B. Millman, & J. G. Langrod (Eds.), *Substance abuse: A comprehensive textbook.* Philadelphia: Lippincott/Williams & Wilkins.

Gross, J. J. (1998). Antecedent and response-focused emotion regulation: Divergent consequences for experience, expression, and physiology. *Journal of Personality and Social Psychology, 74,* 224–237.

Gross, J. J. (2001). Emotion regulation in adulthood: Timing is everything. *Current Directions in Psychological Science, 10,* 214–219.

Grossman, J. B., & Ruiz, P. (2004). Shall we make a leap-of-faith to disulfiram (Antabuse)? *Addictive Disorders & Their Treatment, 3*(3), 129–132.

Grossman, R. P., & Till, B. D. (1998). The persistence of classically conditioned brand attitudes. *Journal of Advertising, 27,* 23–31.

Grossman, S. P., Dacey, D., Halaris, A. E., Collier, T., & Routtenberg, A. (1978). Aphagia and adipsia after preferential destruction of nerve cell bodies in hypothalamus. *Science, 202,* 537–539.

Grossmann, K. E., & Grossmann, K. (1990). The wider concept of attachment in cross-cultural research. *Human Development, 33,* 31–47.

Grotevant, H. (1997). Adolescent development in family contexts. In N. Eisenberg (Ed.), *Handbook of child psychology, Vol. 3: Social, emotional, and personality development* (5th ed., pp. 1097–1149). New York: Wiley.

Groth-Marnat, G. (1997). *Handbook of psychological assessment.* New York: Wiley.

Grubin, D., & Madsen, L. (2005). Lie detection and the polygraph: A historical review. *Journal of Forensic Psychiatry & Psychology, 16,* 357–369.

Gruen, R. J. (1993). Stress and depression: Toward the development of integrative models. In L. Goldberger & S. Breznitz (Eds.), *Handbook of stress: Theoretical and clinical aspects.* New York: Free Press.

Gruenberg, A. M., & Goldstein, R. D. (2003). Mood disorders: Depression. In A. Tasman, J. Kay, & J. A. Lieberman (Eds.), *Psychiatry.* New York: Wiley.

Grunberg, N. E., Faraday, M. M., & Rahman, M. A. (2001). The psychobiology of nicotine self-administration. In A. Baum, T. A. Revenson, & J. E. Singer (Eds.), *Handbook of health psychology* (pp. 249–262). Mahwah, NJ: Erlbaum.

Guarnaccia, P. J., & Rogler, L. H. (1999). Research on culture-bound syndromes: New directions. *American Journal of Psychiatry, 156,* 1322–1327.

Gudjonsson, G. H. (2001). Recovered memories: Effects upon the family and community. In G. M. Davies & T. Dalgleish (Eds.), *Recovered memories: Seeking the middle ground.* Chichester, England: Wiley.

Guenther, K. (1988). Mood and memory. In G. M. Davies & D. M. Thomson (Eds.), *Memory in context: Context in memory.* New York: Wiley.

Guggenheim, F. G. (2000). Somatoform disorders. In B. J. Sadock & V. A. Sadock (Eds.), *Kaplan and Sadock's comprehensive textbook of psychiatry* (7th ed., Vol. 1, pp. 1504–1532). Philadelphia: Lippincott/Williams & Wilkins.

Guilbault, R. L., Bryant, F. B., Brockway, J. H., & Posavac, E. J. (2004). A meta-analysis of research on hindsight bias. *Basic & Applied Social Psychology, 26*(2–3), 103–117.

Guilford, J. P. (1959). Three faces of intellect. *American Psychologist, 14,* 469–479.

Guilleminault, C., & Fromherz, S. (2005). Narcolepsy: Diagnosis and management. In M. H. Kryger, T. Roth, & W. C. Dement (Eds.). *Principles and practice of sleep medicine.* Philadelphia: Elsevier Saunders.

Gunnel, D., & Ashby, D. (2004). Antidepressants and suicide: What is the balance of benefit and harm? *British Medical Journal, 329*(7456), 34–38.

Gupta, G. R. (1992). Love, arranged marriage, and the Indian social structure. In J. J. Macionis & N. V. Benokraitis (Eds.), *Seeing ourselves: Classic, contemporary and cross-cultural reading in sociology.* Englewood Cliffs, NJ: Prentice-Hall.

Gureje, O., Simon, G. E., Ustun, T. B., & Goldberg, D. P. (1997). Somatization in cross-cultural perspective: A world health organization study in primary care. *American Journal of Psychiatry, 154,* 989–995.

Guyton, A. C. (1991). *Textbook of medical physiology.* Philadelphia: Saunders.

Güzeldere, G., Flanagan, O., & Hardcastle, V. G. (2000). The nature and function of consciousness: Lessons from blindsight. In M. S. Gazzaniga (Ed.), *The new cognitive neurosciences.* Cambridge, MA: The MIT Press.

Haas, L. (1999). Families and work. In M. B. Sussman, S. K. Steinmetz, & G. W. Peterson (Eds.), *Handbook of marriage and the family* (pp. 571–612). New York: Plenum.

Hackam, D. G., & Anand, S. S. (2003). Emerging risk factors for atherosclerotic vascular disease: A critical review of the evidence. *Journal of the American Medical Association, 290,* 932–940.

Hadaway, C. K., Marler, P. L., & Chaves, M. (1993). What the polls don't show: A closer look at U.S. church attendance. *American Sociological Review, 58,* 741–752.

Hagerty, M. R. (2000). Social comparisons of income in one's community: Evidence from national surveys of income and happiness. *Journal of Personality and Social Psychology, 78,* 764–771.

Hales, D. (1987). *How to sleep like a baby.* New York: Ballantine.

Halford, J. C. G., & Blundell, J. E. (2000). Separate systems for serotonin and leptin in appetite control. *Annals of Medicine, 32,* 222–232.

Halford, J. C. G., Gillespie, J., Brown, V., Pontin, E. E., & Dovey, T. M. (2004). Effect of television advertisements for foods on food consumption in children. *Appetite, 42*(2), 221–225.

Hall, C. C. I. (1997). Cultural malpractice: The growing obsolescence of psychology with the changing U.S. population. *American Psychologist, 52,* 642–651.

Hall, C. S. (1966). *The meaning of dreams.* New York: McGraw-Hill.

Hall, C. S. (1979). The meaning of dreams. In D. Goleman & R. J. Davidson (Eds.), *Consciousness: Brain, states of awareness, and mysticism.* New York: Harper & Row.

Hall, E. (1987). *Growing and changing: What the experts say.* New York: Random House.

Hall, G. S. (1904). *Adolescence.* New York: Appleton.

Hall, J. A., **Carter, J. D.**, & **Horgan, T. G.** (2000). Gender differences in the nonverbal communication of emotion. In A. Fischer (Ed.), *Gender and emotion*. Cambridge, UK: Cambridge University Press.

Halmi, K. A. (2002). Physiology of anorexia nervosa and bulimia nervosa. In C. G. Fairburn & K. D. Brownell (Eds.), *Eating disorders and obesity: A comprehensive handbook*. New York: Guilford.

Halmi, K. A. (2003). Eating disorders: Anorexia nervosa, bulimia nervosa, and obesity. In R. E. Hales & S. C. Yudofsky (Eds.), *Textbook of Clinical Psychiatry*. Washington, DC: American Psychiatric Publishing.

Halpern, D. F. (1992). *Sex differences in cognitive abilities*. Hillsdale, NJ: Erlbaum.

Halpern, D. F. (1997). Sex differences in intelligence: Implications for education. *American Psychologist, 52,* 1091–1102.

Halpern, D. F. (1998). Teaching critical thinking for transfer across domains: Dispositions, skills, structure training, and metacognitive monitoring. *American Psychologist, 53,* 449–455.

Halpern, D. F. (2000). *Sex differences in cognitive abilities*. Mahwah, NJ: Erlbaum.

Halpern, D. F. (2003). *Thought and knowledge: An introduction to critical thinking*. Mahwah, NJ: Erlbaum.

Halpern, D. F. (2004). A cognitive-process taxonomy for sex differences in cognitive abilities. *Current Directions in Psychological Science, 13*(4), 135–139.

Halpern, S. D., **Andrews, T. J.**, & **Purves, D.** (1999). Interindividual variation in human visual performance. *Journal of Cognitive Neuroscience, 11,* 521–534.

Halverson, C. F. Jr., & **Wampler, K. S.** (1997). Family influences on personality development. In R. Hogan, J. Johnson, & S. Briggs (Eds.), *Handbook of personality psychology*. San Diego: Academic Press.

Hamann, S. B., **Ely, T. D.**, **Hoffman, J. M.**, & **Kilts, C. D.** (2002). Ecstasy and agony: Activation of human amygdala in positive and negative emotion. *Psychological Science, 13* (2), 135–141.

Hamill, R., **Wilson T. D.**, & **Nisbett, R. E.** (1980). Insensitivity to sample bias: Generalizing from atypical cases. *Journal of Personality and Social Psychology, 39,* 578–589.

Hamilton, W. D. (1964). The evolution of social behavior. *Journal of Theoretical Biology, 7,* 1–52.

Hamilton, W. D., & **Zuk, M.** (1982). Heritable true fitness and bright birds: A role for parasites. *Science, 218,* 384–387.

Hammen, C. (2003). Mood disorders. In G. Stricker & T. A. Widiger (Eds.), *Handbook of psychology, Vol. 8: Clinical psychology*. New York: Wiley.

Haney, C., **Banks, W. C.**, & **Zimbardo, P. G.** (1973). Interpersonal dynamics in a simulated prison. *International Journal of Criminology and Penology, 1,* 69–97.

Haney, C., & **Zimbardo, P. G.** (1998). The past and future of U.S. prison policy: Twenty-five years after the Stanford Prison Experiment. *American Psychologist, 53,* 709–727.

Hankin, B. L., **Abramson, L. Y.**, **Moffitt, T. E.**, **Silva, P. A.**, **McGee, R.**, & **Angell, K. E.** (1998). Development of depression from preadolescence to young adulthood: Emerging gender differences in a 10-year longitudinal study. *Journal of Abnormal Psychology, 107,* 128–140.

Hannigan, J. H., & **Armant, D. R.** (2000). Alcohol in pregnancy and neonatal outcome. *Seminars in Neonatology, 5,* 243–254.

Happonen, P., **Voutilainen, S.**, & **Salonen, J. T.** (2004). Coffee drinking is dose dependently related to the risk of acute coronary events in middle-aged men. *Journal of Nutrition, 134,* 2381–2386.

Harlow, H. F. (1958). The nature of love. *American Psychologist, 13,* 673–685.

Harlow, H. F. (1959). Love in infant monkeys. *Scientific American, 200*(6), 68–74.

Harmsen, P., **Rosengren, A.**, **Tsipogianni, A.**, & **Wilhelmsen, L.** (1990). Risk factors for stroke in middle-aged men in Goteborg, Sweden. *Stroke, 21,* 23–29.

Harrington, M. E., & **Mistlberger, R. E.** (2000). Anatomy and physiology of the mammalian circadian system. In M. H. Kryger, T. Roth, & W. C. Dement (Eds.), *Principles and practice of sleep medicine*. Philadelphia: Saunders.

Harris, J. E. (1984). Remembering to do things: A forgotten topic. In J. E. Harris & P. E. Morris (Eds.), *Everyday memory, actions, and absent-mindedness*. New York: Academic Press.

Harris, J. R. (1998). *The nurture assumption: Why children turn out the way they do*. New York: Free Press.

Harris, J. R. (2000). Context-specific learning, personality, and birth order. *Current Directions in Psychological Science, 9*(5), 174–177.

Harvey, M. H. (1999). Memory research and clinical practice: A critique of three paradigms and a framework for psychotherapy with trauma survivors. In L. M. Williams & V. L. Banyard (Eds.), *Trauma & memory*. Thousand Oaks, CA: Sage Publications.

Haselton, M. G., & **Buss, D. M.** (2000). Error management theory: A new perspective on biases in cross-sex mind reading. *Journal of Personality and Social Psychology, 78,* 81–91.

Hashibe, M., **Ford, D. E.**, & **Zhang, Z. F.** (2002). Marijauna smoking and head and neck cancer. *Journal of Clinical Pharmacology, 42,* 103S–107S.

Haslam, N. (1997). Evidence that male sexual orientation is a matter of degree. *Journal of Personality and Social Psychology, 73,* 862–870.

Hastorf, A., & **Cantril, H.** (1954). They saw a game: A case study. *Journal of Abnormal and Social Psychology, 49,* 129–134.

Hatfield, E., & **Rapson, R. L.** (1993). *Love, sex, and intimacy: Their psychology, biology, and history*. New York: HarperCollins.

Haugland, G., **Siegel, C.**, **Hopper, K.**, & **Alexander, M. J.** (1997). Mental illness among homeless individuals in a suburban county. *Psychiatric Services, 48,* 504–509.

Hauser, M., & **Carey, S.** (1998). Building a cognitive creature from a set of primitives: Evolutionary and developmental insights. In D. D. Cummins & C. Allen (Eds.), *The evolution of mind*. New York: Oxford University Press.

Hawkins, S. A., & **Hastie, R.** (1990). Hindsight: Biased judgments of past events after the outcomes are known. *Psychological Bulletin, 107,* 311–327.

Haworth-Hoeppner, S. (2000). The critical shapes of body image: The role of culture and family in the production of eating disorders. *Journal of Marriage and the Family, 62,* 212–227.

Hays, K. F. (1999). *Working it out: Using exercise in psychotherapy*. Washington, DC: American Psychological Association.

Haywood, T. W., **Kravitz, H. M.**, **Grossman, L. S.**, **Cavanaugh, J. L., Jr.**, **Davis, J. M.**, & **Lewis, D. A.** (1995). Predicting the "revolving door" phenomenon among patients with schizophrenic, schizoaffective, and affective disorders. *American Journal of Psychiatry, 152,* 861–956.

Hazan, C., & **Shaver, P.** (1986). *Parental caregiving style questionnaire*. Unpublished questionnaire.

Hazan, C., & **Shaver, P.** (1987). Romantic love conceptualized as an attachment process. *Journal of Personality and Social Psychology, 52,* 511–524.

He, J., **Ogden, L. G.**, **Vupputuri, S.**, **Bazzano, L. A.**, **Loria, C.**, & **Whelton, P. K.** (1999). Dietary sodium intake and subsequent risk of cardiovascular disease in overweight adults. *Journal of the American Medical Association, 282,* 2027–2034.

Healy, D. (2004). *Let them eat Prozac: The unhealthy relationship between the pharmaceutical industry and depression*. New York: NYU Press.

Healy, D., & **Whitaker, C.** (2003). Antidepressants and suicide: Risk-benefit conundrums. *Journal of Psychiatry & Neuroscience, 28*(5), 28.

Heaps, C. M., & **Nash, M.** (2001). Comparing recollective experience in true and false autobiographical memories. *Journal of Experimental Psychology: Learning, Memory, and Cognition, 27,* 920–930.

Hearst, E. (1988). Fundamentals of learning and conditioning. In R. C. Atkinson, R. J. Herrnstein, G. Lindzey, & R. D. Luce (Eds.), *Stevens' handbook of experimental psychology*. New York: Wiley.

Heatherton, T. F., **Striepe, M.**, & **Wittenberg, L.** (1998). Emotional distress and disinhibited eating: The role of self. *Personality and Social Psychology Bulletin, 24,* 301–313.

Heiby, E. M. (2002). It is time for a moratorium on legislation enabling prescription privileges for psychologists. *Clinical Psychology: Science & Practice, 9*(3), 256–258.

Heider, F. (1958). *The psychology of interpersonal relations*. New York: Wiley.

Heine, S. J., & **Renshaw, K.** (2002). Interjudge agreement, self-enhancement, and liking: Cross-cultural divergences. *Personality and Social Psychology Bulletin, 28*(5), 578–587.

Heinrichs, R. W. (2005). The primacy of cognition in schizophrenia. *American Psychologist, 60,* 229–242.

Hellige, J. B. (1990). Hemispheric asymmetry. *Annual Review of Psychology, 41,* 55–80.

Hellige, J. B. (1993a). Unity of thought and action: Varieties of interaction between left and right cerebral hemispheres. *Current Directions in Psychological Science, 2*(1), 21–25.

Hellige, J. B. (1993b). *Hemispheric asymmetry: What's right and what's left*. Cambridge, MA: Harvard University Press.

Helmholtz, H. von. (1852). On the theory of compound colors. *Philosophical Magazine, 4,* 519–534.

Helmholtz, H. von. (1863). *On the sensations of tone as a physiological basis for the theory of music* (A. J. Ellis, Trans.). New York: Dover.

Helson, R., **Jones, C.**, & **Kwan, V. S. Y.** (2002). Personality change over 40 years of adulthood: Hierarchical linear modeling analyses of two longitudinal studies. *Journal of Personality & Social Psychology, 83,* 752–766.

Hemenover, S. H. (2003). The good, the bad, and the healthy: Impacts of emotional disclosure of trauma on resilient self-concept and psychological distress. *Personality and Social Psychology Bulletin, 29,* 1236–1244.

Hendrick, S. S., & **Hendrick, C.** (1992). *Liking, loving, and relating* (2nd ed.). Pacific Grove, CA: Brooks/Cole.

Hendrick, S. S., & **Hendrick, C.** (2000). Romantic love. In S. S. Hendrick & C. Hendrick (Eds.), *Close relationships*. Thousand Oaks, CA: Sage.

Hennessy, D. A., & **Wiesenthal, D. L.** (1999). Traffic congestion, driver stress, and driver aggression. *Aggressive Behavior, 25,* 409–423.

Henriksson, M. M., Aro, H. M., Marttunen, M. J., Heikkinen, M. E., Isometsa, E. T., Kuoppasalmi, K. I., & Lonnqvist, J. K. (1993). Mental disorders and comorbidity of suicide. *American Journal of Psychiatry, 150,* 935–940.

Henry, K. R. (1984). Cochlear damage resulting from exposure to four different octave bands of noise at three different ages. *Behavioral Neuroscience, 1,* 107–117.

Henry, P. J., Sternberg, R. J., & Grigorenko, E. L. (2005). Capturing successful intelligence through measures of analytic, creative, and practical skills. In O. Wilhelm & R. W. Engle (Eds.), *Handbook of understanding and measuring intelligence.* Thousand Oaks, CA: Sage.

Hepper, P. (2003). *Prenatal psychological and behavioural development.* Thousand Oaks, CA: Sage.

Herek, G. M. (1996). Heterosexism and homophobia. In R. P. Cabaj & T. S. Stein (Eds.), *Textbook of homosexuality and mental health.* Washington, DC: American Psychiatric Press.

Herek, G. M. (2000). The psychology of sexual prejudice. *Current Directions in Psychological Science, 9,* 19–22.

Hering, E. (1878). *Zür lehre vom lichtsinne.* Vienna: Gerold.

Herman, J. L. (1994). Presuming to know the truth. *Nieman Reports, 48,* 43–45.

Hermann, R. C., Dorwart, R. A., Hoover, C. W., & Brody, J. (1995). Variation in ECT use in the United States. *American Journal of Psychiatry, 152,* 869–875.

Hermann, R. C., Ettner, S. L., Dorwart, R. A., Hoover, C. W., & Yeung, E. (1998). Characteristics of psychiatrists who perform ECT. *American Journal of Psychiatry, 155,* 889–894.

Hermans, H. J. M., & Kempen, H. J. G. (1998). Moving cultures: The perilous problems of cultural dichotomies in a globalizing society. *American Psychologist, 53,* 1111–1120.

Herrett-Skjellum, J., & Allen, M. (1996). Television programming and sex stereotyping: A meta-analysis. In B. R. Burleson (Ed.), *Communication yearbook 19* (pp. 157–185). Thousand Oaks, CA: Sage.

Herrmann, D., Raybeck, D., & Gruneberg, M. (2002). *Improving memory and study skills: Advances in theory and practice.* Ashland, OH: Hogrefe & Huber.

Herrnstein, R. J., & Murray, C. (1994). *The bell curve: Intelligence and class structure in American life.* New York: Free Press.

Hersh, S. M. (2004, May 10). Torture at Abu Ghraib. *New Yorker, 80*(17), 54–67.

Hertwig, R., Barron, G., Weber, E. U., & Erev, I. (2004). Decisions from experience and the effect of rare events in risky choice. *Psychological Science, 15,* 534–539.

Herzog, D. B., & Delinski, S. S. (2001). Classification of eating disorders. In R. H. Striegel-Moore & L. Smolak (Eds.), *Eating disorders* (pp. 31–50). Washington, DC: American Psychological Association.

Herzog, H. A. (2005). Dealing with the animal research controversy. In C. K. Akins, S. Panicker, & C. L. Cunningham (Eds.), *Laboratory animals in research and teaching: Ethics, care and methods.* Washington, DC: American Psychological Association.

Herzog, T. A., Abrams, D. B., Emmons, K. M., Linnan, L. A., & Shadel, W. G. (1999). Do processes of change predict smoking stage movements? A prospective analysis of the transtheoretical model. *Health Psychology, 18,* 369–375.

Heshka, S., & Heymsfield, S. B. (2002). Pharmacological treatments on the horizon. In C. G. Fairburn & K. D. Brownell (Eds.), *Eating disorders and obesity: A comprehensive handbook* (pp. 557–561). New York: Guilford.

Heszen-Niejodek, I. (1997). Coping style and its role in coping with stressful encounters. *European Psychologist, 2,* 342–351.

Hetherington, E. M. (1999). Should we stay together for the sake of the children? In E. M. Hetherington (Ed.), *Coping with divorce, single parenting, and remarriage.* Mahwah, NJ: Erlbaum.

Hetherington, E. M. (2003). Intimate pathways: Changing patterns in close personal relationships across time. *Family Relations: Interdisciplinary Journal of Applied Family Studies, 52,* 318–331.

Hetherington, E. M., Reiss, D., & Plomin, R. (1994). *Separate social worlds of siblings: The impact of nonshared environment on development.* Hillsdale, NJ: Erlbaum.

Hetherington, M. M., & Rolls, B. J. (1996). Sensory-specific satiety: Theoretical frameworks and central characteristics. In E. D. Capaldi (Ed.), *Why we eat what we eat: The psychology of eating* (pp. 267–290). Washington, DC: American Psychological Association.

Hettema, J. M., Neale, M. C., & Kendler, K. S. (2001). A review and meta-analysis of the genetic epidemiology of anxiety disorders. *American Journal of Psychiatry, 158,* 1568–1578.

Hettich, P. I. (1998). *Learning skills for college and career.* Pacific Grove, CA: Brooks/Cole.

Hewstone, M. (1990). The "ultimate attribution error"? A review of the literature on intergroup causal attribution. *European Journal of Social Psychology, 20,* 311–335.

Higgins, E. T. (2004). Making a theory useful: Lessons handed down. *Personality and Social Psychology Review, 8*(2), 138–145.

Highhouse, S., Beadle, D., Gallo, A., & Miller, L. (1998). Get 'em while they last! Effects of scarcity information in job advertisements. *Journal of Applied Social Psychology, 28,* 779–795.

Hilgard, E. R. (1965). *Hypnotic susceptibility.* New York: Harcourt, Brace & World.

Hilgard, E. R. (1986). *Divided consciousness: Multiple controls in human thought and action.* New York: Wiley.

Hilgard, E. R. (1987). *Psychology in America: A historical survey.* San Diego: Harcourt Brace Jovanovich.

Hilgard, E. R. (1992). Dissociation and theories of hypnosis. In E. Fromm & M. R. Nash (Eds.), *Contemporary hypnosis research.* New York: Guilford.

Hill, C. E., & Lambert, M. J. (2004). Methodological issues in studying psychotherapy processes and outcomes. In M. J. Lambert (Ed.), *Bergin and Garfield's handbook of psychotherapy and behavior change.* New York: Wiley.

Hilton, J. L., & von Hippel, W. (1996). Stereotypes. *Annual Review of Psychology, 47,* 237–271.

Hirsh, I. J., & Watson, C. S. (1996). Auditory psychophysics and perception. *Annual Review of Psychology, 47,* 461–484.

Ho, B., Black, D. W., & Andreasen, N. C. (2003). Schizophrenia and other psychotic disorders. In R. E. Hales & S. C. Yudofsky (Eds.), *Textbook of clinical psychiatry.* Washington, DC: American Psychiatric Publishing.

Hobson, C. J., & Delunas, L. (2001). National norms and life-event frequencies for the revised Social Readjustment Rating Scale. *International Journal of Stress Management, 8*(4), 299–314.

Hobson, J. A. (1988). *The dreaming brain.* New York: Basic Books.

Hobson, J. A. (1989). *Sleep.* New York: Scientific American Library.

Hobson, J. A. (2002). *Dreaming: An introduction to the science of sleep.* New York: Oxford University Press.

Hobson, J. A., & McCarley, R. W. (1977). The brain as a dream state generator: An activation-synthesis hypothesis of the dream process. *American Journal of Psychiatry, 134,* 1335–1348.

Hocevar, D., & Bachelor, P. (1989). A taxonomy and critique of measurements used in the study of creativity. In J. A. Glover, R. R. Ronning, & C. R. Reynolds (Eds.), *Handbook of creativity.* New York: Plenum.

Hochberg, J. (1988). Visual perception. In R. C. Atkinson, R. J. Herrnstein, G. Lindzey, & R. D. Luce (Eds.), *Stevens' handbook of experimental psychology* (2nd ed., Vol. 1). New York: Wiley.

Hodgkin, A. L., & Huxley, A. F. (1952). Currents carried by sodium and potassium ions through the membrane of the giant axon of Loligo. *Journal of Physiology, 116,* 449–472.

Hoek, H. W. (2002). Distribution of eating disorders. In C. G. Fairburn & K. D. Brownell (Eds.), *Eating disorders and obesity: A comprehensive handbook.* New York: Guilford.

Hofbauer, R. K., Rainville, P., Duncan, G. H., & Bushnell, M. C. (2001). Cortical representation of the sensory dimension of pain. *Journal of Neurophysiology, 86,* 402–411.

Hoffman, E. (1994). *The drive for self: Alfred Adler and the founding of individual psychology.* Reading, MA: Addison-Wesley.

Hoffstein, V. (2005). Snoring and upper airway resistance. In M. H. Kryger, T. Roth, & W. C. Dement (Eds.). *Principles and practice of sleep medicine.* Philadelphia: Elsevier Saunders.

Hofstede, G. (1980). *Culture's consequences: International differences in work-related values.* Beverly Hills, CA: Sage.

Hofstede, G. (1983). Dimensions of national cultures in fifty countries and three regions. In J. Deregowski, S. Dziurawiec, & R. Annis (Eds.), *Explications in cross-cultural psychology.* Lisse: Swets and Zeitlinger.

Hofstede, G. (2001). *Culture's consequences: Comparing values, behaviors, institutions, and organizations across nations.* Thousand Oaks, CA: Sage.

Hogan, M. F., & Morrison, A. K. (2003). Organization and financing of mental health care. In A. Tasman, J. Kay, & J. A. Lieberman (Eds.), *Psychiatry.* New York: Wiley.

Holahan, C. J., & Moos, R. H. (1990). Life stressors, resistance factors, and improved psychological functioning: An extension of the stress resistance paradigm. *Journal of Personality and Social Psychology, 58,* 909–917.

Holahan, C. J., & Moos, R. H. (1994). Life stressors and mental health: Advances in conceptualizing stress resistance. In W. R. Avison & J. H. Gotlib (Eds.), *Stress and mental health: Contemporary issues and prospects for the future.* New York: Plenum.

Holden, C. (1986, October). The rational optimist. *Psychology Today,* pp. 55–60.

Holden, C. (2004). FDA weighs suicide risk in children on antidepressants. *Science, 303,* 745.

Holden, G. W. (2002). Perspectives on the effects of corporal punishment: Comment on Gershoff. *Psychological Bulletin, 128,* 590–595.

Holen, A. (2000). Posttraumatic stress disorder, delayed. In G. Fink (Ed.), *Encyclopedia of stress* (Vol. 3, pp. 179–180). San Diego: Academic Press.

Hollander, E., & Simeon, D. (2003). Anxiety disorders. In R. E. Hales & S. C. Yudofsky (Eds.), *Textbook of clinical psychiatry.* Washington, DC: American Psychiatric Publishing.

Hollands, C. (1989). Trivial and questionable research on animals. In G. Langley (Ed.), *Animal experimentation: The consensus changes.* New York: Chapman & Hall.

Hollingworth, L. S. (1914). *Functional periodicity: An experimental study of the mental and motor abilities of women during menstruation.* New York: Teachers College, Columbia University.

Hollingworth, L. S. (1916). Sex differences in mental tests. *Psychological Bulletin, 13,* 377–383.

Hollis, K. L. (1997). Contemporary research on Pavlovian conditioning: A "new" functional analysis. *American Psychologist, 52,* 956–965.

Hollon, S. D., & Beck, A. T. (2004). Cognitive and cognitive behavioral therapies. In M. J. Lambert (Ed.), *Bergin and Garfields handbook of psychotherapy and behavior change.* New York: Wiley.

Holmes, D. S. (1987). The influence of meditation versus rest on physiological arousal: A second examination. In M. A. West (Ed.), *The psychology of meditation.* Oxford: Clarendon Press.

Holmes, T. H., & Rahe, R. H. (1967). The Social Readjustment Rating Scale. *Journal of Psychosomatic Research, 11,* 213–218.

Holtgraves, T. (2004). Social desirability and self-reports: Testing models of socially desirable responding. *Personality and Social Psychology Bulletin, 30,* 161–172.

Holyoak, K. J. (2005). Analogy. In K. J. Holyoak & R. G. Morrison (Eds.), *The Cambridge handbook of thinking and reasoning.* New York: Cambridge University Press.

Hong, G. K., Garcia, M., & Soriano, M. (2000). Responding to the challenge: Preparing mental health professionals for the new millennium. In I. Cuellar & F. A. Paniagua (Eds.), *Handbook of multicultural mental health: Assessment and treatment of diverse populations.* San Diego: Academic Press.

Honig, W. K., & Alsop, B. (1992). Operant behavior. In L. R. Squire (Ed.), *Encyclopedia of learning and memory.* New York: Macmillan.

Hooley, J. M. (2004). Do psychiatric patients do better clinically if they live with certain kinds of families? *Current Directions in Psychological Science, 13*(5), 202–205.

Hooley, J. M., & Candela, S. F. (1999). Interpersonal functioning in schizophrenia. In T. Millon, P. H. Blaney, & R. D. Davis (Eds.), *Oxford textbook of psychopathology* (pp. 311–338). New York: Oxford University Press.

Hooley, J. M., & Hiller, J. B. (1998). Expressed emotion and the pathogenesis of relapse in schizophrenia. In M. F. Lenzenweger & R. H. Dworkin (Eds.), *Origins and development of schizophrenia: Advances in experimental psychopathology.* Washington DC: American Psychological Association.

Hooper, J., & Teresi, D. (1986). *The 3-pound universe—The brain.* New York: Laurel.

Hopko, D. R., Crittendon, J. A., Grant, E., & Wilson, S. A. (2005). The impact of anxiety on performance IQ. *Anxiety, Stress, & Coping: An International Journal, 18*(1), 17–35.

Horn, J. L. (2002). Selections of evidence, misleading assumptions, and oversimplifications: The political message of *The Bell Curve.* In J. M. Fish (Ed.), *Race and intelligence: Separating science from myth* (pp. 297–326). Mahwah, NJ: Erlbaum.

Hornstein, G. A. (1992). The return of the repressed: Psychology's problematic relations with psychoanalysis, 1909–1960. *American Psychologist, 47,* 254–263.

Horowitz, F. D. (1992). John B. Watson's legacy: Learning and environment. *Developmental Psychology, 28,* 360–367.

Horwath, E., & Weissman, M. M. (2000). Anxiety disorders: Epidemiology. In B. J. Sadock & V. A. Sadock (Eds.), *Kaplan and Sadock's comprehensive textbook of psychiatry* (7th ed., Vol. 1, pp. 1441–1449). Philadelphia: Lippincott/Williams & Wilkins.

Hossain, J. L., & Shapiro, C. M. (1999). Considerations and possible consequences of shift work. *Journal of Psychosomatic Research, 47,* 293–296.

Hotopf, M. (2004). Preventing somatization. *Psychological Medicine, 34*(2), 195–198.

Howard, A., Pion, G. M., Gottfredson, G. D., Flattau, P. E., Oskamp, S., Pfafflin, S. M., Bray, D. W., & Burstein, A. G. (1986). The changing face of American psychology: A report from the committee on employment and human resources. *American Psychologist, 41,* 1311–1327.

Howard, D. J. (1995). "Chaining" the use of influence strategies for producing compliance behavior. *Journal of Social Behavior and Personality, 10,* 169–185.

Howard, M. S., & Medway, F. J. (2004). Adolescents' attachment and coping with stress. *Psychology in Schools, 41,* 391–402.

Howard, R., Castle, D., Wessely, S., & Murray, R. (1993). A comparative study of 470 cases of early-onset and late-onset schizophrenia. *British Journal of Psychiatry, 163,* 352–357.

Hrdy, S. B. (1997). Raising Darwin's consciousness: Female sexuality and the prehominid origins of patriarchy. *Human Nature: An Interdisciplinary Biosocial Perspective, 8,* 1–49.

Hsee, C. K., & Zhang, J. (2004). Distinction bias: Misprediction and mischoice due to joint evaluation. *Journal of Personality and Social Psychology, 86,* 680–695.

Hsee, C. K., Zhang, J., & Chen, J. (2004). Internal and substantive inconsistencies in decision making. In D. J. Koehler & N. Harvey (Eds.), *Blackwell handbook of judgment and decision making.* Malden, MA: Blackwell Publishing.

Hsu, L. K. G. (1990). *Eating disorders.* New York: Guilford.

Hsu, L. K. G. (1995). Outcome of bulimia nervosa. In K. D. Brownell & C. G. Fairburn (Eds.), *Eating disorders and obesity: A comprehensive handbook.* New York: Guilford.

Hu, F. B., & Willett, W. C. (2002). Optimal diets for prevention of coronary heart disease. *Journal of the American Medical Association, 288,* 2569–2578.

Hua, J. Y., & Smith, S. J. (2004). Neural activity and the dynamics of central nervous system development. *Nature Neuroscience, 7,* 327–332.

Hubbard, J. R., & Workman, E. A. (1998). *Handbook of stress medicine: An organ system approach.* New York: CRC Press.

Hubel, D. H., & Wiesel, T. N. (1962). Receptive fields, binocular interaction and functional architecture in the cat's visual cortex. *Journal of Physiology, 160,* 106–154.

Hubel, D. H., & Wiesel, T. N. (1963). Receptive fields of cells in striate cortex of very young visually inexperienced kittens. *Journal of Neurophysiology, 26,* 994–1002.

Hubel, D. H., & Wiesel, T. N. (1979). Brain mechanisms of vision. In Scientific American (Eds.), *The brain.* San Franciso: W. H. Freeman.

Hubel, D. H., & Wiesel, T. N. (1998). Early exploration of the visual cortex. *Neuron, 20,* 401–412.

Hudson, W. (1960). Pictorial depth perception in sub-cultural groups in Africa. *Journal of Social Psychology, 52,* 183–208.

Hudson, W. (1967). The study of the problem of pictorial perception among unacculturated groups. *International Journal of Psychology, 2,* 89–107.

Hudspeth, A. J. (2000). Sensory transduction in the ear. In E. R. Kandel, J. H. Schwartz, & T. M. Jessell (Eds.), *Principles of neural science.* New York: McGraw-Hill.

Huesmann, L. R. (1986). Psychological processes promoting the relation between exposure to media violence and aggressive behavior by the viewer. *Journal of Social Issues, 42,* 125–139.

Huesmann, L. R., & Miller, L. S. (1994). Long-term effects of repeated exposure to media violence in childhood. In L. R. Huesmann (Ed.), *Aggressive behavior: Current perspectives.* New York: Plenum Press.

Huesmann, L. R., Moise-Titus, J., Podolski, C. L., & Eron, L. D. (2003). Longitudinal relations between children's exposure to TV violence and their aggressive and violent behavior in young adulthood: 1977–1992. *Developmental Psychology, 39,* 201–221.

Huettel, S. A., Mack, P. B., McCarthy, G., Hua, J. Y., & Smith, S. J. (2002). Perceiving patterns in random series: Dynamic processing of sequence in prefrontal cortex. *Nature Neuroscience, 5,* 485–490.

Hughes, J., Smith, T. W., Kosterlitz, H. W., Fothergill, L. A., Morgan, B. A., & Morris, H. R. (1975). Identification of two related pentapeptides from the brain with the potent opiate agonist activity. *Nature, 258,* 577–579.

Hull, C. L. (1943). *Principles of behavior.* New York: Appleton.

Hunsley, J., Lee, C. M., & Wood, J. M. (2003). Controversial and questionable assessment techniques. In S. O. Lilienfeld, S. J. Lynn, & J. M. Lohr (Eds.), *Science and pseudoscience in clinical psychology.* New York: Guilford.

Hunt, E. (2001). Multiple views of multiple intelligence [Review of the book *Intelligence reframed: Multiple intelligence in the 21st century*]. *Contemporary Psychology, 46,* 5–7.

Hunt, E., Streissguth, A. P., Kerr, B., & Olsen, H. C. (1995). Mothers' alcohol consumption during pregnancy: Effects on spatial-visual reasoning in 14-year-old children. *Psychological Science, 6,* 339–342.

Hunt, H. (1989). *The multiplicity of dreams: Memory, imagination and consciousness.* New Haven: Yale University Press.

Hunt, J. M., Smith, M. F., & Kernan, J. B. (1985). The effects of expectancy disconfirmation and argument strength on message processing level: An application to personal selling. In E. C. Hirschman & M. B. Holbrook (Eds.), *Advances in consumer research* (Vol. 12). Provo, UT: Association for Consumer Research.

Huntsinger, E. T., & Luecken, L. J. (2004). Attachment relationships and health behavior: The mediational role of self-esteem. *Psychology & Health, 19,* 515–526.

Hurvich, L. M. (1981). *Color vision.* Sunderland, MA: Sinnauer Associates.

Huttenlocher, P. R. (1994). Synaptogenesis in human cerebral cortex. In G. Dawson & K. W. Fischer (Eds.), *Human behavior and the developing brain.* New York: Guilford.

Huttenlocher, P. R. (2002). *Neural plasticity: The effects of environment on the development of the cerebral cortex.* Cambridge, MA: Harvard University Press.

Hyde, J. S., Fennema, E., & Lamon, S. J. (1990). Gender differences in mathematics performance: A meta-analysis. *Psychological Bulletin, 107,* 139–155.

Hyman, I. A. (1996). Using research to change policy: Reflections on 20 years of effort to eliminate corporal punishment in the schools. *Pediatrics, 98,* 818–821.

Hyman, I. E., Jr., Husband, T. H., & Billings, J. F. (1995). False memories of childhood experiences. *Applied Cognitive Psychology, 9,* 181–197.

Hyman, I. E., Jr., & Kleinknecht, E. E. (1999). False childhood memories: Research, theory, and applications. In L. M. Williams, & V. L. Banyard (Eds.), *Trauma & memory.* Thousand Oaks, CA: Sage Publications.

Iacono, W. G., & Lykken, D. T. (1997). The validity of the lie detector: Two surveys of scientific opinion. *Journal of Applied Psychology, 82,* 426–433.

Iacono, W. G., & Patrick, C. J. (1999). Polygraph ("lie detector") testing: The state of the art. In A. K. Hess & I. B. Weiner (Eds.), *The handbook of forensic psychology* (pp. 440–473). New York: Wiley.

Iams, J. D. (2002). Preterm birth. In S. G. Gabbe, J. R. Niebyl, & J. L. Simpson (Eds.), *Obstetrics: Normal and problem pregnancies.* New York: Churchill Livingstone.

Ickovics, J. R., Thayaparan, B., & Ethier, K. A. (2001). Women and AIDS: A contextual analysis. In A. Baum, T. A. Revenson, & J. E. Singer (Eds.), *Handbook of health psychology* (pp. 817–840). Mahwah, NJ: Erlbaum.

Iezzi, T., Duckworth, M. P., & Adams, H. E. (2001). Somatoform and factitious disorders. In P. B. Sutker & H. E. Adams (Eds.), *Comprehensive handbook of psychopathology* (3rd ed., pp. 211–258). New York: Kluwer Academic/Plenum Publishers.

Infante, J. R., Torres-Avisbal, M., Pinel, P., Vallejo. J. A., Peran, F., Gonzalez, F., Contreras, P., Pacheco, C., Roldan, A., & Latre, J. M. (2001). Catecholamine levels in practitioners of the transcendental meditation technique. *Physiology & Behavior, 72*(1-2), 141–146.

Inglehart, R. (1990). *Culture shift in advanced industrial society.* Princeton, NJ: Princeton University Press.

Ingram, R. E., Scott, W., & Siegle, G. (1999). Depression: Social and cognitive aspects. In T. Millon, P. H. Blaney, & R. D. Davis (Eds.), *Oxford textbook of psychopathology* (pp. 203–226). New York: Oxford University Press.

Innocenti, G. M. (1994). Some new trends in the study of the corpus callosum. *Behavioral and Brain Research, 64,* 1–8.

Iribarren, C., Sidney, S., Bild, D. E., Liu, K., Markovitz, J. H., Roseman, J. M., & Matthews, K. (2000). Association of hostility with coronary artery calcification in young adults: The CARDIA study. *Journal of the American Medical Association, 283,* 2546–2551.

Irvine, S. H., & Berry, J. W. (1988). *Human abilities in cultural context.* New York: Cambridge University Press.

Irwin, S., & Irwin, T. (2001). *The crocodile hunter: The incredible life and adventures of Steve and Terri Irwin.* New York: Penguin.

Isabella, R. A. (1995). The origins of infant-mother attachment: Maternal behavior and infant development. In R. Vasta (Ed.), *Annals of child development.* London: Jessica Kingsley.

Isenberg, K. E., & Zorumski, C. F. (2000). Electroconvulsive therapy. In B. J. Sadock & V. A. Sadock (Eds.), *Kaplan and Sadock's Comprehensive textbook of psychiatry* (7th ed., Vol. 1, pp. 2503–2515). Philadelphia: Lippincott/Williams & Wilkins.

Ismail, M. A. (1993). Maternal-fetal infections. In C. Lin, M. S. Verp, & R. E. Sabbagha (Eds.), *The high-risk fetus: Pathophysiology, diagnosis, management.* New York: Springer-Verlag.

Isometsa, E. T., Heikkinen, M. E., Marttunen, M. J., Henriksson, M. M., Aro, H. M., & Lonnqvist, J. K. (1995). The last appointment before suicide: Is suicide intent communicated? *American Journal of Psychiatry, 152,* 919–922.

Iversen, S., Iversen, L., & Saper, C. B. (2000). The autonomic nervous system and the hypothalamus. In E. R. Kandel, J. H. Schwartz, & T. M. Jessell (Eds.), *Principles of neural science* (pp. 960–981). New York: McGraw-Hill.

Iwao, S. (1993). *The Japanese woman: Traditional image and changing reality.* New York: Free Press.

Iwawaki, S., & Vernon, P. E. (1988). Japanese abilities and achievements. In S. H. Irvine & J. W. Berry (Eds.), *Human abilities in cultural context.* New York: Cambridge University Press.

Izard, C. E. (1984). Emotion-cognition relationships and human development. In C. E. Izard, J. Kagan, & R. B. Zajonc (Eds.), *Emotions, cognition and behavior.* Cambridge, England: Cambridge University Press.

Izard, C. E. (1990). Facial expressions and the regulation of emotions. *Journal of Personality and Social Psychology, 58,* 487–498.

Izard, C. E. (1991). *The psychology of emotions.* New York: Plenum.

Izard, C. E. (1994). Innate and universal facial expressions: Evidence from developmental and cross-cultural research. *Psychological Bulletin, 115,* 288–299.

Izard, C. E., & Saxton, P. M. (1988). Emotions. In R. C. Atkinson, R. J. Herrnstein, G. Lindzey, & R. D. Luce (Eds.), *Stevens' handbook of experimental psychology* (Vol. 1). New York: Wiley.

Jablensky, A. (1999). The 100-year epidemiology of schizophrenia. *Schizophrenia Research, 28,* 111–125.

Jackson, L. A., Sullivan, L. A., & Hodge, C. N. (1993). Stereotype effects on attributions, predictions, and evaluations: No two social judgments are quite alike. *Journal of Personality and Social Psychology, 65,* 69–84.

Jacob, R. G., & Pelham, W. H. (2000). Behavior therapy. In B. J. Sadock & V. A. Sadock (Eds.), *Kaplan and Sadock's comprehensive textbook of psychiatry* (7th ed., Vol. 1, pp. 2080–2127). Philadelphia: Lippincott/Williams & Wilkins.

Jacobs, B. L. (2004). Depression: The brain finally gets into the act. *Current Directions in Psychological Science, 13*(3), 103–106.

Jacobs, D. F. (2004). Youth gambling in North America: Long-term trends and future prospects. In J. L. Derevensky & R. Gupta (Eds.), *Gambling problems in youth: Theoretical and applied perspectives* (pp. 1-24). New York: Kluwer/Plenum.

Jacobs, H. S. (2001). Idea of male menopause is not useful. *Medical Crossfire, 3,* 52–55.

Jacobsen, T., Edelstein, W., & Hoffman, V. (1994). A longitudinal study of the relations between representation of attachment in childhood and cognitive function in childhood and adolescence. *Developmental Psychology, 30,* 112–124.

Jacoby, L. L., Hessels, S., & Bopp, K. (2001). Proactive and retroactive effects in memory performance: Dissociating recollection and accessibility bias. In H. L. Roediger, J. S. Nairne, I. Neath, & A. M. Surprenant (Eds.), *The nature of remembering: Essays in honor of Robert G. Crowder* (pp. 35–54). Washington, DC: American Psychological Association.

Jain, S. P., Buchanan, B., & Maheswaran, D. (2000). Comparative versus noncomparative advertising. *Journal of Consumer Psychology, 9,* 201–211.

James, J. E. (2004). Critical review of dietary caffeine and blood pressure: A relationship that should be taken more seriously. *Psychosomatic Medicine, 66*(1), 63–71.

James, W. (1884). What is emotion? *Mind, 19,* 188–205.

James, W. (1890). *The principles of psychology.* New York: Holt.

James, W. (1902). *The varieties of religious experience.* New York: Modern Library.

Jamison, K. R. (1988). Manic-depressive illness and accomplishment: Creativity, leadership, and social class. In F. K. Goodwin & K. R. Jamison (Eds.), *Manic-depressive illness.* Oxford, England: Oxford University Press.

Janig, W. (2003). The autonomic nervous system and its coordination by the brain. In R. J. Davidson, K. R. Scherer, & H. H. Goldsmith (Eds.), *Handbook of affective sciences.* New York: Oxford University Press.

Janis, I. L. (1958). *Psychological stress.* New York: Wiley.

Janis, I. L. (1972). *Victims of groupthink.* Boston: Houghton Mifflin.

Janis, I. L. (1993). Decision making under stress. In L. Goldberger & S. Breznitz (Eds.), *Handbook of stress: Theoretical and clinical aspects* (2nd ed.). New York: Free Press.

Janis, I. L., & Mann, L. (1977). *Decision making: A psychological analysis of conflict, choice, and commitment.* New York: Free Press.

Jaroff, L. (1993, November 29). Lies of the mind. *Time,* pp. 52–59.

Jefferson, J. W., & Greist, J. H. (2000). Lithium. In B. J. Sadock & V. A. Sadock (Eds.), *Kaplan and Sadock's comprehensive textbook of psychiatry* (7th ed., Vol. 1, pp. 2377–2389). Philadelphia: Lippincott/Williams & Wilkins.

Jemmott, J. B., III, & Magloire, K. (1988). Academic stress, social support, and secretory immunoglobin A. *Journal of Personality and Social Psychology, 55,* 803–810.

Jensen, A. R. (1969). How much can we boost IQ and scholastic achievement? *Harvard Educational Review, 39,* 1–23.

Jensen, A. R. (1980). *Bias in mental testing.* New York: Free Press.

Jensen, A. R. (1982). Reaction time and psychometric g. In H. J. Eysenck (Ed.), *A model for intelligence.* New York: Springer-Verlag.

Jensen, A. R. (1987). Process differences and individual difference in some cognitive tasks. *Intelligence, 11,* 107–136.

Jensen, A. R. (1992). The importance of intraindividual variation in reaction time. *Personality and Individual Differences, 13,* 869–881.

Jensen, A. R. (1993a). Test validity: *g* versus "tacit knowledge." *Current Directions in Psychological Science, 2*(1), 9–10.

Jensen, A. R. (1993b). Why is reaction time correlated with psychometric *g*? *Current Directions in Psychological Science, 2*(2), 53–56.

Jensen, A. R. (1998). *The g factor: The science of mental ability.* Westport, CT: Praeger.

Jensen, E. (2000). *Brain-based learning.* San Diego: Brain Store.

Jenson, J. D. (2004). It's the information age, so where's the information? *College Teaching, 52*(3), 107–112.

Jessell, T. M., & Kelly, D. D. (1991). Pain and analgesia. In E. R. Kandel, J. H. Schwartz, & T. M. Jessell (Eds.), *Principles of neural science* (3rd ed.). New York: Elsevier.

Jex, S. M., Bliese, P. D., Buzzell, S., & Primeau, J. (2001). The impact of self-efficacy on stressor-strain relations: Coping style as an explanatory mechanism. *Journal of Applied Psychology, 86*, 401–409.

Ji, L.-J., Peng, K., & Nisbett, R. E. (2000). Culture, control, and perception of relationships in the environment. *Journal of Personality and Social Psychology, 78*, 943–955.

Jick, H., Kaye, J. A., & Jick, S. S. (2004). Antidepressants and the risk of suicidal behaviors. *Journal of the American Medical Association, 292*, 338–343.

John, O. P., & Srivastava, S. (1999). The big five trait taxonomy: History, measurement, and theoretical perspectives. In L. A. Pervin & O. P. John (Eds.), *Handbook of personality: Theory and research.* New York: Guilford.

Johnson, A. (2003). Procedural memory and skill acquisition. In A. F. Healy & R. W. Proctor (Eds.), *Handbook of psychology, Vol. 4: Experimental psychology.* New York: Wiley.

Johnson, B. A., & Ait-Daoud, N. (2005). Alcohol: Clinical aspects. In J. H. Lowinson, P. Ruiz, R. B. Millman, & J. G. Langrod (Eds.), *Substance abuse: A comprehensive textbook.* Philadelphia: Lippincott/Williams & Wilkins.

Johnson, B. T. (1994). Effects of outcome-relevant involvement and prior information on persuasion. *Journal of Experimental Social Psychology, 30*, 556–579.

Johnson, B. T., Maio, G. R., & Smith-McLallen, A. (2005). Communication and attitude change: Causes, processes, and effects. In D. Albarracin, B. T. Johnson, & M. P. Zanna (Eds.), *The handbook of attitudes.* Mahwah, NJ: Erlbaum.

Johnson, C., & Mullen, B. (1994). Evidence for the accessibility of paired distinctiveness in distinctiveness-based illusory correlation in stereotyping. *Personality and Social Psychology Bulletin, 20*, 65–70.

Johnson, D. (1990). Animal rights and human lives: Time for scientists to right the balance. *Psychological Science, 1*, 213–214.

Johnson, J. G., & Sherman, M. F. (1997). Daily hassles mediate the relationship between major life events and psychiatric symptomatology: Longitudinal findings from an adolescent sample. *Journal of Social and Clinical Psychology, 16*, 389–404.

Johnson, M. K. (1996). Fact, fantasy, and public policy. In D. J. Herrmann, C. McEvoy, C. Hertzog, P. Hertel, & M. K. Johnson (Eds.), *Basic and applied memory research: Theory in context* (Vol. 1). Mahwah, NJ: Erlbaum.

Johnson, M. K., Hashtroudi, S., & Lindsay, D. S. (1993). Source monitoring. *Psychological Bulletin, 114,* 3–28.

Johnson, S. B., & Carlson, D. N. (2004). Medical regimen adherence: Concepts assessment, and inter-ventions. In J. M. Raczynski & L. C. Leviton (Eds.), *Handbook of clinical health psychology: Vol 2. Disorders of behavior and health.* Washington, DC: American Psychological Association.

Johnston, J. C., & McClelland, J. L. (1974). Perception of letters in words: Seek not and ye shall find. *Science, 184,* 1192–1194.

Joiner, T. E. (2002). Depression in its interpersonal context. In I. H. Gotlib & C. L. Hammen (Eds.), *Handbook of depression.* New York: Guilford.

Joiner, T. E., & Katz, J. (1999). Contagion of depressive symptoms and mood: Meta-analytic review and explanations from cognitive, behavioral, and interpersonal viewpoints. *Clinical Psychology: Science and Practice, 6,* 149–164.

Joiner, T. E., Jr., & Metalsky, G. I. (1995). A prospective test of an integrative interpersonal theory of depression: A naturalistic study of college students. *Journal of Personality and Social Psychology, 69,* 778–788.

Jones, B. C., Little, A. C., Penton-Voak, I. S., Tiddeman, B. P., Burt, D. M., & Perrett, D. I. (2001). Facial symmetry and judgments of apparent health: Support for a "good genes" explanation of the attractiveness-symmetry relationship. *Evolution and Human Behavior, 22,* 417–429.

Jones, E. E., & Davis, K. E. (1965). From acts to dispositions: The attribution process in person perception. In L. Berkowitz (Ed.), *Advances in experimental social psychology* (Vol. 2). New York: Academic Press.

Jones, E. E., & Nisbett, R. E. (1971). The actor and the observer: Divergent perceptions of the causes of behavior. In E. E. Jones, D. E. Kanouse, H. H. Kelley, R. E. Nisbett, S. Valins, & B. Weiner (Eds.), *Attribution: Perceiving the causes of behavior.* Morristown, NJ: General Learning Press.

Jones, F., & Kinman, G. (2001). Approaches to studying stress. In F. Jones & J. Bright (Eds.), *Stress: Myth, theory, and research.* Harlow, UK: Pearson Education.

Jones, G. V. (1990). Misremembering a common object: When left is not right. *Memory & Cognition, 18*(2), 174–182.

Jordan, B. (1983). *Birth in four cultures.* Quebec, Canada: Eden Press.

Jorgensen, R. S., Johnson, B. T., Kolodziej, M. E., & Schreer, G. E. (1996). Elevated blood pressure and personality: A meta-analytic review. *Psychological Bulletin, 120,* 293–320.

Joseph, R. (1992). *The right brain and the unconscious.* New York: Plenum.

Josse, G., & Tzourio-Mazoyer, N. (2004). Hemispheric specialization for language. *Brain Research Reviews, 44,* 1–12.

Judge, T. A., & Cable, D. M. (2004). The effect of physical height on workplace success and income: Preliminary test of a theoretical model. *Journal of Applied Psychology, 89,* 428–441.

Julien, R. M. (2001). *A primer of drug action.* New York: Freeman.

Jung, C. G. (1917/1953). *On the psychology of the unconscious.* In H. Read, M. Fordham, & G. Adler (Eds.), *Collected works of C. G. Jung* (Vol. 7). Princeton, NJ: Princeton University Press.

Jung, C. G. (1921/1960). *Psychological types.* In H. Read, M. Fordham, & G. Adler (Eds.), *Collected works of C. G. Jung* (Vol. 6). Princeton, NJ: Princeton University Press.

Jung, C. G. (1933). *Modern man in search of a soul.* New York: Harcourt, Brace & World.

Kaas, J. H. (2000). The reorganization of sensory and motor maps after injury in adult mammals. In M. S. Gazzaniga (Ed.), *The new cognitive neurosciences.* Cambridge, MA: The MIT Press.

Kagan, J. (1998, November/December). A parent's influence is peerless. *Harvard Education Letter.*

Kahneman, D. (1999). Objective happiness. In D. Kahneman, E. Diener, & N. Schwarz (Eds.), *Well-being: The foundations of hedonic psychology.* New York: Russell Sage Foundation.

Kahneman, D. (2003). A perspective on judgment and choice: Mapping bounded rationality. *American Psychologist, 58,* 697–720.

Kahneman, D., & Frederick, S. (2005). A model of heuristic judgment. In K. J. Holyoak & R. G. Morrison (Eds.), *The Cambridge handbook of thinking and reasoning.* New York: Cambridge University Press.

Kahneman, D., & Tversky, A. (1973). On the psychology of prediction. *Psychological Review, 80,* 237–251.

Kahneman, D., & Tversky, A. (1982). Subjective probability: A judgment of representativeness. In D. Kahneman, P. Slovic, & A. Tversky (Eds.), *Judgment under uncertainty: Heuristics and biases.* Cambridge: Cambridge University Press.

Kahneman, D., & Tversky, A. (2000). *Choices, values, and frames.* New York: Cambridge University Press.

Kales, J. D., Kales, A., Bixler, E. O., Soldatos, C. R., Cadieux, R. J., Kashurba, G. J., & Vela-Bueno, A. (1984). Biopsychobehavioral correlates of insomnia: V. Clinical characteristics and behavioral correlates. *American Journal of Psychiatry, 141,* 1371–1376.

Kalichman, S. C. (1995). *Understanding AIDS: A guide for mental health professionals.* Washington, DC: American Psychological Association.

Kalidindi, S., & McGuffin, P. (2003). The genetics of affective disorders: Present and future. In R. Plomin, J. C. Defries, I. W. Craig, & P. McGuffin (Eds.), *Behavioral genetics in the postgenomic era.* Washington, DC: American Psychological Association.

Kalmijn, M. (1998). Intermarriage and homogamy: Causes, patterns, trends. *Annual Review of Sociology, 24,* 395–421.

Kandel, E. R. (2000). Nerve cells and behavior. In E. R. Kandel, J. H. Schwartz, & T. M. Jessell (Eds.), *Principles of neural science* (pp. 19–35). New York: McGraw-Hill.

Kandel, E. R. (2001). The molecular biology of memory storage: A dialogue between genes and synapses. *Science, 294,* 1030–1038.

Kandel, E. R., & Jessell, T. M. (1991). Touch. In E. R. Kandel, J. H. Schwartz, & T. M. Jessell (Eds.), *Principles of neural science* (3rd ed.). New York: Elsevier.

Kandel, E. R., & Schwartz, J. H. (1982). Molecular biology of learning: Modification of transmitter release. *Science, 218,* 433–442.

Kandel, E. R., & Siegelbaum, S. A. (2000). Synaptic integration. In E. R. Kandel, J. H. Schwartz & T. M. Jessell (Eds.), *Principles of neural science* (pp. 207–228). New York: McGraw-Hill.

Kandel, E. R., & Wurtz, R. H. (2000). Constructing visual images. E. R. Kandel, J. H. Schwartz, & T. M. Jessell (Eds.), *Principles of neural science.* New York: McGraw-Hill.

Kandell, J. J. (1998). Internet addiction on campus: The vulnerability of college students. *CyberPsychology and Behavior, 1*(1), 11–17.

Kane, J. (1991). *Be sick well: A healthy approach to chronic illness.* Oakland, CA: New Harbinger Publications.

Kane, M. J., & Engle, R. W. (2002). The role of prefrontal cortex in working-memory capacity, executive attention, and general fluid intelligence: An individual-differences perspective. *Psychonomic Bulletin & Review, 9,* 637–671.

Kane, T. D., Marks, M. A., Zaccaro, S. J., & Blair, V. (1996). Self-efficacy, personal goals, and wrestlers' self-regulation. *Journal of Sport & Exercise Psychology, 18,* 36–48.

Kaplan, H., & Dove, H. (1987). Infant development among the Ache of Eastern Paraguay. *Developmental Psychology, 23,* 190–198.

Karau, S. J., & Williams, K. D. (1993). Social loafing: A meta-analytic review and theoretical integration. *Journal of Personality and Social Psychology, 65,* 681–706.

Karau, S. J., & Williams, K. D. (1995). Social loafing: Research findings, implications, and future directions. *Current Directions in Psychological Science, 4,* 134–140.

Kassel, J. D., Stroud, L. R., & Paronis, C. A. (2003). Smoking, stress, and negative affect: Correlation, causation, and context across stages of smoking. *Psychological Bulletin, 129,* 270–304.

Kasser, T. (2002). *The high prices of materialism.* Cambridge, MA: MIT Press.

Kasser, T., Ryan, R. M., Couchman, C. E., & Sheldon, K. M. (2004). Materialistic values: Their causes and consequences. In T. Kasser & A. D. Kanner (Eds.), *Psychology and consumer culture: The struggle for a good life in a materialistic world.* Washington, DC: American Psychological Association.

Kasser, T., & Sharma, Y. S. (1999). Reproductive freedom, educational equality, and females' preference for resource-aquisition characteristics in mates. *Psychological Science, 10,* 374–377.

Kassin, S. M., Tubb, V. A., Hosch, H. M., & Memon, A. (2001). On the "general acceptance" of eyewitness testimony research: A new survey of the experts. *American Psychologist, 56,* 405–416.

Katigbak, M. S., Church, A. T., Guanzon-Lapena, M. A., Carlota, A. J. & del Pilar, G. H. (2002). Are indigenous personality dimensions culture specific? Philippine inventories and the five-factor model. *Journal of Personality and Social Psychology, 82,* 89–101.

Kaufman, A. S. (2000). Tests of intelligence. In R. J. Sternberg (Ed.), *Handbook of intelligence* (pp. 445–476). New York: Cambridge University Press.

Kaufman, J. C., & Baer, J. (2002). Could Steven Spielberg manage the Yankees?: Creative thinking in different domains. *Korean Journal of Thinking & Problem Solving, 12*(2), 5–14.

Kaufman, J. C., & Baer, J. (2004). Hawking's haiku, Madonna's math: Why it is hard to be creative in every room of the house. In R. J. Sternberg, E. L. Grigorenko, & J. L. Singer (Eds.), *Creativity: From potential to realization.* Washington, DC: American Psychological Association.

Kaufman, L., & Rock, I. (1962). The moon illusion I. *Science, 136,* 953–961.

Kay, J., & Kay, R. I. (2003). Individual psychoanalytic psychotherapy. In A. Tasman, J. Kay, & J. A. Lieberman (Eds.), *Psychiatry.* New York: Wiley.

Kazdin, A. (2001). *Behavior modification in applied settings.* Belmont: Wadsworth.

Kazdin, A., & Benjet, C. (2003). Spanking children: Evidence and issues. *Current Directions in Psychological Science, 12*(3), 99–103.

Kazdin, A. E. (1994). Methodology, design, and evaluation in psychotherapy research. In A. E. Bergin & S. L. Garfield (Eds.), *Handbook of psychotherapy and behavior change* (4th ed.). New York: Wiley.

Keating, D. P. (2004). Cognitive and brain development. In R. M. Lerner & L. Steinberg (Eds.), *Handbook of adolescent psychology.* New York: Wiley.

Keefauver, S. P., & Guilleminault, C. (1994). Sleep terrors and sleepwalking. In M. H. Kryger, T. Roth, & W. C. Dement (Eds.), *Principles and practice of sleep medicine* (2nd ed.). Philadelphia: Saunders.

Keesey, R. E., & Powley, T. L. (1975). Hypothalamic regulation of body weight. *American Scientist, 63,* 558–565.

Kehoe, E. J., & Macrae, M. (1998). Classical conditioning. In W. O'Donohue (Ed.), *Learning and behavior therapy.* Boston, Allyn & Bacon.

Keller, H. E., & Lee, S. (2003). Ethical issues surrounding human participants research using the Internet. *Ethics & Behavior, 13*(3), 211–219.

Keller, P. A., & Block, L. G. (1999). The effect of affect-based dissonance versus cognition-based dissonance on motivated reasoning and health-related persuasion. *Journal of Experimental Psychology: Applied, 5,* 302–313.

Kelley, B. D., Feeney, L., O'Callaghan, E., Browne, R., Byrne, M., Mulryan, N., Scully, A., Morris, M., Kinsella, A., Takei, N., McNeil, T., Walsh, D., & Larkin, C. (2004). Obstetric adversity and age at first presentation with schizophrenia: Evidence of a dose-response relationship. *American Journal of Psychiatry, 161,* 920–922.

Kelley, H. H. (1950). The warm-cold variable in first impressions of persons. *Journal of Personality, 18,* 431–439.

Kelley, H. H. (1967). Attributional theory in social psychology. *Nebraska Symposium on Motivation, 15,* 192–241.

Kelly, K. M., & Schramke, C. J. (2000). Epilepsy. In G. Fink (Ed.), *Encyclopedia of stress* (pp. 66–70). San Diego: Academic Press.

Kelman, H. C. (1967). Human use of human subjects: The problem of deception in social psychological experiments. *Psychological Bulletin, 67,* 1–11.

Kelman, H. C. (1982). Ethical issues in different social science methods. In T. L. Beauchamp, R. R. Faden, R. J. Wallace, Jr., & L. Walters (Eds.), *Ethical issues in social science research.* Baltimore: Johns Hopkins University Press.

Kendall, P. C., Holmbeck, G., & Verduin, T. (2004). Methodology, design, and evaluation in psychotherapy research. In M. J. Lambert (Ed.), *Bergin and Garfield's handbook of psychotherapy and behavior change.* New York: Wiley.

Kendler, K. S. (2000). Schizophrenia: Genetics. In B. J. Sadock & V. A. Sadock (Eds.), *Kaplan and Sadock's comprehensive textbook of psychiatry* (7th ed., Vol. 1, pp. 1147–1158). Philadelphia: Lippincott/Williams & Wilkins.

Kendler, K. S., & Gardner, C. O., Jr. (1998). Boundaries of major depression: An evaluation of DSM-IV criteria. *American Journal of Psychiatry, 155,* 172–177.

Kendler, K. S., Kuhn, J., & Prescott, C. A. (2004). The interrelationship of neuroticism, sex, and stressful life events in the prediction of episodes of major depression. *American Journal of Psychiatry, 161,* 631–636.

Kendler, K. S., Myers, J., & Prescott, C. A. (2005). Sex differences in the relationship between social support and risk for major depression: A longitudinal study of opposite-sex twin pairs. *American Journal of Psychiatry, 162,* 250–256.

Kendler, K. S., Thornton, L. M., Gilman, S. E., & Kessler, R. C. (2000). Sexual orientation in a U.S. national sample of twin and nontwin sibling pairs. *American Journal of Psychiatry, 157,* 1843–1846.

Kennedy, T. E., Hawkins, R. D., & Kandel, E. R. (1992). Molecular interrelationships between short- and long-term memory. In L. R. Squire & N. Butters (Eds.), *Neuropsychology of Memory* (2nd ed.). New York: Wiley.

Kenrick, D. T., & Gutierres, S. E. (1980). Contrast effects and judgments of physical attractiveness: When beauty becomes a social problem. *Journal of Personality and Social Psychology, 38,* 131–140.

Kessen, W. (1996). American psychology just before Piaget. *Psychological Science, 7,* 196–199.

Kessler, R. C. (1997). The effects of stressful life events on depression. *Annual Review of Psychology, 48,* 191–214.

Kessler, R. C. (2002). Epidemiology of depression. In I. H. Gotlib & C. L. Hammen (Eds.), *Handbook of depression.* New York: Guilford.

Kessler, R. C., Berglund, P., Demler, O., Jin, R., & Walters, E. E. (2005a). Lifetime prevalence and age-of-onset distributions of DSM-IV disorders in the national comorbidity survey replication. *Archives of General Psychiatry, 62,* 593–602.

Kessler, R. C., Demier, O., Frank, R. G., Olfson, M., Pincus, H. A., Walters, E. E., Wang, P., Wells, K. B., & Zaslavsky, A. M. (2005b). Prevalence and treatment of mental disorders: 1990–2003. *New England Journal of Medicine, 352,* 2515–2523.

Kessler, R. C., Olfson, M., & Berglund, P. A. (1998). Patterns and predictors of treatment contact after first onset of psychiatric disorders. *American Journal of Psychiatry, 155,* 62–69.

Khot, U. N., Khot, M. B., Bajzer, C. T., Sapp, S. K., Ohman, E. M., Brener, S. J., Ellis, S. G., Lincoff, M. A., & Topol, E. J. (2003). Prevalence of conventional risk factors in patients with coronary heart disease. *Journal of the American Medical Association, 290,* 898–904.

Kiecolt-Glaser, J. K., Garner, W., Speicher, C., Penn, G. M., Holliday, J., & Glaser, R. (1984). Psychosocial modifiers of immunocompetence in medical students. *Psychosomatic Medicine, 46*(1), 7–14.

Kiecolt-Glaser, J. K., & Glaser, R. (1995). Measurement of immune response. In S. Cohen, R. C. Kessler, & L. U. Gordon (Eds.), *Measuring stress: A guide for health and social scientists.* New York: Oxford University Press.

Kieseppa, T., Partonen, T., Huakka, J., Kaprio, J., & Lonnqvist, J. (2004). High concordance of bipolar 1 disorder in a nationwide sample of twins. *American Journal of Psychiatry, 161,* 1814–1821.

Kiesler, C. A. (1992). U.S. mental health policy: Doomed to fail. *American Psychologist, 47,* 1077–1082.

Kiesler, C. A. (2000). The next wave of change for psychology and mental health services in the health care revolution. *American Psychologist, 55,* 481–487.

Kiesler, D. J. (1999). *Beyond the disease model of mental disorders.* New York: Praeger Publishers.

Kihlstrom, J. F. (1985). Hypnosis. *Annual Review of Psychology, 36,* 385–418.

Kihlstrom, J. F. (1998a). Dissociations and dissociation theory in hypnosis: Comment on Kirsch and Lynn (1998). *Psychological Bulletin, 123,* 186–191.

Kihlstrom, J. F. (1998b). Exhumed memory. In S. J. Lynn & K. M. McConkey (Eds.), *Truth in memory.* New York: Guilford.

Kihlstrom, J. F. (2001). Dissociative disorders. In P. B. Sutker & H. E. Adams (Eds.), *Comprehensive handbook of psychopathology* (3rd ed., pp. 259–276). New York: Kluwer Academic/Plenum Publishers.

Kihlstrom, J. F. (2004). An unbalanced balancing act: Blocked, recovered, and false memories in the laboratory and clinic. *Clinical Psychology: Science & Practice, 11*(1), 34–41.

Killeen, P. R. (1981). Learning as causal inference. In M. L. Commons & J. A. Nevin (Eds.), *Quantitative analyses of behavior, Vol. 1: Discriminative properties of reinforcement schedules*. Cambridge, MA: Ballinger.

Kim, H., & Markus, H. R. (1999). Deviance or uniqueness, harmony or conformity? A cultural analysis. *Journal of Personality and Social Psychology, 77*, 785–800.

Kim, K., & Spelke, E. S. (1992). Infants' sensitivity to effects of gravity on visible object motion. *Journal of Experimental Psychology: Human Perception and Performance, 18*, 385–393.

Kimura, D. (1973). The asymmetry of the human brain. *Scientific American, 228*, 70–78.

Kimura, D., & Hampson, E. (1993). Neural and hormonal mechanisms mediating sex differences in cognition. In P. A. Vernon (Ed.), *Biological approaches to the study of human intelligence*. Norwood, NJ: Ablex.

King, A. C., Oman, R. F., Brassington, G. S., Bliwise, D. L., & Haskell, W. L. (1997). Moderate-intensity exercise and self-rated quality of sleep in older adults: A randomized controlled trial. *Journal of the American Medical Association, 277*, 32–37.

King, G. R., & Ellinwood Jr., E. H. (2005). Amphetamines and other stimulants. In J. H. Lowinson, P. Ruiz, R. B. Millman, & J. G. Langrod (Eds.), *Substance abuse: A comprehensive textbook*. Philadelphia: Lippincott/Williams & Wilkins.

King, L. A., & Emmons, R. A. (1990). Conflict over emotional expression: Psychological and physical correlates. *Journal of Personality and Social Psychology, 58*, 864–877.

King, L. A., & Emmons, R. A. (1991). Psychological, physical, and interpersonal correlates of emotional expressiveness, conflict and control. *European Journal of Personality, 5*, 131–150.

King, N. J., Eleonora, G., & Ollendick, T. H. (1998). Etiology of childhood phobias: Current status of Rachman's three pathways theory. *Behaviour Research and Therapy, 36*, 297–309.

Kinsbourne, M. (1980). If sex differences in brain lateralization exist, they have yet to be discovered. *Behavioral and Brain Sciences, 3*, 241–242.

Kinsbourne, M. (1997). What qualifies a representation for a role in consciousness? In J. D. Cohen & J. W. Schooler (Eds.), *Scientific approaches to consciousness*. Mahwah, NJ: Erlbaum.

Kinsey, A. C., Pomeroy, W. B., & Martin, C. E. (1948). *Sexual behavior in the human male*. Philadelphia: Saunders.

Kinsey, A. C., Pomeroy, W. B., Martin, C. E., & Gebhard, P. H. (1953). *Sexual behavior in the human female*. Philadelphia: Saunders.

Kirkpatrick, L. A. (1999). Attachment and religious representations and behavior. In J. Cassidy & P. R. Shaver (Eds.), *Handbook of attachment: Theory, research and clinical applications*. New York: Guilford.

Kirkpatrick, L. A. (2005). *Attachment, evolution, and the psychology of religion*. New York: Guilford.

Kirsch, I. (1997). Response expectancy theory and application: A decennial review. *Applied and Preventive Psychology, 6*, 69–79.

Kirsch, I., & Lynn, S. J. (1998). Dissociation theories of hypnosis. *Psychological Bulletin, 123*, 100–115.

Kitchens, A. (1991). Left brain/right brain theory: Implications for developmental math instruction. *Review of Research in Developmental Education, 8*, 20–23.

Kittler, P. G., & Sucher, K. P. (1998). *Food and culture in America: A nutrition handbook*. St. Paul: West.

Klein, M. (1948). *Contributions to psychoanalysis*. London: Hogarth.

Klein, P. D. (1997). Multiplying the problems of intelligence by eight: A critique of Gardner's theory. *Canadian Journal of Education, 22*, 377–394.

Klein, T. W., Friedman, H., & Specter, S. (1998). Marijauna, immunity and infection. *Journal of Neuroimmunology, 83*, 102–115.

Kleinke, C. L., Peterson, T. R., & Rutledge, T. R. (1998). Effects of self-generated facial expressions on mood. *Journal of Personality and Social Psychology, 74*, 272–279.

Kleinmuntz, B. (1980). *Essentials of abnormal psychology*. San Francisco: Harper & Row.

Klerman, E. B., Davis, J. B., Duffy, J. F., Dijk, D., & Kronauer, R. E. (2004). Older people awaken more frequently but fall back asleep at the same rate as younger people. *Sleep: Journal of Sleep & Sleep Disorders Research, 27*, 793–798.

Kline, P. (1991). *Intelligence: The psychometric view*. New York: Routledge, Chapman, & Hall.

Kline, P. (1995). A critical review of the measurement of personality and intelligence. In D. H. Saklofske & M. Zeidner (Eds.), *International handbook of personality and intelligence*. New York: Plenum.

Klosch, G., & Kraft, U. (2005). Sweet dreams are made of this. *Scientific American Mind, 16*(2), 38–45.

Kluegel, J. R. (1990). Trends in whites' explanations of the black-white gap in socioeconomic status. *American Sociological Review, 55*, 512–525.

Kluft, R. P. (1996). Dissociative identity disorder. In L. K. Michelson & W. J. Ray (Eds.), *Handbook of dissociation: Theoretical, empirical, and clinical perspectives*. New York: Plenum.

Kluft, R. P. (1999). True lies, false truths, and naturalistic raw data: Applying clinical research findings to the false memory debate. In L. M. Williams & V. L. Banyard (Eds.), *Trauma & memory*. Thousand Oaks, CA: Sage Publications.

Knecht, S., Drager, B., Floel, A., Lohmann, H., Breitenstein, C., Henningsen, H., & Ringelstein, E. B. (2001). Behavioural relevance of atypical language lateralization in healthy subjects. *Brain, 124*, 1657–1665.

Knecht, S., Fioel, A., Drager, B., Breitenstein, C., Sommer, J., Henningsen, H., Ringelstein, E. B., & Pascual-Leone, A. (2002). Degree of language lateralization determines susceptibility to unilateral brain lesions. *Nature Neuroscience, 5*, 695–699.

Knight, J. (2004). The truth about lying. *Nature, 428*, 692–694.

Kochanska, G. (2001). Emotional development in children with different attachment histories: The first three years. *Child Development, 72*, 474–490.

Koehler, J. J. (1996). The base rate fallacy reconsidered: Descriptive, normative, and methodological challenges. *Behavioral Brain Sciences, 19*, 1–53.

Koester, J., & Siegelbaum, S. A. (2000). Propagated signaling: The action potential. In E. R. Kandel, J. H. Schwartz, & T. M. Jessell (Eds.), *Principles of neural science* (pp. 150–174). New York: McGraw-Hill.

Kohlberg, L. (1963). The development of children's orientations toward a moral order: I. Sequence in the development of moral thought. *Vita Humana, 6*, 11–33.

Kohlberg, L. (1969). Stage and sequence: The cognitive-developmental approach to socialization. In D. A. Goslin (Ed.), *Handbook of socialization theory and research*. Chicago: Rand McNally.

Kohlberg, L. (1976). Moral stages and moralization: Cognitive-developmental approach. In T. Lickona (Ed.), *Moral development and behavior: Theory, research and social issues*. New York: Holt, Rinehart & Winston.

Kohlberg, L. (1984). *Essays on moral development, Vol. 2: The psychology of moral development*. San Francisco: Harper & Row.

Kohut, H. (1971). *Analysis of the self*. New York: International Universities Press.

Kolb, B., Gibb, R., & Robinson, T. E. (2003). Brain plasticity and behavior. *Current Directions in Psychological Science, 12*, 1–5.

Kolb, B., & Whishaw, I. Q. (1998). Brain plasticity and behavior. *Annual Review of Psychology, 49*, 43–64.

Kop, W. J., Gottdiener, J. S., & Krantz, D. S. (2001). Stress and silent ischemia. In A. Baum, T. A. Revenson, & J. E. Singer (Eds.), *Handbook of health psychology* (pp. 669–682). Mahwah, NJ: Erlbaum.

Kopta, S. M., Lueger, R. J., Saunders, S. M., & Howard, K. I. (1999). Individual psychotherapy outcome and process research: Challenges leading to greater turmoil or a positive transition? *Annual Review of Psychology, 50*, 441–69.

Koren, D., Arnon, I., & Klein, E. (1999). Acute stress response and posttraumatic stress disorder in traffic accident victims: A one-year prospective, follow-up study. *American Journal of Psychiatry, 156*, 367–373.

Koriat, A., & Bjork, R. A. (2005). Illusions of competence in monitoring one's knowledge during study. *Journal of Experimental Psychology: Learning, Memory, and Cognition, 31*(2), 187–194.

Koriat, A., Goldsmith, M., & Pansky, A. (2000). Toward a psychology of memory accuracy. *Annual Review of Psychology, 51*, 481–537.

Koriat, A., Lichtenstein, S., & Fischhoff, B. (1980). Reasons for confidence. *Journal of Experimental Psychology, 6*, 107–118.

Korn, J. H. (1987). Judgments of acceptability of deception in psychological research. *Journal of General Psychology, 114*, 205–216.

Korn, J. H. (1997). *Illusions of reality: A history of deception in social psychology*. Albany: State University of New York Press.

Kornhaber, M. L. (2004). Multiple intelligences: From the ivory tower to the dusty classroom—But why? *Teachers College Record, 106*(1), 57–76.

Kostreva, M., McNelis, E., & Clemens, E. (2002). Using a circadian rhythms model to evaluate shift schedules. *Ergonomics, 45*, 739–763.

Kotovsky, K., Hayes, J. R., & Simon, H. A. (1985). Why are some problems hard? Evidence from Tower of Hanoi. *Cognitive Psychology, 17*, 248–294.

Kotulak, R. (1996). *Inside the brain: Revolutionary discoveries of how the mind works*. Kansas City: Andrews McMeel.

Kracke, W. (1991). Myths in dreams, thought in images: An Amazonian contribution to the psychoanalytic theory of primary process. In B. Tedlock (Ed.), *Dreaming: Anthropological and psychological interpretations*. Santa Fe, NM: School of American Research Press.

Kracke, W. (1992). Languages of dreaming: Anthropological approaches to the study of dreaming in other cultures. In J. Gackenback & A. Sheik (Eds.), *Dream images: A call to mental arms*. Amityville, NY: Baywood.

Krakauer, D., & Dallenbach, K. M. (1937). Gustatory adaptation to sweet, sour, and bitter. *American Journal of Psychology, 49*, 469–475.

Krakauer, J. (1998). *Into thin air: A personal account of the Mount Everest disaster*. New York: Villard.

Kramer, M. (1994). The scientific study of dreaming. In M. H. Kryger, T. Roth, & W. C. Dement (Eds.),

Principles and practice of sleep medicine (2nd ed.). Philadelphia: Saunders.

Kransny, L., Williams, B. J., Provencal, S., & Ozonoff, S. (2003). Social skills interventions for the autism spectrum: Essential ingredients and a model curriculum. *Child and Adolescent Psychiatric Clinics of North America, 12*(1), 107–122.

Krantz, D. S., & McCeney, M. K. (2002). Effects of psychological and social factors on organic disease: A critical assessment of research on coronary heart disease. *Annual Review of Psychology, 53,* 341–369.

Krantz, D. S., Sheps, D. S., Carney, R. M., & Natelson, B. H. (2000). Effects of mental stress in patients with coronary artery disease. *Journal of the American Medical Association, 283,* 1800–1802.

Krebs, D. L., & Denton, K. (1997). Social illusions and self-deception: The evolution of biases in person perception. In J. A. Simpson & D. T. Kenrick (Eds.), *Evolutionary social psychology.* Mahwah, NJ: Erlbaum.

Kroger, J. (1995). The differentiation of "firm" and "developmental" foreclosure identity statuses: A longitudinal study. *Journal of Adolescent Research, 10,* 317–337.

Kroger, J. (1996). Identity, regression, and development. *Journal of Adolescence, 19,* 203–222.

Kroger, J. (2003). Identity development during adolescence. In G. R. Adams & M. D. Berzonsky (Eds.), *Blackwell handbook of adolescence.* Malden, MA: Blackwell Publishing.

Krosnick, J. A. (1999). Survey research. *Annual Review Psychology, 50,* 537–567.

Krosnick, J. A., & Fabrigar, L. R. (1998). *Designing good questionnaires: Insights from psychology.* New York: Oxford University Press.

Krueger, J. (1996). Personal beliefs and cultural stereotypes about racial characteristics. *Journal of Personality and Social Psychology, 71,* 536–548.

Krueger, J., Ham, J. J., & Linford, K. M. (1996). Perceptions of behavioral consistency: Are people aware of the actor-observer effect? *Psychological Science, 7,* 259–264.

Krueger, W. C. F. (1929). The effect of overlearning on retention. *Journal of Experimental Psychology, 12,* 71–78.

Kruglanski, A. W., & Stroebe, W. (2005). The influence of beliefs and goals on attitudes: Issues of structure, function, and dynamics. In D. Albarracin, B. T. Johnson, & M. P. Zanna (Eds.), *The handbook of attitudes.* Mahwah, NJ: Erlbaum.

Krull, D. S. (2001). On partitioning the fundamental attribution error: Dispositionalism and the correspondence bias. In G. B. Moskowitz (Ed.), *Cognitive social psychology: The Princeton Symposium on the legacy and future of social cognition.* Mahwah, NJ: Erlbaum.

Krull, D. S., & Erickson, D. J. (1995). Inferential hopscotch: How people draw social inferences from behavior. *Current Directions in Psychological Science, 4,* 35–38.

Kryger, M. H. (1993). Snoring. In M. A. Carskadon (Ed.), *Encyclopedia of sleep and dreaming.* New York: Macmillan.

Kryger, M. H., Roth, T., & Dement, W. C. (2005). *Principles and practice of sleep medicine.* Philadelphia: Elsevier Saunders.

Kulick, A. R., Pope, H. G., & Keck, P. E. (1990). Lycanthropy and self-identification. *Journal of Nervous & Mental Disease, 178*(2), 134–137.

Kumar, V. M. (2004). Body temperature and sleep: Are they controlled by the same mechanism? *Sleep & Biological Rhythms, 2*(2), 103–125.

Kupfermann, I., Kandel, E. R., & Iversen, S. (2000). Motivational and addictive states. In E. R. Kandel, J. H. Schwartz, & T. M. Jessell (Eds.), *Principles of neural science.* New York: McGraw-Hill.

Kutchins, H., & Kirk, S. A. (1997). *Making us crazy: DSM—The psychiatric Bible and the creation of mental disorders.* New York: Free Press.

La Cerra, P., & Kurzban, R. (1995). The structure of scientific revolutions and the nature of the adapted mind. *Psychological Inquiry, 6,* 62–65.

LaBar, K. S., & LeDoux, J. E. (2003). Emotional learning circuits in animals and humans. In R. J. Davidson, K. R. Scherer, & H. H. Goldsmith (Eds.), *Handbook of affective sciences.* New York: Oxford University Press.

LaBine, S. J., & LaBine, G. (1996). Determinations of negligence and the hindsight bias. *Law & Human Behavior, 20,* 501–516.

Lachman, S. J. (1996). Processes in perception: Psychological transformations of highly structured stimulus material. *Perceptual and Motor Skills, 83,* 411–418.

Lachter, J., Forster, K. I., & Ruthruff, E. (2004). Forty-five years after Broadbent (1958): Still no identification without attention. *Psychological Review, 111,* 880–913.

Laitinen, J., Ek, E., & Sovio, U. (2002). Stress-related eating and drinking behavior and body mass index and predictors of this behavior. *Preventive Medicine: An International Journal Devoted to Practice & Theory, 34,* 29–39.

Lakein, A. (1996). *How to get control of your time and your life.* New York: New American Library.

Lamb, H. R. (1998). Deinstitutionalization at the beginning of the new millenium. *Harvard Review of Psychiatry, 6,* 1–10.

Lamb, M. E., Hwang, C. P., Ketterlinus, R. D., & Fracasso, M. P. (1999). Parent-child relationships: Development in the context of the family. In M. H. Bornstein & M. E. Lamb (Eds.), *Developmental psychology and advanced textbook.* Mahwah, NJ: Erlbaum.

Lamb, M. E., Ketterlinus, R. D., & Fracasso, M. P. (1992). Parent-child relationships. In M. H. Bornstein & M. E. Lamb (Eds.), *Developmental psychology: An advanced textbook* (3rd ed.). Hillsdale, NJ: Erlbaum.

Lambert, M. J., & Barley, D. E. (2001). Research summary on the therapeutic relationship and psychotherapy outcome. *Psychotherapy: Theory, Research, Practice, Training, 38,* 357–361.

Lambert, M. J., & Bergin, A. E. (1992). Achievements and limitations of psychotherapy research. In D. K. Freedheim (Ed.), *History of psychotherapy: A century of change.* Washington, DC: American Psychological Association.

Lambert, M. J., Bergin, A. E., & Garfield, S. L. (2004). Introduction and historical overview. In M. J. Lambert (Ed.), *Bergin and Garfield's handbook of psychotherapy and behavior change.* New York: Wiley.

Lambert, M. J., Hansen, N. B., & Finch, A. E. (2001). Using patient-focused research: Using patient outcome data to enhance treatment effects. *Journal of Counseling and Clinical Psychology, 69,* 159–172.

Lambert, M. J., & Ogles, B. M. (2004). The efficacy and effectiveness of psychotherapy. In M. J. Lambert (Ed.), *Bergin and Garfield's handbook of psychotherapy and behavior change.* New York: Wiley.

Lampe, A., Soellner, W., Krismer, M., Rumpold, G., Kantner-Rumplmair, W., Ogon, M., & Rathner, G. (1998). The impact of stressful life events on exacerbation of chronic low-back pain. *Journal of Psychosomatic Research, 44,* 555–563.

Lampinen, J. M., Neuschatz, J. S., & Payne, D. G. (1999). Source attributions and false memories: A test of the demand characteristics account. *Psychonomic Bulletin & Review, 6,* 130–135.

Landabaso, M. A., Iraurgi, I., Sanz, J., Calle, R., Ruiz de Apodaka, J., Jimenez-Lerma, J. M., & Gutierrez-Fraile, M. (1999). Naltrexone in the treatment of alcoholism. Two-year follow up results. *European Journal of Psychiatry, 13,* 97–105.

Landel-Graham, J., Yount, S. E., & Rudnicki, S. R. (2003). Diabetes mellitus. In A. M. Nezu, C. M. Nezu, & P. A. Geller (Eds.). *Handbook of psychology, Vol. 9: Health psychology.* New York: Wiley.

Lang, P. J. (1995). The emotion probe: Studies of motivation and attention. *American Psychologist, 50,* 372–385.

Langdon, P. E., Yagueez, L., Brown, J., & Hope, A. (2001). Who walks through the "revolving door" of a British psychiatric hospital? *Journal of Mental Health (UK), 10,* 525–533.

Lange, C. (1885). One leuds beveegelser. In K. Dunlap (Ed.), *The emotions.* Baltimore: Williams & Wilkins.

Langlois, J. H., Kalakanis, L., Rubenstein, A. J., Larson, A., Hallam, M., & Smoot, M. (2000). Maxims or myths of beauty? A meta-analytic and theoretical review. *Psychological Bulletin, 126,* 390–423.

Lanyon, R. I., & Goodstein, L. D. (1997). *Personality assessment.* New York: Wiley.

Lapierre, Y. D. (2003). Suicidality with selective serotonin reuptake inhibitors: Valid claim? *Journal of Psychiatry & Neuroscience, 28,* 340–347.

Lareau, A. (2003). *Unequal childhoods: Class, race, and family life.* Berkeley: University of California Press.

Larsen, J. T., McGraw, A. P., Mellers, B. A., & Cacioppo, J. T. (2004). The agony of victory and thrill of defeat: Mixed emotional reactions to disappointing wins and relieving losses. *Psychological Science, 15,* 325–330.

Larson, R., Richards, M., Moneta, G., Holmbeck, G., & Duckett, E. (1996). Changes in adolescents' daily interactions with their families from ages 10 to 18: Disengagement and transformation. *Developmental Psychology, 32,* 744–754.

Latané, B. (1981). The psychology of social impact. *American Psychologist, 36,* 343–356.

Latané, B., & Nida, S. A. (1981). Ten years of research on group size and helping. *Psychological Bulletin, 89,* 308–324.

Latané, B., Williams, K., & Harkins, S. (1979). Many hands make light the work: The causes and consequences of social loafing. *Journal of Personality and Social Psychology, 37,* 822–832.

Lattal, K. A. (1992). B. F. Skinner and psychology [Introduction to the Special Issue]. *American Psychologist, 27,* 1269–1272.

Latz, S., Wolf, A. W., & Lozoff, B. (1999). Cosleeping in context: Sleep practices and problems in young children in Japan and United States. *Archives of Pediatrics & Adolescent Medicine, 153,* 339–346.

Laughlin, H. (1967). *The neuroses.* Washington, DC: Butterworth.

Laughlin, H. (1979). *The ego and its defenses.* New York: Aronson.

Laumann, E. O., Gagnon, J. H., Michael, R. T., & Michaels, S. (1994). *The social organization of sexuality: Sexual practices in the United States.* Chicago: University of Chicago Press.

Laursen, B., Coy, K. C., & Collins, W. A. (1998). Reconsidering changes in parent-child conflict across adolescence: A meta-analysis. *Child Development, 69,* 817–832.

Lavie, P. (2001). Sleep-wake as a biological rhythm. *Annual Review of Psychology, 52,* 277–303.

Lavin, C., & Kavesh, L. (1988). *Tales from the front.* New York: Doubleday.

Lavine, H., Sweeney, D., & Wagner, S. H. (1999). Depicting women as sex objects in television advertising: Effects on body dissatisfaction. *Personality and Social Psychology Bulletin, 25,* 1049–1058.

Lawless, H. T. (2001). Taste. In E. B. Goldstein (Ed.), *Blackwell handbook of perception.* Malden, MA: Blackwell.

Lazarus, A. A. (1995). Different types of eclecticism and integration: Let's be aware of the dangers. *Journal of Psychotherapy Integration, 5,* 27–39.

Lazarus, R. S. (1991). *Emotion and adaptation.* New York: Oxford University Press.

Lazarus, R. S. (1993). Why we should think of stress as a subset of emotion. In L. Goldberger & S. Breznitz (Eds.), *Handbook of stress: Theoretical and clinical aspects* (2nd ed.). New York: Free Press.

Lazarus, R. S. (1999). *Stress and emotion: A new synthesis.* New York: Springer Publishing Company.

Lazarus, R. S. (2003). Does the positive psychology movement have legs? *Psychological Inquiry, 14*(2), 93–109.

Leahey, T. H. (1992). The mythical revolutions of American psychology. *American Psychologist, 47,* 308–318.

Leavitt, F. (1995). *Drugs and behavior* (3rd ed.). Thousand Oaks, CA: Sage.

Leavitt, F. (2001). Iatrogenic recovered memories: Examining the empirical evidence. *American Journal of Forensic Psychology, 19*(2), 21–32.

LeBoeuf, R. A., & Shafir, E. B. (2005). Decision making. In K. J. Holyoak & R. G. Morrison (Eds.), *The Cambridge handbook of thinking and reasoning.* New York: Cambridge University Press.

LeDoux, J. E. (1994). Emotion, memory and the brain. *Scientific American, 270,* 50–57.

LeDoux, J. E. (1995). Emotion: Clues from the brain. *Annual Review of Psychology, 46,* 209–235.

LeDoux, J. E. (1996). *The emotional brain.* New York: Simon & Schuster.

LeDoux, J. E. (2000). Emotion circuits in the brain. *Annual Review of Neuroscience, 23,* 155–184.

Lee, I.-M., Karon, J. M., Selik, R., Neal, J. J., & Fleming, P. L. (2001b). Survival after AIDS diagnosis in adolescents and adults during the treatment era, United States, 1984–1997. *Journal of the American Medical Association, 285,* 1308–1315.

Lee, I.-M., Rexrode, K. M., Cook, N. R., Manson, J. E., & Buring, J. E. (2001a). Physical activity and coronary heart disease in women: Is "no pain, no gain" passé? *Journal of the American Medical Association, 285,* 1447–1454.

Lee, I.-M., & Skerrett, P. J. (2001). Physical activity and all-cause mortality: What is the dose-response relation? *Medicine and Science in Sports and Exercise, 33,* S459–S471.

Lee, R. M., & Ramirez, M. (2000). The history, current status, and future of multicultural psychotherapy. In I. Cuellar & F. A. Paniagua (Eds.), *Handbook of multicultural mental health: Assessment and treatment of diverse populations.* San Diego: Academic Press.

Lee, S. (2000) *Wild thing.* [Web Page]. Retrieved July 2, 2002 from http://www.usaweekend.com/00_issues/000618/000618croc_hunter.html.

Lee, S., & Katzman, M. A. (2002). Cross-cultural perspectives on eating disorders. In C. G. Fairburn & K. D. Brownell (Eds.), *Eating disorders and obesity: A comprehensive handbook.* New York: Guilford.

Leeper, R. W. (1935). A study of a neglected portion of the field of learning: The development of sensory organization. *Journal of Genetic Psychology, 46,* 41–75.

Lefcourt, H. M. (2001). The humor solution. In C. R. Snyder (Ed.), *Coping with stress: Effective people and processes* (pp. 68–92). New York: Oxford University Press.

Lefcourt, H. M., Davidson, K., Shepherd, R., Phillips, M., Prkachin, K., & Mills, D. (1995). Perspective-taking humor: Accounting for stress moderation. *Journal of Social and Clinical Psychology, 14,* 373–391.

Leff, J., & Vaughn, C. (1985). *Expressed emotion in families.* New York: Guilford.

Leff, J., Trieman, N., & Gooch, C. (1996). Team for the Assessment of Psychiatric Services (TAPS) Project 33: Prospective follow-up study of long-stay patients discharged from two psychiatric hospitals. *American Journal of Psychiatry, 153,* 1318–1324.

Lehman, D. R., Chiu, C., & Schaller, M. (2004). Psychology and culture. *Annual Review of Psychology, 55,* 689–714.

Lehrer, P. M., & Woolfolk, R. L. (1984). Are stress reduction techniques interchangeable, or do they have specific effects? A review of the comparative empirical literature. In R. L. Woolfolk & P. M. Lehrer (Eds.), *Principles and practice of stress management.* New York: Guilford.

Lehrer, P. M., & Woolfolk, R. L. (1993). Specific effects of stress management techniques. In P. M. Lehrer & R. L. Woolfolk (Eds.), *Principles and practice of stress management* (2nd ed.). New York: Guilford.

Leibovic, K. N. (1990). Vertebrate photoreceptors. In K. N. Leibovic (Ed.), *Science of vision.* New York: Springer-Verlag.

Leighton, J. P., & Sternberg, R. J. (2003). Reasoning and problem solving. In A. F. Healy & R. W. Proctor (Eds.), *Handbook of psychology, Vol. 4: Experimental psychology.* New York: Wiley.

LeMagnen, J. (1981). The metabolic basis of dual periodicity of feeding in rats. *Behavioral and Brain Sciences, 4,* 561–607.

Lemme, B. H. (1999). *Development in adulthood.* Boston: Allyn & Bacon.

Lennie, P. (2000). Color vision. In E. R. Kandel, J. H. Schwartz, & T. M. Jessell (Eds.), *Principles of neural science.* New York: McGraw-Hill.

Leo, J. (1987, January). Exploring the traits of twins. *Time,* p. 63.

Lepine, R., Barrouillet, P., & Camos, V. (2005). What makes working memory spans so predictive of high-level cognition? *Psychonomic Bulletin & Review, 12*(1), 165–170.

Lerman, H. (1986). *A mote in Freud's eye: From psychoanalysis to the psychology of women.* New York: Springer.

Lerner, J. S., Small, D. A., & Loewenstein, G. (2004). Heart strings and purse strings: Carryover effects of emotions on economic decisions. *Psychological Science, 15,* 337–341.

Lett, H. S., Blumenthal, J. A., Babyak, M. A., Sherwood, A., Strauman, T., Robbins, C., & Newman, M. F. (2004). Depression as a risk factor for coronary artery disease: Evidence, mechanisms, and treatment. *Psychosomatic Medicine, 66,* 305–315.

LeVay, S. (1996). *Queer science: The use and abuse of research into homosexuality.* Cambridge, MA: MIT Press.

Levenson, R. W. (1992). Autonomic nervous system differences among emotions. *Psychological Science, 3,* 23–27.

Levenson, R. W. (2003). Autonomic specificity and emotion. In R. J. Davidson, K. R. Scherer, & H. H. Goldsmith (Eds.), *Handbook of affective sciences.* New York: Oxford University Press.

Leventhal, H. & Tomarken, A. J. (1986). Emotions: Today's problems. *Annual Review of Psychology, 37,* 565–610.

Levin, S., Henry, P. J., Pratto, F., & Sidanius, J. (2003). Social dominance and social identity in Lebanon: Implications for support of violence against the West. *Group Processes and Intergroup Relations, 6,* 353–368.

Levine, J. M. (1999). Solomon Asch's legacy for group research. *Personality and Social Psychology Review, 3,* 358–364.

Levine, M. W. (2001). Principles of neural processing. In E. B. Goldstein (Ed.), *Blackwell handbook of perception.* Malden, MA: Blackwell.

Levine, R., & Norenzayan, A. (1999). The pace of life in 31 countries. *Journal of Cross-Cultural Psychology, 30,* 178–205.

Levine, R., Sata, S., Hashimoto, T., & Verma, J. (1995). Love and marriage in eleven cultures. *Journal of Cross-Cultural Psychology, 26,* 554–571.

Levinson, D. J., with Darrow, C. M., Klein, E. G., Levinson, M. H., & McKee, B. (1978). *The seasons of a man's life.* New York: Knopf.

Levinthal, C. F. (2002). *Drugs, behavior, and modern society.* Boston: Allyn & Bacon.

Levis, D. J. (1989). The case for a return to a two-factor theory of avoidance: The failure of non-fear interpretations. In S. B. Klein & R. R. Bowrer (Eds.), *Contemporary learning theories: Pavlovian conditioning and the status of traditional learning theory.* Hillsdale NJ: Erlbaum.

Levy, G. D., Taylor, M. G., & Gelman, S. A. (1995). Traditional and evaluative aspects of flexibility in gender roles, social conventions, moral rules, and physical laws. *Child Development, 66,* 515–531.

Levy, J. (1985, May). Right brain, left brain: Fact or fiction. *Psychology Today,* 38–44.

Levy, J., Trevarthen, C., & Sperry, R. W. (1972). Perception of bilateral chimeric figures following hemispheric disconnection. *Brain, 95,* 61–78.

Lewandowsky, S., Duncan, M., & Brown, G. D. A. (2004). Time does not cause forgetting in short-term serial recall. *Psychonomic Bulletin & Review, 11*(5), 771–790.

Lewin, K. (1935). *A dynamic theory of personality.* New York: McGraw-Hill.

Lewis, D. O., Yeager, C. A., Swica, Y., Pincus, J. H., & Lewis, M. (1997). Objective documentation of child abuse and dissociation in 12 murderers with dissociative identity disorder. *American Journal of Psychiatry, 154,* 1703–1710.

Li, N. P., Bailey, J. M., Kenrick, D. T., & Linsenmeier, J. A. W. (2002). The necessities and luxuries of mate preferences: Testing the tradeoffs. *Journal of Personality and Social Psychology, 82,* 947–955.

Libby, P., Ridker, P. M., & Maseri, A. (2002). Inflammation and atherosclerosis. *Circulation, 105,* 1135–1143.

Lichtenstein, S., Fischhoff, B., & Phillips, L. (1982). Calibration of probabilities: The state of the art to 1980. In D. Kahneman, P. Slovic, & A. Tversky (Eds.), *Judgment under uncertainty: Heuristics and biases.* Cambridge, England: Cambridge University Press.

Lickey, M. E., & Gordon, B. (1991). *Medicine and mental illness: The use of drugs in psychiatry.* New York: W. H. Freeman.

Lickliter, R., & Honeycutt, H. (2003). Developmental dynamics: Toward a biologically plausible evolutionary psychology. *Psychological Bulletin, 129,* 819–835.

Lieberman, J. A., Tollefson, G., Tohen, M., Green, A. I., Gur, R. E., Kahn, R., McEvoy, J., Perkins, D., Sharma, T., Zipursky, R., Wei, H., Hamer, R. M., & HGDH Group Study. (2003). Comparative efficacy and safety of atypical and conventional antipsychotic drugs in first-episode psychosis: A randomized double-blind trial of olazapine versus haloperidol. *American Journal of Psychiatry, 160,* 1396–1404.

Liebert, R. M., & Liebert, L. L. (1998). *Liebert & Spiegler's personality strategies and issues.* Pacific Grove: Brooks/Cole.

Lilienfeld, S. O., & Lynn, S. J. (2003). Dissociative identity disorder: Multiple personalities, multiple controversies. In S. O. Lilienfeld, S. J. Lynn, & J. M. Lohr (Eds.), *Science and pseudoscience in clinical psychology.* New York: Guilford.

Lilienfeld, S. O., Lynn, S. J., Kirsch, I., Chaves, J. F., Sarbin, T. R., Ganaway, G. K., & Powell, R. A. (1999). Dissociative identity disorder and the sociocognitive model: Recalling the lessons of the past. *Psychological Bulletin, 125,* 507–523.

Lilienfeld, S. O., Wood, J. M., & Garb, H. N. (2000). The scientific status of projective tests. *Psychological Science in the Public Interest, 1*(2), 27–66.

Lin, S. W., & Anthnelli, R. M. (2005). Genetic factors in the risk for substance use disorders. In J. H. Lowinson, P. Ruiz, R. B. Millman, & J. G. Langrod (Eds.), *Substance abuse: A comprehensive textbook.* Philadelphia: Lippincott/Williams & Wilkins.

Lindgren, H. C. (1969). *The psychology of college success: A dynamic approach.* New York: Wiley.

Lindsay, M., & Lester, D. (2004). *Suicide by cop: Committing suicide by provoking police to shoot you (death, value and meaning).* Amityville, NY: Baywood Publishing.

Lindsay, P. H., & Norman, D. A. (1977). *Human information processing.* New York: Academic Press.

Lindsay, S. D., Allen, B. P., Chan, J. C. K., & Dahl, L. C. (2004). Eyewitness suggestibility and source similarity: Intrusions of details from one event into memory reports of another event. *Journal of Memory & Language, 50*(1), 96–111.

Lindsay, S. D., & Read, J. D. (2001). The recovered memories controversy: Where do we go from here? In G. M. Davies & T. Dalgleish (Eds.), *Recovered memories: Seeking the middle ground.* Chichester, England: Wiley.

Linnet, K. M., Dalsgaard, S., Obel, C., Wisborg, K., Henriksen, T. B., Rodriguez, A., Kotimaa, A., Moilanen, I., Thomsen, P. H., Olsen, J., & Jarvelin, M. (2003). Maternal lifestyle factors in pregnancy risk of attention deficit hyperactivity disorder and associated behaviors: Review of the current evidence. *American Journal of Psychiatry, 160,* 1028–1040.

Lippa, R. A. (1994). *Introduction to social psychology.* Pacific Grove, CA: Brooks/Cole.

Lisanby, S. H., Maddox, J. H., Prudic, J., Devanand, D. P., & Sackeim, H. A. (2000). The effects of electro-convulsive therapy on memory of autobiographical and public events. *General Psychiatry, 57,* 581–590.

Livesley, W. J., Jang, K. L., & Vernon, P. A. (2003). Genetic basis of personality structure. In T. Millon & M. J. Lerner (Eds.), *Handbook of psychology, Vol. 5: Personality and social psychology.* New York: Wiley.

Lizarraga, M. L. S., & Ganuza, J. M. G. (2003). Improvement of mental rotation in girls and boys. *Sex Roles, 40,* 277–286.

Lockhart, R. S. (1992). Measurement of memory. In L. R. Squire (Ed.), *Encyclopedia of learning and memory.* New York: Macmillan.

Lockhart, R. S. (2000). Methods of memory research. In E. Tulving & F. I. M. Craik (Eds.), *The Oxford handbook of memory* (pp. 45–58). New York: Oxford University Press.

Lockhart, R. S., & Craik, F. I. (1990). Levels of processing: A retrospective commentary on a framework for memory research. *Canadian Journal of Psychology, 44*(1), 87–112.

Locurto, C. (1990). The malleability of IQ as judged from adoption studies. *Intelligence, 14,* 275–292.

Loehlin, J. C. (1992). *Genes and environment in personality development.* Newbury Park, CA: Sage.

Loehlin, J. C. (2000). Group differences in intelligence. In R. J. Sternberg (Ed.), *Handbook of intelligence* (pp. 176–195). New York: Cambridge University Press.

Loehlin, J. C., Horn, J. M., & Willerman, L. (1997). Heredity, environment, and IQ in the Texas Adoption Project. In R. J. Sternberg & E. L. Grigorenko (Eds.), *Intelligence, heredity, and environment.* New York: Cambridge University Press.

Loewenstein, R. J. (1996). Dissociative amnesia and dissociative fugue. In L. K. Michelson & W. J. Ray (Eds.), *Handbook of dissociation: Theoretical, empirical, and clinical perspectives.* New York: Plenum.

Loftus, E. F. (1979). *Eyewitness testimony.* Cambridge, MA: Harvard University Press.

Loftus, E. F. (1992). When a lie becomes memory's truth: Memory distortion after exposure to misinformation. *Current Directions in Psychological Science, 1,* 121–123.

Loftus, E. F. (1993). Psychologist in the eyewitness world. *American Psychologist, 48,* 550–552.

Loftus, E. F. (1994). The repressed memory controversy. *American Psychologist, 49,* 443–445.

Loftus, E. F. (1997, September). Creating false memories. *Scientific American,* 71–75.

Loftus, E. F. (1998). Remembering dangerously. In R. A. Baker (Ed.), *Child sexual abuse and false memory syndrome.* Amherst, NY: Prometheus Books.

Loftus, E. F. (2003). Make believe memories. *American Psychologist, 58,* 864–873.

Loftus, E. F. (2004). Memories of things unseen. *Current Directions in Psychological Science, 13*(4), 145–147.

Loftus, E. F., & Bernstein, D. M. (2005). Rich false memories: The royal road to success. In A. F. Healy (Ed.), *Experimental cognitive psychology and its applications.* Washington, DC: American Psychological Association.

Loftus, E. F., & Ketcham, K. (1994). *The myth of repressed memory: False memories and allegations of sexual abuse.* New York: St. Martin's Press.

Loftus, E. F., & Palmer, J. C. (1974). Reconstruction of automobile destruction: An example of the interaction between language and memory. *Journal of Verbal Learning and Verbal Behavior, 13,* 585–589.

Logie, R. H., Zucco, G. M., & Baddelely, A. D. (1990). Interference with visual short-term-memory. *Acta Psycholgica, 75,* 55–74.

Logue, A. W. (1991). *The psychology of eating and drinking* (2nd ed.). New York: W. H. Freeman.

Long, J. E., Jr. (2005). Power to prescribe: The debate over prescription privileges for psychologists and the legal issues implicated. *Law & Psychology, 29,* 243–260.

Longman, D. G., & Atkinson, R. H. (2002). *College learning and study skills.* Belmont, CA: Wadsworth.

Lott, B. (1987). *Women's lives.* Pacific Grove, CA: Brooks/Cole.

Lott, B. (2002). Cognitive and behavioral distancing from the poor. *American Psychologist, 57,* 100–110.

Lowden, A., Akerstedt, T., & Wibom, R. (2004). Suppression of sleepiness and melatonin by bright light exposure during breaks in night work. *Journal of Sleep Research, 12*(1), 37–43.

Lowinson, J. H., Ruiz, P., Millman, R. B., & Langrod, J. G. (2005). *Substance abuse: A comprehensive textbook.* Philadelphia: Lippincott/Williams & Wilkins.

Luborsky, L., Rosenthal, R., Diguer, L., Andrusyna, T. P., Berman, J. S., Levitt, J. T., Seligman, D. A., & Krause, E. D. (2002). The dodo bird verdict is alive and well—mostly. *Clinical Psychology: Science & Practice, 9,* 2–12.

Luborsky, L., Singer, B., & Luborsky, L. (1975). Comparative studies of psychotherapies: Is it true that everyone has won and all must have prizes? *Archives of General Psychiatry, 32,* 995–1008.

Lucas, R. E., Clark, A. E., Georgellis, Y., & Diener, E. (2003). Reexamining adaptation and set point model of happiness: Reactions to changes in marital status. *Journal of Personality and Social Psychology, 84,* 527–539.

Lucas, R. E., Clark, A. E., Georgellis, Y., & Diener, E. (2004). Unemployment alters the set point for life satisfaction. *Psychological Science, 15*(1), 8–13.

Lucas, R. E., Diener, E., & Suh, E. (1996). Discriminant validity of well-being measures. *Journal of Personality and Social Psychology, 71,* 616–628.

Luchins, A. S. (1942). Mechanization in problem solving. *Psychological Monographs, 54* (6, Whole No. 248).

Ludwig, A. M. (1994). Mental illness and creative activity in female writers. *American Journal of Psychiatry, 151,* 1650–1656.

Ludwig, A. M. (1995). *The price of greatness: Resolving the creativity and madness controversy.* New York: Guilford.

Ludwig, A. M. (1998). Method and madness in the arts and sciences. *Creativity Research Journal, 11,* 93–101.

Ludwig, D. S., Pereira, M. A., Kroenke, C. H., Hilner, J. E., Van Horn, L., Slattery, M. L., & Jacobs, D. R., Jr. (1999). Dietary fiber, weight gain, and cardiovascular disease risk factors in young adults. *Journal of the American Medical Association, 282,* 1539–1546.

Luecke-Aleksa, D., Anderson, D. R., Collins, P. A., & Schmitt, K. L. (1995). Gender constancy and television viewing. *Developmental Psychology, 31,* 773–780.

Luft, A. R., Buitrago, M. M., Ringer, T., Schulz, J. B., & Dichgans, J. (2004). Motor skill learning depends on protein synthesis in motor cortex after training. *Journal of Neuroscience, 24,* 6515–6520.

Lugaresi, E., Cirignotta, F., Montagna, P., & Sforza, E. (1994). Snoring: Pathogenic, clinical, and therapeutic aspects. In M. H. Kryger, T. Roth, & W. C.

Dement (Eds.), *Principles and practice of sleep medicine* (2nd ed.). Philadelphia: Saunders.

Luh, C. W. (1922). The conditions of retention. *Psychological Monographs, 31*.

Lundberg, U. (2000). Catecholamines. In G. Fink (Ed.), *Encyclopedia of stress* (Vol. 1, pp. 408–413). San Diego: Academic Press.

Luo, S., & Klohen, E. C. (2005). Assortative mating and marital quality in newlyweds: A couple-centered approach. *Journal of Personality and Social Psychology, 88*, 304–326.

Lutz, C. (1987). Goals, events and understanding in Ifaluk emotion theory. In N. Quinn & D. Holland (Eds.), *Cultural models in language and thought.* Cambridge, England: Cambridge University Press.

Lutz, D. J., & Sternberg, R. J. (1999). Cognitive development. In M. H. Bornstein & M. E. Lamb (Eds.), *Developmental psychology: An advanced textbook.* Mahwah, NJ: Erlbaum.

Lye, D. N., & Biblarz, T. J. (1993). The effects of attitudes toward family life and gender roles on marital satisfaction. *Journal of Family Issues, 14*, 157–188.

Lykken, D. T. (1998). *A tremor in the blood: Uses and abuses of the lie detector.* New York: Plenum Press.

Lykken, D. T., McGue, M., Tellegen, A., & Bouchard, T. J., Jr. (1992). Emergenesis: Genetic traits that may not run in families. *American Psychologist, 47*, 1565–1577.

Lykken, D. T., & Tellegen, A. (1996). Happiness is a stochastic phenomenon. *Psychological Science, 7*, 186–189.

Lynn, D. J., & Vaillant, G. E. (1998). Anonymity, neutrality, and confidentiality in the actual methods of Sigmund Freud: A review of 43 cases, 1907–1939. *American Journal of Psychiatry, 155*, 163–171.

Lynn, M. (1992). Scarcity's enhancement of desirability: The role of naive economic theories. *Basic & Applied Social Psychology, 13*, 67–78.

Lynn, S. J., Kirsch, I., Barabasz, A., Cardena, E., & Patterson, D. (2000). Hypnosis as an empirically supported clinical intervention: The state of the evidence and a look to the future. *International Journal of Clinical & Experimental Hypnosis, 48*, 239–259.

Lynn, S. J., & Nash, M. (1994). Truth in memory: Ramifications for psychotherapy and hypnotherapy. *Journal of Clinical Hypnosis, 36*, 194–208.

Lytton, H. (1997). Physical punishment is a problem, whether conduct disorder is endogenous or not. *Psychological Inquiry, 8*, 211–214.

Maas, J. B. (1998). *Power sleep.* New York: Harper Perennial.

Maccoby, E. E. (2000). Parenting and its effects on children: On reading and misreading behavior genetics. *Annual Review of Psychology, 51*, 1–27.

MacCoun, R. J. (1998). Biases in the interpretation and use of research results. *Annual Review Psychology, 49*, 259–287.

MacDonald, K. (1998). Evolution, culture, and the five-factor model. *Journal of Cross-Cultural Psychology, 29*, 119–149.

Macht, M., & Simons, G. (2000). Emotions and eating in everyday life. *Appetite, 35*, 65–71.

Mack, A. (2003). Inattentional blindness: Looking without seeing. *Current Directions in Psychological Science, 12*(5), 180–184.

Mack, A., & Rock, I. (1998). *Inattentional blindness.* Cambridge, MA: MIT Press.

Mack, A. H., Franklin Jr., J. E., & Frances, R. J. (2003). Substance use disorders. In R. E. Hales & S. C. Yudofsky (Eds.), *Textbook of clinical psychiatry.* Washington, DC: American Psychiatric Publishing.

MacLean, P. D. (1954). Studies on limbic system ("viosceal brain") and their bearing on psychosomatic problems. In E. D. Wittkower & R. A. Cleghorn (Eds.), *Recent developments in psychosomatic medicine.* Philadelphia: Lippincott.

MacLean, P. D. (1993). Cerebral evolution of emotion. In M. Lewis & J. M. Haviland (Eds.), *Handbook of emotions.* New York: Guilford.

MacMillan, H. L., Fleming, J. E., Streiner, D. L., Lin, E., Boyle, M. H., Jamieson, E., Duku, E. K., Walsh, C. A., Wong, M. Y. Y., & Beardslee, W. R. (2001). Childhood abuse and lifetime psychopathology in a community sample. *American Journal of Psychiatry, 158*, 1878–1883.

MacMillan, H. L., Fleming, J. E., Trocme, N., Boyle, M. H., Wong, M., Racine, Y. A., Beardslee, W. R., & Offord, D. R. (1997). Prevalence of child physical and sexual abuse in the community: Results from the Ontario health supplement. *Journal of the American Medical Association, 278*, 131–135.

Macmillan, M. (1991). *Freud evaluated: The completed arc.* Amsterdam: North-Holland.

Macrae, C. N., & Bodenhausen, G. V. (2000). Social cognition: Thinking categorically about others. *Annual Review of Psychology, 51*, 93–120.

Maddi, S. R. (1989). *Personality theories: A comparative analysis.* Chicago, IL: Dorsey Press.

Madon, S., Guyll, M., Aboufadel, K., Montiel, E., Smith, A., Palumbo, P., & Jussim, L. (2001). Ethnic and national stereotypes: The Princeton trilogy revisited and revised. *Personality and Social Psychology Bulletin, 27*, 996–1010.

Madsen, K. B. (1968). *Theories of motivation.* Copenhagen: Munksgaard.

Madsen, K. B. (1973). Theories of motivation. In B. B. Wolman (Ed.), *Handbook of general psychology.* Englewood Cliffs, NJ: Prentice-Hall.

Maguire, W., Weisstein, N., & Klymenko, V. (1990). From visual structure to perceptual function. In K. N. Leibovic (Ed.), *Science of vision.* New York: Springer-Verlag.

Maher, B. A. (2001). Delusions. In P. B. Sutker & H. E. Adams (Eds.), *Comprehensive handbook of psychopathology* (3rd ed., pp. 309–370). New York: Kluwer Academic/Plenum Publishers.

Mahoney, M. J. (1974). *Cognition and behavior modification.* Cambridge, MA: Ballinger.

Mahowald, M. W. (1993). Sleepwalking. In M. A. Carskadon (Ed.), *Encyclopedia of sleep and dreaming.* New York: Macmillan.

Maier, N. R. F. (1931). Reasoning and learning. *Psychological Review, 38*, 332–346.

Main, T. (1998). How to think about homelessness: Balancing structural and individual causes. *Journal of Social Distress & the Homeless, 7*, 41–54.

Malcolm, J. (1980: Pt. 1, Nov. 24; Pt. 2, Dec. 1). The impossible profession. *The New Yorker*, pp. 55–133, 54–152.

Maldonado, J. R., & Spiegel, D. (2003). Dissociative disorders. In R. E. Hales & S. C. Yudofsky (Eds.), *Textbook of clinical psychiatry.* Washington, DC: American Psychiatric Publishing.

Maletzky, B. M. (2002). The paraphilias: Research and treatment. In P. E. Nathan & J. M. Gorman (Eds.), *A guide to treatments that work.* London: Oxford University Press.

Maltzman, I. (1994). Why alcoholism is a disease. *Journal of Psychoactive Drugs, 26*, 13–31.

Mandler, G. (1984). *Mind and body.* New York: Norton.

Mandler, G. (1993). Thought, memory, and learning: Effects of emotional stress. In L. Goldberger &

S. Breznitz (Eds.), *Handbook of stress: Theoretical and clinical aspects* (2nd ed.). New York: Free Press.

Mandler, G. (2002). Origins of the cognitive revolution. *Journal of the History of the Behavioral Sciences, 38*, 339–353.

Mangelsdorf, S., Gunnar, M., Kestenbaum, R., Lang, S., & Andreas, D. (1990). Infant proneness-to-distress temperament, maternal personality, and mother-infant attachment: Associations and goodness of fit. *Child Development, 61*, 830–831.

Marangell, L. B., Silver, J. M., Goff, D. C., & Yudofsky, S. C. (2003). Psychopharmacology and electroconvulsive therapy. In R. E. Hales & S. C. Yudofsky (Eds.), *Textbook of clinical psychiatry.* Washington, DC: American Psychiatric Publishing.

Marcelino, A. S., Adam, A. S., Couronne, T., Koester, E. P., & Sieffermann, J. M. (2001). Internal and external determinants of eating initiation in humans. *Appetite, 36*, 9–14.

Marcenes, W. G., & Sheiham, A. (1992). The relationship between work stress and oral health status. *Social Science and Medicine, 35*, 1511.

Marcia, J. E. (1966). Development and validation of ego identity status. *Journal of Personality and Social Psychology, 3*, 551–558.

Marcia, J. E. (1980). Identity in adolescence. In J. Adelson (Ed.), *Handbook of adolescent psychology.* New York: Wiley.

Marcia, J. E. (1994). The empirical study of ego identity. In H. A. Bosma, T. L. G. Graafsma, H. D. Grotevant, & D. J. de Levita (Eds.), *Identity and development: An interdisciplinary approach.* Thousand Oaks, CA: Sage.

Marder, S. R. (2000). Schizophrenia: Somatic treatment. In B. J. Sadock & V. A. Sadock (Eds.), *Kaplan and Sadock's comprehensive textbook of psychiatry* (7th ed., Vol. 1, pp. 1199–1209). Philadelphia: Lippincott/Williams & Wilkins.

Marder, S. R., & van Kammen, D. P. (2000). Dopamine receptor antagonists (typical antipsychotics). In B. J. Sadock & V. A. Sadock (Eds.), *Kaplan and Sadock's comprehensive textbook of psychiatry* (7th ed., Vol. 1, pp. 2356–2376). Philadelphia: Lippincott/Williams & Wilkins.

Maris, R. W., Berman, A. L., & Silverman, M. M. (2000). *Comprehensive textbook of suicidology.* New York: Guilford.

Markowitsch, H. J. (2000). Neuroanatomy of memory. In E. Tulving & F. I. M. Craik (Eds.), *The Oxford handbook of memory* (pp. 465–484). New York: Oxford University Press.

Markus, H. R., & Kitayama, S. (1991). Culture and the self: Implications for cognition, emotion, and motivation. *Psychological Review, 98*, 224–253.

Markus, H. R., & Kitayama, S. (1994). The cultural construction of self and emotion: Implications for social behavior. In S. Kitayama & H. R. Markus (Eds.), *Emotions and culture: Empirical studies of mutual influence.* Washington, DC: American Psychological Association.

Marteau, T. M., & Weinman, J. (2004). Communicating about health threats and treatments. In S. Sutton, A. Baum, & M. Johnston (Ed), *The Sage handbook of health psychology.* Thousand Oaks, CA: Sage.

Martin, C. L., & Ruble, D. (2004). Children's search for gender cues: Cognitive perspectives on gender development. *Current Directions in Psychological Science, 13*(2), 67–70.

Martin, R., & Leventhal, H. (2004). Symptom perception and health care-seeking behavior. In J. M. Raczynski & L. C. Leviton (Eds.), *Handbook of clinical health psychology, Vol. 2: Disorders of behavior and health*. Washington, DC: American Psychological Association.

Martin, R. A. (2002). IS laughter the best medicine? Humor, laughter, and physical health. *Current Directions in Psychological Science, 11*(6), 216–220.

Maslow, A. H. (1954). *Motivation and personality*. New York: Harper & Row.

Maslow, A. H. (1968). *Toward a psychology of being*. New York: Van Nostrand.

Maslow, A. H. (1970). *Motivation and personality*. New York: Harper & Row.

Maslow, A. H. (1971). *Farther reaches of human nature*. New York: Viking Penguin.

Massaro, D. W., & Loftus, G. R. (1996). Sensory and perceptual storage: Data and theory. In E. L. Bjork & R. A. Bjork (Eds.), *Memory*. San Diego: Academic Press.

Masters, W. H., & Johnson, V. E. (1966). *Human sexual response*. Boston: Little, Brown.

Masters, W. H., & Johnson, V. E. (1970). *Human sexual inadequacy*. Boston: Little, Brown.

Masuda, T., & Nisbett, R. E. (2001). Attending holistically versus analytically: Comparing the context sensitivity of Japanese and Americans. *Journal of Personality and Social Psychology, 81*, 922–934.

Matsumoto, D. (1994). *People: Psychology from a cultural perspective*. Pacific Grove, CA: Brooks/Cole.

Matsumoto, D. (2003). Cross-cultural research. In S. F. Davis (Ed.), *Handbook of research methods in experimental psychology*. Malden, MA: Blackwell Publishers.

Matthey, S. (1998). P<.05—But is it clinically *significant*?: Practical examples for clinicians. *Behaviour Change, 15*, 140–146.

Matusov, E., & Hayes, R. (2000). Sociocultural critique of Piaget and Vygotsky. *New Ideas in Psychology, 18*(2–3), 215–239.

Matute, H., & Miller, R. R. (1998). Detecting causal relations. In W. O'Donohue (Ed.), *Learning and behavior therapy*. Boston, Allyn & Bacon.

Mayer, J. (1955). Regulation of energy intake and the body weight: The glucostatic theory and the lipostatic hypothesis. *Annals of the New York Academy of Science, 63*, 15–43.

Mayer, J. (1968). *Overweight: Causes and control*. Englewood Cliffs, NJ: Prentice-Hall.

Mays, V. M., Rubin, J., Sabourin, M., & Walker, L. (1996). Moving toward a global psychology: Changing theories and practice to meet the needs of a changing world. *American Psychologist, 51*, 485–487.

McBride-Chang, C., & Jacklin, C. N. (1993). Early play arousal, sex-typed play, and activity level as precursors to later rough-and-tumble play. *Early Education & Development, 4*, 99–108.

McBurney, D. H. (1996). *How to think like a psychologist: Critical thinking in psychology*. Upper Saddle River, NJ: Prentice-Hall.

McCarley, R. W. (1994). Dreams and the biology of sleep. In M. H. Kryger, T. Roth, & W. C. Dement (Eds.), *Principles and practice of sleep medicine* (2nd ed.). Philadelphia: Saunders.

McCauley, M. E., Eskes, G., & Moscovitch, M. (1996). The effect of imagery on explicit and implicit tests of memory in young and old people: A double dissociation. *Canadian Journal of Experimental Psychology, 50*, 34–41.

McClelland, D. C. (1975). *Power: The inner experience*. New York: Irvington.

McClelland, D. C. (1985). How motives, skills and values determine what people do. *American Psychologist, 40*, 812–825.

McClelland, D. C. (1987). Characteristics of successful entrepreneurs. *Journal of Creative Behavior, 3*, 219–233.

McClelland, D. C., Atkinson, J. W., Clark, R. A., & Lowell, E. L. (1953). *The achievement motive*. New York: Appleton-Century-Crofts.

McClelland, D. C., & Boyatzis, R. E. (1982). The leadership motive pattern and long-term success in management. *Journal of Applied Psychology, 67*, 737–743.

McClelland, D. C., & Koestner, R. (1992). The achievement motive. In C. P. Smith (Ed.), *Motivation and personality: Handbook of thematic content analysis*. New York: Cambridge University Press.

McClelland, J. L. (1992). Parallel-distributed processing models of memory. In L. R. Squire (Ed.), *Encyclopedia of learning and memory*. New York: Macmillan.

McClelland, J. L. (2000). Connectionist models of memory. In E. Tulving & F. I. M. Craik (Eds.), *The Oxford handbook of memory* (pp. 583–596). New York: Oxford University Press.

McClelland, J. L., & Rogers, T. T. (2003). The parallel distributed processing approach to semantic cognition. *Nature Reviews Neuroscience, 4*, 310–322.

McClelland, J. L., & Rumelhart, D. E. (1985). Distributed memory and the representation of general and specific information. *Journal of Experimental Psychology: General, 114*, 159–188.

McClure, E. B. (2000). A meta-analytic review of sex differences in facial expression processing and their development in infants, children, and adolescents. *Psychological Bulletin, 126*, 424–453.

McConnell, J. V. (1962). Memory transfer through cannibalism in planarians. *Journal of Neuropsychiatry, 3*(Suppl. 1), 542–548.

McCrae, R. R. (1984). Situational determinants of coping responses: Loss, threat and challenge. *Journal of Personality and Social Psychology, 46*, 919–928.

McCrae, R. R. (2005). Personality structure. In V. A. Derlega, B. A. Winstead, & W. H. Jones (Eds.), *Personality: Contemporary theory and research*. Belmont, CA: Wadsworth.

McCrae, R. R., & Costa, P. T., Jr. (1987). Validation of the five-factor model of personality across instruments and observers. *Journal of Personality and Social Psychology, 52*, 81–90.

McCrae, R. R., & Costa, P. T., Jr. (1990). *Personality in adulthood*. New York: Guilford.

McCrae, R. R., & Costa, P. T., Jr. (1997). Personality trait structure as a human universal. *American Psychologist, 52*, 509–516.

McCrae, R. R., & Costa, P. T., Jr. (1999). A five-factor theory of personality. In L. A. Pervin & O. P. John (Eds.), *Handbook of personality: Theory and research*. New York: Guilford.

McCrae, R. R., & Costa, P. T., Jr. (2003). *Personality in adulthood: A five-factor theory perspective*. New York: Guilford.

McCrae, R. R., Terracciano, A., & 78 members of the Personality Profiles of Cultures Project. (2005). Universal features of personality traits from the observer's perspective: Data from 50 cultures. *Journal of Personality and Social Psychology, 88*, 547–561.

McCrink, K., & Wynn, K. (2004). Large-number addition and subtraction by 9-month-old infants. *Psychological Science, 15*, 776–781.

McCullough, M. E. (2001). Forgiving. In C. R. Snyder (Ed.), *Coping with stress: Effective people and processes* (pp. 93–113). New York: Oxford University Press.

McCullough, M. E., Bellah, C. G., Kilpatrick, S. D., & Johnson, J. L. (2001). Vengefulness: Relationships with forgiveness, rumination, well-being, and the Big Five. *Personality and Social Psychology Bulletin, 27*, 601–610.

McCullough, M. E., & Witvliet, C. V. (2002). The psychology of forgiveness. In C. R. Synder & S. J. Lopez (Eds.), *Handbook of positive psychology*. New York: Oxford University Press.

McDaniel, M. A. (2005). Big-brained people are smarter: A meta–analysis of the relationship between *in vivo* brain volume and intelligence. *Intelligence, 33*, 337–346.

McDaniel, M. A., Waddill, P. J., & Shakesby, P. S. (1996). Study strategies, interest, and learning from text: The application of material appropriate processing. In D. J. Herrmann, C. McEvoy, C. Hertzog, P. Hertel, & M. K. Johnson (Eds.), *Basic and applied memory research: Theory in context* (Vol. 1). Mahwah, NJ: Erlbaum.

McDonald, C., & Murphy, K. C. (2003). The new genetics of schizophrenia. *Psychiatric Clinics of North America, 26*(1), 41–63.

McDonald, W. M., Thompson, T. R., McCall W. V., & Zormuski, C. F. (2004). Electroconvulsive therapy. In A. F. Schatzberg & C. B. Nemeroff (Eds.), *Textbook of psychopharmacology*. Washington, DC: American Psychiatric Publishing.

McGaugh, J. L. (1995). Emotional activation, neuromodulatory systems, and memory. In D. L. Schacter, J. T. Coyle, G. D. Fischbach, M. Mesulam, & L. E. Sullivan (Eds.), *Memory distortion*. Cambridge, MA: Harvard University Press.

McGaugh, J. L. (2002). The amygdala regulates memory consolidation. In L. R. Squire & D. L. Schacter (Eds.), *Neuropsychology of memory*. New York: Guilford.

McGaugh, J. L. (2004). The amygdala modulates the consolidation of memories of emotionally arousing experiences. *Annual Review of Neuroscience, 27*, 1–28.

McGeoch, J. A., & McDonald, W. T. (1931). Meaningful relation and retroactive inhibition. *American Journal of Psychology, 43*, 579–588.

McGlashan, T. H., & Fenton, W. S. (1992). The positive-negative distinction in schizophrenia: Review of natural history validators. *Archives of General Psychiatry, 49*, 63–72.

McGlashan, T. H., & Hoffman, R. E. (2000). Schizophrenia: Psychodynamic to neurodynamic theories. In B. J. Sadock & V. A. Sadock (Eds.), *Kaplan and Sadock's comprehensive textbook of psychiatry* (7th ed., Vol. 1, pp. 1159–1168). Philadelphia: Lippincott/Williams & Wilkins.

McGregor, H. A., Lieberman, J. D., Greenberg, J., Solomon, S., Arndt, J., Simon, L., & Pyszczynski, T. (1998). Terror management and aggression: Evidence that mortality salience motivates aggression against worldview-threatening others. *Journal of Personality and Social Psychology, 74*, 590–605.

McGrew, J. H., Wright, E. R., Pescosolido, B. A., & McDonel, E. C. (1999). The closing of Central State Hospital: Long-term outcomes for persons with severe mental illness. *Journal of Behavioral Health Services & Research, 26*, 246–261.

McGue, M., Bouchard, T. J., Jr., Iacono, W. G., & Lykken, D. T. (1993). Behavioral genetics of cognitive ability: A life-span perspective. In R. Plomin & G. E. McClearn (Eds.), *Nature, nurture and psychology*. Washington, DC: American Psychological Association.

McHale, S. M., Crouter, A. C., & Whiteman, S. D. (2003). The family contexts of gender development in childhood and adolescence. *Social Development, 12*, 125–148.

McHugh, P. R. (1995). Dissociative identity disorder as a socially constructed artifact. *Journal of Practical Psychiatry and Behavioral Health, 1,* 158–166.

McKean, K. (1985, June). Decisions, decisions. *Discover,* pp. 22–31.

McKelvie, P., & Low, J. (2002). Listening to Mozart does not improve children's spatial ability: Final curtains for the Mozart effect. *British Journal of Development Psychology, 20,* 241–258.

McKenna, J. J. (1993). Co-sleeping. In M. A. Carskadon (Ed.), *Encyclopedia of sleep and dreaming.* New York: Macmillan.

McKenna, K. Y. A., & Bargh, J. A. (1998). Coming out in the age of the Internet: Identity "demarginalization" through virtual group participation. *Journal of Personality and Social Psychology, 75,* 681–694.

McLean, D. E., & Link, B. G. (1994). Unraveling complexity: Strategies to refine concepts, measures, and research designs in the study of life events and mental health. In W. R. Avison & I. H. Gotlib (Eds.), *Stress and mental health: Contemporary issues and prospects for the future.* New York: Plenum.

McLellan, A. T., Lewis, D. C., O'Brien, C. P., & Kleber, H. D. (2000). Drug dependence, a chronic mental illness: Implications for treatment, insurance, and outcome evaluation. *Journal of the American Medical Association, 284,* 1689–1695.

McLoughlin, K., & Paquet, M. (2005, December 14). Gambling led Hogan to robbery, lawyer says. *Lehigh University's The Brown and White.* Retrieved March 21, 2006 from http://www.bw.lehigh.edu/story.asp?ID=19313.

McLoyd, V. C. (1998). Socioeconomic disadvantage and child development. *American Psychologist, 53,* 185–204.

McNally, R. J. (1994). Cognitive bias in panic disorder. *Current Directions in Psychological Science, 3,* 129–132.

McNally, R. J. (1996). *Panic disorder: A critical analysis.* New York: Guilford.

McNally, R. J. (1999). Posttraumatic stress disorder. In T. Millon, P. H. Blaney, & R. D. Davis (Eds.), *Oxford textbook of psychopathology* (pp. 144–165). New York: Oxford University Press.

McNally, R. J. (2003). *Remembering trauma.* Cambridge, MA: Belknap Press/Harvard University Press.

McNeil, T. F., Cantor-Graae, E., & Ismail, B. (2000). Obstetrics complications and congenital malformation in schizophrenia. *Brain Research Reviews, 31,* 166–178.

Mechanic, D. (1980). *Mental health and social policy.* Englewood Cliffs, NJ: Prentice-Hall.

Mechanic, D. (1999). Mental health and mental illness. In A. V. Horvitz & T. L. Scheid (Eds.), *A handbook for the study of mental health: Social contexts, theories, and systems.* New York: Cambridge University Press.

Mednick, S. A., Machon, R. A., Huttunen, M. O., & Bonett, D. (1988). Adult schizophrenia following prenatal exposure to an influenza epidemic. *Archives of General Psychiatry, 45,* 189–192.

Mednick, S. A., Watson, J. B., Huttunen, M., Cannon, T. D., Katila, H., Machon, R., Mednick, B., Hollister, M., Parnas, J., Schulsinger, F., Sajaniemi, N., Voldsgaard, P., Pyhala, R., Gutkind, D., & Wang, X. (1998). A two-hit working model of the etiology of schizophrenia. In M. F. Lenzenweger & R. H. Dworkin (Eds.), *Origins and development of schizophrenia: Advances in experimental psychopathology.* Washington DC: American Psychological Association.

Medora, N. P., Larson, J. H., Hortacsu, N., & Dave, P. (2002). Perceived attitudes towards romanticism: A cross-cultural study of American, Asian-Indian, and Turkish young adults. *Journal of Comparative Family Studies, 33,* 155–178.

Meeus, W. (1996). Studies on identity development in adolescence: An overview of research and some new data. *Journal of Youth & Adolescence, 25,* 569–598.

Meeus, W., Iedema, J., Helsen, M., & Vollebergh, W. (1999). Patterns of adolescent identity development: Review of literature and longitudinal analysis. *Developmental Review, 19,* 419–461.

Mega, M. S., Cummings, J. L., Salloway, S., & Malloy, P. (1997). The limbic system: An anatomic, phylogenetic, and clinical perspective. *Journal of Neuropsychiatry & Clinical Neurosciences, 9,* 315–330.

Meichenbaum, D. H. (1977). *Cognitive-behavior modification.* New York: Plenum.

Meilman, P. W. (1979). Cross-sectional age changes in ego identity status during adolescence. *Developmental Psychology, 15,* 230–231.

Mellor, D. (2003). Contemporary racism in Australia: The experiences of Aborigines. *Personality and Social Psychology Bulletin, 29,* 474–486.

Meltzer, H. Y., Davidson, M., Glassman, A. H., & Vieweg, V. R. (2002). Assessing cardiovascular risks versus clinical benefits of atypical antipsychotic drug treatment. *Journal of Clinical Psychiatry, 63*(9), 25–29.

Melzack, R., & Wall, P. D. (1965). Pain mechanisms: A new theory. *Science, 150,* 971–979.

Melzack, R., & Wall, P. D. (1982). *The challenge of pain.* New York: Basic Books.

Mendelson, W. B. (2005). Hypnotic medications: Mechanisms of action and pharmacologic effects. In M. H. Kryger, T. Roth, & W. C. Dement (Eds.). *Principles and practice of sleep medicine.* Philadelphia: Elsevier Saunders.

Mennella, J. A., & Beauchamp, G. K. (1996). The early development of human flavor preferences. In E. D. Capaldi (Ed.), *Why we eat what we eat: The psychology of eating* (pp. 83–112). Washington, DC: American Psychological Association.

Mennella, J. A., Pepino, M. Y., & Reed, D. R. (2005). Genetic and environmental determinants of bitter perception and sweet preferences. *Pediatrics, 115,* 216–222.

Mentzer, R. L. (1982). Response biases in multiple-choice test item files. *Educational and Psychological Measurement, 42,* 437–448.

Merikangas, K. R., & Risch, N. (2003). Will the genomics revolution revolutionize psychiatry? *American Journal of Psychiatry, 160,* 625–635.

Merikle, P. M., & Daneman, M. (1996). Memory for unconsciously perceived events: Evidence from anesthetized patients. *Conciousness & Cognition: An International Journal, 5,* 525–541.

Mesquita, B. (2001). Culture and emotion: Different approaches to the question. In T. J. Mayne & G. A. Bonanno (Eds.), *Emotions: Current issues and future directions.* New York: Guilford.

Mesquita, B. (2003). Emotions as dynamic cultural phenomena. In R. J. Davidson, K. R. Scherer, & H. H. Goldsmith (Eds.), *Handbook of affective sciences.* New York: Oxford University Press.

Metzger, E. D. (1999). Electroconvulsive therapy. In A. M. Nicholi (Ed.), *The Harvard guide to psychiatry.* Cambridge, MA: Harvard University Press.

Meyer, D. E., & Schvaneveldt, R. W. (1976). Meaning, memory structure, and mental processes. *Science, 192,* 27–33.

Meyer, R. E. (1996). The disease called addiction: Emerging evidence in a 200-year debate. *The Lancet, 347,* 162–166.

Meyer, R. G. (1992). *Practical clinical hypnosis: Techniques and applications.* New York: Lexington Books.

Meyer-Bahlburg, H. F. L., Ehrhardt, A. A., Rosen, L. R., Gruen, R. S., Veridiano, N. P., Vann, F. H., & Neuwalder, H. F. (1995). Prenatal estrogens and the development of homosexual orientation. *Developmental Psychology, 31,* 12–21.

Mezulis, A. H., Abramson, L. Y., Hyde, J. S., & Hankin, B. L. (2004). Is there a universal positivity bias in attributions? A meta-analytic review of individual, developmental and cultural differences in the self-serving attributional bias. *Psychological Bulletin, 130,* 711–747.

Mezzich, J. E., Lewis-Fernandez, R., & Ruiperez, M. A. (2003). The cultural framework of psychiatric disorders. In A. Tasman, J. Kay, & J. A. Lieberman (Eds.), *Psychiatry.* New York: Wiley.

Michaels, S. (1996). The prevelance of homosexuality in the United States. In R. P. Cabaj & T. S. Stein (Eds.), *Textbook of homosexuality and mental health.* Washington, DC: American Psychiatric Press.

Mickelson, K. D., Kessler, R. C., & Shaver, P. R. (1997). Adult attachment in a nationally representative sample. *Journal of Personality and Social Psychology, 73,* 1092–1106.

Mignot, E. (2005). Narcolepsy: Diagnosis and management. In M. H. Kryger, T. Roth, & W. C. Dement (Eds.), *Principles and practice of sleep medicine.* Philadelphia: Elsevier Saunders.

Mikulincer, M., & Shaver, P. R. (2005). Attachment security, compassion, and altruism. *Current Directions in Psychological Science, 14*(1), 34–38.

Milar, K. S. (2000). The first generation of women psychologists and the psychology of women. *American Psychologist, 55,* 616–619.

Milgram, S. (1963). Behavioral study of obedience. *Journal of Abnormal and Social Psychology, 67,* 371–378.

Milgram, S. (1964). Issues in the study of obedience. *American Psychologist, 19,* 848–852.

Milgram, S. (1968). Reply to the critics. *International Journal of Psychiatry, 6,* 294–295.

Milgram, S. (1974). *Obedience to authority.* New York: Harper & Row.

Miller, A. G. (1986). *The obedience experiments: A case study of controversy in social science.* New York: Praeger.

Miller, G. A. (1956). The magical number seven, plus or minus two: Some limits on our capacity for processing information. *Psychological Review, 63,* 81–97.

Miller, G. A. (2003). The cognitive revolution: A historical perspective. *Trends in Cognitive Sciences, 7*(3), 141–144.

Miller, I. J. (1996). Managed care is harmful to outpatient mental health services: A call for accountability. *Professional Psychology: Research and Practice, 27,* 349–363.

Miller, I. J., & Reedy, F. E. Jr. (1990). Variations in human taste-bud density and taste intensity perception. *Physiological Behavior, 47,* 1213–1219.

Miller, J. G. (1999). Cultural psychology: Implications for basic psychological theory. *Psychological Science, 10,* 85–91.

Miller, J. G. (2001). Culture and moral development. In D. Matsumoto (Ed.), *The handbook of culture and psychology* (pp. 151–170). New York: Oxford University Press.

Miller, N. E. (1944). Experimental studies of conflict. In J. M. Hunt (Ed.), *Personality and the behavior disorders* (Vol. 1). New York: Ronald.

Miller, N. E. (1959). Liberalization of basic S-R concepts: Extension to conflict behavior, motivation, and social learning. In S. Koch (Ed.), *Psychology: A study of a science* (Vol. 2). New York: McGraw-Hill.

Miller, N. E. (1985). The value of behavioral research on animals. *American Psychologist, 40,* 423–440.

Miller, R. R., & Grace, R. C. (2003). Conditioning and learning. In A. F. Healy & R. W. Proctor (Eds.), *Handbook of psychology, Vol. 4: Experimental psychology.* New York: Wiley.

Millman, J., Bishop, C. H., & Ebel, R. (1965). An analysis of test-wiseness. *Educational and Psychological Measurement, 25,* 707–726.

Millstone, E. (1989). Methods and practices of animal experimentation. In G. Langley (Ed.), *Animal experimentation: The consensus changes.* New York: Chapman & Hall.

Minuchin, S., Rosman, B. L., & Baker, L. (1978). *Psychosomatic families: Anorexia nervosa in context.* Cambridge, MA: Harvard University Press.

Miranda, J., Bernal, G., Lau, A., Kohn, L., Hwang, W., & LaFromboise, T. (2005). State of the science on psychosocial interventions for ethnic minorities. *Annual Review of Clinical Psychology, 1,* 113–42.

Mischel, W. (1961). Delay of gratification, need for achievement, and acquiescence in another culture. *Journal of Abnormal and Social Psychology, 62,* 543–552.

Mischel, W. (1968). *Personality and assessment.* New York: Wiley.

Mischel, W. (1973). Toward a cognitive social learning conceptualization of personality. *Psychological Review, 80,* 252–283.

Mischel, W. (1984). Convergences and challenges in the search for consistency. *American Psychologist, 39,* 351–364.

Mishra, R. C. (2001). Cognition across cultures. In D. Matsumoto (Ed.), *The handbook of culture and psychology* (pp. 119–136). New York: Oxford University Press.

Mitchell, K. J., & Johnson, M. K. (2000). Source monitoring: Attributing mental experiences. In E. Tulving & F. I. M. Craik (Eds.), *The Oxford handbook of memory* (pp. 179–196). New York: Oxford University Press.

Miyamoto, S., Lieberman, J. A., Fleishhacker, W. W., Aoba, A., & Marder, S. R. (2003). Antipsychotic drugs. In A. Tasman, J. Kay, & J. A. Lieberman (Eds.), *Psychiatry.* New York: Wiley.

Moak, D. H., & Anton, R. F. (1999). Alcohol. In B. S. McCrady & E. E. Epstein (Eds.), *Addictions: A comprehensive guidebook.* New York: Oxford University Press.

Modestin, J. (1992). Multiple personality disorder in Switzerland. *American Journal of Psychiatry, 149,* 88–92.

Modestin, J., Huber, A., Satiri, E., Malti, T., & Hell, D. (2003). Long-term course of schizophrenic illness: Bleuler's study reconsidered. *American Journal of Psychiatry, 160,* 2202–2208.

Moe, A., & De Bini, R. (2004). Studying passages with the loci method: Are subject-generated more effective than experimenter-supplied loci pathways? *Journal of Mental Imagery, 28*(3–4), 75–86.

Moghaddam, F. M., Taylor, D. M., & Wright, S. C. (1993). *Social psychology in cross-cultural perspective.* New York: W. H. Freeman.

Mojtabai, R. (2005). Perceived reasons for loss of housing and continued homelessness among homeless persons with mental illness. *Psychiatric Services, 56*(2), 172–178.

Moline, M. L. (1993). Jet lag. In M. A. Carskadon (Ed.), *Encyclopedia of sleep and dreaming.* New York: Macmillan.

Möller, J., Hallqvist, J., Diderichsen, F., Theorell, T., Reuterwall, C., & Ahlbom, A. (1999). Do episodes of anger trigger myocardial infarction? A case-crossover analysis in the Stockholm heart epidemiology program (SHEEP). *Psychosomatic Medicine, 61,* 842–849.

Mollon, J. D. (1989). "Tho' she kneel'd in that place where they grew . . ." *Journal of Experimental Biology, 146,* 21–38.

Moncrieff, J. (2001). Are antidepressants overrated? A review of methodological problems in antidepressant trials. *Journal of Nervous and Mental Disorders, 189,* 288–295.

Monk, T. H. (2000). Shift work. In M. H. Kryger, T. Roth, & W. C. Dement (Eds.), *Principles and practice of sleep medicine.* Philadelphia: Saunders.

Monroe, S. M., & Hadjiyannakis, K. (2002). The social environment and depression: Focusing on severe life stress. In I. H. Gotlib & C. L. Hammen (Eds.), *Handbook of depression.* New York: Guilford.

Moore, B. C. J. (2001). Basic auditory processes. In E. B. Goldstein (Ed.), *Blackwell handbook of perception.* Malden, MA: Blackwell.

Moore, K. L., & Persaud, T. V. N. (1998). *Before we are born.* Philadelphia: Saunders.

Moos, R. H., & Schaefer, J. A. (1993). Coping resources and processes: Current concepts and measures. In L. Goldberger & S. Breznitz (Eds.), *Handbook of stress: Theoretical and clinical aspects* (2nd ed.). New York: Free Press.

Morahan-Martin, J., & Schumacher, P. (2000). Incidence and correlates of pathological Internet use among college students. *Computers in Human Behavior, 16*(1), 13–29.

Morgan, H. (1996). An analysis of Gardner's theory of multiple intelligence. *Roeper Review, 18,* 263–269.

Morgan, M. J. (2000). Ecstacy (MDMA): A review of its possible persistent psychological effects. *Psychopharmacology, 152,* 230–248.

Morley, J. E. (2001). Male menopause is underdiagnosed and undertreated. *Medical Crossfire, 3*(1), 46–47, 51.

Morokoff, P. J., Quina, K., Harlow, L. L., Whitmire, L., Grimley, D. M., Gibson, P. R., & Burkholder, G. J. (1997). Sexual assertivenes scale (SAS) for women: Development and validation. *Journal of Personality and Social Psychology, 73,* 790–804.

Morrison, A. R. (2003). The brain on night shift. *Cerebrum, 5*(3), 23–36.

Morton, A. (1998). *Diana: Her true story. The commemorative edition.* New York: Pocket Books.

Moseman, S. E., Freeman, M. P., Misiazek, J., & Gelenberg, A. J. (2003). Mood stabilizers. In A. Tasman, J. Kay, & J. A. Lieberman (Eds.), *Psychiatry.* New York: Wiley.

Most, S. B., Simons, D. J., Scholl, B. J., Jimenez, R., Clifford, E., & Chabris, C. F. (2001). How not to be seen: The contribution of similarity and selective ignoring to sustained inattentional blindness. *Psychological Science, 12*(1), 9–17.

Mountcastle, V. B., & Powell, T. P. S. (1959). Neural mechanisms subserving cutaneous sensibility, with special reference to the role of afferent inhibition in sensory perception and discrimination. *Bulletin of the Johns Hopkins Hospital, 105,* 201–232.

Mowrer, O. H. (1947). On the dual nature of learning: A reinterpretation of "conditioning" and "problem-solving." *Harvard Educational Review, 17,* 102–150.

Mozell, M. M., Smith, B. P., Smith, P. E., Sullivan, R. L., & Swender, P. (1969). Nasal chemoreception in flavor identification. *Archives of Otolaryngology, 90,* 367–373.

Mrdjenovic, G., & Levitsky, D. A. (2005). Children eat what they are served: The imprecise regulation of energy intake. *Appetite, 3,* 273–282.

Mulligan, N. W. (1998). The role of attention during encoding in implicit and explicit memory. *Journal of Experimental Psychology: Learning, Memory, & Cognition, 24,* 27–47.

Munck, A. (2000). Corticosteroids and stress. In G. Fink (Ed.), *Encyclopedia of stress* (Vol. 1, pp. 570–577). San Diego: Academic Press.

Munk-Jorgensen, P. (1999). Has deinstitutionalization gone too far? *European Archives of Psychiatry & Clinical Neuroscience, 249*(3), 136–143.

Murdock, B. (2001). Analysis of the serial position curve. In H. L. Roediger III, J. S. Nairne, I. Neath, & A. M. Surprenant (Eds.), *The nature of remembering: Essays in honor of Robert G. Crowder* (pp. 151–170). Washington, DC: American Psychological Association.

Murphy, K. R. (2002). Can conflicting perspectives on the role of *g* in personnel selection be resolved? *Human Performance, 15,* 173–186.

Murray, H. A. (1938). *Explorations in personality.* New York: Oxford University Press.

Murray, S. L., Holmes, J. G., Bellavia, G., Griffin, D. W., & Dolderman, D. (2002). Kindred spirits? The benefits of egocentrism in close relationships. *Journal of Personality and Social Psychology, 82,* 563–581.

Murray, S. L., Holmes, J. G., & Griffin, D. W. (1996a). The benefits of positive illusions: Idealization and the construction of satisfaction in close relationships. *Journal of Personality and Social Psychology, 70,* 79–98.

Murray, S. L., Holmes, J. G., & Griffin, D. W. (1996b). The self-fulfilling nature of positive illusions in romantic relationships: Love is not blind, but prescient. *Journal of Personality and Social Psychology, 71,* 1155–1180.

Murstein, B. I., & Fontaine, P. A. (1993). The public's knowledge about psychologists and other mental health professionals. *American Psychologist, 48,* 839–845.

Mustanski, B. S., Chivers, M. L., & Bailey, J. M. (2002). A critical review of recent biological research on human sexual orientation. *Annual Review of Sex Research, 12,* 89–140.

Myers, D. G. (1992). *The pursuit of happiness: Who is happy—and why.* New York: Morrow.

Myers, D. G. (1999). Close relationships and quality of life. In D. Kahneman, E. Diener, & N. Schwarz (Eds.), *Well-being: The foundations of hedonic psychology.* New York: Russell Sage Foundation.

Myers, D. G. (2001). Do we fear the right things? *American Psychological Society Observer, 14*(10), 3.

Myers, D. G., & Diener, E. (1995). Who is happy? *Psychological Science, 6,* 10–19.

Myers, D. G., & Diener, E. (1997). The pursuit of happiness. *Scientific American Special Issue, 7,* 40–43.

Myers, D. G., & Lamm, H. (1976). The group polarization phenomenon. *Psychological Bulletin, 83,* 602–627.

Mynatt, C. R., Doherty, M. E., & Tweney, R. D. (1978). Consequences of confirmation and disconfirmation in a simulated research environment. *Quarterly Journal of Experimental Psychology, 30,* 395–406.

Nairne, J. S. (2002). Remembering over the short-term: The case against the standard model. *Annual Review of Psychology, 53,* 53–81.

Nairne, J. S. (2003). Sensory and working memory. In A. F. Healy & R. W. Proctor (Eds.), *Handbook of psychology, Vol. 4: Experimental psychology*. New York: Wiley.

Nakajima, S., & Patterson, R. L. (1997). The involvement of dopamine D2 receptors, but not D3 or D4 receptors, in the rewarding effect of brain stimulation in the rat. *Brain Research, 760*, 74–79.

Narumoto, J., Okada, T., Sadato, N., Fukui, K., & Yonekura, Y. (2001). Attention to emotion modulates fMRI activity in human right superior temporal sulcus. *Cognitive Brain Research, 12*, 225–231.

Nash, M. R. (2001, July). The truth and hype of hypnosis. *Scientific American, 285*, 36–43.

Neiss, R. (1988). Reconceptualizing arousal: Psychobiological states in motor performance. *Psychological Bulletin, 103*, 345–366.

Neiss, R. (1990). Ending arousal's reign of error: A reply to Anderson. *Psychological Bulletin, 107*, 101–105.

Neisser, U. (1967). *Cognitive psychology*. New York: Appleton-Century-Crofts.

Neisser, U. (1998). Introduction: Rising test scores and what they mean. In U. Neisser (Ed.), *The rising curve: Long-term gains in IQ and related measures*. Washington, DC: American Psychological Association.

Neisser, U., Boodoo, G., Bouchard, T. J., Jr., Boykin, A. W., Brody, N., Ceci, S. J., Halpern, D. F., Loehlin, J. C., Perloff, R., Sternberg, R. J., & Urbina, S. (1996). Intelligence: Knowns and unknowns. *American Psychologist, 51*, 77–101.

Neisser, U., & Harsch, N. (1992). Phantom flashbulbs: False recollections of hearing the news about *Challenger*. In E. Winograd & U. Neisser (Eds.), *Affect and accuracy in recall: Studies of "flashbulb" memories*. New York: Cambridge University Press.

Nelson, C. A., Bloom, F. E., Cameron, J. L., Amaral, D., Dahl, R. E., & Pine, D. (2002). An integrative, multidisciplinary approach to the study of brain-behavior relations in the context of typical and atypical development. *Development and Psychopathology, 14*, 499–520.

Nemeth, C., & Chiles, C. (1988). Modelling courage: The role of dissent in fostering independence. *European Journal of Social Psychology, 18*, 275–280.

Nestler, E. J., & Malenka, R. C. (2004). The addicted brain. *Scientific American, 290*(3), 78–85.

Newcombe, N., & Huttenlocher, J. (1992). Children's early ability to solve perspective-taking problems. *Developmental Psychology, 28*, 635–643.

Niaura, R., Todaro, J. F., Stroud, L., Spiro, A., Ward, K. D., & Weiss, S. (2002). Hostility, the metabolic syndrome, and incident coronary heart disease. *Health Psychology, 21*, 588–593.

Nickerson, C., Schwarz, N., Diener, E., & Kahneman, D. (2003). Zeroing in on the dark side of the American dream: A closer look at the negative consequences of the goal for financial success. *Psychological Science, 14*, 531–536.

Nickerson, R. S., & Adams, M. J. (1979). Long-term memory for a common object. *Cognitive Psychology, 11*, 287–307.

Niebyl, J. R. (2002). Drugs in pregnancy and lactation. In S. G. Gabbe, J. R. Niebyl, & J. L. Simpson (Eds.), *Obstetrics: Normal and problem pregnancies*. New York: Churchill Livingstone.

Nielsen Media Research. (1998). *Report on television: 1998*. New York: Author.

Nielsen, T. A., Zadra, A. L., Simard, V., Saucier, S., Stenstrom, P., Smith, C., & Kuiken, D. (2003). The typical dreams of Canadian university students. *Dreaming, 13*(4), 211–235.

Nikelly, A. G. (1994). Alcoholism: Social as well as psycho-medical problem—The missing "big picture." *Journal of Alcohol & Drug Education, 39*, 1–12.

Nisbett, R. E. (2005). Heredity, environment, and race differences in IQ: A commentary on Rushton and Jensen. *Psychology, Public Policy, and the Law, 11*, 302–310.

Nisbett, R. E., Peng, K., Choi, I., & Norenzayan, A. (2001). Culture and systems of thought: Holistic versus analytic cognition. *Psychological Review, 108*, 291–310.

Nishino, S., Mignot, E., & Dement, W. C. (1995). Sedative-hypnotics. In A. F. Schatzberg & C. B. Nemeroff (Eds.), *American Psychiatric Press textbook of psychopharmacology*. Washington, DC: American Psychiatric Press.

Nist, S. L., & Holschuh, J. L. (2000). Comprehension strategies at the college level. In R. F. Flippo & D. C. Caverly (Eds.), *Handbook of college reading and study strategy research*. Mahwah, NJ: Erlbaum.

Nolen-Hoeksema, S. (1991). Responses to depression and their effects on the duration of depressive episodes. *Journal of Abnormal Psychology, 100*, 569–582.

Nolen-Hoeksema, S. (1995). Gender differences in coping with depression across the lifespan. *Depression, 3*, 81–90.

Nolen-Hoeksema, S. (2000). The role of rumination in depressive disorders and mixed anxiety/depressive symptoms. *Journal of Abnormal Psychology, 109*, 504–511.

Nolen-Hoeksema, S. (2001). Gender differences in depression. *Current Directions in Psychological Science, 10*, 173–176.

Nolen-Hoeksema, S. (2002). Gender differences in depression. In I. H. Gotlib & C. L. Hammen (Eds.), *Handbook of depression*. New York: Guilford.

Nomaguchi, K. M., & Milkie, M. A. (2003). Costs and rewards of children: The effects of becoming a parent on adults' lives. *Journal of Marriage and the Family, 65*, 356–374.

Norcross, J. C. (1995). Dispelling the dodo bird verdict and the exclusivity myth in psychotherapy. *Psychotherapy, 32*, 500–504.

Norfleet, M. A. (2002). Responding to society's needs: Prescription privileges for psychologists. *Journal of Clinical Psychology, 58*, 599–610.

Norman, R. M. G., & Malla, A. K. (1995). Prodromal symptoms of relapse in schizophrenia: A review. *Schizophrenia Bulletin, 21*, 527–539.

Norris, F. H., with Byrne, C. M., Diaz, E., & Kaniasty, K. (2001). *Risk factors for adverse outcomes in natural and human-caused disasters: A review of the empirical literature*. Retrieved November 21, 2001 from U.S. Department of Veterans Affairs National Center for PTSD website: http://www.ncptsd.org/facts/disasters/fs_riskfactors.html.

North, C. S., Eyrich, K. M., Pollio, D. E., & Spitznagel, E. L. (2004). Are rates of psychiatric disorders in the homeless population changing? *American Journal of Public Health, 94*(1), 103–108.

Novick, L. R., & Bassok, M. (2005). Problem solving. In K. J. Holyoak & R. G. Morrison (Eds.), *The Cambridge handbook of thinking and reasoning*. New York: Cambridge University Press.

Noyes, R., Clarkson, C., Crowe, R. R., Yates, W. R., & McChesney, C. M. (1987). A family study of generalized anxiety disorder. *American Journal of Psychiatry, 144*, 1019–1024.

Noyes, R., Jr., Stuart, S. P., Lanbehn, D. R., Happel, R., Longley, S. L., Muller, B. A., & Yagla, S. J. (2003). Test of an interpersonal model of hypochondriasis. *Psychosomatic Medicine, 65*, 292–300.

Noyes, R., Jr., Watson, D. B., Letuchy, E. M., Longley, S. L., Black, D. W., Carney, C. P., & Doebbeling, B. N. (2005). Relationship between hypochondriacal concerns and personality dimensions and traits in a military population. *Journal of Nervous and Mental Disease, 193*(2), 110–118.

Nucci, L. P. (2002). The development of moral reasoning. In U. Goswami (Eds.), *Blackwell handbook of childhood cognitive development*. Malden, MA: Blackwell Publishing.

Oakes, M. E., & Slotterback, C. S. (2000). Self-reported measures of appetite in relation to verbal cues about many foods. *Current Psychology: Developmental, Learning, Personality, Social, 19*, 137–142.

Ochse, R. (1990). *Before the gates of excellence: The determinants of creative genius*. Cambridge, England: Cambridge University Press.

O'Donohue, W. (1998). Conditioning and third-generation behavior therapy. In W. O'Donohue (Ed.), *Learning and behavior therapy*. Boston: Allyn & Bacon.

Ohayon, M. M., Carskadon, M. A., Guilleminault, C., & Vitiello, M. V. (2004). Meta-analysis of quantitative sleep parameters from childhood to old age in healthy individuals: Developing normative sleep values across the human lifespan. *Sleep: Journal of Sleep & Sleep Disorders Research, 27*, 1255–1273.

Ohman, A., & Mineka, S. (2003). The malicious serpent: Snakes as a prototypical stimulus for an evolved module of fear. *Current Directions in Psychological Science, 12*, 5–9.

Ohman, A., & Wiens, S. (2003). On the automaticity of autonomic responses in emotion: An evolutionary perspective. In R. J. Davidson, K. R. Scherer, & H. H. Goldsmith (Eds.), *Handbook of affective sciences*. New York: Oxford University Press.

Okami, P., & Shackelford, T. K. (2001). Human sex differences in sexual psychology and behavior. *Annual Review of Sex Research, 12*, 186–241.

Okami, P., Weisner, T., & Olmstead, R. (2002). Outcome correlates of parent-child bedsharing: An eighteen-year longitudinal study. *Journal of Developmental & Behavioral Pediatrics, 23*, 244–253.

Olds, J., & Milner, P. (1954). Positive reinforcement produced by electrical stimulation of the septal area and other regions of the rat brain. *Journal of Comparative and Physiological Psychology, 47*, 419–427.

Olds, M. E., & Fobe, J. L. (1981). The central basis of motivation: Intracranial self-stimulation studies. *Annual Review of Psychology, 32*, 523–574.

O'Leary, K. D., Kent, R. N., & Kanowitz, J. (1975). Shaping data collection congruent with experimental hypotheses. *Journal of Applied Behavior Analysis, 8*, 43–51.

Olfson, M., Marcus, S. C., Druss, B. , & Pincus, H. A. (2002). National trends in the use of outpatient psychotherapy. *American Journal of Psychiatry, 159*, 1914–1920.

Olfson, M., Marcus, S. C., & Pincus, H. A. (1999). Trends in office-based psychiatric practice. *American Journal of Psychiatry, 156*, 451–457.

Olfson, M., Shaffer, D., Marcus, S. C., & Greenberg, T. (2003). Relationship between antidepressant medication treatment and suicide in adolescents. *Archives of General Psychiatry, 60*, 978–982.

Oliver, M. B., & Hyde, J. S. (1993). Gender differences in sexuality: A meta-analysis. *Psychological Bulletin, 114*, 29–51.

Oliveri, M., Turriziani, P., Carlesimo, G. A., Koch, G., Tomaiuolo, F., Panella, M., & Caltagirone, C. (2001). Parieto-frontal interactions in visual-object and visual-spatial working memory: Evidence from transcranial magnetic stimulation, *Cortex, 11,* 606–618.

Olson, J. M., & Maio, G. R. (2003). Persuasion and attitude change. In T. Millon & M. J. Lerner (Eds.), *Handbook of psychology, Vol. 5: Personality and social psychology.* New York: Wiley.

Olson, J. M., Roese, N. J., & Zanna, M. P. (1996). Expectancies. In E. T. Higgins & A. W. Kruglanski (Eds.), *Social psychology: Handbook of basic principles.* New York: Guilford.

Olson, J. M., & Stone, J. (2005). The influence of behavior on attitudes. In D. Albarracin, B. T. Johnson, & M. P. Zanna (Eds.), *The handbook of attitudes.* Mahwah, NJ: Erlbaum.

Olson, J. M., & Zanna, M. P. (1993). Attitudes and attitude change. *Annual Review of Psychology, 44,* 117–154.

Olson, M. A., & Fazio, R. H. (2001). Implicit attitude formation through classical conditioning. *Psychological Science, 12,* 413–417.

Olson, M. A., & Fazio, R. H. (2002). Implicit acquisition and manifestation of classically conditioned attitudes. *Social Cognition, 20*(2), 89–104.

Ones, D. S., Viswesvaran, C., & Dilchert, S. (2005). Cognitive ability in selection decisions. In O. Wilhelm & R. W. Engle (Eds.), *Handbook of understanding and measuring intelligence.* Thousand Oaks, CA: Sage.

Operario, D., & Fiske, S. T. (2001). Stereotypes: Content, structures, processes, and context. In R. Brown & S. L. Gaertner (Eds.), *Blackwell handbook of social psychology: Interpersonal processes.* Malden, MA: Blackwell.

Organista, P. B., & Miranda, J. (1991). Psychosomatic symptoms in medical outpatients: An investigation of self-handicapping theory. *Health Psychology, 10,* 427–431.

Orne, M. T. (1951). The mechanisms of hypnotic age regression: An experimental study. *Journal of Abnormal and Social Psychology, 46,* 213–225.

Orne, M. T., & Dinges, D. F. (1989). Hypnosis. In H. I. Kaplan & B. J. Sadock (Eds.), *Comprehensive textbook of psychiatry* (5th ed., Vol. 2). Baltimore: Williams & Wilkins.

Orne, M. T., & Holland, C. C. (1968). On the ecological validity of laboratory deceptions. *International Journal of Psychiatry, 6,* 282–293.

Ornstein, R. E. (1977). *The psychology of consciousness.* New York: Harcourt Brace Jovanovich.

Ornstein, R. E., & Dewan, T. (1991). *The evolution of consciousness: Of Darwin, Freud, and cranial fire—The origins of the way we think.* New York: Prentice-Hall.

Ortmann, A., & Hertwig, R. (1997). Is deception acceptable? *American Psychologist, 52,* 746–747.

Oskamp, S. (1991). *Attitudes and opinions.* Englewood Cliffs, NJ: Prentice-Hall.

Ostovich, J. M., & Sabini, J. (2004). How are sociosexuality, sex drive, and lifetime number of sexual partners related? *Personality and Social Psychology Bulletin, 30,* 1255–1266.

Ott, P. J., Tarter, R. E., & Ammerman, R. T. (1999). *Sourcebook on substance abuse: Etiology, epidemiology, assessment, and treatment.* Boston: Allyn & Bacon.

Outtz, J. L. (2002). The role of cognitive ability tests in employment selection. *Human Performance, 15,* 161–171.

Ozer, E. J., Best, S. R., Lipsey, T. L., & Weiss, D. S. (2003). Predictors of posttraumatic stress disorder and symptoms in adults: A meta-analysis. *Psychological Bulletin, 129,* 52–73.

Pace-Schott, E. F. (2005). The neurobiology of dreaming. In M. H. Kryger, T. Roth, & W. C. Dement (Eds.). *Principles and practice of sleep medicine.* Philadelphia: Elsevier Saunders.

Padgett, D. A., & Sheridan, J. F. (2000). Herpesviruses. In G. Fink (Ed.), *Encyclopedia of stress* (pp. 357–363). San Diego: Academic Press.

Paivio, A. (1969). Mental imagery in associative learning and memory. *Psychological Review, 76,* 241–263.

Paivio, A. (1986). *Mental representations: A dual coding approach.* New York: Oxford University Press.

Paivio, A., Khan, M., & Begg, I. (2000). Concreteness of relational effects on recall of adjective-noun pairs. *Canadian Journal of Experimental Psychology, 54*(3), 149–160.

Paivio, A., Smythe, P. E., & Yuille, J. C. (1968). Imagery versus meaningfulness of nouns in paired-associate learning. *Canadian Journal of Psychology, 22,* 427–441.

Palladino, J. J., & Carducci, B. J. (1984). Students' knowledge of sleep and dreams. *Teaching of Psychology, 11,* 189–191.

Palmer, S. E. (2003). Visual perception of objects. In A. F. Healy & R. W. Proctor (Eds.), *Handbook of psychology, Vol. 4: Experimental psychology.* New York: Wiley.

Palmere, M., Benton, S. L., Glover, J. A., & Ronning, R. (1983). Elaboration and recall of main ideas in prose. *Journal of Educational Psychology, 75,* 898–907.

Panksepp, J. (1991). Affective neuroscience: A conceptual framework for the neurobiological study of emotions. In K. T. Strongman (Ed.), *International review of studies on emotion.* Chichester, England: Wiley.

Paradiso, S. P., Robinson, R. G., Andreasen, N. C., Downhill, J. E., Davidson, R. J., Kirchner, P. T., Watkins, G. L., Boles Ponto, L. L., & Hichwa, R. D. (1997). Emotional activation of limbic circuitry in elderly normal subjects in a PET study. *American Journal of Psychiatry, 154,* 384–389.

Park, C. L., & Fenster, J. R. (2004). Stress-related growth: Predictors of occurrence and correlates with psychological adjustment. *Journal of Social and Clinical Psychology, 23,* 195–215.

Parrot, A. C. (2000). Human research on MDMA (3,4-Methylene-dioxymethamphetamine) neurotoxicity: Cognitive and behavioral indices of change. *Neuropsychobiology, 42*(1), 17–24.

Partinen, M., & Hublin, C. (2005). Epidemiology of sleep disorders. In M. H. Kryger, T. Roth, & W. C. Dement (Eds.). *Principles and practice of sleep medicine.* Philadelphia: Elsevier Saunders.

Pashler, H., Johnston, J. C., & Ruthruff, E. (2001). Attention and performance. *Annual Review of Psychology, 52,* 629–651.

Patel, J. K., Pinals, D. A., & Breier, A. (2003). Schizophrenia and other psychoses. In A. Tasman, J. Kay, & J. A. Lieberman (Eds.), *Psychiatry.* New York: Wiley.

Pato, M. T., Eisen, J. L., & Phillips, K. A. (2003). Obsessive-compulsive disorder. In A Tasman, J. Kay, & J. A. Lieberman (Eds.), *Psychiatry.* New York: Wiley.

Patrick, H., Nicklas, T. A., Hughes, S. O., & Morales, M. (2005). The benefits of authoritative feeding style: Caregiver feeding styles and children's food consumption patterns. *Appetite, 44,* 243–249.

Patterson, D. R., & Jensen, M. P. (2003). Hypnosis and clinical pain. *Psychological Bulletin, 129,* 495–521.

Paulhus, D. L. (1991). Measurement and control of response bias. In J. P. Robinson, P. Shaver, & L. S. Wrightsman (Eds.), *Measures of personality and social psychological attitudes.* San Diego: Academic Press.

Paulos, J. A. (1995). *A mathematician reads the newspaper.* New York: Doubleday.

Paunonen, S. V. (2003). Big-Five factors of personality and replicated predictions of behavior. *Journal of Personality and Social Psychology, 84,* 411–424.

Pavlov, I. P. (1906). The scientific investigation of psychical faculties or processes in the higher animals. *Science, 24,* 613–619.

Pavlov, I. P. (1927). *Conditioned reflexes* (G. V. Anrep, Trans.). London: Oxford University Press.

Payne, D. G., & Blackwell, J. M. (1998). Truth in memory: Caveat emptor. In S. J. Lynn & K. M. McConkey (Eds.), *Truth in memory.* New York: Guilford.

Payne, D. G., & Wenger, M. J. (1996). Practice effects in memory: Data, theory, and unanswered questions. In D. J. Herrmann, C. McEvoy, C. Hertzog, P. Hertel, & M. K. Johnson (Eds.), *Basic and applied memory research: Practical applications* (Vol. 2). Mahwah, NJ: Erlbaum.

Payne, J. W., & Bettman, J. R. (2004). Walking with the scarecrow: The information-processing approach to decision research. In D. J. Koehler & N. Harvey (Ed.), *Blackwell handbook of judgment and decision making.* Malden, MA: Blackwell Publishing.

Pearce, L. (1974). Duck! It's the new journalism. *New Times, 2*(10), 40–41.

Pedersen, P. (1994). A culture-centered approach to counseling. In W. J. Lonner & R. Malpass (Eds.), *Psychology and culture.* Boston: Allyn & Bacon.

Peele, S. (1989). *Diseasing of America: Addiction treatment out of control.* Lexington, MA: Lexington Books.

Peele, S. (2000). What addiction is and is not: The impact of mistaken notions of addiction. *Addiction Research, 8,* 599–607.

Peladeau, N., Forget, J., & Gagne, F. (2003). Effect of paced and unpaced practice on skill application and retention: How much is enough? *American Educational Research Journal, 40,* 769–801.

Pennebaker, J. W., Colder, M., & Sharp, L. K. (1990). Accelerating the coping process. *Journal of Personality and Social Psychology, 58,* 528–537.

Peplau, L. A. (2003). Human sexuality: How do men and women differ? *Current Directions in Psychological Science, 12*(2), 37–40.

Perlman, M. D., & Kaufman, A. S. (1990). Assessment of child intelligence. In G. Goldstein & M. Hersen (Eds.), *Handbook of psychological assessment.* New York: Pergamon Press.

Perone, M., Galizio, M., & Baron, A. (1988). The relevance of animal-based principles in the laboratory study of human operant conditioning. In G. Davey & C. Cullen (Eds.), *Human operant conditioning and behavior modification.* New York: Wiley.

Perry, W., & Braff, D. L. (1994). Information-processing deficits and thought disorder in schizophrenia. *American Journal of Psychiatry, 151,* 363–367.

Person, E. S. (1990). The influence of values in psychoanalysis: The case of female psychology. In C. Zanardi (Ed.), *Essential papers in psychoanalysis.* New York: New York University Press.

Pert, C. B., & Snyder, S. H. (1973). Opiate receptor: Demonstration in the nervous tissue. *Science, 179,* 1011–1014.

Perugini, E. M., Kirsch, I., Allen, S. T., Coldwell, E., Meredith, J. M., Montgomery, G. H., & Sheehan, J. (1998). Surreptitious observation of response to hypnotically suggested hallucinations: A test of the compliance hypothesis. *International Journal of Clinical & Experimental Hypnosis, 46*, 191–203.

Petersen, A. C., Compas, B. E., Brooks-Gunn, J., Stemmler, M., Ey, S., & Grant, K. E. (1993). Depression in adolescence. *American Psychologist, 48*, 155–168.

Peterson, C. (2000). The future of optimism. *American Psychologist, 55*(1), 44–55.

Peterson, C., & Bossio, L. M. (2001). Optimism and physical well-being. In E. C. Chang (Ed.), *Optimism and pessimism: Implications for theory, research, and practice* (pp. 127–146). Washington, DC: American Psychological Association.

Peterson, C., Seligman, M. E. P., & Vaillant, G. E. (1988). Pessimistic explanatory style is a risk factor for physical illness: A thirty-five-year longitudinal study. *Journal of Personality and Social Psychology, 55*, 23–27.

Peterson, C., Seligman, M. E. P., Yurko, K. H., Martin, L. R., & Friedman, H. S. (1998). Catastrophizing and untimely death. *Psychological Science, 9*, 127–130.

Peterson, L. R., & Peterson, M. J. (1959). Short-term retention of individual verbal items. *Journal of Experimental Psychology, 58*, 193–198.

Petrie, K. J., & Pennebaker, J. W. (2004). Health-related cognitions. In S. Sutton, A. Baum, & M. Johnston (Eds.), *The Sage handbook of health psychology.* Thousand Oaks, CA: Sage.

Petrie, K. J., Booth, R. J., & Pennebaker, J. W. (1998). The immunological effects of thought suppression. *Journal of Personality and Social Psychology, 75*, 1264–1272.

Petrie, M. (1994). Improved growth and survival of offspring of peacocks with more elaborate trains. *Nature, 371*, 585–586.

Petrill, S. A. (2005). Behavioral genetics and intelligence. In O. Wilhelm & R. W. Engle (Eds.), *Handbook of understanding and measuring intelligence.* Thousand Oaks, CA: Sage.

Petry, N. M. (2005). *Pathological gambling: Etiology, comorbidity, and treatment.* Washington, D.C.: American Psychological Association.

Petty, R. E., & Cacioppo, J. T. (1986). *Communication and persuasion: Central and peripheral routes to attitude change.* New York: Springer-Verlag.

Petty, R. E., & Wegener, D. T. (1998). Attitude change: Multiple roles for persuasion variables. In D. T. Gilbert, S. T. Fiske, & G. Lindzey (Eds.), *The handbook of social psychology.* New York: McGraw-Hill.

Petty, R. E., & Wegener, D. T. (1999). The elaboration likelihood model: Current status and controversies. In S. Chaiken & Y. Trope (Eds.), *Dual-process theories in social psychology.* New York: Guilford.

Petty, R. E., Wegener, D. T., & Fabrigar, L. R. (1997). Attitudes and attitude change. *Annual Review of Psychology, 48*, 609–647.

Petty, R. E., Wheeler, S. C., & Tormala, Z. L. (2003). Persuasion and attitude change. In T. Millon & M. J. Lerner (Eds.), *Handbook of psychology, vol. 5: Personality and social psychology.* New York: Wiley.

Pezdek, K. (2003). Event memory and autobiographical memory for the events of September 11, 2001. *Applied Cognitive Psychology, 17*, 1033–1045.

Pfaffmann, C. (1978). The vertebrate phylogeny, neural code, and integrative process of taste. In C. Carterette & M. P. Friedman (Eds.), *Handbook of perception* (Vol. 6A). New York: Academic Press.

Pfau, M., Kenski, H. C., Nitz, M., & Sorenson, J. (1990). Efficacy of inoculation strategies in promoting resistance to political attack messages: Application to direct mail. *Communication Monographs, 57*, 25–43.

Pfaus, J. G., Kippin, T. E., & Centeno, S. (2001). Conditioning and sexual behavior: A review. *Hormones & Behavior, 40*, 291–321.

Phares, V. (1996). *Fathers and developmental psychopathology.* New York: Wiley.

Phillips, W. T., Kiernan, M., & King, A. C. (2001). The effects of physical activity on physical and psychological health. In A. Baum, T. A. Revenson, & J. E. Singer (Eds.), *Handbook of health psychology* (pp. 627–660). Mahwah, NJ: Erlbaum.

Pi, E. H., & Simpson, G. M. (2001). Medication-induced movement disorders. In B. J. Sadock & V. A. Sadock (Eds.), *Kaplan and Sadock's comprehensive textbook of psychiatry* (7th ed., Vol. 2). Philadelphia: Lippincott/Williams & Wilkins.

Piaget, J. (1929). *The child's conception of the world.* New York: Harcourt, Brace.

Piaget, J. (1932). *The moral judgment of the child.* Glencoe, IL: Free Press.

Piaget, J. (1952). *The origins of intelligence in children.* New York: International Universities Press.

Piaget, J. (1954). *The construction of reality in the child.* New York: Basic Books.

Piaget, J. (1983). Piaget's theory. In P. H. Mussen (Ed.), *Handbook of child psychology* (Vol. 1). New York: Wiley.

Pike, A., Manke, B., Reiss, D., & Plomin, R. (2000). A genetic analysis of differential experiences of adolescent siblings across three years. *Social Development, 9*, 96–114.

Pike, K. M., & Rodin, J. (1991). Mothers, daughters, and disordered eating. *Journal of Abnormal Psychology, 100*, 198–294.

Pilcher, J. J., Ginter, D. R., & Sadowsky, B. (1997). Sleep quality versus sleep quantity: Relationships between sleep and measures of health, well-being and sleepiness in college students. *Journal of Psychosomatic Research, 42*, 583–596.

Pilcher, J. J., & Walters, A. S. (1997). How sleep deprivation affects psychological variables related to college students' cognitive performance. *Journal of American College Health, 46*, 121–126.

Pillow, D. R., Zautra, A. J., & Sandler, I. (1996). Major life events and minor stressors: Identifying mediational links in the stress process. *Journal of Personality and Social Psychology, 70*, 381–394.

Pilowsky, I. (1993). Aspects of abnormal illness behaviour. *Psychotherapy and Psychosomatics, 60*, 62–74.

Pine, D. S. (2000). Anxiety disorders: Clinical features. In B. J. Sadock & V. A. Sadock (Eds.), *Kaplan and Sadock's comprehensive textbook of psychiatry* (7th ed., Vol. 1, pp. 1476–1489). Philadelphia: Lippincott/Williams & Wilkins.

Pines, A. M. (2004). Adult attachment styles and their relationship to burnout: A preliminary, cross-cultural investigation. *Work & Stress, 18*(1), 66–80.

Pittenger, D. J. (2003). Internet research: An opportunity to revisit classic ethical problems in behavioral research. *Ethics & Behavior, 13*(1), 45–60.

Pittman, F., III. (1994, January/February). A buyer's guide to psychotherapy. *Psychology Today*, 50–53, 74–81.

Plante, T. G. (1999a). *Contemporary clinical psychology.* New York: Wiley.

Plante, T. G. (1999b). Could the perception of fitness account for many of the mental and physical health benefits of exercise? *Advances in Mind-Body Medicine, 15*, 291–295.

Plante, T. G., Caputo, D., & Chizmar, L. (2000). Perceived fitness and responses to laboratory-induced stress. *International Journal of Stress Management, 7*(1), 61–73.

Pliner, P., & Mann, N. (2004). Influence of social norms and palatability on amount consumed and food choice. *Appetite, 42*, 227–237.

Plomin, R. (1993). Nature and nurture: Perspective and prospective. In R. Plomin & G. E. McClearn (Eds.), *Nature, nurture and psychology.* Washington, DC: American Psychological Association.

Plomin, R. (1994). Nature, nurture, and development. In R. J. Sternberg (Ed.), *Encyclopedia of human intelligence.* New York: Macmillan.

Plomin, R. (2003). General cognitive ability. In R. Plomin & J. C. DeFries (Eds.), *Behavioral genetics in the postgenomic era.* Washinton, DC: American Psychological Association.

Plomin, R. (2004). Genetics and developmental psychology. *Merrill-Palmer Quarterly, 50*, 341–352.

Plomin, R., DeFries, J. C., McClearn, G. E., & McGuffin, P. (2001). *Behavioral genetics.* New York: Freeman.

Plomin, R., & Spinath, F. M. (2004). Intelligence: Genetics, genes, and genomics. *Journal of Personality & Social Psychology, 86*, 112–129.

Plotkin, H. (1998). *Evolution in mind: An introduction to evolutionary psychology.* Cambridge, MA: Harvard University Press.

Plotkin, H. (2004). *Evolutionary thought in psychology: A brief history.* Malden, MA: Blackwell Publishing.

Plucker, J. A., & Renzulli, J. S. (1999). Psychometric approaches to the study of human creativity. In R. J. Sternberg (Ed.), *Handbook of creativity.* New York: Cambridge University Press.

Plutchik, R. (1984). Emotions: A general psychoevolutionary theory. In K. R. Scherer & P. Ekman (Eds.), *Approaches to emotion.* Hillsdale, NJ: Erlbaum.

Plutchik, R. (1993). Emotions and their vicissitudes: Emotions and psychopathology. In M. Lewis & J. M. Haviland (Eds.), *Handbook of emotions.* New York: Guilford.

Policastro, E., & Gardner, H. (1999). From case studies to robust generalizations: An approach to the study of creativity. In R. J. Sternberg (Ed.), *Handbook of creativity.* New York: Cambridge University Press.

Pomeroy, C., & Mitchell, J. E. (2002). Medical complications of anorexia nervosa and bulimia nervosa. In C. G. Fairburn & K. D. Brownell (Eds.), *Eating disorders and obesity: A comprehensive handbook.* New York: Guilford.

Ponterotto, J. G., & Pedersen, P. B. (1993). *Preventing prejudice: A guide for counselors and educators.* Newbury Park, CA: Sage.

Pope, H. G., Gruber, A. J., Hudson, J. I., Huestis, M. A., & Yurgelun-Todd, D. (2001). Neuropsychological performance in long-term cannabis users. *Archives of General Psychiatry, 58*, 909–915.

Pope, H. G., Gruber, A. J., & Yurgelun-Todd, D. (2001). Residual neuropsychologic effects of cannabis. *Current Psychiatry Report, 3*, 507–512.

Pope, K. S., Keith-Spiegel, P., & Tabachnick, B. G. (1986). Sexual attraction to clients. *American Psychologist, 41*, 147–158.

Popenoe, D. (1996). *Life without father.* New York: Pressler Press.

Pornpitakpan, C. (2004). The persuasiveness of source credibility: A critical review of five decades' evidence. *Journal of Applied Social Psychology, 34,* 243–281.

Porter, S., Yuille, J. C., & Lehman, D. R. (1999). The nature of real, implanted, and fabricated memories for emotional childhood events: Implications for the recovered memory debate. *Law and Human Behavior, 23,* 517–537.

Post, F. (1996). Verbal creativity, depression and alcoholism: An investigation of one hundred American and British writers. *British Journal of Psychiatry, 168,* 545–555.

Postman, L. (1985). Human learning and memory. In G. A. Kimble & K. Schlesinger (Eds.), *Topics in the history of psychology.* Hillsdale, NJ: Erlbaum.

Potthoff, J. G., Holahan, C. J., & Joiner, T. E., Jr. (1995). Reassurance-seeking, stress generation, and depressive symptoms: An integrative model. *Journal of Personality and Social Psychology, 68,* 664–670.

Powell, R. A., & Boer, D. P. (1995). Did Freud misinterpret reported memories of sexual abuse as fantasies? *Psychological Reports, 77,* 563–570.

Powell, R. A., & Gee, T. L. (1999). The effects of hypnosis on dissociative identity disorder: A reexamination of the evidence. *Canadian Journal of Psychiatry, 44,* 914–916.

Pratt, L. A., Ford, D. E., Crum, R. M., Armenian, H. K., Gallo, J. J., & Eaton, W. W. (1996). Depression, psychotropic medication, and risk of myocardial infarction: Prospective data from Baltimore ECA follow-up. *Archives of Internal Medicine, 94,* 3123–3129.

Priester, J. R., & Petty, R. E. (1995). Source attributions and persuasion; Perceived honesty as a determinant of message scrutiny. *Personality and Social Psychology Bulletin, 21,* 637–654.

Priester, J. R., & Petty, R. E. (2001). Extending the bases of subjective attitudinal ambivalence: Interpersonal and intrapersonal antecedents of evaluative tension. *Journal of Personality and Social Psychology, 80,* 19–34.

Priester, J. R., & Petty, R. E. (2003). The influence of spokesperson trustworthiness on message elaboration, attitude strength, and advertising. *Journal of Consumer Psychology, 13,* 408–421.

Prifitera, A. (1994). Wechsler scales of intelligence. In R. J. Sternberg (Ed.), *Encyclopedia of human intelligence.* New York: Macmillan.

Prochaska, J. O. (1994). Strong and weak principles for progressing from precontemplation to action on the basis of twelve problem behaviors. *Health Psychology, 13,* 47–51.

Proffitt, D. R., & Caudek, C. (2003). Depth perception and the perception of events. In A. F. Healy & R. W. Proctor (Eds.), *Handbook of psychology, Vol. 4: Experimental psychology.* New York: Wiley.

Pronin, E., Gilovich, T., & Ross, L. (2004). Objectivity in the eye of the beholder: Divergent perceptions of bias in self versus others. *Psychological Review, 111,* 781–799.

Pronin, E., Lin, D. Y., & Ross, L. (2002). The bias blind spot: Perceptions of bias in self versus others. *Personality and Social Psychology Bulletin, 28,* 369–381.

Prudic, J., & Sackeim, H. A. (1999). Electroconvulsive therapy and suicide risk. *Journal of Clinical Psychiatry, 60,* 104–110.

Pruitt, D. G. (1971). Choice shifts in group discussion: An introductory review. *Journal of Personality and Social Psychology, 20,* 339–360.

Purves, D., Lotto, B., & Polger, T. (2000). Color vision and the four-color-map problem. *Journal of Cognitive Neuroscience, 12,* 233–237.

Pyszczynski, T., Greenberg, J., & Solomon, S. (1999). A dual-process model of defense against conscious and unconscious death-related thoughts: An extension of terror management theory. *Psychological Review, 106,* 835–845.

Pyszczynski, T., Greenberg, J., Solomon, S., Arndt, J., & Schimel, J. (2004). Why do people need self-esteem? A theoretical and empirical review. *Psychological Bulletin, 130,* 435–468.

Pyszczynski, T., Solomon, S., & Greenberg, J. (2003). *In the wake of 9/11: The psychology of terror.* Washington, DC: American Psychological Association.

Quinn, K. A., Macrae, C. N., & Bodenhausen, G. V. (2003). Stereotyping and impression formation: How categorical thinking shapes person perception. In M. A. Hogg & J. Cooper (Eds.), *The Sage handbook of social psychology.* Thousand Oaks, CA: Sage.

Quitkin, F. M. (1999). Placebos, drug effects, and study design: A clinician's guide. *American Journal of Psychiatry, 156,* 829–836.

Rabins, P. V., Lyketsos, C. G., & Steele, C. D. (1999). *Practical dementia care.* New York: Oxford University Press.

Rachman, S. J. (1992). Behavior therapy. In L. R. Squire (Ed.), *Encyclopedia of learning and memory.* New York: Macmillan.

Ragland, D. R., & Brand, R. J. (1988). Type A behavior and mortality from coronary heart disease. *The New England Journal of Medicine, 318*(2), 65–69.

Rains, G. D. (2002). *Principles of human neuropsychology.* New York: McGraw-Hill.

Raj, A., & Sheehan, D. (2004). Benzodiazepines. In A. F. Schatzberg & C. B. Nemeroff (Eds.), *Textbook of psychopharmacology.* Washington, DC: American Psychiatric Publishing.

Rakic, P., Bourgeois, J. P., & Goldman-Rakic, P. S. (1994). Synaptic development of the cerebral cortex: Implications for learning, memory, and mental illness. *Progress in brain research, 102,* 227–243.

Ramadan, N. M. (2000). Migraine. In G. Fink (Ed.), *Encyclopedia of stress* (pp. 757–770). San Diego: Academic Press.

Ramey, C. T., & Ramey, S. L. (2004). Early educational interventions and intelligence. In E. Zigler & S. J. Styfco (Eds.), *The Head Start debate.* Baltimore: Paul H. Brookes Publishing.

Ramey, S. L. (1999). Head Start and preschool education: Toward continued improvement. *American Psychologist, 54,* 344–346.

Ramsay, D. S., Seeley, R. J., Bolles, R. C., & Woods, S. C. (1996). Ingestive homeostasis: The primacy of learning. In E. D. Capaldi (Ed.), *Why we eat what we eat: The psychology of eating* (pp. 11–29). Washington, DC: American Psychological Association.

Rapee, R. M., & Barlow, D. H. (2001). Generalized anxiety disorders, panic disorders, and phobias. In P. B. Sutker & H. E. Adams (Eds.), *Comprehensive handbook of psychopathology* (3rd ed., pp. 131–154). New York: Kluwer Academic/Plenum Publishers.

Raphael, B., & Dobson, M. (2000). Effects of public disasters. In G. Fink (Ed.), *Encyclopedia of stress* (Vol. 1, pp. 699–705). San Diego: Academic Press.

Rasmussen, C., Knapp, T. J., & Garner, L. (2000). Driving-induced stress in urban college students. *Perceptual & Motor Skills, 90,* 437–443.

Rauscher, F. H., Shaw, G. L., & Ky, K. N. (1993). Music and spatial task performance. *Nature, 365,* 611.

Rauscher, F. H., Shaw, G. L., & Ky, K. N. (1995). Listening to Mozart enhances spatial-temporal reasoning: Towards a neurophysiological basis. *Neuroscience Letters, 185,* 44–47.

Raynor, H. A., & Epstein, L. H. (2001). Dietary variety, energy regulation, and obesity. *Psychological Bulletin, 127,* 325–341.

Raynor, J. O., & Entin, E. E. (1982). Future orientation and achievement motivation. In J. O. Raynor & E. E. Entin (Eds.), *Motivation, career striving, and aging.* New York: Hemisphere.

Read, C. R. (1991). Achievement and career choices: Comparisons of males and females. *Roeper Review, 13,* 188–193.

Real, L. (1991). Animal choice behavior and the evolution of cognitive architecture. *Science, 253,* 980–986.

Reber, R. (2004). Availability. In F. P. Rudiger (Ed.), *Cognitive illusions.* New York: Psychology Press.

Recanzone, G. H. (2000). Cerebral cortical plasticity: Perception and skill acquisition. In M. S. Gazzaniga (Ed.), *The new cognitive neurosciences.* Cambridge, MA: The MIT Press.

Recht, L. D., Lew, R. A., & Schwartz, W. J. (1995). Baseball teams beaten by jet lag. *Nature, 377,* 583.

Rechtschaffen, A. (1994). Sleep onset: Conceptual issues. In R. D. Ogilvie & J. R. Harsh (Eds.), *Sleep onset: Normal and abnormal processes.* Washington, DC: American Psychological Association.

Reddy, B. S. (1999). Role of dietary fiber in colon cancer: An overview. *American Journal of Medicine, 106*(1A), 16S–19S.

Reed, J. G., & Baxter P. M. (2003). *Library use: A handbook for psychology.* Washington, DC: American Psychological Association.

Rees, C. J., & Metcalfe, B. (2003). The faking of personality questionnaire results: Who's kidding whom? *Journal of Managerial Psychology, 18*(2), 156–165.

Reeve, C. L., & Hakel, M. D. (2002). Asking the right questions about *g. Human Performance, 15,* 47–74.

Regan, P. C. (1998). What if you can't get what you want? Willingness to compromise ideal mate selection standards as a function of sex, mate value, and relationship context. *Personality and Social Psychology Bulletin, 24,* 1294–1303.

Regan, P. C. (2003). *The mating game: A primer on love, sex, and marriage.* Thousand Oaks, CA: Sage.

Regan, T. (1997). The rights of humans and other animals. *Ethics & Behavior, 7*(2), 103–111.

Regier, D. A., & Burke, J. D. (2000). Epidemiology. In B. J. Sadock & V. A. Sadock (Eds.), *Kaplan and Sadock's comprehensive textbook of psychiatry.* Philadelphia: Lippincott/Williams & Wilkins.

Rehm, L. P., Wagner, A., & Ivens-Tyndal, Co. (2001). Mood disorders: Unipolar and bipolar. In P. B. Sutker & H. E. Adams (Eds.), *Comprehensive handbook of psychopathology* (pp. 277–308). New York: Kluwer Academic/Plenum.

Reibel, D. K., Greeson, J. M., Brainard, G. C., & Rosenzweig, S. (2001). Mindfulness-based stress reduction and health-related quality of life in a heterogeneous patient population. *General Hospital Psychiatry, 23*(4), 183–192.

Reichert, T. (2003). The prevalence of sexual imagery in ads targeted to young adults. *Journal of Consumer Affairs, 37,* 403–412.

Reichert, T., Heckler, S. E., & Jackson, S. (2001). The effects of sexual social marketing appeals on cognitive processing and persuasion. *Journal of Advertising, 30*(1), 13–27.

Reichert, T., & Lambiase, J. (2003). How to get "kissably close": Examining how advertisers appeal to consumers' sexual needs and desires. *Sexuality & Culture: An Interdisciplinary Quarterly, 7*(3), 120–136.

Reinharz, D., Lesage, A. D., & Contandriopoulos, A. P. (2000). Cost-effectiveness analysis of psychiatric deinstitutionalization. *Canadian Journal of Psychiatry, 45,* 533–538.

Reisner, A. D. (1998). Repressed memories: True and false. In R. A. Baker (Ed.), *Child sexual abuse and false memory syndrome.* Amherst, NY: Prometheus Books.

Rennie, D., & Luft, H. S. (2000). Making them transparent, making them credible. *Journal of the American Medical Association, 283,* 2516–2521.

Repetto, M., & Gold, M. S. (2005). Cocaine and crack: Neurobiology. In J. H. Lowinson, P. Ruiz, R. B. Millman, & J. G. Langrod (Eds.), *Substance abuse: A comprehensive textbook.* Philadelphia: Lippincott/Williams & Wilkins.

Rescorla, R. A. (1978). Some implications of a cognitive perspective on Pavlovian conditioning. In S. H. Hulse, H. Fowler, & W. K. Honig (Eds.), *Cognitive processes in animal behavior.* Hillsdale, NJ: Erlbaum.

Rescorla, R. A. (1980). *Pavlovian second-order conditioning.* Hillsdale, NJ: Erlbaum.

Rescorla, R. A., & Wagner, A. R. (1972). A theory of Pavlovian conditioning: Variations in the effectiveness of reinforcement and nonreinforcement. In A. H. Black & W. F. Prokasky (Eds.), *Classical conditioning: II. Current research and theory.* New York: Appleton-Century-Crofts.

Rest, J. R. (1986). *Moral development: Advances in research and theory.* New York: Praeger.

Reuter-Lorenz, P. A., & Miller, A. C. (1998). The cognitive neuroscience of human laterality: Lessons from the bisected brain. *Current Directions in Psychological Science, 7,* 15–20.

Reynolds, A. J., Temple, J. T., Robertson, D. L., & Mann, E. A. (2001). Long-term effects of an early childhood intervention on educational achievement and juvenile arrest: A 15-year follow-up of low-income children in public schools. *Journal of the American Medical Association, 285,* 2339–2346.

Richardson, C. R., Kriska, A. M., Lantz, P. M., & Hayword, R. A. (2004). Physical activity and mortality across cardiovascular disease risk groups. *Medicine and Science in Sports and Exercise, 36,* 1923–1929.

Richardson, G. S. (1993). Circadian rhythms. In M. A. Carskadon (Ed.), *Encyclopedia of sleep and dreaming.* New York: Macmillan.

Ridker, P. M. (2001). High-sensitivity C-reactive protein: Potential adjunct for global risk assessment in the primary prevention of cardiovascular disease. *Circulation, 103,* 1813–1818.

Rieber, R. W. (1998). The assimilation of psychoanalysis in America: From popularization to vulgarization. In R. W. Rieber & K. D. Salzinger (Eds.), *Psychology: Theoretical-historical perspectives.* Washington, DC: American Psychological Association.

Rieskamp, J., & Hoffrage, U. (1999). When do people use simple heuristics, and how can we tell? In G. Gigerenzer, P. M. Todd, & ABC Research Group (Eds.), *Simple heuristics that make us smart* (pp. 141–168). New York: Oxford University Press.

Rihmer, Z. (2003). Do SSRI's increase the risk of suicide among depressives even if they are only taking placebo? *Psychotherapy & Psychosomatics, 72,* 357–358.

Riis, J., Loewenstein, G., Baron, J., Jepson, C., Fagerlin, A., & Ubel, P. A. (2005). Ignorance of hedonic adaptation to hemodialysis: A study using ecological momentary assessment. *Journal of Experimental Psychology: General, 134*(1), 3–9.

Rilling, M. (1996). The mystery of the vanished citations: James McConnell's forgotten 1960s quest for planarian learning, a biochemical engram, and celebrity. *American Psychologist, 51,* 589–598.

Rilling, M. (2000). John Watson's paradoxical struggle to explain Freud. *American Psychologist, 55,* 301–312.

Rimal R. N. (2001). Longitudinal influences of knowledge and self-efficacy on exercise behavior: Tests of a mutual reinforcement model. *Journal of Health Psychology, 6,* 31–46.

Riskind, J. H. (2005). Cognitive mechanisms in generalized anxiety disorder: A second generation of theoretical perspectives. *Cognitive Therapy & Research, 29*(1), 1–5.

Roberts, B. W., & DelVecchio, W. F. (2000). The rank-order consistency of personality traits from childhood to old age: A quantitative review of longitudinal studies. *Psychological Bulletin, 126,* 3–25.

Roberts, B. W., & Pomerantz, E. M. (2004). On traits, situations, and their integration: A developmental perspective. *Personality and Social Psychology Review, 8,* 402–416.

Roberts, P., & Newton, P. M. (1987). Levinsonian studies of women's adult development. *Psychology and Aging, 2,* 154–163.

Robiner, W. N., Bearman, D. L., Berman, M., Grove, W. M., Colon, E., Armstrong, J., Mareck, S., & Tanenbaum, R. L. (2003). Prescriptive authority for psychologists: Despite deficits in education and knowledge. *Journal of Clinical Psychology in Medical Settings, 10*(3), 211–212.

Robins, R. W., Gosling, S. D., & Craik, K. H. (1999). An empirical analysis of trends in psychology. *American Psychologist, 54,* 117–128.

Robinson, D. G., Woerner, M. G., McMeniman, M., Mendelowitz, A., & Bilder, R. M. (2004). Symptomatic and functional recovery from a first episode of schizophrenia or schizoaffective disorder. *American Journal of Psychiatry, 161,* 473–479.

Robinson, F. P. (1970). *Effective study* (4th ed.). New York: Harper & Row.

Rockey, D. L., Jr., Beason, K. R., Howington, E. B., Rockey, C. M., & Gilbert, J. D. (2005). Gambling by Greek-affiliated college students: An association between affiliation and gambling. *Journal of College Student Development, 46,* 75-87.

Rodgers, J. E. (1982). The malleable memory of eyewitnesses. *Science Digest, 3,* 32–35.

Rodgers, J., Buchanan, T., Scholey, A. B., Heffernan, T. M., Ling, J., & Parrott, A. C. (2003). Patterns of drug use and the influence of gender on self-reports of memory ability in ecstasy users: A web-based study. *Journal of Psychopharmacology, 17,* 389–396.

Rodin, J. (1985). Insulin levels, hunger, and food intake: An example of feedback loops in body weight regulation. *Health Psychology, 4,* 1–24.

Roediger, H. L., III. (1980). Memory metaphors in cognitive psychology. *Memory & Cognition, 8,* 231–246.

Roediger, H. L. III, Gallo, D. A., & Geraci, L. (2002). Processing approaches to cognition: The impetus from the levels-of-processing framework. *Memory, 10,* 319–332.

Roediger, H. L., III, & McDermott, K. B. (1995). Creating false memories: Remembering words not presented in lists. *Journal of Experimental Psychology: Learning, Memory, and Cognition, 21,* 803–814.

Roediger, H. L., III, & McDermott, K. B. (2000). Tricks of memory. *Current Directions in Psychological Science, 9,* 123–127.

Roediger, H. L., III, Wheeler, M. A., & Rajaram, S. (1993). Remembering, knowing, and reconstructing the past. In D. L. Medin (Ed.), *The psychology of learning and motivation: Advances in research and theory.* San Diego: Academic Press.

Roehrs, T., Carskadon, M. A., Dement, W. C., & Roth, T. (2005). Daytime sleepiness and alertness. In M. H. Kryger, T. Roth, & W. C. Dement (Eds.). *Principles and practice of sleep medicine.* Philadelphia: Elsevier Saunders.

Roehrs, T., & Roth, T. (2000). Hypnotics: Efficacy and adverse effects. In M. H. Kryger, T. Roth, & W. C. Dement (Eds.), *Principles and practice of sleep medicine.* Philadelphia: Saunders.

Roehrs, T., & Roth, T. (2004). "Hypnotic" prescription patterns in a large managed-care population. *Sleep Medicine, 5,* 463–466.

Roffwarg, H. P., Muzio, J. N., & Dement, W. C. (1966). Ontogenetic development of the human sleep-dream cycle. *Science, 152,* 604–619.

Rogers, C. R. (1951). *Client-centered therapy: Its current practice, implications, and theory.* Boston: Houghton Mifflin.

Rogers, C. R. (1961). *On becoming a person: A therapist's view of psychotherapy.* Boston: Houghton Mifflin.

Rogers, C. R. (1980). *A way of being.* Boston: Houghton Mifflin.

Rogers, C. R. (1986). Client-centered therapy. In I. L. Kutash & A. Wolf (Eds.), *Psychotherapist's casebook.* San Francisco: Jossey-Bass.

Rogers, N. L., & Dinges, D. F. (2002). Shiftwork, circadian disruption, and consequences. *Primary Psychiatry, 9*(8), 50.

Rogers, W. T., & Yang, P. (1996). Test-wiseness: Its nature and application. *European Journal of Psychological Assessment, 12,* 247–259.

Rogoff, B. (1990). *Apprenticeship in thinking.* New York: Oxford University Press.

Rogoff, B. (1998). Cognition as a collaborative process. In D. Kuhn & R. S. Siegler (Eds.), *Handbook of child psychology, Vol. 2: Cognition perception, and language.* New York: Wiley.

Rohner, R. P., & Veneziano, R. A. (2001). The importance of father love: History and contemporary evidence. *Review of General Psychology, 5,* 382–405.

Rohrer, D., Taylor, K., Pashler, H., Wixted, J. T., & Capeda, N. J. (2005). The effect of overlearning on long-term retention. *Applied Cognitive Psychology, 19,* 361–374.

Rojahn, K., & Pettigrew, T. F. (1992). Memory for schema-relevant information: A meta-analytic resolution. *British Journal of Social Psychology, 31,* 81–109.

Rolls, E. T. (1990). A theory of emotion, and its application to understanding the neural basis of emotion. *Cognition and Emotion, 4,* 161–190.

Rolls, E. T., & Tovee, M. T. (1995). Sparseness of the neuronal representation of stimuli in the primate temporal visual cortex. *Journal of Neurophysiology, 73,* 713–726.

Romano, S. J., & Quinn, L. (2001). Evaluation and treatment of bulimia nervosa. *Primary Psychiatry, 8*(2), 57–62.

Rose, D. P. (1997). Dietary fatty acids and cancer. *American Journal of Clinical Nutrition, 66,* 998S–1003S.

Rose, D., Wykes, T., Leese, M., Bindman, J., & Fleischmann, P. (2003). Patient's perspectives on electroconvulsive therapy: Systematic review. *British Medical Journal, 326,* 1363–1365.

Rose, H., & Rose, S. E. (2000). *Alas, poor Darwin: Arguments against evolutionary psychology.* New York: Harmony Books.

Rosenberg, P. S., & Biggar, R. J. (1998). Trends in HIV incidence among young adults in the United

States. *Journal of the American Medical Association, 279,* 1894–1899.

Rosenberg, S. D., Rosenberg, H. J., & Farrell, M. P. (1999). Midlife crisis revisited. In S. L. Willis & J. D. Reid (Eds.), *Life in the middle: Psychological and social development in middle age* (pp. 47–70). San Diego, CA: Academic Press.

Rosenblatt, A., Greenberg, J., Solomon, S., Pyszczynski, T., & Lyon, D. (1989). Evidence for terror management theory: I. The effect of mortality salience on reactions to those who violate or uphold cultural values. *Journal of Personality and Social Psychology, 57,* 681–690.

Rosenthal, R. (1976). *Experimenter effects in behavioral research.* New York: Halsted.

Rosenthal, R. (1994). Interpersonal expectancy effects: A 30–year perspective. *Current Directions in Psychological Science, 3,* 176–179.

Rosenthal, R. (2002). Experimenter and clinical effects in scientific inquiry and clinical practice. *Prevention & Treatment, 5*(38).

Rosenthal, R., & Fode, K. L. (1963). Three experiments in experimenter bias. *Psychological Reports, 12,* 491–511.

Rosenzweig, M. R., & Bennet, E. L. (1996). Psychobiology of plasticity: Effects of training and experience on brain and behavior. *Behavioural Brain Research, 78*(5), 57–65.

Rosenzweig, M. R., Krech, D., & Bennett, E. L. (1961). Heredity, environment, brain biochemistry, and learning. In *Current trends in psychological theory.* Pittsburgh: University of Pittsburgh Press.

Rosenzweig, M., Krech, D., Bennett, E. L., & Diamond, M. (1962). Effects of environmental complexity and training on brain chemistry and anatomy: A replication and extension. *Journal of Comparative and Physiological Psychology, 55,* 429–437.

Rosenzweig, S. (1985). Freud and experimental psychology: The emergence of idiodynamics. In S. Koch & D. E. Leary (Eds.), *A century of psychology as a science.* New York: McGraw-Hill.

Ross, B. (1991). William James: Spoiled child of American psychology. In G. A. Kimble, M. Wertheimer, & C. White (Eds.), *Portraits of pioneers in psychology.* Hillsdale, NJ: Erlbaum.

Rosso, I. M., Cannon, T. D., Huttunen, T., Huttunen, M. O., Lönnqvist, J., & Gasperoni, T. L. (2000). Obstetric risk factors for early-onset schizophrenia in a Finnish birth cohort. *American Journal of Psychiatry, 157,* 801–807.

Roter, D. L., Hall, J. A., Merisca, R., Nordstrom, B., Cretin, D., & Svarstad, B. (1998). Effectiveness of interventions to promote patient compliance. *Medical Care, 36,* 1138–1161.

Rothblum, E. D., Solomon, L. J., & Albee, G. W. (1986). A sociopolitical perspective of DSM-III. In T. Million & G. L. Klerman (Eds.), *Contemporary directions in psychopathology: Toward the DSM-IV.* New York: Guilford.

Rotter, J. B. (1982). *The development and application of social learning theory.* New York: Praeger.

Routh, D. K., & Reisman, J. M. (2003). Clinical psychology. In D. K. Freedheim (Ed.), *Handbook of psychology, Vol. 1: History of psychology.* New York: Wiley.

Rowatt, W. C., Cunningham, M. R., & Druen, P. B. (1999). Lying to get a date: The effect of facial physical attractiveness on the willingness to deceive prospective dating partners. *Journal of Social & Personal Relationships, 16,* 209–223.

Rowe, D. (1994). *The limits of family influence: Genes, experience, and behavior.* New York: Guilford.

Rowe, D., & van den Oord, E. J. C. G. (2005). Genetic and environmental influences. In V. A. Derlega, B. A. Winstead, & W. H. Jones (Eds.), *Personality: Contemporary theory and research.* Belmont, CA: Wadsworth.

Rowe, S. M., & Wertsch, J. V. (2002). Vygotsky's model of cognitive development. In U. Goswami (Ed.), *Blackwell handbook of childhood cognitive development.* Malden, MA: Blackwell Publishing.

Rozin, P. (1990). The importance of social factors in understanding the acquisition of food habits. In E. D. Capaldi & T. L. Powley (Eds.), *Taste, experience, and feeding.* Washington, DC: American Psychological Association.

Rozin, P., Dow, S., Moscovitch, M., & Rajaram, S. (1998). What causes humans to begin and end a meal? A role for memory for what has been eaten, as evidenced by a study of multiple meal eating in amnesic patients. *Psychological Science, 9,* 392–396.

Rozin, P., Kabnick, K., Pete, E., Fischler, C., & Shields, C. (2003). The ecology of eating: Smaller portion sizes in France than in the United States help explain the French paradox. *Psychological Science, 14,* 450–454.

Ruble, D. N., & Martin, C. L. (1998). Gender development. In W. Damon (Ed.), *Handbook of child psychology (Vol. 3): Social, emotional, and personality development.* New York: Wiley.

Rudisch, B., & Nemeroff, C. B. (2003). Epidemiology of comorbid coronary artery disease and depression. *Biological Psychiatry, 54,* 227–240.

Rudorfer, M. V., Henry, M. E., & Sackheim, H. A. (2003). Electroconvulsive therapy. In A. Tasman, J. Kay, & J. A. Lieberman (Eds.), *Psychiatry.* New York: Wiley.

Ruiter, R. A., Abraham, C., & Kok, G. (2001). Scary warnings and rational precautions: A review of the psychology of fear appeals. *Psychology & Health, 16,* 613–630.

Ruscio, J. (2002). *Clear thinking with psychology: Separating sense from nonsense.* Belmont, CA: Wadsworth.

Rush, A. J. (1984). Cognitive therapy. In T. B. Karasu (Ed.), *The psychiatric therapies.* Washington, DC: American Psychiatric Press.

Rush, A. J. (2000). Mood disorders: Treatment of depression. In B. J. Sadock & V. A. Sadock (Eds.), *Kaplan and Sadock's comprehensive textbook of psychiatry* (7th ed., Vol. 1, pp. 1377–1384). Philadelphia: Lippincott/Williams and Wilkins.

Rush, A. J., & Beck, A. T. (2000). Cognitive therapy. In B. J. Sadock & V. A. Sadock (Eds.), *Kaplan and Sadock's comprehensive textbook of psychiatry* (7th ed., Vol. 1, pp. 2167–2177). Philadelphia: Lippincott/Williams & Wilkins.

Rushton, J. P. (2003). Race differences in *g* and the "Jensen effect." In H. Nyborg (Ed.), *The scientific study of general intelligence: Tribute to Arthur R. Jensen.* Oxford, UK: Pergamon.

Rushton, J. P., & Jensen, A. R. (2005). Thirty years of research on race differences in cognitive ability. *Psychology, Public Policy, and Law, 11,* 235–294.

Russell, G. F. M. (1995). Anorexia nervosa through time. In G. Szmukler, C. Dare, & J. Treasure (Eds.), *Handbook of eating disorders: Theory, treatment, and research.* New York: Wiley.

Russell, G. F. M. (1997). The history of bulimia nervosa. In D. M. Garner & P. E. Garfinkel (Eds.), *Handbook of treatment for eating disorders.* New York: Guilford.

Russell, J. A. (1991). Culture and the categorization of emotions. *Psychological Bulletin, 110,* 426–450.

Russo, N. F., & Denmark, F. L. (1987). Contributions of women to psychology. *Annual Review of Psychology, 38,* 279–298.

Rutherford, A. (2000). Radical behaviorism and psychology's public: B. F. Skinner in the popular press, 1934–1990. *History of Psychology, 3,* 371–395.

Rutherford, W. (1886). A new theory of hearing. *Journal of Anatomy and Physiology, 21,* 166–168.

Rutledge, T., Reis, S. E., Olson, M., Owens, J., Kelsey, S. F., Pepine, C. J., Mankad, S., Rogers, W. J., Merz, C. N. B., Sopko, G., Cornell, C. E., Sharaf, B., & Matthews, K. A. (2004). Social networks are associated with lower mortality rates among women with suspected coronary disease: The National Heart Lung, and Blood Institute–sponsored women's ischemia syndrome evaluation study. *Psychosomatic Medicine, 66,* 882–888.

Rutter, M., & Silberg, J. (2002). Gene-environment interplay relation to emotional and behavioral disturbance. *Annual Review of Psychology, 53,* 463–490.

Ryan, R. M., & Deci, E. L. (2001). On happiness and human potentials: A review of research on hedonic and eudaimonic well-being. *Annual Review of Psychology, 52,* 141–166.

Ryckeley, R. (2005, May). Don't send in the clowns. *The Citizen.*

Sack, A. T., Hubl, D., Prvulovic, D., Formisano, E., Jandl, M., Zanella, F. E., Maurer, K., Goebel, R., Dierks, T., & Linden, D. E. J. (2002). The experimental combination of r TMS and fMRI reveals the functional relevance of parietal cortex for visuospatial functions. *Cognitive Brain Resarch, 13,* 85–93.

Sack, A. T., & Linden, D. E. J. (2003). Combining transcranial magnetic stimulation and functional imaging in cognitive brain research: Possibilities and limitations. *Brain Research Reviews, 43*(1), 41–56.

Sackeim, H. A., Haskett, R. F., Mulsant, B. H., Thase, M. E., Mann, J. J., Pettinati, H. M., Greenberg, R. M., Crowe, R. R., Cooper, T. B., & Prudic, J. (2001). Continuation pharmacotherapy in the prevention of relapse following electroconvulsive therapy: A randomized controlled trial. *Journal of the American Medical Association, 285,* 1299–1307.

Sacks, O. (1987). *The man who mistook his wife for a hat.* New York: Harper & Row.

Sadker, M., & Sadker, D. (1994). *Failing at fairness: How America's schools cheat girls.* New York: Scribners.

Salkovskis, P. M., & Warwick, H. M. C. (2001). Meaning, misinterpretations, and medicine: A cognitive-behavioral approach to understanding health anxiety and hypochondriasis. In V. Starcevic & D. R. Lipsitt (Eds.), *Hypochondriasis: Modern perspectives on an ancient malady.* New York: Oxford University Press.

Salthouse, T. A. (1996). The processing-speed theory of adult age differences in cognition. *Psychological Review, 103,* 403–428.

Salthouse, T. A. (2000). Aging and measures of processing speed. *Biological Psychology, 54,* 35–54.

Salthouse, T. A. (2003). Memory aging from 18–80. *Alzheimer Disease & Associated Disorders, 17*(3), 162–167.

Salthouse, T. A. (2004). What and when of cognitive aging. *Current Directions in Psychological Science, 13*(4), 140–144.

Salvendy, J. T. (1993). Selection and preparation of patients and organization of the group. In H. I. Kaplan & B. J. Sadock (Eds.), *Comprehensive group psychotherapy.* Baltimore: Williams & Wilkins.

Samelson, F. (1981). Struggle for scientific authority: The reception of Watson's behaviorism, 1913–1920. *Journal of the History of the Behavioral Sciences, 17,* 399–425.

Samelson, F. (1994). John B. Watson in 1913: Rhetoric and practice. In J. T. Todd & E. K. Morris (Eds.), *Modern perspectives on John B. Watson and classical behaviorism.* Westport, CT: Greenwood Press.

Samet, J. M. (1992). The health benefits of smoking cessation. *Medical Clinics of North America, 76,* 399–414.

Sanchez, I. M., & Turner, S. M. (2003). Practicing psychology in the era of managed care: Implications for practice and training. *American Psychologist, 58*(2), 116–129.

Sande, M. A., & Ronald, A. (2004). Treatment of HIV/AIDS: Do the dilemmas only increase? *Journal of the American Medical Association, 292,* 224–236.

Sanderson, W. C., & Barlow, D. H. (1990). A description of patients diagnosed with DSM-III-R generalized anxiety disorder. *Journal of Nervous and Mental Disease, 178,* 588–591.

Sandin, B., Chorot, P., Santed, M. A., & Valiente, R. M. (2004). Differences in negative life events between patients with anxiety disorders, depression and hypochondriasis. *Anxiety, Stress & Coping: An International Journal, 17*(1), 37–47.

Sanger, D. J. (2004). The pharmacology and mechanisms of action of new generation, nonbenzodiazepine hypnotic agents. *CNS Drugs, 18*(Suppl1), 9–15.

Sanislow, C. A., & Carson, R. C. (2001). Schizophrenia: A critical examination. In P. B. Sutker & H. E. Adams (Eds.), *Comprehensive handbook of psychopathology* (3rd ed., pp. 403–444). New York: Kluwer Academic/Plenum.

Saper, C. B. (2000). Brain stem, reflexive behavior, and the cranial nerves. In E. R. Kandel, J. H. Schwartz, & T. M. Jessell (Eds.), *Principles of neural science* (pp. 873–888). New York: McGraw-Hill.

Saxe, L. (1994). Detection of deception: Polygraph and integrity tests. *Current Directions in Psychological Science, 3,* 69–73.

Saxe, L., & Ben-Shakhar, G. (1999). Admissibility of polygraph tests: The application of scientific standards post-Daubert. *Psychology, Public Policy, and Law, 5,* 203–223.

Sayers, S. L. (2004). Depression and heart disease: The interrelationship between these two common disorders is complex and requires careful diagnostic and treatment methods. *Psychiatric Annals, 34*(4), 282–288.

Scarr, S. (1997). Behavior-genetic and socialization theories of intelligence: Truce and reconciliation. In R. J. Sternberg & E. L. Grigorenko (Eds.), *Intelligence, heredity, and environment.* New York: Cambridge University Press.

Scarr, S., & Weinberg, R. A. (1977). Intellectual similarities within families of both adopted and biological children. *Intelligence, 32,* 170–190.

Scarr, S., & Weinberg, R. A. (1983). The Minnesota adoption studies: Genetic differences and malleability. *Child Development, 54,* 260–267.

Schachter, S. (1959). *The psychology of affiliation.* Stanford, CA: Stanford University Press.

Schachter, S. (1964). The interaction of cognitive and physiological determinants of emotional state. In L. Berkowitz (Ed.), *Advances in experimental social psychology* (Vol. 1). New York: Academic Press.

Schachter, S., & Singer, J. E. (1962). Cognitive, social and physiological determinants of emotional state. *Psychological Review, 69,* 379–399.

Schachter, S., & Singer, J. E. (1979). Comments on the Maslach and Marshall-Zimbardo experiments. *Journal of Personality and Social Psychology, 37,* 989–995.

Schacter, D. L. (1996). *Searching for memory: The brain, the mind, and the past.* New York: Basic Books.

Schacter, D. L. (2001). *The seven sins of memory: How the mind forgets and remembers.* Boston, MA: Houghton Mifflin.

Schaeffer, N. C. (2000). Asking questions about threatening topics: A selective overview. In A. A. Stone, J. S. Turkkan, C. A. Bachrach, J. B. Jobe, H. S. Kurtzman, & V. Cain (Eds.), *The science of self-report: Implications for research and practice.* Mahwah, NJ: Erlbaum.

Schafe, G. E., & Bernstein, I. E. (1996). Taste aversion learning. In E. D. Capaldi (Ed.), *Why we eat what we eat: The psychology of eating* (pp. 31–52). Washington, DC: American Psychological Association.

Schaie, K. W. (1990). Intellectual development in adulthood. In J. E. Birren & K. W. Schaie (Eds.), *Handbook of the psychology of aging* (3rd ed.). San Diego: Academic Press.

Schaie, K. W. (1994). The course of adult intellectual development. *American Psychologist, 49,* 304–313.

Schaie, K. W. (1996). *Adult intellectual development: The Seattle longitudinal study.* New York: Cambridge University Press.

Scheier, M. F., & Carver, C. S. (1985). Optimism, coping and health: Assessment and implications of generalized expectancies. *Health Psychology, 4,* 219–247.

Scherer, K. R., & Wallbott, H. G. (1994). Evidence for universality and cultural variation of differential emotion response patterning. *Journal of Personality and Social Psychology, 66,* 310–328.

Schiff, M., & Lewontin, R. (1986). *Education and class: The irrelevance of IQ genetic studies.* Oxford: Clarendon Press.

Schiffman, J., Ekstrom, M., LaBrie, J., Schulsinger, F., Sorenson, H., & Mednick, S. (2002). Minor physical anomalies and schizophrenia spectrum disorders: A prospective investigation. *American Journal of Psychiatry, 159,* 238–243.

Schiffman, S. S., Graham, B. G., Sattely-Miller, E. A., & Warwick, Z. S. (1998). Orosensory perception of dietary fat. *Current Directions in Psychological Science, 7,* 137–143.

Schildkraut, J. J., Hirshfeld, A. J., & Murphy, J. M. (1994). Mind and mood in modern art, II: Depressive disorders, spirituality, and early deaths in the abstract expressionist artists of the New York School. *American Journal of Psychiatry, 151,* 482–488.

Schimel, J., Simon, L., Greenberg, J., Pyszczynski, T., Solomon, S., Waxmonsky, J., & Arndt, J. (1999). Stereotypes and terror management: Evidence that mortality salience enhances stereotypic thinking and preference. *Journal of Personality and Social Psychology, 77,* 905–926.

Schimmack, U., & Crites, S. L. (2005). The structure of affect. In D. Albarracin, B. T. Johnson, & M. P. Zanna (Eds.), *The handbook of attitudes* . Mahwah, NJ: Erlbaum.

Schlosberg, H. (1954). Three dimensions of emotion. *Psychological Review, 61,* 81–88.

Schmidt, F. L. (2002). The role of general cognitive ability and job performance: Why there cannot be a debate. *Human Performance, 15,* 187–210.

Schmidt, F. L., & Hunter, J. (2004). General mental ability in the world of work: Occupational attainment and job performance. *Journal of Personality and Social Psychology, 86,* 162–173.

Schmithorst, V. J., Wilke, M., Dardzinski, B. J., & Holland, S. K. (2002). Correlation of white matter diffusivity and anisotropy with age during childhood and adolescence: A cross-sectional diffusion-tensor MR imaging study. *Radiology, 222,* 212–218.

Schmitt, D. P. (2005). Fundamentals of human mating strategies. In D. M. Buss (Ed.), *The handbook of evolutionary psychology.* New York: Wiley.

Schmitt, D. P., & 121 members of the International Sexuality Description Project. (2004). Patterns and universals of mate poaching across 53 nations: The effects of sex, culture, and personality on romantically attracting another person's partner. *Journal of Personality and Social Psychology, 86,* 560–584.

Schmitt, M. T., & Maes, J. (2002). Stereotypic ingroup bias as self-defense against relative deprivation: Evidence from a longitudinal study of the German unification process. *European Journal of Social Psychology, 32,* 309–326.

Schmitz, J. M., & DeLaune, K. A. (2005). Nicotine. In J. H. Lowinson, P. Ruiz, R. B. Millman, & J. G. Langrod (Eds.), *Substance abuse: A comprehensive textbook.* Philadelphia: Lippincott/Williams & Williams.

Schneider, F., & Deldin, P. J. (2001). Genetics and schizophrenia. In P. B. Sutker & H. E. Adams (Eds.), *Comprehensive handbook of psychopathology* (3rd ed., pp. 371–402). New York: Kluwer Academic/Plenum.

Scholey, A. B., Parrott, A. C., Buchanan, T., Heffernan, T. M., Ling, J., & Rodgers, J. (2004). Increased intensity of Ecstasy and polydrug usage in the more experienced recreational Ecstasy/MDMA users: A WWW study. *Addictive Behaviors, 29,* 743–752.

Schreiber, F. R. (1973). *Sybil.* New York: Warner.

Schuit, A. J., Feskens, E. J., Launer, L. J., & Kromhaut, D. (2001). Physical activity and cognitive decline, the role of the apolipoprotein e4 allele. *Medicine and Science in Sports and Exercise, 33,* 772–777.

Schulz-Hardt, S., Frey, D., Luethgens, C., & Moscovici, S. (2000). Biased information search in group decision making. *Journal of Personality & Social Psychology, 78,* 655–669.

Schuman, H., & Kalton, G. (1985). Survey methods. In G. Lindzey & E. Aronson (Eds.), *Handbook of social psychology* (3rd ed.). New York: Random House.

Schwartz, B. L. (1999). Sparkling at the end of the tongue: The etiology of tip-of-the-tongue phenomenology. *Psychonomic Bulletin & Review, 6,* 379–393.

Schwartz, B., & Robbins, S. J. (1995). *Psychology of learning and behavior* (4th ed.). New York: Norton.

Schwartz, J. H. (2000). Neurotransmitters. In E. R. Kandel, J. H. Schwartz, & T. M. Jessell (Eds.), *Principles of neural science.* New York: McGraw-Hill.

Schwartz, J. H., & Westbrook, G. L. (2000). The cytology of neurons. In E. R. Kandel, J. H. Schwartz, & T. M. Jessell (Eds.), *Principles of neural science* (pp. 67–104). New York: McGraw-Hill.

Schwartz, J. P., Waldo, M., & Higgins, A. J. (2004). Attachment styles: Relationship to masculine gender role conflict in college men. *Psychology of Men & Masculinity, 5*(2), 143–146.

Schwartz, L., Slater, M. A., & Birchler, G. R. (1994). Interpersonal stress and pain behaviors in patients with chronic pain. *Journal of Consulting and Clinical Psychology, 62,* 861–864.

Schwartz, M. W., Peskind, E., Raskind, M., Nicolson, M., Moore, J., Morawiecki, A., Boyko, E. J., & Porte, D. J. (1996). Cerebrospinal fluid leptin levels: Relationship to plasma levels and to adiposity in humans. *Nature Medicine, 2,* 589–593.

Schwartz, M. W., Woods, S. C., Porte, D., Seeley, R. J., & Baskin, D. G. (2000). Central nervous system control of food intake. *Nature, 404,* 661–671.

Schwarz, N. (1999). Self-reports: How the questions shape the answers. *American Psychologist, 54,* 93–105.

Schwarz, N., & Strack, F. (1999). Reports of subjective well-being: Judgmental processes and their methodological implications. In D. Kahneman, E. Diener, & N. Schwarz (Eds.), *Well-being: The foundations of hedonic psychology.* New York: Russell Sage Foundation.

Scoville, W. B., & Milner, B. (1957). Loss of recent memory after bilateral hippocampal lesions. *Journal of Neurology, Neurosurgery & Psychiatry, 20,* 11–21.

Scroppo, J. C., Drob, S. L., Weinberger, J. L., & Eagle, P. (1998). Identifying dissociative identity disorder: A self-report and projective study. *Journal of Abnormal Psychology, 107,* 272–284.

Scull, A. (1990). Deinstitutionalization: Cycles of despair. *The Journal of Mind and Behavior, 11*(3/4), 301–312.

Scully, J. A., Tosi, H., & Banning, K. (2000). Life event checklists: Revisiting the social readjustment rating scale after 30 years. *Educational & Psychological Measurement, 60,* 864–876.

Seabrook, R., Brown, G. D. A., & Solity, J. E. (2005). Distributed and massed practice: From laboratory to classroom. *Applied Cognitive Psychology, 19*(1), 107–122.

Searle, A., & Bennett, P. (2001). Psychological factors and inflammatory bowel disease: A review of a decade of literature. *Psychology, Health and Medicine, 6,* 121–135.

Searleman, A. (1996). Personality variables and prospective memory performance. In D. J. Herrmann, C. McEvoy, C. Hertzog, P. Hertel, & M. K. Johnson (Eds.), *Basic and applied memory research: Practical applications* (Vol. 2). Mahwah, NJ: Erlbaum.

Searleman, A., & Herrmann, D. (1994). *Memory from a broader perspective.* New York: McGraw-Hill.

Sears, D. O. (1975). Political socialization. In F. I. Greenstein & N. W. Polsby (Eds.), *Handbook of political science* (Vol. 2). Reading, MA: Addison-Wesley.

Sedikides, C., Gaertner, L., & Toguchi, Y. (2003). Pancultural self-enhancement. *Journal of Personality and Social Psychology, 84,* 60–79.

Sedikides, C., & Strube, M. J. (1997). Self-evaluation: To thine own self be good, to thine own self be sure, to thine own self be true, and to thine own self be better. In M. P. Zanna (Ed.), *Advances in experimental social psychology.* New York: Academic Press.

Seeley, R. J., & Schwartz, M. W. (1997). Regulation of energy balance: Peripheral endocrine signals and hypothalamic neuropeptides. *Current Directions in Psychological Science, 6,* 39–44.

Segall, M. H., Campbell, D. T., Herskovits, M. J. (1966). *The influence of culture on visual perception.* Indianapolis: Bobbs-Merrill.

Segall, M. H., Dasen, P. R., Berry, J. W., & Poortinga, Y. H. (1990). *Human behavior in global perspective: An introduction to cross-cultural psychology.* New York: Pergamon Press.

Segerstrom, S. C., & Miller, G. E. (2004). Psychological stress and the human immune system: A meta-analytic study of 30 years of inquiry. *Psychological Bulletin, 130,* 601–630.

Segerstrom, S. C., Taylor, S. E., Kemeny, M. E., & Fahey, J. L. (1998). Optimism is associated with mood, coping and immune change in response to stress. *Journal of Personality and Social Psychology, 74,* 1646–1655.

Seidlitz, L., & Diener, E. (1993). Memory for positive versus negative life events: Theories for the differences between happy and unhappy persons. *Journal of Personality and Social Psychology, 64,* 654–664.

Seifer, R. (2001). Socioeconomic status, multiple risks, and development of intelligence. In R. J. Sternberg & E. L. Grigorenko (Eds.), *Environmental effects on cognitive abilities* (pp. 59–82). Mahwah, NJ: Erlbaum.

Seifer, R., Schiller, M., Sameroff, A. J., Resnick, S., & Riordan, K. (1996). Attachment, maternal sensitivity, and infant temperament during the first year of life. *Developmental Psychology, 32,* 12–25.

Seligman, M. E. P. (1971). Phobias and preparedness. *Behavior Therapy, 2,* 307–321.

Seligman, M. E. P. (1974). Depression and learned helplessness. In R. J. Friedman & M. M. Katz (Eds.), *The psychology of depression: Contemporary theory and research.* New York: Wiley.

Seligman, M. E. P. (1990). *Learned optimism.* New York: Pocket Books.

Seligman, M. E. P. (1992). *Helplessness: On depression, development, and death.* New York: Freeman.

Seligman, M. E. P. (1995). The effectiveness of psychotherapy. *American Psychologist, 50,* 965–974.

Seligman, M. E. P. (2002). Positive psychology, positive prevention, and positive therapy. In C. R. Snyder & S. J. Lopez (Eds.), *Handbook of positive psychology* (pp. 3–11). New York: Oxford University Press.

Seligman, M. E. P. (2003). The past and future of positive psychology. In C. L. M. Keyes & J. Haidt (Eds.), *Flourishing: Positive psychology and the life well-lived.* Washington, DC: American Psychological Association.

Seligman, M. E. P., & Csikszentmihalyi, M. (2000). Positive psychology: An introduction. *American Psychologist, 55,* 5–14.

Seligman, M. E. P., & Hager, J. L. (1972, August). Biological boundaries of learning (the sauce béarnaise syndrome). *Psychology Today,* pp. 59–61, 84–87.

Seligman, M. E. P., & Isaacowitz, D. M. (2000). Learned helplessness. In G. Fink (Ed.), *Encyclopedia of stress* (Vol. 2, pp. 599–602). San Diego: Academic Press.

Seligman, M. E. P., & Levant, R. F. (1998). Managed care policies rely on inadequate science. *Professional Psychology: Research and Practice, 29,* 211–212.

Selye, H. (1936). A syndrome produced by diverse nocuous agents. *Nature, 138,* 32.

Selye, H. (1956). *The stress of life.* New York: McGraw-Hill.

Selye, H. (1973). The evolution of the stress concept. *American Scientist, 61*(6), 672–699.

Selye, H. (1974). *Stress without distress.* New York: Lippincott.

Selye, H. (1982). History and present status of the stress concept. In L. Goldberger & S. Breznitz (Eds.), *Handbook of stress: Theoretical and clinical aspects.* New York: Free Press.

Semmer, N. K., McGrath, J. E., & Beehr, T. A. (2005). Conceptual issues in research on stress and health. In C. L. Cooper (Ed.), *Handbook of stress medicine and health.* Boca Raton, FL: CRC Press.

Servan-Schreiber, D., Kolb, R., & Tabas, G. (1999). The somatizing patient. *Primary Care, 26,* 225–242.

Seta, J. J., Seta, C. E., & McElroy, T. (2002). Strategies for reducing the stress of negative life experiences: An average/summation analysis. *Personality and Social Psychology Bulletin, 28,* 1574–1585.

Seta, J. J., Seta, C. E., & Wang, M. A. (1991). Feelings of negativity and stress: An averaging-summation analysis of impressions of negative life experiences. *Personality and Social Psychology Bulletin, 17,* 376–384.

Shackelford, T. K., Schmitt, D. P., & Buss, D. M. (2005). Universal dimensions of human mate preferences. *Personality & Individual Differences, 39,* 447–458.

Shafir, E., & LeBoeuf, R. A. (2002). Rationality. *Annual Review of Psychology, 53,* 491–517.

Shafir, E., & LeBoeuf, R. A. (2004). Context and conflict in multiattribute choice. In D. J. Koehler & N. Harvey (Ed), *Blackwell handbook of judgment and decision making.* Malden, MA: Blackwell Publishing.

Shalev, A. Y. (2001). Posttraumatic stress disorder. *Primary Psychiatry, 8*(10), 41–46.

Shapiro, A. F., Gottman, J. M., & Carrère. (2000). The baby and marriage: Identifying factors that buffer against decline in marital satisfaction after the first baby arrives. *Journal of Family Psychology, 14,* 59–70.

Shapiro, D. H., Jr. (1984). Overview: Clinical and physiological comparison of meditation with other self-control strategies. In D. H. Shapiro, Jr., & R. N. Walsh (Eds.), *Meditation: Classic and contemporary perspectives.* New York: Aldine.

Shapiro, S. L., Schwartz, G. E. R., & Santerre, C. (2002). Meditation and positive psychology. In C. R. Snyder & S. J. Lopez (Eds.), *Handbook of positive psychology.* New York: Oxford University Press.

Sharpe, D., Adair, J. G., & Roese, N. J. (1992). Twenty years of deception research: A decline in subjects' trust? *Personality and Social Psychology Bulletin, 18,* 585–590.

Sharps, M. J., & Wertheimer, M. (2000). Gestalt perspectives on cognitive science and on experimental psychology. *Review of General Psychology, 4,* 315–336.

Shatz, C. J. (1992, September). The developing brain. *Scientific American,* 60–67.

Shaver, P. R., Schachner, D. A., & Mikulincer, M. (2005). Attachment style, excessive reassurance seeking, relationship processes, and depression. *Personality and Social Psychology Bulletin, 31*(3), 343–359.

Shavitt, S., Sanbonmatsu, D. M., Smittipatana, S., & Posavac, S. S. (1999). Broadening the conditions for illusory correlation formation: Implications for judging minority groups. *Basic & Applied Social Psychology, 21,* 263–279.

Shear, J., & Jevning, R. (1999). Pure consciousness: Scientific exploration of meditation techniques. *Journal of Consciousness Studies, 6,* 189–209.

Shear, M. K., & Beidel, D. C. (1998). Psychotherapy in the overall management strategy for social anxiety disorder. *Journal of Clinical Psychiatry, 59,* 39–46.

Shearer, B. (2004). Multiple intelligences theory after 20 years. *Teachers College Record, 106*(1), 2–16.

Shedler, J., Mayman, M., & Manis, M. (1993). The illusion of mental health. *American Psychologist, 48,* 1117–1131.

Sheehan, S. (1982). *Is there no place on earth for me?* Boston: Houghton Mifflin.

Shepard, R. N. (1990). *Mind sights.* New York: W. H. Freeman.

Sher, L., & Mann, J. J. (2003). Psychiatric pathophysiology: Mood disorders. In A. Tasman, J. Kay, & J. A. Lieberman (Eds.), *Psychiatry.* New York: Wiley.

Sherif, M., Harvey, O., White, B., Hood, W., & Sherif, C. (1961). *Intergroup conflict and cooperation: The Robber's Cave experiment.* Norman: University of Oklahoma, Institute of Group Behavior.

Sherman, D. K., Nelson, L. D., & Ross, L. D. (2003). Naive realism and affirmative action: Adversaries are more similar than they think. *Basic and Applied Social Psychology, 25,* 275–289.

Sherman, M., & Key, C. B. (1932). The intelligence of isolated mountain children. *Child Development, 3,* 279–290.

Shermer, M. (1997). *Why people believe weird things: Pseudoscience, superstition, and other confusions of our time.* New York: W. H. Freeman.

Shermer, M. (2004, March). None so blind. *Scientific American,* p. 42.

Sherry, D. F. (1992). Evolution and learning. In L. R. Squire (Ed.), *Encyclopedia of learning and memory.* New York: Macmillan.

Shettleworth, S. J. (1998). *Cognition, evolution, and behavior.* New York: Oxford University Press.

Shike, M. (1999). Diet and lifestyle in the prevention of colorectal cancer: An overview. *American Journal of Medicine, 106*(1A), 11S–15S, 50S–51S.

Shimamura, A. P. (1995). Memory and the prefrontal cortex. In J. Grafman, K. J. Holyoak, & F. Boller (Eds), *Structure and functions of the human prefrontal cortex.* New York: New York Academy of Sciences.

Shimamura, A. P., Berry, J. M., Mangels, J. A., Rusting, C. L., & Jurica, P. J. (1995). Memory and cognitive abilities in university professors: Evidence for successful aging. *Psychological Science, 6,* 271–277.

Shimp, T. A., Stuart, E. W., & Engle, R. W. (1991). A program of classical conditioning experiments testing variations in the conditioned stimulus and context. *Journal of Consumer Research, 18,* 1–12.

Shobe, K. K., & Schooler, J. W. (2001). Discovering fact and fiction: Case-based analyses of authentic and fabricated discovered memories of abuse. In G. M. Davies & T. Dalgleish (Eds.), *Recovered memories: Seeking the middle ground.* Chichester, England: Wiley.

Shulman, R. B. (2001). Response versus remission in the treatment of depression: Understanding residual symptoms. *Primary Psychiatry, 8*(5), 28–30, 34.

Siebert, A. (1995). *Student success: How to succeed in college and still have time for your friends.* Fort Worth: Harcourt Brace Jovanovich.

Siegler, R. S. (1992). The other Alfred Binet. *Developmental Psychology, 28,* 179–190.

Siegler, R. S. (1994). Cognitive variability: A key to understanding cognitive development. *Current Directions in Psychological Science, 3*(1), 1–5.

Sigel, I. E. (2004). Head Start—Revisiting a historical psychoeducational intervention: A revisionist perspective. In E. Zigler & S. J. Styfco (Eds.), *The Head Start debate.* Baltimore: Paul H. Brookes Publishing.

Sigman, M., & Whaley, S. E. (1998). The role of nutrition in the development of intelligence. In U. Neisser (Ed.), *The rising curve: Long-term gains in IQ and related measures.* Washington, DC: American Psychological Association.

Signorielli, N. (2001). Television's gender role images and contribution to stereotyping: Past present future. In D. G. Singer & J. L. Singer (Eds.), *Handbook of children and the media.* Thousand Oaks, CA: Sage.

Signorielli, N., McLeod, D., & Healy, E. (1994). Gender stereotypes in MTV commercials: The beat goes on. *Journal of Broadcasting & Electronic Media, 38,* 91–101.

Silberman, E. K. (1998). Psychiatrists' and internists' beliefs. *Primary Psychiatry, 5,* 65–71.

Silver, E., Cirincion, C., & Stead-man, H. J. (1994). Demythologizing inaccurate perceptions of the insanity defense. *Law & Human Behavior, 18,* 63–70.

Silverman, I., & Choi, J. (2005). Locating places. In D. M. Buss (Ed.), *The handbook of evolutionary psychology.* New York: Wiley.

Silverman, I., Choi, J., Mackewn, A., Fisher, M., Moro, J., & Olshansky, E. (2000). Evolved mechanisms underlying wayfinding: Further studies on the hunter-gatherer theory of spatial sex differences. *Evolution and Human Behavior, 21,* 201–213.

Silverman, I., & Eals, M. (1992). Sex differences in spatial ability: Evolutionary theory and data. In J. Barkow, L. Cosmides, & J. Tooby (Eds.), *The adapted mind.* New York: Oxford University Press.

Silverman, I., & Phillips, K. (1998). The evolutionary psychology of spatial sex differences. In C. Crawford & D. L. Krebs (Eds.), *Handbook of evolutionary psychology: Ideas, issues, and applications.* Mahwah, NJ: Erlbaum.

Silverstein, L. B., & Auerbach, C. F. (1999). Deconstructing the essential father. *American Psychologist, 54,* 397–407.

Simon, H. A. (1957). *Models of man.* New York: Wiley.

Simon, H. A. (1974). How big is a chunk? *Science, 183,* 482–488.

Simons, D. K., & Chabris, C. F. (1999). Gorillas in our midst: Sustained inattentional blindness for dynamic events. *Perception, 28,* 1059–1074.

Simonton, D. K. (1990). Creativity and wisdom in aging. In J. E. Birren & K. W. Schaie (Eds.), *Handbook of the psychology of aging.* San Diego: Academic Press.

Simonton, D. K. (1997). Creative productivity: A predictive and explanatory model of career trajectories and landmarks. *Psychological Review, 104,* 66–89.

Simonton, D. K. (1999a). Creativity and genius. In L. A. Pervin & O. John (Eds.), *Handbook of personality theory and research.* New York: Guilford.

Simonton, D. K. (1999b). Talent and its development: An emergenic and epigenetic model. *Psychological Review, 106,* 435–457.

Simpson, J. A., Fletcher, G. J. O., & Campbell, L. (2001). The structure and function of ideal standards in close relationships. In G. J. O. Fletcher & M. S. Clark (Eds.), *Blackwell handbook of social psychology: Interpersonal processes.* Malden, MA: Blackwell.

Simpson, J. L. (2002). Fetal wastage. In S. G. Gabbe, J. R. Niebyl, & J. L. Simpson (Eds.), *Obstetrics: Normal and problem pregnancies.* New York: Churchill Livingstone.

Simpson, J. L., & Niebyl, J. R. (2002). Occupational and environmental perspectives on birth defects. In S. G. Gabbe, J. R. Niebyl, & J. L. Simpson (Eds.), *Obstetrics: Normal and problem pregnancies.* New York: Churchill Livingstone.

Simpson, S. (2001) Interview with Crocodile Hunter Steve Irwin [Web Page]. Retrieved July 2, 2002 from http://www.sciam.com/article.cfm?articleID=000679 84-6FE2-1C70-84A9809EC588EF21&pageNumber= 1&catID=2.

Sinclair, D. (1981). *Mechanisms of cutaneous stimulation.* Oxford, England: Oxford University Press.

Sinclair, R. C., Hoffman, C., Mark, M. M., Martin, L. L., & Pickering, T. L. (1994). Construct accessibility and the misattribution of arousal: Schachter and Singer revisited. *Psychological Science, 5,* 15-19.

Sinclair, S., Dunn, R., & Lowery, B. S. (2005). The relationship between parental racial attitudes and children's implicit prejudice. *Journal of Experimental Social Psychology, 41,* 283–289.

Singer, L. T., Arendt, R., Minnes, S., Farkas, K., Salvator, A., Kirchner, H. L., & Kliegman, R. (2002). Cognitive and motor outcomes of cocaine-exposed infants. *Journal of the American Medical Association, 287,* 1952–1960.

Singer, L. T., Minnes, S., Short, E., Arendt, R., Farkas, K., Lewis, B., Klein, N., Russ, S., Min, M. O., & Kirchner, H. L. (2004). Cognitive outcomes of preschool children with prenatal cocaine exposure. *Journal of the American Medical Association, 291,* 2448–2456.

Singer, M. T., & Lalich, J. (1996). *Crazy therapies: What are they? Do they work?* San Francisco: Jossey-Bass.

Sinha, D. (1983). Human assessment in the Indian context. In S. H. Irvine & J. W. Berry (Eds.), *Human assessment and cultural factors.* New York: Plenum.

SJB. (2006, March 6). Overcoming problem gambling [Why?]. Message posted to http://www.gamcare.org.uk/forum/index.php?tid=7193.

Skinner, A. E. G. (2001). Recovered memories of abuse: Effects on the individual. In G. M. Davies, & T. Dalgleish (Eds.), *Recovered memories: Seeking the middle ground.* Chichester, England: Wiley.

Skinner, B. F. (1938). *The behavior of organisms.* New York: Appleton-Century-Crofts.

Skinner, B. F. (1953). *Science and human behavior.* New York: Macmillan.

Skinner, B. F. (1957). *Verbal behavior.* New York: Appleton-Century-Crofts.

Skinner, B. F. (1969). *Contingencies of reinforcement.* New York: Appleton-Century-Crofts.

Skinner, B. F. (1971). *Beyond freedom and dignity.* New York: Knopf.

Skinner, B. F. (1984). Selection by consequences. *Behavioral and Brain Sciences, 7*(4), 477–510.

Skinner, B. F., Solomon, H. C., & Lindsley, O. R. (1953). *Studies in behavior therapy: Status report I.* Waltham, MA: Unpublished report, Metropolitan State Hospital.

Skolnick, P. (2003). Psychiatric pathophysiology: Anxiety disorders. In A. Tasman, J. Kay, & J. A. Lieberman (Eds.), *Psychiatry.* New York: Wiley.

Slamecka, N. J. (1985). Ebbinghaus: Some associations. *Journal of Experimental Psychology: Learning, Memory and Cognition, 11,* 414–435.

Slamecka, N. J. (1992). Forgetting. In L. R. Squire (Ed.), *Encyclopedia of learning and memory.* New York: Macmillan.

Slatcher, R. B., & Pennebaker, J. W. (2005). Emotional processing of traumatic events. In C. L. Cooper (Ed.), *Handbook of stress medicine and health.* Boca Raton, FL: CRC Press.

Slater, E., & Shields, J. (1969). Genetical aspects of anxiety. In M. H. Lader (Ed.), *Studies of anxiety.* Ashford, England: Headley Brothers.

Slaughter, M. (1990). The vertebrate retina. In K. N. Leibovic (Ed.), *Science of vision.* New York: Springer-Verlag.

Slobin, D. I. (1992). *The crosslinguistic study of language acquisition.* Hillsdale, NJ: Erlbaum.

Sloman, S. A. (2002). Two systems of reasoning. In T. Gilovich, D. Griffin, & D. Kahneman (Eds.), *Heuristics and biases.* New York: Cambridge University Press.

Slovic, P. (1990). Choice. In D. N. Osherson & E. E. Smith (Eds.), *Thinking: An invitation to cognitive science* (Vol. 3). Cambridge, MA: MIT Press.

Slovic, P., & Fischhoff, B. (1977). On the psychology of experimental surprises. *Journal of Experimental Psychology: Human Perception and Performance, 3,* 544–551.

Slovic, P., Fischhoff, B., & Lichtenstein, S. (1982). Facts versus fears: Understanding perceived risk. In

D. Kahneman, P. Slovic, & A. Tversky (Eds.), *Judgment under uncertainty: Heuristics and biases.* Cambridge, England: Cambridge University Press.

Slovic, P., Lichtenstein, S., & Fischhoff, B. (1988). Decision making. In R. C. Atkinson, R. J. Herrnstein, G. Lindzey, & R. D. Luce (Eds.), *Stevens' handbook of experimental psychology* (Vol. 2). New York: Wiley.

Smedley, S. R., & Eisner, T. (1996). Sodium: A male moth's gift to its offspring. *Proceedings of the National Academy of Sciences, 93,* 809–813.

Smith, C. A., & Lazarus, R. S. (1993). Appraisal components, core relational themes, and the emotions. *Cognition and Emotion, 7,* 233–269.

Smith, C. P. (1992). Reliability issues. In C. P. Smith (Ed.), *Motivation and personality: Handbook of thematic content analysis.* New York: Cambridge University Press.

Smith, F. J., & Campfield, L. A. (1993). Meal initiation occurs after experimental induction of transient declines in blood glucose. *American Journal of Physiology, 265,* 1423–1429.

Smith, G., Bartlett, A., & King, M. (2004). Treatments of homosexuality in Britain since the 1950's— An oral history: The experience of patients. *British Medical Journal USA, 4,* 143–144.

Smith, J. C. (1975). Meditation and psychotherapy: A review of the literature. *Psychological Bulletin, 32,* 553–564.

Smith, M., & Pazder, L. (1980). *Michelle remembers.* New York: Pocket Books.

Smith, M. L., & Glass, G. V. (1977). Meta-analysis of psychotherapy outcome studies. *American Psychologist, 32,* 752–760.

Smith, P. B. (2001). Cross-cultural studies of social influence. In D. Matsumoto (Ed.), *The handbook of culture and psychology.* New York: Oxford University Press.

Smith, P. B., & Bond, M. H. (1994). *Social psychology across cultures: Analysis and perspectives.* Boston: Allyn & Bacon.

Smith, S. (1988). Environmental context-dependent memory. In G. M. Davies & D. M. Thomson (Eds.), *Memory in context: Context in memory.* New York: Wiley.

Smith, S. B. (2000). *Diana in search of herself: Portrait of a troubled princess.* New York: Signet.

Smith, S. M. (1995). Getting into and out of mental ruts: A theory of fixation, incubation, and insight. In R. J. Sternberg & J. E. Davidson (Eds.), *The nature of insight* (pp. 229–251). Cambridge, MA: MIT Press.

Smith, S. M., McIntosh, W. D., & Bazzini, D. G. (1999). Are the beautiful good in Hollywood? An investigation of the beauty-and-goodness stereotype on film. *Basic & Applied Social Psychology, 21,* 69–80.

Smith, T. W. (1999). *The emerging 21st century American family.* Chicago: University of Chicago, National Opinion Research Center.

Smith, T. W., & Gallo, L. C. (2001). Personality traits as risk factors for physical illness. In A. Baum, T. A. Revenson, & J. E. Singer (Eds.), *Handbook of health psychology* (pp. 139–174). Mahwah, NJ: Erlbaum.

Smolak, L., & Murnen, S. K. (2001). Gender and eating problems. In R. H. Striegel-Moore & L. Smolak (Eds.), *Eating disorders: Innovative directions in research and practice* (pp. 91–110). Washington, DC: American Psychological Association.

Smyth, J. M., & Pennebaker, J. W. (1999). Sharing one's story: Translating emotional experiences into words as a coping tool. In C. R. Snyder (Ed.), *Coping: The psychology of what works.* New York: Oxford University Press.

Smyth, J. M., & Pennebaker, J. W. (2001). What are the health effects of disclosure? In A. Baum, T. A. Revenson & J. E. Singer (Eds.), *Handbook of health psychology* (pp. 339–348). Mahwah, NJ: Erlbaum.

Smyth, J., Litcher, L., Hurewitz, A., & Stone, A. (2001). Relaxation training and cortisol secretion in adult asthmatics. *Journal of Health Psychology, 6,* 217–227.

Snow, R. E. (1986). Individual differences in the design of educational programs. *American Psychologist, 41,* 1029–1039.

Snowden, L. R., & Hu, T. W. (1996). Outpatient service use in minority-serving mental health programs. *Administration and Policy in Mental Health, 24,* 149–159.

Snowden, L. R., & Yamada, A. (2005). Cultural differences in access to care. *Annual Review of Clinical Psychology, 1,* 143–166.

Snowdon, D. (2001). *Aging with grace: What the Nun Study teaches us about leading longer, healthier, and more meaningful lives.* New York: Bantam Books.

Snyder, S. H. (2002). Forty years of neurotransmitters: A personal account. *Archives of General Psychiatry, 59,* 983–994.

Snyder, S. H., & Ferris, C. D. (2000). Novel neurotransmitters and their neuropsychiatric relevance. *American Journal of Psychiatry, 157,* 1738–1751.

Sobal, J. (1995). Social influences on body weight. In K. D. Brownell & C. G. Fairburn (Eds.), *Eating disorders and obesity: A comprehensive handbook.* New York: Guilford.

Solberg, E. C., Diener, E., Wirtz, D., Lucas, R. E., & Oishi, S. (2002). Wanting, having, and satisfaction: Examining the role of desire discrepancies in satisfaction with income. *Journal of Personality and Social Psychology, 83,* 725–734.

Soldatos, C. R., Allaert, F. A., Ohta, T., & Dikeos, D. G. (2005). How do individuals sleep around the world? Results from a single-day survey in ten countries. *Sleep Medicine, 6,* 5–13.

Soler, C., Nunez, M., Gutierrez, R., Nunez, J., Medina, P., Sancho, M., Alvarez, J., & Nunez, A. (2003). Facial attractiveness in men provides clues to semen quality. *Evolution and Human Behavior, 24,* 199–207.

Solms, M. (2000). Freudian dream theory today. *Psychologist, 13,* 618–619.

Solms, M. (2004). Freud returns. *Scientific American, 290*(5), 83–88.

Solomon, D. A., Keller, M. B., Leon, A. C., Mueller, T. I., Lavori, P. W., Shea, M. T., Coryell, W., Warshaw, M., Turvey, C., Maser, J. D., & Endicott, J. (2000). Multiple recurrences of major depressive disorder. *American Journal of Psychiatry, 157,* 229–233.

Solomon, D. A., Keller, M. B., Leon, A. C., Mueller, T. I., Shea, M. T., Warshaw, M., Maser, J. D., Coryell, W., & Endicott, J. (1997). Recovery from major depression: A 10-year prospective follow-up across multiple episodes. *Archives of General Psychiatry, 54,* 1001–1006.

Solomon, S., Greenberg, J., & Pyszczynski, T. (1991). A terror management theory of social behavior: The psychological functions of self-esteem and cultural worldviews. In M. Zanna (Ed.), *Advances in experimental social psychology* (Vol. 24). Orlando, FL: Academic Press.

Solomon, S., Greenberg, J., & Pyszczynski, T. (2004a). Lethal consumption: Death-denying materialism. In T. Kasser, & A. D. Kanner (Eds.), *Psychology and consumer culture: The struggle for a good life in a materialistic world.* Washington, DC: American Psychological Association.

Solomon, S., Greenberg, J., & Pyszczynski, T. (2004b). The cultural animal: Twenty years of terror management. In J. Greenberg, S. L. Koole, & T. Pyszczynski (Eds.), *Handbook of experimental existential psychology.* New York: Guilford.

Solowij, N., Stephens, R. S., Roffman, R. A., Babor, T., Kadden, R., Miller, M., Christiansen. K., McRee, B., & Vendetti, J. (2002). Cognitive functioning of long-term heavy cannabis users seeking treatment. *Journal of the American Medical Association, 287,* 1123–1131.

Solso, R. L. (1994). *Cognition and the visual arts.* Cambridge, MA: MIT Press.

Song, S., Sjostrom, P. J., Reigl, M., Nelson, S., & Chklovskii, D. B. (2005). Highly nonrandom features of synaptic connectivity in local cortical circuits. *PLoS Biol, 3*(3), 1–13.

Sorensen, J. L., Haug, N. A., & Batki, S. L. (2005). Psychosocial issues of HIV/AIDS among drug users in treatment. In J. H. Lowinson, P. Ruiz, R. B. Millman, & J. G. Langrod (Eds.), *Substance abuse: A comprehensive textbook.* Philadelphia: Lippincott/Williams & Williams.

Sotiriou, P. E. (2002). *Integrating college study skills: Reasoning in reading, listening, and writing.* Belmont, CA: Wadsworth.

Sousa, D. A. (2000). *How the brain learns: A classroom teacher's guide.* Thousand Oaks, CA: Corwin Press.

Sowell, E. R., Trauner, D. A., Gamst, A., & Jernigan, T. L. (2002). Development of cortical and subcortical brain structures in childhood and adolescence: A structural MRI study. *Developmental Medicine and Child Neurology, 44*(1), 4–16.

Spangler, W. D. (1992). Validity of questionnaire and TAT measures of need for achievement: Two meta-analyses. *Psychological Bulletin, 112,* 140–154.

Spanos, N. P. (1986). Hypnotic behavior: A social-psychological interpretation of amnesia, analgesia, and "trance logic." *Behavioral & Brain Sciences, 9*(3), 449–467.

Spanos, N. P. (1994). Multiple identity enactments and multiple personality disorder: A sociocognitive perspective. *Psychological Bulletin, 116,* 143–165.

Spanos, N. P. (1996). *Multiple identities and false memories.* Washington, DC: American Psychological Association.

Spanos, N. P., & Coe, W. C. (1992). A social-psychological approach to hypnosis. In E. Fromm & M. R. Nash (Eds.), *Contemporary hypnosis research.* New York: Guilford.

Spear, P. (2000). The adolescent brain and age-related behavioral manifestations. *Neuroscience and Biobehavioral Reviews, 24,* 417–463.

Speed, A., & Gangestad, S. W. (1997). Romantic popularity and mate preferences: A peer-nomination study. *Personality and Social Psychology Bulletin, 23,* 928–936.

Spelke, E. S. (1994). Initial knowledge: Six suggestions. *Cognition, 50,* 431–455.

Spelke, E. S., & Newport, E. L. (1998). Nativism, empiricism, and the development of knowledge. In W. Damon (Ed.), *Handbook of child psychology (Vol. 1): Theoretical models of human development.* New York: Wiley.

Sperling, G. (1960). The information available in brief visual presentations. *Psychological Monographs, 74*(11, Whole No. 498).

Sperry, R. W. (1982). Some effects of disconnecting the cerebral hemispheres. *Science, 217,* 1223–1226, 1250.

Spiegel, D. (1995). Hypnosis, dissociation, and trauma: Hidden and overt observers. In J. L. Singer (Ed.), *Repression and dissociation: Implications for personality theory, psychopathology, and health.* Chicago: University of Chicago Press.

Spiegel, D. (2003a). Hypnosis and traumatic dissociation: Therapeutic opportunities. *Journal of Trauma & Dissociation, 4*(3), 73–90.

Spiegel, D. (2003b). Negative and positive visual hypnotic hallucinations: Attending inside and out. *International Journal of Clinical & Experimental Hypnosis, 51*(2), 130–146.

Spiegel, D., Cutcomb, S., Ren, C., & Pribram, K. (1985). Hypnotic hallucination alters evoked potentials. *Journal of Abnormal Psychology, 94*, 249–255.

Spiegel, H., Greenleaf, M., & Spiegel, D. (2000). Hypnosis. In B. J. Sadock & V. A. Sadock (Eds.), *Kaplan and Sadock's comprehensive textbook of psychiatry.* Philadelphia: Lippincott/Williams & Wilkins.

Spiegler, M. D., & Guevremont, D. C. (1998). *Contemporary behavior therapy.* Pacific Grove, CA: Brooks/Cole.

Spiegler, M. D., & Guevremont, D. C. (2003). *Contemporary behavior therapy.* Belmont, CA: Wadsworth.

Sprecher, S. (1998). Insiders' perspectives on reasons for attraction to a close other. *Social Psychology Quarterly, 61*, 287–300.

Sprecher, S. (1999). "I love you more today than yesterday": Romantic partners' perceptions of changes in love and related affect over time. *Journal of Personality and Social Psychology, 76*, 46–53.

Sprecher, S., & Duck, S. (1994). Sweet talk: The importance of perceived communication for romantic and friendship attraction experienced during a get-acquainted date. *Personality and Social Psychology Bulletin, 20*, 391–400.

Sprenger, M. (2001). *Becoming a "wiz" at brain-based teaching: From translation to application.* Thousand Oaks, CA: Corwin Press.

Springer, S. P., & Deutsch, G. (1998). *Left brain, right brain.* New York: W. H. Freeman.

Squire, L. R. (2004). Memory systems of the brain: A brief history and current perspective. *Neurobiology of Learning & Memory, 82*(3), 171–177.

Squire, L. R., & Knowlton, B. J. (2000). The medial temporal lobe, the hippocampus, and the memory systems of the brain. In M. S. Gazzaniga (Ed.), *The new cognitive neurosciences* (2nd ed., pp. 765–780). Cambridge, MA: MIT Press.

Squire, L. R., Knowlton, B., & Musen, G. (1993). The structure and organization of memory. *Annual Review of Psychology, 44*, 453–495.

Stainton, J. (1999). *The crocodile hunter: Steve's story* (Videotape). Santa Monica, CA: Artisan Home Entertainment.

Stajkovic, A. D., & Luthans, F. (1998). Self-efficacy and work-related performance: A meta-analysis. *Psychological Bulletin, 124*, 240–261.

Stamler, J., Daviglus, M. L., Garside, D. B., Dyer, A. R., Greenland, P., & Neaton, J. D. (2000). Relationship of baseline serum cholesterol levels in three large cohorts of younger men to long-term coronary, cardiovascular, and all-cause mortality and to longevity. *Journal of the American Medical Association, 284*, 311–318.

Stanovich, K. E. (2003). The fundamental computational biases of human cognition: Heuristics that (sometimes) impair decision making and problem solving. In J. E. Davidson & R. J. Sternberg (Eds.), *The psychology of problem solving.* New York: Cambridge University Press.

Stanovich, K. E. (2004). *How to think straight about psychology.* Boston: Allyn & Bacon.

Stanovich, K. E., & West, R. F. (2002). Individual differences in reasoning: Implications for the rationality debate. In T. Gilovich, D. Griffin, & D. Kahneman (Eds.), *Heuristics and biases.* New York: Cambridge University Press.

Starcevic, V. (2001). Clinical features and diagnosis of hypochondriasis. In V. Starcevic & D. R. Lipsitt (Eds.), *Hypochondriasis: Modern perspectives on an ancient malady.* New York: Oxford University Press.

Steele, K. M. (2003). Do rats show a Mozart effect? *Music Perception, 21*, 251–265.

Steiger, H., Bruce, K. R., & Israel, M. (2003). Eating disorders. In G. Stricker & T. A. Widiger (Eds.), *Handbook of psychology, Vol. 8: Clinical psychology.* New York: Wiley.

Steiger, H., & Seguin, J. R. (1999). Eating disorders: Anorexia nervosa and bulimia nervosa. In T. Millon, P. H. Blaney, & R. D. Davis (Eds.), *Oxford textbook of psychopathology* (pp. 365–389). New York: Oxford University Press.

Stein, B. E., & Meredith, M. A. (1993). *Vision, touch, and audition: Making sense of it all.* Cambridge, MA: MIT Press.

Stein, B. E., Wallace, M. T., & Stanford, T. R. (2001). Brain mechanisms for synthesizing information from different sensory modalities. In E. B. Goldstein (Ed.), *Blackwell handbook of perception.* Malden, MA: Blackwell.

Stein, M. B., Walker, J. R., Hazen, A. L., & Forde, D. R. (1997b). Full and partial posttraumatic stress disorder: Findings from a community survey. *American Journal of Psychiatry, 154*, 1114–1119.

Steinberg, L. (2001). We know some things: Adolescent-parent relationships in retrospect and prospect. *Journal of Research on Adolescence, 11*, 1–20.

Steinberg, L., & Levine, A. (1997). *You and your adolescent: A parents' guide for ages 10 to 20.* New York: Harper Perennial.

Steinberg, L., & Morris, A. S. (2001). Adolescent development. *Annual Review of Psychology, 52*, 83–110.

Steinberg, L., & Steinberg, W. (1994). *Crossing paths: How your child's adolescence triggers your own crisis.* New York: Simon & Schuster.

Steinhausen, H. (2002). The outcome of anorexia nervosa in the 20th century. *American Journal of Psychiatry, 159*, 1284–1293.

Steinmetz, J. E. (1998). The localization of a simple type of learning and memory: The cerebellum and classical eyeblink conditioning. *Current Directions in Psychological Science, 7*, 72–77.

Stekel, W. (1950). *Techniques of analytical psychotherapy.* New York: Liveright.

Stellar, E. (1954). The physiology of motivation. *Psychological Review, 61*, 5–22.

Stern, W. (1914). *The psychological method of testing intelligence.* Baltimore: Warwick & York.

Sternberg, R. J. (1985). *Beyond IQ: A triarchic theory of human intelligence.* New York: Cambridge University Press.

Sternberg, R. J. (1986). *Intelligence applied: Understanding and increasing your intellectual skills.* New York: Harcourt Brace Jovanovich.

Sternberg, R. J. (1988a). A three-facet model of creativity. In R. J. Sternberg (Ed.), *The nature of creativity: Contemporary psychological perspectives.* Cambridge, England: Cambridge University Press.

Sternberg, R. J. (1988b). *The triarchic mind: A new theory of human intelligence.* New York: Viking.

Sternberg, R. J. (1988c). Triangulating love. In R. J. Sternberg & M. L. Barnes (Eds.), *The psychology of love.* New Haven, CT: Yale University Press.

Sternberg, R. J. (1991). Theory-based testing of intellectual abilities: Rationale for the triarchic abilities test. In H. A. H. Rowe (Ed.), *Intelligence: Reconceptualization and measurement.* Hillsdale, NJ: Erlbaum.

Sternberg, R. J. (1998). How intelligent is intelligence testing? *Scientific American Presents Exploring Intelligence, 9*, 12–17.

Sternberg, R. J. (1999). The theory of successful intelligence. *Review of General Psychology, 3*, 292–316.

Sternberg, R. J. (2000a). Creativity is a decision. In A. L. Costa (Ed.), *Teaching for intelligence II* (pp. 85–106). Arlington Heights, IL: Skylight Training.

Sternberg, R. J. (2000b). Successful intelligence: A unified view of giftedness. In C. F. M. van Lieshout & P. G. Heymans (Eds.), *Developing talent across the life span* (pp. 43–65). Philadelphia: Psychology Press.

Sternberg, R. J. (2003a). Construct validity of the theory of successful intelligence. In R. J. Sternberg, J. Lautrey, & T. I. Lubart (Eds.), *Models of intelligence: International perspectives.* Washington, DC: American Psychological Association.

Sternberg, R. J. (2003b). My house is a very, very, very fine house—But it is not the only house. In H. Nyborg (Ed.), *The scientific study of general intelligence: Tribute to Arthur R. Jensen.* Oxford, UK: Pergamon.

Sternberg, R. J. (2004). Culture and Intelligence. *American Psychologist, 59*, 325–338.

Sternberg, R. J. (2005). There are no public policy implications: A reply to Rushton and Jensen. *Psychology, Public Policy, and the Law, 11*, 295–301.

Sternberg, R. J., Conway, B. E., Ketron, J. L., & Bernstein, M. (1981). People's conceptions of intelligence. *Journal of Personality and Social Psychology, 41*, 37–55.

Sternberg, R. J., Grigorenko, E. L., & Kidd, K. K. (2005). Intelligence, race, and genetics. *American Psychologist, 60*, 45–69.

Sternberg, R. J., & Hedlund, J. (2002). Practical intelligence, *g*, and work psychology. *Human Performance, 15*, 143–160.

Sternberg, R. J., & Kaufman, J. C. (1998). Human abilities. *Annual Review of Psychology, 49*, 479–502.

Sternberg, R. J., & Lubart, T. I. (1992). Buy low and sell high: An investment approach to creativity. *Current Directions in Psychological Science, 1*(1), 1-5.

Sternberg, R. J., & O'Hara, L. A. (1999). Creativity and intelligence. In R. J. Sternberg (Ed.), *Handbook of creativity.* New York: Cambridge University Press.

Stevens, S. S. (1955). The measurement of loudness. *Journal of the Acoustical Society of America, 27*, 815–819.

Stewart-Williams, S. (2004). The placebo puzzle: Putting the pieces together. *Health Psychology, 23*, 198–206.

Stice, E. (2001). Risk factors for eating pathology: Recent advances and future directions. In R. H. Striegel-Moore & L. Smolak (Eds.), *Eating disorders: Innovative directions in research and practice* (pp. 51–74). Washington, DC: American Psychological Association.

Stich, S. P. (1990). Rationality. In D. N. Osherson & E. E. Smith (Eds.), *Thinking: An invitation to cognitive science* (Vol. 3). Cambridge, MA: MIT Press.

Stickgold, R. (2001). Toward a cognitive neuroscience of sleep. *Sleep Medicine Reviews, 5*, 417–421.

Stickgold, R. (2005). Why we dream. In M. H. Kryger, T. Roth, & W. C. Dement (Eds.). *Principles and practice of sleep medicine*. Philadelphia: Elsevier Saunders.

Stickgold, R., & Walker, M. P. (2004). To sleep, perchance to gain creative insight. *Trends in Cognitive Sciences, 8*(5), 191–192.

Stoddard, G. (1943). *The meaning of intelligence*. New York: Macmillan.

Stone, A. A., Bovbjerg, D. H., Neale, J. M., Napoli, A., Valdimarsdottir, H., Cox, D., Hayden, F. G., & Gwaltney, J. M. (1992). Development of the common cold symptoms following experimental rhinovirus infection is related to prior stressful events. *Behavioral Medicine, 18,* 115–120.

Stone, L. (1977). *The family, sex and marriage in England 1500–1800*. New York: Harper & Row.

Stone, W. N. (2003). Group psychotherapy. In A. Tasman, J. Kay, & J. A. Lieberman (Eds.), *Psychiatry*. New York: Wiley.

Stoner, J. A. F. (1961). *A comparison of individual and group decisions involving risk*. Unpublished master's thesis, Massachusetts Institute of Technology.

Stoney, C. M. (2003). Gender and cardiovascular disease: A psychobiological and integrative approach. *Current Directions in Psychological Science, 12*(4), 129–133.

Stoohs, R. A., Blum, H. C., Haselhorst, M., Duchna, H. W., Guilleminault, C., & Dement, W. C. (1998). Normative data on snoring: A comparison between younger and older adults. *European Respiratory Journal, 11,* 451–457.

Stoolmiller, M. (1999). Implications of the restricted range of family environments for estimates of heritability and nonshared environment in behavior-genetic adoption studies. *Psychological Bulletin, 125,* 392–409.

Straus, M. A. (2000). Corporal punishment and primary prevention of physical abuse. *Child Abuse & Neglect, 24,* 1109–1114.

Straus, M. A., & Stewart, J. H. (1999). Corporal punishment by American parents: National data on prevalence, chronicity, severity, and duration, in relation to child family characteristics. *Clinical Child & Family Psychology Review, 2*(2), 55–70.

Strayer, D. L., & Johnston, W. A. (2001). Driven to distraction: Dual-task studies of simulated driving and conversing on a cellular telephone. *Psychological Science, 12,* 462–466.

Streissguth, A. P., Barr, H. M., Bookstein, F. L., Sampson, P. D., & Olson, H. C. (1999). The long-term neurocognitive consequences of prenatal alcohol exposure: A 14-year study. *Psychological Science, 10,* 186–190.

Striegel-Moore, R. H., Silberstein, L. R., & Rodin, J. (1993). The social self in bulimia nervosa: Public self-consciousness, social anxiety, and perceived fraudulence. *Journal of Abnormal Psychology, 102.*

Strupp, H. H. (1996). The tripartite model and the *Consumer Reports* study. *American Psychologist, 51,* 1017–1024.

Stumpf, H., & Stanley, J. C. (1996). Gender-related differences on the College Board's Advanced Placement and Achievement Tests, 1982–1992. *Journal of Educational Psychology, 88,* 353–364.

Sturgis, E. T. (1993). Obsessive-compulsive disorders. In P. B. Sutker & H. E. Adams (Eds.), *Comprehensive handbook of psychopathology* (2nd ed.). New York: Plenum.

Sue, D. W., & Sue, D. (1999). *Counseling the culturally different: Theory and practice*. New York: Wiley.

Sue, S. (2003). In defense of cultural competency in psychotherapy and treatment. *American Psychologist, 58,* 964–970.

Sue, S., Zane, N., & Young, K. (1994). Research on psychotherapy with culturally diverse populations. In A. E. Bergin & S. L. Garfield (Eds.), *Handbook of psychotherapy and behavior change* (4th ed.). New York: Wiley.

Sugiyama, L. S. (2005). Physical attractiveness in adaptionist perspective. In D. M. Buss (Ed.), *The handbook of evolutionary psychology*. New York: Wiley.

Sullivan, G. M., & Coplan, J. D. (2000). Anxiety disorders: Biochemical aspects. In B. J. Sadock & V. A. Sadock (Eds.), *Kaplan and Sadock's comprehensive textbook of psychiatry*, (7th ed., Vol. 1). Philadelphia: Lippincott/Williams & Wilkins.

Sullivan, G., Burnam, A., & Koegel, P. (2000). Pathways to homelessness among the mentally ill. *Social Psychiatry & Psychiatric Epidemiology, 35,* 444–450.

Sullivan, P. F., Neale, M. C., & Kendler, K. S. (2000). Genetic epidemiology of major depression: Review and meta-analysis. *American Journal of Psychiatry, 157,* 1552–1562.

Super, C. M. (1976). Environmental effects on motor development: A case of African infant precocity. *Developmental Medicine and Child Neurology, 18,* 561–567.

Susman, E. J., Dorn, L. D., & Schiefelbein, V. L. (2003). Puberty, sexuality, and health. In R. M. Lerner, M. A. Easterbrooks, & J. Mistry (Eds.), *Handbook of psychology, Vol. 6: Developmental psychology*. New York: Wiley.

Susman, E. J., & Rogol, A. (2004). Puberty and psychological development. In R. M. Lerner & L. Steinberg (Eds.), *Handbook of adolescent psychology*. New York: Wiley.

Susser, E. B., Brown, A., & Matte, T. D. (1999). Prenatal factors and adult mental and physical health. *Canadian Journal of Psychiatry, 44,* 326–334.

Susser, E. B., Neugebauer, R., Hoek, H. W., Brown, A. S., Lin, S., Labovitz, D., & Gorman, J. M. (1996). Schizophrenia after prenatal famine: Further evidence. *Archives of General Psychiatry, 53,* 25–31.

Suzuki, L. A., & Vraniak, D. A. (1994). Ethnicity, race, and measured intelligence. In R. J. Sternberg (Ed.), *Encyclopedia of human intelligence*. New York: Macmillan.

Swan, G. E., Hudmon, K. S., & Khroyan, T. V. (2003). Tobacco dependence. In A. M. Nezu, C. M. Nezu, & P. A. Geller (Eds.), *Handbook of psychology, Vol. 9: Health Psychology*. New York: Wiley.

Swim, J. K. (1994). Perceived versus meta-analytic effect sizes: An assessment of the accuracy of gender stereotypes. *Journal of Personality and Social Psychology, 66,* 21–36.

Swim, J. K., & Sanna, L. J. (1996). He's skilled, she's lucky: A meta-analysis of observers' attributions for women's and men's successes and failures. *Personality and Social Psychology Bulletin, 22,* 507–519.

Szasz, T. (1974). *The myth of mental illness*. New York: Harper & Row.

Szasz, T. (1990). Law and psychiatry: The problems that will not go away. *The Journal of Mind and Behavior, 11*(3/4), 557–564.

Szegedy-Maszak, M. (2005, August 8). In gambling's grip. *Los Angeles Times*. Retrieved March 10, 2006, from http://www.latimes.com/features/printedition/health/la-he-gamble8aug08,1,3002368.story?coll=la-headlines-pe-health.

Szmukler, G. I., & Patton, G. (1995). Sociocultural models of eating disorders. In G. Szmukler, C. Dare, & J. Treasure (Eds.), *Handbook of eating disorders: Theory, treatment, and research*. New York: Wiley.

Tajfel, H., & Turner, J. C. (1979). An integrative theory of intergroup conflict. In W. G. Austin & S. Worchel (Eds.), *The social psychology of intergroup relations*. Monterey, CA: Brooks/Cole.

Takahashi, M., Nakata, A., Haratani, T., Ogawa, Y., & Arito, H. (2004). Post-lunch nap as a worksite intervention to promote alertness on the job. *Ergonomics, 47,* 1003–1013.

Takahashi, T., Sasaki, M., Itoh, H., Yamadera, W., Ozone, M., Obuchi, K., Hayashida, K., Matsunaga, N., & Sano, H. (2002). Melatonin alleviates jet lag symptoms caused by an 11-hour eastward flight. *Psychiatry & Clinical Neurosciences, 56,* 301–302.

Talbott, J. A. (2004). Deinstitutionalization: Avoiding the disasters of the past. *Psychiatric Services, 55,* 1112–1115.

Talwar, S. K., Xu, S., Hawley, E. S., Weiss, S. A., Moxon, K. A., & Chapin, J. K. (2002). Behavioural neuroscience: Rat navigation guided by remote control. *Nature, 417,* 37–38.

Tamminga, C. A. (1999). Principles of the pharmacotherapy of schizophrenia. In D. S. Charney, E. J. Nestler, & B. S. Bunney (Eds.), *Neurobiology of mental illness* (pp. 272–290). New York: Oxford University Press.

Tamminga, C. A., & Carlsson A. (2003). Psychiatric pathophysiology: Schizophrenia. In A. Tasman, J. Kay, & J. A. Lieberman (Eds.), *Psychiatry*. New York: Wiley.

Tanaka-Matsumi, J. (2001). Abnormal psychology and culture. In D. Matsumoto (Ed.), *The handbook of culture & psychology*. New York: Oxford University Press.

Tanner, J. M. (1978). *Fetus into man: Physical growth from conception to maturity*. Cambridge, MA: Harvard University Press.

Tardiff, K., Marzuk, P. M., & Leon, A. C. (2002). Role of antidepressants in murder and suicide. *American Journal of Psychiatry, 159,* 1248–1249.

Tart, C. T. (1988). From spontaneous event to lucidity: A review of attempts to consciously control nocturnal dreaming. In J. Gackenbach & S. LaBerge (Eds.), *Conscious mind, sleeping brain: Perspectives on lucid dreaming*. New York: Plenum.

Tashkin, D. P., Baldwin, G. C., Sarafian, T., Dubinett, S., & Roth, M. D. (2002). Respiratory and immunologic consequences of marijuana smoking. *Journal of Clinical Pharmacology, 42,* 71S–81S.

Tavris, C. (1998, September 13). Peer pressure (Review of *The Nurture Assumption*). *The New York Times Book Review, 103,* p. 14.

Taylor, E. (1999). An intellectual renaissance of humanistic psychology. *Journal of Humanistic Psychology, 39,* 7–25.

Taylor, E. (2001). Positive psychology and humanistic psychology: A reply to Seligman. *Journal of Humanistic Psychology, 41*(1), 13–29.

Taylor, J. H., & Walker, L. J. (1997). Moral climate and the development of moral reasoning: The effects of dyadic discussions between young offenders. *Journal of Moral Education, 26,* 21–43.

Taylor, S. E., & Brown, J. D. (1988). Illusion and well-being: A social psychological perspective on mental health. *Psychological Bulletin, 103,* 193–210.

Taylor, S. E., & Brown, J. D. (1994). Positive illusions and well-being revisited: Separating fact from fiction. *Psychological Bulletin, 116,* 21–27.

Teachman, J. D., Polonko, K. A., & Scanzoni, J. (1999). Demography and families. In M. B. Sussman, S. K. Steinmetz, & G. W. Peterson (Eds.), *Handbook of marriage and the family* (pp. 39–76). New York: Plenum.

Tedeschi, R. G., Park, C. L., & Calhoun, L. G. (1998). Posttraumatic growth: Conceptual issues. In R. G. Tedeschi, C. L. Park, & L. G. Calhoun (Eds.), *Posttraumatic growth: Positive changes in the aftermath of crisis* (pp. 1–22). Mahwah, NJ: Erlbaum.

Tedlock, L. B. (1992). Zuni and Quiche dream sharing and interpreting. In B. Tedlock (Ed.), *Dreaming: Anthropological and psychological interpretations.* Santa Fe, NM: School of American Research Press.

Teigen, K. H. (2004). Judgments by representativeness. In F. P. Rudiger (Ed.), *Cognitive illusions.* New York: Psychology Press.

Tellegen, A., Lykken, D. T., Bouchard, T. J., Jr., Wilcox, K. J., Segal, N. L., & Rich, S. (1988). Personality similarity in twins reared apart and together. *Journal of Personality and Social Psychology, 54,* 1031–1039.

Tennen, H., & Affleck, G. (1999). Finding benefits in adversity. In C. R. Snyder (Ed.), *Coping: The psychology of what works.* New York: Oxford University Press.

Tenopyr, M. L. (2002). Theory versus reality: Evaluation of *g* in the workplace. *Human Performance, 15,* 107–122.

Tepper, B. J., & Nurse, R. J. (1997). Fat perception is related to PROP taster status. *Physiology & Behavior, 61,* 949–954.

Terman, L. M. (1916). *The measurement of intelligence.* Boston: Houghton Mifflin.

Terr, L. (1994). *Unchained memories.* New York: Basic Books.

Tessier-Lavigne, M. (2000). Visual processing by the retina. In E. R. Kandel, J. H. Schwartz, & T. M. Jessell (Eds.), *Principles of neural science.* New York: McGraw-Hill.

Testa, K. (1996). Church to pay $1 million in false-memory case. *San Jose Mercury News,* 8A.

Teuber, M. (1974). Sources of ambiguity in the prints of Maurits C. Escher. *Scientific American, 231,* 90–104.

Thase, M. E., Jindal, R., & Howland, R. H. (2002). Biological aspects of depression. In I. H. Gotlib & C. L. Hammen (Eds.), *Handbook of depression.* New York: Guilford.

Thase, M. E., Jindal, R., & Howland, R. H. (2002). Biological aspects of depression. In I. H. Gotlib & C. L. Hammen (Eds.), *Handbook of depression.* New York: Guilford.

Thayer, R. E. (1996). *The origin of everyday moods.* New York: Oxford University Press.

Thelen, E. (1995). Motor development: A new synthesis. *American Psychologist, 50,* 79–95.

Thomas, A., & Chess, S. (1977). *Temperament and development.* New York: Brunner/Mazel.

Thomas, A. J., Kalaria, R. N., & O'Brien, J. T. (2004). Depression and vascular disease: What is the relationship? *Journal of Affective Disorders, 79*(1–3), 81–95.

Thomas, D. R. (1992). Discrimination and generalization. In L. R. Squire (Ed.), *Encyclopedia of learning and memory.* New York: Macmillan.

Thomas, R. M. (2005). *Comparing theories of child development.* Belmont, CA: Wadsworth.

Thompson, J. K., & Kinder, B. (2003). Eating disorders. In M. Hersen, & S. Turner (Eds.), *Handbook of adult psychopathology.* New York: Plenum Press.

Thompson, J. K., & Stice, E. (2001). Thin-ideal internalization: Mounting evidence for a new risk factor for body-image disturbance and eating pathology. *Current Directions in Psychological Science, 10*(5), 181–183.

Thompson, R. A., & Nelson, C. A. (2001). Developmental science and the media: Early brain development. *American Psychologist, 56,* 5–15.

Thompson, R. F. (1989). A model system approach to memory. In P. R. Solomon, G. R. Goethals, C. M. Kelley, & B. R. Stephens (Eds.), *Memory: Interdisciplinary approaches.* New York: Springer-Verlag.

Thompson, R. F. (1992). Memory. *Current Opinion in Neurobiology, 2,* 203–208.

Thompson, R. F. (2005). In search of memory traces. *Annual Review of Psychology, 56,* 1–23.

Thompson, R. F., & Zola, S. M. (2003). In D. K. Freedheim (Ed.), *Handbook of psychology* (Vol. 2): New York: Wiley.

Thorne, B. M., & Henley, T. B. (1997). *Connections in the history and systems of psychology.* Boston: Houghton Mifflin.

Thornhill, R. (1976). Sexual selection and nuptial feeding behavior in *Bittacus apicalis* (Insecta: Mecoptera). *American Naturalist, 110,* 529–548.

Thornton, B., & Moore, S. (1993). Physical attractiveness contrast effect: Implications for self-esteem and evaluations of the social self. *Personality and Social Psychology Bulletin, 19,* 474–480.

Thorpy, M., & Yager, J. (2001). *Sleeping well: The sourcebook for sleep and sleep disorders.* New York: Checkmark Books.

Thun, M. J., Apicella, L. F., & Henley, S. J. (2000). Smoking vs. other risk factors as the cause of smoking-attributable deaths: Confounding in the courtroom. *Journal of the American Medical Association, 284,* 706–712.

Thune, I., & Furberg, A. (2001). Physical activity and cancer risk: Dose-response and cancer, all sites and site specific. *Medicine and Science in Sports and Exercise, 33,* S530–S550.

Tibbo, P., Hanstock, C., Valiakalayil, A., & Allen, P. (2004). 3-T proton MRS investigation and glutamine in adolescents at high genetic risk for schizophrenia. *American Journal of Psychiatry, 161,* 1116–1118.

Tice, D. M., Bratslavsky, E., & Baumeister, R. F. (2001). Emotional distress regulation takes precedence over impulse control: If you feel bad, do it! *Journal of Personality and Social Psychology, 80,* 53–67.

Till, B. D., & Priluck, R. L. (2000). Stimulus generalization in classical conditioning: An initial investigation and extension. *Psychology and Marketing, 17,* 55–72.

Tindale, R. S., Kameda, T., & Hinsz, V. B. (2003). Group decision making. In M. A. Hogg & J. Cooper (Eds.), *The Sage handbook of social psychology.* Thousand Oaks, CA: Sage.

Titsworth, B. S., & Kiewra, K. A. (2004). Spoken organizational lecture cues and student notetaking as facilitators of student learning. *Contemporary Educational Psychology, 29,* 447–461.

Todd, J. T., & Morris, E. K. (1992). Case histories in the great power of steady misrepresentation. *American Psychologist, 47,* 1441–1453.

Todd, P. M., & Gigerenzer, G. (2000). Precis of simple heuristics that make us smart. *Behavioral & Brain Sciences, 23,* 727–780.

Tolman, D. L., & Diamond, L. M. (2001). Desegregating sexuality research: Cultural and biological perspectives on gender and desire. *Annual Review of Sex Research, 12,* 33–74.

Tolman, E. C. (1932). *Purposive behavior in animals and men.* New York: Appleton-Century-Crofts.

Tolman, E. C. (1938). The determiners of behavior at a choice point. *Psychological Review, 45,* 1–41.

Tolman, E. C. (1948). Cognitive maps in rats and men. *Psychological Review, 55,* 189–208.

Tolman, E. C., & Honzik, C. H. (1930). Introduction and removal of reward, and maze performance in rats. *University of California Publications in Psychology, 4,* 257–275.

Tomkins, S. S. (1980). Affect as amplification: Some modifications in theory. In R. Plutchik & H. Kellerman (Eds.), *Emotion: Theory, research and experience* (Vol. 1). New York: Academic Press.

Tomkins, S. S. (1991). *Affect, imagery, consciousness: 3. Anger and fear.* New York: Springer-Verlag.

Tooby, J., & Cosmides, L. (1989). Evolutionary psychology and the generation of culture: Part 1. Theoretical considerations. *Ethology and Sociobiology, 10,* 29–49.

Torgersen, S. (1979). The nature and origin of common phobic fears. *British Journal of Psychiatry, 119,* 343–351.

Torgersen, S. (1983). Genetic factors in anxiety disorders. *Archives of General Psychiatry, 40,* 1085–1089.

Torrey, E. F. (1992). *Freudian fraud: The malignant effect of Freud's theory on American thought and culture.* New York: Harper Perennial.

Torrey, E. F. (1996). *Out of the shadows.* New York: Wiley.

Toufexis, A. (1990, December 17). Drowsy America. *Time,* pp. 78–85.

Trachtenberg, J. D., & Sande, M. A. (2002). Emerging resistance to nonnucleoside reverse transcriptase inhibitors: A warning and a challenge. *Journal of the American Medical Association, 288,* 239–241.

Trasti, N., Vik, T., Jacobson, G., & Bakketeig, L. S. (1999). Smoking in pregnancy and children's mental and motor development at age 1 and 5 years. *Early Human Development, 55,* 137–147.

Travis, F. (2001). Autonomic and EEG patterns distinguish transcending from other experiences during Transcendental Meditation practice. *International Journal of Psychophysiology, 42,* 1–9.

Travis, F., & Pearson, C. (2000). Pure consciousness: Distinct phenomenological and physiological correlates of "consciousness itself." *International Journal of Neuroscience, 100*(1-4), 77–89.

Treisman, G. J. (1999). AIDS education for psychiatrists. *Primary Psychiatry, 6*(5), 71–73.

Triandis, H. C. (1989). Self and social behavior in differing cultural contexts. *Psychological Review, 96,* 269–289.

Triandis, H. C. (1994). *Culture and social behavior.* New York: McGraw-Hill.

Triandis, H. C. (2001). Individualism and collectivism: Past, present, and future. In D. Matsumoto (Ed.), *The handbook of culture and psychology.* New York: Oxford University Press.

Trivers, R. L. (1971). The evolution of reciprocal altruism. *Quarterly Review of Biology, 46,* 35–57.

Trivers, R. L. (1972). Parental investment and sexual selection. In B. Campbell (Ed.), *Sexual selection and the descent of man.* Chicago: Aldine.

Trotter, R. J. (1986, September). The three faces of love. *Psychology Today,* pp. 46–54.

Tsai, J. L., Butcher, J. N., Muñoz, R. F., & Vitousek, K. (2001). Culture, ethnicity, and psychopathology. In P. B. Sutker & H. E. Adams (Eds.), *Comprehensive handbook of psychopathology.* New York: Kluwer Academic/Plenum.

Tsigos, C., Kyrou, I., & Chrousos, G. P. (2005). Stress, endocrine manifestations and diseases. In C. L. Cooper (Ed.), *Handbook of stress medicine and health*. Boca Raton, FL: CRC Press.

Tsuang, M. T., Glatt, S. J., & Faraone, S. V. (2003). Genetics and genomics in schizophrenia. *Primary Psychiatry, 10*(3), 37–40, 50.

Tugade, M. M., & Fredrickson, B. L. (2004). Resilient individuals use positive emotions to bounce back from negative emotional experiences. *Journal of Personality and Social Psychology, 86*, 320–333.

Tulving, E. (1986). What kind of a hypothesis is the distinction between episodic and semantic memory? *Journal of Experimental Psychology: Learning, Memory and Cognition, 12*, 307–311.

Tulving, E. (1993). What is episodic memory? *Current Directions in Psychological Science, 2*(3), 67–70.

Tulving, E. (2001). Origin of autonoesis in episodic memory. In H. L. Roediger III, J. S. Nairne, I. Neath, & A. M. Surprenant (Eds.), *The nature of remembering: Essays in honor of Robert G. Crowder* (pp. 17–34). Washington, DC: American Psychological Association.

Tulving, E. (2002). Episodic memory: From mind to brain. *Annual Review of Psychology, 53*, 1–25.

Tulving, E., & Schacter, D. L. (1990). Priming and human memory systems. *Science, 247*, 301–306.

Tulving, E., & Thomson, D. M. (1973). Encoding specificity and retrieval processes in episodic memory. *Psychological Review, 80*, 352–373.

Turek, F. W., & Gillette, M. U. (2004). Melatonin, sleep, and circadian rhythms: Rationale for development of specific melatonin agonists. *Sleep Medicine, 5*, 523–532.

Turk, D. C., & Okifuji, A. (2003). Pain management. In A. M. Nezu, C. M. Nezu, & P. A. Geller (Eds.), *Handbook of psychology, Vol. 9: Health psychology*. New York: Wiley.

Turkheimer, E. (1991). Individual and group differences in adoption studies of IQ. *Psychological Bulletin, 110*, 392–405.

Turkheimer, E., Haley, A., Waldron, M., D'Onofrio, B., & Gottesman, I. I. (2003). Socioeconomic status modifies heritability of IQ in young children. *Psychological Science, 14*, 623–628.

Turkheimer, E., & Waldron, M. (2000). Nonshared environment: A theoretical, methodological, and quantitative review. *Psychological Bulletin, 126*, 78–108.

Turkkan, J. S. (1989). Classical conditioning: The new hegemony. *Behavioral and Brain Sciences, 12*, 121–179.

Turner, J. C., & Reynolds, K. J. (2001). The social identity perspective in intergroup relations: Theories, themes, and controversies. In R. Brown & S. L. Gaertner (Eds.), *Blackwell handbook of social psychology: Intergroup processes*. Malden, MA: Blackwell Publishing.

Turner, J. G., Hogg, M. A., Oakes, P. J., Reicher, S. D., & Wetherell, M. S. (1987). *Rediscovering the social group: A self-categorization theory*. Oxford, UK: Basil Blackwell.

Turner, J. R., & Wheaton, B. (1995). Checklist measurement of stressful life events. In S. Cohen, R. C. Kessler, & L. U. Gordon (Eds.), *Measuring stress: A guide for health and social scientists*. New York: Oxford University Press.

Turner, S. M., Beidel, D. C., Stanley, M. A., & Heiser, N. (2001). Obsessive-compulsive disorder. In P. B. Sutker & H. E. Adams (Eds.), *Comprehensive textbook of psychiatry* (3rd ed., pp. 155–182). New York: Kluwer Academic/Plenum.

Tversky, A. (1972). Elimination by aspects: A theory of choice. *Psychological Review, 79*, 281–299.

Tversky, A., & Kahneman, D. (1973). Availability: A heuristic for judging frequency and probability. *Cognitive Psychology, 5*, 207–232.

Tversky, A., & Kahneman, D. (1974). Judgments under uncertainty: Heuristics and biases. *Science, 185*, 1124–1131.

Tversky, A., & Kahneman, D. (1982). Judgment under uncertainty: Heuristics and biases. In D. Kahneman, P. Slovic, & A. Tversky (Eds.), *Judgment under uncertainty: Heuristics and biases*. New York: Cambridge University Press.

Tversky, A., & Kahneman, D. (1983). Extensional versus intuitive reasoning: The conjunction fallacy in probability judgment. *Psychological Review, 90*, 283–315.

Twenge, J. M., Campbell, W. K., & Foster, C. A. (2003). Parenthood and marital satisfaction: A meta-analytic review. *Journal of Marriage and the Family, 65*, 574–583.

Uchino, B. N. (2004). *Social support and physical health outcomes: Understanding the health consequences of our relationships*. New Haven, CT: University Press.

Uchino, B. N., Uno, D., & Holt-Lunstad, J. (1999). Social support, physiological processes, and health. *Current Directions in Psychological Science, 8*, 145–148.

Ulrich, R. E. (1991). Animal rights, animal wrongs and the question of balance. *Psychological Science, 2*, 197–201.

Underwood, B. J. (1961). Ten years of massed practice on distributed practice. *Psychological Review, 68*, 229–247.

Underwood, B. J. (1970). A breakdown of the total-time law in free-recall learning. *Journal of Verbal Learning and Verbal Behavior, 9*, 573–580.

Unger, R. K., & Crawford, M. (1992). *Women and gender: A feminist psychology*. New York: McGraw-Hill.

Ungerleider, L. G., & Haxby, J. V. (1994). "What" and "where" in the human brain. *Current Opinion in Neurobiology, 4*, 157–165.

Ursano, R. J., Fullerton, C. S., & Norwood, A. E. (2001). *Psychiatric dimensions of disaster: Patient care, community consultation, and preventive medicine*. Retrieved November 20, 2001 from American Psychiatric Association Web site: http:www.psych.org/pract_of_psych/disaster.cfm.

Ursano, R. J., & Silberman, E. K. (1999). Psychoanalysis, psychoanalytic psychotherapy, and supportive psychotherapy. In R. E. Hales, S. C. Yudofsky, & J. A. Talbott (Eds.), *American Psychiatric Press textbook of psychiatry*. Washington, DC: American Psychiatric Press.

U.S. Department of Health and Human Services. (1999). *Mental health: A report of the Surgeon General*. Washington, DC: U.S. Government Printing Office.

Vaillant, G. E. (1994). Ego mechanisms of defense and personality psychopathology. *Journal of Abnormal Psychology, 103*, 44–50.

Vaillant, G. E. (2000). Adaptive mental mechanisms: Their role in a positive psychology. *American Psychologist, 55*, 89–98.

Valenstein, E. S. (1973). *Brain control*. New York: Wiley.

Van de Castle, R. L. (1994). *Our dreaming mind*. New York: Ballantine Books.

van den Boom, D. C. (1994). The influence of temperament and mothering on attachment and exploration: An experimental manipulation of sensitive responsiveness among lower-class mothers and irritable infants. *Child Development, 65*, 1457–1477.

Vandereycken, W. (2002). History of anorexia nervosa and bulimia nervosa. In C. G. Fairburn, & K. D. Brownell (Eds.), *Eating disorders and obesity*. New York: Guilford.

van der Post, L. (1975). *Jung and the story of our time*. New York: Vintage Books.

Vandewater, K., & Vickers, Z. (1996). Higher-protein foods produce greater sensory-specific satiety. *Physiology & Behavior, 59*, 579–583.

Van Dongen, H. P. A., Baynard, M. D., Maislin, G., & Dinges, D. F. (2004). Systematic interindividual differences in neurobehavioral impairment from sleep loss: Evidence of trait-like differential vulnerability. *Sleep: Journal of Sleep & Sleep Disorders Research, 27*, 423–433.

Van Dongen, H. P. A., & Dinges, D. F. (2005). Circadian rhythms in sleepiness, alertness, and performance. In M. H. Kryger, T. Roth, & W. C. Dement (Eds.), *Principles and practice of sleep medicine*. Philadelphia: Elsevier Saunders.

Van Dongen, H. P. A., Maislin, G., Mullington, J. M., & Dinges, D. F. (2003). The cumulative cost of additional wakefulness: Dose-response effects on neurobehavioral functions and sleep physiology from chronic sleep restriction and total sleep deprivation. *Sleep: Journal of Sleep & Sleep Disorders Research, 26*, 117–126.

van Eck, M., Nicolson, N. A., & Berkhof, J. (1998). Effects of stressful daily events on mood states: Relationship to global perceived stress. *Journal of Personality and Social Psychology, 75*, 1572–1585.

Van Gelder, T. (2005). Teaching critical thinking: Some lessons from cognitive science. *College Teaching, 53*(1), 41–46.

van Ijzendoorn, M. H., & Sagi, A. (1999). Cross-cultural patterns of attachment: Universal and contextual dimensions. In J. Cassidy & P. R. Shaver (Eds.), *Handbook of attachment: Theory, research, and clinical applications*. New York: Guilford.

Vase, L. R., Riley, I. J., & Price, D. (2002). A comparison of placebo effects in clinical analgesic trials versus studies of placebo analgesia. *Pain, 99*, 443–452.

Vaughn, B. E., & Bost, K. K. (1999). Attachment and temperament: Redundant, independent, or interacting influences on interpersonal adaptation and personality development? In J. Cassidy & P. R. Shaver (Eds.), *Handbook of attachment: Theory, research, and clinical applications*. New York: Guilford.

Vazquez, C., Munoz, M., & Sanz, J. (1997). Lifetime and 12-month prevalence of DSM-III-R mental disorders among the homeless in Madrid: A European study using the CIDI. *Acta Psychiatrica Scandinavica, 95*, 523–530.

Vecera, S. P., Vogel, E. K., & Woodman, G. F. (2002). Lower region: A new cue for figure-ground assignment. *Journal of Experimental Psychology: General, 131*, 194–205.

Veenhoven, R. (1993). *Happiness in nations*. Rotterdam, Netherlands: Risbo.

Vega, W. A., Kolody, B., Aguilar-Gaxiola, S., & Catalano, R. (1999). Gaps in service utilization by Mexican Americans with mental health problems. *American Journal of Psychiatry, 156*, 928–934.

Venturello, S., Barzega, G., Maina, G., & Bogetto, F. (2002). Premorbid conditions and precipitating events in early-onset panic disorder. *Comprehensive Psychiatry, 43*(1), 28–36.

Vermeeren, A. (2004). Residual effects of hypnotics: Epidemiology and clinical implications. *CNS Drugs, 18*(5), 297–328.

Vernberg, E. M., La Greca, A. M., Silverman, W. K., & Prinstein, M. J. (1996). Prediction of posttraumatic stress symptoms in children after Hurricane Andrew. *Journal of Abnormal Psychology, 105,* 237–248.

Vernon, P. A., Wickett, J. C., Bazana, G. P., & Stelmack, R. M. (2000). The neuropsychology and psychophysiology of human intelligence. In R. J. Sternberg (Ed.), *Handbook of intelligence.* Cambridge, UK: Cambridge University Press.

Videbech, P., & Ravnkilde, B. (2004). Hippocampal volume and depression: A meta-analysis of MRI studies. *American Journal of Psychiatry, 161,* 1957–1966.

Viglione, D. J., & Rivera, B. (2003). Assessing personality and psychopathology with projective methods. In J. R. Graham & J. A. Naglieri (Eds.), *Handbook of psychology, Vol. 10: Assessment psychology.* New York: Wiley.

Vinogradov, S., Cox. P. D., & Yalom, I. D. (2003). Group therapy. In R. E. Hales & S. C. Yudofsky (Eds.), *Textbook of clinical psychiatry.* Washington, DC: American Psychiatric Publishing.

Vinters, H. V. (2001). Aging and the human nervous system. In J. E. Birren & K. W. Schaie (Eds.), *Handbook of the psychology of aging* (5th ed., pp. 134–159). San Diego, CA: Academic Press.

Visser, P. S., & Cooper, J. (2003). Attitude change. In M. A. Hogg & J. Cooper (Eds.), *The Sage handbook of social psychology.* Thousand Oaks, CA: Sage.

Vodelholzer, U., Homyak, M., Thiel, B., Huwig-Poppe, C., Kiemen, A., Konig, A., Backhaus, J., Reimann, D., Berger, M., & Hohagen, R. (1998). Impact of experimentally induced serotonin deficiency by tryptophan depletion on sleep EEG in healthy subjects. *Neuropsychopharmacology, 18,* 112–124.

Volavka, J., Czobor, P., Sheitman, B., Lindenmayer, J. P., Citrome, L., McEvoy, J. P., Cooper, T. B. , Chakos, M., & Lieberman, J. A. (2002). Clozapine, olanzapine, risperidone, haloperidol in the treatment of patients with chronic schizophrenia and schizoaffective disorder. *American Journal of Psychiatry, 159,* 255–262.

Volkow, N. D., Fowler, J. S., & Wang, G. J. (2004). The addicted human brain viewed in the light of imaging studies: Brain circuits and treatment strategies. *Neuropharmacology, 47,* 3–13.

Vollmer, W. M., Sacks, F. M., Ard, J., Appel, L. J., Bray, G. A., Simons-Morton, D. G., Conlin, P. R., Svetkey, L. P., Erlinger, T. P., Moore, T. J., & Karanja, N. (2001). Effects of diet and sodium intake on blood pressure: Subgroup anlaysis of the DASH-sodium trial. *Annals of Internal Medicine, 18,* 1019–1028.

Voyer, D. (1996). On the magnitude of laterality effects and sex differences in functional lateralities. *Laterality, 1,* 51–83.

Voyer, D., Nolan, C., & Voyer, S. (2000). The relation between experience and spatial performance in men and women. *Sex Roles, 43,* 891–915.

Voyer, D., Voyer, S., & Bryden, M. P. (1995). Magnitude of sex differences in spatial abilities: A meta-analysis and consideration of critical variables. *Psychological Bulletin, 117,* 250–270.

Vygotsky, L. S. (1934/1986). *Thought and language.* A. Kozulin (Trans). Cambridge, MA: MIT Press.

Vyse, S. A. (2000). *Believing in magic: The psychology of superstition.* New York: Oxford University Press.

Wagner, H. (1989). The physiological differentiation of emotions. In H. Wagner & A. Manstead (Eds), *Handbook of social psychophysiology.* New York: Wiley.

Wagner, U., Gais, H., Haider, H., Verleger, R., & Born, J. (2004). Sleep inspires insight. *Nature, 427,* 352–355.

Wahlsten, D. (1997). The malleability of intelligence is not constrained by heritability. In B. Devlin, S. E. Fienberg, D. P. Resnick, & K. Roeder (Eds.), *Intelligence, genes, and success: Scientists respond to The Bell Curve.* New York: Springer-Verlag.

Wald, G. (1964). The receptors of human color vision. *Science, 145,* 1007–1017.

Waldrop, D., Lightsey, O. R., Ethington, C. A., Woemmel, C. A., & Coke, A. L. (2001). Self-efficacy, optimism, health competence, and recovery from orthopedic surgery. *Journal of Counseling Psychology, 48,* 233–238.

Walker, E., Kestler, L., Bollini, A., & Hochman, K. M. (2004). Schizophrenia: Etiology and course. *Annual Review of Psychology, 55,* 401–430.

Walker, L. J. (1988). The development of moral reasoning. In R. Vasta (Ed.), *Annals of child development* (Vol. 5). Greenwich, CT: JAI Press.

Walker, L. J. (1989). A longitudinal study of moral reasoning. *Child Development, 60,* 157–166.

Walker, L. J., & Taylor, J. H. (1991). Strange transitions in moral reasoning: A longitudinal study of developmental processes. *Developmental Psychology, 27,* 330–337.

Walker, M. P., Brakefield, T., Morgan, A., Hobson, J. A., & Stickgold, R. (2002). Practice with sleep makes perfect: Sleep dependent motor skill learning. *Neuron, 35,* 205–211.

Walker, M. P., & Stickgold, R. (2004). Sleep-dependent learning and memory consolidation. *Neuron, 44,* 121–133.

Wallace, B., & Fisher, L. E. (1999). *Consciousness and behavior.* Boston: Allyn & Bacon.

Wallen, K. (1989). Mate selection: Economics and affection. *Behavioral and Brain Sciences, 12,* 37–38.

Walraven, J., Enroth-Cugell, C., Hood, D. C., MacLeod, D. I. A., & Schnapf, J. L. (1990). The control of visual sensitivity: Receptoral and postreceptoral processes. In L. Spillmann & J. S. Werner (Eds.), *Visual perception: The neurophysiological foundations.* San Diego: Academic Press.

Walsh, B. T. (2003). Eating disorders. In A. Tasman, J. Kay, & J. A. Lieberman (Eds.), *Psychiatry.* New York: Wiley.

Walsh, B. T., Seidman, S. N., Sysko, R., & Gould, M. (2002). Placebo response studies of major depression: Variable, substantial and growing. *Journal of the American Medical Association, 287,* 1840–1847.

Walsh, J. K., Dement, W. C., & Dinges, D. F. (2005). Sleep medicine, public policy, and public health. In M. H. Kryger, T. Roth, & W. C. Dement (Eds.). *Principles and practice of sleep medicine.* Philadelphia: Elsevier Saunders.

Walter, C. A. (2000). The psychological meaning of menopause: Women's experiences. *Journal of Women and Aging, 12*(3–4), 117–131.

Walters, E. E., & Kendler, K. S. (1995). Anorexia nervosa and anorexic-like syndromes in a population-based female twin sample. *American Journal of Psychiatry, 152,* 64–71.

Walther, E., & Grigoriadis, S. (2003). Why sad people like shoes better: The influence of mood on the evaluative conditioning of consumer attitudes. *Psychology & Marketing, 10,* 755–775.

Walton, M. E., Devlin, J. T., & Rushworth, M. F. S. (2004). Interactions between decision making and performance monitoring within prefrontal cortex. *Nature Neuroscience, 7,* 1259–1265.

Wampold, B. E. (2001). *The great psychotherapy debate.* Mahwah, NJ: Erlbaum.

Wang, P. S., Berglund, P., Olfson, M., Pincus, H. A., Wells, K. B., & Kessler, R. C. (2005). Failure and delay in initial treatment contact after first onset of mental disorders in the National Comorbidity Survey Replication. *Archives of General Psychiatry, 62,* 603–613.

Wang, P. S., Lane, M., Olfson, M., Pincus, H. A., Wells, K. B., & Kessler, R. C. (2005). Twelve-month use of mental health services in the United States: Results from the National Comorbidity Survey Replication. *Archives of General Psychiatry, 62,* 629–640.

Wangensteen, O. H., & Carlson, A. J. (1931). Hunger sensation after total gastrectomy. *Proceedings of the Society for Experimental Biology, 28,* 545–547.

Warr, P. (1999). Well-being and the workplace. In D. Kahneman, E. Diener, & N. Schwarz (Eds.), *Well-being: The foundations of hedonic psychology.* New York: Russell Sage Foundation.

Waterman, A., & Archer, S. (1990). A life-span perspective on identity formation: Development in form, function, and process. In P. B. Baltes, D. L. Featherman, & R. M. Lerner (Eds.), *Life-span development and behavior* (Vol. 10). Hillsdale, NJ: Erlbaum.

Watkins, L. R., & Maier, S. F. (2002). Beyond neurons: Evidence that immune and glial cells contribute to pathological pain states. *Physiological Reviews, 82,* 981–1011.

Watkins, L. R., & Maier, S. F. (2003). When good pain turns bad. *Current Directions in Psychological Science, 12,* 232–236.

Watson, D., David, J. P., & Suls, J. (1999). Personality, affectivity, and coping. In C. R. Snyder (Ed.), *Coping: The psychology of what works.* New York: Oxford University Press.

Watson, D., Klohen, E. C., Casillas, A., Nus Simms, E., Haig, J., & Berry, D. S. (2004). Match makers and deal breakers: Analyses of assortative mating in newlywed couples. *Journal of Personality, 72,* 1029–1068.

Watson, D., & Pennebaker, J. W. (1989). Health complaints, stress, and distress: Exploring the central role of negative affectivity. *Psychological Review, 96,* 234–254.

Watson, D., Suls, J., & Haig, J. (2002). Global self-esteem in relation to structural models of personality and affectivity. *Journal of Personality and Social Psychology, 83,* 185–197.

Watson, D. L., & Tharp, R. G. (2007). *Self-directed behavior: Self-modification for personal adjustment.* Belmont, CA: Wadsworth.

Watson, J. B. (1913). Psychology as the behaviorist views it. *Psychological Review, 20,* 158–177.

Watson, J. B. (1919). *Psychology from the standpoint of a behaviorist.* Philadelphia: Lippincott.

Watson, J. B. (1924). *Behaviorism.* New York: Norton.

Watson, J. B. (1930). *Behaviorism.* New York: Norton.

Watson, J. B., & Rayner, R. (1920). Conditioned emotional reactions. *Journal of Experimental Psychology, 3,* 1–14.

Waugh, N. C., & Norman, D. A. (1965). Primary memory. *Psychological Review, 72,* 89–104.

Weaver, C. A., & Krug, K. S. (2004). Consolidation-like effects in flashbulb memories: Evidence from September 11, 2001. *American Journal of Psychology, 117,* 517–530.

Weaver, M. F., & Schnoll, S. H. (1999). Stimulants: Amphetamines and cocaine. In B. S. McCrady & E. E. Epstein (Eds.), *Addictions: A comprehensive guidebook.* New York: Oxford University Press.

Webb, W. B. (1992a). Developmental aspects and a behavioral model of human sleep. In C. Stampi (Ed.), *Why we nap: Evolution, chronobiology, and functions of polyphasic and ultrashort sleep.* Boston: Birkhaeuser.

Webb, W. B. (1992b). *Sleep: The gentle tyrant*. Bolton, MA: Anker.

Webb, W. B., & Dinges, D. F. (1989). Cultural perspectives on napping and the siesta. In D. F. Dinges & R. J. Broughton (Eds.), *Sleep and alertness: Chronobiological, behavioral, and medical aspects of napping*. New York: Raven.

Wechsler, D. (1939). *The measurement of adult intelligence*. Baltimore: Williams & Wilkins.

Wechsler, H., Lee J. E., Kuo, M., Seibring, M., Nelson, T. F., & Lee, H. (2002). Trends in college binge drinking during a period of increased prevention efforts. *Journal of American College Health, 50*(5), 203–217.

Wegner, D. M. (1997). Why the mind wanders. In J. D. Cohen & J. W. Schooler (Eds.), *Scientific approaches to consciousness*. Mahwah, NJ: Erlbaum.

Wegner, D. M., Wenzlaff, R. M., & Kozak, M. (2004). Dream rebound: The return of suppressed thoughts in dreams. *Psychological Science, 15*(4), 232–236.

Weinberg, R. A. (1989). Intelligence and IQ: Landmark issues and great debates. *American Psychologist, 44*, 98–104.

Weinberger, J. (1995). Common factors aren't so common: The common factors dilemma. *Clinical Psychology: Science and Practice, 2*, 45–69.

Weiner, B. (Ed.). (1974). *Achievement motivation and attribution theory*. Morristown, NJ: General Learning Press.

Weiner, B. (1980). *Human motivation*. New York: Holt, Rinehart & Winston.

Weiner, B. (1986). *An attributional theory of motivation and emotion*. New York: Springer-Verlag.

Weiner, B. (1994). Integrating social and personal theories of achievement striving. *Review of Educational Research, 64*, 557–573.

Weiner, R. D. (2000). Retrograde amnesia with eletroconvulsive therapy: Characteristics and implications. *General Psychiatry, 57*, 591–592.

Weinfield, N. S., Sroufe, L. A., Egeland, B., & Carlson, E. A. (1999). The nature of individual differences in infant-caregiver attachment. In J. Cassidy & P. R. Shaver (Eds.), *Handbook of attachment: Theory, research, and clinical applications*. New York: Guilford.

Weisberg, R. W. (1986). *Creativity: Genius and other myths*. New York: W. H. Freeman.

Weisberg, R. W. (1993). *Creativity: Beyond the myth of genius*. New York: W. H. Freeman.

Weisberg, R. W. (1999). Creativity and knowledge: A challenge to theories. In R. J. Sternberg (Ed.), *Handbook of creativity*. New York: Cambridge University Press.

Weiten, W. (1984). Violation of selected item-construction principles in educational measurement. *Journal of Experimental Education, 51*, 46–50.

Weiten W. (1988a). Objective features of introductory psychology textbooks as related to professors' impressions. *Teaching of Psychology, 15*, 10–16.

Weiten, W. (1988b). Pressure as a form of stress and its relationship to psychological symptomatology. *Journal of Social and Clinical Psychology, 6*(1), 127–139.

Weiten, W. (1998). Pressure, major life events, and psychological symptoms. *Journal of Social Behavior and Personality, 13*, 51–68.

Weiten, W. Guadagno R. E., & Beck, C. A. (1996). Students' perceptions of textbook pedagogical aids. *Teaching of Psychology, 23*, 105–107.

Weiten, W., & Diamond, S. S. (1979). A critical review of the jury-simulation paradigm: The case of defendant characteristics. *Law and Human Behavior, 3*, 71–93.

Weiten, W., & Wight, R. D. (1992). Portraits of a discipline: An examination of introductory psychology textbooks in America. In A. E. Puente, J. R. Matthews, & C. L. Brewer (Eds.), *Teaching psychology in America: A history*. Washington, DC: American Psychological Association.

Wells, G. L., & Bradfield, A. L. (1998). "Good, you identified the suspect": Feedback to eyewitnesses disorts their reports of the witnessing experience. *Journal of Applied Psychology, 83*, 360–376.

Wells, G. L., & Olson, E. A. (2003). Eyewitness testimony. *Annual Review of Psychology, 54*, 277–295.

Wells, G. L., Olson, E. A., & Charman, S. D. (2002). The confidence of eyewitnesses in their identifications from lineups. *Current Directions in Psychological Science, 11*(5), 151–154.

Wells, K., Klap, R., Koike, A., & Sherbourne, C. (2001). Ethnic disparities in unmet need for alcoholism, drug abuse, and mental health care. *American Journal of Psychiatry, 158*, 2027–2032.

Welsh, R. S. (2003). Prescription privileges: Pro or con. *Clinical Psychology: Science & Practice, 10*, 371–372.

Wenzlaff, R. M., & Wegner, D. M. (2000). Thought suppression. *Annual Review of Psychology, 51*, 51–91.

Wertheimer, M. (1912). Experiment-elle studien über das sehen von bewegung. *Zeitschrift für Psychologie, 60*, 312–378.

Wessely, S., & Kerwin, R. (2004). Suicide risk and the SSRI's. *Journal of the American Medical Association, 292*, 379–381.

Wesson, D. R., Smith, D. E., Ling, W., & Seymour, R. B. (2005). Sedative-hypnotics. In M. H. Kryger, T. Roth, & W. C. Dement (Eds.). *Principles and practice of sleep medicine*. Philadelphia: Elsevier Saunders.

Westen, D. (1998). The scientific legacy of Sigmund Freud: Toward a psychodynamically informed psychological science. *Psychological Bulletin, 124*, 333–371.

Westen, D., & Gabbard, G. O. (1999). Psychoanalytic approaches to personality. In L. A. Pervin & O. P. John (Eds.), *Handbook of personality: Theory and research*. New York: Guilford.

Wethington, E. (2000). Life events scale. In G. Fink (Ed.), *Encyclopedia of stress* (Vol. 1, pp. 618–622). San Diego: Academic Press.

Wever, E. G., & Bray, C. W. (1937). The perception of low tones and the resonance-volley theory. *Journal of Psychology, 3*, 101–114.

Wexler, B. E., Gottschalk, C. H., Fulbright, R. K., Prohovnik, I., Lacadie, C. M., Rounsaville, B. J., & Gore, J. C. (2001). Functional magnetic resonance imaging of cocaine craving. *American Journal of Psychiatry, 158*, 86–95.

Wheeler, L., & Kim, Y. (1997). What is beautiful is culturally good: The physical attractiveness stereotype has different content in collectivistic cultures. *Personality and Social Psychology Bulletin, 23*, 795–800.

Whitaker, R. (2002). *Mad in America: Bad science, bad medicine, and the enduring mistreatment of the mentally ill*. New York: Perseus Publishing.

Whitbourne, S. K. (1999). Physical changes. In J. C. Cavanaugh & S. K. Whitbourne (Eds.), *Gerontology: Interdisciplinary perspectives* (pp. 91–122). New York: Oxford University Press.

Whitbourne, S. K., Zuschlag, M. K., Elliot, L. B., & Waterman, A. S. (1992). Psychosocial development in adulthood: A 22-year sequential study. *Journal of Personality and Social Psychology, 63*, 260–271.

White, S. H. (2000). Conceptual foundations of IQ testing. *Psychology, Public Policy, and Law, 6*, 33–43.

White, W. (1997) Croco%#@! Dundee [Web Page]. Retrieved July 2, 2002 from http://www.outsidemag.com/magazine/1197/9711out.html.

Whitfield, C. L. (1995). *Memory and abuse: Remembering and healing the effects of trauma*. Deerfield Beach, FL: Health Communications.

Widiger, T. A., & Sankis, L. M. (2000). Adult psychopathology: Issues and controversies. *Annual Review of Psychology, 51*, 377–404.

Wigboldus, D. H. J., Dijksterhuis, A., & van Knippenberg, A. (2003). When stereotypes get in the way: Stereotypes obstruct stereotype-inconsistent trait inferences. *Journal of Personality and Social Psychology, 84*, 470–484.

Wikaitis, J., Mulvihill, T., & Nasrallah, H. A. (2004). Classic antipsychotic medications. In A. F. Schatzberg & C. B. Nemeroff (Eds.), *Textbook of psychopharmacology*. Washington, DC: American Psychiatric Publishing.

Wilding, J., & Valentine, E. (1996). Memory expertise. In D. J. Herrmann, C. McEvoy, C. Hertzog, P. Hertel, & M. K. Johnson (Eds.), *Basic and applied memory research: Theory in context* (Vol. 1). Mahwah, NJ: Erlbaum.

Williams, A., & Giles, H. (1998). Communication of ageism. In M. C. Hecht (Ed.), *Communicating prejudice* (pp. 136–160). Thousand Oaks, CA: Sage.

Williams, B. A. (1988). Reinforcement, choice, and response strength. In R. C. Atkinson, R. J. Herrnstein, G. Lindzey, & R. D. Luce (Eds.), *Stevens' handbook of experimental psychology*. New York: Wiley.

Williams, C. G., Gagne, M., Ryan, R. M., & Deci, E. L. (2002). Facilitating autonomous motivation for smoking cessation. *Health Psychology, 21*, 40–50.

Williams, G. C. (1966). *Adaptation and natural selection*. Princeton, NJ: Princeton University Press.

Williams, J. B. W. (1999). Psychiatric classification. In R. E. Hales, S. C. Yudofsky, & J. A. Talbott (Eds.), *American Psychiatric Press textbook of psychiatry* (3rd ed.). Washington, DC: American Psychiatric Press.

Williams, J. E., Paton, C. C., Siegler, I. C., Eigenbrodt, M. L., Neito, F. J., & Tyroler, H. A. (2000). Anger proneness predicts coronary heart disease risk. *Circulation, 101*, 2034–2039.

Williams, K. E., & Bond, M. J. (2002). The roles of self-efficacy, outcome expectancies and social support in the self-care behaviors of diabetics. *Psychology, Health & Medicine, 7*(2), 127–141.

Williams, M. H. (1992). Exploitation and inference: Mapping the damage from therapist-patient sexual involvement. *American Psychologist, 47*, 412–421.

Williams, N. A., & Deffenbacher, J. L. (1983). Life stress and chronic yeast infections. *Journal of Human Stress, 9*(1), 26–31.

Williams, R. B. (2001). Hostility (and other psychosocial risk factors): Effects on health and the potential for successful behavioral approaches to prevention and treatment. In A. Baum, T. A. Revenson, & J. E. Singer (Eds.), *Handbook of health psychology* (pp. 661–668). Mahwah, NJ: Erlbaum.

Williams, R. B., & Williams, V. P. (2001). Managing hostile thoughts, feelings, and actions: The lifeskills approach. In C. R. Snyder (Ed.), *Coping with stress: Effective people and processes* (pp. 137–153). New York: Oxford University Press.

Williams, R. L., & Eggert, A. (2002). Notetaking predictors of test performance. *Teaching of Psychology, 29*(3), 234–237.

Williams, W. M. (1998). Are we raising smarter children today? School-and-home-related infuences on IQ. In U. Neisser (Ed.), *The rising curve: Long-term gains in IQ and related measures.* Washington, DC: American Psychological Association.

Williams, W. M., & Ceci, S. J. (1997). Are Americans becoming more or less alike?: Trends in race, class, and ability differences in intelligence. *American Psychologist, 52*, 1226–1235.

Williamson, D. A., Zucker, N. L., Martin, C. K., & Smeets, M. A. M. (2001). Etiology and management of eating disorders. In P. B. Sutker & H. E. Adams (Eds.), *Comprehensive handbook of psychopathology.* New York: Kluwer Academic/Plenum.

Willis, W. D. (1985). *The pain system. The neural basis of nococeptive transmission in the mammalian nervous system.* Basel: Karger.

Willoughby, T., Motz, M., & Wood, E. (1997). The impact of interest and strategy use on memory performance for child, adolescent, and adult learners. *Alberta Journal of Educational Research, 43*, 127–141.

Wills, T. A., & Fegan, M. (2001). Social networks and social support. In A. Baum, T. A. Revenson, & J. E. Singer (Eds.), *Handbook of health psychology* (pp. 209–234). Mahwah, NJ: Erlbaum.

Wilsnack, S. C., Wonderlich, S. A., Kristjanson, A. F., Vogeltanz-Holm, N. D., & Wilsnack, R. W. (2002). Self-reports of forgetting and remembering childhood sexual abuse in a nationally representative sample of U.S. women. *Child Abuse and Neglect, 26*(2), 139–147.

Wilson, G. T. (1982). Alcohol and anxiety: Recent evidence on the tension reduction theory of alcohol use and abuse. In K. R. Blankstein & J. Polivy (Eds.), *Self-control and self-modification of emotional behavior.* New York: Plenum.

Wilson, R. S., & Bennett, D. A. (2003). Cognitive activity and risk of Alzheimer's disease. *Current Directions in Psychological Science, 12*(3), 87–91.

Windholz, G. (1997). Ivan P. Pavlov: An overview of his life and psychological work. *American Psychologist, 52*, 941–946.

Winn, P. (1995). The lateral hypothalmus and motivated behavior: An old syndrome reassessed and a new perspective gained. *Current Directions in Psychological Science, 4*, 182–187.

Winsler, A. (2003). Introduction to special issue: Vygotskian perspectives in early childhood education. *Early Education & Development, 14*(3), 253–269.

Winters, K. C., Arthur, N., Leitten, W., & Botzet, A. (2004). Gambling and drug abuse in adolescence. In J. L. Derevensky & R. Gupta (Eds.), *Gambling problems in youth: Theoretical and applied perspectives* (pp. 57–80). New York: Kluwer/Plenum.

Winzelberg, A. J., & Luskin, F. M. (1999). The effect of a meditation training in stress levels in secondary school teachers. *Stress Medicine, 15*, 69–77.

Wise, M. G., Gray, K. F., & Seltzer, B. (1999). Delirium, dementia, and amnestic disorders. In R. E. Hales, S. C. Yudofsky, & J. A. Talbott (Eds.), *The American Psychiatric Press textbook of psychiatry* (3rd ed., pp. 317–362). Washington, DC: American Psychiatric Press.

Wise, R. A. (1999). Animal models of addiction. In D. S. Charney, E. J. Nestler, & B. S. Bunney (Eds.), *Neurobiology of mental illness.* New York: Oxford University Press.

Witkin, H. A. (1950). Individual differences in ease of perception of embedded figures. *Journal of Personality, 19*, 1–15.

Witkin, H. A., Dyk, R. B., Paterson, H. F., Goodenough, D. R., & Karp, S. (1962). *Psychological differentiation.* New York: Wiley.

Wittkower, E. D., & Warnes, H. (1984). Cultural aspects of psychotherapy. In J. E. Mezzich & C. E. Berganza (Eds.), *Culture and psychopathology.* New York: Columbia University Press.

Wolk, A., Manson, J. E., Stampfer, M. J., Colditz, G. A., Hu, F. B., Speizer, F. E., Hennekens, C. H., & Willett, W. C. (1999). Long-term intake of dietary fiber and decreased risk of coronary heart disease among women. *Journal of the American Medical Association, 281*, 1998–2004.

Wolpe, J. (1958). *Psychotherapy by reciprocal inhibition.* Stanford, CA: Stanford University Press.

Wolpe, J. (1990). *The practice of behavior therapy.* Elmsford, NY: Pergamon Press.

Wonderlich, S. A. (2002). Personality and eating disorders. In C. G. Fairburn & K. D. Brownell (Eds.), *Eating disorders and obesity: A comprehensive handbook.* New York: Guilford.

Wood, E., Desmarais, S., & Gugula, S. (2002). The impact of parenting experience on gender stereotyped toy play of children. *Sex Roles, 47*(1–2), 39–49.

Wood, F., Ebert, V., & Kinsbourne, M. (1982). The episodic-semantic memory distinction in memory and amnesia: Clinical and experimental observations. In L. Cermak (Ed.), *Human memory and amnesia.* Hillsdale, NJ: Erlbaum.

Woodhead, M. (2004). When psychology informs public policy: The case. In E. Zigler & S. J. Styfco (Eds.), *The Head Start debate.* Baltimore: Paul H. Brookes Publishing.

Woods, S. C., Schwartz, M. W., Baskin, D. G., & Seeley, R. J. (2000). Food intake and the regulation of body weight. *Annual Review of Psychology, 51*, 255–277.

Woolfolk, R. L., & Richardson, F. C. (1978). *Stress, sanity and survival.* New York: Sovereign/Monarch.

Worthen, J. B., & Wade, C. E. (1999). Direction of travel and visiting team athletic performance: Support for a circadian dysrhythmia hypothesis. *Journal of Sport Behavior, 22*, 279–287.

Worthington, E. L., Jr., & Scherer, M. (2004). Forgiveness is an emotion-focused coping strategy that can reduce health risks and promote health resilience: Theory, review, and hypotheses. *Psychology and Health, 19*, 385-405.

Wright, J. H., Beck, A. T., & Thase, M. E. (2003). Cognitive therapy. In R. E. Hales & S. C. Yudofsky (Eds.), *Textbook of clinical psychiatry.* Washington, DC: American Psychiatric Publishing.

Wundt, W. (1874/1904). *Principles of physiological psychology.* Leipzig: Engelmann.

Wylie, M. S. (1998). The shadow of a doubt. In R. A. Baker (Ed.), *Child sexual abuse and false memory syndrome.* Amherst, NY: Prometheus Books.

Wynder, E. L., Cohen, L. A., Muscat, J. E., Winters, B., Dwyer, J. T., & Blackburn, G. (1997). Breast cancer: Weighing the evidence for a promoting role of dietary fat. *Journal of the National Cancer Institute, 89*, 766–775.

Wynn, K. (1992). Addition and subtraction by human infants. *Nature, 358*, 749–750.

Wynn, K. (1996). Infants' individuation and enumeration of sequential actions. *Psychological Science, 7*, 164–169.

Wynn, K. (1998). An evolved capacity for number. In D. D. Cummins & C. Allen (Eds.), *The evolution of mind.* New York: Oxford University Press.

Xiaghe, X., & Whyte, M. K. (1990). Love matches and arranged marriages: A Chinese replication. *Journal of Marriage and the Family, 52*, 709–722.

Yamamoto, J., Silva, J. A., Justice, L. R., Chang, C. Y., & Leong, G. B. (1993). Cross-cultural psychotherapy. In A. C. Gaw (Ed.), *Culture, ethnicity, and mental illness.* Washington, DC: American Psychiatric Press.

Yang, H., Liu, T., & Zang, D. (2000). A study of stressful life events before the onset of hypothyroidism. *Chinese Mental Health Journal, 14*, 201–202.

Yates, F. A. (1966). *The art of memory.* London: Routledge & Kegan Paul.

Ybarra, O., Stephan, W. G., & Schaberg, L. (2000). Misanthropic memory for the behavior of group members. *Personality and Social Psychology Bulletin, 26*, 1515–1525.

Yerkes, R. M., & Morgulis, S. (1909). The method of Pavlov in animal psychology. *Psychological Bulletin, 6*, 257–273.

Yi, H., Stinson, F. S., Williams, G. D., & Dufour, M. C. (1999). *Surveillance report #53: Trends in alcohol-related fatal traffic crashes, United States, 1977–1998.* Rockville, MD: National Institute on Alcohol Abuse and Alcoholism.

Yost, W. A. (2000). *Fundamentals of hearing: An introduction.* San Diego, CA: Academic Press.

Young, K. S. (1996, August). *Internet addiction: The emergence of a new clinical disorder.* Paper presented at the meeting of the American Psychological Association: Toronto, Ontario, Canada.

Young, K. S. (1998). *Caught in the net: How to recognize the signs of Internet addiction—and a winning strategy for recovery.* New York: Wiley.

Zajonc, R. B. (1980). Feeling and thinking: Preferences need no inferences. *American Psychologist, 35*, 151–175.

Zane, N., Hall, G. C. N., Sue, S., Young, K., & Nunez, J. (2004). Research on psychotherapy with culturally diverse populations. In M. J. Lambert (Ed.), *Bergin and Garfield's handbook of psychotherapy and behavior change.* New York: Wiley.

Zarate, M. A., Garcia, B., Garza, A. A., & Hitlan, R. T. (2004). Cultural threat and perceived realistic group conflict as dual predictors of prejudice. *Journal of Experimental Social Psychology, 40*, 99–105.

Zarcone, V. P., Jr. (2000). Sleep hygiene. In M. H. Kryger, T. Roth, & W. C. Dement (Eds.), *Principles and practice of sleep medicine.* Philadelphia: Saunders.

Zatzick, D. F. (1999). Managed care and psychiatry. In R. E. Hales, S. C. Yudofsky, & J. A. Talbott (Eds.), *American Psychiatric Press textbook of psychiatry.* Washington, DC: American Psychiatric Press.

Zatzick, D. F., & Dimsdale, J. E. (1990). Cultural variations in response to painful stimuli. *Psychosomatic Medicine, 52*(5), 544–557.

Zautra, A. J., & Smith, B. W. (2001). Depression and reactivity to stress in older women with rheumatoid arthritis and osteoarthritis. *Psychosomatic Medicine, 63*, 687–696.

Zechmeister, E. B., & Nyberg, S. E. (1982). *Human memory: An introduction to research and theory.* Pacific Grove, CA: Brooks/Cole.

Zeiler, M. (1977). Schedules of reinforcement: The controlling variables. In W. K. Honig & J. E. R. Staddon (Eds.), *Handbook of operant behavior.* Englewood Cliffs, NJ: Prentice-Hall.

Zenhausen, R. (1978). Imagery, cerebral dominance and style of thinking: A unified field model. *Bulletin of the Psychonomic Society, 12,* 381–384.

Zepelin, H. (1993). Internal alarm clock. In M. A. Carskadon (Ed.), *Encyclopedia of sleep and dreaming.* New York: Macmillan.

Zepelin, H., Siegel, J. M., & Tobler, I. (2005). Mammalian sleep. In M. H. Kryger, T. Roth, & W. C. Dement (Eds.). *Principles and practice of sleep medicine.* Philadelphia: Elsevier Saunders.

Zillmer, E. A., & Spiers, M. V. (2001). *Principles of neuropsychology.* Belmont, CA: Wadsworth.

Zimbardo, P. G. (2004, May 9). Power turns good soldiers into "bad apples." *Boston Globe.* Retrieved from http://www.boston.com/news/globe/ editorial_opinion/oped/articles/2004/05/09.

Zimbardo, P. G. (2005, June). The psychology of power and evil: All power to the person? To the situation? To the system? [Presentation for the course, The Psychology of Terrorism, organized by the faculty of the National Center on the Psychology of Terrorism]. Unpublished manuscript retrieved from http://www.prisonexp.org/pdf/powerevil.pdf.

Zimbardo, P. G., Haney, C., & Banks, W. C. (1973, April 8). The mind is a formidable jailer: A Pirandellian prison. *New York Times Magazine,* Section 6, p. 36.

Zimmerman, I. L., & Woo-Sam, J. M. (1984). Intellectual assessment of children. In G. Goldstein & M. Hersen (Eds.), *Handbook of psychological assessment.* New York: Pergamon Press.

Zola, S. M., & Squire, L. R. (2000). The medial temporal lobe and the hippocampus. In E. Tulving & F. I. M. Craik (Eds.), *The Oxford handbook of memory* (pp. 485–500). New York: Oxford University Press.

Zorick, F. J., & Walsh, J. K. (2000). Evaluation and management of insomnia: An overview. In M. H. Kryger, T. Roth, & W. C. Dement (Eds.), *Principles and practice of sleep medicine.* Philadelphia: Saunders.

Zrenner, E., Abramov, I., Akita, M., Cowey, A., Livingstone, M., & Valberg, A. (1990). Color perception: Retina to cortex. In L. Spillman & J. S. Werner (Eds.), *Visual perception: The neurophysiological foundations.* San Diego: Academic Press.

Zuckerman, M. (1971). Dimensions of sensation seeking. *Journal of Consulting and Clinical Psychology, 36,* 45–52.

Zurbriggen, E. L., & Sturman, T. S. (2002). Linking motives and emotions: A test of McClelland's hypothesis. *Personality & Social Psychology Bulletin, 28,* 521–535.

Forsyth, D. R., 461, 472, 493
Foster, C. A., 327
Foster, R. G., 139
Foulkes, D., 152, 163
Fowler, J. S., 160
Fox, G. L., 327
Fozard, J. L., 327
Fraley, R. C., 478
Frame, S., 216
Framtom, C., 267
Francasso, M. P., 311
Frances, R. J., 160
Francis, G., 210
Francis, M. E., 396
Frank, J., 460
Frank, J. B., 443
Frank, J. D., 443
Frank, L. K., 366
Frank, L. R., 451
Franklin, J. E., Jr., 160
Franks, C. M., 444
Franzen, M. D., 254
Fraser, S. C., 463, 499
Frasure-Smith, N., 385
Frazer, A., 70
Frederick, S., 250, 299
Frederickson, B. L., 289, 378, 395
Frederickson, B., 16
Fredriks, A. M., 322
Freedman, J. L., 298, 463, 499
Freud, S., 6, 9, 14, 15, 20, 21, 138, 149, 151, 152, 163, 220, 312, 341–347, 349, 358, 382, 436, 438–440, 452
Frey, B. S., 297
Frey, K. S., 333
Friedkin, N. E., 492
Friedman, H., 160
Friedman, M., 384
Friedman, S. R., 161
Friesen, W., 292, 293, 328
Frieze, I. H., 469
Frijda, N. H., 292
Frishman, L. J., 100
Fromherz, S., 148
Fromm, E., 154
Fuchs, A. H., 3
Fujita, F., 297
Fuller, S. R., 493
Fullerton, C. S., 408
Fullilove, M., 308
Funder, D. C., 352, 361
Furberg, A., 390
Furumoto, L., 5
Fuster, J. M., 78
Fyer, A. J., 409
Fyrberg, D., 51

G

Gabbard, G. O., 348, 349
Gabrielli, J. D. E., 224
Gaddis, C., 169
Gaertner, S. L., 474, 495
Gaeth, C. J., 237
Gage, F. H., 79, 416
Gagne, F., 228
Gagnon, A., 496
Gais, S., 147
Galaburda, A. M., 332
Galambos, N. L., 333
Galati, B., 292
Galderisi, S., 420
Galizio, M., 183
Gallagher, S. N., 291
Gallo, D. A., 207
Gallo, L. C., 384, 387

Galton, F., 22
Gambone, J. C., 392
Gangestad, S. W., 475
Gangi, B. K., 460
Gantt, W. H., 170
Ganuza, J. M. G., 29
Garb, H. N., 367
Garcia, B. F., 351
Garcia, J., 190
Garcia, M., 455
Garcia, S. D., 475
Gardner, C. O., Jr., 414
Gardner, E. P., 125
Gardner, H., 11, 91, 263–264, 266
Gardner, W. L., 288
Garfield, S. L., 443, 460
Garner, L., 375
Garnett, N., 52
Garry, M., 216
Gartrell, N. K., 285
Gawronski, B., 472
Gazzaniga, M. S., 11, 80, 81, 82
Gearon, J. S., 422
Geddes, J. R., 449, 451
Gee, T. L., 413
Geiger, M. A., 26
Geller, J. L., 457
Geller, L., 355
Gelman, S. A., 333
George, J. M., 327
Geraci, L., 207
Gergen, K. J., 12
German, T. P., 238
Gershoff, E. T., 188
Gershon, E. S., 416
Geschwind, N., 332
Getchell, M. L., 124
Getchell, T. Y., 124
Ghez, C., 76
Gibb, R., 78
Gigerenzer, G., 249
Gilbert, D. T., 472, 473
Giles, H., 496
Giles, T. R., 454
Gilgen, A. R., 9
Gilhooly, K. J., 240
Gillberg, M., 146, 162
Gillette, M. U., 148
Gillham, J. E., 388
Gilovich, T., 23
Ginter, D. R., 139
Girgus, J. S., 117
Gitlin, M., 448, 449
Gladue, B. A., 285
Glaser, R., 386
Glass, C. R., 444
Glass, R. M., 451
Glassman, A., 385
Glassner, B., 248
Glatt, S. J., 421
Gleaves, D. H., 222, 413
Goeders, N. E., 382
Goff, D. C., 456
Gold, M. S., 69, 160
Golden, C. J., 254
Goldenberg, H., 10, 11
Goldin, L. R., 416
Goldman-Rakic, P. S., 93
Goldsmith, H. H., 312
Goldsmith, M., 215
Goldstein, D. G., 249
Goldstein, E., 221
Goldstein, E. B., 122
Goldstein, H. W., 255
Goldstein, I. L., 255
Goldstein, R. D., 414

Goldstein, W. M., 244, 248
Gonzalez, C. A., 427
Gooch, C., 457
Goodenough, D. R., 163
Goodstein, L. D., 366, 367
Goodwin, C. J., 171
Goodwin, F. K., 415, 416
Gooley, J. J., 139
Gordon, B., 450
Gordon, H. W., 91
Gordon, J., 107
Gordon, J. U., 387
Gordon-Salant, S., 327
Gorski, R. A., 83
Gosling, S. D., 11
Gottdiener, J. S., 385
Gottesman, I. I., 84, 86, 421
Gottfredson, L. S., 254, 255, 260, 263
Gottman, J. M., 327
Gottschall, J., 479
Gould, E., 79
Gould, R., 325
Gould, S. J., 13, 87
Gouras, P., 107
Gourevitch, M. N., 160
Gouzoulis-Mayfrank, E., 161
Graber, J. A., 321
Grace, R. C., 174
Graf, P., 226
Granberg, G., 49
Grant, I., 386
Gratton, A., 77
Gray, J. R., 289
Gray, K. F., 328
Gray, W. D., 218
Green, B., 173
Green, C., 8
Green, J. P., 154
Greenberg, J. L., 361–363
Greenberg, J. S., 397
Greenberg, M. A., 396
Greenberg, R. P., 151, 349, 462
Greene, R. L., 218, 227
Greenfield, D. N., 382
Greenfield, P., 259
Greenland, P., 384
Greenleaf, M., 153
Greeno, C. G., 279
Greeno, J., 236
Greenough, W. T., 92
Greenson, R. R., 439
Gregory, R. L., 112, 117
Greist, J. H., 449
Grencavage, L. M., 443
Griffin, D. W., 476
Griffith, E. E., 427
Griffiths, M., 382
Grigerenko, E. L., 22, 256, 258, 261
Grigoriadis, S., 201
Grinspoon, L., 160
Grob, C. S., 161
Grose-Fifer, J., 308
Gross, C. G., 79
Gross, C. P., 450
Gross, J. J., 395
Grossman, J. B., 446
Grossman, R. P., 201
Grossman, S. P., 76
Grossmann, K., 312
Grossmann, K. E., 312
Grotevant, H., 327
Groth-Marnat, 366
Grove, W. M., 367
Gruber, A. J., 160
Grubin, D., 291
Gruen, R. J., 376

Hummel, J. E., 111
Hunsley, J., 367
Hunt, E., 309
Hunt, H., 151
Hunt, J. M., 481
Hunter, J., 254, 255
Huntsinger, E. T., 478
Hurvich, L. M., 108
Husband, T. H., 221
Huttenlocher, P. R., 68, 93
Huxley, A., 65
Hyde, J. S., 331
Hyde, T. M., 422, 423, 448
Hyman, I. E., Jr., 221

I

Iacono, W. G., 291, 413
Ickovics, J. R., 390
Iezzi, T., 411
Infante, J. R., 156
Inglehart, R., 297
Ingram, R. E., 418
Innocenti, G. M., 332
Irabarren, C., 384
Irvine, S. H., 256
Irwin, S., 339
Isaacowitz, D. M., 381
Isabella, R. A., 312
Isenberg, K. E., 451
Ismail, B., 423
Ismail, M. A., 309
Isometsa, E. T., 45, 46
Israel, M., 429
Ivens-Tyndal, C. O., 414, 417
Iversen, L., 76
Iversen, S., 76, 77
Iwao, S., 478
Iwawaki, S., 256
Izard, C. E., 291, 292, 295

J

Jablensky, A., 418
Jacklin, C., 15, 333
Jackson, D. C., 291
Jackson, L.A., 496
Jackson, S., 201
Jacob, R. G., 447
Jacobs, B. L., 416
Jacobs, D. F., 1
Jacobs, G. H., 108
Jacobs, H. S., 328
Jacobs, R. L., 417
Jacobsen, T., 312
Jacobson, G., 308
Jacoby, L. L., 219
Jain, S. P., 482
James, J. E., 390
James, W., 4–5, 13, 14, 138, 293
Jamison, K. R., 267, 415, 416
Jang, K. L., 357
Janig, W., 289, 294
Janis, I. L., 374, 378, 492–493
Janssen, R. S., 390
Jaroff, L., 221
Jefferson, J. W., 449
Jemmott, J. B., 387
Jensen, A. R., 256, 258, 260–261, 262, 268
Jensen, E., 92
Jensen, M. P., 153
Jessell, T. M., 70, 125, 127
Jevning, R., 156
Jex, S. M., 351
Ji, L.-J., 242
Jick, H., 449
Jick, S. S., 449
Jindal, K., 416

Jindal, R., 69
Johansen, C., 386
John, O. P., 341, 476
Johnson, A., 224
Johnson, B. A., 164
Johnson, B. T., 481, 482
Johnson, C., 470
Johnson, D., 52
Johnson, J. A., 392, 393
Johnson, M. K., 216
Johnson, S. B., 392, 393
Johnson, V., 279–280
Johnston, J. C., 110, 206
Johnston, W. A., 206
Joiner, T. E., Jr., 418
Jones, B. C., 479
Jones, C., 325
Jones, E. E., 471, 472
Jones, F., 376
Jordan, B., 126
Joseph, R., 90
Josse, G., 91
Judge, T., 46, 55
Julien, R. M., 156
Jung, C. G., 6, 9, 347–348, 440

K

Kaas, J. H., 79
Kagan, J., 369
Kahneman, D., 245–246, 247, 250, 299, 431
Kaiser, P., 105
Kalaria, R. N., 385
Kales, J. D., 163
Kalichman, S. C., 391
Kalidindi, S., 416
Kalin, N. H., 291
Kalmijn, M., 475
Kalton, G., 49
Kameda, T., 492
Kamin, L, 261
Kandall, S. R., 308
Kandel, E. R., 66, 67, 68, 70, 77, 105, 125, 224
Kandell, J. J., 382
Kane, J., 392
Kane, J. M., 448
Kane, M. J., 78
Kane, T. D., 351
Kanowitz, J., 50
Kaplan, H., 310
Karau, S. J., 491
Kassel, J. D., 382
Kasser, T., 283, 297T., 355
Kassim, S. M. , 230, 497
Katigbak, M. S., 363
Katz, J., 418
Katzman, M. A., 429
Kaufman, A. S., 253, 260
Kaufman, J. C., 256, 266
Kaufman, L., 118
Kavesh, L., 467
Kay, J., 440
Kay, R. L., 440
Kaye, J. A., 449
Kazdin, A., 188, 197, 436
Keating, D. P., 322
Keck, P. E., 419
Keefauver, S. P., 149
Keefe, F. J., 386
Keefer, L., 386
Keesey, R. E., 76
Kehoe, E. J., 174
Keith-Spiegel, P., 460
Keller, H. E., 51
Keller, M. B., 449
Keller, P. A., 484
Kelley, B. D., 423
Kelley, H. H., 471

Kelly, J., 327
Kelly, J. A., 390
Kelly, J. P., 127
Kelly, K. M., 386
Kelly, P. J., 145
Kelman, H. C., 51, 488
Keltner, D., 476
Kempen, H. J. G., 12
Kendall, P. C., 442
Kendler, K. S., 285, 409, 414, 418, 421, 429
Kennedy, T. E., 224
Kenrick, D. T., 133, 331
Kent, R. N., 50
Kernan, J. B., 481
Kerwin, R., 449
Kessler, R. C., 387, 408, 415, 436, 437, 478
Kester, J. D., 206
Ketcham, K., 220
Ketterlinus, R. D., 311
Key, C. B., 258
Khalsa, S., 139
Khan, M., 208
Khersonsky, D., 475
Khot, U. N., 384
Khroyan, T. V., 389
Kidd, K. K., 256
Kiecolt-Glaser, J. K., 386
Kiernan, M., 390
Kieseppa, T., 416
Kiesler, C. A., 403, 454, 457
Kiewra, K. A., 26
Kihlstrom, J. F., 155, 220, 413
Kilbey, M. M., 43
Killeen, P. R., 192
Killiany, R. J., 328
Kim, A., 488
Kim, K., 318
Kim, Y., 468
Kimmel, A. J., 51
Kimura, D., 91, 332
Kinder, B., 429
King, A. C., 162, 390
King, G. R., 69
King, L., 375
King, M., 407
King, N. J., 409
Kinman, G., 376
Kinsbourne, M., 138, 226, 332
Kinsey, A., 283, 284
Kippin, T. E., 174
Kirk, S. A., 407
Kirkpatrick, L. A., 312, 478
Kirsch, I., 154, 155
Kitayama, S., 363–364
Kitchens, A., 90
Kittler, P. G., 123, 278
Klein, E., 408
Klein, M., 440
Klein, T. W., 160
Kleinke, C. L., 292
Kleinknecht, E. E., 221
Kleinmuntz, B., 415
Kleitman, N., 137, 141, 142
Klerman, E. B., 143
Kline, P., 254, 365
Klipper, M. Z., 396
Klohnen, E. C., 475
Klosch, G., 163
Kluegel, J. R., 496
Kluft, R. P., 222, 413
Klymenko, V., 105
Knapp, T. J., 375
Knecht, S., 74, 91
Knight, J., 290
Knowlton, B. J., 77, 224, 225
Kochanska, G., 312
Koegel, P., 458
Koehler, J. J., 246

approach-avoidance conflict, 375
Arapesh, 151
archetypes, 347, 348
archival records, as data source, 36
Archives of the History of American Psychology (AHAP), 12
arguments
  components of, 300–301
  evaluating, 301
  one-sided versus two-sided, 481
arithmetic, infants and, 318
arousal
  autonomic, 289, 293, 294
  emotional, 378–379, 395, 396
  optimal level of, 379
  sexual, 174, 279
arrangement, problems of, 236
art, perceptual principles and, 128–131
arthritis, stress and, 385
articles, journal, 54–57
artists, mental illness and, 267
Asian Americans, 13
assertiveness, measuring, 365
associations
  learned, 170
  response-outcome, 181
assumptions, 300
asylums, 403, 456
atherosclerosis, 383–384
attachment
  biological basis for, 311–312
  culture and, 312, 313
  in infants, 310–312
  love and, 477–478
  patterns of, 312
  theories of, 310–311
attachment styles, 477–478
attention
  divided, 206
  lack of, 218
  marijuana use and, 160
  memory encoding and, 206
  observational learning and, 193
  pain perception and, 126
  selective, 109, 227
  sleep deprivation and, 147
  in working memory, 211
attitude alignment, 475
attitudes, 467, 480–484
  ambivalent, 481
  behavior and, 480
  changing, 481–482
  components of, 480–481
  conditioning of, 200, 482, 483
  defined, 480
  dimensions of, 480
  existing, 482
  formation of, 482–483, 496
  observational learning of, 483
  prejudiced, 494–497
  similarity in, 475
  strength of, 480
attraction, 467, 475–480
  tactics of, 479–480
attractiveness
  cultural standards for, 479
  eating disorders and, 429
  happiness and, 297
  impressions and, 468–469, 470
  interpersonal attraction and, 475
  judgments of, 133
  mate preferences and, 282–283
attribution processes, 467, 471–474
attributions, 471
  bias in, 471–472, 496
  culture and, 473–474
  external, 471, 472, 473, 496
  internal, 471, 472, 473, 496

stable-unstable dimension of, 471, 472, 496
  for success and failure, 471, 472–473, 496
atypical antipsychotic drugs, 448
auditory cortex, 78, 79
auditory hallucinations, 419
auditory nerves, 122
auditory processing, in brain, 78, 80
auditory sensory storage, 210
auditory system, 119–122
authority, obedience to, 486–488
autonomic arousal, 289–290
autonomic nervous system (ANS), 71–72, 76, 83, 289–290, 380
autonomic specificity, 294
autonomy versus shame and doubt, 314
availability heuristic, 245–246, 431
aversion therapy, 445–446
aversive stimulus, 185–186
avoidance behavior, 198
avoidance learning, 186
avoidance response, 409
avoidance-avoidance conflict, 375
avoidant attachment, 312, 477–478
awareness, levels of, 138, 342–343
axon(s), 64, 65, 66
  olfactory, 125
  in optic nerve, 102
  squid, 65

B

back pain, stress and, 385
balance, 76
Bantus, 117
barbiturates, 157
base rates, 398–399
  ignoring, 246–247
baseline data, 198
basilar membrane, 121, 122
Bay of Pigs, 492
Beck Institute of Cognitive Therapy and Research, 447
bedtime, ideal, 139
behavior
  cultural factors in, 21–22
  defined, 7
  evolution of, 88–89
  multifactorial causation of, 21, 89, 158, 296, 399, 427
  observable, 87
behavior modification, 24, 197–199, 446, 461
behavior therapies, 436, 444–447, 452–453, 461
  aversion therapy, 445–446
  cognitive therapy, 446–447, 452–453
  effectiveness of, 447
  social skills training, 446
  systematic desensitization, 444–445, 452–453
behavioral contract, 199
behavioral disengagement, 381
behavioral genetics, 357, 360
behavioral maneuvers, 88, 89
behavioral perspective, 9, 11
  evaluation of, 352
  on personality, 349–352, 358
behavioral rehearsal, 446
behavioral traits, evolution of, 88
behaviorism, 7–9, 349
beliefs, 480, 494
Bell Curve, The (Herrnstein & Murray), 260, 261, 268
Bellini, Gentile and Giovanni, 128
bell-shaped curve, 251, A-10
Belvedere (Escher), 130
benzodiazepines, 147–148
beta waves, 138, 142
Beyond Freedom and Dignity (Skinner), 8
bias
  in attributions, 471–472, 496

confirmation, 493
  experimenter, 49–50
  in person perception, 470
  sampling, 48, 58
  self-effacing, 474
  self-serving, 472–473
  social desirability, 49, 366
Big Five traits, 340–341
  cross-cultural studies of, 363
  evolutionary perspective on, 361, 369
  heritability of, 360
  measurement of, 365
  twin studies of, 357
Binet-Simon intelligence scale, 250
binge drinking, 158
binge eating/purging, 428
binocular cues, to depth perception, 114–115
biological constraints, on conditioning, 189–190
biological drives, 346
biological motives, 275
biological perspective(s), 9, 11–12
  evaluation of, 361
  Eysenck's, 357, 358
  on personality, 356–357, 358–359, 360
biological rhythms, 139–141
biomedical therapies, 436,
biopsychosocial model, 373, 394
bipolar cells, in retina, 101, 102
bipolar disorder, 414, 449
bird and train problem, 241–242
birth defects, 307
bisexuals, 283, 390
blind spot, 100, 101
blindness, inattentional, 109
blood, glucose levels in, 277
blood-brain barrier, 72
blood flow, in brain, 73–74
blood pressure (hypertension), 384, 385, 389, 398
Bobo doll, 196
body image, disturbed, 428
body language, 292
body temperature, 139, 140, 274
Boggs, Wade, 169
bottom-up processing, 110
bounded rationality, theory of, 243
brain
  in adolescence, 322
  blood flow in, 73–74
  deterioration of, 328
  development of, 92
  drug effects on, 159
  electrical stimulation of, 73
  lesioning of, 73
  lobes of, 78, 79
  number of neurons in, 70
  percentage "in use," 70
  "reward pathway" in, 159
  plasticity of, 78–79
  structure of, 74–79
  study of, 73–75
  ventricles of, 423–424
  visual pathways in, 103–105
  weight of, 72, 328
brain abnormalities, schizophrenia and, 422–423
brain activity, consciousness and, 138–139
brain-based learning, 92
brain damage, 79
brain-imaging procedures, 73–75
brain organization, gender differences in, 332
brain size, intelligence and, 262
brain surgery, 73
brain waves, 138–139
"brainedness," 90, 91
brainstem, 75, 125
breast size, men's preferences for, 369
brightness, of colors, 98, 105–106
Broca's area, 80

brontophobia, 407
bulimia nervosa, 428, 429
business negotiations, classical conditioning in, 201
Byrd, James, Jr., 494
bystander effect, 490, 491

C

C fibers, 126
C-reactive protein, 384
caffeine, 157, 162, 390
Cambridge, Center for Behavioral Studies, 183
cancer, 373
 cell phones and, 399
 diet and, 390
 exercise and, 390
 smoking and, 388
cannabis, 157, 158, 159, 160
Cannon-Bard theory, 294
capsaicin, 124
cardiovascular disease, 384
career success, 287
caregivers, attachment to, 310–312
caregiving styles, 477
case histories, 221
case studies, 45–46, 47, 349
catastrophic thinking, 381, 394, 411
catatonic schizophrenia, 420
catecholamines, 380
catharsis, 382
causation
 correlation and, 42, 43–44, 398
 experimental research and, 40
 multifactorial, 21, 89, 158, 296, 399, 427
cell membrane, of neuron, 65, 66, 67
cell phones, 206, 399
cells
 brain, 79
 genetic material in, 84
 in nervous system, 63–64
 in retina, 100, 101, 102
 See also neurons
cellular immune responses, 386
center-surround arrangement, 102–103, 125
Centers for Disease Control and Prevention, 392
central nervous system, 71, 72
 see also brain; spinal cord
central tendency, measures of, A-8–A-9
centration, 316
cephalocaudal trend, 309
cerebellum, 76, 224
cerebral cortex, 75, 76, 77–78
cerebral hemispheres, 77–78, 79, 80, 332
cerebral laterality, 80–82
cerebral specialization, 90–91
 gender differences in, 332
cerebrospinal fluid (CSF), 72, 423
cerebrum, 75, 76, 77–78
chance, in statistical results, A-14
change, as source of stress, 375–376
channel, in persuasion, 481
Charles, Prince, 305–306
chat rooms, 51
child abuse
 multiple personality and, 413
 repressed memories of, 220–223
childbirth, pain in, 126
childlessness, 326
childrearing, 360
 cultural differences in, 473
children
 aggression in, 193, 196
 cognitive development in, 314–319
 deciding whether to have, 326
 effect of father absence on, 334–335
 environmental deprivation and, 261
 food preferences of, 123, 124, 278

fostering independence in, 363
gender-role socialization of, 333–463
imitation of models by, 351
media violence and, 193, 196
moral development in, 319–320
motor development in, 309–310
parental love for, 353
personality development in, 314, 345–347
physical punishment of, 187–188
China (Chinese), 256, 294
chlorpromazine, 448
choices
 conflict and, 375
 factors in, 243–250
 see also decision making
cholesterol, 384, 389
chromosomes, 84, 306
chronic diseases, 373–374
chunks, in short-term memory, 210
cigarettes, 200, 388
cigars, 388
circadian rhythms, 139–140
circular reasoning, 165, 301
clarification, in client-centered therapy, 441
class attendance, grades and, 25, 26
classical conditioning, 170–176
 acquisition in, 174, 175, 182
 in advertising, 200
 of anxiety, 409, 444–445
 of attitudes, 482
 aversion therapy and, 445
 avoidance learning and, 186
 basic processes in, 174–176
 in business negotiations, 201
 discrimination in, 176, 182
 of emotions, 172, 173
 in everyday life, 172–174
 extinction in, 174–175, 182
 of food preferences, 278
 generalization in, 175–176, 182
 overview of, 194–195
 Pavlov's formulation of, 170
 of physiological responses, 173–174
 in politics, 201
 spontaneous recovery in, 175
 terminology and procedures for, 170–172
classical music, for infants, 92, 93
claustrophobia, 407
client-centered therapy, 440–442, 452–453, 461
clinical psychologists, 46, 438
clinical psychology, 10, 17, 18
clinical social workers, 438
clitoris, 280
closure, as Gestalt principle, 111, 112, 129
Clouser, Ronald, 230
cocaine, 157–158, 159, 160
 neurotransmitters and, 69
 prenatal development and, 308
cochlea, 121
coefficient of determination, A-12, A-13
cognition, 11, 235
cognitive abilities, 11
 aging and, 328–329
 gender differences in, 29, 330–331
 marijuana use and, 160
cognitive appraisal, of stressful events, 377
cognitive-behavioral therapy, 446–447, 452–453
cognitive development, 314–319
 attachment style and, 312
 moral development and, 319
 Piaget's stage theory of, 314–317
 sociocultural theory of, 317–318
cognitive dissonance, 483–484
cognitive maps, 191
cognitive perspective, 9, 11
 on conditioning, 190–192
 on emotions, 289
 on intelligence, 262–263

cognitive psychology, 17, 18
cognitive revolution, 235
cognitive schemas, 495
cognitive style, 90, 91
 depression and, 417
 culture and, 242–243
cognitive tasks, hemispheres and, 90
cognitive therapy, 446–447, 452–453, 461
collective unconscious, 347
collectivism, 363, 473–474, 491
 conformity and, 488
 marriage and, 478
college admissions tests, 43
college students
 alcohol and, 158
 gambling among, 1–2
colleges, psychology laboratories at, 3–4
color blindness, 107
color mixing, 106
color solid, 105–106
color vision, 100, 105–108
 opponent process theory of, 107–108
 trichromatic theory of, 106–107
Columbia space shuttle, 368
commitment, 323, 477
common sense, versus scientific approach, 37
communication
 on dates, 475
 in groups, 490
 with health providers, 392
 nonverbal, 292
 persuasive, 481–482
communities, positive, 16
community mental health centers, 455, 460
community mental health movement, 456
co-morbidity, 430
companionate love, 476–477
comparative evaluations, 244
comparison to others, happiness and, 299
comparitors, 132–133
compensation, 348
competence, attractiveness and, 468
competition
 between groups, 496
 individualism and, 474
complementary colors, 107
compliance
 with authority, 486–488
 with group, 485–486
 with medical advice, 392–393
composers, mental illness and, 267
compulsions, 408
concepts, semantic networks of, 213–214
conclusions, 300
concordance rates
 for anxiety disorders, 409
 for mood disorders, 416
 for schizophrenia, 421, 425
concrete operational period, 315, 316
conditionability, 357
conditioned reinforcers, 182, 311
conditioned response (CR), 171, 172, 173, 174, 176, 409, 444, 445
conditioned stimulus (CS), 171, 172, 173, 174, 176, 186, 409, 444, 445
 ecologically relevant, 190
 predictive value of, 192
conditioning, 169
 biological constraints on, 189–190
 cognitive processes in, 190–192
 contingencies and, 192
 evaluative, 200, 482, 483
 personality and, 350–351
 rapid, 190
 see also classical conditioning; operant conditioning
cones, 100–101, 108
confirmation bias, 493

physical, 309–310, 321–322, 327–329
  prenatal, 306–309
  sexual, 321
developmental norms, 310
developmental psychology, 17, 18
deviance, as criterion for abnormality, 403, 404
deviation IQ scores, 252–253
diabetes, 386, 399
diagnosis, 404
Diagnostic and Statistical Manual of Mental Disorders (DSM), 405–406
diazepam, 447
dichromats, 107
diet, quality of, 389–390
dieting, 279
diffusion of responsibility, 490, 491
digestive system, hunger and, 277
disagreement
  as punishment, 483
  perceptions in, 34–35, 36
discipline, parental, 187
disclosure, emotional, 396
disconfirming evidence, 231
discrimination
  in classical conditioning, 176, 182
  in operant conditioning, 181–182
discrimination (social)
  against homosexuals, 286
  prejudice and, 494, 495
discriminative stimuli, 181
disease(s)
  biopsychosocial model of, 373
  prenatal development and, 309
  psychosomatic, 383
  see also illness
disinhibition, with hypnosis, 153
disorganized schizophrenia, 420
displacement, 344, 345
display rules, 294
dissociation, in hypnosis, 154–155
dissociative amnesia, 412–413
dissociative disorders, 412–413
dissociative fugue, 412
dissociative identity disorder (DID), 412–413, 418
dissonance theory, 483–484
distributed practice, 228, 229
distribution
  normal, 251–252, 253, A-10–A-11
  skewed, A-9
divergent thinking, 266
diversity, cultural, 22
division of labor, 331
divorce, 298, 334, 335, 396
Dix, Dorothea, 455, 456
dizygotic twins, 85
DNA, 84
dolphins, 142
door-in-the-face technique, 132
dopamine, 68, 69, 76, 77, 159, 448
dopamine hypothesis, of schizophrenia, 422
double-blind procedure, 50
doubt, 314
Doyle, Arthur Conan, 235
dream analysis, 348, 439
dreams/dreaming, 149–152, 163, 364
  common themes in, 150, 151
  content of, 149–150, 163
  culture and, 151
  interpretation of, 163
  links with waking life, 150–151
  recall for, 163, 151
  REM and, 137, 142–143
  shocking, 163
  symbolism in, 163
  theories of, 151–152
drinking
  on college campuses, 158
  stress and, 382

see also alcohol
drive reduction, 274
drives, 274, 355
  biological, 76
  Freud's view of, 344
driving
  alcohol and, 76
  cell phone use and, 206
drowsiness, 147
drug companies, 450
drug dependence, 159, 160
drug therapies
  deinstitutionalization and, 456–457
  effectiveness of, 450
  for psychological disorders, 447–450, 452–453
drug use and abuse, 156–161
  during pregnancy, 308
  stress and, 382
drunk driving, test for, 76
DSM-IV, 405–406
dual-coding theory, 208
dual-process theories, of decision making, 250

E

ear, sensory processing in, 120–111
eardrum, 120, 121
early maturation, 322
eating behavior
  biological factors in, 276–277
  with eating disorders, 428
  environmental cues to, 277–278
  neurotransmitters and, 69
  observational learning and, 278
  in rats, 88
  regulation of, 76
  stress and, 279, 382
eating disorders, 406, 427–429
eating habits
  poor, 389–390
  sleep and, 162
ecologically relevant conditioned stimuli, 190–240
ecstasy, 158, 161
education, mental health services utilization and, 437
educational/school psychology, 17, 18
efferent nerve fibers, 71
efficiency, in groups, 490–491
effort justification, 484
egg cell, 306
ego, 342, 343
egocentrism, 316, 317
Eichman, Adolf, 486
ejaculation, 321
elaboration, in encoding, 207
elaboration likelihood model, 484–485
Elavil, 449
election campaign ads, 201
electrical stimulation of the brain (ESB), 11, 73, 77
electrocardiograph (EKG), 141
electroconvulsive therapy (ECT), 450–451
electrodes, 73, 138, 450
electroencephalograph (EEG), 138–139
electromyograph (EMG), 141
electrooculograph (EOG), 141
elicited responses, 171
elimination by aspects, 244
embryonic stage, 306–307, 308
emetic drugs, 445
emotion(s), 288–293
  attitudes and, 480, 494
  autonomic nervous system and, 71–72
  behavioral component of, 292–293
  Cannon-Bard theory of, 294
  categorization of, 293
  cognitive component of, 288–289

conditioned, 172, 173, 200, 482, 483
control of, 289
culture and, 292–293
decision making and, 244
defined, 288
Ellis's model of, 394–395395
evolutionary perspective on, 295
expressed, 426
facial expressions for, 292, 293
fundamental, 292, 295
heart disease and, 384–385
hemispheric specialization and, 82
James-Lange theory of, 293–294
limbic system and, 77
manipulation of, 200, 201
motivation and, 287–288
negative, 279, 289, 378, 414
physiological component of, 289–292
positive, 16, 289, 378, 395
release of, 382, 395–396
in schizophrenia, 419
stress and, 377–378
suppression of, 395–396
theories of, 293–295
two-factor theory of, 294–295
words for, 293
emotional arousal, 378–379, 395, 396
emotional development., 310–312
empathy, of therapist, 441
empiricism, 20, 53, 89
  in social psychology, 493–494
  statistics and, A-7, A-14
empty nest, 327
encoding, 205, 206–208
  enriching, 207–208, 229
  ineffective, 218
encoding specificity principle, 219–220
endocrine system, 76, 83
  stress and, 380
  see also hormones
endorphins, 69, 70, 160
English tit-mouse, 193
environment
  heredity and, 8, 22, 86, 89, 197, 329, 331
  intelligence and, 258–259, 265
environments, enriched, 92, 93, 259
epilepsy, surgery for, 82
episodic memory system, 225–226, 329
equilibrium, 76, 274
escape learning, 185–186
Escher, M. C., 130, 131
Eskimos, 294
essay tests, 217
ethics
  APA standards for, 52, 53
  in research, 51–52, 488
  personal, 320
ethnic groups
  IQ scores and, 260–262
  mental health services utilization by, 437
  in U.S. population, 13
ethnic stereotypes, 469, 495
etiology, 404
euphoria
  in bipolar disorders, 415
  from drugs, 157, 158
evaluative conditioning, 200, 482, 483
evidence
  anecdotal, 58–58
  disconfirming, 231
  lack of, 268
evolutionary biology, 13
evolutionary perspective, 9, 12–13, 87–89
  on cognitive abilities, 319
  on color vision, 105, 109
  on conditioned taste aversion, 190
  on consciousness, 138, 139
  criticism of, 13, 283, 332

motivation (cotinued)
  observational learning and, 193
  of hunger and eating, 276–279
  sexual, 279–286
motives, 274, 275
motor cortex, 78, 79
motor development, 309–310
motor neurons, 68
Mount Everest, 273
movement
  coordination of, 76
  illusion of, 110–111
  motor cortex and, 78
Mozart effect, 93
MRI (magnetic resonance imaging), 73, 74, 262
Müller-Lyer illusion, 117, 188–119
multiaxial system, 405–406
multicultural sensitivity, in psychotherapy, 455
multifactorial causation, 21, 89, 158, 296, 394, 427
multimodal therapy, 461
multiple personality disorder, 412–413
multiple sclerosis, 64
multiple-choice tests, 26–27, 217
muscles
  nerves and, 71
  neurotransmitters and, 68
myelin sheath, 64

N

naive realism, 34
names, remembering, 206
napping, 145–146, 162
narcolepsy, 148
narcotics, 156–157, 159, 308
narrative methods, 229
NASA, 368
Nash, John, 421
National Alliance for the Mentally Ill, 405
National Institute of Mental Health, 409
National Institute on Drug Abuse, 160
National Sleep Foundation, 147
National Television Violence Study, 196
Native Americans, IQ scores of, 260
nativists, 318
natural selection, 5, 12–13, 87, 88, 331
  face recognition and, 105
  of cognitive abilities, 319
  of personality traits, 361
  person perception and, 470
naturalistic observation, 44–45, 47
nature versus nurture, 8, 22
  in gender differences, 331
  in intelligence, 256–262
  in learning, 197
  see also environment; heredity
Nazi Germany, 201, 486
nearsightedness, 99–100
Necker cube, 113, 130
need for achievement, 286–288
need for self-actualization, 355
need for affiliation, 287
needs
  basic, 355
  biological, 275
  gratification of, 345
  Maslow's hierarchy of, 354–355
negative correlation, 42, 43, A-11
negative feedback systems, 83
negative reinforcement, 185–186, 187, 198
negative self-talk, 381, 394
negative symptoms, of schizophrenia, 420
negative thinking, 447
  depressive disorder and, 417
negatively skewed distribution, A-9
negligence lawsuits, 369
NEO Personality Inventory, 365

nerve endings, 125
nerves, 71
nervous system
  autonomic, 71–72, 76, 83, 289–290, 380
  organization of, 70–72
  peripheral, 71–72
neural circuits, for memory, 224
neural impulse, 65–66
neural networks, 67–68
neurodevelopmental hypothesis, 423
neurogenesis, 417
neurons, 63–64, 65, 66
  aging and, 328
  as feature detectors, 104, 105
  motor, 68
  myelination of, 322
  new, , 79 416
  number of in brain, 70
  resting potential of, 65
  structure of, 64
  in visual cortex, 104
neuropeptide Y, 276, 380
Neuropsychology Central, 64
neuroses, 439
neuroticism, 340, 360, 361, 387, 391, 411
neurotransmitters, 66, 67, 68–70
  anxiety disorders and, 409
  drug action and, 159–160
  hormones and, 83
  in hunger, 276
  memory and, 224
  monamine, 68–69
  mood disorders and, 416
  in schizophrenia, 422
newborns, sleep cycle of, 143, 144
nicotine, 68, 157, 388
night vision, 101
nightmares, 408
nine-dot problem, 239, 241
nominal fallacy, 165
non sequitur, 301
nondeclarative memory system, 225
non-REM (NREM) sleep, 143, 144–145
nonsense syllables, 216
nonverbal behavior, 292
  gender differences in, 331
norepinephrine (NE), 68, 69, 159, 416, 449
normal distribution, 251–252, 253, A-10–A-11
normality, versus abnormality, 404–405
nose, smell and, 124–125
note taking, during lectures, 26
nucleus accumbens, 159
null hypothesis, A-14
Nun Study, 328
Nurture Assumption, The (Harris), 369
nutrition
  poor, 389-390
  prenatal development and, 308

O

obedience, 468, 486–488
obesity, 390
  fear of, 428
object permanence, 315, 317
object recognition, background consistency and, 114
observation
  direct, 36
  naturalistic, 44–45, 47
  precise, A-7
  via Internet, 51–52
observational learning, 192–193, 196
  of attitudes, 483
  eating behavior and, 278
  of gender roles, 333
  overview of, 194–195
  personality and, 351

of prejudice, 496
observers, biases of, 472
obsessions, 408
obsessive-compulsive disorder, 408
  etiology of, 409
  prevalence of, 408
  therapy for, 461
occipital lobe, 78, 79, 103, 104
occupational attainment, IQ scores and, 254–255
occupational stereotypes, 469–470
octopus, 63
odds, gambling, 247
odors, types of, 125
Oedipal complex, 346
Office of Research Integrity (ORI), 51
offspring, parental investment in, 281
olfactory bulb, 125
olfactory cilia, 124, 125
olfactory system, 124–125
omega 3 fatty acids, 389
openness to experience, 340, 360, 361
operant chamber, 178
operant conditioning, 177–188
  acquisition in, 179, 182
  of anxiety responses, 409
  of attitudes, 482–483
  basic processes in, 179–182
  discrimination in, 181–182
  extinction in, 180–181, 182
  of gender roles, 333
  generalization in, 181–182
  observational learning and, 193
  overview of, 194–195
  personality and, 350
  of prejudice, 496
  shaping in, 180
  Skinner's conception of, 177–179
  terminology and procedures for, 178–179
operational definitions, 35
operations, mental, 316
opiates, 77, 156–157, 159
opinions, 498
opponent process theory, of color vision, 107–108
optic chiasm, 103, 104
optic disk, 99, 100
optic nerve, 99, 101, 102
optical illusions, 117–119, 130
optimal level of arousal, 379
optimism, 9, 298, 352, 354
  stress reduction and, 387–388
optimistic explanatory style, 388
options, choosing among, 318–244
oral stage, 346
orders, obeying, 486–488
orgasm, 280
ossicles, of ear, 121
osteoporosis, 428
outgroup derogation, 497
outgroups, 470
outlining, 228
oval window, 121
ovaries, 321
overcompensation, 348
overconfidence, 231
overdose, drug, 159, 160
overeating, 278, 428
overextrapolations, 93
overlearning, 227

P

pace of life, culture and, 42–43
Pagano, Bernard, 230
pain
  chronic, 126, 127
  endorphins and, 70
  perception of, 125–126
paintings, perceptual principles and, 128–131

palatability, of food, 278
pancultural view, of psychological disorders, 426
panic disorder, 407
  etiology of, 409
  therapy for, 461
papillae, 123
Pappenheim, Bertha, 436
parallel distributed processing (PDP), 214
paralysis
  in conversion disorder, 411
  from spinal cord damage, 72
paranoid schizophrenia, 419–420
parasympathetic division, of autonomic
    nervous system, 72, 290
paraventricular nucleus (PVN), 276, 277
parent-child attachment, 310–312
parental investment, 280, 282
parenthood, 326–327
  happiness and, 297
parents
  caregiving styles of, 477
  children's personality and, 360, 369
  conflict with adolescents, 327
  disciplinary procedures of, 187–188
  as source of prejudicial attitudes, 496
  unconditional love from, 353
  see also children; family
parietal lobe, 78, 79, 125
Parkinsonism, 68, 76, 328
paroxetine, 449
participants, in research, 35, 39, 51
passion, 477
passionate love, 476–477, 478
patriotism, 362
patterns, perception of, 108–114
Pauley, Jane, 414
Pavlovian conditioning, 170
Paxil, 449
peacocks, 89
Pearson product-moment correlation, A-12
peer review process, 37
penis, 280, 321
penis envy, 346, 349
pennies, 205
People for the Ethical Treatment of Animals
    (PETA), 52
percentile scores, 325, A-10
perception
  auditory, 121–122
  defined, 97
  of depth, 114–117
  of forms and patterns, 108–114
  Gestalt principles of, 110–112, 129
  of pain, 1125–127
  person, 467, 468–470
  study of, 4
  subjectivity of, 22–23, 109, 127, 470, 494, 495
  of taste, 124
perceptual asymmetries, 82, 91
perceptual constancies, 117
perceptual hypotheses, 112–114, 118, 119
perceptual motor tasks, 225
perceptual set, 109
perfectionism, 429
performance
  academic, 23
  individual vs. group, 491
  sleep deprivation and, 147
performance pressure, 377
Pergament, Moshe, 1
peripheral nervous system, 71–72
peripheral vision, 101
persecution, delusions of, 419
person-centered theory, of personality,
    353–354, 358
person-centered therapy, 440
person perception, 467, 468–470
  evolutionary perspective on, 470

expectations and, 23
  prejudice and, 494–496
  subjectivity in, 470
person-situation controversy, 351–352
personal distress, as criterion for abnormality,
    404–405
personal growth, 10
personal unconscious, 347
personality
  Adler's theory of, 348
  attractiveness and, 468
  behavioral perspectives on, 349–352, 358
  biological perspectives on, 356–357, 358–359,
    360
  compliance with medical advice and, 393
  consistency of, 340
  culture and, 363–364
  distinctiveness of, 340
  evolutionary perspective on, 369
  five-factor model of, 340–341
  Freud's psychoanalytic theory of, 341–347,
    358
  genetic basis for, 357, 360
  happiness and, 298
  healthy, 355
  heart disease and, 383–384
  heredity and, 86
  hindsight and, 368–369
  humanistic perspectives on, 352–356, 358
  Jung's theory of, 347–348
  Maslow's view of, 354–355
  nature of, 340–341
  observational learning and, 351
  psychodynamic perspectives on, 341–349, 358
  Rogers's person-centered theory of, 353–354,
    358
  somatoform disorders and, 411
  stability of, 324–325
personality development, 310–312, 312–314,
    324–325
  Freud's stages of, 345–347
  Rogers's view of, 353, 358
  Skinner's view of, 350, 348
personality disorders, 406
Personality Project, 355
personality psychology, 17, 18
personality structure, 341
  Eysenck's view of, 357, 358
  Freud's view of, 342
  Rogers's view of, 353
  Skinner's view of, 350, 358
personality tests, 286, 287, 325, 340, 365–367
  basic, 340–341, 357
  creativity and, 267
  culture and, 363
  eating disorders and, 429
  evolution and, 361
  heritability of, 360
  testing of, 365, 504
persuasion, 481–482
  central route to, 484–485
  classical conditioning and, 200–201
  peripheral route to, 484–485
  resistance to, 482
  techniques of, 132, 498–499
pessimistic explanatory style, 387–388, 417,
    418
PET (positron emission tomography) scans,
    73–7–74
pets, stress and, 387
phallic stage, 346
pharmaceutical industry, 450
phi phenomenon, 110–111
phobias, 170, 218, 407
  conditioning of, 186, 409
  therapy for, 461
  treatment for, 444–445
phobic disorder, 407

phonemic encoding, 207, 218
phonological loop, 211
physical appearance, person perception and,
    468–469
physical attractiveness. *See* attractiveness
physical dependence, on drugs, 148, 159, 160
physical fitness, 390, 397
physiological arousal, 71–72, 289
physiological psychology, 17, 18
physiological recording, as data collection
    method, 36
physiology, psychology and, 3
Picasso, Pablo, 129
pictorial depth cues, 115
pineal gland, 139
pinna, 120, 121
pitch, 119, 120
  perception of, 121–122
pituitary gland, 75, 77, 83, 380
place theory, of hearing, 121–122
placebo, 48
placebo effects, 48–49, 126
  in therapy, 462, 463
  meditation and, 156
placenta, 306, 309
plateau phase, of sexual response cycle, 280
play, aggressive, 196
pleasure centers, in brain, 77, 159
pleasure principle, 342, 343
Poggendorff illusion, 117
point prevalence rates, 430
pointillism, 129
poker, online, 1
political agenda, 335
political debates, 34, 37
political views, 362
politics, classical conditioning and, 201
polygenic traits, 84
polygraph, 290–291
pons, 76, 163
Ponzo illusion, 117
population, representative samples from, 48,
    A-13, A-14
positive correlation, 42, 43, A-11
positive illusions, 383
positive psychology movement, 13, 16, 289,
    355, 388
positive symptoms, of schizophrenia, 420
positively skewed distribution, A-9
postconventional level, 319, 320
posthypnotic suggestion, 153–154
postpartum depression, 326
postsynaptic neuron, 66, 67, 159
postsynaptic potential (PSP), 67
posttraumatic stress disorder (PTSD), 408, 220
potassium ions, 65
poverty, 335
  happiness and, 297
  use of mental health services and, 455
practical intelligence, 254, 255, 263
Pragnanz, 111
preconscious, 342
preconventional level, 319
predators, avoiding, 88, 89
prediction, as goal of scientific approach, 33
preferences, making choices about, 243–245
prefrontal cortex, 78, 159, 291, 322
pregnancy, 306–309, 423
prejudice, 494–497
  cultural worldviews and, 362
  defined, 494
  learning of, 496
premises, 300
prenatal development, 306–309
  environmental factors in, 308
  hormones in, 83, 285, 332
  maternal drug use and, 308
  maternal illness and, 308, 423

Type A personality, 384
Type B personality, 384

U

ultraviolet spectrum, 98
uncertainty
  decision making and, 245
  reducing, 399
unconditional positive regard, 441
unconditioned response (UCR), 171, 172, 173, 174, 176, 409, 444, 445
unconditioned stimulus (UCS), 171, 172, 173, 174, 176, 189–190, 409, 444, 445
unconscious
  Freud's view of, 6, 220, 342, 439
  Jung's view of, 347
understanding, as goal of scientific approach, 33
undifferentiated schizophrenia, 420
unemployment, 298
unipolar disorder. *See* depressive disorder
universalistic view, of psychological disorders, 426
universities, psychology laboratories at, 3–4
University of Leipzig, 3
University of Minnesota Center for Twin and Adoption Research, 356, 357
upside-down T, 117

V

vacillation, 375
vagus nerve, 277
validity, of IQ tests, 254
Valium, 409, 447, 448
valproate, 450
value, expected, 245
variability, of data, A-9–A-10
variable-interval schedules of reinforcement, 183, 184
variable-ratio schedules of reinforcement, 183, 184
variables, 33–34
  confounding of, 39
  correlations between, 42–44, A-11
  in experiments, 38
  extraneous, 39
Vasarely, Victor, 130, 131
vasocongestion, 279–280

vengefulness, 396
ventricles, of brain, 423–424
ventromedial nucleus of the hypothalamus (VMH), 276, 277
verbal aggression, 331
verbal intelligence, 254, 255
verbal material, brain hemispheres and, 90
verbal mnemonics, 228–229
verbal skills, gender differences in, 331
verifiability, of scientific claims, 7
Veterans Administration (VA), 10–11
viability, age of, 307
Victorian era, 364
video games, 196
Vienna Psychoanalytic Society, 348
violence, in media, 193, 196
violent crimes, 158, 331
Violin and Grapes (Picasso), 129
Visible Human Project, 76
Vision Science, 99
vision, 98–119
  aging and, 327
  color, 100, 105–108
  night, 101
  perceptual constancies in, 117
  peripheral, 101
  stimulus for, 98
visual ability, individual differences in, 103
visual acuity, 100
visual agnosia, 97
visual cortex, 78, 79, 103–105
visual fields, in brain, 80, 81, 103
visual illusions, 117–119, 130
visual imagery, memory and, 208, 229
visual processing, in brain, 78
visual-spatial ability, 29, 331
visuospatial sketchpad, 211
vocational success, IQ scores and, 254–255
voltage, in neuron, 65, 67
vomiting, 428
vulnerability, to schizophrenia, 86

W

waist-to-hip ratio, 479
walking speed, 42
water jar problem, 237, 238, 241
Waterfall (Escher), 130, 131

wavelength
  of light waves, 98, 105, 108
  of sound waves, 119, 120
wealth, happiness and, 297
Web of Addictions, 157
Wechsler Adult Intelligence Scale (WAIS), 251, 252
weight, preoccupation with, 428
well-being, subjective, 296–299
Wellesley College, 5
Wernicke's area, 80
what and where pathways, 105
Whole Brain Atlas, 78
windigo, 427
wine tasting, 122, 123, 124
Winfrey, Oprah, 255
wish fulfillment, dreams as, 151, 152
wishful thinking, 383
witches, 404
withdrawal illness, 160
women, in history of psychology, 5
work shifts, rotating, 140
work
  happiness and, 298
  nighttime, 146
workaholics, 384
working memory, 78, 211-212, 329
World War II, 10–11, 21
worldviews, cultural, 361–363
worrying, 407
writers, mental illness and, 267

X

X rays, of brain, 73
Xanax, 447, 448

Y

Yoruba (Nigeria), 293
youthfulness, mate preferences and, 282

Z

Zollner illusion, 117
Zoloft, 449
zolpidem, 148
Zulu, 119
zygote, 306

> Credits

Photo Credits

This page constitutes an extension of the copyright page. We have made every effort to trace the ownership of all copyrighted material and to secure permission from copyright holders. In the event of any question arising as to the use of any material, we will be pleased to make the necessary corrections in future printings. Thanks are due to the following authors, publishers, and agents for permission to use the material indicated.

Cover: © Flip Chalfant/Getty Images

Contents: xxix: © Caroline Schiff/zefa/Corbis; xxx: © Josh Westrich/zefa/Corbis xxxi: © Royalty-Free/Corbis; xxxii: © Michael Freeman/Digital Vision/Getty Images; xxxiii: © Nevada Wier/Corbis; xxxiv: © David H. Wells/Corbis; xxxv: © C. Lyttle/zefa/Corbis; xxxvi: © Andersen Ross/Blend Images/Alamy; xxxvii: © ER Productions/Corbis; xxxviii: © Reza/Webistan/Corbis; xxxix: © Bryan F. Peterson/Corbis; xl: © Alan Schein Photography/Corbis; xli: © Klaus Hackenberg/zefa/Corbis; xlii: © Dennis Cooper/zefa/Corbis; xliii: © Dennis Stock/Magnum Photos

Chapter Opener 1. xlviii: © Caroline Schiff/zefa/Corbis

Chapter Opener 2. 32: © Josh Westrich/zefa/Corbis

Chapter Opener 3. 62: © Royalty-Free/Corbis

Chapter Opener 4. 96: © Michael Freeman/Digital Vision/Getty Images

Chapter Opener 5. 136: © Nevada Wier/Corbis

Chapter Opener 6. 168: © David H. Wells/Corbis

Chapter Opener 7. 204: © C. Lyttle/zefa/Corbis

Chapter Opener 8. 234: © Andersen Ross/Blend Images/Alamy

Chapter Opener 9. 272: © ER Productions/Corbis

Chapter Opener 10. 304: © Reza/Webistan/Corbis

Chapter Opener 11. 338: © Bryan F. Peterson/Corbis

Chapter Opener 12. 372: © Alan Schein Photography/Corbis

Chapter Opener 13. 402: © Klaus Hackenberg/zefa/Corbis

Chapter Opener 14. 434: © Dennis Cooper/zefa/Corbis

Chapter Opener 15. 466: © Dennis Stock/Magnum Photos

Chapter 1 1: right, © Associated Press/AP 1: left, © Michael Newman/PhotoEdit 5: center, Archives of the History of American Psychology, University of Akron 5: right, Archives of the History of American Psychology, University of Akron 5: left, Photo courtesy of Archives of the History of American Psychology, University of Akron, Akron, Ohio 9: left, Copyright © 1971 Time Inc. Reprinted by permission. Getty Images. 13: © Michael & Patricia Fogden/Corbis 14: (Pavlov lab) Bettmann/Corbis 14: (Freud and others) Compliments of Clark University, Worcester, Massachusetts 14: (Hollingworth) Archives of the History of American Psychology, University of Akron 14: (Washburn) Archives of the History of American Psychology, University of Akron 14: (Wundt & others) Archives of the History of American Psychology, University of Akron 14: (airplane) Stock Montage, Inc. 14: (intelligence test) Bettmann/Corbis 14: (telephone) Culver Pictures, Inc. 15: (Atomic bomb) Culver Pictures, Inc. 15: (Erikson) AP/Wide World Photos 15: bottom, (Kahneman) Courtesy of Daniel Kahneman 15: (Kenneth Clark) © Bettmann Corbis 15: (Loftus) Courtesy of Elizabeth Loftus 15: (Maccoby) Chuck Pointer/Stanford News Service 15: (Seligman) Courtesy of Martin E. P. Seligman 15: (Shuttle liftoff) NASA 15: (Vietnam) © Associated Press/AP 22: © Steve Raymer/Corbis 25: © Martin Heiter/Stock Connection Distribution/Alamy 27: inset, © Rob Gage/Taxi/Getty Images

Chapter 2 37: © Lara Jo Regan/Liaison/Getty Images 45: © Carl & Ann Purcell/Corbis 50: Courtesy of Robert Rosenthal 52: Courtesy of Neal Miller 59: © Mark Bolster

Chapter 3 68: Courtesy of Solomon Snyder 69: © Associated Press/AP 70: Courtesy of Candace Pert 73: left, (Figure 3.8a photo) © Alvis Upitis/ Image Bank /Getty Images 73: right, (Figure 3.8c photo) © Dan McCoy/Rainbow 74: top right, (Figure 3.10 photo) © Wellcome Dept of Cognitive Neurology /Science Photo Library/Photo Researchers, Inc. 74: top left, (Figure 3.9 photo) © ISM- Sovereign/PhotoTake 75: top left, (Figure 3.12 photo) Wadsworth Collection 80: Photo by Bob Paz/Caltech, Courtesy of Roger Sperry 85: © Barbara Penoyar/Photodisc Green/Getty Images 86: bottom left, Photo courtesy of Tara McKearney 87: © Bettmann/Corbis 89: Courtesy of John Alcock 91: © Peter Beck/Corbis

Chapter 4 97: © Steve Cole/Photodisc Green/Getty Images 100: center, (Figure 4.3 photos) Craig McClain 104: Courtesy of David Hubel 106: right, (Figure 4.10 photo) Courtesy of BASF 111: top right, Archives of the History of American Psychology, The University of Akron 111: bottom right, © Tony Freeman/PhotoEdit 115: bottom right, (Figure 4.26 photo) U.S. Department of Energy 115: bottom center, (Figure 4.26 photo) © Chris George/Alamy 115: top center, (Figure 4.26 photo) © Jean-Marc Truchet/Getty Images 115: top right, (Figure 4.26 photo) © Ron Fehling/Masterfile 115: top left, (Figure 4.26 photo) © Royalty Free/Corbis 115: bottom left, (Figure 4.26photo) © Jose Fuste Raga/zefa/Corbis 116: Vincent van Gogh (Dutch, 1853-1890), A Corridor in the Asylum, late May or early June 1889. Black chalk and gouache on pink Ingres paper; 25-5/8 x 19-5/16 in. (65.1 x 49.1 cm): "The Metropolitan Museum of Art, Bequest of Abby Aldrich

Rockefeller, 1948 (48.190.2) Photograph © 1998 The Metropolitan Museum of Art." 119: © Alan Evrard/Robert Harding/Getty Images 120: inset, (Figure 4.34 photo) © Betts Anderson Loman/PhotoEdit 123: © Michael Mahovlich/Masterfile 124: Courtesy of Linda Bartoshuk 128: bottom, Brera Predica di S. Marco Pinaocteca, by Gentile and Giovanni Belini in Egitto. Scala/Art Resource, New York 128: top, Maestro della cattura di Cristo, Cattura di Cristo, parte centrale, Assisi, S. Francisco. Scala/Art Resource, New York 129: top, Georges Seurat, French, 1859-1891, *A Sunday Afternoon on La Grande Jatte* - 1884, 1884–86, oil on canvas, 81¾ × 121¼ in. (207.5 × 308.1 cm) (and detail), Helen Birch Bartlett Memorial Collection, 1926.224 combination of quadrant captures F1, F2, G1, G2. The Art Institute of Chicago. Photography © The Art Institute of Chicago. 129: Pablo Picasso, *Violin and Grapes, Céret and Sorgues* (spring-early fall 1912), oil on canvas, 20 × 24 inches (50.6 × 61 cm), collection, The Museum of Modern Art, New York, Mrs. David M. Levy Bequest. Digital image © The Museum of Modern Art/Licensed by SCALA/Art Resource, NY. © 2007 Estate of Pablo Picasso/Artists Rights Society (ARS), New York. 130: Salvador Dali, *The Slave Market with the Disappearing Bust of Voltaire*, (1940), Oil on canvas, 18¼ × 25⅜ inches. Collection of The Salvador Dali Museum, St. Petersburg, FL. Copyright © 2006 The Salvador Dali Museum, Inc. © 2007 Salvador Dali, Gala-Salvador Dali Foundation/Artists Rights Society (ARS), New York. 131: Vasarely, Victor (1908–1997) *Tukoer-Ter-Ur*, 1989. Acrylic on canvas, 220 × 220 cm. Private Collection, Monaco. © Erich Lessing/Art Resource, NY. Copyright © 2007 Artists Rights Society (ARS), New York/ADAGP, Paris. 131: top left, (Figure 4.46 photo) M. C. Escher's Waterval 1961. © 2006 The M. C. Escher Company-Holland. All rights reserved. www.mcescher.com 131: top right, (Figure 4.47 photo) M. C. Escher's Waterval 1958. © 2006 The M. C. Escher Company-Holland. All rights reserved. www.mcescher.com 131: bottom right, (Figure 4.48 photo) Vasarely, Victor (1908-1997) Tukoer-Ter-Ur, 1989. Acrylic on canvas, 220 x 220 cm. Private Collection, Monaco. © Erich Lessing / Art Resource, NY. Copyright © 2006 Artists Rights Society (ARS), New York/ADAGP, Paris. 131: (Figure 4.49) Magritte, Rene, *Les Promenades d'Euclide,* The Minneapolis Institute of Arts, The William Hood Dunwoody Fund. Copyright © 2007 Charly Herscovic, Brussels/Artists Rights Society (ARS) New York.

Chapter 5 141: © Richard T. Nowitz /PhotoTake, Inc./Alamy Images 142: © Steve Bloom Images/Alamy 146: © Associated Press/AP 147: Courtesy of William Dement 150: center right, (Figure 5.7 photo) © Chris Gregory/Alamy 150: top right, (Figure 5.7 photo) © Image Source/Alamy 150: top left, (Figure 5.7 photo) © mediacolor's/Alamy 151: bottom, Courtesy of Harvard Medical School Division of Sleep Medicine 151: center, Courtesy of Rosalind Cartwright 151: top, National Library of Medicine 154: bottom left, Chuck Painter/Stanford News Service 154: top left, Courtesy of X. Ted Barber 154: bottom center, © Associated Press/AP 155: inset, (Figure 5.10 photo) © RF/Corbis

Chapter 6 170: right, © Bettmann/Corbis 170: left, © Bettmann/Corbis 173: inset, (Figure 6.4 photo) © Craig McClain 175: Archives of the History of American Psychology, University of Akron 176:

inset, (Figure 6.8 photo) Archives of the History of American Psychology, The University of Akron **178:** Courtesy of B. F. Skinner **179:** inset, (figure 6.10 photo) © Richard Wood/Index Stock Imagery **180:** left, Courtesy of Animal Behavior Enterprises, Inc. **180:** right, © Gerald Davis by permission of Karen Davis **184:** top left, (Figure 6.12 photo) © Andy Sacks/Photographer's Choice/Getty Images **184:** top right, (Figure 6.12 photo) © David Falconer/Folio, Inc. **184:** bottom left, (Figure 6.12 photo) © David Woods /Stock Market/Corbis **184:** bottom right, (Figure 6.12 photo) © Rick Doyle **190:** Courtesy of John Garcia **191:** Archives of the History of American Psychology, The University of Akron **192:** Courtesy of Robert Rescorla **193:** center right, Photo by Keeble, courtesy of Albert Bandura **193:** top right, © J. Markham/Bruce Coleman, Inc. **193:** top left, © Frank Siteman/Index Stock Imagery, Inc. **195:** (Pavlov dog) Bettmann/Corbis **195:** (Little Albert) Archives of the History of American Psychology, University of Akron **195:** (Pig) Courtesy of Animal Behavior Enterprises, Inc. **195:** (bird) © J. Markham/Bruce Coleman, Inc. **195:** (gambling) © David Falconer/Folio, Inc. **195:** © Frank Siteman/Index Stock Imagery, Inc. **197:** © Bob Daemmrich/ The Image Works **200:** inset, (Figure 6.24 photo) © Bill Aron/Photo Edit

Chapter 7 **209:** © Wayne Weiten **210:** © 2001 Pryde Brown Photographs, Princeton, N.J. Courtesy of George A. Miller **211:** Courtesy of Alan Baddeley **212:** right, © Associated Press/AP **213:** Courtesy of W. F. Brewer. Brewer, W. F., and Treyens, J. C., "Role of schemata in memory of places," Cognitive Psychology, 1981, 13, 207-230. **215:** Courtesy of Elizabeth Loftus **216:** Courtesy of Marcia K. Johnson **217:** © Bettmann/Corbis **221:** © Associated Press/AP **223:** The Montreal Neurological Insitute, McGill University **224:** Courtesy of Eric Kandel **226:** Courtesy of Endel Tulving **230:** left, © UPI/Bettmann/Corbis **230:** right, © UPI/Bettmann/Corbis **231:** © Bill Fritsch/ Brand X Pictures/Alamy

Chapter 8 **235:** Carnegie-Melon University, courtesy University Relations **240:** inset, Craig McClain **242:** Craig McClain **244:** © Boris Roessler/DPA/epa/ Corbis **245:** Courtesy of Barbara Tversky **245:** bottom, Courtesy of Daniel Kahneman **248:** © Associated Press/AP **251:** bottom, Archives of the History of American Psychology, University of Akron **251:** top, © Bettmann/Corbis **253:** Archives of the History of American Psychology, University of Akron **255:** left, © Associated Press/AP **255:** right, © Rufus F. Folkks/ Corbis **255:** center, © Spencer Platt/Getty Images **259:** Courtesy of Sandra Scarr **260:** Courtesy of Arthur R. Jensen **262:** Courtesy of Robert Sternberg **263:** Courtesy of Howard Gardner, photo © Jay Gardner **264:** © Associated Press/AP **268:** © Simon Marsden/marsdenarchive.com **269:** Cover of Naked in Cyberspace by Carole A. Lane: Reproduced by courtesy and permission of Information Today, Inc., Medford, NJ

Chapter 9 **273:** Copyright © by Klev Schoening **276:** © Yoav Levy/PhotoTake **278:** © James Marshall/ The Image Works **279:** © Owen Franken/Corbis **280:** © Bettmann/Corbis **283:** Courtesy of David M. Buss **286:** © John Lazar/Los Angeles Daily News/Corbis Sygma **287:** Boston University Photo Services, courtesy of David C. McClelland **289:** © LWA-Dann Tardif/ Corbis **290:** inset, Figure 9.14 photo © Mark C. Burnett/Stock, Boston **291:** Courtesy of Joseph LeDoux, New York University **291:** inset, Figure 9.15 (snake) © C. H. Wooley **293:** Photos for Figure 9.16: From

Unmasking the Face, © 1975 by Paul Ekman. Photograph courtesy of Paul Ekman **294:** © Bill Apple, courtesy of Stanley Schachter **299:** © Stuart Hughes/ Corbis

Chapter 10 © Bill Freeman / PhotoEdit © Don Hammond/ Design Pics Inc. / Alamy © LWA-Dann Tardif/Corbis **305:** © Tim Graham/Corbis **307:** bottom left, © Petit Format/Guigoz/ Science Source/ Photo Researchers, Inc. **307:** right, © Petit Format/ Nestle/Science Source/Photo Researchers, Inc. **307:** top left, © Petit Format/Science Source/Photo Researchers, Inc. **311:** top right, Archives of the History of American Psychology, University of Akron **311:** top left, © Konner/AnthroPhoto **311:** bottom, © Martin Rogers/Stock, Boston/IPN Stock **311:** center right, © Sir Richard Bowlby Bt. **312:** Erik Hesse **314:** bottom, © Farrell Grehan/Corbis **314:** top, © Ted Streshinsky/Corbis **317:** Archives of the History of American Psychology, University of Akron **319:** Harvard University Archives, Call #UAV 605.295.8p Kohlberg **322:** © Kevin Cooley/Taxi/Getty Images **326:** inset, (Figure 10.17 photo) © RF/Corbis **329:** Courtesy of Wayne Weiten **334:** © Royalty Free/Corbis

Chapter 11 © Andy Sacks/Stone/Getty Images **339:** © Associated Press/AP **342:** National Library of Medicine **343:** © Peter Aprahamian/Corbis **346:** © Michael Newman/PhotoEdit **347:** Images from C. G. Jung Bild Und Wort, © Walter-Verlag AG, Olten, Switzerland, 1977 **347:** top right, © Bettmann/Corbis **348:** bottom left, © Bettmann/Corbis **348:** top, © Bettmann/Corbis **350:** top left, Courtesy of B. F. Skinner **350:** inset, Figure 11.6 photo © Jacobs Stock Photography/Corbis **351:** Photo by Keeble, courtesy of Albert Bandura **352:** University photographer Joe Pineiro, Columbia University **353:** Courtesy of Carl Rogers Memorial Library **354:** Wadsworth Thomson Collection **357:** By permission from the H. J. Eysenck Memorial Fund **358:** inset, Figure 11.12 photo © Daly & Newton/Stone/Getty Images **361:** center, Courtesy of Hazel Rose Markus **361:** bottom right, Courtesy of Shinobu Kitayama **361:** top, © Cheryl Maeder/Corbis **362:** (Freud's couch) © Peter Aprahamian/Corbis **362:** (Lab tech and rat) © Richard Wood/Index Stock Imagery **362:** (Therapy) © Tom Stewart/Corbis **362:** (Twins) © Daly & Newton/ Stone/Getty Images **363:** (Father) © Stephanie Rausser/Taxi/Getty Images **363:** (Potty) © Michael Newman/PhotoEdit **363:** (women laughing) © Jacobs Stock Photography/Corbis **367:** Reprinted by permission of the publishers from Henry A. Murray, Thematic Apperception Test, Cambridge, Mass.: Harvard University Press, Copyright © 1943 by The President and Fellows of Harvard College, © 1971 by Henry A. Murray. **368:** © Paul S. Howell/Getty Images

Chapter 12 **374:** Courtesy of Richard S. Lazarus **379:** © Bettmann/Corbis **381:** Courtesy, Albert Ellis Institute **382:** top, © Paul Thomas/The Image Bank/ Getty Images **383:** Courtesy of Shelley Taylor **384:** © Arlene Collins **385:** inset, Figure 12.6 photo Digital Vision/Getty Images **388:** Courtesy of Martin E. P. Seligman **389:** inset, Figure 12.8 photo © Bonnie Kamin/Photo Edit **389:** © Ryan McVay/Getty Images **392:** Courtesy of University of California, Riverside **393:** © Adamsmith/SuperStock/Alamy **396:** © Acey Harper/Time Life Pictures/Getty Images **397:** inset, Figure 12.14 photo © Paul Francis Photo **397:** inset, Figure 12.15 (golfer photo) © Paul Francis Photo **397:** inset, Figure 12.15 (jogging photo) © Michael Newman/PhotoEdit **397:** inset, Figure 12.15 (lounge photo) © C. H. Wooley

Chapter 13 **404:** top center, Culver Pictures, Inc. **404:** center, St. Catherine of Siena Exorcising a Possessed Woman, c. 1500–1510 (detail). Girolamo Di Benvenuto. Denver Art Museum Collection, Gift of Samuel H. Kress Foundation Collection, 1961.171 © Denver Art Museum 2006. All rights reserved **404:** bottom, © David Lees/Corbis **408:** bottom center, © Associated Press/AP **408:** left, © Bettmann/Corbis **414:** right, © Graeme Robertson/Getty Images **414:** left, © Katy Winn/Corbis **417:** Courtesy of Susan Nolen-Hoeksema **420:** Courtesy of Nancy Andreasen. M.D. **421:** © Reuters/Corbis **424:** (top right) Munch, Edvard: The Scream. National Gallery, Oslo, Norway, SCALA/Art Resource/NY; © 2007 The Munch Museum/The Munch-Ellingsen Group/Artists Rights Society (ARS), NY **424:** center left, van Gogh, Vincent: Portrait of Dr. Gachet. Musee d'Orsay, Paris. © Erich Lessing/Art Resource, NY **424:** top right, © Bettmann/Corbis **424:** bottom left, © Derek Bayes/Aspect Picture Library **424:** center right, © Graeme Robertson/Getty Images **424:** bottom right, © Reuters/Corbis **428:** © Ed Quinn/Corbis

Chapter 14 **435:** Warner Bros./Shooting Star **436:** Mary Evans/Sigmund Freud Copyrights **439:** National Library of Medicine **440:** © Bruce Ayres/ Stone/Getty Images **441:** top right, Courtesy of Carl Rogers Memorial Library **441:** bottom, © Zigy Kaluzny/Stone/Getty Images **442:** © Manchan/ Photodisc Red/Getty Images **444:** Courtesy of Joseph Wolpe **445:** inset, (Figure 14.8 photo) © Robert Harding Picture Library **445:** top left, © Kent News & Picture/Corbis Sygma **446:** Courtesy of Aaron T. Beck **451:** © James Wilson/Woodfin Camp & Associates, all rights reserved **452:** (Beck) Courtesy of Aaron T. Beck **452:** (Freud) National Library of Medicine **452:** (Rogers) Courtesy of Carl Rogers Memorial Library **452:** (Wolpe) Courtesy of Joseph Wolpe **453:** (2nd down) © Zigy Kaluzny/Stone/Getty Images **453:** (3rd down) © Kent News & Picture/Corbis Sygma **453:** (4th down) © Manchan/Photodisc Red/Getty Images **453:** (bottom left) © James Wilson/Woodfin Camp & Associates, all rights reserved **453:** (bottom right) © PhotoDisc, Inc. **453:** (top) © Bruce Ayres/Stone/ Getty Images **455:** © Michael Newman/PhotoEdit **456:** inset, (inset) Detail of painting in Harrisburg State Hospital, photo by Ken Smith/LLR Collection **456:** right, Culver Pictures, Inc. **458:** © Associated Press/AP **459:** © Tom McCarthy/SKA **462:** © International Stock/Robert Harding Picture Library **463:** © Tony Freeman/PhotoEdit

Chapter 15 **469:** inset, © image100/Alamy **471:** University Archives, Spencer Research Library, University of Kansas **473:** © Ian Waldie/Getty Images **475:** © Stockbyte Platinum/Alamy **476:** bottom left, Courtesy of Elaine Hatfield **476:** top left, Courtesy of Ellen Berscheid **479:** top, © DPA/The Image Works **480:** inset, (Figure 15.7 photo) © Associated Press/AP **483:** right, Courtesy of Prof. Jerry Suls **483:** inset, Figure 16.11 photo © Associated Press/AP **486:** Courtesy of University of Pennsylvania, University Communications **487:** right, Photos © 1965 by Stanley Milgram. From the film Obedience, distributed by Penn State Media Sales. Reprinted by permission of Alexandra Milgram. **487:** right, © 1981 Eric Kroll, courtesy of Alexandra Milgram **488:** Courtesy of Philip Zimbardo **489:** From A Simulation Study of the Psychology of Imprisonment Conducted at Stanford University, 1971. Copyright © Philip Zimbardo. Reproduced with permission. **489:** right, © AFP /Getty Images **492:** © Pictor International/ ImageState /Alamy **495:** © Associated Press/AP **499:** © Tony Freeman/Photo Edit

Figure Credits

Chapter 1 11: Figure 1.3: Adapted from Robins, E. W., Gosling, S. D., & Craik, K. H. (1999) "An Empirical Analysis of Trends in Psychology," American Psychologist, 54 (2), 117-128. Copyright © 1999 by the American Psychological Association. Reprinted by permission of the publisher and author. 26: DOONESBURY © by G. B. Trudeau. Dist. by UNIVERSAL PRESS SYNDICATE. Reprinted with permission. All rights reserved. 28: Cartoon NON SEQUITUR © 2004 by Wiley Miller. Dist. by UNIVERSAL PRESS SYNDICATE. Reprinted with permission. All rights reserved.

Chapter 2 34: ScienceCartoonsPlus.com 36: Figure 2.2 From Sherman, D. K., Nelson, L. D., & Ross, L. D., "Naïve Realism and Affirmative Action: Adversaries Are More Similar Than They Think," Basic and Applied Social Psychology, 25, 275-289. Copyright 2003 Lawrence Erlbaum Associates, Inc. Reprinted by permission. 43: ScienceCartoonsPlus.com 45: Figure 2.9: Adapted from Levine, R. V., and Norenzayan, A., "The Pace of Life in 31 Countries", 1999, Journal of Cross-Cultural Psychology, 30 (2), 178-205 . Copyright © 1999 Sage Publications. Reprinted by permission of Sage Publications. 55: Figure 2.13: Sample record reprinted with permission of the American Psychological Association, publisher of the PsycINFO (r) database. Copyright © 1887-present, American Psychological Association. All rights reserved. For more information contact psycinfo.apa.org. 56: Figure 2.14: Sample record reprinted with permission of the American Psychological Association, publisher of the PsycINFO (r) database. Copyright © 1887–present, American Psychological Association. All rights reserved. For more information contact psycinfo.apa. org. 58: DILBERT: © Scott Adams/Dist. by United Feature Syndicate, Inc.

Chapter 3 74: © Bryan Christie Design [on page credit: From Bremmer, J. D. (2005). Brain Imaging Handbook, New York: W. W. Norton, p. 34. Illustration © by Bryan Christie Design.] 81: bottom, Cartoon © 1988. Used by permission of John L. Hart FLP, and Creators Syndicate, Inc. 86: Cartoon © 2006 Leo Cullum from the cartoonbank.com. All rights reserved. 89: Table 3.2: Adapted from Animal Behavior by John Alcock, 1998, p. 463. Copyright © 1998 John Alcock. Reprinted by permission of Sinauer Associates and the author. 90: Figure 3.21: Cartoon courtesy of Roy Doty.

Chapter 4 108: Figure 4.13: Based on data from Wald, G., & Brown, P. K. (1965) "Human Color Vision and Color Blindness," Symposium Cold Spring Harbor Laboratory of Quantitative Biology, 30, 345-359 (p. 351). Copyright © 1965. Reprinted by permission of the author. 109: Figure 4.15: From Fliegende Blatter, October 23, 1892, p. 147. 113: Attributed to W. E. Hill, 1915 from a German 1888 postcard. 114: Figure 4.24: "Figures of 2 Tricycles," from The Thinking Eye, the Seeing Brain: Explorations in Visual Cognition by James T. Enns (p. 204). Copyright © 2004 by W. W. Norton. Used by permission of W. W. Norton & Company, Inc. 114: From J. L. Davenport and M. C. Potter, "Scene consistency in object and background perception," 2004, Psychological Science, 15 Vol 8 (6), 559-564. Reprinted by permission of the author. 116: Cartoon BIZARRO © Dan Piraro. King Features Syndicate. 116: Figure 4.27: Adapted by permission from an illustration by Ilil Arbel on page 83 of "Pictorial Perception and Culture," by Jan B. Deregowski in Scientific American, 227 (5) November 1972. Copyright © 1972 by Scientific American, Inc. All rights reserved. 118: Figure 4.31: Ponzo illustration from Mind Sights by Roger N. Shepard, © 1990 by Roger N. Shepard. Reprinted by permission of Henry Holt & Co., LLC. 120: Figure 4.34: Decibel level examples from Atkinson, R. L., Atkinson R. C., Smith, E. F., & Hilgard, E. R., Introduction to Psychology, Ninth Edition, San Diego: Harcourt, copyright © 1987. Reprinted by permission of Wadsworth Publishing. 123: Figure 4.37: Data from Bartoshuk, L. M. (1993) "Genetic and Pathological Taste Variation: What Can We Learn from Animal Models and Human Disease?." In D. Chadwick, J. Marsh & J. Goode (Eds.), The Molecular Basis of Smell and Taste Tranduction, pp. 251-267. John Wiley & Sons, Inc. 133: Figure 4.51: From Alber, Joseph, Interaction of Color. Copyright © 1963 and Reprinted by permission of the publisher, Yale University Press.

Chapter 5 140: Figure 5-1: Circadian rhythms adapted from Wide Awake at 3:00 AM, by Richard M. Coleman. Copyright © 1986 by Richard M. Coleman. Reprinted by permission of Henry Holt & Co., LLC. 142: Figure 5.2: Figure from Hauri, P., "Current Concepts The Sleep Disorders," 1982, The Upjohn Company, Kalamazoo, Michigan. Reprinted by permission. 144: Figure 5.4: Figure adapted from an updated revision of a figure in Roffwarg, H. P., Muzio, J N., and Dement, W. C., "Ontogenetic Development of Human Sleep Dream Cycle," 1966. Science, 152, 604-609. Adapted and revised by permission of the author. 148: Cartoon © 2006 Joe Dator from cartoonbank.com. All rights reserved. 149: ScienceCartoonsPlus.com 150: Figure 5.7: From Nielsen, T.A., Zadra, A. L., Simard, V., Saucier, S., Stenstrom, P., Smith, C., & Kuiken, D. (2003), "The Typical Dreams of Canadian University Students," Dreaming, 13, 211-235 (from Table 1, p. 217). Copyright © 2003 by the Association for the Study of Dreams. 153: Figure 5.9: Adapted from Nash, M. R. (2001, July), "The Truth and the Hype of Hypnosis." Scientific American, 285, 46-55 (53). Copyright © 2001 by Scientific American. All rights reserved. 155: Figure 5.10: (Redrawn) from illustration on p. 86 by Lorelle A. Raboni, Scientific American, 226, 85-90, February 1972. From "The Physiology of Meditation," by R. K. Wallace and H. Benson. Copyright © 1972 by Scientific American, Inc. Redrawn by permission of L. A. Raboni. 157: ScienceCartoonsPlus.com 159: Figure 5.11: Adapted from Kalat, J. W. (2001). Biological Psychology. © 2001 Wadsworth. Reprinted by permission. 163: Figure 5.12: Adapted from Sleep, the Gentle Tyrant, 2nd Ed. by Wilse B. Webb, 1992. Copyright © 1992 by Anker Publishing Co., Bolton, Ma. Adapted by permission. 163: Figure 5.13: Adapted from Power Sleep by James B. Maas, copyright © 1998 by James B. Mass, Ph. D. Used by permission of Villard Books, a division of Random House, Inc. 165: Figure 5.14: From Health and Wellness, Third edition by Edlin and Golanty, 1992, p. 286. Copyright © 1992 by Jones & Bartlett Publishers, Inc., Sudbury, MA. www.jbpub.com. Reprinted by permission.

Chapter 6 171: Figure 6.1: Adapted from Yerkes, R. M., & Morgulis, S. (1909), "The Method of Pavlov in Animal Psychology," Psychological Bulletin, 6, 257-273. American Psychological Association. Inset: From Goodwin, C. J., "Misportraying Pavlov's Apparatus," 1991. American Journal of Psychology 104 (1), pp. 135-141. © 1991 by the Board of Trustees of the University of Illinois. 171: ScienceCartoonsPlus.com 181: Figure 6.11: © 2002 Time, Inc. Reprinted by permission 182: Cartoon @ The Family Circus-BILL KEANE, Inc. King Features Syndicate 196: Cartoon CALVIN AND HOBBES © 1995 by Bill Watterson. Distributed by UNIVERSAL PRESS SYNDICATE. Reprinted with permission. All rights reserved.

Chapter 7 205: Figure 7.1: Reprinted from Cognitive Psychology, 11, by Nickerson, R. S., and Adams, M. J., "Long-Term Memory for a Common Object," 287-307, Copyright © 1979, with permission from Elsevier. 212: Cartoon © The New Yorker Collection 1983 by Ed Fisher from cartoonbank.com. All rights reserved. 214: Figure 7.8: Adapted from Collins, A. M. & Loftus (1975) "A Spreading Activation Theory of Semantic Processing, " Psychological Review, 82, 407-428. Copyright © 1975 by the American Psychological Association. Adapted by permission of the publisher and author. 215: Figure 7.9: Based on Lofuts, E. F., & Palmer, J. C., (1974) "Reconstruction of Automobile Destruction: An Example of Interaction Between Language and Memory," Journal of Verbal Learning and Verbal Behavior," 13, 585-589. Academic Press, Inc. 221: Figure 7.13: From "Lies of the Mind," Time, 11/29/93. Copyright © 1993 Time Inc. Reprinted by permission. 222: Cartoon DOONESBURY © 1994 by G. B. Trudeau. Reprinted with permission of Universal Press Syndicate. All rights reserved. 228: Figure 7.19: Adapted from Rundus, D. (1971) "Analysis of Rehearsal Processes in Free Recall," Journal of Experimental Psychology, 89, 63-77. Copyright © 1971 by the American Psychological Association. Adapted by permission of the publisher and author. 229: Figure 7.20: Reprinted (adapted) from Journal of Verbal Learning and Verbal Behavior (now Journal of Memory and Language), 9, by B. J. Underwood, "A Breakdown of the Total-Time Law in Free-Recall Learning," 573-580, Copyright © 1970 with permission from Elsevier. 229: Figure 7.21: From Bower, G. H., (1970) "Analysis of a Mnemonic Device," American Scientist, 58, Sept-Oct., 496-499. Copyright © 1970 by Scientific Research Society. Reprinted by permission.

Chapter 8 236: DILBERT: © Scott Adams/Dist. by United Feature Syndication, Inc. 238: Figure 8.4: Based on Luchins, A. S. (1942) "Mechanization in Problem Solving," Psychological Monographs, 54 (Whole No. 248). 239: Figure 8.5: From Conceptual Blockbusting: A Guide to Better Ideas, by James L. Adams, pp. 17-18. Copyright © 1980 by James L. Adams. Reprinted by permission of W. H. Freeman 239: Figure 8.6: From Kendler, Howard H. (1974) Basic Psychology 3rd Edition, pp. 403, 404. Copyright © 1974 The Benjamin-Cummings Publishing Co. Adapted by permission of Howard H. Kendler. 240: Cartoon Calvin & Hobbes © by Bill Watterson. Reprinted with permission of Universal Press Syndicate. All rights reserved. 241: Figure 8.10: From Kendler, Howard H. (1974) Basic Psychology 3rd Edition, pp. 403, 404. Copyright © 1974 The Benjamin-Cummings Publishing Co. Adapted by permission of Howard H. Kendler. 241: Figure 8.8: Based on by Luchins, A. S. (1942), "Mechanization in Problem Solving," Psychological Monographs, 54 (Whole No. 248). 241: Figure 8.9: From Conceptual Blockbusting: A Guide to Better Ideas, by James L. Adams, pp. 17-18. Copyright © 1980 by James L. Adams. Reprinted by permission of W. H. Freeman 246: Cartoon © 2005 Steve Kelley. The Times-Picayune. Reprinted with permisson. 255: Figure 8.17: Adapted from Sternberg, R. J., Conway, B. E., Keton, J. L. & Bernstein, M. (1981), "People's Conceptions of Intelligence," Journal of Personality and Social Psychology, 41 (1), p. 45. Copyright © 1981 by the American Psychological Association. Adapted by permission of the publisher and author. **256:** ScienceCartoonsPlus.com **258:** Cartoon © The New Yorker Collection 1994 Charles Barsotti from the cartoonbank.com. All rights reserved. **264:** Table 8.4: Adapted from Gardner, H. & Hatch, T., (1989) "Multiple Intelligences Go to School: Educational Implications of the Theory of Multiple Intelligences," Educational Researcher, 18 (8), 4–10. American Educational Research Association. Additional data from Gardner, 1998

Chapter 9 280: Figure 9.4: Data based on Masters, W. H., & Johnson, V. E., 1966, Human Sexual Response. Little Brown and Company. **282:** Cartoon BIZARRO © Dan Piraro. King Features Syndicate. **282:** Figure 9.8: From Buss, D. M., & Schmitt, D. P. (1993) "Sexual Strategies Theory: An Evolutionary Perspective on Human Mating," Psychological Review, 100, 204-232. Copyright © 1993 by the American Psychological Association. Reprinted by permission of the publisher and author. **287:** Figure 9.12: Descriptions reprinted by permission of Dr. David McClelland. **293:** Figure 9.16: Data from Ekman, P., & Friesen, W. V. (1975). Unmasking the Face, © 1975 by Paul Ekman, Prentice-Hall. **297:** Cartoon © The New Yorker Collection 1987 Mischa Richter from the cartoonbank.com. All rights reserved. **298:** Figure 9.20: Reproduced from (Figure 19.1 Marital status and happiness, p. 378) "Close relationship and quality of life," by David G. Myers. In Well-Being: The Foundations of Hedonic Psychology, edited by Daniel Kahneman, Ed Diener, and Norbert Schwarz. Copyright © 1999 Russell Sage Foundation, 112 East 64th Street, New York, NY 10021. Reprinted with permission. **300:** Figure 9.22: From Halpern, D. F., (1996) Thought & Knowledge: An Introduction to Critical Thinking, p. 181, figure 5.1. Copyright © 2003, 1996 Lawrence Erlbaum Associates. Reprinted by permission of Lawrence Erlbaum Associates.

Chapter 10 Cartoon Non Sequitur © 2002 by Wiley. Reprinted with permission of Universal Press Syndicate. All rights reserved. **308:** Figure 10.2: Reprinted (adapted) from Before We Are Born: Essentials of Embryology and Birth Defects by Moore, K. L. & Persaud, T. V. N , 5/E., Copyright © 1998, with permission from Elsevier. **313:** Figure 11.8 Adapted from Van IJzendoom, Marinus H., Kroonenberg, Pieter M. (1988), "Cross-cultural Patterns of Attachment: A Meta-analysis of the Strange Situation," Child Development, 59(1) 147-156. **318:** Figure 10.9: From Wynn, K. "Addition and Subtraction by Human Infants," (1992), Nature, 358, 749-750. Copyright © 1992 Macmillan Magazines, Ltd. Reprinted with permission from Nature and the author. **323:** Figure 10.15: Adapted from "Identity in Adolescence," by J. E. Marcia, 1980. In J. Adelson (Ed.), Handbook of Adolescent Psychology, pp. 159–210. Copyright © 1980 by John Wiley & Sons, Inc. Adapted by permission of John Wiley & Sons, Inc. **324:** Figure 10.15: Adapted from Meilman, P. W. (1979). "Cross-sectional Age Changes in Ego Identity Status During Adolescence," Developmental Psychology, 15, 230-231. Copyright © American Psychological Association. Reprinted by permission of the publisher and author. **327:** Cartoon SALLY FORTH © Howard and Mac. King Features Syndicate. **329:** Figure 10.19: Reprinted from Biological Psychology, 54, (1–3), by Salthouse, T. A. , "Aging and Measures of Processing Speed," 35–54, Copyright © 2000, with permission from Elsevier. **330:** Table 10.1: Adapted from Ruble, T. L. (1983) "Sex Stereotypes: Issues of Change in the 70s", Sex Roles, 9, 397-402. Copyright © 1983 Plenum Publishing Group. Adapted by per-

mission. With kind permission of Springer Science and Business Media. **331:** Cartoon CATHY © 1986 by Cathy Guisewite. Dist. by UNIVERSAL PRESS SYNDICATE. Reprinted with permission. All rights reserved.

Chapter 11 344: bottom, ScienceCartoonsPlus.com **355:** bottom, Cartoon PEANUTS © United Feature Syndicate, Inc. **355:** Figure 11.10: Adapted from Potkay, C. R., & Allen, B. P. (1986), Personality Theory, Research and Application, p. 246. Brooks/Cole Publishing Company. Copyright © 1986 by C.R. Potkay & Bem Allen. Adapted by permission of the authors. **357:** Figure 11.11: From Eysenck, H. J. (1976) The Biological Basis of Personality, 1st Ed., p. 36. Courtesy of Charles C. Thomas, Publisher, Springfield, Illinois. Reprinted by permission of the publisher. **363:** (Eysenck's model) From Eysenck, H. J. (1976) The Biological Basis of Personality, 1st Ed., p. 36. Courtesy of Charles C. Thomas, Publisher, Springfield, Illinois. Reprinted by permission of the publisher. **364:** Figure 11.14: Adapted from Markus, H. R., & Kitayama, S. (1991) "Culture and the Self: Implications for Cognition, Emotion, and Motivation," Psychological Review, 98, 224–253. Copyright © 1991 by the American Psychological Association. Adapted by permission of the author. **367:** Data derived from: Handbook for the Sixteen Personality Factor Questionnaire and based on the 16PF Version, 4, Copyright © 1970, 1988, 1992 by the Institute for Personality and Ability Testing, Inc. (IPAT), Champaign, Illinois, USA. All rights reserved.

Chapter 12 376: Table 12.1: Reprinted from Journal of Psychosomatic Research, 11, by T. H. Holmes and R. Rahe, 213–218, in "The Social Readjustment Rating Scale," Copyright © 1967, with permission from Elsevier. **380:** top, DILBERT: © Scott Adams/Dist. by United Feature Syndicate, Inc. **382:** top, Cartoon CATHY © 1981 by Cathy Guisewite. Reprinted with permission of Universal Press Syndicate. All rights reserved. **391:** Figure 12.10: Adapted from Kalichman, S. C., (1995) Understanding AIDS: A Guide for Mental Health Professionals. Copyright © 1995 American Psychological Association. Reproduced by permission of the publisher and author. **397:** Figure 12.14: "Relaxation Procedure" from The Relaxation Response, by Herbert Benson, M.D. and Miriam Z. Klipper. Copyright © 1975 by William Morrow & Company, Inc. By permission of HarperCollins Publishers, Inc. **397:** Figure 12.15: Adapted from Blair, S. N., Kohl, W. H., Paffenbarger, R. S., Clark, D. G. , Cooper, K. H. , & Gibbons, L. W., (1989) " Physical Fitness and All-Cause Mortality," Journal of the American Medical Association, 262, 2395–2401. Copyright © 1989 American Medical Association. Reprinted by permission. **398:** bottom, Cartoon Copyright @ Borgman. King Features Syndicate.

Chapter 13 406: Figure 13.2: Reprinted with permission from the Diagnostic and Statistical Manual of Mental Disorders, DSM-TR Text Revision. Copyright © 2000 American Psychiatric Association. **407:** top left, ScienceCartoonsPlus.com **411:** top left, Cartoon Copyright © by Patrick Hardin, www.CartoonStock.com **415:** Table 13.1: From Sarason, I. G., & Sarason, B. G. (1987) Abnormal Psychology: The Problem of Maladaptive Behavior, 5/E, © 1987, p. 283. Reprinted by permission of Prentice-Hall, Inc., Englewood Cliffs, NJ. **416:** Figure 13.8: From Figure 6–1, "Age of Onset for Bipolar Mood Disorder," from Manic-Depressive Illness, by Frederick K. Goodwin and Kay R. Jamison [p. 132]. Copyright © 1990 by

Oxford University Press., Inc. Used by permission of Oxford University Press, Inc.

Chapter 14 443: Cartoon INSIDE WOODY ALLEN © Stuart Hample. King Features Syndicate. **443:** Figure 14.5: Adapted from Lambert, M. J., Hansen, N. B., & Finch A. E. (2001), "Patient-focused Research: Using Patient Outcome Data to Enhance Treatment Effects," Journal of Consulting and Clinical Psychology, 69, 159–172. Copyright © 2001 by the American Psychological Association. Adapted by permission of the publisher and author. **445:** Figure 14.7: From Rudestam K. E. (1980) Methods of Self-Change: An ABC Primer, pp. 42-43, Copyright © 1980 by Wadsworth, Inc. Reprinted by permission of the author. **448:** Figure 14.10: From data in NIMH-PSC Collaborative Study I and reported in "Drugs in the Treatment of Psychosis," by J. O. Cole, S. C. Goldberg & J. M. Davis, 1966, 1985. In P. Solomon (Ed.) Psychiatric Drugs, Grune & Stratton. Reprinted by permission of J. M. Davis. **450:** Cartoon © The New Yorker Collection 2000 Frank Cotham from cartoonbank.com. All rights reserved. **457:** Cartoon Doonesbury © 1986 by G. B. Trudeau. Reprinted with permission of Universal Press Syndicate. All rights reserved. **461:** Figure 14.14: Adapted from Smith, M. L. and Glass, G. V. (1977) "Meta Analysis of Psychotherapy Outcome Series," American Psychologist, 32 (Sept), 752–760. Copyright © 1977 by the American Psychological Association. Adapted by permission of the publisher and author.

Chapter 15 467: Excerpt from: Tales from the Front by Cheryl Lavin and Laura Kavesh, © copyright 1988 by Cheryl Lavin and Laura Kavesh. Used by permission of Doubleday, a division of Random House, Inc. and with permission from The Aaron Priest Literary Agency. **468:** Cartoon © The New Yorker Collection 2005 Marisa Acocello Marchetto from cartoonbank.com. All rights reserved. **469:** DILBERT: © Scott Adams/Dist. by United Feature Syndicate, Inc. **474:** Figure 15.4: Adapted from Hofstede, G. (2001). Culture's Consequences, 2/e, p. 215. Copyright © 2001 Sage Publications. Adapted by permission of Dr. Geert Hofstede. **476:** Cartoon © The New Yorker Collection 2002 Alex Gregory from cartoonbank.com. All rights reserved. **479:** Cartoon BIZARRO © Dan Piraro. King Features Syndicate. **481:** Figure 15.8: Based on Lippa, R. A. (1994) Introduction to Social Psychology, Brooks/Cole Publishing Company. Copyright © 1994 by Wadsworth. Reprinted by permission. **485:** Figure 15.12: Adapted from Asch, Solomon (1955) "Opinion and Social Pressure," Scientific American, November 1955, from an illustration by Sara Love on p. 32. Copyright © 1955 by Scientific American, Inc. All rights reserved. **486:** Figure 15.13: Adapted from Asch, Solomon (1955) "Opinion and Social Pressure," Scientific American, November 1955, from an illustration by Sara Love on p. 35. Copyright © 1955 by Scientific American, Inc. All rights reserved. **491:** Figure 15.15: Adapted from Latane, B., Williams, K., & Harkins, S. (1979) "Many Hands Make Light the Work: The Causes and Consequences of Social Loafing," Journal of Personality and Social Psychology, 37, 822-832. Copyright © 1979 by the American Psychological Association. Adapted by permission of the publisher and author. **493:** Figure 15.17: Adapted with permission of The Free Press, a Division of Simon & Schuster Adult Publishing Group, from DECISION MAKING: A Psychological Analysis of Conflict, Choice and Commitment, by Irving J. Janis and Leon Mann. Copyright © 1977 by The Free Press. All rights reserved.

TO THE OWNER OF THIS BOOK:

I hope that you have found *Psychology: Themes and Variations, Briefer Version,* Seventh Edition, useful. So that this book can be improved in a future edition, would you take the time to complete this sheet and return it? Thank you.

School and address: _____

_____

Department: _____

Instructor's name: _____

1. What I like most about this book is: _____

_____

_____

2. What I like least about this book is: _____

_____

_____

3. My general reaction to this book is: _____

_____

_____

4. The name of the course in which I used this book is: _____

_____

5. Were all of the chapters of the book assigned for you to read? _____

   If not, which ones weren't? _____

6. In the space below, or on a separate sheet of paper, please write specific suggestions for improving this book and anything else you'd care to share about your experience in using this book.

_____

_____

_____

_____

_____

_____

DO NOT STAPLE.   TAPE HERE

FOLD HERE

THOMSON
★
WADSWORTH

NO POSTAGE
NECESSARY
IF MAILED
IN THE
UNITED STATES

BUSINESS REPLY MAIL
FIRST-CLASS MAIL   PERMIT NO. 34   BELMONT CA

POSTAGE WILL BE PAID BY ADDRESSEE

Attn: Michele Sordi, Psychology Editor

Thomson Wadsworth
10 Davis Drive
Belmont CA 94002-9801

FOLD HERE

OPTIONAL:

Your name: _____ Date: _____

May we quote you, either in promotion for *Psychology: Themes and Variations, Briefer Version,* Seventh Edition, or in future publishing ventures?

Yes: _____ No: _____

Sincerely yours,

Wayne Weiten

DO NOT STAPLE.   TAPE HERE